# TEXTS AND CONTEXTS

# TEXTS AND CONTEXTS

## BIBLICAL TEXTS IN THEIR
## TEXTUAL AND SITUATIONAL CONTEXTS

ESSAYS IN HONOR OF

## LARS HARTMAN

EDITED BY

### TORD FORNBERG
AND
### DAVID HELLHOLM

ASSISTED BY

CHRISTER D. HELLHOLM

### SCANDINAVIAN UNIVERSITY PRESS
Oslo - Copenhagen - Stockholm - Boston

Scandinavian University Press (Universitetsforlaget AS),
P.O. Box 2959 Tøyen, N-0608 Oslo, Norway
Fax +47 22 57 53 53

Stockholm office
SCUP, Scandinavian University Press
P.O. Box 3255, S-103 65 Stockholm, Sweden
Fax +46 8 20 99 82

Copenhagen office
Scandinavian University Press AS
P.O. Box 54, DK-1002 København K, Denmark
Fax +45 33 32 05 70

Boston office
Scandinavian University Press North America
875-81 Massachusetts Avenue, Cambridge MA 02139, USA
Fax +1 617 354 68 75

The Laser fonts Super Hebrew, Symbol Greek and Coptic LS used to print parts of this
work are available from Linguist's Software, Inc., P. O. Box 580 Edmonds,
WA 98020-0580, USA (1-206-775-1130).

Typeset by Christer D. Hellholm
Jacket design: Astrid E. Jørgensen
Jacket illustration: Codex argenteus. The Silver Bible. Mark 4: 21–28.
(Uppsala Univertitetsbibliotek)
Printed in Norway by ROTANOR Bokproduksjon AS 1995

# Preface

Dear Lars Hartman

Friends, colleagues and students of yours are happy to congratulate you on the occasion of your 65th birthday on 2 March 1995 by presenting the following studies in your honor.

In your academic teaching as well as in your scholarly work you have constantly emphasized the importance of the context for the interpretation of biblical texts; you have done so out of the conviction that the textual as well as the situational contexts are of utmost importance for the semantic interpretation as well as for the pragmatic-communicative function of biblical texts. Consequently it seemed appropriate to ask the contributors to let their essays focus on "Texts and Contexts" as is also indicated in the title of this Festschrift. In the analyses of a variety of texts they have in manifold ways succeeded in putting contextuality on the agenda in a way and to an extent that reflects your own diverse interests and engagements in the subject-matter over the years.

This volume has been in the making for some time and we are grateful to all who have collaborated in this undertaking. At the same time, however, we deeply deplore the premature death of one contributor, Professor Georg Strecker (Göttingen), and of two colleagues, who had declared themselves willing to present essays in your honor, Professor Fritzleo Lentzen-Deis, SJ (Rome) and Professor Willem Vorster (Pretoria).

The willingness of so many to collaborate with us in this project is the indisputable proof of a deep appreciation and gratitude toward you as a friend, colleague and wise teacher.

*Ad multos annos!*

Uppsala/Oslo/Hammarö, 15 October 1994

Tord Fornberg      David Hellholm

# Table of Contents

Contributors . . . . . . . . . . . . . . . . . . . . . . . . . . . . . . . . . . . . . . . . xvii

Abbreviations . . . . . . . . . . . . . . . . . . . . . . . . . . . . . . . . . . . . . . xxi

## PART I

### BIBLICAL TEXTS IN THEIR TEXTUAL CONTEXTS

## SECTION A

### INTRA-TEXTUAL RELATIONS

BERTIL ALBREKTSON, Ezekiel 30:16 — A Conjecture . . . . . . . . . . . . . . . . . . . .5

DAVID HELLHOLM, Substitutionelle Gliederungsmerkmale und die Kompo-
   sition des Matthäusevangeliums . . . . . . . . . . . . . . . . . . . . . . . . . . . . . . .11
   1. Einige Strukturmerkmale an der Textoberfläche des Matthäusevangeliums 11 —
   2. Sprachwissenschaftliche Grundlagenüberlegungen 15 — 3. Einige substitutionelle
   Gliederungsmerkmale im Matthäusevangelium 33 — 4. Zusammenfassung 64.

DONALD A. HAGNER, Imminence and Parousia in the Gospel of Matthew . . . . . . .77
   1. Introduction 77 — 2. The Disciples' Question 78 — 3. The Imminence Sayings 79
   — 4. Imminence and the Required Interim Period 81 — 5. Matthew's εὐθέως: Immediately After What? 82 — 6. The Relation of the Fall of Jerusalem to the Eschatological
   Judgment 86 — 7. The Date of Matthew 88 — 8. Conclusion 89.

FRANÇOIS VOUGA, "Habt Glauben an Gott". Der Theozentrismus der
   Verkündigung des Evangeliums und des christlichen Glaubens im
   Markusevangelium . . . . . . . . . . . . . . . . . . . . . . . . . . . . . . . . . . . . . . .93
   1. Zur Auslegungstradition des Markusevangeliums 93 — 2. Jesus als Zeuge eines
   Gottesglaubens 95 — 3. Die Bedeutung der Thematisierung von πίστις und πιστεύειν im Markusevangelium 98 — 4. 'Nachfolge' im Markusevangelium 103 —
   5. Zusammenfassung 106.

ADELA YARBRO COLLINS, Establishing the Text: Mark 1:1 . . . . . . . . . . . . . . . . .111
   1. Introduction 111 — 2. The Readings 112 — 3. The Source-Variants 114 —
   4. External Evidence 117 — 5. Internal Evidence 121 — 6. Conclusion 125.

Lucien Legrand, The "Visitation" in Context . . . . . . . . . . . . . . . . . . . . . . .129
    1. The Immediate Context 129 — 2. An Integrated Structure (Luke 1:26-56) 132 —
    3. General Structure of Luke 1-2 137 — 4. The General Context of Luke-Acts 141.

Hartwig Thyen, Noch einmal: Johannes 21 und "der Jünger, den Jesus
    liebte". . . . . . . . . . . . . . . . . . . . . . . . . . . . . . . . . . . . . . . . . . .147
    1. Ein Konsensus wankt 147 — 2. Die Funktion von Joh 20,30f. 148 — 3. Petrus
    und der geliebte Jünger in Joh 21 155 — 4. Struktur und Intention von Joh 21 166
    — 5. Der geliebte Jünger als der ideale Evangelist 170.

Ernst Baasland, Rhetorischer Kontext in Apg 15,13-21. Statuslehre und
    die Actareden . . . . . . . . . . . . . . . . . . . . . . . . . . . . . . . . . . . . . .191
    1. Einleitung 191 — 2. Apg 15,13-21 und die Kontexte 193 — 3. Apg 15,13ff. und
    die Statuslehre 196 — 4. Die Stasis im erzählten Kontext 200 — 5. Exegetisches zum
    Text Apg 15,13-21 205 — 6. Zusammenfassung 220.

Jacob Jervell, Das Aposteldekret in der lukanischen Theologie . . . . . . . . . . . . .227
    1. Wozu das Dekret? 227 — 2. Das Dekret in der Komposition 229 — 3. Die Kon-
    texte 231 — 4. Apg 10-11 und 15 232 — 5. Das Dekret, das Gesetz, und die luka-
    nische Theologie 235.

Andreas Lindemann, Die Christuspredigt des Paulus in Athen
    (Act 17,16-33) . . . . . . . . . . . . . . . . . . . . . . . . . . . . . . . . . . . . . .245

Karl-Gustav Sandelin, 'Do Not Be Idolaters!' (1 Cor 10:7). . . . . . . . . . . . . .257
    1. The Problem 257 — 2. Analysis of 1 Cor 10:1-10 262 — 3. Paul's Utilization of
    the Pre-Pauline Injunction. 266 — 4. Conclusion 271.

Jan Lambrecht, S.J., The Most Eminent Way: A Study of 1 Corin-
    thians 13 . . . . . . . . . . . . . . . . . . . . . . . . . . . . . . . . . . . . . . . . .275
    1. Introductory Remarks 275 — 2. Text and Context 276 — 3. A Reading of
    1 Corinthians 13 283 — 4. Eschatology? 292.

Folker Siegert, Die Makrosyntax des Hebräerbriefs . . . . . . . . . . . . . . . . . . .305
    1. Einleitung 305 — 2. Gliederung des Hebräerbriefs 307 — 3. Konklusion 314.

# Section B

## Inter-Textual Relations

Nils A. Dahl, Benediction and Congratulation . . . . . . . . . . . . . . . . . . . . . . .319
    1. Introduction 319 — 2. Congratulatory and other Benedictions in the Hebrew
    Scriptures 321 — 3. Conclusions and Outlook 328.

George W. E. Nickelsburg, Scripture in *1 Enoch* and *1 Enoch* as
    Scripture . . . . . . . . . . . . . . . . . . . . . . . . . . . . . . . . . . . . . . . . .333
    1. Introduction 333 — 2. Scripture in 1 Enoch 334 — 3. 1 Enoch as Scripture 343 —
    4. Some Implications 350.

BIRGER A. PEARSON, *1 Enoch* in the Apocryphon of John . . . . . . . . . . . . . . . . . .355
    1. Introduction 355 — 2. *1 Enoch* 356 — 3. The Apocryphon of John 359 —
    4. Intertextuality 360 — 5. Conclusions 364.

PEDER BORGEN, Man's Sovereignty over Animals and Nature According to
    Philo of Alexandria. . . . . . . . . . . . . . . . . . . . . . . . . . . . . . . . . . . . . . . . . .369
    1. The Problem of Method 369 — 2. The Interpretation of Gen 1:26/28 in *Op.* 83-84
    372 — 3. The Actual Sovereignty 375 — 4. Jewish Criteria in a "Greek" Debate 376 —
    5. Dominion over the created world in general 377 — 6. Greed, Idolatry and Vices
    Now 379 — 7. Conditioned Eschatological Realization 381 — 8. Cosmos, Humanity
    and Israel 384 — 9. Conclusion 387.

MICHAEL GOULDER, The Phasing of the Future . . . . . . . . . . . . . . . . . . . . . . .391
    1. The Phasing Movement among the Paulines 391 — 2. Mark 13 397 — 3. The Apo-
    calypse 402.

PETR POKORNÝ, Die Bedeutung des Markusevangeliums für die Entstehung
    der christlichen Bibel . . . . . . . . . . . . . . . . . . . . . . . . . . . . . . . . . . . . . . . .409
    1. Markus als Gründer einer neuen literarischen (Unter)Gattung 409 — 2. Die durch
    spätere Tradition beeinflußte Deutung seiner Leistung 410 — 3. Die kritische Beur-
    teilung der Rolle des Markusevangeliums als einer grundsätzlichen Umdeutung der
    Jesus-Traditionen 411 — 4. Markus und die älteren christologischen Formeln 413
    — 5. Markus und die Passionsgeschichte 414 — 6. Das Messiasgeheimnis und die
    Gleichnisse bei Markus 416 — 7. Die erste Zwischenbilanz 417 — 8. Markus und
    die Logienquelle (Q) 418 — 9. Die zweite Zwischenbilanz 420 — 10. Der narrative
    Rahmen und seine theologische Bedeutung 421 — 11. Die Folgen für die Entstehung
    der Idee eines christlichen Kanons 423.

HENDRIKUS W. BOERS, A Context for Interpreting Paul . . . . . . . . . . . . . . . . .429
    1. Introduction 429 — 2. The Problem of the Center of Paul's Thought 429 —
    3. Context in the Interpretation of Texts 431 — 4. The Problem with Justification
    by Faith as the Center for Understanding Paul 433 — 5. The Question of a Structure
    of Convictions as the Foundation of Paul's Thought 436 — 6. Methodological Back-
    ground 437 — 7. Justification of the Gentiles as the Interpretive Center of Galatians
    and Romans 439 — 8. In Search of an Interpretive Context for Paul 442 — 9. Pro-
    posed Method 444 — 10. A Structure which Comes to Expression as the Negation
    of Human Distinctions in Christ 444 — 11. The Function of Words from the Stem
    πιστ- in Paul's Thought 449.

JAMES D. G. DUNN, Was Paul Against the Law? The Law in Galatians and
    Romans: A Test-Case of Text in Context . . . . . . . . . . . . . . . . . . . . . . . . . .455
    1. Introduction 455 — 2. The Law in Galatians 457 — 3. The Law in Romans 465 —
    4. Conclusion 471.

TROELS ENGBERG-PEDERSEN, Galatians in Romans 5-8 and Paul's
    Construction of the Identity of Christ Believers . . . . . . . . . . . . . . . . . . . . .477
    1. Two Issues 477 — 2. Theology and Ethics 477 — 3. Romans 5-8 — The Structure
    479 — 4. Romans 5-8 — The Theme 482 — 5. Paul's Writing of Romans 485 —
    6. Galatians in Romans 6:1-8:13 487 — 7. Galatians in Romans 5:1-11 and 8:14-39
    489 — 8. Galatians in Romans 5-8 — The Baptism Cluster 492 — 9. Romans 5-8
    Within the Letter as a Whole 493 — 10. Net Results 494.

Hans Dieter Betz, Paul's "Second Presence" in Colossians. . . . . . . . . . . . . . .507
1. Introduction 507 — 2. Goethe's Concept of "Second Presence" 508 —
3. Epistolary Formulae in Paul's Letters 510 — 4. A Pauline Formula in
Colossians 512 — 5. Paul's Literary Portrait 515 — 6. Conclusion 517.

Bruce C. Johanson, 1 Thessalonians 2:15-16: Prophetic Woe-Oracle
with ἔφθασεν as Proleptic Aorist . . . . . . . . . . . . . . . . . . . . . .519
1. Introductory 519 — 2. Summary and Critique of Some Important Options of
Interpretation Regarding ἔφθασεν 521 — 3. Preliminary Motivations for Investigating
ἔφθασεν as a Proleptic Aorist 522 — 4. The Woe-Oracle as a Prophetic Form Mediated
by Sacred Text 525 — 5. The Woe-Oracular Character of 1 Thessalonians 2:15-16 528
— 6. Ἔφθασεν as a Proleptic Aorist 529 — 7. Summary and Conclusion 531.

Wiard Popkes, James and Paraenesis, Reconsidered . . . . . . . . . . . . . . . . . .535
1. The Heritage of Martin Dibelius 535 — 2. Research on Paraenesis 537 —
3. Characteristics of Paraenesis 543 — 4. Observations in James 546 —
5. Consequences 547.

# Part II

## Biblical Texts in Their Situational Contexts

# Section C

## Biblical Texts and Their Historical Background

Joseph A. Fitzmyer, The Palestinian Background of "Son of God" as a
Title for Jesus . . . . . . . . . . . . . . . . . . . . . . . . . . . . . . . .567
1. The Problem 567 — 2. Old Testament Data Bearing on the Title "Son of God" 569
— 3. The New Palestinian Jewish Material 571 — 4. The Implications of the New
Material for Various New Testament Passages 573.

John J. Collins, Asking for the Meaning of a Fragmentary Qumran Text.
The Referential Background of 4QAaron A . . . . . . . . . . . . . . . . . . . . .579
1. Introduction 579 — 2. The Suffering Servant in Isaiah 581 — 3. The Servant
in Pre-Christian Judaism 582 — 4. The Text from Qumran 583 — 5. A Sectarian
Background 586 — 6. Conclusion 588.

Lars Rydbeck, ΕΥΣΕΒΕΙΑΝ ΕΔΕΙΞΕΝ ΤΟΙΣ ΑΝΘΡΩΠΟΙΣ.
The Significance of the Bilingual Asoka Inscription for New Testament
Philology and for Research into the Notion of Hellenism. . . . . . . . . . . . . . .591
1. Introductory Remarks 591 — 2. The Greek-Aramaic Inscription of Asoka from
Kandahar (Afghanistan) 592 — 3. The Greek Portion of the Inscription of Asoka 593
— 4. Commentary on the Inscription 594.

SEÁN FREYNE, Jesus and the Urban Culture of Galilee......................597
1. Introduction 597 — 2. Galilean Regional Geography and Jesus 600 — 3. The Role
of Sepphoris and Tiberias 604 — 4. Jesus in Galilee 610 — 5. Conclusion 619.

EDVIN LARSSON, The Resurrection of Jesus and the Rise of Christology........623
1. Jesus and Christology: Continuity or Discontinuity? 623 — 2. The Resurrection
of Jesus 628 — 3. The Resurrection of Jesus and the Rise of Christology 632 —
4. Christ as Preexistent Co-creator 639 — 5. Some Concluding Remarks 640.

MOGENS MÜLLER, The Hidden Context. Some Observations to the
Concept of the New Covenant in the New Testament ....................649
1. "The Unparallelled Discovery" 649 — 2. The Congregation as the Omnipresent
Context 651 — 3. The Impact of the New Covenant 653.

ARLAND J. HULTGREN, Liturgy and Literature: The Liturgical Factor in
Matthew's Literary and Communicative Art..........................659
1. Introductory Remarks 659 — 2. Liturgically Formed Materials 660 —
3. Literary and Communicative Functions 666 — 4. Closing Remarks 670.

RENÉ KIEFFER, Traditions juives selon Mc 7,1-23 ........................675
1. Introduction 675 — 2. L'état synoptique de notre texte 675 — 3. Le texte
de Marc 678 — 4. Quelques réflexions herméneutiques 685.

GERD THEISSEN, Urchristlicher Liebeskommunismus. Zum 'Sitz im Leben'
des Topos ἄπαντα κοινά in Apg 2,44 und 4,32.......................689
1. Der Stand der Diskussion 689 — 2. Das Bild der Apostelgeschichte 693 —
3. Vier Argumente historischer Skepsis 696 — 4. Versuch einer neuen Lösung 706.

GEORG STRECKER†/TORSTEN NOLTING, Der vorchristliche Paulus.
Überlegungen zum biographischen Kontext biblischer Überlieferung
— zugleich eine Antwort an Martin Hengel..........................713
1. Einleitung 713 — 2. Die Position Martin Hengels 714 — 3. Die neutestamentlichen
Notizen über den vorchristlichen Paulus. Tarsos oder Jerusalem 718 — 4. Diasporapharisäer und Gelehrtenschüler 732 — 5. Folgerungen: Der vorchristliche Paulus 737.

HEIKKI RÄISÄNEN, Romans 9-11 and the "History of Early Christian
Religion" ....................................................743
1. Introduction 743 — 2. On the Early Reception of Romans 9-11 744 — 3. The Place
of Romans 9-11 in Modern "New Testament Theologies" 745 — 4. A Brief Analysis of
Romans 9-11 748 — 5. Paul's Theological and Social Problems as the Background of
Romans 9-11 752 — 6. Romans 9-11 in a History of Early Christian Religion 756 —
7. On the History of Influence 758 — 8. Toward a Personal Appreciation 760.

BENGT HOLMBERG, Paul and Commensality...........................767
1. Introduction 767 — 2. Commensality Decoded 768 — 3. Commensality
Delimited 771 — 4. Commensality Demanded 778.

JARL ULRICHSEN, Die Auferstehungsleugner in Korinth: Was meinten sie
eigentlich? .................................................781
1. Das exegetische Problem 781 — 2. Das methodische Problem 783 — 3. Das Material
784 — 4. Kritische Beurteilung der Lösungsvorschläge 788 — 5. Zusammenfassung 797.

WAYNE A. MEEKS, The Temporary Reign of the Son: 1 Cor 15:23-28 . . . . . . . . .801

ABRAHAM J. MALHERBE, Paul's Self-Sufficiency (Philippians 4:11) . . . . . . . . . . . . .813
1. Introduction 813 — 2. Friendship Language in Philippians 814 — 3. Friendship
Language in Philippians 4:10-20 815 — 4. A More General View of Αὐτάρκεια 818
— 5. Friendship and Self-Sufficiency 821 — 6. Philippians 4 822.

BIRGER OLSSON, A Social-Scientific Criticism of 1 Peter . . . . . . . . . . . . . . . . . .827
1. Introductory Remarks 827 — 2. A Sociological Exegesis 828 — 3. A Periphrastic
Outline of 1 Peter 832 — 4. Theory-Bound Observations and Overinterpretations 836
— 5. The Role of the Literary Dimension 840 — 6. The Evaluation of the Analysis 1990
842 — 7. The New Subdiscipline 1993 844.

EINAR THOMASSEN, Λόγος ἀπὸ σιγῆς προελθών (Ignatius, _Mag._ 8:2) . . . . . . . . .847
1. Introduction 847 — 2. Traditio-historical Elements 849 — 3. The Context of
the Theme in Ignatius 857.

# SECTION D

## HISTORY OF INTERPRETATION AND PRESENT-DAY HERMENEUTICS

FRANÇOIS BOVON, Jesus' Missionary Speech as Interpreted in the Patristic
Commentaries and the Apocryphal Narratives . . . . . . . . . . . . . . . . . . . . . . . .871
1. Introduction 871 — 2. The Patristic Commentators 872 — 3. The Apocryphal
Narratives 875 — 4. The Comparability of the Patristic Interpretations and the
Apocryphal Narratives 880 — 5. Conclusion 884.

TORD FORNBERG, God, the Fathers, and the Prophets. The Use of Heb 1:1
in Recent Theology of Religions . . . . . . . . . . . . . . . . . . . . . . . . . . . . . . . .887
1. Introduction 887 — 2. The History of Interpretation 887 — 3. Heb 1:1 in Modern
Indian Catholicism 890 — 4. The Use of Heb 1:1 by the Vatican 893 — 5. Additional
Texts in Hebrews 894 — 6. Evaluation and Conclusions 895.

HANS HÜBNER, Eine hermeneutisch unverzichtbare Unterscheidung:
Vetus Testamentum und Vetus Testamentum in Novo receptum . . . . . . . . . . .901
1. Die Trias "historisch – theologisch – hermeneutisch" 901 — 2. Contra und pro:
Die theologisch und historisch eigenständige Größe "Vetus Testamentum in Novo
receptum" 902 — 3. Geschichtlicher Horizont und Wirklichkeitsverständnis 906.

HARALD RIESENFELD, A Basic Code in the New Testament . . . . . . . . . . . . . . . . .911

WILHELM WUELLNER, Death and Rebirth of Rhetoric in Late Twentieth
Century Biblical Exegesis . . . . . . . . . . . . . . . . . . . . . . . . . . . . . . . . . . . .917
1. Introduction 917 — 2. Rhetoric's Demise in Modern Biblical Interpretation 918 —
3. Rhetoric's Rebirth in Late 20th Century Biblical Interpretation 919 — 4. Assessment and Outlook 922.

PETER LAMPE, Identification with Christ. A Psychological View of Pauline
Theology . . . . . . . . . . . . . . . . . . . . . . . . . . . . . . . . . . . . . . . . . . . . . . . .931
1. Introduction 931 — 2. Soteriologically Oriented Statements 932 — 3. The Ethically-
Oriented Chain of Statements: Identification as Basis for a New Christian Life Style 933
— 4. Conclusion 941.

BERNARD LATEGAN, The Function of Biblical Texts in a Modern Situational
Context . . . . . . . . . . . . . . . . . . . . . . . . . . . . . . . . . . . . . . . . . . . . . . . . .945
1. Introduction 945 — 2. The Variables in Theological Discourse 947 — 3. Addressing
the Third Public in the South African Context 951 — 4. Proposal for an Interactive,
Constructive Mode of Theological Discourse in the Public Arena 955.

THOR STRANDENÆS, John 2:4 in a Chinese Cultural Context: Unnecessary
Stumbling Block for Filial Piety? . . . . . . . . . . . . . . . . . . . . . . . . . . . . .959
1. Necessary and Unnecessary Stumbling Blocks in the New Testament 959 —
2. Τί ἐμοὶ καὶ σοί, γύναι; οὔπω ἥκει ἡ ὥρα μου — in Chinese and in Greek 963
— 3. Γύναι 965 — 4. Τί ἐμοὶ καὶ σοί, γύναι... 968 — 5. Οὔπω ἥκει ἡ ὥρα μου 973
— 6. Conclusion 974.

WOLFGANG SCHENK, Römer 13, 'Obrigkeit' und 'Kirche im Sozialismus' . . . . . . .979
1. Die Christenheit im Deutschland des 'Dritten Reiches' 980 — 2. Die Christenheit
im Deutschland der 'Diktatur des Proletariats' 984 — 3. Konsequenzen 992.

JOSEPH PATHRAPANKAL, Apostolic Commitment and "Remembering
the Poor". A Study in Gal 2:10 . . . . . . . . . . . . . . . . . . . . . . . . . . . . . . .1001
1. Introduction 1001 — 2. The Context of Gal 2:10 1004 — 3. The Request made
by the 'Pillars' (Gal 2:10a) 1004 — 4. Paul's Commitment to the Cause of the Poor
(Gal 2:10b) 1009 — 5. Paul's Anxiety about the Destiny of the Relief Fund 1012 —
6. The Message of Gal 2:10 1014.

TORD FORNBERG, Selected Bibliography—Lars Hartman . . . . . . . . . . . . . . . . .1019

Index of Passages (Selective) . . . . . . . . . . . . . . . . . . . . . . . . . . . . . . . . .1029

# Contributors

Bertil Albrektson
Bibelkommissionen
Åsgränd 1
S–753 10 Uppsala, Sweden

Ernst Baasland
The Free Faculty of Theology
Gydas vei 4
N–0363 Oslo, Norway

Hans Dieter Betz
The Divinity School
Swift Hall
The University of Chicago
Chicago, IL 60637, USA

Hendrikus W. Boers
Candler School of Theology
Emory University
Atlanta, GA 30322, USA

Peder Borgen
University of Trondheim
Department of Religious Studies
N–7055 Dragvoll–Trondheim, Norway

François Bovon
Harvard University
The Divinity School
45 Francis Avenue
Cambridge, MA 02138, USA

Adela Yarbro Collins
The Divinity School
Swift Hall
University of Chicago
Chicago, IL 60637, USA

John J. Collins
The Divinity School
Swift Hall
University of Chicago
Chicago, IL 60637, USA

Nils A. Dahl
Rektorhaugen 17
N-0876 Oslo, Norway

James D. G. Dunn
Department of Theology
Abbey House, Palace Green
Durham DH1 3RS, England

Troels Engberg-Pedersen
University of Copenhagen
Institute of Biblical Exegesis
Købmagergade 46
DK–1150 Copenhagen K, Denmark

Joseph A. Fitzmyer, S.J.
Jesuit Community
Georgetown University
37th & O Streets, NW
Washington, DC 20057, USA

*Tord Fornberg*
University of Uppsala
Department of Theology
Box 1604
S–751 46 Uppsala, Sweden

*Seán Freyne*
School of Hebrew,
Biblical and Theological Studies
University of Dublin
Trinity College
Dublin 2, Ireland

*Michael Goulder*
University of Birmingham
P. O. Box 363
Birmingham B15 2TT, England

*Donald A. Hagner*
Fuller Theological Seminary
135 North Oakland Avenue
Pasadena, CA 91182, USA

*David Hellholm*
University of Oslo
Institute for Biblical Studies
P. O. Box 1023, Blindern
N–0315 Oslo, Norway

*Bengt Holmberg*
University of Lund
Department of Theology
Allhelgona Kyrkogata 8
S–223 62 Lund, Sweden

*Hans Hübner*
Georg-August-Universität Göttingen
Platz der Göttinger Sieben 2
D–37073 Göttingen, Germany

*Arland J. Hultgren*
Luther Seminary
2481 Como Avenue
St. Paul, MN 55108, USA

*Jacob Jervell*
Sæterstoa
N–2150 Årnes, Norway

*Bruce C. Johanson*
1030 Highland Park Drive
College Place
Walla Walla, WA 99324, USA

*René Kieffer*
University of Uppsala
Department of Theology
Box 1604
S–751 46 Uppsala, Sweden

*Jan Lambrecht S.J.*
Minderbroedersstraat 11
B–3000 Leuven, Belgium

*Peter Lampe*
Theologische Fakultät
Christian-Albrechts-Universität
Leibniz-Straße N50a
D–24118 Kiel, Germany

*Edvin Larsson*
Tiundagatan 41
S–752 30 Uppsala, Sweden

*Bernard Lategan*
University of Stellenbosch
Faculty of Arts
Stellenbosch 7600, RSA

*Lucien Legrand*
St. Peter's Pontifical Seminary
Malleswaram West P.O.
Bangalore 560 055, India

*Andreas Lindemann*
Kirchliche Hochschule Bethel
Postfach 13 01 40
D–33544 Bielefeld, Germany

*Abraham J. Malherbe*
Yale Divinity School
409 Prospect Street
New Haven, CT 06511-2167, USA

*Wayne A. Meeks*
Yale University
Department of Religious Studies
P. O. Box 2160 Yale Station
New Haven, CT 06520-2160, USA

*Mogens Müller*
University of Copenhagen
Institute of Biblical Exegesis
Købmagergade 46
DK–1150 Copenhagen K, Denmark

*George W. E. Nickelsburg*
School of Religion
Gilmore Hall, University of Iowa
Iowa City, IA 52240, USA

*Torsten Nolting*
Georg-August-Universität Göttingen
Platz der Göttinger Sieben 2
D–37073 Göttingen, Germany

*Birger Olsson*
University of Lund
Department of Theology
Allhelgona Kyrkogata 8
S–223 62 Lund, Sweden

*Joseph Pathrapankal, C.M.I.*
Dharmaram Pontifical Institute
Bangalore 560 029, India

*Birger Pearson*
27345 E. Vine Avenue
Escalon, CA 95320, USA

*Petr Pokorný*
Charles University
The Protestant Theological Faculty
Jungmannova 9
P. O. Box 529
CZ–115 55 Praha 1, Czech Republic

*Wiard Popkes*
Theologisches Seminar des Bundes
Evangelisch-Freikirchlicher Gemein-
den in Deutschland K.d.ö.R. in
Hamburg-Horn
Rennbahnstraße 115
D–22111 Hamburg, Germany

*Heikki Räisänen*
Department of Biblical Exegetics
P.O. Box 37
FIN-00014 University of Helsinki
Finland

*Harald Riesenfeld*
University of Uppsala
Department of Theology
Box 1604
S–751 46 Uppsala, Sweden

*Lars Rydbeck*
University of Lund
Department of Theology
Allhelgona Kyrkogata 8
S–223 62 Lund, Sweden

*Karl-Gustav Sandelin*
Åbo Akademi
Biskopsgatan 16
FIN–20500 Åbo, Finland

*Wolfgang Schenk*
Mittelstraße 3
D–66125 Saarbrücken, Germany

*Folker Siegert*
Université de Neuchâtel
Faculté de théologie
Faubourg de l'Hôpital 41
CH–2000 Neuchâtel, Switzerland

*Thor Strandenæs*
Misjonshøgskolen
Misjonsveien 34
N–4024 Stavanger, Norway

*Georg Strecker* †

*Gerd Theißen*
Ruprecht-Karls-Universität
Wissenschaftl.-Theologisches Seminar
Kisselgasse 1
D–69117 Heidelberg, Germany

*Einar Thomassen*
University of Bergen
Department of Religious Studies
Sydnesplass 9
N–5007 Bergen, Norway

*Hartwig Thyen*
Adalbert-Seifriz-Straße 16
D–69151 Neckargemünd, Germany

*Jarl Ulrichsen*
University of Trondheim
Department of Religious Studies
N–7055 Dragvoll–Trondheim, Norway

*François Vouga*
Kirchliche Hochschule Bethel
Postfach 13 01 40
D–33544 Bielefeld, Germany

*Wilhelm Wuellner*
Pacific School of Religion
1798 Scenic Avenue
Berkeley, CA 94709, USA

# Abbreviations

## 1. Abbreviations of Biblical Books et cetera

For the abbreviations of names for Biblical Books with the Apocrypha, Pseudepigraphical and Early Patristic Books, Dead Sea Scrolls and related texts, Other Jewish texts, and Nag Hammadi texts the following two systems have been utilized:

(a) The system of the *Journal of Biblical Literature (JBL): Instructions for Contributors* has been adopted for the essays in *English*;

(b) The system of the *Theologische Realenzyklopädie (TRE): Abkürzungsverzeichnis*, ed. S. Schwertner, 2nd edition, Berlin/New York: de Gruyter 1994 has been used for the essays in *German*.

## 2. Abbreviations of Periodicals and Series

For the abbreviations of Periodicals, Reference Works, Series et cetera the system of the *TRE* has been adopted for *all essays*; for the sake of convenience these are listed below. In those cases where no abbreviations are found in *TRE* the full titles have been given in the bibliographies.

| | |
|---|---|
| AAAbo | Acta Academiae Aboensis |
| *AAS* | *Acta Apostolicae Sedis* |
| AASF | Annales Academiae Scientiarum Fennicae |
| *ABR* | *Australian biblical review* |
| AGJU | Arbeiten zur Geschichte des antiken Judentums und des Urchristentums |
| AGWG.PH | Abhandlungen der (K.) Gesellschaft der Wissenschaften zu Göttingen. Philologisch–historische Klasse |
| AHAW.PH | Abhandlungen der Heidelberger Akademie der Wissenschaften. Philologisch–historische Klasse |
| *AJBI* | *Annual of the Japanese Biblical Institute* |
| *AJP* | *American journal of philology* |
| *AJTh* | *Asia journal of theology* |
| AMNSU | Arbeiten und Mitteilungen aus dem Neutestamentlichen Seminar zu Uppsala |

| AnASU | Annales Academiae R. Scientiarum Upsaliensis |
| AnBib | Analecta biblica |
| AncB | Anchor Bible |
| *ARNW* | *Aufstieg und Niedergang der römischen Welt* |
| ARW | Archiv für Religionswissenschaft |
| *ASeign* | *Assemblées du Seigneur* |
| ASNU | Acta Seminarii Neotestamentici Upsaliensis |
| ATD | Das Alte Testament Deutsch |
| AThANT | Abhandlungen zur Theologie des Alten und Neuen Testaments |
| *ATJ* | *Africa theological journal* |
| AuA | Antike und Abendland |
| AUU | Acta Universitatis Upsaliensis |
| *BASOR* | *Bulletin of the American Schools of Oriental Research* |
| BBB | Bonner biblische Beiträge |
| *BCSBS* | *Bulletin of the Canadian Society of Biblical Studies* |
| *BeO* | *Bibbia e oriente* |
| BET | Beiträge zur biblischen Exegese und Theologie |
| BEThL | Bibliotheca Ephemeridum theologicarum Lovaniensium |
| BEvTh | Beiträge zur evangelischen Theologie |
| BFChTh | Beiträge zur Förderung christlicher Theologie |
| BHTh | Beiträge zur historischen Theologie |
| BGBE | Beiträge zur Geschichte biblischer Exegese |
| *Bib.* | *Biblica* |
| *BiTr* | *Bible Translator* |
| *BJRL* | *Bulletin of the John Rylands Library* |
| BK | Biblischer Kommentar |
| BN | Biblische Notizen |
| BNTC | Black's New Testament Commentaries |
| *BR* | *Biblical research* |
| *BS* | *Bibliotheca sacra* |
| *BSNC* | *Bulletin. Secretariatus pro Non Christianis* |
| *BSNTS* | *Bulletin of the Studiorum Novi Testamenti Societas* |
| *BTB* | *Biblical theology bulletin* |
| *BTN* | *Bibliotheca theologica Norvegica* |
| BU | Biblische Untersuchungen |
| BWANT | Beiträge zur Wissenschaft vom Alten und Neuen Testament |
| *BZ* | *Biblische Zeitschrift* |
| BZAW | Beihefte zur Zeitschrift für die alttestamentliche Wissenschaft |
| BZNW | Beihefte zur Zeitschrift für die neutestamentliche Wissenschaft |

| | |
|---|---|
| CB.NT | Coniectanea biblica. New Testament series |
| CB.OT | —. Old Testament series |
| *CBG* | *Collationes Brugenses et Gandavenses* |
| *CBQ* | *Catholic biblical quarterly* |
| CBQ.MS | —. Monograph series |
| CJAn | Christianity and Judaism in antiquity |
| CNT | Coniectanea neotestamentica |
| CNT(N) | Commentaire du Nouveau Testament. Neuchâtel |
| *CoTh* | *Collectanea theologica* |
| CRI | Compendia rerum Iudaicarum ad novum testamentum |
| *CQR* | *Church quarterly review* |
| *CTJ* | *Calvin theological journal* |
| | |
| *DTT* | *Dansk teologisk tidsskrift* |
| | |
| EdF | Erträge der Forschung |
| *EeV* | *Esprit et vie* |
| *EHPhR* | *Études d'histoire et de philosophie religieuses* |
| EHS | Einleitung in die Heilige Schrift |
| EKK | Evangelisch–katholischer Kommentar zum Neuen Testament |
| *EKL* | *Evangelisches Kirchenlexikon* |
| *ET* | *Expository times* |
| EtB | Études bibliques |
| *EThL* | *Ephemerides theologicae Lovanienses* |
| EThS | Erfurter theologische Schriften |
| *EuA* | *Erbe und Auftrag* |
| *EvQ* | *Evangelical quarterly* |
| *EvTh* | *Evangelische Theologie* |
| *EWNT* | *Exegetisches Wörterbuch zum NT* |
| | |
| FBESG | Forschungen und Berichte der Evangelischen Studiengemeinschaft |
| FKDG | Forschungen zur Kirchen– und Dogmengeschichte |
| FRLANT | Forschungen zur Religion und Literatur des Alten und Neuen Testaments |
| *FrRu* | *Freiburger Rundbrief* |
| FzB | Forschung zur Bibel |
| fzb | Forschungen zur Bibel |
| | |
| GCS | Die griechischen christlichen Schriftsteller der ersten drei Jahrhunderte |

| GLB | de Gruyter Lehrbuch |
| GNT | Grundrisse zum Neuen Testament |
| *GPM* | *Göttinger Predigtmeditationen* |
| GTA | Göttinger theologische Arbeiten |
| GTBS | Gütersloher Taschenbücher Siebenstern |
| *GThT* | *Gereformeerd Theologische Tijdschrift* |

| HAT | Handbuch zum Alten Testament |
| HDR | Harvard dissertations in religion |
| *Hesp.* | *Hesperia* |
| *HibJ* | *Hibbert journal* |
| HK | Handkommentar zum Alten Testament |
| HNT | Handbuch zum Neuen Testament |
| HThK | Herders theologischer Kommentar zum Neuen Testament |
| HThR | Harvard theological review |
| HThS | Harvard theological studies |
| *HTS* | *Hervormde teologiese studies* |
| *HUCA* | *Hebrew Union College annual* |
| HUTh | Hermeneutische Untersuchungen zur Theologie |
| HWP | Historisches Wörterbuch der Philosophie |

| ICC | International critical commentary |
| *IDB* | *The Interpreter's dictionary of the Bible* |
| *IEJ* | *Israel exploration journal* |
| *IntB* | *The Interpreter's Bible* |
| *Interp.* | *Interpretation* |
| *ITS* | *Indian theological studies* |

| *JAAR* | *Journal of the American Academy of Religion* |
| *JAC* | *Jahrbuch für Antike und Christentum* |
| *JAOS* | *Journal of the American Oriental Society* |
| *JBL* | *Journal of biblical literature* |
| *JBR* | *Journal of Bible and religion* |
| *JBTh* | *Jahrbuch für biblische Theologie* |
| *JEH* | *Journal of ecclesiastical history* |
| *JETS* | *Journal of the Evangelical Theological Society* |
| *JJS* | *Journal of Jewish studies* |
| *JP* | *Journal of philology* |
| *JQR* | *Jewish quarterly review* |
| *JR* | *Journal of religion* |
| *JRT* | *Journal of religious thought* |

| | |
|---|---|
| JSHRZ | Jüdische Schriften aus hellenistisch–römischer Zeit |
| *JSJ* | *Journal for the study of Judaism in the Persian, Hellenistic and Roman period* |
| *JSNT* | *Journal for the study of the New Testament* |
| JSNT.S | —. Supplement series |
| JSOT.S | Journal for the Study of the Old Testament. Supplement series |
| JSPE.S | Journal for the study of the pseudepigrapha. Supplement series |
| *JThS* | *Journal of theological studies* |
| *JTSA* | *Journal of theology for Southern Africa* |
| JudChr | Judaica and Christiana |
| | |
| KAT | Kommentar zum Alten Testament |
| KAV | Kommentar zu den apostolischen Vätern |
| KEK | Kritisch–exegetischer Kommentar über das Neue Testament |
| KHC | Kurzer Hand–Commentar zum Alten Testament |
| *KiZ* | *Kirche in der Zeit* |
| KNT | Kommentar zum Neuen Testament |
| KuD | Kerygma und Dogma |
| KVR | Kleine Vandenhoeck–Reihe |
| | |
| *LAW* | *Lexikon der Alten Welt* |
| LCC | Library of Christian classics |
| LCL | Loeb classical library |
| LeDiv | Lectio divina |
| *LingBibl* | *Linguistica biblica* |
| *LThK* | *Lexikon für Theologie und Kirche* |
| *LuthQ* | *Lutheran quarterly* |
| | |
| MSS | Münchener Studien zur Sprachwissenschaft |
| MSSNTS | Monograph series. Society for New Testament Studies |
| MThSt | Marburger theologische Studien |
| *MThZ* | *Münchener theologische Zeitschrift* |
| *MySal* | *Mysterium Salutis* |
| | |
| NABPR.SS | National Association of Baptist Professors of Religion. Special studies series |
| NCeB | New Century Bible |
| NEB | Neue Echter Bibel |
| *NedThT* | *Nederlands theologisch tijdschrift* |
| *Neotest.* | *Neotestamentica* |
| *NHS* | *Nag Hammadi Studies* |

NIC            New international commentary
NIGTC          New international Greek Testament commentary
*NKZ*          *Neue kirchliche Zeitschrift*
NLC            New London commentary on the New Testament
*NT*           *Novum Testamentum*
NT.S           —. Supplements
NTA            Neutestamentliche Abhandlungen
*NTAb*         *New Testament Abstracts*
NTCom          New Testament commentaries
NTD            Das Neue Testament Deutsch
NTG            Neue theologische Grundrisse
NTOA           Novum testamentum et orbis antiquus
*NTS*          *New testament studies*
*NTT*          *Norsk teologisk tidsskrift*
NTTS           New Testament tools and studies
*NV*           *Nova et vetera*

OBO            Orbis biblicus et orientalis
ÖTBK           Ökumenischer Taschenbuch–Kommentar zum Neuen Testament
OTL            Old Testament library

*PEQ*          *Palestine exploration quarterly*
PG             Migne, Patrologiae cursus completus. Series Graeca
PNTC           Pelical New testament commentaries
PO             Patrologia orientalis

*QD*           *Quaestiones disputatae*

*RAC*          *Reallexikon für Antike und Christentum*
*RB*           *Revue biblique*
*RdQ*          *Revue de Qumran*
*RE*           *Realencyklopädie für protestantische Theologie und Kirche*
*REJ*          *Revue des études juives*
*RevBib*       *Revista biblica*
*RevSR*        *Revue des sciences religieuses*
*RExp*         *Review and expositor*
*RHR*          *Revue de l'histoire des religions*
RNT            Regensburger Neues Testament
*RoB*          *Religion och bibel*
*RSR*          *Recherches de science religieuse*
*RStR*         *Religious Studies Review*

| | |
|---|---|
| *RThPh* | *Revue de théologie et de philosophie* |
| RVV | Religionsgeschichtliche Versuche und Vorarbeiten |
| | |
| SBB | Stuttgarter biblische Beiträge |
| *SBFLA* | *Studii Biblici Franciscani liber annuus* |
| SBi | Sources bibliques |
| SBL.DS | Society of biblical literature. Dissertation series |
| SBL.MS | —. Monograph series |
| SBL.SBS | —. Sources for biblical studies |
| SBL.SP | —. Seminar papers |
| SBL.TT | —. Texts and translations |
| SBM | Stuttgarter biblische Monographien |
| SBS | Stuttgarter Bibelstudien |
| SBT | Studies in biblical theology |
| *SBTh* | *Studia biblica et theologica* |
| SC | Sources chrétiennes |
| SCHNT | Studia ad corpus Hellenisticum novi testamenti |
| *SEÅ* | *Svensk exegetisk årsbok* |
| SHAW.PH | Sitzungsberichte der Heidelberger Akademie der Wissenschaften. Philosophisch–Historische Klasse |
| SHR | Studies in the history of religions |
| SHVU | Skrifter utgivna av K. Humanistiska Vetenskapssamfundet i Uppsala |
| SJ | Studia judaica |
| *SJTh* | *Scottish journal of theology* |
| SMHVL | Scripta minora. K. Humanistiska Vetenskapssamfundet i Lund |
| SMRT | Studies in medieval and reformation thought |
| SO.S | Symbolae Osloenses. Fasciculus suppletionis |
| SPAW.PH | Sitzungsberichte der Preußischen Akademie der Wissenschaften. Philosophisch–historische Klasse |
| SPIB | Scripta Pontificii Instituti Biblici |
| StANT | Studien zum Alten und Neuen Testament |
| StD | Studies and documents |
| *StEv* | *Studia evangelica* |
| StNT | Studien zum Neuen Testament |
| *StTh* | *Studia theologica* |
| StUNT | Studien zur Umwelt des Neuen Testaments |
| SUC | Schriften des Urchristentums |
| *SvTK* | *Svensk teologisk kvartalskrift* |
| SVTP | Studia in veteris testamenti pseudepigrapha |

| | |
|---|---|
| *SyBU* | *Symbolae biblicae Upsalienses* |
| SWJT | Southwestern journal of theology |
| TANZ | Texte und Arbeiten zum neutestamentlichen Zeitalter |
| TB | Theologische Bücherei |
| TBAW | Tübinger Beiträge zur Altertumswissenschaft |
| *TDNT* | *Theological dictionary of the New Testament* |
| TEH | Theologische Existenz heute |
| ThA | Theologische Arbeiten |
| *ThD* | *Theology Digest* |
| ThDiss | Theologische Dissertationen |
| ThHK | Theologischer Handkommentar zum Neuen Testament |
| *ThLZ* | *Theologische Literaturzeitung* |
| *ThQ* | *Theologische Quartalschrift* |
| *ThR* | *Theologische Rundschau* |
| ThSt(B) | Theologische Studien (ed. K. Barth) |
| *ThStKr* | *Theologische Studien und Kritiken* |
| *ThV* | *Theologische Versuche* |
| ThW | Theologische Wissenschaft |
| *ThWNT* | *Theologisches Wörterbuch zum Neuen Testament* |
| *ThZ* | *Theologische Zeitschrift* |
| TNTC | Tyndale New Testament commentaries |
| *TRE* | *Theologische Realencyklopädie* |
| *TS* | *Theological studies* |
| *TTh* | *Tijdschrift voor theologie* |
| *TThZ* | *Trierer theologische Zeitschrift* |
| *TTK* | *Tidsskrift for teologi og kirke* |
| *TU* | *Texte und Untersuchungen zur Geschichte der altchristlichen Literatur* |
| *TynB* | *Tyndale bulletin* |
| *TZTh* | *Tübinger Zeitschrift für Theologie* |
| | |
| UB | Urban Taschenbücher |
| UBS.MS | United Bible Societies. Monograph series |
| UNT | Untersuchungen zum Neuen Testament |
| UTB | Uni–Taschenbücher |
| | |
| *VF* | *Verkündigung und Forschung* |
| *VigChr* | *Vigiliae Christianae* |
| | |
| WdF | Wege der Forschung |

| WMANT | Wissenschaftliche Monographien zum Alten und Neuen Testament |
| *WuA* | *Wort und Antwort* |
| WUNT | Wissenschaftliche Untersuchungen zum Neuen Testament |
| YCS | Yale classical studies |
| ZAW | Zeitschrift für die alttestamentliche Wissenschaft |
| *ZBK* | *Zürcher Bibelkommentar* |
| *ZDPW* | *Zeitschrift des deutschen Palästina–Vereins* |
| *ZKG* | *Zeitschrift für Kirchengeschichte* |
| *ZKTh* | *Zeitschrift für katholische Theologie* |
| *ZM* | *Zeitschrift für Missionswissenschaft* |
| *ZNW* | *Zeitschrift für die neutestamentliche Wissenschaft* |
| *ZRGG* | *Zeitschrift für Religions– und Geistesgeschichte* |
| *ZThK* | *Zeitschrift für Theologie und Kirche* |

# Part I

## Biblical Texts in Their Textual Contexts

# SECTION A

## INTRA-TEXTUAL RELATIONS

# Ezekiel 30:16 — A Conjecture

## Bertil Albrektson

It has long been recognized that the last words of the Hebrew text of Ezek 30:16 are obscure and probably corrupt. The purpose of the present paper is to suggest a new emendation which involves only a minor change of the consonants of the MT and which makes acceptable sense in the context.

The difficult passage is part of an oracle in which Yahweh threatens to destroy Egypt. His judgement will affect various cities in Egypt. In v. 16 it is said that Yahweh "will set fire to Egypt; Sin (Pelusium?) shall be in great agony; No (Thebes) shall be breached", and the verse ends with the obscure and disputed words ונף צרי יומם, literally "and Noph (Memphis) adversaries of daytime".

Most commentators are agreed that the MT is impossible as it stands. There are, however, exceptions. The construction with an adverb serving as a *nomen rectum* after a *nomen regens* in the construct state has been defended by, for instance, Rosenmüller[1] and Barthélemy[2] with reference to cases like 1 Kgs 2:31 and Prov 26:2, where the word חנם "without cause" is found in a similar position. It is however doubtful if this reference is sufficient to save the wording of the MT. The instances adduced both include חנם, which may indicate that the construction is possible only with this particular word: no case containing an adverb of time like יומם is found in biblical Hebrew. But this is not the most serious objection to the formulation of the MT: the wording is suspect even if one is prepared to accept the construct phrase צרי יומם (in which case it might be preferable to regard יומם as a noun rather than as an adverb—cf. Jer 15:9; 33:20, 25). To make sense, the MT "requires a verb to be supplied".[3] As it now stands, it would seem to mean something like "and Noph (shall be) adversaries of daytime", which is nonsense. It is difficult to avoid the conclusion almost unanimously drawn in the commentaries that the MT is corrupt and must be emended.

---

[1] Rosenmüller 1810, 395.
[2] Barthélemy 1992, 249.
[3] Cooke 1936, 334.

The witness of the ancient versions points in a similar direction; at least they show traces of textual confusion in the Hebrew text at an early stage. Even Barthélemy, a stout defender of the MT, allows for "un éventuel accident textuel".[4] The Septuagint reads καὶ διαχυθήσεται ὕδατα "and waters shall be poured out", which may be an attempt "to give an approximate sense to a slightly changed sequence of consonants" ("einen ungefähren Sinn in eine leicht veränderte Konsonantenfolge zu bringen")[5] and looks more like an awkward effort to handle a difficult text than a testimony to the correct original wording. The Syriac translation has even less to contribute: *wmps thwᵓ lmpwltᵓ* "and Memphis shall become a ruin"—a general phrase which appears to reveal the translator's perplexity rather than his *Vorlage*. Possibly the beginning of v. 17 in the Peshitta, *wᵓyk myᵓ* "and like water", should also be regarded as part of the translation of the disputed Hebrew text; as in the Septuagint the consonantal sequence מים seems to be presupposed instead of יומם in the MT. Both the Vulgate and the Targum appear to reflect a Hebrew text identical with the MT.

Thus the ancient versions do not contribute much to the emendation of the corrupt text; they present no variant which could have serious claims to represent a correct and original reading. The Septuagint, however, and perhaps also the Peshitta, is not without significance as evidence that the Hebrew text was already in disorder at an early stage.

Under such circumstances it is not surprising that a number of conjectures have been suggested. One of the more influential proposals is that of Cornill,[6] ונפרצו חומתיה "and its walls shall be broken down", which is reproduced in the critical apparatus of BHK and BHS and accepted by, among others, Herrmann,[7] Cooke,[8] Fohrer,[9] May,[10] and Eichrodt.[11] This is certainly a possible text, but it involves more rewriting of the consonants than is desirable and so must be considered to have a fairly low probability; Eichrodt rightly characterizes it as a "Geistreiche, aber ganz unsichere Deutung".[12] The editor of Ezekiel in BHK, Bewer, suggests a phrase found in 2 Sam 5:20 and 1 Chr 14:11, כפרץ מים "like a bursting flood". It can claim partial support from the Septuagint but does not appear to fit the context

---

[4] Barthélemy 1992, 249.
[5] Zimmerli 1969, 727.
[6] Cornill 1886, 370f.
[7] Herrmann 1924, 190.
[8] Cooke 1936, 334, 337.
[9] Fohrer 1955, 171f.
[10] May 1956, 231.
[11] Eichrodt 1966, 284.
[12] ibid., n. 8.

particularly well. Smend's proposal[13] keeps closer to the wording of the Septuagint: ונפצו מימם "and its waters will be spread about", but this too seems unsatisfactory from the point of view of content, and, as Cornill[14] observed, the verb פוץ is never used of water (Prov 5:16 is different). G. R. Driver[15] has suggested ומים יפרצון "and the waters shall burst in", which is perhaps more attractive, as it "exactly uses up the letters of the M.T.",[16] but the consonants are redistributed in a way which is not entirely convincing. Still another restoration, also worth considering though perhaps not immediately persuasive, is Wevers'[17] suggestion, offered with due caution and provided with a question-mark, that the original text may have run ונפרץ מוסד/יסוד "and the foundation breached".

More acceptable, perhaps, is the minimal change from צרי to צרו suggested in a version of the Book of Ezekiel published in 1986 as part of the new official Danish translation of the Bible.[18] This emendation results in the rendering "og angriber Nof ved højlys dag", i.e. "and attack Noph in broad daylight". It is not entirely clear to me whether the translators assume the Hebrew verb to be צור I "confine", "besiege", or צור II "show hostility to". The first verb is more common and frequently used about cities, though it is normally construed with a preposition. The choice of Danish equivalent, "angribe", points perhaps to the second alternative, as does the fact that the verb takes a direct object. In both cases, however, the qualification "by day" arouses suspicion: sieges are normally carried on day and night, and it seems rather pointless to specify a threat of attack against the city in this way. A further weakness of the graphically highly attractive Danish solution is its use of the suffix conjugation of the verb: the immediately preceding statements about Sin and No are in the prefix conjugation, and one would have expected the same form to be used here.

The above list of emendations is not exhaustive,[19] but even this limited number may be sufficient to show both that the problem is difficult and that no obvious solution is available. As matters stand, it may be justifiable to suggest yet another restoration of the recalcitrant text.

As the adverb יומם "by day" seems not to fit particularly well in the context, it is perhaps possible to interpret the word instead as the ordinary noun יום "day" with a suffix for 3rd masc. plur., "their day" (as for instance in Ezek 21:34, E.T. v. 29). This

---

[13] Quoted in Bertholet 1897, 158.

[14] Cornill 1886, 371

[15] Driver 1938, 177.

[16] ibid.

[17] Wevers 1969, 165.

[18] Hezekiels Bog 1986, 79, 133.

[19] Some more are listed in Barthélemy 1922, 247.

is a suggestion found in the commentary by Kraetzschmar.[20] What could be said in this connection about the "day" of the inhabitants of Noph? Perhaps that it shall be darkened, an idea which is expressed in v. 18; the passage about the clouds in v. 3 may also be compared. Kraetzschmar looks in this direction and suggests יעוף from a verb עוף II "be dark". The existence of such a verb is however in dispute: the only instance, Job 11:17, is questionable from a text-critical point of view.[21]

But Kraetzschmar's interpretation of יומם and his general understanding of the passage seem worthy of consideration, and a solution may be suggested which retains the advantages of Kraetzschmar's emendation without sharing its weakness. There is a verb with a meaning similar to that of the verb proposed by Kraetzschmar, a verb whose existence is less dubious and whose consonants, moreover, are closer to the letters preserved in the MT. It is the verb צלל III "be shady, grow dark", of the same root as the common noun צל "shadow", "shade". Admittedly the instances in the Old Testament are few. The Qal form is found only once, in Neh 13:19, and the interpretation is a controversial issue. It is possible that צללו in that passage should not be derived from צלל "grow dark" but taken instead as a form of a homonym with the sense "be cleared", "become empty",[22] suggested by its Syriac cognate and by the renderings of the ancient versions. The traditional translation may still, however, be regarded as a serious alternative: "When it began to be dark in the gates of Jerusalem". But if the Qal form in Nehemiah is uncertain, there is a clear case of the Hiphil form found in the very same section of the Book of Ezekiel, in 31:3, where it means "to shadow", "to shade". So the existence of this verbal stem in biblical Hebrew seems secured; at the same time its comparative rarity could explain why it was misrepresented by scribes.

Thus it may be suggested that the original wording of Ezek 30:16 could have been ונף יצל יומם "and Noph, their day grows dark", i.e. "the day of (the inhabitants of) Noph grows dark", with *casus pendens* according to a common syntactical construction.[23] It is hardly a valid argument against the proposed emendation that a similar description of the judgement occurs in v. 18, "At Tehaphnehes the day shall be dark" (reading חשׁך with many Hebrew manuscripts and the ancient versions instead of חשׂך), as the section vv. 13–19 is indeed repetitive:[24] "set fire" is used in v. 14 as well as in v. 16, "execute judgement" both in v. 14 and in v. 19.

This conjecture results in a text which (a) is graphically quite close to the consonants of the MT; (b) makes good sense in the context; (c) adopts a mode of expres-

---

[20] Kraetzschmar 1900, 226.

[21] Cf., e.g., Clines 1989, 256.

[22] Cf. Rudolph 1949, 206f.; Clines 1984, 244; Blenkinsopp 1989, 357f.

[23] Gesenius–Kautzsch–Cowley 1910, §143; Joüon 1923, §156.

[24] See Zimmerli 1969, 734.

sion found elsewhere in this author; and (d) uses words known from other passages in the Book of Ezekiel.

\* \* \*

It is a pleasure to dedicate this short note in appreciation and friendship to Lars Hartman. I need not fear that he will look down on such preoccupation with minor textual details: in his work he has clearly shown that he recognizes the fundamental role of philology for sound exegesis. So I salute him with the wise words of Cornill[25] in the preface to his commentary on Ezekiel 1886: "dass es sich hier nicht um kleinliche Wortklaubereien handelt, sondern dass wir, auch wenn wir dem Buchstaben unsere Mühe und unsere Sorgfalt zuwenden, doch für den Geist schaffen".

## Bibliography

Barthélemy, D. 1992: *Critique textuelle de l'Ancien Testament*. Tome 3. Ézéchiel, Daniel et les 12 Prophètes (Orbis biblicus et orientalis 50/3), Fribourg: Éditions universitaires & Göttingen: Vandenhoeck & Ruprecht 1992.

Bertholet, A. 1897: *Das Buch Hesekiel* (KHC XII), Freiburg i. B., Leipzig & Tübingen: Mohr (Siebeck) 1897.

Blenkinsopp, J. 1989: *Ezra–Nehemiah*. A Commentary (OTL), London: SCM Press 1989.

Clines, D. J. A. 1984: *Ezra, Nehemiah, Esther* (NCeB), Grand Rapids: Eerdmans & London: Marshall, Morgan & Scott 1984.

— 1989: *Job 1–20* (Word Biblical Commentary 17), Dallas: Word Books 1989.

Cooke, G. A. 1936: *A Critical and Exegetical Commentary on the Book of Ezekiel* (ICC), Edinburgh: T. & T. Clark 1936.

Cornill, C. H. 1886: *Das Buch des Propheten Ezechiel*, Leipzig: Hinrichs'sche Buchhandlung 1886.

Driver, G. R. 1938: "Linguistic and textual Problems: Ezekiel", in: *Bib*. 19 (1938) 175–87.

Eichrodt, W. 1966: *Der Prophet Hezekiel*. Kapitel 19–48 (ATD 22/2), Göttingen: Vandenhoeck & Ruprecht 1966.

Fohrer, G. 1955: *Ezechiel* (HAT I:13), Tübingen: Mohr (Siebeck) 1955.

Gesenius–Kautzsch–Cowley 1910: *Gesenius' Hebrew Grammar*, ed. by E. Kautzsch, transl. by A. E. Cowley, 2nd ed., Oxford: Clarendon Press 1910.

Herrmann, J. 1924: *Ezechiel* (KAT XI), Leipzig & Erlangen: Deichertsche Verlagsbuchhandlung Dr. Werner Scholl 1924.

Hezekiels Bog 1986: *Hezekiels Bog*. Det gamle Testamente i ny oversættelse, København: Det danske Bibelselskab 1986.

---

[25] Cornill 1886, V.

Joüon, P. 1923: *Grammaire de l'hébreu biblique*, Rome: Institut biblique pontifical 1923.

Kraetzschmar, R. 1900: *Das Buch Ezechiel* (HK III:3:1), Göttingen: Vandenhoeck & Ruprecht 1900.

May, H. G. 1956: "The Book of Ezechiel. Introduction and Exegesis", in: *IntB* VI, 1956, 39–338.

Rosenmüller, E. F. C. 1810: *Scholia in Vetus Testamentum*, VI:2, Lipsiae: Sumtibus Ioh. Ambros. Barthii 1810.

Rudolph, W. 1949: *Esra und Nehemia samt 3. Esra* (HAT I:20), Tübingen: Mohr (Siebeck) 1949.

Wevers, J. W. 1969: *Ezekiel* (NCeB), London: Oliphants 1969.

Zimmerli, W. 1969: *Ezechiel*. 2. Teilband. Ezechiel 25–48 (BK.AT XIII/2), Neukirchen-Vluyn: Neukirchener Verlag 1969.

# Substitutionelle Gliederungsmerkmale und die Komposition des Matthäusevangeliums

David Hellholm

Bei der Behandlung des Themas werde ich wie folgt vorgehen: *erstens* wird eine kurze Beschreibung einiger an der Textoberfläche erkennbarer und schon öfters beobachteter Strukturelemente im Matthäusevangelium gegeben; *zweitens* werden sprachwissenschaftliche Grundlagenprobleme im Hinblick auf Kompositionsanalysen im allgemeinen diskutiert; *drittens* werden die sog. "substitutionellen Gliederungsmerkmale" im Matthäusevangelium einer eingehenden Analyse unterzogen und *viertens* folgt eine knappe Zusammenfassung der bisherigen Überlegungen.

## 1. Einige Strukturmerkmale an der Textoberfläche des Matthäusevangeliums

### 1.1. Gliederungsmodelle des Matthäusevangeliums

Die Kompositionsanalyse des Matthäusevangeliums ist mit großen Problemen behaftet[1], u.zw. liegt dies z.T. daran, daß der Text selbst unterschiedliche Strukturen aufzuweisen scheint, z.T. aber auch daran, daß die Exegeten, die diesen Text analysieren, nicht nur unterschiedliche Besonderheiten in der Formulierung des Evangelisten bzw. seiner Quellen beobachten, sondern auch daran, daß keine Klarheit darüber zu herrschen scheint, wie die vorhandenen Sachverhalte zu bewerten bzw. einander zuzuordnen sind[2].

In seinem großangelegten Kommentar zum Matthäusevangelium hat Ulrich Luz dankenswerterweise die bisherigen Gliederungsversuche in drei Grundtypen eingeteilt, und ich gebrauche in meinem Referat der Einfachheit halber die von Luz ver-

---

[1] Vgl. U. Luz 1985, 15-28; W. D. Davies/D. C. Allison, Jr. 1988, 58-72; D. A. Hagner 1993, l-liii.

[2] Wie verhält sich z.B. die Funktion der fünf Redekompositionen zu der Funktion der Dreiteilung des Evangeliums? Vgl. hierzu die Diskussion bei D. R. Bauer 1988, 44f., 55, 129ff.

wendeten Benennungen[3], ohne darauf einzugehen, ob sie adequat sind bzw. ob es noch weitere Grundtypen gibt[4].

(1) *Das Modell der fünf Bücher*: Dieses Modell basiert auf den fünf großen Reden in Kap. 5-7, 10, 13, 18, 23-25 mit den von Matthäus stammenden Abschlußwendungen: καὶ ἐγένετο ὅτε ἐτέλεσεν ὁ Ἰησοῦς τοὺς λόγους τούτους oder ähnlichen Formulierungen[5].

(2) *Das Zentrum-Modell*: Dieses besagt, daß das Matthäusevangelium chiastisch um ein Zentrum herum aufgebaut ist[6]. Entweder dient dabei Kap. 11[7] oder Kap. 13[8] als angebliches Zentrum.

(3) *Das markinische Gliederungsmodell*: Die entscheidende Zäsur liegt demzufolge zwischen 16,20 und 16,21, d.h. nach dem Petrusbekenntnis bei Caesarea Philippi[9]. Bedeutungsvoll ist demnach die Formulierung: ἀπὸ τότε ἤρξατο ὁ Ἰησοῦς δεικνύειν τοῖς μαθηταῖς αὐτοῦ κτλ., die derjenigen von 4,17 entspricht, wo es heißt: ἀπὸ τότε ἤρξατο ὁ Ἰησοῦς κηρύσσειν κτλ. Diesem Modell entsprechend zerfällt das Matthäusevangelium also in zwei Hauptteile, die in etwa den Hauptteilen des Markusevangeliums entsprechen[10]. Als dritter Teil kommt noch der Einleitungsteil (1,1-4,16) hinzu, der die Präsentation Jesu beinhaltet[11].

Wie diese Gliederungsmodelle mit ihren jeweiligen Strukturierungsmerkmalen

---

[3] Luz 1985, 17f.; vgl. jetzt auch S. Byrskog 1994, 345-47.

[4] Davies/Allison 1988, 59-61 führen fünf Grundtypen auf; zu den von Luz, ibid. erwähnten drei fügen sie noch zwei hinzu: (a) "M. D. Goulder's lectionary hypothesis" (Goulder 1974) und (b) "R. H. Gundry's indefinite plan" (Gundry 1982). Vgl. auch D. R. Bauer 1988, 21-55: "Geographical-chronological Structures", "Topical Structures", "Conceptual Structures".

[5] Dieses Modell basiert auf der Pentateuch-Hypothese von B. W. Bacon 1930; hierzu D. R. Bauer 1988, 27-35. Eine Variante davon ist C. D. Allisons (1992, 1208) Modell von abwechselnd sechs narrativen (N) und fünf diskursiven (D) Einheiten: N (1-4), D (5-7). N (8-9), D (10), N (11-12), D (13), N (14-17), D (18), N (19-23), D (24-25) und N (26-28); ferner J. P. Meier 1992, 627-37. S. auch die Einschätzung dieser Reden seitens J. D. Kingsburys 1988 *innerhalb des markinischen Gliederungsmodells*, wenn er aufgrund der Beobachtung, "that they contain sayings that seemingly are without relevance for the characters in the story to whom they are addressed" (p. 107), die Konklusion zieht, daß die eigentlichen Adressaten die 'implizierten Leser' sind (p. 107-13, esp. 109ff.); ähnlich schon N. A. Dahl 1973, 146 und jetzt H. D. Betz 1992, 277 und 283.

[6] Vgl. D. R. Bauer 1988, 36-40.

[7] So z.B. H. B. Green 1968.

[8] So z.B. C. H. Lohr 1961, 427; P. F. Ellis 1974, 12-13; H. J. B. Combrink 1983, 71.

[9] Diese Gliederung des Markusevangeliums ist allerdings auch umstritten, vgl. z.B. D.-A. Koch 1983, 145-66 sowie die Arbeit meines Schülers J. G. Cook 1985 (forthcoming). S. auch D. Lührmann 1987, 23: "Mk gibt freilich keine Gliederung seines Werkes".

[10] Aufbauend auf Vorgänger wie E. Lohmeyer/W. Schmauch 1958, 1, 64, 264 und E. Krentz 1964 wurde dieses Modell von J. D. Kingsbury 1975, 7-25 herausgearbeitet. Zur Vor- bzw. Nachgeschichte dieses Modells s. ferner D. R. Bauer 1988 passim sowie F. Neirynck 1988, 21-25.

[11] Vgl. Kingsbury 1988, 43-58.

einander zu- bzw. unterzuordnen sind, m.a.W. wie sie in Relation zu einander zu setzen sind, ist immer noch nicht klargestellt. Bei einer solchen Untersuchung der Gesamtstruktur des Matthäusevangeliums müssen zumindest folgende Problemkreise umrissen werden[12]: (a) die Bedeutung der geographischen und chronologischen Referenzen; (b) die Relation zwischen narrativen und diskursiven Elementen mit Einbeziehung der Redewendungen, die sich am Ende der fünf großen Redekompositionen befinden (7,28; 11,1; 13,53; 19,1; 26,1); (c) die Bedeutung der sog. formelhaften Satzanfänge in 4,17 bzw. 16,21 und ihre Beziehung zu den soeben angeführten fünf Redeschlußwendungen; (d) der extensionale Bezugsumfang des Titels (1,1); (e) die Relevanz und Funktion charakteristischer matthäischer literarischer Mittel wie Chiasmus, Inklusio, numerische Anordnungen etc. für die *texttypologische Makro-Struktur* dieses Evangeliums; (f) die mögliche Existenz von thematischen Einheiten und ihre Interrelation innerhalb einer *semantischen Makro-Struktur;* (g) die Relation zwischen thematischen Einheiten und Teiltexten verschiedenen Grades auf der mikro-semantischen Ebene sowie diejenige zwischen der globalen makro-semantischen Struktur und der text-typologischen makro-textuellen Struktur[13].

## 1.2. Gliederungsindizien im Matthäusevangelium

Die erste und dritte Hypothese sind für mein jetziges Thema von besonderem Interesse, da sie meist mit Hinweis auf Indizien in der Oberflächenstruktur des Textes begründet werden. Gerade diesem Phänomen möchte ich im folgenden nachgehen, in dem ich "Abschlußwendungen", "Formelhafte Satzanfänge" sowie "Summarien" bzw. "Kopfstücke" einer näheren Analyse unterziehe:

(a) *Abschlußwendungen:* Ich fange dabei mit den sog. Abschlußwendungen der Reden an, da diese einheitlicher in der Formulierung und auffälliger in der Gesamtkomposition des Evangeliums sind[14]. Diese Formulierungen, die sich wie oben schon angegeben wurde 7,28; 11,1; 13,53; 19,1 und 26,1 jeweils am Ende einer größeren Rede bzw. Redekomposition Jesu befinden, werden von den Exegeten gene-

---

[12] Vgl. hierzu auch D. R. Bauer 1988, 55.

[13] Unter *semantischem Makro-Struktur* verstehe ich mit T. A. van Dijk 1980, 41 die abstrakte Repräsentation der "globale(n) *Bedeutungs*struktur eines Textes", d.h. eine semantische Texttiefenstruktur (Hervorheb. von mir; vgl. auch van Dijk 1985, 115ff.); unter *texttypologischer Makro-Struktur* verstehe ich ebenfalls mit van Dijk, ibid., 128 "solche globalen Strukturen die den *Typ* eines Textes *kennzeichnen*", d.h. eine Textoberflächenstruktur. Zusammenfassend drückt van Dijk diesen Unterschied so aus: "eine Superstruktur [in meiner Terminologie: texttypologische Makro-Struktur –DH] ist eine Art *Textform,* deren Gegenstand, Thema, d.h.: Makro-Struktur [in meiner Terminologie: semantische Makro-Struktur –DH], der *Textinhalt* ist" (ibid.).

rell als Redewendungen[15], spezieller dann als Schluß-, Abschluß-, oder sogar Redeschlußwendungen bzw. -formeln[16] einerseits, oder als Überleitungs- bzw. Übergangsformeln[17] andererseits bezeichnet. Daß Matthäus hier eine besonders geprägte Formulierung verwendet, ist schon längst erkannt, gleich ob man sie für eine
Schöpfung des Evangelisten oder einer seiner Quellen hält. Der textgrammatische
Charakter dieser Wendungen aber ist m.W. bisher noch nicht untersucht, geschweige denn geklärt worden[18].

(b) *Formelhafte Satzanfänge oder besser: Teiltextanfänge*[19]: Diese kommen in
der Formulierung, wie sie oben § 1.1 (3) zitiert worden sind – wie schon gesagt –,
nur an zwei Stellen vor: in 4,17 und 16,21. Dieser "sprachlich eigenartige Ausdruck"[20] hat laut einigen Exegeten textdelimitierende Funktion[21], ohne daß sein
textgrammatischer Charakter überhaupt diskutiert worden ist. Auf keinen Fall kann
man sich m.E. mit der wenig präzisen Charakterisierung "formelhafte Satzanfänge"
begnügen[22].

(c) *Die sogenannten Summarien oder Kopfstücke*: Zwei einander entsprechende
Textabschnitte, die als Summarien[23] oder als Kopfstücke[24] bezeichnet werden, finden sich 4,23 und 9,35 (man vgl. aber die ganzen Abschnitte 4,23-25 sowie 9,35-
38), wo es heißt: καὶ περιῆγεν ὁ Ἰησοῦς ἐν ὅλῃ τῇ Γαλιλαίᾳ [bzw. τὰς πόλεις πάσας καὶ τὰς κώμας (9,35)] διδάσκων ἐν ταῖς συναγωγαῖς αὐτῶν καὶ κηρύσσων
τὸ εὐαγγέλιον τῆς βασιλείας καὶ θεραπεύων πᾶσαν νόσον καὶ πᾶσαν μαλακίαν

---

[14] Vgl. z.B. T. Fornberg 1989, 18, 129; D. C. Allison 1992, 1203; Meier 1992, 627; B. Standaert
1992, 1239: "Nous avons manifestement affaire à une procédé intentionnel: la répétition avec de mi-
nimes variantes et surtout la force conclusive de l'ultime formulation «quand Jésus eut achevé *tous*
ces discours» (26,1), obligent à reconnaître ici une structuration qui affecte tout l'évangile mattheen"
und ferner M. A. Powell 1990, 45: "... the great speeches that Jesus gives are remarkable for the
amount of discourse time devoted to them" sowie unten Anm. 120. Siehe aber demgegenüber
Krentz's Einschätzung unten 157.

[15] So H. Conzelmann/A. Lindemann 1980, 263.

[16] So z.B. R. Bultmann 1964, 359; Ph. Vielhauer 1975, 357; Luz 1985, 19; J. Gnilka 1986, 283.
Davies/Allison 1988, 725: "closing formula".

[17] So z.B. W. Wilkens 1985, 24 et passim; vgl. auch Luz, ibid. und Gnilka, ibid.

[18] Auch nicht im Kommentar zu den Textkonstituenten im Matthäusevangelium von dem sprach-
wissenschaftlich orientierten Neutestamentler W. Schenk 1987, 440f. S. dazu unten § 3.1.

[19] In der Tat handelt es sich nämlich nicht ausschließlich um *Satzanfänge*, sondern um Anfänge
zu *satzübergreifenden* Texteinheiten.

[20] Bibelkommissionen 1981, Fußnote zu Matt. 4,17: "Samma språkligt egenartade uttryck an-
vänder grundtexten i 16:21".

[21] Bibelkommissionen 1981, ibid.; W. G. Kümmel 1973, 76f.; J. D. Kingsbury 1975, 7ff.; Wilkens 1985, 30; mit Vorbehalt Luz 1985, 18 und idem 1990, 484f. Anders Davies/Allison 1988, 387.

[22] Darin ist Luz 1985, 18 Recht zu geben. S. dazu unten § 3.2.2.1.

[23] So W. Grundmann 1968, 111; Vielhauer 1975, 359.

[24] So Wilkens 1985, 25 et passim.

[ἐν τῷ λαῷ (nur 4,23)] (4,23). Auch diese sog. Summarien oder Kopfstücke spielen in der Exegese für die Gliederung des Matthäusevangeliums – wie wir noch sehen werden[25] – eine wesentliche Rolle, obwohl auch hier Schwierigkeiten bei der Beurteilung ihrer Funktion bestehen.

Bei dieser Gelegenheit muß ich mich auf diese drei Merkmalsgruppen beschränken und die sog. *Episodenmerkmale*[26], die bei Matthäus eine so große Rolle spielen, im wesentlichen außer Acht lassen. Ehe ich die substitutionellen Gliederungsmerkmale einer näheren Analyse unterziehen kann, ist es aber erforderlich, die sprachwissenschaftlichen Grundlagen dafür etwas näher darzustellen.

## 2. Sprachwissenschaftliche Grundlagenüberlegungen

### 2.1. Suppositio formalis versus suppositio materialis

Eine der grundlegenden Einsichten der Sprachphilosophie sowie der Linguistik ist die Feststellung verschiedener Stufen oder Ebenen eines jeden Sprach- bzw. Textsystems. Dabei unterscheidet man vorerst zwischen *Objektsprache* bzw. *Primärsprache*[27] und *Metasprache*[28] oder adäquater zwischen verschiedenen objekt- und metasprachlichen Ebenen[29]. Wie bedeutungsvoll diese Unterscheidung ist, geht schon aus der Tatsache hervor, daß sie "heute bereits zum theoretischen Arsenal der Methodologie der Wissenschaften" gehört[30].

Seit der mittelalterlichen Scholastik redet man von verschiedenen *suppositiones*[31] und unterscheidet zunächst zwischen *suppositio formalis* ('formaler' Voraussetzung, d.h. "Anwendung eines Wortes auf etwas von ihm Verschiedenes"[32]) und *suppositio materialis* ('sachlicher' Voraussetzung, d.h. "Anwendung des Wortes

---

[25] S. dazu unten § 3.2.2.2.

[26] S. hierzu E. Gülich/W. Raible 1977a, 143f.; D. Hellholm 1980, 91-3; idem 1986, 41.

[27] E. Coseriu spricht von Primärsprache anstatt von Objektsprache (z.B. idem 1981, 64 sowie idem 1988a, 15).

[28] A. Tarski 19[43/44]/70, bes. 15-17, 21-3; idem 19[35]/83, bes. 167; R. Carnap 1956, 4 und 44; Raible 1972, 10-13, 221-41; F. von Kutschera 1975, 29f.; A. Menne 1980, 64f.; J. Lyons 1977, 10-13; Th. Rentsch 1980, 1301-03; A. J. Greimas/J. Courtés 1982, 188-90; und in der alttestamentlichen Exegese z.B. A. Gibson 1981, 50-9, 129-30.

[29] R. Harweg 1981, 285-92; idem 1981a, 111-39.

[30] G. Klaus 1975a, 791.

[31] Vgl. A. Wedberg 1968, 182: "Daß ein Zeichen für eine Sache supponiert, bedeutet wörtlich, daß das Zeichen anstelle von der Sache tritt" (Übers. von mir); s. ausführlich dazu W. Kneal/M. Kneal 1978, 246-74; Menne 1973, 19-23; idem 1980, 60-65; Raible 1972, 11; Coseriu 1975, 151-52, 157-60; idem 1988a, 15f.; Klaus 1975c, 1187, und idem 1975d, 1193.

[32] Klaus 1975d, 1193.

auf sich selbst"[33]).

Diese Differenzierung findet sich, wie bes. der Sprachwissenschaftler Eugenio Coseriu nachgewiesen hat, zuerst – wenn auch nur ansatzweise – in Augustins Dialog *"De magistro"*[34], wo u.a. dargelegt wird, "daß lat. *verbum* genau wie z.B. *flumen* »Fluß« ein Wort IST und daß es »Wort« BEDEUTET, während *flumen* zwar ein Wort ist, aber nicht »Wort« bedeutet"[35]. In der englischsprachlichen Literatur werden hierfür seit W. V. Quine[36] die Bezeichnungen *'use'* und *'mention'* verwendet[37].

Der Logiker Albert Menne formuliert die Relation zwischen Objektsprache/Metasprache auf der einen Seite und formaler/materialer Supposition auf der anderen folgendermaßen[38]: "Bei der *Objektsprache* werden die Worte in *formaler Supposition* gebraucht, stehen also für Objekte, die etwas anderes sind als das Wort, durch das sie bezeichnet werden", z.B. das Wort Macintosh steht hier für den Computer, mit dessen Hilfe dieser Aufsatz niedergeschrieben worden ist. Das Wort bezieht sich also auf ein außersprachliches Objekt. "Bei der *Metasprache,*" fährt Menne fort, "stehen die Worte in *materialer Supposition*, da sie für Worte gebraucht werden, genauer: für die Worte der Objektsprache", z.B. (a) wenn das Wort 'Macintosh' sich auf das Wort selbst, das aus neun Buchstaben besteht, bzw. dreisilbig ist, bezieht, (b) wenn über die 'Ausdrucksmittel einer Sprache', wie z.B. in Form von grammatischen Benennungen gesprochen wird, oder (c) wenn in einer syntagmatischen Relation ein Text über einen anderen handelt[39]. Mit Menne muß außerdem noch festgehalten werden, daß "dabei die Ausdrucksmittel der Metasprache genau wie die der Objektsprache der Umgangssprache entnommen sein (können)"[40].

Der Unterschied zwischen Objekt- bzw. Primärsprache und verschiedenen Arten von Metasprachen kann durch folgende Figur veranschaulicht werden[41], wobei zu beachten ist, daß die *metasprachlichen* Beispiele sich in zwei Kategorien einteilen lassen: die vier ersten sind *paradigmatischer*, während das letzte *syntagmatischer* Art ist (s. *Figur 1*):

---

[33] Klaus ibid.; vgl. auch Wedberg, ibid.: "Im Satz: 'Mensch ist ein Substantiv' hat dasselbe Wort (sc. Mensch, das im vorherigen Satz in *persönlicher Supposition* gebraucht worden war –DH) *materielle Supposition*, denn es supponiert für das ausgesprochene oder geschriebene Wort 'Mensch' selbst" (Übers. von mir).

[34] Coseriu 1975, 126-39, bes. 129ff. Text bei E. Schadel 1975, 64; zur problemgeschichtlichen Einführung s. ibid. 46-55.

[35] Coseriu 1988a, 15; idem 1975, 157ff.

[36] Quine 1951, § 4; s. von Kutschera 1975, 29 Anm. 2.

[37] Vgl. z.B. Lyons 1977, 5-10; Menne 1980, 60f.; idem 1985, 34.

[38] Menne 1980, 64; vgl. auch J. M. Bocheński/A. Menne 1983, 23f.; Menne 1985, 34 sowie Coseriu 1981, 64.

[39] Vgl. P. Hellwig 1984, 16: "Die Relation Metatext zu Objekttext liegt vor, wenn ersterer über letzteren handelt"; vgl. auch L. Hartman 1987, 63; ferner unten Anm. 44-46.

[40] Menne 1985, 34.

## Figur 1

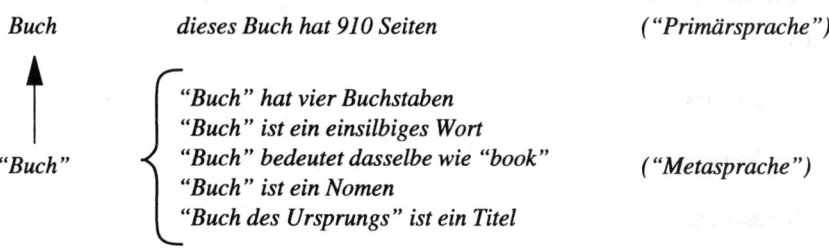

Ein instruktives Beispiel, das Menne anführt, ist die mittelalterliche Gewohnheit, "in liturgischen Büchern … die zu betenden Texte schwarz zu schreiben, die metasprachlichen [bzw. metakommunikativen –DH], nicht zu sprechenden Texte, die Handlungsanweisungen enthielten, z.B. laut oder leise, kniend oder sitzend zu sprechen, wurden rot geschrieben. Daher die Bezeichnung 'Rubriken' für liturgische Regeln und Handlungsanweisungen"[42].

Am zweiten Beispiel sowie an den verschiedenen Kategorien im *Figur 1* zeigt sich schon, daß die Unterscheidung zwischen Objektsprache bzw. -text und Metasprache bzw. -text nicht differenziert genug ist, denn die 'Rubriken' beziehen sich ja nicht auf den Gebetstext selbst, sondern auf die außertextliche Vortragsweise des Liturgen. Hier tritt der unten zu beschreibende Unterschied zwischen text-*externen* und text-*internen* metasprachlichen Textebenen mit aller Deutlichkeit hervor[43].

Man muß sich ferner darüber im klaren sein, daß der Begriff "Objekt- bzw. Primärsprache" *keine absolute* Sprach- bzw. Textstufe bezeichnet. Im Gegenteil, er bezeichnet vielmehr *nur relative* Sprach- bzw. Textstufen[44], denn eine Metasprache oder ein Metatext kann seinerseits wiederum zur Objekt- bzw. Primärsprache oder zum Objekt- bzw. Primärtext für Metasprachen oder Metatexte höherer Dignität werden usw.[45] Der Sprachwissenschaftler Roland Harweg hat dafür den Terminus "Treppenstufensystem" im Gegensatz zum absoluten und in mancher Beziehung inadäquateren "Leiterstufensystem" vorgeschlagen[46], wie *Figur 2* aufzeigt:

---

[41] Vgl. hierzu die Figur bei Coseriu 1988a, 15, wo allerdings kein syntagmatisches Beispiel gegeben wird. S. ferner Heger 1992, 6: "Eine Illustration zu diesen Unterarten sowie zu der prinzipiellen Iterierbarkeit der Gegenüberstellung von *mention* and *use* biete(t) … der Kalauer '*ein Hund hat je vier Beine, Buchstaben und Kasus*'".

[42] Menne 1980, 64; vgl. die Rubriken, die sich in der Liturgieinstruktion der Did. 9,1-3 finden und s. die Textzitate unten Anm. 230. Ein weiteres Beispiel stellen diejenigen Deiktika dar, die "als Textdeiktika, d.h. als Deiktika, deren Deixisobjekt ein Textsegment ist" (Harweg 1979, 167), gelten; vgl. ferner die Darstellung in Hellholm 1980, 51f.

[43] S. unten § 2.1.II.(4).

[44] Harweg 1981, 289f.

# Figur 2:

## 1. DAS LEITERSTUFENSYSTEM

usw.

⋮

Zweite Metasprache

⋮

Erste Metasprache

⋮

Objektsprache

⋮

Welt

## 2. DAS TREPPENSTUFENSYSTEM

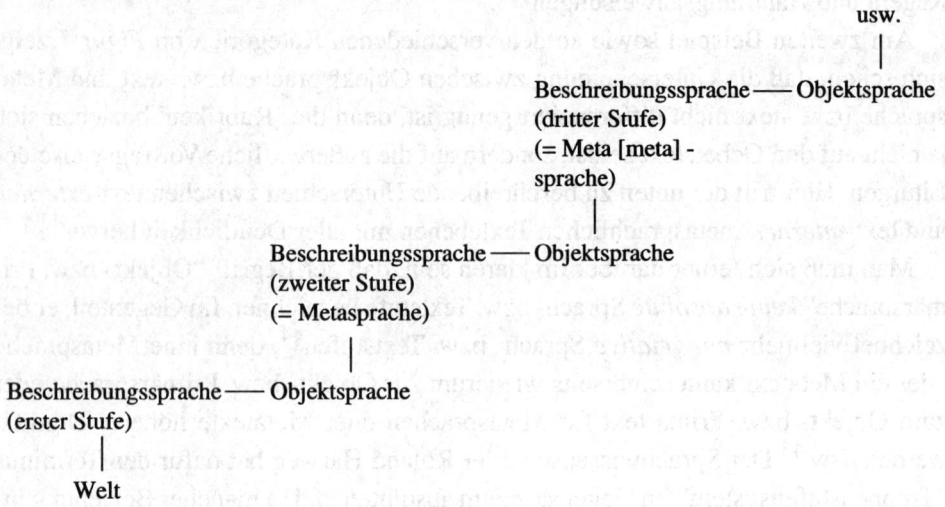

Nun ist diese grundlegende, aber hauptsächlich paradigmatische Unterscheidung zwischen *formaler* und *materialer Supposition* bei Analysen von größeren Texten ergänzungsbedürftig, und zwar in syntagmatischer Hinsicht[47], wie Harwegs Treppenstufensystem schon andeutet. Aus dem Grunde werde ich zunächst zwischen vier Ebenen unterscheiden, die sich wiederum in zwei Hauptgruppen subsumieren lassen:

I. ERSTE HAUPTGRUPPE: *textexterne* Ebenen bezüglich der direkten oder indirekten Referenz auf die *außersprachlichen* Gegenstände und Sachverhalte:

(1) Die *Objektebene* oder *Primärebene*[48], in der auf die außersprachlichen Gegenstände und Sachverhalte *direkt* referiert wird, z.B. auf Jesu Lehr- bzw. Heiltätigkeit oder auf das Matthäusevangelium als das erste unter den kanonischen Evan-

---

[45] Vgl. Klaus 1973, 44: "In dieser Hierarchie von Sprachen bezeichnen wir die Sprache, über die gesprochen wird, als *Objektsprache*, die Sprache, in der über die Objektsprache gesprochen wird, als *Metasprache*. Die Metasprache bildet also stets die nächsthöhere Stufe zur Objektsprache. So ist die Sprache erster Stufe die Objektsprache für die Sprache zweiter Stufe. Für diese wiederum ist die Sprache dritter Stufe die Metasprache usw."; ferner idem 1975a, 791: "Die Unterscheidung zwischen Objekt- und Metasprache läßt sich dadurch beliebig weitertreiben, daß die Metasprache einer Objektsprache selbst wieder zum Objekt der Untersuchung in einer Metasprache 2. Stufe gemacht wird usw."; ähnlich auch Coseriu 1981, 64: "Die Unterscheidung zwischen *primärer Sprache* und *Metasprache* wird überhaupt nicht innerhalb der Ausrichtung der Sprache auf die verschiedenen den Redeakt konstituierenden Elemente getroffen, sie betrifft vielmehr eines dieser Elemente selbst, nämlich die Realität. Sie klassifiziert die Fakten innerhalb der Realität danach, ob sie zur Sprache gehören oder nicht"; ferner Heger 1992, 6: "… müssen natürliche Sprachen eine Möglichkeit enthalten …, die Möglichkeit nämlich, Aussagen über sich selbst formulieren zu lassen; oder noch technischer: als ihre eigenen Metasprachen zu fungieren, und dies nicht nur einmal, sondern innerhalb entsprechender Hierarchien von Metasprachen *ad infinitum*".
Dies gilt freilich auch umgekehrt, denn "eine Sprache, die in einem Zusammenhang Metasprache ist, kann in einem anderen Zusammenhang – wenn sie selbst untersucht wird – auch Objektsprache sein" (Klaus 1975b, 886).

[46] Harweg 1981, 291f.; idem 1981a, 137.

[47] Für die Unterscheidung zwischen paradigmatischen und syntagmatischen Relationen vgl. z.B. Lyons 1973, 75ff.; Harweg 1979, 20-35; H. E. Brekle 1972, 81-84; M. A. K. Halliday/R. D. Huddleston 1981, 18-53; H. Schnelle 1973, 168; Hellholm 1980, 84 mit Anm. 42; idem 1986, 33f. und idem 1991, 151-57; Coseriu 1988a, 141-58: "Auf der syntagmatischen Achse ist die Beziehung zwischen den sprachlichen Elementen »kopulativ« (sowohl *a* als auch *b*), da es sich um eine Beziehung *in praesentia* handelt; auf der paradigmatischen Achse dagegen ist sie »disjunktiv« oder »ausschließend« (»entweder x oder y« oder »wenn x, dann nicht y«, und umgekehrt); denn es geht hier um eine Beziehung zwischen einem »gegenwärtigen« (»gewählten«) Element und anderen »abwesenden« (»nicht gewählten« oder »ausgeschlossenen«) Elementen derselben Klasse sprachlicher Einheiten" (ibid., 141f.).

[48] So Coseriu 1981, 64 und idem 1988a.

gelien[49].

(2) Die *Textebene*, in der auf die außersprachlichen "Gegenstände und Sachverhalte" *indirekt* durch mikro-syntagmatische Substitution[50], d.h. durch vermittelnde Referenz[51], referiert wird, z.B. in dem Satz: "Das Matthäusevangelium, das fünf große Reden Jesu enthält, ist ein strukturell komplexes Gebilde", in dem das Relativpronomen nur *indirekt* auf das Objekt selbst mittels des Korrelats Bezug nimmt. Auf der Textebene wird hingegen durch das Relativpronomen *direkt* auf das als Korrelat funktionierende Nomen Bezug genommen. Diese Doppelfunktion gilt nicht nur für Relativpronomina, sondern auch für alle Anaphora und für diejenigen Kataphora, die als satzinterne Relatoren funktionieren[52], sowie für diejenigen Deiktika, die als Real-Deiktika gelten[53]. Diese Distinktion zwischen *direktem* und *indirektem* Bezug wurde schon vom alexandrinischen Grammatiker Apollonios Dyskolos (2. Jh. n. Chr.) erkannt und πρώτη γνῶσις bzw. δευτέρα γνῶσις genannt[54]. Die Textebene liegt in der Tat auf der Grenze zwischen text-*externer* und text-*interner* Ebene. Ausschlaggebend für die Zuordnung der jeweiligen Ebene ist dabei die Fragestellung.

II. ZWEITE HAUPTGRUPPE: *textinterne* Ebenen bezüglich der reinen oder milderen Referenz auf *den ganzen Text* bzw. auf *Teiltexte* verschiedenen Grades:

(3) Die *Abstraktionsebenen* verschiedenen Grades, in denen auf Teiltexte bzw. Sätze durch mikro- oder makrosyntagmatische Substitution Bezug genommen

---

[49] In diesem Falle, wenn das Zeichen sich außerhalb des Textes selbst befindet und nicht einen Teil davon ausmacht, ist die Referenz auf einen Text nicht meta-substitutionell, sondern objekt-reell; es handelt sich in solchen Fällen also nicht um materiale, sondern vielmehr um formale Supposition (vgl. im Gegensatz dazu unten II.4).

[50] Siehe Hellholm 1980, 84f.; idem 1986, 36 mit Anm. 43.

[51] Siehe Hellholm 1980, 41 mit Lit. und 49 mit Anm. 204. Hierzu vgl. schon K. Bühler 1934/78, 390: "Was die anaphorischen Pfeile direkt treffen, sind nicht die Dinge, von denen die Rede ist, sondern es sind entweder die sprachlichen Fassungen dieser Dinge, also Sätze oder Satzteile, wie es [Hermann] Paul schon völlig korrekt angibt. Oder es sind doch die Dinge, aber so wie sie gefaßt sind: die Dinge und Sachverhalte also, wie sie von den Gesprächspartnern bereits als das und das charakterisiert worden sind".

[52] Diejenigen kataphorischen Ausdrücke, die sich oberhalb der Satzeinheit befinden, kommen nur als metakommunikative bzw. metasprachliche Ausdrücke vor; vgl. Gülich/Raible 1977, 44; Raible 1972, 154, 159f.; Hellholm 1980, 31.

[53] S. Hellholm 1980, 51f. mit Lit. Für die metasprachlichen *Text-deiktika* s. das Zitat aus Harweg 1979, 167 oben Anm. 42 sowie ibid. 168: "Wir sagen deshalb genauer, daß die Textdeixis im Dienste metasprachlicher Anaphora oder allgemeiner: metasprachlicher syntagmatischer Substitution stehen". Die syntagmatische Substitution, um die es sich hier handelt, ist ausschließlich von *mik-roformat*, s. dazu z.B. Raible in Gülich/ Raible 1977, 117f. sowie oben Anm. 51.

[54] *de pron.* 77b; *de synt.* 98,26; vgl. Hellholm 1980, 49; ferner, allerdings ohne Hinweis auf Apollonios Dyskolos, J. Palm 1960, 8ff.

wird[55], z.B. durch die Wendung in Didache 4,14b: αὕτη ἐστὶν ἡ ὁδὸς τῆς ζωῆς [*Dies* ist der Weg des Lebens], wobei αὕτη sich anaphorisch auf den Textabschnitt 1,2-4,14a bezieht; oder 7,1: ταῦτα πάντα προειπόντες βαπτίσατε κτλ. [Nachdem ihr vorher *dies alles* mitgeteilt habt, tauft usw.], wobei ταῦτα πάντα sich anaphorisch auf die sechs ersten Kapitel des Buches bezieht, also auf einen Teiltext der Didache; ferner die ähnliche Formulierung in 11,1: ταῦτα πάντα τὰ προειρημένα [*all das* vorher Mitgeteilte], wobei die abstrakte Substitution ταῦτα πάντα sich in diesem Falle anaphorisch entweder auf den Textabschnitt 7,1-10,8 oder wahrscheinlicher auf den ganzen Textabschnitt 1,1-10,8 bezieht[56]. Hier ist noch zu bemerken, daß die Teiltexte Kap. 1,2-4,14a; 1-6 sowie 7-10 bzw. 1-10 de facto *Objekt(texte)* im Harwegs Treppenstufensystem darstellen; Objekte für die Abstraktionswendungen sind also in erster Linie Teiltexte und nicht primär die außersprachlichen Gegenstände und Sachverhalte als solche.

(4) Die *Metaebenen* verschiedenen Grades, in denen *textintern* auf Gattungen, Gesamttexte oder gegebenenfalls Teiltexte mit Hilfe von *makrosyntagmatischer* Substitution referiert wird[57]; Beispiele hierfür sind: (a) die *Erzähltextebene* in den Evangelien als Metaebene für die Redetextebene, (b) *Gattungsbenennungen* wie Evangelium, Historischer Roman bzw. Monographie, Administrativer oder Apologetischer Brief, Apokalypse etc., oft in Kombination mit Titeln, wie z.B. bei den Prologen der Johannesoffenbarung (1,1-3)[58] oder der Didache (*incipit*); (c) *Textnamen* wie das Matthäus-, Markus-, Lukas- oder Johannesevangelium, oder (d) *Teiltextbenennungen* wie die erste, zweite, dritte oder vierte Vision im Hirten des Hermas[59] oder Teilüberschriften in der Didache wie z.B.: ἡ μὲν οὖν ὁδὸς τῆς ζωῆς ἐστιν *αὕτη* [*Dies* also ist der Weg des Lebens] (1,2a); ἡ δὲ τοῦ θανάτου ὁδός ἐστιν *αὕτη* [*Dies* aber ist der Weg des Todes] (5,1a); τούτων δὲ τῶν λόγων ἡ διδαχή ἐστιν *αὕτη* [*Dies* aber ist die Lehre dieser Worte] (1,3), wobei αὕτη an all diesen Stellen – im Gegensatz zu 4,14b[60] – kataphorischen Bezug hat[61]; ferner auch die Teilüberschriften eingeleitet mit περί + Genitiv des Haupwortes: περὶ δὲ τοῦ βαπτίσματος [Was aber die Taufe betrifft] (7,1) sowie περὶ δὲ τῆς εὐχαριστίας [Was aber die Eucharistie betrifft] (9,1)[62]; all diese Benennungen bzw. Namen beziehen sich textintern, d.h. syntagmatisch, auf Gattungskorpora, Gesamt- oder Teiltexte als Objekte

---

[55] S. Hellholm 1980, 86f. mit Literaturverweisen.

[56] Vgl. Kl. Wengst 1984, 16f. und jetzt K. Niederwimmer 1989, 158-60, 212, bes. aber meine Analyse in Hellholm 1995a.

[57] S. Harweg 1973, bes. 69; Gülich/Raible 1977, 119-21; Hellholm 1980, 75f., 84f.; vgl. auch Hellwig 1984, 7ff., 16f.

[58] Dazu ausführlich Hellholm 1990.

[59] S. Hellholm 1980, 149, 156, 183, 192-94.

[60] Vgl. dazu in diesem Paragraphen oben II. (3).

[61] Vgl. Niederwimmer 1989, 89, 146 und 92.

für die Metawendungen und nicht auf die außersprachlichen Gegenstände und Sachverhalte, die in diesen größeren oder kleineren Texteinheiten thematisiert werden.

Die text-*externe* Metaebene tritt in solchen Fällen auf, wo beispielsweise Handlungsanweisungen an text-*externe* Personen, z.B. an Liturgen im Text eines liturgischen Handbuches gegeben werden[63]. Diese text-*externe* Metaebene spielt aber bei Textdelimitationen in den meisten Fällen allerhöchstens eine bescheidene oder gar keine Rolle.

*Zusammenfassend* können wir also feststellen, daß wir es bei Textanalysen mit zunächst vier Stufen zu tun haben, von denen drei Abstraktionsstufen verschiedenen Grades darstellen: (1) Objektebene oder Primärebene (welche in sich selbst eine Abstraktion der Wirklichkeit darstellt[64]), (2) Textebene, sowie verschiedene (3) Abstraktions- bzw. (4) Metaebenen text-*interner* Art, die alle für die Textdelimitation von ausschlaggebender Bedeutung sind.

## 2.2. Substitutionelle Gliederungsmerkmale

Wie wir oben gesehen haben, orientieren sich zwei von den exegetischen Gliederungsmodellen, das *Modell der fünf Bücher* sowie das sog. *markinische Gliederungsmodell*, an Indizien in der Oberflächenstruktur des Matthäusevangeliums. Hier fallen tatsächlich exegetische Beobachtungen mit gewissen textlinguistischen zusammen, die besagen, daß die Makro-Struktur[65] eines Textes an der Textoberfläche erkennbar sein muß[66]. Werner Kallmeyer und Reinhard Meyer-Hermann haben

---

[62] Vgl. Niederwimmer 1989, 11, 69, 159, 176; ferner s. unten Anm. 230; s. auch die ähnlichen Metaformulierungen mit περί im 1 Kor. 7,1.25; 8,1; 12,1; 16,1.12; dazu J. Weiß 1910/70, 169f. und zuletzt die Untersuchung von M. Mitchell 1989 mit der für unseren Zweck wichtigen Bestätigung, daß "περὶ δέ … is one of the ways in which Paul introduces the topic of the next argument or sub-argument" (p. 256). Nur muß festgestellt werden, daß eine Formula περὶ δέ nicht zu belegen ist, denn diese Substitution auf Metaebene besteht aus περί + Genitiv des Hauptwortes; die Konjunktion δέ dient lediglich der allerdings gewichtigen Funktion, einen Satz mit dem Vorhergehenden zu verbinden; s. das Zitat aus J. Blomqvist 1981, 59 unten ad Anm. 183. Strikt gesagt, leitet die Wendung περὶ δέ + Genitiv des Hauptwortes textuell *kontextbezogene* Sub-Texte ein, während περί + Genitiv textuell *kontextlose* Texte einleitet bzw. markierte Teiltexteinschnitte delimitiert. Mitchell selber gibt mehrere Beispiele, in denen περί + Genitiv ohne δέ als Meta-Äußerung funktioniert. Ein asyndetisches Beispiel aus dem Neuen Testament stellt im Hebr. der Abschnitt, der mit 5,11 anfängt, dar: περὶ οὗ ….

[63] S. Mennes Beispiel oben ad Anm. 42.

[64] S. Raible 1980, 321; idem 1981, 27; Gülich/Raible 1977, 57.

[65] van Dijk 1980, 128-59 verwendet, wie wir schon oben Anm. 13 gesehen haben, hierfür den Terminus "Superstruktur", um den Unterschied zu den "semantischen Makrostrukturen" deutlich hervortreten zu lassen. Vgl. auch Combrink 1983, 68f.

[66] Für Diskussion und Referenzen s. Hellholm 1980, 76f. und idem 1986, 31f.

mit Recht hervorgehoben, daß "die Gliederung von Texten nach Sinn- oder Funkti-
onsabschnitten immer schon ein Gegenstand der Textwissenschaft und der Rhetorik", und – das muß man als Bibelwissenschaftler hinzufügen – der Exegese "gewesen ist". Bei der speziellen Behandlung der Textgliederung im Rahmen der Textlinguistik tritt, laut Kallmeyer/Meyer-Hermann, "jedoch ein bis dahin nicht zentraler
Aspekt hervor: die Aufmerksamkeit richtet sich auf die *Markierung von Grenzen*
und die *Gestaltung von Übergängen* als eine gesonderte Komponente der Textkonstitution"[67]. Dieser bedeutungsvolle Aspekt stellt in der Exegese nur teilweise etwas Neues dar, denn er ist stets ein wichtiges Hilfsmittel gewesen sowohl bei
literarkritischen als auch bei form- und redaktionsgeschichtlichen Analysen *diachroner* Art von alttestamentlichen[68] sowie neutestamentlichen[69] Texten. Bei *syn-
chronen* Kompositionsanalysen von *Gesamttexten* spielen solche Grenzmarkie-run-
gen in der Exegese allerdings erst in letzter Zeit eine zentralere Rolle[70]. Hierzu hat

---

[67] W. Kallmeyer/R. Meyer-Hermann 1980, 251.

[68] Vgl. in bezug auf das Alte Testament, z.B. Ch. Hardmeier 1978, 34: "Das Interesse des Exegeten an einer befriedigenden und umfassenden Definition der sprachlichen Einheit 'Text' dürfte allein schon in der klassischen Frage der Literarkritik nach der Abgrenzbarkeit von Texteinheiten im
biblischen Schrifttum hinreichend begründet sein", ferner die Kritik ibid., 70; Kl. Koch 1974, 20; W.
Richter 1971, 49-72; G. Fohrer/H. W. Hoffmann/F. Huber/L. Markert/G. Wanke 1976, 44-57. O. H.
Steck 1989, 8-14, 45-61.

[69] Als Beispiel auf der Ebene der neutestamentlichen Literarkritik kann, unter Verweis u.A. auf
"harte Übergänge", die Teilungshypothesen der Paulusbriefe dienen: so z.B. G. Bornkamm 1971,
172: "Der Bruch zwischen beiden Teilen des überlieferten Briefganzen [sc. 2. Kor. 1-7 bzw. 10-13
–DH] ist so eklatant, daß, wie bereits erwähnt, längst schon die auch mir einleuchtende These vertreten worden ist, die letzten vier Kapitel seien nicht gleichzeitig mit den ersten abgefaßt und abge-
sandt, sondern seien ein Fragment des dort erwähnten Schmerzenbriefes"; ferner ibid., 176: "...
noch auf eine andere Bruchstelle unseres Briefes ... Schon im zweiten Kapitel [sc. 2,12 –DH] ...
bricht die Erzählung jäh ab, um erst im 7. Kapitel (fast sieben Seiten des Nestle Textes später!) [7,5f.
–DH] ebenso unvermittelt in der Erzählung fortzufahren"; vgl. auch Vielhauer 1975, 150-55, 160-
66. Betz 1985, 26 stellt zuerst fest, daß "three kinds of observations seem to underlie whatever proposals are found in these works [sc. die literarkritischen Arbeiten zum 2. Kor. –DH]: (1) breaks in
the train of thought, (2) discontinuities in reports of events, (3) sudden changes in the tone of the
presentation", fährt dann aber fort mit der kritischen Bemerkung: "None of these arguments operates
at the level of the text itself, but on hypothetical constructions lying beneath the text: the train of
thought, the plan of the letter, the course of events, and psychology. One of the few scholars to have
complained about the lack of methodological reflection in the debate was Anton Halmel [1904 –DH]
... Halmel was one of the few scholars who engaged in formal arguments pertaining to the text itself
... But investigations of what modern text linguistics calls 'Gliederungsmerkmale' (signs of demar-
cation [mit Verweis auf Gülich/Raible 1977, 54 in Anm. 240 –DH]) remained the exception, and
Halmel's methodological complaints went altogether unnoticed".

[70] In der alttestamentlichen Forschung z.B. Hardmeier 1978; B. Wiklander 1984; Kl. Koch 1983/
89, und in der neutestamentlichen Forschung, z.B. Kl. Berger 1977, 17-27; Hellholm 1980, 1986 und
1995; Hartman 1980 und 1987; J. C. Cook 1985; B. C. Johanson 1987.

gewiß der zunehmende Einfluß der Textlinguistik Entscheidendes beigetragen.

Solche Grenzen bzw. Übergänge werden in Texten durch sog. Gliederungs-merkmale gekennzeichnet[71]. In früheren Publikationen habe ich im Anschluß an Elisabeth Gülich und Wolfgang Raible[72] ausführlich über solche Gliederungsmerk-male und ihre Hierarchisierung für die Teiltextanalyse von narrativen Texten gehan-delt und weise hier nur darauf hin[73]. Für meine jetzigen Zwecke kann ich mich auf die *substitutionellen* Gliederungsmerkmale und ihre Probleme bei der Textgliede-rung des Matthäusevangeliums beschränken.

Ehe ich auf das Matthäusevangelium eingehen kann, müssen jedoch, im An-schluß an die Diskussion oben über *formale* und *materiale Supposition,* zwei Typen von substitutionellen Gliederungsmerkmalen näher charakterisiert werden:

(a) *Substitution auf Metaebene (SM):* Im Unterschied zu den syntagmatischen Substitutionen auf *Textebene*, die der Verkettung von Sätzen bzw. der Mikro-Struk-tur von Texten dienen, sind die syntagmatischen Substitutionen auf *Metaebene* Ma-nifestationen (a) von unterschiedlichen *generischen* Konzepten wie Erzählung, Evangelium, Parabel usw. oder (b) von *Einzeltexten* bzw. *Teiltexten* verschiedenen Grades, die entweder *neutral* wie Kapitel, Abschnitt, Paragraph oder *inhaltsbezo-gen* bzw. *generisch* wie Vision, Himmelsbrief, Gleichnis, Wundererzählung, Rede etc. sein können[74].

Durch vorhergehende bzw. nachfolgende Nomina oder Sätze können also ganze Sätze, Textsequenzen, die wir Teiltexte genannt haben, oder sogar ganze Texte bzw.

---

[71] Zu ihrer Funktion vgl. E. Gülich/U. Quasthoff 1985, 177: "The structuring into subtexts is established at the surface level of the narrative text by hierarchically ordered discourse markers. Thus it is the process of comprehension, that is, the listener's [or: reader's –DH] activity of recon-structing the narrative structure, that serves as an argument for the functional explanation of surface-level markers"; vgl. jetzt auch D. Schiffrin 1987, die von "sequential dependence" im Zusammen-hang mit 'discourse markers' redet, um dadurch anzugeben, daß "markers are devices that work on a discourse level: they are not dependent on the smaller units of talk of which discourse is composed" (S. 37). Wie so viele anglo-sachsische Linguisten nimmt Schiffrin aber keine Notiz, von dem was im deutschen Sprachraum erarbeitet worden ist; sie scheint, sehr zu ihrem Nachteil, die grundlegenden Arbeiten von Gülich/Raible mit ihrer Hierarchisierung von Gliederungsmerkmalen überhaupt nicht zu kennen (!); vgl die scharfe Kritik G. Hammarströms an "a great number of English speaking 'for-mal' or 'theoretical' linguists of the last few decades [who –DH] cannot read these languages [sc. Spanish, German or French –DH] either" (1988, 138).

[72] Gülich/Raible 1975 und 1977a.

[73] Hellholm 1980, 78-95 und dort angegebene Lit.; idem 1986, 38-42. Vgl. ferner L. Hartman 1980, 130.

[74] Vgl. Hellwig 1984, 6: "In der Regel zeigen sie (sc. die Überschriften) den Inhalt des nachfol-genden [Textes bzw. –DH] Textteils an … Es gibt Überschriften, die nichts anderes als eine formale Einteilung des Textes bewirken sollen, wie z.B. *Vorbemerkung, Einleitung, erster Teil* und *zweiter Teil …*"; ferner schon Raible 1972, 209.

Gattungen substituiert werden. "Wird nun bei einer Substitution ein Text als Ganzes oder werden Teile des Textes als Bestandteil eines Kommunikationsprozesses bezeichnet", so sprechen wir mit E. Gülich und W. Raible von "Substitution *auf Metaebene*". "Hierbei werden metakommunikative Nomina, gegebenenfalls in Verbindung mit metakommunikativen Verben [d.h. *verba dicendi* bei geäußerten, *verba sentiendi, cogitandi* oder auch *agendi* bei nicht-geäußerten Kommunikationsakten – DH[75]] verwendet, beispielsweise dann, wenn ein Text oder Teiltext als 'Rede' oder 'Erzählung' bezeichnet wird"[76]. Dabei muß beachtet werden, daß "mit einer Substitution auf Meta-Ebene ... auf folgende oder auf vorausgegangene Erzähltexte oder Teiltexte verwiesen werden (kann)"[77].

Da nicht nur der intensionale Bedeutungsumfang (aristotelisch-stoisch: λεκτόν oder σημαινόμενον), sondern auch der extensionale Bezugs- oder Referenzumfang (aristotelisch-stoisch: τυγχάνον oder πρᾶγμα) dieses Gliederungsmerkmals variabel ist, ist eine Gradierung in Rängen $SM^0$, $SM^1$, $SM^2$, $SM^3$ etc. erforderlich. Diese Rangordnung der Substitutionen auf Metaebene kann leicht durch das Dezimalklassifikationssystem, von dem ich in diesem Aufsatz Gebrauch mache, demonstriert werden[78]: Kapitel 1, 2, 3 usw.; Abschnitt 1.1, 1.2 ..., 2.1, 2.2 usw.; Paragraph 1.1.1, 1.1.2 ..., 2.1.1, 2.1.2 usw.; Absatz 1.1.1.1, 1.1.1.2 ..., 1.2.1.1, 1.2.1.2 usw.

Diese metakommunikativen Nomina bzw. Sätze stehen also in *materialer Supposition* zu den Gattungen, Texten bzw. Textabschnitten, auf welche sie sich gegebenenfalls beziehen und sie referieren somit auf Gattungskorpora, Texte oder Teiltexte und nicht auf die außersprachlichen Gegenstände und Sachverhalte als solche. Dies soll verdeutlicht werden durch eine etwas detailliertere Darstellung der unteren rechten Trapezecke in Hegers semantischem Trapez-Modell[79] (*Figur 4*). Durch diese Verdeutlichung soll veranschaulicht werden, daß nicht nur "Gegenstände" wie Textklassen, Texte und Teiltexte und "Sachverhalte" auf der text-*externen* Ebene, sondern auch "Textklassen", "Texte" und "Teiltexte" auf der text-*internen* Ebene Referenzobjekte darstellen können. Zum besseren Verständnis dieser Veranschaulichung ist es aber notwendig, zuerst das Trapez-Modell selbst, u.zw. mit einigen Verdeutlichungen vorzuführen (*Figur 3*):

---

[75] Vgl. Gülich/Raible 1977a, 138; und weiter Hellholm 1980, 80f.

[76] Gülich/Raible 1977a, 141; E. Gülich 1976, 242.

[77] Gülich 1976, 245.

[78] Zu M. Deweys Dezimalklassifikationssystem s. Menne 1980, 97ff.

[79] K. Heger 1976, 38-60, bes. 58; vgl. auch Kubczak 1975, 28-33; idem 1978, 26-32 sowie Baldinger 1980, 139ff., 260-82.

# Figur 3:

## HEGERS TRAPEZIUM (IN VON MIR VERDEUTLICHTER FORM)

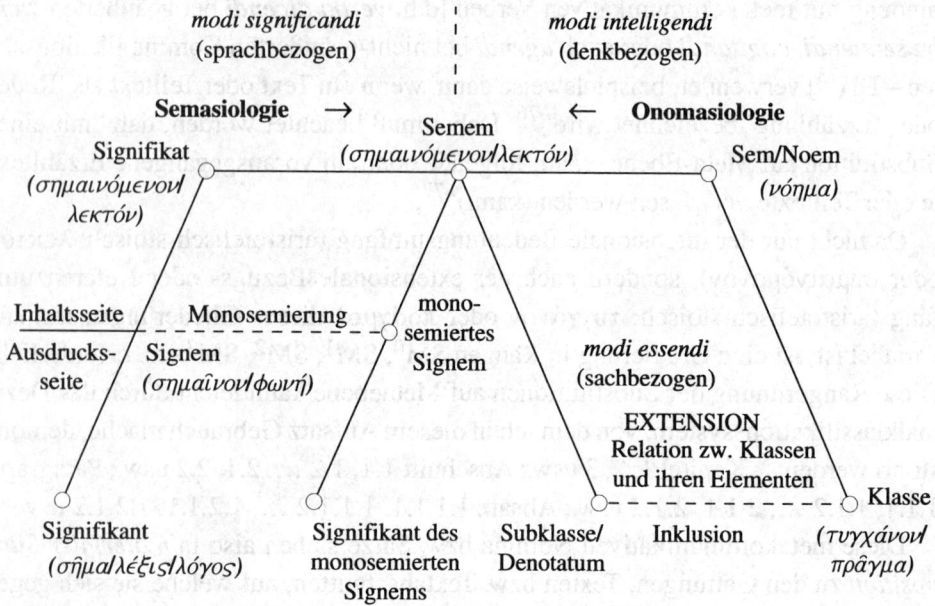

## Exkurs: Erläuterungen zum verdeutlichten Trapezium

Das Trapez-Modell selbst mit dem eingebauten Dreieck ist folgendermaßen anwendbar:
(1) Auf den *Ebenen der Parole, der Σ-parole sowie der Langue;* auf der *Parole*-Ebene genügt das Dreieck, da hier die Monosemierung (durch den Kontext) vorausgesetzt ist; auf der *Σ-parole*-Ebene genügt das Trapezium ohne Dreieck, da hier keine Monosemierung vorgesehen ist und das einfache Trapezium lediglich für paradigmatische *Signem*-Analysen gebraucht werden kann; lediglich auf der *Langue*-Ebene ist das vollständige Trapezium mit Dreieck erforderlich, denn das Dreieck-Modell vermag nicht auf der *ersten Metaebene* das Phänomen Synonymie oder Polysemie zu erklären, und bei *Langue*-Analysen ist eine Monosemierung mit Hilfe der syntagmatischen Umgebung (in Form von *Linguemen* des Ranges Rn ±1) vorausgesetzt[80]. Das Signifikat wird laut Heger definiert als eine dem Signem entsprechende Einheit der Inhaltsseite, die "sowohl polysem als auch mit Signifikaten anderer Signeme partiell synonym sein kann"[81]; hinzu kommt, daß auf der *zweiten Metaebene* das Dreieck-Modell eine Definition von Semasiologie und Onomasiologie nicht zuläßt, die "nicht als tautologische Spiegelbilder von einander erscheinen"[82]. (2) Anwendbar ist

---

[80] Heger 1969, 171, 175; idem 1976, 53ff.
[81] Heger 1976, 41.
[82] Heger 1969, 169.

ferner das Trapez-Modell sowohl auf der *einzelsprachlichen als auch auf der außereinzel-sprachlichen Ebene*, da es nicht nur *Seme*, sondern auch *Noeme* berücksichtigt. *Seme* sind dabei als kleinste distinktive Einheiten definiert, die folglich in den meisten Fällen auf einzelsprachlich gebundene *Sememe* bezogen werden; *Noeme* dagegen stellen intensional definierte Begriffe dar, die von einzelsprachlichen Bedingungen frei sind, d.h. sie sind außer-einzelsprachlichen Charakters. "The distinction between *seme* and *noeme* helps avoid misunderstanding. *Seme* corresponds to an internal analysis of a given language; *noeme* corresponds to a comparative analysis, whether of two different languages or of two different stages of the same language"[83]. (3) Durch die Verwendung des *Signems* wird ausdrücklich betont, daß das Modell "nicht nur für signifikative Minimaleinheiten (*Moneme*), sondern auch für signifikative Einheiten höherer hierarchischer Ränge ... brauchbar sein soll"[84]. Die Ersetzung des Monems mit Signem im Trapezium hat also wie Baldinger bemerkt weitgehende Konsequenzen: "the model becomes applicable to the complete hierarchy of meaningful units (from the moneme to the sentence, and even further, to the text = *ascending analysis* or *descending analysis*, depending on the direction of the analysis)"[85].

Als gedankliche Hilfe bei der Erklärung des Trapeziums kann die scholastische Unterscheidung zwischen *"modi significandi"*, *"modi intelligendi"* und *"modi essendi"* dienen. Sie bestand in der Unterscheidung zwischen sprachbezogenen (*voces*), denkbezogenen (*intellectus*) und sachbezogenen (*res*) Aspekten[86]. Die *modi significandi* wurden teils passivisch als "Eigenschaften der Sache, so, wie sie durch die Sprache bezeichnet wird", teils aktivisch als "Eigenschaften der sprachlichen Formen (bzw. der Sprache), die Eigenschaft der Sprache, eine Sache zu 'bedeuten'" verstanden; die *modi intelligendi* dagegen teils passivisch "als Eigenschaften der Sachen als vom Verstand erfaßt", teils aktivisch "als Eigenschaften des Verstandes selbst, der etwas erfaßt"[87] verstanden.

Zur Unterscheidung zwischen *"Semasiologie"* und *"Onomasiologie"*, siehe bes. die Ausführungen bei Heger und Baldinger[88]. Heger stellt dabei klar, daß im *Semem* "sich die einzelsprachliche linke mit der außereinzelsprachlichen rechten Seite" des Trapeziums trifft[89]. Baldinger seinerseits unterscheidet zuerst zwischen der *Struktur* einer Einzelsprache und dem *System* einer außereinzelsprachlichen Einheit, wobei das System *per definitionem* abstrakter ist als die Struktur. Sprache ist laut ihm einerseits "un système où tout se tient"[90], andererseits aber mit Mario Wandruszka "ein System [laut Baldinger besser: eine

---

[83] Baldinger 1980, 267; vgl. auch Heger 1983 und idem 1987, 427; ferner Raible 1983, 1-9 und idem 1989, 107.

[84] Heger 1976, 40; ferner ibid., 29, 40-41; jetzt auch idem 1992, 11f.

[85] Baldinger 1980, 262ff. (Zitat von S. 262).

[86] Vgl. Coseriu 1975, 153-57; ferner J. Lyons 1973, 274ff., 446ff.; H. Arens 1980, 99f.; J. Pinborg 1984, 68-72 und Raible 1983, 6f.; idem 1987, bes. 504f.

[87] Coseriu 1975, 155.

[88] Baldinger 1980, 110ff., 277-309 [= deutsch 1978, 372-401]; Heger 1969; vgl. auch Hellholm 1986, 23.

[89] Heger 1969, 168.

[90] Baldinger, ibid. 141.

Struktur] von Programmen in verschiedenen Registern, mit vielfältiger Defizienz und Red-undanz, mit Mangel und Überfluß"[91]. Diese Unterscheidung entspricht derjenigen zwischen onomasiologischen und semasiologischen Aspekten[92]. Das Verhältnis dieser beiden Unterscheidungen zu einander wird dann von Baldinger so formuliert, daß es die beiden Hälfte des Trapeziums erhellt und erklärt: "In fact, the [imperfect –DH] structure realized in a given language is always the starting-point for semasiology. The coherent [and perfect –DH] system, on the other hand, is the starting-point for onomasiology. The *structure* or structures are always the structure or structures of a given language. The *system* is always of a conceptual order, going beyond any given language"[93]. Auch aus kommunikativer Sicht verhält es sich ähnlich, wie Baldinger hervorhebt, denn im Kommunikationsprozeß bleibt die Bipolarität zwischen Sender und Empfänger, Sprecher und Hörer eine grundlegende Struktur: "These two poles correspond exactly to the opposition ... between semasiology and onomasiology. The hearer receives from his interlocutor forms, the meaning of which he must determine in order to understand them. Thus, the hearer's task is semasiological. The speaker, on the other hand, has to communicate mental objects (concepts). He must select designations from the vocabulary placed at his disposal by his memory; he must link concepts to acoustic images, so converting them into *signifiants*; that is, his task is onomasiological"[94].

Zur von mir hinzugefügten aristotelischen bzw. stoischen Terminologie, siehe zu ersterer Klaus Oehler[95], der unter Hinweis auf "die zeichentheoretisch wichtigste Stelle bei Aristoteles" (*De int.* 1.16a 3-8: *Die stimmlichen Äußerungen sind Symbole der Widerfahrnisse in der Seele, und das Geschriebene ist Symbol für die stimmlichen Äußerungen. Und wie nicht alle dieselbe Schrift haben, so haben auch nicht alle dieselben Laute. Wofür jedoch diese erstlich Zeichen sind, nämlich für die Widerfahrnisse in der Seele, die sind bei allen dieselben, und ebenso sind die Dinge dieselben, von denen die Widerfahrnisse der Seele Abbildungen sind;* Ἔστι μὲν οὖν τὰ ἐν τῇ φωνῇ τῶν ἐν τῇ ψυχῇ παθημάτων σύμβολα, καὶ τὰ γραφόμενα τῶν ἐν τῇ φωνῇ· καὶ ὥσπερ οὐδὲ γράμματα πᾶσι τὰ αὐτά, οὐδέ φωναὶ αἱ αὐταί· ὧν μέντοι ταῦτα σημεῖα πρώτως, ταὐτὰ πᾶσι παθήματα τῆς ψυχῆς, καὶ ὧν ταῦτα ὁμοιώματα πράγματα ἤδη ταὐτά [ibid., 251]), mit Recht darauf aufmerksam macht, daß "die anscheinend unsterbliche Fable convenue, erst die Stoiker hätten das, was ausgesagt wird oder werden kann (σημαινόμενον = λεκτόν), d.h. die Bedeutung, einerseits von dem Sprachzeichen (σημαίνον) und andererseits von dem Gegenstand (τυγχάνον) unterschieden, wird durch Aristoteles ganz einfach widerlegt ... Im triadischen Zeichenbegriff des Aristoteles wird erstmals in der griechischen Philosophie die Differenz zwischen der Bedeutung und dem Gegenstandsbezug sprachlicher Ausdrücke thematisiert". Zur stoischen Terminologie bzw. Sprachphilosophie verweise ich auf die Ausführungen bei Cose-

---

[91] M. Wandruszka 1967, 3-7.
[92] Baldinger 1980, 142.
[93] Ibid. 151. Vgl. hierzu auch Coseriu 1988a, 250-65; idem 1988b, bes. 89-132, 132-58.
[94] Baldinger 1980, 132.
[95] Oehler 1986, 255f.; so auch v. Kutschera 1975, 45f. Anm. 32.

riu u.A.[96].

Auf die konträre Interpretation der linken Triangel- bzw. Trapez-Seite bei Coseriu auf der einen Seite, der eine *Identifikation* zwischen Aristoteles 'semiotischem Dreieck' und de Saussures Unterscheidung zwischen 'Ausdrucks- und Inhaltsseite' vertritt[97], und bei Hans-Heinrich Lieb und Klaus Oehler andererseits, welche eine *Differenz* zwischen dem auf Aristoteles aufgebauten 'semiotischen Dreieck' bei Ogden und Richards[98] und die *'signifiant-signifié'*-Ellipse' (= Wortform – Wortinhalt) bei de Saussure[99] vertreten[100], kann in diesem Zusammenhang nicht mehr eingegangen werden.

Zur Unterscheidung zwischen 'Extension' und 'Denotatum', ist die Klarstellung bei der Logikerin S. Stebbing hilfreich, wenn sie feststellt, daß "the extension of a term signifying a class-property is all the varieties distinguished as subclasses. The extension, therefore, are *classes*, not individuals; the denotation is the *membership of the classes*, not the classes"[101].

Das Vorkommen von Klassen sowie von Denotata in der unteren rechten Trapez-Ecke entspricht dem Vorkommen von *Semen* und *Noemen* in der oberen rechten Trapez-Ecke, und zeigt somit an, daß in Wirklichkeit hier "zwei verschiedene Trapeze" vorliegen.[102] Die Möglichkeit sowohl Denotata als auch extensionale Klassen in der unteren rechten Trapez-Ecke einzubeziehen wird jetzt von Heger zugestanden: "Für das Trapez-Modell selbst sehe ich daher heute keinen Hinderungsgrund, für die rechte untere Ecke zu einer sowohl die 'Sache' als auch den extensionalen Aspekt der 'Klasse' berücksichtigenden Besetzung mit der extensional zu interpretierenden 'Element-Klasse-Relation' überzugehen".[103]

Wie oben dargelegt wurde, soll durch eine etwas detailliertere Darstellung der unteren rechten Trapezecke in Hegers semantischem Trapez-Modell jetzt (in *Figur 4*) verdeutlicht werden, daß nicht nur "Gegenstände" wie "Textklassen", "Texte" und "Teiltexte" sowie "Sachverhalte" auf der textexternen *suppositio-formalis*-Ebene, sondern auch "Textklassen", "Texte" und "Teiltexte" auf der textinternen *suppositio-materialis*-Ebene Referenzobjekte darstellen können:

---

[96] Coseriu 1975, 113-22; ferner H. Geckeler 1971, 80; von Kutschera 1975, 38-46 sowie H. E. Brekle 1985, 44-67 mit weiterer Lit.

[97] Coseriu 1975, 74-91; idem 1988a, 14f.

[98] C. K. Ogden/I. A. Richards 1946, 11.

[99] F. de Saussure 19[16]/67, 76ff.

[100] H. H. Lieb 1981, bes. 146, 154; Kl. Oehler 1986, 257.

[101] S. Stebbing 1965, 105; so auch Heger 1969, 163f.; idem 1976, 35-7 sowie Kubczak 1975, 84ff.

[102] Heger 1987, 427.

[103] Heger 1987, 429 mit Hinweis auf Heger-Mudersbach 1984, 27-39 [§ 2.5].

## Figur 4:

### DAS "ALIQUO" DES KLASSISCHEN "ALIQUID STAT PRO ALIQUO"

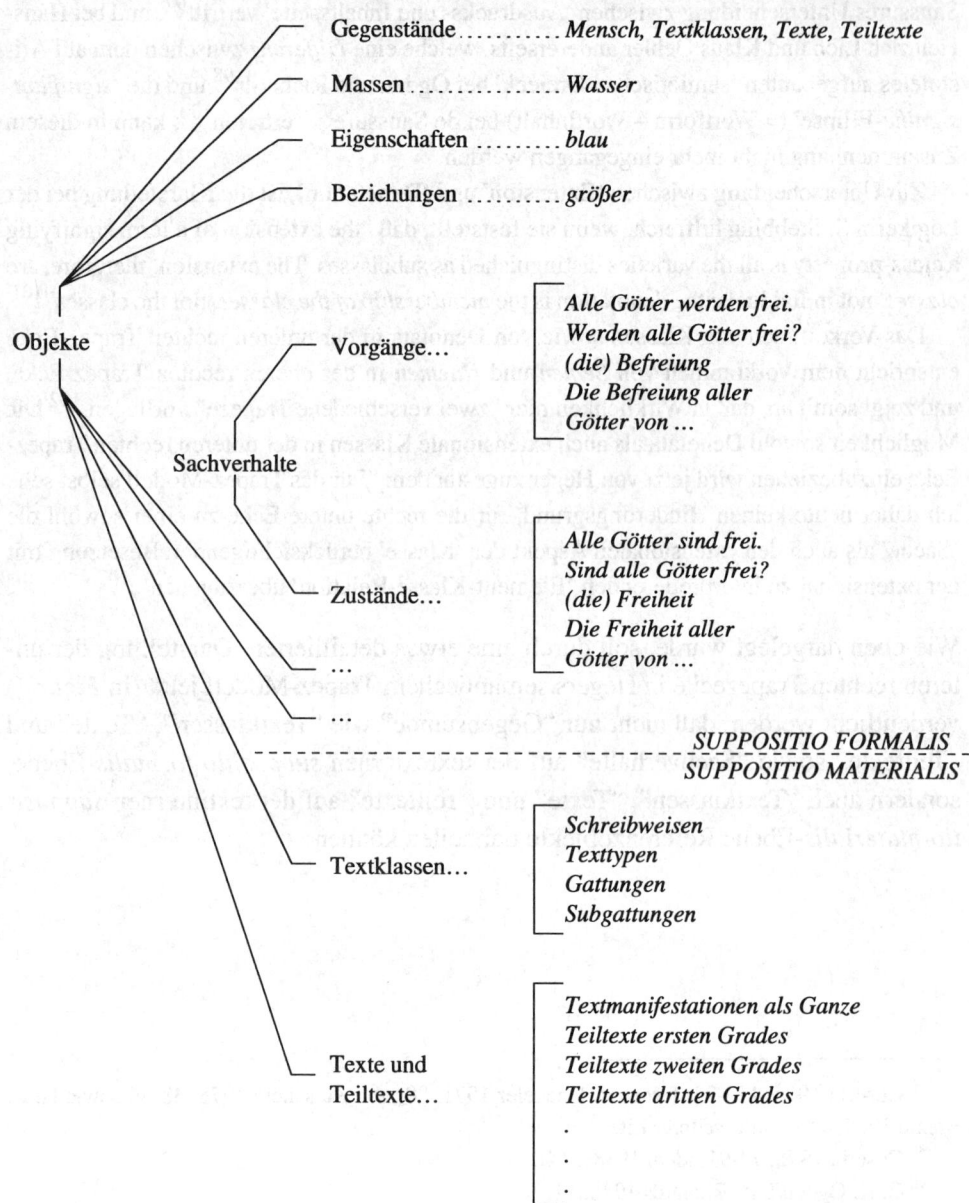

Gegenstände........... *Mensch, Textklassen, Texte, Teiltexte*

Massen................ *Wasser*

Eigenschaften ......... *blau*

Beziehungen .......... *größer*

Objekte

Vorgänge...
*Alle Götter werden frei.*
*Werden alle Götter frei?*
*(die) Befreiung*
*Die Befreiung aller*
*Götter von ...*

Sachverhalte

Zustände...
*Alle Götter sind frei.*
*Sind alle Götter frei?*
*(die) Freiheit*
*Die Freiheit aller*
*Götter von ...*

...

...

*SUPPOSITIO FORMALIS*
*SUPPOSITIO MATERIALIS*

Textklassen...
*Schreibweisen*
*Texttypen*
*Gattungen*
*Subgattungen*

Texte und
Teiltexte...
*Textmanifestationen als Ganze*
*Teiltexte ersten Grades*
*Teiltexte zweiten Grades*
*Teiltexte dritten Grades*

**Exkurs: Erläuterungen zum *aliquo* des klassischen *aliquid stat pro aliquo***

Dieses Schema ist Hartmut Kubczak[104] entnommen und durch die Gegenstandsmengen *Textklassen, Texte* und *Teiltexte* in bezug auf die formale Supposition sowie durch zwei Objekttypen *Textklassen, Texte* und *Teiltexte* in bezug auf die materiale Supposition erweitert worden. Kubczaks Spezifizierung des *"aliquo"* qua *suppositio formalis* fällt z.T. mit Aristoteles Verständnis von πράγματα zusammen, die "sich auf alle Entitäten, die im Rahmen der aristotelischen Ontologie vorkommen können ... also nicht nur auf räumlich ausgedehnte, sinnlich wahrnehmbare *Gegenstände,* sondern auch auf *Sachverhalte, Handlungen, Eigenschaften, Klassen (Gattungen und Arten), Klassenmerkmale etc.* (beziehen)"[105]; vgl. schon J. L. Ackrill, der in seiner Interpretation von *de int.* 16b 19 bemerkt: "The word here (and elsewhere) [sc. ... τοῦ πράγματος ... –DH] translated by 'actual thing' applies to *deeds, facts, states of affairs,* &c., as well as to *objects"*[106].

*(b) Substitution auf Abstraktionsebene (SA):* Von der Substitution auf Metaebene ist die Substitution auf Abstraktionsebene zu unterscheiden. Damit ist ein Typ von Wiederaufnahme gemeint, "bei welcher das Substituens einen größeren Bedeutungsumfang hat als das Substituendum", allerdings ohne auf einer reinen Metaebene im Verhältnis zum ersetzten Textabschnitt zu stehen[107]. "Eine solche Substitution auf Abstraktionsebene läge z.B. vor, wenn eine größere Anzahl von Sätzen oder Textabschnitten zusammengefaßt würde durch '*Diese Ereignisse* veranlaßten X usw.'"[108].

Der Sprachwissenschaftler Wolfgang Raible hat eine Typologie von 4 bzw. 5 solchen Substitutionsarten auf Abstraktionsebene aufgestellt, von denen in diesem Zusammenhang nur zwei von Bedeutung sind:

"Typ A: 'X schwieg sehr lange. *Sein (dieses, das) Schweigen* hat sich gelohnt'"[109]. Bei diesem Substitutionstyp liegt, worauf Raible hinweist, der Fall vor, den der Indogermanist Walter Porzig schon 1940 an Beispielen aus dem Altgriechischen als "Namen für Satzinhalte" bezeichnet hatte[110]. Porzig schreibt: "Hier handelt es sich ... um Sätze, in denen der Inhalt eines anderen Satzes, dargestellt durch ein abstraktes Nomen, beurteilt wird. Oft geht der Satz [man könnte hinzufügen: der Textabschnitt –DH], über den geurteilt wird, unmittelbar vorher, so daß ihn das abstrakte Nomen aufnimmt"[111].

---

[104] Kubczak 1975, 69; idem 1978, 34.

[105] Oehler 1986, 256 (Hervorheb. von mir).

[106] J. L. Ackrill 1963, 122 (Hervorheb. von mir).

[107] Gülich/Raible 1977a, 142; Raible 1972, 150.

[108] Gülich/Raible 1977a, 142.

[109] Raible 1972, 195; s. auch die Analyse ibid., 196.

[110] Vgl. Raible 1972, 182.

[111] W. Porzig 1942, 75; vgl. auch Palm 1960, 14.

"Typ B: 'Balzac arbeitete für zwei. *Er tat dies (es)* wegen seiner Schulden'"[112]. Hier "wird einem Verb₁ ein Verb₂ + pronominale Form (oder Pronomen) substituiert. Das zweite Verb muß dabei ein Verb auf Abstraktionsebene sein ..."[113]. Das abstrakte Verb ist hier 'tun'.

Die Abstraktionsebene "stellt eine – stets relative – Zwischenstufe zwischen den beiden Polen Text und Metatext dar"[114]. Es handelt sich um eine Reduktion von Texten, Teiltexten bzw. Sätzen durch ein "Abstraktum" (das nicht direkt meta-narrativ ist) mitunter, wie schon Porzig beobachtet hat, in Verbindung mit einem "Verb des Aufhörens"[115] und/oder mit einem gleichwertigen Präpositionsausdruck bzw. einem temporalen Nebensatz. In Ergänzung zu den Stellen aus der Didache, die oben § 2.1. II (3) zitiert wurden, gebe ich vier Beispiele aus Hermas: ἐτέλεσεν οὖν τὴν ἐξήγησιν τοῦ πύργου [So *hatte* sie *die Erklärung* des Turmes *vollendet*] (15,4); μετὰ τὸ λαλῆσαι αὐτὴν τὰ ῥήματα ταῦτα κτλ. [*Als* sie *diese Worte gesprochen hatte* usw.] (2,1); μετὰ τὸ παῆναι αὐτῆς τὰ ῥήματα ταῦτα κτλ. [*Nachdem diese* ihre *Worte zu Ende gekommen waren* usw.] (3,3); ὅτε οὖν ἐπαυσάμην ἐρωτῶν αὐτὴν περὶ πάντων τούτων κτλ. [*Als* ich nun mit meinen Fragen über *dies alles zu Ende gekommen war* usw.] (16,1)[116]. Diese Beispiele zeigen klar, wie die SA zwischen den Polen Text und Metatext oszillieren können: περὶ πάντων τούτων steht der Textebene, τὰ ῥήματα ταῦτα der Metaebene am nächsten, während τὴν ἐξήγησιν τοῦ πύργου sich dazwischen befindet, aber doch eindeutig näher an der Metaebene als an der Textebene.

Auch diese Substitutionsart kann gliedernde Funktion haben, jedoch nicht auf derselben Ebene wie die Substitution auf Metaebene, "sondern je nach Umfang des substituierten Textpassus auf einer der nachfolgenden Stufen"[117]; sie sind nämlich diese untergeordnet, was ausschlaggebend sein wird bei der Gesamtdelimitation bzw. der Kompositionsanalyse des Matthäusevangeliums. Bedeutungsvoll ist außerdem noch die Feststellung, daß auch diese Substitutionsart nicht in erster Linie auf außersprachliche Phänomene Bezug nimmt, sondern hauptsächlich eine mildere Form von *materialer Supposition* darstellt[118].

Nachdem wir so die beiden Substitutionsarten näher charakterisiert haben, können wir jetzt einen Teil der substitutionellen Gliederungsmerkmale im Matthäus-

---

[112] Raible 1972, 195.

[113] Raible, ibid., 197; s. auch die weitere Analyse ibid.

[114] Raible, ibid., 13; vgl. den ganzen Abschnitt ibid.,13-21.

[115] Porzig 1942, 46ff.; vgl. auch Palm 1960, 14: "In dieser Hinsicht [sc. Demonstrativa als Attribut – DH] hat sich also bei Thuk. ein fester Anordnungstypus entwickelt. Meistenteils finden wir ihn in Sätzen, die einen Abschnitt abschließen und zu einem neuen hinüberleite[n]".

[116] S. Hellholm 1980, 86f. mit weiteren Beispielen.

[117] S. Gülich/Raible 1977a, 142 und ferner die Bemerkungen unten ad Anm. 142.

[118] Vgl. Harweg 1980, 306 mit Anm. 27 auf Seite 327.

evangelium einer eingehenden sprachwissenschaftlichen Analyse unterziehen.

## 3. Einige substitutionelle Gliederungsmerkmale im Matthäusevangelium

Bei der Analyse der substitutionellen Gliederungsmerkmale im Matthäusevange-lium werde ich diese in der umgekehrten Reihenfolge behandeln, wie ich sie oben dargestellt habe.

### 3.1. Substitutionen auf Abstraktionsebene

Diejenigen redaktionellen Redewendungen[119], die am Ende der fünf großen von Matthäus thematisierten Redekompositionen[120] Jesu zu finden sind, sehen in einer Zusammenstellung wie folgt aus:

7,28   καὶ ἐγένετο ὅτε <u>ἐτέλεσεν</u> ὁ Ἰησοῦς <u>τοὺς λόγους τούτους</u> κτλ.

11,1   καὶ ἐγένετο ὅτε <u>ἐτέλεσεν</u> ὁ Ἰησοῦς <u>διατάσσων</u> τοῖς δώδεκα μαθηταῖς αὐτοῦ κτλ.

13,53 καὶ ἐγένετο ὅτε <u>ἐτέλεσεν</u> ὁ Ἰησοῦς <u>τὰς παραβολὰς ταύτας</u> κτλ.

19,1   καὶ ἐγένετο ὅτε <u>ἐτέλεσεν</u> ὁ Ἰησοῦς <u>τοὺς λόγους τούτους</u> κτλ.

26,1   καὶ ἐγένετο ὅτε <u>ἐτέλεσεν</u> ὁ Ἰησοῦς <u>πάντας τοὺς λόγους τούτους</u> κτλ.

Ihre textgrammatische Struktur kann, nach unserer Charakterisierung oben, nicht mehr zweifelhaft sein. Es handelt sich, u.zw. eindeutig, um *Substitutionen auf Ab-straktionsebene*, denn hier finden sich: (a) *abstrakte Nomina* bzw. in einem Fall ein *abstraktes Verb* zusammen mit Demonstrativpronomina: (πάντας) τοὺς λόγους τούτους, τὰς παραβολὰς ταύτας bzw. διατάσσων; (b) in allen Fällen befinden sich diese abstrakten Nomina bzw. das abstrakte Verb in Verbindung mit einem *Verb des Aufhörens* (τελεῖν; vgl. die Beispiele aus Hermas oben § 2.2 (b): 3,3: παῆναι und 16,1: παύεσθαι und Lukas 7,1 [s. unten Anm. 121]: πληροῦν sowie προειρεῖν bzw. προείρησθαι in Didache 7,1 und 11,1 zitiert oben § 2.1. II (3))[121]. Die jeweiligen Substitutionswendungen nehmen Bezug auf die jeweils vorhergehende Rede, auf die—entweder in sehr abstrakter Form durch λόγοι[122], oder weniger abstrakt durch παραβολαί bzw. διατάσσων—referiert wird. Von diesen fünf Substitutionen auf

---

[119] Vgl. B. H. Streeter 1924, 262 als einen der ersten Entdecker dieser formelhaften Wendung und s. ferner Betz 1992, 277-79 sowie die Kommentare ad. loc.

[120] Vgl. D. R. Bauer 1988, 132: "it is ... true that the five great discourses are explicitly noted by Matthew in the transitional statements; by this means, *he draws attention to them*" (meine Hervor-heb.); H. Koester 1990, 329: "Matthew, though following for the most part Mark's narrative, high-lights the discourses of Jesus. They become the center of Jesus' ministry ... the speeches constitute the focus of Jesus' ministry. The miracles and other narratives from Mark have been drastically shor-tened in Matthew's text".

Abstraktionsebene entsprechen die 1., 3., 4. und 5. dem Typ A von Raible[123], den Porzig "Namen für Satzinhalte" genannt hatte, während die 2. dem Typ B von Raible entspricht. Das Substituens besteht in diesem Falle aus dem abstrakten Verb διατάσσειν, das zwar weniger abstrakt ist als *tun* aber genau den abstrakten Verben ἀναγινώσκειν bzw. λαλεῖν in den Wendungen ὅτε ἐτέλεσεν ἀναγινώσκουσα κτλ. bzw. ὅτε οὖν ἐπαύσατο μετ᾽ ἐμοῦ λαλοῦσα κτλ. in Hermas 4,1 bzw. 18,1 entspricht[124]. In allen fünf Fällen können wir feststellen, daß die Substituentia sich sehr nahe an meta-narrativen Abstrakta befinden, was mit Raibles Feststellung von deren relativer Zwischenstufe zwischen Text und Metatext nur übereinstimmt. Dieser meta-narrative Charakter erklärt sich in diesen Sätzen natürlich durch ihre Funktion als Abschluß-Signale für die fünf großen *Reden* Jesu in diesem Evangelium.

Auf zwei Besonderheiten, die öfters diskutiert worden sind, möchte ich noch

---

[121] Vgl. Porzig 1942, 54f.; bes. interessant ist der parallele Abschluß der lukanischen Feldrede 7,1: Ἐπειδὴ ἐπλήρωσεν πάντα τὰ ῥήματα αὐτοῦ εἰς τὰς ἀκοὰς τοῦ λαοῦ, εἰσῆλθεν εἰς Καφαρναούμ. Der historisch bedeutungsvollen diachronen Frage, die sich aufgrund der Ähnlichkeit zwischen Matt. 7,28 und Luk. 7,1 einstellt, ob Matt. diese SA aus einer seiner Quellen übernommen und adaptiert hat, kann hier nicht nachgegangen werden; *unter Voraussetzung der Q-Grundlage* für die Berg- sowie für die Feldpredigt (Matt. 5,1-7,29 bzw. Luk. 6,20-49), vgl. z.B. Streeter 1924, 268; E. Klostermann 1929/75, 85f.; E. Schweizer 1973, 123; Luz 1985, 415; Gnilka 1986, 283; Schürmann 1969, 391; Schenk 1987, 440 und nunmehr auch die Q-Synopse von Kloppenborg 1988, 48-50: "The lack of significant agreement between Matthew and Luke, coupled with the presence of Matthean and Lukan elements and Markan influence suggests that both evangelists have thoroughly reworked Q at this point" (Zitat von S. 50). *Abhängigkeit von Q wird bestritten* von Frankemölle 1974, 334. Die lukanische Redaktion von 7,1 betonen J. Jeremias 1980, 151; Luz, ibid., Davies/Allison 1988, 724 und zuletzt F. Bovon 1989, 347, der sowohl eine materiale als auch eine formale Suppositiondeutung vertritt, wenn er schreibt: "Πληρόω weist nicht nur auf das Ende der Feldrede (τελέω [? –DH]), sondern auch auf die Fülle der Worte Jesu: Jesus hat alles gesagt, was er sagen wollte"; Bovon stellt aber gleichzeitig fest, daß "Lukas ... das Wort πληρόω zwar häufig, aber nirgendwo sonst für das Ende einer Rede (verwendet)" (ibid. Anm. 13), also im Zusammenhang mit einer SA (sic!). Im Unterschied zum Abschluß der Bergpredigt wird hier ein kataphorischer Hinweis auf das, was im Text folgt, gegeben; vgl. unten Anm. 138.

[122] Der Plural οἱ λόγοι wird hier polysemisch gebraucht: erstens in der Bedeutung "eine zusammenhängende Rede" (s. W. Bauer 1988, 969 [s.v. 1aδ]), aufgefaßt als *suppositio formalis*; zweitens aber auch in der durch das Demonstrativum indizierten Bedeutung "geschriebene Worte u. Reden" (s. Bauer, ibid., 970 [s.v. 1aζ]), u.U. aufgefaßt als *suppositio materialis*. Bauer verzeichnet hier u.A. zurecht Apk. 1,3; 22,7. 9f. 18f. Er registriert indessen keine der Redeabschlußwendungen unter der zweiten Bedeutung, was darauf hindeutet, daß er ihre textgrammatische Funktion als SA mit Referenz auf die *Redekompositionen* nicht beachtet hat, was ein weiteres Indizium für ihre Zwischenstellung zwischen Text und Metatext ausmacht.

[123] Vgl. Raible 1972, 203: "Typisch für alle Fälle [des Substitutionstyps A –DH] ist der stets zusammen mit den auf Abstraktionsebene substituierenden Nomina vorkommende anaphorische/deiktische Artikel ...."

[124] S. Hellholm 1980, 87.

kurz eingehen:

(1) Es ist schon längst beobachtet worden, daß die letzte Rede Jesu eigentlich aus zwei Reden besteht, die Matthäus zusammengefügt hat und durch die letzte Substitution auf Abstraktionsebene hat beenden lassen. Dies ist in der Tat durch die Sonderform der Wendung selbst in 26,1 angegeben, wenn es dort heißt: πάντας τοὺς λόγους τούτους. Πάντας bezieht sich demzufolge nicht, jedenfalls nicht ausschließlich bzw. in erster Linie, wie Luz und andere vor und nach ihm meinen, auf "alle fünf Reden"[125], sondern auf die beiden Kompositionsteile in Kapp. 23-25, die von Matthäus als nur eine, aber dafür sehr lange Rede gehalten werden. Das nachgestellte[126] Demonstrativpronomen τούτους referiert hier mit Hilfe seines abstrakten Hauptwortes (τοὺς λόγους) textdeiktisch auf eine oder mehrere Teil-texte[127]. "Durch das Dem[onstrativum] wird der in dem Hauptwort liegende Begriff mit einem im Zusammenhang vorkommenden identifiziert"[128]. Diese 'Identifikation' zwischen einem abstrakten Hauptwort und Teiltexten oder Sätzen ist das – wie oben betont wurde – was eine Substitution auf Abstraktionsebene (SA) konstituiert. Das prädikative πάντας gibt den extensionalen Bezugsumfang der Substitution an, ist aber in diesem Falle zweideutig: von der obigen Zusammenstellung der substitutionellen Redeschlußwendungen (SA) her, gewinnt man leicht den Eindruck, daß in der letzten SA Matthäus mit Hilfe von πάντας *"alle"* Reden Jesu zusammenfassen möchte, wobei dem πάντας ein sehr weiter Bezugsumfang beigemessen wird; geht man hingegen von der Tatsache aus, daß jede der fünf über das gesamte Evangelium verstreuten Reden mit ihrer jeweils eigenen Substitution beendet wird, so läge es wohl näher, anzunehmen, daß πάντας auf die *"ganze"* letzte, u.zw. aus zwei Teilen zusammengesetzte, Rede Jesu, aber auch *nur* auf diese, referiert; damit wird für diese Substitution (SA) ein begrenzterer Bezugsumfang vorausgesetzt[129]. Hierfür spricht (a) die Tatsache, daß der erste Teil dieser Rede, der tatsächlich eine eigene Rede darstellt (vgl. die Situationsbeschreibung 24,1-3!), mit keiner Substitutions-

---

[125] Luz 1985, 415 Anm. 3; vgl. u.a. auch Klostermann 1927/71, 207, Grundmann 1968, 530f. und jetzt auch Gnilka 1986, 283, idem 1988, 383: "Damit sind vom Ende her alle Redekompositionen nochmals verbunden" sowie D. R. Bauer 1988, 132, Koester 1990, 330: "... the last discourse ends with 'and it happened, when Jesus had finished *all* these words ...'" und Standaert 1992, 1239, who translates: "quand Jésus eut achevé *tous* ces discours".

[126] Dazu vor allem Palm 1960.

[127] S. Hellholm 1980, 51f. mit Lit.; vgl. auch Palm, ibid., 8ff.

[128] Palm, ibid., 8.

[129] So auch die schwedische Übersetzung von 1981: "När Jesus hade avslutat *hela* detta tal ... [Als Jesus diese *ganze* Rede beendet hatte ...]" (Übers. und Hervorheb. von mir); und jetzt Byrskog 1994, 207 Anm. 6 unter Verweis auf meine Beobachtung in Hellholm 1986/87, 87f. Weniger wahrscheinlich ist der Bezug "auf die letzten von Kap. 21 an als 'alle Jerusalamer Reden'", so Schenk 1987, 440; indirekt dagegen jetzt auch Davies/Allison 1988, 61 Anm. 31 (s. folgende Anm.).

formel beendet wird, was im Matt. singulär wäre[130]; subsidiäres Argument für die Auffassung von Kap. 23-25 als eine einzige Rede ist ferner die Tatsache, daß *auch* im ersten Teil dieser Rede (23,1-38) Jesus, wie in all den anderen Reden, nicht nur die Volksmenge oder die vorösterlichen Jünger, sondern auch und vor allem den implizierten Leser anredet; dieser ist ja irgendein Jünger, der in der Periode zwischen Jesu Auferstehung und seiner Parusie das Evangelium hört: "To hear and to internalize Jesus' speeches is to be conformed to the shape of his life. This, then, is the chief purpose of Jesus' great speeches: to bring the life of the disciple, or the implied reader, into conformity with the shape of Jesus' life" (cf. 23:12!);[131](b) die Tatsache, daß Lukas in dem oben Anm. 121 zitierten Redeabschluß seiner Feldrede (7,1) den Ausdruck πάντα τὰ ῥήματα[132] auf die *ganze* Feldrede und nicht auf eine Reihe von Reden referieren lassen kann; (c) die formgeschichtliche bzw. linguistische Bestimmung dieser Sätze als Substitutionen auf Abstraktionsebene mit dem schon erwähnten begleitenden Umstand, daß "der Satz [bzw. der Textabschnitt – DH], über den geurteilt wird [d.h. das Substituendum –DH], (oft) *unmittelbar vorher(geht)*"[133].

Nachdem die Argumente für sowie gegen einen umfangreicheren Bezugs- bzw. Bedeutungsumfang angegeben worden sind, scheint mir schon an dieser Stelle im Matt. eine sowohl semantisch als auch sigmatisch doppeldeutige Aussage vorzuliegen, die zum einen die *ganze* letzte, sehr umfangsreiche Rede abschließt und gleichzeitig angibt, daß damit auch *alle* Reden Jesu nun zu einem Ende gekommen sind: die polysemisch angegebenen Bedeutungsumfänge sowie die entsprechenden Bezugsumfänge wären somit Rechnung getragen.

(2) Im Streit um die Benennung dieses Substitutionstyps unter den Exegeten ist der *Funktionsaspekt* von bes. Bedeutung: Handelt es sich um "Abschlußwendungen"[134] oder um "Überleitungs- bzw. Übergangsformeln" wie schon Streeter und nach ihm u.a. Kingsbury, Luz, Wilkens, Gnilka, Schenk und D. R. Bauer meinen[135]? Bei der Beantwortung dieser Frage muß dreierlei bedacht werden: (a) die

---

[130] Vgl. auch Davies/Allison 1988, ibid.: "Mt 23, which is clearly separate from the eschatological discourse in 24-5 (note the new beginning in 24.1), does not constitute a sixth discourse. It lacks the fixed formula found at the end of 5-7, 10, 13, 18, and 24-5"; so erneut Allison 1992, 1208, wo er das Matt. in abwechselnd sechs narrative und fünf diskursive Einheiten einteilt. Diesem Kapitel aber den Redecharakter abzusprechen ist wenig einleuchtend. Die oben vorgeschlagene Deutung bietet m.E. auch die beste Lösung zum Ausbleiben der Substitutionsformel nach Kap. 23; dadurch wird die abwechselnd narrative und diskursive Struktur, die Allison befürwortet, jedoch nicht beeinträchtigt!

[131] Kingsbury 1988, 111; zum zweiten Teil dieses ersten Redeteils s. E. Haenchen 1965b, 50ff.

[132] Zur Bedeutung "Verkündigung" von τὰ ῥήματα bei Lukas, s. Jeremias 1980, 54 und 151.

[133] S. oben Anm. 111 (Hervorheb. von mir).

[134] So die meisten Kommentatoren.

*Substitutionen selbst* beziehen sich ausdrücklich auf die vorhergehenden Reden durch die abstrakten Nomina bzw. das abstrakte Verb sowie durch deren Verbindung mit einem Verb des Aufhörens; (b) die der Substitutionswendung vorangehende stereotype, septuagintierende[136] Formulierung καὶ ἐγένετο weist zwar kataphorisch auf etwas im Nachtext hin, nicht unbedingt aber auf einen Textabschnitt in Form einer *suppositio materialis*, die wohl zunächst als *Substitution auf Metaebene* aufzufassen wäre (so vor allem 11,1[137]), sondern bisweilen, wie 7,28 deutlich zeigt, begrenzt auf ein Geschehen, das im Redeschluß selbst zur Erwähnung kommt, also in Form einer *suppositio formalis;* (c) diejenigen *Sätze*, von denen die Substitutionswendungen einen Teil darstellen, sind – wie soeben erwähnt wurde – nicht einheitlich: in 7,28 gibt es im ganzen Satz (καὶ ἐγένετο inbegriffen!) keinen Bezug auf den folgenden Text[138], wie die Formulierung zeigt: καὶ ἐγένετο ὅτε ἐτέλεσεν ὁ Ἰησοῦς τοὺς λόγους τούτους ἐξεπλήσσοντο οἱ ὄχλοι ἐπὶ τῇ διδαχῇ αὐτοῦ· ἦν γὰρ διδάσκων αὐτοὺς ὡς ἐξουσίαν ἔχων καὶ οὐχ ὡς οἱ γραμματεῖς αὐτῶν. Der ganze Satz ist ein anaphorischer Verweis auf die Bergpredigt, wie die Verwunderung des Publikums über Jesu διδαχή eindeutig belegt[139]. Die anderen vier Sätze am Ende der Reden weisen dagegen kataphorisch auf das hin, was noch folgt, z.B. 11,1: καὶ ἐγένετο ὅτε ἐτέλεσεν ὁ Ἰησοῦς διατάσσων τοῖς δώδεκα μαθηταῖς αὐτοῦ, μετέβη ἐκεῖθεν τοῦ διδάσκειν καὶ κηρύσσειν ἐν ταῖς πόλεσιν αὐτῶν. Der Hauptsatz weist hier zweifellos nach vorwärts, allerdings ist seine Formulierung so vage, daß man erst nach einer eingehenden Analyse entscheiden kann, ob er als *materiale* oder als *formale* Supposition einzuschätzen ist, ein Problem, dem wir unten mehrmals begegnen werden[140]. Wir können also feststellen, daß die SA selbst das Vorhergehende abschließt, ohne notwendigerweise dadurch einen Übergang zu etwas Neuem zu implizieren; dies kann durchaus der Fall sein, aber dann nur in Verbindung mit dem restlichen Satz, der somit als ganzer zu einem Überleitungs- oder Übergangsvers bzw. -perikope wird[141].

*Zusammenfassend* können wir bei diesen sog. Redeschlußwendungen eindeutig feststellen, daß es sich *textgrammatisch* um Substitutionen auf Abstraktionsebene (SA), die SM sehr nahe kommen, handelt, und daß diese jeweils auf einen vorher-

---

[135] Streeter 1924, 262: "Its emphasis is not on the 'Here endeth' but on the 'Here beginneth'; it is a formula of *transition from discourse to narrative"*; Kingsbury 1975, 6; Luz 1985, 19; Wilkens 1985, 24; Gnilka 1986, 283; Schenk 1987, 440; D. R. Bauer 1988, 129 und 132; Standaert 1992, 1224f., 1241-44.

[136] Dazu Davies/Allison 1988, 82 und bes. J. Fitzmyer 1981, 119.

[137] S. unten § 3.2.2.2. Ende.

[138] Darauf habe ich schon in Hellholm 1986-87, 88f. hingewiesen; s. jetzt auch Byrskog 1994, 345 unter Verweis auf meine Analyse ibid. Ob diese Singularität im Matt. im Unterschied zum Abschluß der Feldrede des Lukas (s. oben Anm. 121) irgendwie mit der Quellenlage der Bergpredigt (als Epitome!) zusammenhängt, kann an dieser Stelle nicht erörtert werden.

gehenden Teiltext, der eine Redekomposition darstellt, und nicht direkt auf die außersprachliche Wirksamkeit Jesu referieren. Sie stehen also teilweise[142] in materialer Supposition zu den vorhergehenden Teiltexten und funktionieren demzufolge
als echte Gliederungsmerkmale (die ja nicht nur Abschluß-, sondern auch Überlei-
tungswendungen darstellen[143]) an der Textoberfläche; in welchem hierarchischen
Rang im Vergleich mit anderen Gliederungsmerkmalen aber, bleibt noch zu überle-
gen[144]. Doch, soviel dürfte allein aus der formalen Beschreibung der Substitutionen
auf Abstraktionsebene hervorgegangen sein, daß dieses Gliederungsmerkmal nicht
ganz derselben Bedeutung wie dem der Substitutionen auf Metaebene zugemessen

---

[139] Daraus, wie aus Punkt (a) oben, geht hervor, daß es textgrammatisch nicht korrekt ist, wenn
Luz 1985, 19 schreibt: "Die Redeschlußwendung καὶ ἐγένετο ὅτε ἐτέλεσεν etc. ... schließt syntaktisch nicht eine Rede ab, sondern leitet eine neue Etappe der Erzählung *ein!*"; Falsch auch D. R.
Bauer 1988, 129, wenn er, nachdem er festgestellt hat, daß der temporale Nebensatz als einen unter-
geordneten Satz im Verhältnis zum Hauptsatz dient, behauptet: "In each case, the subordinate clause
points back to the discourse, while the main clause points ahead to the material that follows"; (wenn
Bauer, ibid. außerdem schreibt, daß "the formula consists of a temporal clause, introduced with the
temporal particle 'when' (τότε [sic! –DH]), followed by the main clause", dann fragt man sich, ob
hier in der Tat nicht eine fälschliche Rückübersetzung ins Griechische aus dem Englischen, wo
"when" sowohl Zeitadverb als auch Zeitkonjunktion sein kann, vorliegt, denn der *Nebensatz* wird
[und kann (!)] ja nicht durch das Zeitadverb τότε, sondern nur durch die Zeitkonjunktion ὅτε eingeleitet [werden]!). Zur Sache vgl. auch Hermas 15,4: ἐτέλεσεν οὖν τὴν ἐξήγησιν τοῦ πύργου, wo
nicht einmal auf eine außertextliche Reaktion verwiesen wird. Korrekt dagegen jetzt auch (s. vorhe-
rige Anm.) Davies/Allison 1988, 725: "Despite the significant parallels with the conclusions to the
other major discourses, 7.28-9 stands out as atypical. This is because it is the only conclusion which
does not carry the story forward. 11.1; 13.54; 19.1; and 26.1 all immediately immerse the reader
back into the narrative flow". Ein singuläres Phänomen stellt dieser Hinweis auf ein außertextliches
Handeln (im Sinne einer *suppositio formalis* Formulierung) im Zusammenhang mit solch einer SA
allerdings nicht dar, wie z.B. 2 (syr) Bar 87, 1 belegt: "Und es geschah, als ich alle Worte dieses Briefes beendet und ihn sorgfältig zu Ende geschrieben hatte, da faltete ich ihn zusammen, siegelte ihn
behutsam und band ihn an den Hals des Adlers" (Übers. A. F. J. Klijn 1976, 184 [leicht modifiziert]).

[140] Vgl. z.B. unten § 3.2.2.2.(b).

[141] Vgl. das Zitat von Kallmeyer/Meyer-Hermann oben § 2.2 Anfang mit den Anm. 67ff.; von
Palm oben Anm. 115; ferner Gülich/Raible 1977, 54, die ausgerechnet im Zusammenhang mit Gliederungsmerkmalen schreiben: "Es zeigt sich dabei auf jeden Fall, daß für die Konstitution und die
Enkodierung bzw. für die Dekodierung eines Textes von entscheidender Wichtigkeit die *Übergänge*
zwischen verschiedenen Teiltexten und generell die textinternen Relationen ... sind" (Hervorheb.
bei Gülich/Raible), sowie Raible 1979, 70: "Die Abgrenzung solcher Sinneinheiten oder Teiltexte
... wird dadurch möglich gemacht, daß es Signale gibt, die den Übergang von einer Sinneinheit zur
anderen markieren. Zu den 'Gliederungssignalen' ... , die solche Übergänge kennzeichnen, gehört
beispielsweise die Überlappung mehrerer Kohärenzmittel an einer bestimmten Stelle des Textes";
ferner Hellholm 1986, 54 [§ 4.2.2.2.4 #(2)].

[142] Vgl. Raibles Feststellung (zitiert oben ad Anm. 117), daß die SA sich auf einer gleitenden
Skala zwischen Text und Metatext, d.h. zwischen formaler und materialer Supposition, befinden.

[143] Vgl. oben § 3.1.(2).

werden kann, da diese Substitution sich nicht auf derselben Ebene befindet, sondern jener untergeordnet ist[145]. Diese Beobachtung wird bei der noch ausstehenden Gesamtdelimitation bzw. der Kompositionsanalyse des Matthäusevangeliums ausschlaggebend sein, denn sie spricht einerseits m.E. gegen Bacons Modell der fünf Bücher als *übergeordnetem* Kompositionsprinzip[146]. Wie die hier vorliegende Nähe dieses Substitutionstyps zu den Substitutionen auf Metaebene zeigt bedeutet dieses Urteil andererseits keineswegs, daß diese Kompositionsstruktur weniger bedeutungsvoll bzw. vom Evangelisten Matthäus weniger ausgearbeitet sein sollte; im Gegenteil, sie ist zweifellos originär matthäisch, liegt aber auf einer anderen Ebene und hat eine andere Funktion als die liniere narrative Struktur. Der liniere narrative Struktur ist in einem narrativen Text des Texttyps "Erzählung" übergeordnet und der Wechsel zwischen narrativer und diskursiver Struktur bleibt der narrativen Struktur untergeordnet.[147] Diese beiden Kompositionsstrukturen komplementieren sich aber gegenseitig.[148] Schon hier gibt es also erste entscheidende Anzeichen für die Durchtriebenheit dieses Evangelisten bei der Komposition seines Evangeliums.

---

[144] In welcher hierarchischen Rangordnung diese SA sich im Vergleich mit anderen substitutionellen und episodären Delimitationsmerkmalen im Matt. befinden, kann im Rahmen dieses Aufsatzes nicht näher behandelt, sondern muß einer weiteren Behandlung vorbehalten werden.

[145] Vgl. oben ad Anm. 117.

[146] Anders neuerdings Fornberg 1989, 18, der die Baconsche Hypothese übernimmt und mit der an und für sich richtigen Feststellung begründet, daß die "formelle Struktur mit alternierendem Erzähl- und Redestoff in einer sehr distinkten Weise das ganze Matt. prägt und im wesentlichen als Matthäus eigene Konstruktion anzusehen ist" (Übers. von mir); so auch Standaert 1992, 1239f. und Allison 1992, 1203: "My sympathies lie with Bacon and his followers. Mt 4,17 and 16,21 just cannot, despite recurrent attempts to show otherwise, bear the literary weight which has been placed upon them"; ferner J. P. Meier 1992, 628: "Matthew's editorial hand is clear not only in this overall pattern of narrative plus discourse but also in the redactional formula he uses both to close the five major discourses and to provide a transition back to the narrative". Daraus können aber m.E. keine Konsequenzen für die *erste* Stufe des Gesamtaufbaus vom Matt. gezogen werden, denn dazu bedarf es des Nachweises, daß im Matt. dieser Strukturanweiser auf Abstraktionsebene demjenigen auf Metaebene übergeordnet ist, was schwerlich gelingen wird. So auch Powell 1990, 46: "The great speeches of Jesus must be viewed as serving some subsidiary purpose in the narrative, for they do not define the overall development of the story", sowie jetzt Hagner 1993, li: "… the fivefold discours structure should be recognized as a subsidiary structure rather than the primary one".

[147] S. dazu Hellholm 1995, bes. den Paragraphen "Commentary on the Embedment of Dialogues within the Text-Internal Narrative Structure". Ferner in bezug auf Matthäus, Powell 1990, 46: "The speeches certainly represent a slowing of discourse time that directs the reader to consider the material as possessing special significance. At the same time, however, the reader of Matthew's story realizes that Jesus has not come to give speeches but to give his life. He has come to save people from their sin and he will accomplish this not through the speeches but through the blood of the covenant, which is 'poured out for many for the forgiveness of sins' (26:28)".

## 3.2. Substitutionen auf Metaebene

### 3.2.1. Außermatthäische Beispiele aus dem Neuen Testament

Um der Problemstellung sowie der Allgemeingültigkeit dieses Substitutionstyps willen, gebe ich vorerst zwei Beispiele aus anderen, vieldiskutierten neutestamentlichen Texten als dem Matthäusevangelium:

(1) Apg. 1,8: ἀλλὰ λήμψεσθε δύναμιν ἐπελθόντος τοῦ ἁγίου πνεύματος ἐφ' ὑμᾶς καὶ ἔσεσθέ μου μάρτυρες ἔν τε Ἰερουσαλὴμ καὶ ἐν πάσῃ τῇ Ἰουδαίᾳ καὶ Σαμαρείᾳ καὶ ἕως ἐσχάτου τῆς γῆς. Dazu schreiben Conzelmann/Lindemann: "Im übrigen wird die Gliederung des Buches bereits in 1,8 angedeutet, wo Jesus als letztes Wort vor der Himmelfahrt den Jüngern verheißt, sie sollten seine Zeugen sein 'in Jerusalem, in ganz Judäa und Samaria und bis zum Ende der Erde'. Entsprechend dieser Ankündigung handelt der erste Abschnitt Apg 1-5 von der Gemeinde in Jerusalem, der zweite Teil 6-12 von der Mission in Judäa und Samaria und der dritte Teil 13-28 von der 'Weltmission' des Paulus, die diesen bis nach Rom führt"[149]. Hier wird ohne nähere theoretische Diskussion vorausgesetzt, daß V. 8 in *materialer Supposition* zum folgenden Text bzw. zu den drei Teiltexten der Apostelgeschichte steht und nicht, zumindest nicht direkt, auf die außertextliche Missionstätigkeit der Zeugen referiert. V. 8 wird also als Substitution auf Metaebene für den Rest der Apg. bzw. für seine Teile und somit als Dispositionsschema aufgefaßt[150]. Dabei formuliert Lukas als Verfasser, wie Vielhauer mit Recht betont hat, "die Inhaltsangabe des Fortsetzungswerkes *nicht als eigene Aussage* – etwa als zweiten Teil des Proömiums –, sondern er legt sie dem Auferstandenen in den Mund und legitimiert damit sein ungewöhnliches Vorhaben ebenso beiläufig wie wirksam"[151].

---

[148] S. Kingsbury 1988, 113: "Contrary to what many scholars have claimed over the years, the great speeches of Jesus do not constitute the climactic feature of Matthew's Gospel nor do they stand apart from the rest of the story being told. On the contrary, each speech can be seen to be appropriately situated within the story's plot. One of the unique features of these speeches is that Jesus can be found at places to speak past the story-audience, the crowds or the disciples, and to address directly the implied reader in his or her own situation in the time between the ressurection and the Parousia".

[149] Conzelmann/Lindemann 1991, 310.

[150] So schon M. Dibelius 1968, 164. Von einem Dispositionsschema spricht ausdrücklich Conzelmann 1963, 22: "8b enthält Programm und Dispositionsschema des Buches"; ähnlich u.a. E. Haenchen 1965a, 112f.; W. G. Kümmel 1973, 132; G. Schneider 1980, 66-68, 203; G. Schille 1983, 72; E. Larsson 1983, 15 und 21; R. Pesch 1986, 37 und 69f.; G. Lüdemann 1987, 32; E. Lövestam 1988a, 1 und 6; idem 1988b, 38.

[151] Vielhauer 1975, 385 (Hervorheb. von mir); vgl. auch R. I. Pervo 1987, 72: "The Book of Acts opens with a prediction of the risen Lord that serves as a geographical outline (Acts 1:8) of the work".

(2) Apk. 1,19: γράψον οὖν ἃ εἶδες καὶ ἃ εἰσὶν καὶ ἃ μέλλει γενέσθαι μετὰ ταῦτα. Auch dieser Satz wird von den meisten Auslegern ohne weiteres als *materiale Suppositionsaussage* interpretiert. Ernst Lohmeyer z.B. meint: "Die drei Relativsätze skizzieren flüchtig Inhalt und Ordnung des Buches; der 1. = 1,9-20, der 2. = c. 2.3, der 3. (in 4,1 wieder aufgenommen) = c. 4-21"[152], und schon Wilhelm Bousset sprach ausdrücklich von einer *Dispositionsangabe,* als er schrieb: "1,19 ist also eine Disposition des folgenden gegeben, die in 4,1 deutlich wieder aufgenommen wird"[153]. Es handelt sich laut diesen beiden Exegeten und nicht nur ihnen[154] in 1,19 um eine *Substitution auf Metaebene,* die als Metatext und somit als echtes Gliederungsmerkmal zu charakterisieren ist.

Ob diese beiden Beispielssätze mit Recht oder Unrecht[155] als in *materialer Supposition* stehend aufgefaßt wurden bzw. werden, sei in diesem Zusammenhang dahingestellt, da es uns nur darauf ankam, das methodische Vorgehen an bekannten außermatthäischen Beispielen zu exemplifizieren.

---

[152] Lohmeyer 1953/70, 19.

[153] W. Bousset 1906/66, 198.

[154] So auch u.a. R. H. Charles 1920, 33; H. Kraft 1974, 49; U. B. Müller 1984, 86; Conzelmann/ Lindemann 1991, 360; Vielhauer 1975, 498.

[155] Für die *Lukasstelle* meint Larsson, ibid., daß die Dispositionsdeutung nicht absolutiert werden darf; ähnlich auch J. Roloff 1981, 13, 24 und jetzt Lövestam 1988b, 38, der eine Kombination von Objekt- und Metaaussage befürwortet, wenn er schreibt: "Die geographischen Markierungen in V. 8 dienen nicht nur zur Veranschaulichung vom Gang des Wortes von Jerusalem und über die Welt hinaus. Sie geben auch die Disposition des Buches an ..." (Übers. von mir).

Für die *Apokalypse* bestreiten die Dispositionsdeutung u.a. E. Schüssler Fiorenza 1985, 58 Anm. 22 (im Anschluß an G. B. Caird 1966, 26) und Roloff 1984, 45: "Diese [sc. die Dreizeitenformel – DH] ist schwerlich als Inhaltsangabe der Apk. zu verstehen ..."; so auch J. Lambrecht 1980, 79f. und M. Karrer 1986, 158 mit Anm. 84.

Hierdurch bestätigt sich allerdings nur, wie aktuell und bedeutungsvoll die prinzipielle Unterscheidung zwischen *suppositio materialis* und *suppositio formalis* für die Beantwortung des strukturellen Aufbaus neutestamentlicher Texte in der Tat ist.

## 3.2.2. Einige Substitutionen auf Metaebene im Matthäusevangelium

### 3.2.2.1. Die formelhaften Satz- bzw. Teiltextanfänge in 4,17 und 16,21

Die beiden Textabschnitte lauten in synoptischer Gegenüberstellung:

| Matthäus 4,17 | Matthäus 16,21 |
|---|---|
| ἀπὸ τότε ἤρξατο ὁ Ἰησοῦς κηρύσσειν καὶ λέγειν· μετανοεῖτε· ἤγγικεν γὰρ ἡ βασιλεία τῶν οὐρανῶν. | ἀπὸ τότε ἤρξατο ὁ Ἰησοῦς δεικνύειν τοῖς μαθηταῖς αὐτοῦ ὅτι δεῖ αὐτὸν εἰς Ἱεροσόλυμα ἀπελθεῖν καὶ πολλὰ παθεῖν ... καὶ ἀποκτανθῆναι καὶ τῇ τρίτῃ ἡμέρᾳ ἐγερθῆναι. |

Wie schon oben § 1.2.(b) erwähnt, betrachten einige wenige[156] Exegeten diese Satz- bzw. Teiltextanfänge als bedeutsames Gliederungsmerkmal für die Gesamtkomposition des Matthäusevangeliums[157], ohne jedoch ihre textgrammatische Struktur näher zu bestimmen. Die Frage ist nun einerseits aus welchem Grunde und andererseits mit welchem Recht diese Satz- bzw. Teiltextanfänge als Delimitationssignale aufgefaßt werden?

Als Grund kann die Formelhaftigkeit allein auf keinen Fall genügen. Als Delimitationsmerkmale höchsten Grades[158] können diese formelhaften Satz- bzw. Teiltextanfänge nämlich nur dann dienen, wenn man glaubhaft machen kann, daß wir es in der Tat mit *Substitutionen auf Metaebene* bzw. deren *Surrogaten* zu tun haben. Dies wird nun in erster Linie von den gebrauchten Verben abhängen. Können die

---

[156] Vgl. die forschungsgeschichtliche Feststellung von D. R. Bauer 1988, 85: "The history of the investigation into this passage [sc. 4,17 –DH] could be written in short compass; scholars have generally ignored it ... Many commentators remark that the formula indicates a turning point in the ministry of Jesus [= *suppositio formalis* Deutung –DH], but for reasons usually unexplained they fail to draw structural implications [= *suppositio materialis* Deutung –DH] from this observation". Dieser Sachverhalt hängt m.E. mit der Unfähigkeit der Exegeten zusammen, methodisch zwischen objekt-sprachlichen und meta-sprachlichen Äußerungen zu unterscheiden.

[157] Z.B. Lohmeyer/Schmauch 1958, 9*-10*, 65, 264f.; Krentz 1964, 411: "This parallelism of form is as striking as the closing formula of the five discourses noted by Bacon"; M. A. Powell 1992, 193: "... the verses have obvious significance from a literary perspective: they serve as the narrator's own explicit indicators of narrative flow. They serve to inform the reader of major new developments in the overall flow of the story"; vgl. weiter Kümmel 1973, 75-77; Kingsbury 1975, 7-25; Combrink 1983, 70; Gnilka 1986, 99; Schenk 1987, 36 und mit gewißem Vorbehalt auch Luz 1985, 24-26 sowie idem 1990, 484f.

[158] Für die notwendige Hierarchisierung von Gliederungsmerkmalen, s. Hellholm 1980, 78-80 mit Referenzen.

*verba dicendi:* κηρύσσειν, λέγειν und δεικνύειν[159] (letzteres nicht nur in der Bedeutung: erklären[160], sondern auch als *verbum agendi* in der Bedeutung: zeigen[161]) in diesen Sätzen eindeutig als *materiale Suppositionsindikatoren* für Teiltexte unten angegebener Extension und nicht nur, wie die *verba dicendi* in 4,17a gedeutet werden könnten[162], ausschließlich für das direkte Zitat in 4,17b, verstanden werden? Dies ist selbstverständlich nur dann möglich, wenn auch das direkte (4,17) bzw. indirekte (16,21) Zitat, als auf einer Metaebene zu den jeweils folgenden Teiltexten stehend, interpretierbar sind, was einer ernsthaften Überprüfung wert ist[163]: μετα-νοεῖτε· ἤγγικεν γὰρ ἡ βασιλεία τῶν οὐρανῶν würde dann auf den Teiltext 4,18 bis 16,13/20 Bezug nehmen, während die erste Leidensankündigung (16,21) mit den Verben ἀπελθεῖν, παθεῖν, ἀποκτανθῆναι und ἐγερθῆναι auf den Teiltext 16,22 bis 28,15/20 (nicht notwendigerweise aber auf extensional distinkt abgrenzbare Teilabschnitte innerhalb dieses Teiltextes) referieren würde[164]. Bezüglich 4,17b als metasprachlicher Überschrift, d.h. *Substitution auf Metaebene,* muß festgestellt werden,

---

[159] Die Markusvorlage hat das einfache *verbum dicendi:* διδάσκειν; Matthäus hat also ein komplexeres Verb eingesetzt.

[160] So die Übersetzung in Bibelkommissionen 1981, ibid.; ähnlich W. Bauer 1988, 345 s.v. 3: *'nachweisen, dartun, klarmachen';* H. Schlier, 1935, 27: *lehren, belehren*; Vgl. Liddell/Scott/Jones 1966, 373, s.v. 3: *'show, make known,* esp. by words, *explain'.*

[161] So bes. D. R. Bauer 1988, 104: "Rather, this term means 'present' or 'show', which may include verbal description, but in the New Testament always includes more than simply speech ... If we place 'show' in 16.21 within the context of the flow of the narrative throughout 16.21-28.20, it becomes evident that Jesus shows his disciples the necessity of his passion not only by what he says, but also by what he does, especially by himself undertaking the journey to Jerusalem." Luz 1990, 488: "Δεικνύειν setzt er, weil διδάσκω (Mk 8,31) bei ihm vor allem ethische Unterweisung meint; man sollte das seltene Wort nicht theologisch überfrachten". Eine apokalyptische Interpretation vom Verb δεικνύειν findet sich m.E. zu Unrecht z.B. bei Lohmeyer-Schmauch 1958, 264 und Grundmann 1968, 397; dagegen jetzt auch Luz, ibid, Anm. 10.

[162] Schenk 1987, 266 s.v. κηρύσσω: "4,17(=Mk) ist das Vb. (sc. κηρύσσειν –DH) als metakommunikative jesuanische Redeeinleitung samt der inhaltl. Redefüllung übernommen ...". Das *verbum agendi* δεικνύειν in 16,21 kann jedenfalls nicht in gleichem Maße eingeschränkt werden, wie (möglicherweise aber weniger wahrscheinlich) die *verba dicendi* κηρύσσειν und λέγειν in 4,17!

[163] Eine Analyse dieser sowie anderer Teiltexte unter dem Aspekt: *suppositio formalis/suppositio materialis?* ist in Vorbereitung. S. vorläufig Krenz 1964, 410f.: "At 4:17 Jesus' first preaching is summarized. The verse opens ἀπὸ τότε ἤρξατο ὁ Ἰησοῦς, followed by the infinitives κηρύσσειν and λέγειν, *plus a summary of the content of his preaching.* Formally 16:21 parallels this structure completely. It opens ἀπὸ τότε ἤρξατο ὁ Ἰησοῦς Χριστός, followed by the infinitive δεικνύειν *with an object clause giving the content of the new message"* ... "This unique parallelism of form together with summary of content suggests that these two verses serve as *headings, almost titles,* for the two great divisions of Jesus ministry that he found in Mark" (Hervorheb. von mir); aufgenommen von Kingsbury 1975/89, s. unten ad Anm. 170ff.: "superscriptions".

[164] Vgl. auch die Zitate aus Gnilka 1988, 81 und Hagner 1993, 71 unten in Anm. 170.

daß hier eine Analogie zu Apg. 1,8 insofern vorliegt[165], als die Inhaltsangabe (V. 17b) nicht als eigene Aussage des Matthäus formuliert ist, sondern als direktes Jesuswort. Die Parallellaussage 16,21 ist zwar von Matthäus formuliert, aber auch hier als Jesuswort, allerdings in indirekter Rede. Aus diesen Gründen sollte man bezüglich der beiden Textstellen vielleicht lieber von *Surrogaten von Substitutionen auf Metaebene* sprechen.

Wie schwierig es anscheinend ist, die *formale* oder *materiale* Supposition diesen beiden Versen zuzuordnen, geht aus der Formulierung in einer Fußnote zu der neuen schwedischen Übersetzung hervor, wenn es dort in bezug auf 4,17 und 16,21 heißt: "Auf diese Weise werden zwei Hauptabschnitte in der *Wirksamkeit Jesu* markiert: einer, wenn er das Himmelreich für alle verkündet und der andere, wenn er seinen engsten Jüngern seine Aufgabe als der leidende Heiland erklärt"[166]. Hier wird von "zwei Hauptabschnitten" gesprochen, aber nicht im Matthäusevangelium, obwohl die Formulierung es nahe gelegt hätte, sondern "in der Wirksamkeit Jesu"; damit wird möglicherweise angedeutet, daß diese Verse als in *formaler Supposition* stehend interpretiert worden sind, oder liegt hier vielleicht nur eine lässige Formulierung vor, d.h. steht 'in der Wirksamkeit Jesu' eigentlich für 'in der Darstellung der Wirksamkeit Jesu'? Explizit als in *suppositio materialis* stehend mit Bezug auf das Matthäusevangelium versteht diese "Wendungen" jedoch Joachim Gnilka, wenn er schreibt: "Wie Jesus zunächst die Himmelsherrschaft zu verkündigen beginnt, hebt er im zweiten Teil *des Evangeliums* an von seinen Leiden zu sprechen"[167]. Beide Formulierungen weisen allerdings nicht nur auf zwei Perioden hin, sondern charakterisieren diese Abschnitte außerdem noch vom Inhaltlichen her, u.zw. in einer Weise, die einer materialen Suppositionsaussage nahe kommt. Wenn Wolfgang Schenk diese beiden Wendungen als "entscheidende Gliederungsmerkmale" kennzeichnet und sie in einer näheren Bestimmung mit folgenden Worten charakterisiert: "Mit der volleren Wendung 'von da an begann Jesus' + Inf. des Redeverbs ... leitet 4,17 ... *den ersten Buchteil* als die Periode des Umkehrsrufes Jesu und seiner Schüler ein, wie ebenso 16,21 ... *den zweiten* als die Periode der Verwerfungs- und Rehabilitierungs-Vorhersagen und deren Eintreten"[168], so versteht er zwar – wie Gnilka – diese Gliederungsmerkmale als Textgliederungsmerkmale auf

---

[165] Vgl. das Zitat von Vielhauer oben ad Anm. 151.

[166] Zu 4,17 (Übers. und Hervorheb. von mir).

[167] Gnilka 1986, 99 (Hervorheb. von mir); so auch idem 1988, 81. Unklar in bezug auf die Art von Supposition ist die Formulierung Klostermanns: "schwerlich will Mt hiermit eine erste Predigtzeit von einer späteren 16,21 unterscheiden" (1927/71, 29); genau so unklar ist E. Schweizer: "Matthäus ... weist mit 'von da an' auf die ganze jetzt folgende Zeit" (1973, 224).

[168] Schenk 1987, 36 s.v. ἀπὸ τότε (Hervorheb. von mir).

Metaebene ("... den ersten Buchteil ...")[169], aber deren genauerer linguistischer Charakter wird auch von ihm leider nicht explizit dargelegt. Ausdrücklich als *Substitution auf Metaebene* versteht vor allem Jack Dean Kingsbury diese formelhafte Wendungen, wenn sie laut ihm "sentences that serve as veritable superscriptions for whole sections of the Gospel"[170] darstellen. "Thus 4,17 describes Jesus as publicly presenting himself to Israel and summoning it to the Kingdom of Heaven. By the same token 16,21 describes him as revealing to his disciples that it is God's will that he go to Jerusalem to suffer, die, and be raised"[171]; und wiederholt wenn er an anderer Stelle feststellt, daß "the *'superscription'* 16,21 alerts us to the theme of this section: the suffering, death, and resurrection of Jesus Messiah"[172].

Ein anderer aber kaum weniger komplexer Weg zur Lösung der diesbezüglichen Schwierigkeiten dieser formelhaften Satz- bzw. Teiltextanfänge wäre, sie ausschließlich als temporale (und lokale) (ἀπὸ τότε ἤρξατο ...) *Episodenmerkmale* ersten Grades (EM[1])[173] – anstatt als Suppositionen auf Metaebene – zu deuten und sie den makro-suppositionalen Gliederungsmerkmalen hierarchisch *neben-* bzw. *unterzuordnen*[174]. Wie gesagt, ist aber auch diese Lösung nicht so unproblematisch, wie sie im ersten Moment erscheinen mag, denn zumindest müssen zwei elementare Fragen gestellt werden: (a) Erstens worauf sich die Zeitangabe ἀπὸ τότε bezieht?

---

[169] Vgl. Schenk 1987, 58 s.v. ἄρχομαι: "... Buchgliederungsstellen ... [= 4,17 und 16,21 –DH]"; s. das vollständige Zitat unten Anm. 184.

[170] Kingsbury 1975, 9 (meine Hervorheb.); so auch schon Krentz 1964, 411: "headings, almost titles" und nunmehr D. R. Bauer 1988, 87 unter Verwendung der unglücklichen, weil unklaren, Term 'particularized' und Gnilka 1988, 81: "Überschrift" sowie Hagner 1993, 71 zu 4:12-17: "This quotation serves as a rubric for the entire Galilean ministry of Jesus. The final verse clearly marks a dividing point in the entire narrative and finds its counter-part in another dividing point that is introduced with the very same words, ἀπὸ τότε ἤρξατο ὁ Ἰησοῦς (16:21)".

[171] Kingsbury, ibid. Inkonsequenterweise drückt sich Kingsbury im neuen Vorwort zur zweiten Auflage seines Buches (1975/89) so aus, als verstände er die formelhaften Satz- bzw. Teiltextanfänge als formale Suppositionsaussage, wenn er schreibt: "... the consistency in my use of 4:17 and 16:21 lies in the fact that I regard these two passages as making the two main turning points *in Jesus Life:* at 4:17, Jesus begins his public ministry to Israel; at 16:21, he turns toward Jerusalem, where he suffers, dies, and is raised" (s. xvii; Hervorheb. von mir); tatsächlich dürfte es sich um eine lässige Formulierung handeln, wie es vermutlich auch bei der Formulierung der schwedischen Bibelkommission 1981, wie wir oben gesehen haben, der Fall war.

[172] Kingsbury, ibid., 21 (meine Hervorheb.); so auch D. R. Bauer ibid., 96. S. auch Kingsbury 1988, 78: "The second literary device Matthew employs to lend cohesion to this third part of his story is the passion-prediction. There are three such predictions (16:21; 17:22-23; 20:17-19), and these, in turn, are supplemented by a verse in the passion account itself which calls them to mind (26:2). These three passion-predictions are the counterpart to the major summary-passages found in the second part of Matthew's story (4:23; 9:35; 11:1)".

Dabei muß man sich merken, daß es eben nicht ἀπὸ τοῦ νῦν (von jetzt an)[175], sondern in der Tat ἀπὸ τότε (von jener Zeit an, oder: von da an)[176] heißt. 'Απὸ τότε bezieht sich in beiden Fällen in erster Linie anaphorisch auf präzise angegebene
Zeitpunkte im jeweils vorhergehenden Text: in 4,17 bzw. 16,21 werden nicht nur
auf Zeitpunkte, sondern auch auf Ortsangaben in den Teiltexten 4,12-13 bzw. 16,13
durch anaphorische Verweise hingewiesen[177]. Einmalige Zeit- sowie Ortsverände-
rungen werden dort angegeben und thematisiert: in 4,12-13 nach der Hinrichtung
Johannes des Täufers und im Zusammenhang mit der Rückkehr Jesu nach Galiläa
und mit seiner Niederlassung in Kapharnaum am galiläischen Meer nach der Übersiedlung von Nazareth (᾽Ακούσας δὲ ὅτι ᾽Ιωάννης παρεδόθη ἀνεχώρησεν εἰς τὴν
Γαλιλαίαν. καὶ καταλιπὼν τὴν Ναζαρὰ ἐλθὼν κατῴκησεν εἰς Καφαρναοὺμ τὴν

---

[173] Dagegen kann hier nicht damit argumentiert werden, "that ἀπὸ τότε recurs not only in 16.21
but also in 26.16, and that ἤρξατο is again used of Jesus in 11.7 and 20 (this last with τότε)" (so Da-
vies/Allison 1988, 387 und 287; ähnlich F. Neirynck 1988, 33 und Standaert 1992, 1242), denn bei
dieser formelhaften Wendung geht es ja nicht um das Vorkommen der einzelnen Lexeme für sich,
sondern um das des *Gesamtsyntagmas: ἀπὸ τότε ἤρξατο + Infinitiv des Redeverbs* (so mit Recht
Schenk, ibid. sowie Krentz 1964, 410; D. R. Bauer 1988, 44, 85 und Kingsbury 1975/89, xviii Anm.
29), das im Matthäusevangelium in der Tat nur an den zwei oben diskutierten Stellen vorkommt. Es
ist ferner logisch unerlaubt, wie Neirynck (1988, 33) das tut, in der Weise zu argumentieren, daß man
zuerst feststellt, daß Judas und nicht Jesus Subjekt des Verbums ἐζήτει in 26,16 ist, um darauf aber
diese Feststellung dadurch zu nivellieren, daß man auf den Zusammenhang der Geschichte Judas mit
der Geschichte Jesu hinweist. Dieser Hinweis ist an und für sich natürlich richtig, aber es ist gleichzeitig notwendig festzustellen, daß diese beiden *Strukturmerkmale* sowie diese beiden *Geschichten
auf verschiedenen Ebenen liegen*, wie Kingsbury das tut, wenn er damit konkludiert, daß "one does
best, therefore, to construe the passion account, not as a main part in its own right, but as the *climactic subsection* of the end of Matthew's story (16:21-28:20)" (1988, xviii Anm. 29 von S. xvii;
Hervorheb. von mir). Ferner muß ausdrücklich festgestellt werden, daß während die Teiltextanfänge
in 4,17 und 16,21 *suppositio-materialis*-Aussagen in Form von Substitutionen auf Metaebene darstellen, so ist die Wendung in 26,16 nur als *suppositio-formalis*-Aussage verständlich, da die *verba
dicendi* bzw. *agendi* hier fehlen.
   [174] Episodenmerkmale (dazu Hellholm 1980, 93f. mit Literaturhinweisen; idem 1986, 41), auf
die ich hier leider nicht mehr ausführlich eingehen kann, spielen für die Komposition des Matt. eine
überaus große Rolle. Erst nach einer Gesamtanalyse des Matt. kann aber die hierarchische Relation
zwischen den verschiedenen Merkmalen bestimmt werden.
   [175] Vgl. hierzu W. Bauer 1988, 1104 s.v. νῦν 3.b.; ferner Neirynck 1988, 38.
   [176] Vgl. hierzu W. Bauer 1988, 1642, s.v. τότε 1; ferner F. Blaß/A. Debrunner/F. Rehkopf 1976,
§ 459,3.
   [177] Darauf verweist jetzt auch Standaert 1992, 1244: "Ici l'ἀπὸ τότε ne peut servir d'appui pour
justifier une dite césure narrative entre 4,16 et 4,17. S'il y a du nouveau, c'est dans la succession de
Jésus après le Baptist (cf. 4,12). Mais le propre de Matthieu sera d'insister en même temps sur la
continuité: Jésus qui «commence à prêcher»; dit ici exactement la même chose que Jean (3,2)!";
*ibid.*, 1243: " L'ἀπὸ τότε renoue ainsi avec le contexte antérieur, plus exactement avec le début du
paragraphe que précède (16,13)"; vgl. auch Allison 1992, 1203.

παραθαλασσίαν ἐν ὁρίοις Ζαβουλῶν καὶ Νεφθαλίμ); in 16,13 nach dem Verlassen von Galiläa und im Zusammenhang mit dem außerpalästinensischen Aufenthalt in der Umgebung von Caesarea Philippi (Ἐλθὼν δὲ ὁ Ἰησοῦς εἰς τὰ μέρη Καισαρείας τῆς Φιλίππου …). Derjenige Teil der Wendung, der aus der Präposition ἀπό in Kombination mit dem Zeitadverb τότε besteht, spricht also einerseits für eine Anknüpfung nach rückwärts, und zeigt somit eine *verbindende Funktion* auf,[178] schließt aber andererseits keinesfalls einen Neueinsatz aus, sondern setzt durch die Präposition ἀπὸ in der Tat einen solchen voraus. (b) Zweitens muß man sich aber auch fragen, warum diese formelhafte Wendung als Verbindungsglied asyndetisch formuliert ist (ἀπὸ τότε ἤρξατο …, nicht aber καὶ ἀπὸ τότε ἤρξατο …) und außerdem noch eine Renominalisierung[179] des Namens Jesu bringt? Jack Dean Kingsbury[180] und David R. Bauer[181] haben auf den asyndetischen Charakter von 4,17 und 16,21 nicht nur im Unterschied zu der Textstelle 26,16, sondern auch zum textuellen Kontext dieser beiden Stellen aufmerksam gemacht und mit Recht daraus den "formulaic character of this phrase at 4.17 and 16.21"[182] gefolgert; ihre Folgerung wird bestätigt durch die satz-syntaktische Grammatik des Griechischen, welche "forbids asyndetical juxtaposition of sentences" und die besagt, daß "every sentence must open with a particle that indicates its relationship to the preceding

---

[178] So Frankemölle 1974, 344; vgl. Luz 1985, 168: "… ἀπὸ τότε will gerade die Verbindung zu V 12-16 herstellen"; ferner ibid., 173; Davies/Allison 1988, 387: "… ἀπὸ τότε links what follows with what precedes …" und Standaert 1992, 1241: "En effet, comme nous l'avons noté plus haut [S. 1224f. u.a. mit Verweis auf Lukians Traktat: Πῶς δεῖ Ἱστορίαν συγγράφειν § 55–DH], les anciens ne cherchaient point à marquer des césures ni à établir des divisions. Leur effort littéraire était bien plutôt celui d'unir, d'effacer les traces de toute séparation antérieure et de montrer les liens que rapprochent chaque élément de la construction". Auf denselben Lukiantraktat verweist schon M. A. Tolbert 1989, 109; Dieser lautet in Wielands Übers.: "Alles sey durchaus mit gleichem Fleiß ausgearbeitet und vollendet, so daß, wenn er mit dem ersten Stücke fertig ist, das andere haarscharf in dasselbe passe, und so alle Theile wie eine Kette in einander greiffen, ohne daß die Erzählung jemals abbreche, oder das Ganze aus vielen zusammengestellten Erzählungen bestehe, sondern das Vorhergehende immer mit dem folgenden so genau und unmerklich verbunden sey, daß alles aus einem Stücke gearbeitet zu seyn scheine" (1971, Bd II, Teil 4, S. 138f.).

[179] Dazu s. Hellholm 1980, 94f. mit dort angegebener Lit.: "Auf die Gliederungsmerkmale mit textexternem Analogon folgen diejenigen Merkmale, die kein direktes Analogon im textexternem Bereich besitzen. Von diesen Merkmalen tritt die Renominalisierung an erste Stelle … Unter Renominalisierung (versteht man) die Wiederaufnahme eines Nomens oder Eigennamens im Text, nachdem vorher im Textverlauf eine pronominale Bezeichnung der Person verwendet worden ist". Zu den beiden Matthäusstellen vgl. schon Lohmeyer/Schmauch, 1958, 62; ferner Kingsbury 1975/89, 15f.; D. R. Bauer 1988, 84.

[180] Kingsbury 1975/89, 8 Anm. 43 und xx: "Asyndetic *apo tote* signals that 4:17 and 16:21 stand apart form the preceding pericopes 4:12-16 and 16:13-20".

[181] D. R. Bauer 1988, 44 und 85.

[182] D. R. Bauer 1988, 86.

sentence. Omission of the particle is allowed only under clearly defined circumstances"[183]. Der asyndetische Charakter der Formulierung sowie die Renominalisierung deutet nun aber – teilweise im Unterschied zur indirekten Zeitangabe ἀπὸ τότε – auf einen funktionalen *Neueinsatz* hin. *Als Episodenmerkmal* hat die syntagmatische Formulierung ἀπὸ τότε ἤρξατο ὁ Ἰησοῦς ... also eine Doppeltfunktion: (a) ἀπὸ τότε weist zuallererst *anaphorisch* auf die bestimmten Zeit- bzw. Ortsangaben in 4,12-13 bzw. 16,13, aber außerdem noch *kataphorisch* auf das was folgt, hin, während (b) die asyndetische Konstruktion, das finite Hilfsverb ἤρξατο[184] zusammen mit den dazugehörigen Infinitivverben sowie die Renominalisierung von ὁ Ἰησοῦς in 4,17 bzw. 16,21 eindeutig *kataphorisch* auf das, was folgt, hinweist[185]. Auf diese Weise bilden die beiden Teiltexte 4,12-17 bzw. 16,13-21/23 und nicht allein die Verse 4,17 bzw. 16,21 Episodeneinheiten, die den gesamten Matthäustext an zwei Stellen delimitieren, u.zw. in der Weise, daß die direkten Episodenmerkmale am Anfang, während die indirekten anaphorischen zusammen mit den kataphorischen am Ende dieser Episodeneinheiten erscheinen[186].

Diese Doppeltheit kommt gerade in der synoptischen Zusammenstellung des Matthäustextes mit dessen Markusvorlage, wie sie bei Neirynck zu finden ist und hier wiederholt vorgelegt wird, am deutlichsten zutage[187]:

---

[183] Blomqvist 1981, 59; vgl. auch idem 1969, 19; idem 1991, 267 [§ 300.8a-d] und s. ferner J. D. Denniston 1954, xliii-xlvi.

[184] Wie vor allem J. W. Hunkin 1924 in einer eindringlichen Studie nachgewiesen hat, gebraucht Matthäus – im Unterschied zu Markus – ἄρχομαι nie ausschließlich pleonastisch, sondern immer in der konkreten und prägnanten Bedeutung: beginnen, anfangen. Vgl. dazu ferner Schenk 1987, 58 s.v. ἄρχομαι: "Mt übernimmt oder setzt es da wo er wirklich den *Beginn* einer Handlung und deren Fortdauer bezeichnen oder besonders hervorheben will. Das markieren besonders die Buchgliederungsstellen mit dem Zusatz *von da an* 4,17 (= Mk)"; N. Turner, in: J. H. Moulton/W. F. Howard/N. Turner 1976 (IV), 32; Kingsbury 1975, 8; D. R. Bauer 1988, 86. Kritisch zum pleonastischen Verständnis von ἄρχομαι + Infinitiv im Markusevangelium äußert sich, unter Hinweis auf andere, Neirynck 1988, 36-41. Damit ändert sich jedoch Nichts für den ingressiven Gebrauch im Syntagma ἀπὸ τότε ἤρξατο + Infinitiv im Matthäusevangelium.

[185] Zu Unrecht spielt leider Kingsbury die beiden Funktionen: anaphorische Verbindung und kataphorischen Neueinsatz gegeneinander aus, wenn er u.a. gegen Neirynck darauf beharrt, daß "Asyndetic *apo tote* signals that 4:17 and 16:21 stand apart from the preceding pericopes 4:12-16 and 16:13-20" (1975/89, xx).

[186] Vgl. W. Dressler 1973, 65f.: "Das Vorhandensein von Übergängen erschwert freilich das präzise Erkennen der genauen Grenzen von Textabschnitten" (S. 65).

[187] Neirynck 1988, 31.

| Matthäus 4,12.17 | Markus 1,14-15 |
|---|---|

12 Ἀκούσας δὲ
ὅτι Ἰωάννης παρεδόθη
ἀνεχώρησεν
εἰς τὴν Γαλιλαίαν. ( ... )

14 Μετὰ δὲ
τὸ παραδοθῆναι τὸν Ἰωάννην
ἦλθεν ὁ Ἰησοῦς
εἰς τὴν Γαλιλαίαν

17 *ἀπὸ τότε ἤρξατο ὁ Ἰησοῦς*
κηρύσσειν
καὶ λέγειν

κηρύσσων *τὸ εὐαγγέλιον τοῦ θεοῦ*
15 καὶ λέγων ὅτι

( ... ) ἤγγικεν ἡ βασιλεία τοῦ
θεοῦ·

μετανοεῖτε·
ἤγγικεν γὰρ ἡ βασιλεία
τῶν οὐρανῶν.

μετανοεῖτε ( ... ).

Es ist zweifelsohne richtig, wie Neirynck betont, daß man die Markusvorlage sofort im Matthäustext wiedererkennen kann, aber damit ist – gegen Neirynck – nicht gesagt, daß Matthäus den Text so verstanden hat wie Markus[188], oder daß die urchristlichen Leser bzw. Hörer die Gelegenheit, bzw. die Fähigkeit gehabt haben die Markusvorlage zu vergleichen bzw. daraus interpretatorische Schlüsse zu ziehen.

Die Partizipien κηρύσσων und λέγων bei Markus sind vom finiten Verb ἦλθεν abhängig und auf diese Weise wird bei Markus angegeben, daß die ganze Aussage in 1,14-15 auf engste zusammengehört. Dies ist aber anders bei Matthäus, wo ἀπὸ τότε ἤρξατο zwar indirekt auf den Zeit- und Ortswechsel in V. 12 hinweist, wodurch aber gerade das *Neue* gegenüber Markus hervorgehoben wird: die Infinitivverben κηρύσσειν und λέγειν sind bei Matthäus vom finiten Verb ἤρξατο abhängig und leiten somit etwas Neues ein, genauso wie die oben genannte asyndetische Konstruktion sowie die Renominalisierung von ὁ Ἰησοῦς.

Nun besteht in bezug auf Feststellungen von Gliederungsmerkmalen allerdings keine Notwendigkeit, diese formelhaften Satz-bzw. Teiltextanfänge entweder als SM oder als EM (p ∨ q) zu verstehen. Im Gegenteil, man könnte den Evangelisten

---

[188] Hierzu gehört u.a. die Beobachtung von Betz, daß Matt. offenbar Schwierigkeiten mit der Markus-Vorlage hatte wegen des Inhalts der Verkündigung vom εὐαγγέλιον τοῦ θεοῦ: "Mark in fact fails to give any explanation at this point, so Matthew felt he should set the record straight. Accordingly, when Jesus »*began* to preach« (ἤρξατο ... κηρύσσειν) he called for repentance and justified it by the nearness of »the kindom of the heavens« just as John had done" ... "Matthew's solution is contained in his peculiar term τὸ εὐαγγέλιον τῆς βασιλείας (»the gospel of the kingdom«), which is clearly a Mattheanism" ... "Matthew found it unacceptable when Mark attributed the term εὐαγγέλιον to Jesus' message before his death and resurrection" (1992, 280f.).

Matthäus eine hochraffinierte Verkoppelung von zwei Gliederungsmerkmalen in jeweils einem einzigen, aber komplexen Teiltext an zwei Delimitationsstellen des
Evangeliums sehr wohl zutrauen: *als Substitutionsmerkmal* mit *kataphorischer*
Substitutionsrichtung leitet, wie wir oben gesehen haben, 4,17 *den ersten Buchteil*
als die Periode des Umkehrsrufes Jesu und seiner Schüler ein, wie ebenso 16,21 *den*
*zweiten* als die Periode der Verwerfungs- und Rehabilitierungs-Vorhersagen und deren Eintreten[189]; als *Episodenmerkmal* mit sowohl *kataphorischem* als auch *ana-*
*phorischem* Hinweis, wird zuerst auf das was folgt hingewiesen, aber dieser
Neueinsatz knüpft gleichzeitig an das unmittelbar Vorhergehende an. Dabei liegt
auf der *literarischen Ebene*[190] jedoch das Hauptgewicht auf den *funktionalen Neu-*
*einsatz,* wie die Substitutionsaussage in Kombination mit dem kataphorischen Episodenmerkmal mit aller Deutlichkeit zeigt[191]. Wir hätten es dann mit einer Merkmalskombination an der Textoberfläche zu tun, deren Merkmale sich bei der
Textdelimitation komplementieren ($p \land q$), und deshalb umso bedeutungsvoller anzusehen wären[192].

Ein weiteres Raffinement, das im Blick auf den Kommunikationsprozeß zu erwarten ist, würde in der Annahme bestehen, daß Matthäus durch seine Formulierung die beiden Ebenen: materiale und formale Supposition gewissermaßen ver-
mengt hat, um auf diese Weise die Erzähltextebene mit der Objektebene möglichst
zu identifizieren. Solch eine "Vermengung" der beiden Ebenen liegt in bezug auf
*narrative* Texte ohnehin nahe. Die Durchtriebenheit des Matthäus gegenüber Mar-

---

[189] Die Verbindung der beiden Buchteile (4,17-16,20 bzw. 16,21-28,20) wird durch das Phänomen der "causation" hergestellt, wie Bauer 1988, 73-108 nachgewiesen hat; zustimmend Powell
1990, 46: "Matthew tells the story of Jesus' ministry of teaching, preaching, and healing in a way
that explains why Israel rejected and crucified its Messiah".

[190] Methodisch dürfen die literarischen und historischen Ebenen nicht verwechselt werden.

[191] Vgl. Kingsbury 1988, 77: "The one device is that of the 'journey.' In 16:21, Matthew reports
that it is God's will that Jesus go to Jerusalem. As far as the travels of Jesus are concerned, 16:21
stands out as a watershed. Already prior to 16:21, Jesus has begun those travels that will ultimately
bring him to Jerusalem (12:15; 14:13). But these travels prior to 16:21 are of a decidedly different
nature from those that follow it. Prior to 16:21, Jesus' travels have ... the character of 'withdrawal
in the face of danger,' whether it be a conspiracy on the part of the religious leaders to kill him
(12:14-15) or Herod's beheading of John the Baptist (14:13a). From 16:21 on, Jesus' travels assume
the character of a 'divinely ordained journey to Jerusalem'".

[192] Sachlich argumentiert in ähnlicher Weise jetzt auch Gnilka 1988, 81, indem er folgende Delimitationsmerkmale in 16,21 herausstellt: (a) die "zeitliche Bemerkung" als erster Bestandteil eines
Episodenmerkmals; (b) der "Ortswechsel" von Galiläa zum Jerusalem als zweiter Bestandteil des
Episodenmerkmals; (c) der "Themawechsel" von 4,17: "die Verkündigung der Herrschaft der Himmel in Galiläa, zu 16,21: "das Aufzeigen der Notwendigkeit des Leidens Jesu in Jerusalem"; (d) und
schließlich die Hervorheb. der Funktion dieses einleitenden Verses als "Überschrift". Vgl. die ähnliche Merkmalskombination OrSib IV, 48: νῦν δ' ὅσ' ἀπὸ πρώτης γενεῆς ἔσται, τάδε λέξω· zur Beurteilung vom Meta-Charakter dieser Stelle, s. Hartman unten Anm. 230 und Anm. 231.

kus an dieser Stelle besteht gerade darin, daß er es verstanden hat, die eindeutige *suppositio formalis*-Aussage in Mark. 1,14-15[193] in eine mehrdeutige *suppositio formalis/materialis*-Aussage, d.h. wohl in ein *Surrogat einer Substitution auf Metaebene*, zu verwandeln[194]. Als ausführliches, durch Merkmalskombination hergestelltes Delimitationsmerkmal, müßte dann nicht nur die formelhaften Wendungen in 4,17 bzw. 16,21, sondern die ganzen Teiltexte 4,12-17 bzw. 16,13-21/23 dienen.

Grundsätzlich bin ich jedoch der Meinung, daß man erst nach einer eingehenden linguistischen Kompositionsanalyse des ganzen Evangeliums, die hier nicht geboten werden kann, zu einem begründeten Urteil kommen kann. Wie die Forschungsgeschichte zur Komposition des Ersten Evangeliums zeigt, darf man aber die Fragestellung: *materiale* oder *formale Supposition?* auf keinen Fall vernachlässigen[195]. Genausowenig aber darf man die Möglichkeit von *Merkmalskombinationen* in delimitierenden Texteinheiten außer Acht lassen[196].

---

[193] Zu den Summarien im Mark. als *suppositio formalis*-Aussagen s. Ch. W. Hedricks Zusammenfassung, die trotz Unklarheit in der Begriffsbestimmung richtig sein dürfte (vgl. Vielhauers Definition unten ad Anm. 200): "They are not summaries in the narrow sense that they summarize episodes that precede or follow in the narrative [was entweder als *suppositio materialis* Aussagen oder als *suppositio formalis* Aussagen interpretiert werden kann –DH], rather they summarize new activities over broad general geographical areas and indefinite periods of time [was wohl nur als *suppositio formalis* Aussagen zu verstehen ist –DH]. The action narrated in the summary is clearly distinguishable from that narrated in the episodes" (1984, 303f.; vgl. auch 294f. sowie Davies/Allison unten Anm. 201 und W. Egger 1990, 155-58).

[194] Vgl. die beiden folgenden Anm. Zur matthäischen Redaktion von 4,12-17 s. die Ausführungen bei Luz 1985, 168: "Entscheidend ist ..., daß unser Abschnitt dem markinischen Summar 1,14f entspricht. Mk 1,14 hat seine Entsprechung in Mt 4,12, Mk 1,15 in Mt 4,17. Dazwischen hat Mt V 13, die Übersiedlung Jesu von Nazareth nach Kafarnaum, und V 14f, das dazugehörige Erfüllungszitat, eingeschoben ... Der Text ist also dreiteilig: V 12 bildet den Übergang und bereitet vor. V 17 enthält die Hauptaussage, den Beginn der Verkündigung Jesu mit seinem ersten Verkündigungswort, herausgehoben durch zwei Verben: κηρύσσειν καὶ λέγειν. V 13-16 nennt die entscheidende Voraussetzung der V 17 einsetzende Jesusverkündigung". Vgl. hierzu ferner Davies/Allison 1988, 374f.

[195] Ausgerechnet diese Frage aber wird bei der Analyse dieser beiden sog. "formelhaften Satzanfänge" von den meisten Kommentatoren, einschließlich Luz 1985 und 1990, Neirynck 1988 und Davies/Allison 1988 und 1991 nicht direkt gestellt! Ausnahmen sind etwa Krentz 1964, Kingsbury 1975, Gnilka 1988 und D. R. Bauer 1988. Zur Bedeutung der Frequenz metakommunikativer Sätze für die Bestimmung der Teiltextstruktur s. R. Ludwig 1987, 29f.: "... je weniger metakommunikativer Sätze gebraucht werden, desto geringer die Einschnitte in der (Teil-)Textstruktur".

[196] Vgl. Ludwig, ibid., 30: "Wichtig ist nun, daß sowohl bestimmte Kausaljunktoren, die primär als Satzverknüpfer funktionieren, sowie natürlich erst recht metakommunikative Verweise der Herstellung typisch schriftlicher, weiter gespannter, komplexer Teiltextebenen dienen".

## 3.2.2.2. Die sogenannten Summarien oder Kopfstücke

Von den sog. Summarien oder Kopfstücken kann ich in diesem Zusammenhang nur zwei behandeln, u.zw. die beinahe gleichlautenden Sätze im Kap. 4 bzw. im Kap. 9, die von Prof. Birger Gerhardsson als die "zweifellos wichtigsten Summarien im ganzen Evangelium" bezeichnet worden sind[197]. Dort heißt es:

| Matthäus 4,23 | Matthäus 9,35 |
|---|---|
| καὶ **περιῆγεν** ἐν ὅλῃ τῇ Γαλιλαίᾳ | καὶ **περιῆγεν** <u>ὁ Ἰησοῦς</u> τὰς πόλεις πάσας καὶ τὰς κώμας |
| **διδάσκων** ἐν ταῖς συναγωγαῖς αὐτῶν καὶ **κηρύσσων** τὸ εὐαγγέλιον τῆς βασιλείας | **διδάσκων** ἐν ταῖς συναγωγαῖς αὐτῶν καὶ **κηρύσσων** τὸ εὐαγγέλιον τῆς βασιλείας |
| καὶ **θεραπεύων** πᾶσαν νόσον καὶ πᾶσαν μαλακίαν ἐν τῷ λαῷ. | καὶ **θεραπεύων** πᾶσαν νόσον καὶ πᾶσαν μαλακίαν. |

Vor allem der Text aus 4,23-25 wird als Sammelbericht/Summar[198] oder als Kopfstück[199] bezeichnet. Aber was heißt hier Summar oder Kopfstück? Unter "Summar" versteht man gewöhnlicherweise eine zusammenfassende Formulierung des Evangelisten von der Lehre oder den Taten Jesu[200]. So verstanden, fassen die Summarien in den Evangelien die außersprachliche bzw. außertextliche Tätigkeit Jesu (in Wort und Tat) zusammen, und so werden diese Summarien in vielen Fällen, u.zw. teilweise wohl mit Recht, verstanden[201]. Die Benennung "Kopfstück" dagegen zeigt unzweideutig, daß dieser Textabschnitt als eine Metaformulierung aufgefaßt wird.

Nun zeigt sich aber, daß die beiden referierten Sätze aus 4,23 und 9,35 von den meisten Exegeten nicht als sich auf die Ebene der außersprachlichen 'Wirklichkeit' im dargestellten Leben Jesu beziehend, d.h. als Summarien im eigtl. Sinne, sondern

---

[197] B. Gerhardsson 1991, 31 (Übers. von mir); idem 1979, 23; Dahl 1973, 60 macht darauf aufmerksam, daß "nur hier (4,23) und 9,35 karakterisiert Matt Jesu Botschaft direkt als Evangelium (vgl. 24,14; 26:13)". Vgl. auch Betz 1992, 280f. (zitiert oben in Anm. 188).

[198] Als Sammelbericht, z.B. Klostermann 1927/71, 31; als Summar z.B. Lohmeyer/ Schmauch ·1958, 71-72; Grundmann 1968, 111; Gerhardsson 1979, 22-24; idem 1991, 28-51; Conzelmann/Lindemann 1991, 292; Vielhauer 1975, 359; Luz 1985, 179; Gnilka 1986, 106; Davies/ Allison 1988, 412; Betz 1992, 281-83. Bei diesen Formulierungen wird nicht klar, ob es sich um einen Sammelbericht/ein Summar eines außertextlichen Verhaltens Jesu (*suppositio formalis*) oder eines innertextlichen Textabschnitts (*suppositio materialis*) handelt (vgl. dazu oben Anm. 193).

[199] So Wilkens 1985, 25.

[200] Vgl. Vielhauer 1975, 338f.

vielmehr als auf den Text bzw. auf Teiltexte des Matthäusevangeliums interpretiert werden. Ich zitiere hier nur Rudolf Bultmann, der im "Ergänzungsheft" zu seiner "Geschichte der synoptischen Tradition" schreibt: "In 4,23-25 hat Mt durch die Stichworte κηρύσσειν und θεραπεύειν sozusagen die Disposition der folgenden Kapp. angegeben: 5,1-7,29 handelt vom κηρύσσειν, 8,1-9,34 vom θεραπεύειν"[202].

Zu beachten ist ferner, daß Matthäus auch hier (wie in 4,17 im Verhältnis zu Mark 1,14f.) die eindeutige *suppositio formalis*-Aussage in Markus 1,39 (καὶ ἦλθεν κηρύσσων εἰς τὰς συναγωγὰς αὐτῶν εἰς ὅλην τὴν Γαλιλαίαν καὶ τὰ δαιμόνια ἐκβάλλων) in, wie es scheint, mehr oder weniger eindeutige *suppositio materialis*-Aussagen verwandelt hat[203].

Bultmann und viele Ausleger mit ihm interpretieren also diese Summarien de facto nicht als Summarien im eigentlichen Sinn (d.h. als sich auf die außertextlichen Ereignisse im Leben Jesu beziehend), sondern als Delimitationsmerkmale auf Metaebene, d.h. als *Dispositionsschemata*. Die textdelimitierende Funktion kommt dabei den metakommunikativen Verben (διδάσκειν, κηρύσσειν und θεραπεύειν) zu, u.zw. in der Weise wie Günther Bornkamm es formuliert hat, nämlich daß "Matthäus die Wundergeschichten, die Mk 1 und 2, 4 und 5 bieten, bereits im Anschluß an die Bergrede folgen (läßt) und sie zu einer Folge zusammen(stellt), deren Anordnungsprinzip durch die gleichen Sätze 4,23 und 9,35 einleitend und abschließend gekennzeichnet ist"[204].

Es stellt sich aber weiter heraus, daß selbst unter den Exegeten, die sich darüber einig sind, daß es sich hier um Metawendungen handelt, keine Einigkeit darüber

---

[201] So z.B., Davies/Allison 1988, 412: "Observe that, in addition to the introductory summary, 4.23-5, there are at least two typifying résumés between each of the five great Matthean discourses (cf. Theissen, *Stories* [1983 –DH], p. 205 [= G. Theißen 1974, 205 –DH]). These do not primarily just 'summarize' what has gone before or what will come after [was entweder als *suppositio materialis* Aussagen oder als *suppositio formalis* Aussagen interpretiert werden kann –DH]; instead do they supply narrative continuity, lengthen narrative, time, expand the geographical setting, create a picture of movement ... highlight central themes, and tell us that the material in Matthew represents only a selection ... [was wohl nur als *suppositio formalis* Aussagen zu verstehen ist –DH]". S. ferner das Zitat von Hedrick 1984 oben Anm. 193.

[202] R. Bultmann 1971, 120 (Bultmann selbst (!), s. idem 1958, 50). Vgl. Luz 1985, 179: "Der entscheidende *Titelsatz* V 23 ..." (Hervorheb. von mir).

[203] Wiederum hat Matt. die Schwierigkeit in der Markus-Vorlage beseitigt; siehe dazu Betz 1992, 281: "When Matthew characterizes Jesus' activities in the summaries in 4:23 and 9:35, the evangelist is again critical of the description of Mark in 1:39. Mark's claim that Jesus preached (κηρύσσειν) in the Galilean synagogues apparently looks anachronistic to Matthew, and he, therefore, reformulated it by letting Jesus do three things: He *taught* (διδάσκειν) in the synagogues, but he *preached* (κηρύσσειν) »the gospel of the kingdom« outside where also the *healings* took place (4:23)".

[204] G. Bornkamm 1961, 49.

herrscht, ob die zweite Substitution in 9,35 anaphorisch auf den Vortext oder kataphorisch auf den Nachtext zu beziehen ist[205]. *Anaphorisch* wird sie u.a. von Bornkamm, Luz, Davies/Allison et alii interpretiert, wenn diese die beiden sehr ähnlich formulierten Substitutionen auf Metaebene als "einleitend und abschließend" (Bornkamm im Zitat oben) bezeichnen und somit als Inklusionsmerkmal für 5,1-9,34 verstehen[206]. Die anaphorische Deutung von 9,35 sei, laut Vielhauer, sicherlich auch durch die matthäische Systematik bei der Komposition der Bergpredigt (5-7) und vom Tatenzyklus (8-9) beeinflußt worden[207]. *Kataphorisch* wird 9,35f. indessen von Bultmann gedeutet, wenn er diese Substitution als "Situationsangabe ... für die Instruktionsrede"[208] bzw. als "Einleitung der Missionsrede"[209] kennzeichnet. Die Ausgaben von Nestle/Aland[24-26] sowie die Synopse von H. Greeven drucken beide den Text so ab, daß 9,35 eindeutig als kataphorischer Verweis gekennzeichnet wird.

Leider findet sich in der Formulierung 9,35 keine eindeutige Angabe für die Substitutionsrichtung, wohl aber ein paar andeutende Indizien. Der Tempusgebrauch hilft uns nur bedingt weiter, da das Griechische wie bekannt keine *consecutio temporum* kennt und die Handlungen nur in Relation zum Zeitpunkt des Redners ge-

---

[205] Eine Doppeltfunktion befürwortet Dahl 1973, 60: "V. 23 wird fast wörtlich wiederholt in 9,35; diese Verse stellen eine Einrahmung von der grundlegenden Schilderung der Lehre und des Wirkens Jesu in Kap. 5-7 und 8-9 dar", und ferner 134: "V. 35 ist ein Sammelbericht, der als Abschluß des Vorhergehenden und gleichzeitig als Übergang und Einleitung zu Kap. 10 dient" (Übers. von mir); so auch Gerhardsson 1991, wenn er, wie Dahl, zuerst die Inklusion feststellt: "Die erste vollständige Zusammenfassung von Jesu Wirksamkeit findet sich 4,23(-25). Sie wird fast wörtlich in 9,35 wiederholt. Diese beiden Notizen umschliessen drei Kapitel über Jesu Unterricht (5-7) und zwei über seine Machttaten (8-9) und deuten kurz an, was in diesen fünf dazwischenliegenden Kapiteln berichtet worden ist" (S.31). Später aber wird 9,35 auch kataphorisch gedeutet, wenn es heißt: "Das Summar in 9,35 stellt nicht nur den Abschluß der Komposition 4,23-9,35 dar, sondern gleichzeitig auch den Übergang zum nächsten Abschnitt, der davon handelt, daß die Jünger den Auftrag erhalten und ausgesandt werden, 9,36-10,42" (S. 41; Übers. von mir); vgl. idem 1979, 22f.; 30. Ähnlich Gnilka 1988, 351. Unklar ist Grundmann 1968, 283-85.

[206] Luz 1985, 24f., 178; idem 1990, 64: "Der Kreis schließt sich: Der Evangelist wiederholt 4,23 mit geringen Variationen. Der Leser/innen blicken zurück auf Kap. 5-9". Zur Inklusio-Deutung vgl. u.a. auch schon K. L. Schmidt (s. unten Anm. 208); ferner: H. J. Held 1961, 237; Schweizer 1973, 150f.; Frankemölle 1974, 380; Combrink 1983, 80; Gnilka 1986, 106. So offenbar auch Schenk 1987, 265: "Mt ist in seiner Verwendung ganz von der Mk-Red. abhängig, dessen doppelte Verwendung 1,14f er zu der rahmenden inclusio 4,23, 9,35 gedehnt hat"; vgl. auch ibid., 107; auch Davies/Allison 1988, 92, 411f. sowie 1991, 143, 146, 158 vertreten eine Inklusio-Deutung, obwohl sie im übrigen die *suppositio formalis* Deutung vorauszusetzen scheinen (s. oben Anm. 201 und unten Anm. 208); zuletzt J. M Robinson 1992, 370: "This summary is used twice, so as to surround the Inaugural Sermon and the Matthean collection of healings (Mt 8-9) that was specifically constructed to document Q 7,22" und Hagner 1993, 259: "... a summarizing inclusio ...."

[207] Vielhauer 1975, 359; vgl. auch Combrink 1983, 71 und 80; D. R. Bauer 1988, 89.

setzt werden. "Vorzeitigkeit und Nachzeitigkeit in der erzählenden Rede werden jedoch in der Regel durch den bloßen Kontext zum Ausdruck gebracht"[210]. In 9,35 sowie in 4,23 ist das Tempus Imperfekt: περιῆγεν! Beim anaphorischen Verständnis von 9,35 als materiale Suppositionsaussage spielt in der Übersetzung das Tempus eine bedeutungsvolle Rolle. In diesem Falle müßte das Plusquamperfekt ("Und Jesus *war* in allen Städten und Dörfern *umhergezogen* ...") und nicht das Imperfekt ("Und Jesus *zog* in allen Städten und Dörfern *umher* ...") gewählt werden, was m.W. in keiner Übersetzung zu finden ist[211]. Dieser Unterschied im Tempus kommt allerdings im griechischen Text nicht zum Ausdruck, da "das griechische Plusquamperfekt ... dem lateinischen Plusquamperfekt nicht zu vergleichen (ist)"[212]. Immerhin gibt es im Griechischen die Möglichkeit, die Vorvergangenheit zum Ausdruck zu bringen: Entweder eine "Periphrase mit dem Aoristpartizip", z.B. *καὶ περιαγαγὼν ἦν ὁ Ἰησοῦς ... διδάσκων ... καὶ κηρύσσων ... καὶ θεραπεύων κτλ.*, die dem lateinischen oder deutschen Plusquamperfekt entspricht und somit die Vorvergangenheit klar zum Ausdruck brächte[213], denn "in der Umschreibung mit Aoristpartizip hat sich das Griechische ein Gegenstück des Lateinischen historischen

---

[208] Bultmann 1964, 355; so schon A. H. McNeile 1915, 46: "After the account of the second stay at Capharnaum (ix. 1-34), the *résumé* is again inserted (v. 35) as an introduction to the similar work to which the disciples were sent out" und später auch Klostermann 1927/71, 85: "... scheint Mt 35 nicht Unterschrift unter einen früheren Abschnitt (so KL Schmidt [1919/64, 69 –DH]), sondern Beginn der Einleitung zur Instruktionsrede sein zu sollen"; J. Schmid 1965, 175; G. Strecker 1971, 175; Wilkens 1985, 25: "Das Kopfstück 9. 35-38 leitet zur Senderede Kap. 10 über", D. Patte 1987, 138: "A new section of the Gospel begins with an almost verbatim repetition in 9:35 of the description of Jesus' overall ministry–teaching, preaching, healing–found in 4:23". Eine Schwäche der neuerschienenen Kommentare von Davies/Allison 1988, 412 und 1991, 146 sowie Luz 1985, 24f., 178 und 1990, 64 ist erstens bei Davies/Allison die Negligierung der *Suppositio*-Frage und zweitens bei Davies/Allison sowie bei Luz, daß zu der Stelle 9,35 Alands und Greevens kataphorische Text-Gliederung sowie McNeile's, Bultmanns, Klostermanns, Schmids, Streckers, Wilkens und Patte's kataphorische Deutung merkwürdigerweise nicht nur nicht diskutiert, sondern nicht einmal erwähnt werden; es wird einfach nur dekretiert, daß es sich um eine *"inclusio* created by the two verses" handle (so Davies/Allison 1991, 146; s. oben in dieser Anm. sowie Anm. 201).

[209] Ibid., 359; so auch Grundmann 1968, 283ff.

[210] H. Weinrich 1977, 290; vgl. J. Wackernagel 1926, 151, 185; E. Schwyzer 1950, 254.

[211] Doch vgl. jetzt die Paraphrase bei Davies/Allison 1991, 147: "Having travelled through cities and villages (v. 35) Jesus knows the condition of the multitudes ...".

[212] Weinrich, ibid.

[213] Vgl. G. Björk 1940, 74ff.: "Als vorläufig frühestes Beispiel ... können wir nunmehr eine N.T.-Stelle einreihen: Lk. 23,19: ὅστις (sc. Barabbas) ἦν διὰ στάσιν τινὰ γενομένην ἐν τῇ πόλει καὶ φόνον βληθεὶς ἐν τῇ φυλακῇ ... Die Variante βεβλημένος muß (auch im Hinblick auf Lk. 23,25, Joh. 3,24) als Lectio facilior gelten, während das von cod. B [und jetzt auch 𝔓[75] –DH] verbürgte βληθείς den präzisen Sinn gibt: »er war seinerseits wegen Straßenunruhen mit Totschlag ins Gefängnis geworfen *worden*»" (S. 77); Vgl. ferner Blaß/Debrunner/Rehkopf 1976, § 355; W. Bauer 1988, 452 s.v. εἰμί II.4.c. sowie W. Dietrich 1973, 178.

Plusquamperfekts geschaffen"[214] oder eine Substitution auf Abstraktionsebene
(SA) hätte hier eine eindeutige richtungsweisende Aussage gebracht. Weder der einen noch der anderen Möglichkeit hat sich Matthäus jedoch bedient.

Bei Voraussetzung der materialen Supposition scheint die Analyse der Komposition vom Inhaltlichen her: Lehre (Kapp. 5-7) und Tat (Kapp. 8-9)[215] eher für ein
anaphorisches und somit inklusives, die philologische und textgrammatische Analyse der Substitution selbst indessen eher für ein kataphorisches Verständnis von
9,35 zu sprechen. Für die kataphorische Referenz sprechen (1) daß hier im Unterschied zu 4,23 eine Renominalisierung des Jesus-Namens (καὶ περιῆγεν ὁ Ἰησοῦς)
vorliegt[216], die erst 10,5 im Zusammenhang mit dem Zitatformel zur Aussendungsrede wiederholt wird, wenn es dort heißt: τούτους τοὺς δώδεκα ἀπέστειλεν ὁ
Ἰησοῦς παραγγείλας αὐτοῖς λέγων; in 9,36-38 bzw. in 10,1-4, die von allen Kommentatoren zum folgenden Text gezogen werden, findet sich dagegen keine Renominalisierung[217]; (2) daß der Textabschnitt 9,36-38, der unmittelbar an 9,35
anschließt[218], sich eindeutig auf die folgende Aussendungsrede bezieht[219] und
nicht auf den vorhergehenden Textabschnitt 4,23-9,34; (3) daß die Formulierung
der Vollmacht in 10,1 direkt auf 9,35 zurückgreift[220]; (4) "daß hier im Unterschied
zu 4,23 nicht mehr Galiläa als Bereich der Tätigkeit Jesu genannt wird", was "viel-

---

[214] Björk, ibid., der weiter vermerkt, daß "natürlich keine Rede davon sein (kann), daß die ganze
Erscheinung ihrem Ursprung nach ein Latinismus sei", gleichzeitig aber hinzufügt, daß "das Lateinische ganz auszuschalten … ebensowenig angängig (ist)" (S. 78).

[215] Eine ebenso klare und deutliche Unterscheidung zwischen Lehre und Tat findet sich im Nachtext der Substitution 9,35, so weit ich sehe, nicht; sie ist jedoch vorhanden, worauf u.a. Strecker
1971, 175 hingewiesen hat: "Auf den Redekomplex der Bergpredigt (5,1-7,29) folgt die Darstellung
der zehn Wunder, die in 8,1-9,34 gegen den Markusaufriß zusammengestellt und durch einen Chorschluß als einheitliches Ganzes vom folgenden abgegrenzt sind. Ähnlich stehen anschließend Aussendungsrede (9,35-11,1) und der Hinweis auf die Taten Jesu nebeneinander (11,2-6. 19.20ff.)"; vgl.
jetzt auch Allison 1992, 1205 und 1217ff. in bezug auf die Aussendung der Jünger.

[216] Zur Renominalisierung vgl. oben Anm. 179.

[217] Daß "ὁ Ἰησοῦς nach 9,33f. nötig (ist)" (so Luz 1991, 64 Anm.1) ist an und für sich richtig,
legt indessen nur eine notwendige, wohl aber keine hinreichende Bedingung für die Renominalisierung bloß.

Daß in 4,23 und 9,35 eine konjunktionale Kopplung durch καί mit dem Kontext vorliegt und keine asyndetische wie in 4,17 und 16,21, zeigt nur an, daß diese Stellen einen höheren Rang besitzen
als jene.

[218] S. Luz 1990, 80: "V. 36a schließt an das vorangehende Summar direkt an".

[219] Vgl. Luz, ibid., der zuerst feststellt, daß "die beiden Abschnitte 9,36-38 und 10,1-5a durch
keine gemeinsamen Stichworte aufeinander bezogen und auch inhaltlich verschieden (sind)", dann
aber hervorhebt, daß "ein impliziter inhaltlicher Zusammenhang beiden Abschnitten zugrunde
(-liegt)"; Gnilka 1988, 351: "Die VV 36-38 sind bereits auf die folgende Aussendungsrede gerichtet".

leicht als Andeutung des Evangelisten zu verstehen (ist), daß der Bereich des Wirkens Jesu sich nun weiter ausdehnte"[221] und (5) daß m.E. außerdem noch zwei weitere Substitutionen[222] im Nachtext vorliegen, die sich beide auf 9,35 beziehen, und, was an und für sich nur logisch ist, auf einer niedrigeren Ebene als diese stehen:

(a) Die *Substitution auf Metaebene niedrigeren Grades* in der Einleitung zur Aussendungsrede 10,1, wo es heißt: καὶ προσκαλεσάμενος τοὺς δώδεκα μαθητὰς αὐτοῦ ἔδωκεν αὐτοῖς ἐξουσίαν πνευμάτων ἀκαθάρτων ὥστε ἐκβάλλειν αὐτὰ καὶ θεραπεύειν πᾶσαν νόσον καὶ πᾶσαν μαλακίαν. Hier wird die Formulierung von 9,35b (θεραπεύειν πᾶσαν νόσον καὶ πᾶσαν μαλακίαν) aufgenommen und auf die Jünger übertragen[223]. 10,1 ist mit Hilfe des *verbum agendi* ἔδωκεν als *kataphorische* Substitution auf Metaebene für das, was folgt[224], für Matthäus theologisch so wichtig, weil die Jünger dadurch "an Jesu eigenes Handeln angeglichen [werden], wie es in 4,23 und 9,35 sichtbar wird und in 8,1-9,34 ausgeführt war"[225]. Der extensionale Bezug dieses ersten Metasatzes niedrigeren Grades reicht, wie die abschließende Substitution auf Abstraktionsebene in 11,1 zeigt, von 10,2 bis 10,42[226].

(b) Die *Substitution auf Metaebene niedrigeren Grades* im Anschluß an die Substitution auf Abstraktionsebene am Ende der Aussendungsrede 11,1b, wo es heißt: ... μετέβη ἐκεῖθεν τοῦ διδάσκειν καὶ κηρύσσειν ἐν ταῖς πόλεσιν αὐτῶν. Hier

---

[220] Gnilka 1988, 351: "(Man) darf V 35 nicht von den VV 36-38 trennen, weil das in ihm aufklingende Motiv der Krankenheilungen in 10,1 in wörtlicher Übereinstimmung aufgegriffen ist: καὶ θεραπεύων πᾶσαν νόσον καὶ πᾶσαν μαλακίαν.

Wenn Luz 1990, 82 meint "V.1bc greift zurück auf 4,23; 9,35" (so auch Gerhardsson 1991, 41f.; idem 1979, 31), so ist das inhaltlich natürlich richtig. Syntagmatisch gesehen dürfte es indessen klar sein, daß allein durch die Nähe zu 9,35 die Beziehung in erster Linie zu diesem Text vom Autor beabsichtigt ist bzw. vom Leser so aufgefaßt werden muß. S. ausführlich dazu unten im folgenden Absatz.

[221] So Schmid 1965, 175.

[222] Falls es sich tatsächlich, wie ich meine, um *suppositio materialis*-Sätze handelt.

[223] S. oben Anm. 215 und ferner Held 1961, 237-39; Strecker 1971, 175: "Bezeichnend ist auch, daß in der summarischen Zusammenfassung der Tätigkeit Jesu bzw. der Jünger θεραπεύ-ειν neben κηρύσσειν und διδάσκειν wiederkehrt (4,23f.; 9,35; 10,7f.)"; vgl. auch Combrink 1983, 81; so auch Luz 1990, 82: "Die Formulierung der Vollmacht in V 1bc greift zurück auf 4,23; 9,35"; Davies/Allison 1991, 153: "Matthew now repeats a phrase used of Jesus in both 4.23 (q.v.) and 9.35 and thereby drives home once again the correlation between Jesus' deeds and those of his followers: the disciples do what their master did". Schenk 1987, 294 konstatiert zwar den redaktionellen Charakter von 10,1, bemerkt aber nicht die substitutionelle Metafunktion der redaktionellen Verdoppelung von θεραπεύειν (vgl. 10, 8) im Zusammenhang des Schülerauftrags.

[224] Die Metafunktion wird jetzt auch bemerkt von Davies/Allison 1991, 150, wenn sie feststellen, daß 10,1 "a heading for the discourse that follows" konstituiert.

wird mit aller Deutlichkeit auf die Formulierung von 9,35a (διδάσκων ... καὶ κηρύσσων) Bezug genommen[227]. Die Deutung von 11,1b als rubrikaler Satz findet sich zumindest angedeutet bei Luz sowie bei Davies/Allison[228], ohne daß der extensionale Bezug genau festgestellt wird bzw. werden kann.

Auf diese Weise wird die angenommene kataphorische Substitution auf Metaebene in 9,35 durch zwei weitere daran anknüpfende, aber hierarchisch subordinierende kataphorische Substitutionen auf Metaebene aufgenommen und weitergeführt: (a) durch den Hinweis auf die folgende Instruktionsrede in 10,1 und (b) durch den Hinweis auf Jesu weitere Wirksamkeit in Wort und Tat im folgenden Teiltext in 11,1b[229].

### 3.2.2.3. Grade von Substitutionen auf Metaebene im Matthäusevangelium

Zum Schluß soll noch erwähnt werden, daß es im ersten Evangelium, zusätzlich zu den schon oben analysierten, eine Reihe 'Substitutionen auf Metaebene' verschiedenen Grades[230] gibt, die im Rahmen dieses Aufsatzes nicht behandelt werden konnten. Eine solche Substitution sollte zumindest nicht unerwähnt bleiben, nämlich diejenige ersten Grades (SM[1]), die ganz am Anfang des Evangeliums steht: βί-

---

[225] Grundmann 1968, 287; so auch Gnilka 1988, 355: "Die Vollmachtsübertragung ist zwar von E (sc. dem Evangelisten –DH) als geschichtliches Ereignis konzipiert. Der Jüngerbegriff aber deutet an, daß diese Vollmacht in der Gemeinde fortlebt und fortwirkt"; Luz 1990, 83: "Die Jünger partizipieren an seiner (sc. Jesu) eigenen Vollmacht; das machen die Rückverweise auf 4,23; 9,35 und 8,16 deutlich"; sowie Gerhardsson 1991, 41: "Die Jünger erhalten hier genau die Aufgabe die Jesus selbst hat" (Übers. von mir); idem 1979, 31; und Davies/Allison 1991, 150: "The *imitatio Christi* is implicit", und s. ferner das Zitat von ibid. S. 153 oben Anm. 223. S. jetzt die Zusammenstellung der Korrelation zwischen Ereignissen die Jesus auf der einen Seite und solchen, die seine Jünger auf der anderen betreffen bei Allison 1992, 1217.

[226] S. dazu oben § 3.1.(2) sowie Luz 1990, 83: "δώδεκα μαθηταί bildet mit 11,1 eine Inklusion. Die kompositionelle Verklammerung, die Mt durch den Eingangsvers erreicht, ist also sehr intensiv"; ibid. 153: "V 1a weist auf 10,1, V 1b auf 9,35 zurück".

[227] Die anaphorische *tiefenstrukturelle* Anknüpfung an 4,23 und 9,35 wird mit Recht von Schenk 1987, 266 betont, obwohl er die *oberflächenstrukturelle* Metafunktion von 11,1 nicht registriert: "Zwischen die beiden Schülerkomplexe hat Mt 11,1 red. nochmals ein abs. verwendetes κ. [κηρύσσειν –DH] Jesu als Summarium eingefügt, das als verkürzte Dubl. ohnehin auf die beiden voranstehenden Summarien 4,23 und 9,35 zurückweist und als Slot in der semant. Tiefenstruktur wiederum klar inhaltlich gefüllt erscheint". D. R. Bauer 1988, 89 vergleicht zwar 11,1 mit 4,25 und 9,35, unterläßt dabei aber, die Ähnlichkeit mit 10,1 zu notieren.

[228] Luz 1990, 153: "V 1b deutet zugleich die allgemeine Szene für *die folgende Kapitel* an" (Hervorheb. von mir); Davies/Allison 1991, 238: "This redactional verse simultaneously concludes the preceding discourse and resubmerges the reader *in the narrative flow*" (Hervorheb. von mir); Hagner 1993, 295: "11:1 is a *transitional* verse, closing off the discourse and preparing for the pericope that begins in 11:2" (Hervorheb. von mir).

[229] Vgl. hierzu auch das oben Anm. 215 gegebene Zitat aus Strecker 1971, 175.

βλος γενέσεως Ἰησοῦ Χριστοῦ υἱοῦ Δαυὶδ υἱοῦ Ἀβραάμ (1,1). Dieser Vers ist m.E. eindeutig eine SM und funktioniert als Titel[231], aber ihr extensionaler Bezugsumfang ist problematisch u.zw. deswegen, weil ihre intensionale Bedeutung unklar bzw. polysem ist. Βίβλος γενέσεως kann nämlich, je nach der *Bedeutung* bzw. den *Bedeutungen (Intension[en])* von den Lexemen βίβλος und γένεσις bzw. vom Syntagma βίβλος γενέσεως, die wir voraussetzen können[232], bzw. die in der Forschung

---

[230] Zu 'Substitutionen auf Metaebene' verschiedenen Grades, vgl. z.B. Did. 9,1: περὶ δὲ τῆς εὐχαριστίας, οὕτως εὐχαριστήσατε· [Was aber die Eucharistie betrifft, sagt folgendermaßen Dank: ...] einerseits und 9,2: πρῶτον περὶ τοῦ ποτηρίου· [Zuerst in bezug auf den Kelch: ...] bzw. 9,3: περὶ δὲ τοῦ κλάσματος· [In bezug auf das (gebrochene) Brot aber: ...] andererseits, und vgl. dazu Niederwimmer 1989, 181 bzw. 185; ferner: OrSib IV, 1-23 (SM[1]) [s. dazu das Zitat von Hartman unten Anm. 231] mit IV, 48 (SM[2]): νῦν δ' ὅσ' ἀπὸ πρώτης γενεῆς ἔσται, τάδε λέξω· [Jetzt aber das, was vom ersten Geschlecht sein wird, das will ich sagen]; vgl. dazu Hartman 1987, 67: "V. 48 introduziert (auf Metaebene) und markiert für den Leser was kommt" (Übers. von mir). Hartman hat hier de facto zwei verschiedene Grade von 'Substitutionen auf Metaebene' mit je unterschiedlichem Denotatumsumfang aufgezeigt, ohne jedoch ausdrücklich darauf hingewiesen bzw. die beiden explizite in Beziehung zu einander gesetzt zu haben.

[231] So auch D. Dormeyer 1992, 1361ff.; vgl. Hellwig 1984, 16: "Titel sind Metatexte, da sie auf einen Ko-Text Bezug nehmen und ihn nach Art und Inhalt charakterisieren" sowie Hartman 1987, 63f., der bei der Analyse von OrSib IV schreibt: "Hier [sc. V. 1 – DH] fängt die Einleitung an, die bis zum V. 23 reicht. *Es ist ein Text über den folgenden Text* und er steht folglich auf eine *Metaebene* im Verhältnis zu diesem" (Zitat: S. 63; Übers. und Hervorheb. von mir; vgl. auch oben Anm. 192). Als Titel stellt Matt. 1,1 allerdings keinen Namen dar, denn ein Name des Buches ist erst später durch die *Inscriptio* hinzugekommen. Zu dieser Problematik vgl. meine Analyse von Apk 1,1-3 in Hellholm 1990.

Zu Matt. 1,1 s. Davies/Allison 1988, 151f: "The question of whether 1.1 is a general title should take into account this consideration: it was custom in the prophetic, didactic and apocalyptic writings of Judaism to open with an independent titular sentence announcing the content of the work. Illustrations include the following: Proverbs, Ecclesiastes, Canticles, Hosea, Amos, Joel, Nahum, Tobit, Baruch, the Community Rule, the War Rule, the Testaments of the Twelve Patriarchs, Jubilees, 1 Enoch, 2 Enoch (in some mss), the Testament of Job, and the Apocalypse of Abraham. Even more telling than this, however, is the introductory use of *seper* or βίβλος or βιβλίον in ancient Jewish and Christian literature ...: a. Nahum 1.1 ... b. Tobit 1.1 ... c. Baruch 1.1 ... d. T. Job 1.1 ... e. Apoc. Abraham, title ... f. 2 Esdras 1.1-3 ... g. Sepher Ha-Razim, preface ... Beyond a common use of *seper* or βίβλος or βιβλίον, it is noteworthy that several of these openings have an anarthrous βίβλος or βιβλίον (a,b,d) and further that in five out of seven instances a υἱός-formula follows the first mention of the author or subject (b,c,e,f,g). Now because Mt 1.1 likewise opens with an anarthrous βίβλος which is immediately followed by a υἱός-formula and then a genealogy, the texts cited offer firm support for understanding 1.1 as a general title. When the first evangelist began his book with βίβλος, he was evidently following custom". Gegen 1,1 als Titel s. jetzt G. N. Stanton 1992, 1188-90 and 1196.

[232] Hierbei spielen die *kommunikativen Präsuppositionen* beim Sender und seinen damaligen Adressaten, die wir zu rekonstruieren versuchen müssen, eine entscheidende Rolle.

vorausgesetzt worden sind, *extensional* entweder (a) auf die Verse 2-17 von Kapitel 1[233], (b) auf den Abschnitt 1,2-25[234]; (c) auf den Abschnitt 1,2-2,23[235], (d) auf den sog. Prolog 1,2-4,16[236], (e) auf das ganze Matthäusevangelium[237] oder (f) möglicherweise auf (a), (b), (c), (d) und (e) bzw. variable Konstellationen davon zugleich referieren[238].

In den sechs oben angegebenen Alternativen des Bezugsumfanges müßten wir dann zusammen (A) mindestens drei verschiedene Bedeutungen des *Lexems* βίβλος: [1] *Semem$_{A:1}$*: Urkunde = Verzeichnis[239], [2] *Semem$_{A:2}$*: Buch[240], [3] *Semem$_{A:3}$*: Teil eines Buches = Abschnitt oder Teiltext[241], bzw. (B) fünf verschiedene Bedeutungen des *Lexems* γένεσις: [1] *Semem$_{B:1}$*: Ursprung = Genealogie[242], [2] *Semem$_{B:2}$*: Ursprung = Geburt[243], [3] *Semem$_{B:3}$*: Geschichte ≈ Schicksal[244], [4] *Semem$_{B:4}$*: (göttliche) Vaterschaft[245] oder [5] *Semem$_{B:5}$*: als "Name eines Buches" = Genesis[246] voraussetzen.

Diese Bedeutungsvarianten können dann (1) entweder *durch Monosemierung* des *Syntagmas* βίβλος γενέσεως mittels Kombinationen der angegebenen *Sememe*, die im Syntagma als *Seme* funktionieren, in der oben gegebenen Sememreihenfolge zugunsten folgender Varianten unterschieden werden[247]:

---

[233] So u.a. Lohmeyer/Schmauch 1958, 4 mit Anm. 1; Schmid 1965, 35; O. Eißfeld 1966, 465; Strecker 1971, 53 mit Anm. 1 sowie 247; W. B. Tatum 1977, 526; H. Balz 1980, 524. Als eine von zwei Alternativen bei Stanton 1992, 1189.

[234] So u.a. A. Vögtle 1971, 73 und Luz 1985, 88 mit Hinweis auf Gen. 2,4a und 5,1a; Patte 1987, 16; Neirynck 1988, 27 Anm. 32. Als eine zweite Alternative bei Stanton 1992, 1190.

[235] So u.a. A. Plummer 1909, 1 und W. C. Allen 1912, 1-2.

[236] Krentz 1964, 411: "This view of 4:17 and 16:21 [s. oben Anm. 157 –DH] suggests that 1:1 ( ... ) may serve in similar fashion for 1:1-4:16 and thus mark off the first section of the gospel". Mit Bezug auf Gen. 2,4a und 5,1a meint Kingsbury (1975, 11 im Anschluß an Krentz 1964, 411 und 414): "'Book of the Origin' is an elastic expression that can introduce at once a genealogy and the narration of circumstances attendant to that genealogy"; so jetzt auch D. R. Bauer 1988, 75. Methodisch korrekt stellt jedoch Schenk 1987, 303f. (gegen u.a. Kingsbury und Luz) fest, daß der Bezug auf das Vorkommen des Syntagmas in Gen. 2,4 und 5,1 "nur als Voraussetzung, nicht aber als Grund und Entscheidungskriterium für Mt. fungieren (kann)"; diese Interpretation des Syntagmas βίβλος γενέσεως mag trotzdem korrekt sein, vgl. meine Diskussion unten.

[237] So Th. Zahn 1903, 40; Klostermann 1927/71, 1; W. D. Davies 1966, 68-69; Frankemölle 1974, 363; Davies/Allison 1988, 149-54; Dormeyer 1992, 1363.

[238] So oder ähnlich z.B. Grundmann 1968, 61; J. C. Fenton 1977, 36; Davies/Allison 1988, 153f.

[239] Für diese Bedeutung, s. die Belege bei Preisigke 1915, #3919.8; idem 1925, 268. Für das hebräische ספר in dieser Bedeutung s. Eißfeld 1966, 464, der auf Jes. 29,1 (Brief) und Neh. 7,5 (Verzeichnis) hinweist; ferner Luz 1985, 88 Anm. 3; Davies/Allison 1988, 154; Hagner 1993, 3, 9.

[240] Die Bedeutung "Buch" ist die bei weitestem frequenteste, s. nur W. Bauer 1988, 282 s.v.; Lampe 1968, 297 s.v., sowie die Belege bei Davies/Allison 1988, 151f.; so auch Dormeyer 1992, 1362. Unter Verweis auf Texte wie Tob 1,1; 1QS 1,1; 1QM 1,1; ApkAbr, Prol. möchte Schenk 1987, 304 sowie Frankemölle 1974, 363 die Bedeutung "Buch" als "Offenbarungsbuch" spezifizieren.

(a) der Bedeutung "Genealogieverzeichnis" (*Semem*$_{A:1}$ + *Semem*$_{B:1}$) "Jesu Christi"[248] als Überschrift für den Denotatumsbereich 1,2-17;

(b) der Bedeutung "Geburtsverzeichnis" oder "Urkunde des Ursprungs" *(Semem $_{A:1}$ + Semem$_{B:2}$)* "Jesu Christi"[249] als Überschrift für den Denotatumsbereich 1,2-25;

(c) der Bedeutung "Geschichtsbuch" *(Semem*$_{A:2}$ + *Semem*$_{B:3}$) "Jesu Christi"[250]

---

[241] Belege für die Bedeutung: "a *division* of a book" finden sich bei Liddell/Scott/Jones [LSJ] 1966, 333 s.v. 4. Das hebräische ספר allerdings bedeutet "niemals 'Kapitel' oder 'Abschnitt'", sondern "(bezeichnet) immer ein selbständiges Schriftstück" (Eißfeld 1966, 464 im Anschluß an G. von Rad). Die Behauptung von Davies/Allison 1988, daß das griechische Lexem "βίβλος means nothing save 'book'" (S. 151) ist nicht nur angesichts der Belege bei LSJ, sondern auch angesichts ihrer eigenen Belege, von denen zwei ein hebräisches ספר voraussetzen: "but it (sc. βίβλος) (or βιβλίον) could also designate a 'letter' (1 Kgs 21.8) or a 'record' (Gen 2.4; 5.1; Tob 7.13)" (S. 154), nur teilweise korrekt. Die Bestreitung der *Bedeutungsvariante:* 'Buch-Teil' bzw. 'Abschnitt' bei Davies/ Allison ist deshalb bedeutungsvoll, weil sie mit ihrer Auffassung des *Denotatumsumfangs* verbunden wird, wenn es heißt: "Now because neither Mt 1.2-17 nor even Mt 1.2-2.23 or 1.2-4.16 could plausibly be labelled a 'book', the βίβλος of 1.1 most naturally encompasses the gospel as a whole" (ibid.).

[242] Diese Bedeutung des *griechischen Lexems* γένεσις ist m.W. nicht zu belegen, sondern nur aus dem *Syntagma* βίβλος γενέσεως als Übersetzung des hebräischen ספר תלדות (Gen. 5,1) bzw. aus dem *hebräischen Lexem* תלדות (Gen. 2,4a etc.) abzuleiten; s. z.B. McNeile 1915, 1; Lohmeyer/ Schmauch 1958, 4; Schmid 1965, 35; K. Stendahl 1962, 770; Eißfeld 1966, 465; Trilling 1964, 93; Tatum 1977, 526; Hagner 1993, 3, 9.

[243] Zu dieser Bedeutung, s. z.B. W. Bauer 1988, 309 s.v.; Lampe 1968, 310 s.v. 1 bzw. 6.

[244] Für die Bedeutung "fate, destiny" von γένεσις, s. Lampe 1968, 310 s.v. 8; Diese Bedeutungsvariante von 'Geschichte' ist von den Kommentatoren m.W. bisher übersehen worden, vielleicht mit Ausnahme von Fenton 1977, 36, der jedenfalls die Bedeutung "life story" erwähnt. Vgl. dazu die Bedeutung "Lebenslauf" von ὁ τροχὸς τῆς γενέσεως in Jak. 3,6 (s. W. Bauer 1988, 310 s.v. 4).

[245] Zu dieser Bedeutung, s. – unter Verweis auf R. Lane Fox 1979, 712 – Schenk 1987, 303-05 mit lexikalischen Belegen: Herodot 2, 146; Sophokles, *Trach.* 380; Kallist, *Frag.* 14 Z. 24; Arrian, *Anab.* 3,3.2 und 7,29.3.

[246] Zu dieser Bedeutung in Zusammenhang mit dem 1. Buch Mose, s. Lampe 1968, 310 s.v. 4; ferner bes. Davies/Allison 1988, 151: "The title of the first book of the OT in the LXX had already been fixed as 'Genesis' by the time of Matthew ... That Γένεσις had already before Matthew's time become the standard title of the Greek Torah's first book is obviously rather important for the interpretation of Mt 1.1–perhaps even as important as the occurrences of βίβλος γενέσεως in Gen 2.4 and 5.1"; s. die Belege ibid.; ähnlich auch Schenk 1984, 304.

[247] Weitere monosemierte Bedeutungsvarianten kommen deshalb nicht in Frage, weil andere *Semem*-Kombinationen von βίβλος bzw. γένεσις mit einander unvereinbar sind.

[248] So G. Schrenk 1933, 615; Balz 1980, 524 und Gnilka 1986, 7. S. jetzt die Einwände von Davies/Allison 1988, 150.

[249] So Vögtle 1971, 73; Luz 1985, 88: "Urkunde des Ursprungs".

[250] So Th. Zahn 1903, 40; Klostermann 1927/71, 1; W. D. Davies 1966, 68-69 und Frankemölle 1974, 363.

als Überschrift für den Denotatumsbereich 1,2-28,20;

(d) der Bedeutung "[Offenbarungs]Buch der göttlichen Vaterschaft" *(Semem$_{A:2}$ + Semem$_{B:4}$)* "Jesu Christi"[251] als Überschrift für den Denotatumsbereich 1,2-28,20;

(e) der Bedeutung "Genesisbuch" *(Semem$_{A:2}$ + Semem$_{B:5}$)* "Jesu Christi"[252] als Überschrift für den Denotatumsbereich 1,2-28,20;

(f) der Bedeutung "Genealogieabschnitt" *(Semem$_{A:3}$ + Semem$_{B:1}$)* "Jesu Christi"[253] als Überschrift für den Denotatumsbereich 1,2-17;

(g) der Bedeutung "Geburtsabschnitt" *(Semem$_{A:3}$ + Semem$_{B:2}$)* "Jesu Christi"[254] als Überschrift für den Denotatumsbereich 1,2-25;

(h) der Bedeutung "Buchteil von der Genealogie, Geburt und Jugend" *(Semem$_{A:3}$ + Semem$_{B:1/2}$ mit dem Sondersem:* Jugend]) "Jesu Christi"[255] als Überschrift für den Denotatumsbereich 1,2-2,23;

(i) der Bedeutung "Buchteil des Ursprungs" *(Semem$_{A:3}$ + Semem$_{B:2}$* [mit den *Sondersemen des Syntagmas:* Genealogie + weitere begleitenden Umständen dazu]) "Jesu Christi"[256] als Überschrift für den Denotatumsbereich 1,2-4,16;

(2) oder aber durch verschiedene Kombinationen der angegebenen Alternative als Bedeutungsvarianten, die auf unterschiedliche Denotatabereiche referieren, *ohne* bzw. *nur durch teilweise Monosemierung* nebeneinander stehen gelassen werden, u.zw. zugunsten etwa folgender Variationen:

(j) der Bedeutungen "Offenbarungsbuch der wahren göttl. Vaterschaft über den Messiasköning Jesu ... der zugleich auch Nachkomme Davids und Nachkomme Abrahams ist"[257], wobei [j1] die Hauptüberschrift sich auf das ganze Evangelium [1,2-28,20] *((d): Semem$_{A:2}$ + Semem$_{B:4}$)* bezieht und lediglich [j2] die

---

[251] So als Hauptbedeutung: Schenk 1987, 303-05; s. ferner oben Anm. 245 und Anm. 250 sowie unten zu (j) mit Anm. 257f.

[252] So als Hauptbedeutung: Davies/Allison 1988, 150-53; s. ferner unten zu (k) mit Anm. 259.

[253] Dies stellt nun freilich eine Subvariante zur Bedeutungsvariante (1:a): "Genealogieverzeichnis" dar, u.zw. als Teiltextrubrik anstatt als Rubrik eines selbständigen Schriftstücks. Insofern ist das griechische βίβλος in seiner Bedeutung flexibler als das hebräische ספר, was natürlich in bes. Maße für das *Syntagma* βίβλος γενέσεως gilt.

[254] *Mutatis mutandis* gilt für diese Subvariante dasselbe wie für die vorige; s. Anm. 241.

[255] So Plummer 1909, 1; Allen 1912, 1-2: "It seems probable that the title should be taken as covering not the whole Gospel, but only that portion of it which gives Christ's ancestry and the circumstances of His birth and childhood".

[256] So etwa Kingsbury (1975, 11 im Anschluß an Krentz 1964, 411 und 414), s. oben Anm. 236; ferner jetzt auch D. R. Bauer unter Verweis auf die Superscriptio in Gen. 5,1b, wo die Wendung "introduces a genealogy (5.1-32) and the following narrative material (6.1-8). This section of Genesis closes with another superscription introducing the next division. Therefore, the use of the phrase in Gen. 5.1b introduces a section of both genealogical and narrative material within a book" (1988, 75).

[257] So Schenk 1987, 304f.; ähnlich Dormeyer 1992 passim, bes. 1382.

"beiden Näherbestimmungen [υἱοῦ Δαυὶδ υἱοῦ Ἀβραάμ –DH] … die spezielle Überschrift für das 1,2-17 angeschlossene Segment im engeren Sinne (bilden)"[258] *((a): Semem$_{A:1}$ + Semem$_{B:1}$)* oder

(k) der Bedeutungen [k1a] "Genesisbuch" *((e): Semem$_{A:2}$ + Semem$_{B:5}$)*[259] oder
[k1b] "Geschichtsbuch" *((c): Semem$_{A:2}$ + Semem$_{B:3}$)*[260] mit Bezug auf den
Denotatumsbereich 1,2-28,20 und [k2] "Genealogieverzeichnis" *((a): Semem
$_{A:1}$ + Semem$_{B:1}$)* mit Bezug auf den Denotatumsbereich 1,2-17 sowie [k3] "Geburtsverzeichnis" bzw. "Urkunde des Ursprungs" *((b): Semem $_{A:1}$ + Semem
$_{B:2}$)* mit Bezug auf den Denotatumsbereich 1,2-25 oder

(l) der Bedeutungen [l1a] "Genesisbuch von der göttlichen Vaterschaft" *((e) + (d):
Semem$_{A:2}$ + Semem$_{B:5/4}$)* mit Bezug auf den Denotatumsbereich 1,2-28,20
oder [l1b] "Genisisbuch vom Schicksal/von der Geschichte Jesu Christi" *((e)
+ (c): Semem$_{A:2}$ + Semem$_{B:5/3}$)* mit Bezug auf den Denotatumsbereich 1,2-
28,20 sowie [l2] "Erster Buchteil" mit u.a. durch den Nebenbestimmungen
υἱὸς Δαυίδ, υἱὸς Ἀβραάμ angegebenen und mit der Lektüre sich je erweitern-
den Bedeutungsumfängen[261] [l2a]: "Genealogieverzeichnis" *((a) Semem $_{A:1}$ +
Semem$_{B:1}$)* mit Bezug auf den Denotatumsbereich 1,2-17; [l2b]: "Geburtsabschnitt" *((g) Semem$_{A:3}$ + Semem$_{B:2}$)* mit Bezug auf den Denotatumsbereich
1,2-25; [l2c]: "Buchteil der Genealogie, Geburt und Jugend" *((h) Semem$_{A:3}$ +
Semem$_{B:1/2}$ [mit dem *Sondersem:* Jugend])* mit Bezug auf den Denotatumsbereich 1,2-2,23; [l2d]: "Buchteil von der Präsentation Jesu Christi" *((i) Seme-
m$_{A:3}$ + Semem$_{B:2}$ [mit den *Sondersemen des Syntagmas:* weitere begleitenden
Umständen dazu])* mit Bezug auf den Denotatumsbereich 1,2-4,16.

Hier ist nicht der Ort, eine Entscheidung zu treffen, obwohl ich zu einer Lösung in
Richtung der Alternative (j), (k) bzw. bevorzugsweise (l) neige, da Matthäus offenbar, wie wir schon öfters beobachten konnten, *mehrdeutige* Formulierungen bevor-

---

[258] Ibid., 305. Ähnlich schon Grundmann 1968, 61; Frankemölle 1974, 360-65 und A. Kretzer
1980, 583.

[259] So als sekundärer Bedeutungsumfang Davies/Allison 1988, 153f.: "Certainty is here unob-
tainable, but perhaps it would not be rash to conclude that our evangelist intended his opening words
to have more than one evocation … Such a happy interpretation is not, we think, over subtle; and it
has the two-fold advantage of harmonizing conflicting observations and of agreeing with what has
been termed Matthew's tendency to cater to different levels of comprehension at the same time".

[260] So Fenton 1977, 36: Der Titel in 1,1 ist "telescopic: it can be extended to include more and
more of what Matthew is beginning to write about. First, it can cover the genealogy which immediately follows it; then, it can refer to the account of the birth of Jesus …; thirdly, it can mean 'history'
or 'life story' …".

[261] Diese Synthese wird m.W. hier zum ersten Male als *hypothetische* Lösung des Problems vorgeschlagen. Sie setzt allerdings ein raffiniertes Kommunikationsspiel zwischen Sender und damaligen Empfängern seines Evangeliums voraus.

zugt. Meine Absicht war es nur, diese Substitution auf Metaebene ersten Grades (SM[1]) als interessantes Beispiel für die problematische aber höchst bedeutungsvolle Interrelation zwischen intensionalem Bedeutungsumfang und extensionalem Bezugsumfang bei substitutionalen Gliederungsmerkmalen darzulegen.

Durch die vorgeführten Beispiele habe ich zeigen wollen, daß es verschiedene Grade von Substitutionen auf Metaebene gibt. Eine Hierarchisierung dieser Substitutionen kann hier nicht erfolgen, u.zw. aus dem Grunde, weil eine solche nicht durch deduktive Überlegungen erschlossen, sondern nur durch induktive Analysen der Gesamtkomposition erarbeitet werden kann. Diese Analysearbeit aber steht in der hier dargelegten Form vorläufig noch aus.

## 4. Zusammenfassung

Abschließend fasse ich kurz zusammen:

(1) Um zu möglichst sicheren Ergebnissen bei der Herausarbeitung von Gliederungsmerkmalen zu gelangen, ist es erforderlich, zwischen verschiedenen Ebenen im Text zu unterscheiden, u.zw. beginnend mit der Differenzierung zwischen *suppositio formalis* und *suppositio materialis* und spezifizierend mit der Differenzierung zwischen den text-*externen* Objekt- bzw. Textebenen und den text-*internen* Abstraktions- bzw. Metaebenen.

(2) Die vorhandenen Gliederungsmerkmale an der Textoberfläche müssen als Ausgangspunkt für jede Textgliederung von sowohl narrativen als auch argumentativen Texten dienen; so auch bei der Analyse von Evangelientexten.

(3) Im Matthäusevangelium finden wir Substitutionen sowohl auf Metaebene als auch auf Abstraktionsebene. In konsequenter, ja fast stereotyper Weise hat Matthäus sich den SA beim Abschluß seiner fünf großen Reden im Munde Jesu bedient. Problematisch scheint vorläufig noch die Herausarbeitung der Substitutionen auf Metaebene zu sein, entweder

(a)  weil die Redewendungen sich z. T. nicht eindeutig der formalen bzw. der materialen Supposition zuordnen lassen, oder

(b)  weil der extensionale Bezugsumfang manchmal nicht eindeutig festgelegt werden kann, da der intensionale Bedeutungsumfang vage ist, bzw. die Lexeme und Syntagmen polysem sind, oder

(c)  weil die Substitutionsrichtung unter Umständen entweder anaphorisch oder kataphorisch sein kann.

Durch schärfere Analysen im Einzelnen sowie vor allem bezüglich der Gesamtstruktur dieses Evangeliums, in denen auch andere Delimitationssignale sowie Merkmalskombinationen berücksichtigt werden müssen, werden sich m. E. diese Schwierigkeiten allerdings bewältigen lassen, u.zw., wie ich es für notwendig halte, in einer kommunikationstheoretisch befriedigenden Weise.

(4) Besonders signifikant für das Matthäusevangelium scheint die Benutzung von direkt intensional sowie direkt bzw. indirekt extensional mehrdeutigen Substitutionen an bewußt strategisch bedeutsamen Delimitationsstellen zu sein.

(5) Obwohl ich hier noch keinen strikt wissenschaftlich durchgeführten Gliederungsvorschlag für das Matthäusevangelium vorlegen kann, hoffe ich indes durch Beobachtungen zum Phänomen "Intra-textualität von metasprachlichen Äußerungen", auf Probleme bei der Kompositionsanalyse dieses Evangeliums hingewiesen zu haben, die zuallererst einer sprachwissenschaftlichen Lösung harren.

## *Bibliographie*

### I. TEXTAUSGABEN, LEXICA UND GRAMMATIKEN

*Novum Testamentum Graece*, eds. E. Nestle/K. Aland, Stuttgart: Württembergische Bibelanstalt [24]1960; [26]1979.

*Synopse der drei ersten Evangelien*, ed. A. Huck/H. Greeven, Tübingen: Mohr (Siebeck) [13]1981.

*Q-Parallels. Synopsis, Critical Notes & Concordance* (Foundations & Facets), ed. J. S. Kloppenborg, Sonoma, CA: Polebridge 1988.

*Die Apostolischen Väter*. Griechisch-deutsche Parallelausgabe auf der Grundlage der Ausgaben von Franz Xaver Funk/ Karl Bihlmeyer und Molly Whittaker mit Übersetzungen von M. Dibelius und D.-A. Koch neu übersetzt und herausgegeben von Andreas Lindemann und Henning Paulsen, Tübingen: Mohr (Siebeck) 1992.

*La Doctrine des Douze Apôtre (Didachè)* (SC 248), eds. W. Rordorf/A. Tuilier, Paris: Cerf 1978.

*Didache (Apostellehre), Barnabasbrief, Zweiter Klemensbrief, Schrift an Diognet* (SUC II), ed. Kl. Wengst, Darmstadt: Wissenschaftliche Buchgesellschaft 1984.

*Didache. Zwölf-Apostel-Lehre/Traditio Apostolica. Apostolische Überlieferung: Griechisch, Latein, Deutsch* (Fontes Christiani), eds. G. Schöllgen/W. Geerlings, Freiburg i. Br.: Herder 1991.

*Der Hirt des Hermas* (GCS 48), ed. M. Whittaker, Berlin: Akademie Verlag [2]1967.

*Die Oracula Sibyllina* (GCS), ed. J. Geffcken, Leipzig: Hinrichs'sche 1902 [= [2]1967].

*Die syrische Baruch-Apokalypse* (JSHRZ V/2), übers. A. F. J. Klijn, Gütersloh: Mohn 1976, 107-84.

Bauer, W. 1988: *Griechisch-deutsches Wörterbuch zu den Schriften des Neuen Testaments und der frühchristlichen Literatur*, hrsg. von Kurt und Barbara Aland, Berlin: de Gruyter [6]1988.

Björk, G. 1940: *HN ΔΙΔΑΣΚΩΝ. Die periphrastischen Konstruktionen im Griechischen* (SHVU 1940 32:2), Uppsala/Leipzig: Almqvist & Wiksell/Harrassowitz 1940.

Blomqvist, J. 1969: *Greek Particles in Hellenistic Prose*, Lund: Gleerup 1969.

— 1981: *On Adversative Coordination in Ancient Greek and as a Universal Linguistic Phenomenon* (AUU. Acta Societatis Linguisticae Upsaliensis. Nova Series 3:2), Stockholm: Almqvist & Wiksell 1981.

Blomqvist, J. & Jastrup, P. O. 1991: *Grekisk – Græsk Grammatik*, København: Akademisk Forlag 1991.

Denniston, J. D. 1954: *The Greek Particles*, Oxford: Clarendon [2]1954.

Lampe, G. W. H. 1968: *A Patristic Greek Lexicon*, Oxford: Clarendon 1968 [= 1961].

Liddell, H. G./Scott, R./Jones, H. S. 1940: *A Greek-English Lexicon*, Oxford: Clarendon [9]1940.

Preisigke, F. 1915/74: *Sammelbuch Griechischer Urkunden aus Ägypten, Band I*, Straßburg: Trübner 1915 [= Berlin/New York: de Gruyter 1974].

— 1931: *Wörterbuch der griechischen Papyrusurkunden, Band I-III*, Berlin: Eigner Verlag 1925-1931.

Blaß, F./Debrunner, A./Rehkopf, F. 1976: *Grammatik des neutestamentlichen Griechisch*, Göttingen: Vandenhoeck & Ruprecht [14]1976.

Schwyzer, E. 1950: *Griechische Grammatik* (Handbuch der Altertumswissenschaft 2:2), München: Beck 1950.

Turner, N. 1976: *A Grammar of New Testament Greek*. 4 Vol. by J. H. Moulton/W. F. Howard/N. Turner. *Vol. 4: Style,* Edinburgh: Clark 1976.

Wackernagel, J. 1926: *Vorlesungen über Syntax mit besonderer Berücksichtigung von Griechisch, Lateinisch und Deutsch, 1. Teil,* Basel: Emil Birkhäuser [2]1926.

Wieland, Ch. M. 1971: *Lucian von Samosata: Sämtliche Werke. Aus dem Griechischen übersetzt und mit Anmerkungen und Erläuterungen versehen.* Zweiter Band: Dritter und Vierter Teil, Darmstadt: Wissenschaftliche Buchgesellschaft 1971 [= 1788/89].

## II. EXEGETISCHE ARBEITEN

Allen, W. C. 1912: *The Gospel According to S. Matthew* (ICC), Edinburgh: Clark [3]1912.

Allison, D. C. 1992: "Matthew: Structure, Biographical Impulse and the Imitatio Christi", in: Van Segbroeck/Tuckett/Van Belle/Verheyden (eds.) 1992, 1203-21.

Bacon, B. W. 1930: *Studies in Matthew*, New York/London: Holt 1930.

Balz, H. 1980: "Βίβλος", in: H. Balz/G. Schneider (eds.), *EWNT* 1, Stuttgart etc.: Kohlhammer 1980, 524-25.

Bauer, D. R. 1988: *The Structure of Matthew's Gospel. A Study in Literary Design* (JSNT.S 31), Sheffield: Almond 1988.

Berger, Kl. 1977: *Exegese des Neuen Testaments*. Neue Wege vom Text zur Auslegung (UTB 658), Heidelberg: Quelle & Meyer 1977.

Betz, H. D. 1985: *2 Corinthians 8 and 9. A Commentary on Two Administrative Letters of the Apostle Paul* (Hermeneia), Philadelphia, PA: Fortress 1985.

— 1992: "The Sermon on the Mount in Matthew's Interpretation", in: idem, *Synoptische Studien. Gesammelte Aufsätze II*, Tübingen: Mohr (Siebeck) 1992, 270-89.

Bibelkommissionen 1981: *Bibelkommissionens översättning av Nya testamentet* med noter [Schwedische Übersetzung des Neuen Testaments], Stockholm: Verbum 1981.

Bornkamm, G. 1961: "Die Sturmstillung im Matthäusevangelium", in: Bornkamm/Barth/Held 1961, 48-53.

— 1971: "Die Vorgeschichte des sogenannten zweiten Korintherbriefes", in: idem, *Geschichte und Glaube. Zweiter Teil. Gesammelte Aufsätze Band IV* (BEvTh 53), München: Kaiser 1971, 162-94.

Bornkamm, G./Barth, G./Held, H. J. 1961: *Überlieferung und Auslegung im Matthäusevangelium* (WMANT 1), Neukirchen-Vluyn: Neukirchener [2]1961.

Bousset, W. 1906/66: *Die Offenbarung des Johannis* (KEK 16), Göttingen: Vandenhoeck & Ruprecht [2]1906 [= Neudruck 1966].

Bultmann, R.1931/64: *Die Geschichte der synoptischen Tradition* (FRLANT NF 12), Göttingen: Vandenhoeck & Ruprecht [6]1964 [= [2]1931].

— 1958: *Ergänzungsheft* [zur Geschichte der synoptischen Tradition], Göttingen: Vandenhoeck & Ruprecht [3]1958.

— 1971: *Ergänzungsheft* [zur Geschichte der synoptischen Tradition], bearbeitet von G. Theißen und Ph. Vielhauer, Göttingen: Vandenhoeck & Ruprecht [4]1971.

Byrskog, S. 1994: *Jesus the Only Teacher. Didactic Authority and Transmission in Ancient Israel, Ancient Judaism and the Matthean Community* (CB.NT 24), Stockholm: Almqvist & Wiksell 1994.

Caird, G. B. 1966: *The Revelation of St. John the Divine* (Harper New Testament Commentary), New York: Harper 1966.

Charles, R. H. 1920: *The Revelation of St. John, Vol. I* (ICC), Edinburgh: T. & T. Clark 1920.

Combrink, H. J. B. 1983: "The Structure of the Gospel of Matthew as Narrative", in: *TynB* 34 (1983) 61-90.

Conzelmann, H. 1963: *Die Apostelgeschichte* (HNT 7), Tübingen: Mohr (Siebeck) 1963.

Conzelmann, H./Lindemann, A. 1991: *Arbeitsbuch zum Neuen Testament* (UTB 52), Tübingen: Mohr (Siebeck) [10]1991.

Cook, J. G. 1985: *A Text Linguistic Approach to the Gospel of Mark* (Ph.D. Diss., Emory University), Atlanta, GA 1985 (forthcoming).

Dahl, N. A. 1973: *Matteusevangeliet, Del 1,* Oslo etc.: Universitetsforlaget [2]1973.

Davies, W. D. 1966: *The Setting of the Sermon on the Mount,* Cambridge: Cambridge University Press [2]1966.

Davies, W. D./Allison, Jr. D. C. 1988: *The Gospel According to Saint Matthew. Vol. I: Introduction and Commentary on Matthew I-VII* (ICC), Edinburgh: T. & T. Clark 1988.

— 1991: *The Gospel According to Saint Matthew. Vol. II: Commentary on Matthew VIII-XVIII* (ICC), Edinburgh: T. & T. Clark 1991.

Dibelius, M. 1968: *Aufsätze zur Apostelgeschichte* (FRLANT NF 42), Göttingen: Vandenhoeck & Ruprecht [5]1968.

Dormeyer, D. 1992: "Mt 1,1 als Überschrift zur Gattung und Christologie des Matthäus-Evangeliums", in: Van Segbroeck/Tuckett/Van Belle/Verheyden (eds.) 1992, 1361-83.

Egger, W. 1990: *Methodenlehre zum Neuen Testament. Einführung in linguistische und historisch-kritische Methoden,* Freiburg i. Br./Basel/Wien: Herder [2]1990.

Ellis, P. F. 1974: *Matthew: His Mind and His Message,* Collegeville: Liturgical 1974.

Eißfeld, O. 1966: "Biblos Geneseos", in: idem, *Kleine Schriften. Dritter Band*, Tübingen: Mohr (Siebeck) 1966, 458-70.

Fenton, J. C. 1977: *The Gospel of St. Matthew* (PNTC), revised ed., Harmondworth: Penguin 1977.

Fitzmyer, J. 1981: *The Gospel According to Luke, Vol. I* (AncB 28), Garden City, NY: Doubleday 1981.

Fohrer, G./Hoffmann, H. W./Huber, F../Markert, L./Wanke, G. 1976: *Exegese des Alten Testaments. Einführung in die Methodik* (UTB 267), Heidelberg: Quelle & Meyer 1976.

Fornberg, T. 1989: *Matteusevangeliet 1:1-13:52* (Kommentar till Nya testamentet 1A), Uppsala: EFS-förlaget 1989.

Frankemölle, H. 1974: *Jahwebund und Kirche Christi* (NTA 10), Münster: Aschendorff 1974.

Gerhardsson, B. 1979: *The Mighty Acts of Jesus According to Matthew* (SMHVL 1978-79:5), Lund: Gleerup 1979.

— 1991: *Jesu maktgärningar i Matteusevangeliet*, Lund: Novapress 1991.

Gibson, A. 1981: *Biblical Semantic Logic*. A Preliminary Analysis, Oxford: Blackwell 1981.

Gnilka, J. 1986: *Das Matthäusevangelium. I. Teil* (HThK I/1), Freiburg/Basel/Wien: Herder 1986.

— 1988: *Das Matthäusevangelium. II. Teil* (HThK I/2), Freiburg/Basel/Wien: Herder 1988.

Goulder, M. D. 1974: *Midrash and Lection in Matthew*, London: SPCK 1974.

Green, H. B. 1968: "The Structure of St. Matthew's Gospel", in: F. L. Cross (ed.), *Studia Evangelica IV: Papers Presented to the Third International Congress on New Testament Studies. Part I: The New Testament Scriptures* (TU 102), Berlin: Akademie-Verlag 1968, 47-59.

Grundmann, W. 1968: *Das Evangelium nach Matthäus* (ThHK 1), Berlin: Evangelische Verlagsanstalt 1968.

Gundry, R. H. 1982: *Matthew: A Commentary on His Literary and Theological Art*, Grand Rapids, MI: Eerdmans 1982.

Haenchen, E. 1965a: *Die Apostelgeschichte* (KEK 3), Göttingen: Vandenhoeck & Ruprecht [6]1965.

— 1965b: "Matthäus 23", in: idem, *Gott und Mensch. Gesammelte Aufsätze*, Tübingen: Mohr (Siebeck) 1965, 29-54.

Hagner, D. A. 1993: *Matthew 1-13* (Word Biblical Commentary 33A), Dallas, TX: Word Books 1993.

Halmel, A. 1904: *Der zweite Korintherbrief des Apostels Paulus*, Halle: Niemeyer 1904.

Hardmeier, Ch. 1978: *Texttheorie und biblische Exegese. Zur rhetorischen Funktion der Trauermetaphorik in der Prophetie* (BEvTh 79), München: Kaiser 1978.

Hartman, L. 1980: "Form and Message. A Preliminary Discussion of 'Partial Texts' in Rev 1-3 and 22,6ff.", in: Lambrecht (ed.) 1980, 129-49.

— 1987: "Vad säger Sibyllan? Byggnad och budskap i de sibyllinska oraklens fjärde bok", in: P. W. Bøckman/R. E. Kristiansen (eds.), *Context. Essays in Honour of P. J. Borgen* («Relieff» 24), Trondheim: Tapir 1987, 61-74. [Engl. trans. in: L. Hartman, *On Reading Others' Letters. Collected Essays*. Ed. by David Hellholm 1995.]

Hedrick, Ch. W. 1984: "The Role of 'Summary Statements' in the Composition of the Gospel of Mark: A Dialog with Karl Schmidt and Norman Perrin", in: *NT* 26 (1984) 289-311.

Held, H. J. 1961: "Matthäus als Interpret der Wundergeschichten", in: Bornkamm/ Barth/Held 1961, 155-287.

Hellholm, D. 1980: *Das Visionenbuch des Hermas als Apokalypse. Formgeschichtliche und text-theoretische Studien zu einer literarischen Gattung. Band I: Methodologische Vorüber-legungen und makrostrukturelle Textanalyse* (CB.NT 13:1), Lund: Gleerup 1980.

— 1986: "The Problem of Apocalyptic Genre and the Apocalypse of John", in: A.Y. Collins (ed.), *Early Christian Apocalypticism: Genre and Social Setting* (= *Semeia* 36), Decatur, GA: Scholars Press 1986, 13-64.

— 1986-87: "En textgrammatisk konstruktion i Matteusevangeliet", in: *SEÅ* 51-52 (1986-87) 80-9.

— 1990: "The Visions He Saw or: To Encode the Future in Writing. An Analysis of the Prologue of John's Apocalyptic Letter", in: Th.W. Jennings, Jr. (ed.), *Text and Logos. The Humanistic Interpretation of the New Testament* [FS Hendrikus Boers] (Scholars Press. Humanistic Series), Atlanta, GA: Scholars Press 1990, 109-46.

— 1991: "Methodological Reflections on the Problem of Definition of Generic Texts", in: J. J. Collins/J. H. Charlesworth (eds.), *Mysteries and Revelations. Apocalyptic Studies since the Uppsala Colloquium* (JSP.S 9), Sheffield: JSOT 1991, 135-63.

— 1995: *Lucian's Icaromenippos. A Textlinguistic and Generic Investigation.* (SO.S. XXVIII), Oslo: Norwegian University Press 1995 (forthcoming).

— 1995a: "Från judisk tvåvägslära till kristen dopkatekes. En inblick i tillkomsten av en första kyrkoordning", in: R. Hvalvik/H. Kvalbein (eds.), *Ad Acta. Studier til Apostlenes gjerninger og urkristendommens historie.* FS Edvin Larsson, Oslo: Verbum 1995, 109-139.

Hunkin, J. W. 1924: "'Pleonastic archomai' in the New Testament", in: *JThS* 25 (1924) 391-95.

Jeremias, J. 1980: *Die Sprache des Lukasevangeliums* (KEK. Sonderband), Göttingen: Vandenhoeck & Ruprecht 1980.

Johanson, B. C. 1987: *To All the Brethren. A Text-Linguistic and Rhetorical Approach to I Thessalonians* (CB.NT 16), Stockholm: Almqvist & Wiksell 1987.

Karrer, M. 1986: *Die Johannesoffenbarung als Brief. Studien zu ihrem literarischen, historischen und theologischen Ort* (FRLANT 140), Göttingen: Vandenhoeck & Ruprecht 1986.

Kingsbury, J. D. 1975/89: *Matthew: Structure, Christology, Kingdom*, Philadelphia, PA: Fortress 1975, [2]1989.

— 1988: *Matthew as Story*, Philadelphia, PA: Fortress [2]1988.

Kloppenborg, J. S. 1988: siehe unter Textausgaben etc.

Klostermann, E. 1927/71: *Das Matthäusevangelium* (HNT 4), Tübingen: Mohr (Siebeck) [4]1971 [= [3]1927].

— 1929/75: *Das Lukasevangelium* (HNT 5), Tübingen: Mohr (Siebeck) [3]1975 [= [2]1929].

Koch, D.-A. 1983: "Inhaltliche Gliederung und geographischer Aufriß im Markusevangelium", in: *NTS* 29 (1983) 145-66.

Koch, Kl. 1974: *Was ist Formgeschichte?*, Neukirchen/Vluyn: Neukirchener [3]1974.

— 1983/89: "Vom profetischen zum apokalyptischen Visionsbericht", in: D. Hellholm (ed.), *Apocalypticism in the Mediterranean World and the Near East,* Tübingen: Mohr (Siebeck) 1983/[2]1989, 413-46.

Koester, H. 1990: *Ancient Christian Gospels. Their History and Development*, London/Philadelphia, PA: SCM/Trinity 1990.

Kraft, H. 1974: *Die Offenbarung des Johannes* (HNT 16a), Tübingen: Mohr (Siebeck) 1974.

Krentz, E. 1964: "The Extent of Matthew's Prologue. Toward the Structure of the First Gospel", in: *JBL* 83 (1964) 409-14.

Kretzer, A. 1980: "γένεσις", in: H. Balz/G. Schneider (eds.), *EWNT* 1, Stuttgart etc.: Kohlhammer 1980, 582-84.

Kümmel, W. G. 1973: *Einleitung in das Neue Testament*, Heidelberg: Quelle & Meyer [17]1973.

Lambrecht, J. (ed.) 1980: *L'Apocalypse johannique et l'Apocalyptique dans le Nouveau Testament* (BEThL 53), Gembloux/Leuven: University – Peeters 1980.

— 1980: "A Structuration of Revelation 4,1-22,5", in: Lambrecht (ed.) 1980, 77-104.

Lane Fox, R. 1979: *Alexander der Große*, Düsseldorf: [2]1979.

Larsson, E. 1983: *Apostlagärningarna, Band I* (Kommentar till Nya Testamentet 5A), Uppsala: EFS-förlaget 1983.

Lövestam, E. 1988a: "Apostlagärningarnas ärende", in: *SvTK* 64 (1988) 1-6.

— 1988b: *Apostlagärningarna* (Tolkning av Nya testamentet 5), Stockholm: Verbum 1988.

Lohmeyer, E./Schmauch, W. 1958: *Das Evangelium des Matthäus* (KEK, Sonderband), Göttingen: Vandenhoeck & Ruprecht [2]1958.

— 1953/70: *Die Offenbarung des Johannes* (HNT 16), Tübingen: Mohr (Siebeck) 1970 [= [2]1953].

Lohr, C. H. 1961: "Oral Techniques in the Gospel of Matthew", in: *CBQ* 23 (1961) 403-35.

Lüdemann, G. 1987: *Das frühe Christentum nach den Traditionen der Apostelgeschichte. Ein Kommentar*, Göttingen: Vandenhoeck & Ruprecht 1987.

Lührmann, D. 1987: *Das Markusevangelium* (HNT 3), Tübingen: Mohr (Siebeck) 1987.

Luz, U. 1985: *Das Evangelium nach Matthäus (Mt 1-7)* (EKK 1:1), Zürich/Neukirchen-Vluyn: Benziger/Neukirchener 1985.

— 1990: *Das Evangelium nach Matthäus (Mt 8-17)* (EKK 1:2), Zürich/Neukirchen-Vluyn: Benziger/Neukirchener 1990.

McNeile, A. H. 1915: *The Gospel according to St. Matthew*, London: Macmillan 1915.

Meier, J. P. 1992: "Matthew, Gospel of", in: D. N. Freedman (ed.), *Anchor Bible Dictionary*, Vol. 4, New York etc.: Doubleday 1992, 622-41.

Mitchell, M. M. 1989: "Concerning ΠΕΡΙ ΔΕ in 1 Corinthians", in: *NT* 31 (1989) 229-56.

Müller, U. B. 1984: *Die Offenbarung des Johannes* (ÖTBK 19), Gütersloh/Würzburg: Mohn/Echter 1984.

Neirynck, F. 1988: "Ἀπὸ τότε ἤρξατο and the Structure of Matthew", in: *EThL* 64, Leuven: University – Peeters 1988, 21-59.

Niederwimmer, K. 1989: *Die Didache* (KAV 1), Göttingen: Vandenhoeck & Ruprecht 1989.

Patte, D. 1987: *The Gospel According to Matthew. A Structural Commentary on Matthew's Faith*, Philadelphia, PA: Fortress 1987.

Pesch, R. 1986: *Die Apostelgeschichte* (EKK 5:1), Zürich/Neukirchen-Vluyn: Benziger/Neukirchener 1986.

Pervo, R. I. 1987: *Profit with Delight.* The Literary Genre of the Acts of the Apostles, Philadelphia, PA: Fortress 1987.

Plummer, A. 1909: *An Exegetical Commentary on the Gospel according to St. Matthew*, London: Scott 1909.

Powell, M. A. 1990: *What is Narrative Criticism?* (Guides to Biblical Scholarship. New Testament Series), Minneapolis, MN: Fortress 1990.

— 1992: "The Plot and Subplots of Matthew's Gospel", in: *NTS* 38 (1992) 187-204.

Richter, W. 1971: *Exegese als Literaturwissenschaft. Entwurf einer alttestamentlichen Literaturtheorie und Methodologie,* Göttingen: Vandenhoeck & Ruprecht 1971.

Robinson, J. M. 1992: "The Sayings Gospel Q", in: Van Segbroeck/Tuckett/Van Belle/Verheyden (eds.) 1992, 361-88.

Roloff, J. 1981: *Die Apostelgeschichte* (NTD 5), Göttingen: Vandenhoeck & Ruprecht 1981.

— 1984: *Die Offenbarung des Johannes* (ZBK.NT 18), Zürich: Theologischer Verlag 1984.

Schenk, W. 1987: *Die Sprache des Matthäus. Die Textkonstituenten in ihren makro- und mikrostrukturellen Relationen,* Göttingen: Vandenhoeck & Ruprecht 1987.

Schille, G. 1983: *Die Apostelgeschichte des Lukas* (ThHK 5), Berlin: Evangelische Verlagsanstalt 1983.

Schlier, H. 1935: "δείκνυμι κτλ.", in: *ThWNT* II, Stuttgart: Kohlhammer 1935, 26-33.

Schmid, J. 1965: *Das Evangelium nach Markus* (RNT 1), Regensburg: Pustet 1965.

Schmidt, K. L. 1919/64: *Der Rahmen der Geschichte Jesu. Literarkritische Untersuchungen zur ältesten Jesusüberlieferung,* Berlin: Trowitzsch 1919 [= Neudruck: Darmstadt: Wissenschaftliche Buchgesellschaft 1964].

Schneider, G. 1980: *Die Apostelgeschichte* (HThK V/1), Freiburg/Basel/Wien: Herder 1980.

Schrenk, G. 1933: "βίβλος, βιβλίον", in: *ThWNT* I, Stuttgart: Kohlhammer 1933, 613-20.

Schürmann, H. 1969: *Das Lukasevangelium. Erster Teil* (HThK III/1), Freiburg/ Basel/Wien: Herder 1969.

Schüssler Fiorenza, E. 1985: *The Book of Revelation. Justice and Judgment*, Philadelphia, PA: Fortress 1985.

Schweizer, E. 1973: *Das Evangelium nach Matthäus* (NTD 2), Göttingen: Vandenhoeck & Ruprecht 1973.

Van Segbroeck, F./Tuckett, C. M/Van Belle, G./Verheyden, J. (eds.), *The Four Gospels 1992. FS Frans Neirynck, Vol. II* (BEThL 100-B), Leuven: University – Peeters 1992.

Standaert, B. 1992: "L'évangile selon Matthieu. Composition et genre littéraire", in: Van Segbroeck/Tuckett/Van Belle/Verheyden (eds.) 1992, 1223-50.

Stanton, G. N. 1992: "Matthew: *ΒΙΒΛΟΣ, ΕΥΑΓΓΕΛΙΟΝ, OR ΒΙΟΣ?*" in: Van Segbroeck/ Tuckett/ Van Belle/Verheyden (eds.) 1992, 1187-1201.

Steck, O. H. 1989: *Exegese des Alten Testaments. Leitfaden der Methodik,* Neukirchen-Vluyn: Neukirchener [12]1989.

Stendahl, K. 1962: "Matthew", in: H. H. Rowley/M. Black (eds.), *PCB*, Surrey: Nelson 1962, 769-98.

Strecker, G. 1971: *Der Weg der Gerechtigkeit. Untersuchung zur Theologie des Matthäus* (FRLANT 82), Göttingen: Vandenhoeck & Ruprecht [3]1971.

Streeter, B. H. 1924: *The Four Gospels: A Study of Origins*, London: Macmillan 1924.

Tatum, W. B. 1977: "'The Origin of Jesus Messiah' (Matt 1:1, 18a): Matthew's Use of the Infancy Traditions", in: *JBL* 96 (1977) 523-35.

Theißen, G. 1974: *Urchristliche Wundergeschichten. Ein Beitrag zur formgeschichtlichen Erforschung der synoptischen Evangelien* (StNT 8), Gütersloh: Mohn 1974.

— 1983: *The Miracle Stories of Early Christian Tradition* (Studies in the New Testament and its World), Edinburgh: T. & T. Clark 1983.

Tolbert, M. A. 1989: *Sowing the Gospel. Mark's World in Literary-Historical Perspective,* Minneapolis, MN: Fortress 1989.

Trilling, W. 1964: *Das wahre Israel* (StANT 10), München: Kösel [3]1964.

Vielhauer, Ph. 1975: *Geschichte der Urchristlichen Literatur. Einleitung in das Neue Testament, die Apokryphen und die Apostolischen Väter* (GLB), Berlin: de Gruyter 1975.

Vögtle, A. 1971: "Die Genealogie Mt 1,2-16 und die matthäische Kindheitsgeschichte", in: idem, *Das Evangelium und die Evangelien*, Düsseldorf: Patmos 1971, 57-102.

Weiß, J. 1910/70: *Der erste Korintherbrief* (KEK 5), Göttingen: Vandenhoeck & Ruprecht 1910 [= Neudruck 1970].

Wengst, Kl. 1984: siehe unter Textausgaben etc.

Wiklander, B. 1984: *Prophecy as Literature. A Text-Linguistic and Rhetorical Approach to Isaiah 2-4* (CB.OT 22), Lund: Gleerup 1984.

Wilkens, W. 1985: "Die Komposition des Matthäus-Evangeliums", in: *NTS* 31 (1985) 24-38.

Zahn, Th. 1903: *Das Evangelium nach Matthäus* (KNT 1), Leipzig: Deichert 1903.

## III. PHILOSOPHISCHE UND SPRACHWISSENSCHAFTLICHE ARBEITEN

Ackrill, J. L. 1963: *Aristotle's Categories and De Interpretatione*. Translated with Notes (Clarendon Aristotle Series), Oxford: Clarendon 1963.

Arens, H. 1980: "Geschichte der Linguistik", in: H. P. Althaus/H. Henne/H. E. Wiegand (eds.), *Lexikon der germanistischen Linguistik,* Tübingen: Niemeyer [2]1980, 97-107.

Baldinger, K. 1978: "Semasiologie und Onomasiologie", in: H. Geckeler (ed.), *Strukturelle Bedeutungslehre* (WdF 126), Darmstadt: Wissenschaftliche Buchgesellschaft 1978, 372-401.

— 1980: *Semantic Theory*. Towards a Modern Semantics, Oxford/New York: Blackwell/St. Martin 1980.

Bocheński, I. M./Menne, A. 1983: *Grundriß der formalen Logik* (UTB 59), Paderborn: Schöningh [5]1983.

Brekle, H. E. 1972: *Semantik* (UTB 102), München: Fink [2]1972.

Bühler, K. 19[34]/78: *Sprachtheorie. Die Darstellungsfunktion der Sprache,* Jena: Fischer 1934 [= Frankfurt/Main: Ullstein 1978].

Bungarten, Th. (ed.) 1981: *Wissenschaftssprache. Beiträge zur Methodologie, theoretischen Fundierung und Deskription,* München: Fink 1981.

Carnap, R. 1958: *Meaning and Necessity. A Study in Semantics and Modal Logic,* Chicago/London: University of Chicago Press [2]1958.

Coseriu, E. 1975: *Die Geschichte der Sprachphilosophie von der Antike bis zur Gegenwart. Eine Übersicht. Teil I: Von der Antike bis Leibniz* (Tübinger Beiträge zur Linguistik 11), Tübingen: Narr 1975.

— 1981: *Textlinguistik. Eine Einführung* (Tübinger Beiträge zur Linguistik 109), Tübingen: Narr [2]1981.

— 1988a: *Einführung in die Allgemeine Sprachwissenschaft* (UTB 1372), Tübingen: Franke 1988.

— 1988b: *Sprachkompetenz. Grundzüge der Theorie des Sprechens.* Bearb. u. hrsg. von H. Weber (UTB 1481), Tübingen: Franke 1988.

Dietrich, W. 1973: *Der periphrastische Verbalaspekt in den romanischen Sprachen* (Beihefte zur Zeitschrift für romanische Philologie 140), Tübingen: Niemeyer 1973.

van Dijk, T. A. 1980: *Textwissenschaft. Eine interdisziplinäre Einführung* (dtv wissenschaft 4364), Tübingen/München: Niemeyer/Deutscher Taschenbuch Verlag 1980.

— 1985: "Semantic Discourse Analysis", in: T. A. van Dijk (ed.), *Handbook of Discourse Analysis. Vol. 2: Dimensions of Discourse,* London: Academic Press 1985, 103-36.

van Dijk, T. A./Petöfi, J. S. (eds.) 1977: *Grammars and Descriptions* (Research in Text Theory 1), Berlin: de Gruyter 1977.

Dressler, W. 1973: *Einführung in die Textlinguistik* (Konzepte der Sprach- und Literaturwissenschaft 13), Tübingen: Niemeyer [2]1973.

Geckeler, H. 1971: *Strukturelle Semantik und Wortfeldtheorie,* München: Fink 1971.

Gibson, A. 1981: siehe unter II. Exegetische Arbeiten.

Greimas, A. J./Courtés, J. 1982: *Semiotics and Language. An Analytical Dictionary,* Bloomington, IN: Indiana University Press 1982.

Gülich, E. 1976: "Ansätze zu einer kommunikationsorientierten Erzähltextanalyse (am Beispiel mündlicher und schriftlicher Erzähltexte)", in: W. Haubrichs (ed.), *Erzähltextforschung 1 (= Zeitschrift für Literaturwissenschaft und Linguistik Beiheft 4),* Göttingen: Vandenhoeck & Ruprecht 1976, 224-56.

Gülich, E./Quasthoff, U. M. 1985: "Narrative Analysis", in: T. van Dijk (ed.), *Handbook of Discourse Analysis. Vol. 2: Dimensions of Discourse,* London: Akademic Press 1985, 169-97.

Gülich, E./Raible, W. 1975: "Textsorten-Probleme", in: H. Moser (ed.), *Linguistische Probleme der Textanalyse* (Jahrbuch des Instituts für deutsche Sprache 35), Düsseldorf: Schwann 1975, 144-97.

— 1977: *Linguistische Textmodelle* (UTB 130), München: Fink 1977.

— 1977a: "Überlegungen zu einer makrostrukturellen Textanalyse: J. Thurber, The Lover and His Lass", in: van Dijk/Petöfi (eds.) 1977, 132-75.

Halliday, M. A. K./Huddleston, R. D. 1981: "Paradigmatic and syntagmatic relations", in: M. A. K. Halliday/J. R. Martin (eds.), *Readings in Systemic Linguistics,* London: Batsford 1981, 17-53.

Hammarström, G. 1988: "Synchrony, diachrony and communicative aspects", in: J. Albrecht/J. Lüdtke/H. Thun (eds.), *Energeia und Ergon. Sprachliche Variation – Sprachgeschichte – Sprachtypologie. Studia in honorem Eugenio Coseriu, Band II,* (Tübinger Beiträge zur Linguistik 300), Tübingen: Narr 1988, 135-41.

Harweg, R. 1973: "Text grammar and literary texts: Remarks on a grammatical science of litera-ture", in: *Poetics* 9 (1973) 65-91.

— 1979: *Pronomina und Textkonstitution* (Beihefte zu Poetica 2), München: Fink ²1979.

— 1980: "Meta-assertorische, meta-propositionale und meta-ontologische Aussagen. Ein Beitrag zur Typo- und Textologie metakommunikativer Rede", in: *Folia Linguistica* 14 (1980) 283-328.

— 1981: "Verwendung und Erwähnung und die Unterscheidung von Objekt- und Metasprache", in: *Zeitschrift für Phonetik, Sprachwissenschaft und Kommunikationsforschung* 34 (1981) 285-92.

— 1981a: "Strukturen und Probleme linguistischer Rede. Zeichen- und abbildungstheoretische Be-merkungen zur Sprache der Linguistik", in: Bungarten (ed.) 1981, 111-39.

Heger, Kl. 1969: "Die Semantik und die Dichotomie von Langue und Parole – Neue Beiträge zur theoretischen Standortbestimmung von Semasiologie und Onomasiologie", in: *Zeitschrift für romanische Philologie* 85 (1969) 144-215.

— 1976: *Monem, Wort, Satz und Text* (Konzepte der Sprach- und Literaturwissenschaft 8), Tübin-gen: Niemeyer ²1976.

— 1983: "'Concepts' and 'Noemes'", in: H. Seiler/G. Brettschneider (eds.), *Language Invariants and Mental Operations*. International Interdisciplinary Conference held at Gummers-bach/Cologne, Germany September 18-23, 1983, Tübingen: Narr 1983, 97-101.

— 1987: "Von Dreiecken, Trapezen und anderen Polygonen", in: G. Lüdi/H. Stricker/J. Wüest (eds.), *"Romania ingeniosa"*. *Festschrift G. Hilty,* Bern/Frankfurt am Main/New York/ Paris: Lang 1987, 421-42.

— 1992: "Langue und Parole", in: V. Agel/R. Hessky (eds.), *Offene Fragen – offene Antworten in der Sprachgermanistik* (Reihe Germanistische Linguistik 128), Tübingen: Niemeyer 1992, 1-13.

Heger, Kl./Mudersbach, Kl. 1984: *Aktantenmodelle. Aufgabestellung und Aufbauregeln* (AHAW. PH Klasse 1984:4), Heidelberg/Birkenau: Bitsch 1984.

Hellwig, P. 1984: "Titulus oder Über den Zusammenhang von Titeln und Texten", in: *Zeitschrift für germanistische Linguistik* 12 (1984) 1-20.

Kallmeyer, W./Meyer-Hermann, R. 1980: "Textlinguistik", in: H. P. Althaus/H. Henne/H. E. Wie-gand (eds.), *Lexikon der germanistischen Linguistik,* Tübingen: Niemeyer ²1980, 242-58.

Klaus, G. 1973: *Semiotik und Erkenntnistheorie*, München: Fink ⁴1973.

— 1975a: "Metasprache", in: *Philosophisches Wörterbuch* II, Leipzig: VEB Bibliographisches In-stitut ¹¹1975, 792f.

— 1975b: "Objektsprache", in: ibid., 886f.

— 1975c: "Stufentheorie, semantische", in: ibid., 1187.

— 1975d: "Supposition", in: ibid., 1193.

Kneal, W./Kneal, M. 1978: *The Development of Logic,* Oxford: Clarendon 1978.

Kubczak, H. 1975: *Das Verhältnis von Intension und Extension als sprachwissenschaftliches Problem* (Forschungsberichte des Instituts für deutsche Sprache 23), Tübingen: Narr 1975.

— 1978: *Die Metapher. Beiträge zur Interpretation und semantischen Struktur der Metapher auf der Basis einer referentialen Bedeutungsdefinition,* Heidelberg: Winter 1978.

von Kutschera, F. 1975: *Sprachphilosophie* (UTB 80), München: Fink [2]1975.

Lieb, H. H. 1981: "Das 'semiotische Dreieck' bei Ogden und Richards: eine Neuformulierung des Zeichenmodells von Aristoteles", in: H. Geckeler et al. (eds.), *Logos semantikos: studia linguistica in honorem Eugenio Coseriu 1921-1981*; Vol. I: J. Trabant (ed.): *Geschichte der Sprachphilosophie und der Sprachwissenschaft,* Berlin/New York/Madrid: de Gruyter/Editorial Gredos 1981, 137-56.

Ludwig, R. 1987: "Mündlichkeit und Schriftlichkeit. Felder der Forschung und Ansätze zu einer Merkmalssystematik im Französischen", in: *Romanistisches Jahrbuch* 37 (1986), Berlin/New York: de Gruyter 1987, 15-45.

Lyons, J. 1973: *Einführung in die moderne Linguistik,* München: Beck [3]1973.

— 1977: *Semantics,* Vol. I, Cambridge: Cambridge University Press 1977.

Menne, A. 1973: *Einführung in die Logik* (UTB 34), München: Francke [2]1973.

— 1980: *Einführung in die Methodologie. Elementare allgemeine wissenschaftliche Denkmethoden im Überblick* (Die Philosophie), Darmstadt: Wissenschaftliche Buchgesellschaft 1980.

— 1985: *Einführung in die formale Logik. Eine Orientierung über die Lehre von der Folgerichtigkeit, ihre Geschichte, Strukturen und Anwendungen* (Die Philosophie), Darmstadt: Wissenschaftliche Buchgesellschaft 1985.

Oehler, Kl. 1986: *Aristoteles Kategorien. Übersetzt und erläutert* (Aristoteles Werke in deutscher Übersetzung I/1), Berlin/Darmstadt: Akademie-Verlag/Wissenschaftliche Buchgesellschaft [2]1986.

Ogden, C. K./Richards, I. A. 1946: *The Meaning of Meaning. A Study of the Influence of Language upon Thought and of the Science of Symbolism,* New York: Harcourt, Brace & World [8]1946.

Palm, J. 1960: *Zur Funktion und Stellung des attributiven Demonstrativums im Griechischen* (Scripta Minora. Regiae Societatis Humaniorum Litterarum Lundensis 1959-1960:2), Lund: Gleerup 1960.

Pinborg, J. 1984: "Modus significandi", in: J. Ritter/K. Gründer (eds.), *Historisches Wörterbuch der Philosophie,* Band 6, Basel/Stuttgart/Darmstadt: Schwabe/Wissenschaftliche Buchgesellschaft 1984, 68-72.

Porzig, W. 1942: *Die Namen für Satzinhalte im Griechischen und im Indogermanischen* (Untersuchungen zur indogermanischen Sprach- und Kulturwissenschaft 10), Berlin: de Gruyter 1942.

Quine, W. V. 1951: *Mathematical Logic,* Cambridge, MA: Harvard University Press 1951.

Raible, W. 1972: *Satz und Text.* Untersuchungen zu vier romanischen Sprachen (Beihefte zur Zeitschrift für romanische Philologie 132), Tübingen: Niemeyer 1972.

— 1979: "Zum Textbegriff und zur Textlinguistik", in: J. S. Petöfi (ed.), *Text vs Sentence*. Basic Questions of Textlinguistics. Second Part (Papiere zur Text-linguistik/Papers in Textlinguistics 20.2), Hamburg: Buske 1979, 63-73.

— 1980: "Was sind Gattungen? Eine Antwort aus semiotischer und textlinguistischer Sicht", in: *Poetica* 12 (1980) 320-49.

— 1981: "Rechtssprache – Von den Tugenden und den Untugenden einer Fachsprache", in: I. Radtke (ed.), *Die Sprache des Rechts und der Verwaltung*, Stuttgart: Klett-Cotta 1981, 20-43.

— 1983: "Zur Einleitung", in: H. Stimm/W. Raible (eds.), *Zur Semantik des Französischen. Beiträge zum Regensburger Romanistentag* (Zeitschrift für französische Sprache und Literatur—Beiheft 9), Wiesbaden: Steiner 1983, 1-24.

— 1987: "Comment integrer la syntaxe dans la semantique? La solution des grammairiens scolastiques", in: G. Lüdi/H. Stricker/J. Wüest (eds.), *"Romania ingeniosa". Festschrift für Prof. Dr. Gerold Hilty zum 60. Geburtstag*, Bern etc.: Lang 1987, 497-510.

— 1989: "Phänomenologische Textwissenschaft. Zum Beitrag von Katsuhiko Hatakeyama, János S. Petöfi und Emel Sözer (Text, Konnexität, Kohärenz)", in: M.-E., Conte (ed.), *Kontinuität und Diskontinuität in Texten und Sachverhalts-Konfigurationen. Diskussion über Konnexität, Kohäsion und Kohärenz* (Papiere zur Textlinguistik 50), Hamburg: Buske 1989, 101-10.

Rentsch, Th. 1984: "Metasprache/Objektsprache", in: J. Ritter/K. Gründer (eds.), *Historisches Wörterbuch der Philosophie*, Band 5, Basel/Stuttgart/Darmstadt: Schwabe/Wissenschaftliche Buchgesellschaft 1984, 1301-03.

de Saussure, F. 19[16]/67: *Grundfragen der allgemeinen Sprachwissenschaft*, Berlin: de Gruyter [2]1967 [Französisch: *Cour de linguistique général*, Lausanne/Paris: Payot 1916].

Schadel, E. 1975: *Aurelius Augustinus, De magistro. Einführung, Übersetzung und Kommentar* (Diss. Würzburg 1975), Bamberg 1975.

Schiffrin, D. 1987: *Discourse markers* (Studies in Interactional Sociolinguistics 5), Cambridge etc.: Cambridge University Press 1987.

Schnelle, H. 1973: *Sprachphilosophie und Linguistik* (rororo studium 30), Reinbek b. Hamburg: Rowohlt 1973.

Stebbing, S. 1965: *A Modern Elementary Logic*, Revised by C. W. K. Mundle, London: Methuen & Co. [5]1965.

Tarski, A. 19[43/44/]70: "The Semantic Conception of Truth", in: L. Linsky (ed.), *Semantics and the Philosophy of Language. A Collection of Readings,* Urbana, IL/Chicago, IL/London: University of Illinois Press 1970 [= 1952], 13-47 (Zuerst erschienen in: *Philosophy and Phenomenological Research* 4 [1943/44], 341-75).

— 19[35]/83: "The Concept of Truth in Formalized Languages", in: idem, *Logic, Semantics, Metamathematics. Papers from 1923-1938,* Indianapolis, IN: Hackett [2]1983, 152-278 [Deutsch in: *Studia Philosophica* I (1935) 261-405].

Wandruszka, M. 1967: "Die maschinelle Übersetzung und die Dichtung", in: *Poetica* 1 (1967) 3-7.

Wedberg, A. 1968: *Filosofins historia. Antiken och medeltiden,* Stockholm: Bonniers [2]1968.

Weinrich, H. 1977: *Tempus. Besprochene und erzählte Welt,* Stuttgart: Kohlhammer [3]1977.

# Imminence and Parousia in the Gospel of Matthew

Donald A. Hagner

## 1. Introduction

1.1. At many important points the Gospel of Matthew presents a particularly diffi-cult challenge so far as intra-textual coherence is concerned. Thus perhaps with re-gard to Matthew more than any other Gospel, scholars have been tempted to conclude that the evangelist has combined discrete elements from the traditions available to him that are in fact not compatible. In this connection we may mention such well known polarities as Matthew's particularism and universalism, and his portrayal of Jesus as both loyal to and yet as transcending the Torah.

1.2. One such problem, although hardly unique to Matthew, concerns the vexing question of the time of the parousia. At different points in the Gospel the parousia is said to be imminent,[1] to occur in the indeterminate future, or to be unknown. It is, of course, possible to understand some of these references in more than one way and thus by a process of harmonizing to circumvent the problem. More often than not, however, such harmonizing results in forced exegesis. The difficulty of the problem is only further compounded by various references or allusions to the de-struction of Jerusalem. How has this state of affairs come about in the Gospel tradi-tion? How is the complexity of the data to be explained? Is it possible to speak of intra-textual coherence on this confusing subject so far as the mind of the evangelist Matthew is concerned?

1.3. The present essay takes as its starting point the twofold question of the disciples in response to Jesus' announcement of the destruction of the temple, and hence the fall of Jerusalem, at the beginning of the eschatological discourse: "Tell us, when will this be, and what will be the sign of your coming and the end of the age?"

---

[1] Throughout this essay by "imminent" I mean not immediacy, or happening at any moment, but rather in the sense of happening within the lifetime of at least some of Jesus' contemporaries.

(24:3). The following hypothesis will be under review: When Jesus spoke of imminence it was only in reference to the destruction of Jerusalem; he spoke of the parousia, on the other hand, only as involving a delay or as being in the indefinite future.[2] It was then the inability of the disciples to separate the two events that led them to transfer the idea of imminence from the fall of Jerusalem to the parousia and the end of the age.

## 2. The Disciples' Question

2.1. The question of the disciples at the beginning of the eschatological discourse in Mark indicates their confusion: "Tell when will this be [lit. 'these things' (ταῦτα), i.e. the destruction of the temple], and what will be the sign that all these things are about to be accomplished (ταῦτα συντελεῖσθαι πάντα)" (Mark 13:4). The use of συντελέω points rather clearly to eschatological consummation. Having heard of the destruction of the temple, the four disciples of the inner core of the twelve, Peter, James, John and Andrew, put the question to Jesus privately (κατ' ἰδίαν), which itself indicates that they considered themselves to be asking for privileged information, namely information about the time of the end of the age.[3] Matthew's redaction of Mark makes the confusion even more conspicuous: "Tell us, when will this be [lit. "these things" (ταῦτα), i.e. the destruction of the temple] and what will be the sign of your coming and the end of the age (τὸ σημεῖον τῆς σῆς παρουσίας καὶ συντελείας τοῦ αἰῶνος)" (Matt 24:3; for the last phrase, cf. 13:39, 40, 49, in reference to the final judgment).[4] Matthew has added the specific reference to the parousia and altered Mark's verb to the noun συντέλεια, modified by τοῦ αἰῶνος. This unmistakable emphasis indicates that the evangelist shared the conviction of the disciples about the inseparability of the events of the fall of Jerusalem and the parousia.[5]

---

[2] Although my purpose here is not apologetic, this essay does in effect challenge the conclusion of F. W. Beare that "On any approach, we cannot relieve Jesus of the burden—if such it is—of this error [i.e. of "anticipating the end of the world within the generation that witnessed the fall of Jerusalem"]." Beare 1972, 120.

[3] See E. Gräßer 1957, 154f.

[4] Some have argued that there is no reference to the fall of the temple in the question of verse 3, taking the καί as epexegetical. Thus R. Walker 1967, 59, followed by F. W. Burnett 1981, 207. So too I. Broer 1993, 212. It seems very difficult to believe, however, that readers encountering the ταῦτα in the question of verse 3 would not immediately think of the antecedent prophecy of the destruction of the temple in verse 2.

[5] Thus Hartman: "The composition must reflect thinking in which the fall of Jerusalem is a phase in the eschatology and the Parousia is also expected to occur soon." Hartman 1966, 241.

2.2. We do not have to look far for an explanation of the disciples' expectation. As the honoree of the present volume has shown,[6] the Markan apocalypse is dependent on Daniel, and indeed to a considerable extent functions as a kind of midrash of the Danielic texts. In view in Daniel 12 is not merely the end of the temple, but a shattering of the nation and the accomplishing of all things, that is, the end of the age (Dan 12:6-7). If the second temple was to be destroyed, the end of the present world order was also necessarily in the offing.[7] The result of this conviction was that the disciples would have been prone to take the imminence sayings that referred to Jerusalem and apply them also to the end of the age, and thus to the parousia of the Son of Man. The temple had once been destroyed and the people had been taken into captivity; if now the second temple was to be destroyed this must surely signal the tribulation of the end of the age, the birth pains of the Messiah, and accordingly entail the long expected turning of the aeons.

## 3. The Imminence Sayings

3.1. If Jesus can have predicted the destruction of the temple, which was to take place in AD 70,[8] then we have a fixed point in time that can logically be regarded as the referent of the various imminence sayings. Several of these sayings fit such an understanding particularly well, at least from the standpoint of the length of time itself. A few sayings thus contain a reference to "this generation" (23:36; 24:34).[9] These are very probably to be put together with 16:28 with its reference to "some standing here who will not taste death before ..." A period of some forty years after the death of Jesus is an appropriate length of time that makes good sense of these sayings. With them we should probably also put 10:23 with its reference to having "gone through all the towns of Israel." We have available, therefore, an historical event that coincides particularly well with the imminence sayings. There is thus an obvious a priori chronological suitability in understanding these passages as referring to the destruction of Jerusalem.

   3.2.1. The question that must be asked, of course, is whether the language used

---

   [6] Hartman 1966, 145ff., 220f. "We may find parallels in Jewish texts both for the ideas of the destruction of the Temple and the City, regarded as a judgement, and for the combination of these ideas with the eschatology" (222).

   [7] "As surely as Daniel suggests no great time gap between the attack on the city and the end, so it is with the eschatological discourse." D. Ford 1979, 73.

   [8] The a priori convictions of many scholars prohibit the possibility of such a prediction of a specific historical event. As Hartman indicates, however, the predictions of the fall of Jerusalem "bear hardly any traces of having come into existence ex eventu." Hartman 1966, 240.

   [9] For the view that 24:34 refers to the fall of Jerusalem, see D. Wenham 1982. Cf. A. R. Moore 1966, 131-36.

to denote the termini in these passages can fairly be taken as referring to the destruction of Jerusalem. Unfortunately none of the passages states this specifically. The closest is 23:36, which refers to judgment that will come upon "this generation" (τὴν γενεὰν ταύτην). The fact that this is followed directly by a lament for Jerusalem and then the prophecy of the destruction of the temple in 24:2 leads easily to the conclusion that the fall of Jerusalem may have been originally in view.

3.2.2. The other passages are more difficult. The terminus for 10:23 is "before the Son of Man comes" (ἕως ἂν ἔλθῃ ὁ υἱὸς τοῦ ἀνθρώπου), while that for 16:28 is "before they see the Son of Man coming in his kingdom" (ἕως ἂν ἴδωσιν τὸν υἱὸν τοῦ ἀνθρώπου ἐρχόμενον ἐν τῇ βασιλείᾳ αὐτοῦ). It is by no means impossible to take the former as a reference to the destruction of Jerusalem, i.e., that in view is a coming of the Son of Man in judgment.[10] The Son of Man comes to bring the renewal (παλιγγενεσία) of all things and to assume a throne of glory, but that throne is also a throne associated with judgment (19:28). A main function of the glorious Son of Man is that of judgment (cf. 25:31ff.). Since the fall of Jerusalem is a foreshadowing of the final judgment, it has eschatological connotations and can be regarded as the proleptic work of the Son of Man. If this is an admissible interpretation, it is also a possible way to understand the latter passage.[11] To be sure, the words ἐν τῇ βασιλείᾳ have then to be taken in a slightly unusual sense.

3.2.3. On the other hand, however, it may be that the evangelist understood the latter passage, or both passages, as referring to the parousia and the end of the age. The reason this cannot be excluded is that the author of Matthew apparently believed with the disciples that the parousia was to follow very closely after the destruction of Jerusalem. This is an almost unavoidable conclusion from the redactional insertion of εὐθέως in 24:29, unless one takes the immediately preceding material as referring to troubles at the end time rather than the destruction of Jerusalem (which in my opinion is in view in 24:15ff.). The evangelist seems clearly to have believed that the parousia and the end of the age were to occur in that generation. Whether Jesus believed this, however, is another question.

---

[10] Among commentators that have drawn this conclusion are Bullinger, Lenski, Lagrange, and Benoit. See too esp. A. Feuillet 1961, and J. A. T. Robinson 1979. Cf. R. Schnackenburg 1963: "This passage about the persecution of the prophets which is realized in the disciples of Jesus and will be 'avenged on this generation' (23:36) is followed by the announcement of the destruction of Jerusalem (vv. 37-39; in Luke in another context, 13:34 seq.). This may indicate that the evangelist had it in mind also in Matt. 10:23" (205). See also the discussion in D. A. Hagner 1993, 278-80.

[11] Cf. Schnackenburg 1963, 20.

## 4. Imminence and the Required Interim Period

4.1. There are three important reasons why it is highly unlikely that Jesus ever spoke of his parousia as imminent to that generation.

4.1.1. The first is the logion Jesu that is supremely important to the subject before us: "But about that day and hour no one knows, neither the angels of heaven, nor the Son, but only the Father" (24:36). Because this logion was almost certainly not created by the early church but goes back to Jesus himself, we have what must be regarded as a lodestar in finding our way through the difficulties before us. The force of the statement is not that Jesus is ignorant only of the precise hour or day (and not the week, month or year), but that he does not know the time at all. The language is formulaic and simply refers to the time itself of the end of the age.[12] Jesus, therefore, does not know the time of the end. But if Jesus acknowledged ignorance of the time of his parousia, then it is extremely unlikely that he also spoke of the imminence of his parousia. The imminence sayings must accordingly be understood with reference to another terminus, and thus the probability increases that what was originally in view in these sayings was the destruction of Jerusalem, especially given the exceptionally appropriate length of time. To this logion should be added the several other related sayings that indicate the impossibility of knowing the time of the parousia of the Son of Man (24:42, 44; cf. 24:50; 25:13), and naturally all of the sayings about the uncertainty of the time of the parousia and the consequent necessity of being prepared for it at any time.

4.1.2. The second reason is that a number of the sayings of Jesus presuppose an interim period of unspecified length between his death and the parousia. Here we may point generally to the choosing of his disciples (4:19), the building of his church (16:18f.; 18:18), and his promise as the risen one to be with them to the end of the age (18:20; 28:20). Especially significant, of course, is the necessity of the gospel being preached to the nations (24:14; 28:19; cf. 26:13; 10:18). In the eschatological discourse itself, there are indications of certain things, e.g., tribulation, persecution, and deception, that must take place before the end (cf. 24:6-8, 9f., 23-26). The key question here is whether the evangelist would have regarded the forty year interim period between the death of Jesus and the destruction of Jerusalem as a sufficient period of time for the fulfillment of these expectations. Although we do not know, we can by no means exclude this possibility, as we shall see (in 5.3.2).

4.1.3. Thirdly, there is a strong note of delay in the three successive parables that

---

[12] See esp. Beasley-Murray 1993, 456ff. He correctly concludes that "we surely misconstrue [in Mark 13] the denotation of v. 32 if we attempt to force it into the context of v. 30. This means that we must allow v. 32 to stand on its own feet and not subordinate it to v. 30, as is so constantly done in contemporary exposition" (458; cf. the further discussion on 459-61).

precede the dramatic picture of the final judgment in 25:31ff. The wicked servant acts unrighteously, believing that his master "is delayed (χρονίζει)" (24:48); the ten maidens become drowsy because "the bridegroom was delayed (χρονίζοντος)" (25:5); and in the parable of the talents, the master is described as one who goes on a journey to return only "after a long time (μετὰ πολὺν χρόνον)" (25:19). To this material may be joined the accompanying warnings that since the time of the end is unknown, it will be unexpected (24:42, 44, 50; 25:13).

4.2. If we combine the well-established point of the agnosticism of Jesus on the question of the time of his parousia with the requirement of a lengthy, unspecified interim period, and the emphasis on delay and unexpectedness, it becomes practically impossible to believe that Jesus ever spoke of his parousia as imminent. On the other hand, because the length of time in the termini of the imminence sayings ("this generation"; "some standing here who will not die") fits the fall of Jerusalem so well, the conclusion becomes a more probable one that the imminence logia of Jesus originally referred only to the destruction of Jerusalem.

## 5. Matthew's εὐθέως: Immediately After What?

5.1. Matthew's redactional addition of εὐθέως in 24:29, already mentioned above, is obviously by its meaning an indicator of imminence, but also a reference to the parousia. The words governed by εὐθέως are "after the suffering of those days (μετὰ τὴν θλῖψιν τῶν ἡμερῶν ἐκείνων)." But what tribulation is in view?

5.2. The difficulty of 24:4-28 is evident from the fact that commentators have given diametrically opposed interpretations of this material. Some have argued, for example, that the entire passage—indeed, including even 24:29-35—refers exclusively to the fall of Jerusalem.[13] This view, however, requires a particularly difficult shift in the understanding of the traditional apocalyptic language, both in these verses and in the question of verse 3.[14] Much more common, on the other hand, is the view that the entire passage has in mind the parousia and the end of the age, so that, in

---

[13] Feuillet 1956; Tasker 1961, 223-31; Gaston 1970, 483-85; Brown 1979, 12-14; France 1985, 333-46: "Thus when the significance of the Old Testament imagery is appreciated, vv 29-31 may be recognized, as the context virtually demanded, as a highly symbolic description of the theological significance of the coming destruction of the temple and its consequences" (345f.). So too, Garland, 1993. For a detailed refutation of this view, see the excellent appendix, "Mark 13:24-27 not the second coming?", in D. Wenham 1982, 138-42.

[14] See Burnett (1981), 218-24. Donaldson's (1985) comment is apropos: "But if the *parousia* is past, the injunctions to watch lose all their force, and the whole discourse collapses" (164).

particular, verses 15-28 refer to an event still to take place in the future, just prior to the parousia. J. Gnilka provides an example of this view. He finds in verse 15 a reference to "ein großer Frevel ..., eine Aufgipfelung des Bösen in einem noch nicht dagewesenen Maß," to be related to the Antichrist and the Man of Lawlessness or the Son of Perdition, of which we read in Paul (2 Thess 2:3) as well as in the apocalyptic literature. The majority of commentators also hold to this view: e.g., A. H. McNeile (1938), W. Grundmann (1972), D. Hill (1972), E. Schweizer (1975), F. W. Burnett (1981), R. H. Gundry (1982), D. Patte (1987), D. J. Harrington (1991), and I. Broer (1993).

5.2.1. The interpretation of 24:15ff. as referring to a future manifestation of the Antichrist nevertheless has some difficulties. To begin with, if this interpretation of the passage is true, then apparently nowhere in the discourse is the initial question about the destruction of the temple or the fall of Jerusalem addressed[15]—which seems at least exceptionally odd.[16] The passage would furthermore no longer have had relevance to the readers of Matthew, but only to a time long after them. It would seem also to demand, for example, a future rebuilding of the temple (Matthew's replacement of Mark's ὅπου οὐ δεῖ [13:14] with ἐν τόπῳ ἁγίῳ [24:15] points more clearly to the temple; cf. Acts 6:13; 21:28). It is unnatural to take this phrase as meaning something such as the Holy Land or the community of God[17] and it is methodologically questionable to read the passage in the light of 2 Thess 2:4 or 1 John 2:18.

5.3. The section beginning in 24:15 refers, in my opinion, to the desecration of the temple in connection with the destruction of Jerusalem in A.D. 70.[18] Among those who have also drawn this conclusion, whether Matthew is dated pre- or post-70, are: A. Plummer (1909), W. C. Allen (1912), J. Lambrecht (1972), D. A. Carson (1984), T. L. Donaldson (1985), P. F. Ellis (1985), C. L. Blomberg (1992), D. Wenham

---

[15] See, however, footnote 4, above. This is one reason I. Broer (1993, 214) insists that the disciples' question concerns only the time of the parousia.

[16] To argue as does D. R. A. Hare that Matthew "totally ignores the first question [about the time of the destruction of the temple], which for his generation is no longer vital, and makes the discourse as a whole an answer to the second [about the end of the age]" is to predetermine the conclusion (Hare 1967, 178; see the same argument in Broer 1993, 224). It is extremely difficult to believe that Matthew's first post-70 readers, if not his very first readers, would not have thought of the recent destruction of Jerusalem immediately upon encountering the allusion to the "desolating sacrilege" in 24:15. See further Burnett (1981) 220.

[17] Matthew "envisions a new desecration of a new 'holy place,' the sanctuaries of Jesus-Sophia." Burnett 1981, 334.

[18] Contra Broer 1993.

(1982) and L. Morris (1992)[19]. The redaction of Mark 13:14ff., Matthew's source for the passage in question, in Luke 21:20ff. indicates that Luke understood the passage as referring to that historical event *post eventum*. If Luke understood the Markan passage as referring to the fall of Jerusalem, there is perhaps even more reason why Matthew might have understood it this way if he were writing *before* the event. There is furthermore a good question about what 24:23-28, with its warning concerning false messiahs and false prophets, is meant to refer to. Even if 24:15-22 *does* refer to the fall of Jerusalem in 70, there is no guarantee that the focus does not shift in verses 23-28 to some other, later time frame (see 5.4 below).

5.3.1. The problems sometimes mentioned in connection with this understanding of 24:15ff. can be answered. A key problem noted by many is the description of the great tribulation (θλῖψις μεγάλη) in verse 21 as involving suffering "such as has not been from the beginning of the world until now, no, and never will be (οἵα οὐ γέγονεν ἀπ᾽ ἀρχῆς κόσμου ἕως τοῦ νῦν οὐδ᾽ οὐ μὴ γένηται)." As G. R. Beasley-Murray has shown, however, this is traditional and formulaic language used to describe exceptional suffering, and hence is not to be taken literally. He cites as examples, Exod 9:18; 10:14 and 11:6 and, indeed, Dan 12:1 (cf. Josephus, *War*, proem 4).[20] It is furthermore often noted that the details of the passage do not correspond exactly with the actual events of the fall of Jerusalem in AD 70. It is unlikely, for example, that a statue of Titus was erected on the site of the destroyed temple[21] (cf. Eusebius, *E.H.* III.5.4 who depends on Josephus). Further, the command to flee into the mountains (24:16) hardly corresponds to the tradition (from Eusebius, *E H.* III. 5.3) that the Christians fled to Pella in the northern valley of the Jordan.[22] Still, it is to be noted that the evidence of Eusebius may not be altogether reliable.[23] The lack of detailed correspondence between the actual events and the prophecies in both Mark and Matthew, however, may merely be a further indication that the latter were not written *ex post facto*.[24]

5.3.2. A further problem that we must now address is the required interim period before the end. As we have noted above, the evangelist knows well that the end cannot occur before certain things happen. Jesus, after all, chose disciples to carry on his work, to preserve and hand on his teaching, to build his community, the church;

---

[19] We may add G. R. Beasley-Murray 1993 here because of his conclusions concerning the interpretation of Matthew's source, the parallel passage in Mark 13:14ff. (cf. 411).

[20] Beasley-Murray 1993, 419.

[21] See D. Ford 1979, 158. Ford finds only a general correspondence to the events of AD 70 in "the invading Roman Armies" (166).

[22] See e.g., M. Hengel 1985, 16f.

[23] See Beasley-Murray, 1993, 412f.

[24] "There is not a syllable which reflects knowledge of events which took place in the Jewish War, still less of the actual destruction of the city and temple." Beasley-Murray 1993, 407.

they were also to experience a time of tribulation and severe persecution. But above all, the disciples had a mission to accomplish before the end, even among the Gentiles, and this is stated unequivocally: "And this gospel of the kingdom will be preached throughout the whole world, as a testimony to all nations (πᾶσιν τοῖς ἔθνησιν), and then the end (τὸ τέλος) will come" (24:14; to which compare especially 26:13 and 28:19). Can the evangelist have believed that all this could have been accomplished within a forty year period? Obviously the only really problematic issue here is the worldwide mission to the Gentiles. Even here, however, it is by no means impossible that the evangelist can have believed that the mission had been essentially accomplished by 70, for the world in view was that of the Mediterranean basin, not the world as we know it. To be compared with this is the statement of Paul in Rom 10:18 (quoting LXX Ps 18:5), in which he likens the spread of the gospel to the universal availability of general revelation. The gospel indeed had already been made available to the Jews of the dispersion.[25] If Paul could express himself this way already in the fifties, it is not at all impossible that our evangelist could have held a similar perspective.

5.3.3. A final problem to consider is whether the forty year period is sufficiently long enough in the evangelist's mind to account for the unique emphasis on the delay of the return of the master, i.e., of the Son of Man. I see no reason why it cannot be. In the atmosphere of a heightened eschatological awareness where the dawning of the kingdom had been so dramatically announced, the consummation of the age must have been thought to be in the very near future (cf. Acts 1:6). The delay of a generation under those circumstances must indeed have seemed long to wait. And the delay material, furthermore, is quite consonant with the various warnings of 24:5-13, which in my view the evangelist regards as taking place before the fall of Jerusalem.

5.4. The content of 24:23-28 corresponds closely to that of verses 4-14, which together serve as a kind of frame for verses 15-22. Neither passage has time limits; in view is apparently only the danger of false messiahs and prophets in the indeterminate future. The only specific event in the whole of 24:4-28 is found in the middle passage of verses 15-22 with their reference to the desecration of the temple and the accompanying instructions about fleeing. To my mind, the εὐθέως of 24:29 requires relationship to something definite in the preceding context.[26] It hardly makes much

---

[25] Cf. J. A. Fitzmyer 1993, 599: "Thus, in effect, Paul asserts the universal character of the preaching of the gospel and denies that Israel has lacked the opportunity to believe in Christ. Like the whole world, Israel has heard the good news."

[26] Contra Donaldson 1985, 165, who like many others finds in the language "a vague time reference" to a future period of suffering.

sense to say "immediately after" something general in the indeterminate future.[27] The phrase by its nature requires something more specific. The only *specific* item in the preceding context that could correspond to "the suffering of those days" (note the definite article: τὴν θλῖψιν and the demonstrative pronoun: τῶν ἡμερῶν ἐκείνων) in 24:29 is the desecration of the temple in 24:15. Thus it is arguably most probable that the evangelist's redactional addition refers to the destruction of the temple, alluded to in 24:15 and earlier in 24:2.

5.4.1. If this conclusion is true, then the evangelist shared the perspective of the disciples that the end of the temple meant the end of the world. The one would follow the other immediately, and thus we have the Matthean insertion of εὐθέως to emphasize the point.

## 6. The Relation of the Fall of Jerusalem to the Eschatological Judgment

6.1. A further complicating factor in making sense of the Olivet Discourse and sorting out the issues we have been discussing is that the historical event of the fall of Jerusalem is also a foreshadowing of the final judgment. The manner in which this is formulated, however, and the exegetical conclusions that are drawn are very important.

6.2. A number of scholars argue for what must be called a deliberate double reference in 24:15ff. They assert that the passage actually refers *both* to the event of AD 70 and to the Antichrist of the yet future eschatological judgment. As representatives here we may note the following: C. E. B. Cranfield (1972),[28] D. Ford (1979),[29] V. K. Agbanou (1982),[30] and F. D. Bruner (1990).[31] Others seem to make the same point. Thus J. P. Meier concludes his discussion of the passage with the statement

---

[27] Wenham 1982, 130, rightly notes that in Mark 13 the "close verbal link between verses 19 and 24 shows that the tribulation associated with the desolating sacrilege is the immediate prelude to the end." But then he proceeds in effect to cancel out the meaning of the word "immediate" in the quoted sentence by arguing that this event is to be regarded as only "inaugurating a final period leading up to the end" (131). Wenham ignores Matthew's εὐθέως (24:29) in his discussion.

[28] Cranfield 1972, concerning Mk 13:14-20: "It seems then that neither an exclusively historical nor an exclusively eschatological interpretation is satisfactory, and that we must allow for a double reference, for a mingling of historical and eschatological" (402). Cranfield is followed by G. E. Ladd 1974, 310f.

[29] "Thus it is likely that the βδέλυγμα τῆς ἐρημώσεως *is a comprehensive term applying first to the armies of Rome, but including later manifestations of Antichrist*" (163, italics as in original).

[30] Agbanou 1983, 81: "Car au-delà des avertissements donnés aux chrétiens sur la chute imminente de Jérusalem et les précautions à prendre, il faut voir, dans la perspective matthéenne, des instructions qui se rapportent à la catastrophe universelle de la fin du monde."

that "this pericope on the great tribulation speaks both of the church's past and of its future."[32] L. Hartman also writes, if somewhat tentatively: "Bearing the context in mind, both in the Gospels and in Daniel (which was interpreted eschatologically), it seems probable that the symbol in question refers to some form of blasphemy which will characterize the last days. In addition, at least in the text as it now stands, it seems that the devastation of Jerusalem and Judaea was associated with it."[33]

6.3. As I have already mentioned above, and as I will argue below in 6.4, it is clear that there is a theological relationship between the fall of Jerusalem and the final judgment of which it is a foreshadowing. One distinct advantage of such a perspective is that it may enable us to explain the strange, mixed character of the entire apocalyptic discourse. Thus Mark and Matthew can have moved from the historical to the eschatological more or less at will, in this way causing our problem of disentangling the material. The question that must be dealt with carefully, however, is the actual intention of the evangelist Matthew, insofar as we can determine it.

6.3.1. In my opinion, the perception of the theological interrelatedness between the fall of Jerusalem and yet future eschatological events is much easier from our position than, by the nature of things, it would or could have been to Matthew or his readers. Can the evangelist really have had in mind—have really intended for his readers—a double reference in 24:15ff.? This seems very unlikely to me, especially given the conclusions I have argued above. Matthew's εὐθέως in 24:29 leaves no time for a secondary reference to something yet lying in the future that must occur before the parousia. For the evangelist the fall of Jerusalem is to be followed directly by the end of the age. For us, on the other hand, who know of the lengthening interim period between the two, the idea of a double reference seems not only possible, but plausible.

6.4. There is no question, however, that from *our* perspective the fall of Jerusalem is an anticipation and foreshadowing of the final judgment. The description of the fall of Jerusalem in 24:15ff. has unmistakable eschatological associations. It cannot have been otherwise, since the evangelist himself perceived the fall of Jerusalem as immediately preceding the eschatological judgment. The two were to be understood together. From our perspective, the desolating sacrilege of 24:15 and the time of in-

---

[31] Speaking the desolating sacrilege of 24:15, Bruner 1990, 2:858f., who speaks explicitly of a "double reference," writes: "Something like the abomination of desolation in Daniel's time did in fact recur in Jesus' time (the Roman destruction of the temple); and something like the abomination of desolation in Jesus' time may happen at the end of time."

[32] Meier 1980, 284.

[33] Hartman 1966, 152.

tense suffering that is cut short for the sake of the elect (24:21f.) refer to the catastrophe of AD 70, but also suggest a time of future crisis that truly brings us to the
brink of the eschaton. The succession of images that come to mind with reference
to Daniel's βδέλυγμα τῆς ἐρημώσεως (Dan 9:27; 11:31; 12:11), beginning with that
of Antiochus Epiphanes in 167 BC (1 Macc 1:54), and including those of Caligula
in AD 39-40 and the Roman invaders of AD 70, leads easily to the notion of the Antichrist of the end time (cf. esp. 2 Thess 2:3-4). In short, we are able to see an additional level of reference in Matt 24:15ff. that the evangelist and his first readers
could not have seen.[34]

## 7. The Date of Matthew

7.1. The conclusions argued for in this essay have significant implications for the
dating of the Gospel.[35] To my mind, Matthew's insertion of εὐθέως in 24:29 to describe the parousia of the Son of Man and the end of the age can only mean that he
regarded the end of the age as following directly upon the desolation of the temple.[36] This means, of course, that we must therefore put the writing of the Gospel
before 70, or possibly only shortly thereafter.[37] The consensus of a date for Matthew in the eighties deserves therefore to be challenged.

7.2. It is worth reminding ourselves how little hard evidence we have for the dating
of the Gospels. Two key pieces of evidence in the traditional dating of Matthew are
by no means compelling. First, the reference in 22:7 to the king sending his troops
and burning the city is not necessarily a reference to the literal destruction of Jerusalem in AD 70.[38] Second, the decisions of Yavneh in the eighties, about which we

---

[34] Cf. the remarks of Beasley-Murray 1993, 416, on the Markan parallel passage.

[35] Well might Beare, placing the Gospel as much as thirty years after the fall of Jerusalem, comment that "it is most remarkable that it should still be possible for a Christian writer to link it [the
fall of Jerusalem] so closely with the Parousia of Jesus as Son of man and with the end of the age."
Beare 1972, 125. No explanation is forthcoming from Beare, who on other grounds feels compelled
to a late date for the Gospel.

[36] Lambrecht 1972, 323 n.40: "εὐθέως: can the end of Jerusalem and the parousia be brought
closer in time? Perhaps this should warn us against placing the date of Mt. too long after 70."

[37] J. A. T. Robinson 1976, 24: "So conscious was Harnack of this difficulty [the εὐθέως] that he
insisted that the interval could not be extended more than five years (or ten at the very most), thus
dating Matthew c. 70-75. He would rather believe that Matthew wrote before the fall of Jerusalem
than stretch the meaning of εὐθέως further. It seems a curious exercise to stretch it at all!"

[38] See K. H. Rengstorf 1960, for the conventional character of the language concerning punitive
expeditions, and B. Reicke 1972, 123, for an effective indication of the incongruities in relating the
parable to the fall of Jerusalem. See further, Hagner 1993, lxxiiif.

know very little indeed, hardly constitute a watershed in Jewish-Christian relations. The remarkable hostility to the Pharisees in Matthew is not at all unthinkable at an earlier time, say in the sixties.[39] Nor, we may add, is Matthew's dependence upon Mark a problem, since there is no reason why Matthew may not have been written fairly soon after Mark. And, finally, as for certain aspects of Matthew's developed theology, e.g., christology and ecclesiology, these are already found in the Pauline letters quite a few years earlier than even our dating of Matthew.

7.3. To be considered on the positive side for a pre-70 date of Matthew are the following observations. Several redactional additions of Matthew refer to the temple (the altar, 5:23-24; the temple tax, 17:24-27; swearing by the sanctuary, 23:16-22) and these make more sense if the temple were still standing when Matthew wrote. Furthermore, the redactional addition of "pray that your flight may not be in winter or on a sabbath" (24:20) makes little sense if the destruction of the temple had already occurred.[40]

7.4. There is, in short, no invincible reason why Matthew must be dated after 70. On the other hand, it is of course equally impossible to demonstrate an early date for the Gospel. It is only maintained here that openness of mind on the question may make for a more satisfactory understanding of a number of aspects of the Gospel, not least of which the striking addition of εὐθέως in 24:29.

## 8. Conclusion

8.1. It is not possible to prove the thesis that has been under examination here. The materials with which we must work are both limited in scope and difficult. What I hope that I have done here is to present at least a plausible explanation of what is after all a perplexing problem in the Gospel of Matthew. According to this hypothesis, if Jesus spoke in imminent terms only with respect to the fall of Jerusalem, and if then imminence became attached almost inevitably to the parousia of the Son of Man, we can account for all the data, including the difficult Gospel logia concerning an imminent parousia now found in the Gospels.

8.2. The argument of this essay rests upon two fixed pillars. The first is that Jesus did not know the time of the coming of the Son of Man, i.e., of his own future pa-

---

[39] See Hagner 1985, 246-54 for a defense of these statements.

[40] See further, J. A. T. Robinson 1976, 103ff. For a recent, strong defence of an early date (pre-70) for Matthew, see Gundry 1982.

rousia (Matt 24:36; Mark 13:32). The second is that the disciples were unable to contemplate the destruction of the temple without thinking also of the end of the age and the coming of the Messiah (Matt 24:3). The one, therefore, was surely to be followed immediately by the other (Matt 24:29). With these two pillars in place, it is possible to make sense of the various logia, and at the same time to address the issue of intra-textual coherence in the Gospel of Matthew. Matthew is coherent only if it was written before AD 70, or not long after this date, because only then can the imminence logia have had meaning *both* in reference to Jerusalem *and* to the parousia. The common late dating of the Gospel, on the other hand, leaves no convincing way to assimilate the imminence logia that refer to the parousia, which thus remain foreign elements unassimilated by the evangelist.

8.3. The church of the first century had to learn that it was not to be the generation that witnessed the parousia. Those Christians doubtless would have been astonished to think that their successors in the *twentieth*, and soon the *twenty-first* century, would still be waiting for the return of the Son of Man. But in the same way that they soon began to lean more and more on the logia that truly reflected the perspective of Jesus concerning the parousia—those concerning the unknowableness of the time, the delay and the consequent unexpectedness of the time of the end—so too the church of every generation down to the present has looked to those same passages. The signs of the end have been present to every generation, and thus the church of every generation, even as the interim period has continued to lengthen, has been right to stand in readiness, and faithfully to keep its watch.

## Bibliography

Agbanou, V. K. 1983: *Le discours eschatologique de Matthieu 24-25: tradition et rédaction*, Paris: Gabalda 1983.

Allen, W. C. 1912: *A Critical and Exegetical Commentary on the Gospel According to S. Matthew*, 3rd ed., Edinburgh: T. & T. Clark 1912.

Beare, F. W. 1972: "The Synoptic Apocalypse: Matthean Version," in: J. Reumann (ed.), *Understanding the Sacred Text. Essays in honor of Morton S. Enslin on the Hebrew Bible and Christian Beginnings*, Valley Forge: Judson 1972, 117-33.

Beasley-Murray, G. R. 1993: *Jesus and the Last Days: The Interpretation of the Olivet Discourse*, Peabody, MA: Hendrickson 1993.

Blomberg, C. L. 1992: *Matthew* (New American Commentary 22), Nashville, TN: Broadman 1992.

Broer, I. 1993: "Redaktionsgeschichtliche Aspekte von Mt. 24:1-28," in: *NT* 35 (1993) 209-33.

Brown, S. 1979: "The Matthean Apocalypse," in: *JSNT* 4 (1979) 2-27.

Bruner, F. D. 1990: *Matthew: A Commentary*, 2 vols., Dallas, TX: Word 1990.

Burnett, F. W. 1981: *The Testament of Jesus-Sophia. A Redaction-Critical Study of the Eschatological Discourse in Matthew*, Lanham, MD: University Press of America 1981.

Carson, D. A. 1984: "Matthew", in: F. E. Gaebelein (ed.), *Expositor's Bible Commentary*, 8:1-599, Grand Rapids, MI: Zondervan 1984.

Cranfield, C. E. B. 1972: *The Gospel According to Saint Mark*, Cambridge: Cambridge University Press 1972.

Donaldson, T. L. 1985: *Jesus on the Mountain. A Study in Matthean Theology* (JSNT.S 8), Sheffield: JSOT 1985.

Ellis, P. F. 1985: *Matthew: His Mind and His Message*, Collegeville, MN: Liturgical Press 1985.

Feuillet, A. 1956: "Le sens du mot Parousie dans l'Évangile de Matthieu: Comparaison entre Mt 24 et Jc 5, 1-11," in: W. D. Davies and D. Daube (eds.), *The Background of the New Testament and its Eschatology,* FS C. H. Dodd, Cambridge: Cambridge University Press 1956, 261-80.

— 1961: "Les origins et la signification de Mt 10.23b: Contribution à l'étude du problème eschatologique," in: *CBQ* 23 (1961) 182-98.

Fitzmyer, J. A. 1993: *Romans* (AncB 33), New York: Doubleday 1993.

Ford, D. 1979: *The Abomination of Desolation in Biblical Eschatology*, Washington DC: University Press of America 1979.

France, R. T. 1985: *Matthew* (TNTC), Leicester/Grand Rapids: Intervarsity Press/Eerdmans 1985.

Garland, D. E. 1993: *Reading Matthew. A Literary and Theological Commentary on the First Gospel*, New York: Crossroad 1993.

Gaston, L. 1970: *No Stone on Another: Studies in the Significance of the Fall of Jerusalem in the Synoptic Gospels* (NT.S 23), Leiden: Brill 1970.

Gräßer, E. 1957: *Das Problem der Parusieverzögerung in den synoptischen Evangelien und in der Apostelgeschichte* (BZNW 22), 2nd ed., Berlin: De Gruyter 1960.

Grundmann, W. 1972: *Das Evangelium nach Matthäus* (ThHK 1), Berlin: Evangelische Verlags-anstalt 1972.

Gundry, R. H. 1982: *Matthew. A Commentary on His Literary and Theological Art*, Grand Rapids, MI: Eerdmans 1982.

Hagner, D. A. 1985: "The *Sitz im Leben* of the Gospel of Matthew," in: *SBL 1985 Seminar Papers*, Atlanta, GA: Scholars 1985, 243-69.

— 1993: *Matthew 1-13* (Word Biblical Commentary 33A), Dallas TX: Word 1993.

Hare, D. R. A. 1967: *The Theme of the Jewish Persecution of Christians in the Gospel According to Matthew* (MSSNTS 6), Cambridge: Cambridge University Press 1967.

Harrington, D. J. 1991: *The Gospel of Matthew* (Sacra Pagina 1), Collegeville, MN: Liturgical Press 1991.

Hartman, L. 1966: *Prophecy Interpreted. The Formation of Some Jewish Apocalyptic Texts and of the Eschatological Discourse Mark 13 par.* (CB.NT 1), Lund: Gleerup 1966.

Hengel, M. 1985: *Studies in the Gospel of Mark*, Philadelphia, PA: Fortress 1985.

Hill, D. 1972: *The Gospel of Matthew* (NCeB), London: Oliphants 1972.

Ladd, G. E. 1974: *The Presence of the Future. The Eschatology of Biblical Realism*, Grand Rapids, MI: Eerdmans 1974.

Lambrecht, J. 1972: "The Parousia Discourse. Composition and Content in Mt., XXIV-XXV," in: M. Didier (ed.), *L'Évangile selon Matthieu. Rédaction et Théologie* (BEThL 29), Gembloux: Duculot 1972, 309-42.

McNeile, A. H. 1938: *The Gospel According to St. Matthew*, London: Macmillan 1938.

Meier, J. P. 1980: *Matthew* (New Testament Message 3), Wilmington, DE: Glazier 1980.

Moore, A. R. 1966: *The Parousia in the New Testament* (NT.S 13), Leiden: Brill 1966.

Morris, L. 1992: *The Gospel According to Matthew*, Grand Rapids, MI: Eerdmans 1992.

Patte, D. 1987: *The Gospel According to Matthew. A Structural Commentary on Matthew's Faith*, Philadelphia, PA: Fortress 1987.

Plummer, A. 1909: *An Exegetical Commentary on the Gospel According to S. Matthew*, London: Stock 1909.

Reicke, B. 1972: "Synoptic Prophecies on the Destruction of Jerusalem," in: D. E. Aune (ed.), *Studies in New Testament and Early Christian Literature* (NT.S 33), Leiden: Brill 1972, 121-34.

Rengstorf, K. H. 1960: "Die Stadt der Mörder (Matt. 22:7)," in: W. Eltester (ed.), *Judentum, Urchristentum, Kirche*. FS J. Jeremias (BZNW 26), Berlin: Töpelmann 1960, 106-29.

Robinson, J. A. T. 1976: *Redating the New Testament*, Philadelphia, PA: Westminster 1976.

— 1979: *Jesus and His Coming*, 2nd ed., Philadelphia, PA: Fortress 1979.

Schnackenburg, R. 1963: *God's Rule and Kingdom*, New York: Herder and Herder 1963.

Schweizer, E. 1975: *The Good News According to Matthew*, Atlanta, GA: John Knox 1975.

Tasker, R. V. G. 1961: *The Gospel According to Saint Matthew. An Introduction and Commentary*, (TNTC), London: Intervarsity 1961.

Walker, R. 1967: *Die Heilsgeschichte im ersten Evangelium* (FRLANT 91), Göttingen: Vandenhoeck & Ruprecht 1967.

Wenham D. 1982: "'This generation will not pass …' A Study of Jesus' Future Expectation in Mark 13," in: H. H. Rowdon (ed.), *Christ the Lord*. FS D. Guthrie, Leicester: Intervarsity 1982, 127-50.

# "Habt Glauben an Gott".
## Der Theozentrismus der Verkündigung des Evangeliums und des christlichen Glaubens im Markusevangelium

François Vouga

Nimmt man an, daß der Verfasser des Markusevangeliums nicht nur der Sammler ihm bereits vorliegender Traditionen und theologischer Vorstellungen war[1], sondern seine Erzählung durch ein eigenes, theologisches Profil gestaltet hat[2], so kommt man zu einem gewissen Konsens: Zentral ist die Verbindung der Verkündigung der βασιλεία mit der geheimnisvollen Offenbarung des Gottessohnes, die durch den Begriff des 'Evangeliums' hergestellt wird, – korrelativ dazu – die Interpretation des christlichen Glaubens durch das Thema der Nachfolge. Diese Kreuzestheologie setzt den zentralen Platz der Christologie voraus, von woher die menschliche Befindlichkeit und die existentiellen Haltungen thematisiert und beurteilt werden[3].

### 1. Zur Auslegungstradition des Markusevangeliums

Diese Auslegungstradition des Markusevangeliums, die das Evangelium in der Rezeptionsgeschichte der paulinischen Theologie mehr oder weniger verortet, setzt Zusammenhänge voraus, die der Text des Evangeliums weder enthält noch impliziert:

1. Jesus ist zwar der Verkünder der βασιλεία (Mk 1,14f.; vgl. vielleicht auch Mk 4,26. 30), mit seiner Person ist aber die βασιλεία keineswegs verbunden. Er bringt die frohe Botschaft, daß die βασιλεία nahe ist (Mk 1,15), Menschen warten auf sie

---

[1] Verwiesen sei hier auf H. Räisänen 1973 und idem 1976 und auf R. Pesch 1976 und idem 1977.

[2] Zum Beispiel: E. Best 1981; J. D. Kingsbury 1983; D.-A. Koch 1975; K.-G. Reploh 1969; J. Schreiber 1967; Chr. Senft 1991; D. O. Via 1985; H. Weinacht 1972. In anderen Perspektiven: H. C. Kee, 1977; B. L. Mack 1988; J. Marcus 1986; E. Trocmé 1963.

[3] Programmatisch: J. Schreiber 1967; Chr. Senft 1991 und, nach W. Schmithals 1979, für die sogenannte Grundschrift.

(15,43), kommen in ihre Nähe (Mk 12,34) und den Jüngern wird ihr Geheimnis gegeben (Mk 4,11[4]), was wahrscheinlich bedeutet, daß ihnen verkündigt wird, wie
man in die βασιλεία hineingeht (Mk 9,47; 10,14f.23f.). Sie wächst in ihrer Gegenwart (4,26. 30), einigen, die Jesu nachfolgen, wird sie bereits mit Macht erscheinen
(Mk 9,1) und Jesus verspricht den Zwölf, mit ihnen den Wein nach seinem Tod in
der βασιλεία zu trinken (Mk 14,25), was, laut Mk 14,28; 16,7, auf die unmittelbare
Zeit nach Ostern verweist. Kurzum: Die βασιλεία ist eine Größe, die sich auf Erden
gegenwärtig gemacht hat, und die durch die Verkündigung Jesu bezeugt wird, ohne
daß sie mit der Person Jesu anders verbunden sei, als daß Jesus ihre Nähe verkündigt.[5]

2. Ist die βασιλεία an die Person Jesu keineswegs gebunden, so ist sie genausowenig mit dem apokalyptischen Kommen des Menschensohnes in Verbindung gebracht. Dies ist sowohl aus Mk 8,34 - 9,1 als auch aus Mk 13 (vgl. vor allem Mk
13,24-27), wo der Verfasser des Markusevangeliums konsequent vermeidet, von
der βασιλεία in bezug auf die 'Parusie' zu sprechen, ersichtlich[6]. Auch mit dem
letzten Tag und mit der letzten Stunde hat die βασιλεία nichts zu tun (Mk 13,28-
37). Kurzum: Einen theologischen Zusammenhang zwischen der präsentisch-
eschatologischen Größe der βασιλεία und der Christologie sieht wohl die Auslegungstradition des Markusevangeliums, aber nicht sein Text selbst.

3. In einer ähnlichen Weise ist der Gottessohn nur mittelbar Gegenstand des
christlichen Glaubens, wie ihn das Markusevangelium darstellt: Geglaubt werden
soll und wird an die Fähigkeit, die ihm gegeben ist, zu heilen und zu 'retten' (Mk
2,5; 5,34. 36; 6,6; 9,19. 23f. 42; 10,52; 15,32 und, *via negationis*, 13,21). Jesus fordert deshalb die Jünger auf, Glaube an Gott zu haben (Mk 11,22!), was zur Konsequenz haben wird, daß ihnen die gleiche Macht zuteil werden wird (Mk 11,23f.),
die in den Wundern und Heilungen Jesu wirksam ist (Mk 9,19. 29): Dem Gebet (Mk
9,29) bzw. dem Gebet des Glaubens (Mk 11,22-24; vgl. Mk 9,19) wird die Erhörung
versprochen. Der Glaube an das Evangelium (Mk 1,15) besteht offenbar darin, daß
an die geheimnisvolle und wunderbare Kraft Gottes geglaubt wird, die in Jesus bereits gegenwärtig ist[7]. Die paulinische These, nach welcher der Mensch durch den

---

[4] So B. van Iersel 1993, 126f.

[5] Für die Interpretation des Begriffes der markinischen βασιλεία bietet M. Hauser 1993 ein neues Paradigma, das sich an Chr. Blumhardt und L. Ragaz orientiert. Es fällt in der Forschungsgeschichte auf, daß die Bedeutung und die Funktion der βασιλεία im Rahmen der Predigt Jesu
regelmäßig zurückprojiziert wird, die Rezeption des Begriffes im literarischen und theologischen
Zusammenhang des Markusevangeliums nur von W. Kelber 1974 und M. Hauser 1993 genau untersucht wurde.

[6] So mit Recht M. Hauser 1993.

[7] Mit Recht stellt A. Lindemann 1991, 199 Anm. 102 fest, daß das Markusevangelium nirgendwo
einen Zusammenhang zwischen βασιλεία und Wunder herstellt. Anders Lk 11,20 // Mt 12,28.

Glauben an Jesus Christus gerechtfertigt sei (Röm 3,21-31 usw.), findet kein Äquivalent in der markinischen Erzählung[8]. Gegenstand des Glaubens ist vielmehr Gott, der allein gut ist (Mk 10,18) und der als einziger Gott geliebt werden soll (Mk 12,29f. mit Zitat von Dt 6,4 und 5).

## 2. Jesus als Zeuge eines Gottesglaubens

Abgesehen von der Aufforderung, an Gott zu glauben (Mk 11,22), kommt der Begriff des 'Glaubens' (πίστις) nur innerhalb von Wundererzählungen vor. Jesus sieht den Glauben der Menschen, die ihm den Gelähmten durch das Dach bringen (Mk 2,5), stellt fest, daß der Glaube der an Blutfluß leidenden Frau (Mk 5,34) und des blinden Sohnes des Timaios (Mk 10,52) sie gerettet haben (ἡ πίστις σου σέσωκέν σε – zweimal), aber auch, daß die Jünger noch keinen Glauben haben (Mk 4,40), nachdem ihnen gesagt worden war, daß ihnen das Geheimnis der βασιλεία gegeben worden sei (Mk 4,10-12[9])

In Mk 2,5 genauso wie in Mk 5,34 und 10,52 erscheint der Glaube als Motiv der Wundererzählung und kann formgeschichtlich erklärt werden: Das Vertrauen in die Kraft des Wundertäters ist Bestandteil der Gattung[10]. Diese Betrachtung ist aber rein formalistisch. Der Glaube ist nämlich deswegen Bestandteil der Wundererzählungen, weil Wundererzählungen einen argumentativen Charakter haben und gerade die Funktion erfüllen, den Glauben hervorzurufen, zu verstärken oder zu verteidigen. Dies gilt nicht nur für die Stoffe der Jesus-Tradition, die auf die Autorität Jesu (Mk 1,21f. 27; 2,10), auf die Kraft Gottes (Lk 5,17) oder auf die Einheit des Vaters und des Sohnes (das Johannesevangelium hat offenbar den Begriff σημεῖον von Mk 8,11 als ein Interpretament der Wundererzählungen Jesu rezipiert und thematisiert[11]) verweisen, sondern auch für die nicht-christlichen Texte und Inschriften. Unter dem Begriff des 'Glaubens' können zwar sehr verschiedene Überzeugungen bzw. Überzeugungssysteme verstanden werden: Die Gottessohnschaft Jesu (im Johannesevangelium), die Kraft des Heilgottes und die Glaubwürdigkeit seines Heiligtums (in Epidauros) oder die besonderen Fähigkeiten des Apollonius von Tyana (bei Philostrat). Regelmäßig geht es aber darum, die menschliche Bereitschaft, an das Wunderbare zu glauben, so mit philosophischen, ideologischen oder religiösen Thesen in Verbindung zu bringen, daß das Wunder als Argument, das eine neue Struktur der Wirklichkeit begründen soll, oder als Argument, das auf der

---

[8] Anders Chr. Senft 1991.

[9] Zur grammatikalischen Konstruktion, vgl. B. van Iersel 1993, 126f.

[10] Bultmann 1921, 234-236; G. Theißen 1974, 64f.

[11] Begründung, historische Deutung und Interpretation in F. Vouga 1992.

Struktur der Wirklichkeit basiert, verwendet wird[12]. Im ersten Fall ist die Funktion der Wundererzählung diejenige der Propaganda und der Werbung (der Aufforderung zum Glauben), im zweiten Fall handelt es sich um die Verstärkung der vorhandenen Überzeugungen (um die Selbstbestätigung des Glaubens) oder um ihr genaueres Verständnis (Wundererzählungen sind funktionalisiert und bilden den Rahmen für Unterweisungen, *wie* man glauben soll[13]).

Wenn die Wundererzählungen die argumentative Funktion haben, Überzeugungen bzw. Glauben hervorzurufen oder zu verstärken, und wenn das Markusevangelium dies in Mk 2,5; 4,40; 5,34 und 10,52 explizit mit dem Begriff πίστις thematisiert, mit welchen Thesen oder mit welchen Vorstellungen will es die Übereinstimmung des Lesers hervorrufen oder verstärken? Die explizite Antwort in Mk 1,15 und die implizite Antwort in Mk 4,40 lauten: Der Leser soll eine Haltung einnehmen, die als Glauben an das 'Evangelium' bzw. als Glauben bezeichnet und positiv bewertet wird. Was dieser Glaube bedeutet bzw. woran geglaubt werden soll, und worin dieser Akt des Glaubens besteht, läßt sich zunächst am besten von folgenden Beobachtungen her interpretieren:

1. Durch den Begriff des Glaubens bzw. durch den Verweis auf den Glauben, der rettet (Mk 5,34; 10,52), wird nicht die Heilung bzw. die Rettung mit der Person Jesu, sondern mit einer Bereitschaft bzw. mit einer Fähigkeit, die verschiedene Menschen bereits in sich haben, in Verbindung gebracht. Die Kraft des Wunders ist nämlich nicht nur durch die ἐξουσία Jesu bestimmt, sondern durch die Haltung und die Handlungen der unmittelbar oder mittelbar betroffenen Menschen (unmittelbar: 5,34; 10,52; mittelbar: 2,5). Dies wird bestätigt durch den Bericht des Aufenthaltes Jesu in seiner Heimat (Mk 6,1-6a): Jesus kann dort kaum einige Wunder tun, und zwar deswegen, weil seine Mitbürger keinen Glauben haben. Fazit: Der Glaube, zu dem das Markusevangelium den Leser auffordert, ist eine Haltung, die Handlungen hervorruft, und die zusammen Voraussetzungen für Heilungen und Wunder bilden. Diese Haltung wird nicht als Glauben *an Jesus* dargestellt, sondern als eigener Glaube des Menschen. Damit ist die Frage allerdings nicht beantwortet, woran bzw. an wen der Glaube, der hervorgerufen bzw. verstärkt werden soll, glauben soll.

2. Als einziger Gegenstand des Glaubens (πίστις) wird Gott in Mk 11,22 genannt. Präziser formuliert: Als Deutung seines öffentlichen Auftritts in Jerusalem fordert Jesus seine Jünger auf, Glauben an Gott zu haben. Von der Form her betrach-

---

[12] Die Unterscheidung der Argumente in die beiden Klassen 'association' und 'dissociation', und die Unterteilung der ersten Klasse in "arguments basés sur la structure du réel", "arguments qui fondent la structure du réel" und "arguments quasi logiques" entnehme ich Ch. Perelman 1970 und idem 1980.

[13] Texte der Inschriften von Epidauros: R. Herzog 1931; zur Interpretation und formgeschichtlichen Auswertung, vgl. M. Wolter 1992.

tet ist die Unterweisung von Mk 11,22-25 eine Sonderbelehrung der Jünger. Der Verfasser des Markusevangeliums wiederholt eine Struktur, die er in Mk 4,1-9 und 4,10-32; 7,1-15 und 7,17-23; 9,14-27 und 9,28f.; 10,1-9 und 10,10-12; 10,17-22 und 10,23-31 verwendet hatte: Eine öffentliche Rede oder eine öffentliche Handlung wird für die Jünger zu Hause bzw. privat erläutert. Dadurch erfüllt sich das Programm von Mk 4,10-12 und 4,33f.: Die 'Aussenseiter' bekommen alles als Gleichnis bzw. als indirekte Rede[14], während die Worte und Taten Jesu für die Jünger und für die *insiders* als τὸ μυστήριον ( ... ) τῆς βασιλείας τοῦ θεοῦ interpretiert werden[15]. Was in Mk 11,22-25 den Jüngern erläutert wird, ist die Verfluchung des Feigenbaums (Mk 11,12-14 und 11,20), wobei Jesus eine Frage des Petrus beantwortet (Mk 11,21), die in Mk 11,14 bereits vorbereitet worden war. Die Bedeutung dieser symbolischen Handlung ergibt sich einerseits aus der Jüngerbelehrung von Mk 11,22-25, andererseits aus der Erzählung einer zweiten symbolischen Handlung (= der sogenannten Tempelreinigung), die mit der Geschichte des Feigenbaums (= des ungläubigen Feigenbaums?) eingerahmt wird. Auch hier wiederholt das Markusevangelium eine Struktur, die für seine Darstellungsweise typisch ist (Mk 3,20-35; 5,21-43 usw.[16]). Damit interpretieren sich die beiden Erzählungsabschnitte gegenseitig. Genauso wie der Feigenbaum hätte Früchte tragen sollen, auch wenn es nicht die Zeit für Feigen war (Mk 11,12-14), genauso hätte der Tempel ein Haus des Gebetes für alle Völker sein sollen[17]. Kurzum: Die markinische Komposition von Mk 11,12-25 verbindet zwei Themen, die in Mk 9,14-29 bereits kombiniert waren, nämlich die Aufforderung zum Glauben, der das Unmögliche für möglich hält (Mk 9,23f.; 11,24) und möglich macht (Mk 9,28f.: hätte möglich gemacht und macht möglich; Mk 11,23), und die Aufforderung zum Gebet, das als Mittel zu dieser möglichen Unmöglichkeit dargestellt wird (Mk 9,28f.; 11,24). In beiden Fällen ist die unmögliche Möglichkeit, Heilungen und Wunder zu tun, dem Glauben versprochen (Mk 9,19; 11,22-24) und durch das Gebet gegeben (Mk 9,28f.; 11,24). Voraussetzung dafür ist nicht die Person Jesu, und auch nicht die persönliche Verbindung zu Jesus, sondern ein Glaube, der als Glauben an Gott von Jesus hervorgerufen wird (Mk 11,22). Anders formuliert: Jesus ist nicht der Vermittler, sondern der Veranlasser des Glaubens[18], der als Gottesglauben definiert wird. Den Jüngern hat Jesus zwar die Macht über die unreinen Geister gegeben (Mk 6,7), aber dies geschieht da-

---

[14] Der markinische Begriff παραβολή ist von E. Cuvillier 1993 redaktionsgeschichtlich und theologisch untersucht worden.

[15] B. van Iersel 1993, 126f.

[16] B. Standaert 1978, 174-262.

[17] Zur Interpretation s. D. Lührmann 1987, 191-194: "Die eigentliche Funktion des Tempels".

[18] Ich verweise auf die Unterscheidung, die S. Kierkegaard 1844 und idem 1849 zwischen Sokrates und Jesus als Lehrer vornimmt.

durch, daß ihnen das Geheimnis der βασιλεία τοῦ θεοῦ gegeben wird (Mk 4,11). Fazit: Jesus ist der Verkünder einer βασιλεία und der Zeuge eines Glaubens, die den Jüngern die geheimnisvolle Macht geben, das Unmögliche für möglich zu halten und zu tun. Alles ist möglich dem, der glaubt (Mk 9,23), das heißt: der an Gott glaubt (Mk 11,22-25).

### 3. Die Bedeutung der Thematisierung von πίστις und πιστεύειν im Markusevangelium

Neben dem Begriff des 'Glaubens' (πίστις, Mk 2,5; 5,43; 10,52; 11,22) kommen noch das Substantiv des 'Unglaubens' (ἀπιστία, Mk 6,6a und 9,24), das Adjektiv 'ungläubig' (ἄπιστος, Mk 9,19) und das Verb 'glauben' (πιστεύειν, Mk 1,15; 5,36; 9,23f. 42; 11,23f. 31; 13,21 und 15,32) vor. Ἀπιστία und ἄπιστος bedürfen insofern keiner besonderen Untersuchung, als sie in Zusammenhängen vorkommen, die bereits besprochen worden sind oder in bezug auf die Begriffsanalyse von πιστεύειν noch zu interpretieren sind. Das Verb πιστεύειν kommt (a) in der Sonderbelehrung der Jünger von Mk 11,22-25 (V. 23f.) und in den zwei Wundererzählungen von Mk 5,21-43 (V. 36) und Mk 9,14-29 (V. 23f.) vor, die alle bereits erwähnt worden sind. Thematisiert wird in Mk 9,23f., daß der Glaube kein Besitz des religiösen Menschen bzw. keine Weltanschauung ist, sondern daß er vielmehr in dem Augenblick dem Zweifel bzw. dem Unglauben geschenkt wird[19]. Πιστεύειν erscheint (b) in einer partizipialen Form im Dialog zwischen Jesus und Johannes bzw. in den Gemeinderegeln von Mk 9,38-50 (V. 42): Die Jünger sollen die Kleinen, die glauben, nicht verführen. Das Verb wird absolut verwendet[20] und bezeichnet die Gläubigen als die soziale Gruppe der Anhänger Jesu (bzw. der christlichen Gemeinden). Für die Interpretation des markinischen Verständnisses des christlichen Glaubens hat diese Stelle nur insofern eine Relevanz, als das Verb πιστεύειν genauso wie ἀκολουθεῖν die bloße Zugehörigkeit zu den Jüngern bzw. zu den Schülern bedeuten kann (Mk 9,38[21]). Übrig bleiben (c) die programmatische Verkündigung Jesu von Mk 1,14f., die zur Bekehrung und zum Glauben an das Evangelium auffordert (Mk 1,15), (d) die Warnung vor Leuten, die die Jünger bzw. die Schüler Jesu verführen werden, indem sie ihnen sagen werden: "Siehe, hier ist der Christus, siehe dort" (Mk 13,14-23 [V. 21]), und (e) Überlegungen von Hohenpriestern, Schriftgelehrten und Ältesten, die mit der ironischen Frage der Kontinuität zwischen Johannes dem

---

[19] R. Bultmann 1933, 228.

[20] Die Variante πιστευόντων εἰς ἐμέ ist quantitativ gut bezeugt, läßt sich aber als Angleichung an Mt 18,6 hinreichend erklären. Vgl. B. M. Metzger 1975, 101f.

[21] In beiden Fällen bezeichnen 'glauben' und 'nachfolgen' die christliche Sozialisation, das heißt: Die Zugehörigkeit zur christlichen Gemeinde.

Täufer und Jesus konfrontiert werden (Mk 11,27-12,12, in Mk 11,31) und von Hohenpriestern, die sich den Schriftgelehrten anschließen, um zu erwarten, daß Jesus vom Kreuz herabsteige, damit sie sehen und glauben (Mk 15,32).

1. Die Aufforderung, an das Evangelium zu glauben (Mk 1,15), ist Bestandteil einer Bekehrungspredigt[22]: Die Schlußfolgerung, die sich aus der Verkündigung des 'Evangeliums', nämlich aus der guten Nachricht, daß die Zeit erfüllt und die βασιλεία nahe ist, ableiten läßt, ist die Empfehlung[23], umzukehren und an das 'Evangelium' zu glauben. Was mit 'Evangelium' gemeint ist, wird zunächst in der Formulierung der Ankündigung von Mk 1,14 deutlich: Die Nachricht, nach welcher die Zeit erfüllt und die βασιλεία nahe ist, wird als 'Evangelium Gottes' (τὸ εὐαγγέλιον τοῦ θεοῦ[24]) bezeichnet. Die frohe Botschaft, die Jesus bringt, ist die Nachricht, daß Gottes Reich genaht ist[25]. Jesus ist hier eindeutig der Verkünder und nicht der Inhalt des 'Evangeliums'. Genausowenig wird das 'Evangelium', das an alle Völker vor der apokalyptischen Erscheinung des Menschensohnes verkündigt werden soll, mit der Person Jesu in Verbindung gebracht (Mk 13,10). Zweimal werden allerdings die Person Jesu und das 'Evangelium' im Markusevangelium assoziiert: In Mk 8,35 geht es um die Verheißung, daß derjenige seine Seele retten wird, der sie "wegen meiner und wegen des Evangeliums" verliert (ἕνεκεν ἐμοῦ καὶ τοῦ εὐαγγελίου), und in Mk 10,29 um diejenigen, die allerlei "wegen meiner und wegen des Evangeliums" (ἕνεκεν ἐμοῦ καὶ ἕνεκεν τοῦ εὐαγγελίου) aufgegeben haben, und die es hundertfach empfangen werden. Aus dieser Bindung wird geschlossen, daß Jesus Bestandteil des Evangeliums selber sei[26]. Dabei wird aber übersehen, daß die Assoziation der beiden Begriffe ihre Unterscheidung voraussetzt, und daß der eine mit dem anderen nicht identifiziert werden darf. Verwiesen wird einerseits auf die Verantwortung Jesu, der das Evangelium Gottes verkündigt (so eindeutig Mk 1,14f.), und andererseits auf die frohe Botschaft der Nähe der βασιλεία, die eine Entscheidung des Menschen verlangt. Schwieriger sind die beiden letzten Stellen des Markusevangeliums, wo der Begriff εὐαγγέλιον noch vorkommt. Die erste Stelle ist der Titel des Buchs. Die kaum entscheidbare Frage, ob "Anfang des Evangeliums von Jesus Christus" (Ἀρχὴ τοῦ εὐαγγελίου Ἰησοῦ Χριστοῦ, Mk 1,1) die Gattung der markinischen Erzählung oder die christliche Verkündigung (wie bei Paulus) bezeichnet, ändert nichts an der Tatsache, daß

---

[22] D. Lührmann 1987, 42.

[23] Zur Logik der moralischen Sprache und zur Unterscheidung zwischen dem Imperativ und der Empfehlung, die einer Begründung bedürftig ist, s. R. M. Hare 1952.

[24] D. Lührmann 1987,41 schreibt ohne Begründung: "Mk bindet die Nähe des Reiches Gottes exklusiv an das Wort Jesu", kommentiert aber richtig: "Die Nähe wird vermittelt durch das εὐαγγέλιον, das zu verkündigen ist, nicht unmittelbar durch die Ausgesandten".

[25] B. van Iersel, 1993, 89.

[26] Zum Beispiel: D. Lührmann 1987, 42.

'Evangelium' auf das Buch, und nicht auf den Inhalt der Predigt Jesu verweist: Das Buch erzählt den Ursprung der Verkündigung der Botschaft von Jesus Christus, wie sie begann[27]. Präziser formuliert: Das Markusevangelium ist insofern 'Evangelium', als es die frohe Botschaft Jesu berichtet, das heißt: als es berichtet, daß und wie Jesus das Gottesevangelium durch seine Worten und Taten verkündigt hat. Inhalt des Evangeliums ist die von Jesus gepredigte Nähe der βασιλεία, nicht die Person Jesu selber. Als hermeneutischen Schlüssel für das markinische Verständnis des 'Evangeliums' hat man die letzte Stelle betrachtet, wo εὐαγγέλιον vorkommt: Mk 14,9[28] (Wo immer das Evangelium in die ganze Welt hinein verkündigt wird, wird auch gesagt werden, wie eine Frau Jesus in Bethanien gesalbt hat, in Erinnerung an sie). Mit dem Verb κηρύσσειν zusammen, verweist 'Evangelium' kaum auf das Buch des Markus. Eher scheint der Erzähler an die apostolische Verkündigung zu denken, die den Tod (vgl. Mk 14,8: "Sie hat meinen Leib vorweg zur Bestattung gesalbt") und die Auferstehung Jesu zum Thema hat[29]. Daß das Markusevangelium die Szene von Mk 14,3-9 innerhalb des Zusammenhangs von Mk 14,1-11 als Vorbereitung der Passionsgeschichte verstanden hat, ist kaum zu bezweifeln. Dies setzt aber nicht ohne weiteres voraus, daß der Begriff 'Evangelium' den paulinischen Sinn des "Wort des Kreuzes" (1 Kor 1,17ff.) für Markus hat. Vorsichtiger läßt sich feststellen, daß auch das, was in der Passion Jesu geschieht, von der Verkündigung der Nähe der βασιλεία her zu verstehen sei[30]. Bestandteil der Gegenwart der βασιλεία sind die Konflikte, die sie provoziert und die sowohl Jesus (Mk 8,31: δεῖ) als auch seine Jünger und Schüler (Mk 4,16f.; 10,30; 13,9-13) treffen können, aber zu ihrer Verkündigung gehören auch Berichte von Taten und symbolischen Handlungen, die ihre Nähe bezeugen.

Fazit: Aus der Analyse des markinischen Sprachgebrauchs des Begriffes 'Evangelium'[31] ergibt sich, daß die Predigt Jesu als Verkündigung der Nähe der βασιλεία und als Aufforderung, an die frohe Botschaft dieser Nähe zu glauben, programmatisch dargestellt wird. "An das Evangelium glauben" bedeutet nicht: An Jesus glauben, sondern: An die Nähe der βασιλεία (vgl. Mk 11,22: An Gott).

2. In der Warnung vor der Verkündigung von Verführern (Mk 13,21-23) hat πιστεύειν den bloßen Sinn von "für wahr halten": Falsch ist die Aussage, die die eschatologische Erscheinung des Christus und die Ereignisse, auf welche Mk

---

[27] B. van Iersel 1993, 89.

[28] Th. Söding 1985.

[29] Zum Beispiel H. J. Holtzmann 1889, 273; A. Loisy 1912, 390f.

[30] D.Lührmann 1987, 233: "Vielmehr stellt Mk hier am Beginn der Passionsgeschichte wie in Mk 1,14f am Beginn des ganzen Evangeliums noch einmal heraus, daß auch das, was nun in der Passion Jesu geschieht, Teil des Evangeliums als der Nähe des Reiches Gottes im Wort Jesu ist".

[31] Diskussion mit R. Bultmann 1921, 372f., und J. Schreiber 1967, in D. Lührmann 1987, 40f.

13,14-20 verweist (die Caligula-Krise[32], der jüdische Krieg, die Zerstörung des Tempels[33], wie Mk 13,1f. es nahelegt?) in Zusammenhang bringt. Die Stelle hat nur deswegen eine Relevanz für die Analyse des markinischen Verständnisses von πιστεύειν, weil sie sich mit der Frage der Christologie direkt auseinandersetzt. Fraglich ist, ob mit den Pseudochristussen und mit den Pseudopropheten die gleichen Personen gemeint sind (Mk 13,22), und inwiefern die Leute, die das eschatologische Kommen Christi mit den erwähnten historischen Ereignissen in Verbindung gebracht haben, und deren christologische Vorstellung in Mk 13,21 widerlegt wird (μὴ πιστεύετε), mit den Pseudopropheten (und mit den Pseudochristussen?) identifiziert werden können[34]. Sinnvoll wäre es, die Verführer von Mk 13,21 und die Pseudopropheten von Mk 13,22 als eine einzige Gruppe zu betrachten, die das endzeitliche Auftreten Christi (Mk 13,21) mit historischen Figuren (die Pseudochristusse) in Verbindung bringen. Die Warnung vor 'Pseudopropheten' ist ein traditioneller Topos, der aus der Diskussion über die wahre Prophetie und der Polemik gegen vermeintliche abweichende Lehren übernommen wird. Der Begriff der 'Pseudochristusse' ist in Mk 13,22 zum ersten Mal literarisch belegt (vgl. Mt 24,24), und könnte die Leute bezeichnen, die nach Mk 13,6 im Namen Jesu auftreten sollen und behaupten, daß sie es sind (ἐγώ εἰμι). Wer diese 'Pseudochristusse' bzw. diese Menschen, die sich als Christus vorstellen, sind, und welche christologische Vorstellungen sie voraussetzen, läßt sich vom Markusevangelium her nicht rekonstruieren. Abgelehnt wird eine Form der Christologie, die eine vermeintliche Präsenz Christi in einer als eschatologisch gedeuteten Gegenwart bekennt bzw. die sich auf eine Offenbarungstradition beruft bzw. welche sich als die Stimme des Erlösers oder des erhöhten Christus versteht[35]. Die Tendenz der eigenen Argumentation der markinischen Erzählung ist klar: Das Evangelium Gottes, das heißt: Die Verkündigung der Nähe der βασιλεία ist so deutlich wie möglich von der Erwartung der apokalyptischen Erscheinung des Menschensohnes abgekoppelt (Mk 13,24-27[36]).

3. Der Verlauf der Auseinandersetzung zwischen Jesus und den Hohenpriestern, den Schriftgelehrten und den Ältesten in Mk 11,27-12,12 ist in mehrerer Hinsicht verblüffend. Vorausgesetzt wird zunächst die öffentliche Bedeutung und die – auch von den Gesprächspartnern Jesu – anerkannte religiöse Autorität des Täufers. Ho-

---

[32] G. Theißen 1989, 133-211.

[33] Konsequente Interpretation des Markusevangeliums im Horizont des jüdischen Krieges in Ch. Masson 1968.

[34] So zum Beispiel A. Loisy 1908, 426.

[35] Am einfachsten läßt sich diese Tendenz in der Logienquelle (s. W. H. Kelber 1983, 90-139) und in der johanneischen Offenbarungstradition (s. F. Vouga 1990) belegen.

[36] Einzelanalyse und Auswertung in H. Conzelmann 1959 und M. Hauser 1993.

henpriester, Schriftgelehrte und Älteste befinden sich nur deswegen in einem Dilemma, weil sie vor der Bevölkerung Angst haben, und zwar insofern, als alle den Johannes für einen Propheten halten (Mk 11,32f.). Daß Jesus auch vom Volk für einen Propheten gehalten wird (Mk 6,14f.; 8,28), und daß die öffentliche Meinung ihn auch vor seinen 'Gegnern' schützen kann (Mk 11,18; 12,12; 14,2), wird hier nicht in Betracht genommen. Eine größere Autorität scheint der Täufer zu haben, und darauf verweist Jesus selber (Mk 11,30), der die Kontinuität zwischen Johannes und sich selbst in Anspruch nimmt: Falls sie dem Täufer glauben (Mk 11,31), dann müssen sie die Autorität Jesu als Verkünder des Gottesevangeliums auch anerkennen (Mk 11,28; vgl. Mk 1,4-11). Hier besteht aber das zweite verblüffende Moment der Erzählung: Wenn Jesus – der die Gesichtspunkte des Erzählers vertritt[37] – zum Glauben auffordert, dann geht es um den Glauben an Gott (Mk 11,22) oder an sein Evangelium (Mk 1,15). Weiterhin gibt das Markusevangelium einen dritten empfehlenswerten Gegenstand des Glaubens an, und dieser Gegenstand besteht in der Figur des Johannes: Geglaubt werden soll an das Gottesevangelium (Mk 1,15), an Gott (Mk 11, 31) und an Johannes den Täufer (11,31). Von der Erzählung wird nämlich vorausgesetzt, daß Jesus mit der Vollmacht des Himmels handelt, genauso wie die Taufe des Johannes vom Himmel, und nicht von Menschen war (Mk 11,28 und 30f.), und daß die Hohenpriester, die Schriftgelehrten und die Ältesten dem Täufer Glauben schenken sollten.

Fazit: Gegenstand des christlichen Glaubens ist im Markusevangelium Gott, die Nähe seiner βασιλεία, aber auch Johannes der Täufer, der den Herrschaftswechsel proklamiert, aber nicht die Person Jesu. Die These, nach welcher das Thema des Markusevangeliums die Christologie und, entsprechend, der Christusglaube sei, muß insofern revidiert werden, als die Christologie Funktion der Theologie bleibt, und das doppelte Zentrum der Verkündigung des markinischen Jesus und des Buchs der markinischen Erzählung das Gottesevangelium der nahen βασιλεία τοῦ θεοῦ ist.

4. Die Inszenierung des Spottes der Hohenpriester und der Schriftgelehrten in Mk 15,32 ist ironisch im gleichen Sinne wie die Frage des Blinden in Joh 9,27: Als rhetorisches Spiel wird angenommen, daß die Hohenpriester und Schriftgelehrten 'sehen' und 'glauben' möchten. Was sie angeblich erwarten, ist, daß Jesus vom Kreuz herabsteigt: Dann würden sie ihn als Christus und als König Israels anerkennen dürfen. Diese Forderung eines Zeichens, das die Verkündigung Jesu legitimieren soll, hat Parallelen in Mk 8,11: Jesus soll die Nähe der βασιλεία durch ein Zeichen des Himmels ausweisen, was vom Markusevangelium insofern als Versuchung dargestellt wird, als die Wirklichkeit der βασιλεία dadurch völlig mißver-

---

[37] D. Rhoads and D. Michie 1982, 35-44.

standen wäre. Gegen ein ähnliches Mißverständnis wehrt sich Jesus in Mk 8,33. Indem sie Jesus ironisch als Christus und als König Israels bezeichnen, verweisen Hohenpriester und Schriftgelehrte auf die in Mk 15,26 erwähnte Tafel, die die Hinrichtung offiziell begründet: Die Tatsache, daß Jesus auf dem Kreuz bleibt und stirbt, bestätigt, daß es nichts zu sehen gibt, und daß es auch keinen Grund gibt, zu glauben. Was sie zu glauben hätten, wird nicht ausgeführt: πιστεύειν wird absolut gebraucht, und hat einen ähnlichen Sinn wie in 9,42: sich wegen der Nähe der βασιλεία bekehren und zum Kreis der Jünger und Schüler Jesu bzw. zu der christlichen Gemeinde gehören.

Fazit: Der 'Glaube', die Aufforderungen, zu glauben, und die Thematisierung dessen, was πίστις bzw. πιστεύειν bedeuten, spielen eine beträchtliche Rolle in der markinischen Erzählung des Evangeliums. Die Vorstellungen der markinischen Theologie setzen aber eigene Zusammenhänge voraus, die sich von der paulinischen und von der johanneischen Theologie deutlich unterscheiden. Im Johannesevangelium ist der Glaube an den Erlöser Bedingung des eschatologischen Lebens, in der paulinischen Brieftheologie ist der Glaube an Jesus Christus die Voraussetzung für die Rechtfertigung[38]. Im Markusevangelium bezeichnet der Glaube die existentielle Haltung des Menschen, der das Gottesevangelium, das heißt: die frohe Botschaft der Nähe der βασιλεία, empfängt und von den unmöglichen Möglichkeiten, die seine Gegenwart ermöglicht und fordert, lebt und handelt.

## 4. 'Nachfolge' im Markusevangelium

Dieses Ergebnis, das der markinische Christologie eine funktionelle, und keine zentrale Bedeutung gibt, wird durch die Analyse der markinischen Vorstellung des Begriffes der 'Nachfolge' noch bestätigt. Ἀκολουθεῖν kommt 18mal im Markusevangelium vor. Wenn man von Mk 9,38 und von 14,13, der für die Untersuchung keine Relevanz haben, weil ἀκολουθεῖν nicht auf Jesus bezogen ist, absieht, ergibt sich folgendes Bild des markinischen Sprachgebrauchs:

1. Ἀκολουθεῖν kommt dreimal im Rahmen der Berufungsgeschichten der Jünger vor (Mk 1,18; 2,14. 15) und einmal in bezug darauf (Mk 10,28: Die Jünger haben alles aufgegeben und sind Jesu nachgefolgt). Genauso wie in Lk 9,57. 59 (// Mt 8,19. 22) werden Traditionen der Wanderpredigt aufgenommen und nach dem Muster der Berufungsgeschichte von Elisa literarisch – und in Mk 1,16-20 hagiographisch – bearbeitet. Die doppelte Begrifflichkeit der 'Nachfolge' (ἀκολουθεῖν) und der Aufforderung, Jesu zu folgen (ὀπίσω μου), sind von III Reg 19,19-21 übernom-

---

[38] Wobei Röm 11,32 zeigt, daß die These der Rechtfertigung durch den Glauben sich mit der Allversöhnungslehre vereinbaren läßt.

men: Genauso wie Elia einen anderen Propheten beruft, der sein Schüler sein wird, genauso beruft Jesus seine Jünger bzw. Schüler, die ihn in seiner Predigt der Nähe der βασιλεία begleiten werden. Die 'Nachfolge' setzt nicht den Glauben an Jesus, sondern an Gott und an die Nähe seiner βασιλεία voraus.

2. Dreimal beschreibt ἀκολουθεῖν die Anziehungskraft, die die Verkündigung der βασιλεία in den Worten und in den Taten Jesu auf die Öffentlichkeit hat (Mk 2,15; 3,7; 5,24), und zweimal verweist er darauf (Mk 10,32; 11,9). Viele Zöllner und Sünder lagen mit Jesus und seinen Jüngern zu Tisch, und folgten ihm (Mk 2,15), eine große Menge aus Galiläa, aus Judäa, aus Jerusalem, aus Idumäa, aus Transjordanien und aus der Gegend um Tyros und Sidon folgte Jesus nach, als er sich an den See zurückzog (Mk 3,7), und viele Leute folgten ihm und umdrängten ihn, als er in dem Boot von dem Gebiet der Gerasener nach Galiläa zurückgekommen war (Mk 5,24). Eine andere theologische Bedeutung, als daß Leute sich um Jesus versammeln, um ihn zu hören, hat hier ἀκολουθεῖν nicht. Daß gleiche gilt für Mk 10,32 (diejenigen, die Jesus nachfolgen bzw. begleiten, sind durch die dritte Leidensankündigung erschrocken) und für Mk 11,9: Die Voraufgehenden und die Nachfolgenden schreien: "Hosanna, gelobt sei, der im Namen des Herrn kommt, gelobt sei das kommende Reich unseres Vaters David, hosanna in der Höhe". Zum einen ist die Bezugsfigur Gott (hier: Der Herr) bzw. seine βασιλεία, und nicht Jesus. Zum anderen ist ἀκολουθεῖν, hier mit προάγειν verbunden, kein *terminus technicus* der 'Nachfolge'.

3. Dreimal wird von Jüngern berichtet, daß sie Jesus nachfolgen. Einmal geht es darum, daß Jesus in seine Heimatstadt kommt, und daß seine Jünger ihm dorthin folgen (Mk 6,1). Der Begriff hat hier offensichtlich keine theologische, sondern nur eine geographische Bedeutung. Von Petrus wird dann erzählt, daß er Jesus von weitem bis hinein in die Residenz des Hohenpriesters folgte (Mk 14,54), und von Frauen, die ihm nachgefolgt waren, als er in Galiläa war, daß sie von weitem zuschauten, als Jesus starb (Mk 15,41). Wenn die Bemerkung über Petrus nicht kraß ironisch auf Mk 8,34 verweist, hat ἀκολουθεῖν in Mk 14,54 die gleiche harmlose Bedeutung wie in Mk 6,1. Eindeutig ist jedenfalls der Sinn in Mk 15,41: Die Frauen sind Jesus nachgefolgt "als er in Galiläa war", und nicht auf seinem Weg nach Jerusalem, wie die Aufforderung von Mk 8,34 es implizieren würde.

4. Der Aphorismus, der die Unterweisung von Mk 8,34-9,1 einführt, ist eine markinische Variation des Logions, das sich in parallelen Fassungen in der Logienquelle (Lk 14,26f. // Mt 10,37f.), im Thomasevangelium (EvTh 55; vgl. EvTh 101) und im Apokryphen Brief des Jakobus (NHC I,2 5,31ff.) befindet[39]. Die markinische Fassung nimmt auf den Dialog zwischen Jesus und Petrus (Mk 8,32f.) un-

---

[39] Zum Logion und seinen Variationen J. D. Crossan 1983,131-137.

mittelbar bezug: Jesus fordert Petrus auf, ihm nachzufolgen (ὀπίσω μου; vgl. Mk 1,17. 20), und Mk 8,34 thematisiert die Bedingungen dieser 'Nachfolge'. Genauer formuliert: Drei Bedingungen werden vorausgesetzt, um hinter Jesus zu kommen[40]. Die erste Bedingung ist die Bereitschaft, sich selbst zu verleugnen, die zweite, sein Kreuz auf sich zu nehmen, und die dritte, Nachfolger Jesu zu werden. Die beiden ersten weisen auf die Entscheidung hin, die Konsequenzen der Gegenwart der βα-σιλεία in seiner Existenz und in seinen Handlungen zu tragen[41]. "Sein Kreuz auf sich nehmen" ist zwar eine Metaphorik, die vom Tode Jesu her entstanden und verständlich ist[42]; sie ist aber keine Aufforderung zur Nachfolge des Menschensohnes, der am Kreuz sterben wird, sondern zu der Bereitschaft, aufgrund der βασιλεία eigene Risiken einzugehen[43]. Getragen werden soll das eigene Kreuz, nicht das Kreuz von Golgotha. Die dritte Bedingung, um ὀπίσω μου ἐλθεῖν, besteht im ἀκο-λουθεῖν. Die beiden Begriffe, die in III Reg 19,19-21 (und vielleicht in Mk 1,16-20) unmittelbar kombiniert sind, werden hier insofern unterschieden, als der eine den anderen voraussetzt. Ἀκολουθεῖν hat deswegen wahrscheinlich den gleichen Sinn wie in Mk 1,18 und 2,14, nämlich: Der Verkündigung bzw. der Lehre Jesu als Jünger bzw. als Schüler zuzuhören[44].

5. Übrig bleiben zwei Stellen, in denen der reiche Mann aufgefordert wird, Jesus nachzufolgen, um das ewige Leben zu erben (Mk 10, 21) und der Blinde sich entschließt, Jesus nachzufolgen (Mk 10, 52). Die Einladung von Mk 10,21 und die Absage des Reichen werden in Mk 10,23-31, das heißt in einer Sonderbelehrung der Jünger, kommentiert: Anders als der Reiche haben die Jünger tatsächlich alles aufgegeben, um Jesus nachzufolgen. Der Ruf, der an den Reichen adressiert wird, ist insofern kein anderer, als derjenige, der den Jüngern in Mk 1,16-20 erteilt worden ist. Dies wird im Dialog zwischen Jesus und den Jüngern sofort bestätigt: Thema ist die Schwierigkeit, in die βασιλεία einzutreten. Die Wundererzählung von Mk 10,46-53 hat andererseits die Funktion, den Übergang zwischen Mk 8,27-10,45 und Mk 11,1-16,7 zu bilden[45]. Der Blinde erfüllt insofern das markinische Programm, indem er den 'Glauben' hat, der ihn retten kann (Mk 10,52; vgl. Mk 11,22-25), und indem er Jesus 'nachfolgt', das heißt: indem er Jünger bzw. Schüler Jesu, das heißt: Jünger der βασιλεία τοῦ θεοῦ wird.

---

[40] V. Taylor 1966, 381.

[41] V. Taylor 1966, 381.

[42] D. Lührmann 1987, 152.

[43] So mit Recht M. Hauser 1993. Anders D. Lührmann 1987, 152.

[44] Der Begriff 'Jünger' ist insofern unpräzis, als die Notwendigkeit einer persönlichen Bindung an Jesus als Bestimmung des markinischen Verständnisses der Befindlichkeit des christlichen Glaubens voraussetzen kann. So zum Beispiel V. Taylor 1966, 380.

[45] B. Standaert 1978, 119-126; B. van Iersel 1993, 70f.

## 5. Zusammenfassung

Fassen wir die Ergebnisse der Sprachanalyse von βασιλεία, πίστις bzw. πιστεύειν, εὐαγγέλιον und ἀκολουθεῖν im Markusevangelium zusammen:

1. Die βασιλεία ist eine eschatologische Größe, die hier und jetzt gegenwärtig wird, wenn Menschen durch ihre Nähe erfaßt werden. Sie ist nicht an die Person Jesu gebunden, und ihr Kommen mit Macht (Mk 9,1) steht in keinem Zusammenhang mit der apokalyptischen Erscheinung des Menschensohnes (Mk 13,24-27).

2. Werden die Menschen, die Schüler oder die Jünger Jesu aufgefordert, zu glauben, dann sollen sie an Gott (Mk 11,22), an sein Evangelium der Nähe der βασιλεία (Mk 1,15), an Johannes den Täufer, der den Herrschaftswechsel ankündigt (Mk 11,31; vgl. Mk 1,4-11), oder an die Macht, zu heilen und zu retten, die in Jesus und durch das Gebet wirksam ist, glauben. Genauso wenig wie die βασιλεία ist der Glaube an die Person Jesu gebunden.

3. Das Gleiche gilt paradoxerweise für die 'Nachfolge': Menschen werden aufgefordert, Jesus nachzufolgen, oder sie entschließen sich, ihm zu folgen. Damit gemeint ist, daß sie seine Schüler bzw. die Jünger der βασιλεία werden: Jesus ist hier auch der Veranlasser, und nicht die Bedingung des christlichen Glaubens[46]. Das interpretative Modell für das Verhältnis zwischen Jesus und seinen Schülern ist durch die prophetische Tradition gegeben (III Reg 19,19-21; vgl. Mk 1,16-20; 2,14, aber auch Mk 10,21. 28 und 10,52, die auf die Berufungsgeschichten direkt oder indirekt verweisen). Ein *terminus technicus* der Nachfolge als "Nachfolge des Menschensohnes auf seinem Weg nach Jerusalem und bis zum Kreuz" läßt sich im Markusevangelium nicht finden. Thema ist vielmehr die Bereitschaft, Schüler Jesu, das heißt: Jünger der βασιλεία, deren Nähe er verkündigt, zu werden, und die entsprechenden Risiken auf sich zu nehmen (Mk 8,34).

4. Gibt die alttestamentliche, prophetische Tradition das Interpretationsmodell für das Verhältnis zwischen Jesus und seinen Jüngern (das Verhältnis Jesus/'Jünger' ist als Äquivalent zum Verhältnis Elia/Elisa zu verstehen) her, so liefert sie auch den hermeneutischen Rahmen für das Verständnis des Herrschaftswechsels, für das Ver-

---

[46] Die Frage ist: Wie verhalten sich Christologie und Theologie zueinander? Im Johannesevangelium ist die Theologie Funktion der Christologie: Der Erlöser ist der Sohn, und der Vater begründet seine Autorität. Bei Paulus wird die Theologie christologisch definiert (vgl. Röm 3,21-31; 1 Kor 1,17-3,4: Das Kreuz ist als Offenbarung Gottes verstanden), so daß die Christologie Interpretament der Theologie ist. In dieser Hinsicht ist die markinische Perspektive ähnlich. Der Unterschied besteht in der Vorstellung, daß es keinen anderen Weg zum johanneischen Vater gibt, als den Sohn, und daß das Kreuzesereignis die von Gott gewählte Strategie ist, um sich vom Menschen anerkennen zu lassen (1 Kor 1,18-26; vgl. die Argumentation von Röm 1,18-3,31). Eine ähnlich Bindung der βασιλεία an den markinischen Gottessohn gibt es nicht, auch wenn sich die Nähe der βασιλεία in seinen Worten und Taten offenbart.

ständnis seines Geheimnisses und für das Verständnis der konfliktvollen Geschichte der βασιλεία in der Welt der Menschen, das heißt: in der Welt der Hohenpriester, der Schriftgelehrten und der Ältesten. Nicht nur die Figur Elias spielt dabei eine entscheidende Rolle (Mk 1,4-11; 6,14-29; 9,2-8. 9-11; 15,34f.), sondern auch der Prophet Jesaja. Genannt und zitiert wird er am Anfang des Buches (Mk 1,2f.), wo er die Nähe Gottes und seiner βασιλεία ankündigt, aber auch in Mk 7,6f. um die Gegnerschaft zu der βασιλεία zu erklären, und der Missionsauftrag seiner Berufungsgeschichte (Jes 6,9f.) wird als Interpretament für die Verstockung verwendet, die die Verkündigung der Nähe der βασιλεία in der Welt der Menschen verursacht (Mk 4,10-12). Das eigentliche Thema und das Zentrum des Markusevangeliums ist nämlich nicht die Christologie, sondern τὸ μυστήριον τῆς βασιλείας τοῦ θεοῦ und der Anfang ihrer Verkündigung und ihrer Geschichte unter den Menschen.

## Bibliographie

Best, E. 1981: *Following Jesus. Discipleship in the Gospel of Mark* (JSNT.S 4), Sheffield: JSOT Press 1981.

Bultmann, R. 1921: *Die Geschichte der synoptischen Tradition* (FRLANT 29), Göttingen: Vandenhoeck & Ruprecht 1921.

— 1933: "Zur Frage des Wunders", in: idem, *Glauben und Verstehen* I, Tübingen: Mohr (Siebeck) 1933, 214-228.

Conzelmann, H. 1959: "Geschichte und Eschaton nach Mc. 13", in: *ZNW* 50 (1959) 210-221.

Crossan, J. D. 1983: *In Fragments. The Aphorisms of Jesus*, San Francisco: Harper & Row 1983.

Cuvillier, E. 1993: *Le concept de παραβολή dans le second évangile. Son arrière-plan littéraire, sa signification dans le cadre de la rédaction marcienne, son utilisation dans la tradition de Jésus* (EtB Nouvelle Série 19), Paris: Gabalda 1993.

Hare, R. M. 1952: *The Language of Morals*, Oxford: Clarendon Press 1952.

Herzog, R. 1931: *Die Wunderheilungen von Epidauros* (Philologus Suppl. XXII 3), Leipzig: Dieterich'sche Verlagsbuchhandlung 1931.

Hauser, M. 1993: *Die βασιλεία τοῦ θεοῦ im Markusevangelium*, Diss., Bielefeld 1993.

Holtzmann, H. J. 1889: *Die Synoptiker – Die Apostelgeschichte* (Hand-Commentar zum Neuen Testament), Freiburg: J. C. B. Mohr 1889.

van Iersel, B. 1993: *Markus: Kommentar*, Düsseldorf: Patmos 1993.

Kee, H. C. 1977: *Community of the New Age. Studies in Mark's Gospel*, Philadelphia, PA: Westminster 1977.

Kelber, W. H. 1974: *The Kingdom in Mark. A New Place and a New Time*, Philadelphia, PA: Fortress Press 1974.

— 1983: *The Oral and the Written Gospel. The Hermeneutics of Speaking and Writing in the Synoptic Tradition, Mark, Paul, and Q*, Philadelphia, PA: Fortress Press 1983.

Kierkegaard S. 1844: *Philosophische Brocken* (GTBS 607), Gütersloh: Gerd Mohn [2]1985.

— 1849: *Einübung im Christentum und anderes*, Köln und Olten: Jakob Hegner 1951.

Kingsbury, J. D. 1983: *The Christology of Mark's Gospel*, Philadelphia, PA: Fortress Press 1983.

Koch, D.-A. 1975: *Die Bedeutung der Wundererzählungen für die Christologie des Markusevangeliums* (BZNW 42), Berlin: de Gruyter 1975.

Lindemann, A. 1991: "Die Erzählung der Machttaten Jesu in Markus 4,35-6,6a. Erwägungen zum formgeschichtlichen und zum hermeneutischen Problem", in: Breytenbach C. und Paulsen H. (Hrsg.), *Anfänge der Christologie. Festschrift für Ferdinand Hahn zum 65. Geburtstag*, Göttingen: Vandenhoeck & Ruprecht 1991, 185-208.

Lührmann, D. 1987: *Das Markusevangelium* (HNT 3), Tübingen: Mohr (Siebeck) 1987.

Loisy, A. 1908: *Les évangiles synoptiques II*, Paris: chez l'auteur 1908.

— 1912: *L'Évangile selon Marc*, Paris: Emile Nourry 1912.

Mack, B. L. 1988: *A Myth of Innocence. Mark and Christian Origins*, Philadelphia, PA: Fortress Press 1988.

Marcus, J. 1986: *The Mystery of the Kingdom of God* (SBL.DS 90), Atlanta, GA: Scholars Press 1986.

Masson, Ch. 1968: *L'Évangile de Marc et l'Église de Rome*, Neuchâtel: Delachaux & Niestlé 1968.

Metzger, B. M. 1975: *Textual Commentary on the Greek New Testament*, Stuttgart: United Bible Societies [3]1975.

Perelman, Ch. 1970: *Traité de l'Argumentation. La nouvelle rhétorique* (Collection de sociologie générale et de philosophie sociale), Bruxelles: Éditions de l'Institut de Sociologie, Université Libre de Bruxelles [2]1970.

— 1980: *Das Reich der Rhetorik. Rhetorik und Argumentation* (Beck'sche Schwarze Reihe 212), München: Beck 1980.

Pesch, R. 1976: *Das Markusevangelium* I (HThK II/1), Freiburg: Herder 1976.

— 1977: *Das Markusevangelium* (HThK II/2), Freiburg: Herder 1977.

Räisänen H. 1973: *Die Parabeltheorie im Markusevangelium* (Schriften der Finnischen Exegetischen Gesellschaft 26), Helsinki: Finnish Exegetical Society 1973.

— 1976: *Das 'Messiasgeheimnis' im Markusevangelium* (Schriften der Finnischen Exegetischen Gesellschaft 28), Helsinki: Finnish Exegetical Society 1976.

Reploh, K.-G. 1969: *Markus – Lehrer der Gemeinde. Eine redaktionsgeschichtliche Studie zu den Jüngerperikopen des Markus-Evangeliums* (SBM 9), Stuttgart: Katholisches Bibelwerk 1969.

Rhoads, D. and Michie, D. 1982: *Mark as Story. An Introduction to the Narrative of a Gospel*, Philadelphia: Fortress Press 1982.

Schmithals, W. 1979: *Das Evangelium nach Markus* (ÖTBK 2/1 und 2/2), Gütersloh: Gerd Mohn 1979.

Schreiber, J. 1967: *Theologie des Vertrauens. Eine redaktionsgeschichtliche Untersuchung des Markusevangeliums*, Hamburg: Furche 1967.

Senft, Chr. 1991: *L'évangile selon Marc* (Essais bibliques 19), Genève: Labor et Fides 1991.

Söding, Th. 1985: *Glaube bei Markus. Glaube an das Evangelium, Gebetsglaube und Wunderglaube im Kontext der markinischen Basileiatheologie und Christologie* (SBB 12), Stuttgart: Katholisches Bibelwerk 1985.

Standaert, B. 1978: *L'Évangile selon Marc. Composition et genre littéraire*, Nijmegen: Stickting Studentenpres 1978.

Taylor, V. 1966: *The Gospel According to St. Mark*, London: Macmillan ²1966.

Theißen, G. 1974: *Urchristliche Wundergeschichten. Ein Beitrag zur formgeschichtlichen Erforschung der synoptischen Evangelien* (StNT 8), Gütersloh: Gerd Mohn 1974.

— 1989: *Lokalkolorit und Zeitgeschichte in den Evangelien. Ein Beitrag zur Geschichte der synoptischen Tradition* (NTOA 8), Göttingen: Vandenhoeck & Ruprecht/Freiburg: Éditions Universitaires 1989.

Trocmé, E. 1963: *La formation de l'évangile selon Marc* (EHPhR 57), Paris: Presses Universitaires de France 1963.

Via, D. O. 1985: *The Ethics of Mark's Gospel in the Middle of Time*, Philadelphia, PA: Fortress Press 1985.

Vouga, F. 1990: *Die Johannesbriefe* (HNT 15/III), Tübingen: Mohr (Siebeck) 1990.

— 1992: "Le quatrième évangile comme interprète de la tradition synoptique: Jean 6", in: Denaux, A. (ed.), *John and the Synoptics* (BEThL 101), Leuven: Leuven University Press – Peeters 1992, 261-280.

Weinacht, H. 1972: *Die Menschwerdung des Sohnes Gottes im Markusevangelium. Studien zur Christologie des Markusevangeliums* (HUTh 13), Tübingen: Mohr (Siebeck) 1972.

Wolter, M. 1992: "Inschriftliche Heilungsberichte und neutestamentliche Wundererzählungen. Überlieferungs- und formgeschichtliche Betrachtungen", in: Berger, K., Vouga, F., Wolter, M., Zeller, D., *Studien und Texte zur Formgeschichte* (TANZ 7), Tübingen: Francke 1992, 135-175.

# Establishing the Text: Mark 1:1[1]

Adela Yarbro Collins

## 1. Introduction

Part of the process of intra-textual and inter-textual interpretation is the decision which manuscript or manuscripts to follow in establishing the wording of the text to be interpreted. Some textual problems of this type are more significant than others. Assuming that the inscriptions (titles) of New Testament texts are secondary, the opening units of the actual texts provide important signals about the genre of the work as a whole and crucial information about the author's intention. The *incipit* of the Gospel of Mark (1:1) characterizes either the following text-unit or, more likely, the Gospel as a whole as "The beginning of the Gospel of Jesus Christ [son of God]." The question of the presence or absence of the words characterizing Jesus Christ as (the) son of God is important for the reasons just stated and for the question of how the theme of the identity of Jesus unfolds from the point of view of the reader. The following article examines the evidence for the variants in an effort to determine the earliest recoverable wording of this verse and thus make a contribution to the resolution of the literary issues mentioned above.

[1] I am happy to offer this study as a token of esteem for Professor Lars Hartman from whom I have learned much, beginning with the academic year 1968-69 when he was a visiting professor at the Harvard Divinity School. I would also like to thank Bart Ehrman and Peter Head for their comments on an earlier draft, as well as Eldon Jay Epp for helpful suggestions. I am grateful to Tjitze Baarda for making available to me an unpublished discussion of this problem by Heinrich Greeven and for helpful suggestions.

## 2. *The Readings*

2.1. The important readings are as follows:[2]

(I)   Ἰησοῦ       28*

(II)  Ἰησοῦ       Χριστοῦ S.01*[3] Θ.038 28[corr] 1555*[4] sy[pal] ms[5] arm[mss6] geo[ad] sa[ms7] Origen[gr, lat] (d. 254) Serapion (d. 362) Cyril of Jerusalem (d. 386)[8]

(III) [κυρίου  Ἰησοῦ Χριστοῦ] sy[pal mss9]

(IV)  Ἰησοῦ       Χριστοῦ υἱοῦ θεοῦ S.01[a] B.03 D.05 L.019 W.032 Severian (d. 408)

(V)   Ἰησοῦ       Χριστοῦ υἱοῦ τοῦ θεοῦ A.02 E.07 F.09 G.011[suppl] H.013 K.017 M.021 S.028 U.030 V.031 Y.034 Γ.036 Δ.037 Π041 Σ.042 Φ.043 Ω045 047 all but three known Greek minuscules[10] Byzantine lectionary (Menologion, 3 Jan.) Cyril of Alexandria

---

[2] Cf. Alexander Globe 1982, 214-15, and Peter M. Head 1991, 622-23.

[3] The siglum S.01 is used here for Codex Sinaiticus in accordance with the suggestion of Leon Vaganay and Christian-Bernard Amphoux (Vaganay/Amphoux 1991, 14) that an uncial be designated by its number preceded by a zero, with its letter first and with a full stop between the letter and the number. This usage will be followed here for all the uncials cited.

[4] Globe points out that, although MS 255 is cited in support of this variant by Westcott and Hort who were followed by Legg and several commentators, the number now refers to a manuscript of the Acts and Epistles. In the nineteenth century the number applied to a manuscript from Mount Athos (now Athos, Vatopediu 918) dated to the twelfth or thirteenth century which Globe designates as codex 1555 (Globe 1982, 214, n. 15); this MS is not listed in Appendix I of Nestle[26]. Tischendorf also cited MS 255 in support of this variant (Tischendorf 1869, 1. 214).

[5] Codex Climaci rescriptus; this manuscript was edited by Agnes Smith Lewis 1909; for a brief description see Vaganay/Amphoux 1991, 35.

[6] Variant (II) is attested by Codex Matenadaran 6200 (formerly Codex 1111 of the Lazarev Institute in Moscow; MS M in Künzle's edition) dated to 887 CE and by Codex Matenadaran 2374 (formerly Ejmiacin 229; MS E in Künzle's edition) dated to 989 CE; see Beda O. Künzle 1984. The former manuscript is MS 991 in the report of Erroll Rhodes (1959). According to Head (1991, 622) variant (II) is attested by nine Armenian manuscripts.

[7] This variant is attested by a Sahidic MS which was probably written in the first half of the fifth century, no. 182 in the Palau-Ribes collection of the papyrological institute of the Theological Faculty of the University of Barcelona. It was published by Hans Quecke, who gave it the siglum P in his edition (Quecke 1972; on the date see p. 59).

[8] Although Jerome otherwise attests variant (VI), he attests variant (II) in a letter to Pammachius written in 395 CE (Jerome *Letters* 57.9; see the edition by Isidore Hilberg 1910, 518).

[9] The three witnesses to the Palestinian Syriac version that attest this reading are Cod. Vaticanus Syr. 19 (1030 CE), Cod. Sinaiticus, St. Catherine's Monastery (1104 CE), Cod. Sinaiticus, St. Catherine's monastery (1118 CE). See Agnes Smith Lewis and Margaret Dunlop Gibson 1899, ix-xii, 262.

[10] According to Greeven (see note 1), the three minuscules are 237[sch], 238[sch], 259[sch].

(d. 444)

(VI) ['Ιησοῦ    Χριστοῦ υἱοῦ θεοῦ] or ['Ιησοῦ Χριστοῦ υἱοῦ τοῦ θεοῦ] it (all
extant mss) vg syr[p, h] cop[sa, bo] the remainder of the arm mss
geo[op, tb] eth goth arab pers pers harmony Irenaeus[lat], arm (d.
202) Victorinus of Pettau (d. 304) Ambrose (d. 397) Jerome (d.
420) Augustine (d. 430)

(VII) Ἰησοῦ    Χριστοῦ υἱοῦ τοῦ κυρίου 1241

2.2. In support of variant (II), Tischendorf cited Irenaeus, *Against Heresies* 3.11.8
(preserved in Greek and Latin translation). Against Tischendorf, C. H. Turner argued that Irenaeus was concerned in this passage to compare the openings of the
four canonical gospels and to show how each corresponded to one of the faces of
the cherubim as described in Rev 4:7. Since he associated the Gospel of Mark with
the fourth living creature ("like a flying eagle") and interpreted the eagle in terms
of the Spirit hovering with its wings over the church, Irenaeus "hurries on to the prophetic reference" ("as it is written in Isaiah the prophet"). Since the words υἱοῦ
θεοῦ do not contribute anything to his point, he simply drops them.[11] Alexander
Globe took up this argument and described all of the quotations in this passage as
"truncated."[12] He is correct in stating that Irenaeus cited only vss 1 and 3 from John
1 and only vss 1 and 18 from Matthew 1. The paraphrase of Luke 1, however, must
include at least vs 8, as well as vs 5, because only vs 8 mentions Zachary's offering
sacrifice to God. Globe's statement that Irenaeus omits the quotation from Malachi
in Mark 1:2 is misleading, because it implies that the following quotation from Isaiah is cited. It is not. In fact, the quotations of Irenaeus are selections, not "contrac-
tions." He does not omit any words or phrases between the opening and closing
words of the other quotations.[13] Thus, if he indeed had the phrase υἱοῦ θεοῦ in his
text and omitted it, this procedure would be unique in this passage.

Turner mentioned that Irenaeus had included the words υἱοῦ θεοῦ in two other
citations of Mark 1:1.[14] Globe gave the references as Irenaeus *Against Heresies*

---

[11] Turner 1927, 150. Accepting the Latin translation as an accurate witness to the original, A.
Souter argued that Irenaeus omitted not only υἱοῦ θεοῦ but also Ἰησοῦ Χριστοῦ in *Against Heresies*
3.11.8. He assumed, however, that Irenaeus "had the fuller text" of Mark. It is not clear whether
Souter meant that the words υἱοῦ θεοῦ were also part of this "fuller text" (Souter 1923, cxxix; cf. p.
44).

[12] Globe 1982, 212.

[13] Head argued that Irenaeus was quoting accurately and selectively and pointed out that he indicated the end of one quotation from a particular work and the beginning of another from the same
work by prefixing the word καί to the subsequent quotation (Head 1991, 625; see W. Wigan Harvey,
1857, 2. 47-49; Adolf Stieren 1853, 1. 467-71).

[14] Turner 1927, 150.

3.10.5 (Latin) and 3.16.3 (Latin and Armenian).[15] He argued that the context favored the longer text. This is in fact the case, especially in 3.16.3. It is possible that the Latin translator or a later scribe added the equivalent of the phrase υἱοῦ θεοῦ in 3.10.5. The discussion of God in the context could have been based originally on God's role as the speaker in the prophetic quotation cited from Mark 1:2 and as the subject of the quotation cited from Mark 1:3. In 3.16.3, however, one would have to suppose that the translator added, not only the whole reference to Mark 1:1, since the preceding discussion deals specifically with Jesus as Son of God, but also the following section which shows how the prophets announced that Jesus was the Son of God. It is striking that Mark 1:1-2 is understood differently in 3.10.5 and 3.16.3.[16] In the former passage, the clause "as it is written in the prophets" is connected with the prophetic quotations that follow. In the latter passage, which lacks the prophetic citations given in Mark, it is connected with the preceding phrases "Jesus Christ, the Son of God." This discrepancy could be taken as a sign that the whole section dealing with Mark 1:1-2 in 3.16.3 is a later addition, but it may be an indication of Irenaeus' flexibility in interpreting Scripture, depending on his immediate goal. Another possibility is that Irenaeus used one text of Mark in composing 3.11.8 (the passage about the connection between the gospels and the cherubim) and another in composing 3.10.5 and 3.16.3.[17] But it is unlikely that an author would use two different texts of the Gospel in passages within the same book of the same work. It seems more prudent, therefore, to take Irenaeus as a witness for variant (VI), in agreement with Turner and Globe, than for variant (II).

## 3. The Source-Variants

3.1. The next step in dealing with this problematic passage is to determine the source-variants, i.e., one or two variants from which the others derived.[18] According to Globe, who apparently consulted a facsimile or microfilm of codex 28,[19] the scribe of this minuscule originally wrote only the abbreviation of Ἰησοῦ in Mark 1:1, but later added the abbreviation for Χριστοῦ as a superscript after the former

---

[15] Globe 1982, 211, n. 6.

[16] Both passages read "as it is written in the prophets," rather than "as it is written in the book of Isaiah the prophet." The change was made apparently because the first quotation is from Malachi and only the second from Isaiah.

[17] This seems to be Head's conclusion (Head 1991, 625). Greeven concluded that Irenaeus read a text of Mark 1:1 lacking υἱοῦ θεοῦ (reflected accurately in *Against Heresies* 3.11.8) and that he himself expanded the text by adding the two words in the other passages (3.10.5 and 3.16.3); see note 1 above.

[18] The term "source-variant" is taken from Vaganay/Amphoux 1991, 82.

[19] Globe 1982, 214, n. 15 and 215.

abbreviation in the large, blank space between the title (inscription) of Mark and the first verse. If it is the case that the original scribe carefully returned to this passage to correct it, it is probable that the exemplar read Ἰησοῦ Χριστοῦ and lacked υἱοῦ θεοῦ. Thus the source-variant of (I) is probably (II).

3.2. Variant (III) is attested by three manuscripts of a Syro-Palestinian (Aramaic) lectionary (sy^pal abc), which is an Evangeliary,[20] dating from the eleventh or twelfth century.[21] As Globe has argued, following Colwell and Riddle, the equivalent of the word "Lord" is a secondary, reverential addition.[22] This argument is supported by the fact that a Syro-Palestinian manuscript which apparently gives a continuous text of Mark, Codex Climaci rescriptus, lacks both the equivalents of "Lord" and "Son of God."[23] This manuscript thus supports variant (II). It is clear then that variant (II) is the source-variant for variant (III).

3.3. Variant (V) differs from variant (IV) only in the presence of the article before θεοῦ. Globe argued, following Westcott and Hort, that this addition of the article is a typical Byzantine revision, elevating the idiom of the phrase "Son of God" to proper Attic style.[24] If such were the case, however, one would expect the article before υἱοῦ as well. The source of variant (V) may be the desire of one or more scribes to specify the one (true) God. If either of these arguments is correct, then variants (V) and (VI) derive from variant (IV).

3.4. Variant (VII), Ἰησοῦ Χριστοῦ υἱοῦ τοῦ κυρίου, probably also derives from variant (IV). It is likely that the abbreviation of κυρίου was either deliberately (perhaps under the influence of liturgical usage) or inadvertently substituted for the abbreviation of θεοῦ.

3.5. Two variants remain, (II) and (IV). It is notoriously difficult to decide which is the source of the other.[25] The absence of υἱοῦ θεοῦ could be explained as an accidental omission. That is, in copying the sequence ΙΗΣΟΥΧΡΙΣΤΟΥΥΙΟΥΘΕΟΥ or ΙΥΧΥΥΥΘΥ a scribe's eye could have skipped from ΧΡΙΣΤΟΥ to ΘΕΟΥ or from ΧΥ to ΘΥ.[26] If such an omission occurred, variant (II) would derive from variant (IV). It has been objected that it is unlikely that a scribe would have made such an error so near the beginning of a work.[27] Heinrich Greeven doubted that a scribe's

---

[20] See Vaganay/Amphoux 1991, 24.

[21] Kirsopp Lake, Robert P. Blake, and Silva New 1928, 313-15; cf. Vaganay/Amphoux 1991, 35-36.

[22] Globe 1982, 215. On the subject of reverential alterations to the text of the Synoptic Gospels in relation to Christology, see Peter M. Head 1993, 105-129.

[23] Lake, Blake, and New 1928, 314-15; cf. Vaganay/Amphoux 1991, 35.

[24] Globe 1982, 215.

[25] See the brief history of scholarship on this point in ibid., 209-11.

[26] B.03, however, reads ΙΥΧΥΥΙΟΥΘΥ (see *Bibliorum SS. Graecorum* 1904, 1277 (= p. 43).

[27] So Bart D. Ehrman (1991, 150-51) and Head (1991, 629).

eye would have jumped or wandered from the $\overline{Y}$ of $\overline{XY}$ to the $\overline{Y}$ of $\overline{\Theta Y}$, since there are only three letters in between. If there had been a sequence of eight letters with the accompanying supralinear strokes, signifying abbreviations, in his exemplar, the scribe would have paid special attention to these in order to copy them correctly. Greeven did not exclude the possibility of such an error, but held it to be unlikely.[28] If Globe's analysis of the situation in codex 28 is correct (see 3.1. above), it answers these objections. The situation in Codex Sinaiticus may be analogous. On folio 18 verso line two, the original hand wrote OYΠYXYKAΘΩCΓE. Between lines one and two and above KA, the letters $\overline{YY\Theta Y}$ were added.[29] It is difficult to tell from the photograph whether the addition was by the original scribe or a later hand. Kirsopp Lake argued that four different scribes were involved in writing the New Testament portion of the manuscript (including Barnabas and Hermas). He defined the oldest group of corrections as the A group and distinguished six correctors within this group. On Plate II he gave five to sixteen examples of each of these correctors' work, plus four doubtful cases. The particular correction of interest here was not included in any of these categories. On the same plate, examples were given of the work of some correctors from the groups labeled B and C, who also made corrections to the gospels, but 18v 2 is not among them. The use of the siglum ℵ[1] in Nestle[26] and of ℵ[a] in UBS[3] for this variant is an indication of the scholarly tradition that the correction was made by a scribe in group A. According to Lake, some of the correctors of group A did their work before the manuscript left the scriptorium.[30] If the phrase υἱοῦ θεοῦ was added to S.01 before it left the scriptorium, this state of affairs may indicate that the phrase was in the manuscript from which S.01 was copied and that the original scribe omitted it accidentally. It is also possible that the original scribe corrected the copy in light of another manuscript. Given the possibility, however, that the words υἱοῦ θεοῦ were accidentally omitted and that this error was soon corrected, it is probably not prudent to consider S.01 as a strong witness for variant (II).

3.6. The other explanation is that the presence of the phrase υἱοῦ θεοῦ is due to a scribe's deliberate expansion of the reference to Jesus Christ. This explanation is supported by the tendency of scribes to expand titles (inscriptions or superscriptions) and quasi-titles (*incipits*) of books. The title of the book of Revelation is sometimes cited as an example.[31] Peter M. Head pointed out a number of other passages in the New Testament in which the phrase "Son of God" was apparently added

---

[28] See note 1 above.

[29] See Helen and Kirsopp Lake 1911, 18v.

[30] K. Lake, ibid., xxii; cf. Bruce M. Metzger 1992, 15, 46. Metzger uses the siglum ℵ[a] for readings introduced by correctors who worked within the scriptorium.

[31] Bruce M. Metzger 1971, 73; cf. 731.

by one or more scribes.[32] Globe suggested that a factor in the omission of the phrase υἱοῦ θεοῦ from the critical Greek New Testaments of Tischendorf, Westcott-Hort, and Nestle was their suspicion of theological elements that did not seem to be primitive.[33] Whereas Globe rejected this argument, Bart Ehrman accepted and developed it, arguing that the phrase υἱοῦ θεοῦ is an orthodox corruption, added to combat the adoptionists' reading of Mark.[34]

3.7. The search for a single source-variant in the case of Mark 1:1 leads to the conclusion that it is somewhat more likely that variant (II) is the source of variant (IV) than vice versa. It is unlikely that an accidental omission of the words υἱοῦ θεοῦ or their abbreviations would have gone undetected. Whereas such errors of omission are attested in Sinaiticus and 28, they were apparently corrected very soon after they were made. Other approaches may be brought to bear on the case to see if they support this tentative conclusion.

## 4. External Evidence

4.1. In the rather unlikely event that the accidental omission of the phrase υἱοῦ θεοῦ or its abbreviations remained undetected until the manuscript in question began to be copied, one would expect the error to be confined to a single group of manuscripts with a genealogical relationship. The problem with this approach is that little is known about the genealogical relationships of the manuscripts of the New Testament. The genealogical method of classical philology, the attempt to establish a stemma illustrating the transmission of a work, has in large part been abandoned by critics of the text of the New Testament, due to the complexity of the evidence. The attempt to establish relationships among a smaller group of manuscripts (a "family"), however, is still recognized as a valid enterprise.[35] Furthermore, it is worthwhile to define larger relationships among texts which may be designated "textual groups" or "textual clusters."[36]

4.2. In light of this situation, one may address the question to what degree the manuscripts attesting the two source-variants are independent of one another. The texts attesting variant (II) will be discussed first. As indicated earlier, S.01* is not strong evidence for variant (II). Θ.038 (Codex Koridethi, ninth century), along with

---

[32] Head 1991, 627; see also idem 1993, 115-16.

[33] Globe 1982, 209. John William Burgon and Edward Miller (1896, 286) argued, against Tischendorf, that the phrase υἱοῦ θεοῦ was fraudulently removed from certain copies of the Gospel by precursors of the Gnostic sect.

[34] Ehrman 1991, 152; this suggestion is discussed below.

[35] See the discussion in Eldon Jay Epp 1980, 139 and the literature cited in n. 22.

[36] See the proposal by Eldon Jay Epp 1989, 84-101.

minuscules 565 and 700, is a primary representative of a group (the "C" text group) that stands between the "B" text group and the "D" text group (the texts representing what has historically been called the "Western" text-type). According to Larry Hurtado, the quantity of Western readings in Θ, 565 and 700 suggest that the text represented by these manuscripts is a form of Western text as it was shaped in the East.[37] Codex 28, along with Codex Koridethi, is still assigned by some scholars to a recension that issued in the Caesarean text-type.[38] Kurt and Barbara Aland classify it as having an independent text in Mark only.[39] Ms 1555 was given the number ε 1341 by von Soden. He placed it in his I[r] class, a group with sporadic Western readings.[40] But 1555 has a different reading in Mark 1:1 from that of D.05, the old Latin and the Vulgate, the major representatives of the "Western" text-group attested for this verse. According to the Alands, the Palestinian Syriac (actually an Aramaic dialect used by Christians) verion is, for the most part, a normal Koine type with occasional Alexandrian readings.[41] Bruce Metzger has noted that, unlike both the earlier and later Syriac lectionary systems, the Palestinian Syriac lectionary is modeled directly on a typical Greek lectionary. Furthermore, the text of the Palestinian Syriac version is quite independent of the Old Syriac and the Peshitta.[42] The Armenian manuscripts that attest variant (II) include the two oldest, which represent the first translation of the New Testament into Armenian. This version was probably based on the Old Syriac version (attested by sy[c] and sy[s]).[43] Geo[ad] attests the first translation of the New Testament into Old Georgian, G[1], and represents the Adysh Gospels, a Georgian manuscript written in 897. This version was probably based on the oldest Armenian version.[44]

As noted earlier, one manuscript of the Sahidic Coptic version attests variant (II), PPalau Rib (designated "P" by its editor). It is not yet clear to what text-group it belongs. The editor offered only general observations, for example, that it follows the other Sahidic manuscripts by and large. P occasionally has readings that have been

---

[37] Larry W. Hurtado 1981, 88-89.

[38] Vaganay and Amphoux date this recension to the second century (1991, 104). The Caesarean text-type was identified by B. H. Streeter (1924) and Kirsopp Lake, R. P. Blake, and S. New (Lake/Blake 1923, 267-86; Lake, Blake, and New 1928). The existence of a Caesarean text-type has been disputed by Eldon Jay Epp (1974, 393-96) and Larry Hurtado has refuted the case for a pre-Caesarean text (1981, 22-23, 43-45, 62, 86-89).

[39] Kurt Aland and Barbara Aland 1987, 129, 155; see also Head 1991, 624.

[40] Globe 1982, 216.

[41] Aland/Aland 1987, 195. Lake, Blake, and New had argued that the Palestinian Syriac version was based ultimately on Greek manuscripts of the Caesarean text-type (Lake, Blake and New 1928, 320-21).

[42] Bruce Metzger 1977, 79, 82.

[43] Aland/Aland 1987, 200-1.

[44] Aland/Aland 1987, 201. See also Robert P. Blake 1929, 445-46.

identified as "Egyptian;" less often, "Western" readings. Sometimes, however, P has an "Egyptian" or "Koine" reading in places where the majority of the Sahidic mss have a "Western" reading. It likewise follows the "Egyptian" or "Koine" text-type at times when the majority have a "Caesarean" reading.[45]

The New Testament text cited by Cyril of Jerusalem (d. 386) has several agreements with S.01 and with manuscripts of the so-called Caesarean text-type in Mark,[46] but we do not know what manuscripts he actually used. Origen (d. 254) consistently cited Mark 1:1 without the words υἱοῦ θεοῦ in works composed both in Alexandria and in Caesarea.[47] He may have taken this reading from manuscripts representing the "B" text-group or from others of another group or both. In any case, he must be taken as an independent witness. It may be that Serapion of Thmuis of Egypt (d. 362) and Cyril of Jerusalem are dependent on Origen for this reading.[48] Another possibility is that one or both of these authors were dependent in this case on Irenaeus *Against Heresies* 3.11.8.[49]

4.3. Variant (II) is thus attested by six witnesses, which, in light of present knowledge, seem to be independent of one another: Θ.038; 28; 1555; the Palestinian Syriac version; one manuscript of the Sahidic Coptic version; and Origen. The evidence is insufficient to establish genealogical relationships among these witnesses. Codex Koridethi represents the "C" text-group. If the Palestinian Syriac represents the Koine text-type, and if that text-type is conflate, this reading must derive ultimately either from a text of group "B" or "D." The same is probably true of the Sahidic manuscript. The question of the geographical origins of these text-groups must remain open.[50] This range of independent external evidence does call into question the hypothesis that variant (II) derives from variant (IV) by accidental omission. To the argument that several scribes made the same error independently, one must respond that it is odd that the error does not seem to have occurred in the vast number of manuscripts of the Koine or Byzantine type.[51]

---

[45] Quecke 1972, 48-56.

[46] Globe 1982, 211, n. 6.

[47] Ibid., 213.

[48] On the frequent dependence of early Christian writers on their predecessors, see Bruce M. Metzger 1971/72, 396-97. Head (1991, 624) and John William Burgon and Edward Miller (1896, 281) conclude that Serapion was dependent on Origen for this reading. Burgon and Miller reach the same conclusion regarding Cyril of Jerusalem (282). In both cases they argue that the two later writers took over the text of Origen along with his argument against those who attribute the Old Testament to a different God from that of the New Testament.

[49] Head made a general comment to this effect (1991, 625).

[50] See Eldon Jay Epp 1991.

[51] So also Ehrman 1991, 150. The reading is questionable only in 237, 238, and 259, as Greeven pointed out (see note 1).

4.4. Variant (IV) is attested by two of the major text-groups, "B" (B.03, S.01$^a$ and L.019)[52] and "D" (D.05, all the Old Latin and most of the Vulgate manuscripts). It is also supported by W.032, which has an independent form of text with an affinity to the "Western" text-type in the first four or five chapters of Mark.[53] It is a pity that Mark 1:1 is not attested by p$^{45}$, since this text has significant agreement with W.032[54] and could clarify the age and origin of the reading. This variant is also attested by Irenaeus, an important witness of the second century, the Koine text-type, part of the Syriac tradition (the Peshitta and the Harclean), parts of the Coptic, Armenian, and Georgian tradition, and the Gothic, Arabic, and Persian traditions. The other patristic witnesses include Victorinus of Pettau, Ambrose, Severian, who was bishop of Gabala in western Syria around 400 CE, Jerome, and Augustine.

4.5. Irenaeus is not necessarily an independent witness, since his quotations generally agree with the "D" text-group or "Western" text-type.[55] Many of the other patristic citations could be dependent on him or also on the "Western" text-type or group. Cyril of Alexandria may be accepted as an independent witness.[56] Counting Cyril and the relevant portions of the Syriac and Coptic traditions, variant (IV) is supported by seven probably independent witnesses. The external evidence thus favors variant (IV). The quantitative external evidence is strongly in favor of variant (IV), but when probably independent witnesses alone are counted, the balance is only slightly in its favor.

4.6. The question of the qualitative character of the external evidence must be raised as well. The intrinsic quality of Codex Vaticanus is high and the combination of its testimony with that of Codex Bezae is weighty. Nevertheless, it would be far too circular to argue that, because many of Codex Vaticanus' readings are superior, its readings should always be judged original. The combination of Codex B.03 and D.05 cannot be taken as infallible. Apart from patristic citations, the earliest evidence for variant (II) is fifth century and for variant (IV), fourth century. But both variants have early patristic support; Origen (third) for (II) and Irenaeus (second) for (IV). It would be fallacious to argue that a second century attestation (as opposed

---

[52] The "B" group is represented primarily by p$^{75}$ and B.03 (Codex Vaticanus); see the discussion by Epp (1980, 87, 92-97). Vaganay and Amphoux argue that S.01 represents one of the great recensions of the Greek text made during the second half of the third century and the early fourth century, which resulted in the Egyptian or Alexandrian text-type (except for John 1-7 which has a "Western" text; Vaganay/Amphoux 1991, 106-08). Gordon D. Fee, however, has argued that the notion of a scholarly recension of the NT text in Alexandria either in the fourth or the second century, either as a created or carefully edited text, is a myth (Fee 1974).

[53] See Hurtado 1981, 22-23, 86-87; cf. Vaganay/Amphoux 1991, 97.

[54] Hurtado 1981, 65-66.

[55] See Vaganay/Amphoux 1991, 47.

[56] Ibid., 48.

to a third) is proof of originality. Nevertheless, whereas the search for a single source-variant slightly favored variant (II), the external evidence slightly favors variant (IV). A further approach remains to be explored, internal criticism.

## 5. Internal Evidence

5.1. The aim of internal criticism is to weigh the intrinsic value of the variants according to the text and its context.[57] Globe argued that Mark's first verse stands as a summary of important themes for the entire book.[58] In making a case for this conclusion, he stated that the phrase "Son of God" occurs only sixteen times in the synoptics and always under Markan influence. This statement is incorrect. The phrase occurs in Luke 1:35, the speech of Gabriel to Mary, a passage that has no parallel in Mark. The Greek phrase is very similar to variant (IV) of Mark 1:1, since both nouns lack the article. The phrase also occurs twice in the Q-form of the temptation (Matt 4:3, 6//Luke 4:3, 9) in a form similar to variant (V) of Mark 1:1. These occurrences are also independent of Mark. There are also passages in which Matthew or Luke have the phrase and Mark does not (Matt 14:33, 16:16, 26:63; Luke 22:70). Globe's main point is that the idea of Jesus' sonship with God forms a crucial theme in Mark (1:11; 3:11; 8:38; 9:7; 12:6; 13:32; 14:36, 61; and 15:39). He is certainly right that this is an important theme in Mark, but the presence of this theme only shows that the words υἱοῦ θεοῦ *may* have stood in the original form of Mark 1:1, not that they in fact did.[59]

5.2. Globe also argued that the evangelist modeled his first verse on several Greek superscriptions of the Septuagint which have a similar formula including:

> (a) a noun without the article specifying the type of proclamation, (A) sometimes, as in Mark, with a second noun in the genitive; (b) the name of the person who transmits the proclamation, (B) sometimes, as in Mark, in the genitive; and (c) the filial relationship of the person transmitting the proclamation, (C) sometimes, as in Mark, in a genitive phrase ('son of NAME') without any articles.[60]

A problem with this thesis arises already with regard to the first element of the alleged formula. Nine of the twelve examples (not counting Mark and counting the two *incipits* of Hosea and Nahum separately) open with a noun that gives, more or

---

[57] See, e.g., Vaganay/Amphoux 1991, 79.

[58] Globe 1982, 217.

[59] Head probably went too far in arguing that the shorter reading is to be preferred as the more difficult reading because of the harmony of the longer reading with Mark's presentation of Jesus as the Son of God elsewhere, but he has a point (1991, 626-27).

[60] Globe 1982, 217-18.

less accurately, the literary form of the work or its constituent parts.[61] But this is not the type of noun that occurs as the first element of Mark 1:1. Ἀρχή marks the beginning of the work which is then labeled as "good news" in the second element (a second noun and in the genitive). Only one of the twelve examples from the Septuagint opens in this way: ἀρχὴ λόγου (Hos 1:2 LXX). The correspondence between Mark 1:1 and Hos 1:2 hardly constitutes a "formula."

In Globe's alleged formula, the nature and function of the optional second noun is unspecified. This lack of specification calls into question the hypothesis that there was a formula that Mark adapted. The second noun, in the examples that have it, has diverse characteristics and functions. In three cases, it gives the alleged human author of the work (Prov 1:1, Eccl 1:1, and Amos 1:1). In three cases, it gives a literary form or description of the content of the work (Cant 1:1, Nah 1:1b, Mal 1:1 and Hos 1:2, the latter being the only one really similar to Mark). In another three examples, the second noun names the divine author of the work (Hos 1:1, Joel 1:1, and Zeph 1:1).

Globe's definition of the second element of the formula as "the name of the person who transmits the proclamation" begs the question whether Ἰησοῦ Χριστοῦ in Mark 1:1 is a subjective or objective genitive. Even if it is taken as a subjective genitive, there is a significant difference between Mark and the examples cited by Globe. In the texts from the Septuagint, authorship of the work in question by the person named is implied. There is no such implication in Mark.

The third element of the alleged formula states the filial relationship of the author of the work. One of Globe's examples, Nah 1:1, should not be listed for this part of the formula, since it gives the town of the prophet, not his father's name. Given the weak correspondence of Mark with the first two parts of the formula, it is not at all clear that the evangelist modeled the phrase "Son of God" on the statements of filial relation at the beginning of some books of the Septuagint, as Globe claims. This argument does not provide significant support for the hypothesis that the phrase υἱοῦ θεοῦ was part of the original text of Mark.[62]

5.3. Globe presented a further argument of an internal critical sort, namely, that if a scribe had added the phrase "Son of God" to Mark 1:1, one would expect the scribe to have modeled the phrase on the Attic grammatical standard and to have used one or two articles.[63] Globe presumed too much knowledge about the hypo-

---

[61] Two of the examples begin with the word λῆμμα (Nahum 1:1a, Mal 1:1); this word seems to describe the content of the work that follows. Εὐαγγελίου in Mark 1:1 seems also to describe the content rather than the form of the work.

[62] Heinrich Greeven also rejected this argument and pointed out that the "filial relationship" is lacking in Cant 1:1, Hos 1:2, Amos 1:1 and Mal 1:1 (see note 1).

[63] Globe 1982, 217.

thetical scribe and his style. A scribe attempting to imitate Mark's style could have reproduced the phrase as it appears in Mark 3:11 with two articles or as it appears in 15:39 with no articles. Thus, this argument is without weight.[64]

5.4. As noted briefly above, Ehrman suggested that variant (IV) (including υἱοῦ θεοῦ) originated in the context of the various readings of Mark current in the early church before orthodoxy established a normative reading. He stated that "[a]s far back as our earliest records we find Christians who claimed that Jesus was adopted to be the Son of God at his baptism...."[65] Adoptianism proper is a heresy that originated in the eighth century in Spain. But through the influence of Adolf Harnack's *Dogmengeschichte*, the term (usually spelled "Adoptionism") has also been applied to a point of view that appears in various forms in early Greek theology according to which Jesus was a human being gifted with divine powers. This point of view has been ascribed to the Ebionites and the Monarchians.[66]

According to Irenaeus, Cerinthus taught that Jesus was the son of Joseph and Mary, but surpassed all men in *justitia, prudentia,* and *sapientia.*[67] Christ descended upon Jesus in the form of a dove after his baptism, and left him before his death.[68] In other passages, Irenaeus indicates that Cerinthus and the Ebionites differed in their beliefs about Christ. He also stated that the Ebionites preferred (or used only) the Gospel according to Matthew, whereas "[t]hose again who distinguish between Jesus and Christ and say that Christ cannot have suffered, but that actually only Jesus suffered" prefer Mark.[69]

Hippolytus says that Theodotus of Byzantium took his ideas about Christ "from the school of the Gnostics, Cerinthus and Ebion" and that he described the appearance of Christ in the following way:

> Jesus was a man [ἄνθρωπον] born of a virgin according to the counsel of the Father. He lived together with all men [ἀνθρώποις] and became pre-eminently pious. He subsequently, at his baptism in the river Jordan received Christ from above, who descended in the form of a dove. And this was the reason why powers did not operate in him prior to the manifestation in him of that Spirit which descended and which proclaimed him to be Christ (*refutatio omn. haer.* 7.35.1-2).[70]

---

[64] Head also rejects this argument (1991, 628). See also the comment by Gordon Fee that scribes may have preferred Koine, and especially Septuagintal, idioms to classical ones (1974, 41).

[65] Ehrman 1991, 146.

[66] "Adoptianism" 1974, 18-19.

[67] Irenaeus *adv. haer.* 1.26.1; see A. F. J. Klijn and G. J. Reinink 1973, 3, 102-5.

[68] Irenaeus *adv. haer.* 1.26.2, 3.11.7; Klijn/Reinink 1973, 20, 104-7.

[69] "Those" are apparently Cerinthus and Carpocrates; Irenaeus *adv. haer.* 3.11.7; Klijn/Reinink 1973, 20. Cf. Irenaeus ibid., 1.24.4 on Basilides, 1.25.1 on Carpocrates; the baptism of Jesus is not mentioned in these passages, however.

It is unlikely that Theodotus used primarily the Gospel of Mark, since he mentions the virgin birth as well as the baptism of Jesus.

The earliest *direct* association of such an interpretation of the baptism of Jesus with the Ebionites is found in Epiphanius. He does not seem to have had any independent information about the Ebionites, but based his description of them on Irenaeus, Pseudo-Tertullian, and Eusebius. His account goes beyond theirs because he had access to some Jewish Christian documents and attributed the ideas in them to the Ebionites. These books included a Gospel (whose title is uncertain), the *Periodoi Petrou*, and the *Anabathmoi Jakobou*. Epiphanius says that the gospel used by the Ebionites begins with the baptism of John:

> The reason for this is that they insist that Jesus was really man [ἄνθρωπον], as I said, and that Christ came into being in him because he descended in the form of a dove, as we have also already found in other heresies (*panarion* 30.14.4).[71]

Epiphanius says that both the Ebionites and the Cerinthians used the Gospel of Matthew, but this conclusion may result from his misreading of the passage in Irenaeus cited above (*adv. haer.* 3.11.7).[72] The gospel that Epiphanius associated with the Ebionites could be (1) a gospel otherwise unknown; (2) a harmony of several gospels; (3) a form of Matthew from which the genealogies and infancy narratives have been removed;[73] (4) some form of Mark. The citation introducing John the Baptist does not agree with any of the canonical gospels (Epiphanius *panarion* 30.14.3). The indications of who was king and who was high priest at the time of his appearance constitute an analogy to Luke, but the data are different. The quotation of the scene in which Jesus' relatives ask for him looks like a harmony of Matthew (12:47-50) and Luke (8:20-21; Epiphanius *panarion*, 30.14.5).

Ehrman's thesis is that a scribe added the phrase υἱοῦ θεοῦ to Mark 1:1 in order to preclude an adoptionistic reading of the account of the baptism later in the chapter. The scribe's intention was to indicate that Jesus was already the Son of God before his baptism.[74] This is an interesting thesis, but difficult to demonstrate. A problem with it is that the Gospel of Mark was soon overshadowed by the Gospels

---

[70] Klijn/Reinink 1973, 22-23, 112-13; see also Hippolytus *refutatio omn. haer.* 10.23.1-2; Klijn/Reinink 1973, 120-23.

[71] Ibid., 28-38; translation cited is on p. 181, Greek text on p. 180.

[72] Epiphanius *panarion* 30.3.7; see Klijn/Reinink 1973, 10-11, 178-79. Filaster says that Cerinthus accepted the Gospel of Matthew and rejected the other three, but he is probably dependent on Epiphanius for this view (Filaster *div. her. liber* 36; Klijn/Reinink 1973, 15, 230-31).

[73] See Epiphanius *panarion* 30.13.1-14.3. Compare Tatian's *Diatessaron* from which the genealogies, but not the infancy narratives, were removed (for discussion see Peter M. Head 1992, 121-37).

[74] Ehrman 1991, 152.

of Matthew and Luke. But Irenaeus' remark that those who distinguish between Jesus and Christ prefer the Gospel of Mark (see above) is significant support for it.

## 6. Conclusion

On the one hand, the search for a single source-variant slightly favors variant (II), which lacks the words υἱοῦ θεοῦ. On the other hand, the weight of the external evidence supports variant (IV), which has these words. Internal criticism and the study of the historical context tip the scales in favor of variant (II). It is far easier to explain why a scribe would add these words than it is to explain their deliberate omission. It is probably not coincidental that the earliest witness for the longer reading is Irenaeus, whose major work was written against heresies in the early Christian movement. It is rather unlikely that the words were omitted by accident. But it is quite credible that they were added, either out of piety or to combat too human an understanding of Jesus. The addition probably occurred sometime in the second century.

## Bibliography

"Adoptianism" 1974: "Adoptianism", in: F. L. Cross and E. A. Livingstone (eds.), *The Oxford Dictionary of the Christian Church*, 2nd rev. ed., Oxford-New York: Oxford University Press 1974, 18-19.

Aland, K./Aland, B. 1987: *The Text of the New Testament*, Grand Rapids, MI/Leiden: Eerdmans/ Brill 1987.

*Bibliorum SS. Graecorum* 1904: *Bibliorum SS. Graecorum Codex Vaticanus 1209 (Cod. B)*, Pars Altera: *Testamentum Novum*, Milan: Vatican Library-Ulricum Hoepli 1904.

Blake, R. P. 1929: *The Old Georgian Version of the Gospel of Mark: From the Adysh Gospels with the Variants of the Opiza and Tbet' Gospels With a Latin Translation* (PO 20.3), Paris: Firmin-Didot 1929, 435-574.

Burgon, J. W./Miller, E. 1896: *The Traditional Text of the Holy Gospels*, London/Cambridge: George Bell and Sons/Deighton, Bell and Co. 1896.

Ehrman, B. D. 1991: "The Text of Mark in the Hands of the Orthodox", in: *LuthQ* 5 (1991) 143-56. Also published in: M. S. Burrows and P. Rorem (eds.), *Biblical Hermeneutics in Historical Perspective: Studies in Honor of Karlfried Froehlich on His Sixtieth Birthday*, Grand Rapids, MI: Eerdmans 1991, 19-31; citations are from *LuthQ*.

Epp, E. J. 1974: "The Twentieth Century Interlude in New Testament Textual Criticism", in: *JBL* 93 (1974) 386-414.

— 1980: "A Continuing Interlude in New Testament Textual Criticism?" in: *HThR* 73 (1980) 131-51.

— 1989: "The Significance of the Papyri for Determining the Nature of the New Testament Text in the Second Century: A Dynamic View of Textual Transmission", in: W. L. Petersen (ed.), *Gospel Traditions in the Second Century* (CJAn 3), Notre Dame, IN: University of Notre Dame Press 1989, 71-103.

— 1991: "New Testament Papyrus Manuscripts and Letter Carrying in Greco-Roman Times", in: B. A. Pearson (ed.), *The Future of Early Christianity: Essays in Honor of Helmut Koester*, Minneapolis, MN: Fortress 1991, 35-56.

Fee, G. D. 1974: "P75, P66, and Origen: The Myth of Early Textual Recension in Alexandria", in: R. N. Longenecker and M. C. Tenney (eds.), *New Dimensions in New Testament Study*, Grand Rapids, MI: Zondervan 1974, 19-45.

Globe, A. 1982: "The Caesarean Omission of the Phrase 'Son of God' in Mark 1:1", in: *HThR* 75 (1982) 209-18.

Harvey, W. W. 1857: *Sancti Irenaei Episcopi Lugdunensis: Libros quinque adversus Haereses*, Vol. I-II, Cambridge: Cambridge University Press 1857.

Head, P. M. 1991: "A Text-Critical Study of Mark 1.1: 'The Beginning of the Gospel of Jesus Christ'", in: *NTS* 37 (1991) 621-29.

— 1992: "Tatian's Christology and Its Influence on the Composition of the Diatessaron", in: *TynB* 43 (1992) 121-37.

— 1993: "Christology and Textual Transmission: Reverential Alterations in the Synoptic Gospels", in: *NT* 35 (1993) 105-129.

Hilberg, I. 1910: *Sancti Eusebii Hieronymi Epistulae*, Pars I: *Epistulae I-LXX* (CSEL 54), Vienna/ Leipzig: Tempsky/Freytag 1910.

Hurtado, L. W. 1981: *Text-Critical Methodology and the Pre-Caesarean Text: Codex W in the Gospel of Mark* (StD 43), Grand Rapids, MI: Eerdmans 1981.

Klijn, A. F. J./Reinink, G. J. 1973: *Patristic Evidence for Jewish-Christian Sects*, (NT.S 36), Leiden: Brill 1973.

Künzle, B. O. 1984: *Das altarmenische Evangelium*, vol. 1: *Edition zweier altarmenischer Handschriften*, vol. 2: *Lexikon*, (EHS. 21.33), Bern/Frankfurt a.M./Nancy/New York: Peter Lang 1984. (The work is bilingual with facing pages in French and German.)

Lake, H./Lake, K. 1911: *Codex Sinaiticus Petropolitanus: The New Testament, the Epistle of Barnabas and the Shepherd of Hermas*, Oxford: Clarendon 1911.

Lake, K./Blake, R. P. 1923: "The Text of the Gospels and the Koridethi Codex", in: *HThR* 16 (1923) 267-86.

Lake, K./Blake, R. P./New, S. 1928: "The Caesarean Text of the Gospel of Mark", in: *HThR* 21 (1928) 207-404.

Lewis, A. S. 1909: *Codex Climaci rescriptus: Fragments of Sixth Century Palestinian Syriac Texts of the Gospels, of the Acts of the Apostles, and of St. Paul's Epistles*, Cambridge: Cambridge University Press 1909.

Lewis, A. S. and Gibson, M. D. 1899: *The Palestinian Syriac Lectionary of the Gospels*, London: Kegan Paul, Trench, Trübner, & Co. 1899.

Metzger, B. M. 1971: *A Textual Commentary on the Greek New Testament: A Companion Volume to the United Bible Societies' Greek New Testament (third edition)*, London-New York: United Bible Societies 1971.

— 1971/72: "Patristic Evidence and the Textual Criticism of the New Testament", in: *NTS* 18 (1971/72) 379-400.

— 1977: *The Early Versions of the New Testament: Their Origin, Transmission, and Limitations*, Oxford: Clarendon 1977.

— 1992: *The Text of the New Testament: Its Transmission, Corruption, and Restoration*, 3rd rev. ed., New York-Oxford: Oxford University Press 1992.

Quecke, H. 1972: *Das Markusevangelium Saïdisch: Text der Handschrift PPalau Rib. Inv.-Nr. 182 mit den Varianten der Handschrift M 569*, Barcelona: Papyrologica Castroctaviana 1972.

Rhodes, E. F. 1959: *An Annotated List of Armenian New Testament Manuscripts* (Annual Report of Theology Monograph Series 1), Tokyo: Rikkyo (St. Paul's) University 1959.

Souter, A. 1923: "The New Testament Text of Irenaeus", in: W. Sanday/C. H. Turner (eds.), *Nouum Testamentum Sancti Irenaei Episcopi Lugdunensis*, Oxford: Clarendon 1923.

Stieren, A. 1853: *Sancti Irenaei Episcopi Lugdunensis quae supersunt omnia*, Vol. I-II, Leipzig: Weigel 1853.

Streeter, B. H. 1924: *The Four Gospels: A Study of Origins*, London: Macmillan 1924.

Tischendorf, C. 1869: *Novum Testamentum Graece*, Vol. I, 8th ed., Leipzig: Giesecke & Devrient 1869.

Turner, C. H. 1927: "A Textual Commentary on Mark 1", in: *JThS* 28 (1927) 145-58.

Vaganay, L./Amphoux, C.-B. 1991: *An Introduction to New Testament Textual Criticism*, Cambridge-New York: Cambridge University Press 1991.

# The "Visitation" in Context

Lucien Legrand

Many attempts have been made to identify the structure of Luke 1-2.[1] They are based mostly on the obvious parallelism between the infancies of John the Baptist and of Jesus: the two Annunciations (Luke 1:8-25 and 1:26-38), the two Birth stories (1:57-79 and 2:1-21) and the two reports on the "growth" of the boys (1:80 and 2:40, 52). But a few pericopae seem to resist this paralleling treatment and find no counterpart in the opposite section. One can see this particularly with the "Visitation" (1:39-56) and the two episodes of Jesus in the Temple (2:22-39, 41-52). Commentators classify them as "supplements" (Lyonnet) or "complements" (Laurentin). But this labelling does not explain in which way they "supplement" or "complement" the context. In this paper I intend to situate the pericope of the "Visitation" in its context. I will examine it first in its immediate context following the Annunciation to Mary, then in its broader context of the Lukan Infancy narrative and finally in its general context of the Lukan work.[2]

## 1. The Immediate Context

In the present Lukan redaction, the two pericopae of the Visitation and of the Annunciation are closely connected.

The participle ἀναστᾶσα that forms the transition between the two episodes in the beginning of v.39 is a typical Lukan word.[3] It is often expletive (11:7, 8; 15:18, 20; 17:19; Acts 8:27; 9:39; 10:13, 20, 23 etc.); but in other cases it suggests an immediate response to an event or to a challenge (Luke 4:29; 5:28; 6:8; Acts 5:6; 9:18; 22:16). Especially noteworthy are Luke 4:39 and 5:25 where ἀναστάς is connected

---

[1] A synopsis of the various reconstructions can be found in Brown 1977, 248f.

[2] I am particularly indebted for several insights developed in the present paper to lively discussions with Prof. B. Hubsch, Professor at the Institut Supérieur de Théologie de Madagascar and at the Institut Catholique de Lyon.

[3] Used 36 times in Luke-Acts; cf. Jeremias 1980, 55; Hawkins 1909, 35f.

with παραχρῆμα as here in 1:39 it is qualified by the synonymous μετὰ σπουδῆς.

Ἐν ταῖς ἡμέραις ταύταις is also typical of Luke,[4] The phrase can connote a vague time setting (Luke 6:12; Acts 6:1) or it can indicate a precise chronological connection (Luke 23:7; 24:18) and mean "precisely at that time." In Acts 1:15 and 11:27 as in Luke 1:39, the phrase is used by way of transition to form a contextual link. In Luke 1:39 the translation of GNB ("soon afterwards") or of the NAB ("thereupon") conveys the mood of the text better than the NEB ("about that time"), the NIV ("at that time") or the RSV/NRSV ("in those days"): Luke indicates very specifically that Mary started "with haste". This "haste" emphasises the consequent dependence of the Visitation upon the Annunciation.

The meaning of this "haste" has been explained in different ways. The rhetorical explanation of Ambrose of Milan is well known: "*quasi laeta pro voto, religiosa pro officio, festina pro gaudio*": Mary exhibits a joyful eagerness to see her relative, a pious readiness to help and a hurry to share in the common joy.[5] This psychologising exegesis fails to take the context into account. In Luke-Acts, "haste" characterizes a response to an announcement or a call: Zacchaeus "hastens" to come down from the tree in answer to Jesus' call (Luke 19:5f.); in Acts 22:18, Paul is invited to leave Jerusalem "in haste" to undertake his particular vocation to the Nations. Closely related to our context is the "haste" of the shepherds in Luke 2:16 to go and verify the "sign", given by the angel, of the child in the manger (2:12). There is a definite parallelism with the haste of Mary. She too has been given the sign, by an angel, of the pregnancy of Elizabeth. Like the shepherds, she hurries to respond in "obedience to the plan revealed to her by the angel, a plan which included the pregnancy of Elizabeth (1:36-37)."[6] This haste should not "be used to analyse Mary's psychology. It suggests the proper reaction to the heavenly sign that has just been given."[7]

The text that follows continues the close connection with the previous pericope.

---

[4] Cf. Jeremias 1980, 55: "occurs only in the Lukan double work: four times in the Gospel and thrice in the Acts."

[5] Quoted by Lagrange 1948, 41. See other psychological explanations listed in Brown 1977, 331 and Schürmann 1982, 66.

[6] Brown 1977, 331; Karris 1991, 681; Marshall 1978, 80: "Mary's haste reflects her obedience to the angelic message."

[7] Fitzmyer 1981, 362. We leave aside the question of whether σπουδή means actually haste or "a serious mood of mind" as suggested by Hospodar 1956.

The greeting of Elizabeth in v. 42 echoes the angel's words in vv. 28-33:

| 1:42 | 1:28-33 |
|---|---|
| Blessed... | Favored one... |
| the fruit of your womb | You will conceive in your womb |

while her last word recalls Mary's final response to the angel:

| 1:45 | 1:38 |
|---|---|
| she who believed... | the servant |
| there will be fulfilment | let it be |
| of the things said | according to your word |
| by the Lord | ... of the Lord |

It is true that the wording is different and that the parallelism is more thematic than verbal. Yet, as Schürmann says: "Gehört die Szenen mit der vorigen ... eng zusammen."[8]

As for the Song of Mary, it is solidly anchored in the context through v. 48, commonly accepted as a Lukan addition to an existing hymn. The "low estate" of the "handmaid" refers explicitly to v. 38 and the "blessing of all generations" echoes v. 45.

Apart from v. 48, the style[9] as well as the contents of the Magnificat suggest a distinct origin, more likely Judaeo-Christian[10] than Jewish[11] or Baptist.[12] R. E. Brown remarks that "without the Magnificat, vv. 39-45. 56 cease to be so clearly an autonomous scene and can be regarded as an epilogue of the annunciation of Mary."[13] He suggests that the parallel of the two annunciations to Zechariah and to

---

[8] Schürmann 1982, 64; cf. Evans 1990, 169. E. Burrows 1940, 47 rightly remarks that the words of Elizabeth can be considered either as an imitation or a commentary of the angel's greeting.

[9] Jeremias 1980, 60 attributes v. 48 to Lukan redaction. Except 2 Cor 7:11, ἰδοὺ γάρ occurs only in the Lukan double work (Luke 1:44, 48; 2:10; 6:23; 17:21; Acts 9:11) and so also ἀπὸ τοῦ νῦν (Luke 1:48; 5:10; 12:52; 22:18, 69; Acts 18:6). 2 Cor 5:16 constitutes the only exception mentioned by Jeremias (But see also John 8:11). Apart from v. 48, Jeremias' stylistic analysis classifies the entire text of the Magnificat as "traditional" (60-63) and concludes: "Das Magnificat läßt an keiner Stelle mit Sicherheit einen Eingriff der Redaktion erkennen." Yet note the dissenting view of Marshall 1978, 83 and the reserved opinion of Schürmann 1982, 74, 77. The latter prefers to see in vv. 51-55 a secondary generalisation of the personal feelings expressed by Mary in the first part of the canticle.

[10] Cf. Jones 1968, 28.

[11] As suggested by Gunkel, Spitta, Klostermann, Bultmann, Hahn, Winter.

[12] According to the views of Lohmeyer, Rengstorf, Kraeling, Dibelius, Vielhauer, Kümmel.

[13] Brown 1977, 339.

Mary be extended to the "epilogue" in which Elizabeth reflects on the favour she has received (1:24f.) and proclaims the grace conferred on Mary the believer (vv.39-45). The addition of the canticle would belong to a latter stage, yet also Lukan.[14] Whichever may be the case, the present composition must be accounted for as it is, all the more so if it is specifically Lukan. According to Brown, Luke would have "sacrificed some of the perfect balance of his diptych construction in order to strengthen the theological message of the scene."[15] We have now to see what this "theological message" was and whether by sacrificing a "perfect balance" Luke did not achieve another balance.

## 2. An Integrated Structure (Luke 1:26-56)

Once we see the annunciation to Mary and the visit to Elizabeth as linked together to form a unit, we can examine the structure of this unit.

### 2.1. A Word Event

Note first that the narrative focuses on the mutual greeting of the two women. Mary greets her cousin (1:46) and is greeted by her (vv. 44f.). Mary responds to Elizabeth's greeting by a song (vv. 46-55). The title of "visitation" often given to the episode is in fact misleading. First, it makes Mary the single main character of the story whereas the role of Elizabeth is equally important. Secondly, it supposes that the point of the story resides in the visit of Mary with her relative, whereas the visit is just alluded to in a short concluding verse, totally void of any descriptive element (v. 56). Indeed, the way the pericope concludes might even give the impression that Mary had left by the time of the delivery. It is as though the whole arduous journey from Nazareth to the highlands of Judea had been undertaken simply for the exchange of blessings between the two women. This observation eliminates any psychologizing, moralizing or anecdotal interpretation. The purpose of the narrative is not to emphasize the charity of Mary, rushing to the help of her pregnant cousin. The narrative intends to bring the two expectant mothers face to face, interpreting for each other, and for the reader, the significance of what happened to them. The whole burden of the pericope lies on the two women exchanging their faith percep-

---

[14] Brown 1977, 339f.
[15] Brown 1977, 339.

tion. The narrative goes beyond the level of the mere event to its faith contents, beyond the story of the pregnancies to the revelation imparted to the protagonists. What happens to the women becomes a word event. The transcendent ῥῆμα communicated by the angel (1:38) now becomes a dialogue between two daughters of Israel. The episode of the "visitation" is related to that annunciation as the earthly confession of faith to the heavenly revelation.[16]

## 2.2. A Revelation

Since Mary had already received her revelation from the angel in Nazareth, it is now Elizabeth's turn to receive a message from on high. As seen above, it would be wrong to make vv. 39-40 the key to the interpretation of the passage. More significant is the double divine intervention reported in v. 41:

(a) "The child leaped in her womb": John the prophet begins his ministry in which he will announce the good news (cf.3:10) of the coming of the "greater One" (3:16).

(b) Elizabeth is "filled with the Holy Spirit": she too becomes a prophetess. In Gen 25:22 Rebecca had been unable to understand the movement of her children in her womb. But now the time has come when the Spirit will teach the faithful from within (cf. Luke 12:12) in order to make them witnesses (Luke 24:49; Acts 1:8; 2:4; 4:8, etc.). The babe and Elizabeth anticipate the community of the "little ones" to whom has been revealed the mystery of the Son, a mystery hidden from those who go only by science and wisdom (Luke 10:21f.). Elizabeth has received the divine revelation that enables her to transcend the mere external facts, to have access to faith and, in the Spirit, to become a prophetic witness to the advent of the "Lord."

## 2.3. The Public Confession (vv. 42-45)

In the power of the Spirit, Elizabeth "cried with a loud voice" (v. 42). Crying with a loud voice "may be a formal mark of inspired utterance (Mark 9:24; John 1:15; 7:28,37; Rom 8:15; 9:27; Gal 4:6) or joyful praise (1 Chr 16:4f.; Ps 66:1; Isa 40:9) or simply public proclamation,"[17] says Marshall, who thinks that the first two senses are present here. But the third meaning need not be excluded. Elizabeth had kept

---

[16] Bengel 1855, 212f. thinks that the conception of Jesus would have taken place at the time of the Visitation: thus would Jesus be really of Juda. Surprising as it may be, this conjecture brings our attention to the fact that the Annunciation story does not report in conclusion that Mary conceived (in contrast with 1:24). The whole burden of the text consists in the Word, communicated by the angel, received in faith by Mary and shared with Elizabeth: "Le récit de l'annonce à Marie se passe tout en parole ... (Marie) passe de la parole de l'ange qu'elle accepte à la parole de sa cousine" (Delorme, 1991, 193).

[17] Marshall 1978, 81.

secret what the Lord had done for her (1:24f.). Now the silence is broken: the mystery realised in the silence of the annunciation is now made manifest.

But which kind of "inspired utterance" does Elizabeth express? From the point of view of its literary form, Elizabeth's pronouncement is complex. For Plummer, the words form a canticle made of two stanzas (vv. 42f.; 44f.) each stanza having two distichs.[18] R. E. Brown also speaks of "a canticle of praise" in "hymnic form."[19] But Lagrange had early on expressed reservations.[20] Closer analysis shows that, after "the poetical blessing, the text turns to prose with the rhetorical question of v. 43 and the summary of v. 44 (resuming v. 41) ... Then again, in v. 45, the poetical inspiration returns with a fine macarism."[21] The revelation received is framed by a blessing and a macarism. The blessing refers to Mary's motherhood; the macarism concerns the faith of the πιστεύσασα. The former pertains to the order of God-given fecundity (cf. Gen 1:22, 28; 5:2; 17:16; 24:60, etc.); the latter evokes the messianic happiness granted to those who have received the Good News (cf. Isa 40:9ff.; 61:1ff.; 52:7ff.; Luke 6:20ff.; 10:23; 11:27). Moving from the one to the other, there is a climactic construction and the revelation made to Elizabeth that Mary's child is "the Lord" forms the transition between the two. Because Mary is the mother of the Lord and because she accepts it in faith, the ancient blessing of motherhood turns into the eschatological blessedness of those who have opened their hearts and lives to God's word. The parallelism with 11:27f. is obvious. Both passages of Luke, 1:42-45 and 11:27f., express the double level of Mary's relationship with Jesus or, more deeply, the dialectic relationship between event and word in the Gospel. Through Elizabeth's words the basic Gospel insight expressed in Luke 11:27f. is rooted in the very origins of Jesus himself.[22]

In the acclamation of Elizabeth, the initial blessing and the concluding macarism frame a confession of faith. For the first time, the gift of the Spirit leads to the confession of Jesus' lordship (cf. 1 Cor 12:3; Rom 10:9). "Elizabeth's words are much

---

[18] Plummer 1986, 27.

[19] Brown 1977, 333, 342. J. McHugh 1975, 71 would even suggest that the words of Elisabeth could have been already "a prayer commonly used by Christians of the day to the mother of Jesus": the Catholic Hail Mary would go back to the early Church!

[20] Lagrange 1948, 42f.: "les distiques de la première strophe seraient beaucoup trop courts;" cf. Evans 1990, 72, who finds that "Plummer's arrangement ... is not convincing."

[21] Bovon 1989, 86. See a similar opinion of Fitzmyer 1981, 358.

[22] Another parallel can be found in the way in which Luke links Jesus' hymn of jubilation in 10:21f. (= Matt 11:25ff) with the macarism of the disciples (Luke 10:23f. =Matt 13:16f.). In Mark's construction, the "revelation" to the little ones "confessed" (ἐξομολογοῦμαι) leads to a call to discipleship. In Luke, the outcome of the confessed revelation will be the blessedness of the disciples who have seen and heard. To Elizabeth and Mary already it had been given to "hear", and to the shepherds (Luke 2:15f.) and Simeon (2:30) were given the eyes to see.

more than the return of a greeting; they are also confession of faith and interpretation of an event. The first acknowledgement of Christ here is totally inspired by the Spirit (cf. 1 Cor 12:2): it leads to an homologesis inviting everybody to commitment."[23]

## 2.4. Hymn and Celebration (vv. 46-55)

Stylistically, Mary's response is more homogeneous than the pronouncement of Elizabeth. It is a poetical canticle, more specifically a hymn of praise.

Though the Magnificat may have come from a different setting, it is well integrated into the present redaction of the text.[24] In the vast perspectives it evokes and in the strong socio-political overtones it contains, the song of Mary seems to go beyond the humble confines of a village girl's pregnancy. But the context had already enlarged the perspectives beyond those confines: a word event underlay the mere fact of begetting. Mary was not just to become a mother but the mother of the "Lord." Her true beatitude was due to her faith that accepted the fulfilment of the Lord's words. It was to be a messianic blessedness, and therefore her story, her joy and the praise she deserved assumed the grander dimensions of God's plan in time, space and human society:

• *in time*: on the one hand, the perspectives extend to "all the generations" (v. 48) and "for ever" (v. 55); towards the past, they encompass "the dealings of God, from the time of Abraham, with Israel, his poor Servant."[25]

• *in space*: centred on the seed of Abraham (v. 55), the vision extends to "all who fear him" (v. 50): "the text looks beyond the boundaries of the Jewish people to the Nations that will accept the Gospel (cf. Acts 10:35)."[26]

• *in human society*: Mary becomes the type of the "poor", the "lowly", the "hungry" whom God's messianic intervention is going to uplift and to fill with good things, while their opponents are cast down and sent away empty.

By thus extending the perspectives, the song of Mary, in good hymnic tradition, gives fuller meaning to the word event underlying the historical fact. Dupont has compared the function of the Magnificat to "that of the chorus in the classic tragedies which suspended the unfolding of the action, so as to score the significance of

---

[23] Schürmann 1982, 67.

[24] On the links between the Magnificat and its context in the present redaction, see Delorme 1991, 190f.

[25] Lohfink 1990, 19. See pp. 17-19 for the discussion on the meaning of the stories in Mary's canticle. But Lohfink may be too rigid in restricting the references to the past of Israel in a narrow sense excluding the Gentiles. Israel's sense of election is not basically exclusivistic. See also Delorme 1991, 198f., 242.

[26] Bovon 1989, 89; pace Lohfink 1990, 21f.

what happens ... Unnecessary from the point of view of the development of the plot, it has a different function: that of clarifying the meaning of the event which has just been narrated."[27]

In the song of Mary, the word event which has been revealed and confessed through Elizabeth is now celebrated in a celebration which, following the biblical line, does not become atemporal or purely archetypical but is deeply rooted in the concrete history of a struggling people.

## 2.5. An Integrated Structure

Can we better define the integrated structure formed by the annunciation stories to Zechariah and Mary and the encounter of the two mothers? In a passing observation that deserves further analysis, B. Standaert detects in the Lukan work the application of the rhetorics of Greek drama: "The narrative starts in two different ways, in two separate scenes, apparently disconnected, and the circumstances ... lead to a third stage where the double plots cross each other and find a denouement in the encounter."[28] This kind of structure in which two annunciations or revelations are linked by an encounter can be found in the story of the centurion Cornelius in Acts 10-11, in the vocation of Paul in Acts 9, in the meeting of Philip with the Ethiopian minister in Acts 8, in the episode of Simeon and Anna in Luke 2 and in the resurrection at Nain in Luke 7.[29]

An important element of the denouement (λύσις) is the recognition or discovery (ἀναγνώρισις) in which, for better (comedy) or for worse (tragedy), the parties recognize each other, like Orestes or Iphigenia.[30]

This is also the plot of Luke 1. First Zechariah and Elizabeth, but most prominently John the Baptist, appear on the scene. But it is in the secret of a heavenly annunciation, and the identity of John remains hidden: Zechariah is "reduced to silence and unable to speak" and Elizabeth "hides herself." Then the scene shifts to Nazareth where Mary receives the promise of the birth of a child. But again nothing is manifested outwardly: even the text does not mention explicitly that Mary became pregnant. It all remains within the silence of God and of Mary's secret acceptance of his word. The inspired shout of Elizabeth reveals the secret, and now, in the encounter of the two women, the "discovery", the double ἀναγνώρισις takes place. John will be the prophet recognizing the Lord and pointing to him; the child of Mary will be the Lord himself.

---

[27] Dupont 1985, 957.
[28] Standaert 1985, 332.
[29] Standaert 1985, 333.
[30] Aristotle, *De Poetica*, 11.

It remains for the chorus to sing the significance of what happens through the song of Mary. This choral function of the Magnificat could explain the vagueness of its attribution. The textual problem concerning the attribution of the song is well known.[31] In spite of "an overwhelming preponderance of evidence,"[32] assigning the song to Mary, the antiquity of the few but very ancient versions and patristic witnesses mentioning rather Elizabeth remains impressive. Indeed the Committee responsible for the UBS edition of the New Testament acknowledges a sympathy "to the supposition that perhaps neither name was present in the original text."[33] This hypothesis would correspond quite well with the anonymous and generic character of the chorus in Greek tragedy. Nonetheless, even if the attribution to Mary is maintained, the mere mention of "Mary" as subject without any descriptive note stands in sharp contrast to the elaborate introduction to Elizabeth's speech. By contrast, the individuality of Mary seems to disappear. She becomes simply the voice of the believing community associated to the mystery now taking place. This was in fact the role of the ancient chorus, to link the audience to the tragedy.

We may therefore trace in Luke 1:26-56 the basic elements of plot, denouement and recognition, punctuated by a choral song. But more fundamental than this literary structure is the underlying theological pattern. In terms of literary criticism, the "recognition" (of Jesus as Lord) takes place by the operation of a *deus ex machina* ("filled with the Holy Spirit"). But from the point of view of Luke, the Spirit is not an outward adjuvant, a heavenly artifice supplying the deficiencies of the plot. He is the real protagonist of the entire double work. The literary "recognition" is indeed a "revelation." It is not Elizabeth who discovers the truth but the Spirit himself who manifests the underlying reality. Elizabeth receives this revelation and proclaims it in a confession; the choral song of Mary responds to it in hymnic celebration.

## 3. General Structure of Luke 1-2

This pattern of revelation, confession and celebration is solidly embedded in Lukan theology and literary composition. Thus, in Acts 2, the coming of the Spirit in vv. 1-3 is followed by the preaching of Peter (vv. 14-36), resulting in the emergence of a community characterised by sharing and the celebration of the Temple cult, of the breaking of the bread, of prayer and praise (vv. 42-46).[34] Again in Acts 3-4, the healing of the paralytic and the subsequent trial by the Sanhedrin are the occasion

---

[31] From the time of A. von Harnack 1931; see bibliography on the debate in Marshall 1978, 79; McHugh 1975, 445; Laurentin 1982, 13-22.

[32] Metzger et al. 1971, 130.

[33] Metzger et al. 1971, 131.

[34] Cf. Legrand 1982, 193-209.

of another double proclamation of the Gospel (3:12-16; 4:8-12). This also results in the multiple prayer of thanksgiving of the paralytic himself (3:8f.) and of the people (4:21), and concludes with the hymn of the community (4:24-30). Later on, the entangled concentration of visions of Acts 10 gives Peter the opportunity to evangelize Cornelius (10:24-43). The outcome will be the coming of the Spirit opening the mouth of "pagan nations" to "speak in tongues extolling God" (10:44-46).

In the third Gospel, apart from the Infancy Narratives, the motive of the celebration appears more as a theme than as a structural element. "Giving glory to God" is the frequent conclusion of Lukan pericopae (5:25f.; 7:16; 13:13; 18:43). The miracle of the Ten Lepers is quite revealing. The saving action has failed to reach its purpose if it does not result in praise of God: "rendering glory to God" is the sign of genuine faith (17:15, 18). The stress on "joy" in Luke 15 should also be noted. In the parable of the "prodigal child", the final point is not just the generosity of the father or the jealousy of the son. Rather, it consists in the extravagant celebration organised for the return of the spendthrift. In fact, of the 22 verses of the parable (15:11-32), a full eleven (vv. 22-32) deal with the final celebration and its repercussions.

It is in the Infancy narratives that the structure Revelation-Proclaimed Confession-Celebration appears the most clearly. After the sequence which we have just analysed, the same basic structure recurs in the subsequent pericopae. In the account of the birth of the Baptist (1:57-79), great stress is laid in the manifestation of the name of John (vv. 59-63) after the event of the birth is reported in vv. 57f. The name of John is highlighted. It had constituted the opening statement of the angel's message in 1:13.[35] The very name ("the Lord has given grace") implies that, with the birth of the child, God's saving action was to begin. This is further developed in the following verses (1:16f.).[36] The manifestation of the name is also significant. The revelatory and prophetical character of this proclamation of the name by both parents is brought out by the fact that Elizabeth could not have come to know of this name from Zechariah since "he had been silent and unable to speak" (v. 20): the

---

[35] A heaven-imposed name "… implies that the child will have a role in the drama of God's salvation" (Fitzmyer 1981, 325).

[36] All commentators would not agree that Luke presupposed the etymological meaning of the name Johannan. For Lagrange 1948, 16 "le nom symbolise le rôle de Jean ou le dessein de Dieu." But Bovon 1989, 54, thinks that "wahrscheinlich hat die Etymologie … in der ersten Überlieferung der Tradition mitgeklungen … Für Lukas spielt sie keine Rolle mehr." Brown, while suspicious of overly elaborate etymological constructions in the Lukan Infancy narrative (against Laurentin 1982, 209f.) notes that, in general in the Bible, "the name is given before birth to signify that God has a special role for the child" (1977, 272).

context suggests that it was through revelation that she came to know of the name.[37] The narrative structure emphasizes the name giving and makes the event such a divine manifestation that "fear came on all their neighbours" and that all who heard said: "What then will the child be?" (vv. 65f.). Whichever may have been the etymological significance Luke perceived or wanted the reader to perceive in the name of John, Luke viewed the giving of the name to the child as a portent of what the child would be. For him, the episode is a *rhema* to be "laid up in the heart" (v. 66).

The revelation and proclamation of the name is followed by a choral doxology, intoned by Zechariah (1:64). It is echoed in the cry of wonderment of the people (1:65f.) and solemnly developed in the Benedictus, explicitly referred to as a "prophecy" (v. 67).

In the subsequent pericope of Jesus' birth, there is a double celebration, one in heaven by the angelic chorus and then on earth by the shepherds. After the event has been narrated (2:1-7), a revelation is given by the angels (2:8-12) accompanied by an angelic doxology (2:13f.). Then, in close parallelism to Mary's visit to Elizabeth, the shepherds "hasten" to see and verify the angelic revelation and relay it in a human proclamation (vv. 15-18).[38] The meditative prayer of Mary and the singing of God's glory conclude the section (vv. 19f.).

Finally, the episode of the Presentation of Jesus in the Temple offers one of the most explicit examples of the Lukan pattern. The narrative is reduced to its minimum in 2:22ff. There follows a double mention of the Holy Spirit and the use of the technical term for divine revelation and communication (κεχρηματισμένον: cf. Matt 2:12, 22; Acts 10:22; Heb 8:5; 11:7; cf. Jer 25:30; 31:2; Job 40:8) to introduce the revelation of "Christ the Lord" (vv. 25-28). The canticle of Simeon will be the first reaction. The celebration (vv. 29-32) anticipates the prophetical proclamation (vv. 34f.), but *logos* and *hymnos* belong together, according to the typical Lukan pattern.

In this episode of the Presentation, commentators are inclined to perceive a complex process of tradition and redaction, or of successive levels of Lukan redaction.[39] It is all the more significant therefore that the final stage of Lukan composition was accomplished in such a way that, out of composite "material of different origins,"[40] there resulted a typical sequence of revelation, celebration and prophetical procla-

---

[37] Plummer 1986, 36 suggests that Zechariah would have told Elisabeth in writing of the angelic intervention in the Temple. But this historicising interpretation misses the trend of the narrative. The style of the passage emphasizes the marvellous intervention of God in the events and the theological context stresses the prophetical inspiration of the characters, especially of Elizabeth (cf. 1:41).

[38] Cf. Legrand 1968, 176-81.

[39] Brown 1977, 446 suggests that the *Nunc Dimittis* belongs to a "second stage of Lukan composition in which the canticles were added."

[40] Brown 1977, 447.

mation.

This proposal for the structure explains the significance of the reference to Anna in vv. 36-38. In this puzzling narrative the heroin does not do anything and does not in any apparent way contribute to the development of the story. She is a "prophetess" (2:36) but she utters no oracles. Such a lengthy account of her old age, widowhood, Temple piety would normally prepare the reader for a description either of the rewards of her virtue or of the scandal of undeserved trials. But she is only there, just "at that time", to "praise God" and "speak of him to those who were looking for the redemption of Jerusalem" (v. 38). It has been remarked that Anna, pious and poor widow, is a typical representative of "the *anawim* of the Infancy narratives ... so close to the Jerusalem community of Acts."[41] It has also been observed that Luke "pairs off his *dramatis personae* in terms of men and women," as he does also for Zechariah and Elizabeth, Naaman and the widow of Sarepta (4:25f.), Simon and the sinful woman (7:36-50).[42] By so doing he demonstrates the fulfilment of the prophecy of Joel 3:1f. and of the pentecostal event (Acts 2:17): "Your sons and daughters will prophecy."[43] All this is true. But there remains the apparently incomplete narrative in which a lengthy preparation tapers into a mere presence to "praise God publicly" (ἀνθωμολογεῖτο) and "to speak of him." The indeterminacy of the complement "of him" (is it God or Jesus?) leaves the impression that the verb is more important than the complement. Anna is there to "praise" and "to speak." We think again of the Greek chorus and its role of explaining and singing rather than contributing to the action. We think also of "word and prayer", the two main aspects of the prophetical ministry according to Acts 6:4. Note also that Anna addresses "those who were looking for the redemption of Jerusalem", thus pairing with Simeon who was "looking for the consolation of Israel" (2:25). All this suggests a triple choral ring around the child brought to the Temple by his parents. First, there are the two choregoi, Simeon and Anna, in dialogue of *logos* and *hymnos*. Then, around them, appears the circle of those who looked "for the redemption of Israel." Finally, the third circle is made of the believers, readers of the Gospel, invited to join in the celebration of the mystery revealed and announced.

The sequence revelation-confession-celebration seems to be a recurring feature of the Infancy narrative. Can it be taken as a basic structural principle for the entire Lukan Genesis? It is only in the final episode of Jesus in the Temple that it does not appear. Shall we therefore consider that Luke 1-2 forms a kind of drama in four acts (I. The Annunciations; II. A first Birth; III. A second Birth; IV. In the Temple) ending with an "episode" (Jesus in the Temple at the age of twelve)?

---

[41] Brown 1977, 466.

[42] Fitzmyer 1981, 423.

[43] Brown 1977, 466.

A disadvantage of this organisation of the text is its departure from the usually accepted construction based on the obvious parallelism of the two infancies. But the fact remains that the construction in parallelism, fairly rigorous in the diptych of the Annunciation, is less close for the story of the births and circumcisions, and vanishes completely in the last two scenes in the Temple in Luke 2:22-38. The parallel structure is indeed an element but not the ultimate principle of composition of Luke 1-2. Let us say rather that, within the formal framework of a parallelism, Luke's thought moves along the lines of his basic theological insight. Parallelism provides a general pattern but it is freely manipulated to express the Christian response to the events in word and prayer. By a literary device recalling the Greek chorus, Luke introduces a dialogue of confession and praise. Under the internal pressure of this theological element the parallelism develops quite a few fissures. From the view point of source criticism, these homologetical and hymnal additions might appear as "secondary" or "complementary." But, in the Lukan perspective, this faith response was ultimately the heart of the matter. Events become Christ events only when transformed into *logos*, *homologesis* and *hymnos*, by the divine revelation and the faith of the participants.

## 4. The General Context of Luke-Acts

We have seen above that the clearest parallels to the construction of Luke 1:5-56 can be found in Acts. But the Infancy story represents the most rigorous application of the pattern. In the main body of the Gospel of Luke, the linking of revelation, confession and celebration provides more a pervading theme than a structural principle. The conclusion is therefore that the successive scenes of Luke 1-2, at least in their present form, must have been written at the end of the lengthy process of composition of the double work. They represent the clear formulation of a trend of thought which was progressively taking shape in the mind of the author as he proceeded with the composition of his work. As is frequently the case in writing books, the basic intuition grows in precision as the work progresses. The preface written in a final stage presents the vision in its totality which had clearly dominated the process from the beginning. The structure found in Luke 1-2 provides the author's key to the understanding of the Christ event and of the life of the Church. Far from being a heterogeneous addition, the first chapters constitute the ultimate expression of the Lukan outlook.[44]

In this global context, the double pericope of the Annunciation and of the Visitation plays the role of anticipatory episode. If the Annunciation represents the fun-

---

[44] See bibliography and discussion in Legrand 1981, 25-29.

damental revelation that provides the basic key for an understanding of the Christ event,[45] the encounter of the two mothers in the "Visitation" constitutes the primordial response of faith to that revelation. In Luke 1:26-38, it was God who through the angel unveiled his plan and revealed his Son; Mary was largely passive, an ear to listen and a will to obey. But v. 39 sets things and people in motion. The "handmaid" "arises" and "goes"; she moves to the hill country, visits her relative and sings a stirring if not outright revolutionary poem. Elizabeth, whom Mary meets, is equally active. So also the babe in her womb as it leaps for joy. This manifold activity contrasts sharply with the hieratic, divine, quasi-monologue of the previous episode, broken only by Mary's submissive query and answer in 1:34, 38. If the Annunciation unfolds in the vertical line of the descent of God's message to the world, the scene of the encounter follows the horizontal course of human interaction. Apocalypse has entered history.

Thus, after the descent of the Spirit on Jesus at the baptism (Luke 3:22), Jesus goes to Galilee (4:14), announces the Good News (4:16-21) and stirs the proverbial hornets' nest among the audience (4:22-30). Thus again, in Acts 2, the vertical descent of the Spirit sends the apostles into the streets to encounter the crowds. That same Spirit creates a new community characterised by an active response of worship and sharing. These pericopae of Luke 4 and Acts 2 have been recognised as "programmatic accounts"[46] summarizing the whole ministry of Jesus and of his apostles. But it is not only the course of the ministry which is foreshadowed in these inaugural episodes; it is the God-given power of the Spirit which is manifested. Luke 4 and Acts 2 not only constitute an epitome of the "growth of the Word", they disclose the power abiding in this Word. More than programmatic, they are revelatory, "apocalyptic" in the sense in which they unveil the eschatological "mystery of (God's) will ... the immeasurable greatness of his power" (cf. Eph 1:9, 19) underlying the human course of Jesus' and of the apostles' mission.

This is also the meaning of the twin episode formed by Luke 1:26-56. It reports the divine revelation of Jesus, Son of God and Lord, to Mary and Elizabeth and their response in confession and celebration. The revelation of the Messiah, Son of God coming in the power of the Spirit (Luke 1:35) to Mary is the fundamental apocalypse unveiling the ultimate divine reality abiding in Jesus and his words. The prophetic responses of Mary and Elizabeth become the type of the evangelical activity that the Gospels and the Acts will describe. On the one hand, the central mystery of the Lord's eschatological action is manifested; on the other hand, the profile is already sketched of the human mediations that will prolong the divine deed on

---

[45] Concerning apocalyptic trends in Luke's Infancy narrative, see F. Kattenbusch 1930; F. Neirynck 1959; Schürmann 1982, 23f.; Legrand 1981, 86f., 134-40, 347-51.

[46] Karris 1991, 689.

earth.[47] The narrative thus fulfils the Lucan purpose of "relating the on-going history of the world, in which the Christ event was staged, with the new world of God which Christ brought."[48] The "new world of God": it is the Son of God coming in the power of the Spirit and revealed to Mary; "the on-going history of the world": it is Nazareth and the journey to the hill country, the small "cities" and the country "houses", the homely, unpretentious stories of pregnancies, of visits between relatives, of women's small talk, of childbirth and impending motherhood. All of this is transfigured by a faith expressed in confession and prayer, as the whole world listens in, making the "Visitation" a proto-epiphany.

A final observation. To the pattern Revelation-Confession-Celebration, conversion should normally have been added. Either put in terms of μετανοεῖν/μετάνοια (Luke 9+5; Acts 5+6) or of ἐπιστρέφειν/ἐπιστροφή (in the religious sense Luke 4; Acts 9+1), conversion is an important Lukan theme. This conversion may have radical social implications as shown in the conversion of Zachaeus (Luke 19:8), in the social programme of John the Baptist (Luke 3:10-14) or of the early communities (Acts 2:44f.; 4:32-35). The full Lukan pattern would then seem to be: Revelation-Conversion-Confession-Revolution-Celebration. But there is no conversion explicitly mentioned in Luke 1. The reason is simply that there was no need for it. From the outset, Elizabeth is presented as "righteous before God, living blamelessly according to the commandments and the regulations of the Lord" (Luke 1:6). As for Mary, if no such moral righteousness is predicated of her,[49] her whole picture is of a perfectly transparent faith in God's word (Luke 1:38). J. Dupont has shown that, in the Acts, the Christian proclamation can be addressed to three kinds of audience: to the Jerusalem Jews who bear the responsibility for the crucifixion, or to the Gentiles guilty of idolatry, but also to a third category of honest and decent people, like Cornelius, "a devout man who feared God" (Acts 10:2) or to the Jews of Pisidian Antioch who could in no way bear the responsibility of the Jerusalem events (Acts 13:27ff.). From these latter, faith alone was required (13:38).[50] Mary and Elizabeth belong to this group. Dupont insists that a diffuse sense of sin must have moved even the righteous figures of the Acts and that "the call to faith always implies a sense of sin and a desire for forgiveness."[51] He may have been too systematic.[52] For Elizabeth, her sense of ὄνειδος (1:25) and for Mary her ταπείνωσις (1:48) played the role of openness to God's action that repentance might have

---

[47] Cf. Bovon 1974, 23-39.

[48] Flender 1967, 164.

[49] For an analysis and an explanation of this dissymmetry, see Legrand 1981, 67-72.

[50] Cf. Dupont 1967, 440f.

[51] Dupont 1967a, 461.

[52] As remarked by Bovon 1978, 295.

played for others. "Who exalt themselves will be humbled and all who humble themselves will be exalted" (Luke 18:14), said Jesus as the conclusion of the parable of the Publican. The song of Mary had already voiced the same sentiment: "He has put down the mighty ... exalted the lowly" (1:52).

Unlike Zacchaeus, neither Mary nor Elizabeth had any wealth to divide. But they did express the joy of the poor in welcoming a Lord who would take away the "disgrace" of humiliated women (1:25), a Saviour who would embrace the cause of the lowly and hungry (1:52f.). The social upheaval described in the Song of Mary is also "the world of God"[53] The house setting was different but the joy is the same as in the case of Zacchaeus: "Today salvation has come to this house" (Luke 19:9). This exclamation of joy could replace the misleading title of "Visitation" given to the episode of the first manifestation of the "Lord" to Elizabeth.

Far from being a "supplement" or a "complement", the Visitation constitutes the "linchpin from both a literary and theological point of view of the narrative of the conceptions and births of John and Jesus in parallel."[54] But its full meaning appears only if it is seen in relationship with the Annunciation. Both pericopae constitute together a single word-event. In the Annunciation the saving Word manifests itself in its vertical "apocalyptic" or revelatory form; in the Visitation, the same Word unfolds itself horizontally and finds human expression in the response of a faith shared, confessed and celebrated.

From the literary point of view, the "revelation" and "celebration" play a role similar to that of the "discovery" and of the "chorus" in Greek dramaturgy. But a major difference consists precisely in that, for Luke, the "discovery" is "revelation", a gift of God who is the real protagonist of the story. Therefore the outcome is not the Greek "tragic pleasure which comes from pity and fear"[55] but the evangelical "joy" born of confidence in "God the Saviour" (Luke 1:47).

We reach here the heart of Lukan rhetoric and theology. The pattern of revelation-confession-celebration underlies the composition of the Infancy narratives and will often recur in the Lukan work. It underlies Luke's theological perception of salvation history as the "growth" of the *Logos* (cf. Acts 6:7; 12:24; 19:20), "sent", "announced as Good News" (Acts 10:37) and "demonstrated" (Acts 2:22) by Jesus, confessed, proclaimed, celebrated and lived in the Church (Acts 2:37-47). Ultimately the twin episode of the Annunciation and of the Visitation is indeed the "linchpin from both a literary and theological point of view" not only of the Infancy story but of the Lukan work as a whole.

---

[53] Cf. Flender 1967, 164; Lohfink 1990, 13; R. A. Horsley 1989, 107-23. Surprisingly the Magnificat is not studied in the basic study of B. J. Degenhardt 1965.

[54] Evans 1990, 168.

[55] Aristotle, *De Poetica*, 14.

# Bibliography

Bengel, J. A. 1855: *Gnomon Novi Testamenti*, Tübingen: Fues [3]1855.

Bovon, F. 1974: "L'importance des médiations dans le projet théologique de Luc", in: *NTS* 21 (1974) 23-39.

— 1978: *Luc le Théologien. Vingt Cinq Ans de Recherches (1959-1975)*, Neuchâtel: Delachaux et Niestlé 1978.

— 1989: *Das Evangelium nach Lukas (Lukas 1,1-9,50)* (EKK III/1), Zürich/Neukirchen-Vluyn: Benziger/Neukirchener Verlag 1989.

Brown, R. E. 1977: *The Birth of the Messiah*, London: Chapman 1977.

Burrows, E. 1940: *The Gospel of Infancy*, London: Burns and Oates 1940.

Degenhardt, B. J. 1965: *Lukas Evangelist der Armen*, Stuttgart: Katholisches Bibelwerk 1965.

Delorme, J. 1991: *Au Risque de la Parole*, Paris: Seuil 1991.

Dupont. J. 1967: "Repentir et Conversion d'après les Actes des Apôtres", in: idem, *Études sur les Actes des Apôtres* (LeDiv 45), Paris: Cerf 1967, 421-57.

— 1967a: "La Conversion dans les Actes des Apôtres", in: idem, *Études sur les Actes des Apôtres* (LeDiv 45), Paris: Cerf 1967, 459-76.

— 1985: "Le Magnificat comme Discours de Dieu", in: idem, *Études sur les Evangiles Synoptiques II*, Leuven: University Press 1985, 953-75.

Evans, C. F. 1990: *Saint Luke* (NTCom), London: SCM Press 1990.

Fitzmyer, J. A. 1981/85: *The Gospel according to Luke* (AncB 28-28A), New York: Doubleday 1981-1985.

Flender, H. 1967: *St Luke Theologian of Redemptive History*, London: SPCK 1967.

von Harnack, A. 1931: "Das Magnificat der Elisabet (Luk 1,46-55) nebst einigen Bemerkungen zu Luk 1 und 2", in: idem, *Studien zur Geschichte des Neuen Testaments und der Alten Kirche* I, Berlin: de Gruyter 1931, 62-85.

Hawkins, J. 1909: *Horae Synopticae*, Oxford: Clarendon 1909.

Horsley, R. A. 1989: *The Liberation of Christmas*, New York: Crossroads 1989.

Hospodar, B. 1956: "*Meta spoudês* in Luke 1,39", in: *CBQ* 18 (1956) 14-18.

Jeremias, J. 1980: *Die Sprache des Lukasevangeliums* (KEK. Sonderband), Göttingen: Vandenhoeck & Ruprecht 1980.

Jones, D. 1968: "The Background and Character of the Lukan Psalms", in: *JThS* 19 (1968) 19-50.

Karris, R. J. 1991: "The Gospel according to Luke", in: R. E. Brown/J. A. Fitzmyer/R. E. Murphy (eds.), *The New Jerome Biblical Commentary*, Englewood Cliffs, NJ: Prentice Hall 1991, 675-721.

Kattenbusch, F. 1930: "Die Geburtsgeschichte Jesu als Haggada der Urchristologie", in: *ThStKr* 102 (1930) 454-74.

Lagrange, J.-M. 1948: *Évangile selon Saint Luc* (EtB), Paris: Gabalda [8]1948.

Laurentin, R. 1982: *Les Évangiles de l'Enfance du Christ*, Tournai: Desclée 1982.

Legrand, L. 1968: "L'Évangile aux Bergers. Essai sur le Genre Littéraire de Luc II,8-20", in: *RB* 75 (1968) 161-87.

— 1981: *L'Annonce à Marie (Lc 1,26-38). Une Apocalypse aux origines de l'Évangile* (LeDiv 106), Paris: Cerf 1981.

— 1982: "The Structure of Acts 2", in: *ITS* 19 (1982) 193-209.

Lohfink, N. 1990: *Lobgesänge der Armen. Studien zur Magnificat, den Hodajot von Qumran und einigen späten Psalmen* (SBS 143), Stuttgart: Katholisches Bibelwerk 1990.

Marshall, I. H. 1978: *The Gospel of Luke* (NIGTC), Exeter: Paternoster 1978.

McHugh, J. 1975: *The Mother of Jesus in the New Testament*, London: Darton, Longmans and Todd 1975.

Metzger, B. M. et al. 1971: *A Textual Commentary on the Greek New Testament*, London-New York: United Bible Societies 1971.

Neirynck, F. 1959: "Maria bewaarde al de Worden in haar Hart, Lk 2,19.51 in hun Context verklaard," *CBG* 5 (1959) 433-66.

Plummer, A. 1986: *The Gospel according to S. Luke* (ICC); Edinburgh: T. & T. Clark 1986.

Schürmann, H. 1982: *Das Lukasevangelium* (HThK III/1), Freiburg i Br.: Herder [2]1982.

Standaert, B. 1985: "L'art de composer dans l'œuvre de Luc", in: F. Refoulé (ed.), *A Cause de l'Évangile: Mélanges J. Dupont* (LeDiv 123) Paris: Cerf 1985, 323-47.

# Noch einmal: Johannes 21 und "der Jünger, den Jesus liebte"

## Hartwig Thyen

*... Doch 'Gott ist tot' heißt Ende der Auslegungen, der Erklärungsfunktion von Mythen, Geschichten, Symbolen an der Universität; Tod der sinntragenden Buchstaben, Tod dessen, was man allgemein – aber auch sehr exakt – Heilige Schriften nennen kann. Aufgrund einer bemerkenswerten Ausnahmeregelung blieben einige olympische Mythen von der Entmythologisierung verschont, thronen, wie der Ödipus-Mythos, weiterhin dort oben, regen das Denken an, zu neuen Dimensionen vorzustoßen, und 'geben zu denken'. Doch eine Exegese der Heiligen Schrift als ganzer findet nicht mehr statt. Statt ihrer Exegese betreibt man das Studium ihrer Genese. Man sucht nach ihrer Ursache, Urformel oder Struktur, als gehörte sie in den Bereich ethnologischer Tatsachen ...* (E. Lévinas 1991: 81).

## 1. Ein Konsensus wankt

Fast unisono – und zumeist wenig liebevoll – behandelt die "kritische Forschung" das 21. Kapitel des Johannesevangeliums als den sekundären "Nachtrag" irgendeines "kirchlichen" oder "johanneischen Redaktors". Es gilt ihr als "the key and cornerstone for any redactional theory" (Smith 1965: 234). Ja, die Verfechter solcher Theorien wähnen sich ihrer Sache so sicher und ihr Einfluß reicht so weit, daß dem ahnungslosen Leser einer viersprachigen "Hotelbibel" das gesamte Kapitel und damit ein für die Lektüre des Johannesevangeliums schlechthin konstitutives Moment glatt unterschlagen wird (Wittler 1980). Doch aus der nahezu unübersehbaren Masse der ziemlich homogenen Literatur über Joh 21 ragen zwei ebenso kurze wie gehaltvolle Beiträge deutlich heraus, nämlich die Untersuchung der *"Original Functions of John 21"* von Paul S. Minear (1983) und der etwa gleichzeitig entstandene *"Attempt at a Text-Centered Exegesis of John 21"* von Lars Hartman (1984). Sie haben den bestehenden und mir zutiefst fragwürdigen Konsensus über den sekundären Charakter von Joh 21 so gründlich erschüttert, daß man annehmen sollte, er werde sich davon wohl kaum je wieder erholen. Stattdessen aber ist dieses mehr als mittlere Erdbeben, das die Landschaft in meinen Augen völlig verändert hat, öffentlich kaum je registriert worden. Denn auch in der Johannesforschung wird der Lauf der Dinge offenbar bestimmt durch Eugen Roths Einsicht, "Der Mensch lebt noch mit vieler List, in einer Welt, die nicht mehr ist". Wohl aufgrund solcher Erfahrung hat Paul Minear seinen Freunden und Kollegen in Harvard und anderswo den Ertrag seiner lebenslangen Johannesstudien mit den ironischen Worten gewidmet: "To my Duodecim friends who, as usual, will think otherwise"[1].

Mit erheblichem *understatement* hat Lars Hartman seine genannte Studie nur einen "attempt" genannt. Trotz einiger Bedenken, die gleich zur Sprache kommen müssen, sehe ich darin jedoch weit mehr als den bloßen "Versuch", Joh 21 als unabdingbaren "Teil des vierten Evangeliums" zu erweisen. Wie bei Minear's Beitrag handelt es sich vielmehr um ein geglücktes "Experiment", durch das die Hypothese, daß derjenige, der den Text von Joh 1-21 einst veröffentlichte, dieses Ganze als sinnvolle Einheit begriffen sehen wollte ("as a text that he considered made sense"), ihre eindrucksvolle Bestätigung erfahren hat[2]. Darum möchte ich hier, um Lars Hartman zu ehren, dankbar an seinen Beitrag anknüpfen und mich so zu seinem Hermeneuten machen, damit das Ins-Ohr-Gesagte vielleicht endlich von den Dächern schalle.

## 2. Die Funktion von Joh 20,30f.

Das vielen unwiderstehlich erscheinende Hauptargument für den sekundären Charakter von Joh 21 ist der vermeintlich "ursprüngliche Buchschluß" in den Versen 30 und 31 des vorausgehenden 20. Kapitels. Ihm soll daher zunächst unsere Aufmerksamkeit gelten. Daß durch den ausdrücklichen Hinweis auf *"dieses Buch"* und auf sein *"Geschriebensein"* (20,30) dem impliziten Leser suggeriert werden soll, hier endet das Evangelium, läßt sich schwer bestreiten. Und Hartman sieht ganz richtig, daß dieses Problem durch die enge Bindung der folgenden Erzählung vom wunderbaren Fischzug an die beiden vorausgegangenen Begegnungen des Auferstandenen mit seinen Jüngern (20,19-23 und 24-29) durch μετὰ ταῦτα und πάλιν (21,1), sowie zumal durch die ausdrückliche Zählung dieser neuen Erscheinung als der Dritten

---

[1] Paul S. Minear 1984.

[2] Hartman 1984: 29. Im Rahmen einer "text-centered exegesis" kann sich freilich das Lexem *"considered"* nicht unmittelbar auf die extratextuale Größe des realen Autors und seiner "Intention" seinem vermeintlichen "Erstpublikum" gegenüber beziehen. Denn soll die Exegese wirklich "text-zentriert" bleiben, dann muß *"considered"* vielmehr die überprüfbare Korrespondenz zwischen dem "impliziten Autor" und seinem "idealen (oder impliziten) Leser" ausdrücken. Denn nur diese sind beschreibbare Phänomene des Textes selbst. Von dem empirischen, längst verstorbenen Autor unseres Evangeliums, der sich dazu noch absichtsvoll in der pseudonymen Anonymität "des Jüngers, den Jesus liebte" verborgen hat, können wir dagegen so wenig wissen wie von dessen einstigen "Absichten", von seinem mutmaßlichen "Erstpublikum" ganz zu schweigen.

(21,14) noch erheblich verschärft wird. Hartman meint nun aber – und dafür beruft er sich auf einen frühen Beitrag von mir[3] –, gerade die Art der Fortsetzung der Erzählung in 21,1ff. nötige den Leser dazu, seine Meinung, die er sich soeben über 20,30f. gebildet habe, zu revidieren, die Passage also nicht mehr als Zweckbestimmung des ganzen Evangeliums, sondern als den spezifischen Kommentar über die Thomasgeschichte und zumal über Jesu Seligpreisung derer zu begreifen, die nicht sehen und dennoch glauben (20,29).

Ähnlich, wenngleich differenzierter, urteilt Minear. Nachdem er daran erinnert hat, daß es für den sekundären Charakter von Joh 21 weder irgendeine handschriftliche Evidenz gibt, noch auf ein heterogenes Vokabular oder auf stilistische Abweichungen des Kapitels vom Rest des Evangeliums gegründete Argumente[4], wendet auch er sich 20,30f. zu. Doch obwohl diese beiden Verse zunächst jedem Leser so offensichtlich und nahezu "irrefutable" als der intendierte Abschluß des gesamten Dokuments erscheinen müßten, so daß er in ihrem Licht alles Folgende nur noch als "afterthought", "appendix" oder "postscript" begreifen könne (87), will auch Minear die fraglichen Verse 20,30f., die durch das Thema von *Sehen und Glauben* sehr eng mit Joh 20 und zumal mit 20,29 verbunden seien, gegen diesen ersten Eindruck "as a conclusion of that chapter alone rather than of the whole book" verstanden wissen (87-90).

So lebhaft ich das Ziel begrüße, Joh 21 als wesentlichen und unabdingbaren Teil des Evangeliums zu erweisen, muß ich doch gestehen, daß mir der Weg, den Hartman und Minear dahin einschlagen, in die Irre zu führen scheint. Denn der Wortlaut von Joh 20,30f. läßt es m.E. nicht zu, die Passage lediglich als Schluß der Thomasepisode (Hartman) oder auch des gesamten 20. Kapitels (Minear) zu begreifen. Dazu verknüpft das Syntagma σημεῖα ποιεῖν dieses τέλος der Zeichen doch zu eng und zu deutlich mit ihrer ἀρχή in 2,1-11 (vgl. 2,11!), und ebenso ist γεγραμμένα ἐν τῷ βιβλίῳ τούτῳ ja wohl schwerlich auf Joh 20 oder gar allein auf die Erzählung vom zweifelnden Thomas zu begrenzen[5]. Minear sieht diesen Einwand natürlich

---

[3] Hartwig Thyen 1977; vgl. dazu jetzt aber H. Thyen 1992d.

[4] Minear 1983b: 86f. Zur sprachlichen Homogenität von Joh 1,1-21,25 vgl. jetzt E. Ruckstuhl und P. Dschulnigg 1991. – M.-E. Boismard (1947) meint dagegen, derartige Kriterien aufweisen zu können.

[5] Gerade die signifikante Formulierung von 20,30f. und die Wiederaufnahme des seit Joh 12,37 nicht mehr gebrauchten Lexems σημεῖον haben doch Bultmann (1959, z.St.) und in seiner Nachfolge zumal J. Becker (1969 u. 1991) und R. T. Fortna (1988) dazu veranlaßt, Joh 20,30f. als den "ursprünglichen Schluß" der von ihnen postulierten "Semeia-Quelle" anzusehen. Auch wenn mir diese These, wie überhaupt die Existenz einer derartigen "Semeiaquelle", die Joh. zur Darstellung seiner Geschichte Jesu ausgeschrieben und deren Christologie er dabei zugleich kritisiert haben soll, eine bloße "Legende der Kritik" zu sein scheint (vgl. H. Thyen 1992a), läßt sich der innere Zusammenhang von Joh 20,30f. mit den 2,1ff. einsetzenden "Zeichen Jesu" doch nicht übersehen.

und ist deshalb sehr intensiv und "with some care" (88) um seine Entkräftung bemüht. Dazu hebt er zunächst hervor, daß Jesus die Zeichen, von denen 20,30f. die Rede sei, *"vor seinen Jüngern"* getan habe. Stillschweigend unterstellt er dabei der Wendung ἐνώπιον τῶν μαθητῶν αὐτοῦ einen exklusiven Sinn, als seien durch sie andere Zeugen als die Jünger oder solche neben den Jüngern prinzipiell ausgeschlossen. Da nun aber alle zuvor im Evangelium erzählten Zeichen Jesu nicht in solcher Ausschließlichkeit "vor seinen Jüngern", sondern zugleich vor einer mehr oder minder breiten *Öffentlichkeit* geschehen seien, könne sich 20,30f. nur auf die Zeichen beziehen, von denen in Joh 20 berichtet werde, nämlich auf den weggerollten Stein, auf die geordneten Grabtücher, auf Marias Begegnung zunächst mit den Grabesengeln und dann mit dem vermeintlichen Gärtner und endlich auf die Versammlung der Jünger hinter verschlossenen Türen (88f.). Trotz ihrer Eleganz will mir diese Konstruktion nicht einleuchten. Denn einmal scheint mir das exklusive Verständnis von "vor seinen Jüngern" ein höchst willkürliches Postulat zu sein; zum andern fehlt allen Zügen der Erzählung von Joh 20, die Minear als die in 20,30f. zusammengefaßten *"Zeichen"* erweisen möchte, ausgerechnet die Bezeichnung mit dem bei Joh so prominenten Lexem σημεῖον, so daß wohl kaum zufällig vor ihm noch kein Leser des Evangeliums auf diese Idee gekommen ist; und endlich sind selbst diese mutmaßlichen σημεῖα in Joh 20 ja gar nicht ausnahmslos "vor seinen Jüngern" geschehen, denn nach 21,14 (!) gilt das weder für die Entdeckung des leeren Grabes durch Maria, noch für deren Begegnung mit den Engeln und dann mit dem Auferstandenen[6].

Ich meine deshalb, daß man gar nicht darum herumkommt, in Joh 20,30f. ein Resümee aller sieben in diesem Evangelium erzählten Zeichen zu sehen. Denn völlig unabhängig von der jeweiligen Reaktion der *dramatis personae* auf diese σημεῖα, die Minear m.E. zu Unrecht seiner These dienstbar zu machen sucht, sind sie doch gerade mit diesen Reaktionen allzumal dazu *"geschrieben"*, daß sie den Lesern Anstoß werden zum Glauben und damit zur Wahrnehmung ihres auferstandenen Herrn in ihrer jeweiligen Gegenwart. Als die *Sieben Zeichen* des Evangeliums, die seinen sieben prädizierten Ich-Bin-Worten korrespondieren[7], verstehe ich (1) ihre ἀρχή bei der Hochzeit in Kana (2,1-11), (2) die Rettung des Sohnes des Königlichen (4,46-54), (3) die Heilung des Lahmen (5,1-16), (4) die wunderbare Speisung der Fünftausend (Joh 6), (5) die Heilung des Blindgeborenen (Joh 9), (6) die Erzählung

---

[6] Vgl. Hartman 1984: 30, Anm. 6. Völlig unbegreiflich ist mir vor allem Minear's Auslegung von Joh 20,8. Da wird das solenne *"Er sah und glaubte"*, darauf reduziert, daß der geliebte Jünger (samt Petrus!) sich jetzt durch eigenen Augenschein von der Wahrheit der Nachricht Marias überzeugt hat: "They now 'believed' in Mary's report and thus joined in her confession of ignorance, 'we don't know where'" (Minear 1976: 127).

[7] Vgl. H. Thyen 1992c.

von Tod und Auferweckung des Lazarus (Joh 11) und endlich (7) das im 6. Zeichen schon vorabgebildete letzte und größte Zeichen, nämlich die Geschichte von Verhaftung, Verurteilung, Hinrichtung und Auferstehung Jesu (Joh 18-20)[8]. Alle diese "Zeichen" sind längere, oft von Diskursen unterbrochene *Erzählungen* und nie solche symbolischen Einzelzüge wie etwa die sechs steinernen Krüge bei der Kanahochzeit, der weggerollte Stein am Grabe Jesu oder die geordneten Grabtücher[9]. Daß die Reihe der "Zeichen" Jesu nicht – wie meist behauptet wird – mit dem Lazaruswunder als ihrem siebten beendet sein kann[10], erweisen gerade die umstrittenen Verse 20,30f. Denn da kein Erzähler seinem Gegenüber zumuten kann, bei der Rede von den *"vielen anderen Zeichen, die Jesus vor seinen Jüngern getan hat"* über die langen Kapitel 12-20 hinweg an die schon im Lazaruszeichen (Joh 11) endende Reihe von Wundererzählungen zu denken, müssen die Worte "viele andere Zeichen" das unmittelbar Vorausgegangene einschließen[11]. Zudem gibt es im Evangelium selbst "one significant reference to signs ... that clearly anticipates that later passage"[12], nämlich die Zeichenforderung der Juden nach der Tempelreinigung mit Jesu Antwort: "Zerstört diesen Tempel, und in drei Tagen werde ich ihn wieder aufrichten (ἐγερῶ αὐτόν). Darauf entgegneten die Juden: Dieser Tempel ward in 46 Jahren erbaut und du willst ihn in drei Tagen (wieder) errichten? Er redete aber von dem Tempel seines Leibes. Als er dann von den Toten auferstanden war, da erinnerten sich seine Jünger, daß er dies gesagt hatte, und sie glaubten der Schrift und dem Wort, das Jesus gesprochen hatte" (2,18-22).

Minear sieht die "zentrale Funktion" von Joh 20 darin, den vom Auferstandenen selbst seliggepriesenen *Lesern* des Evangeliums (20,29-31) als *Jüngern zweiter Hand* die Gewißheit zu vermitteln, daß sie, die doch selbst nicht mehr sehen, sondern ihren Glauben nur noch auf das verläßliche Zeugnis jener unmittelbaren Augenzeugen und das *geschriebene* Evangelium gründen könnten, deswegen keinesfalls unterprivilegiert seien. Das werde ihnen gerade durch die Erzählung von den

---

[8] Vgl. H. Thyen 1992b.

[9] Da Jesu Seewandel (Joh 6,16-25) nicht eigens als σημεῖον bezeichnet wird, habe ich ihn auch nicht als solches gezählt, sondern Joh 6 als Einheit begriffen.

[10] Dabei wird dann entgegen dem in Anm. 9 Gesagten der Seewandel Jesu in der Regel als sechstes Zeichen gezählt.

[11] Darin liegt fraglos das *relative* Recht Minear's, 20,30f. auf Joh 20 zu beziehen (1976). Auf die mit Lazarus endende Wunderreihe kommen kann hier eigentlich nur der Literarkritiker in seinem Wahn, endlich den "ursprünglichen Schluß" seiner "Semeiaquelle" wiedergefunden zu haben (freilich muß der Evangelist solchen Scharfsinn seines Kritikers mit dem hohen Preis seines dazu umgekehrt-proportional *schwachen Sinnes* bezahlen).

[12] Minear (1976: 90) zu Joh 2,18-22. Es liegt gerade von dieser Stelle aus freilich viel näher, das hier angekündigte "Zeichen" von Zerstörung und Wiederaufrichtung des "Tempels", nämlich des Leibes Jesu, in den Kapitels 18-20 insgesamt zu sehen, statt in Joh 20 allein.

unzureichenden und hilflosen Reaktionen der *dramatis personae* auf die Zeichen am Grabe Jesu, ja selbst auf deren Begegnungen mit ihrem auferstandenen Herrn, anschaulich vor Augen geführt[13]. Da ich mich selbst nicht als einen derart sehunfähigen Jünger aus einem *second hand shop* zu begreifen vermag, auch die Thomaserzählung nicht als mehr oder minder abschreckendes Beispiel lesen und nicht nur glauben will und kann, weil andere vor mir geglaubt haben, sondern mit Thomas auf Autopsie (Kierkegaard) insistieren muß, kann ich diesem Vorschlag zur Lektüre von Joh 20 nicht folgen. Gerade aus Minear's ebenso revolutionärer wie überzeugender Interpretation der Idee der Inkarnation im Ersten Johannesbrief[14] habe ich gelernt, daß Inkarnation keine bloße Episode in der Geschichte eines himmlischen Logoswesens ist, sondern die Weise, wie der auferstandene Gekreuzigte, durch den Geist-Parakleten vermittelt, im Abschied ewig bei den Seinen *bleiben* will. Die österlichen Begegnungen mit seinen Jüngern dürfen nicht durch ihre Historisierung eingefroren werden. Zumal die Abschiedsreden unseres Evangeliums erweisen Jesus als den Herrn der Zeit. Er ist nicht zeitunterworfenes *Subjekt*. Darum ist sein unzeitig erscheinendes Wort: "In der Welt habt ihr Angst, aber seid getrost, ich habe die Welt überwunden!" (16,33), nicht lediglich die literarische Figur einer *Prolepse*. Vielmehr erklingt darin die zeitenthobene Stimme des Auferstandenen[15], der vor Abraham war (8,59) und dessen Herrlichkeit Jesaja gesehen hat (12,41). Auch das geschriebene Evangelium kann für die späteren Jünger den Glauben so wenig begründen, wie die darin erzählten Zeichen das für die früheren vermochten. Es kann nur zu dem rufen, dahin wo der seine "Bleibe" hat, der da sagt: "Kommt und seht" (1,38f.), damit am Ende jeder noch so späte Jünger sagen muß: "Ich glaube jetzt nicht mehr wegen deiner Rede, sondern weil ich selbst gehört und erkannt habe, daß dieser der Retter der Welt ist" (4,42) und: "Wir sahen seine Herrlichkeit, eine Herrlichkeit als des Eingeborenen vom Vater" (1,14)[16].

---

[13] "Many of them must surely have been inclined to envy that first core of followers who, unlike themselves, had had the privilege of direct encounters with the risen Lord. 'How fortunate must have been those earlier witnesses to see the hands and side of the Crucified'. 'Not so', said the glorified Lord. 'Not so', echoed the Evangelist. ..." (Minear 1976: 89).

[14] P. S. Minear 1970.

[15] Vgl. dazu den schönen Beitrag von Gail R. O'Day (1991) und siehe auch F. W. Marquardt 1993: 362-65.

[16] "Es gibt keinen Schüler zweiter Hand. Wesentlich gesehen sind der erste und der letzte gleich, nur daß die spätere Generation in dem Bericht des Gleichzeitigen die Veranlassung hat, während die gleichzeitige sie in seiner unmittelbaren Gleichzeitigkeit hat und insofern keiner Generation etwas schuldet. Aber diese unmittelbare Gleichzeitigkeit ist bloß die Veranlassung, und dies kann wohl nicht stärker ausgedrückt werden als dadurch, daß der Schüler, wenn er sich selbst verstünde, gerade wünschen müßte, sie möge dadurch aufhören, daß der Gott die Erde wieder verlasse" (Kierkegaard 1976: 123). Ashton 1991: 437-42.

Deswegen ist für die Thomasgeschichte, die Joh mir eigens dazu aus der knappen Notiz οἱ δὲ ἐδίστασαν von Mt 28,17 herausgesponnen zu haben scheint[17], doch wohl etwa die folgende Lesart geboten:

Nun laß dich daran erinnern, daß in diesem Zusammenhang der Thomas steht. Ein Jünger, der sehen lernen will: nicht allein durch Hören oder Sehen, sondern auch durch Anfassen. – Hören, Sehen und Berühren machen erst den ganzen Glauben. Leibhaftig der Auferstandene, leibhaftig auch die Erfahrung mit ihm. – Ja an diesen Zusammenhang muß erinnert werden, damit Thomas nicht so erscheint, wie er sonst immer gesehen wird: daß er nämlich nicht um des reinen Glaubens willen glauben, sondern sehen will. Aber um diese falsche Reinheit geht es gar nicht. Und Thomas will ja nicht nur sehen, sondern auch anfassen. Selber will er seine Erfahrung machen, will nicht glauben, weil andere erfahren haben. Diesen Thomas darf sich keiner schenken.
Oft wird von Theologen gesagt, daß wir vom Auferstandenen keine 'objektiven' Zeugen haben, sondern nur solche Zeugen, die auch zum Glauben gelangten durch ihr Sehen. Das ist richtig – und bleibt doch eine unwahre Behauptung, weil man damit sagt, daß einer heute den Auferstandenen nicht sehen könne. Und so zweifelt man insgeheim auch, ob er denn je gesehen wurde. – Daß es den Thomas geben muß, liegt eben daran, daß er den Zweifel festhält. Gäbe es diesen Zweifel nicht in einer Geschichte, die vom auferstandenen Herrn erzählt, so kämen wir alle nicht vor. Die wir zweifeln müssen, solange wir nicht erfahren haben. …
Zu tadeln ist Thomas nicht, weil er seinen Herrn so nah haben wollte. Damit macht er nur aufmerksam auf den Zusammenhang, der besteht zwischen Geist, Seele und Leib. Daß es um die ganze, unteilbare Wirklichkeit im Glauben zu tun ist. – Sondern zu tadeln ist, daß Thomas etwas zur Bedingung seines Glaubens macht. *Wenn ich nicht …, kann ich nicht glauben (20,25).* Verständlich, daß Thomas so redet, denn er will nicht ausgeschlossen sein von der Erfahrung der anderen Jünger. Und dennoch verschließt er sich so die Möglichkeit, den Auferstandenen zu sehen. … Der Auferstandene läßt sich gleichwohl in der Erzählung auf die (falsche Bedingungs-) Logik des Zweifels ein. Er ahmt den Sprachbau des Thomas (*weil – darum*) in der Antwort nach. *Weil du mich gesehen hast, Thomas, darum glaubst du.* Und dann folgt der berühmte Satz, der in seinem Zusammenhang mit dem vorigen erst seinen Sinn gewinnt: *Selig sind, die nicht sehen und doch glauben!*
So klärt Jesus den kritischen Zweifel darüber auf, daß seine Intention des Sehens verkehrt war. Der Zweifel, der sich vom Glauben ausnehmen will, um durch etwas anderes als Glauben zum Glauben zu kommen, ist ein Widerspruch in sich und kommt nie ans Ziel. Zur schlechten statt zur wahren Vergegenständlichung führt dann das Sehen und Anfassen. Man will sich distanzierend von der Nähe des Auferstandenen überzeugen. So berührt man und fühlt doch nicht; sieht und erkennt nicht; hört und versteht nicht. Der Abstand des Zweifelnden verhindert die Naherfahrung. Die Nähe, die der Zweifelnde doch sucht. So hat Thomas nicht richtig sehen wollen und kam doch zum Glauben! Dafür sorgt ja der Lebendige, daß die falsche Fragestellung des Zweifels nicht fehlschlägt. Er spricht mit Thomas und führt seinen Fin-

---

[17] Vgl. H. Thyen 1992d: 105.

ger. Damit konnte der Zweifler nicht rechnen, der doch *'selber'* sehen und anfassen wollte …[18].

Wer – und sei er der letzte Jünger – so wie Thomas bei seinem Herrn angekommen ist und seine Gegenwart selbst erfahren hat, der hat in der "κοινωνία mit dem Vater und mit seinem Sohne Jesus Christus" seine Bleibe gefunden und kann mit den Jüngern aller Generationen sagen: "Was von Anfang war, was wir im Ohr haben und was uns vor Augen steht, was wir gesehen und mit unseren Händen berührt haben, … das verkündigen wir auch euch, damit auch ihr an unserer Gemeinschaft teil habt. …" (1Joh 1,1-4)[19]. Das gilt auch für die Evangelien. Denn "die Christen der Gemeinden, in denen die Evangelien 'geschrieben' wurden, verstanden sich als gleichzeitig mit dem Auferstandenen lebend. Sie haben ihre Erfahrung mit dem Auferstandenen als die Erfahrung seiner Jünger – historisch gesagt – 'eingetragen'"[20].

Zur Begründung dafür, daß ich dem Vorschlag nicht folgen kann, Joh 20,30f. als den Abschluß lediglich des 20. Kapitels zu interpretieren, mögen diese Erwägungen und das breiter ausgeführte Beispiel der Thomaserzählung genügen. Derart limitiert, werden die Verse 20,30f. zu Unrecht heruntergespielt. Darum muß ich in ihnen mit der Mehrheit ihrer Ausleger den absichtsvollen und solennen Schluß des Corpus des Evangeliums erblicken. Damit ist freilich noch nichts über den sekundären Charakter von Joh 21 gesagt. Im Gegenteil! Da es jedem möglichen Redaktor ja ein Leichtes gewesen wäre, seine Ergänzungen unbemerkt zwischen Joh 20,29 und

---

[18] Lothar Steiger 1993: 100f.

[19] Unter der Überschrift: "Die Belehrung der Unbelehrbaren" behauptet J. Kügler (1988b: 249): "Bekanntlich (!) erhebt der Autor von 1 Joh zu Beginn des Briefes für sich und die Gruppe, der er zugehört, den Anspruch, Augen- und Ohrenzeugen (!) zu sein. … Zwar hat etwa Bultmann versucht, diesen Anspruch auf ein geistig-geistliches Sehen und Hören zu reduzieren, aber dieses Verständnis hat sich nicht durchgesetzt …". Nun, man sollte das leibliche Hören, Sehen, Anfassen und Schmekken der Glaubenden gewiß nicht spiritualisieren, aber deswegen ist noch lange nicht falsch, was "sich nicht durchgesetzt hat". Kügler klassifiziert den 1 Joh als einen Fall "anonymer Pseudepigraphie", in der er die ultima ratio eines Autors sieht, seine in ihrem Insistieren auf ihrem Geistbesitz "unbelehrbaren" Adressaten dennoch zu belehren: "Einem der selbst dabei war, eignet eben eine Autorität, die aus der allgemeinen Geistbegabung herausragt und relativ unabhängig von ihr ist" (253f.). Ich kann da nur hoffen, daß sich diese Sicht des 1 Joh nicht auch noch "durchsetzen" wird. Denn jedem nicht gänzlich Unbelehrbaren müßten doch die neutrische Formulierung und zumal die Perfektformen von 1 Joh 1,1ff. zeigen, daß es hier nicht um Augenzeugenschaft vergangener Historie geht, sondern um die Autopsie der Präsenz des lebendigen Fleischgewordenen; vgl. dazu Minear 1970. In dem "Wir" stellt sich nicht eine Gruppe von "Augenzeugen" autoritär ihren enthusiastischen Adressaten gegenüber, sondern damit werden Leser eingeladen zur Teilhabe an der κοινωνία der Glaubenden. Auch Ashton (1991: 437f.), insistiert m.E. zu Unrecht auf historischer Augenzeugenschaft der "Wir" von Joh 1,14 und 1 Joh 1,1-4.

[20] Steiger 1993: 118f.

20,30f. *ein-*, statt sie an 20,30f. *anzufügen*, wird dem Leser durch die offenbar eigens dazu geschaffenen Verse 20,30f. signalisiert, daß dem durch seinen *Prolog* (1,1-18) eingeleiteten und hier abgeschlossenen *Corpus* des Evangeliums gegenüber mit Kapitel 21 jetzt sein spezifischer *Epilog* als etwas Neues folgt[21]. Ja, so betrachtet haben die Verse Joh 20,30f. geradezu eine Brückenfunktion: Sie schließen nicht nur das Zeugnis des Evangeliums für Jesus ab, sondern leiten zugleich das nun folgende Zeugnis Jesu für dieses Evangelium ein. "Kap. 21 kommt als scheinbarer Nachtrag besser zur Geltung und zur Anerkennung seiner besonderen Bedeutung, als wenn es sich unmittelbar an 20,29 anschlösse. Je weniger streng man aber 20,30f. als Schluß des Evangeliums auffaßt, um so weniger braucht man dann auch Umstände zu machen, 21,24f. richtig zu fassen, d.h. wiederum als Schluß zum ganzen Evangelium, nicht etwa nur zu Kap. 21"[22].

## 3. Petrus und der geliebte Jünger in Joh 21

Das ist jetzt formal und inhaltlich zu begründen, und dazu wende ich mich erneut den Texten zu, die von dem "Jünger, den Jesus liebte" und seiner eigentümlichen Beziehung zu Petrus erzählen. Noch allzusehr im Banne einer literarkritischen Schere-und-Kleister-Methode, deren *"Resultate"* sich aber aus meiner heutigen Sicht der Dinge weder literarisch noch stilistisch zureichend begründen lassen, hatte ich vor Jahren gemeint, erweisen zu können, daß *alle* Texte des Evangeliums, die von dem geliebten Jünger reden, von dem Autor von Joh 21 geschaffen sind und erst in diesem Schlußkapitel, ohne das sie unbefriedigende Fragmente blieben, ihre Klimax erreichen[23]. Dabei hielt ich den Verfasser von Joh 21 zugleich für den Redaktor einer die Kapitel 1-20 umfassenden "Grundschrift". Da aber ein Evangelium ohne diese Figur des geliebten Jüngers alles andere als das uns vertraute *Johannesevangelium* wäre, hatte ich damals vorgeschlagen, fortan nicht mehr den ominösen Verfasser einer vermeintlichen "Grundschrift" oder irgendeines "Predecessors" unseres Evangeliums, sondern diesen Redaktor und Autor von Joh 21 den "vierten

---

[21] Overbeck kann dazu sogar erklären: "Der stärkste Grund gegen die Echtheit von Kap. 21 läge in 20,30f., wenn diese Worte nicht als Schluß des ganzen Evangeliums gemeint wären. Allein eben das ist vielmehr der Fall" (1911: 439).

[22] Overbeck 1911: 435; vgl. ebd. 434-55, wo Overbeck Joh 20,30-21,25 unter der Überschrift "Der Abschluß" behandelt. Sehr schön hat I. de la Potterie (1986) durch den Aufweis des chiastischen Spiels mit den Motiven *"geschrieben"* – *"nicht geschrieben"* in den Rahmenversen dieses "Abschlußes" dessen Kohärenz erwiesen. A: "… die nicht geschrieben sind" (20,30) – B: "Diese aber sind geschrieben …" (20,31) – B': "… dies ist der Jünger, … der dieses geschrieben hat" (21,24) – A': "… wollte man das alles im Einzelnen niederschreiben …", also wiederum *"nicht geschrieben"* (21,25). – Ganz ähnlich: Segovia 1991: 175.

[23] Thyen 1977; vgl. dazu jetzt Minear 1983b: 91ff.

Evangelisten" zu nennen, zumal ja alle derartigen Vorläufer, wenn überhaupt, dann doch immer nur höchst partiell und hypothetisch rekonstruierbare und damit unauslegbare Texte sind. Meine These, der Autor von Joh 21 sei der *Schöpfer* der Figur des geliebten Jüngers, hat mittlerweile Eingang in den Kommentar von J. Becker[24] und in die große Monographie von J. Kügler (1988a) gefunden, die freilich beide noch meinen, sie auch literarkritisch als das sekundäre Werk eines "kirchlichen" (Becker) oder "johanneischen Redaktors" (Kügler) ausweisen und dessen "Intentionen" von denen seiner Vorgänger unterscheiden zu können. Neuerdings hat Bonsack (1988: 55f.) den Nachweis der These vom Autor von Joh 21 als Schöpfer der Texte vom geliebten Jünger als das gelungenste Stück der Literarkritik in Beckers Kommentar bezeichnet. Dazu ist aber daran zu erinnern, daß schon Bultmann die fraglichen Texte aufgrund ähnlicher Beobachtungen insofern als "sekundär" angesehen hatte, als er meinte, sie als *Einfügungen* des Evangelisten in seine Quellen erweisen zu können. Aber begründet der eigentümlich schwebende Charakter dieser Texte und der sie bestimmenden geheimnisvollen Jüngerfigur, die für den Fortgang der Handlung wie der Erzählung nirgendwo eine Rolle spielt, so daß sich die entsprechenden Textpassagen (ähnlich wie die vielerörterten Paraklet-Sprüche) aus ihren jeweiligen Kontexten ohne spürbaren Verlust herauslösen lassen, wirklich die Lizenz zur Literarkritik? Ich bestreite das entschieden und meine, daß dieser Charakter der Texte, der auf der formalen Ebene so exakt demjenigen der Figur des geliebten Jüngers, von dem sie handeln, auf der inhaltlichen Ebene entspricht, sich gerade im Zusammenhang mit Joh 21 viel ungezwungener als ein literarischer Kunstgriff des Autors erklärt[25].

Alle Versuche, für das Rätsel der Identität des "Jüngers, den Jesus liebte" und damit für die Frage nach der Person des vierten Evangelisten (ὁ γράψας ταῦτα: Joh 21,24!) eine befriedigende Lösung zu finden, firmierten jahrhundertelang unter dem Titel "Die johanneische Frage". Das zutiefst Unbefriedigende nahezu aller dieser Unternehmungen – einschließlich des neuesten Wiederbelebungsversuches der alten *johanneischen Frage* durch Martin Hengel[26] – hat seinen Grund darin, daß ihre Autoren die literarische Ebene des Textes als dessen "Welt" nicht zureichend von

---

[24] Becker 1991, z.St

[25] Das bestätigen im übrigen sehr schön, wenn auch gegen seine literarkritische Beurteilung der Texte als "Einfügungen", die Beobachtungen über den "Jünger, der dabei war, ohne dabeigewesen zu sein" bei Bonsack 1988: 56ff.

[26] M. Hengel 1993. Das Buch ist (vgl. S.1f.) als erweiterte und verbesserte Auflage der zuvor schon in englischer Sprache erschienen Studie (Hengel 1989), anzusehen. Wie E. Betti (1962 und 1967) und E. D. Hirsch (1972) scheint auch Hengel noch unverdrossen auf die *Autorenintention* als die einzig *objektive* Sinninstanz von Texten zu setzen und zu meinen, diese historisch-kritisch eruieren zu können. In diesem Sinne hat er jetzt den obskuren Namen des papianischen πρεσβύτερος Ἰωάννης als neuen "Lösungsversuch" der uralten "johanneischen Frage" präsentiert.

der realen Welt seiner möglichen Referenz unterscheiden. Sehr kurzschlüssig – mit den bekannten Folgen des totalen Lichtausfalls – wird da der "implizite Autor" seines Werkes einfach mit dessen fiktionalem Erzähler/Schreiber und dieser wiederum umstandslos mit dem realen Verfasser des Textes identifiziert[27]. Aber das Johannesevangelium ist weder eine historische Chronik der laufenden Ereignisse der Geschichte Jesu, noch ist es als das *quasi* naturwüchsig entstandene Produkt eines Kollektivs das simple Spiegelbild der realen Nöte und Bedürfnisse dieser heute zumeist "johanneische Gemeinde" genannten Gruppe. Es ist vielmehr das anspruchsvolle literarische Opus eines anonymen Dichters, der zugunsten der pseudepigraphen Zuschreibung seines Werkes an die von ihm fingierte auktoriale Erzähler-/Schreiberfigur des "Jüngers, den Jesus liebte" für immer im Dunkel der Geschichte versunken ist, so daß als Rest der alten "johanneischen Frage" nur noch das von Generation zu Generation jedem Leser absichtsvoll erneut aufgegebene Rätsel bleibt, wer aus dem Kreis der Jünger Jesu denn wohl der fingierte Autor dieses Evangeliums sei. Ihre Kennzeichnung als *johanneische* hat diese Rätselfrage daher, daß das vierte Evangelium spätestens seit den Tagen des Irenäus dem Zebedaiden Johannes zugeschrieben wird[28] und seit der Anfertigung der uns als p[66] bekannten Handschrift die Inscriptio εὐαγγέλιον κατὰ Ἰωάννην trägt[29]. Ist die hier vorgetragene Hypothese richtig, dann heißt der "Jünger, den Jesus liebte" nicht "Johannes", weil sich irgendwelche älteren Leute in einer "johanneischen Gemeinde" noch an den beliebten Träger dieses Namens in ihrer Mitte und an ihre Verstörung über seinen

---

[27] Vgl. die Explikation des zugrundeliegenden texttheoretischen Modells durch Staley (1988: 21-49).

[28] Adv. haer. 3,1.1 (=Eus. h.e. 5,8.4): "Zuletzt gab Johannes, der Jünger des Herrn, der auch an seiner Brust gelegen hatte, sein Evangelium in Ephesus ... heraus". Ein drei Jahrzehnte älteres Zeugnis für unser überliefertes JohEv und für *Johannes* als seinen Verfasser ist wohl die Epist. Apost., deren intime Kenntnis des JohEvs (und der Johannesbriefe) der Voranstellung von Johannes und Thomas, sowie der Aufnahme Nathanaels in den Apostelkatalog (2.[13]) korrespondiert; vgl. dazu Hengel 1993: 59ff.

[29] Sollte das vierte Evangelium – wie Hengel (1993: 31-33 u. 204-09) vermutet – vom Augenblick seiner ersten *Publikation* an durch die *Inscriptio* εὐαγγέλιον κατὰ Ἰωάννην und/oder die *Subscriptio* κατὰ Ἰωάννην bezeichnet gewesen sein (wie in p[66]), dann müßte sein Autor zugleich der Schöpfer unseres Vierevangelienkanons sein. Denn der denkwürdige Gebrauch des Lexems εὐαγγέλιον als *Gattungsname* und die ebenso ungewöhnliche Zuschreibung eines Exemplars dieser Gattung an einen Autor durch κατά mit nachfolgendem Namen kann nur der Feder des Herausgebers einer Reihe solcher "Evangelien" und dessen Absicht entstammen, sie so unterscheidbar und damit auch zitierbar zu machen; vgl. Kurt Aland 1965: 5. Zu solcher *Einschreibung* des JohEvs in einen Evangelienkanon würde sein souveränes Spiel mit den synoptischen Texten ebenso passen wie sein Schlußvers 21,25, der sich mit seinem Verweis auf *Bücher* (!) ja wirklich ausnimmt wie "das höchst charakteristische Schlußwort der urchristlichen Evangelienschriftstellerei", das alle weiteren Versuche dazu "entmutigt" oder ihnen doch zumindest "das Gehör der Gläubigen (verschließt)" (Overbeck 1911: 455; vgl. ebd. 409).

unerwarteten Tod vor der Parusie Jesu erinnern konnten, sondern weil *Leser* des Evangeliums in dem Namen des *Zebedaiden Johannes* die Lösung des Rätsels um den geliebten Jünger gefunden zu haben glaubten[30].

Daß diese Leser sich auf ihre Johanneslektüre verstanden und damit einer von dem impliziten Autor selbst gelegten Spur folgten, muß nun gezeigt werden. Die Rezeptiongeschichte läßt erkennen, daß erst der kommentierende Satz: "Dies ist der Jünger, der von diesen Geschehnissen zeugt, und der dieses (Evangelium) geschrieben hat. Und wir wissen, daß sein Zeugnis wahr ist" (21,24), die Frage nach der Identität des geliebten Jüngers wirklich brennend macht. Deshalb fragen wir zunächst nach möglichen Hinweisen darauf in Joh 21. Als die Akteure des wunderbaren Fischzugs werden gleich zu Anfang sieben Jünger genannt, nämlich Petrus als ihr Anführer, Thomas und Nathanael, die (Söhne) des Zebedäus und zwei weitere Jünger, die namentlich nicht benannt werden (21,2). Damit gerät das Rätselraten um den geliebten Jünger in eine heiße Phase. Mußten die Leser ihn nämlich in Joh 13 noch unter den Zwölf mit Ausnahme von Petrus und Judas, also unter zehn Jüngern suchen[31], so kann er jetzt – bei Licht betrachtet – nur noch einer von vieren sein, denn da auch hier Petrus, Thomas und Nathanael leicht auszuschließen sind, bleiben nur noch die beiden Namenlosen und "die des Zebedäus", deren Nennung in dieser Formulierung voraussetzt, daß die Leser sie als Johannes und Jakobus zu identifizieren wissen. Ich hatte früher gemeint, auch die beiden Zebedaiden ausscheiden zu können mit dem Argument, sie seien einfach als Akteure der *Vorlage* (Lk 5,4-11) und nur zur Vollendung der symbolischen Siebenzahl in den Text geraten, so daß mir als Kandidaten nur noch die beiden Namenlosen geblieben waren. Dazu schienen mir die durchgehend festgehaltene Anonymität des geliebten Jüngers und die signifikante Namenlosigkeit des einen der beiden Erstberufenen von Joh 1,35ff. trefflich zu passen[32]. Doch das Argument erscheint mir heute mehr als schwach. Denn gefragt werden muß doch, *warum* Johannes, der doch seinem Werk nirgendwo beliebige Vorlagen und deren Personal gedankenlos einverleibt, die bis-

---

[30] Overbeck (1911: 409-55) hat diese Hypothese ohne Seitenblicke auf die vermeintliche Historie allein aus dem Text des Evangeliums so sorgfältig und vorbildlich begründet, daß ich sie für eine bloße *Hypothese* nicht mehr halten kann.

[31] Mit der gesamten Tradition setze ich voraus, daß der geliebte Jünger als derjenige, der bei letzten Mahl an der Brust seines Herrn lag, keinesfalls außerhalb des Kreises der Zwölf gesucht werden darf. Denn allein sie waren Teilnehmer dieses Mahles. In *diesem* Punkt kann und will auch Johannes seinen Lesern, die er ja immer wieder in sein intertextuelles Spiel mit den synoptischen Evangelien verwickelt, kein X für ein U vormachen. Sie wissen, daß seit Jesu σκληρὸς λόγος von der Lebensnotwendigkeit, "das Fleisch des Menschensohnes zu kauen und sein Blut zu trinken" (6,52ff.) nur noch die Zwölf bei ihm *geblieben* waren (Joh 6,60ff.). Deshalb sind Figuren wie *Johannes Markus* (W. Eckle 1991), *Paulus* (M. Goulder 1993) oder der papianische *Presbyter Johannes* (Hengel 1993: 264ff.; u.pass.) rigoros von der Kandidatenliste zu streichen.

her nie genannten Zebedaiden gerade hier ganz am Ende so unvermittelt in seine Erzählung einführt. Zudem wäre ja selbst dann noch zu fragen, warum er es im Unterschied zu Lk 5,10 seinen Lesern überläßt, die *Namen* der Zebedäussöhne zu erraten. Könnte nicht gerade das ein Hinweis auf den ja ebenfalls *namenlosen* Jünger sein, "den Jesus liebte"?

Ehe wir das Ratespiel unter den vier verbliebenen Kandidaten fortsetzen, blicken wir zunächst noch einmal auf den Schluß unseres Kapitels, der uns ja durch seine Präsentation des geliebten Jüngers als des Evangelisten so neugierig gemacht hatte. Nach der schmerzhaften Rehabilitation von den Folgen seiner dreifachen Verleugnung Jesu durch dessen dreifache Frage nach seiner Liebe und seine dreifache Einsetzung in das Hirtenamt, worin er sich durch das Sterben für die ihm anvertraute Herde als "guter Hirte" bewähren soll und wird, ruft Jesus Petrus erneut in seine Nachfolge: ἀκολούθει μοι[33]. Als der so neuberufene Petrus sich umwendet, bemerkt er, daß er auf seinem Weg nicht allein ist, denn als einen, der auch *nachfolgt* (ἀκολουθοῦντα)[34], erblickt er "den Jünger, den Jesus liebte". Daß der Erzähler ihn jetzt noch einmal ausführlich charakterisiert als den, "der beim Mahl an der Brust Jesu gelegen und ihn gefragt hatte, Herr, wer ist es, der dich ausliefern wird?" (21,20), ist ein auffälliges Signal, das den Leser daran erinnert, daß es ja Petrus war, der beim letzten Mahl den geliebten Jünger zu jener Frage nach dem Verräter aufgefordert hatte und dann selbst als Verleugner zum Quasi-Verräter geworden war. Und mit dem Leser wird sich ja wohl auch der erzählte Petrus erinnern (13,24)[35]. Hatte er nicht schon bei seinem ersten Versuch der Nachfolge (ἠκολούθει τῷ Ἰησοῦ, 18,15), die dann in der dreifachen Verleugnung Jesu kläglich gescheitert

---

[32] Thyen 1977: 263. Auch Hengel (1993) sieht die Funktion der beiden Namenlosen darin, "das Inkognito des Lieblingsjüngers (zu) sichern" (82), und erklärt: "selbst im Zusatzkapitel 21 (!), wo man sein Inkognito hätte lüften können, wenn man es gewollt hätte, wird eine eindeutige Kennzeichnung durch den Hinweis auf die anonymen 'zwei seiner Jünger' (21,2) bewußt unmöglich gemacht" (214); vgl. Kügler 1988a: 391f.

[33] Daß damit absichtsvoll an die Szene mit der Ankündigung der dreifachen Verleugnung Jesu durch Petrus noch vor dem Hahnenschrei (13,36-38) angeknüpft und daß Petrus jetzt zu jener Art von "*Nachfolge*" ermächtigt wird, die er zuvor noch nicht zu leisten vermochte, ist wohl evident. Der Erzähler stellt die Verbindung zwischen der verlorenen und der wiedergewonnenen Liebe des Petrus zu seinem Herrn auch dadurch her, daß er Verlust wie neuen Gewinn an einem "Kohlenfeuer" geschehen läßt (18,18 und 21,9 jeweils mit dem seltenen Lexem ἀνθρακία). – Vgl. zu Joh 21,15-19: L. Steiger 1990: 53-63.

[34] Ich frage mich, ob nicht schon das seit Joh 13,36-38 und nun erst recht durch 21,18f. mit Zügen des Martyriums aufgeladene Lexem ἀκολουθεῖν als Hinweis auf den Märtyrertod auch des geliebten Jüngers gelesen sein will, so daß Petrus Jesus dann nach dessen *Aufgabe* und nicht nach seinem *Schicksal* fragte.

[35] Dennoch hatte damals, wie 13,28f. zeigt, außer dem geliebten Jünger (und dem Leser, der ja schon seit 6,71 darum weiß) keiner die Identität des Verräters erfahren.

war, einen Begleiter gehabt auf dem Weg der Nachfolge, nämlich jenen *"anderen Jünger"*, der *"zusammen mit Jesus"* schon vor ihm den feindlichen Ort betreten hatte (συνεισῆλθεν τῷ Ἰησοῦ εἰς τὴν αὐλὴν τοῦ ἀρχιερέως), während er, Petrus, draußen vor der Tür (πρὸς τῇ θύρᾳ ἔξω) stehenbleiben mußte? Und hatte ihm nicht erst dieser andere durch seine Fürsprache bei der Türhüterin (θυρωρός) überhaupt den Zutritt verschafft und ihn dann hereingeführt (εἰσήγαγεν)? Daß dieser "andere" trotz des Fehlens seiner stereotypen Bezeichnung als "der Jünger, den Jesus liebte" dennoch nur dieser sein kann, hat Frans Neirynck vor allem unter Verweis auf die analoge Struktur der Wettlaufszene von Joh 20,3-8 sorgfältig begründet[36]. Sein Quasi-Pseudonym dürfte hier ausgelassen sein, weil es damit in eine fragwürdige Konkurrenz geraten wäre mit seiner für diese Episode notwendigen Näherbestimmung als eines "Bekannten des Hohenpriesters" (ἦν γνωστὸς τῷ ἀρχιερεῖ). Im Gegensatz zu vielen Auslegern seit der Zeit der Alten Kirche bis hin zu Martin Hengel kann ich diese "Bekanntschaft" unseres fingierten Jünger/Erzählers mit dem Hohenpriester freilich nicht für eine "historische Nachricht" halten, die sich entsprechend ausschlachten ließe. Ich muß in ihr vielmehr ein glänzend erfundenes Mittel der *narratio verisimilis* sehen, das es dem Erzähler erlaubt, den geliebten Jünger ungehindert eintreten zu lassen, damit er dann Petrus den Zutritt verschaffen kann[37]. Da aber die Umständlichkeit der Szeneneinführung und das gehäufte Auftreten des Vokabulars aus der Hirtenrede von Joh 10 (αὐλή, θύρα, θυρωρός, ἀκολουθεῖν, εἰσάγειν, συνεισέρχεσθαι) signalisieren, daß die Szene voller symbolischer Obertöne ist, könnte man ja fragen, ob das nicht auch von der "Be-

---

[36] Neirynck 1975; vgl. M. Hengel 1993: 215f. J. Kügler (1988b: 224-28) bietet zwar eine lange Liste derer, die den "anderen" mit dem "geliebten Jünger" identifizieren, bestreitet diese Möglichkeit selbst jedoch vehement. In der Figur des "anderen Jüngers" sieht er keinen Helfer, sondern eher einen Verführer, eine Art "Halbjünger" à la Nikodemus, dessen schlechtes Beispiel die guten Sitten des Petrus verderbe. Hier solle gezeigt werden, "wohin Petrus gerät, wenn er sich der Führung der falschen Leute anvertraut" (427). Abgesehen davon, daß mir auch Nikodemus bei Johannes sehr viel positiver gezeichnet zu sein scheint, als Kügler ihn sieht, kann ich erst recht an dem "anderen Jünger" nicht den geringsten Makel entdecken.

[37] Vgl. Lausberg 1973: 165f. – Zur Legitimation ihrer eigenen spezifisch *priesterlichen* Ansprüche haben wohl schon die Bischöfe des zweiten Jahrhunderts Johannes aufgrund der Notiz von seiner *Bekanntschaft mit dem Hohenpriester* zum "Träger des priesterlichen Stirnschildes" (Lev 8,9) gemacht (so etwa um 190 Polykrates von Ephesus in seinem Brief an Victor von Rom im Zusammenhang des Passafest-Streites; Text bei Euseb, h.e. 5,24,3. Wie alle Väter bezieht Polykrates Joh 18,16 freilich auf den *Zebedaiden* Johannes als einen der Zwölf). Hengel überträgt dessen angeblich priesterlichen Status umstandslos auf seinen "Presbyter Johannes", der bei ihm zu einem Mitglied der Jerusalemer Priesteraristokratie wird und als dort ansässiger Hausbesitzer nach Jesu Tod dessen Mutter bei sich aufnimmt (Joh 19,27; 1993: 321ff.). Ich kann nicht verhehlen, daß ich solche Historisierung so hochsymbolischer Texte wie Joh 18,15ff. und 19,25ff. nur als deren Banalisierung empfinden kann. Vgl. dagegen zu Joh 19,25-27: Minear 1984: 143ff.

kanntschaft" des "anderen Jüngers" mit dem Hohenpriester gilt. Denn immerhin ist das ja nicht irgendeine Bekanntschaft, sondern die mit dem Inhaber des höchsten von Gott verliehenen Priesteramtes, kraft dessen der Hohepriester "weissagt", durch sein Votum den Todesbeschluß des Synhedriums herbeiführt und so, wie Judas, zum Mitvollstrecker von Gottes Heilsplan wird (Joh 11,47ff.). Doch das ist vielleicht ein Zuviel der Spekulation über ein bloßes *Verisimile*.

Kehren wir deshalb aus der Erinnerung in die Gegenwart des erzählten Petrus zurück! Sich umwendend erblickt der soeben zu Nachfolge und Martyrium Bestimmte den geliebten Jünger, ebenfalls auf dem Weg der Nachfolge, und fragt Jesus: "Herr, was aber ist es um diesen?" Und der Erzähler läßt seinen Jesus diese Frage, absichtsvoll ambivalent, so beantworten: "Wenn ich will, daß er bleibt, bis ich komme, was geht das dich an? Du jedenfalls sollst mir nachfolgen!" Da für ein "johanneisches Mißverständnis" dieses Satzes kein Publikum da ist, muß der Erzähler es sich erst eigens schaffen: "Da verbreitete sich unter den Brüdern das Gerücht[38]: Dieser Jünger stirbt nicht. Doch Jesus hatte ihm ja gar nicht gesagt, daß er nicht sterben werde, sondern: 'Wenn ich will, daß er bleibt, bis ich komme, was geht das dich an?'" (21,20-23). Da diese Sätze m.E. Ursprung der gesamten ephesinischen Johanneslegende und aller ihrer modernen Varianten sind, erfordern sie eine äußerst sorgfältige und ohne alle Seitenblicke auf eine vermeintliche Realwelt vorgehende "*textcentered exegesis*". Die gegenwärtigen Varianten jener Johanneslegende aus dem Ephesus des zweiten Jahrhunderts haben die folgende Grundgestalt: Nach den zitierten Versen soll der geliebte Jünger, Augenzeuge der Geschichte Jesu seit dessen Jerusalemer Todespassah und als solcher der durch die besondere Liebe seines Herrn legitimierte "Traditionsgarant", sowie das verehrte "Schulhaupt" einer spezifisch "johanneischen Gemeinde" gewesen sein. Obwohl bereits in hohem Alter habe sein plötzliches Sterben "seine Gemeinde" aufs Tiefste verstört, weil sie mit seinem Tod nicht nur den Verlust ihres geliebten Lehrers, sondern dazu noch das offenkundige Scheitern einer Verheißung ihres himmlischen Herrn zu verschmerzen gehabt habe. Deshalb seien die posthumen "Herausgeber" seines Evangeliums, die sich in den "Wir" von Vers 24 zu Wort melden sollen, darum bemüht, die verstörte Gemeinde zu trösten und durch ihre Reinterpretation des Jesuswortes auch jeden Schatten eines Verdachtes gegen die Verläßlichkeit seiner Verheißungen

---

[38] Seit der Auferstandene am Ostermorgen *seinen* Vater zum Vater und Gott auch seiner Jünger erklärt und gemacht hat (Joh 20,17) heißen und sind diese fortan *"Jesu Brüder"*. Deshalb erscheint mir die extratextuale Deutung des Lexems ἀδελφοί auf "Mißverstehende ... Nicht-Johanneer" durch Bonsack (1988: 61) ebenso abwegig wie die um das Problem der Referenz *literarischer Werke* völlig unbekümmerte Identifikation der *erzählten* ἀδελφοί mit dem Phantom einer *"johanneischen Gemeinde"*.

auszuräumen[39].

Angesichts dieser alles andere als "textzentrierten" Konstruktion, die – freilich unter der durch die kritische Forschung der letzten beiden Jahrhunderte erzwungenen Preisgabe der Autorschaft des galiläischen Fischers Johannes Zebedäus – nichts anderes ist als die Repetition der alten ephesinischen Legende unter neuen Bedingungen, fragt man sich doch zunächst, wozu denn das ganze raffiniert eingefädelte Ratespiel um die Identität des geliebten Jüngers im Evangelium überhaupt veranstaltet wird, wenn er doch eine in der sogenannten "johanneischen Gemeinde" jedermann bekannte Person gewesen sein soll[40]. Weiter stellt sich die Frage, wo denn jene "herausgebenden Schüler" eigentlich ihre Hand im Spiel haben und wo nicht. Entstammt ihrer Feder etwa auch das "Wir" in Joh 1,14 und anderswo? Und soll ihr vermeintlicher Lehrer und Gemeindegründer womöglich sich selbst als "der Jünger, den Jesus liebte" bezeichnet haben. Das ist doch wohl ein unmöglicher Gedanke, weil der so Bezeichnete damit sich und sein Reden von der Liebe aufs Tiefste diskreditierte. Als Lösung bliebe dann wohl nur, daß seine "Schüler" das gesamte Evangelium in seiner uns überlieferten Gestalt "herausgegeben" haben müßten.

Die durch Küglers Resümee, "Ich glaube es nicht", und durch seine gesamte Monographie erzwungene neue Lektüre aller einschlägigen Texte hat mich überzeugt: Auch wenn Joh 21,22f. den Tod des geliebten Jüngers vorauszusetzen scheint, so kann es sich bei diesem Toten doch keinesfalls um den verehrten Gründer und allseits bekannten Lehrer, um den Traditionsgaranten und das Schulhaupt einer spezi-

---

[39] Mit der Variation, daß mit der fiktionalen, erst von der "johanneischen Redaktion" geschaffenen Lieblingsjünger–Figur auf der Ebene des Evangelientextes gleichwohl einer realen Person aus der Geschichte der "johanneischen Gemeinde", nämlich ihrem "geistbegabten Überlieferungsgaranten und geachteten Lehrer" ein "literarisches Denkmal" habe gesetzt werden sollen, hatte ich selbst noch 1975 in Leuven die alte ephesinische Legende erneuert (Thyen 1977). Doch zu Recht fragt Kügler zu dieser und ähnlichen Konstruktionen: "Könnte es so gewesen sein?", um dann mit schwer widerlegbaren Gründen zu antworten: "Ich glaube es nicht" (1988a: 479).

[40] Overbeck sieht in den Anspielungen auf die Person des Evangelisten, die das ganze Evangelium und zumal sein 21. Kapitel durchziehen, "zwei ganz entgegengesetzte Interessen des Verfassers unzertrennlich ineinandergeflochten, von denen das eine darauf ausgeht, uns den Evangelisten ebenso sicher zu verbergen, wie das andere, ihn uns erraten zu lassen" (1911: 240f.). Längst vor der Ausbildung einer narratologischen Texttheorie samt der ihr entsprechenden Terminologie unterscheidet Overbeck bereits äußerst scharfsinnig zwischen dem "*Evangelisten im vierten Evangelium*" und seinem "*wahren Verfasser*". Nur die Frage nach dem ersteren – wir würden heute sagen, die Frage nach dem vom realen Autor geschaffenen "*Erzähler*" oder nach dem "*fiktiven Autor*" (der keinesfalls mit dem "*impliziten Autor*" verwechselt werden darf) – hält Overbeck für sinnvoll, die Frage nach dem letzteren dagegen für "bare Absurdität" (241). Seine Überlegungen zum Ursprungsort des Evangeliums haben für Overbeck die Konsequenz, daß der vierte Evangelist – selbst wenn er in Kleinasien geschrieben haben sollte – "in der Hauptsache als der Begründer oder Schöpfer der kleinasiatischen Johannessage betrachtet werden" muß und sie darum "nur vor sich und nicht hinter sich haben" kann (362).

fisch "johanneischen Gemeinde" handeln, die in ihrem tiefen Betroffensein über dieses unerwartete Sterben hätte getröstet werden müssen. Denn dieser "geliebte Jünger" ist außerhalb des Textes, d.h. in der Welt seiner Leser – und zwar des sogenannten "Erstpublikums" wie aller späteren Leser des Evangeliums – ein *Unbekannter*. Das macht die Art seiner Einführung in die evangelische Erzählung unübersehbar: "The Beloved Disciple, somewhat surprisingly, is introduced as a character unknown to the reader (13,23; 21,24). He is first referred to as 'one of his disciples, whom Jesus loved' (13,23), not '*the* disciple whom Jesus loved' as he is in 19,26; 20,2; 21,7. 20. The difference is slight but shows that the reader is not expected to recognize the Beloved Disciple. At the end, the reader must also be told that it was the Beloved Disciple who bore witness to, and wrote, these things (21,24)"[41]. Das deiktische οὗτος, das diesen Vers 21,24 einleitet, hat außerhalb des Textes keine Referenz, es verweist dessen Leser vielmehr auf die bei der Lektüre vor seinen Augen innerhalb des Textes und mit dessen Mitteln geschaffene Figur jenes "Jüngers, den Jesus liebte"[42].

Küglers kritischer Destruktion der außertextlichen Existenz des geliebten Jüngers als des Gründers und Lehrers einer besonderen "johanneischen Gemeinde" kann ich nur voll zustimmen. Sie ist mir indes bei weitem noch nicht konsequent und radikal genug. Bedenkt man nämlich, daß das neuerdings verbreitete Reden von einem "johanneischen Schulhaupt" überhaupt nur aufgekommen ist und entstehen konnte, weil man gemeint hatte, diese Person im *Spiegel* der Textpassagen um den geliebten Jünger als deren reales Modell entschlüsseln zu können, so begreife ich nicht, warum Kügler überhaupt noch an diesem Gedanken festhalten und zumal, wie er ihn begründen will, nachdem er ihm mit den Lieblingsjüngertexten doch jegliche Basis entzogen hat[43]. Zudem scheint mir in seinem Fazit, der im Evangelium als ein "Jünger Jesu und Verfasser des Joh" dargestellte "geliebte Jünger" sei "*historisch* ... keines von beiden" gewesen (483), insofern ein Kurzschluß zu stecken, als er damit die schlechthin inkommensurablen Größen des realen Verfassers eines

---

[41] Culpepper 1983: 215; vgl. Kügler (1988a: 481) und siehe das ebd. grundsätzlich zu Textanfängen, sowie speziell zum Eingang des JohEvs Gesagte.

[42] Vgl. Kügler 1988a: 482.

[43] "Die Existenz einer apostolischen Lehrer- und Gründergestalt, die am Beginn des johanneischen Christentums steht oder zumindest in der Gemeindegeschichte eine wichtige Rolle gespielt hat, kann natürlich nicht bestritten werden. Unbestreitbar ist ferner die Möglichkeit, daß die Redaktion diese Gestalt kannte und bei der Gestaltung der Lieblingsjüngerfigur an diese dachte ...." (Kügler 1988a: 482). Doch abgesehen davon, daß der reale Autor eine solche Figur fingiert und sie als den (fiktiven) "Autor" seines Werkes an den Anfang von dessen Lektüre gestellt hat, kann ich für das, was Kügler "unbestreitbar" nennt, keine Indizien entdecken. Das hängt freilich damit zusammen, daß ich seiner Konstruktion der Geschichte des johanneischen Christentums und zumal deren literarkritischer Fundierung nicht zu folgen vermag.

Werkes und eine fiktionale Figur aus dessen "Welt" auf ein und dieselbe Ebene
stellt. Das gilt erst recht für seinen Geniestreich, das stets als sicheres Indiz für die
reale Existenz des geliebten Jüngers und seines Todes in Anspruch genommene
"Gerücht", Jesus habe ihm zugesagt, daß er vor seiner Parusie nicht sterben werde,
"für eine literarische Fiktion zu halten" (484). Denn auch wenn das Gerücht – und
wer wollte das für seine vorliegende Gestalt bestreiten – eine "literarische Fiktion"
ist, so besagt solche Feststellung doch noch lange nichts über die historische Existenz oder Nichtexistenz desjenigen, dessen Verfasserschaft hier durch Pseudepigraphie fingiert wird. Da aber das Mittel der Pseudepigraphie in aller Regel dazu
dient, das unter ihrem Mantel verfaßte Werk durch seinen ihm untergeschobenen
Verfasser zu autorisieren, dürfte diesem Zweck eine bloß erdichtete Figur kaum jemals genügen. Zumindest muß sie in der kulturellen Welt, in der das Werk erscheint,
als eine reale Person *gelten*. Das heißt in unserem Fall, der "geliebte Jünger" muß
einer der Zwölf sein. Außerdem setzt das Spiel mit dem ambivalenten Orakel Jesu
über dessen Bestimmung (21,22f.) m.E. doch zwingend seinen Tod voraus, wie immer es dabei um den "Logos" stehen mag, der sich unter den "Brüdern" verbreitet
haben soll. Und auch das darf ja wohl als für die Pseudepigraphie typisch gelten:
Keiner, der zu diesem Mittel greift, wird riskieren, daß ihm sein fingierter Autor eines Tages als lebendiger Kritiker gegenübertritt. Liegt die Lösung des Rätsels um
den geliebten Jünger, wie die Väter des zweiten Jahrhunderts gemeint haben, in
dem Namen des Zebedaiden Johannes, dann ist er von Petrus nicht durch die Art
seines Todes, sondern durch seine *Aufgabe* zu Lebzeiten unterschieden. Denn wie
Petrus, so sind nach Mk 10,35-40 parr. doch wohl auch die *beiden* Zebedaiden als
Märtyrer gestorben, wenn auch aufgrund von Apg 12,2 im Vergleich mit Gal 2,9
nicht gleichzeitig, wie Eduard Schwartz einst postulierte[44].

Doch noch einmal zurück zu dem unter den Brüdern verbreiteten Gerücht: "Dieser Jünger stirbt nicht". Abgesehen davon, daß es in seiner vorliegenden Gestalt als
ein typisch "johanneisches Mißverständnis" das literarische Mittel in der Hand des
Autors ist, das es ihm erlaubt zu sagen, worauf er mit dem ganzen 21. Kapitel hinaus
will – darauf nämlich, daß kein anderer als Jesus selbst dieses Evangelium als das

---

[44] Gegen Zuntz (1991), der in der Auseinandersetzung mit E. Schwartz (1904 und 1910) das Jo-
hannesmartyrium als späte Legende erweisen will, argumentiert M. Hengel (1993: 88-95) – mir sehr
einleuchtend – genau umgekehrt: Die frühen Spuren des Johannesmartyriums als die "lectio diffcil-
ior" seien durch die spätere Sage vom friedlichen Sterben des uralten Zebedaiden in Ephesus fast
völlig verdrängt worden. Ähnlich, wenngleich immer noch im Schatten der von Overbeck beklagten
Apologetik, erklärt Gnilka: "Die historische Frage nach dem Martertod des Johannes … wird durch
später aufkommende Überlieferungen sehr schwer beantwortbar, ist aber heute einer Lösung im an-
gedeuteten Sinn (sc. Martyrium beider Zebedaiden!) eher zugänglich, nachdem sich die Auffassung
durchgesetzt hat, daß 'der Jünger, den Jesus liebte' des vierten Evangeliums nicht der Zebedäide gewesen sei" (1979: 102). Vgl. noch W. Bauer 1933: 241-44.

bleibende und wahre Zeugnis seines geliebten Jüngers autorisiert hat –, ließe sich ja dennoch fragen, ob nicht über den Zebedaiden Johannes tatsächlich einst ein derartiges Gerücht im Umlauf gewesen sein könnte. Nach Mk 9,1 parr. sagt Jesus zu seinen Jüngern: "Wahrlich, ich sage euch, einige von denen, die jetzt hier stehen, werden den Tod nicht schmecken, ehe sie nicht das machtvolle Gekommensein der Gottesherrschaft (βασιλείαν ἐληλυθυῖαν) gesehen haben". Im Kontext des Markusevangeliums wird rasch klar, daß es Petrus, Jakobus und Johannes sind, die noch vor ihrem Tode die gekommene Gottesherrschaft auf dem Verklärungsberg sehen dürfen. Die Formulierung, μὴ γεύσωνται θανάτου, mit der dabei von ihrem Sterben gesprochen wird, legt es nahe, an das Martyrium dieser drei Zeugen der himmlischen Welt zu denken. Sollte das Logion aber, ehe Markus es auf diese Weise seinem Evangelium einverleibte, schon als isoliertes Jesuswort mündlich tradiert worden sein, dann *könnte* es sich nach den Martyrien seiner beiden Gefährten ja durchaus an den überlebenden *Johannes* geheftet haben[45]. Und die "Brüder", unter denen es sich verbreitet hatte, wären eben jene ersten Jünger Jesu gewesen, zu denen Maria im Auftrag ihres auferstandenen Herrn mit der Osterbotschaft gekommen war (Joh 20,17f.), nicht aber irgendeine "johanneische Gemeinde" am Ende des ersten Jahrhunderts[46]. Doch mehr als ein immerhin möglicher Gedanke kann diese Erwägung freilich nicht sein.

In schroffem Gegensatz zu dieser Sicht und auch zu Küglers großer Monographie, die er aber gar nicht zu kennen scheint, oder jedenfalls mit keiner Silbe auch nur der geringsten *Erwähnung* würdigt, hat sich jüngst Richard Bauckham (1993) zur Frage nach dem geliebten Jünger geäußert[47]. Er knüpft an Hengels Versuch einer neuen Lösung der alten Rätselfrage nach dem geliebten Jünger an. Doch was bei Hengel aufgrund der schillernden Ambivalenzen des Textes noch ein behutsamer "Vorschlag" ist, wird ihm zur unerschütterlichen *Tatsache*. Der geliebte Jünger und Autor des Johannesevangeliums *ist* der papianische Presbyter *Johannes*. Hatte Hengel im Text des Evangeliums noch Signale wahrgenommen, die auf die Person des Zebedaiden verwiesen, und daraus geschlossen, dieser werde hier mit dem Presbyter Johannes zur idealen Jüngerfigur verschmolzen, so sieht Bauckham darin nur eine "unnötige Komplikation" und erklärt den Zebedaiden rundweg zu einem "Phantom", "which needs to be finally and completely exorcised" (24). Vehement bestreitet er jeglichen Rätselcharakter dieser Figur und gewinnt seine Gewißheit, daß für

---

[45] Vgl. W. Bauer 1933: 239.

[46] Ganz zutreffend konstatiert Kügler: "Schließlich weist die Formulierung in V.23 ("unter den Brüdern") darauf hin, daß der implizite Autor den Verbreitungskreis des Gerüchts von seinen Adressaten unterscheidet, die der Erzähler ja sonst direkt anreden kann" (1988a: 484).

[47] In engem Anschluß an Minear weist Bauckham zunächst die unauflösbare Zusammengehörigkeit von Joh 21 mit dem Rest des Evangeliums auf und zeigt dann, daß die Einführung des geliebten Jüngers von vornherein allein dem Zweck dient, ihn dem Leser am Ende als den Autor des Werkes zu präsentieren.

die vermeintlichen Erstleser in der "johanneischen Schule" oder "Gemeinde" über die Frage nach der Identität dieses ihnen "certainly" und "very well" bekannten Jünger-Autors niemals auch nur der geringste Zweifel bestanden habe (29), allein aus dem oben erörterten *Gerücht*, daß der geliebte Jünger vor der Parusie nicht sterben werde: "That the beloved disciple, as a rare, perhaps finally unique, survivor should at the end of his life have been rumoured to be the subject of a personalized version of Mk 9,1 is easily credible. The rumour would certainly be of no interest if the beloved disciple were regarded as an unknown disciple. ..." (29). Von dieser mir äußerst fragwürdigen Identifikation abgesehen, weiß Bauckham jedoch aus den einschlägigen Texten einleuchtend zu begründen[48], daß die Einführung des geliebten Jüngers in den Evangelientext von vorneherein und danach Schritt um Schritt einzig dem Ziel dient, ihn als ebenso "idealen" wie tatsächlichen "Autor" dieses Buches darzustellen und nicht etwa nur als den Typus eines "idealen Jüngers" oder echten Vertreters "johanneischen Christentums" (33-39).

## *4. Struktur und Intention von Joh 21*

Ehe wir uns im letzten und fünften Teil noch den bisher unerörtert gebliebenen Texten über den geliebten Jünger zuwenden, um so die fehlenden Farben und Konturen in seinem Bild zu ergänzen, sind hier noch einmal Struktur und Intention von Joh 21 ins Auge zu fassen. Das Kapitel wird eröffnet durch eine dritte österliche Begegnung Jesu mit seinen Jüngern (1-14). Ort der Handlung ist der "See von Tiberias" in Galiläa. Aber es geht nicht einfach um die Anfügung einer weiteren Ostererzählung, weil aller guten Dinge drei wären, oder weil der Erzähler einen Ausgleich zwischen galiläischer und Jerusalemer Auferstehungtradition hätte schaffen wollen. Denn der Leser hat doch wohl nicht vergessen, daß dieser galiläischen Epiphanie ja die solenne Szene mit der Verleihung des Geistes an die Jünger, ihrer Bevollmächtigung, Sünde zu vergeben oder zu behalten, und der Sendung der so Ausgerüsteten vorausgegangen war (20,19-23). Wie Mk 16,7f. ist Galiläa der Ort des Glaubens und seiner Bewährung im Alltag, Ort der glückenden österlichen Wiederholung alles dessen, was da zuvor mißlungen war[49]. Die zahlreichen und schon oft beobachteten symbolischen Obertöne der Erzählung[50] machen deutlich, daß es die zu

---

[48] Zu diesen Texten zählt Bauckham mit guten Gründen neben Joh 18,15-18 auch Joh 1,35-42, d.h. er sieht in dem mit Andreas und noch vor Petrus erstberufenen Anonymus den geliebten Jünger. Darüber hinaus will er ihn mit der Mehrheit der Ausleger auch mit dem Zeugen unter dem Kreuz identifizieren, der Blut und Wasser aus der durchbohrten Seite Jesu fließen sah (Joh 19,35). Das scheint mir jedoch seit der Studie von Minear (1983a) unmöglich, wie unten zu zeigen sein wird.

[49] Wie die Legende vom Tod des uralten Zebedaiden in Ephesus mir nichts als eine "Lesefrucht" aus Joh 21,22ff. zu sein scheint, so dürfte auch die geläufige Rede von "galiläischen Ostererscheinungen" nur die Frucht der Lektüre von Mk 16,7 sein, deren Ernte längst vor der modernen Forschung bereits Matthäus eröffnet hat; vgl. Steinseifer 1971.

[50] Vgl. Ruckstuhl 1977. Zur Tag-und-Nacht Symbolik siehe auch Segovia 1991: 178f.

"Menschenfischern" bestimmten Jünger sind, die an ihrem ergebnislosen nächtlichen Fang die Wahrheit von Jesu Wort lernen müssen: "Ohne mich könnt ihr nichts tun" (15,5). Erst auf Jesu Wort hin, im Licht seines Tages und seiner Präsenz glückt dann der Fang[51]. Außer in der Kontrastszene, wo er Petrus den Zutritt zur Aula des hohepriesterlichen Palastes und damit zum Ort von dessen dreifacher Verleugnung seines Herrn am Kohlenfeuer (ἀνθρακία) verschafft hatte (Joh 18,15-18 u. 25-27), greift der geliebte Jünger nur hier in den Handlungsablauf (*plot*) des Evangeliums ein. Nachdem er sich ja schon am Grabe Jesu als ein des Lesens der Zeichen seines Herrn Kundiger erwiesen hatte (20,8), eröffnet er Petrus durch sein Wort: *"Es ist der Herr"* (21,7), den Weg zur glückenden *Wiederholung* seines Versagens und – wiederum am *Kohlenfeuer* – zum Wiedergewinn seiner verlorenen Liebe (vgl. H. Thyen 1994/95). Denn auf sein Wort hin bekleidet sich Petrus mit seinem Obergewand, "denn er war nackt" (21,7), und macht sich über den See hinweg auf den Weg zu seinem Herrn. Angesichts des häufigen und sublimen Spiels des Johannes mit den Texten seiner synoptischen Vorläufer habe ich keine Bedenken, diesen Aufbruch des Petrus über das Wasser als die nun glückende Wiederholung seines einst im Versinken kläglich gescheiterten Versuchs zu lesen (Mt 14,26ff.). Über die geheimnisvolle Zahl der *einhundertdreiundfünfzig* großen Fische ist bereits so viel gerätselt worden, daß die Zahl der Lösungsvorschläge bald jener der Fische entsprechen dürfte[52]. Darum übe ich hier Enthaltsamkeit. Auffällig ist aber, daß diese Fische trotz 21,5 weniger die *Materie*, als vielmehr die *Quasi-Genossen* eines Mahles zu sein scheinen, das sich deutlich als Wiederholung der wunderbaren Speisung von Joh 6 zu erkennen gibt.

Overbeck (1911) sieht die "unverkennbare Absicht" des nun folgenden, durch Joh 21,1-14 vorbereiteten Gesprächs zwischen Jesus und Petrus (21,15-24) darin, "das 4. Evangelium zu legitimieren". Ja, das gesamte 21. Kapitel erscheint ihm "zureichend definiert", wenn man es als einen "Anhang, der dem 4. Evangelium beigegeben ist zum Zwecke seiner Legitimierung" bestimmt (436). Auch wenn Petrus insofern im Zentrum des Geschehens zu stehen scheint, als er der alleinige *Partner* des Gesprächs mit Jesus ist und der geliebte Jünger nur dessen *Gegenstand*, muß er – hier wie auch sonst im Evangelium – in Wahrheit doch nur dem anderen Jünger als "Folie" dienen. Dabei kann freilich von irgendeiner Art von "Antipetrinismus" des Johannesevangeliums als Spiegel einer vermeintlichen Rivalität zwischen "petrinischen" und "johanneischen Gemeinden" auch nicht entfernt die Rede sein.

---

[51] Dazu, daß und wie Joh hier Texte des Lukasevangeliums verarbeitet, vgl. Neirynck 1990.

[52] 153 ist eine der in der Antike beliebten "Dreieckszahlen", nämlich die Summe der Zahlen von 1-17. Neben zahlreichen Versuchen, das Rätsel mit Hilfe solcher Zahlensymbolik zu lösen, beruhen viele andere auf der *Gematrie*, d.h. auf der Suche nach Wörtern oder Syntagmen, deren Buchstabenwert der Zahl 153 entspricht.

Denn nicht ein vorsätzlich geschwächter, sondern nur ein starker Petrus, der in den Fußstapfen seines Herrn als ein guter Hirte für seine Schafe sterben wird, kann der Autorisierung des anonymen Jüngers und seines Werkes erfolgreich dienen[53]. Der Dialog zwischen Petrus und seinem Herrn verläuft in zwei Gängen, deren erster Weg und Geschick des Petrus (15-18) und deren zweiter die Bestimmung des geliebten Jüngers thematisiert (20-22). Beide Phasen des Gesprächs enden mit einem ambivalenten Orakel Jesu, zunächst über Petrus (v.18) und dann über den anderen Jünger (v.22). In beiden Fällen hebt der allwissende Erzähler jedoch durch seine unmittelbar an die mißverständlichen Orakel angeschlossenen Kommentare (Vers 19 und Verse 23-25) deren Ambivalenzen sogleich auf. Also hatte Jesus mit seinem Wort über Petrus (v.18) nicht etwa Sturm und Drang von dessen Jugend mit der Hilflosigkeit seines Greisenalters kontrastiert, sondern vielmehr dem ganzen Leben des Petrus metaphorisch bereits sein Sterben als Märtyrer gegenübergestellt. Und im Unterschied zu seinem Wort über Petrus und gegen dessen Wißbegier hatte Jesus über den geliebten Jünger (v.22) – wie die Verse 23-25 klären – gerade *nicht* von dessen Leben und Sterben oder auch Nichtsterben gesprochen, sondern gesagt, der solle bis ans Ende der Tage (ἕως ἔρχομαι) als der wahrhafte Zeuge (ὁ μαρτυρῶν) und Exeget seines Herrn (vgl. 1,18 mit 13,23 und der nachdrücklichen Erinnerung daran in 21,20!) *bleiben*. Einerlei also, ob er lebt oder ob er stirbt, nach dem letzten Willen seines Herrn[54] soll er bleiben und schreiben, soll schreiben und damit in seinem geschriebenen Zeugnis bleiben.

Damit ist bereits gesagt, daß hier allen Autoren, die die Verse 24 und 25 als die sekundären Zusätze von "Redaktoren" oder "Editoren" des Evangeliums vom Rest von Joh 21 abtrennen wollen, aufs entschiedenste zu widersprechen ist. Denn das gesamte Kapitel, ja – wie die 21,20 absichtsvoll rekapitulierte erste Einführung des

---

[53] "Ganz im Gegenteil ist die Höhe des Petrus der Fußsockel für die des Johannes" (Overbeck 1911: 458; vgl. ebd. 456-459; und siehe Kragerud 1959: 53f.). – Ruckstuhl, der trotz seiner besseren Einsicht (in die literarische Einheit des Johannesevangeliums!) an dem redaktionellen Charakter von Joh 21 festhält (oder besser, der bis zur Publikation von "Stilkritik und Verfasserfrage" [1991] daran *festhielt*), hat gemeint, mit diesem "Nachtrag" wolle dessen Verfasser "petrinischen Gemeinden" dieses "johanneische" Evangelium empfehlen (1977: 356, Anm. 28 u. 360f.; ähnlich R. E. Brown 1979: 161f.). "Merkwürdig" gegenüber dieser vermeintlich "starken Rücksichtnahme unseres Kapitels auf Petrus, petrinische Gemeinden und Überlieferung" empfindet Ruckstuhl "die Vernachlässigung des paulinischen Christentums und Missionsgebietes" und zieht daraus den "geographischen" Schluß, daß es "von daher unwahrscheinlich (sei), daß die johanneische Kirche in Ephesus lebte. Sie dürfte zur Zeit des Verfassers in Syrien oder 'jenseits des Jordan' gelebt haben" (1977: 361). Kügler hält diese Konstruktion zu Recht für "anachronistisch" (1988a: 484). Ich kann außer der Verarbeitung der synoptischen Petrusüberlieferung keinerlei Verbeugung vor irgendeiner Art von "Petrinismus" erkennen und empfände es umgekehrt mehr als "merkwürdig", wenn in einem *Evangelium* (!) Paulus und sein Missionsgebiet erkennbar würden. – Die Rede über den vermeintlichen "Antipetrinismus des Joh ist in der Literatur weit verbreitet; vgl. z.B. nur Snyder 1971.

geliebten Jüngers in 13,23ff. zeigt – das ganze Evangelium läuft auf die unlösbar zusammengehörigen Verse 23-25 hinaus, so daß "jede Herauslösung dieser beiden Schlußverse 24 und 25 aus dem 21. Kapitel auch nur durch Alinea absolut grundlos ist"[55]. Ich erspare es mir, die Namen der sicher auch bald "153 großen" Autoren zu nennen, die Harnacks willkürlicher Abtrennung von Joh 21,24f. vom Rest des Kapitels gefolgt sind[56]. Der fast unausrottbare Grund für die Neigung, den Vers 24 vom Vorausgehenden abzutrennen, liegt ja wohl darin, daß unmittelbar nach der Identifikation des geliebten Jüngers mit dem Evangelisten (οὗτός ἐστιν ... ὁ γράψας ταῦτα), die zugleich sein Schreiben als den Zweck seines Bleibens enthüllte, in den "Wir" des οἴδαμεν eine unbestimmte Mehrzahl von Zeugen für die Wahrheit seines Zeugnisses einzutreten scheint. Da nun aber der Evangelist aufgrund der vermeintlich durch sein Sterben notwendig gewordenen *Umdeutung* des unter den "*Brüdern*" verbreiteten *Logos* ja bereits tot sein soll, werden diese Zeugen flugs mit

---

[54] Mit dem konditionalen "Wenn ich will ..." (ἐὰν αὐτὸν θέλω μένειν), läßt Jesus nicht etwa offen, was und ob er will oder nicht will, wie vielfach und neuerdings wieder von Beasley-Murray (1987: 412) behauptet wird, sondern damit erklärt er gerade seinen unverbrüchlichen Willen. Denn jede Deutung, die sich derart auf die konditionale Form des Satzes stützt, übersieht, daß mit dem fraglichen Satz ja *Petrus* angeredet, wegen seiner ungehörigen Einmischung in die Frage nach dem Geschick des geliebten Jüngers schroff zurückgewiesen und an seine eigene Bestimmung erinnert wird. "Das θέλω in dem Falle des Johannes ist nämlich nichts anderes als der Ersatz für den Imperativ im Falle des Petrus, und die Notwendigkeit dieses Ersatzes ist einfach durch den Umstand herbeigeführt, daß der Gesamtanlage der Erzählung gemäß nur die für Petrus bestimmte Willenserklärung sich an diesen direkt richtet. Zugleich aber erklärt sich nun auch das diesem θέλω vorgesetzte ἐάν. Auch dieses ist lediglich durch den Umstand herbeigeführt, daß die für Johannes bestimmten Jesusworte nicht als direkte Anrede an Johannes auftreten, sondern in der Form einer Zurechtweisung des Petrus" (Overbeck 1911: 450). Übersetzt in eine Anrede an den geliebten Jünger, müßte der Satz darum lauten: "Du sollst bleiben und schreiben; schreiben und darin bleiben!"

[55] Overbeck 1911: 453. Gegen diese Einsicht verstoßen die Herausgeber sowohl des *The Greek New Testament*[3] als auch des Nestle-Aland[26], die durch das Druckbild anstelle des Textes eine fragwürdige und irreführende *Interpretation* desselben bieten. Zwar fehlte der Vers 25 im Sinaiticus prima manu zunächst, doch dabei handelt es sich ganz fraglos um ein bloßes Versehen des Schreibers, das er durch das Löschen der dem Vers 24 folgenden *Corona* und *Subscriptio*: εὐαγγέλιον κατὰ Ἰωάννην, sowie durch deren neue Setzung nach dem nun hinzugefügten Vers 25 *eigenhändig* sofort korrigiert hat (vgl. Milne and Skeat 1938: 12f.).

[56] Harnack 1897: 659-680, wonach erst Spätere, in "einem dunklen Wir" verborgen, das Werk des papianischen Presbyters Johannes, durch Joh 21,24f. eigenmächtig ergänzt und ihn selbst als Verfasser des Evangeliums mit dem Zebedaiden identifiziert haben sollen (675f.). Fast bis in alle Einzelheiten hat jetzt M. Hengel (1993) Harnacks Ansichten wiederholt. – Wohin solche Abtrennung der Verse 24f. führt, zeigt die Studie von Wiarda (1992), der nach meinem Eindruck nicht etwa *Johannes*, sondern ein durchaus "*anderes Evangelium*" (ὃ οὐκ ἔστιν ἄλλο: Gal 1,7) auslegt. – Völlig unverständlich ist mir, wie ausgerechnet Bauckham (1993: 30f.), der doch wohl ohne Joh 21,24 schwerlich jemals auf seine treffende Nachzeichnung des geliebten Jüngers als des "*idealen Autors*" gekommen wäre, gerade diesen entscheidenden Vers für sekundär erklären kann.

seinen *Schülern* identifiziert, die sein Evangelium nach dem Tode des Meisters herausgeben und ihm auch noch Vers 25, "die mächtigste Hyperbel, die je ein Buch schließen kann"[57], hinzugefügt haben sollen. Doch abgesehen von dem schwer vorstellbaren schreibenden Kollektiv beruht diese Konstruktion auf der bereits erörterten unmöglichen Voraussetzung, daß mit dem geliebten Jünger entgegen der ihm anhaftenden Verheißung Jesu ein allseits *bekannter* und verehrter Lehrer der "johanneischen Gemeinde" verstorben sei. Diese Voraussetzung ist deshalb unmöglich, weil sie mit dem kunstvollen Spiel um die Anonymität des geliebten Jüngers und mit dem Rätsel seines Namens einen der wesentlichen Reize dieses Evangeliums zerstört. Der "Jünger, den Jesus liebte", dessen Bild bei der Lektüre des Johannesevangeliums vor den Augen seiner ersten wie aller späteren Leser überhaupt erst entsteht, ist also der fiktionale und keinesfalls der reale "Evangelist". Darum besteht zwischen dem "geliebten Jünger" und dem qumranischen "Lehrer der Gerechtigkeit" als einer realen Person von Fleisch und Blut auch nicht die allerentfernteste Analogie[58]. Fällt aber das vermeintliche "Schulhaupt", dann wankt auch das Fundament der ja wesentlich darauf gegründeten und neuerdings so beliebten "johanneischen Schule"[59]. Lassen wir uns also von dem Plural in οἴδαμεν nicht irreführen! Wie Joh 1,14 und 1 Joh 1,1ff. greift darin der implizite Autor zu dem bewährten Instrument des *plural auctoris*. "Mit diesem seinem 'Wir wissen' spricht der Verfasser nur den Glauben aus, mit dem er den Leser seiner Schrift zu entlassen wünscht. Es ist das Glaubensbekenntnis, in dem er sich und den Leser, den er durch seine Schrift gewonnen hat, eins weiß. Als Zeugnis eines Fremden an Fremde könnte es nur das Evangelium verdächtigen"[60]. Weil natürlich auch er sich unter der Maxime weiß, "Wenn ich für mich selbst zeugte, so wäre mein Zeugnis nicht wahr" (Joh 5,31), bleibt ihm gar keine andere Wahl als die *dieses* auktorialen Plurals.

## 5. Der geliebte Jünger als der ideale Evangelist

War mit Joh 21,24 endlich ausgesprochen, daß der geliebte Jünger und verläßliche Wahrheitszeuge kein anderer ist als derjenige, der im Auftrag seines Herrn dies (Evangelium) geschrieben hat, daß er also der überall gegenwärtige und allwissende Erzähler ist, der auch die verborgensten Gedanken seiner Akteure, sowie das ge-

---

[57] J. G. Herder 1829: 273; zitiert bei Overbeck 1911: 454.

[58] So J. Roloff 1968.

[59] Vgl. die einflußreiche Untersuchung von Culpepper (1975). Siehe etwa: "The community regarded the BD as its head in much the same way as ancient schools regarded their founders. The BD may also have been regarded as the representative of the community; and as such his authority is held above Peter's, who may at times serve as the representative of Petrine Christianity" (267).

[60] Overbeck 1911: 454.

heimnisvolle Woher und Wohin seines Protagonisten von Anfang an kennt, dann kann er nicht irgend ein zufälliger Zeuge nur der letzten Tage Jesu in Jerusalem sein. Bedingung dafür, daß sich in, mit und unter seinem Zeugnis kein anderer als der von Jesus selbst gesandte und von ihm zeugende parakletische Geist der Wahrheit zu Wort meldet, ist vielmehr, daß er deren einer ist, von denen gilt: ὅτι ἀπ' ἀρχῆς μετ' ἐμοῦ ἐστε (15,27f.). Daß er *explizit*, nämlich als einer seiner Jünger, "den Jesus liebte", erst bei der Erzählung von Fußwaschung und letztem Mahl in die Erzählung eingeführt wird, kann also keinesfalls bedeuten, daß er ungenannt nicht immer schon als aufmerksamer Zeuge dabeigewesen wäre[61]. Unser fiktionaler Evangelist muß also, mit Lukas gesagt, zu denen gehören, die ἀπ' ἀρχῆς αὐτόπται καὶ ὑπηρέται τοῦ λογοῦ (Lk 1,2) waren, "von Anfang an", nämlich: ἀρξάμενος ἀπὸ τοῦ βαπτίσματος Ἰωάννου (Apg 1,22). Deshalb bin ich trotz des Einspruchs von Frans Neirynck (1991) mehr und mehr davon überzeugt, daß unser Erzähler schon ganz zu Anfang (1,35-42) dadurch, daß er den einen der beiden Erstberufenen in der Anonymität beließ, absichtsvoll eine Leerstelle geschaffen hat, in die sein Leser den geliebten Jünger einsetzen soll[62]. Natürlich hat er diese Identifikation nicht selbst vollzogen – insoweit hat Neirynck ganz recht –, denn damit hätte er ja das erst seinen Lesern aufgegebene Rätsel um seinen Anonymus schon im Ansatz zerstört.

Der geliebte Jünger war ausgezeichnet durch sein *Bleiben* auf dem Weg der Nachfolge. Er war nicht aus dem Garten nach Hause entflohen und hatte seinen Herrn nicht "allein gelassen" (16,32), sondern war ihm nachgefolgt, zuerst bis in den Hof des Hohenpriesters (18,15-18) und endlich in der "Stunde" Jesu bis unter das Kreuz von Golgatha (19,25-27). Ich kann es nicht für bloßen Zufall halten, daß auch die Szene der Berufung der beiden ersten Jünger unter dem Signum des *Bleibens* steht. Als zwei Jünger Johannes (des Täufers)[63] sein Zeugnis, "Siehe das Lamm Gottes", gehört haben, folgen sie Jesus nach (ἠκολούθησαν τῷ Ἰησοῦ: 1,37). Dabei war die knappe Äußerung, "Siehe, das Lamm Gottes", für sie wohl eine Art Aide-mémoire an die gewichtige μαρτυρία ihres Meisters vom Vortag, die er mit dem Satz, "Siehe, das Lamm Gottes, *das der Welt Sünde trägt*", eröffnet und mit dem Bekenntnis, "Dieser ist der Sohn Gottes" beschlossen hatte (1,29-34)[64].

---

[61] Bonsack (1988: 57) macht auf die "sorgfältig gewählte Wortfolge" in 13,23 aufmerksam: "'Einer seiner Jünger lag beim Mahl im Schoß Jesu …, den Jesus lieb hatte': nicht 'nämlich der, welchen Jesus lieb hatte', sondern eher ähnlich deutschem 'und ihn hatte Jesus lieb'". Der Jünger ist also kein Neuer in dieser Szene, neu ist vielmehr nur seine Charakterisierung.

[62] Vgl. H. Thyen (1992b: 2050).

[63] Sein charakteristischer Beiname "der Täufer" fehlt bei Joh. Da hier aber keiner der Jünger als *Johannes* bezeichnet wird, macht ihn schon sein bloßer Name, der auf höchst solenne Weise bereits im Prolog eingeführt wird, unverwechselbar.

[64] Mit diesem Bekenntnis hat Johannes die Rolle der Himmelsstimme aus der ja erkennbar im Hintergrund stehenden synoptischen Tauferzählung übernommen.

Mit diesem Zeugnis im Ohr folgen sie also Jesus nach, "der aber wendet sich um, sieht sie nachfolgen und fragt sie: Was sucht ihr?" Ihre Antwort ist die Gegenfrage, "ποῦ μένεις;": Wo wohnst du? Wir suchen deine *Bleibe*. Und Jesus fordert sie auf: "Kommt und seht! So kamen sie also und sahen, wo seine Bleibe war (ποῦ μένει), und blieben (ἔμειναν) jenen Tag bei ihm. Das war aber um die zehnte Stunde" (1,35-39). Nicht die Frage, *wie* hier die Stunden gezählt werden, ist wichtig – das ist lediglich eine Frage nach dem Verisimile der Erzählung –, sondern *daß* diese Stunde gezählt wird, markiert ihre Unvergeßlichkeit. Denn indem die beiden Nachfolgenden Jesu Bleibe gesehen und bei ihm geblieben waren, haben sie mehr gefunden, als sie suchten: nämlich den Messias und ein neues Leben in seinem Zeugendienst (1,40-42). Und indem Johannes so zwei seiner Jünger zu Nachfolgern Jesu gemacht hat, beginnen sich schon hier sein Wort und seine Bestimmung zu erfüllen: "Er muß wachsen, ich aber abnehmen" (3,30).

Und nun folgt dieser Satz: ἦν Ἀνδρέας ὁ ἀδελφὸς Σίμωνος Πέτρου εἷς ἐκ τῶν δύο τῶν ἀκουσάντων παρὰ Ἰωάννου καὶ ἀκολουθησάντων αὐτῷ (1,40). Schon die bedächtige Art, wie hier der Petrusbruder Andreas als der *eine* der beiden von Johannes angestifteten ersten Nachfolger Jesu identifiziert wird, erweckt die Neugier auf die Identität des anderen. Die Fortsetzung steigert sie: εὑρίσκει οὗτος πρῶτον τὸν ἀδελφὸν τὸν ἴδιον Σίμωνα καὶ λέγει αὐτῷ· εὑρήκαμεν τὸν Μεσσίαν .... Der *Sinaiticus prima manu* bietet hier statt des πρῶτον ein πρῶτος. Der Schreiber oder schon der Verfertiger von dessen Vorlage hat die Sache also wohl so verstanden, daß zunächst Andreas *seinen*[65] Bruder und danach *Johannes* – wie er nach der *Inscriptio* den Evangelisten nennt – den seinen, nämlich Jakobus, gefunden und zu Jesus gebracht hat. Da diese beiden Brüderpaare als die engsten Vertrauten Jesu unter seinen ersten Jüngern waren – und das wußten die Leser des Joh –, haben sich wohl viele diesen *Reim* auf das Rätsel gemacht, zumal das hier ungenannte Brüderpaar dann am Ende ja noch unter denen genannt wird, in deren Mitte der geliebte Jünger sein muß (21,2). Und auch wenn das adverbiale πρῶτον die ursprüngliche Lesart sein sollte und das τὸν ἴδιον gut hellenistisch nur ein αὐτοῦ verträte, bliebe ja mit der Frage nach dem Zweiten das Rätsel dennoch aufgegeben: κύριε, οὗτος δὲ τί; (21,21). Denn daß unser Erzähler, der drei mal betont, es seien *zwei* Jünger gewesen, die Jesus nachfolgten, den Anderen *vergessen* haben könnte, will ja wohl keiner behaupten wollen. Aber da ist noch mehr, das auf die Lösung verweist, die ich eben dem Schreiber des *Sinaiticus* unterstellt habe. Auch hier, wie im Hof des Hohenpriesters und am Grabe Jesu, wäre der geliebte Jünger schon vor Petrus als ἀπ' ἀρχῆς αὐτόπτης bei seinem Herrn gewesen; und auch hier müßte der Kommentar des Erzählers, wenn es ihm nicht vor allem um sein Rätsel ginge, als Antwort

---

[65] τὸν ἴδιον dann emphatisch und nicht einfach als Synonym von αὐτοῦ gebraucht. Vgl. M. Hengel 1993: 216.

auf Jesu ἔρχεσθε καὶ ὄψεσθε wohl lauten: καὶ εἶδεν καὶ ἐπίστευσεν (20,8)[66]. Und sind da nicht noch weitere Klammern, die Anfang und Ende verbinden, und für die Lösung des Rätsels in die hier eingeschlagene Richtung weisen? Mit dem freudigen Bekenntnis, "Wir haben des Messias gefunden!" hatte Andreas seinen Bruder Simon zu Jesus geführt, und der hatte ihn empfangen mit diesen Worten: σὺ εἶ Σίμων ὁ υἱὸς Ἰωάννου, σὺ κληθήσῃ Κηφᾶς, ὃ ἑρμηνεύεται Πέτρος (1,41f.), einem unverkennbaren Spiel mit Mt 16,16ff. Denn wie da Jesu Verheißungswort, "Du bist Petrus ..." (v.18), dem zuvor geäußertem Bekenntnis des Petrus, "Du bist der Christus ..." (v.16) korrespondiert, so ist hier Jesu Wort an Petrus quasi die Antwort auf das Messiasbekenntnis des Andreas. Diese Korrespondenz und das Gewicht beider Äußerungen wird durch das jeweils hinzugefügte ὅ ἐστιν μεθερμηνευόμενον Χριστός bzw. ὃ ἑρμηνεύεται Πέτρος nachdrücklich unterstrichen. Und eben diese erste Begegnung des Petrus mit Jesus ruft der Erzähler dadurch in Erinnerung, daß er Jesus den drei mal nach seiner Liebe Gefragten drei mal Σίμων Ἰωάννου anreden und so zugleich seine Bestimmung als "Felsen" restituieren läßt (21,15-17). Und schließlich heißt es gegen Ende: ἐπιστραφεὶς ὁ Πέτρος βλέπει τὸν μαθητὴν ὃν ἠγάπα ὁ Ἰησοῦς ἀκολουθοῦντα ... λέγει τῷ Ἰησοῦ κτλ. (21,20f.). Es ist hier der gerade neu in die Nachfolge – in die spezifische Nachfolge des Hirten der Schafe bis ins Martyrium – eingewiesene *Petrus*, der sich umwendet und den geliebten Jünger als einen bereits und wie schon immer *Nachfolgenden* erblickt. Denn ganz fraglos sagt das durch alles Vorausgehende geprägte und geladene ἀκολουθοῦντα hier mehr, als daß der andere Jünger bloß hinter Petrus herginge. Und am Anfang als die beiden Täuferjünger Jesus als Erste *nachfolgen*, heißt es: στραφεὶς δὲ ὁ Ἰησοῦς καὶ θεασάμενος αὐτοὺς ἀκολουθοῦντας λέγει αὐτοῖς κτλ. (1,38). Diese frappante Analogie der Formulierung ließe sich natürlich einfach als die typische Schreibweise unseres Evangelisten abtun, wenn nicht die genannten anderen Hinweise Zweifel an ihrer bloßen Zufälligkeit erweckten. Zu diesen Zeichen der Verbindung von Anfang und Ende gehört endlich auch der Umstand, daß derjenige, der auf das Wort, "Siehe das Lamm Gottes", seines Lehrers Johannes hin Jesus nachge-

---

[66] Leider muß ich mich hier unter die "zwölf Freunde" gesellen, "die wie gewöhnlich anders denken" als Minear (1976), der den geliebten Jünger in 20,8 (wegen 20,9f.) nicht wirklich *glauben*, sondern nur das bestürzte "we don't know where" der Maria (20,2) *für wahr halten* lassen will. Das erscheint mir jedoch aus mehreren Gründen als eine unmögliche Interpretation. *Sehen* und *Glauben* gehören bei Johannes trotz des Makarismus von 20,29 untrennbar zusammen (vgl. nur 1,14 und siehe das oben zur Thomaserzählung Gesagte). Die Zeit des Glaubens kann nicht derart mit der Kalenderzeit verrechnet werden, wie Minear das tut (vgl. nur 2,11). Trotz seiner Zugehörigkeit als "einer von ihnen" kann sich der allwissende und stets schon glaubende Erzähler-Jünger, wie 13,28 zeigt, von den anderen distanzieren, so daß das begründende γάρ von 20,9 *zugleich* den Unglauben des Petrus, wie das Wunder des *"vorzeitigen"* Glaubens des geliebten Jüngers erklären kann. Vgl. Byrne 1985.

folgt war, nicht eben nur "jenen Tag", sondern bis in die Stunde und an den Ort des Sterbens dieses Lammes für die Sünden der Welt bei seinem Herrn *geblieben* ist (19,25ff.) und auf seine Weise *bleiben* soll, ἕως ἔρχομαι (21,22f.).

Blicken wir deshalb jetzt endlich noch auf die Rolle des geliebten Jüngers in der entscheidenden Szene der Kreuzigung Jesu (Joh 19,25-37). Nur hier erscheint er nicht zusammen mit Petrus, sondern steht "bei der Mutter Jesu". Und doch bringt auch hier gerade die unerwartete Anwesenheit des geliebten Jüngers in dieser Stunde dem Leser Petrus' Abwesenheit erst so recht zum Bewußtsein. Daß im Johannesevangelium außer dem "Jünger, den Jesus liebte" nur "seine Mutter" nie mit ihrem Namen genannt wird, ist schon oft beobachtet worden. Sie tritt im ganzen Evangelium nur zwei mal in Erscheinung, nämlich bei der ἀρχή der Zeichen in Kana (2,1-11) und bei deren τέλος, als er in Golgatha sein τετέλεσται spricht und den Geist hingibt (19,30). Beide Male heißt sie nur "die Mutter Jesu" und beide Male redet Jesus sie mit dem befremdlichen "γύναι" an. Wohl muß sie sich in Kana sagen lassen: τί ἐμοὶ καὶ σοί, γύναι; οὔπω ἥκει ἡ ὥρα μου (2,4)[67]. Und doch ist es dann gerade auch ihr Verhalten, das schon jene Hochzeit zu einer erfüllten Prolepse der "Stunde Jesu" macht: *"Und er offenbarte seine Herrlichkeit und seine Jünger glaubten an ihn"* (2,11). Und als die hier nur vorabgebildete Stunde der Verherrlichung des Vaters durch den Sohn und des Sohnes durch den Vater dann wirklich gekommen ist, ist "seine Mutter" erneut zur Stelle. Bei der Kanahochzeit gehört sie zu der jüdischen "Familie", während Jesus und seine Jünger geladene Hochzeitsgäste waren (2,2). Sie läßt sich durch Jesu brüske Zurückweisung an ihrer Rolle nicht irremachen und gebietet den "Dienern: ὅ τι ἂν λέγῃ ὑμῖν ποιήσατε. Birger Olsson hat einleuchtend gezeigt, wie die Erzählung von Joh 1,14-2,11, deren Abschnitte jeweils durch τῇ ἐπαύριον (1,29. 35. 43) und τῇ ἡμέρᾳ τῇ τρίτῃ (2,1; vgl. Ex 19,10f. 16) zu einem Sechs-Tage-Schema verbunden sind, vor dem Hintergrund des Sinaigeschehens von Ex 19-24 als dessen typologische Entsprechung gestaltet ist[68]. Die

---

[67] Das τί ἐμοὶ καὶ σοί, γύναι; darf man wohl als Teil eines geistvollen Spiels mit der Erzählung von Elia und der Witwe von Sarephta ansehen (1 Kön 17,7-24). Wie Elia dort Mehl und Öl wunderbar mehrt, so behebt Jesus hier den Mangel an Wein, damit die Freude der Hochzeitsleute vollkommen sei (vgl. 15,11). Fährt dort die über den Tod ihres Sohnes bekümmerte Mutter Elia an mit den Worten: τί ἐμοὶ καὶ σοί, ἄνθρωπε θεοῦ; (17,18), so tadelt hier umgekehrt Jesus seine Mutter so: τί ἐμοὶ καὶ σοί, γύναι; Und wie dort Elia den Sohn der Witwe erweckte und ihn seiner Mutter übergab mit den Worten: βλέπε, ζῇ ὁ υἱός σου (17,23), so rettet Jesus – wiederum in Kana! – den Sohn des königlichen Beamten durch sein Wort: ὁ υἱός σου ζῇ (4,50). Von hier aus wird deutlich, warum Johannes bei seinem fast förmlichen *Verhör* "feierlich bekannt und nicht verleugnet hatte" (καὶ ὡμολόγησεν καὶ οὐκ ἠρνήσατο, καὶ ὡμολόγησεν), daß er auch nicht *Elia* sei (1,19-21). Denn er mußte auch diesen Platz dem mit Jesus gekommenen, neuen und größeren Elia freihalten.

[68] B. Olsson 1974: 102ff. Olsson spricht vom "Sinai Screen": "I use 'screen' and not 'pattern' or 'structure' or 'motif' because of its dynamic character and its usefulness in an analysis of the semantic structure of a text and the postsemantic processes … behind a text" (102).

jüdische Tradition stellt das Geschehen der Offenbarung der Herrlichkeit Jhwhs am "dritten Tage", des sechsten in der Reihe der Tage der Bereitung, oft als die Hochzeit Jhwhs mit Israel dar[69]. Wie ein *Cantus firmus* zieht sich von Ex 19,8 an das Versprechen des Volkes durch die Erzählung: πάντα, ὅσα εἶπεν ὁ θεός, ποιήσομεν καὶ ἀκουσόμεθα (vgl. 24,3. 7). Mit ihrer Weisung an die "Diener", ὅ τι ἂν λέγῃ ὑμῖν ποιήσατε, nimmt "Jesu Mutter" dieses alte Treuversprechen ihres Volkes auf. Und weil die διάκονοι dann gehorsam "tun", was der Herr ihnen gebietet, "wissen" sie – im Unterschied zu dem ahnungslosen ἀρχιτρίκλινος – um das "Woher" (πόθεν) des köstlichen Weines (2,9; vgl. 7,17!). Darum kann ich Paul S. Minear nur zustimmen, wenn er die namenlose "Mutter Jesu" im Johannesevangelium weder als die "Mutter Kirche", noch als Vertreterin des "Judenchristentums", sondern – ähnlich wie Nathanael, den "Israeliten, an dem kein Falsch ist" (1,45ff.) – als die symbolische Repräsentantin der toratreuen Synagoge verstehen will: "The beloved disciple welcomed the Messiah's mother into the community of those reborn as God's children. The word of the Crucified cancels out any anti-Semitism among his disciples by means of a pro-Semitic command, an inescapable 'Love your enemies!' This word of the Messiah cancels out the brutality of his first word to his mother: 'What have you to do with me? My hour has not yet come (2,4)'. After Jesus' hour had come she had a new son and his disciple(s) had a new mother"[70]. So erinnern diese letzten Worte Jesu als sein teuerstes Vermächtnis seine Kirche bleibend daran, daß ihr Heil von den Juden kommt (4,22), und zugleich zeigen sie uns, daß wir alle noch einen langen Weg vor uns haben, bis auch aus uns Jünger werden, die Jesus liebt[71].

Als letztem der Texte, in denen der geliebte Jünger eine Rolle zu spielen scheint, müssen wir uns nun endlich noch der Erzählung von Jesu Sterben (19,28-35) zuwenden. Sie schließt – mit μετὰ τοῦτο verbunden – unmittelbar an die eben erörterte Szene der Kundgabe des letzten Willens Jesu an. War schon durch dieses Vermächtnis Jesu irdisches Werk vollendet (πάντα τετέλεσται: 19,28), so sagt er nun, um als letzte seiner ewigen Aufgaben noch *die Schrift zu erfüllen*: "Mich dürstet!" Auf dieses Wort hin reichen sie ihm auf einem Ysopstengel einen mit Essig getränkten Schwamm, wie die Schrift sagt: καὶ εἰς τὴν δίψαν μου ἐπότισάν με ὄξος (Ps 69,22). Und als Jesus den Essig getrunken hat, sagt er "Sie ist erfüllt (τε-

---

[69] Vgl. Olsson 1974: 107f.

[70] Minear 1984: 150; vgl. ebd. 143ff. – Daß die Mutter Jesu hier – wie sonst Petrus – das in den Augen des Evangelisten vermeintlich nur halbgläubige *Judenchristentum* repräsentiere, während der geliebte Jünger für den wahren Glauben der *Heidenchristen* stehe, hatte R. Bultmann (1959: 520f.) m.E. allzu sicher ("ohne Zweifel") behauptet. Je auf ihre Weise haben neuerdings einerseits M. Pamment (1983) und andererseits M. Goulder (1993) diese These aufgenommen und erheblich verschärft. Daß und warum sie jedoch verfehlt ist, kann nur im Rahmen einer sorgfältigen Analyse der Rolle des νόμος, der ἐντολή und der Ἰουδαῖοι bei Joh erwiesen werden, die hier nicht zu leisten ist.

[71] Vgl. H. Thyen 1990: 704f.

τέλεσται) und neigte sein Haupt und gab den Geist hin (παρέδωκεν τὸ πνεῦμα)"[72].

Jesus stirbt – nach dem Wort des Johannes – als das *"Lamm Gottes, das der Welt Sünde trägt"* (1,29). Neben den betonten Nennungen der *Nähe* des Passah seit 11,55 weist auch der *Ysop*, auf dem sie ihm soeben den Essig reichten, darauf hin, daß an diesem Kreuz in eben der Stunde, da im Tempel die Passahlämmer geschlachtet werden, das wahre Passahlamm stirbt[73]. Vollends deutlich wird das in der folgenden Szene: Als die Soldaten, die auf die Intervention der Juden bei Pilatus hin an den Gekreuzigten das *Crurifragium* vollziehen, zu Jesus kommen und erkennen, daß er bereits tot ist,

> *da zerschlugen sie ihm nicht die Schenkel. Vielmehr stieß ihm einer der Soldaten seine Lanze in die Seite, und sogleich flossen Wasser und Blut heraus. Und der das gesehen hat, der hat es bezeugt. Und sein Zeugnis ist wahr. Und 'jener' weiß, daß (d)er die Wahrheit sagt, damit auch ihr am Glauben festhaltet. Denn das (alles) ist geschehen, damit die Schrift erfüllt werde: Kein Knochen soll ihm gebrochen werden (Ex 12,10; Ps 34,21). Und wiederum eine andere Schrift(stelle) (die da) sagt: Sie werden auf den schauen, den sie*

---

[72] Gewiß ist παρέδωκεν τὸ πνεῦμα auch ein Euphemismus für *Sterben*, doch das Verbum weist darauf hin, daß hier symbolische Obertöne im Spiel sind. Es ist der Geist, den Johannes "wie eine Taube auf ihn herabkommen und *auf ihm bleiben* sah" (1,32), den er nun hingibt, an alle, die an ihn glauben (vgl. 16,7). Siehe dazu Hoskyns 1947: 533 und S. D. Moore (1989: 8ff.), der sehr scharfsinnig beobachtet, wie in diesem Schrei, *"Mich dürstet!"*, die – etwa von G. O'Day (1986) als bloß literarisches Instrument der Offenbarung gedeutete – *johanneische Ironie* total in sich zusammenbricht. Als einer, der vermeinte, sich auf den "johanneischen Dualismus" und das ihm entsprechende Unterscheiden zwischen Literal- und Figuralsinn zu verstehen, konnte der Leser sich bis zu diesem Schrei auf Kosten von Nikodemus, der Frau am Jakobsbrunnen oder der satten Menge von Joh 6 im Gefühl überlegenen Wissens sonnen. Doch in diesem Schrei nach nichts anderem als purem Wasser im literalen Sinn holt die *johanneische Ironie* den Leser ein, rehabilitiert in gewissem Sinn die eben noch Belächelten und macht am Ende den Leser selbst zu ihrem Opfer. Da es aber ohne einen, der sie zu goutieren weiß, keine Ironie gibt, bleibt ihm nichts anderes als erneute Lektüre. Dabei wird er nicht nur wahrnehmen, wie er selbst bei seinem vorausgegangene Lesen zum Opfer der Ironie geworden ist, sondern wird bemerken, wie der Dualismus vom Paradox verschlungen wird und wie der Text, den er zu beherrschen wähnte, zum unausschöpflichen und niemals *"mechanisierbaren"*, sondern stets nur kraft Divination *"motivierbaren"* Verstehenspotential wird; (Schleiermacher; vgl. M. Frank 1977: 247ff.).

[73] Mit der Salbung in Bethanien (12,1-8) beginnt *"sechs Tage vor dem Passah"* die letzte Woche Jesu, die absichtsvoll seiner ersten Woche (1,19-2,11) korrespondiert; vgl. Olsson 1974:23f. Damit wird das in Gegenwart der "Mutter Jesu" geschehene Kanawunder zur unmittelbaren Entsprechung dieser Sterbestunde, so daß der Fülle des köstlichen Weines als eschatologischer Überbietung des καθαρισμὸς τῶν Ἰουδαίων (2,6) dort, der Strom von Wasser und Blut aus der durchbohrten Seite Jesu hier zu entsprechen scheint; zur Entsprechung von Kanawunder und Sterben Jesu vgl. auch Kurz 1989: 104f. – Auf die analoge Konnotation von *Ysop, Blut* und *Wasser* in Hebr 9,19 verweist Hoskyns 1947: 533.

*durchbohrt haben (Sach 12,10).*

Das Zitat von Ex 12,10 (Ps 34,21) bezieht sich deutend auf das (schriftgemäß) unterlassene *Crurifragium* an Jesus, dem als dem Passahlamm kein Bein gebrochen werden darf. Der Streit darüber, ob hier die Passahvorschrift von Ex 12,10 *oder* das Lob von Gottes Erbarmen über den Gerechten aus Ps 34,21 zitiert wird, ist insofern müßig, als Joh in der Tradition jüdischer Exegese darin keine Alternative sehen dürfte. Gerade als der leidende Gerechte, als Gottes Knecht und Sohn (ἰδοὺ συνήσει ὁ παῖς μου καὶ ὑψωθήσεται καὶ δοξασθήσεται σφόδρα: Jes 52,13) ist ihm Jesus das "Lamm Gottes, das der Welt Sünde trägt". Ähnliches gilt für das zweite Zitat aus Sach 12,10, das sich deutend auf den Lanzenstich und seine Folgen bezieht. Wie nämlich schon im biblischen Sacharjabuch[74] selbst eine enge Beziehung zum Jesajabuch, sowie zu Jeremia und Ezechiel besteht, so dürfte auch für Joh im Hintergrund von Sach 12,10 zugleich mit dem gesamten Kontext dieser Stelle (Sach 12,9-14,21 und darin zumal mit dem *"geschlagenen Hirten"* von 13,7f., sowie mit dem Entspringen der *"lebendigen Wasser"* in Jerusalem von 14,8f.) der "um unserer Sünden willen Durchbohrte" von Jes 53,4ff. stehen.

Aber das Sacharja-Zitat erfordert – wie Minear (1983a) gezeigt hat – noch genaueres Hinsehen. Sach 12,9ff. ist als Gottesrede stilisiert. In dieser lautet Vers 10: "Aber über das Haus David und die Bewohner Jerusalems werde ich einen Geist der Erbarmung und des Gebets ausgießen, und sie werden auf den (?) schauen (im hebräischen Text: sie werden auf *mich* schauen; LXX: ἐπιβλέψονται πρὸς με), den sie durchbohrt haben. Ihn werden sie betrauern, wie man um den einzigen Sohn trauert, ihn werden sie bitter beklagen, wie man um den Erstgeborenen klagt". Deutlich ist in diesem Text der Sache nach von Umkehr und Reue die Rede: Vom Geist der Erbarmung und des Gebets erfaßt, werden Mörder umkehren und den, den sie durchbohrt haben, wie einen "einzigen Sohn" betrauern. Da dieses Zitat den Lanzenstich und seine Folgen deuten soll, kann der, "der das gesehen und bezeugt hat" (ὁ ἑωρακὼς μεμαρτύρηκεν: 19,35) deshalb nur der Soldat sein, der den Lanzenstich ausführte, keinesfalls aber der *geliebte Jünger*. Denn das Sacharja-Zitat fordert, daß diejenigen, die ihn durchbohrt haben, mit denen identisch sind, die jetzt vom Geist der Erbarmung erfaßt "auf ihn schauen". Wir haben hier also, mit anderen Worten gesagt, ein intertextuelles Spiel mit dem Bekenntnis des synoptischen Hauptmanns unter dem Kreuz Jesu vor Augen: "The very person who struck the last blow against the Son of Man becomes the first witness to him"[75]. Und doch hat Minear mit dieser einleuchtenden Erkenntnis den fast einhelligen Konsens darüber,

---

[74] Vgl. zur Komposition des Sacharjabuches als kanonischer Schrift B. S. Childs 1979: 472ff.

[75] Minear 1983a: 164; vgl. "the pronoun in v. 35 presupposes an antecedent and the nearest antecedent was this soldier" (163).

daß Joh 19,35 von dem geliebten Jünger die Rede sei, nicht etwa beseitigt. Ich glaube im Gegenteil, daß seine Kritik, die ihn verdrängen wollte, diesem Jünger überhaupt erst den ihm angemessenen Platz eingeräumt hat. Denn schon seit der Zeit der Alten Kirche – und das heißt unter *"native speakers"* der Koine – hat man innerhalb von Vers 35 einen Subjektwechsel wahrgenommen. In diesem Sinn fragt Bultmann völlig angemessen: "Wer ist der ἐκεῖνος? Der Augenzeuge selbst kann es ja nicht sein, sondern nur ein Anderer, der in der Lage ist, für die Wahrheit des Zeugnisses zu bürgen"[76]. Aufgrund von 21,24, wo der geliebte Jünger als der fiktionale Evangelist in seine einladenden Worte: καὶ οἴδαμεν ὅτι ἀληθὴς αὐτοῦ ἡ μαρτυρία ἐστίν, das Zeugnis des Soldaten von 19,35 deutlich erkennbar mithineinnimmt, hege ich keinen Zweifel daran, daß der wissende ἐκεῖνος nur der geliebte Jünger sein kann. Wie auch sonst im Evangelium behält er sein Wissen für sich, bis er es als der, "der dies geschrieben hat", öffentlich bezeugen wird, *"damit auch ihr* (so wie dieser Zeuge!) *glaubt"* (19,35; vgl. 20,31). Die Notwendigkeit, zwischen dem ἑωρακώς und dem ἐκεῖνος zu unterscheiden, wird auch klar aus der fundamentalen Bedeutung des biblischen Zeugenrechts von Dt 19,15 für unser Evangelium, wo selbst Jesu eigenes Zeugnis seine Wahrheit verlöre, wenn er nur für sich selbst zeugte (5,31; vgl. 8,16f. u.ö.). Weil es stets des übereinstimmenden Zeugnisses wenigstens zweier Zeugen bedarf, wird auch in Joh 19,35 die Wahrheit des Zeugnisses des Einen erst durch den ἐκεῖνος als den Anderen verbürgt. Diese Deutung bewahrt endlich auch das Rätsel um die Figur des geliebten Jüngers, der im gesamten Corpus des Evangeliums nie als öffentlicher *Zeuge* seines Herrn hervortritt. Erst im Epilog tritt er dieses ihm bestimmte Zeugenamt an; und zwar zunächst – noch innerhalb der Erzählung – im engeren Jüngerkreis oder zumindest Petrus gegenüber (21,7; vgl. dagegen 13,24-28), und vor aller Welt erst danach durch sein Evangelium, nachdem er ganz am Ende enthüllt hat, daß *er* selbst der Erzähler war, der "es geschrieben hat".

Aber *was* hat der Soldat gesehen und welches ist der Inhalt seines Zeugnisses, um dessen Wahrheit der geliebte Jünger weiß? Auf dem Höhepunkt seiner Auseinandersetzung mit den Juden während des Laubhüttenfestes hatte Jesus erklärt: *"Wenn ihr den Sohn des Menschen erhöht haben werdet, dann werdet ihr erkennen, daß* ICH BIN (absolutes ἐγώ εἰμι), *und daß ich nichts von mir selbst aus tue, sondern nur das sage, was mich der Vater gelehrt hat"* (Joh 8,28)[77]. Dazu stellt Minear (1983a: 163) fest: "This is the only prediction of a lifting up in which knowledge is

---

[76] Bultmann 1959: 526; er fährt fort: "Dann aber kann doch nur Jesus selbst gemeint sein". – Minear (1983a: 170ff.) diskutiert das Problem und plädiert für den *Soldaten* als das identische Subjekt sowohl von ἑωρακώς als auch von ἐκεῖνος οἶδεν.

[77] Vgl. zum absoluten ἐγώ εἰμι als der alttestamentlich-johanneischen "Offenbarungsformel" H. Zimmermann (1960) und siehe zur Relation von Joh 8,28 zu 19,35 Thyen 1992c: 24ff.

to be given to Jesus' *enemies*". Kaum zufällig sind "die Juden" als die *Initiatoren* der Kreuzigung Jesu auch das grammatische Subjekt des Satzes: ὅπου αὐτὸν ἐσταύρωσαν (19,18), wie auch sie es sind, auf deren Intervention hin es zu dem finalen Lanzenstich und dem Strömen von Wasser und Blut aus der durchbohrten Seite Jesu kommt. Das sah der *umkehrende* Soldat, der sie hier als ihr ausführendes Organ gewissermaßen repräsentiert, und erkannte in dem Gekreuzigten den ἐγώ εἰμι[78]. Und da ist wohl noch eine weitere Beziehung zwischen jenem Laubhüttenfest und unserer Szene:

> *Am letzten und höchsten Tag des Festes trat Jesus auf und verkündete mit lauter Stimme: 'Wenn einer dürstet, so komme er zu mir; und es trinke, wer an mich glaubt. Wie die Schrift sagt: Ströme lebendigen Wassers werden aus seinem Leibe fließen'. (Damit redete er von dem Geist, den die empfangen sollten, die an ihn glaubten. Noch gab es den Geist freilich nicht, denn Jesus war ja noch nicht verherrlicht) (7,37-39)[79].*

Auch diese Verheißung erfüllt sich in dieser Stunde der Verherrlichung Jesu vor den Augen des Soldaten, der Zeuge wird, wie in dem Strom von Blut und Wasser aus der durchbohrten Seite Jesu "*ein Quell sich öffnet für das Haus David und alle Bewohner Jerusalems gegen Sünde und Unreinheit*" (Sach 13,1).

Wie viele andere war auch ich einst davon überzeugt, daß die Notiz über das Austreten von Blut und Wasser aus der Seitenwunde Jesu und die nachdrückliche Benennung eines Augenzeugen dafür in antidoketistischer Absicht das wahre Menschsein Jesu und/oder sein tatsächlich erfolgtes Sterben beweisen solle. Doch nach vielfacher neuer Johanneslektüre erscheinen mir heute alle antidoketistischen Deutungen unserer hochsymbolischen Lanzenstich-Szene samt den damit verbun-

---

[78] Man darf wohl annehmen, daß Joh den Text in seiner schwierigen überlieferten Gestalt kannte: "Sie werden auf *mich* schauen, den sie durchbohrt haben". – Wenn ich sagte, der Soldat habe in dem Gekreuzigten den ἐγώ εἰμι erkannt, ist natürlich von der erzählten fiktionalen Figur und nicht von der Psychologie irgendeines römischen Centurio die Rede. Das gleiche gilt von "den Juden als Initiatoren der Kreuzigung Jesu". Auch hier erläge man der *referential fallacy* (und schlimmer noch: dem Antisemitismus), wenn man das Syntagma "die Juden" auf das empirische jüdische Volk statt auf die erzählten und insofern ebenfalls fiktionalen Akteure der Erzählung und ihr erzähltes Verhalten bezöge.

[79] Ich lese Jesu Ruf zum Glauben als einen chiastischen Parallelismus membrorum, verstehe die Wendung καθὼς εἶπεν ἡ γραφή als Ankündigung des *folgenden* Schriftzitates und beziehe das Pronomen αὐτοῦ bei κοιλία auf den Leib *Jesu*. Schwierig ist die Identifikation des Zitates. Mir erscheint immer noch Sach 13,1 und 14,8 (auf dem Hintergrund von Ez 47,1ff. und der Identifikation des Leibes Jesu mit dem Tempel in Joh 2,21) der plausibelste Vorschlag, zumal ja Sach 12,9ff. deutlich im Hintergrund von 19,31ff. steht. Vgl. dazu R. E. Brown 1966: 319ff.

denen Exkursionen in die Gefilde antiker Volksmedizin völlig abwegig[80]. Einen
Zeugen für den jedermann sichtbaren tatsächlich eingetretenen Tod Jesu oder für
seine in der antiken Welt angeblich aus dem Herausfließen von Blut und Wasser aus
seiner Wunde einfach diagnostizierbare *menschliche Natur* würde Joh schwerlich
mit der emphatischen Wendung, καὶ ὁ ἑωρακὼς μεμαρτύρηκεν (19,35) einführen.
Die Täufermartyria: κἀγὼ ἑώρακα καὶ μεμαρτύρηκα ὅτι οὗτός ἐστιν ὁ υἱὸς τοῦ
θεοῦ (1,34), an die sie als Spiel mit der synoptischen Szene vom Bekenntnis des
Hauptmanns kaum zufällig anklingt, und Joh 3,11. 32f. erweisen dieses Syntagma
als geprägten Ausdruck. Wo er erscheint, wird nicht eine jedermann sichtbare Ba-
nalität des Alltags bezeugt, sondern die allein dem Glauben sichtbare himmlische
Welt (Minear 1983a: 164). Auch über Joh 19,35 hinaus sehe ich im gesamten Johannesevangelium nirgendwo auch nur das entfernteste Anzeichen irgendeines *An-
tidoketismus*. Solche Akzente setzten ja einen dem Evangelium vorausgehenden
oder ihm gleichzeitigen *Doketismus* als Problem voraus[81]. Auch wenn ich Käse-
manns berühmter Diagnose eines "naiven Doketismus" bei Johannes keineswegs
zustimmen kann, dürfte er ihn doch zu Recht eher *auf dem Weg in die Gnosis* als
unter ihren Bekämpfern sehen. Denn das Problem, das unser Evangelist zu bearbei-
ten hat, besteht ja gerade darin, daß Jesus ein bloßer Mensch ist, der sich in den Augen seiner Gegner anmaßt, *Gottes Sohn* zu sein (10,33); einer, der behauptet, vom
Himmel herabgestiegen zu sein, obwohl man doch seinen Vater und seine Mutter
genau kennt (6,41f.); einer, der messianische Ansprüche erhebt, wo er doch aus dem
heilsgeschichtlich irrelevanten Nazareth stammt; einer, der elend am Kreuz veren-
det, ohne daß sein "himmlischer Vater" da interveniert hätte. Solchem durch die jüdische Katastrophe des Jahres 70 genährten Zweifel gegenüber wird nun die

---

[80] Vgl. H. Thyen 1977; G. Richter 1977: 120ff.; W. Langbrandtner 1977: passim. Wie Richter,
Langbrandtner u.a. sah ich in den Johannesbriefen damals Zeugnisse der Auseinandersetzung mit ei-
ner christologischen Häresie, deren Vertreter mit ihrer doketistischen und/oder dualistischen Chri-
stologie à la Kerinth die Einheit der Gemeinde bedrohten. Und wir glaubten, im Zuge dieser
Auseinandersetzung habe eine *johanneische Redaktion* auch das Johannesevangelium u.a. durch die
Notiz von 19,35 mit antidoketistischen Akzenten versehen. – Zur Kritik vgl. Minear 1983a: 164.

[81] Um die bereits im Titel angekündigte "antidoketische Christologie im Johannesevangelium"
überhaupt aufweisen und seine These so durchführen zu können, muß Schnelle (1986) neben zahllosen unkontrollierbaren literarkritischen Operationen und Traditionszuweisungen vor allem zu dem
Geniestreich greifen, die *Johannesbriefe* zeitlich *vor* dem Evangelium anzusetzen. Über dieser
höchst fragwürdigen Konstruktion einer "Geschichte des johanneischen Christentums", die ihm zudem weithin zum Maßstab der Textauslegung wird, gerät Schnelle der Poet Johannes (Kermode
1986) dann schließlich zu einem "Quasi-Kirchlichen-Redaktor" seiner vermeintlich "johanneischen
Schultradition". Ich kann zu diesem ganzen Unternehmen – ebenso wie zu dem gewiß nicht minder
fleißigen Beitrag über den geliebten Jünger von Mahoney (1974) – nur mit Lévinas (1991: 81; zitiert
oben S. 147) sagen, daß hier statt der Exegese eines biblischen Textes, das Studium seiner vermeintlichen Genese betrieben wird.

*Gottheit* und göttliche Sendung Jesu in unserem Evangelium in einer Weise betont, daß es da, wo der Boden dazu bereitet ist, zu seiner gnostischen Lektüre durchaus verführen kann und ja tatsächlich auch vielfach dazu verführt hat.

Aus allem bisher Erörterten ergibt sich für die Frage nach der Identität des geliebten Jüngers als oberstes Gebot, daß seine bis zuletzt absichtsvoll durchgehaltene Anonymität respektiert werden muß[82]. Wohl wird am Ende enthüllt, daß er der verläßliche und von keinem geringeren als seinem auferstandenen Herrn selbst autorisierte *Evangelist* ist – und der Leser weiß aus allem, was er aus dem Evangelium über ihn erfahren hat, daß er dazu wie kein anderer der Jünger Jesu qualifiziert ist[83] –, aber dennoch bleibt der Schleier über dem Geheimnis seines *Namens* undurchdringlich. Natürlich hat dieser rätselhafte Umstand von Anfang an die Neugier schon der ersten wie danach aller späteren Leser erweckt, und das sollte er auch. Dazu war er eigens und höchst kunstvoll als der besondere Reiz dieses Evangeliums geschaffen. In der Rezeptionsgeschichte heißt dieses Rätsel: "Die johanneische Frage". Aber keiner, der je versucht, sie zu beantworten und das Rätsel zu lösen, darf dabei übersehen, daß es nicht die Vergeßlichkeit der Nachgeborenen, sondern der Text des Evangeliums selber ist, der ihm das Rätsel aufgibt. Das heißt aber, daß überall da, wo man die ephesinische Legende vom uralten Johannes in welcher ihrer Variationen und apologetischen Abschwächungen auch immer zum *Hintergrund* von Joh 21,23f. macht, alles verdorben und das Evangelium um seinen vorzüglichsten Reiz gebracht wird[84]. Das ganze kunstvoll eingefädelte Rätselspiel um den verborgenen Namen des Evangelisten wird zur öden Spielerei, wenn man – wie das

---

[82] Darin, diesen Respekt neu eingeschärft zu haben, sehe ich das Hauptverdienst der großen Arbeit von J. Kügler 1988a. – Cullmann (1975: 81f.), "findet" sich zwar mit der Namenlosigkeit des geliebten Jüngers "ab", doch muß sie ihm zugleich apologetischen Zwecken dienen: "Jedoch spricht gerade die Anonymität des Lieblingsjüngers für seine historische Existenz. Die apokryphen Evangelien pflegen ihre legendarischen Berichte nicht zu einem anonymen, sondern eher zu bekannten Jüngern in Beziehung zu setzen"; ähnlich Quast 1989: 16.

[83] Bei allen oben genannten Fragwürdigkeiten seiner *historischen Konstruktion* hat Bauckham (1993) mit guten Gründen herausgestellt, daß der geliebte Jünger im Evangelium als "idealer Autor" gezeichnet wird. Wie Jesus, der an der Brust seines Vaters liegt (1,18), dessen einzig authentischer "Exeget" ist, so ist der geliebte Jünger, der beim letzten Mahl an der Brust seines Herrn lag, sein autorisierter Exeget.

[84] Die altkirchliche Zuschreibung des Evangeliums an den Apostel Johannes erscheint mir mit Overbeck (1911: 409ff.) demgegenüber als der glänzende Beleg dafür, daß seinem Autor die Mystifikation mit dem geliebten Jünger durchaus gelungen ist. Das heißt, der (reale) Evangelist muß "in der Hauptsache als der Begründer oder Schöpfer der kleinasiatischen Johannessage betrachtet werden. Er kann sie nur vor sich und nicht hinter sich haben" (362). Das lange Leben des Apostels ist aus Joh 21,23 herausgesponnen. Man sage nicht, das sei unmöglich, denn ein Blick in die einschlägige Literatur belehrt darüber, daß sehr kluge Leute sogar heute noch dergleichen aus Joh 21,23 schließen.

gegenwärtig fast allgemein üblich geworden ist – Joh 21,23 als *Nachricht* vom Tode eines allseits bekannten und beliebten Schulhauptes liest. Mag dieser Vers auch den Tod und möglicherweise sogar den *Märtyrertod* desjenigen Jesusjüngers voraussetzen, den der reale Autor den "geliebten" genannt und zu seinem fiktionalen Evangelisten gemacht hat, so kann doch von dessen Bekanntsein unter den ersten Lesern auch nicht entfernt die Rede sein.

Überhaupt liegt der Fehler vieler Untersuchungen darin, daß ihre Autoren nicht zwischen realem und fiktionalem Autor unterscheiden. Sie beachten nicht, daß sich der reale Autor nach dem Motto des Johannes: "*Er muß wachsen, ich aber muß abnehmen*" absichtsvoll und unwiderruflich an sein eigenes Geschöpf, den "geliebten Jünger", entäußert hat; oder genauer gesagt, daß er aufgegangen ist in seinem *Werk*, in dem das Bild des geliebten Jüngers als seines "Evangelisten" nur ein meisterhaftes Detail ist, das er eigens dazu geschaffen hat, seinem Evangelium die Autorität keines geringeren als die des auferstandenen Jesus selbst zu verleihen. Ist aber die Autorisierung des Evangeliums der Zweck der *Erfindung* der Gestalt des geliebten Jüngers, dann kann dafür kein anderer als nur einer aus dem Kreis der Zwölf Modell gestanden haben. Nur mit dieser Unterscheidung zwischen dem Maler, seinem Modell und seinem Porträt lassen sich die Fragen nach dem "geliebten Jünger" sinnvoll stellen und möglicherweise ein Stück weit beantworten. Der Maler und sein Modell sind fraglos reale Personen, das Porträt natürlich nicht. Noch dazu handelt es sich bei diesem Porträt – wie beim Täufer- und beim Jesusbild unseres Evangelisten – um ein derart abstraktes und idealisiertes Bild, daß sich darin – von den späteren Betrachtern ganz zu schweigen – wohl nicht einmal der Abgebildete wiedererkennen könnte. Aber das braucht er auch nicht. Er ist lange tot und sein Andenken ist bei unserem (realen) Evangelisten gut aufgehoben[85]. Nach der alten Devise: "*De mortuis nil nisi bene*", sah er seine Aufgabe nicht darin, Sichtbares wiederzugeben, sondern das Unsichtbare sichtbar zu machen.

Hat man mit Overbeck (1911: 239), dessen Gründen schwer zu widersprechen sein dürfte, die "johanneische Frage" so auf die Suche nach jenem "Modell" reduziert und Joh 21,23 "rigoros" aus der Reihe derjenigen Stellen ausgeschlossen, die wenigstens *Hinweise* auf dessen Identität geben könnten, so bleiben als mögliche Anhaltspunkte zur Lösung des Rätsels nur noch Joh 1,35-42 und 21,2. Als *Opfer* seiner gelungenen Mystifikation – wozu unser Evangelist sie ja auch ausersehen hatte – haben die Väter des zweiten Jahrhunderts den geliebten Jünger als den realen Autor des vierten Evangeliums angesehen und ihn aufgrund dieser Stellen, so-

---

[85] Das bestätigt schon ein flüchtiger Blick auf die zahllosen bewegenden, meist von Joh 19,25-27 und 13,21-30 angeregten Darstellungen des Apostels Johannes der Kunstgeschichte. Ihre kongenialste ist vielleicht Matthias Grünewalds Vision der beiden johanneischen Johannesfiguren unter dem Kreuz des Isenheimer Altars.

wie der synoptischen Evangelien, wo die Zebedaiden ja zu den engsten Vertrauten Jesu gehören, mit dem Apostel Johannes identifiziert. Und auch wenn wir Kinder der Aufklärung zu ihren einfachen Identifikationen nicht mehr in der Lage sind, sondern – wie ich vorgeschlagen habe – in dieser Sache unterscheiden müssen zwischen *Maler, Modell* und *Porträt*, so erscheint doch auch mir für das "Modell", um das es unter unseren Bedingungen ja allein gehen kann, die von den Vätern gefundene Lösung des Rätsels die bei weitem plausibelste. Und "die plausibelste Lösung" kann ja nur diejenige heißen, die der implizite Autor seinen Lesern mit gleicher Energie sowohl *"sicher verbergen"* wie zu *"erraten"* aufgeben wollte[86].

Doch mit dem Rätsel um den *Namen* des geliebten Jüngers geht es wie mit der russischen Puppe in der Puppe: Kaum glaubt man das erste gelöst zu haben, da geht schon ein weiteres aus ihm hervor. Das hat Overbeck klar gesehen und damit zugleich ein neues Instrument zur Überprüfung der Lösung des ersten Rätsels gewonnen (409-33). Diese *neue johanneische Frage* formuliert er so: "Man begreift vollkommen, daß der Verfasser nur einen Apostel brauchen konnte, *aber warum mußte es gerade Johannes sein?*" Zur Beantwortung dieser Frage führt ihn die Beobachtung, daß nirgendwo in der gesamten übrigen Tradition Gestalt und Rolle Johannes des Täufers "so kühn und willkürlich" behandelt sind wie in unserem Evangelium (416), zu der folgenden Erwägung:

... Nimmt man z.B. an, daß für den Verfasser des Evangeliums der Apostel Johannes für den eben angegebenen Zweck der gegebene Mann war, weil er seinem Evangelisten zu Jesus nach seinem Hinscheiden dieselbe Stellung zu geben gedachte, *wie dem Täufer vorher*, so verstand sich die mysteriöse Einführung des Evangelisten von selbst. Sein Name konnte dann im Evangelium gar kein anderer als ein Geheimname sein. Denn er trug ihn nicht wegen irgend welcher Beziehung zum wirklichen Apostel Johannes, sondern wegen seiner Beziehung zur Idealfigur des Täufers im Kopfe des Verfassers des Evangeliums. Dieser hat selbst seinen Evangelisten unnennbar gemacht, weil er überhaupt nur eine Gestalt seiner Idealwelt ist, nur in dieser lebt und einen Namen hat. Natürlich mußte dieser Jünger einen Namen erhalten, aber ihn unter den ihm gegebenen Aposteln unmittelbar zu finden, konnte der Verfasser selbst nicht denken, sondern es handelt sich für ihn (darum), diesen Namen in den Apostelkreis *hinein* zu praktizieren, d.h. zu seiner Identifikation außerhalb dieses Kreises einzusetzen. Das gelang ihm aber, indem er zu seinem Idealjünger die Täufergestalt seines Evangeliums dazu erfand. Unter den Aposteln ist Johannes der Evangelist dieses Evangeliums nicht um seiner selbst willen, sondern um des Täufers willen als sein Namensvetter, oder anders gesagt: Er heißt Johannes um des ihm in seinem Evangelium zugefallenen Berufs willen und um der inneren Verwandtschaft dieses

---

[86] Overbeck (1911: 241f.; vgl. 409); ebd. wird methodisch vorbildlich gezeigt, daß wir ohne das uns überlieferte "Vorurteil" in dieser Frage niemals weiterkämen. Es gälte vielmehr, den uns von der Tradition zugespielten Namen des Apostels Johannes "mit Hilfe unserer Konjizierungsgabe am Text zu überprüfen".

Berufs willen mit dem des Täufers in der ganzen Oekonomie der Offenbarung des göttlichen Lichts in der Welt nach der Grundvorstellung dieser Oekonomie, auf der laut Prolog das ganze 4. Evangelium beruht (417).

Ich muß zum Schluß kommen und mich hier deshalb leider darauf beschränken, diesen kühnen Gedanken Overbecks wenigstens in Erinnerung zu rufen und ihn der unverdienten Vergessenheit zu entreißen. Denn auch er ist ein uns "von der Tradition" gegebenes "Vorurteil", das darauf wartet, am Text des Evangeliums "mit Hilfe unserer Konjizierungsgabe" überprüft zu werden. Alles, was ich bisher zu solchem Überprüfen unternommen habe[87], macht mich zuversichtlich, daß Overbecks "Vorurteil" diesen Plausibilitätstest bestehen wird; und mehr als möglichst große *Plausibilität* ist ja wohl in der Sache von Textinterpretationen niemals erreichbar. Erkennt man das ganze Evangelium – auch darin der Zeugentora von Dt 19,15 verpflichtet – als das wahre und übereinstimmende Zeugnis dieser *beiden* großen Zeugen, nämlich zunächst des "von Gott gesandten Mannes, mit Namen Johannes", wie er bereits im Prolog feierlich eingeführt wird, und danach des "Jüngers, den Jesus liebte", der als der einstige Schüler und geheimnisvolle Namensvetter des *ersten* sozusagen, oder vielmehr: *"so zu raten"* der zweite *Johannes* ist, so zeigt sich bald, daß diese beiden Figuren nicht nur "im Kopf des Evangelisten", sondern in dem auf der Textebene manifesten Spiel zwischen dem omniszienten Erzähler und seinem idealen Zuhörer miteinander zu kommunizieren beginnen. In diesem Licht erscheint 1,29. 35ff. als der Anfang jener Kommunikation. Denn nicht nur das unmittelbar vorausgehende wahre Zeugnis des Soldaten unter dem Kreuz, sondern auch und erst recht das Zeugnis seines unvergessenen Meisters, "Siehe, das Lamm Gottes, das der Welt Sünde trägt" (1,29. 35) nimmt der geliebte Jünger in sein *geschriebenes Zeugnis* mit hinein, wenn er am Ende, in seinem "wir wissen", gemeinsam mit ihnen und allen, die die frei machende Wahrheit seines Zeugnisses erkennen, einlädt zum Glauben (21,24), zum Eintritt in seine κοινωνία mit dem Vater und mit seinem Sohn Jesus Christus (1 Joh 1,1-4). So *"bleibt"* in und mit seinem Evangelium zusammen mit dem *unbenannten* zweiten Johannes auch der erste Johannes als der von Gott gesandte Zeuge: ἕως ἔρχομαι (21,22). Der Vergleich von 1,34 mit 20,31 und 21,24 zeigt die Übereinstimmung und verbürgt damit die Wahrheit ihres Zeugnisses.

Der Abschluß des "Buches der Täufermartyria", wie ich Joh 1-10 nenne: πάντα δὲ ὅσα εἶπεν Ἰωάννης περὶ τούτου ἀληθῆ ἦν. καὶ πολλοὶ ἐπίστευσαν εἰς αὐτὸν ἐκεῖ (10,41f.), entspricht so genau dem Ende des mit Joh 11 einsetzenden zweiten Buches, daß dessen letzter Satz *unverschlüsselt* lauten könnte: αὕτη ἐστὶν ἡ μαρτυρία τοῦ Ἰωάννου (1,19), καὶ οἴδαμεν ὅτι ἀληθὴς αὐτοῦ ἡ μαρτυρία ἐστιν

---

[87] Vgl. dazu einstweilen Thyen 1992b: 2025ff.

$(21,24)^{88}$.


## Bibliographie

Aland, Kurt 1961: "The Problem of Anonymity and Pseudonymity in Christian Literature of the First Two Centuries", in: *JThS* 12 (1961) 39-49.

Ashton, John 1991: *Understanding the Fourth Gospel*, London: Clarendon 1991.

Bauckham, Richard 1993: "The Beloved Disciple as Ideal Author", in: *JSNT* 49 (1993) 21-44.

Bauer, Walter 1933: *Das Johannesevangelium* (HNT 6), Tübingen: Mohr (Siebeck) ³1933.

Beasley-Murray, George R. 1987: *John* (Word Biblical Commentary 36), Waco, TX: Word Books Publisher 1987.

Becker, Jürgen 1969: "Wunder und Christologie" in: *NTS* 16 (1969/70) 130-48.

— 1991: *Das Evangelium nach Johannes* (ÖTBK 4,1 u. 2), Gütersloh: Mohn ³1991.

Betti, Emilio 1962: *Die Hermeneutik als allgemeine Methodik der Geisteswissenschaften* (Philosophie und Geschichte 78/79), Tübingen: Mohr (Siebeck) ²1962.

— 1967: *Allgemeine Auslegungslehre als Methodik der Geisteswissenschaften*, Tübingen: Mohr (Siebeck) 1967.

Boismard, Marie-Emile 1947: "Le chapître XXI de saint Jean: éssai de critique littéraire", in: *RB* 54 (1947) 473-501.

Bonsack, Bernhard 1988: "Der Presbyteros des dritten Briefs und der geliebte Jünger des Evangeliums nach Johannes", in: *ZNW* 79 (1988) 45-62.

Brown, Raymond E. 1966: *The Gospel according to John* (AncB 29), Vol. I, New York: Doubleday 1966.

— 1970: *The Gospel according to John* (AncB 29A), Vol. II, New York: Doubleday 1970.

— 1979: *The Community of the Beloved Disciple*, New York: Paulist Press 1979.

Bultmann, Rudolf 1959: *Das Evangelium des Johannes* (KEK 2), Göttingen: Vandenhoeck & Ruprecht ¹⁶1959.

Byrne, Brendan 1985: "The Faith of the Beloved Disciple and the Community in John 20", in: *JSNT* 23 (1985) 83-97.

Childs, Brevard S. 1979: *Introduction to the Old Testament as Scripture*, London: SCM 1979.

Cullmann, Oscar 1975: *Der johanneische Kreis*, Tübingen: Mohr (Siebeck) 1975.

---

[88] Dazu, daß die eigentliche Zäsur, die das Evangelium in zwei Bücher gliedert, nicht zwischen Joh 12 und 13, sondern zwischen Joh 10 und 11 in dem mit den Versen 10,40-42 für den Täufer errichteten *Epitaph* liegt, und daß die Erzählung von Tod und Auferweckung des Lazarus mit derjenigen von Jesu eigenem Sterben und Auferstehen die große Inclusio des zweiten Buches bildet, vgl. Thyen 1992b: 2025ff. Dort habe ich mich auch – wie ich hoffe behutsam genug – zur Frage der möglichen Beziehung zwischen Lazarus und dem geliebten Jünger geäußert; s. dazu auch Byrne 1985: 86ff.

Culpepper, Richard Alan 1975: *The Johannine School: An Evaluation of the Johannine-School-Hypothesis Based on an Investigation of the Nature of Ancient Schools* (SBL.DS 26), Missoula, MT: Scholars Press 1975.

— 1983: *Anatomy of the Fourth Gospel*, Philadelphia, PA: Fortress 1983.

de la Potterie, Ignace 1986: "Le témoin qui demeure: Le disciple que Jésus aimait", in: *Bib.* 67 (1986) 343-59.

Eckle, Wolfgang 1991: *Den der Herr liebhatte – Rätsel um den Evangelisten Johannes*, Hamburg: Dr. Kovač 1991.

Fortna, Robert Thomson 1988: *The Fourth Gospel and its Predecessor*, Edinburgh: Clark 1988.

Frank, Manfred 1977: *Das individuelle Allgemeine*, Frankfurt: Suhrkamp 1977.

Gnilka, Joachim 1979: *Das Evangelium nach Markus* (EKK II/2), Neukirchen-Vluyn u. Zürich: Neukirchener Verlag u. Benziger 1979.

Goulder, Michael 1993: "An Old Friend Incognito", in: *SJTh* 45 (1993), 487-513.

Harnack, Adolf von 1897: *Geschichte der altchristlichen Literatur* II/1, Leipzig: Hinrichs 1897.

Hartman, Lars 1984: "An Attempt at a Text-Centered Exegesis of John 21", in: *StTh* 38 (1984) 29-45.

Hengel, Martin 1989: *The Johannine Question*, London: SCM/Philadelphia, PA: Trinity Press 1989.

— 1993: *Die johanneische Frage. Ein Lösungsversuch* (WUNT 67), Tübingen: Mohr (Siebeck) 1993.

Herder, Johann Gottfried 1967: "Von Gottes Sohn, der Welt Heiland. Nach Johannis Evangelium", in: Ders., *Sämtl. Werke* 19, Hildesheim: Olms 1967, 253-424.

Hirsch, E. D. 1972: *Prinzipien der Interpretation* (UTB 104), München: Fink 1972.

Hoskyns, Edwyn Clement 1947: *The Fourth Gospel* (ed. F. C. Davey), London: Faber and Faber 1947.

Kermode, Frank 1986: "St John as Poet", in: *JSNT* 28 (1986) 3-16.

— 1987: "John", in: Alter, R. and Kermode, F. (eds.), *The Literary Guide to the Bible*, London: Collins 1987, 440-65.

Kierkegaard, Sören 1976: *Philosophische Brotsamen und Unwissenschaftliche Nachschrift*, München: Deutscher Taschenbuch Verlag 1976.

Kragerud, Alv 1959: *Der Lieblingsjünger im Johannesevangelium*, Oslo: Osloer Universitätsverlag 1959.

Kügler, Joachim 1988a: *Der Jünger, den Jesus liebte* (SBB 16), Stuttgart: Katholisches Bibelwerk 1988.

— 1988b: "Die Belehrung der Unbelehrbaren", in: *BZ* 32 (1988) 249-54.

Kurz, William S. 1989: "The Beloved Disciple and Implied Readers", in: *BTB* 19 (1989) 100-107.

Langbrandtner, Wolfgang 1977: *Weltferner Gott oder Gott der Liebe* (BET 6), Frankfurt/Bern/Las Vegas: Peter Lang 1977.

Lausberg, Heinrich 1973: *Handbuch der literarischen Rhetorik*, Bd. I, München: Max Hueber Verlag ²1973.

Lévinas, Emmanuel 1991: "Philosophie und Religion", in: Ders., *Außer sich*, München und Wien: Carl Hanser Verlag 1991, 79-92.

Mahoney, Robert 1974: *Two Disciples at the Tomb* (TW 6), Bern/Frankfurt: Peter Lang Verlag 1974.

Marquardt, Friedrich Wilhelm 1993: *Was dürfen wir hoffen, wenn wir hoffen dürfen?*, Gütersloh: Chr.Kaiser/G. Mohn 1993.

Milne, H. J. M. and Skeat, T. C. 1938: *Scribes and Correctors of the Codex Sinaiticus*, London: British Museum 1938.

Minear, Paul S. 1970: "The Idea of Incarnation in First John", in: *Interp.* 24 (1970) 291-302.

— 1976: "'We don't know where …' John 20,2", in: *Interp.* 30 (1976) 125-39.

— 1983a: "Diversity and Unity: A Johannine Case Study", in: U. Luz/H. Weder (eds.), *Die Mitte des Neuen Testaments. Einheit und Vielfalt neutestamentlicher Theologie. FS E. Schweizer*, Göttingen: Vandenhoeck & Ruprecht 1983, 162-75.

— 1983b: "The Original Functions of John 21", in: *JBL* 102 (1983) 85-98.

— 1984: *John. The Martyr's Gospel*, New York: The Pilgrim Press 1984.

Moore, Stephen D. 1989: "Rifts in (a Reading of) the Fourth Gospel, or: Does Johannine Irony still collapse in a Reading that Draws Attention to itself?", in: *Neotestamentica* 23 (1989) 5-17.

Neirynck, Frans 1975: "The 'Other Disciple' in Jn 18,15-16", in: *EThL* 51 (1975) 113-41 [Leuven: University Press/Peeters] = Ders., *Evangelica I* (BEThL 60), Leuven: University Press/Peeters 1982, 335-63 (additional notes ebd. 363-64).

— 1990: "John 21", in: *NTS* 36 (1990) 321-36 (= Neirynck, F., *Evangelica II* (BEThL 99), Leuven: University Press/Peeters 1991, 601-16.

— 1991: "The Anonymous Disciple in John 1", in: *Evangelica II* (BEThL 99), Leuven: University Press/Peeters 1991, 617-49.

O'Day, Gail R. 1986: *Revelation in the Fourth Gospel*, Philadelphia, PA: Fortress 1986.

— 1991 "'I have overcome the World' (John 16:33): Narrative Time in John 13-17", in: *Semeia* 53 (1991) 153-66.

Olsson, Birger 1974: *Structure and Meaning in the Fourth Gospel* (CB.NT 6), Lund: Gleerup 1974.

Overbeck, Franz 1911: *Das Johannesevangelium* (ed. C. A. Bernoulli), Tübingen: Mohr (Siebeck) 1911.

Pamment, Margaret 1983: The Fourth Gospel's Beloved Disciple", in: *ET* 94 (1983) 363-67.

Quast, Kevin 1989: *Peter and the Beloved Disciple* (JSNT.S.\ 32), Sheffield: JSOT-Press 1989.

Richter, Georg 1977: *Studien zum Johannesevangelium* (BU 13), Hg. J. Hainz, Regensburg: Pustet 1977.

Roloff, Jürgen 1968: "Der johanneische 'Lieblingsjünger' und der Lehrer der Gerechtigkeit", in: *NTS* 15 (1968) 129-51.

Ruckstuhl, Eugen 1977: "Zur Aussage und Botschaft von Johannes 21", in: Schnackenburg, R. u.a. (Hgg.), *Die Kirche des Anfangs*. FS H. Schürmann, Leipzig: St. Benno 1977, 339-62.

Ruckstuhl, Eugen und Dschulnigg, Peter 1991: *Stilkritik und Verfasserfrage im Johannesevangelium* (NTOA 17), Freiburg und Göttingen: Universitätsverlag Freiburg/Schweiz u. Vandenhoeck & Ruprecht 1991.

Schnelle, Udo 1987: *Antidoketische Christologie im Johannesevangelium* (FRLANT 144), Göttingen: Vandenhoeck & Ruprecht 1987.

Schwartz, Eduard 1904: *Über den Tod der Söhne Zebedäi* (AGWG.PH. VII/5), Berlin: Weidmannsche Buchhandlung 1904.

— 1910: "Noch einmal der Tod der Söhne Zebedäi", in: *ZNW* 11 (1910) 89-104.

Segovia, Fernando F. 1991: "The Final Farewell of Jesus: A Reading of John 20:30-21:25", in: *Semeia* 53 (1991) 167-90.

Smith, D. Moody 1965: *Composition and Order of the Fourth Gospel*, New Haven, CT: Yale University Press 1965.

Snyder, G. F. 1971: "John 13,16 amd the Anti-Petrinism of the Johannine Tradition", in: *BR* 16 (1971) 5-15.

Staley, Jeffrey L. 1988: *The Print's First Kiss. A Rhetorical Investigation of the Implied Reader in the Fourth Gospel* (SBL.DS 82), Atlanta, GA: Scholars Press 1988.

Steiger, Lothar 1990: *Er geht mit uns*, Freiburg: Herder 1990.

— 1993: *Die Erinnerung nach vorne. Erzählter Glaube. Die Evangelien*, Stuttgart: Radius 1993.

Steinseifer, Bernd 1971: "Der Ort der Erscheinungen des Auferstandenen", in: *ZNW* 62 (1971) 232-65.

Thyen, Hartwig 1977: "Entwicklungen innerhalb der johanneischen Theologie und Kirche im Spiegel von Joh 21 und der Lieblingsjüngertexte des Evangeliums", in: de Jonge, M. (ed.), *L' Évangile de Jean* (BEThL 44), Leuven: University Press/Peeters 1977, 259-99.

— 1990: "Juden und Christen – Kinder eines Vaters", in: Blum, E. u.a. (Hgg.), *Die Hebräische Bibel und ihre zweifache Nachgeschichte*. FS R. Rendtorff, Neukirchen-Vluyn: Neukirchener Verlag 1990, 689-705.

— 1992a: "Rez. Fortna, R. T., The Fourth Gospel and its Predecessor", in: *ThLZ* 117 (1992) 34-39.

— 1992b: "Die Erzählung von den bethanischen Geschwistern (Joh 11,1-12,19) als 'Palimpsest' über synoptischen Texten", in: Van Segbroeck, F. u.a. (eds.), *The Four Gospels 1992*. FS F. Neirynck (BEThL 100), Vol. III, Leuven: University Press/Peeters 1992, 2021-50.

— 1992c: "Ich bin das Licht der Welt. Jesu Ich- und Ich-Bin-Sagen im Johannesevangelium", in: *JAC* 35 (1992) 19-46.

— 1992d: "Johannes und die Synoptiker", in: Denaux, A. (ed.), *John and the Synoptics* (BEThL 101), Leuven: University Press/Peeters 1992, 81-107.

— 1994/95: "Misericordias Domini – 30.4.1995: Johannes 21,15-19" (Predigtmeditation über Joh 21), in: *GPM* 49 Heft 2 (1994/95).

Wiarda, Timothy 1992: "John 21, 1-23: Narrative Unity and its Implications", in: *JSNT* 46 (1992) 53-71.

Wittler, H. H., Bischof von Osnabrück (Hg.) 1980: *Johannes – John – Juan – Giovanni. – Ferienund Hotelbibel in vier Sprachen*. Textauswahl: Rudolf Schackenburg 1980.

Zimmermann, Heinrich 1960: "Das absolute Ἐγώ εἰμι als die neutestamentliche Offenbarungsformel", in: *BZ* 4 (1960) 54-69 und 266-76.

Zuntz, Günther 1991: "Papiana", in: *ZNW* 82 (1991) 242-63.

# Rhetorischer Kontext in Apg 15,13-21[1]
## Statuslehre und die Actareden

### Ernst Baasland

## 1. Einleitung

Der größte Gewinn der rhetorischen Forschung ist, daß hier, gemäß antiken Maßstäben, ein literarischer mit einem sozialgeschichtlichen Zugang kombiniert wird.
Rhetorischer Stil ('Text') ist von der Argumentationssituation ('Kontext') nicht zu
lösen.[2].

Aber gerade hier fangen die Probleme an: Nicht nur muß die soziale und argumentative Situation in den meisten Fällen rekonstruiert[3] werden. Man muß auch
fragen, was 'reale' Argumentationssituationen[4] sind, und ob nicht die Betonung *ei-*

---

[1] Dieser Aufsatz wurde auf einer Konferenz für Neutestamentler der nordischen Länder in Helsinki im Juni 1990 vorgetragen, vgl. P. Luomanen (ed.) 1991. Der Leiter der Gruppe, die die rhetorischen Aspekte von Lukas-Apg diskutierte, war der Jubilar. Hartmans tiefe Verwurzelung in traditionellen exegetischen Arbeitsweisen und seine Offenheit für neue, nicht zuletzt textlinguistische
und rhetorische Zugänge, ist zweifelsohne für die neueste Exegese im Norden und auch über die nordischen Länder hinaus, richtungsweisend gewesen.

[2] Die formgeschichtliche Forschung verfolgte dieselbe doppelte Zielrichtung, indem sie Stil als
eine soziologische Tatsache verstehen wollte. Die Formgeschichte verließ aber bald ihre Basis in der
rhetorischen Forschung und vermochte weder das Interesse an der Textgestalt noch an dem soziolo-
gischen Kontext aufrecht zu halten.

[3] Schon bei den paulinischen Texten bereitet die Rekonstruktion Probleme. Immerhin gibt es in
dem Fall hauptsächlich nur eine argumentative Situation. Es fehlen allerdings nicht in der Paulus-
forschung Hypothesen über Zwei-Fronten-Kämpfe oder auch die These, daß die realen und die in-
tendierten Adressaten deutlich zu unterscheiden sind. Grundsätzlich wird aber eine rhetorische
Situation vorausgesetzt, sei es eine bedrängte Lage, in der Paulus juridisch argumentieren muß (etwa
im Galaterbrief, also eher im Stil der γένος δικανικόν), sei es eine freundschaftliche Atmosphäre,
in der Paulus die Gemeinde/Freunde ermahnen (etwa im 1 Thess., also eher γένος συμβουλευτικόν)
oder loben will (γένος ἐπιδεικτικόν).

[4] Bei den narrativen Texten liegen mindestens zwei vor. Denn die berichtete argumentative Situation (etwa für die Reden der Apostelgeschichte) ist nicht mit der primären rhetorischen Situation
identisch, nämlich der, in welcher die Evangelientexte und Apg gebraucht, oder von den Autoren als
Argumenttexte intendiert wurden.

*ner* rhetorischen Situation zu verhängnisvollen Vereinfachungen führen kann. Denn es ist offensichtlich, was J. E. Barnhardt aphoristisch ausdrückt: "Every Kontext has a Kontext"[5]. Die Kontextfrage ist fast eine unendliche[6].

Die Kontexte konkurrieren um die Aufmerksamkeit der Exegeten. Moden, exegetische Schultraditionen und frühere Vernachlässigungen sind ausschlaggebend, wenn man bestimmte Kontexte hervorhebt, – abgesehen davon, daß Texte je nach Gattung und Inhalt bestimmte Kontexte voraussetzen. Die Konkurrenz kann friedlich-addierend sein, kann aber auch wirklich konkurrierend, antagonistisch sein, indem man einige Kontexte bewußt ausklammert.

Die komplizierte Lage tritt klar hervor, wenn man den schwierigen Text Apg 15,13-21 exegesiert. Hier werde ich nur Kontexte behandeln, die in der Forschung *vernachlässigt* worden sind.

Die Hauptsache ist darum, *die rhetorischen Mittel und Strategien*, die im Text vorliegen, zu analysieren. Das gilt um so mehr, da die neutestamentliche Forschung einen wichtigen Teil der Rhetorik vernachlässigt hat, nämlich die *Statuslehre*. Weil aber die rhetorischen Mittel eng mit Erwägungen zum traditionsgeschichtlichen Kontext verbunden sind, müssen sich diese zwei Kontexte gegenseitig beleuchten.

In diesem Zugang liegt eine Begrenzung. Ich meine aber, daß die Analyse der rhetorischen Mittel Vorrang vor der Rekonstruktion der argumentativen Situation hat, sei es der rhetorischen Situation des Verfassers[7], sei es der historischen oder fiktiven Situation der Jakobusrede[8] auf dem sogenannten Apostelkonzil[9].

---

[4] Ein Verfasser weiß selten, was der reale Leser denkt und fühlt. Paulus fühlt sich nach kurzer Zeit der Lage etwa in Korinth entfremdet, obwohl er die Gemeinde gründete und den Lebenslauf der implizierten Personen relativ gut kannte. Es ist somit immer ein Unterschied zwischen dem, was der Verfasser denkt und noch mehr dem, was er als die Situation darstellt, und der realen Situation der Empfänger. Hier hat die Rezeptionskritik zu differenzieren versucht (zwischen intendiertem und realem Leser, usw.), was an sich wünschenswert ist, aber selten möglich ist. Immer ist eine Art Fiktion zu berücksichtigen, indem der Verfasser die Situation der Leser gemäß seiner Informationen, nach seinem Wunschbild, seiner Hoffnung, seiner Deutung, usw. schildert. Die rhetorische Forschung hat diesem Element der Fiktion nicht genügend Aufmerksamkeit geschenkt. Deshalb hat man diejenigen Schriften, die pseudepigraphischen Charakter haben, nicht in den Griff nehmen können.

[5] J. E. Barnhardt 1980, 301-313, der sich dieser hermeneutischen Frage von der philosophischen Seite nähert.

[6] Das gilt in erster Linie auf *diachroner* Ebene. Der Hintergrund eines Textes ist auf einem Hintergrund zu sehen, dessen Hintergrund wiederum Hintergründe hat. Aber auch auf *synchroner* Ebene, d.h. wenn man die unmittelbare Umgebung eines Textes analysiert, ist Kontext kein eindeutiges Phänomen. Neben dem erzählten und historisch-rekonstruierten Kontext, ist etwa der breitere sozialgeschichtliche Kontext, der traditionsgeschichtliche und der rhetorische Kontext heranzuziehen.

[7] Diese Perspektive war in der älteren Tendenzkritik vorrangig und kam in der redaktionsgeschichtlichen Forschung wieder zur Geltung. Die Mehrzahl der Analysen zur Apg 15, wie zu Apg überhaupt, sind von diesen Methoden her geschrieben worden.

Das Ziel dieses Aufsatzes ist zu zeigen, daß der Verfasser der Apg. mit der Rhetorik und der Statuslehre vertraut war. Die hellenistische Rhetorik wurde aber im Horizont jüdisch-alttestamentlicher Rechtstraditionen gesehen. Die *Verflechtung* der beiden Kontexte läßt sich anhand einer Analyse von Apg 15,13ff gut zeigen, obwohl andere Actatexte leichter die Bedeutung der Statuslehre illustrieren können.

## 2. Apg 15,13-21 und die Kontexte

### 2.1. 15,13-21 im Rahmen der anderen Reden

Neben den acht größeren Petrus-Reden und acht größeren Paulus-Reden kommen in den Acta-Reden sieben andere Personen zu Wort. Jakob ist einer unter Vielen, dem nur eine Rede zugeteilt wird. In dieser Gruppe sind die absolute Mehrzahl Nicht-Christen (Gamaliel, Tertullus, usw.). Nur Stefanus und Jakobus sind Christen. Ab 15,35ff ist Paulus der einzige christliche Prediger. Die Jakobus-Rede ist also, von Paulus' Predigt abgesehen, die letzte christliche Rede.

---

[8] In der Forschung finden wir vier grundsätzliche Haltungen zur Historizitätsfrage:

a. Die Rede, wie auch das 'Apostelkonzil', sind als Phantasie zu bezeichnen, eine redaktionelle Bildung des Lukas (u.A. E. Haenchen 1961, 396-414).

b. Eine Art Versammlung hat stattgefunden, nicht aber in der von Lukas dargestellten Form. Die Rede trägt judenchristliches Kolorit, ist aber weithin eine Schöpfung des Lukas (vgl. J. Roloff 1981, bes. 224f.).

c. Lukas hat den Tatsachen seine Form gegeben (vgl. J. Munck 1967, 140: "The words of James have been thoroughly reworked"), aber die Rede, wie auch die Erzählung vom 'Apostelkonzil', enthalten historische Erinnerungen.

d. Die Jakobusrede und die Darstellung vom 'Apostelkonzil' liefern echte historische Daten, obwohl natürlich nur ausgewählte Daten wiedergegeben sind (so Th. Zahn 1921, 504-533).

[9] Die historische Rekonstruktion betrifft nicht nur die Rede als solche, da die Rede eng mit den Geschehnissen in Apg 15 verbunden ist, und damit mit der ganzen Problematik des 'Apostelkonzils', und auch mit dem Verhältnis von Apg 15 und Gal 2 und damit mit der Chronologie des Paulus, zusammenhängt.

Die Skepsis gegen die Darstellung des Apostelkonzils in Apg 15 gegenüber Gal 2 hat auf die Analyse der Jakobusrede eingewirkt (vgl. G. Zuntz 1972, 233ff.).

Anders verhält es sich wohl, wenn man die Ereignisse, von denen Gal 2 berichtet, nicht als identisch mit Apg 15 sieht. Dadurch wird die historische Rekonstruktion schwieriger und die Einordnung in die Chronologie des Paulus nicht unbedingt leichter. Andererseits kann man dann Apg 15 eher unvoreingenommen deuten und auswerten.

Die historische Rekonstruktion ist auch von der Einschätzung der inneren Logik in Apg 15 abhängig. Für den modernen Leser erscheinen die Vorgänge und die Argumentation als sehr sprunghaft, und legen eine literarkritische Erklärung nahe (vgl. A. von Harnack 1908, 155-157; 188-199; R. Bultmann 1967, 412-423, hier bes. 417).

Eine andere Frage muß aber zuvor gestellt werden: Konnte der Leser der ersten Jahrhunderte eine Logik in Apg 15 erblicken? Um diese Frage geht es in diesem Aufsatz.

Es ist heute eine Binsenwahrheit in der Forschung, daß eine innere Beziehung zwischen vielen Acta-Reden besteht. Im Fall der Jakobusrede ist die innere Relation zur vorgehenden Petrusrede ganz offensichtlich (s.u.).Aber auch zu anderen Reden gibt es deutliche Relationen, etwa zu Apg 2 und 7.

Apg 2,22: Ἄνδρες Ἰσραηλῖται, ἀ-
κούσατε ... Ἰησοῦν ... εἰς ὑμᾶς
δυνάμεσι καὶ τέρασι καὶ σημείοις
οἷς ἐποίησεν δι' αὐτοῦ ὁ θεὸς ἐν
μέσῳ ὑμῶν καθὼς αὐτοὶ οἴδατε

Apg 15,13: Ἄνδρες ἀδελφοί, ἀκού-
σατέ μου.
Vgl. 15,12: ἐξηγουμένων ὅσα ἐποίησεν ὁ θεὸς σημεῖα καὶ τέρατα ἐν
τοῖς ἔθνεσιν δι' αὐτῶν.

Vgl. Apg 2,25f.: Δαυὶδ γὰρ λέγει ...
ἡ σάρξ μου κατασκηνώσει ἐπ' ἐλπίδι
2,27 ὅτι οὐκ ἐγκαταλείψεις τὴν
ψυχήν μου εἰς ᾅδην οὐδὲ δώσεις ....
2,29: Δαυίδ ... τὸ μνῆμα αὐτοῦ ἔστιν
ἐν ἡμῖν ἄχρι τῆς ἡμέρας ταύτης.

Vgl. 15,15: καθὼς γέγραπται·
15,16: Μετὰ ταῦτα ἀναστρέψω καὶ
ἀνοικοδομήσω τὴν σκηνὴν Δαυὶδ
τὴν πεπτωκυῖαν καὶ ... ἀνοικοδομήσω ....
15,17f.: λέγει κύριος ποιῶν ταῦτα
γνωστὰ ἀπ' αἰῶνος.

Die Parallelen werden noch deutlicher wenn man die Linie zu Apg 7 zieht. Die Davidsthematik ist in vielfältiger Weise vorbereitet (ἕως τῶν ἡμερῶν Δαυίδ, vgl. 13,22)[10], und wird in Apg 7 wie in Apg 15 mit einem Hinweis auf Moses (7,44: Ἡ σκηνὴ τοῦ μαρτυρίου ἦν τοῖς πατράσιν ἡμῶν ἐν τῇ ἐρήμῳ καθὼς διετάξατο ὁ λαλῶν τῷ Μωϋσῇ ποιῆσαι αὐτὴν κατὰ τὸν τύπον ὃν ἑωράκει) verknüpft. Auch die 'Hütte – Tempel' Thematik tritt deutlich hervor. Die Verwendung von σκηνή (neben 7,44 auch 7,46ff.: Δαυίδ ... εὑρεῖν σκήνωμα τῷ οἴκῳ Ἰακώβ. Σολομῶν δὲ οἰκο-δόμησεν αὐτῷ οἶκον. ἀλλ' οὐχ ὁ ὕψιστος ἐν χειροποιήτοις κατοικεῖ) muß in diesem Zusammenhang gesehen werden.

Die Parallele zur Stephanusrede ist besonders wichtig, weil die Argumentation, die den Streit entzündet, eine ähnliche war[11]. In Apg 6-7 liegt mehr ein juridischer Prozeß vor[12], und es geht um wirkliche Vorwürfe[13]. In beiden Fällen geht es aber um die Gefährdung der Sitten (ἔθη) Moses. Apg 7 gibt die prinzipielle und ausführliche Antwort und zwar von der 'Torah' im Sinne der fünf Bücher des Moses und nicht zuletzt vom Deuteronomium her, während es in Apg 15 nur um die Anpassung im

---

[10] Ausführlich J. Jervell 1983, 79-96. Auch E. Richard 1980/83, 195 und idem 1978, 337f.

[11] In beiden Fällen liegt das Schema vor: Probleme entstehen, innere Krise droht, neue Lösungen bahnen sich an.

[12] Nicht nur τὸν λαὸν καὶ τοὺς πρεσβυτέρους καὶ τοὺς γραμματεῖς, sondern auch ἤγαγον εἰς τὸ συνέδριον spricht dafür.

[13] Vgl. λαλοῦντος ῥήματα βλάσφημα εἰς Μωϋσῆν καὶ τὸν θεόν ... λαλῶν ῥήματα κατὰ τοῦ τόπου τοῦ ἁγίου καὶ τοῦ νόμου ... λέγοντος ὅτι Ἰησοῦς ὁ Ναζωραῖος οὗτος καταλύσει τὸν τόπον τοῦτον καὶ ἀλλάξει τὰ ἔθη ἃ παρέδωκεν ἡμῖν Μωϋσῆς.

Rahmen der christlichen Gemeinde, und das Verhältnis von Juden- und Heidenchristen geht.

## 2.2. Rhetorische Gattungen und die Acta-Reden

Bei der Kategorisierung dieser Reden hat die Forschung bisher lediglich folgende Einteilung benutzt: Missionsreden, Verteidigungsreden und Abschiedsreden/Testamente (Apg 20).

Diese Kategorisierung und Einteilung ist sowohl unbefriedigend als auch unvollständig. 'Missionsrede' ist ein moderner Begriff, der in der Forschung nur so lange benutzt werden konnte, wie die Fragen nach Tradition und Quellen hinter den Acta-Reden das dominierende Problem waren; spiegelten sie rein faktisch die urchristliche Missionsverkündigung wieder (C. H. Dodd[14], B. Gärtner[15] u.a.)? Oder hatten sie nur wenig (unter anderem M. Dibelius[16], U. Wilkens[17]) oder sozusagen nichts (E. Haenchen[18] u.a.) mit dieser Verkündigung zu tun?

Dodds und Gärtners Nachweis eines grundlegenden Schemas in diesen Reden machte Eindruck. 'Missionsrede' als formhistorische Gattung war etabliert, und wurde auch dann übernommen, wenn man sich, wie etwa U. Wilkens, kritischer zur Historizität dieser Reden stellte. Die Kategorie 'Missionsrede' wurde immerhin ohne Seitenblick auf die rhetorische Analyse[19] gestaltet.

Neben dem Vorwurf einer Modernisierung und dem fehlenden rhetorischen Bewußtsein, ist außerdem die Differenzierung zwischen Missionsreden und Verteidigungsreden problematisch. Denn die sog. Missionsreden Apg 4,8-12 und 4,19-20; 5,29-32 sind in erster Linie Verteidigungsreden. In den Acta-Erzählungen gibt es drei 'Missionsreden' für Juden (2,14-36/39; 3,12-26 und 13,16-41) und drei für Heiden (10,34-43; 14,15-17 und 17,22-31). Die absolute Mehrzahl wird also als Verteidigungsreden präsentiert: 3 von Petrus (4,8-12.19f; 5,29-32); 3 von Paulus (22,1-21; 24,10-21; 26,2ff.); die Stefanus-Rede; fünf von anderen (Gamaliel, Demetrius, der Stadtschreiber in Ephesus, Tertullus und Festus). Außerdem sind die Petrus- und Jakobus-Reden in den Kapiteln 1-15 (mit Ausnahme von 11,5-17) und

---

[14] Dodd 1962.

[15] Gärtner 1961, 34-54.

[16] Die Reden der Apostelgeschichte und die antike Geschichtsschreibung (1949), in: Dibelius 1953, 120-162.

[17] Wilckens 1961 (1974).

[18] Haenchen 1961, 73ff. et passim.

[19] So Dodd 1962; Gärtner 1961; Noch K. Berger 1984, 72f. Vielleicht läßt sich diesen unbefangene Umgang mit der Kategorie dadurch erklären, daß man noch im Schatten der dominierenden kerygmatischen Theologie lebte, und noch mehr, weil die Kategorie 'Predigt' in der synoptischen Forschung fast überall akzeptiert war. Missionsrede/Missionspredigt ist nur eine leichte Anpassung dieser etablierten Gattungsbezeichnung.

28,17-20 auf Grund von Streitigkeiten entstanden.

Eine etwas bessere Einteilung der Reden gab F. F. Bruce schon 1944[20]. Er unterschied zwischen 4 Typen: 'Evangelistic', 'deliberative' (1,16ff.; 15,7-11.13-21), 'apologetic' (Stefanus-Rede, 11,4-17, 6 Paulus-Reden), 'hortatory' (20,18ff.). Aber auch bei Bruce werden klassische und mehr modern-kirchliche Formen zu dicht verwebt.

Im Ausgangspunkt sollte man sich aber mehr an die klassischen Einteilungen – deliberative (γένος συμβουλευτικόν), judiziale (γένος δικανικόν) und epideiktische Reden (γένος ἐπιδεικτικόν) – halten. Die letzte Kategorie existiert in Apg nicht. In den deliberativen (und auch judizialen) Reden haben wir Einschläge der synagogalen Predigttradition[21]), der Testamenttradition (Apg 20) und also auch Züge der christlichen Missions- und Proselytenverkündigung.

Die Mehrzahl der Reden ist also judizial. In den deliberativen Reden gibt es sogar Einschläge juristischer Argumentation. U.a. fungiert der Schriftbeweis auf diese Weise[22]. Das stimmt mit vielen charakteristischen Zügen in Apg überein: Die Kapitel 16 und 19-28 sind sozusagen von Gerichtsverhandlungen gegen Paulus geprägt, juridische Terminologie kommt häufiger vor als in allen anderen Schriften des Neuen Testaments, und der juridische Begriff Zeuge/Zeugenaussage (μάρτυς, μαρτυρία) prägt die Darstellung der Missionsverkündigung[23]. Man kann wie u.A. R. Morgenthaler[24], und W. C. van Unnik[25] behaupten, daß der ganze 'Zweck (bzw. Absicht)' der Apg. dadurch geprägt sei.

Die Jakobusrede fügt sich gut in diesen Rahmen ein. Ob Jakobus hier in dem entstandenen Streit die zweite Zeugenaussage bringt (vgl. 15,7ff. und Deut 19,15) oder ob er als Richter die Entscheidung fällt (διὸ ἐγὼ κρίνω, 15,19), ist unklar, aber die Argumentation ist juridisch, obwohl die Situation der Rede eher einer deliberativen Rede entspricht.

## 3. Apg 15,13ff. und die Statuslehre

Wenn die meisten Reden judizial sind oder Einschläge der juridischen Argumentation haben, ist es nicht überraschend, daß die Statuslehre in Apg wiederzufinden ist. Ob Lukas diese aus der gewöhnlichen Rechtspraxis oder aus rhetorischen Lehrbü-

---

[20] F. F. Bruce 1942, 5. Es ist aber auffallend, daß die bisherige rhetorische Forschung wenig Interesse an der Rhetorik der Actareden gelenkt hat.

[21] Man braucht das nicht so weit zu führen wie J. W. Bowker 1967/68, 96-111.

[22] Vgl. W. S. Kurz 1980, 171-95.

[23] A. A. Trites 1974, 278-84.

[24] R. Morgenthaler 1949, 7ff.

[25] W. C. van Unnik 1960, 26-59, bes. 54ff.; vgl. auch etwa C. Burchard 1970, 130ff.

chern kannte (z.B. wie sie am deutlichsten von Hermagoras von Temnos entwickelt wurde), ist relativ gleichgültig[26].

Ein Indiz für die Vertrautheit des Lukas ist der Gebrauch der klassischen Wörter der Stasis-Lehre (ζήτημα/ζήτησις, στάσις), den wir gerade bei Lukas – und auffallend häufig in Apg 15 – finden.

Ζήτημα taucht in Apg 15,2; 18,15; 23,29; 25,19; 26,3 auf. Ζήτησις haben wir auch in Apg 15,2.7 und 25,20, ansonsten nur in den Pastoralbriefen (4 mal) und Joh 3,25[27]. Man kann den Begriff vom Hintergrund jüdischer Schriftauslegung (= מדרש) ableiten[28], er ist aber in dem breiteren hellenistischen Kontext zu sehen. Bei Hermagoras hieß die Statuslehre πολιτικὸν ζήτημα, und entsprechend wird sie *civilis quaestio* bei Cicero genannt. Die Statuslehre bezieht sich auf eine öffentliche Angelegenheit, die nach juridischen (oder ethischen und politischen) Maßstäben entschieden wurden.

Ebenso ist στάσις ein ausgeprägtes Lukas-Wort (sonst nur in Mark 15,7; Hebr 9,8)[29]. In Mark 15,7; Luk 23,19.25 bezeichnet es eher einen gewalttätigen Aufruhr, hat aber in Apg 15,2; 19,40; 23,7.10; 24,5 die klassisch-juridischen Bedeutungen: Zwist, der Ausgangspunkt für Rechts- und Kompetenzstreit. συζήτησις kommt nur in Apg 28,29 vor, also gerade am Ende von Apg[30].

## 3.1. Genus rationale

In den Gerichtsverhandlungen gegen Petrus und Paulus spitzt sich der Streit zu. Hinter diesen Texten steckt in der Tat die Statuslehre[31].

Da es hier um juridische Vorgänge geht, muß von *genus rationale* die Rede sein. Im Rahmen rechtlicher Prozesse wurde die eigentliche Statuslehre praktiziert. Die Prozesse wurden einem der folgenden 'Fälle' zugeordnet:

---

[26] Hermagoras (2. J.v.C.) gilt durch sein Werk 'περὶ τῶν στάσεων' als Grundleger der Statuslehre, ist aber heute nur durch die Vermittlung Ciceros, Quintilian und Hermogenes bekannt.

[27] Das Verb ζητέω wird selten technisch-juridisch benutzt.

[28] Vgl. B. Gerhardsson 1961, 250 Anm. 4 mit Hinweis auf H. A. Wolfson (Philo I, [2]1948, 193f.).

[29] Es ist m.E. kein Zufall, daß dieser Begriff in 1 Clem. einen Schlüßelbegriff wird (1,1; 2,6; 3,2; 14,2; 46,9; 51,1; 54,2; 57,1; 63,1). Er hat hier nicht den technisch-rhetorischen Sinn, aber es würde sich lohnen sowohl den Streit wie die Lösung aus der Sicht der antiken Statuslehre zu sehen.

[30] Das Verb συζητέω wird nur in Mark und Lukas/Apg gebraucht. Es hat diesen technischen Gebrauch in Mark 8,11; (9,10); 9,14.16; 12,28 und in Luk 22,23 (24,15); Apg 6,9; 9,29. Bei den beiden letztgenannten sind 'die Hellenisten' in die Debatte/den Zwist verwickelt.

[31] Neben den Primärquellen (Hermagoras, Cicero, Quintilianus, Hermogenes) s. bes. J. Martin 1974, 28-51.

- *status coniecturalis* (στοχασμός), wenn der Angeklagte die ihm vorgeworfene Tat leugnet,
- *status definitivus* (ὅρος), man diskutiert welche Gesetze angewandt werden sollen,
- *status qualitatis* (ποιότης), die Umstände die eine Tat rechtfertigen kann,
- *translatio* (μετάληψις), man versucht die Verhandlung abzuschneiden, um sie bei einem anderen Gericht fortzusetzen.

In der Apg. hat das Gerichtsverfahren keinen kriminellen Hintergrund, und *status coniecturalis* (στοχασμός) und *status qualitatis* (ποιότης) kommen nicht in Frage. Dagegen dreht sich der Streit um *status definitivus* (ὅρος), also die Frage nach der Rechtsgrundlage für eine Anklage. Man diskutiert hier nicht den Inhalt des Gesetzes (*controversia nominis*), sondern ob das, wessen man angeklagt ist, in einem anderen und größeren Zusammenhang gesehen werden muß. Demetrius meinte, daß Paulus' Verkündigung von dem einen, wahren Gott ein Angriff auf die Göttin Artemis darstellte (18,35ff.). Die Oberpriester und die Sadduzäer suchten nach einer Rechtsgrundlage für ihre Anklage: "Welche Kraft und welcher Name gaben euch die Macht, dies zu tun"? (Apg 4,7), während Gamaliel meinte, daß keine definierte Anklage ausgestellt werden könne (Apg 5,34ff.).

Apg zufolge kennt Paulus auch den vierten Status, nämlich *translatio* (μετάληψις) gut. Er will, daß der Prozeß abgebrochen wird, weil er das Gericht nicht anerkennt. Deshalb beruft sich Paulus zum Schluß auf sein Recht: "Ich stehe vor des Kaisers Gericht und hier habe ich ein Recht darauf, mein Urteil zu erhalten. Ich habe den Juden kein Unrecht getan" (25,10).

### Ἀσύστατα

In den Gerichtsverfahren, die Apg beschreibt, ist die Rechtsgrundlage der Anklagen unklar, und der innere Zusammenhang fehlt. Man findet keine echte Grundlage, um ein Urteil über Petrus und Paulus zu fällen. Die Sache kann also nicht im Gericht entschieden werden. Wir haben es damit mit einem ἀσύστατον zu tun.

Hermagoras gibt vier solche ἀσύστατα an, während z.B. Fotunatian, Grillius, Hermogenes und Cicero viele andere aufzählen[32].

In der Darstellung der Prozesse in der Apg. kann man besonders die folgende ἀσύστατα wiederzufinden:

- ἐλλείπουσα, wenn es an einer notwendigen Prämisse der Argumentation fehlt,
- ἰσομερής, wenn die Rechtlage für beide Parteien gleich ist,
- ὑπόθεσις ἄπορος, wenn eine Perspektive eine Anklage oder eine Verteidigung unmöglich macht, bzw. wenn man in unauflösliche Widersprüche geraten ist,
- παρ' ἰστορίαν, wenn der historischen Wahrheit widersprochen wird.

---

[32] Dazu J. Martin 1974, bes. 18-23.

Sowohl Gamaliel (Kap.5) als auch der Stadtschreiber (Kap.18), Felix (Kap.24) und Agrippa (Kap.26) gehen von solchen ἀσύστατα aus. Paulus selber argumentiert mit ihrer Hilfe, etwa Apg 24,12f.19 (ἔδει ἐπὶ σοῦ παρεῖναι καὶ κατηγορεῖν εἴ τι ἔχοιεν πρὸς ἐμέ).

Das zu sehen, *ist wichtig für den eigentlichen 'plot' in Apg*. Denn genau dies treibt die Handlung und die Missionsverkündigung voran, bis Paulus in Rom das Evangelium verkündet.

## 3.2. Genus legale

Apg 15 gibt kein Gerichtverfahren wieder. Deshalb sind *genus rationale* oder die ἀσύστατα-Fragen nicht aktuell. Insofern könnte man leichter die Bedeutung der Statuslehre anhand anderer Reden untersuchen.

Dennoch taucht in Apg diese Art juridischer Sprache auf, und diese Züge haben die Forschung veranlaßt Apg 15 als ein 'Konzil' zu bezeichnen. In der Tat kommt in Apg 15 der zweite Teil der Statuslehre in Frage, nämlich *genus legale*. Dieses Genus ist zwar auch in der gerichtlichen Beredsamkeit beheimatet, wird aber außerhalb des Gerichts häufig verwendet. Denn hier befinden wir uns sozusagen im Vorraum des Gerichtslokals, wo es darum geht, Gesetze und Verordnungen zu verstehen und richtig auszulegen. Auch in andere Situationen des Lebens und Redens kommen solche Gesetze und Verordnungen zur Sprache. Deswegen ist es keineswegs überraschend, daß man das *genus legale* auch in der Apg in nicht-jurikalen Reden entdeckt.

Schon im Rechtsstreit mit Heiden geht es ums *genus legale*, etwa wenn – gemäß Apg – der römische Bürger Paulus als Unruhestifter angeklagt wird. Das *genus legale* ist aber in viel stärkerem Maße im Streit mit jüdischen Behörden und innerhalb der christlichen Gemeinde aktuell. Denn nur in den Reden an die jüdischen Behörden und in der inneren kirchlichen Debatte dreht sich der Rechtsstreit um das AT und AT-Interpretationen.Das *genus legale* wird in hellenistischer Zeit natürlich auch von Juden angewandt, und A. Schwarz[33] und D. Daube[34] haben längst die Ähnlichkeit zwischen Hillelschen Auslegungsprinzipien und der hellenistischen Rhetorik, vor allem bei den 'Beweisen' (πίστεις ἄτεχνοι und ἔντεχνοι) und in der Statuslehre, gesehen.

---

[33] Die Beiträge Schwarz sind in der Forschung leider in Vergessenheit geraten, siehe besonders diejenigen in: A. Schwarz 1913. Er gehörte noch zu den Generationen jüdischer Forscher, die sich sowohl in der jüdischen wie auch im klassisch-griechischen Erbe beheimatet fühlten.

[34] D. Daube 1949, 239-264.

Auch beim *genus legale* operiert Hermagoras mit vier Kategorien[35]:

- ῥητὸν καὶ διάνοια, also das Verhältnis Wortlaut – Bedeutung,
- ἀντινομία, wenn verschiedene Gesetze auf einen und denselben Fall angewandt werden können,
- ἀμφιβολία, wenn verschiedene Auslegungen eines Gesetzes vorliegen,
- συλλογισμός, wenn das Gesetz nichts direkt sagt. Ein Analogieschluß ist aber auf Grund ähnlicher Gesetze möglich.

Meiner Meinung nach lassen diese Prinzipien sich sowohl leicht auf Paulus' Interpretation des ATs im Römer- und Galaterbrief[36] als auch auf die Reden der Apg und nicht zuletzt auf die AT-Zitate in den Acta-Reden anwenden. Durch diesen Zugang wird die rhetorische und traditionsgeschichtliche Analyse eng zusammengebracht. Denn hier geht es um Antinomien, Verlagerungen, Spannungen, die in jeder Tradition vorhanden sind, und die in neuen, aktuellen Fällen durch neue Lösungen und Traditionsbildungen gelöst werden müssen.

Eine derartige Lage schildert Apg 15, was die folgende Analyse noch zeigen will. Schon auf Grund der Terminologie ahnt man, daß es um solche Verhandlungen geht. Die Verben σιγᾶν, συμφωνεῖν, κρίνειν legen diese Behauptung nahe.

## 4. Die Stasis im erzählten Kontext

Apg 15 wird insgesamt als eine Debatte über ἐὰν μὴ περιτμηθῆτε τῷ ἔθει τῷ Μωϋσέως, eingeführt. Die Beschneidung ist der Verordnung des Moses zufolge Pflicht, und der Zwist (στάσεως καὶ ζητήσεως) entsteht, wenn die Frage der Erlösung mit dieser Verordnung verknüpft wird (οὐ δύνασθε σωθῆναι, 15,1). Dies war offensichtlich der Standpunkt der Gläubigen der Pharisäer-Partei, als sie sich gemäß 15,5 folgendermaßen äußerten: "Sie müssen beschnitten und dazu verpflichtet werden, Moses Gesetz zu halten" (δεῖ περιτέμνειν αὐτοὺς παραγγέλλειν τε τηρεῖν τὸν νόμον Μωϋσέως). Nicht nur die messiasgläubigen Judenchristen müssen nach dem Gesetz leben, sondern auch Heidenchristen müssen durch die Beschneidung Juden werden und durch die Gesetzerfüllung als Juden leben, um Christen zu sein.

Man hätte erwarten können, daß die Beschneidung im weiteren Verlauf erwähnt werden würde, wie etwa in der Stephanusrede, Apg 7,8ff. In den Reden in Apg 15

---

[35] Nach Quintilian, *Institutio* III, 6, 60-62. Quintilian führt sofort (*ibid.* III,6, 62ff.), und zwar von Cicero (in erster Linie von '*pulcherrimos illos De Oratore*' her), seine ergänzenden und kritischen Kommentare an. Cicero äußert sich am ausführlichsten zur Statuslehre in *De Inventione*.

[36] Vgl. K. A. Morland 1994 (1991); auch J. S. Vos 1992, 254-270 und E. Baasland 1988, Anm. 34.

wird aber nicht gegen die Ansicht argumentiert, daß die Beschneidung notwendig sei. Nur die Praxisfrage für die Heidenchristen, die Frage nach τηρεῖν τὸν νόμον Μωϋσέως, spielt in der Fortsetzung eine Rolle.

Die Argumentation in Apg 15 ist aber von der Statuslehre her verständlicher, da man die Prinzipien für die Anführung von einander widersprechenden Gesetzen/ Verordnungen kennt. In solchen Fällen muß man herausfinden, ob einige übergeordnet sind oder ob andere in engerem Sinne angewandt werden (*quae abrogatio aut derogatio sit*)[37].

Darum geht es in Apg 15. Schon in der Petrusrede klingt dies in indirekter Weise an. Erst in der Jakobusrede werden die Schriftprinzipien einander gegenüber gestellt.

Die indirekte Argumentation in der Petrusrede liefert aber eine wichtige Prämisse. Wie in Röm 2,11; 3,29f. wird von dem Übergeordneten her argumentiert[38]: Gott behandelt die Menschen nicht unterschiedlich. Das ist der ewige Wille Gottes (vgl. 15, 7: ἀφ' ἡμερῶν ἀρχαίων) und dies zeigt sich in den jüngsten Taten Gottes (vgl. 15,8: καθὼς καὶ ἡμῖν)[39]. Mit dem Axiom, daß Gott, weil er der Gesetzgeber ist, alle rechtfertig behandelt, beruft man sich auf Gott selbst als Zeugen: Er wird hier 'der Herzenskenner' (ὁ καρδιογνώστης θεός) genannt, ein Terminus lukanischer Prägung, der aber gleichzeitig mit Deut 10,16 korrespondiert (καὶ περιτεμεῖσθε τὴν σκληροκαρδίαν ὑμῶν καὶ τὸν τράχηλον ὑμῶν οὐ σκληρυνεῖτε)[40]. Der Term τράχηλον taucht somit in Apg 15,10 auf, ein Begriff der im Zusammenhang sonst etwas unvermittelt wäre. Die Anspielungen auf deuteronomischen Sprachgebrauch sind kaum zufällig, sondern prägen die ganze Argumentation.

## 4.1. Stasis im Verhältnis der beiden Reden in Apg 15

Ehe ich die exegetischen Einzelheiten in der Jakobusrede näher erläutere, muß ein Blick auf die Ähnlichkeiten und Unterschiede der beiden Reden gerichtet werden. Die enge Beziehung zwischen den beiden Reden ist offensichtlich, und die Synopse

---

[37] [Cicero] *Ad Herennium* II, X. 15; auch *De inventione* II, XLIX. 144-47.

[38] Dazu J. M. Bassler 1982, bes. 7-16(-66).

[39] Apg 15,9 korrespondiert mit 10,34: ὅτι οὐκ ἔστιν προσωπολήμπτης ὁ θεός, dem Cornelius-text, dessen Ergebnis bekanntlich in der ganzen Petrusrede weitergeführt wird. Vgl. 15,8: αὐτοῖς δοὺς τὸ πνεῦμα τὸ ἅγιον καθὼς καὶ ἡμῖν (= 10,44.45.47); 15,9: καὶ οὐθὲν διέκρινεν μεταξὺ ἡμῶν τε καὶ αὐτῶν, τῇ πίστει καθαρίσας τὰς καρδίας αὐτῶν (= 10,10ff.); 15,11: διὰ τῆς χάριτος τοῦ κυρίου Ἰησοῦ πιστεύομεν σωθῆναι (= 10,43).

[40] Vgl. Röm 2,29; auch Deut 10,15-17; Deut. 10,16 (vgl. Apg 15,10); Deut 10,15 (vgl. Apg 15,7).

zeigt, daß die Struktur sehr ähnlich ist:

15,6f.: Situation: Verhandlung/Streit
πολλῆς δὲ ζητήσεως γενομένης

15,7: Einleitung/ Übergang

15,7: Anrede: Ἄνδρες ἀδελφοί

15,7: Propositio (ὑμεῖς ἐπίστασθε ὅτι)
(ἀφ' ἡμερῶν ἀρχαίων ἐν ὑμῖν ἐξελέξατο ὁ θεὸς ... ἀκοῦσαι τὰ ἔθνη τὸν
λόγον)

15,8f.: Begründung
(καὶ ὁ καρδιογνώστης θεὸς ἐμαρτύρη-
σεν αὐτοῖς ... καθὼς καὶ ἡμῖν)
(καὶ οὐθὲν διέκρινεν
μεταξὺ ἡμῶν τε καὶ αὐτῶν τῇ πίστει
καθαρίσας τὰς καρδίας αὐτῶν)

15,10f.: Folgerung
(15,10: νῦν οὖν τί πειράζετε τὸν θεὸν
ἐπιθεῖναι ζυγὸν ἐπὶ τὸν τράχηλον τῶν
μαθητῶν ὃν οὔτε οἱ πατέρες ἡμῶν οὔτε
ἡμεῖς ἰσχύσαμεν βαστάσαι;)

(15,11: ἀλλὰ διὰ τῆς χάριτος τοῦ κυρίου Ἰησοῦ πιστεύομεν σωθῆναι καθ' ὃν
τρόπον κἀκεῖνοι)

15,12f.: Situation: Ruhe/neue Reden
Μετὰ δὲ τὸ σιγῆσαι αὐτοὺς

15,13: Einleitung/ Übergang

15,13: Anrede: Ἄνδρες ἀδελφοί, ἀκού-
σατε ...

15,14: Propositio (Συμεὼν ἐξηγήσατο)
(πρῶτον ὁ θεὸς ἐπεσκέψατο λαβεῖν ἐξ
ἐθνῶν λαὸν τῷ ὀνόματι αὐτοῦ)

15,15-18: Schriftzitat
(καὶ τούτῳ συμφωνοῦσιν οἱ λόγοι τῶν
προφητῶν καθὼς γέγραπται)

15,19: Folgerung: (διὸ ἐγὼ κρίνω
μὴ παρενοχλεῖν τοῖς ἀπὸ τῶν ἐθνῶν
ἐπιστρέφουσιν ἐπὶ τὸν θεόν)

15,20: Präzisierung/Begründung
(15,21: Μωϋσῆς γὰρ ἐκ γενεῶν ἀρχαίων κατὰ πόλιν τοὺς κηρύσσοντας αὐτὸν ἔχει ἐν ταῖς συναγωγαῖς κατὰ πᾶν
σάββατον ἀναγινωσκόμενος)

(15,20: ἀλλὰ ἐπιστεῖλαι αὐτοῖς τοῦ
ἀπέχεσθαι ...)

Das Verhältnis zwischen Prämisse/Argumentation/Rechtsbelehrung und Anwen-
dung/Peroratio/Urteil, ist etwas unklar, u.a. weil die zwei Reden so eng zusammengehören; die Jakobusrede baut auf der Petrusrede.

Die Rolle des Jakobus ist in doppeltem Licht zu sehen. Er stellt sich demütig hinter die Interpretation Simons (Simeons) und die Aussage der Schrift. Aber mit seiner anscheinend unangefochtenen Autorität stellt er zunächst fest, daß Simeons
Interpretation (ἐξηγήσατο) und die Schrift übereinstimmen (καὶ τούτῳ συμφωνοῦσιν οἱ λόγοι τῶν προφητῶν), um letztlich auf dieser Grundlage ein Urteil zu
fällen (διὸ ἐγὼ κρίνω = *ego censeo*).

Dieses Urteil kann natürlich zu der Annahme einer überragenden Autorität des
Jakobus führen, was historisch gesehen auch stimmen mag. An dieser Stelle (15,19)
möchte ich aber das Gewicht dieses Anspruches etwas abschwächen.

Zunächst darf nicht übersehen werden, daß die versammelte Gemeinde (πᾶν τὸ
πλῆθος) schon nach der Rede des Petrus und des Paulus (und Barnabas) zur Ruhe
kam. Die Ruhe in einer Situation von ζήτημα/ζήτησις und στάσις bedeutet Zustim-

mung. Jakobus zieht somit nur die Folgerungen. Zweitens liegt eine echte Paralle-lität zwischen den Ausführungen des Petrus und des Paulus vor. Beide bezeugen Gottes Handeln durch ihre Verkündigung[41], und diese zwei ganz und gar überein-stimmenden Zeugen (vgl. Deut 19,15) haben die Versammlung überzeugt.

Wichtiger ist drittens noch, daß die zwei (δια)κρίνειν-Sätze rhetorisch gesehen nicht parallel sind. Petrus spricht vom Urteil Gottes, daß Gott nicht auf das Ansehen der Person achtet, während Jakobus sein Urteil fällt, bzw. das Urteil der Versamm-lung proklamiert.

Dennoch liegt eine gewisse Parallelisierung zwischen den zwei (δια)κρίνειν-Sätzen vor, die nicht unwichtig ist, denn hier liegt die Prämisse für die fast in Verruf gekommene Formulierung in Apg 15,28: "Der heilige Geist und wir" (ἔδοξεν γὰρ τῷ πνεύματι τῷ ἁγίῳ καὶ ἡμῖν). Außerdem folgt in beiden Fällen ein Kommentar zum Gesetz des Moses.

Weil die gemeinsame Struktur der beiden Reden so offensichtlich ist, werde ich hier noch weitere Unterschiede hervorheben, die für die rhetorische Einschätzung wichtig sind.

Die Jakobusrede ist keine eigenständige Rede, sondern knüpft an die Argumen-tation des Petrus an: Simeon hat erklärt (ἐξηγήσατο), wie Gott vor langem (γνωστὰ ἀπ' αἰῶνος). Während die Zeitangabe Simeons unpräzis oder gar irreführend scheint, legt die Angabe des Jakobus bewußt einen rhetorischen Topos zugrunde, den auch Paulus in seinen Briefen reichlich benutzt (Röm 1; 4; Gal 3): Das, was von Anfang an da war, hat Vorrang vor Bräuchen, die später entstanden sind.

In einem, und zwar in dem theologisch entscheidenden Punkt, kann man aber eine Diskrepanz zwischen den beiden Reden sehen: Predigt nicht Petrus die evan-gelische Freiheit vom Gesetz (15,10f.), während Jakobus eine Art Anpassung zum Gesetz fordert (15,20f.)? Es entsteht also die exegetische Frage, ob Lukas gemäß seinem eigenen Anliegen die Botschaft des Petrus von der judenchristlichen Ten-denz des Jakobus überschatten läßt? Diese Frage hängt nicht zuletzt von der Deu-tung der Schlüßelaussagen in 15,10[42] und mit der philologischen Auswertung der Konjunktion ἀλλά ab. Wenn sie in den zwei Reden parallel sind, liegt in der Tat eine Diskrepanz vor.

## 4.2. Traditionsgeschichtlicher Kontext

Die Bezüge der Petrusrede zum Deuteronomium werden noch deutlicher in der Ja-kobusrede[43]. Besonders die folgenden Parallelen kommen in Frage:

---

[41] Vgl. 15,7: ἐξελέξατο ὁ θεὸς διὰ τοῦ στόματός μου ἀκοῦσαι τὰ ἔθνη τὸν λόγον τοῦ εὐαγγε-λίου und 15,12: ὅσα ἐποίησεν ὁ θεὸς σημεῖα καὶ τέρατα ἐν τοῖς ἔθνεσιν δι' αὐτῶν.

[42] Dazu J. A. Nolland 1980, 105-115, der nochmal den positiven Sinn von ζυγόν begründet.

• Die zwei Ausdrücke ἐξ ἐθνῶν λαόν und λαβεῖν τῷ ὀνόματι αὐτοῦ in Apg 15,14 (s.u.).

• Das Gewicht liegt auf suchen/finden; vgl. die Änderung des Amoszitates in Apg 15,17 und etwa Deut 4,29f.: וּבִקַּשְׁתֶּם מִשָּׁם אֶת־יְהוָה אֱלֹהֶיךָ וּמָצָאתָ / καὶ ζητήσετε ἐκεῖ κύριον τὸν θεὸν ὑμῶν καὶ εὑρήσετε (... καὶ εὑρήσουσίν σε πάντες οἱ λόγοι οὗτοι ἐπ' ἐσχάτῳ τῶν ἡμερῶν, καὶ ἐπιστραφήσῃ πρὸς κύριον)[44]. Das deuteronomistische Geschichtsschema ist wie in anderen Actareden[45] auch hier sichtbar.

• Amos 9,11f. steht in großer Nähe zur deuteronomistischen Theologie[46].

• Zwei Zeugnisse müssen übereinstimmen (Deut 19,15ff.). Erst nachdem Peter und Paulus/Barnabas geredet haben, nimmt Jakobus das Wort.

• Eine im Zusammenhang mit Apg 15 übersehene Stelle ist m.E. Deut 21,5. Denn dies ist die einzige Stelle im AT neben Amos 9, wo die Formulierung ἐπὶ τῷ ὀνόματι αὐτοῦ auftaucht. Die Lage die in Deut 21 geschildert wird ähnelt auffallend der Schilderung in Apg 15. Wenn ein Streit entsteht sollen die Priester/Leviten εὐλογεῖν ἐπὶ τῷ ὀνόματι αὐτοῦ / וּלְבָרֵךְ בְּשֵׁם יְהוָה, und aus deren Mund (ἐπὶ τῷ στόματι αὐτῶν) sollen allen Streitigkeiten (πᾶσα ἀντιλογία / כָּל־רִיב) im Volk zu Ende kommen.

• Neuerdings hat u.a. der jüdische Forscher Moshe Weinfeld[47] den Gegensatz zwischen der priesterlichen und (schriftgelehrten – prophetischen) deuteronomistischen Tradition stark unterstrichen. Mittels einer konsequenten 'Desacralization'[48] konnte Deuteronomium die Transzendenz Gottes entsprechend stark betonen. Der Zentralisierung des Kultes liegt eine Betonung des Namens Gottes zugrunde, weil die eigentliche Wohnung Gottes in den Himmel verlagert ist (Deut 26,15: הַשְׁקִיפָה מִמְּעוֹן קָדְשְׁךָ מִן־הַשָּׁמַיִם).

---

[43] Dies gesehen zu haben, ist das Verdienst J. Duponts in seiner Auslegung von Apg 15,14, siehe Dupont 1956/57, aber auch idem 1985a. Neuerdings hat H. v. d. Sandt 1992 zu begründen versucht, daß Deut 4 der eigentliche Hintergrund des Amoszitates sei.

[44] Dazu Sandt 1992, 74f.,91ff. Sandt überspitzt seine These und will u.A. auch die Zeitangabe ἐπ' ἐσχάτῳ τῶν ἡμερῶν, vgl. Apg 15,10.14 aus Deut 4,30 erklären.

[45] Vgl. D. P. Moessner 1988, 49f. (Anm. 29 bringt weitere Hinweise).

[46] Dazu Sandt 1992, und besonders deutlich bei U. Kellermann 1969, 169-183, der den Amosschluß für eine deuteronomistische Interpolation hält.

[47] Besonders M. Weinfeld 1972; idem 1985; und idem 1991. Weinfeld knüpft hier an den Arbeiten G. von Rads an. Über die Schlüsselstellung des Deuteronomiums im AT, bzw. in der Geschichte Israels ist in der neuesten Forschung keine Diskussion mehr, vgl. etwa den Konferenzbericht von N. Lohfink (Hg.) 1985.

[48] M. Weinfeld 1973.

Diese Beobachtungen sind wichtig, auch um Actas doppeltes Verhältnis zur Thora[49] zu verstehen, und sie können auch die Bedeutung der Tempelfrage in Relation zur Gesetzes- und Heidenmissionsdiskussion[50] verständlich machen.

## 5. Exegetisches zum Text Apg 15,13-21

Nur die philologische Exegese kann entscheiden, ob die hier erwogenen rhetorischen und traditionsgeschichtlichen Zusammenhänge plausibel sind. Werden dadurch die Rätseln des Textes gelöst und ist diese Klärung für die damaligen Leser und Hörer sinnvoll? Unter Berücksichtigung der Statuslehre werde ich versuchen hier die Probleme des Textes zu erhellen.

### 5.1. Apg 15,13-21 in der exegetischen Diskussion

In den Kommentaren und Aufsätzen zu dieser Rede stehen das Aposteldekret und die damit verbundenen historischen, textkritischen und exegetischen Probleme im Vordergrund[51]. Das Dekret wird dann im Kontext des sogenannten Apostelkonzils gesehen, aber dadurch wird die Perspektive eingeengt. Erst im Horizont von Lukas Verhältnis zum 'Judentum', zum Gesetz und zur Frage Israels[52] kommt die Problematik des ganzen Textes Apg 15,13ff. zum Vorschein:

(a) Die Hauptfrage in der Forschung ist immer das sogenannte Aposteldekret gewesen, das direkt das Verhältnis von Judenchristen und Heidenchristen berührt[53].
(b) Mit der Deutung von 15,20 hängt das Rätsel in Apg 15,21 zusammen[54], ein Vers der gemäß M. Dibelius "nach Zusammenhang und Bedeutung zu den schwierigsten

---

[49] Akzeptiert als Norm, fordert aber eine kritische Auslegung. Zu den Besonderheiten der lukanischen Gesetzesterminologie, vgl. M. Klinghardt 1988, 115-23. In Apg 15 sind die Besonderheiten deutlich zu sehen: νόμος und Μωϋσῆς, νόμος und ἔθος, scheint identisch zu sein.

[50] Dazu M. Klinghardt 1988, 267ff.

[51] Neben den Kommentaren (wo der Text – von Exkursen über das Aposteldekret abgesehen – innerhalb 2 bis 4 Seiten behandelt wird) s. besonders M. Simon 1969/70, 437-60; A. Weiser 1984, 145-167; N. Taylor 1992, 96-122 (The Question of Law and the Jerusalem Conference); M. Klinghardt 1988, bes. 156-224. Sonst ist die Jakobusrede nur in schwer zugänglichen (auch mir unzugänglichen) Dissertationen ausführlich behandelt; Th. Gomes 1979; S. A. Panimolle 1977; M. Halstad Gates 1940; G. Strothotte 1955. Eine ernsthafte Beschäftigung mit der Rede ist vielfach von einem oft ziemlich schablonenartigen Jakobus-Bild gehemmt, ein Bild das neuerdings (u.A. von M. Hengel 1985) eindrücklich korrigiert worden ist.

[52] J. Jervell 1972; S. G. Wilson 1973 und idem 1983; G. Lohfink 1975; J. T. Sanders 1987; J. B. Tyson 1988.

[53] Die Bibliographie von A. J. / M. B. Mattill 1966, 418ff., zählt 72 Nummern zu diesem Thema.

[54] Grundlegend immer noch J. H. Ropes 1896. Vgl. neuerdings D. R. Schwarz 1987.

des Neuen Testaments gehört"[55]. Was begründet dieser merkwürdige γάρ-Satz? Sind die Judenchristen oder Heidenchristen die primären Adressaten des Wortes?

(c) Natürlich hat das Schriftzitat in Apg 15,16f. Interesse bei den Auslegern erregt[56]. Das Amoszitat bereitet der Exegese Schwierigkeiten schon durch die komplizierte Textüberlieferung, bzw. durch die erheblichen Unterschiede zwischen TM und LXX. Die Deutung dieser Unterschiede wird natürlich die Exegese der Jakobusrede reichlich beeinflussen.

(d) Mit der Schriftauslegung hängen auch die merkwürdigen Zeitangaben in Apg 15,13ff. zusammen: 15,14: πρῶτον; 15,16: μετὰ ταῦτα; 15,18: ἀπ' αἰῶνος; 15,21: ἐκ γενεῶν ἀρχαίων; vgl. 15, 7: ἀφ' ἡμερῶν ἀρχαίων und 15, 10: νῦν.

(e) Dies ist wohl auch der Rahmen, in dem die Deutung von 15,14 (λαβεῖν ἐξ ἐθνῶν λαὸν τῷ ὀνόματι αὐτοῦ, "sich ein Volk von Heiden gewinnen, die seinen Namen ehren sollen") zu sehen ist [57]. Die Interpretation dieses Ausdruckes hängt natürlich am engsten mit der übergeordneten Fragestellung (Lukas Verhältnis zum 'Judentum', zum Gesetz, zur Frage Israel und die Heidenkirche) zusammen.

Ehe ich auf diese exegetischen Fragen eingehe, muß einiges zur Rhetorik der Rede bemerkt werden.

## 5.2. Zur Rhetorik der Jakobusrede

Die Rede tritt nicht als Rede hervor, sondern als eine zusammenfassende Rechtsbelehrung. Deswegen hat K. Berger[58] die Petrus- und Jakobusrede als rhetorische Einheit gelesen, und das Schema *narratio – argumentatio – peroratio* wiedergefunden. Jedenfalls kann man bei keiner der Reden eine wirkliche rhetorische τάξις suchen, obwohl man in der Jakobusrede noch Rudimente davon finden kann.

15,13 ist eine schlichte Anrede ohne *captatio benevolentiae*, etc.

15,14 ist offenbar eine Art *propositio*, die aus der 'Exegese des Petrus' hervorging.

15,15-18 hat Elemente einer *argumentatio*; die Autoritäten, bzw. die Übereinstimmung mehrerer Autoritäten wird betont.

15,19-21 ist in der Tat eine *peroratio*, die drei Schritte vollzieht:

- 15,19: διὸ ἐγὼ κρίνω, die Schlußfolgerung, die wohl aus der Schrift hervorgeht;
- 15,20: ἀλλά, eine Präzisierung, sei es als eine Addierung oder Einschränkung gemeint;
- 15,21: γάρ, die Begründung.

---

[55] M. Dibelius 1951, 87, vgl. 83.

[56] Vgl. T. Holtz 1968, 21-27; E. Richard 1983 (1980), 278ff. und idem 1982, bes. 44-53; J. Dupont 1985b, 19-32; W. C. Kaiser Jr. 1977, 97-111; M. A. Braun 1977, 113-121; H. v. d. Sandt 1992.

[57] Besonders die Beiträge von J. Dupont 1956/57, 47-50 (= 1967, 361-65), und idem 1985a; P. Winter 1957, 399-406; N. A. Dahl 1957/58, 319-27; G. Lohfink 1975, bes. 58f.

[58] K. Berger 1984, 72.

Die Rede ist im Bereich des rhetorischen Stils (λέξις) stärker, aber nicht im Übermaß bearbeitet.

Ein Element ist die *inclusio*:

- 15,14: καθὼς πρῶτον ὁ θεός; 15,15: καθὼς γέγραπται;
- 15,14: καθὼς πρῶτον ὁ θεός; 15,17f.: λέγει κύριος ποιῶν ταῦτα γνωστὰ ἀπ᾽ αἰῶνος;
- 15,16: ἀνοικοδομήσω; 15,16: ἀνοικοδομήσω

Die letzte *inclusio* ist nur ein Teil einer chiastischen Struktur, wo Lukas die LXX-Vorlage bearbeitet, und die Vorsilbe ἀν und überhaupt die ἀ-Alliteration als stilistisches Mittel benutzt:

ἀναστρέψω καὶ
ἀνοικοδομήσω

τὴν σκηνὴν Δαυὶδ τὴν πεπτωκυῖαν
καὶ τὰ κατεσκαμμένα αὐτῆς

ἀνοικοδομήσω καὶ
ἀνορθώσω αὐτήν

Auch im zweiten Teil des Zitats, wo die Perspektive nicht länger Gottes Handeln, sondern die Wirkung unter den Menschen ist[59], haben wir Parallelismen, die aber durch sachliche und weniger durch stilistische Erwägungen bedingt zu sein scheinen:

ὅπως ἂν ἐκζητήσωσιν τὸν κύριον
οἱ κατάλοιποι τῶν ἀνθρώπων καὶ
πάντα τὰ ἔθνη

ἐφ᾽ οὓς ἐπικέκληται τὸ ὄνομά μου ἐπ᾽ αὐτούς

Die Zeitbegriffe scheinen rhetorisch durchdacht zu sein, aber wiederum weniger stilistisch als argumentativ:

15,14  πρῶτον
15,15  καὶ τούτῳ συμφωνοῦσιν οἱ λόγοι τῶν προφητῶν
15,16  Μετὰ ταῦτα
15,18  λέγει κύριος ποιῶν ταῦτα γνωστὰ ἀπ᾽ αἰῶνος
15,19  Μωϋσῆς ἐκ γενεῶν ἀρχαίων

Die Wortstellung am Anfang (oder ganz am Ende eines Satzes in 15,18) zeigt, daß die Zeitbegriffe betont und für die Argumentation wichtig sind.

---

[59] Die anthropozentrische Perspektive kommt durch den Zusatz τὸν κύριον noch deutlicher als in LXX zum Ausdruck.

## 5.3. Die 'propositio' (15,14)

Apg 15,14 ist eine Schlußfolgerung der Exegese Simeons (Συμεὼν ἐξηγήσατο). Wie oben angeführt, liegt keine 'Exegese' vor, sondern ein Hinweis auf die Beschneidung des Herzens und den ewigen Heilswillen Gottes. Wie schon im Deuteronomium geht es um das Verhältnis Wortlaut – Bedeutung, also um die erste Form, das *genus legale* (ῥητὸν καὶ διάνοια). Die Essenz dieser Exegese führt 15,14 in einer Art *propositio* aus, die eine wichtige Konsequenz aus dieser Exegese zieht.

Um die Phrase λαβεῖν ἐξ ἐθνῶν λαὸν τῷ ὀνόματι αὐτοῦ zu verstehen, muß man mit N. A. Dahl vom letzteren λαβεῖν τῷ ὀνόματι αὐτοῦ ausgehen[60]. Die Übersetzung dieser Formulierung[61] hängt mit dem Verständnis vom traditionsgeschichtlichen Hintergrund des τῷ ὀνόματι αὐτοῦ zusammen. Man braucht Dahls These, daß die Phrase aus Sach 2,15 hergeleitet sei und targumischen Ursprung (לשמיה לעם) hat, nicht zu übernehmen, obwohl man eine alternative Erklärung suchen muß, solange man die Formulierung in TM/LXX nicht finden kann. Ist sie vom Amoszitat (ἐπικέκληται τὸ ὄνομά μου ἐπ' αὐτούς) herzuleiten[62]? Dafür spricht die eigenartige Formulierung (קרא שם על), die sehr selten ist und die die Amosstelle mit Deut 28,10 verbindet[63]. An beiden Stellen liegt eine universalistische Perspektive vor, und nur an diesen Stellen im AT wird 'das Volk' und nicht etwa 'heilige Stätte' Objekt dieser Handlung.

Die Nähe des Amostextes zum Deuteronomium ist offensichtlich, und auch die targumischen Texte zeigen die Wirkungsgeschichte der deuteronomistischen שם-Theologie. Dann muß man aber den Hintergrund nicht nur an ein paar Stellen[64] suchen, sondern die deuteronomistische שם-Theologie[65] als ganze vor Augen haben.

Die formelartige Formulierung in Deut 12,11.21; 14,23.24; 16,2.6.11; 26,2 lautet:

---

[60] N. A. Dahl 1957/58, 319ff.

[61] Λαμβάνειν: nehmen, tragen, zuhören, und in seinem Namen, in seiner Herrschaft (J. Roloff 1981, ad loc.).

[62] Von L. Hartman 1981, 1271 angedeutet.

[63] M. Weinfeld 1972, 327. Vgl. B. Nitzan 1994, 77-90. Für die Qumrangemeinde gehört es zu ihrem Selbstbewußtsein, daß sie 'im Namen Gottes' berufen und gesegnet ist (11QBer 15.17r, vgl. Deut 28,10).

[64] Etwa Deut 26,19: ὑπεράνω πάντων τῶν ἐθνῶν, ὡς ἐποίησέν σε ὀνομαστὸν καὶ καύχημα καὶ δόξαστόν, εἶναί σε λαὸν ἅγιον κυρίῳ τῷ θεῷ σου, καθὼς ἐλάλησεν (wo übrigens auch der hebräische Text עם und גוים unterscheidet).

[65] Vgl. L. Hartman 1981, 1271, der mit Recht auf die deuteronomistische Stelle 1 Kön 8,17 hinweist.

ὁ τόπος, ὃν (ἐν τῷ τόπῳ, ᾧ, bzw. εἰς τὸν τόπον, ὃν)
ἂν ἐκλέξηται κύριος ὁ θεὸς ὑμῶν (σου αὐτὸν) ἐπικληθῆναι τὸ ὄνομα αὐτοῦ ἐκεῖ.

Offensichtlich strebte die LXX diese Monotonie bewußt an, denn die hebräische Unterlage ist viel variierter, obwohl zwei Formulierungen sich häufen:

• כָּל־אֲשֶׁר אָנֹכִי מְצַוְּךָ אֶתְכֶם עוֹלְהֵיכֶם שָׁם מַעֲשֵׂר
• לְשַׁכֵּן שְׁמוֹ שָׁם

G. von Rad[66] hat im letzteren Ausdruck eine theologische Neuformulierung gesehen, die die Transzendenz Gottes in neuer Weise ausspricht. M. Weinfeld will noch deutlicher diese 'spiritual Metamorphosis'[67] unterstreichen, und damit auch den Unterschied zwischen der Vorlage in 2 Sam 7 (wo vom Wohnen Gottes im Tempel die Rede ist) und der eigentlichen deuteronomistischen Theologie. Demgemäß ist die Wohnung Gottes im Himmel (2 Sam 7,30.39.43.49; Deut 26,15) während sein Name unter den Menschen wohnt (vgl. לְשַׁכֵּן שְׁמוֹ שָׁם).

Dieselbe Tendenz taucht in der Stephanusrede in verstärkter Form auf[68]. Lukas will für den Leser deutlich machen, daß Gott nicht an den Kultus in Jerusalem gebunden ist. Dennoch ist der Name Gottes durch die Taufe (2,38; 8,16; 10,48) und in Jesus Christus bekannt geworden. Die Formulierung in 4,12 (οὐδὲ γὰρ ὄνομά ἐστιν ἕτερον ὑπὸ τὸν οὐρανὸν τὸ δεδομένον ἐν ἀνθρώποις ἐν ᾧ δεῖ σωθῆναι ἡμᾶς) ist auch in dieser Hinsicht programmatisch. Man kann in Jesus Christus den Namen Gottes auch ohne Tempel anrufen (2,21) und dadurch ist die Öffnung für die messiasgläubigen Heiden ermöglicht.

In dieser Sicht ist dann die Formulierung ἐξ ἐθνῶν λαὸν zu sehen. Die enge Zusammenstellung der zwei Begriffe in einem Präpositionsausdruck – sogar ohne Artikel[69] zu verwenden –, legt die Frage nach dem Verhältnis Israel-Kirche nahe. Ist λαός die Kirche (wie etwa in Apg 18,10)? Liegt hier irgendeine Konzeption vom 'wahren Israel'[70] zugrunde oder ist λαός auch hier das alttestamentliche Gottesvolk?

---

[66] G. von Rad 1963, 38f.

[67] Weinfeld 1972, 324f. und idem 1976, 18-56.

[68] Die 'Hütte' Apg 7,44ff.; gegen den Tempel Salomos 7,47f.

[69] Das fehlende τόν vor λαόν hat die Exegese besonders auffallend gefunden. Man kann unter Umständen diesen Befund so deuten, daß hier nur von einem Volk, bzw. von einem mit Israel verbundenen Volk, gesprochen wird.

[70] G. Lohfink 1975, 60: *"das wahre Israel ist erst dann erreicht, wenn die Heiden in die Gemeinschaft des Gottesvolkes eingebracht worden sind."* Die Hervorhebung dieses Satzes unterstreicht was Lohfink in der Einleitung zu der Analyse von Apg 15,13-18 sagt: "dieser Text ist für die lukanische Ekklesiologie von großer Bedeutung" (s. 58).

Die Deutung hängt nicht nur vom lukanischen Verständnis der Begriffe λαός und ἔθνος ab[71]. Es ist von vornherein anzunehmen, daß τὰ ἔθνη, wie immer bei Lukas, ein neutraler oder positiver Begriff (= Nationen, Völker, nicht etwa Heiden) ist. Abgesehen von Zweifelsfällen, etwa Apg 18,10, hält Lukas den aus LXX hergeleiteten, und auf Israel angewandten, theologischen λαός-Begriff[72], durch.

Die präzisere Deutung muß mit der Präposition ἐξ in 15,14 anfangen. Die meisten Exegeten legen – wenn die Präposition überhaupt behandelt wird – die partitive Deutung zu Grunde. Ein Volk ist auserwählt unter den Völkern[73]. Aber sowohl die Wortstellung als auch der wohl ursprünglichere[74] Gebrauch der Präposition legen ein anderes Verständnis nahe: Mit den Heiden als Ausgangspunkt nahm Gott sich ein Volk. Dieses Verständnis paßt nicht nur zur jahwistischen Tradition, bzw. zur Abrahamgeschichte (bes. Gen 12,2f.)[75], sondern noch besser zur deuteronomistischen Konzeption Deut 7,6/14,2:

ὅτι λαὸς ἅγιος εἶ κυρίῳ τῷ θεῷ σου

כִּי עַם קָדוֹשׁ אַתָּה לַיהוָה אֱלֹהֶיךָ

(καὶ καὶ σὲ προείλατο / ἐξελέξατο κύριος ὁ θεός)

λαὸν περιούσιον ἀπὸ (bzw. παρά...) πάντων τῶν ἐθνῶν τῶν ἐπὶ προσώπου τῆς γῆς

לְעַם סְגֻלָּה מִכֹּל הָעַמִּים אֲשֶׁר עַל־פְּנֵי הָאֲדָמָה

Wie auch Ex 19,5 wird zwar hier עַמִּים im Sinne von גּוֹיִם gebraucht, aber anders als in Ex 19,6 spricht Deut. nicht von מַמְלֶכֶת כֹּהֲנִים וְגוֹי קָדוֹשׁ. Von königlicher Priesterherrschaft ist nicht die Rede. Das Volk ist Volk Gottes, weil man sich von den Göttern abgewandt hat, den Namen des einen Gottes ehrt, und in den Herzen beschnitten worden ist.

Zu diesem erwählten Volk Gottes haben nun auch die Christen – und zwar auch die Heidenchristen – Zugang. Die letzte Präzisierung wird durch andere Autoritäten, die λόγοι τῶν προφητῶν bestätigt.

---

[71] G. Lohfink 1975, 33-62.

[72] Grundlegend immer noch H. Strathmann 1942, 29-39 (und 49-57).

[73] So von G. Lohfink 1975, 59 als selbstverständlich vorausgesetzt: "Auch hier tritt der partitative Aspekt des λαός-Begriffs deutlich zutage: das neue Gottesvolk, von dem Vers 14 die Rede ist, stammt ἐξ ἐθνῶν".

[74] Dazu A. T. Robertson 1919, 596ff., der 'out of', 'from within' als 'Grundbedeutung' und m.R. 'separation' und die Vertauschung mit ἀπό als eine spätere Entwicklung sieht.

[75] N. A. Dahl 1966, 139-158 hat gezeigt, daß die Abrahamgeschichte auch sonst für Lukas wichtig ist.

## 5.4. Explizite Schriftargumentation (15,15-18)

Die Auslegung des problematischsten Zitats[76] aus Amos 9 spitzt sich in der Deutung von σκηνὴ Δαυίδ/אֶת־סֻכַּת דָּוִיד zu. Die Auslegung geht in vier Richtungen[77]:

* Die christologische Deutung[78] die sich auf Apg 7,44 bezieht, und die Hütte Davids als den Leib Jesu, der durch die Auferstehung auferweckt/aufgerichtet wurde, sieht.
* Die Deutung vom eschatologisch restituierten Israel[79], sei es ein durch das Christusgeschehen[80] restituiertes Gottesvolk, das auch Heiden inkorporiert[81], oder sei es das in der Zukunft wiederhergestellte Israel[82].
* Die Deutung, daß die Judenchristen[83] oder gar die Gemeinde in Jerusalem[84], die Hütte Davids repräsentieren.
* Die Deutung, die eindeutig die Kirche als die Hütte Davids, bzw. die Gemeinde aus Juden und Heidenchristen[85] als das wahre, wiederhergestellte Israel sieht.

Allen diesen Deutungen ist die personale Ausrichtung gemeinsam. Individuen, Gruppen, Volk sollen angegeben werden[86]. Dabei kommt aber die Betonung vom souveränen Handeln Gottes[87] und der Schlüsselbegriff σκηνή/סֻכָּה zu kurz. Diesen zweideutigen und eigenartigen Ausdruck[88] in Amos 9 deuten die meisten Ausleger

---

[76] Die historische Einordnung des Amostextes und die traditionsgeschichtlichen Bezüge des Textes, sind recht kompliziert. Zum Forschungsstand, vgl. zuletzt: G. F. Hasel 1991, 105-120. F. I. Andersen/D. N. Freedman 1989; G. V. Smith 1989, 274-84; J. A. Soggins 1987, bes. 149f.

[77] J. Dupont hat 1985b, 20ff. bewußt vereinfachend auf zwei Hauptpositionen, die christologische bzw. die ekklesiologische Deutung, beschränkt.

[78] Neuerdings u.A. E. Haenchen 1961, 389; G. Schneider 1981, 183; F. F. Bruce 1960, 310.

[79] F. Mußner 1988, 93; Lukas denkt vermutlich an die prophetischen Ansagen über den endzeitlichen Einbezug der Heiden in das messianische Heil (PsSal 18,50; Deut 32,43).

[80] H. Conzelmann 1972, 92.

[81] G. Lohfink 1975, 59; R. Pesch 1986, 80. Lohfink legt in seiner Deutung viel Gewicht auf das folgende ὅπως/bzw. לְמַעַן und führt dabei Fragen ein, die der Text nicht exakt beantworten will (etwa: Ist die Eröffnung von Heiden durch die Verstockung oder die Umkehr Israels abhängig?).

[82] So die dispensationalistische Deutung (s.u), die in diesem Punkt mit dem Amostext, bzw. der heutigen Auslegung dieser Stelle, übereinstimmt.

[83] T. Holtz 1968, 21-27 vermutet, daß sich Judenchristen in besonderem Maße gerade auf diese Stelle stützten. Von einem anderen Ausgangspunkt gelangt J. Jervell zur selben Lösung.

[84] J. Schmitt 1953, 209-218.

[85] Vgl. W. Michaelis 1964, 369-396, hier 375: Die Amosstelle bezieht sich auf die Entstehung der christlichen Gemeinde, und in 15,16 sind die Judenchristen, in 15,17 die Heidenchristen gemeint.

[86] Im Lichte der Wirkungsgeschichte des Textes liegt in der Tat diese Deutung nahe, vgl. Billerbeck 1924, 728f.; J. Dupont 1985b, 28-31.

[87] Im Amostext und auch in den späteren – schon von Billerbeck 1924, 728f., angeführten – Auslegungen. CD 7,14ff.; 4Q Flor 1,10ff. (weniger Sanh 96b) bestätigt, daß es eine Initiative Gottes ist.

[88] Dazu J. A. Soggins 1987, 147.

des TM auf Davids Königreich, obwohl der Ausdruck nie mit David verbunden ist, und als Bezeichnung seines Königreichs (= מַמְלָכָה, Amos 7,9.13) nicht geeignet ist. Solange man aber die Nennung von Edom (אֱדוֹם) als ursprüngliche Lesart ansieht, kann man diese Verlegenheitslösung verstehen.

> Das Zelt wird hier freilich nicht konkret (als der Ort, wo eine Familie/Gemeinde sich sammelt), sondern irgendwie metaphorisch gebraucht, sei es für das, was unsicher ist (vgl. Jes 1,8: ὡς σκηνή = כְּסֻכָּה), was vorübergehend existiert, oder für das, was im Gegensatz zum Haus (οἶκος, בית) nicht an einen Ort gebunden ist. Deshalb wird σκηνή meistens als Übersetzung von אהל benutzt, was am häufigsten die Lade Jahves bezeichnet, so auch in Jes 16,5 (ἐν σκηνῇ Δαυίδ = בְּאֹהֶל דָּוִד; vgl. 2 Sam 6,17;7,6, etc.).

Was die Übersetzer der LXX in Amos 9 mit σκηνὴ Δαυίδ meinten, muß offen stehen, aber vieles spricht für die Annahme, daß Apg 15,16 das Zelt der Begegnung/des Zeugnisses, die Lade, meint. Die parallele Stelle in Apg 7,44ff. spricht direkt vom 'Zelt des Zeugnisses', das Moses aufrichtete und das bis zur Zeit Davids Zentrum des Kultes war. Ähnlich der polemischen Spitze im Deuteronomium, wird in Apg der Gegensatz zum Tempelkult in Jerusalem deutlich:

7,42:    καθὼς γέγραπται ἐν βίβλῳ τῶν προφητῶν (= Apg 15,15). Vgl. 7,48: καθὼς ὁ προφήτης λέγει

7,44:    Ἡ σκηνὴ τοῦ μαρτυρίου ἦν τοῖς πατράσιν ἡμῶν ἐν τῇ ἐρήμῳ (vgl. Apg 15,16)

7,45:    ἕως τῶν ἡμερῶν Δαυίδ

7,46:    καὶ ᾐτήσατο εὑρεῖν σκήνωμα τῷ οἴκῳ Ἰακώβ

7,47f.:  Σολομὼν δὲ οἰκοδόμησεν αὐτῷ οἶκον ἀλλ' οὐχ ὁ ὕψιστος ἐν χειροποιή-τοις κατοικεῖ (Vgl. Apg 17,24).

Hinter Apg steckt also der Gedanke, daß Gott ein neues, nicht an einen Ort gebundenes Zelt der Anbetung aufrichtet, wo – gemäß der deuteronomistischen Belehrung – der Name Gottes geehrt werden soll.

Dies erneuerte Israel war in der Verkündung Jesu und der Urkirche nicht vom faktischen Israel zu lösen. Insofern liegt die zweite oben angeführte Deutung, besonders in lukanischer Sicht, am nächsten, muß aber im Rahmen einer fünften Deutung gesehen werden, die von der Vorstellung eines neuen Kultes ausgeht. In dem universalen Kult des Namens Gottes können auch die Heiden einen Platz finden.

Diese Deutung wird durch die Verwendung der Amos-Stelle in CD 7,16 gestärkt. Hier werden die Bücher des Gesetzes als die Hütte des Königs genannt, und zwar mit folgender Begründung; "sowie Er gesagt hat" (= Apg 15,17: λέγει κύριος): "Und ich richte die zerfallene Hütte Davids wieder auf".[89]

Diese Interpretation wird durch die weitere Analyse des Amoszitats bestätigt. Die Punkte, an denen TM und LXX abweichen, treten am deutlichsten in einer Synopse[90] hervor:

| Amos 9,11-12 (TM) | Amos 9,11-12 (LXX) | Apg 15,16-17 |
|---|---|---|
| בַּיּוֹם הַהוּא | ἐν τῇ ἡμέρᾳ ἐκείνῃ | Μετὰ ταῦτα |
| אָקִים | ἀναστήσω | ἀναστρέψω καὶ ἀνοικοδομήσω |
| אֶת־סֻכַּת דָּוִיד | τὴν σκηνὴν Δαυὶδ (÷אֵת) | τὴν σκηνὴν Δαυὶδ |
| הַנֹּפֶלֶת | τὴν πεπτωκυῖαν | τὴν πεπτωκυῖαν |
| וְגָדַרְתִּי | καὶ ἀνοικοδομήσω | |
| אֶת־פִּרְצֵיהֶן | τὰ πεπτωκότα αὐτῆς | |
| וַהֲרִסֹתָיו אָקִים | καὶ τὰ κατεσκαμμένα αὐτῆς ἀναστήσω | καὶ τὰ κατεσκαμμένα αὐτῆς ἀνοικοδομήσω |
| וּבְנִיתִיהָ כִּימֵי עוֹלָם | καὶ ἀνοικοδομήσω αὐτὴν καθὼς αἱ ἡμέραι τοῦ αἰῶνος | καὶ ἀνορθώσω αὐτήν, |
| לְמַעַן יִירְשׁוּ | ὅπως ἐκζητήσωσιν (= יִדְרְשׁוּ) | ὅπως ἂν ἐκζητήσωσιν |
| אֶת־שְׁאֵרִית אֱדוֹם | οἱ κατάλοιποι (÷אֵת) τῶν ἀνθρώπων (= אָדָם) | οἱ κατάλοιποι τῶν ἀνθρώπων **τὸν κύριον** |
| וְכָל־הַגּוֹיִם | καὶ πάντα τὰ ἔθνη, | καὶ πάντα τὰ ἔθνη |
| אֲשֶׁר־נִקְרָא שְׁמִי | ἐφ᾽ οὓς ἐπικέκληται τὸ ὄνομά μου | ἐφ᾽ οὓς ἐπικέκληται τὸ ὄνομά μου |
| עֲלֵיהֶם | ἐπ᾽ αὐτούς, | ἐπ᾽ αὐτούς, |
| נְאֻם־יְהוָה עֹשֶׂה זֹּאת | λέγει κύριος ὁ θεὸς ὁ ποιῶν ταῦτα. | λέγει κύριος ποιῶν ταῦτα |
| | | **γνωστὰ ἀπ᾽ αἰῶνος** |

Angesicht der auffallenden Abweichungen des LXX in 9,11 (bes. אֱדוֹם zu אדם, und יִירְשׁוּ zu יִדְרְשׁוּ), der Apg folgt[91], hat man in der Exegese die Unterschiede zwischen den beiden oft unterschätzt.

---

[89] Die anderen Zitate im frühen Judentum gehen in andere Richtungen, und die direkt messianische Deutung überwiegt, dazu zuletzt J. Dupont 1985b, 28-30, und zwar auch 4 Q Flor 1,12: "wie es geschrieben steht" (= Apg 15,15: καθὼς γέγραπται): "Und ich richte auf die zerfallene Hütte Davids". "Die ist die Hütte Davids ... nachher wird sie stehen, um Israel zu retten".

[90] Die Hervorhebungen geben nur die Unterschiede zwischen LXX und Lukas an: In kursiv die Varianten, ausgehoben ist was der jeweilig Andere nicht hat.

Zunächst ist es verständlich, daß die philologischen Unklarheiten im TM-Text[92], zu verschiedenen Texteditionen und Interpretationen führen konnten. Die Targume und auch die Qumran-Texte[93] zeigen zumindest eine Unsicherheit gegenüber dem Text, den wir als den masoretischen kennen.

Daneben sind die recht deutlichen Unterschiede zwischen Apg und LXX zu beachten. So hat Apg zwei Weglassungen, die mit dem TM-Text übereinstimmen (τὰ πεπτωκότα αὐτῆς und ὁ θεός). Auch die freie rhetorisch-stilistische Bearbeitung des Lukas fällt auf[94]. Wesentlicher sind aber die Verdeutlichung durch τὸν κύριον[95] und die Weglassungen, Zusätze und Abweichungen, die mit den Zeitangaben zusammenhängen:

- 15,16: Μετὰ ταῦτα statt ἐν τῇ ἡμέρᾳ ἐκείνῃ (vgl. Jer 12,15: καὶ ἔσται μετὰ τὸ ἐκβαλεῖν με αὐτοὺς ἐπιστρέψω[96]);
- 15,16: Läßt καθὼς αἱ ἡμέραι τοῦ αἰῶνος weg;
- 15,18: Fügt γνωστὰ ἀπ' αἰῶνος hinzu (vgl. Jes 45,21: ἵνα γνῶσιν ἅμα τίς ἀκουστὰ ἐποίησεν ταῦτα ἀπ' ἀρχῆς. τότε ἀνηγγέλη ὑμῖν Ἐγὼ ὁ θεός);
- Dazu kommen die bewußten Zeitangaben in der ganzen Rede (15,14: πρῶτον, 15,16: Μετὰ ταῦτα, 15,18: ἀπ' αἰῶνος und 15,21: ἐκ γενεῶν ἀρχαίων).

Zweifelsohne wollen sie die Übereinstimmung zwischen dem Beginn und dem, was die Worte des Propheten über die 'letzte' Zeit beschreiben, hervorheben. Die Parallelisierung der Handlungsweise Gottes damals und jetzt kommt außerdem durch den doppelten Gebrauch von καθώς zum Vorschein[97].

Wie fungiert das Zitat nun argumentativ? Hier kann uns die Statuslehre etwas weiter helfen.

Diese als neue Autorität, als λόγοι τῶν προφητῶν introduziert, ist einerseits, etwa in der universellen Ausrichtung, sehr klar. Soll aber die Einschließung der Heiden durch Krieg (TM), durch Studium des Gesetzes (4 Q Flor) oder durch Bekehrung geschehen?

Hier liegt eine Zweideutigkeit vor, also der dritte Status ἀμφιβολία. D.h. ver-

---

[91] Diese Änderungen können eventuell im Lichte vom Deuteronomium gesehen werden. Jedoch bedeutet es nicht viel, daß Edom in Deut positiv gesehen wird (Deut 23,5ff., im Gegensatz zu u.a. Moab). Wichtiger ist das Thema von דרשׁ 'suchen', das im Deuteronomium wichtig ist (vor allem Deut 12,5; 4,29f.), aber auch an den Schlüßelstellen Amos 5,4.14 gebraucht wird.

[92] Neben den Amos-Kommentaren weise ich auf den Aufsatz von M. A. Braun 1977 hin.

[93] Vgl. J. de Waard 1965, 24-26; E. Larsson 1987, 340f.

[94] Vgl. R. Morgenthaler 1949, 87 und J. Dupont 1985b, 25.

[95] Dadurch wird die Zweiteilung des Zitats deutlicher (s.o.).

[96] Zech 2,15 stimmt in der Zeitangabe ἐν τῇ ἡμέρᾳ ἐκείνῃ mit dem LXX-Text (und auch TM-Text = בַּיֹּום הַהוּא) überein, steht aber, wie N. A. Dahl 1957/58 und idem 1966, Anm. 49 eindrücklich gezeigt hat, sachlich Apg. 15,14ff. sehr nahe: ἔσονται αὐτῷ εἰς λαὸν καὶ κατασκηνώσουσιν ἐν μέσῳ σου, καὶ ἐπιγνώσῃ ὅτι κύριος παντοκράτωρ ἐξαπέσταλκέν με πρός σέ.

schiedene Auslegungen eines Gesetzes liegen vor. Amos 9,11f. wird nun in Apg 15,16f. so ausgelegt, daß die Bedeutung der Stelle deutlich wird. Diese klassische Stelle für Israels Wiederaufrichtung wird ihrer Intention gemäß (διάνοια) und auf Grund ihrer Zweideutigkeit (ἀμφιβολία, *controversia ex ambiguo*)[98] dahingehend gedeutet, daß die Heiden von Anfang an in Gottes Erlösungsplan mit eingeschlossen waren. Die Prophetie weist auf eine Zeit hin, wo das wiederaufgerichtete Israel der Ausgangspunkt für eine Heimholung aller Völker (πάντα τὰ ἔθνη) sein soll.

Diese Argumentation kann selbstverständlich nur von den Lesern verstanden werden, die Amos 9,11f. und die eigenartige Deutungsgeschichte, die die Stelle hatte, kennen. Aber im Rahmen von Apg 15 fungiert sie für alle Leser als Gegenargument zu den Einwänden in 15,2 und 15,7. Ein rhetorisch etwas gebildeter Leser wird verstehen, daß es sich in diesem Fall um die Kategorie 'Verordnungen, die einander widersprechen' handelt (ἀντινομία, *controversia ex contrariis legibus*)[99]. Solche Fälle wollte Hillels '*middoth*' lösen, und auch die Stasisdiskussion zielt auf Fälle, wo sich zwei[100] Gesetze widersprechen[101].

## 5.5. Die 'peroratio' mit dem sog. Aposteldekret (15,20)

Die eigentliche *peroratio* in 15,19 ist sehr klar, auch wenn man von der sonderbaren Wortbildung παρ-εν-οχλεῖν nicht absieht. Die Schlußfolgerung (διὸ κρίνω) aus der Amosstelle ist klar: Nicht-Juden, die sich an Jahve wenden, sollen nicht Schwierigkeiten begegnen, bzw. in turbulente Situationen (ὀχλεῖν) geraten.

Der Exegese wäre viel Mühe erspart geblieben, wenn die Jakobusrede mit diesem klaren Satz abgeschlossen hätte. Man ist aber schon auf der richtigen Spur, wenn man das sog. Aposteldekret als eine untergeordnete Präzisierung und keines-

---

[97] Diese durch Änderungen von LXX entstandenen, zeitlichen Angaben, hat die 'covenant-theology' benutzt um die Bünde Gottes in der Heilsgeschichte zu rekonstruieren, während die Dispentationalisten sie für ihre oft extremen Spekulationen anführen. In einer Anmerkung zu Apg 15,16-18 hat die in USA und in den Missionskirchen einflußreiche 'Scofield-Bible' die Jakobusrede zu "the most important passage in the N.T." erklärt, Scofield 1909/1945, ad loc. Nach der dispentationalistischen Lesung ist die Amosstelle nicht durch das Christusgeschehen erfüllt, sondern schildert das zukünftige messianische Kommen Jesu, bezieht sich also auf die Zukunft. Diese Lösung wird noch verteidigt (so W. M. Aldrich 1954), aber allgemein abgelehnt (vgl. W. C. Kaiser 1977; F. F. Bruce 1960, ad loc.).

[98] *Ad Herennium* I. XII. 20.

[99] *Ad Herennium* I. XI. 20

[100] Ich lasse die Frage offen stehen, ob mit λόγοι τῶν προφητῶν ein Verweben von Prophetien gemeint ist, wie viele neuere Forscher meinen, indem man etwa Jer 12,15; Jes 45,21f. und Zef 2,15 vermischt sieht; so u.A. R. Pesch 1986, 8 (mit Hinweis auf weitere Literatur).

[101] Vgl. Cicero: "*Ex ambiguo autem nascitur controversia cum quid senserit scriptor obscurum est, quod scriptum duas pluresve res significat*" (*De Inventione* II, 39, 116).

wegs als die Hauptsache behandelt.

Das wird auch durch den Gebrauch von ἀλλά in 15,20 unterstrichen, was aber nicht deutlich wird, wenn – wie es wohl die Mehrzahl der Exegeten tut – ἀλλά als Adversativ gelesen wird, und damit als eine Einschränkung von 15,19; Die Heiden haben Zugang zu Gott ohne das Gesetz des Moses, von den folgenden Geboten abgesehen.... Man will somit die paulinische Problematik und auch die Szene von Gal 2,1-15, in den lapidaren Satz Apg 15,20 einlesen.

> Für diese konventionelle Lesung spricht natürlich die Wirkungsgeschichte des Textes, auch weil die adversative Bedeutung von ἀλλά unzweifelhaft in der 'Parallele' 15,11 vorliegt.
>
> Dennoch wären einige Fragezeichen zu setzen. Wenn ἀλλά am Anfang eines Satz steht, ist öfter die Übersetzung 'however', 'nevertheless', 'nur', 'mittlerweile', etc. vorzuziehen, auch nach μή[102]. Dazu kommen inhaltliche und weitere syntaktische Erwägungen: Das Gesetz ist in 15,19 überhaupt kein Thema, und man muß, um diesen Bezug aufrechtzuerhalten, 15,20 mit dem folgenden Satz verknüpfen, was zumindest sehr unnatürlich ist. Man kann somit ἀλλά nur mit 15,19 und zwar mit dem Verbum μὴ παρενοχλεῖν (und ἐπιστρέπειν) verbinden; Die Heiden sollen bei der Umkehr zu dem einen Gott (ἐπιστρέφουσιν ἐπὶ τὸν θεόν) nicht gedrängt werden, nur (ἀλλά) will man (schriftlich)[103] auf etwas – wohl Selbstverständliches – hinweisen.

Wenn ἀλλά eher die Bedeutung von δέ – und nicht etwa 'doch wenigstens'[104] – hat, wird in 15,20 wohl eine innere Konsequenz oder eine falsche Schlußfolgerung, und nicht ein zusätzliches Gebot entfaltet. Das wird auch durch das Verb ἀπέχεσθαι (15,20.29) bestätigt, das in den frühchristlichen Texten nie den Sinn von 'Gebot' hat. Der Begriff reflektiert ein Thema der stoischen Ethik[105], nämlich, daß man durch vernünftige Erwägung und durch konsistente Verwendung der eigenen Grundprinzipien auf 'fremde Dinge' verzichten soll.

Die Deutung des Dekrets hängt sowohl von den textkritischen Erwägungen als auch von vermuteter Funktion der Gebote ab. Heute zieht die Mehrzahl der Exegeten den alexandrinischen Text (und 𝔓[45]) gegenüber dem westlichen Text und da-

---

[102] Vgl. J. H. Moulton 1962, 329f. sowie BDR 1976, § 448.5 und 8.

[103] Nach modernem Empfinden ist damit etwas Wichtigeres gesagt. In einer mündlichen Kultur kann eine schriftliche Mitteilung normalerweise nur eine Stütze für die mündliche, direkt persönliche Mitteilung sein. Das Wort τὰ δόγματα in Apg 16,4 zeigt dasselbe. Lukas benutzt das Wort in Luk 2,1 und Apg 17,7 für Verordnungen des Kaisers und beschreibt hier "ethische Verhaltensnormen" (N. Walter 1980, 821).

[104] Wie nach einem Konditionalsatz mit ἐάν, was Apg 15,19 gerade nicht ist.

[105] So R. Bultmann 1912, 97-110, hier 100f. Bultmann macht aber eine sachliche Kategorie, die nicht unbedingt der Terminologie Epiktets entspricht. Vgl. 1 Pet 2,11, wo ἀπέχεσθαι in einem ähnlichen Kontext gebraucht wird.

mit die *kultische* Deutung vor[106]. Auch wort- und traditionsgeschichtliche Erwägungen legen es nahe, καὶ τῆς πορνείας neben den drei offensichtlich kultischen Verordnungen (τῶν ἀλισγημάτων τῶν εἰδώλων καὶ τοῦ πνικτοῦ καὶ τοῦ αἵματος) ebenfalls im kultischen Sinne zu verstehen[107]. Man kann höchstens von καὶ τῆς πορνείας her für eine ethische Zusatzforderung argumentieren.

Schwieriger ist die Frage nach Auswahl und Funktion der Forderungen. Daß sie eine Art von Minimalforderungen sind, ist offensichtlich. Die Funktion dieser Minimalforderungen kann nur im Zusammenhang mit der Auswahl gesehen werden.

Man kann das traditionsgeschichtliche Material nicht umgehen, wenn man erklären will, warum ausgerechnet diese vier Verordnungen genannt werden:

Der Hinweis auf die noachitischen Gebote ist verständlicherweise in der Forschung sehr verbreitet[108] und vor diesem Hintergrund muß man stärker die Universalität der Forderungen herausstellen.

Die Forderungen beanspruchen eine gewisse Allgemeingültigkeit, auch wenn man sie von den jüdischen Proselytenkatechismen her erklärt. Neuerdings hat P. Borgen diese These aufgegriffen und auch die Stärke dieser Erklärung gezeigt[109]. Die Auslassung der Beschneidung, also der Forderung die in den jüdischen Katechismen wesentlich war, steht unmittelbar in Berührung mit dem Konfliktthema in Apg 15.

Noch stärker betont die neuere Forschung die traditionsgeschichtlichen Parallelen zu den גרים-Geboten in Lev 17-18[110]. Bei dieser Analogie beanspruchen die Gebote weniger Universalität, und sollen eher das Verhältnis von Juden- und Heidenchristen in einer bestimmten Lage regulieren.

Eine vierte Position ist m.E. vorzuziehen. G. Strothotte[111] und C. F. Barrett[112]

---

[106] Zur älteren Diskussion bes. G. Resch 1905; H. Lietzmann 1923; J. H. Ropes 1926, 144f., 265-269 und zur neueren Debatte vgl. W. G. Kümmel 1965, 278-288; B. M. Metzger (ed.) 1971, 429-34; M. Klinghardt 1988, 170-176.

[107] Lietzmann 1923, 204-208; M. Klinghardt 1988, 200-204. Bekanntlich hatte A. v. Harnack zunächst diese kultische Deutung entfaltet, hat aber später den westlichen Text und die ethische Deutung zu begründen versucht (auch idem 1908, 188ff.). Die Nachwirkung seiner Begründung ist in der Forschung leicht zu sehen, etwa bei G. Resch 1905 und noch S. G. Wilson 1983, 68ff.

[108] Dazu zuletzt M. Klinghardt 1988, 176-180. Mehr als eine Analogie geben die Parallelen nicht her, vgl. G. Resch 1905, 31ff.

[109] P. Borgen 1988, 126-141, bes. 133ff. Vgl. auch G. Resch 1905, bes. 51-143.

[110] Mit Zustimmung M. Klinghardt 1988, 181-200. Kritisch u.A. G. Resch 1905, 26ff.; S. G. Wilson 1973, 84ff.

[111] Strothotte 1955, nach H. Conzelmann 1972, 92f.

[112] In einem bisher unveröffentlichten Vortrag (The Centre of Acts), als Gastvorlesung u.a. auch in Oslo/ Gemeindefakultät 25.03.92 gehalten, wies er auf pShebi 35,a. 49f.; pSanh 21b,10f.; bPes 25ab; bSanh 74a, hin. Es ist zu erwarten, daß Barrett in seinem ICC- Kommentar (im Druck) diese These weiter entfaltet.

haben auf rabbinische Belege[113] hingewiesen, und zwar auf die Analogie zu den
drei Situationen, in denen ein Jude das Martyrium wählen soll (d.h. wenn er zur Verehrung eines Abbildes, zum Essen (דמים), oder Inzest, gezwungen sei). Die drei Situationen sind keine echten Parallelen zu Apg 15,20, sind aber als Analogien
wichtig. Vor allem, weil sie auf die Beziehung zu theologischen Prinzipien hinweisen.

Apg 15,19f. legt eine ähnliche Erklärung nahe: Die vier Gebote in 15,20 sind die
Umkehrung dessen, was echte Gottesverehrung sei[114]. Gottes Namen zu ehren ist
der Gegensatz zur heidnischen Gottesverehrung, die durch Götterbilder (τῶν ἀλισγημάτων τῶν εἰδώλων, טריפה), Blutgenuß (τοῦ αἵματος, אבילת הדם) Hurerei (τῆς
πορνείας, אוסר ערוה) und in heidnischem Ritual geschlachtete Tiere (τοῦ πνικτοῦ,
נבלה, bzw. טריפה) charakterisiert wird. Dem entspricht auch die Polemik gegen die
Kulte in Deuteronomium und Amos. Gerade weil 15,19f. die Konsequenz aus dem
Zitat von Amos zog, sind an dieser Stelle die Parallelen zum Amosbuch besonders
wichtig.

In den hier genannten Fällen ist kaum die Vierzahl, noch der präzise Inhalt der
Begriffe, entscheidend. Wie in den Pseudo-Klementinen[115] geht es um Einprägung
durch Anschaulichkeit und um Verweilen bei einer Sache durch variierte Ausdrük-
ke.[116]

Vielleicht kann die Statuslehre auch diesen Satz beleuchten. Zunächst ist negativ
festzustellen, daß hier keine neue Autorität, kein Gebot oder Gesetz im Sinne des
*genus legale* präsentiert wird. Höchstens in Apg 15,21 haben wir mit der vierten Kategorie des *genus legale* zu tun, die nie allein eine Argumentation tragen konnte. Es
gab ja im AT kein Gesetz und keine Verordnung, die den Lebenswandel der Heiden
gegenüber Israel nach der Wiederaufrichtung regelten.

Hier wird nur eine Analogie (συλλογισμός) angeführt. Analog mit dem Lebenswandel der Heiden als Fremde in Israel, mit dem jüdischen Proselytenkatechismus,
oder mit den jüdischen Martyrienverpflichtungen, oder – was ich hier als die beste
Analogie vorziehe: Parallel zum jüdischen Verhalten gegenüber heidnischen Kulten, sagen die christlichen 'Gottesfürchtigen' ein Nein zu diesen Kulten.

---

[113] Vgl. Billerbecks Auflistung 1924. B II, 729-739, vgl. auch 721ff. und B III, 421ff.

[114] In dieser Richtung versteht J. Weiß 1917, 235f.; W. G. Kümmel 1965, 285ff. und wohl auch
L. W. Countryman 1988, 71-77 das 'Dekret'. Zur Kritik von Kümmel, siehe S. G. Wilson 1983, 94ff.

[115] Vgl. H. Lietzmann 1923, 207: "der Verfasser der Homilien hat nur etwas ausgiebiger das
Gleiche getan wie sein Muster, der Schöpfer des Dekrets, nämlich den Ausdruck vervielfältigt, um
die Sache kräftig einzuprägen".

[116] In der Rhetorik heißt es *commoratio*. Dieses konkret-anschauliche *rerum sub aspectum sub-
iectio* schildert sowohl Cicero, *De Oratore* 3,202-205 und Quintilianus, *Institutio* IX.1.26ff. sehr lebendig.

## 5.6. Die eigentümliche Begründung (15,21)

Eine Begründung (γάρ) folgt als Abschluß der Rede. Rhetorisch gesehen wäre ein klarer Satz als Abschluß der *peroratio* zu erwarten. Dennoch sehen manche Exegeten hier vielleicht das größte *crux interpretum* in der Jakobusrede. Im Mittelpunkt steht die Frage was γάρ eigentlich begründen soll[117].

• Die naheliegende und traditionelle Deutung sieht 15,21 als eine Begründung der vier 'Gebote' in 15,20, sei es, daß man Calvin oder Overbeck folgt[118]. Nach Calvin u.A. sind diese Gebote für den Umgang mit Juden entscheidend, '*ne illi offendatur*' oder – nach Overbeck – nur als Pietät mit dem Gesetz des Moses, das auch in der Diaspora gelesen wird.

Diese Auffassung stößt aber auf viele Einwände, und hier reicht es, nur eine zu erwähnen: Warum werden nur vereinzelte und recht periphere Gebote aus dem Gesetz des Moses genannt?

• Der γάρ-Satz kann auch 15,19 begründen, sei es, daß man Erasmus oder Giesler folgt. Die seit Erasmus vertretene Deutung besagt, daß die Gesetzesfreiheit der Heidenchristen nicht eine Aufhebung des Gesetzes unter Juden bedeutet. Denn das Gesetz wird jeden Sabbat in aller Welt gelesen[119].

Neuerdings hat aber D. R. Schwarz[120] die fast vergessene Deutung J. K. L. Gieselers erneuert: Jakobus begründet, daß man nach aller Erfahrung nicht das Mosesgesetz auf die Schultern der Heiden legen kann. 15, 20 wird somit analog zum Joch des Gesetzes in 15,10 verstanden.

• Weil durch beide Lösungen Schwierigkeiten entstehen, wollen einige Exegeten, besonders nach Ropes, 15,21 nicht nur auf dem Hintergrund von 15,19, sondern auch von 15,16ff. her, lesen. M. Dibelius wollte "einen kleinen nachgebrachten Midrasch zu der Prophetenstelle" [Amos 9] finden[121], der überall einsichtig werden konnte, weil Moses in aller Welt verkündigt wurde.

Sachlich gesehen, spricht vieles für die beiden letztgenannten Lösungen, dennoch besteht der philologische Einwand, daß ein γάρ-Satz normalerweise den unmittelbar vorgehenden Satz begründet.

Wenn man aber einen deutlichen Argumentationsduktus in der Rede findet, kann

---

[117] J. H. Ropes 1896 gibt 3-4 Auslegungen an, während Johannes Marck (in 1721) schon sechs und später andere Ausleger noch weitere Deutungen aufzählten (ibid., 75), dazu: D. R. Schwartz 1987, 276.

[118] Vgl. Ropes 1896, 76-79.

[119] J. H. Ropes 1896, 79. Auch Th. Zahn 1921, 525f. Nach Chrysostomos begründet der Satz sowohl 15,19 wie auch 15,20, indem 15,21 indirekt erklärt warum das Dekret nur an Heidenchristen und nicht an Juden geschickt wurde.

[120] D. R. Schwartz 1987, 279ff.

[121] M. Dibelius 1953, 88.

man den γάρ-Satz auf 15,20, aber zugleich auch auf den ganzen Argumentations-
zusammenhang in 15,13-20 beziehen.

'Moses' ist damit eher als Verheißung (τοὺς κηρύσσοντας αὐτὸν) zu verstehen,
die, wenn gelesen (ἀναγινωσκόμενος) als Verheißung gedeutet werden muß. Moses ist der Ausgangspunkt aller Stasisdiskussion auch für die ersten Christen. Das
wird durch vier Qualitätsansprüche zum Ausdruck gebracht. Moses

- besitzt den Rang einer alten Verordnung (ἐκ γενεῶν ἀρχαίων);
- ist weit verbreitet (κατὰ πόλιν);
- wird an öffentlichen Stellen (ἐν ταῖς συναγωγαῖς) gelesen, und
- wird ständig wiederholt (κατὰ πᾶν σάββατον).

Inhaltlich sind die fünf Mosebücher gemeint, deren Spitze im Deuteronomium lag,
die Schrift, die wohl zuerst (Neh 8,3ff.) in Israel gelesen wurde. Apg 15,21 ist somit
eine Parallele zu Luk 16,31: "Hört ihr nicht Moses…". Gottes ewiger Heilswille ist
in den Büchern Moses zu lesen.

## 6. Zusammenfassung

Die rhetorische Forschung des Neuen Testaments ist immer noch in ihren Anfängen. Deshalb gibt es immer noch weite Flächen, die auf rhetorische Analyse warten.
In diesem Aufsatz habe ich zwei solche Flächen betreten: Die Reden der Apg. und
die Anwendung der Statuslehre auf neutestamentlichen Schriften.

Die Anwendung der Statuslehre liegt auf der Hand in den dikanischen Reden in
Apg 1-7 und in Apg 24-26, wo es um *genus rationale* geht. Ich habe auch angedeutet, daß die unentschiedene Rechtssituation (die ἀσύστατα) für Apg als Erzählung
von größter Bedeutung ist. Dennoch bin ich nur dem *genus legale* nachgegangen,
und habe versucht sie auf die schwierige Jakobusrede anzuwenden.

Die rhetorische Analyse hat gezeigt, daß die Jakobusrede keine dikanische Rede
ist, aber wohl juridische Argumente enthält. Bisher hat man den Text traditionell-
kirchlich unter dem Gesichtspunkt des 'Konzils' und entsprechend auf das 'Aposteldekret' als das Konzilergebnis verstanden. Diese Deutung isoliert aber 15,20,
statt die Argumentation der Rede als ein Ganzes zu nehmen.

Apg 15 ist eigentlich keine Rede, sondern ein Fragment einer Rede, die eine
*propositio, argumentatio* und *peroratio* hat. Die *propositio* und *peroratio* sind auf
die *argumentatio* hin orientiert, und somit ist die ganze Rede eine Schriftauslegung,
die auf Amos und grundsätzlich auf die Mosebücher, stärker insbesondere aber auf
das Deuteronomium ausgerichtet ist. Die Jakobusrede ist mehr kultisch und in der
deuteronomistischen םש-Theologie gegründet, als man bisher gesehen hat[122]. Die
Tempelproblematik prägt Apg 1-21, und steckt auch hinter der Debatte in Kap 15.

Das 'Aposteldekret' ist kein 'Dekret', sondern eine Konkretisierung der Kritik heidnischer Kulte, die eine Analogie zu ähnlichen jüdischen Auflistungen zeigt. Durch die Statuslehre wird klarer, daß 15,20 keine Gebote, sondern wirklich nur Analogien (im Sinne von συλλογισμός, das vierte *genus legale*) sind. Dagegen bietet das Schriftzitat in 15,16ff. das entscheidende Argument. Hier wird der Sinn des Mosesgesetzes entfaltet, indem die Intention des Mosesgesetzes (im Sinne von διάνοια, das erste *genus legale*) durch das Amoszitat erläutert und jede Zweideutigkeit (im Sinne von ἀντινομία/*leges contrariae* und ἀμφιβολία/*ambiguitas*, also das zweite und dritte *genus legale*) ausgeräumt wird. Insgesamt argumentiert die Jakobusrede nicht für ein neues Gottesvolk, sondern will die Einschließung der Heiden in dem – von Moses und den Propheten geschilderten – Gottesvolk proklamieren.

## *Bibliographie*

*Ad Herennium* = ([Cicero:] *Ad C. Herennium de ratione dicendi*) (LCL 403), ed. H. Caplan, Cambridge, MA: Cambridge University Press [4]1976.

Aldrich, W. M. 1954: "The Interpretation of Acts 15,13-18", in: *BS* 111 (1954) 317-323.

Andersen, F. I./D. N. Freedman 1989: *Amos. A New Translation with Introduction and Commentary*, New York: Doubleday 1989.

Baasland, E. 1988: "Die περί-Formel und die Argumentationssituation des Paulus", in: *StTh* 42 (1988) 69-87.

Barnhardt, J. E. 1980: "Every Kontext has a Kontext", in: *SJTh* 33 (1980) 301-313.

Barrett, C. K. 1987: "Acts and Christian Consensus", in: P. W. Böckmann/R. E. Kristiansen (eds.), *Context*. FS P. J. Borgen, Trondheim: Tapir 1987, 19-34.

Bassler, Jo M. 1982: *Divine Impartiality. Paul and a Theological Axiom* (SBL.DS 59), Chico, CA: Scholars Press 1982.

Berger, Klaus 1984: *Formgeschichte des Neuen Testaments*, Heidelberg: Quelle & Meyer 1984.

[Strack, H. L.] – Billerbeck, Paul 1922-28: *Kommentar zum Neuen Testament aus Talmud und Midrash* I-IV, München: C. H. Beck 1922-28.

Blaß, F. - Debrunner, A. - Rehkopf, F. (=BDR): *Grammatik des neutestamentlichen Griechisch*, Göttingen: Vandenhoeck & Ruprecht [14]1976.

Borgen, Peder J. 1988: "Catalogues of Vices, The Apostolic Decree, and the Jerusalem Meeting", in: J. Neusner, E. S. Frerichs, P. Borgen, R. Horsley (eds.), *The Social World of formative Christianity and Judaism*. FS H. C. Kee, Philadelphia, PA: Fortress Press 1988, 126-141.

Bowker, J. W. 1967/68: "Speeches in Acts: A Study in Poem and Yalammedenu Form", in: *NTS* 14 (1967/68) 96-111.

---

[122] Die Bedeutung der Namen-Theologie hervorgehoben zu haben, ist einen der vielen Einsichten die der Jubilar der neueren Exegese gegeben hat, siehe Hartman 1981 und idem 1992.

Braun, M. A. 1977: "James' Use of Amos at the Jerusalem Council: Steps toward a possible Solution of the textual and theological Problems", in: *JETS* 20 (1977) 113-121.

Bruce, F. F. 1942: *The Speeches in Acts of the Apostles*, London: Tyndale Press 1942.

— 1960: *Commentary on the Book of Acts*, Grand Rapids, MI: Eerdmans 1960.

Bultmann, Rudolf 1912: "Das religiöse Moment in der ethischen Unterweisung des Epiktets und das Neue Testament", in: *ZNW* 13 (1912) 97-110.

— 1967: "Zur Frage nach den Quellen der Apostelgeschichte", in idem, *Exegetica. Aufsätze zur Entstehung des Neuen Testaments*, hrsg. von E. Dinkler, Tübingen: J. C. B. Mohr 1967, 412-423.

Burchard, Christoph 1970: *Der dreizehnte Zeuge: Traditions- und kompositionsgeschichtliche Untersuchungen zu Lukas' Darstellung der Frühzeit des Paulus* (FRLANT 103), Göttingen: Vandenhoeck & Ruprecht 1970.

Cicero: *De Inventione* (LCL 396), ed. H. M. Hubbell, Cambridge, MA: Harvard University Press ⁶1989.

— *De Oratore /Über den Redner*, hrsg. von H. Merklin (Universal-Bibliothek 6884) Stuttgart: Reclam 1976 (= LCL, ed. E.W. Sutton/H. Rackham, Vol. I-II, Cambridge, MA: Harvard University Press 1942).

Conzelmann, Hans 1972: *Die Apostelgeschichte* (HNT 7), Tübingen: J. C. B. Mohr ²1972.

Countryman, L. W. 1988: *Dirt, Greed and Sex*, Philadelphia, PA: Fortress Press 1988.

Dahl, Nils A. 1957/58: "'A People for His Name' (Acts XV,14)", in: *NTS* 4 (1957/58) 319-27.

— 1966: "The Story of Abraham in Luke-Acts", in: L. E. Keck/J. L. Martyn (eds.), *Studies in Luke-Acts*. FS P. Schubert, New York/Nashville, TN: Abingdon Press 1966, 139-158.

Daube, David 1949: "Rabbinic Methods of Interpretation and Hellenistic Rhetoric", in: *HUCA* 22 (1949) 239-264.

Dibelius, Martin 1951: "Die Reden der Apostelgeschichte und die antike Geschichtsschreibung (1949)", in: idem, *Aufsätze zur Apostelgeschichte*, ed. H. Greeven (FRLANT 60), Göttingen: Vandenhoeck & Ruprecht 1951, 120-62.

Dodd, C. H. 1962: *The Apostolic Preaching and its Development: Three Lectures with an Appendix on Eschatology and History*, New York: Harper & Brothers 1962.

Dupont, Jacques 1956/57: "λαός ἐξ ἐθνῶν (Ac 15,14)", in: *NTS* 3 (1956/57) 47-50, auch in: idem, *Études sur les Actes des Apôtres*, Paris: Editions du Cerf 1967, 361-65.

— 1985a: "Un peuple d'entre les nations (Actes 15,14)", in: *NTS* 31 (1985) 321-335.

— 1985b: "Je rebâtirai la cabane de David qui est tombée (Ac 15,16 = Am 9,11)", in: E. Gräßer/O. Merk (Hrsg.), *Glaube und Eschatologie*, FS W. G. Kümmel, Tübingen: J. C. B. Mohr 1985, 19-32.

Gerhardsson, Birger 1961: *Memory and Manuscript. Oral Tradition and Written Transmission in Rabbinic Judaism and Early Christianity* (ASNU 22), Lund/Copenhagen: Gleerup/Munksgaard 1961.

Gomes, Th. 1979: *A People of God from among the Nations. An Interpretation of Acts 15,13-18*, Diss. Gregoriana Rom 1979.

Gärtner, Bertil 1961: "Missionspredikan i Apostlagärningarna", in: *SEÅ* 15 (1961) 34-54.

Haenchen, Ernst 1961: *Die Apostelgeschichte* (KEK III), Göttingen: Vandenhoeck & Ruprecht [13]1961.

Halstad Gates, M. 1940: *The Amos Quotation in Acts 15*, Ph.D. Diss., Dallas Theol. Sem., 1940.

von Harnack, A. 1908: *Die Apostelgeschichte*. Beiträge zur Einleitung in das Neue Testament III, Leipzig: J. C. Hinrichs 1908.

Hartman, Lars 1981: Art. "ὄνομα etc.", in: *EWNT* 2, Stuttgart: Kohlhammer 1981, 1268-1277.

— 1992: *"Auf den Namen des Herrn Jesu". Die Taufe in den neutestamentlichen Schriften* (SBS 148), Stuttgart: Katholisches Bibelwerk 1992.

Hasel, G. F. 1991: *Understanding the Book of Amos*, Grand Rapids, MI: Baker Book House 1991.

Hengel, Martin 1985: "Jakobus der Herrenbruder – der erste 'Papst'?", in: E. Gräßer/O. Merk (Hrsg.), *Glaube und Eschatologie*. FS W. G. Kümmel, Tübingen: J. C. B. Mohr 1985, 71-104.

Hermogenes: περὶ τῶν στάσεων, in: Hermogenes, *Opera*, Hrsg. H. Rabe, Leipzig: Teubner 1913.

Hermagoras: *Fragmente*, Hrsg. D. Matthes, Leipzig: Teubner 1962.

Holtz, Traugott 1968: *Untersuchungen über die alttestamentlichen Zitate bei Lukas* (TU 104), Berlin: Akademie Verlag 1968.

Jervell, Jacob 1972: "James, Defender of Paul", in: idem, *Luke and the People of God; a new Look at Luke-Acts*, Minneapolis, MN: Augsburg Pub. House 1972.

— 1983: "Die Mitte der Schrift. Zum lukanischen Verständnis des Alten Testaments", in: U. Luz/ H. Weder (Hrsg.), *Die Mitte des Neuen Testaments: Einheit und Vielfalt neutestamentlicher Theologie.* FS E. Schweizer, Göttingen: Vandenhoeck & Ruprecht 1983, 79-96.

Kaiser Jr., W. C. 1977: "The Davidic Promise and the Inclusion of the Gentiles (Amos 9,9-15 and Acts 15,13-18): A Test Passage for Theological Systems", in: *JETS* 20 (1977) 97-111.

Kellermann, U. 1969: "Der Amosschluß als Stimme deuteronomistischer Heilshoffnung", in: *EvTh* 29 (1969) 169-183.

Kennedy, G. A. 1984: *New Testament through rhetorical Criticism*, Chapel Hill, NC: University of North Carolina Press 1984.

Klinghardt, Matthias 1988: *Das Gesetz und das Volk Gottes. Das lukanische Verständnis des Gesetzes nach Herkunft, Funktion und seinem Ort in der Geschichte des Urchristentums* (WUNT 2.32), Tübingen: J. C. B. Mohr (Paul Siebeck)1988.

Kümmel, Werner G. 1965: "Die älteste Form des Aposteldekretes", in: idem, *Heilsgeschehen und Geschichte. Gesammelte Aufsätze 1933-64* (MThSt 3), hrsg. v. E. Gräßer, Marburg: Elwer 1965, 278-288.

Kurz, William S. 1980: "Hellenistic Rhetoric in the Christological Proof of Luke-Acts", in: *CBQ* 42 (1980) 171-195.

Larsson, Edvin 1987: *Apostlagärningarna*, Band II (Kommentar till Nya Testamentet 5B), Stockholm: EFS-förlaget 1987.

Lietzmann, Hans 1923: "Der Sinn des Aposteldekrets und seine Textwandlung", in: H. G. Wood (ed.), *Amicitiae Corolla*. FS J. R. Harris, London: University of London Press 1923, 203-211.

Lohfink, Gerhard 1975: *Die Sammlung Israels: eine Untersuchung zur lukanischen Ekklesiologie* (StANT 39), München: Kösel Verlag 1975.

Lohfink, Norbert (ed.) 1985: *Das Deuteronomium. Entstehung, Gestalt und Botschaft* (BEThL 68), Louvain: University Press 1985.

Lohse, Eduard (Hrsg.) 1971: *Die Texte aus Qumran.* Hebräisch und Deutsch, München: Kösel/ Darmstadt: Wissenschaftliche Buchgesellschaft [2]1971.

Luomanen, P (ed.)1991: *Luke – Acts. Scandinavian Perspectives* (Publications of the Finnish Exegetical Society 54) Helsinki /Göttingen: The Finnish Exegetical Society/Vandenhoeck & Ruprecht 1991.

Martin, Josef 1974: *Antike Rhetorik. Technik und Methode* (Handbuch der Altertumswissenschaft 2,3) München: C. H. Beck 1974.

Mattill, A. J. / M. B. 1966: *A Classified Bibliography of Literature on the Acts of the Apostles* (NTTS VII), Leiden: E. J. Brill 1966.

Metzger, Bruce M. (ed.) 1971: *A Textual Commentary on the Greek New Testament,* London: United Bible Societies 1971.

Michaelis, W. 1964: Art. "σκηνή", in: *ThWNT* VII, Stuttgart: Kohlhammer 1964, 369-396.

Moessner, D. P. 1988: "The Ironic Fulfillment of Israel's Glory", in: J. B. Tyson (ed.) 1988, 36-50.

Morgenthaler, R. 1949: *Die lukanische Geschichtsschreibung als Zeugnis: Gestalt und Gehalt der Kunst des Lukas,* Band I-II, Zürich: Zwingli-Verlag 1948-49.

Morland, K. A. 1994 (1991): *The Rhetoric of Curse in Galatians. Paul confronts another Gospel* (Emory Studies in Early Christianity) Atlanta, GA: Scholars Press 1994 (im Druck = Diss. Trondheim 1991).

Moulton, J. H. 1962: *A Grammar of New Testament Greek. Syntax,* Vol. III., Edinburgh: T.& T. Clark 1962.

Munck, J. 1967: *The Acts of the Apostels* (AncB 31), Garden City, N.Y.: Doubleday 1967.

Mußner, F. 1988: *Apostelgeschichte* (Die neue Echter Bibel 5), Würzburg: Echter Verlag [2]1988.

Nitzan, B. 1994: "Benedictions and Instructions for the Eschatological Community (11 Q Ber; 4 Q 285)", in: *RdQ* 16 (1994) 77-90.

Nolland, J. A. 1980: "A Fresh Look at Acts 15,10", in: *NTS* 27 (1980) 105-115.

Panimolle, S. A. 1977: *Il Discorso di Pietro all' assemblea apostolica. II. Parola, fede e spirito* (Studi biblici 2), Bologna: Dehoniane 1977.

Pesch, Rudolf 1986: *Die Apostelgeschichte (Apg 13-28)* (EKK V/2), Zürich: Benziger Verlag/Neukirchen-Vluyn: Neukirchener Verlag 1986.

Quintilianus: *Institutionis Oratoriae/Ausbildung des Redners,* hrsg. von H. Rahn, Band I-II, Darmstadt: Wissenschaftliche Buchgesellschaft 1972-75.

von Rad, Gerhard 1963: *Studies in Deuteronomy* (SBT 9), London: SCM Press 1963 (= idem, *Deuteronomium-Studien* (FRLANT 40), Göttingen: Vandenhoeck & Ruprecht 1947).

Resch, Gotthold 1905: *Das Aposteldekret* (TU 13,3), Leipzig: J. C. Hinrichs 1905.

Richard, Earl 1978: *Acts 6,1-8,4. The Author's Method and Composition* (SBL.DS 41), Missoula, MT: Scholars Press 1978.

— 1980/83: "The Divine Purpose: The Jews and the Gentile Mission (Acts 15)", in: C. H. Talbert (ed.), *Luke–Acts, new Perspectives from the Society of Biblical Literature Seminar*, New York: Crossroad 1983 (= SBL.SP 1980), 278ff.

— 1982: "The Creative Use of Amos by the Author of Acts", in: *NT* 24 (1982) 37-53.

Robertson, A. T. 1919: *A Grammar of New Testament Greek in Light of Historical Reseach,* New York: Hodder & Stoughton ³1919.

Roloff, J. 1981: *Die Apostelgeschichte* (NTD 5), Göttingen: Vandenhoeck & Ruprecht 1981.

Ropes, J. H. 1896: "Acts 15,21", in: *JBL* 15 (1896) 75-81.

— 1926: "The Text of Acts", in: F. J. Foakes Jackson/K. Lake: *The Beginning of Christianity*, Vol. III, London: Macmillan1926, 144f.; 265-269.

Sanders, James T. 1987: *The Jews in Luke-Acts*, Philadelphia, PA: Fortress Press 1987.

v. d. Sandt, H. 1992: "An Explanation of Acts 15.6-21 in Light of Deuteronomy 4,29-35 (LXX)", in: *JSNT* 46 (1992) 73-97.

Schmitt, J. 1953: "L'Église de Jérusalem ou la 'Restauration' d'Israël d'après les cinq premiers Chapitres des Actes", in: *RevSR* 27 (1953) 209-218.

Schneider, Gerhard 1981: *Die Apostelgeschichte* (HThK V.2), Freiburg i. Br.: Herder 1981.

Schwarz, A. 1913: *Die hermeneutische Antinomie in der talmudischen Literatur*, Wien: Israelitisch-Theologische Lehranstalt 1913.

Schwarz, Daniel R. 1987: "The Futility of Preaching Moses (Acts 15,21)", in: *Bib.* 67 (1987) 276-81.

Scofield, Cyrus I. 1909 (1945): *The Scofield Reference Bible: the Holy Bible, containing the Old and New Testament authorized Version, with a new System of connected topical References to all the greater Themes in the Scripture, with Annotations, revised marginal Renderings, Summaries, Definitions, and Index, to which are added Helps at hard Places, Explanations of seeming Discrepancies, and a new System of Paragraphs*, New York: Oxford University Press 1909 (1945).

Simon, M. 1969/70: "The Apostolic Decree and its Setting in the Ancient Church", in: *BJRL* 52 (1969/70) 437-460.

Smith, G. V. 1989: *Amos. A Commentary,* Grand Rapids, MI: Zondervan 1989.

Soggins, J. A. 1987: *The Prophet Amos: A Translation and Commentary,* London: SCM Press 1987.

Strathmann, H. 1942: Art. "λαός", in: *ThWNT* IV, Stuttgart: Kohlhammer 1942, 29-39; 49-57.

Strothotte, G. 1955: *Das Apostelkonzil im Lichte der jüdischen Rechtsgeschichte*, Diss. Erlangen 1955.

Taylor, Nicholas 1992: *Paul, Antioch and Jerusalem. A Study in Relationships and Authority in the Earliest Church* (JSNT.S 66), Sheffield: Sheffield Academic Press 1992.

Trites, A. A. 1974: "The Importance of Legal Scenes and Language in the Book of Acts", in: *NT* 16 (1974) 278-84.

Tyson, J. B. 1988: *Luke–Acts and the Jewish People. Eight Critical Perspectives,* Minneapolis, MN: Augsburg Publishing House 1988.

Unnik, W. C. 1960: "The Book of Acts – the Confirmation of the Gospel", in: *NT* 4 (1960) 26-59.

Vos, J. S. 1992: "Die hermeneutische Antinomie bei Paulus (Galater 3,11-12; Römer 10,5-10)", in: *NTS* 38 (1992) 254-270.

de Waard, J. 1965: *A Comparative Study of the Old Testament Text in the Dead Sea Scrolls,* Leiden: E. J. Brill 1965.

Walter, N. 1980: Art. "δόγμα etc.", in: *EWNT* 1, Stuttgart: Kohlhammer 1980, 819-822.

Weinfeld, Moshe 1972: *Deuteronomium and the Deuteronomistic School.* Oxford: Clarendon Press 1972.

— 1973: "On 'Demythologization and Secularization' in Deuteronomy", in: *IEJ* 23 (1973) 230-233.

— 1976: "Jeremiah and the Spiritual Metamorphosis of Israel", in: *ZAW* 88 (1976) 18-56.

— 1985: "The Emergence of the Deuteronomistic Movement: The Historical Antecedents", in: Norbert Lohfink (ed.) 1985, 76-85.

— 1991: *Deuteronomium 1-11* (AncB 5), New York: Doubleday 1991.

Weiser, A. 1984: "Das 'Apostelkonzil' (Apg 15,1-35): Ereignis, Überlieferung, lukanische Deutung", in: *BZ* 28 (1984) 145-167.

Weiß, Johannes 1917: *Das Urchristentum*, Göttingen: Vandenhoeck & Ruprecht 1917.

Wilkens, Ulrich 1961 (1974): *Die Missionsreden der Apostelgeschichte. Form- und traditionsgeschichtliche Untersuchungen* (WMANT 5), Neukirchen-Vluyn: Neukirchener Verlag (1961) [3]1974.

Wilson, S. G. 1973: *The Gentiles and the Gentile Mission in Luke-Acts* (MSSNTS 23), Cambridge, Eng.: Cambridge University Press 1973.

— 1983: *Luke and the Law,* Cambridge, Eng./New York: Cambridge University Press 1983.

Winter, P. 1957: "Miszellen zur Apostelgeschichte, 2: Acta 15,14 und die lukanische Kompositionstechnik", in: *EvTh* 17 (1957) 399-406.

Zahn, Th. 1919-21: *Die Apostelgeschichte des Lucas* (KNT V), Leipzig/Erlangen: A. Deichert 1919-21.

Zuntz, G. 1972: "An Analysis of the Report about the 'Apostolic Council'", in: idem, *Opuscula Selecta,* Manchester: Manchester University Press 1972, 216-251.

# Das Aposteldekret in der lukanischen Theologie

Jacob Jervell

## 1. Wozu das Dekret?

Wozu eigentlich das Aposteldekret Apg 15,20.29; 16,4; 21,25? Darüber sagt Lukas expressis verbis nichts. Dies kommt bei ihm öfters vor: er erzählt, aber erklärt selten. So ist das kein Wunder, daß die Erklärer verschiedene und dem Text nicht direkt entnommene Absichten anführen. Das Dekret bedeute:

- Ermöglichung der Tischgemeinschaft zwischen Juden und Heiden[1]
- Ablösung des Gesetzes[2]
- Freiheit vom Gesetz[3]
- Auflegung von einzelnen Teilen des Gesetzes[4]
- Kontinuität zum alten Gottesvolk[5]
- Konzession an die Heidenchristen[6] bzw. Judenchristen[7]
- Freiwilliger Verzicht[8]
- Glaubensbewährung[9].

Die Vielfältigkeit der Auslegungen zeigt die Möglichkeiten des historischen Ver-

---

[1] So die herrschende Auffassung: C. L. Blomberg 1984, 66; M.-E. Boismard -A. Lamouille 1990, 2, 66; P. Borgen 1988, 126-144; M. Dibelius 1951, 87; Ph. Esler 1987, 99; L. Goppelt 1954, 91; K. Lake 1933, 204; M. Klinghardt 1988, 156-224; H. Lietzmann 1933, 209; Fr. Mußner 1988, 94; R. Pesch 1988, 81; K. Salo 1991, 252; J. T. Sanders 1991, 452; A. Schlatter 1913/62, 188; G. Schneider 1982, 177 Anm. 124; M. Simon 1969/70, 438, 459; H. Waitz 1936, 231.

[2] H. Conzelmann 1963, 84, 93; cf. Lake 1933, 204 Anm. 1.

[3] F. W. Horn 1983, 275; Schneider 1982, 127 Anm. 24, 184; W. Stählin 1962, 278; R. Wikenhauser 1961, 176f.; S. G. Wilson 1980, 259, 261.

[4] D. R. Catchpole 1976/77, 430; E. Franklin 1975, 128; Lietzmann 1932, 107; J. C. O'Neill 1970, 101f.; F. Overbeck 1870, 229-235; Stählin 1962, 204; Simon 1969/70, 460; A. Strobel 1981, 98.

[5] Conzelmann 1963, 93; Horn 1983, 275; J. Roloff 1988, 227; Schneider 1982, 192; vgl. auch E. Haenchen 1977, 454.

[6] Haenchen 1977, 432; Dibelius 1951, 87; Strobel 1981, 92.

[7] Conzelmann 1963, 84.

[8] R. Knopf 1917, 78.

[9] A. Schlatter 1913/62, 186.

ständnisses. Natürlich ist auch damit zu rechnen, daß in der geschichtlichen Entwicklung mehrere Auslegungen möglich wurden. Das Aposteldekret in dem ursprünglichen historischen Kontext zu erklären ist das Hauptinteresse der Ausleger. Viel schwieriger ist die Frage nach der Bedeutung im Kontext der lukanischen Theologie, was auch schon die Vielfalt der oben angeführte Auffassungen demonstriert[10]. Und wie soll man eigentlich das Aposteldekret mit der heute üblichen und verbreiteten Auffassung von lukanischer Theologie verbinden: die heidenchristliche Attitüde zur Kirche als dem neuen Gottesvolk aus Heiden, das Gesetz als Sittengesetz von dem zeremoniellen Aspekten des frühjüdischen Thoraverständnisses befreit? Das ist an sich unmöglich, das Dekret sei ganz unlukanisch. So kann man es nur auf das Konto des Historiker Lukas überweisen: Es sei überholt und ohne Bedeutung für die heidenchristliche Kirche des Lukas und somit ohne Belang für die eigene Theologie des Lukas[11]. Oder: Die Problematik, die zum Dekret führte, sei nicht diejenige des Lukas[12]. Das Dekret sei nur historisch von einiger Bedeutung, zeige die Anfänge der Kirche auf, habe also heilsgeschichtliche Bedeutung[13]. Die Kontinuität zum alten Israel werde dadurch aufgezeigt[14].

Ob es für Lukas so etwas wie "nur historisch" überhaupt gibt? Das heißt historisch in dem Sinne, daß es nicht mehr eine aktuelle theologische Bedeutung hat. Ist es überhaupt denkbar für Lukas, daß ein apostolisches Dekret nicht mehr Gültigkeit hat? Ist die Geschichte nicht für Lukas norm- und richtunggebend? Es ist m.E. ein Mißverständnis von Lukas als Historiker, wenn man ihn mit den Historikern der Antike gleichstellt, technisch jawohl, aber gar nicht in der Verwendung und Deutung der Geschichte[15]. Man darf den Historiker Lukas nicht von dem Theologen und Schriftausleger trennen. Nun kann man das Problem lösen, indem man die

---

[10] Wilson 1983, 76f. hat es klar gemacht, daß man zwischen der ursprünglichen Fassung und dem Verständnis desselben von Lukas trennen muß; cf. Wedderburn 1993.

[11] O. Bauernfeind 1939, 195.

[12] Lake 1933, 210; cf. Wilson 1980, 260.

[13] Conzelmann 1963, 85.

[14] Wedderburn 1993, 377ff., 383f., versteht Apg 15,29 als die älteste, traditionelle und prälukanische Form des Dekrets, während 15,20 die spezifisch lukanische Um-Interpretation desselben repräsentiere; so vermag er auch bei Lukas eine mehr moralische Auffassung des Dekrets zu finden. Dafür muß er aber in Kauf nehmen, daß "Luke understood the reference and significance of the πνικτά as little as we probably do", oder: "a rather trivial culinary restriction". Und wie soll man es erklären, daß Lukas noch zweimal das Dekret wiedergibt, aber in einer nicht wegzuinterpretierenden kultischen Fassung, 15,29 und 21,25? Und wie ist dann Apg 21,21 als Begründung für das Dekret zu verstehen? Die Auffassung Wedderburns ist auch von der Meinung getragen, daß für Lukas das Gesetz als allgemeines Sittengesetz zu verstehen ist. Wo aber finden wir das in der Apg? Salo 1991, 226 behauptet, wir können aus den Verschiedenheiten der drei Wiedergaben kein redaktionelles Verfahren von Lukas ablesen.

[15] Dazu: J. Jervell 1994 passim.

westliche Textform vorzieht[16]. Denn so stimmt das Dekret mit dem üblichen Verständnis der lukanischen Theologie. Ich halte es nicht für unmöglich, daß gewisse Kreise ein Moraldekret, also die westliche Form, zeremonial umgestaltet haben könnten. Das ist auch bei Lukas selbst denkbar, weil er öfters "liberale" Traditionen "konservativ" umbaut, aber in dem Falle ist die westliche Textform nicht von Lukas vorgezogen. Und wenn man die westliche Form, also das Moraldekret[17], mit den anderen alten Traditionen bei Lukas vergleicht, sieht man, daß dies nicht der Fall sein kann[18]. Denn die alten Traditionen bei Lukas sind von einer Art, die überhaupt kein Moraldekret zulassen. Denn sie reden von einer vollen Freiheit vom Gesetz, die auch in der westlichen Textform nicht da ist. Schwerwiegender sind aber die äußeren Gründe. Eine Umgestaltung eines Moraldekrets in ein zeremoniales ist im ersten, aber nicht im zweiten Jahrhundert denkbar[19]. Somit ist die Geschichte des Dekrets und ihrer Anwendung in der alten Kirche ohne die zeremonial bestimmte Textform nicht zu verstehen[20]. Die Ethizierung des Dekrets ist aus einer Situation, wo die Judenchristen nicht mehr in der Kirche etwas bedeuten, einfach zu verstehen.

Nun aber meine These: Das Gesetz des Mose als das Gesetz des Gottesvolkes bedeutet für Lukas ein Bekenntnis zu dem einen Gott Israels und somit auch Abwehr gegen die Idolatrie. Das Dekret verbindet die Heiden mit dem Gesetz, somit auch mit Israel und soll durch die vier Regeln Idolatrie[21] abwehren und die Reinheit des Gottesvolkes bewahren.

## 2. Das Dekret in der Komposition

Das Dekret kommt viermal bei Lukas vor. Es wird drei Mal zitiert, 15,20.29; 21,25[22], und 16,4 erwähnt[23]. Es hat eine eigenartige Stellung in der Komposition, indem es erst Apg 15 auftaucht. Zu der Zeit hat die Kirche nach Lukas schon eine längere Geschichte hinter sich. Und ganz besonders: Die ersten Heiden sind schon

---

[16] Th. Boman 1964, 26-36; A. C. Clarke 1914, 96f.; P. Glaue 1954; H. C. Scroggs 1960, 36-45; C.-B. Amphoux – L. Vaganay 1986; zu älteren Vertretern: J. H. Ropes 1926, LXXXIV; der westliche Text komme aus einem antijüdischen Milieu: E. J. Epp 1966, 110f.; Ph.-H. Menoud 1951, 26f.

[17] Nach M. Klinghardt 1988,172ff. geht es nicht um eine Ethizierung in der westlichen Textform; vgl. W. A. Strange 1992, 93; Lake 1933, 207.

[18] Vgl. Jervell 1991, 383ff.

[19] Anders A. v. Harnack 1908, 248-263; vgl. auch F. C. Burkitt 1927, 194-199.

[20] Siehe Apok 2,14.20; Justin, Dialog 34,8; Min Felix Octavius 30,6; Euseb Hist Eccl V,1,26; Tertullian, Apol 9;13; PsKlem Hom VII,4,2; 8,1; VIII 19.

[21] Daß die vier Regeln mit Idolatrie zu tun haben, ist ab und zu angenommen, dann aber öfters mit einem ethischen Verständnis verbunden und ohne Bezug auf das Gesetz: W. G. Kümmel 1965, 278-288; Wedderburn 1993, 384-389; Wilson 1983, 92; cf. Strange 1992, 89f.

vorlängst bekehrt worden (Apg 10-11). Von einem längeren Zeitraum zwischen der ersten Heidenbekehrung und dem Konzil redet Lukas deutlich (15,7[24].14). Obwohl das "von uralten Zeiten" grundsätzlich gemeint ist und also die autoritative Bedeutung des Kornelius-Geschehens hervorheben soll, liegt offenbar darin auch ein zeitliches Element. Die ersten Heidenbekehrungen und das Konzil sind ja auch durch die Ereignisse in Apg 12-14 voneinander getrennt. Es ist nicht möglich, das Verhältnis so zu verstehen, daß Apg 15 die Ausführungen Apg 10-11 direkt fortführt und vollendet. Es gab demnach eine Zeit in der Kirche mit Aufnahme von Heiden, aber ohne das Dekret. Nichts in den Ausführungen bis auf Apg 15 deutet auf das Dekret hin oder vorbereitet es. Wir erwarten aber das Dekret tatsächlich schon Apg 10-11, oder aber in Apg 15 ein Hinweis darauf, daß das Dekret schon für die ersten Heiden gültig ist. Die Bekehrung des Kornelius ist ja kein Einzelereignis, sondern bedeutet die Bekehrung der Völkerwelt (10,34; 11,18). Dies Ereignis wird von der Gemeinde in Jerusalem, den christlichen Juden, einfach hingenommen (11,1ff. 18). Das Problem mit der Aufnahme von Heiden in das Gottesvolk ist gelöst: Es gibt keine unreinen Menschen (10,28; 11,9). Jemand, der Gerechtigkeit tut und Gott fürchtet, wird angenommen (10,35). Die Mission des Paulus und Barnabas (Apg 13-14) geht problemlos weiter, d.h. es wird den Heiden von den Juden in der Kirche nichts auferlegt.

Soweit führt uns nichts auf das Dekret zu, weil das Problem mit den Heiden in der Kirche eben kein Problem ist. Teile des mosaischen Gesetzes werden keinem Heiden aufgelegt. Völlig unvorbereitet kommen dann die Forderungen der Pharisäer (Apg 15,1.5): Beschneidung und Gesetzeserfüllung müssen erfordert werden. Von nun ab bestimmt das Dekret das Leben der Kirche, wie wir es aus 16,4 und 21,25 sehen, also in der zweiten Hälfte der Apostelgeschichte. Das Dekret umrahmt die paulinische Mission, Apg 16-21 beschrieben, also die Mission, wo Paulus ohne Barnabas arbeitet (15,36-41). Das Dekret gilt aber nicht nur den – *sit venia verbo* – paulinischen Heiden, sondern allen (21,25).

Die zweite Hälfte der Apg ist u.a. davon bestimmt, daß die Juden in der Kirche das Gesetz in toto einhalten, die Heiden aber nur das für Nicht-Israeliten Notwendige, also das Dekret. Die Komposition zeigt, daß das Dekret das Gesetz nicht ablöst[25]. Das stimmt weder für Juden noch für Heiden. Das geht aus Apg 15 indirekt,

---

[22] Der Wortlaut variiert: (a) εἰδωλόθυτα ersetzt ἀλισγήματα τῶν εἰδώλων; (b) verschiedene Reihenfolge der vier Gebote; (c) der bestimmte Artikel verschwindet und (d) die Mehrzahl πνικτά ist verwendet.

[23] Zur Diskussion über die Traditionsgeschichte des Dekrets: Wedderburn 1993, 372-379.

[24] Es ist gleichgültig ob das ἀφ᾽ ἡμερῶν ἀρχαίων sich auf die historische Rolle des Petrus als Heidenmissionar oder auf die Korneliusepisode bezieht.

[25] Gegen Conzelmann 1963, 84, 93; Lake 1933, 204f. Anm. 1; vgl. auch Horn 1983, 275.

aus Apg 21 direkt hervor. Die christlichen Juden sind "Eiferer für das Gesetz", und der Zusammenhang zeigt, daß es sich um die zeremoniellen Teile handelt[26]. Die Heiden in der Kirche halten vor dem Konzil das Gesetz nicht, sodaß es für sie keine Ablösung des Gesetzes gibt. Endlich 16,3-4, wo das Dekret nicht zitiert, sondern dessen Übergabe an die Gemeinden erzählt wird. Die zweite Epoche der paulinischen Mission fängt hier an, und sie wird überall von dem Dekret bestimmt. Dies gilt zugleich vom Gesetz, indem der Missionar beschnitten wird.

## 3. Die Kontexte

Was die Komposition ergibt, wird von den Kontexten bestätigt. Es geht überall um dasselbe Problem: Das Gesetz und das Gottesvolk. In Apg 15 verlangen die konservativen Judenchristen Beschneidung und Gesetzeserfüllung von den Heiden, sonst können sie nicht gerettet werden (15,1.5). Dies wird von dem Konzil abgelehnt, weil das Heil rein aus der Gnade Gottes kommt (15,11)[27]. Das Heil kommt nicht aus dem Gesetz, aber das Gesetz[28] verbleibt trotzdem als Zeichen des Gottesvolkes, Israel[29]. In toto gültig für Juden, während die Heiden nur "die notwendigen Dinge" davon (15,28) einhalten.

Diese Stellung des Gesetzes hängt mit der Frage des Gottesvolkes zusammen, nämlich mit dem Wiederaufbau Israels und der Zuströmung der Völker (Apg 15,15-18). Das ist aus 15,21 zu sehen, wo die unmittelbare Verbindung zwischen Gesetz und Dekret gegeben ist[30]. V. 21 soll V. 20 begründen[31], das Gesetz begründet das Dekret. Das Dekret ist notwendig weil das Gesetz es fordert[32]. Nicht nur wird das Dekret durch das schriftlich fixierte Gesetz oder gar durch Schriftworte, sondern

---

[26] V. Stolle 1973 sieht Apg 21,18-26 als ein von der lukanischen Komposition bewirktes, störendes Einsprengsel. Wie das nun ist: 21,18-26 ist inhaltlich und sprachlich lukanisch.

[27] Auch innerhalb Apg 15 kommt das Dekret als eine Überraschung. Denn laut dem Vorangehenden sollte alles darauf auslaufen: Die Heiden sind von Beschneidung und Gesetz frei; keine Auflagen dürfen gegeben werden. Schon im Verhältnis zu V. 19 ist das Dekret eine Überraschung.

[28] Zu der neueren Literatur über die Gesetzesfrage in den Lukasschriften: Jervell 1991, 388 Anm. 26.

[29] Es scheint fast unmöglich, einer Interpretation von Lukas in der Gesetzesfrage zu entgehen, wo Lukas immer wieder mit Paulus in seiner soteriologischen Konzeption verglichen, verbunden und kontrastiert wird. Das Gesetz gehört aber für Lukas nicht zur Soteriologie, sondern zur Ekklesiologie.

[30] V. 21 gehöre "nach Zusammenhang und Bedeutung zu den schwierigsten des Neuen Testaments", Dibelius 1955, 87; vgl. M. Dömer 1978, 176; Roloff 1988, 233; E. Trocmé 1957. Schwierig ist V. 21 nur wenn man das Dekret als Gesetzesfreiheit, Konzession an Heidenchristen etc., versteht.

[31] So in fast allen Kommentaren; einige meinen: V. 19 und die Auslegung des Amoszitats: Beg. IV, 177ff.; Trocmé 1957, 160f.; erwogen von Conzelmann 1972, 93.

konkret mit der sabbatlichen Predigt und Lesung von Moses[33] begründet. Die Synagoge ist für Lukas das Haus Gottes, Israels und der Schrift. Somit wird das Dekret doppelt begründet: Einmal "bei den Propheten" (15,15-18), siehe V. 19, sodann bei Moses. Es geht vor allem um Aufnahme der Heiden in Israel als Gottesvolk, siehe V.16 im Verhältnis zu V. 17, sodann um das Zusammenleben von Heiden und Juden in der Kirche und von der Erschaffung von "einem Volk aus den Heiden" (15,14).

So Apg 21,15-26. Paulus muß hier seine Gesetzestreue demonstrieren (21,24) in einem kultischen Akt im Tempel, dem Ort der "exemplarischen Gesetzeserfüllung"[34]. Das gilt gegenüber dem jüdischen Teil der Gemeinde, den "Myriaden" von Gesetzeseiferern unter den christlichen Juden (21,20). Der Kontext ist also von der Gesetzesfrage bestimmt. Und hier kommt eine Bezugnahme auf das Aposteldekret, was nach einer Reihe von Kommentaren hier nicht am Platze ist und wie ein Einsprengsel wirkt[35]. Aber V. 25 ist im Zusammenhang notwendig. Die Anklage gegen Paulus (21,21) dreht sich um das, was er den unter Heiden lebenden Juden lehrt, d.h. offenbar heidnisch zu leben. Die Heiden sind also auch hier im Bilde (siehe auch V. 19) durch die Missionsarbeit des Paulus, die von der Kirche anerkannt wird. Weil es sich hier sowohl um Paulus als auch um die ganze Kirche und die Heidenchristen dreht, muß das Dekret erwähnt werden. Die Kirche ist vom Gesetz bestimmt, auch durch das Dekret.

## 4. Apg 10-11 und 15

Entscheidend für das Verständnis vom Dekret in der lukanischen Theologie ist das Verhältnis zwischen Apg 10-11 und 15. Hätten wir Apg 15 nicht das Dekret, hätten wir auch keine Probleme mit Apg 10-11. Denn das Problem mit der Aufnahme von Heiden in der Kirche ist ja Apg 10-11 gelöst: Es soll den Heiden überhaupt nichts auferlegt werden. Weil die Frage schon Apg 10-11 beantwortet ist, ist es auffallend, daß sie Apg 15 wieder aufgenommen wird, als ob nichts passiert wäre. Doch, Apg 15 wird tatsächlich den Heiden etwas aufgelegt: Das Dekret. Die Frage läßt sich nicht so beantworten, daß Lukas nun eben verschiedene Traditionen und Überliefe-

---

[32] Wenn man das Dekret nicht als eine gesetzliche Auflage versteht, gerät man in unlösliche Schwierigkeiten hinein, nämlich Gesetzesfreiheit und Dekretsregeln zu verbinden. Man sollte nicht mehr bestreiten, daß das Dekret eine Gesetzesverpflichtung bedeutet, so richtig: Lake 1933, 205; Catchpole 1976/77, 430; Franklin 1975, 128; Lietzmann 1932, 107; Klinghardt 1988, 112; Overbeck 1870, 227, 229-235; Salo 1991, 244; Schneider 1982, 226; E. Richard 1980, 269; Stählin, 1970, 278; Strobel 1981, 94,98; A. Weiser 1985, 383.

[33] "Moses" als Bezeichnung für das Gesetz bei Lukas: Klinghardt 1988, 121-123.

[34] Klinghardt 1988, 304.

[35] Statt vieler: Schneider 1982, 311.

rungen besaß, die er unverbunden anführt[36]. Denn er verbindet Apg 15,7-9.14 redaktionell Apg 10-11 mit Apg 15. Lukas sieht keinen Gegensatz zwischen den
Ausführungen Apg 10-11 und 15. Wir haben es also mit Traditionen zu tun, die Lukas aufnimmt und so wiedergibt, wie er sie gefunden hat – inhaltlich, nicht sprachlich – und zugleich bearbeitet und für seine eigene Theologie dienstbar macht. M.E.
hat Lukas eine "liberale" Tradition, die er "konservativ" verarbeitet. Oder: Er besitzt sowohl "liberale" als auch "konservative", bevorzugt aber die letzteren.

Es geht Apg 10-11 um unreines Essen und unreine Tiere (10,10-16; 11,5-9). Es
wird klar ausgedrückt, daß es solche Phänomene nicht mehr gibt, weil Gott sie gereinigt hat (10,15; 11,9). Das Dekret aber rechnet mit unreinem Essen, wie wir sehen werden. In der Anwendung der Traditionen von Apg 10-11 geht es überhaupt
nicht um Essen und Tiere, sondern die Visionen werden so interpretiert, daß es sich
um Menschen dreht (10,28.34f.): Es gibt keine unreinen Menschen; es gibt keinen
Unterschied zwischen Menschen, Juden und Heiden, denn sie sind vor Gott gleich.
So nach dem Beschluß Gottes. Und deshalb werden auch Heiden gerettet (11,18).
Später aber in der Apg gibt es unreine Menschen. Das wird von dem Dekret vorausgesetzt[37]. Die Menschen sind an sich nicht rein, sondern Heiden werden durch den
Geist und Glauben gereinigt (15,8-9). Paulus wird Apg 21,28 angeklagt, den Tempel entweiht zu haben, indem er den Trophimos, einen Unbeschnittenen, angeblich
zum Tempel mitgenommen hat. So wie die Argumentation hier läuft, wird zwischen
reinen und unreinen Menschen unterschieden, was also nach Apg 10-11 unmöglich
sein sollte[38].

Die Gesetzesfrage ist auch Apg 10-11 klar. Weder das Gesetz im ganzen noch
Teile davon kann den Heiden auferlegt werden[39]. Konsequent wird ja auch keine
gesetzliche Anordnung gegeben, denn das würde einen Unterschied zwischen Israel
und den Heiden, Reinen und Unreinen, bedeuten[40]. Zu dieser Tradition gehört die
Beseitigung des Gesetzes, d.h. es führt nicht zum Heil, und deshalb wird es abge-

---

[36] v. Harnack 1908, 193 Anm. 2 findet es unmöglich, daß Lukas Apg 15 an rituelle Speisegebote
denke, denn von solchen sei er schon Apg 10-11 befreit. Deshalb zieht Harnack die westliche Textform vor. Harnack sieht aber nicht die lukanische Verwendung der Tradition in Apg 10-11, wonach
es nicht mehr um unreines Essen, sondern um unreine Menschen geht.

[37] O'Neill 1970, 102 meint, das Dekret solle nicht die Vorstellung von reinen und unreinen Menschen einführen, sondern es gehe nur um die Gültigkeit des Gesetzes. Eine unmögliche Distinktion.
Anders und richtig: Catchpole 1976/77, 430.

[38] Unverständlich Pesch 1981, 115: Apg 15,5 sei eine konsequente Wiederführung von 11,18:
Die Frage von dem Heil der Heiden sei schon gelöst, aber nicht die Tischgemeinschaft und die Gesetzesverpflichtung. Es geht aber Apg 15 eben um das Heil für Heiden (15,1.11).

[39] Wilson 1980, 257: Apg 10-11 bedeute, daß Gott interveniere, um Teile des Gesetzes außer
Kraft zu setzen.

[40] Von Apg 10-11 her werden die Anklagen Apg 6,11.13f. verständlich: Die unreinen Tiere für
rein zu erklären, heißt gerade das Gesetz außer Kraft zu setzen.

schafft (Apg 15,10.19; vgl. 13,38.39): Das Gesetz haben sie nicht halten können; es ist "eine untragbare Last". Auf der anderen Seite wird das Gesetz bestätigt (Apg 6,13f.; 7,38; 21,15-25; 24,17f.; Lk 16,17)[41]. Die jüdischen Christen haben keine Schwierigkeiten mit der Erfüllung des Gesetzes. Und nun wird durch das Dekret Teile von dem Gesetz den Heiden auferlegt, und sie haben früher das Gesetz nicht gehalten.

Diese Gesetzestradition, die Lukas "konservativ" interpretiert, haben wir auch in Verbindung mit dem Tempel. Wie man nun Acta 7 verstehen will, kommt man nicht umhin, daß wir hier tempelkritische Aussagen haben; Gott wohnt nicht "in den von Menschenhänden Gemachten", es geht um den Tempel in Jerusalem (Apg 7,44-50). Der Tempel Apg 7 ist mindestens nicht mehr Gotteshaus. Auf der anderen Seite ist es u.a. aus Lk 1-2; Apg 3; 24,12; 21,15ff. klar, daß der Tempel Gottes Haus ist, in dem er wohnt. In der Tradition stehen sowohl Stephanus als auch Paulus dem Tempel und Gesetz kritisch gegenüber (Apg 6,13,14; 7; 21,28; 26,8). Aber in der lukanischen Anwendung sind sowohl Stephanus als auch Paulus gesetzes- und tempelfromme Juden, die fälschlich angeklagt werden (Apg 6,13f.; 21,27ff., und 24,12ff.).

Auch die Frage der Heidenmission taucht hier auf[42]. In der Tradition bedeutet die jüdische Verwerfung des Evangeliums den Ursprung der Heidenmission (13,46; 18,6). Paulus ist selbst Heidenmissionar (22,15.18.21). Aber für Lukas nehmen besonders die Juden das Evangelium an (2,41; 4,4; 5,14; 6,1.7; 9,42; 12,24; 13,43; 14,1; 17,10ff.; 21,20). Und der Annahme des Evangeliums von den Juden bedeutet das Hinzuströmen der Heiden (Apg 15,15-18). Ablehnung des Evangeliums von Juden heißt neue Hinwendung zu Juden, siehe die Synagogeszenen Apg 13-19. Diese zeigen auch, daß Paulus vor allem Judenmissionar ist, siehe auch 16,17.20. Die Tradition besagt, daß die Heidenmission mit der hellenistischen Mission in Antiochien anfing (Apg 11,20), während für Lukas die Urgemeinde durch Petrus den ersten Anfang machte (Apg 10-11).

Das Dekret gehört zu der "konservativen" Bearbeitung der Tradition. Lukas verarbeitet Traditionen Apg 15. Das Problem ist Beschneidung und Gesetzeserfüllung um das Heil zu erlangen (15,1.5). Die Antwort der Tradition ist auch klar: Wir werden durch die Gnade Gottes gerettet, weil wir gar nicht imstande gewesen sind, das Gesetz zu halten (15,10-11; vgl.13,38f.). Lukas hält daran teilweise fest. Wir werden durch die Gnade gerettet. Wir vermögen aber sehr gut, das Gesetz zu halten, was immer wieder gesagt wird. Und um die Stellung des Gesetzes als Merkmal des

---

[41] Salo 1991, 243: "Ac 15:10 does not match with the legal views we find elsewhere in Luke-Acts".

[42] Schneider 1982, 168: Apg 15 sei eine Wende, weil die gesetzesfreie Heidenmission sich durchsetzte und von den Aposteln in Jerusalem legitimiert werde. Dies ist aber Apg 1,18 geschehen und dort bedingungslos.

Gottesvolkes klarzumachen, kommt das Dekret hinzu. Das heißt nicht, daß Lukas Erfinder des Dekrets ist. Dafür zeugt das Vorkommen des Dekretes in Quellen, die von der Apostelgeschichte unabhängig sind[43]. Die Geschichtlichkeit des Dekrets steht fest; darum geht es also hier nicht. Es geht nur darum, was es in dem lukanischen Rahmen bedeutet. Natürlich kann das Dekret in verschiedenen Traditionen verschiedene Bedeutungen gehabt haben. So könnte vielleicht das Dekret ursprünglich eine Ablösung des Gesetzes bedeuten haben. So versteht es aber Lukas nicht.

## 5. Das Dekret, das Gesetz, und die lukanische Theologie

Bedeutet das Dekret eine gesetzliche Auflage, und wie ist es demnach in der lukanischen Theologie zu verstehen?

Immer wird das Dekret in Verbindung mit dem Gesetz erwähnt[44]. Für Lukas ist das Gesetz Israels Gesetz. Es ist nur Israel gegeben (Apg 7,38.53; vgl. 25,8). Nie wird gesagt, das Gesetz sei auch den Heiden gegeben oder in den Herzen der Heiden geschrieben u.ä. Wenn die Gemeinde für Gesetzesübertretung angeklagt wird, dreht es sich immer um rituelles Vergehen, und Gesetzeskritik ist als Sünde gegen Israel verstanden, so in den Anklagen gegen Jesus, Stephanus und Paulus (Apg 6,11.13f.; 21,28; 25,8; 28,17). Wenn Lukas das Gesetz expressis verbis erwähnt, werden in den überwiegenden Anführungen die rituellen Gebote genannt (Lk 1,6; 2,22.23.24.27.39; 5,14; 20,28; 23,65; Apg 6,13; 7,53; 15,1.5; 21,20.24.28)[45]. Wenn das Dekret auch ganz besonders rituelle Forderungen aufstellt, ist auch dadurch die Nähe zum Gesetz gegeben.

Eine Rede von Freiheit vom Gesetz ist bei Lukas abwegig. Wenn man so etwas überhaupt in der Apg meint finden zu können, dann in den Traditionen Apg 8-14. Denn dort wird den bekehrten Heiden nichts auferlegt. Apg 15,1.5 zeigen, daß bisher von den Heiden keine Gesetzesverpflichtung gefordert worden ist. Teilweise ist eine solche auch in Apg 8-14 gar nicht notwendig, denn die Gottesfürchtigen halten sowieso teilweise das Gesetz, wie das in dem Falle Kornelius paradigmatisch dargestellt wird (10,2.4.22). Die gesetzesfreie Heidenmission gibt es in der Apostelgeschichte nicht, sowie es auch keine heidenchristliche Gemeinden gibt, denn "das Volk aus den Heiden" (Apg 15,14) lebt überall mit den Juden zusammen.

Das Dekret wird 15,28 als "eine Last", βάρος, bezeichnet. Im Zusammenhang

---

[43] Apok 2,14.20; Just Dial 34,8; Min Felix Octavius 30,6; Eus h.e. V,1,26; Tertullian Apol 9,13; PsClem Hom VII,4,2; 8,1; VIII,19.

[44] Sehr intensiv ist neulich die jahrelang vernachläßigte Gesetzesfrage in den Lukasschriften studiert worden; Literatur bei Jervell 1991, 388; zu der konservativ-jüdischen Terminologie des Lukas in der Gesetzesfrage: Jervell, 1972, 136ff.; Klinghardt 1988, 115-123.

[45] Vgl. Jervell 1972, 137ff.

gib es nun nur eine "Last", nämlich das Gesetz (15,10.19). Schon dadurch ist das Dekret als Gesetz bezeichnet. Es geht aber offenbar nur um einen Teil des Gesetzes, nämlich "die notwendigen Dinge", τῶν ἐπάναγκες (15,28). Lukas führt nicht aus, was er unter "notwendig" versteht. Notwendig zum Heil ist es nicht (15,10). "Das Notwendige" kann nur mit Rücksicht auf das Gesetz gesagt sein, also das Notwendige aus dem Gesetz[46]. Das gilt nicht für die Juden, denn für sie ist alles im Gesetz notwendig. Die Schilderung von Paulus in der Apostelgeschichte zeigt, daß er alle Gesetzesforderungen erfüllt. Alle Judenchristen sind "Eiferer für das Gesetz" (Apg 21,20). Anders für die Heiden, denn sie werden nicht beschnitten, verbleiben also Heiden und werden als solche auch gerettet.

Für sie gibt es aber "Notwendiges" im Gesetz, was also in den vier Dekretsgeboten gegeben ist. Was das "Notwendige" ist, hängt nun damit zusammen, wie Lukas das Gesetz versteht.

Bekanntlich hat Lukas keine Zusammenfassung des Gesetzes, so wie wir es in dem Liebesgebot finden (Mt 22,40; Rm 13,9). In der Überlieferung vom doppelten Liebesgebot bezeichnet Lukas nicht dieses Gebot als "das oberste Gebot"( Lk 10,25 im Verhältnis zu Mt 22,36.38.39; Mk 12,29.30.32).

Lukas zeigt aber Apg 7,38ff., was er unter das "Notwendige", also die Absicht des Gesetzes, versteht. Mit der Stephanusrede (Apg 7,2-53) beabsichtigt Lukas, die Anklage gegen Stephanus wegen Gesetzes- und Tempelkritik, zurückzuweisen (6,11.13f.; 7,53). Und 7,38 kommt er auf das Gesetz zu reden, d.h. die Gesetzgebung, in der Mosesequenz der Stephanus-Rede (7,20-43). Hier haben wir offenbar die lukanischen Elemente in der Rede vor uns. Das Gesetz ist "lebendige Worte", λόγια ζῶντα[47], durch Moses an Israel gegeben (7,38). Israel war aber nicht Moses gehorsam, das heißt im Zusammenhang: dem Gesetz (7,39; vgl.7,53). Die Ungehorsamkeit kommt konkret zum Ausdruck: Israel verleugnet Gott als Gott, macht sich neue Götter, denen sie opfern, und sie werden Götzendiener (7,39b-43). Die Anklage gegen Stephanus wegen Gesetzeskritik wendet Lukas in eine Anklage gegen das unbußfertige Israel um. Israel hat das Gesetz nicht erfüllt. Das Gesetz nicht zu erfüllen heißt Götzendienst zu treiben, und folgerichtig: das Gesetz zu erfüllen heißt Gott als Israels Gott zu dienen. Im Zusammenhang: Das Gesetz soll Idolatrie abwehren[48].

Hier haben wir die Brücke zum Dekret. Das Gesetz geht um Idolatrie, und das erste Gebot im Dekret geht auch um Idolatrie[49]. Es ist sinnlos im Zusammenhang

---

[46] Es läßt sich nach Wilson 1983, 82f. nicht entscheiden, ob "das Notwendige" Freiheit vom oder Gebundenheit am Gesetz bedeute.

[47] Salo 1991, 181: "… an emphatically positive statement of the law".

[48] Εἴδωλον nur Apg 7,41 und 15,20 bei Lukas.

[49] Lake 1933, 205; siehe auch oben Anm. 16.

des Dekrets das Essen von Götzenopferfleisch von Idolatrie zu trennen[50]. Die Wiedergabe von dem mehr spezifischen εἰδωλόθυτα (Apg 15,29; 21,25) durch ἀλισγημάτων[51] τῶν εἰδώλων, "Befleckung durch Götzen", ist offenbar richtunggebend[52]. Lukas hat das "Befleckung durch Götzen" sinnvoll vorangestellt als eine Überschrift und Charakteristik über sämtliche Gebote des Dekrets[53]. Er hat also das εἰδωλόθυτα definiert und erweitert: es geht um jede Form von Idolatrie[54]. Bekanntlich ist es öfters aufgezeigt worden, daß alle Gebote des Dekrets als Verbot gegen Idolatrie verstanden werden können[55]. Wir brauchen das nicht nochmals aufzuzeigen, auch nicht die Richtigkeit oder Notwendigkeit dieser Auffassung[56]. Entscheidend ist, daß das Dekret vor allem die Verpflichtung zum Bekenntnis zum Gott Israels den Heiden auferlegt. In dem Zusammenhang geht es nicht oder mindestens nicht nur um Tischgemeinschaft zwischen Juden und Heiden, sondern um den Wiederaufbau des Gottesvolkes Israel als Voraussetzung für das Suchen der Heiden oder der Völker nach dem Gott Israels (15,15-18). Das Problem ist in diesem Zusammenhang die Aufnahme der Heiden in das Volk Israel.

In der Geschichte Israels ist die gröbste Gesetzesübertretung die Idolatrie (Apg 7,41-43). Das wird bei Lukas als die Freude "an dem Werk ihrer Hände" charakterisiert (Apg 7,41). Diese Sünde Israels kennzeichnet auch das Wesen des Heidentums. In den zwei Reden der Apg zu "reinen" Heiden, also nicht zu Gottesfürchtigen, werden die leeren Abgötter mit dem einen, wahren Gott kontrastiert (Apg 14,15f.; 17,22). Die Abgötterei kennzeichnet die Völker, und die Abgötter sind keine richtigen Götter, weil sie ein Werk der Menschenhände sind (Apg 17,29; 19,26 und 7,41)[57]. Das Gesetz, besonders die rituellen Teile ist für Lukas deshalb wichtig,

---

[50] Anders Simon 1969/70, 447. Es ist anders bei Paulus, der das Essen des Opferfleisches an sich von dem Essen desselben in einer heidnischen Kultmahlzeit trennt (1 Kor 8-10).

[51] Zum Begriff: Y. Tissot 1970, 321-346.

[52] Vgl. Tissot 1970, 339-346.

[53] Strange 1992, 103.

[54] Εἰδωλόθυτα dreht sich somit nicht nur um das Essen oder den Kauf von Fleisch von den Opfertieren, sondern um alles, was mit Götzen zu tun hat, vgl. Beg. III, 265-269; Klinghardt 1988, 160ff., 201. Anders Simon 1969/70, 447; man sollte aber nicht mit Simon einwenden, daß die Erwähnung von Idolatrie im Dekret überflüssig sei, weil die Heidenchristen bei der Bekehrung Idolatrie abgesagt haben, op. cit. 446; sogar Israel betet ja fremde Götter an und schafft sich sogar neue (Apg 7,38ff.); wenn Paulus das Essen von Opferfleisch nicht mit Idolatrie identifiziert (1 Kor 8,1-3; 10,28-31; Röm 14,1-13), ist Lukas offenbar anderer Meinung, vgl. Salo 1991, 241.

[55] Kümmel 1965, 278-288; Lake 1933, 205f.; siehe weiter oben Anm. 16.

[56] Besonders zu der Verbindung πορνεία und Idolatrie, J. C. Hurd, Jr. 1965, 253; L. Schenke 1990, 325 (kultische Prostitution); Simon 1969/70, 446; vgl. auch Klinghardt 1988, 201ff.; Salo 1991, 249f. Wenn das ἀλισγήματα für Lukas das mehr spezifische εἰδωλόθυτα ersetzt, folgt nicht daraus, daß man πορνεία als "sexual immorality" verstehen muß, gegen Wedderburn 1993, 378, 383.

weil die Abwehr der Idolatrie das Bekenntnis zu dem Gott Israels bedeutet.

Eine Zusammenfassung des Gesetzes ist das Dekret nicht für Lukas. Es ist aber ein Ausschnitt besonders auf die Heiden zugeschnitten. Und es ist verständlich, warum Lukas die vier Gebote des Dekrets aus Lev 17-18 genommen sieht[58]. Lukas weist nicht direkt auf die Schrift, aber indirekt weil die Begründung des Dekrets 15,21 mit der sabbatlichen Lesung von Moses im Synagogengottesdienst gegeben wird. Es wird also durch Jakobus oder die Apostel nichts Neues gegeben (15,19.23; 21,25).

Es geht Lev 17-18 um die Reinheit des Gottesvolkes (Lev 18,24-30). Wichtig ist, daß die Verpflichtungen der Israeliten auch für die Beisassen gelten (17,1.8.10.13. 15; 18,26). Es geht also um Dinge, die den Juden und Heiden gemeinsam auferlegt werden. Wenn in der Apostelgeschichte nur den Heiden diese Gebote auferlegt werden, so geschieht dies, weil die Israeliten in der Kirche die Thora im ganzen erfüllen[59]. Das Dekret macht es ganz klar, daß der Unterschied Jude – Heide besteht. Der Jude bleibt Jude und der Heide Heide. Der letztere kann gar nicht Jude werden, und von einem "dritten Geschlecht" ist niemals die Rede. Die Absicht des Dekrets ist klar: Die Reinheit des Gottesvolkes, sodaß die Kirche Volk Gottes verbleiben kann. Verheißung und Gesetz wird bei Lukas niemals begrifflich auf einander bezogen, obwohl die lukanische Tradition dies negativ tut (13,28; vgl.15,10).

Die Reinheit des Gottesvolkes ist für Lukas wichtig. Es ist eine entscheidende Frage in Verbindung mit der Aufnahme von Heiden (Apg 10-11): Petrus hat mit Unbeschnittenen gegessen (11,3). Im Zusammenhang wird die Frage dadurch gelöst, daß es keine unreinen Menschen mehr gibt (10,28.34f.; 11,9). Die von Lukas verwendete Tradition besagt: Es gibt ja auch keine unreinen Tiere und kein unreines Essen mehr. Das aber gibt es in dem Dekret.

Die Frage der Unreinheit taucht Apg 15,8-9 wieder auf. Der Besitz des Geistes zeigt, daß Gott jetzt durch den Glauben die Heiden in der Kirche – es geht nicht um alle Heiden, die per definitionem unrein sind! – gereinigt hat. Das kommt für sie nicht mehr durch Beschneidung und totale Gesetzeserfüllung zustande[60]. Die Frage

---

[57] Nicht nur das goldene Kalb, sondern alle Götter scheinen für Lukas von Menschenhänden gemacht zu sein (vgl. Apg 17,29) und zum Anbeten von Menschen (Apg 10,26; 12,22f.; 14,11ff.).

[58] So Bauernfeind 1939, 197; O. Böcher 1989, 325-336; Borgen 1988, 137, 139; Catchpole 1976/77, 429; Conzelmann 1972, 92f.; Esler 1987, 99; Haenchen 1977, 453; J. W. Hunkin 1926, 280f.; Klinghardt 1988, 179-206 (Lev 17f. reiche nicht allein aus); Mußner 1988, 94; O'Neill 1970, 101; Overbeck 1870, 230; Pesch 1986, 81; W. Radl 1991, 56f.; idem 1986, 169-174; Salo 1991, 246f.; Schneider 1982, 187; Simon 1969/70, 450; Strobel 1981, 91; Waitz 1936, 228. Kritisch: Wilson 1983, 84-90, 102; Wedderburn 1993, 362-370.

[59] Es geht im Dekret nicht um die noachitischen Gebote, dazu H. J. Schoeps 1964, 259; Strobel 1981, 92; vgl. Klinghardt 1988, 176-180; Simon 1969/70, 439; Roloff 1988, 227.

[60] Klinghardt 1988, 110f.; Overbeck 1870, 225.

ist so nicht nur das Heil der Heiden (15,1.5), sondern das Verhältnis zwischen Juden und Heiden; 15,9: Gott hat zwischen Juden und Heiden in der Kirche keinen Unterschied gemacht[61]. Israel ist "ein Volk aus den Heiden" beigefügt (Apg 15,14)[62]. Jetzt suchen auch die Heiden den Gott Israels, nachdem das Gottesvolk wiederaufgebaut ist (15.17)[63]. Dadurch kommt ein Neues hinzu: Das Zusammenleben – nicht speziell die Tischgemeinschaft – von Juden und Heiden in der Kirche[64]. Die Frage ist also nunmehr, wie Israel und "das Volk aus den Heiden" zusammenleben können. Weil nun die Kirche Israel ist, kann die Thora nicht abrogiert werden, denn es ist und bleibt das Kennzeichen Israels[65]. Und das Gesetz wird auch gehalten, von den Juden und den Heiden, für die letzteren genau das und soviel von dem Gesetz, was notwendig ist.

Die Apostelgeschichte hindurch bleibt für Lukas der Unterschied zwischen rein und unrein, was nicht zuletzt Apg 21,17ff. zeigt. Neu ist, daß Gott nun die gläubigen Heiden gereinigt und so für das Leben im Gottesvolk fähig macht. Das heißt: falls sie nach dem Dekret leben. Die anderen Heiden sind immer noch unrein. Wenn aber die Heiden durch den Glauben schon gereinigt worden sind, warum dann Gebote über die Reinheit? Die Frage ist abwegig. Die Israeliten, Juden, sind per Definition rein, das heißt weil sie ihre Gebote über Reinheit haben, so auch Lukas (Apg 21,24-26; 24,18). Die Heiden, die Götzenopferfleisch essen, verunreinigen die Juden. Selbstverständlich ist auch ein Gebot gegen Idolatrie notwendig. Das ist ja auch für Juden das erste Gebot und Bekenntnis.

Weil die Kirche ein Anrecht auf Israel hat, ist es wichtig aufzeigen zu können, daß die Kirche das Gesetz erfüllt, während die ungläubigen Juden das Gesetz brechen. Natürlich zeigen auch die Verheißungen das Recht der Kirche, aber darum geht es im Zusammenhang des Dekrets nicht. Rein programmatisch wird gesagt, daß die Juden das Gesetz nicht gehalten haben (Apg 7,53). Dies wird hier mit der Verfolgung von und den Morden auf die Propheten belegt. Nicht daß sie nicht im-

---

[61] Der Vers besage mit 15,10 zusammen, daß das Gesetz weder Juden- noch Heidenchristen verpflichtet, so F. Chr. Baur 1866/67, 135; Haenchen 1977, 428; Overbeck 1870, 226; Conzelmann 1972, 91. Dies wäre richtig, falls wir in V. 10 eine Wesensaussage über das unerfüllbare Gesetz vor uns hätten, was aber nicht der Fall ist, weil die jüdischen Christen nach der Apostelgeschichte keine Schwierigkeiten mit der Erfüllung des Gesetzes haben, es dreht sich um ein Schuldeingeständnis: Wir Juden haben tatsächlich das Gesetz nicht erfüllt (vgl. Apg 7,53), siehe Klinghardt 1988, 110.

[62] Dazu N. A. Dahl 1958, 319-327; J. Dupont 1967, 361-365; G. Lohfink 1975, 59 Anm. 149.

[63] Denn es geht Apg 15,15-18 unmißverständlich um den Wiederaufbau Israels und das Heil der Heiden, und nicht mit Haenchen 1977, 431 und Schneider 1982, 183 um die Auferstehung Jesus als solche.

[64] Vgl. Kümmel 1965, 283.

[65] Anders Horn 1983, 278: "Von einem grundsätzlichen Bleiben der Elemente des Gesetzes kann in Lk/Apg keine Rede sein".

stande waren, das Gesetz zu erfüllen. Es geht 7,53, sowie Apg 7 im ganzen, um Ungehorsam und Unwille. Nichts besagt Apg 7, daß das Gesetz als solches unerfüllbar ist. Sogar der Hohepriester handelt gegen das Gesetz (Apg 23,3). Die Juden haben sogar die gesetzeslosen Heiden benutzt, um den Messias Israels zu töten (Apg 2,23; 4,27). Israel wandte sich an die heidnischen Götter (Apg 7,39ff.). Falsche Zeugen werden von den Juden verwendet (6,11.13.14). Sie sind als Unbeschnittene anzusehen (7,51).

Dagegen wird die Thora von der Kirche ganz streng gehalten. Auch das wird programmatisch gesagt: Die christlichen Juden sind "Eiferer für das Gesetz" (Apg 21,20). Alle Anklagen gegen die Christen wegen Gesetzeskritik sind grundlos (6,11. 13f.; 21,21.28)[66]. Es ist ganz undenkbar, daß die Christen mit Unbeschnittenen verkehren oder etwas unreines essen wollen (Apg 10,14.28; 11,3.8). Paulus, der Missionar par exellence, lebt streng und kompromißlos nach dem Gesetz (18,18; 21,24; 22,3; 23,5.6; 24,14ff.; 25,8; 28,17)[67]. Was über Paulus gesagt wird, gilt für alle Judenchristen, so z.B. 9,36; 16,3.20ff.; 21,12; 22,12. Die Heiden in der Kirche sind gar nicht gesetzeslose, sondern gesetzesfromme, obwohl unbeschnittene (10,1.4. 22.31). Diese Heiden glauben an den Messias Israels, während die ungläubigen Juden ihn töten. Und ihr jüdisches Bekenntnis demonstriert das Dekret.

## Bibliographie

Amphoux, C.-B. – Vaganay, L.1986: *Initiation à la critique textuelle de Nouveau Testament*, Paris: Cerf [2]1986.

Bauernfeind, O.1939: *Die Apostelgeschichte* (ThHK 5), Leipzig: Deichert 1939.

Baur, Fr. Chr.1866/67: *Paulus, der Apostel Jesu Christi*, Leipzig: Fue [2]1866/67.

Beg.: Foakes-Jackson, F. S./Lake, K. (eds.), *The Beginnings of Christianity I. The Acts of the Apostles* I-IV, London: Macmillan 1922-1939.

Blomberg, C. L.1984: "The Law in Luke-Acts", in: *JSNT* 22 (1984) 53-80.

Böcher, O.1989: "Das sogenannte Aposteldekret", in: H. Frankemölle – K. Kertelge (Hgg.), *Vom Urchristentum zu Jesus*, Freiburg: Herder 1989, 325-336.

Boismard, M.-E. – Lamouille, A. 1990: *Les Actes des deux apôtres* (EtB NS 12-14), Paris: Gabalda 1990.

---

[66] Wie u.a. Apg 13,38f. und 15,10 zeigen, ist das eine berechtigte Anklage. Lukas dagegen hält die Anklage für falsch, und Apg 6-7 bestätigt seines Erachtens die kirchliche Treue zum Gesetz, dazu Jervell 1983, 17-32.

[67] Wilson 1980, 257: Die Diskussion über das Gesetz hänge mit der Diskussion über Paulus zusammen, d.h. nicht das Gesetz per se, sondern Paulus sei das Problem. Das stimmt aber nicht mit Apg 6-7 und 10-11, und vor allem natürlich nicht mit dem Lukasevangelium.

Boman, Th. 1964: "Das textkritische Problem des sogenannten Aposteldekrets", in: *NT* 7 (1964) 26-36.

Borgen, P. 1988: "Catalogues of Vices, the Apostolic Decree, and the Jerusalem Meeting", in: J. Neusner, P. Borgen, E. S. Frerichs, R. Horsley (eds.), *The Social World of Formative Christianity and Judaism*, Philadelphia, PA: Fortress 1988, 126-141.

Burkitt, F. C. 1927: "Review of The Beginnings of Christianity Part I. The Acts of the Apostles. Vol. III: The Text of Acts by J. H. Ropes", in: *JThS* 28 (1927) 194-199.

Catchpole, Ph. 1976/77: "Paul, James, and the Apostolic Decree", in: *NTS* 23 (1976/77) 428-444.

Clarke, A. C. 1914: *The Primitive Text of the Gospels and Acts*, Oxford: Clarendon 1914.

Conzelmann, H. 1963/72: *Die Apostelgeschichte* (HNT 7), Tübingen: Mohr (Siebeck) 1963, [2]1972.

Dahl, N. A. 1958: "'A People for His Name' (Acts XV 14)", in: *NTS* 4 (1958) 319-327.

Dibelius, M. 1955: *Aufsätze zur Apostelgeschichte*, hg. H. Greeven (FRLANT 60), Göttingen: Vandenhoeck & Ruprecht 1951; [2]1955.

Dömer, M. 1978: *Das Heil Gottes: Studien zur Theologie des lukanischen Doppelwerkes* (BBB 51), Köln/Bonn: Hanstein 1978.

Dupont, J. 1967: *Études sur les Actes des Apôtres* (LeDiv 45), Paris: Cerf 1967.

Epp, E. J. 1966: *The Theological Tendency of Codex Bezae Cantabrigiensis in Acts* (MSSNTS 3), Cambridge: Cambridge University Press 1966.

Esler, Ph. 1987: *Community and Gospel in Luke-Acts: The Social and Political Motivations of Lucan Theology* (MSSNTS 57), Cambridge: Cambridge University Press 1987.

Franklin, E. 1975: *Christ the Lord. A Study in the Purpose and Theology of Luke-Acts*, London/Philadelphia, PA: SPCK/Westminster 1975.

Glaue, P. 1954: "Der älteste Text der geschichtlichen Bücher des Neuen Testaments", in: *ZNW* 45 (1954) 90-108.

Goppelt, L. 1954: *Christentum und Judentum im ersten und zweiten Jahrhundert. Ein Aufriß der Urgeschichte der Kirche* (BFChTh 55), Gütersloh: Bertelsmann 1954.

Haenchen, E. 1977: *Die Apostelgeschichte* (KEK 3), Göttingen: Vandenhoeck & Ruprecht [7]1977.

von Harnack, A. 1908: *Die Apostelgeschichte: Beiträge zur Einleitung in das NT* 3, Leipzig: Hinrichs'sche Buchhandlung 1908.

Horn, F. W. 1983: *Glaube und Handeln in der Theologie des Lukas* (GTA 26), Göttingen: Vandenhoeck & Ruprecht 1983.

Hunkin, J. W. 1925/26: "The Prohibitions of the Council at Jerusalem", in: *JThS* 27 (1925/26) 272-283.

Hurd, J. C. 1965: *The Origin of I Corinthians*, London: SPCK 1965.

Jervell, J. 1972: *Luke and the People of God. A new Look at Luke-Acts*, Minneapolis, MN: Augsburg 1972.

— 1983: "The Acts of the Apostles and the History of Early Christianity", in: *StTh* 37 (1983) 17-32.

— 1991: "Retrospect and Prospect in Luke-Acts Interpretation", in: *SBLSemPapers 1991*, Atlanta, GA: Scholars Press 1991, 383-404.

— 1994: *The Future of the Past. Luke's Vision of Salvation History and its Bearing on his Writing Salvation History* (B.Witherington, III [ed.], The Acts of the Historians – Acts and Ancient Historiography), Cambridge: Cambridge University Press 1994.

Klinghardt, M. 1988: *Gesetz und Volk Gottes. Das lukanische Verständnis des Gesetzes nach Herkunft, Funktion und seinem Ort in der Geschichte des Urchristentums* (WUNT 2:32), Tübingen: Mohr (Siebeck) 1988.

Knopf, R. 1917: "Die Apostelgeschichte", in: W. Bousset – W. Heitmüller (Hgg.), *Die Schriften des Neuen Testaments III*, Göttingen: Vandenhoeck & Ruprecht ³1917.

Kümmel, W. G. 1965: "Die älteste Form des Aposteldekrets", in: idem, *Heilsgeschehen und Geschichte. Gesammelte Aufsätze 1933-64*, (MThSt 3), Marburg: Elwert 1965, 278-288 [erstmals veröffentlicht 1953].

Lake, K. 1933: "The Apostolic Council of Jerusalem", in: F. J. Jackson – K. Lake (eds.), *The Beginnings of Christianity*, Vol. V, London: Macmillan 1933, 195-212.

Lietzmann, H. 1932: *Geschichte der alten Kirche I*, Berlin: de Gruyter 1932.

— 1933: "Der Sinn des Aposteldekrets und seine Textwandlung", in: H. G. Wood (ed.), *Amicitia Corolla, FS J. Rendel Harris*, London: University of London Press 1933, 203-211.

Lohfink, G. 1975: *Die Sammlung Israels. Eine Untersuchung zur lukanischen Ekklesiologie* (StANT 26), München: Kösel 1975.

Menoud, Ph.-H. 1951: "The Western Text and the Theology of Acts", in: *BSNTS* 2 (1951) 19-32.

Mußner, Fr. 1988: *Apostelgeschichte* (Neue Echter Bibel 5), Würzburg: Echter ²1988.

O'Neill, J. C. 1970: *The Theology of Acts in Its Historical Setting*, London: SPCK ²1970.

Overbeck, F. 1870: *Kurze Erklärung der Apostelgeschichte* (Kurzgefaßtes exeg. Handbuch zum NT von W. L. M. deWette I/4⁴), Leipzig: Weidmann'sche Buchhandlung 1870.

Pesch, R. 1981: "Das Jerusalemer Abkommen und die Lösung des Antiochenischen Konfliktes", in: P. G. Müller/W. Stenger (Hgg.), *Kontinuität und Einheit. FS F. Mußner*, Freiburg: Herder 1981, 105-122.

— 1986: *Die Apostelgeschichte* (EKK 5/2), Zürich/Neukirchen-Vluyn: Benziger/Neukirchener Verlag 1986.

Radl, W. 1986: "Das Gesetz in Apg 15", in: K. Kertelge (Hg.), *Das Gesetz im Neuen Testament*, Freiburg: Herder 1986, 169-174.

— 1991: "Rettung in Israel", in: C. Bußmann – W. Radl (Hg.), *Der Treue Gottes trauen, FS G. Schneider*, Freiburg: Herder 1991, 43-60.

Richard, E. 1980: "The Divine Purpose: The Jews and the Gentile Mission (Acts 15)", in: *SBLSemPapers 1980*, Chico, CA: Scholars Press 1980, 267-280.

Roloff, J. 1988: *Die Apostelgeschichte* (NTD 5), Göttingen: Vandenhoeck & Ruprecht ²1988.

Ropes, J. H. 1926: "The Text of Acts", in: F. J. Jackson – K. Lake (eds.), *The Beginnings of Christianity*, Vol. III, London: Macmillan 1926.

Salo, K. 1991: *Luke's Treatment of the Law. A Redaction-Critical Investigation* (AASF 57), Helsinki: Suomalainen Tiedeakatemia 1991.

Sanders, J. T. 1991: "Who is a Jew and Who is a Gentile in the Book of Acts?", in: *NTS* 37 (1991) 434-455.

Schenke, L. 1990: *Die Urgemeinde: Geschichtliche und theologische Entwicklung*, Stuttgart: Kohlhammer 1990.

Schlatter, A. 1913/62: *Die Apostelgeschichte* (Erläuterungen zum NT 4), Stuttgart: Calwer 1913, <sup>4</sup>1962.

Schneider, G. 1982: *Die Apostelgeschichte II* (HThK V/2), Freiburg: Herder 1982.

Schoeps, H. J. 1964: *Das Judenchristentum. Untersuchungen über Gruppenbildungen und Parteikämpfe in der frühen Christenheit* (Dalp-Taschenbücher), Bern: Francke 1964.

Scroggs, H. C. 1960: "The Composition of the Lucan Writings", in: *HThR* (1960) 36-45.

Simon, M. 1969/70: "The Apostolic Decree and its Setting in the Ancient Church", in: *BJRL* 52 (1969/70) 437-460.

— 1978: "De l'observance rituelle à l'ascèse: recherches sur le Décret Apostolique", in: *RHR* 193 (1978) 27-104.

Stählin, W. 1962: *Die Apostelgeschichte* (NTD 5), Göttingen: Vandenhoeck & Ruprecht 1962; <sup>4</sup>1970.

Stolle, W. 1973: *Der Zeuge als Angeklagter. Untersuchungen zum Paulusbild des Lukas* (BWANT 102), Stuttgart: Kohlhammer 1973.

Strange, W. A. 1992: *The Problem of the Text of Acts* (MSSNTS 71), Cambridge: Cambridge University Press 1992.

Strobel, A. 1981: "Das Aposteldekret als Folge des antiochenischen Streites: Überlegungen zum Verhältnis von Wahrheit und Einheit im Gespräch der Kirchen", in: P. G. Müller/W. Stenger (Hgg.), *Kontinuität und Einheit. FS F. Mußner*, Freiburg: Herder 1981, 81-104.

Tissot, Y. 1970: "Les prescriptions des presbytres (Actes, XV, 41,D)", in: *RB* 77 (1970) 321-346.

Trocmé, É. 1957: *Le Livre des Actes et l'historie* (EHPhR 45), Paris: Presses Universitaires de France 1957.

Waitz, H. 1936: "Das Problem des sogenannten Aposteldekrets und die damit zusammenhängenden literarischen und geschichtlichen Probleme des apostolischen Zeitalters", in: *ZKG* 551 (1936) 228.

Wedderburn, A. J. M. 1993: "The 'Apostolic Decree': Tradition and Redaction", in: *NT* 34 (1993) 362-89.

Weiser, A. 1981: *Die Apostelgeschichte I* (ÖTBK 5/1), Gütersloh/Würzburg: Gerd Mohn/Echter 1981.

— 1985: *Die Apostelgeschichte II* (ÖTBK 5/2), Gütersloh/Würzburg: Gerd Mohn/Echter 1985.

Wikenhauser, R. 1961: *Die Apostelgeschichte* (RNT 5), Regensburg: Pustet <sup>4</sup>1961.

Wilson, S. G. 1980: "Law and Judaism", in: *SBLSemPapers 1980*, Chico, CA: Scholars Press 1980, 251-265.

— 1983: *Luke and the Law* (MSSNTS 50), Cambridge: Cambridge University Press 1983.

# Die Christuspredigt des Paulus in Athen
## (Act 17,16-33)

### Andreas Lindemann

Die Areopagrede, die Lukas in Act 17,22-31 als einzige Missionsrede des Paulus vor einem ausschließlich heidnischen Publikum überliefert[1] und die er wahrscheinlich auch selbst konzipiert hat[2], gilt vielfach als ein geradezu "klassisches" Beispiel für die Spannung, ja für den Gegensatz zwischen der paulinischen und der lukanischen Theologie und damit als charakteristisches Zeugnis für den den wirklichen Paulus verfehlenden "Paulinismus" der Apostelgeschichte[3]. Die Rede wird gesehen als Dokument der lukanischen Rezeption hellenistischen Denkens[4]; und sie gilt, vor allem wegen der erst ganz am Ende folgenden, indirekten christologischen Wendung[5], als ein eher mißglückter Versuch, die authentische paulinische Missionspredigt darzustellen[6]. Dieses Urteil mag richtig sein, wenn man – wie es überwiegend geschieht – die eigentliche wörtliche Rede in 17,22b-31 von ihrem Kontext isoliert;

---

[1] Die kurze Ansprache in Act 14,15-17 dient nur dazu, die göttliche Verehrung der Apostel (14,14) Barnabas und Paulus zurückzuweisen; vgl. Schweizer 1957, 424f.

[2] So die überwiegend in der Exegese vertretene Position; vgl. Conzelmann 1958, 92: "Ich selbst halte die Rede für eine freie Gestaltung des Schriftstellers" – nicht zuletzt deshalb, weil rahmende Szenerie und Rede unmittelbar aufeinander bezogen sind.

[3] So sehr nachdrücklich und die weitere Exegese vielfach bestimmend Vielhauer 1950/51, 10-14. AaO. 13: "Der Verfasser dieser Rede hat aus der Heidenpredigt des Paulus die Christologie eliminiert". S. 14: "Seine Ferne zu Paulus ist ebenso deutlich wie seine Nähe zu den Apologeten".

[4] Nach Dibelius 1939a, 54 ist die Areopagrede "eine hellenistische Rede von der wahren Gotteserkenntnis", "eine hellenistische Rede mit christlichem Schluß".

[5] Schweizer 1957, 425: "Anstelle des Christuszeugnisses tritt hier vor Heiden die Gottesverkündigung"; "die Christusverkündigung ist *strukturell* gesehen nur ein Anhang der Rede" (426; Hervorhebung im Original). Ähnlich schon Dibelius 1939a, 53: "Endlich wird Jesus einmal erwähnt", wobei er aber hinzufügt, das Fehlen des Namens könne "als eine Feinheit des Textes gelten … Die Angabe 17,18 … gibt im voraus den Kommentar dazu" (ebenda A 2). Vgl. Vielhauer 1950/51, 12.

[6] Ich habe selbst die These vertreten, die Areopagrede sei "sachlich nicht von paulinischer Theologie berührt" und zeige keine "Nähe zu einem der Paulusbriefe" (Lindemann 1979, 169 unter Berufung auf Vielhauer). Dieses Urteil ist, wie im folgenden zu zeigen ist, nicht aufrechtzuerhalten.

wird jedoch der Gesamtrahmen der lukanischen Darstellung des Aufenthalts des Paulus in Athen in die Auslegung der Rede einbezogen, so ändert sich das Bild. Gerade bei der Auslegung der Apostelgeschichte ist es wichtig, die "Textwelt" zu erfassen, die Lukas seinen Lesern schildert[7]; in dieser Textwelt aber stellt die Szene "Paulus in Athen" eine Einheit dar, aus der die Areopagrede nicht herausgeschnitten werden darf.

Das Problem einer möglichen Scheidung von Tradition und Redaktion spielt für die folgenden Überlegungen eine allenfalls untergeordnete Rolle. So wird häufig angenommen, in V. 17 und V. 34 zeigten sich Spuren des "Itinerars", dessen karge Angaben – so J. Roloff – von Lukas dazu benutzt worden seien, eine eigene Konzeption zu schaffen, "die von der unverwechselbaren Handschrift ihres Verfassers geprägt ist"[8]. R. Pesch findet in V. 15-17 und V. 34 Notizen des Itinerars; er hält im übrigen aber nur V. 21 für redaktionell lukanisch und führt V. 18-33 auf eine von Lukas bearbeitete Quelle zurück[9]. Zweifellos ist Paulus tatsächlich in Athen gewesen (I Thess 3,1); doch kann die Frage, welcher Quelle Lukas sein Wissen darüber verdankt, hier unerörtert bleiben.

Lukas beginnt (V. 16) seinen Bericht mit einem Hinweis auf das Entsetzen des Paulus[10] über die Götterbilder in Athen, wobei er den diese bezeichnenden Begriff κατείδωλον selbst geschaffen zu haben scheint[11]. V. 17 zufolge nutzt Paulus die offenbar längere Wartezeit bis zum Eintreffen von Silas und Timotheus aus Thessalonich zu Unterredungen[12], und zwar mit Juden und Gottesfürchtigen in der Synagoge, sowie mit zufällig Vorüberkommenden täglich[13] auf der ἀγορά[14]. Über die Reaktionen dieser Gesprächspartner des Paulus wird nichts gesagt, und auch nichts über die Themen dieser Unterredungen. Dann aber heißt es (V.18), daß einige

---

[7] Vgl. die grundsätzlichen Überlegungen zur Auslegung der Apostelgeschichte bei Hartman 1992, 122f., dort bezogen auf das Verhältnis der traditionellen Taufformeln und der lukanischen "Textwelt", in der jene jetzt begegnen.

[8] Roloff 1981, 254.

[9] Pesch 1986, 129-133.

[10] Die Verwendung des Verbs παροξύνεσθαι, zeigt, daß Lukas aus der Perspektive des Paulus heraus formuliert, während der Hinweis auf die Götzenbilder (κατείδωλον) ein Faktum beschreiben soll.

[11] Vgl. Büchsel 1935, 376f. Bemerkenswert ist, wie in der Rede auf dem Areopag selbst derselbe Tatbestand einleitend (V. 22b.23a) als Anlaß einer *captatio benevolentiae* dient, die vom Leser der Apostelgeschichte auf der Grundlage von V. 16 freilich ganz anders wahrgenommen wird als von den Hörern des Paulus in der Erzählung.

[12] Das Verb διαλέγομαι begegnet erstmals in Act 17,2, dann hier und noch achtmal bis Act 24. Lukas scheint geneigt, es immer zweimal kurz nacheinander zu verwenden.

[13] Das κατὰ πᾶσαν ἡμέραν wird implizieren, daß das διαλέγεσθαι in der Synagoge jeweils nur am Sabbat stattfindet; aber ganz sicher ist das nicht.

[14] Zur athenischen Agora vgl. Elliger 1978, 158-173.

der epikuräischen und stoischen Philosophen den Dialog mit Paulus aufnehmen[15]; Lukas teilt nun mit, daß sich einige sehr negativ äußern, indem sie den christlichen Gesprächspartner einen σπερμολόγος nennen[16], der nichts Bedeutsames mitzuteilen wisse[17], während andere interessiert sind und immerhin auf den Inhalt dessen eingehen, wovon Paulus spricht: Er scheine ein καταγγελεύς fremder δαιμόνια zu sein. Die Verwendung des Begriffs καταγγελεύς[18] signalisiert dem Leser der Apostelgeschichte, daß Paulus als Verkündiger einer für Athen fremden Religion eingeordnet wird[19].

Erst an dieser Stelle seines Berichts schiebt Lukas (V. 18 am Schluß) als erläuternden Kommentar den Hinweis ein, Paulus verkündige[20] fortwährend (Imperfekt) "Jesus und die Auferstehung". Diese knappe Notiz hat zu vielfältigen Auslegungen geführt, vor allem im Blick auf ihre Verknüpfung mit der vorangegangenen Charakterisierung des Paulus als eines "Herolds fremder Götter". So wird die These vertreten, die philosophischen Kontrahenten des Paulus hätten "Jesus und die Anastasis" für zwei Götter, geradezu für ein Götterpaar gehalten[21]. Oder es wird erklärt, Lukas habe den Anschein erwecken wollen, die paulinische Predigt sei von den Philosophen in dieser Weise fehlinterpretiert worden, damit deren Unverstand umso deutlicher herausgestellt werde[22]. Solche Auslegungen sind unwahrscheinlich. Daß die philosophischen Hörer das von Paulus Gesagte derart fundamental mißverstanden und Paulus also derart mißverständlich gesprochen haben könnte, ist von Lukas durch nichts angedeutet; man müßte geradezu annehmen, Lukas habe

---

[15] Das Verb συμβάλλειν ist hier wohl synonym mit διαλέγεσθαι, obwohl es an sich einen kritischen Beiklang haben könnte. Zu beachten ist das Imperfekt, das auf einen länger andauernden Vorgang verweisen soll.

[16] Zum Begriff σπερμολόγος vgl. Norden 1913, 333.

[17] Der den Philosophen in den Mund gelegte Satz ist sprachlich kunstvoll gestaltet; vgl. Blaß/Debrunner/Rehkopf 1984, § 385.

[18] Vgl. dazu Schniewind 1933, 71: καταγγελεύς ist der "*Verkünder* nicht im Sinn von 'Lehrer', sondern von *Herold*" (Hervorhebungen im Original).

[19] Zu δαιμόνια vgl. Bauer 1988 s.v. δαιμόνιον.

[20] Der Wechsel von καταγγελεύς zum Verb εὐαγγελίζεσθαι, ist natürlich bewußt vorgenommen worden: Paulus ist nicht einfach "Herold", sondern er verkündigt die "gute Botschaft".

[21] Conzelmann 1958, 94 A 5: Man frage sich, ob Lukas spielerisch "die Zuhörer des Paulus dahin mißverstehen" lassen wolle, daß dieser "ein neues, orientalisches Götterpaar" bringe. Zustimmend Lüdemann 1987, 197; ähnlich Roloff 1981, 258 und auch Pesch 1986, 134. Conzelmann 1972, 105 dagegen differenzierter: "Der christliche Leser jedenfalls versteht, daß hier die zentrale Thematik der christlichen Predigt – im Sinne der lukanischen Theologie – zusammengefaßt ist und vernimmt die folgende Rede als Ausführung derselben." Leider läßt es Conzelmann bei dieser Andeutung bewenden.

[22] So die Vermutung von Külling 1993, 163: Das Thema der Areopagrede sei Gott, und zwar deshalb, weil "die irrtümliche Ansicht" zerstört werden sollte, "als ob es sich bei 'Jesus' und der 'Auferstehung' um Götter nach athenischem oder griechischem Verständnis handle".

der paulinischen Predigt indirekt ein schlechtes Zeugnis hinsichtlich ihrer Versteh-
barkeit ausstellen wollen. Vor allem aber ist zu beachten, daß V. 18fin nicht aus der
Perspektive der philosophischen Disputanten formuliert ist[23], sondern daß der Satz
eine unmittelbar an die Adressaten der Apostelgeschichte gerichtete, objektive Information enthält; kein Leser der Apostelgeschichte aber konnte auf den Gedanken
kommen, "Jesus und die Auferstehung/Anastasis" als Gegenstand paulinischer Predigt könnten zwei Götter gewesen sein. Die Aussage in V. 18fin besagt also nichts
anderes, als daß die Verkündigung des Paulus in seinen Gesprächen mit den
epikuräischen und den stoischen Philosophen Jesus und die Auferstehung zum Inhalt hatte[24], wobei beide Stichworte substantiell vom bisherigen Inhalt der Apostelgeschichte her zu verstehen sind; unklar bleibt lediglich zunächst, ob ἡ ἀνάστασις
die Auferstehung Jesu oder aber die allgemeine Auferstehung (der Toten) meint.
Das zuvor erwähnte Urteil, Paulus spreche von "fremden Göttern", faßt nicht "Jesus
und die Auferstehung" als eine Mehrzahl von Göttern auf, sondern es enthält eine
unspezifische Verallgemeinerung: Die Jesus-Predigt des Paulus führt nach der
Wahrnehmung der Philosophen nicht einen bestimmten neuen Gott ein, sondern sie
spricht einfach von "fremden Göttern" – am Detail ist man nicht interessiert (was
sich jedoch ändern wird)[25]. Entscheidend für diese Auslegung ist die Beobachtung,
daß der erläuternde Satz am Ende von V. 18 im Unterschied zur zweifachen in V. 18
vorangehenden wörtlichen Rede nicht eine subjektive Wertung übermittelt, sondern
daß Lukas hier über einen Tatbestand informiert: Ursache für die zitierten Urteile
war die Predigt des Paulus über Jesus und die Auferstehung. Freilich wird diese
Schlußbemerkung nicht nur das Thema der Debatte mit den Philosophen angeben,
sondern man wird sie auch auf V. 17 zurückbeziehen dürfen – auch die Gespräche
in der Synagoge und auf der Agora hatten Jesus und die Auferstehung zum Gegenstand. So hebt Lukas durch V. 18fin sehr betont die Christus-Bezogenheit der paulinischen Predigt in Athen hervor.

In V. 19-21 wird nun mitgeteilt, daß das Interesse der Athener[26] erwacht, über

---

[23] Lukas schreibt nicht, die Hörer hätten *gemeint*, Paulus rede von zwei Göttern.

[24] So zutreffend, wenn auch knapp, Burchard 1970, 140.

[25] Schille 1983, 355: "Der Plural 'fremde Götter' verlangt nicht unbedingt nach einer Auflösung im Kontext".

[26] Daß in V. 19 nicht mehr speziell von den Philosophen, sondern allgemein von den Bewohnern Athens die Rede ist, zeigt V. 21. Burchard 1970, 140 sieht demgegenüber in V. 19.20 die "'epikuräi-schen und stoischen Philosophen'" als Fragende, die nicht um eine gesonderte Predigt bitten, "son-dern um eine Erläuterung, die das Befremden beseitigt und Einsicht ermöglicht". Es ist aber eher unwahrscheinlich, daß die Aufforderungen in V. 19.20 von denselben Leuten ausgehen sollen, deren Urteile doch unmittelbar zuvor (V. 18) zitiert worden waren. Richtig Schneider 1982, 236: "Die Leu-te nehmen Paulus mit und führen ihn zum Areopag", wobei ἐπιλαμβάνομαι, hier nicht den Aspekt des Gewaltsamen enthalte (ebenda A 49).

die Lehre des Paulus näher informiert zu werden[27]. Wieder ist die Erzählebene zu beachten: Diejenigen, die etwas über die "neue Lehre" des Paulus erfahren wollen (V. 19), kennen offenbar die in V. 18 zitierten Urteile der Epikuräer und der Stoiker; aber sie wollen sich damit nicht zufrieden geben, sondern sie erwarten genauere Informationen[28]. Als kritische Erläuterung fügt Lukas in V. 21 allerdings hinzu, Ursache des Interesses der Athener sei eigentlich nur ihre Neugier, ihre Begeisterung für alles Neue[29]. Ob diese Bemerkung allerdings besagen soll, "die Möglichkeit zu einem echten Dialog" sei von vornherein "verbaut" gewesen[30], ist fraglich; immerhin sieht sich Paulus als Reaktion zu einer längeren Rede veranlaßt, die am Ende beim Publikum zu durchaus unterschiedlichen Konsequenzen führen wird.

In der Rede, die Paulus ἐν μέσῳ τοῦ Ἀρείου πάγου[31] hält, geht es vordergründig fast ausschließlich um "Gott und Mensch", geradezu um eine "natürliche Theologie"; es ist für die Interpretation dieser Rede aber zu beachten, was der Anlaß für diese Rede – nach Lukas! – war, nämlich die Verkündigung Jesu und der Auferstehung. Die Areopagrede steht also im Kontext ganz unter einem christologischen Vorzeichen; sie soll gelesen werden als die für Athen angemessene Form der Ant-

---

[27] In der Exegese wird immer wieder auf Parallelen in der Sokratesüberlieferung verwiesen, vor allem auf die Anklage wegen der Einführung von καινὰ δαιμόνια (Plato *Apol.* 24b; Xenophon *Mem.* I 1,1). Sprachliche Anklänge mögen vorhanden sein (freilich ist an beiden erwähnten Textstellen ausdrücklich von "*anderen* neuen δαιμόνια" die Rede); Lukas erweckt aber in keiner Weise den Anschein, Paulus sei in Athen einer offiziellen Anklage konfrontiert gewesen.

[28] Die Wiederholung V. 19b/V. 20b soll offenbar anzeigen, daß das Interesse ein dringendes ist.

[29] Pesch 1986, 130f. sieht in V. 21 eine lukanische Erläuterung zu einer Quelle, aus der dann nicht nur V. 16-20.22-23 stamme, sondern auch die ganze Areopagrede, da diese mit der Einleitung ja fest verbunden sei (132f.).

[30] So Roloff 1981, 259.

[31] Keinesfalls denkt Lukas beim "Areopag" an eine Behörde oder gar an einen "Gerichtshof", vor dem sich Paulus verteidigen müßte. Unwahrscheinlich und jedenfalls nicht zu belegen ist auch die Erwägung von Pesch 1986, 130, in der Quelle (s.o. A 29) sei "die oberste Behörde Athens" gemeint gewesen, und erst durch V. 21 sei "das – vielleicht schon von Lukas geteilte – Mißverständnis, als sei vom Ares-Hügel die Rede", entstanden. Pesch aaO. 135 liest aus V. 20 heraus, es sei den Philosophen, die Paulus "vor den Areopag führen", "zunächst um die 'Erkenntnis'" gegangen, "dem Areopag wohl auch um die Beurteilung der Erkenntnisse". Um diese Erwägung plausibler zu machen, führt Pesch die Möglichkeit ein, es könne statt des Areopags auch "eine seiner Kommissionen" gemeint sein, wovon im Text nichts zu sehen ist. Peschs Hinweis auf analoge Vorgänge in Philippi (16,19) und Thessalonich (17,6f.) trägt wenig aus, denn dort wird ausdrücklich geschildert, wie die Behörde jeweils reagiert, wovon im Falle Athens nicht die Rede ist. Darauf verweist auch Elliger 1978, 172-175, der zu Recht erklärt, sowohl die Anspielungen auf Sokrates wie auch die Erwähnung des Areopags gehörten "zum szenischen Inventar des historischen Rahmens": "Wollte Lukas ein unverkennbares Bild Athens auch nur in Andeutungen skizzieren, so durfte der bekannteste Bürger der Stadt ebensowenig fehlen wie die berühmte Gerichtsstätte", die es – anders als Agora und Akropolis – nur in Athen gab (aaO. 179.178).

wort auf die in V. 20 gestellte Frage, die sich an der Jesus-Predigt des Paulus (V. 18) entzündet hatte.

Die Areopagrede nimmt explizit das philosophische Interesse am Wesen und der Erkennbarkeit Gottes auf; das in V. 22b-29 Gesagte könnte tatsächlich auch in einer zeitgenössischen philosophischen Erörterung stehen, zumindest im Kontext der Stoa[32]. Lukas will damit aber offensichtlich gerade zeigen, daß dieses Denken dazu geeignet ist, die Predigt des Paulus von Jesus und der Auferstehung philosophisch interessierten Hörern verständlich zu machen. Was der lukanische Paulus in V. 22b-29 über das Wesen Gottes sagt, kann bei den Adressaten (und zwar sowohl bei den Athenern auf der Erzählebene wie auch bei den impliziten Lesern der Apostelgeschichte selbst) nur auf Zustimmung stoßen[33]. Erst in V. 30.31 kommt Paulus, gleichsam nach einer langen "Vorbemerkung", auf das eigentliche Thema bzw. den Anlaß seiner Rede zu sprechen[34]: Der Gott, dessen Wesen von Paulus so eingehend und plausibel dargestellt worden war, läßt jetzt (νῦν) den Menschen die Notwendigkeit der Buße verkündigen, weil er beschlossen hat, die οἰκουμένη in Gerechtigkeit zu richten[35]. Eben darauf, so stellt Paulus in V. 31 fest, bezieht sich seine Botschaft von Jesus und der Auferstehung (V. 18): Gott hat eben diesen Jesus als den endzeitlichen Richter vorgesehen; und um das zu belegen, hat er ihn von den Toten auferweckt. Mit dieser Aussage in V. 31fin schließt sich der mit V. 18 begonnene Kreis; zugleich wird klar, daß ἡ ἀνάστασις in V. 18 offenbar nicht die allgemeine Totenauferstehung bezeichnet hatte, sondern daß von Jesu Auferstehung die Rede gewesen war[36].

Das eigentliche Thema der Areopagrede ist also die Botschaft von der durch seine Auferstehung beglaubigten Stellung Jesu als des von Gott eingesetzten Richters

---

[32] Dies wird betont von Burchard 1970, 140: Es handele sich um eine Rede, "die das verkündigte Neue als längst vertraut, nur verkannt, erklärt". Conzelmann 1958, 94f. hatte gemeint, Lukas knüpfe "nicht an die monotheistischen Elemente der zeitgenössischen Philosophie", insbesondere der Stoa, an, "sondern an ein Motiv der Volksreligion", die auch sonst belegten "den unbekannten Göttern" geweihten Altäre. Aber schon die lukanische Umformulierung der Altarinschrift vom Plural in den Singular zielt offenkundig darauf, den Monotheismus als ein bei den Adressaten heimlich schon vorhandenes religiöses Prinzip zu benennen.

[33] Auf das religionskritische Denken der "epikuräischen Philosophen" (V. 18) geht die Rede nicht ein; Lukas verbindet mit den beiden Schul-Namen offenbar keine bestimmten philosophischen Positionen.

[34] Burchard 1970, 140 betont nachdrücklich den "Umbruch" nach V. 29: "V. 30f. unterscheiden sich inhaltlich und formal vom Vorhergehenden". Anders Conzelmann 1972; 110f.: "Schon die Szenerie hatte auf diesen Inhalt als den zentralen hingewiesen (V. 18), So bilden der erste, biblisch gefärbte Teil der Rede und dieser christologische die Klammer um den anthropologischen Mittelteil".

[35] Schille 1983, 359: Der christologische Schluß komme keineswegs "unvermittelt"; angesichts der "Unwissenheit" gerät die christliche Verkündigung "fast in den Rang einer Naturnotwendigkeit".

am bevorstehenden Tag des Gerichts. Durch die Klammer in V. 18 und V. 30.31 erweist sich diese Rede als eine christologisch-eschatologische Predigt; ihre so breit ausgeführte theologische Akzentuierung soll primär dazu dienen, einem an philosophischem Denken orientierten Publikum das Christus-Kerygma verstehbar zu machen.

Es ist umstritten, ob V. 32 signalisiert, die Rede des Paulus sei von den Hörern unterbrochen worden[37]. Tatsächlich ist durch nichts angedeutet, daß die Paulusrede unvollständig sein könnte; mit V. 30.31 ist das Ziel erreicht, insofern die Aussage von V. 18fin nun hinreichend erklärt worden ist[38]. Dem entspricht es, daß die Predigt unterschiedliche Reaktionen der Hörer zur Folge hat: Bei den einen löst das Stichwort ἀνάστασις νεκρῶν Spott aus, d.h. diese Reaktion ist gegenüber der Ausgangslage (V. 18) unverändert[39]; andere dagegen zeigen sich interessiert, und sie wünschen weitere Belehrung[40]. Damit allerdings ist – so scheint es – der Auftritt des Paulus zuende, "er geht davon" (V. 33)[41]. Doch nun wird – völlig überraschend – nachgetragen, daß "einige", darunter zwei namentlich genannte Personen[42], sich Paulus anschlossen[43] und ihm glaubten (V. 34). Im Anschluß an V. 32.33 scheint die Notiz in V. 34 nachzuklappen; tatsächlich aber steht sie gerade an dieser Stelle sehr

---

[36] Dibelius 1939a, 62 A 1 sieht hier die von ihm regelmäßig beobachtete Spannung zwischen V. 22b-30 einerseits und V. 31 sowie V. 18 andererseits: Nach 17,18 "hat man den Eindruck, daß Jesus und die Auferstehung der Toten die Hauptthemen der Verkündigung seien; die Rede erwähnt Jesus nur am Ende, und ohne Namen, und statt der Totenauferstehung hören wir nur von der Auferstehung Jesu". Um diese aber geht es offensichtlich an beiden Stellen.

[37] So Schneider 1982, 243: Eigentlich hätten die Hörer "nach der Intention des Redners ... an diesem Punkt nach dem Namen des Mannes fragen" sollen, und "dann hätte hier das Christus-Kerygma eingesetzt". Roloff 1981, 266: "Um der dramatischen Pointe willen" werde betont, daß Paulus "zum Abbruch der Rede genötigt" worden sei; doch "in Wirklichkeit ist die Rede ein in sich abgeschlossenes Ganzes". Von einem solchen inneren Widerspruch aber läßt die lukanische Darstellung nichts erkennen; die Hörer reagieren, nachdem Paulus seine das Christus-Kerygma (V. 18fin) explizierende Rede zum Abschluß gebracht hat.

[38] Daß der Name 'Jesus' nicht erwähnt ist, braucht nach V. 18 nicht zu verwundern.

[39] An wen speziell bei den "Spöttern" gedacht sein könnte (Schneider 1982, 243 fragt, ob die Epikuräer gemeint sind), läßt sich nicht sagen (s.o. A 33).

[40] Dibelius 1939a, 66 A 2: "Die Zusage einiger Hörer, den Apostel wieder hören zu wollen, ist als Verlegenheitsauskunft und nicht als ernstes Versprechen gedacht, denn Paulus geht ja gar nicht darauf ein". Noch kritischer Schneider 1982, 244: Die Reaktionen seien beide "letztlich ablehnend". Ähnlich Roloff 1981, 266, der auf Act 2,13; 24,25 als Parallelen verweist. Aber οἱ μὲν ... οἱ δέ signalisiert doch wohl einen wirklichen Unterschied in den Reaktionen der Hörer; und die beiden von Roloff genannten Textstellen enthalten ganz andere Formulierungen.

[41] Nach Schille 1983, 360 meint diese "Regiebemerkung" "weder einen kümmerlichen noch einen glimpflichen Abgang". Nach Schneider 1982, 233 müßte "jetzt die christologische Verkündigung folgen", d.h. die heidnischen Hörer sollten sich näher informieren; stattdessen aber weichen sie aus, und deshalb verläßt Paulus sie.

sinnvoll: Paulus verläßt den Areopag, und erst jetzt stellt sich heraus, daß ihm etliche Hörer und zumindest eine Hörerin folgen. In V. 34 wird also ein Zustand beschrieben, der erst mit dem nicht näher datierten Weggang des Paulus aus Athen (18,1) aus dem Blick gerät[44]. Die Predigt des Paulus auf dem Areopag ist nach dem von Lukas gezeichneten Bild jedenfalls alles andere als erfolglos geblieben[45].

Hat sich Lukas so wie in Act 17,16-33 beschrieben die angemessene christliche Heidenmissionspredigt vorgestellt? M. Dibelius hat das bejaht[46], während etwa H. Conzelmann meint, hier gehe es nicht um eine Musterpredigt, sondern um die Schilderung eines Diskussionserfolges des Paulus über die philosophischen Kontrahenten seiner Zeit[47]. Aber die Feststellung, die Areopagrede sei im Verständnis des Lukas gar keine Predigt[48], trifft den Befund nicht. Zwar handelt es sich tatsächlich gerade nicht um eine Erstinformation über den Inhalt des christlichen Glaubens, denn diese ist schon in V. 16-18 vorangegangen; wohl aber wendet sich der lukanische Paulus in V. 29 und vor allem in V. 30 unmittelbar an die Adressaten, wenn er sagt, daß "alle Menschen" zur Buße aufgerufen sind angesichts des bevorstehenden Gerichts.

Hat Lukas mit seiner Areopagrede die Heidenmissionsverkündigung des authentischen Paulus verfehlt? Die einzige einigermaßen deutliche Bezugnahme des Apostels selbst auf diese Predigt liegt in I Thess 1,9f. vor, wo Paulus vermutlich keine Formel zitiert, sondern in verkürzender Aufnahme des Predigtinhalts an seine ge-

---

[42] Lüdemann 1987, 202 meint, Damaris und Dionysios seien "wohl historisch". Jedenfalls entspricht der Hinweis auf den Status des Dionysios der auch sonst zu beobachtenden Neigung des Lukas, Honoratioren von der Predigt des Paulus überzeugt sein zu lassen; möglicherweise sieht er in Dionysios ein Mitglied der athenischen Stadtverwaltung. Lukanischer Intention entspricht auch die gesonderte, ausdrückliche Erwähnung einer Frau (vgl. Richter Reimer 1992, 253f.).

[43] Daß sich die in V. 34 Erwähnten Paulus zunächst angeschlossen hätten und erst daraufhin "(nach weiterer Belehrung) zum Glauben kamen" (so Schneider 1982, 244), ist im Text durch nichts angedeutet.

[44] Pesch 1986, 133 sieht die "Wirkung" der Areopagrede in V. 32.33 ausgesagt, während V. 34 "den bescheidenen Missionserfolg des Paulus in Athen" erwähne. Aber V. 32-34 bilden eine Einheit, und über die Zahl derer, die sich Paulus anschließen, ist nichts gesagt.

[45] Zum Hintergrund von V. 34 vgl. Lüdemann 1987, 200f. Auch Lüdemann meint, einen "großen Missionserfolg" habe Paulus in Athen vermutlich nicht gehabt, zumal eine athenische Gemeinde auch sonst keine Rolle spiele (aaO. 202). Dibelius 1939a, 68 leitet mit Blick auf die Itinerar-Hypothese aus V. 34 den Gedanken ab, Dionysios und Damaris seien zwar "als willige Hörer" anzusehen, aber nicht als wirkliche Christen. Demgegenüber folgert Schille 1983, 360 aus V. 34 die Gründung einer kleinen Gemeinde (nach Lukas! – nicht historisch). Beides dürfte über das im Text Erkennbare hinausgehen.

[46] Dibelius 1939a, 74 A 1.

[47] Conzelmann 1958, 103.

[48] So Lüdemann 1987, 198.

meindegründende Verkündigung in Thessalonich erinnert[49]. Diese Predigt-Kurz-fassung berührt sich nun freilich doch recht eng mit der lukanischen Szene "Paulus in Athen"[50] – allerdings mit dem Unterschied, daß Paulus in Thessalonich es offen-kundig nicht mit einem philosophisch gebildeten Publikum zu tun hatte und seine Predigt deshalb nicht an einen vorhandenen theoretischen Monotheismus anknüp-fen konnte; er mußte daher die Verkündigung des allein wahren Gottes im Gegen-über zu "den Göttern" zunächst ganz ins Zentrum rücken. Im übrigen aber stimmen, trotz erheblicher Differenzen im theologischen Detail[51], die Predigtthemen hier wie dort erkennbar überein[52]: Es geht um die Rede von Gott und um die Erwartung des von den Toten auferweckten Jesus als des endzeitlichen Richters[53], die im Bekennt-nis dann freilich so formuliert ist, daß Jesus "uns" bewahrt vor diesem künftigen Gericht, was der lukanische Paulus in seiner Predigt vor den Athenern so (noch) nicht sagen kann.

Diese Übereinstimmungen müssen nicht zu dem Schluß führen, daß Lukas den Ersten Thessalonicherbrief gekannt hat, obwohl dies keineswegs ausgeschlossen werden muß[54]. Es kommt vielmehr in erster Linie auf die Feststellung an, daß Lu-kas zumindest die Tendenz der paulinischen Heidenmissionspredigt richtig getrof-fen hat und daß er Paulus in dessen einziger Missionsrede vor heidnischem Publikum durchaus nicht "unpaulinisch" predigen läßt. In vollem Umfang sichtbar wird dies freilich erst, wenn man die Areopagrede nicht aus ihrem literarischen Zu-sammenhang herauslöst, sondern sie im Gegenteil ganz von dem Kontext her liest, für den sie von ihrem Autor geschaffen wurde.

---

[49] Vgl. dazu Holtz 1986, 54-64.

[50] Vgl. dazu Wilckens 1974, 87-91.

[51] Die Differenzen betreffen vor allem das Problem der "natürlichen" Gotteserkenntnis, die der lukanische Paulus eher positiv aufnimmt, während der historische Paulus sie bestreitet (Röm 1), so-wie den bei Paulus selbst gar nicht anklingenden Gedanken einer Gottesverwandtschaft des Men-schen.

[52] Vgl. die Zusammenstellung der Parallelen bzw. Analogien bei Pesch 1986, 141f.

[53] Dieser Aspekt ist stark betont von Burchard 1970, 141.

[54] Vgl. Lindemann 1979, 171: "Die Frage, ob Lukas paulinische Briefe gekannt hat, läßt sich m.E. mit einem vorsichtigen Ja beantworten." Auf das Verhältnis von I Thess 1,9.10 zu Act 17 war ich in meinem Buch allerdings nicht eingegangen.

## Bibliographie

Bauer, W. 1988: *Griechisch-deutsches Wörterbuch zu den Schriften des Neuen Testaments und der frühchristlichen Literatur*, 6. Auflage, hg. von K. Aland und B. Aland, Berlin und New York: de Gruyter 1988.

Blaß, F./Debrunner, A./Rehkopf, F. 1984: *Grammatik des neutestamentlichen Griechisch*, 16. Auflage, Göttingen: Vandenhoeck & Ruprecht 1984.

Büchsel, F. 1935: Art. "εἴδωλον κτλ.", in: *ThWNT* II, Stuttgart: Kohlhammer 1935, 373-377.

Burchard, Chr. 1970: *Der dreizehnte Zeuge. Traditions- und kompositionsgeschichtliche Untersuchungen zu Lukas' Darstellung der Frühzeit des Paulus* (FRLANT 103), Göttingen: Vandenhoeck & Ruprecht 1970.

Conzelmann, H. 1958: "Die Rede des Paulus auf dem Areopag" (1958), in: ders., *Theologie als Schriftauslegung. Aufsätze zum Neuen Testament* (BEvTh 65), München: Chr. Kaiser 1974, 91-105.

— 1972: *Die Apostelgeschichte* (HNT 7), 2. Auflage, Tübingen: Mohr (Siebeck) 1972.

Dibelius, M. 1939a: "Paulus auf dem Areopag" (1939), in: ders., *Aufsätze zur Apostelgeschichte*, hg. von H. Greeven (FRLANT 60), Göttingen: Vandenhoeck & Ruprecht 1951, 29-70.

— 1939b: "Paulus in Athen" (1939), *aaO.*, 71-75.

Elliger, W. 1978: *Paulus in Griechenland. Philippi, Thessaloniki, Athen, Korinth* (SBS 92/93), Stuttgart: Katholisches Bibelwerk 1978.

Haenchen, E. 1965: *Die Apostelgeschichte* (KEK III), 5. Auflage, Göttingen: Vandenhoeck & Ruprecht 1965.

Hartman, L. 1992: *"Auf den Namen des Herrn Jesus". Die Taufe in den neutestamentlichen Schriften* (SBS 148), Stuttgart: Katholisches Bibelwerk 1992.

Holtz, T. 1986: *Der erste Brief an die Thessalonicher* (EKK XIII), Zürich und Neukirchen-Vluyn: Benziger und Neukirchener Verlag 1986.

Külling, H. 1993: *Geoffenbartes Geheimnis. Eine Auslegung von Apostelgeschichte 17,16-34* (AThANT 79), Zürich: Theologischer Verlag 1993.

Lindemann, A. 1979: *Paulus im ältesten Christentum. Das Bild des Apostels und die Rezeption der paulinischen Theologie in der frühchristlichen Literatur bis Marcion* (BHTh 58), Tübingen: Mohr (Siebeck) 1979.

Lüdemann, G. 1987: *Das frühe Christentum nach den Traditionen der Apostelgeschichte. Ein Kommentar*, Göttingen: Vandenhoeck & Ruprecht 1987.

Norden, E. 1913: *Agnostos Theos. Untersuchungen zur Formengeschichte religiöser Rede*, Darmstadt: Wissenschaftliche Buchgesellschaft 1956 (= 1913).

Pesch, R. 1986: *Die Apostelgeschichte*, 2. Teilband Apg 13-28 (EKK V/2), Zürich und Neukirchen-Vluyn: Benziger und Neukirchener Verlag 1986.

Richter Reimer, I. 1992: *Frauen in der Apostelgeschichte des Lukas. Eine feministisch-theologische Exegese*, Gütersloh: Gütersloher Verlagshaus Gerd Mohn 1992.

Roloff, J. 1981: *Die Apostelgeschichte* (NTD 5), Göttingen: Vandenhoeck & Ruprecht 1981.

Schille, G. 1983: *Die Apostelgeschichte des Lukas* (ThHK V), Berlin: Evangelische Verlagsanstalt 1983.

Schneider, G. 1982: *Die Apostelgeschichte*. II. Teil. Kommentar zu Kap. 9,1-28,31 (HThK V/2), Freiburg usw.: Herder 1982.

Schniewind, J. 1933: Art. "ἀγγελία κτλ.", in: *ThWNT* I, Stuttgart: Kohlhammer 1933, 56-71.

Schweizer, E. 1957: "Zu den Reden der Apostelgeschichte" (1957), in: ders., *Neotestamentica. Deutsche und englische Aufsätze 1951-1963. German and English Essays 1951-1963*, Zürich/Stuttgart: Zwingli Verlag 1963, 418-428.

Vielhauer, Ph. 1950/51: "Zum 'Paulinismus' der Apostelgeschichte" (1950/51), in: ders., *Aufsätze zum Neuen Testament* (TB 31), München: Chr. Kaiser 1965, 9-27.

Wilckens, U. 1974: *Die Missionsreden der Apostelgeschichte. Form- und traditionsgeschichtliche Untersuchungen* (WMANT 5), 3. Auflage, Neukirchen-Vluyn: Neukirchener Verlag 1974.

# 'Do Not Be Idolaters!' (1 Cor 10:7)

## Karl-Gustav Sandelin

### 1. The Problem

In several instances Paul reveals his strong Jewish resentment at the polytheistic beliefs prevalent in the Hellenistic world.[1] He praises the Thessalonians who "turned from idols, to be servants of the living and true God" (1 Thess 1:9). He reminds the Galatians that they, before they knew God, "were the slaves of beings which in their nature are no gods" (Gal 4:8). He also refers to the knowledge of the Corinthians concerning their previous pagan life: how they were swept off to the dumb idols (1 Cor 12:2). In the letter to the Romans Paul is even more explicit in his description of idolatry and its consequences (Rom 1:23ff.).

In 1 Cor 10:1-22 Paul warns the Corinthians not to participate in pagan cults. The command "Do not be idolaters!" (1 Cor 10:7) stands in the context of a lengthy description of what befell the fathers in the desert (1 Cor 10:1-10). These had been baptized into Moses (1 Cor 10:2) and had received spiritual food and drink (1 Cor 10:3-4). But God was not pleased with them (1 Cor 10:5) and they were punished for sins they had committed, like idolatry (1 Cor 10:7) and fornication (1 Cor 10:8).

According to many modern standard commentators, this Pauline account was motivated by a current feature in Corinthian community life: some of the Corinthians were over-confident in the effects of the sacraments.[2] The Corinthian "sacramentalists"[3] maintained that baptism[4] and eucharist gave them protection against

---

[1] This article is a contribution resulting from an Inter-Scandinavian project on Hellenistic Judaism and Early Christianity (1988-1993) with Professor Lars Hartman, Professor Peder Borgen, Rev. Per-Jarle Bekken and the present author as participants.

[2] Lietzmann – Kümmel 1969, 45-47; Weiß 1910, 250, 254; Barrett 1968, 25, 220, 227; Conzelmann 1969, 28, 30, 194, 197; Wolff 1982, 39; Lang 1986, 6, 26, 122-124; Klauck 1987, 71.

[3] Such a term is used by Bornkamm 1956, 317. Bornkamm refers to v. Soden 1951, 245-46 (cf. 259), who interprets Paul with the words: "God does not allow that he be used like a talisman". Käsemann 1947/48, 270 and Bandstra 1971, 6 understand the Corinthian position in the same way.

[4] Cf. Carlson 1993, 261.

everything that threatened their future salvation. Therefore they did not see any danger in, for instance, sexual immorality (1 Cor 6:12, 15; 10:8) or participation in pagan cultic activities (1 Cor 8:1, 4; 10:14-22).

Now, according to this standard interpretation, Paul wants the over-confident sacramentalists to understand that something similar to that which befell the fathers could happen to themselves. The events in the desert were written down in order to set a warning example to those who are confronted with the end of times (1 Cor 10:11). As a matter of fact the gift of the sacraments did not give such protection as the over-confident Corinthians believed. Therefore Paul warns the one who thinks that he stands firm lest he should fall (1 Cor 10:12).

In some of the commentaries referred to above Corinthian sacramentalism is seen as a manifestation of attitudes witnessed in other sections of 1 Corinthians, such as being strong (1 Cor 4:10),[5] having freedom to do anything (1 Cor 6:12),[6] possessing knowledge (1 Cor 8:1),[7] and having the Spirit (1 Cor 12:4).[8] The relationship between freedom, knowledge and possession of the Spirit among the Corinthians is described in the following way by Hans Conzelmann: the conduct of the Corinthians "is grounded on a freedom principle (6:12; 10:23); this in turn rests upon 'knowledge' (8:1), and the latter derives from experience of the Spirit (12:4ff.)".[9] But actually 1 Cor 12:1-13 does not describe the position of the Corinthians but that of Paul! And the relationship between freedom in 1 Cor 6:12 and knowledge in 1 Cor 8:1 is not as self-evident as Conzelmann suggests. It can of course be maintained that those in Corinth, who supposed they had the knowledge (γνῶσις) that no idols exist (1 Cor 8:1, 4, 7, 10, 11), based their freedom (ἐξουσία) to eat meat offered through pagan rituals on such knowledge (1 Cor 8:9). This freedom may also have been formulated in the sentence "everything is permitted" (πάντα ἔξεστιν), which Paul cites when discussing the question of idol meat in 1 Cor 10:23-31. But in the context of 1 Cor 6:12, where a similar sentence is cited, no "knowledge" of the kind just mentioned is implied.[10] Thus it is very uncertain if Lietzmann is right when he asserts that the "one who thinks that he stands" (1 Cor 10:12) is the "gnostic" of 1 Cor 6:12 and 8:1, 10 who is sure of his salvation.[11] For

---

[5] Lietzmann – Kümmel 1969, 46; Conzelmann 1969, 197. See also Broer 1989, 317.

[6] Lang 1986, 122.

[7] Lietzmann – Kümmel 1969, 46.

[8] Conzelmann 1969, 197; Lang 1986, 122.

[9] Conzelmann 1988, 14.

[10] Many authors think that the expression πάντα μοι ἔξεστιν "I am free to do anything" could in one way or another originally have emanated from Paul himself. Robertson-Plummer 1911, 121; Weiß 1910, 157; Lietzmann – Kümmel 1969, 27. Conzelmann 1986, 109 states: "The Corinthians apparently derive it from Paul's doctrine of freedom".

[11] Lietzmann – Kümmel 1969, 47.

instance, J. Weiß regards it as a presumption (Vermutung) that 1 Cor 6:12 and 8:1 reflect the principles of the Corinthian "gnostics".[12]

Interpreting 1 Cor 10:1-13 by taking one's point of departure in 1 Cor 8:1-13, where Paul is perhaps discussing with the "gnostics" and therefore using common slogans, has its risks. It is, as a matter of fact, an open question whether Paul is addressing the same problem in the two texts mentioned.[13] In 1 Cor 8 the question causing debate seems to be idol meat,[14] whereas 1 Cor 10:1-22 seems to discuss idolatry in a broader sense (verses 7 and 14).[15] Nevertheless banqueting implying meat offered to idols is also taken up in 1 Cor 10:7, 19-21. In 1 Cor 8:9-13 Paul, with regard to the brother who has a weak conscience,[16] pleads against eating idol meat for instance when visiting a pagan shrine.[17] In 1 Cor 10:27-29 he may have a similar situation in mind or an invitation to a private house where meat is served.[18] In 1 Cor 10:14, 20-21 Paul categorically seems to forbid participation at pagan ritual performances.[19] Because of the intensity with which Paul makes his case in 1 Cor 10:1-22, it is probable that there existed people in the Christian community of Corinth who attended pagan religious occasions. Paul does not, however, name anyone, nor does he say if there were many or few such persons. But are these people the same as those who have such a strong conscience that they are able to eat idol meat? If the plain consumers of idol meat and the attendants at pagan rituals are the same persons, then 1 Cor 10:1-13 may be seen as directed against people claiming that they have the knowledge that no idols exist. But if this were the case, are we here dealing with a phenomenon of boastful knowledge based upon the claim of the possession of the Spirit? In any case it is necessary to study 1 Cor 10:1-13 as such, without taking 1 Cor 8 as a starting-point for the interpretation.

The theory that in 1 Cor 10 Paul is addressing over-confident sacramentalists seems to rest on the following assumptions, which are deductions from the text, not statements in the text itself. First, the admonition in v. 12: "Let the man who thinks that he stands beware lest he should fall" is understood as directed against people

---

[12] Weiß 1910, 157.

[13] The discussion is well described by Broer 1989, 301-04.

[14] See Willis 1985, 110-22.

[15] Cf. Walter 1979, 429-27.

[16] See the discussion of Willis 1985, 89-96, 117-20.

[17] Cf. Willis 1985, 103.

[18] See Willis 1985, 235-39.

[19] Some authors think that the visit to a pagan shrine and eating there in 1 Cor 8:10 is for Paul actually equivalent to the pagan worship Paul has in mind in 1 Cor 10:20-21. Paul condemns both, but uses different arguments in the two cases. See Merklein 1984, 162-69. Others think that Paul differentiates. He accepts the presence of Christians at social gatherings including meals at the shrines, but he does not accept the eating of idol meat at such occasions. See Oster 1992, 64-67.

who believe nothing can threaten their future salvation. Secondly, the sentence is often seen as the goal towards which Paul is aiming in 1 Cor 10:1-11.[20] Thirdly, although verse 12 does not directly say one word about the sacraments, it is understood as a warning against sacramental security.[21] This idea is based on 1 Cor 10:2-4. Paul's words concerning baptism into Moses and spiritual food and drink are understood as referring to the Christian sacraments in two ways: a) the over-confident people in Corinth thought that the Christian sacraments protected them and b) Paul had this in mind when he wrote 1 Cor 10:2-4.

If we give the sentences of Paul the value of known (K) and such derivatives which also serve as explanations for Paul's words the value of unknown (U), we get a short description of the structure of the interpretation: The idea of "the man who thinks he stands..."(K) is Paul's reaction on a Corinthian position meaning "nothing can threaten our salvation" (U) "because we have received the sacraments" (U). Paul argues that the fathers received "sacraments" (U), but still sinned and were punished (K). Therefore the addressees should not sin like the fathers (K). An understanding of verse 12 based on these known and unknown factors then means: "The one who thinks nothing can threaten his future salvation since he has received the sacraments should beware lest he fall, i.e. he should beware lest he sin, because in that case he will be punished with the loss of salvation".

The standard explanation of 1 Cor 10:1-13 has something very logical and consistent about it. But this consistency seems to be a result of the fact that the factors which explain the text are deductions from the text itself. But is an understanding of a text which operates with such a set of unknown factors satisfactory as a reliable exegesis?

Now it cannot of course be denied that 1 Cor 10:12 may be seen as a warning against over-confidence comparable to what we find in Rom 11:20.[22] But even then, if the thought of 1 Cor 10:12 in the mind of Paul may imply that he thinks that his addressees feel too secure, this does not necessarily mean that he thinks that this security derives from "sacramentalism", because Paul does not explicitly say that the Corinthians rely for their security on the sacraments.[23]

In an article published in the Congress volume of the Conference on the New Testament and Hellenistic Judaism held in Aarhus on 5 – 8 February 1992 I chal-

---

[20] According to Barrett 1968, 228 Paul in verse 12 proceeds to make the purpose of the preceding paragraph explicit. Lang 1986, 122 states that verse 12 is the "Skopus" of 1 Cor 10:1-13. Murphy-O'Connor 1990, 807 states concerning verse 12: "This is the point of the whole section".

[21] Barrett 1968, 228; Conzelmann 1969, 199; Lang 1986, 126. Wolff 1982, 39 is very precise at this point: "Die Warnung vor dem Fall in V. 12 läßt erkennen, daß die Korinther meinten, durch Genuß der Sakramente vor dem Abfall zum Götzendienst und seinen Folgen geschützt zu sein".

[22] Cf. Weiß 1910, 254.

lenge the standard view. In my opinion, Paul in 1 Cor 10:1-13 adheres to a pattern found in Old Testament, Jewish and New Testament texts which see the apostasy of the people against the background of the beneficent acts of God (Deut 32:7-27; Exod 32; Neh 9:6-37; Ps 78; 95:8-11; 106; Bar 2:11-15; Philo, *Mos.* 2.271; Heb 3:8-11). Such texts do not, however, contain the thought that the people of Israel sinned because they had the idea that nothing could harm them since God had saved them. Instead the sins, among them idolatry, are signs of the abandoning of God by a people who do not trust in him. Why should Paul refer to such stories in order to admonish people who from his point of view are over-confident? In his account of the fathers in 1 Cor 10:1-10 Paul does not explicitly describe them as over-confident. Paul sees the events in the desert as prefigurations of the Christian sacraments. Just as the fathers were baptized into Moses and received spiritual food and drink, so the Corinthians have become baptized into Christ and have participated in the Lord's supper. These events were gifts from God. Now the Corinthians should take warning and not participate in pagan cults, because this in turn would mean apostasy from faith, as in the case of the fathers.

In the present article I want to take a closer look at the argument of Paul in 1 Cor 10:1-14. If we try to maintain that Paul does not argue against over-confidence in this passage, we have to give another explanation to Paul's words in v. 12 "Let the man who thinks that he stands beware lest he should fall". What does he mean by these words in this context? What is their relation to the preceding statements? Our first task, then, is to analyse 1 Cor 10:1-11. When Paul refers to the events that befell the fathers in the desert by first describing the blissful events and then the punishments, does he create the account by himself, independently using Old Testament tradition? Or is he using an existing text, which he comments upon? If the latter were the case, Paul's possible additions would give us some clues to understanding his own position. The question we have raised has been actualized by W. A. Meeks.

---

[23] Cf. Robertson – Plummer 1911, 208 who admit that security exists among the Corinthians which perhaps makes them feel "secure against contamination from idol-feasts", nevertheless state: "It is less likely that there is a reference to one who thinks that through the sacrament he ipso facto possesses eternal life with God". Also Wendland 1978, 78 is cautious: "Vielleicht hat man sich in Korinth zur Begründung der unbegrenzten Freiheit auch auf die Sakramente berufen..." The idea that the Corinthians built their security on the sacraments is energetically attacked by Schmithals 1969, 370-71. Against v. Soden (1951) Schmithals maintains that the false security of the Corinthians does not derive from their partaking of the sacraments but from their "gnosis". Also Willis 1985, 140-41 argues against the proposed sacramentalism among the Corinthians. In the commentary of Orr – Walther 1976, 244-49, there is no special stress on sacramentalism.

## *2. Analysis of 1 Cor 10:1-10*

W. A. Meeks maintains that in 1 Cor 10:1-13 we may have a separate homily, composed prior to its use in the present context and containing two sets of five similar statements, i.e. five examples of benevolent acts of God in the desert and five examples of rebellion on the part of the fathers. The homily may have been written by Paul himself or by somebody else and later inserted by the apostle at its present place.[24] I think the observations of Meeks concerning the composition of the passage are very fruitful. I would, however, like to develop the idea somewhat differently by taking as my points of departure certain features which regularly reappear in the two series of events presented. I would suggest two basic criteria for pre-pauline origin: (a) Old Testament references and (b) regular features which both stand in contrast to (α) details not having any base in the O.T. and to (β) features which obscure the regularities in the structure. An additional criterion would be the fact that many of the features in the description of the events in the desert have no correspondence with the situation in Corinth insofar as this is known to us from the first letter to the Corinthians.

According to 1 Cor 10:1-4, the five blissful events in the desert, in Paul's words, befell all of "our fathers": the cloud, the baptism into Moses, the sea, the food and the drink. Four of the events also have another feature in common: they are all recorded in the Bible: the cloud (Exod 13:21-22; 14:19, 24; Num 14:14), the sea (Exod 14: 21-22; Num 33:8), the manna (Exod 16: 4, 15; Num 11:6), the drink from the rock (Exod 17:6; Num 20:8). The idea of becoming baptized into Moses is not, however, found in the Old Testament. Nor do we here find the idea that the food and the drink were "spiritual". The "rock" (v. 4) is well known from the Bible (Exod 17:6; Num 20:8-11; Deut 8:15). But the sentence speaking about this rock gives a motivation (γάρ) and in addition contains the ideas that it was spiritual and followed the fathers, statements lacking in the Old Testament. Paul also says that the rock was Christ, a statement which has to be a Christian comment. If we take away the statements that do not have any clear Old Testament base, we are left with four events: (1) our fathers were all under the cloud, (2) they all went through the sea, (3) they all ate the same food and (4) they all drank the same drink from the rock (the rock being mentioned in an explanatory sentence). The rest of the passage is an amplification compared with the Old Testament text.[25] If the series of four blissful events has its counterpart in the series of four examples of rebellion presented in a unified manner, we get two series of four events each. Let us therefore turn to the presenta-

---

[24] Meeks 1982, 64-78. Schüssler Fiorenza 1988, 1181 seems to follow Meeks at this point.

[25] In a previous work I have tried to argue in favour of the commonly held hypothesis that Paul here draws on wisdom-tradition. See Sandelin 1987, 165-72.

tion of the rebellion against God.

The warning has in the last three examples of rebellion (fornication, testing the Lord and grumbling, vv. 8-10) almost the same structure: let us not (viz. do not) commit A, as some of them did (A), and who (therefore) were punished with B. In addition, these examples all refer to events recorded in Numbers (chaps. 11, 14, 21 and 25) although some of the wordings also seem to refer to Exodus (Exod 12:23; 17:2-3) or the Psalms (Ps 78:18; 106:14, 25). In contradistinction to the structure prevalent in verses 8-10 the wording of verse 7 on idolatry is quite different. The first part of the verse is similar in form to verses 8-10: "Do not be idolaters, like some of them". But the word εἰδωλολάτρης does not occur in the LXX, nor do we find it in Philo or Josephus. Further, the latter part of verse 7 does not have a phrase corresponding to the words "as some of them did", but instead says "like some of them, as it is written" and then adds a verbatim citation from Exodus (Exod 32:6). Verse 7 therefore may have originated from Paul himself.[26] Is verse 6 of Pauline origin, too? Here we on the one hand have the same kind of expression at the end as in verses 8-10 ("as they did"), but on the other hand this phrase is introduced by a prepositional infinitive clause: εἰς τὸ μὴ εἶναι ἡμᾶς ἐπιθυμητὰι κακῶν, "not to set our desires on evil things". In verses 7-10 we have clauses with imperatives or subjunctives at this point. This could speak in favour of an original Pauline statement. But the sentence with the infinitive in verse 6 is a result of the preceding sentence, which says that the events occurred as "examples (τύποι) for us". Now Paul makes a similar statement in verse 11, having finished the series of rebellion: "These things happened to them as examples (τυπικῶς) and were written down as a warning for us, ...." Verse 6 can thus be seen as a result of Paul's reshaping of a statement which originally had a form coming close to verses 8-10: "let us not set our desires on evil things, as some of them did, and who therefore were punished with ...." Perhaps the word κακῶν (evil things) is a Pauline addition since the episode referred to lacks this word. The event is recorded in Num 11:4-6, which tells about the desire of the people for meat and other food they had been used to in Egypt instead of the manna. The punishment for this act of rebellion is mentioned in the same chapter, verses 33-34: the people were struck with a severe plague.

If the analysis above is correct, we would have four cases of rebellion all recorded in the book of Numbers and all originally presented in a similar formal manner. Of these four cases only "fornication" has some counterpart in the context of the letter (1 Cor 6:18; 7:2), whereas the ideas of being desirous, testing the Lord and grumbling are confined to 1 Cor 10:6-10 and do not point to the situation in Corinth,[27] which speaks in favour of a pre-Pauline text. Verses 6a (but these events

---

[26] Thus Schüssler Fiorenza 1988, 1182.
[27] Cf. Willis 1985, 151-52; Broer 1989, 313-14.

occurred as examples for us), the word κακῶν (evil things), and 7 (do not be idolaters etc.) would be Pauline additions to the original non-Pauline enumeration of rebellion lying behind vv. 6-10 and corresponding to the four blissful events mentioned in 1 Cor 10:1-4. The name Χριστός in verse 9, if original,[28] would be a Pauline modification, too. Since the first three admonitions are in the first person plural, we may perhaps allow ourselves to suggest this as an original form also for verse 10: μηδὲ γογγύζωμεν (let us not grumble). The second person imperative form in verse 10 may stem from Paul, who uses this in verse 7: μηδὲ εἰδωλολάτραι γίνεσθε (do not be idolaters).

If it is reasonable to postulate that 1 Cor 10:1-4 and 6-10 contains two pre-Pauline lists, one enumerating four blissful events in the desert and the other a set of four examples of rebellion together with warnings not to commit similar sins, then we must ask if verse 5 could contain the original pre-Pauline link between these two lists. We have already noted that both halves of the verse have their counterparts in the Old Testament (Jer 14:10 and Num 14:16, 28-39). Therefore it is possible that 1 Cor 10:5 was a part of the pre-Pauline text.

We have thus reached the point where we can present a possible pre-Pauline text forming a substratum of 1 Cor 10:1-10:

---

[28] If we use external criteria the word Χριστόν receives very strong support from Papyrus 46 (around A.D. 200), although this reading is heavily contested by important textual witnesses having κύριον. The argument based on internal criteria presented by Metzger is reasonable. For some copyists it was difficult to think that Israelites in the wilderness tempted Christ. The ambigous κύριον or the unobjectionable θεόν therefore seemed more suitable. See Metzger 1971, 560.

v. 1.          οἱ πατέρες ἡμῶν
               πάντες ὑπὸ τὴν νεφέλην ἦσαν
      καὶ      πάντες διὰ τῆς θαλάσσης διῆλθον
v. 2.          .........
v. 3.    καὶ   πάντες τὸ αὐτὸ βρῶμα ἔφαγον
v. 4.    καὶ   πάντες τὸ αὐτὸ ἔπιον πόμα.


               .........
v. 5.          ἀλλ' οὐκ ἐν τοῖς πλείοσιν αὐτῶν εὐδόκησεν ὁ θεός,
               κατεστρώθησαν γὰρ ἐν τῇ ἐρήμῳ.

v. 6.          [διὰ τοῦτο] .........
               [μὴ γινώμεθα ἐπιθυμηταὶ]
                     καθὼς [τινες αὐτῶν] ἐπεθύμησαν
                     [καὶ ἐπάταξεν κύριος αὐτοὺς πληγήν.]
v. 7.          .........
v. 8.          μηδὲ πορνεύωμεν,
                     καθὼς τινες αὐτῶν ἐπόρνευσαν
                     καὶ ἔπεσαν μιᾷ ἡμέρᾳ εἴκοσι τρεῖς χιλιάδες.
v. 9.          μηδὲ ἐκπειράζωμεν τὸν κύριον,
                     καθὼς τινες αὐτῶν ἐπείρασαν
                     καὶ ὑπὸ τῶν ὄφεων ἀπώλλυντο.
v. 10.         μηδὲ γογγύζωμεν,
                     καθὼς τινες αὐτῶν ἐγόγγυσαν
                     καὶ ἀπώλοντο ὑπὸ τοῦ ὀλοθρευτοῦ.


Translation:

v. 1.          Our fathers
               were all under the cloud
               and all went through the sea
v. 3.          and all ate the same food
v. 4.          and all drank the same drink.

v. 5.          Nevertheless, God was not pleased with most of them,
               for their bodies were scattered over the desert.

v. 6.          Therefore:
               let us not be desirous,
               as some of them,
               so that the Lord struck them with plague.
v. 8.          And let us not commit fornication,
               as some of them did,
               and twenty-three thousand died in one day.
v. 9.          And let us not put the Lord to the test,
               as some of them did,
               and were destroyed by the serpents.
v. 10.         And let us not grumble,
               as some of them did,
               and were killed by the Destroyer.

As a result of our analysis we may presume that Paul for his own purposes used a Jewish admonition based on the Old Testament not to rebel against God. The pattern containing blessings of God in contraposition to examples of rebellion may be found in several Old Testament, Jewish and New Testament texts (Deut 32:7-27; Exod 32; Neh 9:6-37; Ps 78; 95:8-11; 106; Bar 2:11-15; Philo, *Mos.* 2.271; Heb 3:8-11).[29]

### 3. Paul's Utilization of the Pre-Pauline Injunction.

If it has been correct to assume that Paul is adding his own ideas to a Jewish text, then we ought to be able to see his intentions from these very additions and his subsequent remarks in 1 Cor 10:11-13 (partly also verses 14-22).

According to our view, verse 7 on idolatry is an addition. Since Paul in 1 Cor 10:14 draws the conclusion that the Corinthians should flee from idolatry, the admonition in 1 Cor 10:7 must be one of the central utterances in the whole passage. The pre-Pauline text may be understood as referring to idolatry in the admonition not to commit adultery (1 Cor 10:8) with its reference to the Phinehas-episode in Numbers 25.[30] This feature is given a stronger emphasis by Paul by his adding of 1 Cor 10:7; thus the problem of idolatry in Corinth may be seen as a main reason for Paul to take up the Jewish text. It is also reasonable to think that Paul in the other sinful acts of the fathers could see idolatry because of the close relationship between the pre-Pauline text and Psalms 78 and 106. We find the "testing" of the Lord in Ps 78:18, the "desire" and the "grumbling" in Ps 106:14, 25. Both psalms contain the idea of apostasy to other gods (Ps 78:58; 106:19-20).[31] If Paul has added the word κακῶν (evil things) in 1 Cor 10:6 he may have idolatry in mind.[32]

The citation Paul makes from the episode of the golden calf is chosen with great care: "the people sat down to eat (φαγεῖν) and drink (πεῖν) and rose up to play"

---

[29] Cf. Jeske 1980, 245-55 who also distinguishes between pre-Pauline elements and Pauline additions in 1 Cor 10:1-13. According to Jeske, verses 1-4, 6a, 11, 13, and 16-17 represent a Corinthian position of Christians with a strong ecclesiological identity and eschatological awereness. Paul makes critical corrections by adding verses 5, 6b-10, 12 and 14.

[30] Cf. Meeks 1982, 68-69, who thinks that verse 7 belonged to the original homily because it is hard to imagine a "list of the wilderness generation's sins" without mentioning idolatry. But actually verse 8 (on fornication) contains such a reference. In the Old Testament fornication and idolatry are often associated with one another. See for instance Jer 13: 25-27; Ezek 16:15-16; Hos 2.

[31] Cf. Sandelin 1987, 171.

[32] Cf. Barrett 1968, 224.

(Exod 32:6). The verse actualizes idolatrous eating and drinking,[33] thus pointing forward to 1 Cor 10:21, where Paul stresses the impossibility for a Christian to eat and drink at the table of the demons.[34] But it also points backward to the eating and drinking in the desert.[35] The events that had taken place in the desert were prefigurations for the Christians. They happened that we should not desire evil things (1 Cor 10:6). But they also had a positive aspect. The fathers were baptized into Moses and received spiritual food and spiritual drink from the accompanying rock which was Christ (1 Cor 10:2-4).[36] By adding the words in 1 Cor 10:7 Paul stresses one specific point when he describes the contrast between the gracious gifts of God and the apostasy of the fathers. He particularly contrasts the spiritual food and drink in the desert and the food and drink consumed around the golden calf.[37] Therefore the contrast between the table and cup of the Lord and the table and cup of the demons in 1 Cor 10:21 seems to be implied by Paul already in 1 Cor 10:3-4, 7.

Now Paul says that although all the fathers received something that prefigured Christian sacraments, God was not pleased with most of them (1 Cor 10:1-5a). Why was God not pleased? Nothing in these verses (or in the passages which these verses refer to in the Old Testament) indicates that God was angry with the people because they were over-confident. The reasons for the punishments also manifested in the scattering of the bodies over the desert (1 Cor 10:5b) were different acts of apostasy (1 Cor 10:6-10). Nor do we here have any reference to over-confidence. Paul's interest in these verses is concentrated upon idolatry (1 Cor 10:7).

In 1 Cor 10:11 Paul repeats what he has said in 1 Cor 10:6 by adding a reference to "these things" which have "been written as a warning to us on whom the fulfilment of the ages has come". The idea that the Scriptures were written for the Christians is elsewhere attested in Paul. In 1 Cor 10:11, as in Rom 4:23-24, the thought has a special eschatological nuance and motivation.[38] The Christians are the eschatological people of God (cf. 1 Cor 1:23-24).[39] Thus far the thought of Paul seems

---

[33] Bandstra 1971, 17 states: "This verse does not explicitly mention idolatry, and therefore one needs to see this verse in its context to understand that it referred to an idolatrous banquet followed by idolatrous sport. Here, in order for the quotation to prove the point, the larger context of the quotation must have been operative in Paul's mind; no doubt the context of a quotation is important for understanding the use made of other quotations as well". Cf. Broer 1989, 131; Wolff 1982, 44.

[34] Cf. Weiß 1910, 252; Barrett 1968, 225; Wolff 1982, 44; Lang 1986, 125.

[35] Cf. Conzelmann 1969, 197.

[36] For the rather loose relationship between these gifts to the fathers in the desert and the gifts of the Christian sacraments, see Sandelin 1987, 167-70.

[37] I do not agree with Meeks 1982, 69 that "eat and drink" in verse 7 means the same thing as eating and drinking in verse 3-4.

[38] Cf. Wolff 1982, 45.

[39] Cf. Lang 1986, 30-31.

to be that the Christians, like the fathers, have received benefits from God. But the fathers fell into idolatry and other kinds of sins and were punished. This ought to serve as a warning to the Christians not to fall into idolatry like the fathers.

Now problems arise when we come to 1 Cor 10:12. Why does Paul here seem to make such a strong case against over-confidence? Does he not say: "Let the man, who thinks that he stands believing that he cannot fall, beware. He may fall"? If this is what he means, it looks as if Paul has kept the whole idea hidden up to this point. The standard theory of course presupposes that the Corinthian over-confident people (like the modern exegetes) were at the very beginning of the passage 1 Cor 10:1-13 already supposed to see the implications. Speaking of the baptism into Moses and the spiritual food and drink in the desert, Paul was in an oblique way addressing their over-confident sacramentalism. But if Paul neither refers to sacramentalism nor to over-confidence in 1 Cor 10:1-10, then the injunction against over-confidence in 1 Cor 10:12 looks very odd. One would even be tempted to dismiss 1 Cor 10:12 as a gloss, were it not so strongly attested in the manuscripts!

It is therefore very understandable that exegetes have sought the motive for Paul's words in the Corinthian community. Since Paul apparently criticizes over-confidence in 1 Cor 10:12, it is thought, there must have existed over-confident people in Corinth, probably the same people as the gnostics in 1 Cor 8. In order, then, to find a Corinthian position which would correspond to Paul's words in 1 Cor 10:1-10, exegetes have suggested that some Corinthians based their over-confidence on the salvific effects of the sacraments.

But is the only possible interpretation of 1 Cor 10:12 to see it as an injunction against over-confidence? As such it certainly would have parallels in Paul: "If somebody fancies himself wise ..., let him become a fool" (1 Cor 3:18), "... if a man imagines himself to be something, when he is nothing, he is deluding himself" (Gal 6:3). But can the expression ὁ δοκῶν ἑστάναι (the man who thinks that he stands) only designate such presumption as the examples just mentioned? Philologically there is a slight difference. 1 Cor 3:18 and Gal 6:3 have conditional clauses, whereas Paul in 1 Cor 10:12 uses a participle. The English translation from which the versions of 1 Cor 3:18 and Gal 6:3 above are taken[40] gives a somewhat milder tone to the expression in 1 Cor 10:12: "If you feel sure that you are standing firm".

To "stand" in 1 Cor 10:12 no doubt implies the concept of standing "in faith" (Rom 11:20; 1 Cor 16:13; 2 Cor 1:24; cf. 1 Thess 3:8; 1 Cor 15:1; Phil 4:1).[41] Actually there is a link from this idea of standing in faith in 1 Cor 10:12 to the preceding verse, which talks of "us on whom the fulfilment of the ages has come", i.e. the believers. So, when in 1 Cor 10:11 he has stated that the events described in 1 Cor

---

[40] The New English Bible.

[41] Cf. Wolff 1982, 48; Lang 1986, 126; Broer 1989, 318.

10:1-10 were written as warnings for "us", i.e. the Christians,[42] Paul in verse 12 continues to speak of Christians. In verse 11 he does not limit the relevance of the events in the desert and the warnings to particular Christians. He even includes himself since he speaks of "us". All Christians seem to be in need of warning.

Paul in 1 Cor 10:12 draws a conclusion from what he has said before, a conclusion which ends up with a warning against falling. Is it probable that Paul in verse 12 limits the perspective, thereby applying the words "let the man who thinks that he stands (in faith), beware, lest he should fall" to particular Christians, who in contradistinction to other Christians think that they stand "firm"?[43] I do not think it is necessary to understand Paul in this way. The words "the one who thinks that he stands (in faith)" probably have the same addressees as those for whom the events in the desert were written down as a warning, i.e. all Christians. Paul commends those who stand firm as Christians (2 Cor 1:24; 1 Thess 3:8), and he admonishes the believers to do so (1 Cor 16:13; Gal 5:1; Phil 4:1).

C. Wolff quite correctly observes that the injunction "let the man who thinks that he stands beware lest he should fall" at first sight seems to be formulated in a general way and looks almost as a maxim for life,[44] although Wolff does not take that observation seriously. I. Broer has made a similar observation, but he is of the opinion that the expression ὁ δοκῶν (he who thinks) shows that Paul addresses the gnostics who are certain of their salvation.[45] But Paul may quite well use the verb δοκέω (think) without implying presumption. This is shown by the sentence "I believe (δοκῶ) I too have the spirit of God" (1 Cor 7:40), although this may be an ironical understatement by Paul. 1 Cor 10:12 could thus have the meaning "all, you and we, who think that we stand in faith should beware lest we fall". If Paul in 1 Cor 10:11 states that the events of the desert were written down to warn all of us, then nothing seems to prevent an understanding of 1 Cor 10:12 as an admonition to all believers.

There does, however, exist a clear case in Paul where "standing by faith" is combined with the thought of presumption. Paul speaks of the branches of the olive tree, which designates Israel: "… they were lopped off for lack of faith, and by faith you hold your place. Put away your pride and be on your guard" (Rom 11:20). But here the idea of presumption is clearly articulated, whereas in 1 Cor 10:12 it is not unless we read it into the text. In addition, presumption is only with difficulty applicable

---

[42] Cf. Weiß 1910, 254; Wolff 1982, 45; Willis 1985, 155; Broer 1989, 315-17,

[43] Cf. Broer 1989, 317, who says: "Paulus redet hier nur diejenigen an, die sich als Stehende vor Gott betrachten, und von der Lage in Korinth her ist es dann sehr wahrscheinlich, daß er die Starken anspricht, die auf ihr reines Gewissen pochen und die 'Stärkung' der Gewissen der Schwachen fordern".

[44] Wolff 1982, 48

[45] Broer 1989, 317.

to the context of 1 Cor 10:1-13.

If by "standing" in 1 Cor 10:12 Paul means "standing in faith", what does "falling" mean? Does it mean "falling from faith" (cf. Rom 11:22) or is something more specific intended? Broer suggests that these two possibilities do not have to be mutually exclusive.[46] The specific fall or sin in the context of 1 Cor 10:1-14 no doubt is idolatry.[47] In this case Paul in 1 Cor 10:12 would warn both the Corinthian and all other Christian believers not to fall into idolatry.

The comprehensive perspective continues in 1 Cor 10:13. Paul addresses all Corinthians.[48] Paul states: "So far you have faced no trial (πειρασμός) beyond what man can bear". What kinds of trials or temptations does Paul have in mind? According to Conzelmann, we do not receive any answer to this question.[49] Wolff does, however, point to Pauline passages where it is stated that Satan is the one from whom temptations emanate (1 Cor 7:5; 1 Thess 3:5). Wolff comments: "Through participation in idolatrous banqueting the Corinthians are captured into the realm of the devil, who tries to lead them away from faith".[50] I think this is a correct statement.[51] For Paul the participation in pagan cults means a sharing in the table of the demons (1 Cor 10:21). One possible site for such participation at pagan cultic meals could have been the sanctuary of Demeter and Kore about one kilometre south of the *agora* uphill towards the *Acrocorinth*.[52] Pottery found on the site of the buildings erected during the Roman era[53] suggests that cultic meals were held in the sanctuary then as in classical times.[54]

Paul may in 1 Cor 10:13 also have in mind such texts in the O.T. which see idolatry as a temptation (LXX: πειρασμός), i.e. texts such as Deut 13:2-3 (LXX verses 3-4) and Judg 2:18-3:6, although it is God who lies behind the temptation in these passages. The perspective Paul opens up for the Corinthians is, however, hopeful. He assures them that God will not allow them to be tested above their powers. I think this could mean that the Corinthians do not have to leave the environment of their city, where they are able to witness idolatrous practices all the time. Or to state

---

[46] Broer 1989, 319.

[47] Cf. Walter 1979, 431.

[48] For the discussion which Paul's shift from admonition to comfort has caused among exegetes, see Willis 1985, 157-59 and Broer 1989, 321.

[49] Conzelmann 1969, 199.

[50] Wolff 1982, 48: "Durch die Teilnahme an Götzenopferessen geraten die Korinther in den Bereich des Teufels, der sie vom Glauben abzubringen sucht."

[51] Meeks 1982, 71-72 for his part sees vv. 12-13 as a continuation of the original independent homily, which according to him makes the point about "resistible temptations" rather than idolatry.

[52] See Bookidis – Stroud 1987, especially 3f., 11f., 18-21.

[53] Bookidis – Fischer 1974, 283.

[54] Bookidis – Fischer 1972, 288-304. Cf. Wiseman 1979, 469-72, 509; Gooch 1988, 40-63.

it in Pauline terms: the Corinthians do not have to abandon the world (1 Cor 5:10). Therefore the temptations to fall into idolatry do not cease. But when the Corinthians are confronted with them, God will provide the means to resist them so that the Corinthians are not trapped in them but find their way out. Thus 1 Cor 10:13 may be seen as an integral part of the passage 1 Cor 10:1-13 with its focus on idolatry.

## 4. Conclusion

The result of this investigation is that the apostle Paul in 1 Cor 10:1-13 uses a Jewish text as the base for his warnings to people in Corinth who are in danger of becoming idolaters through participating in pagan banquets. The injunction not to be idolaters, together with the citation of Exod 32:6 in 1 Cor 10:7, is the most important Pauline addition to the pre-pauline text. Therefore it can be seen as containing the central idea of the passage. Nothing seems to make the postulate necessary that Paul is in this passage fighting against over-confident sacramentalists. 1 Cor 10:12 is a warning that can be directed towards every believer. In the world of Paul and his communities anyone may be tempted by idolatry (1 Cor 10:13). But God sides with the faithful.

## *Bibliography*

Bandstra, A. J. 1971: "Interpretation in 1 Corinthians 10:1-11", in: *CTJ* 6 (1971) 5-21.

Barrett, C. K. 1968: *A Commentary on the First Epistle to the Corinthians* (BNTC), London: Black 1968.

Bookidis, N. and Fischer, J. E. 1972: "The Sanctuary of Demeter and Kore on Acrocorinth. Preliminary report IV: 1969-1970", in: *Hesp.* 41 (1972) 283-331.

— 1974: "The Sanctuary of Demeter and Kore on Acrocorinth. Preliminary report V: 1971-73", in: *Hesp.* 43 (1974) 267-307.

Bookidis, N. and Stroud, R. S. 1987: *Demeter and Persephone in Ancient Corinth*, Princeton, NJ: American school of classical studies at Athens 1987.

Bornkamm, G. 1956: "Herrenmahl und Kirche bei Paulus", in: *ZThK* 53 (1956) 312-49 [Reprinted in: idem, *Studien zu Antike und Urchristentum. Gesammelte Aufsätze* II (BEvTh 28), München: Chr. Kaiser, 2nd ed. 1963, 138-76].

Broer, I. 1989: "'Darum: Wer da meint zu stehen, der sehe zu, daß er nicht falle'. 1 Kor 10,12f. im Kontext von 1 Kor 10, 1-13", in: H. Merklein (ed.), *Neues Testament und Ethik. FS R. Schnackenburg*, Freiburg etc.: Herder 1989, 299-325.

Carlson, R. P. 1993: "The role of baptism in Paul's thought", in: *Interp.* 47 (1993) 255-66.

Conzelmann, H. 1969: *Der erste Brief an die Korinther* (KEK 5), Göttingen: Vandenhoeck & Ruprecht 1969 [2nd ed. 1981].

— 1988: *1 Corinthians. A Commentary on the First Epistle to the Corinthians*. Transl. by J. W. Leitch (Hermeneia), Philadelphia, PA: Fortress 1988.

Gooch, P. D. 1988: *Food and the limits of Community: 1 Corinthians 8 to 10* (Diss. typewr. University of Toronto 1988).

Jeske, R. J. 1980: "The Rock was Christ: The Ecclesiology of 1 Cor 10", in: D. Lührmann und G. Strecker (eds.), *Kirche. FS G. Bornkamm*, Tübingen: Mohr (Siebeck) 1980, 245-55.

Käsemann, E. 1947/48: "Anliegen und Eigenart der paulinischen Abendmahlslehre", in: *EvTh* 7 (1947/48) 263-83 [Reprinted in: idem, *Exegetische Versuche und Besinnungen* I, Göttingen: Vandenhoeck & Ruprecht, 2nd ed. 1964, 11-34].

Klauck, H.-J. 1987: *1. Korintherbrief* (NEB), Würzburg: Echter 1987.

Lang, F. 1986: *Die Briefe an die Korinther* (NTD 7), Göttingen: Vandenhoeck & Ruprecht 1986.

Lietzmann, H. – Kümmel, W. G. 1969: *An die Korinther I-II* (HNT 9), Tübingen: Mohr (Siebeck), 5th ed. 1969.

Meeks, W. A. 1982: "'And rose up to play': Midrash and Paraenesis in 1 Corinthians 10:1-22", in: *JSNT* 16 (1982) 64-78.

Merklein, H. 1984: "Die Einheitlichkeit des ersten Korintherbriefes", in: *ZNW* 75 (1984) 153-83.

Metzger, B. E. 1971: *A Textual Commentary to the Greek New Testament*, London and New York: United Bible Societies 1971.

Murphy-O'Connor, J. 1990: "The First Letter to the Corinthians", in: R. Brown et. al. (eds.), *The New Jerome Biblical Commentary*, London: Chapman 1990, 798-815.

*The New English Bible. The New Testament*, Oxford and Cambridge: University Press 1970.

Orr, W. F. and Walther, J. A. 1976: *I Corinthians, A New Translation, Introduction with a Study of the Life of Paul, Notes, and Commentary* (AncB 32), Garden City, NY: Doubleday 1976.

Oster, R. E. Jr. 1992: "Use, Misuse and Neglect of Archaeological Evidence in Some Modern Works on 1 Corinthians (1 Cor 7,1-5; 8,10; 11,2-16; 12,14-26)", in: *ZNW* 83 (1992) 52-73.

Robertson, A. and A. Plummer 1911: *First Epistle of St Paul to the Corinthians* (ICC), Edinburgh: T. & T. Clark 1911.

Sandelin, K.-G. 1987: *Wisdom as Nourisher. A Study of an Old Testament Theme, its Development within Early Judaism and its Impact on Early Christianity*, Åbo: Åbo Akademi 1986 [Published 1987].

Schmithals, W. 1969: *Die Gnosis in Korinth. Eine Untersuchung zu den Korintherbriefen* (FRLANT 48), Göttingen: Vandenhoeck & Ruprecht, 3rd ed. 1969.

Schüssler Fiorenza, E. 1988: "1 Corinthians", in: *Harper's Bible Commentary* (J. L. Mays et al. eds.), San Francisco, CA: Harper & Row 1988, 1168-89.

von Soden, H. 1951: "Sakrament und Ethik bei Paulus", in: idem, *Urchristentum und Geschichte. Gesammelte Aufsätze und Vorträge* I, Tübingen: Mohr (Siebeck) 1951, 239-75.

Walter, N. 1979: "Christusglaube und heidnische Religiosität in paulinischen Gemeinden", in: *NTS* 25 (1979) 422-42.

Weiß, J. 1910: *Der erste Korintherbrief* (KEK 5), Göttingen: Vandenhoeck & Ruprecht 1910 [Reprinted 1970].

Wendland, H.-D. 1978: *Die Briefe an die Korinther* (NTD 7), Göttingen: Vandenhoeck & Ruprecht 1978.

Willis, W. L. 1985: *Idol Meat in Corinth. The Pauline Argument in 1 Corinthians 8 and 10* (SBL.DS 68), Chico, CA: Scholars Press 1985.

Wiseman, J. 1979: "Corinth and Rome I: 228 B.C.- A.D. 267", in: *ANRW* II 7.1., Berlin/New York: de Gruyter 1979, 438-548.

Wolff, C. 1982: *Der erste Brief des Paulus an die Korinther. Zweiter Teil: Auslegung der Kapitel 8-16* (ThHK VII/2), Berlin: Evangelische Verlagsanstalt 1982.

# The Most Eminent Way:
# A Study of 1 Corinthians 13

Jan Lambrecht, S.J.

## 1. Introductory Remarks

The NRSV translation "more excellent" of the expression καθ' ὑπερβολήν in 1 Cor
12:31b is rather free. Paul will show the Corinthians a way "according to excess",
a way par excellence, a way beyond comparison, thus far greater than the way
which even τὰ χαρίσματα μείζονα (v.31a) could provide, the most eminent way.[1]
This study will investigate the well-known chapter thirteen of 1 Corinthians. In current discussion, two specific problems present themselves, one in regard to form,
the other concerning the content. To what degree has Paul been organizing the material of chapter 13, as well as the whole of chapters 12-14, according to a rhetorical
pattern (2.Text and Context)? What is the exact eschatological impact at the end of
chapter 13 (4. Eschatology?)? In between these two major items we will discuss a
number of exegetical difficulties within this pericope (3. A Reading of 1 Cor 13).

---

[1] For the NRSV ("still more excellent") and the REB ("even better") ἔτι qualifies καθ' ὑπερβολήν which is taken as the equivalent of a comparative (cf. Conzelmann 1981, 263: "ein noch aus-
gezeichneterer Weg"; Smit 1993, 248-249). A superlative sense, however, seems preferable and,
most probably, ἔτι goes with the verb δείκνυμι. See Robertson-Plummer 1914, 283: "If ἔτι be taken
with καί, it means 'moreover'"; they translate: "And besides, I show you a supremely excellent
way". A free rendering of verse 31b could be: "Moreover, I am going to show you the most eminent
way". Cf. Wischmeyer 1981, 34; Kieffer 1975a, 42; Holladay 1990, 88 (esp. n. 36). In a study post-
humously published, Van Unnik 1993 maintains the adverbial character of the expression and links
it—it seems to me in a forced way—with what precedes: "Zealously practise the greater gifts 'and
even excessively, or: and even to the highest degree')" (p. 149). —It is for me an honor and deep joy
to be invited to contribute to the *Festschrift* for Lars Hartman, a very respected colleague and, since
almost thirty years, a most faithful friend.

## 2. Text and Context

There is virtual consensus in regard to the relative autonomy of the major section on the spiritual gifts, 1 Cor 12:1-14:40. Most interpreters also accept within this section a kind of ABA' stucture. Chapter 12 deals with diversity in unity within the body of Christ in a rather general way (A); with its focus on love as the most eminent way, chapter 13 interrupts the line of thought (B); chapter 14 comes back to the spiritual gifts, and here Paul provides specific, practical directives (A').[2]

### 2.1. The Context

Recently two authors have been defending a rhetorical disposition within 1 Cor 12-14.

(1) In his 1983 article "Analyse rhétorique des chapitres 12 à 14 de 1 Co", Benoît Standaert proposes the following *dispositio*:[3]

| | |
|---|---|
| 12:1-3: | *propositio* (proposition initiale) |
| 12:4-11: | *exordium* (exorde) |
| 12:12-30: | *narratio* (narration), *similitudo* (comparaison, parabole) |
| 12-13: | en-tête |
| 14-26: | corps de l'exposé |
| 27-30: | conclusion |
| 12:31-13:13: | *digressio* (parenthèse: l'éloge de l'*agapê*) |
| 14:1-36: | *argumentatio* (argumentation proprement dite) |
| 1-5: | exorde |
| 6-36: | la question du don des langues |
| - 6-25: | au niveau des principes |
| - 26-36: | au niveau pratique |
| 14:37-40: | *peroratio* (péroraison), *conclusio* (conclusion). |

In his description Standaert begins with the *argumentatio* which can easily be identified in 14:1-36 and divided into an introduction and twofold treatment of the specific problem of the tongues. The *peroratio* (14:37-40) is brief "comme il se doit".[4] He cites H. Lausberg: "Die Kürze ist selbst ein pathoshaltiges Ausdrucksmittel".[5]

---

[2] For such a description of the content see, e.g., Smit 1991, 196. A concentric stucture is generally admitted for the whole of 1 Cor 12-14. Cf., e.g., Fee 1987, 571: "... the A-B-A pattern noted in previous sections .... This section begins with a more general word (chap. 12), which is followed by a theological interlude (chap. 13) and a very specific response to the matter in hand (chap. 14)". For a comparison of the structure of chaps. 12-14 with chaps. 8-10, see Holladay 1990, 83-84.

[3] Standaert 1983a, 28-34.

[4] Ibid. 29.

[5] Ibid. (see Lausberg 1973, 240).

In this peroration "Paul devotes all the religious authority with which he knows himself invested to the settlement of the dispute .... This corresponds precisely to the *eidos pathêtikon* which is required for the peroration".[6]

Then Standaert discusses the *digressio* of chapter 13. "The digression is rightly placed before the argumentation, exactly as demanded by the then prevailing conventions".[7] He remarks that the content of chapter 13 "has nothing directly exhortative; it is completely praise and description. It is meant to appeal to the Corinthian, to please him ..., perhaps even to make him for a moment forget the problematic situation ...".[8] Standaert concludes that chapter 13 "is not a foreign body inserted afterwards".[9]

Finally the rhetorical qualities of chapter 12 are examined. Verses 1-3 contain "une proposition contrastée et très animée".[10] These verses are loaded with emotion; "this goes well with the opening of a discourse and, in this regard, fits the *eidos pathêtikon* of the conclusion (14:37-40)".[11] In 12:4-11 Standaert finds the *exordium*, "very elegant and apparently neutral regarding the problem which is caused by the glossolalists in the community".[12] He adds: "Paul gives the impression of teaching ... and treating a *quaestio infinita*, notwithstanding the fact that he must soon address the *quaestio finita* of the glossolalists and take disciplinary measures in view of them".[13] The long comparison of 12:12-30 has its own internal structure ("entête, corps, conclusion"). Standaert notes: "such a comparison ..., at this juncture of the exposition, formally corresponds to the *narratio*";[14] and furthermore: "the technique that is used pertains here equally to the *insinuatio*".[15]

What must strike the reader, according to Standaert, is the long detour which Paul takes before addressing the real problem in Corinth. Of course, a *narratio* and a *digressio* are, rhetorically speaking, quite possible and regular. Yet "it is not ... by mere respect of the conventions that Paul has acted as he has done. It would rather seem that he skillfully used a complex instrument so as to reach his aims in the best possible manner".[16]

At first sight the rhetorical analysis of Standaert is very attractive. Although his

---

[6] Standaert 1983a, 29.
[7] Ibid.
[8] Ibid. 30.
[9] Ibid.
[10] Ibid.
[11] Ibid. 31.
[12] Ibid.
[13] Ibid. 31-32.
[14] Ibid. 33.
[15] Ibid.
[16] Ibid. 34.

discussion remains very brief, it respects the way most exegetes understand Paul's way of reasoning, the line of thought. The question, however, is whether Paul has consciously composed his text according to the *dispositio* which Standaert reconstructs. "Was Paul consciously using this ancient rhetorical device or not? And whether he was or was not, how much of this rhetorical analysis consists in supplying technical terms for everyday procedures?"[17] We hesitate to ascribe a too conscious use of rhetorical structures to Paul.[18] Standaert's proposal itself is not without difficulty. One is hardly convinced that 12:1-3 is a *propositio* or that 12:4-11 is an *exordium*. How can a *similitudo* so easily be qualified as a *narratio* (of the facts)? Is 12:27-30 not rather the "application" of the "figurative part", rather than its conclusion? Furthermore, the treatment of a problem must, of course, use some form of argumentation, but why call it, technically, an *argumentatio*? One more remark. The *quaestio finita* of chapter 14 deals with more than just glossolalia; prophecy appears to pose its own problem in the church of Corinth.

(2) Joop Smit has written four recent articles on 1 Cor 12-14. The first one, "Hierarchy in the Church: Rhetorical Analysis of 1 Cor 12"[19] will be investigated in this section; the other three[20] will be discussed later in our study. Smit finds the rhetorical analysis of Standaert too global to be of much help for the solution of the problems in chapter 12.[21] Before the detailed treatment of 1 Cor 12 as well as 13, Smit mentions the threefold division of 1 Cor 12-14.[22] "The whole is included by an introduction (12:1-3) and a conclusion (14:37-40) .... This framework encloses three major parts. The first consists of 12:4-30 and distinguishes itself from the others by the theme of unity-diversity .... The second part comprises 12:31-13:13; it begins with an imperative and the repetition of the key word of the foregoing passage, i.e., χαρίσματα; it distinguishes itself from both other parts by the term ἀγάπη. The third part comprises 14:1-36; this opens with a twofold imperative and the repetition of the key-words of both foregoing parts, i.e., ἀγάπη; πνευματικά; it distinguishes

---

[17] Ibid. 35 (a question asked by J. McHugh as reporter of the English-speaking group in the *Colloquium oecumenicum Paulinum*). Cf. 36 (the same reporter): "... it was suggested that Paul is here talking the rhetoric of the street corner, rather than the polished rhetoric of the legal forum".

[18] Cf. ibid. 44; E. Schweizer (the reporter of "die deutschsprachige Gruppe"): "Benützt Paulus bewusst oder unbewusst ein rhetorisches Schema und rechnet er damit, dass die Leser dies erkennen, was eher abzulehnen ist. Es wurde betont, dass rhetorisches Geschick, rhetorische Kunst durchaus zu unterscheiden wäre von rhetorischen Schemata. Dass Paulus rhetorisch geschickt ist, zeigt sich in 1 Kor 13 sicher, hat aber noch nichts zu tun mit Kenntnis oder Unkenntnis rhetorischer Schemata".

[19] Smit 1989.

[20] Smit 1991, 1992 and 1993.

[21] Smit 1989, 327.

[22] Ibid. 329.

itself from both other parts by the word-group οἰκοδομή – οἰκοδομεῖν".[23]

As for Standaert (who hardly speaks of this matter), for Smit too chapter twelve belongs to the deliberative genre. His division, however, is different from the previous one. According to Smit the *dispositio* of 1 Cor 12 is as follows:[24]

| | |
|---|---|
| 12:1-3 : | *exordium* (= *insinuatio*) |
| 12:4-6 : | *partitio* |
| 12:7-30: | *confirmatio* (*argumentatio*), which contains the three steps of the *partitio* |
| - 7-11 : | the useful gifts (Spirit) |
| - 12-26: | the necessary ministries (Christ) |
| - 27-30: | the hierarchy of the activities (God). |

Smit emphasizes that chapter 13 is no longer deliberative; it belongs to the demonstrative rhetorical genre, of which it possesses all the characteristics.[25]

It is Smit's conviction that "Paul is familiar with classical rhetoric .... For that reason his letters lend themselves very well to rhetorical analysis".[26]

We will have to come back to Smit's vision of chapter 13. According to Smit, his analysis of chapter 12 provides us with the solution of two major problems of content. (1) The *exordium* of 12:1-3 is at the same time an *insinuatio*, i.e., an indirect approach. Through a comparison with the more explicit *conclusio* of 14:37-40—introduction and conclusion form the *inclusio* of the whole section—it becomes evident that Paul, already in the introduction of 12:1-3, not only points to the authority of Jesus, the Lord, but also to that of the apostle of the Lord. In guarded terms Paul in 12:1-3 "insinuates" that the glossolalists must obey him.[27]

(2) According to Smit the three subdivisions of the *confirmatio* correspond with the three verses of the *partitio*. Verses 7-11 deal with the useful gifts of the Spirit (cf. v. 4), verses 12-26 with the necessary ministries in the body of Christ (cf. v. 5), verses 27-30 with the working of God (cf. v. 6). Over against the all-embracing "genus" of God's activities both gifts and ministries are but particular "species". In the whole of verses 7-30 Paul emphasizes a hierarchy. Glossolalia is not a necessary service but only the last (useful) gift and owes, therefore, obedience to the apostle Paul whom God has appointed as first in importance in the Church.[28]

With regard to the rhetorical analysis of both chapter 12 and chapter 13 the same

---

[23] Smit 1991 196; in his study of 1992, 114-115, Smit proposes four parts (within chap. 14 he distinguishes vv. 1-15 and 26-33).

[24] Smit 1989, 330-335.

[25] Cf. Smit 1991 and 1992.

[26] Smit 1991, 215-216. Cf. Smit 1992, 110-111.

[27] Smit 1989, 335-338; cf. also Smit 1991, 196.

[28] Smit 1989, 334-335, 338-341.

question must be asked of Smit as of Standaert. Has Paul consciously organized his writing according to the rules of classical rhetoric? Although 1 Cor 12 is not the immediate topic of this article, a word of evaluation should not be omitted as far as the two problems of content are concerned. (1) It is difficult, if not impossible, to find formal data which would constitute 12:1-3 and 14:37-40 as an *inclusio*. Moreover, from the point of view of content, I cannot detect that Paul in 12:1-3 "insinuates" his own authority over the speakers in tongues. (2) Is 12:4-6 really a *partitio*? Granted that "gifts" in verse 4, "services" in verse 5 and "activities" in verse 6 are not wholly equivalent terms; granted also that it cannot but strike the reader that, in verses 7-30, Paul begins with the Spirit (cf. v. 4), then speaks of Christ (cf. v. 5) and later also mentions God (cf. v. 6). Yet a strict separation between gifts of the Spirit (vv. 7-11), ministries of Christ (vv. 12-26) and working of God (vv. 27-30) does not appear to be intended by Paul.[29] The Spirit is mentioned also in verse 13, and God already in verses 18 and 24. Moreover, verse 12 is connected with what precedes by γάρ; verses 12-26 appear to be an illustrative comparison (with application in vv. 27-30). Furthermore the distinction between gifts (that are only useful) and (necessary) services is most probably forced. Finally, in chapter 12 Paul equally stresses diversity and unity; he defends legitimate diversity, as well as its needed "hierarchical" unity.

Notwithstanding the evident rhetorical qualities of chapters 12-14, it would seem that no clear indication, no sufficient features or markers are present which indicate definitively that Paul intends to structure this section according to a preconceived rhetorical pattern.

## 2.2. The Text

1 Cor 13 contains three parts.[30] Verses 1-3 emphasize that love is the condition without which no gifts are of any value to us; love is indispensable. Verses 4-7 positively and negatively depict the qualities of love. Verses 8-13 constitute the longest part[31] and explain how love, otherwise than the gifts, never ends; part three thus deals with the permanence of love. There is a concentric feature within this chap-

---

[29] But see, most recently, Collins 1993, 79-91, who, with impressive arguments, explains the διακονίαι of 12:5 as ministries which are a commission from the Lord, reserved to apostolic preachers, not everyday deeds or casual actions of individuals within the Corinthian community. He proposes in 12:2-6 a twofold classification of the generic "gifts" (χαρίσματα, v. 4): teaching ministries (διακονίαι, v. 5) and miraculous powers (ἐνεργήματα, v. 6, of which Paul gives examples in vv. 8-10).

[30] Cf., e.g., Weiß 1910, 311; Spicq 1959, 59-60; Holladay 1990, 97.

ter.[32] The second part forms the center (B) and is completely devoted to love; the first and third parts (A and A') contrast the spiritual gifts with love.

One immediately notices that each part contains, at least somewhere within it, a threefold disposition and to a certain extent also a rhythm of three. In the first part we have the three long but similar tripartite sentences in verses 1, 2 and 3: each time ἐάν + verb(s), ἀγάπην δὲ μὴ ἔχω and a conclusive third clause (i.e., a double protasis and an apodosis). In the second part we find an aba'-structure: the eight verbs with οὐ and one verb without οὐ (vv. 4c-6) are framed by verse 4ab and verse 7, both chiastic and with verbs without negation.[33] In the third part verse 8 has εἴτε three times; verse 13 a mentions the triad faith, hope and love. In this third part there is, again, an aba'-structure: verses 8b-12 are framed by verse 8a and verse 13 which both contain the noun "love".[34]

Some exegetes and editions of the New Testament add 12:31b to the first part.[35] Along with others J. Smit even adds the whole of 12:31 to chapter 13.[36] He sees an inclusion in 12:31 and 13:13 because of the presence of μείζων in both verses: the two verses have the same message (love is greater than the greatest gifts); the imperatives of 12:31a and 14:1a each mark the beginning of a new section.[37] These views, however, are hardly correct. It seems to me that 12:31 is a verse of transition which does not yet properly belong to the digression itself; it announces this digression. 12:31a and 31b are better not separated. Verse 31b appears as an afterthought, for Paul somewhat a correction of verse 31a. The καί in καὶ ἔτι of verse 31b pos-

---

[31] That verse 8a introduces a new part becomes evident through a threefold consideration. (1) The πάντα-clauses of verse 7 bring the long listing to a close. (2) Like verse 4a, verse 8a begins with ἡ ἀγάπη and is not linked to the preceding verse by a particle. (3) The δέ after the first εἴτε in verse 8 establishes a connection between verse 8a and what follows. – If verse 8a would still belong to the second part, then the verb must have a moral meaning: love never fails, sins. See Miguens 1975, 78-79 and the long discussion of Lacan 1958 by Neirynck 1963, 599-604. Cf. Sabbe 1965, 298 and 316-317.

[32] See, e.g., Fee 1987, 641: "Thus the argument began with a set of contrasts .... Now, following the lyrical description of *agapê* in vv. 4-7, he [= Paul] brings this argument to its conclusion with another set of contrasts ...".

[33] Neirynck 1963, 602; Smit 1991, 202 and Smit 1992, 112.

[34] Cf. Standaert 1983b, 137: "Le jeu de regroupement ternaire revient également dans la transition du verset suivant (14,1)".

[35] See, e.g., Wolff 1982, 116; Wischmeyer 1981, 36; and the third edition of the Greek N.T.

[36] Smit 1991, 196 and 197; Smit 1992, 109.116 and 118; Smit 1993, 247-255; cf. also Spicq 1959, 52; Lacan, 1973; Carson 1987, 51-58.

[37] See Smit 1992, 109. On pp. 115-116 Smit explains how he sees in the exhortation of 1 Cor 12:31a an ironical *permissio*: "Continue to strive for the greater gifts! It will be your ruin!" In 12:31b, too, he detects an ironical exaggeration: "yes, I will show you a more extraordinary way". Cf. especially Smit 1993, 247-255: 1 Cor 12:31 "is wholly ironic" (253). Such a reading of verse 31, however, is scarcely defensible.

sesses a rather oppositional nuance: yet I will still show you a way beyond comparison. After the δέ of verse 31a Paul could hardly write another δέ.[38] There must not be any doubt that 13:13 still belongs to the third part of the chapter, not to the inclusion. Moreover, the comparative μείζων in verse 13b has the meaning of a superlative while in 12:31a the comparative sense prevails.

One of the positive features of the article by Smit, "The Genre of 1 Corinthians 13 in the Light of Classical Rhetoric", is that in comparing this chapter with the rules of the demonstrative genre the author does not limit himself to the lexical-syntactic level—by itself already a thorough analysis with impressive results.[39] Smit also treats the semantic level.[40] In 1 Cor 13 there is, according to Smit, a personal presentation of charismata and love; there is the description of the "qualities of character" of love and a discussion of the successive stages of love; there is (more or less) the traditional list of virtues. Smit concludes: "The personal framework within which Paul places his subject, the topics which he discusses and the sequence in which he introduces them correspond entirely with the schemes which classical rhetoric has developed".[41] Smit then goes on to the pragmatic level.[42] Rhetorical strategy uses the technique of amplification and minimization. Paul amplifies love and minimizes the charismata. The goal of this strategy is evident. "With the help of 'great' love, Paul demonstrates how small the value of the charismata is so that the fascination with which the Corinthians cherish these extraordinary gifts is diminished. Paul tries to lessen the value of the charismata in the eyes of the Corinthians in order to increase their willingness to set things straight on this point. By devaluating the gifts he prepares for the practical measures which he has in store for them at the end of the present argument".[43]

One of Smit's main (and correct) conclusions is: Originally 1 Cor 13 is not a hymn in praise of love; it is not "a ready-made piece, which on second thought Paul put in this place".[44] No, Paul composed the text while writing on the spiritual gifts; the excursus "fulfills a clear function within the argument of 1 Cor 12-14".[45] In 1 Cor 13 Paul's attention goes to the charisms which he wants to devaluate. Smit even detects in 12:31 and 13:1-3 a decidedly ironical tone which allows him to call the

---

[38] For a good discussion of 12:31 see Wischmeyer 1981, 31-38.

[39] Smit 1991, 195-205; Cf. Smit 1992, 111-112. See also the long rhetorical analysis by Mitchell 1991, 165-171 and 270-279: 1 Corinthians is a *deliberative* argument for unity, "the antidote to factionalism".

[40] Smit 1991, 205-210; Cf. Smit 1992, 112-113.

[41] Smit 1991 210.

[42] Ibid. 210-214.

[43] Ibid. 213; cf. Smit 1992, 113-115.

[44] Smit 1991, 215; cf. Smit 1993, 249.

[45] Smit 1991, 215; cf. Smit 1993, 246.

"demonstrative excursus" (= 1 Cor 13) a kind of satire.[46]

The numerous figures of style, the compositional data and specific choices of words and metaphors without any doubt point to Paul's remarkable stylistic ability. All this is still lexical and syntactic. I do not think, however, that this lexical-syntactic level is able to prove or confirm Paul's conscious use of rhetorical patterns, i.e., his dependence on classical rhetoric. It must be said, moreover, that what is brought forward by Smit in regard to both the semantic and pragmatic level is less than convincing. Quite normal and ordinary items are forced into a so-called conscious rhetorical composition. In addition, a number of observations are less correct. So, e.g., in dealing with minimization (and elsewhere) it is stated that Paul "demonstrates that the gifts are useless, devoid of virtue and provisional".[47] Such a statement is only true in its affirmation of the provisional character of the gifts. Furthermore, can one clearly recognize in 1 Cor 13:4-7 the traditional list of virtues (justice, courage and temperance; with the intended omission of wisdom), as is claimed by Smit?[48]

## 3. A Reading of 1 Corinthians 13

In his characterization of 1 Corinthians 13 J. Dupont speaks of "une autre perspective", a "changement de registre": "On a l'impression de glisser du plan théologique au plan anthropologique".[49] There can be no doubt that there is a change of style at the beginning of 1 Cor 13. The rhetorical analysis remarks that the deliberative

---

[46] Cf. the title of Smit 1992 (song or satire) and 115-118: "'Het hooglied van de liefde' blijkt naar Paulus' bedoeling een spotrede op de eerzucht van de Korintiërs te zijn" (118). For the expression "demonstrative excursus" see pp. 114 and 115, and Smit 1993, passim.

[47] Smit 1991, 215 and cf. 212.

[48] Ibid. 208-210.

[49] Dupont 1983a, 20-21: "Il n'y est fait mention ni de Dieu, ni du Christ, ni de l'Esprit; la dimension commmunautaire cède la place à une attention qui se concentre sur la personne. Il n'est sans doute pas fortuit que le 'Je' passe en premier plan (vv. 1-3, 11, 12b), que la question y soit posée de ce que 'je suis' (v. 2), de 'ce qui *m*'est utile' (v. 3), de ce qu'est *ma* condition présente par rapport à *ma* condition dans le monde à venir (v. 12)" (20). See also Dupont within the discussion of Standaert 1983a, 50: "Je me garderai bien de dire que, par rapport à son contexte anti-individualiste, le chapitre 13 introduit une considération 'individualiste'. Mais je me demande si ce n'est pas là que la personne est reconnue dans sa spécificité propre"; and Dupont 1983b, 279: "Si Jésus Christ n'est pas mentionné explicitement en 1 Cor 13, on doit se demander dans quelle mesure l'éloge que Paul y fait de l'*agapê* serait possible sans la révélation de l'amour divin qui nous a été accordée en lui ...". Cf. Wolff 1982, 119: "... 1 Kor. 13 [kann] nicht anders verstanden werden denn als Zeugnis von der Liebe Gottes in Christus, die in den Glaubenden und durch sie weiterwirken will – auch wenn von Christus hier nicht ausdrücklich die Rede ist". Cf. Wischmeyer 1981, 115-116 (the Christology is implicitly present; with references to Titus 1959 and Conzelmann 1969/1981).

genre of 1 Cor 12 for the time being yields its place to the demonstrative genre. The subject matter, too, clearly indicates that 1 Cor 13 is a digression. Yet this digression is not conceived as a self-contained hymn of love. The excursus functions within the flow of thought of the whole section. The connection between chapters 12 and 13 is manifest. "Tongues" of 13:1 is taken up from 12:28 and 30, and "prophecy" of 13:2 from 12:28 and 29.

### 3.1. 1 Cor 13:1-3

In 13:1-3 Paul uses the first person singular. To what degree is the "I" typical?[50] In his recent study C. R. Holladay, correctly, I think, emphasizes the self-referential character of this "I": "Commentators have long noticed Paul's use of the first person singular here, but it is ordinarily taken in a general rather than a strictly autobiographical sense. In spite of the repeated use of the first person singular in vv. 1-3, these verses are not ordinarily thought to refer to Paul's own apostolic experiences. This may be a classic example of the *sensus literalis* being ignored in favor of a far more problematic interpretation".[51] The seven different items mentioned in verses 1-3 "function as part of Paul's own self-presentation. As such, they are directly anchored in his own apostolic behavior".[52] It would seem that not only in verses 1-3 but also in the whole of chapter 13 (as well as in 12:31b and in chapter 14) the "I" is self-referential.[53]

In a recent study J. H. Petzer[54] rightly defends the reading καυχήσωμαι in verse 3.[55] His interesting analysis of the structure and content of 13:1-3 may help us in our own reading of the passage. We take over his presentation, albeit with some modifications:[56]

---

[50] Cf. Wischmeyer 1981, 90-91: "... ein generalisierendes 'Ich' in einer theologischen Grundsatzrede, die zwar nicht autobiographisch abgezielt ist, wohl aber die eigene Person und die eigene Erfahrung direkt in den Zusammenhang der theologischen Rede einbezieht".

[51] Holladay 1990, 88-89. Paul's self-referential language in chap. 13, which "is grounded in the concrete reality of his own apostolic experience" (98) has a paradigmatic, parenetic function. See also Mitchell 1991, especially 273-274; for the whole of 1 Cor, we may, e.g., mention the remark of p. 303: "... Paul's own recurrent rhetorical strategy of appealing to himself as the example of proper behavior to be imitated ...".

[52] Holladay 1990, 89. Cf. p. 93: "The verses are hypothetical, but they are rendered so because of their hyperbolic form, not because they have an imaginary subject. The first person singular is conspicuous, and the primary referent is Paul. Each of the activities is framed with specific reference to a concrete subject: Paul himself".

[53] Ibid., 82-98.

[54] Petzer 1989.

[55] See, e.g., also Wischmeyer 1981, 81-88; Holladay 1990, 90-91; Smit 1993, 254-255.

*Verse 1*

A  a   Ἐὰν ταῖς γλώσσαις τῶν ἀνθρώπων λαλῶ καὶ τῶν ἀγγέλων,

B      ἀγάπην δὲ μὴ ἔχω,

C            γέγονα χαλκὸς ἠχῶν ἢ κύμβαλον ἀλαλάζον.

*Verse 2*

A  a   καὶ ἐὰν ἔχω προφητείαν

            καὶ εἰδῶ τὰ μυστήρια πάντα καὶ πᾶσαν τὴν γνῶσιν

   b   καὶ ἐὰν ἔχω πᾶσαν τὴν πίστιν ὥστε ὄρη μεθιστάναι,

B      ἀγάπην δὲ μὴ ἔχω,

C            οὐθέν εἰμι.

*Verse 3*

A  a   κἂν ψωμίσω πάντα τὰ ὑπάρχοντά μου

   b   καὶ ἐὰν παραδῶ τὸ σῶμά μου ἵνα καυχήσωμαι,

B      ἀγάπην δὲ μὴ ἔχω,

C            οὐδὲν ὠφελοῦμαι.

The overall parallelistic structure of these first three verses of 1 Cor 13 cannot be denied. We can equally assume that the order in the three A-parts is climactic regarding importance and human involvment. For Paul the gift of tongues is less important and asks less of a person than prophecy (and faith?); again, prophecy is most probably less important and easier than good works and "giving up the body".[57]

Petzer maintains that the A-part of each verse contains a "b" element. For verse 1 this is, according to Petzer, καὶ τῶν ἀγγέλων. This second genitive follows λαλῶ and is thus separated from τῶν ἀνθρώπων, the first genitive phrase.[58] Although the emphatic translation "and *even* of angels" is probably correct,[59] I do not see that the second phrase is by any means the equivalent of the b-clauses of verses 2 and 3. Petzer, moreover, claims that the function of all b-elements consists in pursuing the issue of the corresponding a-part *ad absurdum*.[60] "It is to this effect that the defa-

---

[56] Petzer 1989, 235; Petzer himself refers to Snyman 1986. We may, however, quote Barrett 1968, 299, who reminds us of A. von Harnack's warning: "Many attempts have been made to write out the chapter in the form of verse. This does not seem profitable. The chapter is prose, and its rhythmical patterns are not regular enough to warrant presentation in the form of poetry"; cf. Bornkamm 1985, 223.

[57] Petzer 1989, 237-238.

[58] Ibid. 239-240.

[59] Cf., e.g., Kieffer 1975a, 40: "Si je parle les langues des hommes et *même* des anges"; Wolff 1982, 116: "Wenn ich (nicht nur) mit den Sprachen der Menschen rede, (sondern) *sogar* ..."; Carson 1987, 58.

[60] Petzer 1989, 239-244.

miliarization is being used".[61] "The purpose [of defamiliarization] is to force the reader to rethink or reread a passage, word or phrase, since by his first attempt, the thing sounds strange and unfamiliar".[62] So, according to Petzer, the phrase "and of angels" exaggerates, "defamiliarizes" and puts "the issue of tongues out of the reach of ordinary human beings".[63] Even with the gift of tongues one does not speak like angels. Is Petzer's view correct? Most probably not.[64] Furthermore, is the purpose of the mention of faith in verse 2 "to exaggerate the issue [of prophecy] and to put it out of human reach"?[65] Hardly. Although the wonder-working, mountain-moving faith[66] is more than prophecy and wisdom, it stands here for its own sake, independently alongside prophecy and wisdom.[67] With regard to verse 3 Petzer paraphrases: "even when your willingness to prove your piety through your deeds be perfected to such an extent as giving up, not only your belongings [a-part], but even your own body, with the result that you may be able to (legitimately) boast about it [b-part]".[68] To be sure, the giving up of the body (to suffering, persecution and death)[69] is more than giving away the belongings, but, again, the b-part is not mentioned only, it would seem, in function of the a-part.

Otherwise than Petzer, I also maintain that the forceful threefold repetition in B refers to the whole of A, and, equally, that C refers to the whole of A.[70] As far as C is concerned it should be noticed that γέγονα (v. 1) somewhat corresponds with εἰμί (v. 2), and οὐθέν (v. 2) with οὐδέν (v. 3). Furthermore, in verse 3 ἵνα is rather "re-

---

[61] Ibid. 239.

[62] Ibid. 234.

[63] Ibid. 240.

[64] For the view that the Corinthians and Paul were really thinking of tongues as the language(s) of angels, cf., e.g., Kieffer 1975a, 46; Wischmeyer 1981, 42; Fee 1987, 630-631.

[65] Petzer 1989, 240. Like others, Petzer connects "understanding all mysteries and all knowledge" with "having prophecy". According to Dautzenberg 1975, 150-151, mysteries and knowledge are the content of prophecy, not separate charisms. See, however, the critique of Wischmeyer 1981, 50, n. 61.

[66] Cf. Mark 11:23 and par.

[67] Cf. Wischmeyer 1981, 72: "es handelt sich um das Charisma des Glaubens, der zu Wundertaten befähigt".

[68] Petzer 1989, 241. Cf. Fee 1987, 633-635.

[69] Otherwise Petzer 1989, 242. Petzer sees in the expression a reference to the eucharistic words in Luke's institution narrative: "Thus, παραδῶ τὸ σῶμά μου indeed 'hangs in the air', or one would rather say, is a completed expression on its own, alluding to the giving up of Jesus' body at his death". Yet, in Luke 22:19 the expression is longer and the verb a simplex: τοῦτό ἐστιν τὸ σῶμά μου τὸ ὑπὲρ ὑμῶν διδόμενον. For a pertinent critique of this proposal see Smit 1993, 258.

[70] Cf. Petzer 1989, 235-237.

sultative" (just as ὥστε in verse 2) and the "boasting" here is in itself not negative.[71]

Paul has certainly composed 1 Cor 13:1-3 by means of his impressive A B C pattern and its threefold repetition, but there is, I think, less structure and more variation than Petzer is willing to accept. Moreover, in these verses, just as in the lists of chapter 12, Paul does not limit himself to special gifts of the Spirit, to charisms.

## 3.2. Verses 4-7

The second division of 1 Cor 13 is rightly famous for both its style and structure. In his commentary Fee depicts the general pattern: "The enumeration is basically in three parts: (1) It begins with two positive expressions of love ...; (2) these are followed by eight verbs expressing what love is not like or does not do, the last of which is balanced by its positive counterpart ...; (3) finally, there is a staccato of four verbs, each with the object 'all things'...".[72] The middle part, it would seem, possesses its own rather sophisticated structure. We propose verses 4-7 in structured form as follows:

4   (a)   ἡ ἀγάπη μακροθυμεῖ,

χρηστεύεται ἡ ἀγάπη,

(b)   οὐ ζηλοῖ ἡ ἀγάπη,

οὐ περπερεύεται, οὐ φυσιοῦται,

5   οὐκ ἀσχημονεῖ, οὐ ζητεῖ τὰ ἑαυτῆς,

οὐ παροξύνεται, οὐ λογίζεται τὸ κακόν,

6   οὐ χαίρει ἐπὶ τῇ ἀδικίᾳ, συγχαίρει δὲ τῇ ἀληθείᾳ·

7   (a')   πάντα στέγει,

πάντα πιστεύει, πάντα ἐλπίζει,

πάντα ὑπομένει.

The three parts of this second division appear to possess a concentric structure: a-b-a'. The two elements a and a' frame the longer, central b-part. The last verb of verse 7 ("endures") corresponds in meaning with the first verb of verse 4 ("is patient"). If it can be accepted that verse 7 (just as the two first clauses of v. 4) is chiastic in form (with faith and hope in the middle and στέγει not so different from ὑπομένει), then the first and third parts, moreover, resemble each other also through

---

[71] Cf. Fee 1987, 634-635; Petzer 1989, 243. The interpretation that the ἵνα-clause is a brief parenthesis, a self-exhortation ("let me just for once boast!") by which Paul comments on his argument and, as it were, distances himself from what he himself writes (so Smit 1992, 116-118 and especially Smit 1993, 255-263), is utterly improbable.

[72] Fee 1989, 636.

their chiastic structure.[73] The meaning of πάντα in verse 7 probably oscillates between "all things" (direct object of the first and fourth verb) and "always" (adverbial qualification of the second and third verb).[74]

The third ἀγάπη, that after οὐ ζηλοῖ in verse 4, is text-critically not wholly certain. If it is authentic, it probably goes with οὐ ζηλοῖ, not with οὐ περπερεύεται.[75] The longer clause οὐ ζηλοῖ ἡ ἀγάπη is then the introduction of the second part and stands alone. The eight following verbs appear, it would seem, in four pairs of two. The first pair has the ending –ται, the second the ending –ει, and the third the ending –εται. Moreover, the last verb of the second and third pairs each has a direct object which further enhances the parallelism. All verbs of the first three pairs are preceded by the negation οὐ. The fourth pair (v. 6) possesses a forceful antithetic parallelism, negative in contrast with positive: see οὐ χαίρει – συγχαίρει and ἀδικία – ἀλήθεια;[76] the two clauses, moreover, are about the same in length.

Style is the technique employed in function of structure; the structure itself is subservient to the thought. After the repeated statements in verses 1-3 that, notwithstanding extraordinary gifts and personal endeavor, a person without love is nothing, Paul depicts the nature of that love in verses 4-7. "Über die Liebe lässt sich angemessen ... nur in Begriffen des Handelns sprechen".[77] By means of two verbs Paul first positively mentions two qualities; then, in the second part, he characterizes love negatively with eight verbs. The ninth and last verb is the positive counterpart of the eighth; it leads over to the third part. In this third part Paul, by means of four verbs and a fourfold πάντα, positively and very emphatically concludes his description in verse 7.[78] "Paul does not mean that love always believes the best about everything and everyone, but that love never ceases to have faith; love never loses hope. This is why it can endure".[79]

Holladay claims that in verses 4-7 Paul is referring to himself and to the Corinthians. Paul's personal exemplary life, as well as the harmful attitudes of the Corin-

---

[73] Cf. Neirynck 1963, 603; Bornkamm 1985, 225: "Die positiven Aussagen am Anfang und Ende umrahmen acht negative Satzglieder".

[74] So Neirynck 1963, 603: "always" for the second and third verbs. Cf. Carson 1987, 63: "always" for the four verbs; Martin 1984, 50-51; Fee 1987, 639: "In each case the verb is accompanied by the object 'all things,' a rhetorical repetition which here comes very close to an adverbial use ('in everything,' or 'always')".

[75] Otherwise, e.g., N[26], GNT[3].

[76] Paul seems to favor the combination of these two nouns: see Rom 1:18 and 2:8 (cf. 3:5 and 7).

[77] Wolff 1982, 122 (with reference to H.-D. Wendland).

[78] For two texts from the "Testaments of the Twelve Patriarchs" which provide a similar enumeration and conclude with a πάντα-sentence, see von Rad 1953 and, e.g., Sabbe 1964, 269-273. Moreover, faith, hope and endurance was a traditional Jewish triad (cf., e.g., Wischmeyer 1981, 109).

[79] Fee 1989, 640.

thians, have, as it were, entered this characterization of love. "Those items reflecting his own apostolic behavior serve to illustrate the positive profile that ἀγάπη produces; those negative items depicting unedifying behavior of the Corinthians seem to illustrate the negative profile that results from the absence of ἀγάπη ...".[80]

## 3.3. Verses 8-13

The most difficult and most discussed clause within 1 Cor 13:8-13 is verse 13a. Is the abiding of the well-known triad "faith, hope and love" as a whole eschatological? This specific topic will be dealt with in the last part of this study. The work in this section is rather preparatory. What is the structure and line of thought in these verses? How must we interpret the contrast between "now" and "then"? In verses 8-13 Paul emphasizes the permanence of love. Although ἀγάπη is explicitly mentioned only in verses 8 and 13, the main idea of this third part is that, because of its permanence, love is basically different from the gifts and other human qualities. We may present the Greek text in the following way:

| | | |
|---|---|---|
| 8 | Ἡ ἀγάπη | οὐδέποτε πίπτει· |
| | εἴτε δὲ προφητεῖαι, | καταργηθήσονται· |
| | εἴτε γλῶσσαι, | παύσονται· |
| | εἴτε γνῶσις, | καταργηθήσεται. |
| 9 | ἐκ μέρους γὰρ γινώσκομεν | |
| | καὶ ἐκ μέρους προφητεύομεν· | |
| 10 | | ὅταν δὲ ἔλθῃ τὸ τέλειον, |
| | | τὸ ἐκ μέρους καταργηθήσεται. |
| 11 | ὅτε ἤμην νήπιος, | |
| | ἐλάλουν ὡς νήπιος, | |
| | ἐφρόνουν ὡς νήπιος, | |
| | ἐλογιζόμην ὡς νήπιος· | |
| | | ὅτε γέγονα ἀνήρ, |
| | | κατήργηκα τὰ τοῦ νηπίου. |
| 12 | βλέπομεν γὰρ ἄρτι | |
| | δι᾽ ἐσόπτρου ἐν αἰνίγματι, | |
| | | τότε δὲ πρόσωπον πρὸς πρόσωπον· |
| | ἄρτι γινώσκω ἐκ μέρους, | |
| | | τότε δὲ ἐπιγνώσομαι |
| | | καθὼς καὶ ἐπεγνώσθην. |
| 13 | νυνὶ δὲ μένει πίστις, ἐλπίς, ἀγάπη, τὰ τρία ταῦτα· | |
| | μείζων δὲ τούτων ἡ ἀγάπη. | |

The text in the left column points to activities during Christian life on earth; that in the right column refers to the situation at the end of life and (in v. 12) to life after

---

[80] Holladay 1990, 94-97 (quotation from p. 96).

death. Both parts of the comparison of verse 11 belong, of course, to the period of
earthly existence.

A few words of comment must be given to each of these verses. Verse 8 assumes
that, just as prophecies, tongues and knowledge, love is present in Christian life.
The difference, however (cf. δέ after the first εἴτε), is that love will never end. In
view of the three future tenses within verse 8, one rightly assumes a future nuance
in the present tense πίπτει.[81] The antithetical situation between love and the gifts
requires such an understanding. The two passive aorists of καταργέομαι are best
taken as deponents and therefore active in meaning: "will pass away" (cf. παύσον-
ται: "will cease"). It must strike the reader that prophecies and tongues are mentioned here in different order (compare vv. 1-2: first tongues, then prophecies). As
will be confirmed by the following verses, knowledge in verse 8 (and in the entire
third part) is probably less an extraordinary gift than we had to assume for verse 2.[82]

In verses 9-10 the phrase "in part" is now clearly opposed to "the perfect". Paul
wants to work out and explain (cf. γάρ) what was implied in verse 8. Yet we cannot
avoid the impression that a shift has occurred. While according to verse 8 prophecies, tongues and knowledge will simply disappear, in verses 9-10 prophesying and
knowing will rather be completed; only their partial character will disappear. We
notice that knowledge is now mentioned before prophecy and that the gift of
tongues is no longer spoken of. One should also pay attention to the sudden appearance of the first person plural in verse 9. Verse 10 brings a rather abstract reflection
on the disappearance of what is partial when the perfect comes. The literal translation of ὅταν δὲ ἔλθῃ τὸ τέλειον (v. 10a) should use a *futurum exactum*: "after that
the complete will have come";[83] verse 10b follows: "(then) the partial will disappear".

Verse 11 contains an analogy wherein infancy and adulthood are opposed. Paul
reflects on his own past; he now employs the (autobiographical and at the same time
typical) first person singular. The two ὅτε-constructions are different both from the
ὅταν-construction in the preceding verse and from one another. The first half of
verse 11, with ὅτε ἤμην νήπιος (and more imperfect tenses), means "when I was
child, during that period I was speaking, thinking and reasoning as a child". The nuance in the second half with ὅτε γέγονα ἀνήρ (and one more perfect tense: κατήρ-

---

[81] Cf. Spicq 1959, 93; Wischmeyer 1981, 119: "Adverb und Präsens verleihen πίπτειν als Kennzeichen der ἀγάπη den Zeitwert der 'unendlichen Zeit'-Dauer, wie ihn eben Gott und seine Eigenschaften besitzen".

[82] In verse 2 "all mysteries" and "all knowledge" more or less appear as the contents of prophetic
power (cf. n. 65). This probably is no longer so in the third part.

[83] Is Paul perhaps alluding here to the coming of Christ? Cf., e.g., 1 Cor 4:5: ἕως ἂν ἔλθῃ ὁ Κύριος. See, e.g., Conzelmann 1981, 276; Sabbe 1965, 299.

γηκα, here in the active form) is not exactly the same: "when I became a man, then, at that moment, I put an end to childish ways". Paul looks back not only on his childhood, but also on his becoming an adult.

In verse 12 Paul returns to the situation of the Christians (first person plural) before death (twice ἄρτι: the present life) which stands in sharp contrast to the future completion (twice τότε: the resurrectional life). He explains (γάρ, cf. v. 9) and applies the analogy. The two halves of the verse are parallel. Face-to-face vision and full knowledge correspond to each other.[84] First two metaphors are used: mirror, riddle,[85] yet the seeing itself is not meant metaphorically. There is no need here to enter into the discussion whether Paul means (only) indirect or, more probably, (also) unclear and indistinct seeing over against "face-to-face" vision.[86] Then, in the second half, employing the first person singular, he again refers to partial knowledge which is opposed to future perfect knowledge. The perfection is indicated by the compound verb ἐπιγινώσκω and compared with the way he himself has been known (by God).[87] The shift noted in verse 9 continues. Knowledge does not simply disappear; it is brought to perfection.[88] Moreover, the progressive narrowing of focus also continues, from three gifts in verse 8 to two in verse 9 and to one (knowl-

---

[84] Cf. Miguens 1975, 81 and 83.

[85] The adverbial expression ἐν αἰνίγματι can correctly be translated by "enigmatically" (αἰνιγματικῶς). Cf. Spicq 1959, 100; Miguens 1975, 85; Conzelmann, 1981, 265 ("rätselhaft"), 278, n. 111 ("rätselvoll").

[86] For a state of the question see, e.g., Spicq 1959, 95-102; Sabbe 1975, 306-309. Wischmeyer 1981, 137 remarks that the use of the solemn Septuagintal expression "face to face" suggests the reciprocity which is emphasized in the second part of verse 12.

[87] God knowing us (in the past) is our being elected and converted (and even before the foundation of the world, cf. Rom 8:29). One must take note of the past tense; cf. also 1 Cor 8:3 (perfect) and Gal 4:9 (aorist). Wischmeyer 1981, 139, notes: "Die 1 Kor 13,12 vertretene Meinung, einer schon geschehenen Erkenntnis des Menschen durch Gott werde eine ebensolche endzeitliche Erkenntnis Gottes durch den Menschen entsprechen, findet sich so in keinem der Paralleltexte". See also Bornkamm 1985, 229; Dupont 1960, 51-56, 101-103: "S'il faut donner une précision temporelle à l'expression γνωσθέντες ὑπὸ θεοῦ de Gal., IV, 9, on pourra dire: 'avoir été connu avant la fondation du monde'" (103), and 139: "une connaissance que Dieu a eue de ses élus avant les temps". Fee 1987, 648-649, hesitates to accept this "attractive" suggestion. Spicq 1959, 102, calls the last part of verse 12 a "singulière évocation d'excellence". He notes: "Il faut donner à *kathôs kai* ... sa valeur d'exacte comparaison 'tout comme'". See also Bauer (sub voce καί II, 3) regarding the pleonastic character of καί in "Vergleichssätzen".

[88] Cf. Wischmeyer 1981, 130-131.

edge) in verse 12.[89] One rightly wonders whether partial knowledge in verse 12 is still simply the charism of verses 2 and 8-9.[90]

In verses 8-12 two negative characteristics of the gifts are indicated: they will end; they are partial, imperfect. From verse 8a we learn that love will never end. What about love's perfection? In verse 12 it is vision and knowledge which will become perfect and complete. It would seem that love is present in that seeing and knowing, that it is identical with them.[91]

With verse 13 Paul brings the argument to its conclusion. This verse, however, is loaded with difficulties. Is νυνί the equivalent of ἄρτι? If so, why a δέ? Is μένει the equivalent of οὐδέποτε πίπτει (v. 8)? Why are faith and hope mentioned, so unexpectedly (but see v. 7, and τὰ τρία ταῦτα coins the triad as "these well-known three")?[92] In what does love's "being greater than faith and hope" (μείζων) precisely consist?

## 4. Eschatology?

It would seem that three positions must be set out: no final eschatology in 1 Cor 13; the thoroughly eschatological interpretation of 1 Cor 13:13; and the not strictly eschatological interpretation of 1 Cor 13:13a. What are the arguments? Is it possible for us to motivate our preference and to make a responsible choice?

### 4.1. No Final Eschatology

No less than all early Christians, Paul is convinced that through Jesus Christ "the end of the ages has come" (1 Cor 10:11). Christians live in "the last days". They

---

[89] Some commentators detect in verse 11a an allusion to tongues (cf. 14:20 where Paul, they claim, by νηπιάζω probably refers to tongues) and in verse 12a to prophecy (cf. Num 12:6-8, a passage which deals with prophets). So together with knowledge in verse 12b the three gifts of verse 8 seem to reappear. Cf., e.g., Standaert 1983b, 156. This may, however, be forcing the textual evidence. Cf., e.g., Fee 1987, 646; "Such a view flies full in the face of the argument itself, both here and in 12:4-11 and 14:14".

[90] Otherwise, e.g. Sabbe 1965, 285-286 and 309-310.

[91] Cf. Spicq 1959, 118-120: "Le mouvement de la pensée demande de mettre une certaine équivalence entre l'ἐπίγνωσις céleste ... et l'ἀγάπη indéfectible ..." (118); "il y a donc un lien intrinsèque entre amour et connaissance" (119); Sabbe 1965, 310-312 and 302: "in v. 12b wordt de liefde in een kennisterminologie uitgedrukt".

[92] See (for Paul) 1 Thess 1:3; 5:8. Wischmeyer 1981, 147-153, however, maintains "dass es sich um eine glückliche Formulierung [by Paul], nicht um eine zitierte Formel handelt" (153). Cf. Wischmeyer 1983, 223-230 and, recently, Söding 1992, 38-41 and 63-64 ("paulinische Bildung"): "Der Apostel hat die Trias in seinen Briefen als Kurzformel des Christseins aufgegriffen, die den Gemeinden aus seiner Erstverkündigung bekannt gewesen ist" (41).

have "the first fruits of the Spirit" (Rom 8:23) "as a guarantee" (2 Cor 1:22; 5:5); his gifts or charisms are the undeniable proof of the eschatological quality of Christian existence.

A minority interpretation claims that in 1 Cor 13:8-13 Paul does not refer to the parousia and the ultimate consummation.[93] The main argument of its proponents is, it would seem, that in the same letter to the Corinthians in 2:6-3:4 Paul uses the vocabulary νήπιος – τέλειος (see the terms in 3:1 and 2:6) to distinguish between immaturity and maturity, between "fleshly" and spiritual attitudes in present Christian life (see also 14:20). In 13:8-13 partial and complete (perfect) must therefore be understood as pointing to childhood and adulthood in Christian life before the parousia. E. Miguens argues: In 1 Cor 13:8-13 "we have three pairs of correlatives which, in their turn correspond to each other. They are: *to ek merous – to teleion* (vs. 10; cf. vs. 9); to be a child – to become a man (vs. 11); now – then (vs. 12). They express the same basic concept from different points of view: the gradual development of the Christian life".[94] In his brief contribution to a discussion of the passage, J. Murphy O'Connor states: "I see no compelling reason to understand *arti* and *tote* (v. 12) as denoting a contrast between this present life and the eschaton. It is more likely that he [Paul] is contrasting the present and the immediate future, today and tomorrow".[95] Paul has in mind two stages of the process that takes place in Christians during their earthly life. The major advantage of this interpretation is that the normal meanings of faith and hope in verse 13 can be retained. Verse 13 no longer causes any problem.[96]

Two objections may be raised. (1) What about the "face-to-face" vision of verse 12? Does such a seeing not point to the final eschatological condition? Murphy-O'Connor answers by means of Num 12:6-8, the very OT passage to which 1 Cor 13:12 itself refers. Two forms of revelation are contrasted, that of the prophets and

---

[93] Miguens 1975; J. Murphy-O'Connor in the discussion of Standaert 1983b, 139-142. Cf. the discussion in Carson 1987, 68-72 (without mentioning Miguens or Murphy-O'Connor).

[94] Miguens 1975, 87. See his extensive discussion on pp. 87-91: "The contrast between the child and the grown-up man is not a mere external comparison to illustrate a given idea; it describes the real situation among Christians. ... the pairs partial – total, child – man are correlative — and also *relative*. They mark two different stages of one and the same process which takes place during this life in Christians as individuals rather than as a community. These two different stages are 'now' and 'then,' in the Christian life, which happen sooner or later" (89). It would seem, however, that for Paul the reference to "being a child" and "becoming a man" is in fact no more than a comparison. In Paul this natural process has already taken place. Paul, I think, could hardly claim that he already sees face to face and knows as he has been known by God. Cf. Sabbe 1965 303: "In v. 11 wordt de verleden tijd tegenover de huidige tijd geplaatst. In v. 12 wordt de huidige tijd van de aardse situatie van de christenen een tegenhanger van de toekomstige eschatologische tijd na dit leven".

[95] Murphy O'Connor, in: Standaert 1983b, 140.

[96] Cf. ibid.

that of Moses. The "mouth-to-mouth" nature of Moses' contact, however, is not an immediate vision of God. The relative superiority of God's communication with Moses is not eschatological in the strict sense but still historical.[97] So our future adult seeing "face to face" is not yet the eschatological contemplative vision of God.

(2) Does the disappearance of the gifts as it is announced in verse 8 not point to the eschaton? The proponents of the "no final eschatology" interpretation could reply that in healthy circumstances the gifts can remain during the entire Christian life. Yet in Corinth, because of the situation where gifts are obstructing the practice of love, Paul wishes the gifts "to pass away in order to leave greater scope for the fundamental realities of faith, hope and love".[98]

This present-life interpretation, however, can hardly be correct. The expression οὐδέποτε πίπτει of verse 8, the number of future tenses, the radical disappearance of (τὸ) ἐκ μέρους announced throughout this passage,[99] the contrast between the present and the future life, and more particularly between τότε and ἄρτι in verse 12: all this together makes the historical, not final eschatological understanding simply unacceptable.

Especially the future perfect knowledge which is compared to God's knowledge (v. 12) cannot but point to the strictly eschatological condition. Miguens deals with the last clause of verse 12 in great detail[100] and reasons as follows. The verb ἐπιγνώσομαι, just as γνῶσις in 1 Cor 8:3, is without object. It would be wrong to supply God without ado. 1 Cor 13:2 indicates that the content of the "understanding knowledge" is connected with the "understanding of all mysteries". Because Christians have been known by God,[101] they are able to deepen their understanding and knowledge. The same applies to their future seeing: "The implication is that *blepein* does not express here a vision of some sort in which God is contemplated, but an understanding or intellectual grasping of something else, which cannot be but the

---

[97] Ibid. 140-141. In a more thorough way Miguens 1975, 81-87, examines the term "seeing" and the expressions "enigmatically" and "face to face" against their O.T. background. His hardly correct conclusion is: "... when Paul (1 Cor 13:12a) refers to a *blepein* face to face, he does not speak about a vision of God directly and immediately, but about a Christian *blepein* or understanding of the Christian faith or mysteries (vs. 2) 'then,' which is certainly much clearer and manifest than the *blepein* possible 'now'".

[98] Murphy O'Connor, in Standaert 1983b, 142. Cf. Miguens 1975, 94.

[99] Fee 1987, 643-644, comments on καταργέομαι: "Thus the basic verb chosen to describe the temporal, transitory nature of the *charismata* is an eschatological one, used elsewhere in the letter to refer to the 'passing away' of what belongs merely to the present age" (643). This, of course, does not apply to κατήργηκα of 13:11.

[100] See Miguens 1975, 81-84.90.91-93. Cf. Sabbe 1965, 310-312.

[101] For a discussion of the passive forms and the past tense of 1 Cor 8:3 (perfect) and Gal 4:9 (aorist), see Miguens 1975, 92-93.

object of Christian gnosis, i.e., the 'mysteries' (vs. 2) of the Christian faith".[102]

Yet, although both βλέπομεν and γινώσκω in verse 12 have no direct object and may ask for a seeing and knowing of Christian realities which are not directly God, the expression "face to face" and the clause "even as I have been fully understood (by God)" in the same verse appear to point to God himself.[103] Christians will finally, in the eschaton, see God face to face[104] and know him in the same way as (καθὼς καί) God has directly known them (and still knows them).[105]

D. A. Carson rightly states: "*any* preparousia maturity simply trivializes the language of verse 12".[106] In this context the words of K. Barth are often quoted: "Because the sun rises, all lights go out".[107] The sun will really rise at the parousia, and only then definitely. Then God will "be all in all" (1 Cor 15:28).

## 4.2. Faith, Hope and Love Will Last for Ever

Over against the present-life interpretation of 1 Cor 13:8-13 we find the radical opinion that not only verses 8-12 but also the whole of verse 13 must be understood strictly eschatologically.[108] According to this interpretation Paul states in verse 13a: So then faith, hope and love have no end; all three of them will last and remain for ever. In verse 13b a correction is added: but love is the greatest. This correction, however, in no way denies the eschatological permanence of faith and hope. Four reasons are put forward; they should be taken together.

---

[102] Miguens 1975, 84.

[103] See Spicq 1959, 101, n. 3: "Le contexte ne permet pas de douter que Dieu en personne soit l'objet de la vision ...". Cf. 1 John 3:2: οἴδαμεν ὅτι ἐὰν φανερωθῇ, ὅμοιοι αὐτῷ ἐσόμεθα, ὅτι ὀψόμεθα αὐτὸν καθώς ἐστιν.

[104] Spicq 159, 101, notes: "La substitution du 'face à face' à 'bouche à bouche' de *Nomb.* XII, 8 est peut-être intentionnelle, et se référerait à *Ex* XXXIII, 20 où aucun homme ne peut voir la personne de Iahwé sans mourir".

[105] Cf. the aspect of the perfect tense ἔγνωσται of 1 Cor 8:3. Most probably καθώς in 13:12 is strictly comparative, without any causal nuance. Otherwise Miguens 1975, 93 and, it would seem, Spicq 1959, 102-104.

[106] Carson 1987, 71: "If it is true that the word for 'perfection' is nowhere else used for the entire state of affairs brought about by the parousia, it is also true that it almost always occurs as an adjective. Only here is it a neuter, articular substantive, probably created precisely to serve as a contrast to 'the partial' or 'the imperfect'". Fee 1987, 645, mentions two objections against the "immaturity-maturity" explanation: (1) "... the contrast has to do with the *gifts* being 'partial,' ... not the believers themselves." (2) "One must not give the analogy [v. 11], which is ambiguous at best, precedence of the argument as a whole and the plain statement of v. 12b ...".

[107] Barth 1977, 81. See, e.g., Bornkamm 1985, 228; Carson 1987, 70; Fee 1987, 646 ("Barth's marvelous imagery").

[108] So already Heinrici 1896, 406-407. Cf., e.g., Robertson-Plummer 1914, 287 and 299-300; Lietzmann-Kümmel 1949, 66 and 189.

(1) Verse 13 brings the long digression 1 Cor 13 to a conclusion. In the introductory words νυνὶ δέ the δέ indicates that the opposition between "now" and "then" is finished. This means that νυνί must not be taken temporally in the sense of "(here and) now". That is why Paul no longer uses the exclusively temporal ἄρτι. The meaning of νυνὶ δέ is most probably logical: "So then ...".[109]

(2) By itself, however, the logical meaning of νυνὶ δέ does not decide whether the strictly eschatological or the historical value of the verb μένει which follows must be preferred.[110] According to the proponents of this position the verb μένει of verse 13a corresponds with οὐδέποτε πίπτει (v. 8a).[111] Along with ἀγάπη the two verbs function as an inclusion. The sense "abides" of μένει must therefore be understood as "abides for ever, lasts for ever" which provides the equivalent of "never ends" in verse 8. The verb μένει is strictly eschatological.

(3) Theologically speaking—as it is now often stated—there is no difficulty in the presence of the fundamental dimensions of faith and hope within resurrectional life.[112] What is obtained in the eschaton is not at our disposal. It remains God's benevolence. Our faithful hope in a God who will continue his magnanimity remains

---

[109] Paul quite often employs νυνὶ δέ temporally (cf., e.g., Rom 3:21) as well as logically (cf., e.g., 1 Cor 12:18). Cf. Söding 1992, 635: "Selbstverständlich liesse sich die Wahl des Wortes νυνί in Vers 13, sollte es temporal zu verstehen sein, aus Gründen stilistischer Abwechslung erklären; näher liegt es aber, dass sich νυνί von ἄρτι auch semantisch unterscheidet". Cf. Bornkamm 1985 1985, 230, n. 39: "Der Unterschied zwischen Jetzt (ἄρτι) v. 12 und dem Jetzt (νυνὶ δέ) v. 13 ist wohl zu beachten; das erste hat den Sinn von 'jetzt noch', dem zweiten fehlt die Begrenzung". For a discussion of the logical use, often after an irreal hypothesis, also in Paul, see Neirynck 1963, 606-607. Yet it appears rather far-fetched to find an unexpressed irreal hypothesis in 1 Cor 13:13: "Voorafgaandelijk was spraak van de aardse gaven die moeten vergaan of vervangen worden. Zou dan ook de liefde vergankelijk zijn zoals de charismen? Het is als het ware een onuitgesproken hypothese, onmiddellijk gecorrigeerd in v. 13 ..." (607). Cf. the criticism of Sabbe 1965, 317, n. 53.

[110] Cf. Kieffer 1975a, 68-69; Fee 1987, 650, n. 56; see also Miguens 1975, 77, who for his present-life interpretation also accepts a logical sense: "as it is, these three remain in force ..." (94). Abstractly speaking a logical meaning would equally be possible for our third proposal..

[111] Cf. Neirynck 1963, 609; Bornkamm 1985, 227: "... die positive These, die das Thema der Verse 8-13 abgibt, steht am Anfang (8a) und wird durch den Schluss (13) wiederaufgenommen".

[112] Cf., often with reference to Bultmann, e.g., Lacan 1958, 342; Neirynck 1963, 610-615; Kieffer 1975a, 69; Barrett 1968, 308-311; Conzelmann 1981, 281-282; Bornkamm 1985, 232-233; Carson 1987, 74-75. We may quote a passage from Bornkamm: a person "in der Vollendung" is "auf Gott angewiesen und ohne Ende für ihn offen ..., ständig ein Empfangender, der den Grund seines Lebens nicht in sich selbst hat (πίστις), ständig ein Hoffender, der auf Gott harrt (ἐλπίς)" (232-233); and from Barrett: "Faith, the thankful recognition of the gracious God, will be in place as long as God continues to be gracious; that is, faith is an eternal mark of the true relationship between God and man" (309). Regarding hope, he translates Bultmann, ἐλπίς, in *ThWNT* II, 529: Hope is "a trust in God that looks away from itself and from the world, a trust that waits patiently for God's gift, and, when he has given it, is still not in full (*verfügenden*) possession, but in the serene (*getrosten*) confidence that what God has given God will maintain" (309).

after life.[113] "Die Kennzeichen christlicher Existenz sind von bleibender Gültigkeit, sie werden nicht als Stückwerk beseitigt werden".[114]

(4) A good exegesis, it is asserted, can handle the two Pauline passages which seem to speak against the permanence of faith and hope after the parousia, namely 2 Cor 5:7: "For we walk by faith, not by sight"; and Rom 8:24bc: "Now hope that is seen is not hope. For who hopes for what is seen?" In 2 Cor 5:7 there is—so it is claimed—no real contrast between believing and seeing (διὰ εἴδους does not mean active "sight" but rather "what is seen" – passive); in Rom 8:24bc we have before us popular speculation; the concept of hope here is rather Greek in origin (hope = simple expectation of the future, cf. v. 25) and does not possess the depth of the O.T. (and Pauline) notion.[115]

We hesitate to subscribe to this second and highly eschatological understanding. It would seem that a middle position is to be preferred.

## 4.3. Faith, Hope and Love During this Life

To be sure, according to this third position, just as with the second, love certainly never ends. The permanence of love is without any doubt eschatological. Paul says this clearly at the beginning of verse 8 and, by stressing the charisms as provisional, explains it until the end of verse 12. What is partial will pass away. Not so love! Yet in verse 13a Paul, we think, does not speak of the eschaton but of present-life realities: faith, hope and love. They were already mentioned in verse 7 and there, as it were, in full historical activity. In verse 13b Paul emphasizes that love is the greatest of these three. Why? Of course, because of love's pre-eminent, irreplaceable role in Christian life on earth, but also most probably because of love's unique eschatological nature, its eternal permanence.

What is to be replied to the reasons brought forward by those who defend the second position? How do we argue in favor of our proposal?

(1) As stated above, there can be no doubt that verse 13 brings the excursus to a conclusion. The slightly opposing particle δέ indicates that what is going to be said will be different from the statement in the previous verse. In verse 12 the temporal adverb ἄρτι twice points to an imperfect action in this earthly life in contrast with τότε, i.e., the eschatological fulfillment. It would seem that νυνί in verse 13a is temporal no less than ἄρτι in verse 12; νυνὶ δέ is "une reprise légèrement accentuée de

---

[113] Cf. Sabbe 1965, 322-325.

[114] Wolff 1982, 128. Cf. Söding 1992, 136-139, who stresses "daß sich in der futurisch-eschatologischen Schau Gottes das Glauben und das Hoffen *erfüllen*" (137).

[115] Cf. Dupont 1960, 108-111; Neirynck 1963, 610-614; Sabbe 1965, 304 and 320-321.

ἄρτι ... 'maintenant encore'";[116] νυνί equally points to this earthly life.[117] Yet imperfection is not so much focused upon and there is no longer the explicit opposition between "now" and "then" (no τότε in v. 13b).[118] For that reason Paul most probably changes from ἄρτι to νυνί: "now, i.e., meanwhile, during this life".

(2) We surmise that the verb μένει means "remains now (during this life)".[119] In verse 13a μένει is a present tense (cf. vv. 9 and 12); the verb is not accompanied by the expression εἰς τὸν αἰῶνα (so, e.g., in 2 Cor 9:9). Also elsewhere Paul uses μένω in a non-eschatological sense in, e.g., 1 Cor 3:14; 7:8, 11, 20, 24, 40; and 15:6 (+ ἕως ἄρτι).[120]

At the end of verse 12 Paul writes: "then I will know fully, even as I have been fully known". A future tense (ἐπιγνώσομαι) is followed by a past tense (aorist: ἐπεγνώσθην). Paul compares his eschatological future with his having been known by God before the foundation of the world and, equally, at the time of his historical call: "La πρόγνωσις divine est orientée vers l'eschatologie".[121] It would seem that with νυνὶ δέ μένει Paul is referring to the present time after the past call and before the eschaton.

(3) The question is not so much whether the eschatological permanence of faith and hope is theologically admissible, but rather whether Paul would speak in such a manner. What he clearly states in 2 Cor 5:7 and Rom 8:24-25 appears to contradict such a supposition. Since faith and hope are not charisms in the sense of extraordinary gifts but indispensable attitudes in Christian life, their appearance in verse 13,

---

[116] Spicq 1959, 105.

[117] Fee 1987, 649-650, warns: "... it is difficult under any circumstances to divest the adverb 'now' of some temporal sense. That is, even if its basic thrust is logical (= 'but as it is'), it carries the force 'as it is in the present state of things'. This seems to be all the more so here, given the present tense of the verb 'remain' and the fact that these three opening words [νυνὶ δὲ μένει] stand in immediate conjunction to the eschatological words that have just preceded". Cf. Spicq 1959, 54: "quant à présent"; 104: "maintenant, dans la vie présente".

[118] The double remark of Héring 1949, 121, is to the point: "... il serait ... bien curieux de l'employer (i.e., the expression νυνὶ δέ) pour désigner la permanence éternelle de l'agapè dans l'avenir. De plus ... νυνὶ δέ, pour chaque lecteur non prévenu, s'oppose au τότε du vers. 12b et ne peut par conséquent se revêtir que du sens temporel: *maintenant*".

[119] Some exegetes soften the temporal sense of the verb: the three "remain valid". See, e.g., Grossouw 1954, 516; Senft 1979, 172: "Ce qui demeure, c'est ce qui est à retenir comme essentiel"; Conzelmann 1981, 282 (a suggestion: "gültig bleiben"; he, however, notes: "Dabei geht die eschatologische Intention keineswegs verloren"; ibid.).

[120] Cf. Standaert 1983b, 137: "Le verbe *menei* forme inclusion avec l'ouverture de la troisième strophe (*oudepote piptei*) mais l'accent eschatologique s'est estompé. Paul revient à l'ordre présent, et celui-ci, bien qu'imparfait et destiné à disparaître ..., est qualifé durablement par la foi, l'espérance et *agapê*".

[121] Dupont 1960, 91 (with reference to Rom 8:29).

although somewhat unexpected, is quite understandable.[122]

(4) Whatever the exact nuance of the still future, eschatological διὰ εἴδους in 2 Cor 5:7 may be, it certainly stands in opposition to the present-life condition which Paul characterizes by περιπατοῦμεν διὰ πίστεως. For Paul, there will seemingly no longer be faith after death. One cannot minimize a passage such as Rom 8:23-25 (within 8:18-30). For Paul present Christian life is not yet the eschaton; it is a time of inward groaning, of waiting and hoping.[123] At the time of "the redemption of our bodies", of the final "adoption" Christians will no longer hope; hope will have been fulfilled.

We may draw the conclusion of our argument. In 1 Cor 13:13a Paul most probably deals with the present-day Christian life. Not all Christians are equipped with extraordinary gifts, but in their lives there certainly is the abiding presence of faith, hope and love. Faith and hope will pass away and be replaced by sight and fulfillment. Only eschatological love will remain for ever and will never end.[124] "The quintessential eschatological reality, then, is ἀγάπη, and it is the only such reality to have invaded the now in any absolute sense .... It alone should become the ultimate reality of Christian existence. It alone should be primal".[125]

Does Paul mean love of God or love of neighbor? Although in verse 12 the term "love" is not mentioned, we must assume that the face-to-face vision and the perfect knowledge include love. In this verse, future seeing and knowing of God are spoken of, but love of God is likewise intended. Yet one must remember that in verses 4-7 primarily[126] love of neighbor is depicted: that love is practised during this present life on earth. Love of neighbor must also be meant in verse 13a. However, since in this last clause Paul with faith and hope refers to believing and hoping in God (and Christ), the third term of the triad, love—no doubt love of neighbor—cannot but

---

[122] Cf. Spicq 1959, 105: "L'Apôtre qui vient d'exalter tellement la charité au-dessus des charismes, ne peut pas discréditer implicitement les deux grandes vertus de foi et d'espérance, et c'est dans un souci pastoral et catéchétique qu'il les évoque, comme inséparables ici-bas de l'amour infus de charité. Il donne, par conséquent, à μένειν son sens temporel de 'persévérer, continuer'". See also Guardini 1958, 59-61. At first, one has the impression that this author defends the second explanation: "Alles Irdische vergeht, auch die Charismen, welche in die Ewigkeit reichen" (59); faith and hope possess "den Charakter des Wesentlichen. Ein Mensch kann Christ sein ohne die Charismen, aber nicht ohne den Glauben und die Hoffnung. Diese enthalten schon jetzt Ewiges" (60-61). Yet, when the eschaton comes "werden Glaube und Hoffnung vergehen .... Anders die Liebe" (61).

[123] Cf. Lambrecht 1992, 122-123.

[124] Cf. Fee 1987, 651: "Along with its companions, faith and hope, it [love] abides in the present. But it is greater, at least as the point of this present argument, because it abides on into eternity".

[125] Holladay 1990, 97. For a discussion of the way Paul in verse 13b calls love the greatest of the three, see Söding 1992, 139-142.

[126] Söding 1989, 232-234, and 1992, 128-130, explains how some qualifications of love in verses 4-7 indicate that love of God is also present, already here.

participate in that God direction. Apparently for Paul daily love of neighbor constitutes the only way to attaining authentic, eschatologically enduring love of God and
neighbor.

In verses 4-7 love is personified. In verses 9 and 12a Paul uses the first person
plural, but, by means of the first person singular in verses 1-3, 11 and 12b, he most
probably refers in the first place to himself. What Paul in 1 Cor 13 says about love
is for himself too both a program to be executed and an end goal to be attained.

In chapter 13 of 1 Corinthians God is not explicitly named, nor is Christ. As we
saw, J. Dupont, although not without due reservation, calls this chapter "anthropological" and sees it as complementary to the ecclesiological chapter 12.[127] "The
ἀγάπη consists in what is required from each Christian individually in his or her daily and concrete response which must be given to the Christian call".[128] This does,
however, not mean that a Christian will be able to go that "most eminent way", *via
maxime vialis* (Bengel), without God's grace and the Spirit of Christ.

## Bibliography

Allo, E.-B. 1956: *Saint Paul. Première Epître Aux Corinthiens* (EtB), 2nd ed., Paris: Gabalda 1956.

Bachmann, P. 1921: *Der erste Brief des Paulus an die Korinther* (KNT), Leipzig: Scholl 1921.

Barrett, C. K. 1968: *A Commentary on the First Epistle to the Corinthians* (BNTC), London: Black
     1968.

Barth, K. 1977: *The Resurrection of the Dead,* New York: Arno 1977.

Best, E. 1975: "The Interpretation of Tongues", in: *SJTh* 28 (1975) 46-62.

Bornkamm, G. 1985: "Der köstlichere Weg. 1. Kor. 13", in: idem, *Studien zum Neuen Testament,*
     München: Kaiser 1985, 217-236 (first ed. 1937).

Carson, D. A. 1987: *Showing the Spirit: A Theological Exposition of 1 Corinthians 12-14,* Grand
     Rapids, MI: Baker 1987.

Collins, J. J. 1993: "Ministry as a Distinct Category among Charismata (1 Corinthians 12:4-7), in:
     *Neotestamentica* 27 (1993) 79-91.

Conzelmann, H. 1981: *Der erste Brief an die Korinther* (KEK 5), Göttingen: Vandenhoeck & Rup-
     recht 1969, 2nd ed. 1981. ET of the 1969 ed.: *1 Corinthtians* (Hermeneia), Philadelphia,
     PA: Fortress 1975.

---

[127] Dupont 1983a, 17-21.

[128] Dupont, in the discussion of Standaert 1983a, 50: "L'*agapê* est ce qui est exigé de chaque
chrétien individuellement dans la réponse quotidienne et concrète qu'il a à donner à sa vocation chrétienne".

Dautzenberg, G. 1975: *Urchristliche Prophetie. Ihre Erforschung, ihre Voraussetzungen im Judentum und ihre Struktur im ersten Korintherbrief* (BWANT 104), Stuttgart: Kohlhammer 1975.

Downing, F. G. 1984: "Reflecting the First Century: 1 Corinthians 13:12", in: *ET* 95 (1983-84) 176-177.

Dreyfus, F. 1963: "Maintenant la foi, l'espérance et la charité demeurent toutes les trois (1 Cor. 13,13)", in: *Studia Paulina I* (AnBib 17), Rome: Editrice Pontificio Istituto Biblico 1963, 403-412.

Dupont, J. 1960: *Gnosis. La connaissance religieuse dans les épîtres de saint Paul*, Louvain-Paris: Nauwelaerts-Gabalda 1949, 2nd ed. 1960, esp. 51-148.

— 1983a: "Dimensions du problème des charismes dans 1 Co 12-14", in: L. De Lorenzi (ed.), *Charisma und Agape (1 Ko 12-14)* (Benedictina 7), Rome: Benedictina Editrice 1983, 7-21.

— 1983b: "Conclusions", in: L. De Lorenzi (ed.), *Charisma und Agape (1 Ko 12-14)* (Benedictina 7), Rome: Benedictina Editrice 1983, 286-293.

Elliot, J. K. 1971: "In Favour of καυθήσομαι at I Corinthians 13,3", in: *ZNW* 62 (1971) 297-298.

Fee, G. D. 1987: *The First Epistle to the Corinthians* (NIC), Grand Rapids: Eerdmans 1987.

Fishbane, M. 1986: "Through the Looking Glass: Reflections on Ezek 43:3, Num 12:8 and 1 Cor 13", in: *Hebrew Annual Review* 10 (1986) 63-75.

Gerhardsson, B. 1974: "1 Kor. 13", in: *SEÅ* 39 (1974) 121-133.

— 1978: "Zur Frage von Paulus' rabbinischem Hintergrund", in: E. Bammel, C. K. Barrett & W. D. Davies (eds.), *Donum Gentilicium. FS D. Daube,* Oxford: Clarendon 1978, 185-209.

Giessen, H. 1984: "Apostolische Aktivität ohne Liebe? Zum Verständnis von 1 Kor 13,3b", in: *Theologie der Gegenwart* 27 (1984) 104-111.

Grosheide, F. W. 1957: *De eerste Brief aan de kerk te Korinthe* (Commentaar op het N.T.), Kampen: Kok 1957.

Grossouw, W. 1954: "L'espérance dans le Nouveau Testament", in: *RB* 61 (1954) 508-532 (esp. 516-518).

Guardini, R. 1958: *Drei Schriftauslegungen*, 2nd ed., Würzburg: Werkbund-Verlag 1958, p. 40-68 ("Die christliche Liebe; 1. Korinther 13").

Heinrici, G. 1896: *Der erste Brief an die Korinther* (KEK), Göttingen: Vandenhoeck & Ruprecht 1896.

Héring, J. 1949: *La première épître de saint Paul aux Corinthiens* (CNT(N)) Neuchâtel-Paris: Delachaux & Niestlé 1949.

Holladay, C. R. 1990: "1 Corinthians 13: Paul as Apostolic Paradigm", in: D. L. Balch, E. Ferguson & W. A. Meeks (eds.) *Greeks, Romans, and Christians. FS A. J. Malherbe*, Minneapolis, MN: Fortress 1990, 80-98.

Hugedé, N. 1957: *La métaphore du miroir dans les épîtres de saint Paul dans les épîtres aux Corinthiens*, Neuchâtel: Delachaux & Niestlé 1957.

Iber, G. 1963: "Zum Verständnis von I Cor 12,31", in: *ZNW* 54 (1963) 43-52.

Johansson, N. 1964: "1 Cor. XIII and 1 Cor XIV", in: *NTS* 10 (1963-64) 383-392.

Käsemann, E. 1982: "Unterwegs zum Bleibenden. 1 Korinther 13", in: idem, *Kirchliche Konflikte I*, Göttingen: Vandenhoeck & Ruprecht 1982, 104-115.

Kahlefeld, H. 1971: "Die Rede von der Liebe (1 Kor 13)", in: idem, *Kleine Schriften*, Frankfurt am Main: Knecht 1984, 190-196.

Kieffer, R. 1975a: *Le primat de l'amour* (LeDiv 85), Paris: Cerf 1975.

— 1975b: "'Afin que je sois brûlé' ou bien 'afin que j'en tire orgueil'? (I Cor. XIII.3)", in: *NTS* 22 (1975-76) 95-97.

Klein, W. W. 1986: "Noisy Gong or Acoustic Vase? A Note on 1 Corinthians 13.1", in: *NTS* 32 (1986) 286-289.

Lacan, M. F. 1958: "Les trois qui demeurent. 1 Cor. 13,13", *RSR* 46 (1958) 321-343.

— 1973: "Le mystère de la charité. 1 Co 12,31-13,13", in: *ASeign* 35 (1973) 56-61.

Lambrecht, J. 1992: *The wretched "I" and Its Liberation: Paul in Romans 7 and 8* (Louv. Theol. & Past. Monogr. 14), Leuven: Peeters 1992, 115-133.

Lausberg, H. 1973: *Handbuch der literarischen Rhetorik*, Munich: Hueber, 2nd ed. 1973.

Lietzmann, H. 1949: *An die Korinther* (HNT 9), 4th ed.; ed. by W. G. Kümmel, Tübingen: Mohr 1949.

Louw, J. P. 1988; "The Function of Discourse in a Sociosemiotic Theory of Translation Illustrated by the Translation of *zêloute* in 1 Corinthians 12.31", in: *BiTr* 39 (1988) 329-335.

Lund, N. W. 1931: "The Literary Structure of Paul's Hymn to Love", in: *JBL* 50 (1931) 266-276.

Martin, R. P. 1984: *The Spirit and the Congregation: Studies in 1 Corinthians 12-15*, Grand Rapids, MI: Eerdmans 1984.

Marxsen, W. 1972: "Das 'Bleiben' in I. Kor. 13,13", in: H. Baltensweiler & B. Reicke (eds.), *Neues Testament und Geschichte. Historisches Geschehen und Deutung im Neuen Testament. FS O. Cullmann*, Zürich-Tübingen: Theologischer Verlag – Mohr 1972, 223-230.

Miguens, E. 1975: "1 Cor 13:8-13 Reconsidered", in: *CBQ* 37 (1975) 76-97.

Mitchell, M. M. 1991: *Paul and the Rhetoric of Reconciliation: An Exegetical Investigation of the Language and Composition of 1 Corinthians* (HUTh 28), Tübingen: Mohr 1991.

Neidhart, W. 1984: "Das paulinische Verständnis der Liebe und die Sexualität. Pastoraltheologische Überlegungen", in: *ThZ* 40 (1984) 245-256.

Neirynck, F. 1963: "De grote drie. Bij een nieuwe vertaling van I Cor XIII,13", in: *EThL* 39 (1963) 595-615.

Pedersen, S. 1980: "Agape – der eschatologische Hauptbegriff bei Paulus", in: *Die Paulinische Literatur und Theologie*, Århus-Göttingen: Vandenhoeck & Ruprecht 1980, 159-186.

Petzer, J. H. 1989: "Contextual Evidence in Favour of ΚΑΥΧΗΣΩΜΑΙ in 1 Corinthians 13.3", in: *NTS* 35 (1989) 229-253.

Pop, F. J. 1971: *De eerste Brief van Paulus aan de Corinthiërs* (Prediking van het N.T.), Nijkerk: Callenbach, 2nd ed. 1971.

Riesenfeld, H. 1941: "Etude bibliographique sur la notion biblique d' ἀγάπη, surtout dans 1 Cor 13", in: *CNT* 5 (1941)1-27.

— 1978: "Vorbildliches Martyrium. Zur Frage der Lesarten in I Kor 13,3", in: E. Bammel, C. K. Barrett & W. D. Davies (eds.), *Donum Gentilicium. FS D. Daube*, Oxford: Clarendon 1978, 210-214.

Robertson, A. & A. Plummer 1914: *A Critical and Exegetical Commentary on the First Epistle of St. Paul to the Corinthians* (ICC), 2nd ed., Edinburgh: Clark 1914.

Sabbe, M. 1964/65: "De weg van de liefde (1 Cor. 13)", in: *CBG* 10 (1964) 494-511; 11 (1965) 433-480: repr. in: idem, *Studia neotestamentica. Collected Essays* (BEThL 98), Leuven: University – Peeters 1991, 261-328.

Sanders, J. T. 1966: "First Corinthians 13: Its Interpretation Since the First World War", in: *Interp.* 20 (1966) 159-187.

Sanders, T. K. 1990: "A New Approach to 1 Corinthians 13.1", in: *NTS* 36 (1990) 614-618.

Schindele, M. M. 1972: "Denn unser Erkennen ist Stückwerk (I Kor 13,8)", in: *EuA* 48 (1972) 220-222.

Schlier, H. 1956: "Über die Liebe. – 1 Kor. 13", in: idem, *Zeit der Kirche*, Freiburg: Herder 1956, 186-192.

Schützeichel, H. 1993: "Der Weg der Liebe. Calvins Auslegung von 1 Kor 13", in: *TThZ* 102 (1993) 110-124.

Seaford, R. 1984: "1 Corinthians XIII.12", in: *JThS* 35 (1984) 117-120.

Senft, C. 1979: *La première épître de saint Paul aux Corinthiens* (CNT(N)), Neuchâtel-Paris: Delachaux & Niestlé 1979.

Sisti, P. A. 1968: "L'inno della Carità", in: *BeO* 10 (1968) 39-51.

Smit, J. 1989: "De rangorde in de kerk: Retorische analyse van 1 Kor. 12", in: *TTh* 29 (1989) 325-343.

— 1991: "The Genre of 1 Corinthians 13 in the Light of Classical Rhetoric", in: *NT* 33 (1991) 193-216.

— 1992 (?): "1 Korinte 13: Hooglied of Spotrede?" in: P. Beentjes, J. Maas and T. Wever (eds.), *'Gelukkig de mens'. FS N. Tromp*, Kampen: Kok, s.d., 107-118.

— 1993: "Two Puzzles: 1 Corinthians 12.31 and 13.3: A Rhetorical Solution", in: *NTS* 39 (1993) 246-264.

Snyman, H. 1986: "Remarks on the Stylistic Parallelisms in 1 Corinthians 13", in: J. H. Petzer & P. J. Hartin (eds.), *A South African Perspective on the New Testament. FS B. M. Metzger* (NT Tools & Stud. 15), Leiden: Brill 1986, 203-213.

Söding, T. 1989: "Gottesliebe bei Paulus", in: *ThGl* 79 (1989) 219-242.

— 1992, *Die Trias Glaube, Hoffnung, Liebe bei Paulus. Eine exegetische Studie* (SBS 150), Stuttgart: Katholisches Bibelwerk 1992.

Spicq, C. 1959: *Agapè dans le Nouveau Testament*, Vol. 2, Paris: Gabalda 1959, 53-120.

Standaert, B. 1983a: "Analyse rhétorique des chapitres 12 à 14 de 1 Co", in: L. De Lorenzi (ed.), *Charisma und Agape (1 Ko 12-14)* (Benedictina 7), Rome: Benedictina Editrice 1983, 23-34 (with discussion on 35-50).

— 1983b: "1 Corinthiens 13", in: L. De Lorenzi (ed.), *Charisma und Agape (1 Ko 12-14)* (Benedictina 7), Rome: Benedictina Editrice 1983, 127-139 (with discussion on 139-147).

Stuart, E. 1991: "Love is ... Paul", in: *ET* 102 (1990-91) 264-266.

Thomas, R. L. 1974: "Tongues ... Will Cease", in: *JETS* 17 (1974) 81-89.

Titus, E. L. 1959: "Did Paul Write I Corinthians 13?" in: *JBR* 27 (1959) 299-302.

Van Fleteren, F. 1992: "Per speculum et in aenigmate: I Corinthians 13:12 in the Writings of St. Augustine", in: *Augustinian Studies* 23 (1992) 69-102.

Van Unnik, W. C. 1993: "The Meaning of 1 Corinthians 12:31", in: *NT* 35 (1993) 142-159.

von Rad., G. 1953: "Die Vorgeschichte der Gattung von I. Kor. 13,4-7", in: *Geschichte und Altes Testament. FS A. Alt* (BHTh 16), Tübingen: Mohr 1953, 153-168.

Wagner, C. 1958: "Gotteserkenntnis im Spiegel und Gottesbild in den beiden Korintherbriefen", in: *Bijdragen* 19 (1958) 370-381.

Waters, C. J. 1991: "'Love is ... Paul' – A Response", in: *ET* 103 (1991) 75.

Weiß, J. 1910: *Der erste Korintherbrief* (KEK 5), Göttingen: Vandenhoeck & Ruprecht 1910.

Wischmeyer, O. 1981: *Der höchste Weg. Das 13. Kapitel des 1. Korintherbriefes* (StNT 13), Gütersloh: Mohn 1981.

— 1983: "Traditionsgeschichtliche Untersuchung der paulinischen Aussagen über die Liebe (ἀγάπη)", in: *ZNW* 74 (1983) 222-236.

Wolff, C. 1982: *Der erste Brief des Paulus an die Korinter. Kap. 8-16* (ThHK 7/II), Berlin: Evangelische Verlagsanstalt 1982.

Wong, E. 1992: "1 Corinthians 13:7 and Christian Hope", in: *Louvain Stud.* 17 (1992) 232-242.

# Die Makrosyntax des Hebräerbriefs

Folker Siegert

## 1. Einleitung

Der bescheidene Beitrag der folgenden Seiten gilt der Frage, ob eine von inhaltlichen Erwägungen unabhängige, nur nach objektiv vorhandenen Gliederungsmerkmalen verfahrende Einteilung eines Textganzen wie des Hebräerbriefs möglich sei. Im Kontext des vorliegenden Bandes darf das Bestreben, einer "theologischen" Hermeneutik (was immer das sei) neutrale Beobachtungen als Basis vorzuschalten, auf Sympathien rechnen.

Schlägt man einen der zahllosen biblischen Kommentare auf, wird man meist beim Anblick des Inhaltsverzeichnisses schon gewahr, daß hier keine objektiven Kriterien der Texteinteilung vorherrschen. Der Kommentator konstruiert eine Gliederung gemäß seiner (bereits fertigen) Meinung über Zusammenhänge inhaltlicher Art. Je nach theologischer Gewichtung läßt man neue "Teile", "Perikopen" o.ä. beginnen und enden; man macht Exkurse zur Hauptsache und umgekehrt.

Ein Extrem sind Kommentare, deren Kapitel einfach die Kapitel des Bibeltextes reproduzieren – ein scheinbar objektives Verfahren: man entscheidet nichts. Als ob Stephen Langton im 13. Jahrhundert die Arbeit ein für alle Mal erledigt hätte! – Der weitaus entwickeltere Stand der Textwissenschaft unserer Tage reizte den Unterzeichneten, die Gesamtgliederung einer neutestamentlichen Schrift zu versuchen, die sowohl von bisherigen Lesegewohnheiten als auch von theologischen Wertungen unabhängig ist. Sie muß detailliert genug sein, um mehrere Netze von kata- und anaphorischen Beziehungen zugleich mit den Merkmalen distinktiver Art wiederzugeben; und sie darf nicht so kompliziert sein, daß die Arbeit den Aufwand nicht lohnt (wie an vielen linguistischen Gedankenspielen zu sehen ist).

Unser Beispiel sei der Hebräerbrief. Als Anfangsintuition darf gelten (und wird sich im folgenden bestätigen), daß er ein nahezu einheitliches, wohlformuliertes Ganzes ist, und zwar von der Großgattung 'Diskurs'. Ein Erzähltext zusammengesetzten Charakters wie etwa das Markusevangelium würde andere Analyseschritte nötig machen als die hier zu erprobenden.

Wir werden nun darangehen, die im Hebr., und zwar nur in seinem "Oberflächentext"[1], enthaltenen *Gliederungsmerkmale* festzustellen. Wir kümmern uns (noch) nicht um Inhalte oder Themen; methodisch gesehen, wissen wir noch gar nicht, worauf es dem Autor des vorliegenden Textes am meisten ankommt. Wir lassen uns nicht versuchen, unsere eigenen theologischen Interessen in die Basisarbeit der Textanalyse einzubringen.

Die folgende Analyse berücksichtigt die in der Semiotik wohlbewährte Unterscheidung der drei Ebenen: Syntax, Semantik und Pragmatik. Zum Ausgangspunkt nimmt sie die Syntax, die ja *per definitionem* schon Gliederung und Ordnung ist, und deren Details sich, von Ambiguitäten abgesehen, objektiv feststellen lassen. Da es sich nicht nur um die konventionelle Syntax einzelner Sätze handelt, sondern um die des Textganzen, greifen wir zurück auf die seit den 70-er Jahren mit der nötigen Methodik und Terminologie ausgestattete *Makro-* oder *Textsyntax* [2].

Ein Hauptanliegen der makrosyntaktische Analyse gilt dem Auffinden der *Einbettungen* kleinerer Einheiten in größeren. Die Einbettungen sind feststellbar anhand der *Gliederungssignale,* die in zwei Genera zerfallen:

• Merkmale des *Kontrastes* oder der *Neuheit* (z.B. Wechsel der grammatischen Person, des Tempus, des Modus, auch des Wortfeldes; Adversativpartikeln wie δέ und καί – teilweise wenigstens)[3], und

• Merkmale der *Vertrautheit:* Wiederaufnahmen aller Art, Resümees; typische Partikel: οὖν.

Eine Begründung oder eine nähere Ausführung (typische Partikel: γάρ) wird meist als Kontrast einzustufen sein. Wo sich Gliederungsmerkmale beider Sorten

---

[1] Für Diskurstexte haben sich "Tiefentext"-Hypothesen bis jetzt als wenig ergiebig erwiesen. Wohl kann man mit Greimas' Aktanten-Modell oder mit formallogischen Modellen arbeiten; doch ergeben sich dabei in der Regel keine neuen Strukturmerkmale, die nicht schon im Oberflächentext (im Wortlaut) ausgedrückt wären. Dies gilt insbesondere für Texte, die in dem an Partikeln und an jeglichen Ausdrucksmitteln reichen Griechischen verfaßt sind. Man könnte die Textsorte 'Diskurs' direkt danach definieren, daß (im Idealfall) Oberflächen- und Tiefentext in Deckung sind, und daß ersterer dem letzteren an Explizitheit mindestens gleichkommt. (Eine Ausnahme, die mit dieser Definition identifizierbar würde, wären Texte von verdeckter Argumentation, die – aus welchen Gründen auch immer, und sei es aus Ungeschicklichkeit – eine andere Botschaft transportieren als die ihres Oberflächentextes.)

[2] Wir verfahren nach einer nicht mehr neuen, darum aber nicht weniger guten Methode der Linguisten E. Gülich, K. Heger und W. Raible 1974, insbes. 73-126. Für die Übernahme auf neutestamentliche Diskurstexte vgl. F. Siegert 1985, 98-100 (zur Makrosyntax) und 118f. (Schema des Römerbriefs).

[3] Die Partikeln des Altgriechischen, obwohl es deren viele gibt, dienen selten nur *einem* Zweck. Δέ z.B. markiert oft einen (schwachen) Kontrast, kann aber auch den Rückgriff auf etwas eben schon Genanntes unterstreichen, besonders wenn μέν vorausgegangen ist. In diesem Fall wird man das Moment des Kontrastes (das deswegen nicht fehlt) als weniger bestimmend einstufen.

zugleich finden, muß abgewogen werden, welche die "stärkere" ist, d.h. welches die dominierende, weiterreichende Kontextbeziehung ist. Es ist normal, daß ein Diskurselement sich gleichzeitig in mehreren, und auch noch verschiedenartigen, Beziehungen zu seinem Kontext befindet. Jedes Schema, so detailliert es auch sei, wird die Gegebenheiten des Textes vereinfachen – unter der Maßgabe freilich, das weniger Bestimmende dem stärker Bestimmenden nicht willkürlich vorzuziehen. In Zweifelsfällen müssen hier – soviel ist zuzugeben – semantische, ja auch pragmatische Erwägungen mithelfen. Es gibt keine autonome und von Ambiguitäten freie Syntax, jedenfalls nicht in natürlichen Sprachen.

In der folgenden Analyse werden *Kontraste* durch Einrücken kenntlich gemacht und *Wiederaufnahmen* von Vertrautem durch Rückkehr auf diejenige Stufe der Einrückung, auf der sich das korrespondierende Stück des oberen Kontexts befindet. Weitere Schreibkonventionen sind die folgenden:

<u>Unterstreichung</u> = makrosyntaktisch wirksame Partikel
<u><u>doppelte Unterstreichung</u></u> = korrespondierende Partikeln (μὲν–δέ, οὐκ–ἀλλά)
**Fettschrift** = sonstige Strukturierungsmerkmale
-------- (Trennungsstrich) = Absetzung von Textteilen, die aneinandergereiht, aber nicht näher aufeinander bezogen sind – vgl. den Briefschluß
*Kursivschrift* = Ausdruck, der im unteren Kontext eine Erläuterung finden wird[4];
in Klammern wird auf die entsprechenden Textstellen (auswahlweise) hingewiesen.

Aus Platzgründen wird im folgenden nicht der ganze Text abgeschrieben, sondern nur die für die Strukturanalyse relevanten Teile.

## 2. Gliederung des Hebräerbriefs

| | |
|---|---|
| **1,1** | Πολυμερῶς καὶ πολυτρόπως... |
| 1,2 | <u>ὃν</u> ἔθηκεν *κληρονόμον* (>6,17; 9,15; 11,7f.) πάντων |
| | <u>δι᾽ οὗ</u> καὶ ἐποίησεν |
| 1,3 | <u>ὃς</u> ὢν ἀπαύγασμα ... ἐκάθισεν |
| 1,5 | τίνι <u>γὰρ</u> εἶπεν... |
| | (Zitatenkette, resümiert in V. 14 in einer rhetorischen Frage) |
| **2,1** | <u>Διὰ τοῦτο</u> δεῖ ... **ἡμᾶς** ..., μήποτε παραρυ**ῶμεν** (*propositio*) |
| 2,5 | οὐ <u>γὰρ</u> ἀγγέλοις |
| 2,6 | διεμαρτύρατο <u>δὲ</u> (Schriftbeweise) |
| 2,8b | ἐν τῷ <u>γὰρ</u> «ὑποτάξαι» (Auslegung der Schriftzitate) |
| | <u><u>νῦν δὲ</u></u> οὔπω ὁρῶμεν (Einwand, also Neuheit/ Präzisierung) |

---

[4] Solche erst im Nachhinein erkennbaren kataphorischen Elemente sind eine Besonderheit des Hebr., wie auch des Johannesevangeliums – eine Methode der Insinuation, des unmerklichen Vertrautmachens mit Worten oder Wortbedeutungen, deren Neuheit nicht auffallen soll.

τὸν δὲ … βλέπομεν Ἰησοῦν διὰ τὸ πάθημα … ἐστεφανωμένον

2,10          ἔπρεπεν γὰρ αὐτῷ … διὰ *παθημάτων* (10,32)[5] τελειῶσαι
              (+andere Einbettungen)

2,14     ἐπεὶ οὖν τὰ παιδία (Resümee der Exegese; ebenso unten V. 17)

2,16          οὐ γὰρ δήπου

2.17     ὅθεν ὤφειλεν … ὁμοιωθῆναι (4,15),

              ἵνα … γένηται … *ἀρχιερεὺς* (3,1; 4,14ff.; 5,5; 6,20; 7,26ff. etc.)

2,18     ἐν ᾧ γὰρ *πέπονθεν* (>5,8)

**3,1**  Ὅθεν, **ἀδελφοὶ** ἅγιοι, … κατανοήσατε τὸν ἀπόστολον καὶ ἀρχιερέα

3,3      πλείονος γὰρ οὗτος

3,6b     οὗ[6] οἶκός ἐσμεν **ἡμεῖς**,

              ἐάνπερ τὴν *παρρησίαν* (4,16) καὶ τὸ καύχημα τῆς *ἐλπίδος* (>6,11 etc.) κατάσχωμεν.

3,7f.    Διό, καθὼς λέγει … , «μὴ σκληρύνητε … (der Imperativ zielt mit auf die Briefempfän-
         ger)[7]

3,11     ὡς ὤμοσα … (>6,13.16)· εἰ *εἰσελεύσονται* (>3,18ff. etc.; 9,12) εἰς τὴν *κατάπαυσιν*
         (>4,1.3).»

3,12     Βλέπετε, **ἀδελφοί**, μήποτε ἔσται … *ἀπιστίας*[8] (cf. πίστις negiert 4,2; behauptet 11,1ff.)
              ἐν τῷ ἀποστῆναι ἀπὸ θεοῦ ζῶντος (>9,14; 10,31)

3,13     ἀλλὰ *παρακαλεῖτε* (6,18 etc., 13,22)

3,14          μέτοχοι γὰρ … γεγόναμεν

3,16          τίνες γὰρ … παρεπίκραναν …;

3,17          τίσιν δὲ προσώχθισεν …;

3,18          τίσιν δὲ ὤμοσεν μὴ εἰσελεύσεσθαι … εἰ μὴ τοῖς *ἀπειθήσασιν* (>4,11);

3,19               καὶ (= aber) βλέπομεν ὅτι

**4,1**  Φοβηθῶμεν οὖν, μήποτε καταλειπομένης ἐπαγγελίας … *κατάπαυσιν* (>4,3)

4,2          καὶ γάρ ἐσμεν εὐηγγελισμένοι
              ἀλλ᾽ οὐκ ὠφέλησεν ὁ λόγος … μὴ συγκεκερασμένους τῇ πίστει (>11,1ff.)

4,3      εἰσερχόμεθα γὰρ εἰς τὴν κατάπαυσιν (gleiches γάρ wie in 4,2)
              (Schriftbeweise auf unterschiedlichen Einrückungsstufen)

4,6               ἐπεὶ (= denn) οὖν ἀπολείπεται (Resümee der Schriftbeweise)[9],

4,7          πάλιν … ὁρίζει[10] ἡμέραν

---

[5] Dieser Verweis mag theologisch fragwürdig erscheinen, weil er das einzigartige Leiden Christi mit den Leiden der Christen vergleicht. Es wird jedoch nur der Plural wiederholt, nicht der Singular des V. 9, dessen ἐφάπαξ vom Hebr. hinreichend herausgearbeitet ist.

[6] Dies ist kein echter Relativsatz, sondern ein relativischer Anschluß.

[7] Darum Ausrückung auf die Stufe des Textanfangs.

[8] Dieses Wort resümiert die negativen oder pejorativen Ausdrücke des oberen Kontexts. Verein-zelt kehren Ausdrücke des Bibelzitats (7b-11) wieder; so σήμερον V. 7b > 13.

[9] Zugleich Begründung des Folgenden; darum Einrückung gegenüber 4,7.

[10] Subjekt: der in der Bibel spricht; also Einrückungsstufe von 4,3b.

4,8          εἰ γὰρ αὐτοὺς Ἰησοῦς κατέπαυσεν, (Protasis)

             οὐκ ἂν ἐλάλει (Apodosis)

4,9          ἄρα ἀπολείπεται σαββατισμὸς (Resümee, geht zurück bis 4,3)

4,10         ὁ γὰρ εἰσελθὼν

4,11    Σπουδάσωμεν οὖν εἰσελθεῖν

             ἵνα μὴ ἐν τῷ αὐτῷ τις ὑποδείγματι¹¹ πέσῃ τῆς ἀπειθείας

4,12         ζῶν γὰρ ὁ λόγος

4,14    Ἔχοντες οὖν ἀρχιερέα ..., κρατῶμεν

4,15         οὐ γὰρ ἔχομεν ἀρχιερέα μὴ δυνάμενον

4,16    προσερχώμεθα (>7,25; 12,18) οὖν μετὰ παρρησίας (>10,19) τῷ θρόνῳ (>8,1) τῆς χάριτος

                                                                                        (>12,28)

5,1          πᾶς γὰρ ἀρχιερεὺς ... ἵνα προσφέρῃ ... θυσίας (>9,23.26 etc.) (Bildhälfte der Analo-
             gie)

5,5          οὕτως καὶ ὁ Χριστὸς (Sachhälfte der Analogie)

5,6              καθὼς (Zitat) «... κατὰ τὴν τάξιν Μελχισέδεκ» (>7,1 etc.)

5,7f.        ὃς (Christus) ἐν ταῖς ἡμέραις ... ἔπαθεν (>9,26; 13,12)

5,11    περὶ οὗ πολὺς ἡμῖν ὁ λόγος ..., (Anfangsstufe: der Satz enthält direkte Anrede)¹²

             ἐπεὶ νωθροὶ γεγόνατε

5,12         καὶ γὰρ ... χρείαν ἔχετε

6,1     Διὸ ἀφέντες τὸν τῆς ἀρχῆς ... λόγον ἐπὶ τὴν τελειότητα φερώμεθα¹³

             μὴ πάλιν θεμέλιον καταβαλλόμενοι μετανοίας ... (>V. 6) καὶ πίστεως (>c. 11)¹⁴

6,3     καὶ τοῦτο ποιήσομεν (+frommer Wunsch, *imprecatio*)

6,4          ἀδύνατον γὰρ (nimmt die Negation des V. 1 auf. V. 4-8 sind ein nachträgliches Argu-
             ment)¹⁵

6,7              γῆ γὰρ ἡ πιοῦσα

6,8              ἐκφέρουσα δὲ ἀκάνθας

6,9     πεπείσμεθα δὲ περὶ ὑμῶν

6,10         οὐ γὰρ ἄδικος ὁ Θεὸς ἐπιλαθέσθαι ... (>V. 13.18; 11,1)

6,11    ἐπιθυμοῦμεν δὲ ἕκαστον ὑμῶν ... ἐνδείκνυσθαι σπουδὴν ... ἐλπίδος

6,12         ἵνα ... γένησθε μιμηταὶ τῶν διὰ πίστεως ... (>11,1ff.) κληρονομούντων

6,13             τῷ γὰρ Ἀβραὰμ ... ὁ Θεός ... ὤμοσεν ...

6,16                 ἄνθρωποι γὰρ

6,17                 ἐν ᾧ (= weswegen) ... βουλόμενος ὁ Θεὸς ἐπιδεῖξαι τοῖς κληρονόμοις

---

¹¹ Dieses Wort kehrt zwar wieder, aber in andersartigen (ethischen) Kontexten: 8,5; 9,23.

¹² S. Anm. zu 3,6b.

¹³ *Pluralis modestiae,* nur auf den Autor bezogen.

¹⁴ *Praeteritio,* die das Interesse auf das lenkt, was anscheinend übergangen wird – das beweisen
die hier kursiv gedruckten Wörter, die den unten weiter zu entfaltenden Wortfeldern angehören.

¹⁵ Der Autor ist bemüht, den Sprechakt des Drohens möglichst zu verbergen; dem entspricht
auch die Struktur.

6,18                          ἵνα ... ἰσχυρὰν *παράκλησιν* (>12,5; 13,22) ἔχωμεν ... ἐλπίδος (10,23)

6,19                          ἦν ... ἔχομεν ... εἰσερχομένην[16] ... *καταπετάσματος* (>10,20)

6,20                          ὅπου πρόδρομος ... *εἰσῆλθεν* (>9,12) ᾽Ιησοῦς

                              κατὰ ... Μελχισέδεκ ... ἀρχιερεὺς γενόμενος

7,1                           Οὗτος *γὰρ* ὁ Μελχισέδεκ

[Aus typographischen Gründen überschlagen wir im folgenden 8 Einrückungsstu-
fen. Zur Erinnerung notieren wir die Verszahlen, solange dies gilt, am gegenüberlie-
genden Rand.]

Οὗτος *γὰρ* ὁ Μελχισέδεκ                                                          7,1

Θεωρεῖτε *δὲ* (bleibt auf der Einrückungsstufe des Exkurses)                      7,4

   *καὶ*[17] οἱ *μὲν* ἐκ τῶν υἱῶν Λευὶ                                            7,5

      ὁ *δὲ* μὴ γενεαλογούμενος                                                   7,6

      χωρὶς *δὲ* πάσης ἀντιλογίας                                                 7,7

   εἰ *μὲν* *οὖν* τελείωσις διὰ τῆς Λευιτικῆς ἱερωσύνης ἦν (Protasis)             7,11

   *τίς* *ἔτι* χρεία ... ἕτερον ἀνίστασθαι ἱερέα (Apodosis)

      μετατιθεμένης *γὰρ*                                                         7,12

         ἐφ᾽ ὃν *γὰρ* λέγεται ταῦτα                                              7,13

         *καὶ* περισσότερον                                                       7,15

            μαρτυρεῖται *γὰρ*                                                      7,17

               οὐδὲν *γὰρ* ἐτελείωσεν ὁ νόμος                                     7,19

               ἐπεισαγωγὴ *δὲ* κρείττονος *ἐλπίδος* (10,23; 11,1)

                  *καὶ* *καθ* *ὅσον* οὐ χωρὶς ὁρκωμοσίας                           7,20

                     οἱ *μὲν* *γὰρ* χωρὶς ὁρκωμοσίας

                     οἱ *δὲ* μετὰ ὁρκωμοσίας                                      7,21

                  κατὰ *τοσοῦτο* κρείττονος *διαθήκης* (>8,6ff.)                   7,22

                     *καὶ* οἱ *μὲν* πλείονες                                      7,23

                     ὁ *δὲ*                                                       7,24

                  *ὅθεν* *καὶ* σῴζειν ... δύναται                                 7,25

Τοιοῦτος *γὰρ*[18] ἡμῖν καὶ ἔπρεπεν ἀρχιερεύς                                     7,26

   *ὃς* οὐκ ἔχει καθ᾽ ἡμέραν ἀνάγκην                                             7,27

      τοῦτο *γὰρ* ἐποίησεν *ἐφάπαξ* (>9,12; 10,10)

         ὁ νόμος *γὰρ* ἀνθρώπους καθίστησιν                                       7,28

         ὁ λόγος *δὲ* ... υἱόν

**8,1**    *Κεφάλαιον* *δὲ* ..., τοιοῦτον ἔχομεν ἀρχιερέα,

           *ὃς* ἐκάθισεν ἐν δεξιᾷ

---

[16] Auch dieses Partizip kongruiert mit ἐλπίς, aufgenommen im Akkusativ ἥν.

[17] *καί* *explicativum*.

[18] Hier dient γάρ zur Einführung eines Resümees.

| | |
|---|---|
| 8,3 | πᾶς <u>γὰρ</u> ἀρχιερεύς |
| 8,4 | <u>εἰ</u> μὲν <u>οὖν</u> ἦν ἐπὶ γῆς, (Protasis) |
| | <u>οὐδ᾽ ἂν</u> ἦν ἱερεύς (Apodosis) |
| 8,5 | οἵτινες *ὑποδείγματι* (9,23) καὶ *σκιᾷ* (10,1) λατρεύουσιν τῶν ἐπουρανίων |
| 8,6 | <u>νῦν δὲ</u> διαφορωτέρας τέτυχεν λειτουργίας ... κρείττονός ἐστιν διαθήκης μεσίτης |
| 8,7 | <u>εἰ γὰρ</u> ἡ πρώτη ἐκείνη (Protasis) |
| | <u>οὐκ ἂν</u> δευτέρας (Apodosis) |
| 8,8 | μεμφόμενος <u>γὰρ</u> ... λέγει· |
| | «ἰδοὺ ... *διαθήκην καινήν*» (>9,15) |
| 8,13 | ἐν τῷ λέγειν «καινὴν» πεπαλαίωκεν τὴν πρώτην (nähere Ausführung zu V. 7) |
| **9,1** | εἶχε <u>μὲν οὖν</u> ἡ πρώτη |
| 9,2 | σκηνὴ <u>γὰρ</u> κατεσκευάσθη |
| 9,6 | τούτων <u>δὲ</u> οὕτως κατεσκευασμέν<u>ων</u> εἰς <u>μὲν</u> τὴν πρώτην σκηνὴν ... εἰσίασιν |
| 9,7 | εἰς <u>δὲ</u> τὴν δευτέραν ἅπαξ ... ὁ ἀρχιερεύς, οὐ χωρὶς *αἵματος* (>V. 12ff. etc.) |
| 9,8 | τοῦτο δηλοῦν<u>τος</u> τοῦ πνεύματος ... ἔτι τῆς πρώτης σκηνῆς |
| 9,9 | <u>ἥτις</u> παραβολὴ |
| 9,11f. | Χριστὸς <u>δὲ</u> παραγενόμενος ἀρχιερεύς ... εἰσῆλθεν *ἐφάπαξ* (>10,10) εἰς τὰ ἅγια |
| 9,13 | <u>εἰ γὰρ</u> τὸ αἷμα τράγων (Protasis) |
| 9,14 | <u>πόσῳ μᾶλλον</u> ... εἰς τὸ λατρεύειν *θεῷ ζῶντι*. (>10,31) (Apodosis) |
| 9,15 | <u>καὶ διὰ τοῦτο</u> διαθήκης καινῆς μεσίτης ἐστὶν (Rückgriff auf 8,6) |
| | <u>ὅπως</u> ... λάβωσιν ... αἰωνίου κληρονομίας. |
| 9,16 | ὅπου <u>γὰρ</u> διαθήκη, θάνατον ἀνάγκη |
| 9,18 | <u>ὅθεν</u> οὐδὲ ἡ πρώτη χωρὶς αἵματος |
| 9,19 | λαληθ<u>είσης γὰρ</u> ... κατὰ τὸν νόμον ... ἐρράντισεν |
| 9,22 | <u>καὶ</u>[19] σχεδὸν ἐν αἵματι πάντα καθαρίζεται κατὰ τὸν νόμον |
| 9,23 | ἀνάγκη <u>οὖν</u> τὰ <u>μὲν</u> ὑποδείγματα ... καθαρίζεσθαι αὐτὰ <u>δὲ</u> τὰ ἐπουράνια |
| | κρείττοσιν θυσίαις |
| 9,24 | <u>οὐ γὰρ</u> εἰς χειροποίητα |
| | <u>ἀλλ᾽</u> εἰς αὐτὸν τὸν οὐρανόν |
| 9,25 | οὐδ᾽ <u>ἵνα</u> πολλάκις |
| 9,26b | <u>νυνὶ δὲ</u> ἅπαξ ... διὰ τῆς θυσίας αὐτοῦ πεφανέρωται |
| **10,1** | σκιὰν <u>γὰρ</u>[20] ἔχων ὁ νόμος ..., οὐκ αὐτὴν τὴν εἰκόνα τῶν πραγμάτων |
| 10,5 | <u>διὸ</u> εἰσερχόμενος εἰς τὸν κόσμον λέγει (Subjekt zu denken: der himml. Hohepriester) |
| 10,10 | <u>ἐν ᾧ</u> θελήματι ἡγιασμένοι **ἐσ**μὲν ... ἐφάπαξ |
| 10,11 | <u>καὶ</u> πᾶς <u>μὲν</u> ἱερεὺς |
| 10,12 | οὗτος <u>δὲ</u> μίαν ὑπὲρ ἁμαρτιῶν προσενέγκας θυσίαν |
| 10,14 | μιᾷ <u>γὰρ</u> προσφορᾷ |

---

[19] Führt ein Resümee ein, wie in 9,18 ὅθεν.

[20] Dieses γάρ ist explikativ. Rückkehr zu den semantischen Oppositionen, die die Kapitel 8 bis 10 durchziehen.

10,15              μαρτυρεῖ δὲ ... καὶ τὸ πνεῦμα (Schriftbeweis)

10,18              ὅπου δὲ ἄφεσις (inhaltliche Fortsetzung von V. 12)

10,19    Ἔχοντες οὖν, ἀδελφοί, παρρησίαν ..., (V. 22) προσερχώμεθα

10,23    κατέχωμεν τὴν ὁμολογίαν τῆς ἐλπίδος

10,24    καὶ κατανοῶμεν ἀλλήλους

10,26              ἑκουσίως γὰρ ἁμαρτανόντων ἡμῶν

10,28                        ἀθετήσας τις[21] (Begründung des Vorhergehenden)

10,29    πόσῳ δοκεῖτε χείρονος ἀξιωθήσεται τιμωρίας ὁ ... καταπατήσας[22]

10,30              οἴδαμεν γὰρ τὸν εἰπόντα

10,31    φοβερὸν τὸ ἐμπεσεῖν εἰς χεῖρας θεοῦ ζῶντος (resümierende These)

10,32    Ἀναμιμνῄσκεσθε δὲ τὰς πρότερον ἡμέρας
              ἐν αἷς ... ἄθλησιν *ὑπεμείνατε* (>12,1) παθημάτων

10,34    καὶ γὰρ ... συνεπαθήσατε

10,35    Μὴ ἀποβάλητε οὖν τὴν παρρησίαν

10,36    *ὑπομονῆς* (>12,1) γὰρ ἔχετε χρείαν

10,39    ἡμεῖς δὲ οὐκ ἐσμὲν ὑποστολῆς ... ἀλλὰ *πίστεως* (folgt Definition)

**11**,1              ἔστιν δὲ πίστις ἐλπιζομένων ὑπόστασις

11,2                        ἐν ταύτῃ γὰρ

11,3                        πίστει

11,4                        πίστει etc.: 19 Anaphern auf πίστει, bis V. 31. Als Teilresümee kommt
                        dazwischen:

11,13-16    κατὰ πίστιν ἀπέθανον οὗτοι πάντες

11,17                        πίστει

11,32    καὶ τί ἔτι λέγω; (rhetorische Formel, die die folgende *praeteritio*[23] ankündigt:)
              ἐπιλείψει με γὰρ διηγούμενον ὁ χρόνος

11,35              ἔλαβον

11,36              ἕτεροι δὲ ... ἔλαβον

11,39    καὶ οὗτοι πάντες μαρτυρηθέντες (Zusammenfassung des Exkurses)

**12**,1    Τοιγαροῦν καὶ ἡμεῖς ... δι᾽ ὑπομονῆς τρέχωμεν

12,2              ἀφορῶντες εἰς τὸν τῆς πίστεως ἀρχηγὸν
                        ὃς ... ὑπέμεινεν σταυρὸν

12,3    ἀναλογίσασθε γὰρ[24] τὸν ... ὑπομεμενηκότα

12,4              οὔπω[25] μέχρις αἵματος ἀντικατέστητε

12,5b              (Schriftbeweis, wiederholt das Wort *υἱός* – aufzugreifen in V. 7)

---

[21] Bemerke den Wechsel vom 'wir' zur indefiniten 3. Person.

[22] Hier kehrt die indefinite 3. Person wieder, jedoch untergeordnet, wie mir scheint, der direkten Anrede (2. Pers.), die einen Teil des Plurals der 1. Pers. von 10,24 aufgreift.

[23] *Praeteritio* – ein paradoxes Mittel, um dem vorgeblich Übersprungenen doch die textliche Präsenz zu sichern. Makrosyntaktisch gesehen, ist es eine Digression.

[24] Resümierend. Vokabular von V. 1 und 2 wird aufgegriffen.

12,7    εἰς παιδείαν ὑπομένετε

12,12   διὸ τὰς παρειμένας χεῖρας ... ἀνορθώσατε

12,14   εἰρήνην διώκετε

12,18       οὐ γὰρ προσεληλύθατε

12,19           ἧς ... παρῃτήσαντο (vgl. V. 25)

12,22       ἀλλὰ προσεληλύθατε

12,25   βλέπετε μὴ παραιτήσησθε (siehe V. 19)

            εἰ γὰρ ἐκεῖνοι οὐκ ἐξέφυγον (Protasis)

            πολὺ μᾶλλον ἡμεῖς (Apodosis)

12,26b          (Schriftbeweis)

12,27               τὸ δὲ «ἔτι ἅπαξ» δηλοῖ (Exegese der Beweisstelle)

12,28   διὸ ... ἔχωμεν χάριν

--------

**13,1** Ἡ φιλαδελφία μενέτω (neues Thema, neuer Modus, neue grammatische Person)

13,2    τῆς φιλοξενίας μὴ ἐπιλανθάνεσθε

13,3    μιμνῄσκεσθε

--------

13,4    Τίμιος ὁ γάμος (neues Thema, neuer Modus)

13,5    ἀφιλάργυρος ὁ τρόπος

--------

13,7    Μνημονεύετε τῶν ἡγουμένων ὑμῶν

            ὧν ... μιμεῖσθε τὴν πίστιν.

13,8    Ἰησοῦς Χριστὸς ἐχθὲς καὶ σήμερον ... καὶ εἰς τοὺς αἰῶνας (gleiches Wortfeld)[26]

13,9    Διδαχαῖς ποικίλαις ... μὴ παραφέρεσθε

--------

13,10   Ἔχομεν θυσιαστήριον

13,11       ὧν γὰρ εἰσφέρεται ... τὸ αἷμα ... ἔξω τῆς *παρεμβολῆς*. (>V. 13)

13,12       διὸ καὶ Ἰησοῦς ... ἔξω τῆς πύλης ἔπαθεν.

13,13   Τοίνυν ἐξερχώμεθα[27] πρὸς αὐτὸν ἔξω τῆς παρεμβολῆς

13,14       οὐ γὰρ ἔχομεν

            ἀλλὰ τὴν μέλλουσαν ἐπιζητοῦμεν.

13,15   Δι' αὐτοῦ [οὖν][28] ἀναφέρωμεν

--------

---

[25] Ob mit oder ohne γάρ (s. den Apparat der Ausg. Aland), ich würde die folgenden Verse als Erläuterung (Epexegese) des Begriffs 'Widerstand' im vorigen Vers auffassen.

[26] Diese grammatisch unverbundene These dürfte Erläuterung sein zu πίστις und zum Inhalt des λόγος τοῦ Θεοῦ im vorigen Vers; darum: Einbettung. Hier muß die Semantik die Syntax präzisieren.

[27] Der Konjunktiv der 1. Pers. Plural (Hortativ) erweist, daß wir auf die Anfangsstufe, den Hörerkontakt, zurückkommen.

[28] Mit oder ohne οὖν (vgl. Apparat) ist das αὐτόν des V. 13 wiederaufgenommen.

13,16  Τῆς δὲ εὐποιΐας ... μὴ ἐπιλανθάνεσθε (Fortsetzung der Imperative von 13,2f.; 13,7)
13,17  πείθεσθε
13,18  προσεύχεσθε

--------

13,20f.  Ὁ δὲ θεὸς τῆς εἰρήνης ... καταρτίσαι

--------

13,22  Παρακαλῶ δὲ ὑμᾶς, *ἀδελφοί* (vgl. folgenden Vers)
13,23  γινώσκετε τὸν ἀδελφὸν ἡμῶν Τιμόθεον
13,24  ἀσπάσασθε

--------

13,25 ‘Η χάρις μετὰ πάντων ὑμῶν.

## 3. Konklusion

Das 13. Kapitel bringt vieles, was schon einmal behandelt wurde; es zielt also auf einen Wiedererkennungseffekt (Vertrautheit). Da der Prolog (Kap. 1), diachron-traditionsgeschichtlich gesehen, seinerseits zunächst Vertrautes bringt, entsteht eine Art *inclusio,* wie Barnabas Lindars[29] feststellt: *Hebrews proceeds from the known to the unknown and back to the known at the end.* Formale und inhaltliche Analyse bestätigen sich, wie zu erwarten ist bei einem "guten", d.h. homogenen und von einem kompetenten Sprecher formulierten Text.

Wenn diese Analyse zutrifft, dann wird vieles hinfällig, was in den Kommentaren z.B. über die Struktur der Anfangsabschnitte und über das "Thema" des Briefes zu lesen steht. Das ganze 1. Kapitel ist ein Prolog[30] (über Christus als Gottes endgültige Offenbarung); Kap. 2 benennt nach einem διὰ τοῦτο das paränetische Anliegen, entspricht also einer *propositio;* Kap. 3ff. schließen mit ὅθεν die *argumentatio* an. Diese zerfällt in einen rückblickenden (3-5) und einen vorausblickenden Teil (6-7: Διὸ ἀφέντες ... ἐπὶ τὴν τελειότητα φερώμεθα), innerhalb dessen das Melchisedek-Kapitel (7) eine *digressio* ist. Kapitel 8,1ff. bringt eine ausdrückliche Zusammenfassung (κεφάλαιον ἐπὶ ...)[31], an die sich etliche Erweiterungen in mehr oder weniger gleitenden Übergängen anschließen. Ab 10,19, der neuen Anrede an die "Brüder", wird die in Kapitel 2 begonnene Paränese wieder aufgegriffen

---

[29] B. Lindars 1991, 27.

[30] Die mittelalterliche Einteilung hat hier also das richtige getroffen. Im Unterschied hierzu ist der Einschnitt von 5,1 falsch plaziert; er müßte, wenn schon, bei 4,14 liegen.

[31] Zahlreiche Kommentare und selbst Alands Wörterbuch irren an dieser Stelle, indem sie das ἐπί ignorieren: mit dieser Partikel verknüpft, kann das Wort schlecht 'Hauptsache' bedeuten, eher 'Zusammenfassung'. Vgl. Plutarch, *De defectu oraculorum* 434 E/F: κεφάλαιον ἐπιθεῖναι τῷ λόγῳ 'die Diskussion abschließen'.

und in 12,1ff. (τοιγαροῦν καὶ ἡμεῖς) zu einer *peroratio* geführt, in der die Imperative sich häufen. Im 13. Kapitel werden dann die Strukturen immer einfacher, die Einbettungen immer kürzer: wie schon oft bemerkt worden ist, nähert sich die schriftliche Mahnrede unseres Autors gegen Ende den Konventionen eines Briefes[32], bis hin zur Erwähnung des Timotheus[33], die ihr in weiten Kreisen den Rang eines Paulusbriefes eingetragen hat. Die lose angehängten Schlußvermerke können redaktionell sein (13,22ff.). Vorher gibt es in dieser Hinsicht nichts Verdächtiges.

Der *erste* Schritt zu einem Kommentar ist mit dieser Analyse getan, und eine Menge Material ist gewonnen, noch ehe die Suche nach "Parallelen" begann[34].

Der *nächste* Arbeitsschritt bestünde nun darin, den innertextlichen Querverweisen nachzugehen, die hier durch Kursivdruck einzelner Wörter und durch in Klammern angegebenen Verszahlen nur angedeutet wurden.

Ein *dritter* – und großer – Schritt müßte zu den hier übersprungenen historischen Prolegomena zurückkehren, um das textintern Gewonnene auf die ursprüngliche Kommunikationssituation anzuwenden – womit sich zum ersten Mal der hermeneutische Zirkel schließt. Danach kann die Suche nach Vergleichsmaterial beginnen, aus dem Skelett ein Körper werden.

## *Bibliographie*[35]

Botha, Pieter J. J. 1993: "The Verbal Art of the Pauline Letters: Rhetoric, Performance and Presence", in: Stanley E. Porter and Thomas H. Olbricht (eds.), *Rhetoric and the New Testament: Essays from the 1992 Heidelberg Conference* (JSNT.S 90), Sheffield: JSOT Press 1993, 409-428.

Gülich, Elisabeth und Klaus Heger und Wolfgang Raible 1974: *Linguistische Textanalyse: Überlegungen zur Gliederung von Texten,* Hamburg: Buske 1974.

---

[32] Warum sie dies nicht schon am Anfang tut, darüber kann nun spekuliert werden. Als historische Information sei beigefügt, daß antike Briefe nicht mit der Post kamen, sondern eines Überbringers bedurften. Dieser war im frühen Christentum (dort noch mehr als sonst) ein persönlicher Mittler zwischen dem Absender und der angeredeten Gemeinde. Sein Auftreten und sein mündlicher Beitrag ersetzten, was dem überbrachten Schriftstück an Exordial-Konventionen und Anknüpfungstechniken zu fehlen scheint. – Zum antiken Brief als *mündlicher* Kommunikation vgl. P. Botha 1993.

[33] Die Bekanntheit dieser Person, oder zumindest dieses Namens, ist als Element der Textpragmatik zu werten.

[34] Linguistischer Grundsatz seit de Saussure: das Syntagma rangiert vor dem Paradigma.

[35] Zu spät für eine Berücksichtigung erschien das Buch von George H. Guthrie 1994. Vgl. dort die S. 144. Es ist ein Versuch in struktularer Semantik, ebenso wie die – hier nicht zitierten – Arbeiten von Albert Vanhoye.

Guthrie, George H. 1994: *The Structure of Hebrews: A Text-Linguistic Analysis*, Leiden: Brill 1994.

Lindars, Barnabas 1991: *The Theology of the Letter to the Hebrews*, Cambridge: Cambridge University Press 1991.

Siegert, Folker 1985: *Argumentation bei Paulus* (WUNT 34), Tübingen: Mohr (Siebeck) 1985.

# Section B

## Inter-Textual Relations

# Benediction and Congratulation[1]

## Nils Alstrup Dahl

## 1. Introduction

The ancient rabbis greeted and congratulated one another by praising God. There even existed a standard *beraka*, a blessing or benediction of God which a rabbi should use when he met a scholar of his own people: "Blessed be He, who gives of his wisdom to those who fear him." The rabbis could, however, also appreciate secular learning. Encountering a non-Jewish scholar one should say: "Blessed be He who gives of his wisdom to his creatures." Modern scholars have different customs, they demonstrate their appreciation of a colleague by contributing an essay to a "Festschrift" in his honor.

When I was asked to contribute to a volume of essays in honor of Lars Hartman, it struck me that "Benediction and Congratulation" might be an appropriate topic. A number of notes and a couple of drafts were buried in my files, so that I was happy to be stimulated to present some of my observations in a publishable form. My interest in the theme goes far back. In 1951 I wrote an article on "Adresse und Prooemium des Epheserbriefes" in which I argued that the opening of a letter with a praise of God introduced by a benediction (εὐλογητὸς ὁ θεός or sim.) was likely to be a Jewish variant of the Hellenistic opening of a letter with an assertion of thanksgiving and/or joy, or by other philophronetic phrases that served to establish or confirm good relations between the sender and the addressees.[2] The theory has not been widely accepted, mainly because the evidence for a pre-Christian use of a letter-opening eulogy ("Briefeingangseulogie"), analogous to those in 2 Corinthians,

---

[1] The term "benediction" is here used as a designation of a praise to God that in Hebrew is expressed by derivations of the root *brk* and in Jewish terminology would be called a *beraka*. In translation and paraphrase I have made free use of the RSV retaining the formulation "Blessed be the LORD" for ברוך יהוה and "Blessed are You, LORD" for ברוך אתה יהוה. I have however, capitalized the personal pronouns to make it clear that "He" refers to God and not to a male individual and "You" to God and not to one or several persons.

[2] Dahl 1951.

Ephesians and 1 Peter, is scant. The problem should, however, be reconsidered in a wider perspective.

According to Greek epistolographic theory, a letter is part of a dialogue between persons who are locally separated from one another. Opening and concluding greetings, good wishes and other assertions of appreciation correspond, more or less exactly, to locutions used to greet and/or bid farewell. The same holds good for the eulogies at the beginning of a letter. They are related to the use of benedictions at personal encounters and/or oral reports of good news. Such *situational*, mostly *congratulatory benedictions* are attested at all periods in the history of Israel. If addressed to a corporate body, a letter may substitute for an address which the sender would have given if he had been personally present. We may safely assume that the opening eulogies in three New Testament letters represent a form that on special occasions was also used to address a Christian congregation.

Penetrating studies have dealt with the history and prehistory of the regular synagogue worship and to its importance for early Christian worship, esp. the eucharistic liturgy.[3] Far less attention has been paid to congratulatory and other occasional benedictions (*berakot*) that did not belong to regular worship and/or daily prayer hours. This is also the case in commentaries and special studies on the eulogies in 2 Corinthians, Ephesians and 1 Peter. All three texts, esp. Eph 1:3-14, have various elements in common with Jewish benedictions and prayers, but are also related to a specific epistolary situation. Today few, if any, scholars still hold the view that the eulogy in Ephesians is dependent upon 2 Corinthians and the one in 1 Peter dependent upon Ephesians. Even a variety of attempts to derive the text in Ephesians 1:3-12 (or 14) from an early Christian hymn have failed to carry conviction. Like kerygmatic and credal formulae, even "psalms, hymns, and spiritual songs" are likely to have left room for spontaneity, even if content, form and phraseology were more or less conform to traditional patterns. The same holds true for Jewish *berakot*. The standard rules did not prescribe the exact wording but left room for variation, in the synagogue prayers as well as in benedictions for special occasions.

The present paper was originally intended to contain two parts: I. A comprehensive, but not exhaustive, survey describing the use of benedictions in various situations, tracing a development from early Hebrew Scriptures, through an intermediate period to the liturgy of the synagogue and daily life prescribed in the Mishnah and later sources. II. Comments on the form, function and setting of the benedictions in 2 Corinthians, Ephesians and 1 Peter in the light of the collected comparative material. I have, unfortunately, only been able to complete half of the first part. The complete study would, in any case, have been too long for a Festschrift; I hope to

---

[3] See, e.g., the classical works of Elbogen 1931; Audet 1958; Dix 1945, 50-102; 214-225.

be able to publish it later.

## 2. *Congratulatory and other Benedictions in the Hebrew Scriptures*

In the Hebrew Scriptures blessings of God occur in two distinct contexts. In *historical narratives* they are related to specific events and persons, most often David and Solomon. In *psalms* and *hymns*, benedictions praise God in the context of hymns or prayers of lamentation and thanksgiving. Except in rabbinic texts from the Mishnah onward congratulatory benedictions are only attested in narrative contexts, but even cultic celebrations may provide the occasion for benedictions (see 1 Kgs 8). Overt overlapping of the genres is rare (e.g. Psalm 18 and 2 Samuel 22) and likely to be due to the work of a later editor or redactor. A mixture of the two main forms, occasional and poetic-devotional benedictions, is characteristic of writings that are later than the main parts of the Hebrew Scriptures, e.g. Daniel, the Greek 1 Esdras and Tobit. The *Benedictus* of Zechariah (Luke 1:68-79) as well as the eulogies at the beginning of New Testament letters combine the two forms. In this essay I shall, therefore, pay some attention to the use of benedictions in the Psalms and in later hymns, thanksgivings and prayers, even though liturgical and devotional usage is not in the focus of this study.

How frequently a book attests the use of benedictions of various types is, obviously, contingent upon the literary genre and content. The books of Samuel, Kings and Chronicles only report benedictions that are attributed or pertain to David and Solomon! The majority of benedictions of God has, obviously, never been written down. Even so, it is also clear that an increasing use of benedictions was part of the praxis of communal and personal piety that developed in and after the exile, especially in Hellenistic and early Roman times. In the early period, I would think, benedictions were mainly used when people had a special reason to praise God.

One such occasion could be *military victory*, or *rescue from a hostile attack*. When Abraham had defeated the allied kings and recaptured goods and people, Melchizedek congratulated him by saying: "Blessed be Abram by God Most High (אל עליון), maker (or possessor?) of heaven and earth; and blessed be God Most High, who has delivered your enemies into your hand!" (Gen 14:19-20). A similar congratulatory benediction is attributed to Moses's father-in-law. When Moses had told him about the deliverance from Egypt, Jethro said: "Blessed be the LORD who has delivered you (plur.) out of the hand of the Egyptians and out of the hand of Pharaoh," adding the confession that "Now I know that the LORD is greater than all gods" (Exod 18:10-11). In a third case, the message of Joab's victory over the rebellious troops of Absalom is given the form of a congratulatory benediction: "Blessed be the LORD your God, who has delivered up the men who raised their hand against my lord the king" (2 Sam 18:28). By choosing this form the messenger who first reached David managed to keep silent about the sad part of the news, the death of Absalom.

Another group of congratulatory benedictions pertain to the *installation of a king*. When Solomon at the beginning of his reign requested expert assistance for the building of the temple, king Hiram of Tyre is reported to have rejoiced and exclaimed: "Blessed be the LORD this day, who has given to David a wise son to be over this great people" (1 Kgs 5:7). Variants of this benediction were later on assumed to have been a part of a letter from Hiram (see 2 Chr 2:11-16). The earlier version is likely to imply that the delegates conveyed Hiram's response to Solomon's request both orally and in writing, as a missive (1 Kgs 5:8-9) and only orally reported the benediction. His words do in any case represent the courteous style of diplomatic communication. Before she left, the queen of Sheba paid more cordial, exquisite compliments to king Solomon, concluding with a benediction that is formulated as a wish (יהי יהוה אלהיך ברוך, LXX γένοιτο κύριος ὁ θεός σου εὐλογη-μένος; 1 Kgs 10: 6-9): "Blessed be the LORD your God, who has delighted in you and set you on the throne of Israel! Because the LORD loved Israel for ever, he has made you king, that you may execute justice and righteousness." Minor variants in 2 Chr 9:8 further stress the ties between the king and his god; "who ... set you on his throne as king for the LORD your God! Because your God loved Israel ..." etc.

Whereas the two foreign monarchs hail Solomon with their benedictions, the dying king David primarily expressed his own happiness when he learned that Solomon had been anointed and acclaimed as his successor: "Blessed be the LORD, the God of Israel, who this day has granted one of my offspring to sit on my throne, my own eyes seeing it" (1 Kgs 1:48, with the words "of my offspring" added from 3 Kgs 1:48 LXX). The benediction is only congratulatory in the wider sense that David shares the joy of the jubilant crowd in Jerusalem. In a different way, Solomon's benediction of God, who has fulfilled what he promised to David (1 Kgs 8:16-21) primarily praises God because he has granted Solomon to sit on David's throne and build the temple; by doing so at the consecration of the temple, however, Solomon does at the same time "bless"—or congratulate—all the assembly of Israel (8:14-15). The initial and concluding benedictions form the frame around Solomon's prayer and intercessions at the consecration of the temple (1 Kgs 8:22-53). Their form and function is in many ways similar to the benedictions in psalms, hymns and prayers.

Only the Old Greek version attests that David had blessed the Lord who chose him to be king (2 Kgs 6:21 LXX). The context is the transfer of the ark to the city of David, when David's wife Michal, the daughter of Saul, saw David dance in the festival procession without being properly dressed. When she came and rebuked him, David responded, according to the Greek text: "Before the LORD I will dance! Blessed be the LORD who chose me above your father and above all his house to make me ruler over his people, over Israel!" David insists that he will continue to dance like the maidens who dance uncovered in a hilarious procession, and thus be worthless in the eyes of Michal.[4] In this context, the benediction does not at all convey a congratulation; it has the force of an *oath* or a *curse*. The end of the story is that Michal never had any children. Thus, no pretender of the throne of David could claim to be descendant of Saul as well as of David.

The elaborate story of Abigail and her rich husband Nabal in 1 Samuel 25 includes two benedictions with which David praised God while he was the chief of a mixed gang of warriors. When Abigail went out to David in the wilderness with rich gifts, to make up for her husband's treatment of David and his men and warn him not to take a hasty revenge but leave the retaliation to God, David responded: "Blessed be the Lord … who sent you this day to meet me!" He appends blessings of Abigail, whose discretion has kept him from shedding innocent blood, and lets her return in peace (25:32-35). It is, however, not until he has received the "good news" of Nabal's sudden death that David finally drops the idea of revenging himself and blesses the Lord, who avenged the insult, kept David back from evil, and returned the evildoing of Nabal upon his own head (25:39). The tale has a happy ending: David marries the widowed Abigail. In the form in which we read it, however, the story has a wider significance; in the "deuteronomistic history" it is placed between two incidents at which David spares the life of Saul (1 Samuel 24 and 26) and the words of Abigail anticipate the history of David's reign, teaching him not to take vengeance in his own hand, but trust that God will take care of the retribution (25:28-31). Several later incidents tell how David heeded the lesson.[5]

The Former Prophets (Joshua – Kings) attest no, the other Hebrew Scriptures only few benedictions of God that pertain to *family life*. The words with which the women greet Naomi when Ruth had given birth to Obed, the father of Jesse and grandfather of David, is a good example of a congratulatory benediction: "Blessed be the LORD, who has not left you this day without next of kin (גאל = 'redeemer')"

---

[4] The Greek translation of 1 and 2 Samuel, in Greek 1-2 book of Kings, was made from a Hebrew text that differed considerably from the pre-Masoretic text. In 2 Sam 6:22 most modern translators prefer "in your eyes" (LXX) to "in my eyes" (MT). The omission of "… I will dance. Blessed be the LORD" in 6:21 MT could possibly be due to homoioteleuton, the double occurrence of the Tetragrammaton. In any case, the benediction was part of an early form of the story and is therefore included here.

[5] See 2 Samuel 1-4; 16:5-12; 19:16-30. In several cases, however, David avoided to shed blood himself, but left it to others to do so, see 2 Sam 20:4-22; 21:1-14; 1 Kgs 2:5-9. On the ambiguous portrait of David in the deuteronomistic history, see the stimulating comments of D. Damrosch 1987, 144-260, esp. 209-17 and 250-60.

etc. (Ruth 4:14-15). Another, somewhat different example is part of the narrative about the servant whom Abraham sent to Mesopotamia to find a bride for his son Isaac (Genesis 24). When he had met Rebekah at the well and understood that God had heard his prayer, the servant exclaimed: "Blessed be the LORD, the God of my master Abraham!" and praised God for his faithfulness to his master and the success of his own mission (Gen 24:26-27; cf. vv. 11-14 and 42-48). Both of these stories report events of a special importance with artistic realism: most likely even ordinary persons did "bless" God when a child was born or the right wife had been found. The story about Noah's drunkenness contains the benediction "Blessed be the LORD, the God of Shem!" (Gen 9:26 MT LXX etc.). The blessing of Shem's God implies that Shem is blessed, as Canaan is cursed, but in the context it is clear that curse, blessing and good wishes are realized in the history and the mutual relations between the descendants of Shem (the ancestor of the Israelites), Canaan and Japhet. Not much can be learned about the analogous use of benedictions in everyday life!

The best evidence that even *ordinary people* did bless God in various situations is indirect. When Job received the messages about the disasters that almost simultaneously had hit his animals, his servants, and his sons and daughters, he responded by the famous saying: "The LORD gave, and the LORD has taken away; the name of the LORD be blessed!" (Job 1:21 יהי שם יהוה מברך). This is reported as an extraordinary reaction but presupposes that it was customary to respond to good news by blessing God. A fairly widespread use of benedictions is also indicated by the obscure oracle of doom in Zech 11:4-17, which in a metaphoric language denounces shepherds who do not care for the well-being of the flock, but buy and slay the sheep, and when they sell them they say: "Blessed be the LORD, I have become rich!" (Zech 11:5). The shepherds are, obviously, the religious and political leaders of the postexilic Jewish community, possibly including representatives of Persian (or Seleucid?) government, who pretend to worship God while they enrich themselves by mistreating and exploiting his people.[6] The imagery presumes that the utterance of a benediction-formula because one is happy to have made an unfair gain

---

[6] From Amos onward, prophets had declared sacrifices and other religious ceremonies to be in vain if practiced by people who failed to practice justice and exploited those who were in need of their care. The oracle of doom in Zech 11:4-17 applies the same judgement to leaders who utter pious benedictions while they exploit the flock whose shepherds they should be. Both the time and the interpretation of the oracle has been topics of extended discussions. Apparently, the prophet is himself appointed to be a shepherd. His words and symbolic actions do, however, not bring any relief but imply that the doom will become even more severe before the last wicked shepherd is destroyed. In the context of the proto-apocalyptic oracles of Zechariah 9-11 and 12-14, the oracle in 11:4-17 is best understood as an announcement that the doom has to become even more severe before God will redeem and restore his oppressed and scattered people (see, e.g., 13:7-9 and 10:3-12).

at the expense of others does not perform any genuine praise of God; it is in vain. Such misuse does, however, presuppose that the use of benedictions had become more common than it was before the exile.

Some *later benedictions* from the time after the fall of Jerusalem are also attested in the Old Testament. Ezra received a letter from king Artaxerxes that decreed that the temple in Jerusalem should be made more glorious, and responded by a blessing of "the God of our Fathers," who inspired the decree of the king and commissioned Ezra to implement it (Ezra 7:27-28). The tale of Nebuchadnezzar's dream tells that Daniel blessed the name of God who governs and gives wisdom to wise and reveals mysteries, and continues by thanking and praising God, who gave Daniel wisdom and made the content and the interpretation of the dream known to him (Dan 2:20-23). The following story about the three men in the burning furnace concludes with the words of Nebuchadnezzar: "Blessed be the God of Shadrach, Meshach, and Abednego, who has sent his angel and delivered his servants ..." (Dan 3:28-29). In Ezek 3:12 the benediction "Blessed be the glory of the LORD from his place" is attested both by the Hebrew and the Greek text. Understood as an acclamation by the cherubim, it was frequently repeated, often in combination with the "Holy, holy, holy" in Isa 6:3.

Inserted in the Greek version of the Book of Ezra we find the story of the three men who compete in praising what is strongest. The third of them, identified as Zerubbabel, concludes by praising truth and saying: "Blessed be the God of truth" and adding: "Blessed are You who have given me wisdom ..." (1 Esdras 4:40, 58-60). In the additions of the Greek version(s) of Daniel two extensive songs are attributed to the three men in the furnace. The first begins with a benediction and praise of God, and continues with confession and prayer. The second begins with six benedictions and continues with a call to all beings in heaven and earth to praise the Lord (Dan 3:26-45, 52-90 LXX, Theod = the Song of the Three Young Men).

Examples of *poetic compositions* that include a benediction do, however, already occur in narrative contexts within the Hebrew Scriptures. The report of the transfer of the ark to the city of David in 1 Chronicles 16 omits the encounter of David and Michal and has instead a long thanksgiving and praise that is based upon a combination of Psalm 105 and Psalm 96 with a concluding thanksgiving and benediction from Psalm 106. Instead of "the last words of David" in 2 Sam 23:1-7 a benediction introduces praise of God, confession and prayer in 1 Chr 29:10-19. The best known example is the almost verbatim identity of 2 Samuel 22 with Psalm 18. In both cases the introduction says that the psalm was spoken by David "on the day when the LORD delivered him from the hand of all his enemies and from the hand of Saul." Especially in Chronicles even psalmlike compositions which do not contain any benedictions have been inserted into the narrative framework and, on the other hand, several other psalms are ascribed to a specific situation in the life of David (e.g. Pss 34 and 51).

Here I am not going to analyze the use of benedictions in the Psalms, but shall only point out some of the differences between (a) the typical "situational" benediction uttered by a specific person on a special occasion and (b) the use of benedictions in hymns and psalms. The form "blessed be the LORD" (ברוך יהוה) is regularly used in the Psalms as one among several formulae for praising the Lord. A fairly common alternative is, e.g., "Great is the LORD and greatly to be praised" (Pss 48:1; 96:4; 1 Chr 16:25). The *baruk*-formula is not a constitutive element but occurs in different genres; hymns and psalms of lamentation, prayer and/or thanksgiving.

What is common to the different genres is that they were intended to be *used in worship*; in Psalm 66 and 68 the cultic setting is made explicit. The first of them includes a vow to enter the temple and offer sacrifices, and concludes with a benediction (Ps 66:13-20). The same combination of benediction and sacrifice is also attested in 1 Kings 8 (vv. 15-21 and 55-63) and in 1 Chronicles 16 (vv. 8-36, 1-2 and 40); 1 Chr 29:20-22 and 2 Chr 6:4-11 and 7:1-7. Ps 68 opens with a slightly adapted form of the versicle prescribed for the moving of the ark (Num 10:35). A benediction is followed by a reference to the festival procession into the sanctuary (vv. 19-20, 24-27) and concludes "Blessed be God!" The psalm is, probably, composed for an annual procession, and has clear points of contact with the reports about the transfer of the ark to Jerusalem and the temple in 2 Sam 6:12-15 and 1 Kgs 8:1-11, elaborated in 1 Chronicles 15-16 and 2 Chronicles 5-6. The Chronicler does not only emphasize the assignment of Levites to make music, raise shouts of joy, and praise the LORD (1 Chr 15:16, 28; 16:4-7)—"for His steadfast love endures for ever!" (1 Chr 16:34, 41; 2 Chr 5:13; 7:3, 6). Moreover, we learn that the people responded to longer thanksgivings and prayers by saying "Amen!" and praising the LORD (1 Chr 16:36; 29:20; 2 Chr 7:3-6; see also 2 Chr 29:25-30; Ezra 3:10-11; Neh 9:5-6).

As generally recognized, the conclusion of David's thanksgiving in 1 Chr 16:34-36 is modelled upon Ps 106:1 and 47-48. The entire psalm, including the final benediction and the call for a response, is therefore likely to be earlier than the book of Chronicles. Psalm 106 stands at the end of the fourth of the five books into which the Psalter has been divided, and even the three preceding books concludes with a benediction, Pss 41:13; 72:18-19 and 89:52. Due to the double "Amen! Amen!" they are, like the benediction in Ps 106:48, best understood as liturgical rubrics that point to a response by an assembled community.[7] In two other psalms a benediction comes at the very end, preceded by calls to sing to God (Ps 68:32-35) or to praise

---

[7] Mowinckel 1955, 99 and 226, notes.

the LORD (Ps 135:19-21). The brief form "Blessed be God!" (Ps 135:21) would be a most fitting response. Like Psalm 106 and 1 Chr 16:8-36, quite a few psalms begin with exhortations to praise God, among them Pss 66:1-3; 113:1; 135:1-4, see also 68:4. A response by a benediction or, at least "Amen!" or "Hallelujah!" seems to be called for. The inserted words "let Israel now say" in Ps 124:1 does, likewise, make one expect an acclamation by which the audience would make the benediction (v. 6) its own.

The presence, or at least the possibility, of an *acclamatory response* is characteristic of liturgical benedictions, and so is the absence of formulations that address or refer to contemporary individuals who have been objects of the action for which God is praised. The beneficiaries are indicated by first person forms: God is blessed for what He has done "to me" (Pss 18:46-48; 28:6; 31:21; 66:20; 144:1-2), or "to us" (Ps 124:6; cf. Pss 68:19-20; 135:19-21; 1 Kgs 8:56). Some benedictions are quite general and do not mention beneficiaries (Ps 113:2; 1 Chr 29:10 and texts which—like Ps 106:48—may relate to a response, see above). Even other formulations may be generally applicable, e.g.: "Blessed be the LORD! for He has heard the voice of my supplications" (Ps 28:6; cf. Pss 31:21-22; 68:19). Both the 1. person plural forms and the generalizing tendency is alien to benedictions of God for what He had done in a specific case.

Regardless of type, the great majority of benedictions in the Hebrew Scriptures use the form "Blessed be He!" The only exceptions are the single verse Ps 119:12 and 1 Chr 29:10, where God is addressed with "Blessed are You!" In 2 Chronicles, God is addressed in 2. person sing. throughout the praise, confession and prayer in 29:10-19. Well attested in additions to the Greek Old Testament, i.e. in the hymns inserted in Daniel 3 and in the Book of Tobit, and common in the Qumran Thanksgiving Hymns and the synagogue liturgy, the form must have antedated its earliest literary attestation.[8] In the context of the Psalms, God is mainly addressed as "You" in thanksgiving and prayer (see Pss 28:1-4, 9; 31:1-20; 144:3-11). By contrast, "He" ("the LORD" or sim.) is the only form used in two hymns (Psalms 113 and 124, see also 135:1-12, 14-21; 1 Chr 16:8-34, and the benedictions in 1 Kings 8. In Psalms 18, 66 and 68 the two forms alternate.

Both forms ("He" and "You") can be used to praise God, His attributes and His regular way of acting (e.g. Pss 18:30-34, 25-29; 135:5-7, 13). Reminders of what God has done to His people normally speak *about* God (Pss 66:5-9; 68:5-6; 135:8-12), but words addressed *to* God may be added (Pss 66:10-12; 68:7-10; 135:13). The report of an individual who has been delivered from distress is more often addressed to God (Pss 18:35-45; 31:21-22, but see also Ps 18:4-24). In some cases,

---

[8] W. S. Towner 1968.

the choice of form is dependent upon introductory formulae. One can expect that both God and a human audience will listen, but not address both in the same clauses. In *exhortations* it is, therefore, necessary to speak about God in the 3. person. That does also apply to the first reason added to the call to praise God ("for He is good" or sim.), as well as to formulations like "come and see …" and "come and hear …" (Ps 66:5,16). An addition of "Say to God …" does, however, make it possible to state in direct speech what is to be said to God (Ps 66:3-4; cf. 1 Chr 16:35). In vows about what the speaking subject will say or do, both forms are attested: "I call upon the LORD", and "I will extol You, O LORD" (Ps 18:3 and 49); "I know that the LORD …" and "I know that You, my God …" (Ps 135:5; 1 Chr 29:17). See also Ps 66:13-15 "I will come into Your house with burnt offerings" etc.

An investigation of such introductory formulations, and other matters as well, would have to take account of a much wider material than psalms and songs that contain benedictions as well as of the possibility of antiphonal singing and different speaking voices, perhaps including that an oracle of a temple prophet had its place at the transition from lament to thanksgiving and praise. The purpose of my observations has simply been to illustrate the interrelations and differences between the situational, often congratulatory, benedictions and the liturgical use of the form. The most useful study by C. W. Mitchell seems to prove that this problem has been neglected in Old Testament studies.[9]

## 3. Conclusions and Outlook

The preceding survey should be sufficient to show the difference between the occasional, often congratulatory benedictions in narrative contexts and the more devotional benedictions in Psalms and song. The two types do, however, have some elements in common: Psalms and related texts are more or less comprehensive and include calls to praise God and a variety of reasons to do so, but the actual praise is mainly performed by benedictions at the beginning and/or at the end, less often in the middle. With few exceptions, the form "Blessed is He" has been retained, even

---

[9] Following Westermann 1965, Mitchell 1987, 145, 149-50, 160, 169-70 distinguishes between "spontaneous expressions of thanks and praise" and "doxological praise" which is "a response to the entirety of God's character". This distinction fails to pay attention to the degree to which also the responses to a recent, specific act of God conform to traditional patterns. And why should not a general praise of God be a spontaneous response? Even today, we often use stereotype formulations to extend a cordial, spontaneous congratulation. To say "Blessed be God" is illocutionary simply to praise God. The use of the expression to congratulate another person because of a special event is perlocutionary, and I tend to doubt that this usage is primary. The investigation of Mitchell is mainly lexicographical. It contains a comprehensive and helpful bibliography.

when God is addressed as "You" in other parts of a psalm. Benedictions in early narrative contexts bless God for deliverance from enemies or for what he has done to kings (David and Solomon); Psalm 18 does it because God has given the king vengeance and delivered him from his enemies (see esp. vv. 46-50). Psalm 144 is dependent upon the earlier royal psalm, but the emphasis has shifted from military victory to protection against a hostile attack. Even in psalms the reasons for blessing God are at the same time reasons for rejoicing, here with a joy that is shared by a leader or some other individual and the community. Psalm 144 concludes with a beatitude: "Happy is the people whose God is the LORD!" Other psalms express the confidence that no other God is like the God of Israel (Pss 113, 135 and, e.g., Ps 18:31-33). Thus, an element of congratulation is present even in devotional benedictions.[10]

There is no need here to discuss whether or not one type of benedictions was more original than the other. In the course of time both of them seem to have been "democratized" and more widely used in the life of common people. There is clear evidence that psalms and songs were assigned to specific situations in the life of David, or integrated in a narrative context, and also that devotional benedictions to an increasing degree influenced the form of benedictions used at encounters and other special occasions.

The forms were not always kept separate (see Gen 24:26; Exod 18:10-12); the benedictions of Solomon in 1 Kings 8 are due to a cultic occasion, the dedication of the temple. Solomon is said to have blessed all the assembly of Israel; we may say that he congratulated the people and himself (8:14, 55). In the opening benediction, Solomon praises "the LORD, the God of Israel," who has fulfilled what He promised to David and enabled Solomon to complete the building of the temple. At the conclusion of his intercession, Solomon blesses "the LORD who has given rest to His people Israel" in accordance with the promises given through Moses, and adds prayer wishes and exhortation (1 Kgs 8:15-21, 56-61).

Like the references to God's promises in these benedictions, references to God's past actions in psalms were precedents for God's actions in the present and for the hope that He will act in a similar way in the future. As time went, the Psalms were again and again read and chanted by new generations for whom the benefactions that the Psalms praised became the basis for the trust that God would still act in a similar way and eventually realize the eschatological salvation. What was said about the victory and protection granted to the king, the leaders and the people nourished the messianic hope. Those who read or listen can make the benediction of the God who hears prayers their own.

---

[10] On congratulation in a number of Psalms, see Lipiński 1968.

A number of Jewish texts from Hellenistic times attest the increased use of benedictions. Several new blessings of God are added to the paraphrase of the biblical
story in the Book of Jubilees and the (Pseudo-Philonic) Biblical Antiquities, more
occasionally in the Genesis apocryphon and Palestinian Targumim, and also occur
in the novel of Joseph and Asenath. Benedictions related to war and victory were
reactualized by the Maccabees (1 Macc 4:30-33; 2 Macc 1:17; 15:34). The Dead
Sea War Scroll prescribes benedictions to be pronounced by the High Priest at the
last eschatological battle (1QM 13:2-9; 14:4-7 etc.). Benedictions are also part of
new hymns and psalms (Pss Sol 2:37; 5:19; 6:6; 1QS 11:15-22; 1QH 13:20; 18:14
etc.).

More important for the ordinary Jews was the use of benedictions in daily life.
The Book of Tobit provides an early example of this. The main persons of the story
bless God both in their difficulties and when they experience miraculous help. One
can say that the moral of the whole story is that God is to be blessed both when He
afflicts and when He shows mercy (Tob 11:14; 13:1-2, 5). This theme is spelt out in
Tobit's final "prayer of rejoicing" in chapter 13. Beginning with the benediction in
13:1-2, its first part has a general address, but a second part is a congratulation addressed to Jerusalem, the holy city which God will afflict for the deeds of her sons,
but again show mercy and make glorious. Thus, the story of Tobit and his family
does not only teach a moral lesson but points forward to the eschatological future,
when Jerusalem will resound with the cry of "Hallelujah!" and the benediction
"Blessed be God, who has exalted you for ever!" (13:18). Daily life and eschatology
coexist—not only in the history of Tobit!

The fragments of several of the Dead Sea Scrolls attest benedictions to be used
at various occasions, in daily prayers, at festivals etc. (see 4Q 502, 503, 504, 507,
509, 511, 512). Another set of rules is attested by the Mishnah and later documents
of classical Judaism. The whole system cannot be traced back to the time of Jesus,
but many patterns and phrases certainly do. In addition to the daily prayers and
prayers for special days, even *berakot* to be used on occasions like the observations
of a commandment, the reception of good and bad news and other events, have a
standard nucleus which could be adapted according to the occasion. Some rabbi
maintained that every Jew was obliged to say 100 benedictions to which the particular benedictions were to be added. Most of the *berakot* to be used in regular worship began by "Blessed be You, LORD our God, King of the universe." Short
blessings more often retained the form "Blessed be He," which seems to have been
more common in the rabbinic school houses. The exact wording of the benedictions
was, however, not fixed, and it seems likely that even the "You"-form and the "He"-
form could alternate.

Used as a translation of the Hebrew word ברוך, the Greek word εὐλογητός took on a meaning that differed from ordinary Greek usage. Philo of Alexandria only seldom uses the word and Josephus avoids it. Even early Greek-speaking Christians preferred to use the word and the noun for thanksgiving, εὐχαριστία, which had become virtually synonymous with "blessing" in the meaning praise of God. It is, however, erroneous to think that the formula εὐλογητὸς ὁ θεός simply became obsolete in later Christianity.[11] A glance at a Greek *euchologion* is sufficient to prove that the formula has remained in frequent use until this day. It is also attested in the Apostolic Constitutions, which even include some christianized Jewish prayers. I have also found some examples that the Desert Fathers could still use the ancient form of a congratulatory benediction.

The New Testament contains three examples of the formula "who is blessed for ever!" (Rom 1:25; 9:5; 2 Cor 11:31). The four examples of more extended praise of God introduced with εὐλογητός are all related to a special occasion but are at the same time a more general praise. The *Benedictus* of Zechariah begins by blessing "The Lord, God of Israel," because He visited and redeemed His people, remembering His holy covenant with Abraham. It continues by addressing the child whose birth was the occasion for this hymnic praise (Luke 1:67-79). The three other examples are the letter-opening benedictions in 2 Cor 1:3-7; Eph 1:3-14 and 1 Pet 1:3-7. All three begin with the words: "Blessed be the God and Father of our Lord Jesus Christ." In all of them God is praised for what He has done to "us", but they later shift from first to second pronouns, thus addressing the recipients (2 Cor 1:6; Eph 1:13; 1 Pet 1:4b-5). The common phraseology and the shift to the second person form make it likely that these eulogies reflect a form that was used also by Paul and other preachers.

In 2 Corinthians Paul praises God who has comforted him and enabled him to comfort those who are in affliction. The reason for this is that Paul had been delivered from the deadly peril which he had faced in Asia, but the benediction is a prelude to what Paul later in the letter writes about the power of Christ that is at work in his own weakness. The opening benediction in Ephesians may be read as a congratulation of former Gentiles who have been baptized, sealed with the Holy Spirit and incorporated into the body of Christ. The benediction i 1 Peter congratulates Christians who in the midst of sufferings can rejoice because they have received a share of the salvation about which prophets inquired and angels longed to see.

Most Pauline letters begin with the assertion that Paul gives thanks to God for ·the faith, love (and hope) of the addressees. An opening benediction praises God, the Father of Jesus Christ for what He has done for and to the recipients. In 2 Corinthians God is praised for what He has done to Paul and through him to others, in-

---

[11] The study of J. M. Robinson 1964 does not allow for the statement of R. Deichgräber 1980, 562 that "der Gebrauch des judenchristlichen εὐλογητός ist schon früh zurückgetreten."

cluding the Corinthians. While expressions of thanksgiving and joy are common in official and private hellenistic letters, the opening of a letter with a congratulatory benediction was, no doubt, unusual, although there are some indications that on special occasions it could be used in a Jewish letter. The phraseology in the benedictions has much in common with that of Old Testament and later Jewish benedictions, hymns and prayers, but the continuous subordination of phrases and clauses in Eph 1:3-14 which make the thought move forward like a spiral, is without analogy. A number of questions need to be dealt with in greater detail. I am nevertheless happy to have been able to conclude this fragment of an investigation and to present it to my colleague and friend Lars Hartman. It will be most appropriate to do so with a congratulatory benediction with which Jewish scholars greeted one another: "Blessed be He, who gives of His wisdom to those who fear Him."

## Bibliography

Audet, Jean Paul 1958: "Esquisse historique du genre littéraire de la 'bénédiction' juive et de l'Eucharistie chrétienne", in: *RB* 65 (1958) 371-99.

Dahl, Nils A. 1951: "Adresse und Proömium des Epheserbriefes", in: *ThZ* 7 (1951) 341-64.

Dambrosch, David 1987: *The Narrative Covenant: Transformations of Genre in the Growth of Biblical Literature*, San Francisco, CA: Harper & Row 1987.

Deichgräber, Reinhard 1988: "Benediktionen II, N.T.", in: *TRE* 5, Berlin/New York: de Gruyter 1980, 562-66.

Dix, Gregory 1945: *The Shape of Liturgy*, Glasgow: Dacre Press, 2nd ed. 1945.

Elbogen, Ismar 1931: *Der jüdische Gottesdienst in seiner geschichtlichen Entwicklung*, 3rd ed., Frankfurt/Main: J. Kauffmann Verlag 1931; 4th ed. Hildesheim: Ohlms 1962.

Lipiński, E. 1968: "Macarismes et psaumes de congratulation", in: *RB* 75 (1968) 321-67.

Mitchell, Christopher Wright 1987: *The Meaning of* BRK *"To Bless" in the Old Testament* (SBL.DS 95), Atlanta, GA: Scholars Press 1987.

Mowinckel, Sigmund 1958: *Det Gamle Testamente i ny oversettelse* IV.1 [Norwegian translation with introduction and notes], Oslo: Aschehoug 1955.

Robinson, James M. 1964: "Die Hodajot-Formel in Gebet und Hymnus des Frühchristentums", in: W. Eltester/F. H. Kettler (eds.), *Apophoreta. FS Ernst Haenchen* (BZNW 30), Berlin: Töpelmann 1964, 194-235.

Towner, W. Sibley 1968: "'Blessed be YHWH' and 'Blessed art Thou, YHWH': The Modulation of a Biblical Formula", in: *JAOS* 103 (1968) 386-99.

Westermann, Claus 1965: *The Praise of God in the Psalms*, Richmond, VA: John Knox Press 1965.

# Scripture in *1 Enoch* and *1 Enoch* as Scripture

George W. E. Nickelsburg

## *1. Introduction*

1.1. Since I first became aware of his work in the mid–1960's I have tended to think of Lars Hartman as a "scripture sleuth," one who pores over ancient apocalyptic texts, searching for words, phrases, and motifs that can be traced back to the Hebrew Scriptures, and seeking to discover how they were reinterpreted in the living tradition. His first major venture into scripture sleuthing was *Prophecy Interpreted: The Formation of Some Jewish Apocalyptic Texts and of the Eschatological Discourse Mark 13 Par.*,[1] in which he studied motifs and patterns of thought and the manner in which they embody material from the Hebrew Scriptures. Subsequently, he passed his magnifying glass over *1 Enoch* 10:16–11:2,[2] and then, in *Asking for a Meaning*,[3] he studied *1 Enoch* 1–5 in great detail. The results are impressive and are foundational to all further study; one can see how literate Jewish and Christian apocalypticists were in the language and conceptions of the texts that they considered prophetic and how creative they were in their interpretation of this tradition. A striking element in Hartman's first monograph is the manner in which early Christian apocalypticists worked out of a living tradition that included post–biblical Jewish transformations and combinations of biblical material.

1.2. In this study I shall focus on this Jewish interpretive tradition, as it is attested in *1 Enoch*. Different from Hartman, I shall review almost all of the major parts of *1 Enoch* as repositories of Israel's sacred tradition. In part 2, I shall consider how the Enochic authors gathered and transformed traditions that we know from the Hebrew Bible. In part 3, I shall argue that the editor(s) of *1 Enoch* presented their apocalyptic corpus as itself being scripture—revealed, authoritative, and life–giving in its function, and I shall compare this viewpoint to the approach of some of their con-

---

[1] Hartman 1966.

[2] Hartman 1976–77; idem 1983.

[3] Hartman 1979.

temporaries. Part 4 will suggest a few implications for the study of early Christianity and modern Christian interpretation.

1.3. While it may seem natural to assume that the Jewish authors of *1 Enoch* knew much of the Hebrew Bible, three observations will inform the conclusions in this study. First, *1 Enoch* never *explicitly* refers to the Torah, the Prophets, and the Writings, or to any individual text in the Tanakh. Rather, as Hartman has shown with reference to the sections that he has analyzed, these authors wove into their texts words, phrases, and motifs found in the Hebrew Bible. Second, the Enochic authors made *broad and varied* use of the material we find in Scripture. As we move across large sections of *1 Enoch*, we shall find literary forms and extended traditions that are at home in the Hebrew Bible, and we shall see how the Enochic authors employed a variety of techniques as they interpreted sacred tradition toward a common end: moral exhortation governed by an eschatological perspective. Finally, because *1 Enoch* embodies a multi–layered tradition that developed over three centuries,[4] it is not always clear: (a) whether a particular Enochic text is dependent on a biblical text or a parallel form of the tradition; and (b) whether an Enochic author considers his source to be Scripture. Related to these observations is the fact that instead of appealing to the authority of other texts considered to be Scripture (i.e., the Hebrew Bible or its parts), the final editors of *1 Enoch* claim scriptural authority for their own text.

## 2. Scripture in 1 Enoch

### 2.1. Material Related to Genesis

As one thinks about *1 Enoch*'s use of Scripture, one is naturally drawn to the Book of Genesis. Enoch is, after all, a character taken from the Sethite genealogy in that book, and the Genesis story of the Flood plays a significant role in many strata of *1 Enoch*, from the earliest to the latest.

### 2.1.1. Traditions about the Flood

2.1.1.1. With the exception of the Astronomical Book, the story of the watchers and the women (*1 Enoch* 6–11) embodies the earliest strata of tradition in *1 Enoch*. Although the story is clearly related to the mythic fragment in Gen 6:1–4, the precise nature of their interrelationship is disputed. Is *1 Enoch* 6–11 an interpretation of the Genesis text or does it independently attest the tradition that has been preserved also

---

[4] For a discussion of the various strata in *1 Enoch* and their dating, see Nickelsburg 1981, 47–55, 90–94, 145–151, 214–223.

in Genesis? The latter position has been argued by J. T. Milik[5] and Margaret Barker.[6] In my view neither person proves the case, although I concur with a large number of scholars who believe that Gen 6:1–4 is a fragment of a longer tradition that was interpolated into the text of Genesis.[7] Milik does little more than assert his position for the priority of *1 Enoch* 6–11. Barker's discussion, while considerably more detailed, seems to me much too speculative.[8]

2.1.1.2. The most compelling reason for treating *1 Enoch* 6–11 as an interpretation of Genesis is the fact that it combines the story of the sons of God and the daughters of men with the Flood tradition in the order in which they are combined in Genesis 6–9.[9] If the author of *1 Enoch* 6–11 knows a fuller form of the tradition in Gen 6:1–4, he has combined it with material from Gen 6:5–9:17. My observations here treat the whole of *1 Enoch* 6–11 as such an interpretation. I date this interpretation as a whole to around the year 300 B.C.E.,[10] a time when the Book of Genesis had wide canonical authority.

2.1.1.3. This canonical authority notwithstanding, the author of *1 Enoch* 6–11 treats the Genesis text with great freedom, deleting material, adding other tradition, and giving the whole a tendency very different from that in Genesis.[11] The sketchy story in Genesis, with its reference to the mating of heavenly beings and earthly women and its allusions to *gibborim* and *nefilim*, has become a story of a heavenly revolt and the spawning of a race of demigods who are violent and murderous warriors bent on victimizing creation in general and humanity in particular. The retelling of the Genesis story has four exegetical tendencies.

(a) The story is told not simply as an account of an event from primordial times. *Urzeit* is a paradigm for the present time, which is *Endzeit*. The Flood is a prototype for the great judgment, which will punish the wickedness of the mighty of this earth, who are wreaking havoc in the author's own times. Parodying the ideology of the Hellenistic kings, the author claims that they are sons of rebellious heavenly beings rather than gods like Zeus and Apollo.[12] Through these eschatologizing transformations, the author reads a text about antiquity as prophetic of the end–times and hence relevant to his dispirited contemporaries.

---

[5] Milik 1976, 30–31.

[6] Barker 1987.

[7] See, e.g., von Rad 1972, 113; Westermann 1974, 499–500; Barthelmus 1979, 195.

[8] Nickelsburg 1989.

[9] Detailed support for this and some of the other judgments in this article are worked out in the manuscript of my as yet unpublished commentary on *1 Enoch*.

[10] Nickelsburg 1977, 389–391.

[11] Ibid., 386–401.

[12] Ibid., 396–397.

(b) Moreover, as Hartman has shown,[13] this eschatological interpretation of Genesis has been fleshed out through the use of words and phrases from elsewhere in the Bible. Especially noteworthy is language from Isaiah 65–66, which converts the description of the post–diluvian world in Genesis 8 into a scenario for the eschaton.[14] In the same vein, Sariel becomes the prototype of an eschatological prophet, who transmits to Noah a revelation about the impending end (*1 Enoch* 10:2–3).[15]

(c) Alongside the tendency to interpret Scripture with Scripture, is this author's use of non–Israelite tradition and myth. In addition to an inversion of Hellenistic royal ideology is an inversion of the Prometheus myth. ʿAsael, the tenth of the rebellious heavenly chieftains, brings *evil* to the world through the revelation of the forbidden secrets of mining and metallurgy, which cause bloodshed and sexual immorality (8:1–2). Other of the rebels reveal magic and the astrological arts (8:3; 9:8).[16]

(d) Thus, the eschatological tendency in this interpretation of Genesis 6–9 is enhanced by an ontological dualism not found in Genesis.[17] The origin of evil is not attributed to human beings (though they may be complicitous in it),[18] but to malevolent spirit powers. Although the Enochic authors make reference to the sins of the first parents (32:6) and to Cain's murder of Abel (22:5–7), the primary aetiology of sin, and violence in particular, is expressed in a story about heavenly rebellion. Pitted against the primordial heavenly evil–doers and their supernatural children are the four high holy ones: Sariel, Raphael, Gabriel, and Michael (chaps. 9–10).

2.1.1.4. Thus, this Enochic author takes up the early chapters of Genesis and their emphasis on the sins and the punishment of the first human beings, focuses on an erratic block of material about "the sons of god," and overlays the human story with a scheme that features an eschatological cosmic struggle between evil and good spirit powers.[19] The cosmic dualism and eschatological perspective that will characterize much of Jewish and Christian apocalypticism from Daniel through Revelation provide this author with the hermeneutical key to Genesis, which is aid-

---

[13] Hartman 1983, 21–22.

[14] Isaiah 65–66 appears to stand in the background of a number of other Jewish texts from this period, e.g., *1 Enoch* 26–27; Dan 12:2; *Jub.* 23:26–31; on the latter two texts see Nickelsburg 1972, 20–22, 33.

[15] Cf., e.g., Isa 26:20–21; Zeph 2–3; Rev 6:15–16.

[16] For a discussion of the literature pertaining to the strata of tradition in *1 Enoch* 6–11, see Collins 1978 and Nickelsburg 1978.

[17] On the convergence of complementary dualisms in *1 Enoch*, see Nickelsburg 1991.

[18] The complicity of human beings in the watchers' sins is especially evident in the revelation traditions, particularly in 8:1.

[19] For another example of this tendency, cf. *1 Enoch* 8:1 with Gen 4:22.

ed by a syncretistic use of non–Israelite myth.

2.1.1.5. The story in Genesis 6–11 becomes the fountainhead of an ongoing tradition about the Flood in various strata of *1 Enoch*.[20] *1 Enoch* 106–107 recounts the story of Noah's birth, and chapters 65–67 describe God's revelation to Noah and the angels' construction of the ark. Although chapters 83–84 recount young Enoch's dream about the destruction of the world through a Flood, a number of motifs common to these stories suggest that the stories are crystallizations of a common narrative tradition that posited a typology between Flood and final judgment. The ongoing life of this typological, eschatological interpretation of Genesis is attested in the Son of Man saying attributed to Jesus in Matt 24:37–38 and Luke 17:26–27.

### 2.1.2. The Enoch Legend

2.1.2.1. Although the figure of Enoch is conspicuous by his absence in chapters 6–11, he is central to the rest of *1 Enoch*. The story of the watchers and the women functions as a narrative prologue to the whole corpus, and it is immediately interpreted in chapters 12–16, the account of Enoch's prophetic call.[21] The Flood narratives in chapters 65–67, 83–84, and 106–107 incorporate Enoch as the recipient or the interpreter of revelation.

2.1.2.2. Although we may take these revelatory roles for granted, they represent a significant reinterpretation of the very brief allusion to Enoch in Gen 5:21–24, where his walking with God appears to refer to his righteous life (cf. Wis 4:10–15). This brief, cryptic reference, however, served as the nucleus for a massive tradition ascribed to a single figure, which is paralleled in early Judaism and early Christianity only by the Moses traditions and the four gospels. Three tendencies in this tradition parallel the tendencies we saw in the Flood traditions.

(a) Eschatology is focal in the Enoch traditions, although with fresh nuances. Enoch is a *prophet* of the eschaton. Indeed, his connection with the Flood fades as his revelations in the corpus focus increasingly on the final judgment (preeminently in chaps. 37–71 and 92–105). As the traditions take on a revelatory character, eschatology coalesces with elements from the sapiential tradition, as these are attested in writings like Job and the Wisdom of Solomon. In the accounts of his journeys through heaven and across the earth (chaps. 17–36) and his references back to these journeys (chaps. 92–105), eschatology is undergirded by cosmology.[22] The righteous one of Genesis 5 is reinterpreted as the primordial source of revealed wisdom about the eschaton.

---

[20] Nickelsburg 1984, 93–97.

[21] Ludin Jansen 1939, 115–118.

[22] Stone 1978; Nickelsburg 1981, 54–55.

(b) Complementing the eschatological tendency in the Enoch tradition is its dualism. Different from chapters 6–11, in chapters 12–16, the dead giants release their ghosts, who constitute a world of malevolent spirits, who continue to wreak havoc on humanity until the end–time (15:8–16:1).[23]

(c) The third element corresponding to the Flood traditions is the use of non–Israelite mythology to portray the patriarch. Over the past half century, there has been a developing scholarly consensus that many details in *1 Enoch*, not least those centering around the figure of Enoch, are closely paralleled in Mesopotamian (rather than Hellenistic Greek) texts.[24] In this respect, the Enochic authors follow the cue of Genesis itself, whose story of the Flood reflects ancient near eastern mythology. Once again, however, Enochic authors reshape Genesis stories about primordial times with an eschatological tendency.

## 2.2. Prophetic Material

### 2.2.1. Words, Phrases, and Motifs

It is scarcely surprising that a Jewish work with a heavily predictive element in it employs terminology and motifs from Israel's prophetic Scriptures. Hartman has done an excellent job of detecting and identifying these scriptural nuances and their sources in his studies of *1 Enoch* 1–5 and 10–11.[25] He notes, for example, the parallels to Deuteronomy 33 and Micah 1 in the theophany section in *1 Enoch* 1–5, phraseology from Balaam oracles in the introduction to Enoch's oracle, and elements from Third Isaiah's description of the new earth and new Jerusalem in the eschatological scenarios in chapters 5 and 10.[26] As these and many other examples indicate, the Enochic authors speak with a biblical vocabulary much as a modern preacher may phrase a sermon in the language of the Bible.

### 2.2.2. Prophetic Forms

#### 2.2.2.1. Use of Forms or Genres

More significant, however, is these authors' use of forms or genres at home in Israelite prophecy. The language of Deuteronomy 33 and Micah 1 fleshes out details in a description of the eschatological theophany that is contained in a "salvation–judg-

---

[23] This notion is greatly elaborated in the Book of *Jubilees*; see especially chap. 11; 17:16; 48:2–19.

[24] Ludin Jansen 1939; Grelot 1958; VanderKam 1984.

[25] Hartman 1979; idem 1983.

[26] Hartman 1979, 22–38 especially; idem 1983, 21–22.

ment oracle" that is reminiscent of texts in Third Isaiah.[27] In that oracle the phrases drawn from Isaiah 65–66 inform the author's description of the fates of the righteous and the sinners (i.e., their salvation or judgment), and the language imitating the Balaam oracles expresses the sources of the authority of the seer who utters the oracle. As Ludin Jansen has argued, the account of Enoch's ascent to heaven (chaps. 12–16) has been shaped by biblical accounts of prophetic calls, notably Ezekiel 1–2.[28] The Epistle of Enoch (chaps. 92–105) employs three forms typical of the prophets: woes, exhortations introduced by "fear not," and descriptive vignettes of eschatological events introduced by "in those days."[29] One emerges from a reading of these texts with the distinct impression that these apocalyptic authors intend to speak with a prophetic voice. We shall argue below that they also claim a revelatory authority that parallels that of the prophets (3.3).

## 2.2.2.2. Son of Man Traditions

2.2.2.2.1. Traditions about the "son of man" in *1 Enoch* 37–71 are a special instance of the use of prophetic material. These traditions appear in a set of vignettes that depict heavenly events related to the final judgment. Their sources are: texts about the Chosen One/Servant of YHWH in Isaiah 42, 49, and 52–53 (*1 Enoch* 49:4; 48:2–5; 62–63); oracles about the Davidic king in Isaiah 11 and Psalm 2 (*1 Enoch* 48:8–49:4); and the vision of one like a son of man in Daniel 7 (*1 Enoch* 46–47).[30] Thus this Enochic author employs a technique we have already seen, the conflation of texts believed to be related to one another. In this case, these texts focus in common on an enthroned figure who is God's vice–regent and stands over against the kings of the nations.[31] The Enochic version of the tradition creatively combines into new amalgam elements found uniquely in each of the sources. The figure's role as judge and his possession of the wisdom required for this task are drawn from the Davidic tradition. The kings' astonishment at his exaltation reflects Isaiah 52–53. His identity as a heavenly figure is the contribution of Daniel 7. Governing the whole is the author's belief that in the eschaton, God's justice, exacted by a heavenly figure, will triumph over the demonically inspired oppression enacted by the kings and the

---

[27] For this form, see Hanson 1975, 106–108.

[28] See above, n. 21.

[29] Nickelsburg 1977a, 310–315.

[30] Idem 1987, 56–64.

[31] The nuances are different in each text. In Isaiah 52–53 the kings and the nations witness the Servant's exaltation. In Psalm 2 the kings of the earth rebel against YHWH and his anointed one. In Daniel 7 the beasts represent kingdoms and their horns, kings who oppose the high God; they are judged before the appearance of the one like a son of man. In the Parables of Enoch, the kings and the mighty oppress the righteous and chosen, the clients of the heaven savior figure.

mighty. In a certain way, the author has not strayed far from the viewpoint expressed in chapters 6–11 (see above, 2.1.1.3.(a)).

2.2.2.2.2. The manner in which the son of man traditions have interwoven diverse sources dramatizes the problem of *1 Enoch*'s relationship to Scripture and illustrates the complexity of the Enochic tradition. Elements in Second Isaiah's portrait of the Servant are themselves a revision of Davidic tradition. *1 Enoch* 12–16 has transformed the commissioning account in Ezekiel 1–2, and the throne vision in Daniel 7 reflects the tradition in *1 Enoch* 12–16. The author in *1 Enoch* 37–71 then draws on Daniel 7 to provide a heavenly setting for his interpretation of the Davidic and Servant traditions. Thus, while the Enochic authors doubtless know certain texts as Scripture and employ certain material from them, the Enochic tradition itself is a dynamic one that spawns new variations and then receives them into its system on an equal footing with material and motifs drawn from what we know as the Hebrew Bible.

## 2.3. 1 Enoch and the Writings

2.3.1. The previous paragraphs demonstrate that at least one Enochic author could combine material from the prophets with a text that came to be included in the third section of the Hebrew Bible. Said another way, he considered Daniel to be among the prophets. The same author also draws on Psalm 2 for part of his description of the Chosen One, seeing that Davidic oracle as divine prophecy.

2.3.2. The relationship of *1 Enoch* to the so–called wisdom tradition is complex. An occasional passage like 94:5 appears to reflect the Book of Proverbs (4:4). In general, however, it is better to view the whole of *1 Enoch* as the product of sages who understand themselves to be the latter day bearers of the prophetic tradition. As we shall see below (3.6.3.–3.6.5.) the corpus employs forms, motifs, and concerns that are at home in wisdom texts of the Hebrew Bible and the "Apocrypha."

## 2.4. The Hebrew Bible as a Source for Israel's History: 1 Enoch 85–90

2.4.1. The Animal Vision is the one section of *1 Enoch* whose author appears to have known most of the books of the Hebrew Bible. From this material he has crafted a history of Israel from creation to the eschaton, which he expects imminently during the time of Judas Maccabeus.[32] As sources for his history, he has drawn on the Pentateuch, Joshua through 2 Kings, and probably Ezra or Ezra–Nehemiah.[33] His knowledge of the prophetic corpus is evident in the allegory of the shepherds, the sheep and the wild beasts, which reflects Ezekiel 34 and Zechariah 11, and perhaps

---

[32] Tiller 1993, 61–82.

[33] Cf. 89:72, which knows events recounted in the Book of Ezra.

other texts. His description of the new Jerusalem appears to be dependent on a traditional exposition of Isaiah 60 and 65–66.[34] His knowledge of the Writings apart from Ezra–Nehemiah is impossible to discern. His use of the Chronicler is dubious.[35] He was a contemporary of the author of Daniel and espoused a militant viewpoint quite at odds with that book.[36] Of the rest of the Writings, there is no evidence in the Vision.

2.4.2. In interpreting the Torah, the Deuteronomic history, and Ezra-Nehemiah as an account of Israel's history, this author has also used traditions not found in the Hebrew Bible. Not surprisingly, he draws on the tradition of which he is a part and includes details from the story of the watchers and the women (*1 Enoch* 6–11) as an integral part of his account of the degeneration of humanity and its punishment in the Flood story (86:1–89:9) and of his description of the end–time (90:20–27). Equally interesting are a few non–biblical details in the story of Abel's death (89:4,6), the mingling of the Sethites and Cainites (86:2), and the Exodus story (89:21,25), which appear to reflect the kind of haggadic interpretation of the biblical narrative attested also in the Book of *Jubilees* and the *Genesis Apocryphon*. One detail in the primordial history seems to derive from the pagan myth of the Titanomachia (86:3; cf. Hesiod, *Theogony* 671, 713–26).

2.4.3. Several tendencies govern this author's interpretation of the scriptural texts. The first is the shaping of the whole into a history of humanity. In this enterprise, he interprets Scripture by Scripture, drawing material from the prophets and using one chapter from Ezekiel to develop the major part of his animal allegory. The pattern of sin and punishment that runs through most of his account reflects the same tendency in the Deuteronomic history, which is one of his major sources. However, for some parts of his history, he draws on his own dualistically oriented tradition to explain human sin. It is the heavenly revolt that causes the corruption that leads to the Flood, and in order to explain the troubles of the post–Exilic period, he transforms biblical texts about shepherds, positing the malevolent activity of a second set of rebellious heavenly beings (89:59–90:19). In both cases, as in chapters 6–11, these evil angels are opposed by Sariel, Raphael, Gabriel, and Michael (*1 Enoch* 87–88; 90:21–25). Thus, in the two periods of great violence preceding definitive judgment, events on earth shadow activity in the heavenly realm. History is also eschatologically oriented. Although, the author distinguishes between *Urzeit* and *Endzeit*, the Flood and the final judgment are counterposed, and the story of the watchers concludes only in the end–time. Moreover, the birth of the white bull and the return of the whole human race to its primordial unity and pristine purity

---

[34] See Nickelsburg 1972, 17–23, 28–33 and cf. *1 Enoch* 26–27.

[35] See Tiller 1993, 305.

[36] Ibid., 102–105.

(90:37–38)—made explicit through the animal allegory—indicates that this author views all history in an eschatological perspective.

2.4.4. *In short*, this author's interpretation of Scripture has an historical center that employs non–historical biblical material to support that narrative purpose, that enhances biblical material with non–biblical tradition, and that structures the whole according to a dualistic and eschatological perspective.

2.4.5. A reticence to emphasize the activity of the prophets is a remarkable feature of this author's historical exposition. As noted, material from Isaiah, Ezekiel, and Zechariah is drawn into the narrative, but with no reference to the sources. More striking is the role of Moses. True, he is sent to Pharaoh and speaks in behalf of God (89:17–18), he leads the slaughter of the idolaters (89:35), and he builds the Tabernacle (89:36). Oddly, however, the Sinai story omits any reference to Moses receiving the Torah; revelation came to the Israelites in the wilderness, through no mediator, before they arrived at Sinai (89:28–35). The activity of the rest of the prophets is summarized in three verses (89:51–53). This major omission is remarkable in a text that emphasizes revelation, both by claiming to be revelation received in primordial times before Moses and the prophets and by positing an eschatological revelation as the catalyst of the repentance that triggers the final judgment.

## 2.5. Summary

The Enochic authors are conversant with Scripture and often speak in its idiom and embody their message in its literary forms, though they never explicitly cite Scripture. In their interpretation of scriptural texts, they employ other scriptural material, haggadic tradition (notably that ascribed to Enoch or associated with him), and non–Israelite myth. Their interpretation is governed by a dualism that posits a world that is inhabited by opposing good and evil spirits and by an eschatological perspective that awaits an imminent, final judgment that will resolve the crisis precipitated by the primordial revolt.[37] The lack of any explicit appeal to Scriptural authority is counterpoised with the claim that the Enochic books are the deposit of a revelation given long before the birth of the Bible's first author, Moses, and intended for earth's last generation. This diminution of the authority of the Tanakh and celebration of Enochic authority are linked to the function of the Enochic corpus: it is revealed scripture intended to constitute the eschatological community of the chosen who will endure the final judgment and receive the blessings of eternal life.

---

[37] Nickelsburg 1991.

# 3. 1 Enoch as Scripture

## 3.1. The Corpus as Enoch's Testament

3.1.1. I have argued elsewhere that the penultimate form of *1 Enoch* took the form of a testament ascribed to Enoch.[38] Indicators of this generic identity can be found in 81:1–82:3, where Enoch returns from heaven and instructs Methuselah and his sons in anticipation of his final departure, and in 91:1–3, which reprises the testamentary setting.

3.1.2. On the basis of this orientation, we can identify large parts of *1 Enoch* as constitutive parts of the familiar testamentary genre.[39] The first words of the introduction (1:1) and the subsequent description of the theophany (1:3–7, 9) recall the opening of Moses' testamentary blessing (Deut 33:1–2). The lengthy account of Enoch's cosmic journeys correspond to the narrative, biographical section of the testamentary genre (chaps. 12–36). Skipping the Parables (chaps. 37–71), which are a later addition to the corpus, based on earlier parts of it, we come to the Astronomical chapters (chaps. 72–82), which, judging from Qumran evidence, were originally a separate document.[40] Imbedded in these chapters is a brief section that describes Enoch's final heavenly vision—the books of human deeds (81:1–4)—his return to earth (v 5ab), and the holy ones' command that he prepare for his departure by instructing his children (vv. 5c–10).[41] In 82:1–3, Enoch is speaking to Methuselah and recalling how he has carried out this command. Chapters 83–84 and 85–90 are two major blocks of Enoch's instruction addressed to "Methuselah my son" (83:1; 85:1–2). They focus on the Flood and the history of humanity culminating in the final judgment. Chapter 91 takes up the testamentary scene (vv. 1–3b); in it a summary of the history of humanity is framed by ethical two–ways instruction (vv. 3c–4 I 5–9 I 18–19). This leads to the explicitly exhortatory part of the corpus—Enoch's Epistle (chaps. 92–105), which is addressed to Enoch's sons and to the last generations who will observe truth and peace (92:1). The Apocalypse of Weeks (93:1–10 + 91:11–17) is another capsule history of humanity, said to be derived from the heavenly tablets that Enoch had viewed according to 82:1–4. After another piece of two–ways instruction addressed to "my children" and "the righteous" (94:1–4), the author launches into an extensive set of exhortations and woes ad-

---

[38] Nickelsburg 1981, 150–151.

[39] For a discussion of the vast literature on the testament genre, see Kolenkow 1986 and Collins 1986. For a summary of the formal characteristics mentioned here, see Nickelsburg 1981, 232.

[40] Milik 1976, 5–8.

[41] For the relationship of this section to chapters 1–36, see Nickelsburg 1981, 150–51, but especially Argall 1992, 351–64, who argues that Enoch's vision of the heavenly tablets represents a seventh vision displaced from chaps. 20–36.

dressed to the righteous and sinners of the end time (94:5–104:8) and partly supported by allusions to the visions recounted in chapters 21–32 an 82:1–4. In the
conclusion of the work (104:9–105:2), the author focuses on the Enochic provenance and the book's function. In the end time, Enoch's books will be given to the
righteous, pious, and wise, to teach them the ways of righteous, and they, in turn,
will testify to all sons of the earth. Thus the corpus ends with a self–conscious reference to itself as the embodiment of heavenly wisdom, gotten by Enoch, deposited
with Methuselah, and revealed to the eschatological community of the righteous as
Enoch's testimony—his exhortation to walk in the paths of truth that will lead to
eternal life, both for the nuclear righteous community and for those who heed their
preaching. That this corpus, in one form or another, was thought to serve this function is attested in the Book of *Jubilees* (4:17–19), a text heavily dependent on *1
Enoch* (cf. chap. 5 with *1 Enoch* 6–11).

## 3.2. A Collection of Revelations

There are good reasons to believe that many testamentary works make revelatory
claims.[42] Such a claim is explicit, central, and repeated in the case of *1 Enoch*. If
the Israelite patriarchs based their ethical exhortations on events in their lives,
Enoch bases his on tours that he took through the cosmos in the company of angelic
interpreters. The motif of revelation begins in the first chapter, where Enoch appeals
to his journeys and visions and to the angelic interpretations as the sources of his
authority (1:2; cf. 93:2). That authority is established in the account of his heavenly
ascent, cast in the form of a prophetic call narrative (chaps. 12–16). Thereafter, his
journey accounts are shaped by the form of vision and interpretation (chaps. 17–
36). He has seen the eschatological places and events of which he will later speak,
and he has a definitive angelic interpretation in each instance. His viewing of the
heavenly tablets in 81:1–4 is foundational for his apocalypse in 93:1–10; 91:11–17.
At various points in chapters 94–104, he will remind his readers of what he has
seen: heavenly books, angelic intercessors, and the like.[43] In addition the authors of
chapters 83–84, 85–90 use the form of a dream vision to claim authority for the truth
of his assertions. Thus, through the forms that they use, whether they have prophetic
prototypes or not, the Enochic authors assert the revelatory character of the information that they transmit.

---

[42] Not least the father is able to make detailed predictions of the future.

[43] See, e.g., 98:7–8; 99:3; 104:1; and cf. 102:4–5 with chap. 22 and 103:1–2 with 81:1–4.

## 3.3. A Book of Revealed Wisdom

3.3.1. This revelation is contained and transmitted in writing, a fact that is emphasized in 81:5–82:3, 100:6, and 104:12–13. The testamentary section in 81:5–82:3 is especially important in this respect. Here the editor of the corpus claims that Enoch's books are the embodiment of the heavenly wisdom that has the power to give life. The notion and the language are remarkably close to Sirach 24.[44] According to ben Sira, heavenly wisdom has become resident in the Mosaic Torah. What is important is not the *event* on Sinai when Torah was given to Moses, but the *fact* that the Torah is the embodiment of heavenly wisdom, which is able to give life to those who obey it (Sir 24:13–21). In *1 Enoch*, Enoch's trip to heaven has resulted in the real presence of wisdom in his books, which he has left behind to give life "to all the generations until eternity" (82:1–3; cf. Sir 24:33).

3.3.2. Enoch's wisdom has two components. First, Enoch transmits Torah, which consists of law and moral instruction. Chapters 72–82 reveal the cosmic laws that govern the movement of the heavenly bodies and that justify the solar calendar as the right basis for religious observances.[45] The Epistle of Enoch (chaps. 94–102 in particular) is dominated by a concern about right and wrong human conduct, particularly as it relates to the way that people treat one another. Although the section contains no halakah, its use of the two–ways scheme and its various wisdom forms closely parallel ben Sira's wisdom–shaped Torah instruction. Secondly, Enoch reveals information about the eschaton and about the final judgment, which will be based on human responses to Enoch's Torah. This eschatological instruction is contained both in apocalypses that recount the order of events past, present, and future (chaps. 85–90; 91:5–9; 93:1–10 and 91:11–17) and in descriptions of the places of retribution (chaps. 17–36).

3.3.3. Given this analogy to the Wisdom of ben Sira, one may ask whether it is proper to describe *1 Enoch* as Scripture—an authoritative written text? Before answering that question, we need to remember, first of all, that ben Sira himself claims to transmit revealed instruction which is effective to produce the behavior that receives the covenantal blessing, and he compares his teaching to prophecy. Even if

---

[44] For a detailed comparison of *1 Enoch* and Sirach as two roughly contemporary wisdom writings, see Argall 1992. On the theme of revealed wisdom as such and a comparison of *1 Enoch* 81 and Sirach 24, see ibid., 20–135.

[45] The words "commandment" (*teʾezaz*) and "ordinance" (*šerʿat*) occur with some frequency in chaps. 72–82 with reference to the laws that govern the heavenly bodies (72:2; 73:1; 74:1; 79:1–2), Cf. *1 Enoch* 2:1–5:4 and its comparison of obedience of the works of creation and human disobedience. *1 Enoch* 72–82 says little about calendrical observance as such (but cf. 80:2–8), but provides the theoretical, astronomical undergirding for such observance, which is worked out, e.g., in the Book of *Jubilees*.

his book does not have a communal stamp of approval, its substance has some of the qualities of the canonical texts. However, if we compare ben Sira, who sees himself as an inspired interpreter of the wisdom resident in the Mosaic Torah, with *1 Enoch*, we move a step closer to a kind of canonicity. The Enochic authors do not appeal to the Torah or the Prophets, but base their authority on direct revelatory experience. However one explains the pseudepigraphic device, its claim is clear: the text is based on a prophetic call and on visions of the heavenly and eschatological realia infallibly interpreted by angels.

3.3.4. Thus *1 Enoch* represents a remarkable *tour de force* in the religion of Israel. The authors speak in the language and forms of accepted authoritative Scripture (Torah and Prophets) with all it resonances. However, the explicit authority of the text lies not in these real sources, but in its claim to direct revelation received long before Moses or the prophets lived and spoke. Enoch saw and heard it first and spoke and wrote it first. Enoch's blessing long preceded that of Moses. In an age when antiquity was a virtue, this is a powerful claim.

3.3.5. The fact that *1 Enoch* was not accepted as part of the Jewish canon of the Rabbis should not preempt the question of its status as canonical scripture in some circles. Clearly the text itself claims to be definitive revelation constituting the eschatological community (104:12–13). For those people, the text was scripture. The author of *Jubilees* (4:17–19) and some early Christian usage provides similar, external evidence for such a function (see below 4.1.1).

## 3.4. 1 Enoch's Authority and that of the Hebrew Scriptures

3.4.1. All of this raises an interesting question. Was the Enochic corpus intended to supplant the Mosaic Torah or the emerging Hebrew Bible as authoritative Torah and Scripture? The opening words of the corpus can have the effect of mitigating the power of Moses' blessing by construing it as an echo of Enoch's. The wording in 91:1–3, and indeed the whole structure of chapters 91–93 turns Deuteronomy 31–33 into a reprise of events enacted millennia earlier.[46] The Animal Vision's silence about Moses' receipt of the Torah is striking in this context, given the vision's emphasis on revelation. Nonetheless, there are some counterindications. Perhaps the first is common sense. It does not seem likely that an Israelite of the third to second century would set aside the Torah and the Prophets, while at the same time appropriating a great deal of material from them? Secondly, although the Animal Vision ignores the giving of the Torah, the Apocalypse of weeks mentions it (93:6). Finally, the author of *Jubilees* is an early interpreter of the Enochic writings and holds them in high esteem, placing material from them in a text which is said to be the true form

---

[46] Nickelsburg 1981, 151.

of the revelation that Moses received on Mount Sinai.

3.4.2. Perhaps *Jubilees* and the pseudonymous *Testament of Moses* can help us understand the role and function of *1 Enoch*. While *Jubilees* does not explicitly reject the content or authority of the Pentateuch, its enhancements of Genesis and Exodus and its claim of Mosaic authorship based on angelic dictation that derived in part from heavenly tablets indicate that this author does not consider the Pentateuch to be sufficient and definitive as revealed Torah. Moses heard and wrote more, and this additional revelation was consonant with this author's interpretation of Torah. The author of the *Testament of Moses* held a similar viewpoint, claiming that his book was the true text of Moses' words before his death. One of the most substantial differences between Deuteronomy 30–34 and the *Testament* is the latter's interpretation of Moses' predictions with specific reference to events in the Hellenistic period. Again, the text of Deuteronomy is not sufficient, and one makes up for the lack by attributing a fuller text to Moses.

3.4.3. What the Enochic authors have in common with the pseudo–Mosaic authors is the belief that accepted Scripture is not sufficient and the claim that they present revelation that supersedes that in the Tanakh. The Enochic authors are *more* radical in that they attribute some of the substance of the Hebrew Bible, including the Pentateuch, to Enoch. Along with the writers of *Jubilees* and the *Testament of Moses*, these authors perceive themselves as living in a time of perversity and apostasy. To understand this is, itself, a revelation. They also present their response to their situation as a revelation that constitutes an eschatological community of the chosen.[47] According to the Enochic authors, the eschatological revelation was first given to Enoch who ascended to heaven and returned, as no one had done since.

3.4.4. It is perhaps a moot question whether the Enochic authors wished to displace Torah. In any case, they believed that the ancient seer and sage received revelation not found in the Tanakh. He had foreseen their time, its problems, and its critical place at the end of history and he had received a pointed and explicit message of judgment and salvation that was directed to the people of the last generation. This message was presented, and accepted by some, as authoritative revelation; its self–conscious references to its written character justifies our describing it as scripture in those contexts.

---

[47] For a brief discussion of the interrelationship of these traditions about community founding and their relationship to the Qumran texts, see Nickelsburg 1986, 342–45.

## 3.5. The Perceived Need to Interpret and Supplement the Bible in the Graeco–Roman Period

3.5.1. Our conclusions about *1 Enoch* and works contemporary with it enable us to make some general observations about the ambiguous status of the Hebrew Bible in the last centuries of the common era and the perceived need to interpret and supplement its contents.

3.5.2. Although the Mosaic Torah had widespread canonical authority, authors with a variety of concerns and approaches found it fruitful, or even necessary, to develop written interpretations of the Pentateuchal material. For ben Sira the Mosaic Torah is the repository of heavenly wisdom, but he explicitly states that his interpretive practice is an integral part of the process of transmitting Torah's life–giving wisdom and that the book containing his teaching will provide a deposit "for the generations of eternity" (24:32–33). He likens this teaching to "prophecy" (v. 33). In this respect, ben Sira sees himself and his writing more in continuity with the (authors of) the Hebrew Bible than we might be inclined to recognize. The author of the Book of *Jubilees* also saw a necessity to interpret the Mosaic law for new times and situations, and he attributed his halakah to Moses. Moreover, *Jubilees* attests an ongoing process of interpretation and elaboration of the Pentateuchal narratives for the purpose of halakic exposition or moral exhortation and ascribes this, too, to Moses. Halakic exposition is also attested in the Qumran writings (e.g., CD 9–12), and though these laws are not pseudonymously ascribed to Moses, the laws of community are described as revealed interpretation of Mosaic Torah (1QS 5:7–11).

3.5.3. A range of texts from the Graeco–Roman period also express a concern that scriptural prophecy has not yet been fulfilled. Among writers in the wisdom tradition, Ben Sira longs for the events that will show the prophets to have been trustworthy (36:15–16), and the author of Tobit voices a similar expectation (14:4–5, long text). Among the apocalypticists, the author of Daniel 9 deals explicitly with the problem of unfulfilled prophecy, specifically Jeremiah's prophecy of 70 years (Dan 9:2–27), and because it stands as a word of God, he finds it necessary to reinterpret the text. For the authors of the Qumran *pesharim*, prophecy points to the end–time, their time, and they set about finding the correct meaning of the prophetic texts. In all cases (except Tobit for whom the time of fulfillment is a mystery), these authors assert the validity of their interpretation through an appeal to secondary revelation or inspiration, whether in response to prayer (Sir 39:1, 5–7), an angelic interpreter invoked through prayer (Dan 9:20–23), or the undefined insight of the Teacher of Righteousness and others like him (1QpHab 7:4–8). The author of the *Testament of Moses* adopts a pseudonymous identity and has Moses himself explicate his prophecy with specific reference to the Hellenistic period.

3.5.4. The Enochic authors, however, claim *fresh* revelation. They do not quote the Hebrew Scriptures and interpret or rewrite those Scriptures in their own terms. Instead they cut themselves loose from the received texts and create new ones. Although they may not supplant the old texts, they complement them and invest their new texts with preeminent authority that makes them uniquely binding and superlatively relevant for their times.

3.5.5. Thus, in many and different ways, Jews in the Graeco–Roman period wrestled with both the growing authority of the Hebrew Bible and its obvious deficiencies—with its admitted relevance for their own times and its frustrating failure to get to the point as they understood it.

## 3.6. From Texts to History

Although I have focused my discussion on a set of texts, I have alluded to the *authors* of these texts and to the *situations* they addressed and the *settings* in which they functioned. Here I shall elaborate briefly on these complex matters since they tend to be oversimplified in scholarly discussion.

3.6.1. It is widely assumed that "prophecy was dead" in the Graeco–Roman period. One might agree with this assertion if by a prophet one means certain types of public figures whose proclamations have been preserved in the Hebrew Bible. Even in this case, however, we know far too little to justify lumping all these "prophets" into one or two categories. In any case, the claim that "prophecy was dead" derives from a theological (rather than historical) judgment that links inspiration closely to canonicity. As twentieth century historians we are not justified in concluding that there were no persons in the Graeco–Roman period who could make a plausible case for being prophets. Not only does Josephus falsify such a claim,[48] but a text like 1 Macc 14:41 (like many in the Hebrew Bible) suggests that one's claim to be a prophet could have political ramifications that might result in a negative assessment of the claim which could have lasting influence in the tradition that was shaped by those in power.

3.6.2. A discussion of the issue, however, must move beyond the title of prophet or seer and take into consideration the range of nuances in the texts from the Graeco–Roman period. Ben Sira's rhetoric indicates that this sage saw his teaching to be *similar to* prophecy (24:32–33). Even if he did not claim to be a prophet, he believed that his teaching was inspired (39:5–8). In this respect it may be fruitful to consider Hengel's observations about the relationship between wisdom and prophecy.[49] The sages, scribes, and teachers, by whatever name they called themselves, were the keepers and expounders of both the Torah and the prophets, and it would

---

[48] Horsley 1985.
[49] Hengel 1974, 1:134–35.

appear useful to ask to what extent and in what ways these persons saw their task as *similar to*, and *different from* that of the authors whose texts they interpreted.

3.6.3. We should reconsider the relationship between wisdom literature like Sirach, the Wisdom of Solomon, and Tobit and apocalypses like *1 Enoch*, Daniel, 4 Ezra, and *2 Apoc. Baruch*. The apocalypticists had concerns similar to those of the sages and could express them in similar vocabulary and literary forms.[50] *1 Enoch's* designation for Enoch is "scribe" (12:4; 15:1; 92:1) and the text of *1 Enoch* is said to be "wisdom" (5:8; 37:1; 92:1; 93:10). Dan 12:3 describes the wise teachers in language that recalls Sir 24:32–33. This is not to say that ben Sira was the same kind of scribe as any of the pseudo–Enochic authors, or that the wisdom of the one can be equated with that of the other, but we appear to be dealing with species of the same genus.

3.6.4. It follows from our previous considerations that the old argument as to whether apocalypticism derives from prophecy or wisdom is based on a false dichotomy. If the sages were the interpreters of the prophets and could speak in their idiom, and if apocalypticism is a form of wisdom, then we should expect the apocalypses to reflect a sapiential interpretation of prophecy as well as non–prophetic elements in the sapiential tradition.

3.6.5. In short, a careful comparative reading of sapiential and apocalyptic texts, with close attention to their attitudes toward the Hebrew Scriptures and to the hints that the later texts provide about their social settings, offers considerable potential for an historical reconstruction of the religion and culture of late Second Temple Judaism, both as this related to Judaism of the Persian period and to rabbinic Judaism and nascent Christianity.

## 4. Some Implications

It remains to draw a few connections to the study of early Christianity and to indicate some contemporary implications that provide a rationale for the study of these ancient texts by scholars in Christian communities, even if they do not consider them to be canonical.

### 4.1. Early Christianity

4.1.1. Christians of the first three centuries were not of one mind with respect to *1 Enoch*. Writers from Jude to Origen revered Enoch; some saw him as a prophet, and some quoted the text as Scripture. Others, though they did not cite the source, drew material from the Enochic tradition, especially its interpretation of Gen 6:1–4.[51]

---

[50] Argall 1992, 225–339.

The son of man tradition in the Gospels is a microcosm of the early church's ambivalence about the Enochic writings. The judicial functions that the gospels ascribe to the son of man are derived from the conflated tradition that is attested in the Parables of Enoch and not simply from Daniel.[52] Nonetheless, the clearly identifiable source of the wording in texts like Mark 13:26; 14:62 is Dan 7:13–14. The tradition is reading Daniel in light of the interpretation that we now have in the Parables. This suggests that in *this* Christian tradition the authority of Daniel exceeded that of the Parables of Enoch.

4.1.2. The discussion in 3.6.2.–5. is relevant for a study of the gospels. A considerable part of the study of "Q" has been informed by the untenable dichotomy between wisdom and apocalyptic. If these two types of religious thought are, in fact, two species of the same genus, we need to rethink some hypotheses about the history of "Q" and the community that created it, as well as some hypothetical portraits of the historical Jesus.

4.1.3. Some aspects of our discussion are relevant to the study of early Christianity not because they show us something entirely new, but because they provide Jewish prototypes for tendencies and processes well known in the rise and early development of Christianity.

4.1.3.1. The variety of attitudes toward the Jewish Scriptures that I have highlighted is mirrored in the New Testament. Although writers like Matthew and the author to the Hebrews regularly quote Scripture and cite their sources, many others interweave scriptural words and phrases into their text without attribution. The Apocalypse of John provides the best Christianity analogy to *1 Enoch*, and especially the Parables, not only because of its apocalyptic genre, but also in its unattributed use of words and phrases from Scripture and, interestingly, from the Enochic tradition.[53]

4.1.3.2. Pseudonymity is a point of similarity. The pseudo–Mosaic tradition, with its tendency to elaborate and update parts of the Pentateuch is paralleled in the pseudo–Pauline writings of the New Testament. Just as certain Jewish authors sought authority by speaking in the voices of Enoch, Ezra, Moses, Jeremiah, and Baruch, the names of Peter, Paul, James, John, Jude, Thomas, Phillip, and others were evoked to provide the seal of authority. The same tendency is evident in the scribal practice that led to the apostolic ascriptions of the four gospels. Different from the Jewish texts, this apostolic authority did not derive from a call by the God of Israel or an archangel, but through association with the Son of God.

---

[51] The classic article remains that of Lawlor 1897, although James VanderKam has prepared a new study for the series *Compendia Rerum Iudaicarum ad Novum Testamentum*.

[52] See above, n. 30.

[53] Charles 1912, xcvi–xcix.

4.1.3.3. Finally, the process of developing a new canonical collection (the New Testament) and the creation of Christian literature in the second and third centuries were driven in part by some of the same factors that led to the creation of Jewish literature in the Graeco–Roman period. As Justin's *Dialogue with Trypho* illustrates, the Jewish Scriptures in themselves were not sufficient to serve the Church's apologetic purposes. Moreover, other apologetic and polemical texts and commentaries on New Testament books indicate that even the emerging formation of an expanded canon did not suffice to meet the changing needs of the church as it interacted with its environment. The new scripture also required learned interpretation.

## 4.2. Contemporary Implications

4.2.1. Our overview of Jewish literature in the Graeco–Roman period has demonstrated that the boundary between Scripture and its exposition was not as fixed as one might suppose when one views the period from the perspective of a later time when the Tanakh was accepted as Bible. There was a chronological grey area in which authority was being established and defined. Eventually, canonicity emerged, though in different ways in different places (*1 Enoch* and *Jubilees* are still part of the canon of the Ethiopian Church). With canonicity established, many of the ambiguities resolve themselves as one applies the label "Scripture," and communities forget the painful process of seeking new meanings from texts the nature of whose authority is ambiguous.

4.2.2. However, the problem never really goes away. The dynamics at work among Jewish interpreters in the Graeco–Roman Period are a prototype and a parable of the ongoing history of the Hebrew Bible and the New Testament down to the present time: *time–bound* texts have been invested with ongoing canonical authority to govern the beliefs and practice of communities living in *times that change*. The study of *non–canonical* texts and their authors' struggle with tradition–in–the–process–of–becoming–scripture can perhaps temper an unquestioning adherence to the historically bound canonical decisions of the past—not so that one rejects their intention or the principles that motivated them, but so that one assumes the obligation critically to assess the situation in one's own time and to think and act appropriately and responsibly within the framework of the received tradition. Thus, the religious person and community are engaged in a perennial process of what Lars Hartman has called "Asking for a Meaning."

# Bibliography

Argall, Randal A. 1992: *1 Enoch and Sirach: A Comparative Literary and Conceptual Analysis of the Themes of Revelation, Creation, and Judgment.* Dissertation, The University of Iowa, Ann Arbor, MI: UMI Dissertation Services 1992.

Barker, Margaret 1987: *The Older Testament*, London: SPCK 1987.

Barthelmus, Rüdiger 1979: *Heroentum in Israel und seiner Umwelt* (AThANT 65), Zürich: Theologischer Verlag 1979.

Charles, R. H. 1912: *The Book of Enoch or 1 Enoch,* Oxford: Clarendon 1912.

Collins, John J. 1978: "Methodological Issues in the Study of *1 Enoch*: Reflections on the Articles of P. D. Hanson and G. W. E. Nickelsburg," in: Paul J. Achtemeier (ed.), *SBL 1978 Seminar Papers* (2 vols.) Missoula, MT: Scholars 1978, Vol. 1, 315–22.

— 1986: "The Testamentary Literature in Recent Scholarship," in: Kraft and Nickelsburg (eds.) 1986, 268–85.

Grelot, Pierre 1958: "La légend d'Hénoch dans les apocryphes et dans la Bible: origine et signification," in: *RSR* 46 (1958) 5–26, 181–220.

Hanson, Paul D. 1975: *The Dawn of Apocalyptic: The Historical and Sociological Roots of Jewish Apocalyptic Eschatology*, Philadelphia, PA: Fortress 1975.

Hartman, Lars 1966: *Prophecy Interpreted: The Formation of Some Jewish Apocalyptic Texts and of the Eschatological Discourse Mark 13 Par.* (CB.NT 1), Lund: Gleerup 1966.

— 1976–77: "'Comfort of the Scriptures' – an Early Jewish Interpretation of Noah's Salvation, I En. 10:16–11:2," in: *SEÅ* 41–42 (1976–77) 87–96.

— 1979: *Asking for a Meaning: A Study of 1 Enoch 1–5* (CB.NT 12), Lund: Gleerup 1979.

— 1983: "An early example of Jewish exegesis: *1 Enoch* 10:16–11:2," in: *Neotestamentica* 17 (1983) 16–27.

Hengel, Martin 1974: *Judaism and Hellenism: Studies in their Encounter in Palestine during the Early Hellenistic Period*, 2 vols., Philadelphia, PA: Fortress 1974.

Horsley, Richard A. 1985: *Bandits, Prophets, and Messiahs: Popular Movements in the Time of Jesus*, Minneapolis, MN: Winston 1985.

Kolenkow, Anitra Bingham 1986: "The Literary Genre 'Testament'," in: Kraft and Nickelsburg (eds.) 1986, 257–267.

Kraft, Robert A. and George W. E. Nickelsburg (eds.) 1986: *Early Judaism and its Modern Interpreters*, Philadelphia, PA and Atlanta, GA: Fortress and Scholars 1986.

Lawlor, H. J. 1897: "Early Citations from the Book of Enoch," in: *JP* 25 (1897) 164–225.

Ludin Jansen, H. 1939: *Die Henochgestalt: Eine vergleichende religionsgeschichtliche Untersuchung* (Norske Videnskaps–Akademi i Oslo II. Hist.–Filos. Klasse 1), Oslo: Dybwad 1939.

Milik, J. T. 1976: *The Books of Enoch: Aramaic Fragments from Qumrân Cave 4,* Oxford: Clarendon 1976.

Nickelsburg, George W. E. 1972: *Resurrection, Immortality, and Eternal Life in Intertestamental Judaism* (HThS 26), Cambridge and London: Harvard University 1972.

— 1977: "Apocalyptic and Myth in *1 Enoch* 6–11," in: *JBL* 96 (1977) 383–405.

— 1977a "The Apocalyptic Message of *1 Enoch* 92–105," in: *CBQ* 39 (1977) 309–28.

— 1978: "Reflections upon Reflections: A Response to John Collins' 'Methodological Issues in the Study of *1 Enoch*'," in: *SBL 1978 Seminar Papers* (2 vols.; ed. Paul J. Achtemeier), Missoula, MT: Scholars 1978, Vol. 1, 311–14.

— 1981: *Jewish Literature Between the Bible and the Mishnah*, Philadelphia, PA: Fortress 1981.

— 1984: "Stories of Biblical and Early Post–Biblical Times," in: Michael E. Stone (ed.), *Jewish Writings of the Second Temple Period* (CRI 2:2), Assen/Philadelphia, PA: Van Gorcum/Fortress 1984, 33–87.

— 1986: "*1 Enoch* and Qumran Origins: The State of the Question and Some Prospects for Answers," in: *SBL.SP* 25 (1986) 341–60.

— 1987: "Salvation without and with a Messiah: Developing Beliefs in Writings Ascribed to Enoch," in: Jacob Neusner, William S. Green, and Ernest Frerichs (eds.), *Judaisms and their Messiahs*, Cambridge: Cambridge University Press 1987, 49–68.

— 1989: review of Barker 1987, in: *JBL* 109 (1990) 335–37.

— 1991: "The Apocalyptic Construction of Reality of *1 Enoch*," in: John J. Collins and James H. Charlesworth (eds.), *Mysteries and Revelations: Apocalyptic Studies since the Uppsala Colloquium* (JSPE.S 9), Sheffield: Sheffield Academic Press 1991, 51–64.

Rad, Gerhard von 1972: *Genesis: A Commentary*, Philadelphia, PA: Westminster 1972.

Stone, Michael E. 1978: "The Book of Enoch and Judaism in the Third Century B.C.E.," in: *CBQ* 40 (1978) 479–92.

Tiller, Patrick A. 1993: *A Commentary on the Animal Apocalypse of I Enoch* (SBL Early Judaism and its Literature 4) Atlanta, GA: Scholars 1993.

VanderKam, James C. 1984: *Enoch and the Growth of an Apocalyptic Tradition* (CBQ.MS 16), Washington, DC: Catholic Biblical Association 1984.

Westermann, Klaus 1974: *Genesis* (BK 1.1) Neukirchen-Vluyn: Neukirchener Verlag 1974.

# 1 Enoch in the Apocryphon of John

Birger A. Pearson

## 1. Introduction

A sophisticated term now in vogue in biblical studies is "intertextuality." As might be expected, the term has been borrowed from the critical theorists at work on French, English, and other literatures, among whom intertextuality is touted as "one of the most celebrated concepts of poststructuralism."[1] As also might be expected, this neologism has given rise to other neologisms, such as "internontextuality."[2] Of course, biblical scholars such as our esteemed jubilarian, Lars Hartman, have been carrying out "intertextual" studies for a long time without ever using the currently fashionable term.[3] But they have done so as part of their historical-critical approach to sacred scripture and related writings, not as a substitute for it, as seems now to be the case among scholars celebrating "intertextuality."[4] If doing such work is construed as an aspect of "poststructuralism," I hasten to add that I have gladly entered the world of poststructuralism without ever leaving that of "prestructuralism." (I can report with some satisfaction that some of my English Department colleagues at UCSB assure me that we are now entering the "post-deconstruction" phase, and I'm glad to ride along, again without ever leaving the "pre-deconstruction" phase!). So now, if I should apply the concept of "intertextuality" to the use of *1 Enoch* by the author(s) of the Gnostic *Apocryphon of John*, I affirm most vigorously that I have no intention at all of abandoning the *historical*-critical enterprise.

As to the two writings on which I shall focus in this essay, they are each in its own way exceedingly important texts. *Ap. John* is extant in four fourth-century Coptic manuscripts (NHC II,*1*; III,*1*; IV,*1*; BG,*2*), and a part of what went into its

---

[1] Udo J. Hebel 1989, 1. The term was presumably coined (in French: intertextualité) by the semiotician Julia Kristeva (ibid.). Cf. also Jeanine Parisier Plottel 1978, xiv-xvii.

[2] See Part 4 of Plottel 1978 "Mirrors of Language: Internontextuality" (chaps. 13-15).

[3] See esp. Lars Hartman 1966, and idem 1979.

[4] For the newer approach, which is especially interested in exploring relations between text and modern readers, see e.g. Danna Nolan Fewell (ed.) 1992; and the essays in Sipke Draisma (ed.) 1989.

eventual composition was excerpted by bishop Irenaeus of Lyons in the second century as part of his report on the tenets of "the Gnostics" (*Adversus haereses* 1.29). *Ap. John* contains the clearest and most extensive exposition of the basic Gnostic myth utilized by numerous Gnostic writers and communities of the second century and later, including the illustrious arch-heretic Valentinus.[5]

*1 Enoch* is part of the canonical Old Testament of the Ethiopian Orthodox Church and was evidently regarded as canonical also by the NT writer of the Epistle of Jude, who quotes from it (Jude 14-15). The role played by *1 Enoch* in the development of Jewish and Christian apocalyptic traditions can hardly be overestimated.[6] What has not often been noticed, however, is the "intertextual" relationship between *Ap. John* and *1 Enoch*.[7] I called attention to this in a previous essay of mine,[8] and now wish to elaborate further on this in what follows.

## 2. 1 Enoch

The most obvious point of intersection between *1 Enoch* and *Ap. John* is the myth of the descent of the angels in *1 Enoch* 6-11 and their intercourse with the "daughters of men."[9] I shall therefore concentrate on this myth in the following remarks. The myth in *1 Enoch*, itself an expansion of Gen 6:1-4,[10] is part of what is now known as "the Book of Watchers," one of the oldest parts of the composite document we know as *1 Enoch* (chaps. 1-36).[11] The myth follows immediately upon the lengthy introduction in chaps. 1-5, thoroughly studied by Lars Hartman, which sets the keynote to the Book of Watchers as a whole.[12] The myth provides a basis for the Enoch authors' interpretation of certain evils current in their day, and their expec-

---

[5] Irenaeus informs us that the teachings of the "Gnostics," which he summarizes in *Haer.* 1.29, constituted the basis for the development of the Valentinian teachings (*Haer.* 1.11.1). Valentinus can be seen as having "Christianized" the previously existing Gnostic myth now found in *Ap. John*. See e.g. Gilles Quispel 1980.

[6] Lars Hartman makes this point in 1979, 8-9.

[7] Gerard Luttikhuizen's essay on intertextuality in *Ap. John* makes no mention of it. He concentrates rather on possible reader responses, or non-responses, to the use made of the canonical Old Testament in *Ap. John*. See Luttikhuizen 1989.

[8] Birger A. Pearson 1984, esp. 453-55. See now also Pheme Perkins 1993, 24.

[9] Cf. Madeleine Scopello 1980. For a detailed study of the myth in *1 Enoch* see George W. E. Nickelsburg 1977.

[10] J. T. Milik suggests that Gen 6:1-4 is based on the *1 Enoch* passage, but this view has not found much acceptance. See Milik 1976, 31.

[11] See G. W. E. Nickelsburg 1992. Nickelsburg dates the Book of Watchers to the second half of the third century B.C.E. (ibid., 509).

[12] Hartman 1979, esp. 138-45.

tation of a resolution of evil in the eschatological judgment.[13] The myth as now constituted seems to be a conflation of two separate traditions,[14] but the version known to the author of the related passage in *Ap. John* is presumably the one we now have, i.e. as reflected in the various extant versions.

I quote here the relevant passages in *1 Enoch* 6-11 + 15, using a translation prepared by George Nickelsburg for a forthcoming commentary on *1 Enoch*.[15]

### A. THE ANGELS' PLAN (6:1-6)

6:1. And when the sons of men had multiplied, in those days beautiful and comely daughters were born to them. 2. And the watchers,[16] the sons of heaven, saw them and desired them. And they said to one another, "Come, let us choose for ourselves wives from the daughters of men, and let us beget for ourselves children." 3. And Šemiḥazah, their chief, said to them, "I fear that you will not want to do this deed, and I alone shall be guilty of a great sin." 4. And they all answered him and said, "Let us all swear an oath, and let us all bind one another with a curse, that none of us turn back from this counsel until we fulfil it and do this deed." 5. Then they all swore together and bound one another with a curse. 6. And they were, all of them, two hundred who descended in the days of Jared onto the peak of Mount Hermon.

The text continues with details such as the names of the angels' chiefs (6:6b-8).

### B. THE ANGELS' FORNICATION (7:1)

7:1. These and all the others with them took for themselves wives such as they chose. And they began to go into them, and to defile themselves through them, and to teach them sorcery and charms, and to reveal to them the cutting of roots and plants.

---

[13] Nickelsburg 1992, 509.

[14] So Nickelsburg 1992, 509, and idem 1977. The two cycles feature different angelic chiefs, Šemiḥazah and ʿAsaʾel.

[15] I am very grateful to my old friend George Nickelsburg for allowing me to use his unpublished translation (to appear in the HERMENEIA commentary series), and for his helpful comments on an earlier version of this article. Nickelsburg's translation is eclectic, based not only on the Ethiopic version but also on the Aramaic and Greek fragments. For an accessible translation of the Ethiopic version see that of Ephraim Isaac in James H. Charlesworth (ed.) 1983, vol. 1, 13-89, esp. 15-19. The Qumran fragments of the Aramaic version include *1 Enoch* 6:4-8:1; 10:3-4; and 10:21-11:1 (copy 1) + 6:1-4; 6:7-9:4; 10:8-12 (copy 2); 6:7 (copy 3). See Milik 1976, 150-89. For the Greek fragments of *1 Enoch* see Matthew Black (ed.) 1970.

[16] ἐγρήγοροι in the Greek text preserved by Syncellus (=Aramaic ʿyry) restored in a lacuna by Milik 1976 (p. 165; for extant occurrences of the word ʿyr in the Qumran fragments see Milik's index, p. 387). The Gizeh fragment of the Greek has "angels," followed by the Ethiopic. I assume that the Coptic translator of *Ap. John* used a Greek version of *1 Enoch*, and here he read ἄγγελοι. See discussion below.

## C. The results (7:2-6)

7:2. And they conceived from them and bore to them great giants. And the giants begat Nephilim, and to the Nephilim were born †Elioud† .[17] And they were growing in accordance with their greatness. 3. They were devouring the labor of all the sons of men, and men were not able to supply them, 4. And the giants conspired to kill men and to devour them. 5. And they began to sin against the birds and beasts and creeping things and fish, and to devour one another's flesh. And they drank the blood. 6. Then the earth brought accusation against the lawless ones.

## D. The angels' instruction (8:1-4)

8:1. ʿAsaʾel taught men to make swords of iron and weapons and shields and breastplates and every instrument of war. He showed them metals of the earth and how they should work gold to fashion it apt, and concerning silver, to fashion it for bracelets and ornaments for women. And he showed them concerning antinomy and eyepaint and all manner of precious stones and dyes. And the sons of men made them for themselves and for their daughters, and they transgressed and led astray the holy ones. 2. And there was much godlessness upon the earth, and they made their ways desolate.

The text continues with aspects of magic and astrology attributed to specific angels (8:3), and a report of the cries of the people to heaven (8:4). The Enochic myth also includes an account of the archangels' supplication to God (9:1-11), followed by God's response. God sends Sariel to Noah to warn him of the Flood (10:1-3), and then attends to the punishment of the rebellious angels:

## E. Punishment of the wicked angels (10:4-15)

10:4. And to Raphael he said, "Go, Raphael, and bind ʿAsaʾel hand and foot (and) cast him into the darkness. And make an opening in the wilderness that is in Dudaʾel. 5. And there cast him, and lay beneath him sharp stones and jagged stones. And cover him with darkness, and let him dwell there forever. And cover up his face, and let him not see the light. 6. And on the day of the great judgment, he will be led away to the burning conflagration."

The text continues with further details concerning the punishment of Šemiḥazah, the rest of the Watchers, and their progeny (10:7-15). This is followed by a promise of eschatological blessing (10:16-11:2).

The myth remains incomplete, however, particularly as to its main purpose, which is to explain the origins of present evil. It is picked up again in the next section of the Book of Watchers, i.e. Enoch's dream vision and his commissioning as

---

[17] Nickelsburg follows here the Greek text of Syncellus which, however, is corrupt. The Ethiopic version has "... giants whose heights were three hundred cubits." The Aramaic fragment (4QEnᵃ 1 iii) has a lacuna here; for Milik's attempt at restoring the text see 1976, 150f.

a prophet of judgment (*1 Enoch* 12-16). Enoch is forbidden by God to intercede for the Watchers, for whom no repentance is possible, but rather to pronounce judgment on them. In that context the myth of the fallen angels continues:

F. EVIL SPIRITS AS PROGENY OF THE WATCHERS (15:8-12)

15.8. And now the giants who were begotten by the spirits and flesh —they will call them evil spirits upon the earth, for their dwelling will be upon the earth. 9. The spirits that have gone forth from the body of their flesh are evil spirits, for from men they came into being, and from the holy watchers was the origin of their creation. Evil spirits they will be on the earth and evil spirits they will be called. 10. The spirits of heaven, in heaven is their dwelling; and the spirits begotten in the earth, on earth is their dwelling. 11. And the spirits of the giants <lead astray>, do violence, make desolate, and attack and wrestle and hurl upon the earth and <cause illnesses>. And they eat nothing, but abstain from food and are thirsty and smite. 12. And these spirits (will) rise up against the sons of men and against the women, for they have come forth from them.

The conclusion to this section states that the corrupting work of these evil spirits will persist "until the day of the consummation of the great judgment, when the great age will be consummated" (16:1).

## 3. The Apocryphon of John

The main passage in *Ap. John* that utilizes the myth of the fallen angels in *1 Enoch* is part of a running commentary on the opening chapters of the Book of Genesis, presented in the text as we now have it as part of a dialogue between the Gnostic revealer (Jesus Christ) and his disciple John, son of Zebedee.[18] The immediate context is an answer to the last of ten questions put by the interlocutor John. In response to John's question as to the origins of the "counterfeit spirit," the revealer states first that the chief archon, realizing that the perfect race (of gnostic humans) was superior to him, produced from a liaison with Sophia bitter fate (εἱμαρμένη), which holds humans in thrall (II 27,31-28,32). Repenting from his former creative work, the chief archon plans to bring a flood upon his creation, but Noah and the "immovable race" are saved in a luminous cloud (II 28,32-29,15). The myth of the descent of the angels then follows. I quote from Frederik Wisse's translation of the longer recension in Codex II published in *The Nag Hammadi Library in English*.[19]

---

[18] For my analysis of the structure of *Ap. John* see Pearson 1986, 15-35, esp. 19-25, and idem 1993, esp. 158f.

[19] James M. Robinson and Richard Smith (eds.) 1988. For the Coptic text see Martin Krause 1962; Søren Giversen 1963. For the Coptic text of the BG version see Walter C. Till and Hans-Martin Schenke 1972.

## A. The angels' plan (29,16-25)

And he (the chief archon) made a plan with his powers. He sent his angels to the daughters of men, that they might take some of them for themselves and raise off-spring for their enjoyment. When they had no success, they gathered together again and they made a plan together. They created a counterfeit spirit, who resembles the Spirit who descended, so as to pollute the souls through it.

## B. The angels' fornication (29,26-30)

And the angels changed themselves in their likeness into the likeness of their (the daughters of men) mates, filling them with the spirit of darkness, which they had mixed for them, and with evil.

## C. The angels' instruction (29,30-30,2)

They brought gold and silver and a gift and copper and iron and metal and all kinds of things. And they steered the people who had followed them into great troubles, by leading them astray with many deceptions.[20]

## D. The results (30,2-11)

They (the people) became old without having enjoyment. They died, not having found truth and without knowing the God of truth. And thus the whole creation became enslaved forever, from the foundation of the world until now.[21] And they took women and begot children out of the darkness according to the likeness of their spirit.[22] And they closed their hearts, and they hardened themselves through the hardness of the counterfeit spirit until now.

## 4. Intertextuality

I assume from the foregoing that *Ap. John* is dependent upon a Greek version of *1 Enoch*, despite the numerous differences observable in their respective tellings of the myth of the angels and their liaisons with the daughters of men.[23] Indeed, the context in *Ap. John* is already another case of "intertextuality," a corrective commentary on the opening chapters of Genesis wherein the surface text of Genesis is

---

[20] The versions in Codex III and BG add: "that they might not remember their providence (πρό-νοια) which does not move" (my translation).

[21] This passage, 30,2-7, is found only in Codex II and Codex IV.

[22] Codex III and BG have: "through their counterfeit spirit."

[23] For an important discussion of the myth of the fallen angels in Jewish and Gnostic literature see Gedaliahu A. G. Stroumsa 1984, esp. 15-70. But Stroumsa never goes so far as to argue the case for direct dependence on *1 Enoch*, saying only that the author of *Ap. John* "knew and used the Jewish traditions embodied in various pseudepigraphic works and integrated them into his own version of the myth, albeit not wisely" (p. 38).

explicitly refuted with the repeated refrain, "not as Moses said (or wrote)" (II 13,20; 22,22; 23,3; 29,6).[24] *Ap. John*'s correction of *1 Enoch* is not so blatant, but it is there nevertheless. What is important to note at the outset, however, is that *1 Enoch*, or at least the Book of Watchers, was regarded as important and authoritative enough to supply the author-redactor of *Ap. John* with salient themes in his retelling of the biblical stories. As already noted, the Book of Watchers was a very influential text in Jewish circles, not least because of its aetiology of the origins of evil in the world.

Let us now consider in some detail the respective renditions of the myth of the angels laid out above.

### A. THE ANGELS' PLAN

In *Ap. John* the angels' plan follows upon the Flood, rather than preceding it as in Genesis and *1 Enoch*. The Gnostic author utilizes this myth to show how the chief archon was thwarted in his attempt to destroy the people with the Flood and then had to take additional measures to keep the human race in thrall. *1 Enoch* follows the biblical order of events, and then brings in the account of the evil spirits of the dead giants surviving the Flood and active until the consummation (chaps. 15-16). For *Ap. John* the counterpart to the evil spirits of *1 Enoch* is the "counterfeit spirit" with which the angels corrupt non-Gnostic humankind, working as henchmen of the chief archon. Thus, in *Ap. John*'s telling of the myth the "giants" of *1 Enoch* and Gen 6:4 play no role, at least not here.[25]

The "chief archon" in *Ap. John* is, in one respect, the counterpart to Šemihazah in *1 Enoch*, i.e. in his capacity as leader of the angels. But in another respect he is also the counterpart to God, the biblical creator, referred to elsewhere in the text of *Ap. John* under the names Ialdabaoth, Saklas, and Samael (II 11,15-22).[26] *Ap. John*'s version of the myth in *1 Enoch* is essentially a retelling, showing verbal correspondences in the passage here under consideration only in the words "angels" and "the daughters of men." The latter phrase is ultimately derived from Gen 6:4, but the former is *1 Enoch*'s interpretation of the "sons of God" in Gen 6:2. This is an indication that the author of our passage in *Ap. John* was dependent on *1 Enoch*, i.e. a Greek version thereof.[27]

---

[24] On these passages see Søren Giversen 1963a.

[25] But the chief archon himself can possibly be construed as one of the *nplym* (Gen 6:4), i.e. as an "abortion" (*npl*) of his mother Sophia (II 9,25-10,7). See Stroumsa's discussion of "giants and abortions" in 1984, 65-70.

[26] On these names see my discussion in Pearson 1990, esp. 47-49.

[27] Cf. note 16, above. The exegetical tradition that identifies the *bny hʾelhym* in Genesis as angels is found elsewhere in Jewish literature, but *1 Enoch* would appear to be its earliest attestation. Cf. Stroumsa 1984, 19, and literature cited.

In *Ap. John*'s version one cannot speak of a "fall" of the angels.[28] They are agents of the creator, the "chief archon," who "sends" them, just as God in *1 Enoch* "sends" his archangels to carry out his judgments. One interesting detail in *Ap. John* is that the angels are initially unsuccessful in their attempt to seduce the daughters of men. In order to attain their goal, they create a "counterfeit spirit" (ἀντίμιμον πνεῦμα)[29] as a fake substitute for "the Spirit who descended," i.e. "the Spirit of life" sent by "the Mother" (Sophia) for the salvation of the elect (II 25,2-7). This spirit, which is the functional equivalent of the evil spirits of the giants in *1 Enoch*, has as its main purpose to inspire the desire for sexual intercourse and procreation among human beings, just as it had already inspired Eve to have a sexual liaison with the chief archon (II 24,15-31).[30]

## B. THE ANGELS' FORNICATION

This part of the myth in *Ap. John* modifies the telling of it in *1 Enoch* by picking up another Jewish version of the myth that had already corrected *1 Enoch*'s version. That corrected version is documented in the *Testament of Reuben*, chap. 5. There we read that "women are evil" (5:1) and "easily overcome by the spirit of promiscuity" (5:3). The women of old

> charmed the Watchers, who were before the Flood. As they continued looking at the women, they were filled with desire for them and perpetrated the act in their minds. Then they were transformed into human males, and while the women were cohabiting with their husbands they appeared to them. Since the women's minds were filled with lust for these apparitions, they gave birth to giants. (5:6)[31]

In this version the women are really sleeping with their husbands, but cohabiting with the Watchers in their minds.[32] *Ap. John* modifies this by having the archons themselves doing the deed, as in *1 Enoch*, but accomplishing it by transforming themselves into the shape of the women's husbands. The women are thus less culpable, in traditional Jewish moral terms, in that they do not intend to commit adultery; but in *Ap. John*'s terms they are culpable by the act of intercourse itself. Sexual intercourse and procreation are inherently evil, inspired by the archontic "counterfeit spirit."

An interesting detail found only in Codex II and Codex IV refers to the "counterfeit spirit" as "the spirit of darkness *which they had mixed for them*." The verb for

---

[28] Scopello 1980, 221.

[29] On the ἀντίμιμον πνεῦμα see Alexander Böhlig 1968.

[30] On this myth and its Jewish sources see Pearson 1990a, esp. 99-102; Stroumsa 1984, 38-53.

[31] Howard C. Kee's translation in Charlesworth 1983, 1:784.

[32] Cf. Stroumsa's discussion in 1984, 35-37.

"mix" here is a Copticized form of the Greek κεράννυμι, which would be appropriate to use with an object such as φάρμακον ("drug"), implied in the term φαρμακεία ("use of drugs") in the Greek text of *1 Enoch* 7:1. Of course, the verb is used metaphorically in *Ap. John*.

### C. The angels' instruction

In *1 Enoch* the angels' instruction begins with 7:1 (the passage just now referred to) but is interrupted with an account of the women's pregnancies and the birth of the giants (7:2-6). The instruction then picks up again in 8:1, now said to be the act of another angelic leader, ʿAsaʾel. The ʿAsaʾel passages, including all of the references to angelic instruction, may be a later interpolation into an earlier myth wherein Šemiḥazah plays the chief role.[33] However that may be, the author of *Ap. John* probably knew a version such as we now have in our extant sources, but chose, however, to ignore the story of the birth of the giants and its aftermath. Thus, the angelic instruction follows immediately upon the angels' sexual affair with the daughters of men. This affair itself, in *Ap. John*'s telling, already involved an instruction of sorts, i.e. the inspiration of the women with the "imitation spirit" that put them into a receptive mode.

The overt acts of angelic instruction feature, as in *1 Enoch* 8:1, the introduction of the use of metals such as gold, silver, copper, and iron. Exactly why this detail is found in *Ap. John*, i.e. what purpose it serves in the total narrative, is not altogether clear. But its presence in the text certainly betrays its dependence on *1 Enoch*.[34] More to the point is the spiritual deception of the people promulgated by the angels in the following passage in *Ap. John*, based on *1 Enoch* 8:2. The reference to the depraved people's "hardness of heart" brought about by the imitation spirit probably picks up a detail in *1 Enoch* 16:3, referring to the hardness of the Watchers' hearts and the resultant multiplication of evil on earth.

### D. The results

The results of the fall of the angels in *1 Enoch* is the birth of the giants and its aftermath (7:2-6), including the continuing influence of the evil spirits produced by them

---

[33] So Nickelsburg 1977; cf. n. 14.

[34] Instruction in the arts of civilization ought to be construed positively rather than negatively as in both *1 Enoch* and *Ap. John*. Indeed, the book of *Jubilees* has an interesting passage according to which "the angels of the LORD, who were called Watchers, came down (in the days of Jared) to earth in order to teach the sons of man, and perform judgment and uprightness upon the earth" (*Jub.* 4:15). The same text then goes on to recount the story of the fall of the angels, probably based on the one in the Book of Watchers in *1 Enoch* (*Jub.* 5:1-2). The ʿAsaʾel material in *1 Enoch* is influenced by the Greek myth of Prometheus, according to Nickelsburg (1977, 399-401).

(15:8-12). *Ap. John* presents these results in terms of humanity's natural ignorance of God and the "enslavement" of the entire creation "until now."

### E. PUNISHMENT OF THE WICKED ANGELS

The Enoch version of the myth provides a full account of the judgment of God against the angels and their punishment: Denied repentance, they are thrown into the darkness to be reserved for the everlasting fire that will come with the last judgment (10:4-15). That this part of the myth should be missing from *Ap. John* would come as no surprise, since in *Ap. John* "God" is none other than the wicked "chief archon" himself, the angels' leader, who can hardly be expected to punish the agents of his own bidding! Yet—much to our surprise—the Enoch narrative of the angels' punishment is indeed reflected in *Ap. John*, a final proof of the influence of *1 Enoch* on our Gnostic author. In the text of *Ap. John* as we now have it, as part of a series of instructions pertaining to the destinies of various classes of people, we read the following interchange between the revealer and his interlocutor (27,21-30):

> And I (John) said, "Lord, these also who did not know but have turned away, where will their souls go?" Then he said to me, "To that place where the angels of poverty go they will be taken, the place where there is no repentance. And they will be kept for the day on which those who have blasphemed the spirit will be tortured, and they will be punished with eternal punishment."

There can be no doubt but that this reference to the "angels of poverty" and the human souls held in their sway is inspired by the Enochic myth of the fallen angels. Our Gnostic author thus joins the author of the Book of Watchers and the authors of the other Enochic books reflected in *1 Enoch* in looking forward to a final consummation wherein evil will ultimately be punished and brought to naught. Eschatology is, after all, an integral part of the Gnostic worldview. In the Gnostic case, of course, creation itself, together with its creator, is ultimately brought to naught in accordance with the will of the "God beyond God," the "Invisible Spirit" (cf. *Ap. John* II 2,25-4,6).

## 5. Conclusions

It is a truism that religious texts are written and produced for religious communities. In the case of the Book of Watchers, and eventually *1 Enoch* as a whole, it is evident that we have to do with religious literature meant for an apocalyptic Jewish community. The socio-historical setting of this community in Jewish Palestine is notoriously difficult to pin down, but it is safe to say that it must have had certain resemblances to the Qumran community, both in terms of its interpretation of Torah and its worldview.[35] Its worldview is dominated by dualism: temporal, cosmic, and ontological.[36] Its reinterpretation of Genesis, as seen in its myth of the fallen angels, explains for its community the origins of present evils and invites this community to look forward to an eradication of evil through God's punishment of evil-doers both angelic and human, and a reconstituted cosmos wherein the faithful will dwell in purity and righteousness.

In the case of *Ap. John* we have to do with literature produced for a Gnostic community, or rather a series of them, as reflected in the history of *Ap. John*'s composition.[37] The reinterpretation of the Enochic myth of the angels in the text of *Ap. John* as we now have it is itself done in the process of reinterpreting the Book of Genesis. Here, too, we have to do with a worldview dominated by dualism. The dualism of *Ap. John*, while certainly influenced by that of *1 Enoch* and other Jewish apocalyptic texts, is radical in the extreme, such that we can use *Ap. John* as an illustration of a religio-historical process wherein a completely new "religion" is generated, one that has broken completely out of the boundaries of what can even broadly be called "Judaism."[38] For the readers/hearers of the reinterpreted myth of the angels the message does have certain analogies with that of *1 Enoch*: evil is real and is the product of powerful spiritual forces at work in the world resulting from a primordial fall. The wicked will indeed be punished, and the elect will be saved. What is fundamentally different in *Ap. John*, however, is the view that the biblical creator of the world is himself the problem, and the ultimate solution will come not with a reconstructed cosmos but with an end to the process of human reproduction inspired by the angels, and an end to the cosmos itself.

We began with some remarks about intertextuality and the intertextual relationships between *1 Enoch* and *Ap. John*. We concentrated on a single case, the myth of the angels, but other examples of intertextuality between *1 Enoch* and *Ap. John* could probably be found. Indeed, the Enochic literature as a whole was of considerable importance in the generation and development of Gnostic traditions.[39] But any further discussion of these relationships shall have to be postponed to another occasion.

---

[35] Nickelsburg 1992, 515.

[36] For an extensive discussion of these dualisms see G. W. E. Nickelsburg 1991.

[37] Cf. n. 18, above.

[38] See the Introduction to my book Pearson 1990, and my essay, "Is Gnosticism a Religion?" in: Ugo Bianchi (ed.), *Proceedings of the XVI Congress of the International Association for the History of Religions* (Roma: L'ERMA di Bretschneider, forthcoming).

[39] See Pearson 1984, 451-56.

*Texts and Contexts*

I conclude these remarks with an expression of best wishes to my friend and colleague Lars Hartman on the occasion of his 65th birthday. Må han leva uti hundrade år!

## Bibliography

Black, Matthew 1970: *Apocalypsis Henochi Graece*, Leiden: Brill 1970.

Böhlig, Alexander 1968: "Zum Antimimon Pneuma in den koptisch-gnostischen Texten", in: idem, *Mysterion und Wahrheit. Gesammelte Beiträge zur spätantiken Religionsgeschichte*, Leiden: Brill 1968, 162-74.

Charlesworth, James H. (ed.) 1983: *The Old Testament Pseudepigrapha* 1, Garden City, NY: Doubleday 1983.

Draisma, Sipke (ed.) 1989: *Intertextuality in Biblical Writings: Essays in honour of Bas van Iersel*, Kampen: Kok 1989.

Fewell, Danna Nolan (ed.) 1992: *Reading Between Texts: Intertextuality and the Hebrew Bible* (Literary Currents in Biblical Interpretation), Louisville, KY: Westminster/John Knox 1978.

Giversen, Søren 1963: *Apocryphon Johannis*, København: Munksgaard 1963.

— 1963a: "The Apocryphon of John and Genesis", in: *StTh* 17 (1963) 60-76.

Hartman, Lars 1966: *Prophecy Interpreted. The Formation of Some Jewish Apocalyptic Texts and of the Eschatological Discourse Mark 13 Par* (CB.NT 1), Lund: Gleerup 1966.

— 1979: *Asking for A Meaning: A Study of 1 Enoch 1-5* (CB.NT 12) Lund: Gleerup 1979.

Hebel, Udo J. 1989: *Intertextuality, Allusion, and Quotation: An International Bibliography of Critical Studies*, New York: Greenwood 1989.

Krause, Martin 1962: *Die drei Versionen des Apokryphon des Johannes im koptischen Museum zu Alt-Kairo*, Wiesbaden: Harrassowitz 1962.

Luttikhuizen, Gerard 1989: "Intertextual References in Readers' Responses to the Apocryphon of John", in: Draisma (ed.) 1989, 117-26.

Milik, J. T. 1976: *The Books of Enoch: Aramaic Fragments of Cave 4*, Oxford: Clarendon 1976.

Nickelsburg, George 1977: "Apocalyptic and Myth in 1 Enoch 6-11", in: *JBL* 96 (1977) 383-405.

— 1991: "The Apocalyptic Construction of Reality in *1 Enoch*", in: John J. Collins and James H. Charlesworth (eds.), *Mysteries and Revelations: Apocalyptic Studies since the Uppsala Colloquium* (JSPE.S 9), Sheffield: JSOT Press 1991, 51-64.

—1992: "Enoch, First Book of", in: *The Anchor Bible Dictionary* 2, New York: Doubleday 1992, 508-16.

Pearson, Birger 1984: "Jewish Sources in Gnostic Literature", in: Michael Stone (ed.), *Jewish Writings of the Second Temple Period* (CRJ II/2), Assen: Van Gorcum and Philadelphia, PA: Fortress 1984, 443-81.

— 1986: "The Problem of 'Jewish Gnostic' Literature", in: Charles W. Hedrick and Robert Hodgson (eds.), *Nag Hammadi, Gnosticism, and Early Christianity*, Peabody, MA: Hendrickson 1986, 15-35.

— 1990: "Jewish Haggadic Traditions in *The Testimony of Truth* from Nag Hammadi (CG IX,*3*)", in: idem, *Gnosticism, Judaism, and Egyptian Christianity*, Minneapolis, MN: Fortress 1990, 39-51 (chap. 3).

— 1990a: "Cain and the Cainites", in: idem, *Gnosticism, Judaism, and Early Christianity*, Minneapolis, MN: Fortress 1990, 95-107 (chap. 6).

— 1993: "Apocryphon Johannis Revisited", in: Per Bilde, Helge K. Nielsen and Jørgen P. Sørensen (eds.), *Apocryphon Severini presented to Søren Giversen*, Aarhus: Aarhus University Press 1993, 155-65.

— (forthcoming): "Is Gnosticism a Religion?", in: Ugo Bianchi (ed.), *Proceedings of the XVI Congress of the International Association for the History of Religions*, Rome: L'ERMA di Bretschneider.

Perkins, Pheme 1993: *Gnosticism and the New Testament*, Minneapolis, MN: Fortress 1993.

Plottel, Jeanine Parisier 1978: Introduction to J. P. Plottel and Hanna Charney (eds.), *Intertextuality. New Perspectives in Criticism*, New York: Literary Forum 1978, xiv-xvii.

Quispel, Gilles 1980: "Valentinian Gnosis and the Apocryphon of John", in: Bentley Layton (ed.), *The Rediscovery of Gnosticism. Proceedings of the International Conference on Gnosticism at Yale, New Haven, Connecticut March 28-31*, vol. 1: *The School of Valentinus* (SHR 41), Leiden: Brill 1980, 118-32.

Robinson, James M. and Richard Smith (eds.) 1988: *The Nag Hammadi Library in English*. 3rd ed. rev., San Francisco, CA: Harper & Row 1988.

Scopello, Madeleine 1980: "Le Mythe de la 'chute' des anges dans l'Apocryphon de Jean (II,1) de Nag Hammadi", in: *RSR* 54 (1980) 220-30.

Stroumsa, Gedaliahu A. G. 1984: *Another Seed. Studies in Gnostic Mythology* (NHS 34), Leiden: Brill 1984.

Till, Walter C. and Hans-Martin Schenke 1972: *Die gnostischen Schriften des koptischen Papyrus Berolinensis 8502*. 2nd ed., Berlin: Akademie-Verlag 1972.

# Man's Sovereignty over Animals and Nature According to Philo of Alexandria[1]

Peder Borgen

## 1. The Problem of Method

The problem of method is important for a study of Philo's understanding of man's sovereignty over animals and over the created world in general. It would seem to be natural to collect relevant ideas from Philo's various writings and then try to systematize them. This would be an approach similar to the one used by H. A. Wolfson.[2] According to Wolfson Philo was the first religious thinker to make philosophy a handmaid to revealed religion. Wolfson's study on Philo is part of a comprehensive project under the general title 'Structure and Growth of Philosophic Systems from Plato to Spinoza', and he finds in Philo's writings the "foundations of religious philosophy in Judaism, Christianity, and Islam" as it is said in the sub-title of his two volumes work.

Wolfson's work is a rich collection of important material on Philo, Judaism, Greek philosophy, etc. In spite of his main interest in philosophy of religion, he also pays attention to the actual situation of Hellenistic Judaism, with special reference to Alexandrian Judaism and Philo. Nevertheless, Wolfson's critics are right, when they maintain that he is much more systematic than Philo ever was. Thus a Philonic system rather than Philo himself has been constructed.[3]

Even so, is it possible to avoid the opposite extreme, that of understanding Philo

---

[1] During the last five years I have had the privilege of working together with Lars Hartman and a few others on a Nordic project sponsored by NOS-H. The theme was "New Perspectives on Hellenistic Judaism and the New Testament." Lars Hartman's broad knowledge in the field, his keen interest in questions of method and his great analytic ability, made him play a central role in the work of the group. Many of the meetings were held in Uppsala, and Lars, together with his wife Ulla, were generous and efficient hosts. In honouring him I find it natural to present an essay on a topic taken from the field of Hellenistic Judaism, more specifically from Philo of Alexandria's writings.

[2] Wolfson 1948, 1-2.

[3] See Borgen 1984b, 141-42.

as an eclectic with no uniting core at all? Before answering this question, a brief survey of the writings of Philo should be given. Two exegetical commentaries are extant: a) *Questions and Answers on Genesis and Exodus*, which is a brief commentary in the form of questions and answers on parts of the two first books of the Pentateuch. Most of the Greek original is lost, but the work is preserved in Armenian translation. b) *Allegorical Interpretations of Genesis*, which consists of *Leg. all.* 1-3; *Cher.*; *Sacr.*; *Quod Det.*; *Post.*; *Gig.*; *Quod Deus.*; *Agr.*; *Plant.*; *Ebr.*; *Sobr.*; *Conf.*; *Migr.*; *Heres.*; *Congr.*; *Fuga*; *Mut.*; *Somn. Deo*. This series covers the main parts of Gen 2-41. In both commentaries a verse, verses or parts of a verse are quoted and are followed by an exposition.

Another of Philo's works is most important for the present study, *The Exposition of the Laws of Moses*, of which the extant treatises are: *Op.*; *Abr.*; *Jos.*; *Dec.*; *Spec. leg.*; *Virt.*; *Praem.* The two books *On the Life of Moses* and this Exposition of the Laws of Moses are companion pieces.[4] In these exegetical works, Philo paraphrases and expands or abbreviates the biblical text. Philo's other writings are of varied nature, and are of less importance for the present study.

Most of the material which will be discussed in this essay is found in *The Exposition of the Laws of Moses*. Philo states himself his over all understanding of this work. His outline occurs both in *Mos.* 2:45ff. and in *Praem.* 1ff.[5] In *Mos.* 2:45-46 Philo's summary runs as follows:

> They [the sacred books] consist of two parts, one the historical, the other concerned with commands and prohibitions. One division of the historical side deals with the creation of the world, the other with genealogies.

The summary in *Praem* 1-3 should be quoted more fully:

> The oracles delivered through the prophet Moses are of three kinds. The first deals with the creation of the world, the second with history and the third with legislation. The story of the creation is told throughout with an excellence worthy of the divine subject, beginning with the genesis of Heaven and ending with the framing of man ... The historical part is a record of good and bad lives and of the sentences passed in each generation on both, rewards in one case, punishments in the other. The legislative part has two divisions, one in which the subject matter is more general, the other consisting of the ordinances of specific laws... All these and further the virtues which he assigned to peace and war, have been discussed as fully as was needful in the preceding treatises, and I now proceed in due course to the rewards and punishments which the good and bad have respectively to expect.

In *Praem.* 1-3 Philo divides *The Exposition of the Laws of Moses* into three main

---

[4] See Goodenough 1933, 109-25.

[5] See Borgen 1987, 20; idem 1984a, 233-34.

points, the story of the creation, the historical part and the legislative part. In *Mos.* 2:45ff. two parts are mentioned, the historical and the legislative. The historical part mentioned in *On the Life of Moses* is, however, divided into the creation story and the genealogical part, in accordance with the first two points of the outline given in *Praem.* 1-3. Thus, *The Exposition* can be divided in three parts: the story of creation, the historical part, and the legislative part.

In both summaries Philo characterizes and interprets the Laws of Moses, the Pentateuch. Especially illuminating is the *quaestio* and *solutio* which he gives in *Mos.* 2:47-48: "Why he [Moses] began his lawbook with the history and put the commands and prohibitions in the second place, one must explain" (*Mos.* 2:47). The answer is:

> first that the Father and Maker of the world was in the truest sense also lawgiver; secondly, that he who would observe the laws will accept gladly the duty of following nature and live in accordance with the order of the universe and [his] deeds are in harmony with words and words with deeds (*Mos.* 2:48).

The main point here is the view that God's cosmic laws are seen as identical with the particular laws of Moses given to the Jewish nation, as stated also in *Mos.* 2:52: "Thus whoever will carefully examine the nature of the particular enactments will find that they seek to attain to the harmony of the universe and are in agreement with the principles of eternal nature."

The central passage for our study is found in *Op.* 77-88, that is, in the first treatise of Philo's comprehensive work called The Exposition, and the topic will largely be discussed within the context of this work. The passage has the form of question and answer. This form is widely used by Philo in *The Exposition*, in the *Questions and Answers on Genesis and Exodus*, and in the *Allegorical Laws*.[6]

Gen 1:28 deals in a direct way with human beings' rule over the animals and over nature in general. In the index of the Loeb-edition, volume 10, only two references are given to this Biblical verse, namely *Op.* 84 and 88. One might then think that the topic is peripheral to Philo. This is David Runia's understanding when he writes: "Man has a special place in the cosmos not because of his dominance over the creation, nor because of his cleverness in practical matters, but because he contemplates the worlds of thought and sense and so can reflect on his own nature and situation." In a footnote Runia adds: "Note how Philo plays down this central theme of Gen 1:26-30 in his interpretation in Opif."[7]

---

[6] See Borgen and Skarsten 1976/67, 1-16, also printed in: Borgen 1983, 191-201; Hay 1991.

[7] Runia 1986, 472, and note 372.

## 2. The Interpretation of Gen 1:26/28 in Op. 83-84

In *Op.* 77-88 the problem of an unexpected order and rank in the Pentateuchal story is dealt with in the form of question and answer:[8]

*Op.* 77-88:

*Question*:

(*Op.* 77): One should inquire the reason why man comes last in the world's creation; for, as the sacred writings show, he was the last whom the Father and Maker fashioned.

Four *answers* are given, and a further *comment* is attached. The outline goes as follows:

(1) *Op.* 77-78: God provided first for man's means of living, so that man would find a banquet ready for him when he came.

(2) *Op.* 79-81: Just as man found all provisions needed for life, those who strive for righteousness will experience peace, order and all good things in readiness. Man gave himself to pleasure, however, and so now must work.

(3) *Op.* 82: Man as miniature heaven ties the end of creation to the beginning, heaven.

(4) *Op.* 83-86: Man came after all created things, as king and master.

(5) *Op.* 87-88: Added comment: Man is not inferior because he was created last.

For our analysis it is natural to start with point 4, *Op.* 83-84, because Philo here paraphrases parts of Gen 1:26/28. The first sentence in paragraph 84 ties the paragraphs 83 and 84 together: "for which reason too the Father, having brought him [man] into existence as a living being by nature capable of sovereignty, appointed him, not only in fact but also by verbal election, king of all living beings under the moon..." In *Op.* 83 man's actual sovereignty over the other living beings is demonstrated: "for they were sure, as soon as they saw him, to be amazed and do homage to him as to one who by nature is ruler and despot." Then in paragraph 84a God's explicit and verbal appointment of man as king is referred to, by means of a paraphrase of parts of Gen 1:26/28. In the paragraphs 84b-86 Philo provides proofs of man's rule

---

[8] Also in *Quaes. Gen.* 1:43 the problem of an unexpected order and rank in the Pentateuchal story is dealt with in the form of question and answer.

*Quaes. Gen.* 1:43:

*Question*:

Why, when they hid themselves from the face of God, was not the woman, who first ate of the forbidden fruit, first mentioned but the man; for [Scripture] says, "Adam and his wife hid themselves".

*Answer*:

It was the more imperfect and ignoble element, the female, that made a beginning of transgression and lawlessness, while the male made the beginning of reverence and modesty and all good, since he was better and more perfect.

from experience, that is, from "what is to be seen" (τὰ φαινόμενα).

As already stated, Gen 1:26 and 28 are paraphrased in *Op.* 84a.

Man's nature:

γεννήσας αὐτὸν ὁ πατὴρ ἡγεμονικὸν φύσει ζῷον,

Appointed as king:

οὐκ ἔργῳ μόνον ἀλλὰ καὶ τῇ διὰ λόγου χειροτονίᾳ καθίστη τῶν ὑπὸ σελήνην ἁπάντων βασιλέα

The charge area in detail:

χερσαίων καὶ ἐνύδρων καὶ ἀεροπόρων ὅσα γὰρ θνητὰ ἐν τοῖς τρισὶ στοιχείοις, γῇ, ὕδατι, ἀέρι, πάντα ὑπέταττεν αὐτῷ,

The region not included in the charge:

τὰ κατ' οὐρανὸν ὑπεξελόμενος, ἅτε θειοτέρας μοίρας ἐπιλαχόντα.

Philo's phrasing reflects both Gen 1:26 and 28. It draws specifically on Gen 1:28 in the respect that it refers to the creation of man as an event that has taken place. Gen 1:26 on the other hand reports on God's decision to create man. It draws also specifically on Gen 1:28 in the respect that it refers to the actual charge given man by God, while Gen 1:26 again reports on the background for the giving of this charge. On the other hand, Philo's paraphrase is closer to Gen 1:26 insofar as man's dominion over animals and creation in general is seen against the background of a statement about man's nature. It is to be noticed that the point in Gen 1:28 about man and woman multiplying and filling the earth is not cited by Philo.

Philo draws on a widespread Jewish exegetical tradition when he refers to man's role as ruler as an answer to the question why man was created last. Thus *Gen. Rab.* 19:4 reads, "Yet you were created after everything else, so you should rule over everything that came before."[9] The same point is also made in 4 Ezra 6:53: "On the sixth day you commanded the earth to bring forth before you cattle, beasts and creeping things; and over these you placed Adam as ruler over all the works which you had made."[10]

It is also in agreement with Jewish traditions when Philo specifies the words MT: כבש and רדה and LXX: κατακυριεύω and ἄρχω in Gen 1:28 to mean the rule by a king. A close parallel is found in *Pesiqta Rabbati*, Supplement 21: "And God had in mind to appoint him ruler over His world, and king over all of His creatures, as He said: I am the King of the upper world and man is the king of the lower world."[11]

Philo uses a technical phrase for the appointment of a king: καθίστημι βασιλέα.

---

[9] Neusner 1985, 1, 202.

[10] Metzger 1983, 536.

[11] Cf. Cohn 1962, 1, 58, n. 1.

Both in Philo and in *Pesiqta Rabbati* the same limitation is made for man's rule: He does not rule over heaven, but only over the lower world. Philo (*Op.* 84) states that God "made him king of creatures under the moon" and God "exempted the heavenly beings" from being subject to man. Correspondingly it is said in *Pesikta Rabbati* that God is the king of the upper world, and man is the king of the lower world.

In spite of the fact that Philo in *Op.* 84a draws on Jewish traditions, he formulates these traditions within the context of Greek world view and categories. Thus the list in Gen 1:28 "the fish of the seas and flying creatures of heaven, and all the cattle and all the earth and all the reptiles that creep on the earth" is systematized by him into three of the four elements which in Greek philosophy denoted the four basic components which constituted the physical world. Philo writes: "those living on land (χερσαίων), those living in the sea (ἐνύδρων) and those traversing the air (ἀεροπόρων), for as many mortal beings as are in the three elements, earth, water, air (ἐν τοῖς τρισὶ στοιχείοις, γῆ, ὕδατι, ἀέρι) ..." The Greek ideas of the four elements had influenced Jewish views quite broadly, as can be seen from Wis 7:17 ("... the constitution of the world and the working of the elements ...") and 19:18-21 ("For the elements changed in order with one another ..."); *Num. Rab.* 14:12 end (the four elements, earth, water, air and fire); *Tanhuma Pequde* 3 end (man was made out of the combination of the elements), cf. 4 Macc 12:13 (about man).[12]

Philo applies Greek thought categories already formulated by Aristotle, when he in *Op.* 84a draws the distinction between the sublunar (ὑπὸ σελήνην) air, earth and sea and the supralunar heaven.[13]

In *Op.* 88 Philo has an elaboration of the theme of the mandate given human beings by God according to Gen 1:28. Philo gives examples from experience, with reference to charioteers and pilots without drawing on words from Gen 1:28:

> ... And so the Creator has made man after all things, as a sort of charioteer and driver in order that he may hold the reins and steer the things on earth, having charged him with the care of animals and plants, like a viceroy (ὕπαρχος) of the chief and Great King.

Philo's use elsewhere of the term ὕπαρχος emphasizes the aspects of subordination and obedience, but includes also the idea of participation in the functions of the superiors. The aspect of subordination is in focus in *Legat.* 161 where it is told that Tiberius gave orders to the procurators about what to tell the Jews, and in #207 where it is reported that Gaius gave orders to Petronius, the governor of Syria, to

---

[12] Borgen 1981, 133; Diels 1899, 46, n. 1; Ginzberg 1911, 5, 72.

[13] See Zeller 1911, 198; Nilsson 1950, 674; Pohlenz 1948, 322 (Seneca); 350 (Plutarch and Marc Aurel). See further Cicero, *De natura deorum* II.17.56; *De re publica* VI.17 (end); *Tusculanae disputationes* I.42ff., 60; Seneca, *De ira* III.6.1; *Ad Lucilium epistulae morales* XLIX.16, etc.

guard the passage of the statue of the emperor on its way to Jerusalem. In *Virt.* 55 the emphasis is placed on the aspect of participation. Here it is told that Joshua was distinguished from the multitude and was almost a viceroy to Moses and working together with him in the duties of government. According to *Spec. leg.* 1:19 the heavenly bodies are not gods, but are subordinate under God as his viceroys. Thus, in principle they may be subject to criticism from their superior.

## 3. The Actual Sovereignty

Philo's interpretation of man's rule in Gen 1:26 and 28 in *Op.* 84 as a god-given charge to him as king, is elaborated upon in *Op.* 83 where man's actual royal function is described. Here the phrase ἡγεμὼν φύσει is used, similar to the phrase ἡγεμονικὸν φύσει ζῷον in *O.p* 84a. Instead of βασιλεύς the term δεσπότης, master, lord, despot, is used in #83. Man's royal function is here seen by the way in which the animals acted towards him:

> Man had to come last after all created things, in order that, by appearing suddenly as the last one he might produce consternation (cf. Gen 9:2, ὁ τρόμος, καὶ ὁ φόβος ὑμῶν) in the other living beings. For as soon as they saw him they were sure to be astonished (τέθηκα) and do *proskynesis* (προσκυνέω) to him as to a ruler by nature and a despot.

Thus, the animals, by beholding him, were all tamed, also the most savaged ones. When Philo tells about the homage which the animals made to man, he draws on a Jewish exegetical tradition. In polemic form this tradition is evidenced in *Pirqe Rabbi Eliezer*, ch. 11:

> ... as the creatures saw him [Adam], standing as a representation of God's glory, then they believed that he had created them, and they came to worship him. Then Adam said: You want to prostrate yourselves before me? Not so! I and you, all of us will prostrate ourselves before Him, who has created us ....[14]

In *Op.* 84b-86 Philo refers to examples from experience as a proof of man's rule: a vast number of cattle are led by an ordinary man; a shepherd, a goatherd, and a cowherd lead flocks of sheep and goats and herds of oxen. Bulls are yoked to the plough to plough the land. Rams are laden with wool and give it to the shears. A horse carries the rider on the back and brings him to his wanted destination. Correspondingly, in *Op.* 148 Philo draws the line from present day experience back to the creation: men born many generations after the creation keep safe a torch of sovereignty passed down from the first man. Philo uses here as metaphor the well known picture

---

[14] Cf. Grünbaum 1893, 56, and Cohn 1962, 1, 57, n.3.

of a torch race to illustrate the continuity between Adam and the subsequent generations with regard to their dominion over the animals.

Moreover, when Philo states that the animals were wild but submissive to man already before the Fall, his view is akin with that of some rabbis, although they are
formulated differently. According to *Gen. Rab.* 34:12 the animals' fear and terror of
man, which existed before the Fall, but ceased to exist after the Fall, came back after
the Flood, as seen from Gen 9:2. Correspondingly, in *Quaes. Gen.* 1:56 it is said that
Noah represents creation number two, and he received then the same honour as did
Adam, and was accordingly appointed king of the creatures of the earth.

## 4. Jewish Criteria in a "Greek" Debate

In the passages discussed so far the presence of Jewish traditions has been evident,
although also influenced by Hellenistic ideas of Greek background. A treatise that
is not part of Philo's *Exposition of the Laws of Moses*, the dialogue *De animalibus*
demonstrates how Philo expresses similar views on the basis of Greek terminology
and thought categories. The treatise *De animalibus* is preserved in Armenian translation and an English translation has been provided by Abraham Terian.[15] In the following we mainly draw on his translation and commentary.

Philo's opponent in the dialogue is his nephew Tiberius Iulius Alexander. Terian
thinks that Alexander's views are on the whole genuine. Philo is the single author
of the treatise, however, as can be seen in its composition, which is structured after
the first part of Plato's *Phaedrus*. Alexander and Philo compare human beings and
animals. Alexander argues for their similarity. Like human beings the animals have
reason. Thus there is a moral and juridical relationship between them.

Philo claims that animals do not possess reason. Only rational beings have free
will and can make ethical evaluations and actions. Since the animals are not rational, they do not act ethically, *De animalibus* 77-100. Philo concludes: "to elevate animals to the level of the human race and to grant equality (= ἰσότης ) to unequals (=
ἄνισοι) is the height of injustice (= ἀδικία)," #100.

Although Alexander's views on the rationality of animals were anticipated by
Plato (*Tht.* 189E; *La.* 196E; *Sph.* 263E) they were most probably taken over by Philo from the arguments used by the New Academy, such as Carneades of Cyrene, 2.
century B.C. Such ideas from the New Academy were reiterated by many writers
and are well attested by Sextus Empiricus, *P.* 1:62-77. In his answers to Alexander
Philo draws on arguments used by Stoic philosophers from Chrysippus to Posidon-
ius.

---

[15] Terian 1981. See especially the introduction, pp. 25-64.

As far as vocabulary is concerned there is in this treatise not a word that would suggest a Jewish context. Terian agrees with Leisegang's understanding, however: by arguing for the rationality of animals Alexander is opposing not only the Stoic, but also the Judaeo-biblical view that only man is endowed with the rational spirit. Terian states that by emphasizing the irrationality of animals in contrast to the rationality of human beings, Philo sanctions their use of animals. Thus Philo expresses a view that can be in agreement with the biblical idea of man's dominion over the animals, Gen 1:26-28.

## 5. Dominion over the created world in general

So far the present discussion has centred on human beings' dominion over animals. A further question need be taken up: How does Philo understand man's relationship to the created world in general? Also in this realm Philo draws on traditions which he has in common with sections found in rabbinic literature. Also here *Op.* 77-88 can serve as point of departure. A close parallel to parts of this section is found in *Tosephta Sanhedrin* 8:7 and 9.

The following points show that Philo in parts draws on traditions which he has in common with rabbinic traditions:

The same question, why Adam was created last, occurs in several places in Rabbinic writings.[16] Of special interest is the parallel in *t. Sanh.* 8:7.

Philo, *Op.* 77:

(a) Ἐπιζητήσειε δ' ἄν τις τὴν αἰτίαν, δι' ἣν ὕστατόν ἐστιν ἄνθρωπος τῆς τοῦ κόσμου γενέσεως.

(One should ask the reason why man comes last in the world's creation)

(b) ἐφ' ἅπασι γὰρ τοῖς ἄλλοις αὐτὸν ὁ ποιητὴς καὶ πατήρ, ὥσπερ αἱ ἱεραὶ γραφαὶ μηνύουσιν, εἰργάσατο.

(for, as the sacred writings show, he was the last whom the Father and Maker fashioned)

*Tosephta, Sanhedrin* 8:7 (Tosefta, ed. Zuckermandel):

(b) אדם נברא באחרונה

(Man was created last)

(a) ולמה נברא באחרונה

(And why was he created last?)

Both places the problem is one of unexpected order in the scriptural account: why

---

[16] *Gen. Rab.* 8:1ff.; *Lev. Rab.* 14:1; *Midrash Ps.* 139; *Tanchuma,* ed. Buber, 32; *t. Sanh.* 8:7; *y. Sanh.* 4:9.

was Adam created last? Both places point a) raises the question, while point b) states the fact that man (according to Scriptures) was created last.

The first of Philo's answers is basically the same as one of the answers given in *t. Sanh.* 8:9, and this answer goes beyond the narrative in Gen 1.
*Op.* 78:

> Just as givers of a banquet, then, do not send out the summonses to supper till they have put everything in readiness for the feast ...... in the same way the Ruler of all things, like some provider ... of a banquet, when about to invite man to the enjoyment of a feast ... made ready in beforehand the material ... in order that on coming into the world man might at once find ... a banquet ... full of all things that earth and rivers and sea and air bring forth for use and enjoyment ....

*t. Sanh.* 8:9:

> Another matter: So that he might enter the banquet at once. They have made a parable: To what is the matter comparable? To a king who built a palace and dedicated it and prepared a meal and [only] afterwards invited the guests. And so Scripture says, 'The wisest of women has built her a house' (Prov 9:1). This refers to the King of the kings of kings, blessed be He, who built his world in seven days by wisdom. 'She has hewn out her seven pillars' (Prov 9:1) — these are the seven days of creation. 'She has killed her beasts and mixed her wine' (Prov 9:2) — These are the oceans, rivers, wastes, and all the other things which the world needs ....[17]

In both passages the picture of a banquet is used to explain why Adam was created last. There are even many similarities between Philo and the *Tosephta* in wording:

Philo: καθάπερ οὖν ... τὸν αὐτὸν τρόπον — Tos.: למה הדבר דומה ... כן הוא

Philo: ἐπὶ δεῖπνον ... πρὸς εὐωχίαν ... συμπόσιον ... — Tos.: סעודה

Philo: καλοῦσιν ... καλεῖν ... — Tos.: יכנס ... זימן

Philo: οὐ πρότερον ... προ(ευτρεπίσατο) ... — Tos.: ואחר כך

Philo: εὐτρεπίσαι ... (προ)ευτρεπίσατο ... — Tos.: וחינכה והתקין

Philo: ὁ τῶν ὅλων ἡγεμών ... — Tos.: מלך מלכי המלכים

Philo: γῆ καὶ ποταμοὶ καὶ θάλαττα ... — Tos.: ימים ונהרות ומדברות

Philo: εἰς χρῆσιν καὶ ἀπόλαυσιν ... — Tos.: ושאר צורכי העולם

All these similarities in wording give support to the conclusion that Philo, *Op.* 77-78, and *t. Sanh.* 8:7 and 9 render the same tradition. Moreover, this tradition occurs also in other places in the rabbinic writings, as in *y. Sanh.* 4:9; *b. Sanh.* 38a; *Jalkut, Shemone* 15, cf. *Gen. Rab.* 8:6. The tradition was also used by the Church Fathers, as by Gregor of Nyssa, *De hom. op.*, ch. 2. Thus this tradition was widespread and originated at the time of Philo or before.

---

[17] The translation is taken from Neusner 1981, 224.

This conclusion is strengthened by the fact that Philo explicitly says that he renders the answer of other scholars on the Laws of Moses. Thus, the tradition originated before Philo recorded it in *Op.* 77-78, since he wrote: "Those, then, who have studied more deeply than others the laws of Moses and who examine their contents with all possible minuteness, maintain that ...".[18]

Also with regard to the second answer, *Op.* 79, to the question why man was created last, Philo utilizes Jewish traditions. Here the answer is: "At the moment of his coming into existence man found all provisions for life." This is a repetition of a point already mentioned in his first answer in *Op.* 77: "... He ... made ready for him in beforehand all things in the world ..., since it was His will that when man came into existence he should be at loss for none of the means of living and living well." A close parallel is found in *Gen. Rab.* 8:6: "Only after He had created what was needed for his food He created him." This idea refers to Gen 1:28 where it is said that living beings exist for the sake of human beings. Philo expresses this understanding at several places in his writings, such as in *Prov.* 2:84 (*SVF* 2:149); 91-92; 103; *Mos.* 1:60-62 and *Spec. leg.* 4:119-121.

The idea that the created world exists for the sake of human beings was widespread. Since the Jews understood themselves to be the true human beings, it can be said that the created world exists for the sake of Israel. See 4 Ezra 6:54-59; 7:10f.; 9:13; *2 Bar.* 14:17-19; 15:7 (for the sake of the righteous ones); 21:24; *As. Mos.* 1:12; *Sipre Deut.* 48:85a; *Tanh.B Bereshit* 3ff.; *b. Sanh.* 98b; *b. Ros. Has.* 10b; 11a; *Gen. Rab.* 1:4; *Lev. Rab.* 36:4; *Cant. Rab.* 5:11#4; *Tanh.B Bereshit* 10. The idea that the world existed for the sake of human beings existed among the Stoics, as can be seen in Cicero, *De natura deorum* 2:133; 154ff.; cf. *SVF* 2:527; 1041; 1152-1167; 3:369 and 658. Against this background the question is to be asked: Does Philo refer to human beings in general, or primarily to the Jews as true humanity?

## 6. Greed, Idolatry and Vices Now

This point (that man found all provisions for life) in the second answer on the question why man was created last, stands together with other ideas in *Op.* 79-81. The

---

[18] Runia 1986, 272-74 and 530, discusses *Op* 77-78 under the theme "The encomium of sight", based on Plato's *Timaeus* 47a-c. He finds two Platonic themes in the passage, the gift of the gods and the kinship of man's mind with the heavenly bodies. As for the gifts of the gods, Runia expresses surprise that with the partial exception of *Op* 77-78 Philo ignores this theme.

As a comment to Runia's work, it must be said that his analysis of this passage shows that it needs be supplemented by a study of Jewish exegetical traditions. It is striking that just Philo's use of the (Platonic) theme of the gifts of the gods, is an elaboration of the common Jewish tradition about God making everything ready for man, like a banquet, before man was created.

original ideal conditions of man are pictured, the bad situation of the present, and the possible future restoration of the ideal situation. The ideal is that human beings, like the first man, should spend their days without toil or trouble surrounded by lavish abundance of all that they needed. The present situation forms a contrast to this, however. Due to irrational pleasures (ἡδοναί) gluttony and lust (γαστριμαργία καὶ λαγνεία) desires for glory or wealth or power (αἱ δόξης χρημάτων ἢ ἀρχῆς ἐπιθυμίαι), sorrows (αἱ λῦπαι), fear (φόβος), folly, cowardice and injustice (ἀφροσύνη καὶ δειλία καὶ ἀδικία) and other vices, human beings now suffer penalty and punishments: they have difficulty in obtaining the necessaries of life, and they suffer all kinds of hardships and disasters.

A restoration is possible, however, if men's passions were calmed and brought under control by self-mastery, and the inclination to do wrong was corrected by justice, and life was determined by virtues. Then the warfare of the soul would have been abolished, peace would prevail, and God would provide for the human race good things all coming forth spontaneously and in all readiness.

At other places Philo says that idolatry destroys the cosmic harmony and corrupts man's situation. This point may be illustrated by Philo's interpretation of the first commandment, *Dec.* 52-65. In this section several of the ideas in *Op.* 77-88 re-occur: the four elements, cosmos seen as *megapolis* and human beings' sovereignty over the animals. These agreements are in accordance with Philo's view that the specific written laws where in harmony with the cosmic laws of creation, *Mos.* 2:48.

In *Dec.* 52-65 Philo then offers sharp criticism of those who have deified the four elements, earth, water, air and fire, and others deifying the sun, moon, planets and fixed stars. Some call the earth Kore or Demeter or Pluto, and the sea Poseidon. They call air Hera, fire Hephaestus, the sun Apollo, the moon Artemis, the morning star Aphrodite, etc., *Dec.* 54-55. In contrast to these errors Philo pictures cosmos as a *megapolis* with God as the Creator (ὁ γεννητής), the ruler (ὁ ἄρχων) of *megapolis*, the commander-in-chief of the invincible host army (ὁ στρατάρχης τῆς ἀηττήτου στρατιᾶς), the pilot (ὁ κυβερνήτης) who steers all things in safety, *Dec.* 53. Since the stars are created, they are the brothers of human beings, since all have one Father, the Creator of the universe (ὁ ποιητὴς τῶν ὅλων), *Dec.* 64.

An even sharper criticism is directed to those who worship man-made images, sculptures, paintings, etc., *Dec.* 66-76. The most horrible form of idolatry is the worship of irrational beings, ζῷα ἄλογα, animals, as done by the Egyptians, *Dec.* 76-80. They have even deified the fiercest and most savage of wild animals. Searching in the two elements given by God to man for his use, earth and water, they found on land no creature more savage than the lion nor in water than the crocodile, and these they worship, *Dec.* 78. Philo gives here his own version of the kind of criticism and ridicule of Egyptian animal worship which was quite widespread among non-Egyptians in the Graeco-Roman world.[19] When Philo in *Dec.* 78 writes that the two elements, earth and water, are given by God to man for his use, then he again alludes to Gen 1:26-29 where it says that God has given man the charge of being stewards over animals and plants and to use them for food.

Besides describing Egyptian worship of animals, Philo also internalizes man's conflict with the wild beasts and the warfare among the beasts themselves. He applies this internalization to the Egyptians as a collective entity. A non-Egyptian who sees the Egyptians worshipping wild beasts "regards them with good reason as more miserable than the creatures they honour, as men with souls transformed into the nature of those creatures, so that as they pass before him, they seem beasts in human shape" (*Dec.* 80), cf. *Legat.* 166.

This internalization of the experience of wild animals is given a general application by Philo when he talks about "the wild beasts within the soul", *Praem.* 88, cf. #91. Correspondingly Philo in *Op.* 81 refers to the warfare in the soul.

One might expect that such application of ideas from the animal world to man's inner life should lead to further allegorical internalization of the various species of the reference to animals in the creation story. Philo does this, but on a limited scale. The most elaborate example of such allegorization is found in *Quaes. Gen.* 2:56 where Philo first gives a literal interpretation of Gen 9:1-2 and Gen 1:28 as referring to man's role as king over the animals, and he then presents the deeper meaning which deals with the inner struggle within human beings:

> But as for the deeper meaning, it is to be interpreted as follows: He desires that the souls of intelligent *men increase* in greatness and *multitude* (and) in the form of virtues, and fill the mind with its form, as though it were *the earth*, leaving no part empty and void for follies; and that they should *dominate and rule over the earthly* body and its senses, and *strike terror and fear into beasts*, which is the exercise of the will against evil, for evil is *untamed and savage*. And *over the birds*, (that is) those who are lightly lifted up in thought, those who are (filled) with vain and empty arrogance, (and) having been previously armed, cause great harm, not being restrained *by fear*. Moreover, (over) *the reptiles*, which are a symbol of poisonous passions; for through every soul sense-pleasures and desires and grief and fear *creep*, stabbing and piercing and wounding. And by *the fish* I understand those who eagerly welcome a moist and fluid life but not one that is continent, healthy and lasting.[20]

## 7. Conditioned Eschatological Realization

In *De Praemiis* 79-126 the focus is placed on the future restoration, in ##79-91 centred on the relationship between animals and human beings, and in ##98-126 on

---

[19] Smelik and Hemelrijk 1984, 1852-2000.

[20] English transl. by Marcus, *Philo* 1953, 1, ad loc. See further *Det.* 25-26; *Agr.* 41; 57-58, etc.

man and creation in general with emphasis on man's wealth and health.

It should be repeated here that the treatise *De Praemiis et poenis* is an integral part of *The Exposition of the Laws of Moses*. Against the background of the story of the creation (*Op.*), the stories of the patriarchs as living prototypes of the Laws (*Abr.*, *Jos.*), the Laws themselves interpreted (*Dec.*, *Spec. leg.*), Philo has described their function relative to virtues and vices (*Virt.*), and proceeds now to the different attitudes and actions of men relative to the Laws, and the resulting consequences in on the one hand rewards and blessings and on the other hand in punishments and curses (*Praem.*). In a summary fashion Philo in *Praem.* 9 even refers to the place of human beings in creation as previously stated in *Op.* 77-86: "For from the beginning and simultaneously with the first creation of all things, God provided beforehand, raised from the earth, what was necessary for all living animals and particularly for the human race to which he granted sovereignty over all earthborn creatures" (*Praem.* 9).

In *Praem.* 79-172 blessings and curses are listed. This form is biblical, and Philo draws here extensively on Lev 26 and 28 together with Deut 28. The blessings are conditioned upon obedience to the Laws: "If, he [Moses] says, you keep the divine commandments in obedience to the ordinances and accept his precepts ..., you shall have as a first reward victory over your enemies" (*Praem.* 79). In *Praem.* 85-98 Philo describes this victory. In ##85-91a the theme is man's war with the wild beasts and the victory in the war within man himself.

As shown above, the motif of the war in man himself was present in *Op.* 79-81 where it was said that if men's passions were brought under control, wrongs were checked by righteousness, etc., then the warfare in the soul would have been brought to an end, and ideal conditions would be restored. As for man's conflict with the beasts as pictured in *Praem.* 85-91a, the line can also be drawn back to *Op.*, as can be seen from agreements between *Praem.* 89b-90 and *Op.* 83-84a. In *Praem.* 89b the words about the beasts' fear of man as their master, καταπλαγέντα δ' ὡς ἄρχοντα καὶ φύσει δεσπότην εὐλαβῶς ἔξει, are a close parallel to words in *Op.* 83, κατάπληξιν ... προσκυνεῖν ὡς ἡγεμόνα φύσει καὶ δεσπότην. Both *Praem.* 85-90 and *Op.* 83-86 deal with land-animals and sea-animals.

When Philo in *Praem.* 85-90 pictures the future peace among the animals, he goes beyond his idea about the original situation after creation. According to *Op.* 83, although the animals subordinate themselves under man, they still had fierce conflict among themselves. Philo's future hope, as stated in *Praem.* 85-90, is that even this conflict will end. Thus Philo does not here only draw on his interpretation of Gen 1:26/28, but also to Lev 26:6: "And I will give peace in the land ... and I will remove evil beasts from the land ...." This additional reference does not sufficiently cover Philo's ideas either, when he tells about peace both among the animals and between the animals and human beings. There must therefore be here an influence from Isa 11:6-9:

> The wolf shall dwell with the lamb, and the leopard shall lie down with the kid, and the calf and the lion and the fatling together, and a little child shall lead them. The cow and the bear shall feed; their young shall lie down together; and the lion shall eat straw like the ox. The sucking child shall play over the hole of the asp, and the weaned child shall put his hand on the adder's den. They shall not hurt or destroy in all my holy mountain; for the earth shall be full of the knowledge of the Lord as the waters cover the sea.

Similar ideas were also expressed elsewhere, such as in *Sib. Or.* 3:788-795; Isa 65:25; *2 Bar.* 73:6; Virgil, *Ecloge* 4:18-25.

Just as in Isa 11:6-9 so also in *Praem.* 89-90 bears, lions and leopards are mentioned, but Philo adds elephants and tigers. He lists snake, corresponding to the asp in Isaiah 11. He lacks the domestic animals, cows and bulls, which are mentioned in Isaiah 11. In Isaiah 11 it is said that the animals will graze together (LXX: βόσκω, feed, passive: eat, graze) and Philo expresses the same by the term σύννομος, feeding in herds together, τὸ σύννομον, the being in a herd together. Thus Philo combines the idea from Gen 1:26/28 about man's sovereignty over the animals with ideas from Isa 11:6-9 (and other texts) about peace among the animals. Philo has a longing and a hope for future which he expresses in this way: "Would that this good gift might shine upon our life and that we might be able to see that day ..." (*Praem.* 88).

Philo ties this hope to "some" who are worthy of salvation (ὅταν κρίνῃ τινὰς σωτηρίας ἀξίους). Their personal blessing will then be brought to people in general for all to share, *Praem.* 87. Similarly, the blessings of abundance of food, safe residence, health, etc., will come as a reward to those who keep the Laws, *Praem.* 98-125. Those who practise frugality (ὀλιγόδεια, contentment with little) and practise self-restraint (ἐγκράτεια), will have abundance, *Praem.* 100. Here in *Praem.* 98-125 Philo elaborates on the same expectations of abundance for those obedient to the Laws as he has sketched briefly in *Op.* 79. In *Praem.* 98-125 the direct reference back to the ideal condition of the first human beings is less direct, however. Philo rather draws on various scriptural texts such as Lev 26:3-4: "If you walk in my statutes and observe my commandments and do them, then I will give you your rains in their seasons, and the land shall yield its increase, and the trees of the field shall yield their fruit." In *Praem.* 101 Philo paraphrases these Old Testament verses.

As for the curses, *Praem.* 127-152, they are correspondingly an elaboration of the idea that man's original estate was destroyed by greed and passion. The following two sentences demonstrate the parallelism: *Op.* 80: "That penalty is difficulty in obtaining the necessaries of life." *Praem.* 127: "The first curse ... is poverty ... and lack of necessaries ..." The picture given forms a contrast to man's rule of the animals as pictured in *Op.* 83-84 and in *Praem.* 89: The curse means that God, when he brought forth the universe created the wild animals to warn those who were willing to be rectified and punish the incorrigible, *Praem.* 149. Philo here connects Gen 1:24-25, the creation of the animals, with Lev 26:22: "And I will let loose the wild beasts among you ...."

## 8. Cosmos, Humanity and Israel

The perspective of protology and eschatology must be supplemented by the cosmic place and role of human beings. In *Op.* 82, in the third answer to the question of why man was created last, Philo stated that man was a micro-cosmic being:

> God, being minded to unite in intimate and loving fellowship the beginning and the end of created things, made heaven the beginning and man the end, the one the most perfect of imperishable objects of sense, the other the noblest things earthborn and perishable, being, in very truth, a miniature heaven. He bears within himself many starlike natures ....

In several ways Philo formulates the view that man is a being "in between". Thus in *Op.* 135 Philo draws in particular on Gen 2:7: man is a composite one, made up of earthly substance and of Divine breath. Similarly in *Op.* 146 man's place is between other creatures and God: "Every man, in respect of his mind, is allied to divine reason ... but in the structure of his body he is allied to all the world, for he is compounded of the same things, earth, water, air and fire ...."

Cosmos may be seen as a city, *polis*, and the first man was accordingly a *cosmopolitan*, *Op.* 142-144. This was a Stoic idea, *SVF* 1:262. Philo describes this ideal existence, drawing on Gen 1:26-28, 2:7 and 9:1-2: "The world was his fatherland where he dwelt with full security, being removed from fear, inasmuch as he had been held worthy of the rule of the creatures of the earth, and all things mortal trembled before him, and had been taught or compelled to obey him as their despot. So he lived exposed to no attack amid the comforts of peace unbroken by war" (*Op.* 142).

This *polis* and this constitution must have had citizens before man: "These might justly be termed citizens of the Great City (μεγαπολῖται), having had allotted to them as their dwelling-place the greatest compass, and having been enrolled in the greatest and most perfect commonwealth (πολίτευμα)" (#143). Philo identifies these *megapolites* as heavenly beings, visible stars and noetic beings (probably Philo's interpretation of angels): "And who should these be but rational and divine natures, some incorporeal and visible to mind only, some not without bodies, such as are the stars" (#144).

The first man lived in harmony with this heavenly commonwealth: "Conversing and consorting with these man could not but live in unalloyed bliss, and being of near kin to the Ruler, since the divine Spirit had flowed into him in full current, he earnestly endeavoured in all his words and actions to please the Father and King, following Him step by step in the highways cut out by virtues, since only for souls who regard it as their goal to be fully conformed to God who begat them, is it lawful to draw nigh to Him" (#144). A parallel is found in *Spec. leg.* 1:13-14. Cf. Cicero, *De natura deorum* 154: "For the world is as it were the common dwelling-place for gods and men, or the city that belongs to both; for they alone have the use of reason and live by justice and by law."

Also at several other places Philo pictures man as a being between heaven and earth: *Leg. all.* 3:161; *Quod det.* 84-85; *Conf.* 176ff. *Heres.* 283; *Dec.* 134; *Plant.* 14; 20-22; *Somn.* 1:146, etc.[21]

In general the same understanding of human beings is found in other Jewish sources and also in non-Jewish Hellenistic texts: In Rabbinic texts the place of man is between heaven and earth, usually represented by the angels and the animals. Human beings are akin to the angels in the respect that they have intelligence, walk upright and speak Hebrew. They are similar to the animals in procreation, excretion, eating and drinking. Also man's way of life may be seen within this perspective: When human beings keep the Law of Moses, then they are like angels (or God). If they do not know the Law or they break the Law, then they are like animals. See *Abot R. Nat.* 37; *b. Hag.* 16a; *Pesiq. R.* 43; 179b; *Sipre Deut* .306; 132b; *Tanh.B Bereshit* 17: *Gen. Rab.* 8:11; 12:8; 14:3: 21:5; *Exod. Rab.* 30:16; *Qoh. Rab.* 7:29 #1.

Outside of Judaism it may be said that human beings have aspects in common with the gods and with the irrational animals (Galen, *Protrepticus* 2:4, p. 21 in Kühn's edition). Maximus Tyrius (2. cent. A.D.) thought that man ruled over the animals due to their intelligence and knowledge, but are inferior to the gods due to man's wickedness (*Dial.* VI:1, ed. Hobein). The aim of the Rabbis, Galen and Maximus is to encourage others to live and act in accordance with the divine aspect of their nature. The difference is that in Rabbinic texts the divine knowledge is present in the Law of Moses, while in Hellenistic traditions it is recognized through reason.[22]

When Philo in *Op.* 77-88 discusses the relation between human beings and creation at large, it seems obvious that he speaks about humanity. This passage must be interpreted as part of the "Exposition" as a whole, however. Then one has to ask whether this conclusion is adequately formulated.

---

[21] See Schmidt 1933, 19-21; Meyer 1937, 28-29; cf. p. 78, n. 1; Borgen 1981, 128-30.

[22] Se Dahl 1960, 87-89; Borgen 1981, 127-30.

Above it was shown how man, according to Philo, broke down the order of creation by worshipping many gods. This failure of human beings in general was rectified by the Jewish people. Philo says: "When they went wrong in what was the
most vital matter of all, it is the literal truth that the error which the rest committed
was corrected by the nation of the Jews, which went beyond the created world ...
and chose the service only of the Uncreated and Eternal ..." (*Spec. leg.* 2:166). The
chosen people thus are the true human beings: "... out of the whole human race He
chose of special merit ... those who are in a true sense men (οἱ πρὸς ἀλήθειαν
ἄνθρωποι) and called them to the service of Himself ..." (*Spec. leg.* 1:303). Here
Philo paraphrases the words addressed to Israel in Deut 10:15: "... and chose ...
you above all peoples ...."

Those referred to by Philo in the word "some" in *Praem.* 87 are then, accordingly, those who keep the Laws of Moses. This understanding is in accordance with the
introduction which in *Praem.* 79-84 is given to the larger section on blessings. In
this introduction Philo gives an exposition of Deut 28:1 LXX when he in *Praem.* 79
writes: "If, he [Moses] says, you keep the divine commandments ...." The same
view is expressed in *Praem.* 98 where Philo speaks about those who follow God and
always cleave to His commandments. In *Praem.* 91-97 Philo then tells how the peoples will subjugate themselves under the divine people, either voluntarily or by the
appearance of "a Man" (Num 24:7 LXX), that is, a (Messianic) commander in chief
who shall conquer them.[23]

The key to this combination of universalism and particularism can be seen in
*Mos.* 2:52: "Thus whoever will carefully examine the nature of the particular enactments will find that they seek to attain to the harmony of the universe ...." The cosmic and universal principles are revealed in the Laws of Moses so that the specific
laws are a manifestation of these cosmic principles. From this it becomes evident
that Philo held the view that (the Greek idea about) divine reason is made concrete
in the Laws of Moses. Thus these Laws reveal the cosmic and universal laws which
in principle are the laws which should be followed by all. The people who has the
laws near in speech, thought and action (Deut 30:11-14), "has its dwelling not far
from God; it has the vision of etherial loveliness always before its eyes, and its steps
are guided by a heavenward yearning," *Praem.* 83-84. Thus the chosen people has
accomplished the proper cosmic place intended for human beings.[24]

---

[23] See Borgen 1992, 341-61.
[24] See Borgen 1992, 342-44.

## 9. Conclusion

Methodically it has proved fruitful to take the starting point in a classification of Philo's writings when investigating his views on man's sovereignty. The collection of treatises named *The Exposition of the Laws of Moses* was of central importance, since Philo himself gives clues to his over all understanding of this comprehensive work. The pictures given in *De Praemiis et Poenis* of the future rewards and punishments develop ideas also found in *De Opificio Mundi*. This observation supports the view that the treatise *De Praemiis* is an integral part of Philo's works named *The Exposition of the Laws of Moses*.

The present study has demonstrated that it is a mistaken understanding of Philo to say that man's dominance over the creation had a peripheral place in Philo's thoughts. Although Philo lacks explicit quotations of Gen 1:28, traditions which drew on this verse together with Gen 1:26 and 9:1-3 played a central role in several of his works.

The many Rabbinic and other Jewish parallels to the passages examined, show that Philo has his place within a Jewish context. The impact of Greek/Hellenistic ideas on Philo's texts were stronger than on those parallel texts, however.

Within the context of a cosmic framework Philo finds room for both the proto-logical and eschatological perspectives on the topic of man's sovereignty over animals and nature. In general his ideas are presented in the form of exegesis of parts of the Pentateuch. Within the eschatological outlook he also draws on messianic ideas from Isaiah 11. In *De Animalibus* he discusses the topic of human beings and animals within the context of Greek terminology and categories. Nevertheless Philo's conclusions were basically in harmony with his biblical and Jewish views.

Philo combines the cosmic and universal dimensions with a particularistic concentration on the chosen people who keeps the Laws of Moses. Since the cosmic principles are made manifest in the Laws of Moses, those who keep these Laws are the true human beings. Thus, even when the future blessing is related to the animal world and to nature, the chosen people of the Laws of Moses will play the central role.

In his interpretation of man's dominion over animals and nature Philo does not see man as an autonomous despotic ruler, but as a viceroy of God. Greed, idolatry and lawlessness are central ideas in his description of man's falling away from his original ideal state of being.

# Bibliography

Borgen, P. 1981: *Bread from Heaven*, Leiden: Brill 1965 (repr. 1981).

— 1983: *'Paul Preaches Circumcision and Pleases Men' and Other Essays on Christian Origins*, Trondheim: Tapir 1983.

— 1984a: "Philo of Alexandria", in: M. Stone (ed.), *Jewish Writings of the Second Temple Period* (CRINT 2:2) Assen: Van Gorcum 1984, 233-82.

— 1984b: "Philo of Alexandria. A critical and synthetical survey of research since World War II", in: W. Haase (ed.), *Aufstieg und Niedergang der römischen Welt (ANRW)*, II:21:1, Berlin: Walter de Gruyter 1984, 98-154.

— 1987: *Philo, John and Paul. New Perspectives on Judaism and Early Christianity*, Atlanta, GA: Scholars Press 1987.

— 1992: "There shall come forth a Man", in: J. H. Charlesworth (ed.), *The Messiah*, Minneapolis, MN: Fortress 1992, 341-61.

Borgen, P. and Skarsten, R. 1976/77: "Quaestiones et Solutiones: Some Observations on the Form of Philo's Exegesis", in: *Studia Philonica* 4 (1976/77) 1-16.

Cohn, L. et al. 1962: *Philo in deutscher Übersetzung*, 1, 2nd ed., Berlin: Walter de Gruyter 1962 (1st ed., Breslau: M. and H. Marcus 1909).

Dahl, N. A. 1960: "Imago Dei. Opposisjonsinnlegg ved Jacob Jervells disputas 10.12.1959", in: *NTT* 61 (1960) 65-94.

Diels, H. 1899: *Elementum*, Leipzig: Teubner 1899.

Ginzberg, L. 1911: *The Legend of the Jews*, 5, 8. printing, Philadelphia, PA: The Jewish Publication Society 1968.

Goodenough, E. R. 1933: "Philo's Exposition of the Laws and His De Vita Moses", in: *HThR* 26 (1933) 109-25.

Grünbaum, M. 1893: *Neue Beiträge zur semitischen Sagenkunde*, Leiden: Brill 1893.

Hay, D. M. (ed.) 1991: *Both Literal and Allegorical*, Atlanta, GA: Scholars Press 1991.

Marcus, R. (trans.) 1953, 1: *Philo*, Supplement 1 (LCL), London: Harvard University Press 1953.

Metzger, B. M. (trans.) 1983: "The Fourth Book of Ezra", in: J. H. Charlesworth (ed.), *The Old Testament Pseudepigrapha*, 1, Garden City, NY: Doubleday 1983.

Meyer, R. 1937: *Hellenistisches in der rabbinischen Anthropologie*, Stuttgart: W. Kohlhammer 1937.

Neusner, J. (trans.) 1985: *Genesis Rabbah. The Judaic Commentary to the Book of Genesis. A New American Translation*, 1, Atlanta, GA: Scholars Press 1985.

— 1981: *The Tosefta. Fourth Division: Neziqin*, New York: Ktav 1981.

Nilsson, M. P. 1950: *Geschichte der griechischen Religion*, 5:2:2, München: C. H. Beck 1950.

Pohlenz, M. 1948: *Die Stoa. Geschichte einer geistigen Bewegung*, 1, Göttingen: Vandenhoeck & Rupert 1948.

Runia, D. 1986: *Philo of Alexandria and the Timaeus of Plato*, Leiden: Brill 1986.

Schmidt, H. 1933: *Die Anthropologie Philons von Alexandreia*, Würzburg: Konrad Triltsch 1933.

Smelik, K. A. D. and Hemelrijk, E. A. 1984: "'Who knows not what Monsters Demented Egyptian Worship' – Opinions on Egyptian Worship in Antiquity as Part of the Ancient Conception of Egypt", in: W. Haase (ed.), *Aufstieg und Niedergang der römischen Welt (ANRW)*, II:17:4, Berlin: Walter de Gruyter 1984, 1852-2000.

Terian, A. 1981: *Philonis Alexandrini De Animalibus* (The Armenian Text with Introduction, Translation, and Commentary), Chico, CA: Scholars Press 1981.

Wolfson, H. A. 1948, 1-2: *Philo*, 1-2, 2nd printing, Cambridge, MA: Harvard University Press 1948.

Zeller, E. 1911: *Grundriß der Geschichte der griechischen Philosophie*, 10th ed., Leipzig: O. R. Reisland 1911.

# The Phasing of the Future

Michael Goulder

## 1. The Phasing Movement among the Paulines

Lars Hartman published *Prophecy Interpreted* in 1966, the swallow heralding a fine summer. The core of its findings was the presence of a "midrash", a reinterpretation, of the prophecy of Daniel behind Mark 13 parr., and behind the similar material in the two Thessalonian letters. Other OT passages had been worked over too, drawn in by association, like Deut 13 or Mic 7; but Daniel was primary, and on a large scale. More tentatively Hartman proposed a history of the development of the apocalyptic chapter. He saw a school of interpreters at work developing the tradition, but ultimately it was the thought of one man. Paul appealed in 1 Thess 4:15 to a "word of the Lord", and elsewhere to a παράδοσις, so it seemed natural to think that the basic structure of thought goes back to Jesus.

The work expounding the Danielic background is exemplary, and Hartman was not exaggerating when he spoke of having firm ground under our feet. In the present paper[1] I have attempted to build on that ground, and the structure which emerges is not the same as that proposed in his last chapters; but he will recognize that many of the building blocks are the same, and that it is his work which I am hoping to develop.

In 1 Cor 4:8 Paul writes sarcastically: "Already you are filled! Already you have become rich! Without us you have begun to reign (ἐβασιλεύσατε)! And would that you had begun to reign that we might reign with you!" He goes on to contrast his wretched life as an apostle with their pretensions, and says at the end of the chapter, "For the kingdom (βασιλεία) of God does not consist in talk, but in power" (4:20). The passage for once seems to be clear. There are members of the Corinthian church who think the kingdom of God has arrived, and that they are among those who are

---

[1] I offer the paper with affection to Lars, who has taught me much over the years, and has treated my idiosyncratic views with a kindly respect.

reigning in it. The kingdom is associated with being *filled* (κεκορεσμένοι, sated)[2] and becoming *rich* (ἐπλουτήσατε); probably, as we shall see, the terms imply both spiritual and physical satisfaction and wealth. Paul does not think the kingdom of God has come; his repeated use of the word *already* (ἤδη) in heavy irony shows how absurd he thinks the claim to be. It is all "talk" (4:20). Later on in the letter he will say, "I tell you this, brethren: flesh and blood cannot inherit the kingdom of God, nor does the perishable inherit the imperishable" (15:50). Not only has the kingdom of God not arrived already; it cannot arrive until the End, when the Lord will come and the dead will be raised and we shall be changed.[3]

The first Corinthian letter is invaluable in showing us that there was a wing of early Christianity which thought that the kingdom *had come*, whereas Paul himself thought that it had *not* come. There is none of the dialectical theologian's already-but-not-yet about Paul's position either:[4] he uses the word ἤδη with contempt. We can of course only infer the outlines of the realised doctrine maintained by his opponents. In both 1-4 and 15 the claim of the realised kingdom is associated with claims to be πνευματικοί and in 15 this goes with denial of physical resurrection. The talk of being rich and sated is contrasted by Paul with the rigours of apostolic life, hungry and thirsty and labouring, working with his own hands; so we may think of the opposition as enjoying a comfortable life devoted to prayer, visions, healing, etc., with a shared purse, rather on the model of the Jerusalem church in Acts 2-4. As 1 Cor 4:6 speaks of not being puffed up for *the one* against *the other* (ὑπὲρ τοῦ ἑνὸς κατὰ τοῦ ἑτέρου), there seem to be two real parties rather than the four paraded in 1:12, and we may think of the "realised" group as the Cephas or Christ party—quite suitably if they have a life-style similar to the Jerusalem church.[5] We should have to suppose some sort of future expectation for them as well though: the prayer *Marana tha* must go back to the Aramaic church.

So much inference can do with some support, and we may think that there is

---

[2] Cf. Barrett 1971, 109; Conzelmann 1975, 87f.; Fee 1987, 171f. All three limit the "sating" to spiritual gifts; but Paul contrasts the apostle's hunger and thirst—and kings do not go hungry.

[3] Paul is consistently either negative or future (or both) in his references to the kingdom, which are not very numerous (1 Thess 1:12; 2 Thess 1:5; 1 Cor 4:20; 6:9, 10; 15:24, 50; Gal 5:21; Rom 14:17; [Eph 5:5; Col 1:13; 4:11]). The only text with an apparently present reference is Rom 14:17; but this should be taken in line with 1 Cor 4:20: —

1 Cor 4:20: οὐ γὰρ ἐν λόγῳ ἡ βασιλεία τοῦ θεοῦ ἀλλ᾽ ἐν δυνάμει.
Rom 14:17: οὐ γάρ ἐστιν ἡ βασιλεία τοῦ θεοῦ βρῶσις καὶ πόσις.
      ἀλλὰ δικαιοσύνη καὶ εἰρήνη καὶ χαρὰ …
See my article "Already?" in the forthcoming Festschrift for Robert Gundry.

[4] Of course Paul thinks that *something* has happened already, but it is not the coming of the kingdom of God: and even with the Spirit, he likes expressions like ἀπαρχή and ἀρραβών, which limit the "already" element.

some in the other early Pauline letters, the two Thessalonian epistles.[6] For in both of these we hear of Christians not working, and Paul uses the same phrase as in 1 Cor 4:12, "to work with your own hands" (1 Thess 4:10); the topic is dealt with at length in 2 Thess 3, and both letters say that he told them about this when he was with them (1 Thess 4:11; 2 Thess 3:6, 10). Furthermore the trouble about the Christian's death in 1 Thess 4, which has caused so much grief, and which requires comforting, seems most easily explicable on the basis of a realised kingdom in which the spiritual Christian does not die.[7]

This will certainly have arisen from a misunderstanding; no experienced missionary could have led his converts to expect that they would all escape death. But Cephas-Christians will have thought that they were πνευματικοί, already reigning in the kingdom, inheritors already of the spiritual life which would transcend death, despisers of the flesh that they have already risen above. In their view there would be no ἀνάστασις νεκρῶν, no resurrecting of corpses, but the Christian dead would continue the spiritual life they already possessed. This doctrine, which we can infer from 1 Cor 15,[8] was rather subtle to be taken in in a mission of a few weeks in Thessalonica. There the good news that baptism into Christ gives us victory over death has been understood too simply, to mean that the baptized do not die—especially after the missionaries have left. In this way we can most easily account for the alarm and despondency at Thessalonica when the first Christian did die.

Paul tries at first to counter this disappointment by explaining that "we who are alive, who are left until the coming of the Lord, shall not precede those who have fallen asleep" (4:15). He sets the coming events in a reassuringly confident series ("in a word of the Lord"). The Lord himself will descend with archangel and trumpet call; the dead in Christ will rise first; then we who are alive, who are left, shall be caught up together with them in the clouds to meet the Lord in the air (4:16f.). It's all right: our brother has died, but he has not lost anything. He's just asleep for a little bit, and we'll all be together again with the Lord, when he comes. 1 Thess

---

[5] See Goulder 1991, esp. 516-520. The article argues that Apollos was Paul's ally; that the σοφία of 1-3 is the "wisdom" of life lived by *halakha*, the "taught words of human wisdom" as opposed to plain biblical principles ("not beyond what is written"); and that the ἀνακρίνειν of God's ministers in 4:1-5 is a judging of Paul by comparison with the Jerusalem leadership, as in 9:1-6. The real opposition in 1 Corinthians are those "of Cephas".

[6] Cf. Goulder 1992.

[7] The alternative explanation, that the dead would miss out on the joys of the παρουσία, and perhaps of the millennium, is weak. It is argued for by Klijn 1982, and is supported by Delobel 1990. But *grief* and *comforting* imply something more existential; and we should have expected Paul to write "And so shall we all *share in the Lord's reign*", or something similar, if the Parousia/Millennium were in question.

[8] So Sellin 1987.

tactfully prepares the way for this trouble from the beginning: "remembering ... *your steadfastness of hope in our Lord Jesus*" (1:3); "how you turned to serve a living and true God *and to wait for his Son from heaven*" (1:10). They had been taught to pray *Marana tha*.

Where did Paul's confidence come from? He speaks of the dead as "those who have fallen asleep", of their rising, of the voice of the archangel, and of the times and seasons in which he has instructed them. All of this language is reminiscent of the last chapter of Daniel, where Michael the great angel will arise, and many of those who sleep in the dust of the earth shall rise, after a time of trouble unknown till that time.[9] Paul is telling them this "in a word of the Lord" (ἐν λόγῳ κυρίου), and he is probably drawing, whether directly or indirectly, on Daniel. He speaks of biblical texts as the λόγος of God at 2 Cor 2:17; 4:3, and the phrase λέγει κύριος introduces a verse of scripture at Rom 12:19; 1 Cor 14:21; 2 Cor 6:17, 18; so ἐν λόγῳ κυρίου may mean "in a text from the Bible". If it means "in a word received from Christ in the Spirit",[10] such messages often have a scriptural base, and the language suggests that here. Furthermore, our coming "on clouds" to meet the Lord is probably based on Dan 7:13.[11]

1 Thessalonians is a kindly, pastoral letter, but it did not achieve its object; and soon afterwards Paul[12] had to return to the attack. Three of the principal topics of 1 Thess are resumed in 2 Thess,[13] and in an aggravated form. The persecution of 1 Thess 2:14 has got much worse (2 Thess 1); the false teaching on the day of the Lord

---

[9] So Hartman 1966, 189f.

[10] So Best 1972, 189-194; Holtz 1986, 183f., 196f. It is, of course, an easy matter to ascribe the vital words to a lost saying of the risen Lord, and we may feel hesitant about the process by which such sayings achieved authority. Also, we might have expected a widely accepted word of the risen Christ to have appeared in Mark 13 parr.; and "by Spirit" is distinguished from "by word" in 2 Thess 2:2.

[11] Hartman himself thought in 1966 that ἐν λόγῳ κυρίου referred to a word of the historic Jesus (187f.). This view has not commended itself to recent commentators, largely because the λόγος referred to here does not seem to square with anything in the Marcan apocalypse. The details which agree with Matt 24 are usually seen as Matthew's adaptation of Mark to something like the Thessalonian tradition.

[12] Pauline authorship of 2 Thess is not crucial to my argument: it is enough that the letter comes from the Pauline movement (as its title implies), and that the "phasing" in chap. 2 was already in circulation before Mark.

[13] Hartman 1966, 179 was in a position to assume the authenticity of 2 Thess, in line with virtually all the then commentaries. Today opinion is largely against its authenticity; cf. Collins (ed.) 1990, where a large preponderance of the essayists argue, or assume, that it is non-Pauline; and this is true also of recent commentaries by Trilling 1980, Marxsen 1982 and Laub 1988. Earlier commentaries, including Best 1972, regularly argued for its authenticity; so also Marshall 1983. I have argued for the traditional Pauline ascription in Goulder 1992.

has become entrenched (2 Thess 2:1-12); and the giving up of work (1 Thess 4:10ff.; 5:14) has become endemic (2 Thess 3:6-16).

On the second subject Paul begins, "Now concerning the coming of our Lord Jesus Christ and our assembling to meet him, we beg you, brethren, not to be quickly shaken in mind or excited, either by spirit or by word, or by letter purporting to be from us, to the effect that the day of the Lord has come" (2:1f.). The detail is the same as in the former letter, our assembling to meet the Lord at his coming (παρουσία, 4:15ff.), and the day of the Lord (5:1). The false doctrine is being circulated in three ways: by spirit, that is in messages received in ecstatic utterance; by word, that is by a scriptural text interpreted, in this case perhaps Mal 4:5 or Joel 2:31, both of which speak of the coming ἡμέρα κυρίου; and by letter as from us, that is probably a letter from Paul's fellow evangelist Silas beginning, "Silvanus, Paul and Timothy... ".[14] The wicked deceit leading them astray—that is, the Petrine teaching—is that the day of the Lord, or kingdom of God, *has come* (ἐνέστηκεν).[15] It is the same error Paul derided in 1 Cor 4:8. Silas had been a pillar of the Jerusalem church, according to Acts 15:27, 32; and Paul had had to contest the mistake "when I was still with you" (2 Thess 2:5; cf. 1 Thess 5:1), that is, at a time when Silas was the only other missionary around.

There is nothing for it but to go over the Book of Daniel again ("I told you this", 2:5). What is at work now is "the mystery of lawlessness" (ἀνομία, 2:7), issuing in the persecutions of chap. 1. The classic passage in scripture where the Law is flouted, and God's faithful are persecuted is Daniel. Daniel himself, and Shadrach, Meshech and Abednego, are repeatedly called upon to break the Law, and face martyrdom for their faith. But even in Israel many have been lawless, as we find in Dan 9: "... we have not obeyed the voice of the Lord our God by following his *laws* ... All Israel has transgressed thy *law*" (9:10f.); and mystery (μυστήριον) is a word found almost exclusively in Daniel. Something is "restraining" (τὸ κατέχον, 2:6) the future, indeed someone is restraining (ὁ κατέχων, 2:7) the future; as in Dan 10 Gabriel says that "The prince of the kingdom of Persia withstood me twenty-one days ... and when I am through with him, lo, the prince of Greece will come" (10:13, 20). There are angelic powers in heaven who can hold up the advance of his-

---

[14] See Goulder 1992. Paul began his letters, "Paul, Silvanus and Timothy", and it is not likely that he gave them a veto over the wording. As Paul's teaching over giving up work and over the Christian's survival of death is repeatedly said to go back to the time of the mission (1 Thess 4:11; 5:2; 2 Thess 2:5; 3:6, 10), it is likely that he and Silas were not of one mind, and the "false" teaching was Silas'. Paul is warmer about Timothy than about Silas in 1 Thess 3:6, and Silas soon fades out of the Corinthian mission in Acts 18: Holtz 1986, 13 thinks he may have died.

[15] ἐνέστηκεν means *is present* in Rom 8:38; 1 Cor 3:22; Gal 1:4; but *is imminent* at 1 Cor 7:26. Paul thought the day of the Lord was imminent (coming like a thief in the night, 1 Thess 5:2; cf. 1 Cor 7:26), and he will have objected to any teaching that it was present (so Best 1972, 275ff.).

tory, and it is in Dan 10 that they are mentioned.[16]

A second phase is then foreseen: "Then the lawless one will be revealed, the son of perdition, who opposes and exalts himself against every so-called god or object of worship, so that he takes his seat in the temple of God, proclaiming himself to be God" (2:3f., 8a). Here Paul is thinking of Dan 11, where Antiochus "shall exalt himself and magnify himself above every god, and shall speak astonishing things against the God of gods" (11:36). In Dan 11:31 his forces "shall profane the temple … and they shall set up the abomination that makes desolate": as Paul speaks of the man of lawlessness taking his seat in the temple, it is likely that he thinks of the abomination as a throne. The crisis in which Caligula gave orders for his statue to be placed in the Jerusalem temple was a recent event as Paul wrote, only a decade past, and it was easy to imagine Daniel's Antiochus as taking a similar form in a new Caligula. Then finally "the Lord Jesus will slay him with the breath of his mouth" (2:8b): Antiochus "shall come to his end, with none to help him" at Dan 11:45, but the wording comes from Isa 11:4.[17] Then Dan 12 follows, with the resurrection of those who sleep.

What has happened here is significant for the future. When Paul heard of the grief in the church at the death of one of its members, he wrote to say that dead Christians were only asleep; that the Lord would come soon, suddenly; and that the living should watch. When he realised that the church's shock was based on the false belief that the kingdom had arrived, he wrote again: the Lord will indeed come suddenly, but not before some other things have happened first.[18] The Petrine view that the kingdom *has come* can be confuted only by showing that there are *phases* which have to be fulfilled before it comes; and those phases can only be described with confidence if they can be found in sequence in scripture. They are to be found *in sequence* in Daniel,[19] and especially in Dan 9-12, and it is that which gives Paul his confidence; though he finds himself up against more damaging errors in his later epistles, and does not expound the Daniel texts again.

However once the phasing was set down, its effectiveness appealed to the Pauline movement; and as history lengthened out, the Paulines elaborated the phas-

---

[16] The Greek versions of Daniel use (ἀνθ)ειστήκει for "withstood", but Paul needs the more general word κατέχειν; this is a fish which escaped Hartman's net.

[17] Hartman 1966, 199.

[18] There is a third emphasis in 1 Cor 15 when the "spiritual" opposition is seen as based on a denial of physical resurrection. Paul is a pastor, not a systematic theologian, and exegetes demand of him an unreal consistency which they would never expect of their own minister.

[19] Perhaps because of his very industry, Hartman has failed here to see the wood for the trees: he finds so many Danielic texts that he obscures the sequence. But the sequence is necessary for Paul's argument. The delaying power of the "prince of Greece", understood as the angel of the Roman Empire, is a significant point in the series.

es. We may pause to note here that Paul does not think the error to be a minor matter. Those who are deceived by it "are to perish, because they refused to love the truth and so be saved. Therefore God sends upon them a strong delusion, to make them believe what is false, so that all may be condemned who did not believe the truth but had pleasure in unrighteousness" (2:10ff.). They are going to hell, and God means them to go there.

## 2. Mark 13

We may take two illustrations of the development of the phasing movement among the Paulines, Mark and the Apocalypse. Paul has three basic phases: (1) *Now*, a period of lawlessness, as the future is mysteriously held back, marked with persecution of the Church; (2) *Next*, the appearing of the man of lawlessness, and his session in the temple; (3) *Finally*, the coming of the Lord Jesus, the destruction of the man of lawlessness, and the rising of the dead. Mark divides his apocalypse into the same triple scheme: (1) *the beginning of birth-pangs*, with wars, famines and persecutions of the Church (13:5-13)—during this phase Christians have the duty to *watch* (βλέπετε, 13:5, 9); (2) *when you see the abomination of desolation set up*, the great tribulation will take place, and then Christians must *flee* (13:14-23); (3) *in those days, after that tribulation*, the sun will be darkened, the Son of Man will come and *gather* the elect, and they will have nothing more to do (13:24-27).

The main thrust of Mark 13 is the warning not to believe that the end has come. "*See that no one leads you astray* ... When you hear of wars do not be alarmed: *they must happen but the end is not yet* ... *These things are the beginning of birth-pangs* ... *First* the gospel must be preached to all nations. But you, watch: *I have told you all things in advance*". The question is, What was the position of the false teachers? οὔπω τὸ τέλος: but did they say, "The end is coming any time now", as it is often understood,[20] or "The end is here already"? If it is the former, it is not clear why Mark should rebut it quite so insistently, for he himself thought it was coming in the lifetime of some of Jesus' hearers (9:1; 13:30). If it is the latter, it is the same error which we have seen Paul attacking in 1 Cor 4 and 2 Thess 2; and Mark uses the same three-phase programme as Paul to confound it.

Mark draws on the Thessalonian tradition as he begins: "See that no one lead you astray (μή τις ὑμᾶς πλανήσῃ). Many will come in my name saying, I am he, and will lead many astray ... be not alarmed (μὴ θροεῖσθε)" (13:5ff.). Paul had similarly warned the Thessalonians not to be alarmed (μηδὲ θροεῖσθαι), "Let no man de-

---

[20] Gnilka 1979:2, 188, "Was geschieht, berechtigt nicht zur Auffassung, in den letzten Tagen zu leben"; Hooker 1991, 308, "these disasters are not to be seen as the immediate prelude to the End".

ceive you (μή τις ὑμᾶς ἐξαπατήσῃ) ... a force to lead them astray (ἐνέργειαν πλάνης)" (2 Thess 2:2f., 11). Those coming "in my name" are claiming to be *Christians*; Mark writes elsewhere "Whoever receives one of such children *in my name*", i.e. as a Christian, "no one will be able to do a miracle *in my name*", i.e. claiming to be a Christian, "whoever gives you a cup of water in the name that you are Χριστοῦ", i.e. because you claim to be "of Christ" (9:37-41). It is not easy to think that any Christian could say "I am Messiah", as Matthew interprets it (24:5).[21] It seems better to understand ἐπὶ τῷ ὀνόματί μου to be "those of Christ", referred to in 1 Cor 1:12 and 2 Cor 10:7, since this group did take it upon them to "come in his name". "Saying, I am" will then be the Biblical "I am the one who matters", as in Isa 47:8, 10, where the virgin daughter of Babylon says in her heart, "I am (ἐγώ εἰμι) and there is no one besides me":[22] the Χριστοῦ missionaries of 2 Cor 10f. hit church members across the face, and, in Paul's phrase, enslaved them, so they certainly thought they were the ones who mattered. I follow Baur[23] in thinking that there were substantially two groups in Corinth, the one following Paul and Apollos, the other calling themselves Cephas's group, or Christ's; and if so, this suggests that the deceivers of Mark 13:5f. will be the same as the deceivers of 2 Thess 2, viz. the Petrine missionaries.

The main means which Mark has used to expand the first phase of 2 Thess 2 is the same resource which Paul used, i.e. the Book of Daniel. The disciples' question, "What is the sign when all these things are to be accomplished (ταῦτα συντελεῖσθαι πάντα)?" is an echo of Dan 12:7 LXX, "All these things shall be accomplished (συντελεσθήσεται πάντα ταῦτα)". The insistent "many" comes from Daniel, and so does "it must take place" (δεῖ γενέσθαι, Dan 2:29, 45Θ). The wars and rumours (ἀκοάς) of wars come from Daniel (11:44 ἀκοή/ἀκοαὶ), and so does "nation shall rise against nation and kingdom against kingdom" (ἀναστήσεται βασιλεία ..., Dan 2:39, cf. Isa 19:2). The theme of the faithfulness of the saints and martyrs under persecution comes from Daniel also: "he who endures (ὁ ὑπομείνας) to the end will be saved" (13:13) is related to Dan.12:12Θ, "Blessed is he who endures (ὁ ὑπομένων) and comes to the 1335 days".

---

[21] So also do most modern commentators: Gnilka 1979:2, 186f.; Lührmann 1987, 219; Hooker 1991, 306ff.; Gundry 1993, 737. Hooker suggests that the many led astray in 13:6 differ from the Christians warned against being led astray in 13:5, rather a desperate expedient. But Luke knows better: "See that you are not led astray; *for* many will come in my name saying, I am he, and the time has drawn near" (21:8)—they are arrogant Christians encouraging false expectations of the Parousia. By Luke's time the realised eschatology had faded.

[22] Hartman 1966, 160 says that the echo of Isa 47 carries the overtone of blasphemy; but it is a very vague overtone—the virgin daughter of Babylon did not think that she was God. Rather it is the height of arrogance.

[23] Baur 1831, esp. 116-136.

The persecutions are probably seen against the background of the heroes of Dan 1-6 also: Mark has merely filled out the Daniel scheme which underlies the Thessalonian letters. But the detail that he has used to fill it out is principally from the persecutions endured by Paul. It is he who was handed over to the Sanhedrin (Acts 23), and stood before governors and kings (Felix, Festus, Herod Agrippa II, Acts 24-26, like Daniel and the Three Children before Nebuchadnezzar and Darius); he is the only apostle so to be tried in Acts, and Luke says that at his call he was told he would bear Jesus' name before Gentiles and kings (Acts 9:15; cf. 26:30: "the king and the governor arose"). Mark says that the defence speeches will be "for a testimony to them" (εἰς μαρτύριον αὐτοῖς), and that is exactly how Luke portrays Paul's speeches, especially that in Acts 26, where Agrippa is nearly converted. Paul was beaten five times in synagogues (2 Cor 11:24); and if the gospel had first to be preached to all the nations, it was Paul to whom this mission was entrusted. Paul is one of many early Christians who are filled with the Spirit in the hour of need (Acts 4:8; 5:32; 6:10,15; 13:9). So it seems evident that early Church experience, but especially Paul's endurance of persecution, is in Mark's mind.

Beyond this we may venture some speculations. So many Pauline references raise the reminiscence of *1 Clem.* 5:5ff.: "Through jealousy and strife Paul displayed the prize of endurance (ὑπομονῆς) ... when he had borne his testimony before the rulers, he departed from the world". Clement seems to know a tradition that Paul's death was brought about by the jealousy and quarrelling of fellow-Christians; and this may account for Mark's "Brother shall deliver up brother to death". This is not part of Mic 7:6, some words of which have been appended to it. Hengel suggests plausibly that "you will be hated by all for my name" fits well with the charge of *odium humani generis* levelled at Roman Christians during the Neronic persecution of 64; and that the wars and rumours of war belong well with the military chaos of 68-69.[24] But it is hard to be confident when everything is cloaked in LXX rhetoric, and some points like the earthquakes[25] and famines seem to be nothing more than standard *topoi* (Isa 13:13; Ezek 4, etc.). All we can say with assurance is that the expansions of Phase 1 are principally from Daniel, especially Dan 11-12, and the life of Paul.

Mark moves on to Phase 2 with the call to flee at 13:14. The Pauline "man of lawlessness" in the temple had been based on Antiochus and his abomination of desolation in the temple of Dan 11:31, 36: Mark uses the Danielic expression, "the abomination of desolation", and says that *he* (in the masculine) will be seen stand-

---

[24] Hengel 1985, 21-28. On "Brother shall deliver up brother", Hengel comments, "It is certainly not limited to denunciation and betrayal among blood relations": he himself associates it with Tacitus' report of Christians informing on one another under torture in 64.

[25] Cf. Hartman 1966, 71-77.

ing (ἑστηκότα) where he ought not. The location is not specified, but those *in Judaea* are to flee to the mountains. It is clear that Mark is following the Pauline lead in foreseeing a *man* of iniquity in the Temple[26], no doubt drawing on fears of the mad Nero[27] as well as the mad Caligula. The recommended flight to the mountains follows the pattern of the destruction of Sodom and Gomorrah in Gen 19 (cf. Luke 17:31f.). With his coming Paul had associated a time of apostasy, as he tried to supplant God and his Law. Mark says, "For those days shall be a tribulation such as has not been since the beginning of creation" (13:19); he is interpreting Paul from Dan 12:1, "And there shall be a time of tribulation, tribulation as has not been since there has been a nation on the earth". God's shortening of the days (Mark 13:20) is similarly based on Daniel's reduction of the final week of the world to a time, two times and half a time, 1290 days (Dan 12:11).[28]

It is an error to assimilate the false Christs and false prophets of 13:21f. with the "many" teachers of error of 13:5f. They belong securely in Phase 2, they are not "many", and they perform signs and wonders. In this respect they once more agree with Phase 2 in 2 Thess 2, where the coming of the man of iniquity is "by the activity of Satan with all power and with pretended *signs and wonders*" (2:10, following Deut 13:1f.). The ψευδόχριστοι are not harmless humans like Theudas and John of Gischala (whom Josephus does not call Messiahs). They are demonic extensions of the Antichrist. John writes, "Children, it is the last hour, and as you have heard that Antichrist is coming, so now many antichrists have come to be" (1 John 2:18). To John Antichrist is a spiritual evil power, abroad in many antichrists. To Paul he is the single evil human, the man of iniquity. Mark is close to John.[29]

With Mark's Phase 3 is seen "the Son of Man coming on clouds" (13:26): Paul foresaw the living Christians as rapt with their dead brothers *on clouds* to meet the Lord in the air (1 Thess 4:17). Both texts depend on Dan 7:13, "lo, with the clouds of heaven one like a son of man was coming". In Daniel the one like a son of man

---

[26] Dan 11:31 says, "They will give the abomination of desolation", and the Heb. continues, "He shall seduce with flattery those who violate the covenant" (Gk. "They"). Paul has interpreted the abomination as a throne where the man of iniquity will *sit*; Mark as the man himself, who will *stand*.

[27] Tacitus, *Histories*, 2.8.1f.: Hengel 1985, 26, 135f.

[28] The shortening has been a puzzle to critics. Gnilka 1979:2, 197f., properly refuses reference to Isa 54:7. "For a brief moment I forsook you ...", and says that God "hat im vorhinein (Präteritum!) beschlossen, die Tage abzukürzen"; and Hooker 1991, 316, says that there "is not any alteration in the divine plan": but the point is, where did Mark take the shortening idea from? Hartman 1966, 163f., made a brave attempt with a revocalisation of Dan 12:1, but the half-week scheme seems to me much more convincing.

[29] The same distinction is observed in the Apocalypse. There are Christian teachers of error, Nicolaitans, Jezebels, etc., in Phase 1; the Beast (the Emperor, and so pseudo-Christ) and the false prophet, with multiple demonic spirits, perform signs which deceive the kings of the world in Phase 2 (16:13f.)—see below.

represents the faithful Jews and is being borne on the clouds *up* to God,[30] as Paul has seen; Mark knows that the Lord Jesus is coming *down* from God, and interprets the clouds accordingly.[31] *The Son of Man* is also an interpretation of Dan 7:13: the title was unknown to Paul, but became a christological counter after his death (from Ps 8:4; cf. Heb 2:5-9). He will come "with great power and glory, and will send his angels and gather (ἐπισυνάξει) the elect" (13:26f.): this recalls the general picture of 1 Thess 4:16, and the particular words of 2 Thess 1:7, "the revealing of our Lord Jesus from heaven with *angels* of his *power*", and 2 Thess 2:1, "our ἐπισυναγωγή to him". The angels, and the dominion and glory are already there in Dan 7:10, 14; and further apocalyptic colour is added with the signs in heaven from Isa 13:10; Joel 2:31, and other texts. But essentially Mark is following the three Pauline phases, drawing on the language of the Thessalonian letters and of the texts of Daniel underlying them. As in 1 Thess there is no mention of the destruction of the man of sin (as opposed to 2 Thess); Mark's chapter is an address to the disciples warning them of what *they* have to expect, and for that the destruction of the Abomination is irrelevant. For the same reason Mark does not mention the resurrection of the dead Christians: the concentration, as in 2 Thess 2:1, is on the παρουσία and the ἐπισυναγωγή.

Paul's description of the ἐπισυναγωγή in 1 Thess 4 continued into an exhortation in 5:1-11; its theme was the need to keep awake (γρηγορῶμεν) and not sleep (μὴ καθεύδωμεν), in face of the Day of the Lord coming like a thief in the night. Mark is writing two decades after Paul, and the time perspective has changed a little. He therefore first stresses its *inexorable* development, on the lines of the three phases which he has now expounded; their development is like the inexorable growth of the leaves on the fig-tree, leading on to summer. This little parable is dependent on the setting out of the phases, which are the signs of the approaching Parousia; and must therefore be the creation of the Marcan church, which has provided the detail of the phasing. Secondly he reassures his church that all will be over before Jesus' own generation was dead, i.e. by, say, 85; just as he did at 9:1, "There are some of those standing by ..." A third reassurance follows, that Jesus' words are infallible, though conveniently even he had not been entrusted by God with the exact timing; a piece of manipulation remarked on by Graham Shaw.[32]

The waking/sleeping image remains potent, and Mark develops it. It is not too

---

[30] On this complex question see Casey 1980.

[31] Mark is following the "plot" of the Book of Daniel. He has had the wars, persecutions, etc. of Phase 1 (Dan 1-10), and the tribulation under the abomination of Phase 2 (Dan 11-12:1). He has now reached the resurrection of Dan 12:2f.: Jesus, the son of man who ascended to God in Dan 7, now descends with the dominion, glory and kingship that was given him in Dan 7:14.

[32] Shaw 1983, 196f.

suitable to compare the Lord's coming to that of a thief, so this is suppressed, and the basic, primitive *Marana tha* is exploited instead. *The Lord* of the house *is coming* after an absence away (ἀπόδημος), and the one to *watch* and *not sleep* will therefore be the gatekeeper. The disciples are even so to watch (γρηγορεῖτε)—indeed all Christians are to do so. Paul had warned that the Day of the Lord would come *suddenly* (αἰφνίδιος), so Mark echoes this, "lest he come *suddenly* (ἐξαίφνης) and find you sleeping", and he details the four watches of the night for emphasis. So Mark has followed his Pauline mentor to the end. The three phases are taken from 2 Thess, amplified principally from the Daniel prophecies on which 2 Thess was based; the coming of the Son of Man and the parenesis following are drawn from 1 Thess 4f. The language of Mark 13, as studied by Jan Lambrecht,[33] is predominantly Marcan. The whole thing is the product of the Pauline mission, without remainder.[34]

## 3. The Apocalypse

The same basic scheme underlies the Apocalypse; but whereas Mark was written before 70 (or he would not speak of the abomination as a man), the Seer lived a decade and more later, and he has to extend the "beginning of birth-pangs" to fill in the vacuum. The Beast of 17:3-13 has seven heads: five of them have fallen, one is, the other is not yet come. Since there were three emperors in 68-69, Galba, Otho and Vitellius, who reigned only until another army came and deposed them, we may opt to think that the Seer either does not know about them precisely, or prefers not to count them, in the way that Lady Jane Grey is not counted as queen of England, nor Ahaziah, Joash, Amaziah and Jehoiakim by St Matthew as kings of Judah. The seven emperors will then be Augustus, Tiberius, Caligula, Claudius, Nero, Vespasian and Titus. Titus reigned from 79 to 81, and it is said of the seventh head, "when he comes, he must stay a short while". There is however a "mystery", the beast who was and is not, and is to come up from the Abyss; and of him it is said that he is an eighth and is of the seven, and he can only be Nero (cf. 13:1-4). Dio tells us that Nero was believed to be alive still in the reign of Titus,[35] and the same belief is re-

---

[33] Lambrecht 1967 works with the hypothesis that Mark was editing a version of Mark 13 which is also known to us from Q, the hypothetical source purportedly used by Matthew and Luke. While thinking this theory to be mistaken, I find much of the book impressive, including the linguistic work, which I cannot reproduce here.

[34] I am sorry to be so totally at variance with Robert Gundry 1993, 733-800, who maintains an almost complete dominical tradition behind the Discourse. Other commentators, including Hartman, find at least some words of Jesus underlying it; but the derivation from Paul's reaction to a Jerusalem realised eschatology must exclude that.

[35] 66.19.3.

peatedly testified by the Sibylline Oracles.[36] The same rumour was about earlier and later, but the most widespread evidence associates it with Titus' reign; so we may date the Apocalypse provisionally at around AD 80.

Now there were wicked servants about who said, "My Lord delays", and bridesmaids who slumbered while their Lord delayed, and it is partly to rebuke and to awaken them that the Seer writes (1-3; 22:17). So the opening phase, present history, is extended from one to two heptads, with the Seven Seals continuing into the Seven Trumpets. The second phase is the war waged by the Dragon with the Woman's seed through the Beast and the Second Beast; just as Christians are to *flee* to the mountains in Mark 13:14ff., and there is woe for the *pregnant*, so the Church is seen as like *a pregnant woman about to be delivered*, who flees to the wilderness. Phase 3 in Mark comprised the shaking of the powers in heaven and the coming of the Son of Man: in Rev 15-18 come the Seven Bowls of God's wrath and the judgement of the Great Whore, followed by the coming of the Rider on the White Horse, the Millennium and the New Jerusalem.

The Seer makes his basic divisions plain with impressive scenes in heaven which initiate the trials on earth. Before the Seals we have two chapters in which there is a vision of God's Throne and of the Lamb (4-5); and the Seals themselves are then a coloured version of the preliminary troubles of Mark 13:5-13. There are horsemen bearing bow, sword, scales and death, followed by the martyrs under the altar and an earthquake (Rev 6): the equivalent of the Marcan wars and rumours of war, famines, earthquakes and persecutions of the saints.[37] But the seventh Seal is nothing but the giving of the seven Trumpets to their angels, and the interval between the two series in heaven is but a silence of half an hour (8:1f.). In this way Phase 1 can be subtly extended: the two Sevens are separated by only a brief interval, and the seventh Seal comprises the seven Trumpets, all but their blowing.

Now the 70s were a decade of natural disasters and portents: Pliny the elder records the passing of a great comet in 73,[38] and this is noted also in *Sib. Or.* 5:155-161. The Sibyllines mention a variety of catastrophes: Nero's flight over the Euphrates (as was thought, 68), Titus' burning of Jerusalem (70), earthquakes and tidal waves in Cyprus, the drying of the Maeander and attendant famine, the eruption of Vesuvius (4:119-130, 138-160). Suetonius says that Titus' reign was marked

---

[36] *Sib. Or.* 4:117-139; 5:28-34, 93-110, 137-154, 214-227, 361-385; cf. also *Barn.* 4:4-6; 16:1-5; *Mart. Isa.* 4:1-18. See Reicke 1972. These texts represent Nero as being still alive, and among the Parthians. Tacitus *Hist.* 2:8ff. speaks of him as dead and come to life again in popular rumour, cf. Suetonius, *Nero* 57:2; Dio, loc. cit.; Dio Chrysostom, *Or.* 21:10.

[37] So Sweet 1979, 20: "'the beginning of birth-pangs' ... appear in Revelation under the guise of the Four Horsemen". Sweet gives a similar, but not identical description of the development of the Synoptic apocalypses in Revelation, "John's apocalypse as an updating of his Lord's" (19).

[38] *Nat. Hist.* 2:25.

by much disaster, in particular the eruption of Vesuvius in 79, a fire in Rome and widespread plague; people felt that these events were a sign of the anger of the gods.[39] The Sibyllines are filled with the anger of God;[40] and it is easy to understand that a superstitious age without science, suddenly stricken with the terrifying experience of Vesuvius on top of so much else, should think in eschatological terms.

Now there are four lesser Trumpets, and the fifth and sixth are the two first Woes; the seventh Trumpet is delayed till the end of chap. 11. The first Trumpet is of hail and fire mixed with blood; with the second a great mountain, burning with fire, is thrown into the sea, which sounds like Vesuvius. With the third a great star falls from heaven, poisoning the waters, which sounds like the comet, and the plague. With the fourth a third of the heavenly bodies is darkened. The fifth Trumpet, the first Woe, brings smoke from the bottomless pit darkening the sky, and men are tormented by the stinging locusts: this sounds like the darkening of the sky over Pompeii, and the descent of hot pumice on the inhabitants, interpreted through the imagery of Joel 2.[41] With the sixth Trumpet, the second Woe, the angels on the Euphrates release the Parthian army, two myriad myriads of horsemen; and this is exactly what Nero is expected to lead against the Roman east in the Sibylline texts. So the Trumpets are nothing but the disasters of the 70s, real or expected. The Apocalypse is written about AD 80, when Titus' death began to be expected;[42] the Seer has merely shared in the widespread fear and superstition of the decade, and painted in his Phase 1 (b) in the colours of Amos, Joel and the Exodus.

In Mark's Phase 1 the wars and famines (13:5-8) were kept separate from the persecutions (13:9-13); and the Seer does the same in his Phase 1, with the vision of the persecuted Church in 11:1-13 following the tribulations of 6; 8-9. Already in

---

[39] *Vit. Caes., Divus Titus*, 8:3.

[40] "Be sure that God is no more of tender mercy, but gnashing his teeth in wrath, and destroying at once the whole race of mortals by means of a mighty conflagration" (4:159f.), and *passim*.

[41] Cf. *Sib. Or.* 4:130-139: "But when a firebrand, starting from a deep cavern in the land of Italy, shall reach the broad heaven and burn many a city and consume its men, and clouds of sooty ashes beset the great heaven, and grains fall from the sky like red earth; then recognize the wrath of the God of heaven, because they shall destroy the guiltless race of godly men. And to the west shall come the strife of gathering war, and the exile from Rome, brandishing a mighty sword, crossing the Euphrates with many myriads". It is the same complex of events as Rev 8-9: the smoke from the abyss, the darkening of the luminaries, the descent of hot ashes, the Parthian armies crossing the Euphrates with Nero.

[42] The Seer expected Titus to be succeeded by Nero *redivivus* (17:11, "As for the beast that was and is not, it is an eighth"). 17:10, "Five have fallen, one is, the other has not yet come, and when he comes he must remain only a little while", shifts the time of the prophecy back, and so gains credibility. It is likely that the Apocalypse was in any case re-edited year after year, so perhaps the original version was composed under Vespasian, and in time Domitian was taken to be Nero come to life: but the number of the Second Beast in 13:18 is that of Titus—see below.

7 we have seen a development in the Seer's vision of the Church. It is composed of two wings: first 144 000 "out of every tribe of the *sons of Israel*", which are then named, and sealed to protect them from the coming troubles; and then "a great multitude which no one could number, from *every nation and tribes and peoples and tongues*", which suffer in the tribulation (7:14).[43] There were two missions in the Church, one to the circumcision and one to the Gentiles (Gal 2:8), and the Seer accepts and admires them both.

At first the Jewish church in Palestine escaped persecution (*were sealed*); the first martyrs were Paulines, like Stephen and Paul himself, and the apostles remained in Jerusalem unharmed. But now in 11:1-13 both wings are called on to give their witness. The temple (that is, the Church) is measured (that is, placed under divine providence); but the court without (that is, Jerusalem) is to be given to the nations (that is, the Romans, following a succession of devastating Zealots), and they shall tread the holy city under foot for 42 months (that is, during the siege and fall of Jerusalem, 68-70, grossed up to the Danielic half a week of years). In the meantime two witnesses will prophesy, which are the two olive-trees (the original Jewish olive tree and the grafted Gentile olive tree) and two lampstands (the original Jewish Menorah and the seven-candled Gentile church, as in Asia). One is like Elijah, who was sent to a Gentile (Luke 4:25), with fire at his word to destroy his enemies (2 Kgs 1:10ff.), and power to hold back the rain (1 Kgs 17:1); the other is like Moses, who was sent to the Jews, with power to turn the waters to blood (Exod 7:19) and to smite the earth with every plague (Exod 7-10). When they have finished their testimony, the beast from the Abyss (that is Titus, cf.13:11) shall kill them; and their bodies shall lie in the great city where their Lord was crucified (that is, Jerusalem). No doubt many faithful Christians perished in the catastrophe of 70, Hellenist and Hebrew Christians alike. Perhaps the Seer's picture of their martyrdom is rather idealised, but the detail given makes it clear that it is the massacre in Jerusalem that he is describing, seen from a Christian perspective.

The key to understanding an apocalypse is knowing the point in history where the writer stands. Mark stands at 13:13: he knows about (some of) the trials of the 60s, he does not know about 70 and thinks the Abomination will be a man standing in the Temple. The Seer knows about the Christian martyrs in Jerusalem in 70, and the comet in 73 and Vesuvius in 79 and the expected return of Nero in 80 and the

---

[43] It is common to see the 144 000 and the great multitude in chap. 7 as the same, the universal Church as the ideal numbered Israel. But the same number on Mt Zion, followed by the same *every nation*, etc. in chap. 14 are clearly two communities—the second is evangelized by *another angel*, and it is only the Jewish wing of early Christendom which was ascetic and *did not defile itself with women, for they were virgins* (14:4). chap. 14 requires two missions, and the same is then implied for chap. 7. All interpretations which deny the sexual at 14:4 are forced.

short reign of Titus in 79-81. He thinks that after this Phase 2 will begin, from 11:15, when loud voices in heaven say, "The kingdom of the world has become the kingdom of our Lord and of his Christ".

The Great Tribulation of Phase 2 is conducted in Rev 13 by the Beast from the Sea, who is Nero *redivivus* (13:1-10), and by the "other Beast" from the earth, who exercises all the authority of the first Beast in his presence (13:11-18): this must be the current Emperor—on the grounds that I have urged, Titus.[44] In 13:17f. we hear that this Beast has a number of its name, and it may be suitable to end this essay with a new suggestion for that old riddle.

The text says, "This calls for wisdom; let him who has understanding reckon the number of the Beast"; so it is not likely that we shall solve the riddle by simply adding together the value of the letters—there is some complication which requires σοφία, cleverness. John writes Greek, so the fundamental "reckoning" is probably in Greek, Milesian numbers: and *Sib. Or.* 5:36-40 codes the Emperors according to their initial letters on this basis Vespasian (Οὐεσπασίανος) as 70 (o), Titus as 300 (τ), Domitian as 4 (δ). If we are content simply to add the values of the letters, we find the total for Titus surprisingly near the target. The two τ's make 600, plus 10 for ι makes 610, plus 70 for o makes 680, plus 6 for terminal ς makes 686. This is sufficiently close to make us suspect that we are there if only we can summon a little σοφία; no other Emperor comes anywhere near in the running for 666. Now Titus was a Roman Emperor, and in Latin inscriptions his name stands as TIT; and this must remind anyone who assimilates names and numbers of the Roman XIX, 19— for in Roman counting the prefixed capital I is subtracted from the following digit. On this principle, since Greek ι is 10, TIT = 600-10, 590. Now o has, as we have seen, the value of 70; and terminal sigma, ς, is used for 6; so 590 + 70 + 6 = 666. It does not really call for wisdom, only a little ingenuity.

Lars Hartman picked out almost all the elements of this jigsaw puzzle in 1966, above all the fundamental position of the Daniel prophecies behind Mark, Matthew, Thessalonians and the Apocalypse alike. It was natural at the time to see the single creative mind at work as being that of Jesus. Today's stress on the development of doctrine as a dialectical process out of the work of two competing missions seems to make that less plausible. The Jerusalem mission thought the kingdom had come already, and so probably did Jesus. It was Paul who called in Daniel to mark out the phases of the future; and the Paulines, Mark, Matthew, Luke and the Seer, who developed the Danielic core to plug the increasing gap as the decades passed.

---

[44] Sweet 1979, 214 identifies the second Beast with the false prophet, comparing 16:13 and 19:20. But this is not implied in 13:11-18; and by 19:20 Titus, who had but a short time, was dead. The "great signs, even making fire come down from heaven" (13:13) are unclear, but could be a further reference to the explosion of Vesuvius.

## Bibliography

Barrett, C. K. 1971: *A Commentary on the First Epistle to the Corinthians* (BNTC), London: Black [2]1971.

Baur, F. C. 1831: "Die Christuspartei in der korinthischen Gemeinde, der Gegensatz des petrinischen und paulinischen Christentums in der Ältesten Kirche, der Apostel Petrus in Rom", *TZTh* 3 (1831) 61-206.

Best, E. 1972: *A Commentary on the First and Second Epistles to the Thessalonians* (BNTC), London: Black 1972.

Casey, P. M. 1980: *Son of Man. The interpretation and influence of Daniel*, London: SPCK 1980.

Collins, R. F. (ed.) 1990: *The Thessalonian Correspondence* (BEThL 87), Leuven: Leuven University – Peeters 1990.

Conzelmann, H. 1975: *1 Corinthians* (Hermeneia), Philadelphia, PA: Fortress Press 1975 [= 1st German edn. 1969].

Delobel, J. 1990: "The Fate of the Dead according to 1 Thessalonians 4 and 1 Corinthians 15", in: Collins (ed.) 1990, 340-47.

Fee, G. D. 1987: *The First Epistle to the Corinthians* (NIC), Grand Rapids, MI: Eerdmans 1987.

Gnilka, J. 1979: *Das Evangelium nach Markus* (EKK 2/1-2), Zürich: Benziger/Neukirchen-Vluyn: Neukirchener Verlag 1979.

Goulder, M. D. 1991: "Σοφία in 1 Corinthians", in: *NTS* 37 (1991) 516-534.

— 1992: "Silas in Thessalonica", *JSNT* 48 (1992) 87-106.

Gundry, R. H. 1993: *Mark*, Grand Rapids: MI: Eerdmans 1993.

Hartman, L. 1966: *Prophecy interpreted: The Formation of some Jewish apocalyptic texts and of the eschatological Discourse Mark 13 par.* (CB.NT 1), Lund: Gleerup 1966.

Hengel, M. 1985: *Studies in the Gospel of Mark*, London: SCM Press 1985 [= "Entstehungszeit und Situation des Markusevangeliums", in: H. Cancik (ed.), *Markus-philologie* (WUNT 33), Tübingen: Mohr (Siebeck) 1984, 1-45].

Holtz, T. 1986: *Der erste Brief an die Thessalonicher* (EKK 13), Zürich: Benziger/Neukirchen-Vluyn: Neukirchener Verlag 1986.

Hooker, M. D. 1991: *The Gospel according to St Mark* (BNTC), London: Black 1991.

Klijn, A. F. J. 1982: "1 Thessalonians 4.13-18 and its Background in Apocalyptic Literature", in: M. D. Hooker and S. G. Wilson (eds.), *Paul and Paulinism. FS C. K. Barrett*, London: SPCK 1982, 67-73.

Lambrecht, J. 1967: *Die Redaktion der Markus-Apokalypse* (AnBib 28), Rome: Pontificium Institutum Biblicum 1967.

Laub, F. 1988: *1. und 2. Thessalonicherbrief*, Würzburg: Echter [2]1988.

Lührmann, D. 1987: *Das Markusevangelium* (HNT 3), Tübingen: Mohr (Siebeck) 1987.

Marshall, I. H. 1983: *1 and 2 Thessalonians*, Grand Rapids, MI: Eerdmans 1983.

Marxsen, W. 1982: *Der zweite Thessalonicherbrief* (ZBK 11/2), Zürich: Theologischer Verlag 1982.

Reicke, B. 1972: "Die jüdische Apokalyptik und die johanneische Tiervision", in: *RSR* 60 (1972) 173-192.

Sellin, G. 1987: *Der Streit um die Auferstehung der Toten. Eine religionsgeschichtliche und exegetische Untersuchung von 1. Kor. 15* (FRLANT 138), Göttingen: Vandenhoeck & Ruprecht 1987.

Shaw, G. 1983: *The Cost of Authority*, London: SCM Press 1983.

Sweet, J. P. M. 1979: *Revelation*, London: SCM Press 1979.

Trilling, W. 1980: *Der zweite Brief an die Thessalonicher* (EKK 14), Zürich: Benziger/Neukirchen-Vluyn: Neukirchener Verlag 1980.

# Die Bedeutung des Markusevangeliums für die Entstehung der christlichen Bibel

Petr Pokorný

## 1. Markus als Gründer einer neuen literarischen (Unter)Gattung

Der großen Flut der neueren Studien über das Markusevangelium, die meistens die Zweiquellentheorie vertreten, läßt sich fast als ein Konsensus die Überzeugung entnehmen, wonach diese Schrift eine Wende im Leben der christlichen Kirche markiert und für die Entwicklung der späteren Orthodoxie mit ihrer kanonisierten Sammlung der Schriften (dem Neuen Testament) die Weichen stellt. Das hängt damit zusammen, daß das Markusevangelium als Quelle von Matthäus und Lukas die erste Schrift dieser Art (oder sogar dieser [Unter]Gattung) ist und daß in ihm die spätere theologische Entwicklung vorgeprägt ist. Diese These könnte nur der mögliche Nachweis der Unabhängigkeit des Johannesevangeliums von Markus relativieren, denn die ganze gemeinsame Struktur der Evangelien, ihre *pattern*, müßte dann schon vor Markus vorhanden sein. Diejenigen, die das, wohl sehr behutsam, behaupten[1], haben jedoch eine positive Antwort auf die Frage nach dem Ursprung der gemeinsamen Struktur der kanonischen Evangelien bisher nicht gegeben. Die einzige Lösung hat C. H. Dodd mit seiner Annahme des Urmodells des Evangeliums in Apg 10,36. 38-43 angeboten[2]. Da jedoch die Apostelgeschichte vom Autor des Lukasevangeliums stammt und die Kenntnis des Markusevangeliums voraussetzt, hat diese Hypothese keinen großen Widerhall gefunden[3] und die Stimmen, welche die (mindestens vermittelte) Abhängigkeit des Johannes-evangeliums vom Markusevangelium voraussetzen, sind sehr ernst zu nehmen[4]. Markus hat also eine literarische Untergattung gegründet, die für den christlichen Kanon eine grundlegende Bedeutung gewonnen hat.

---

[1] Schnackenburg 1965, 16; Brown 1985, XLVII.
[2] Dodd 1931-32.
[3] Einwände hat schon Nineham 1955, 228f. erhoben.
[4] Neirynck 1977; Barrett 1990, 33.

## 2. Die durch spätere Tradition beeinflußte Deutung seiner Leistung

Im Rahmen dieses allgemeinen Konsensus sind jedoch recht unterschiedliche Vorstellungen über die Entstehung des Markusevangeliums, über seine Theologie und ihre Bedeutung zu finden. Es gibt zum Beispiel zwei Sammelbände aus Tübingen (P. Stuhlmacher [Hg.], *Das Evangelium und die Evangelien* [1983], und H. Cancik [Hg.] *Markus-Philologie* [1984]), welche die Rolle von Markus sehr positiv einschätzen: Die ziemlich gut erhaltenen Traditionen[5] habe er logisch in ein größeres literarisches Ganzes verbunden, wobei der Begriff εὐαγγέλιον, der zur Interpretation jener Traditionen dient, nachösterlich, aber vorpaulinisch ist[6].

Die letzte Behauptung ist einleuchtend, aber im Ganzen handelt es sich um ein Bild, das zwar einige Züge des Markusevangeliums trefflich wiedergibt, aber seine Funktion im Rahmen des Urchristentums nicht ausdrücken kann. Wie reimt sich die Einrahmung der Worte Jesu in sein Leben, der wir im Markusevangelium begegnen, zu der Anwendung der Worte des Herrn (ursprünglich offensichtlich der Worte des irdischen Jesus) bei Paulus? Paulus hält sie nämlich für Sprüche, die der erhöhte κύριος in der je konkreten Situation als seine entscheidende Richtlinie proklamiert (1Thess 4,15f.; 1Kor 7,10; 9,14) oder die er als Aussagen der Vergangenheit für die Gegenwart authentisiert (1Kor 11,23ff.). Das Thomasevangelium, wo die Sprüche im Prolog als Worte des lebendigen Jesus eingeleitet sind, wurde in den gnostisierenden Endredaktion auch als eine Sammlung aktueller autoritativer Aussage aufgefaßt und James M. Robinson hat schon im Jahre 1971 auch die Spruchquelle der Synoptiker (Q) als eine Sammlung gesehen, die eine solche Auffassung der direkten aktuellen Geltung der Worte Jesu voraussetzt[7], wobei wir jetzt die heftig diskutierte Frage, nämlich, ob die Q eine weisheitliche[8] oder eher eine prophetische[9] Sammlung war, außer Acht lassen können: in jedem Fall war die Autorität solcher Sprüche von ihrer gegenwärtigen Bestätigung durch den auferstandenen Herrn abhängig, während im Markusevangelium die Worte Jesu (auch dort fast ein Drittel des Textes) durch ihre Zugehörigkeit zur irdischen Geschichte des Sohnes Gottes legitimiert werden. Die von Robinson skizzierte alternative Gestaltung christlicher Tradition und von ihr abhängigen Literatur läßt sich kaum als ein nur von den Gnostikern hochgespielter Nebenstrom relativieren, wenn es auch gerade in gnostischem Milieu literarisch weitergelebt hat und in den Dialogen mit den Auferstandenen von Apokryphon des Johannes (BG, NH II/1; III/1; IV/1) bis zur Pistis

---

[5] Lampe – Luz 1983, 430f.

[6] Hengel 1983, 257ff.

[7] Robinson 1971.

[8] Kloppenborg 1987, 238ff.

[9] Sato 1988, 371ff.; s. auch das Gespräch zwischen Robinson 1993 und Sato 1993.

Sophia eine verwandte Untergattung fand. Walter Bauer hat schon vor sechzig Jahren daran aufmerksam gemacht, daß die später kanonisierten Texte mit den früher, in den wirklichen Anfängen geschätzten Traditionen nicht immer identisch sind[10]. Und J. M. Robinson hat m.E. überzeugend nachgewiesen, daß sich die alternative Tradition, welche die Gnosis weiter getragen hat, theologisch mit dem Auferstehungskerygma und der Tradition über die Offenbarungen des Auferstandenen vertragen kann[11].

Die harmonisierende Deutung hat also ihre Schwächen. Aus dem Gesagten geht schon hervor, daß die Entstehung des Markusevangeliums keinesfalls als eine logische Folge der inneren Tendenzen christlicher Tradition zu deuten ist. Seine Entstehung ist mit einer neuen theologischen Entscheidung verbunden, es ist wirklich ein Meilenstein in der Entwicklung sowohl der christlichen Literatur als auch der Theologie überhaupt.

### 3. Die kritische Beurteilung der Rolle des Markusevangeliums als einer grundsätzlichen Umdeutung der Jesus-Traditionen

Auf der anderen Seite gibt es den schon erwähnten anderen Strom, den ich am Beispiel des Buches von B. L. Mack über Markus und die Anfänge des Christentums charakterisieren kann[12], wonach Markus, der mit seiner Schrift einen wesentlichen Beitrag zur Entstehung des Christentums leistete, gleichzeitig das Bild des historischen Jesus und die authentische Jesustradition umgedeutet und verzerrt hat. Mit dieser These müssen wir uns besonders aufmerksam auseinandersetzen. Sie bietet nämlich ein alternatives Bild von Markus und seiner Rolle in den Anfängen des Christentums, das, wie wir sehen werden, unhaltbar ist, aber trotzdem neue Einzelbeobachtungen bringt und zu einem mehr differenzierten Bild des Markusevangeliums im Rahmen der urchristlichen Theologiegeschichte inspiriert. Dieser Auseinandersetzung mit Mack und dem Versuch, die Rolle des Markusevangeliums in mehr umfassenden Zusammenhängen zu definieren, soll dieser Beitrag dienen.

Nach B. L. Mack hat Markus zwar die älteren Traditionen sorgfältig aufbewahrt, aber gleichzeitig in ein radikal neues Ganzes gesetzt. Unter dem Einfluß von Paulus, einem genialen und autoritären neurotischen Visionär, der das Bild von Christus als den für die Sünden der Menschheit geopferten Unschuldigen und seiner Auferstehung entwarf[13], habe Markus sein Buch von Jesus in einer praktisch von ihm

---

[10] Bauer 1934, 231ff.
[11] Robinson 1982.
[12] Mack 1988.
[13] Mack 1988, 98ff., 319f., 323 u.a.

selbst aus kleineren Stücken zusammengestellten Passionsgeschichte gipfeln lassen
und dadurch dem paulinischen Gründungsmythus des Christentums angepaßt[14].
Soweit Mack.

Seine radikale These ist jedoch mit einigen Beobachtungen verbunden, welche
den werdenden Konsensus in einigen Teilbereichen der Forschung widerspiegeln.
Zusammen mit V. K. Robbins hat er sich an der Untersuchung der rhetorischen Formen beteiligt, welche im Neuen Testament, besonders in der synoptischen Tradition
benutzt sind. Es hat sich gezeigt, daß mehrere synoptische Geschichten Jesu, die in
einem Spruch gipfeln (*pronouncement stories*, früher von der Formgeschichtlichen
Schule *Paradigmata* oder *Apophthegmata* genannt), nach den Regeln der griechischen *chreia* überliefert, interpretiert und transformiert sind, was auch einen be-
trächtlichen Teil der Reich-Gottes-Verkündigung Jesu verbunden betrifft[15]. Zusammen mit den Untersuchungen, welche die Authentizität der apokalyptischen Men-
schensohn-Worte Jesu in Frage gestellt haben[16], hat dies die Schlußfolgerung unterstützt, wonach die Verkündigung Jesu nicht ausgesprochen apokalyptisch einge-
stellt war, wie man es unter dem andauerndem Einfluß von Albert Schweitzer behauptet hat.

Wenig überzeugend sind jedoch einige Folgerungen, welche Mack daraus gezogen hat, wie z.B. die These, wonach die apokalyptischen Züge der Verkündigung
Jesu, die man unter dem Einfluß der nachösterlichen apokalyptischen Stimmung
hervorgehoben hat, zum Bild des irdischen Jesus überhaupt nicht gehören. Dies behauptet nicht nur Mack, sondern auch andere amerikanische Forscher, wie z.B.
Marcus J. Borg[17]. Das Werk unseres Jubilars hat die tiefen Wurzeln des urchristlichen eschatologischen Denkens gezeigt[18]. Nach Mack ist dagegen erst Markus der
Vater des apokalyptischen Jesusbildes, das er in das Leben Jesu aus der nachösterlichen Naherwartung eingetragen hat. Markus habe das authentische Bild Jesu un-
terdrückt – das Bild eines Wanderlehrers etwa kynischer Art, dessen Reich-Gottes-
Lehre ein ideales Modell alternativer zwischenmenschlicher Beziehungen war.

In Auseinandersetzung mit dieser Auffassung müssen wir eine unterschiedliche
Darstellung der Rolle des Markusevangeliums in der Geschichte der christlichen
Literatur anbieten und seine Beziehung zu den christlichen literarischen oder vorli-
terarischen Texten seiner Zeit genauer charakterisieren. Es handelt sich um seine

---

[14] Ebd. 308., 323., 363-69 u.a.

[15] Mack – Robbins 1989, 1ff., 31ff., 195ff.

[16] Mehr überzeugend sind die Arbeiten, welche die Worte Jesu im synoptischen Kontext untersucht haben, wie z.B. Perrin 1967, 154-206; Schürmann 1983 oder Wanke 1981, als die Arbeiten,
welche das Thema Menschensohn religionsgeschichtlich (mit uneinheitlichem Ergebnis) behandelt
haben.

[17] Borg 1987; ders. 1991, 13.

[18] Hartman 1966, 244-48.

Beziehung zu den ältesten christlichen Bekenntnisformeln und christologischen Titeln, zu der Passionsgeschichte, den Sammlungen der Gleichnisse Jesu (Mk 4), zur Logienquelle (Q), bzw. auch zum Thomasevangelium, zu Paulus oder zu einigen Texten, die von Markus unabhängige Gestaltungen der Jesus-Tradition sein könnten, und schließlich zu den Synoptikern. Was ich jetzt vorlege, sind keine radikal neue exegetische Beobachtungen, sondern eher ein Versuch, die Beziehungen zwischen den bekannten Beobachtungen zu entdecken und daraus die notwendigen Folgen für das umfassende Bild der Anfänge christlicher Theologie und Literatur zu ziehen.

## 4. Markus und die älteren christologischen Formeln

Es gehört zum Konsensus der Markusforschung, daß der Evangelist mit einigen nachösterlichen christologischen Formeln vertraut war, die in seiner Zeit unter den Anhängern Jesu und unter neuen Christen offensichtlich schon ziemlich weit verbreitet waren. Mit einer Anspielung auf die sog.Pistisformel aus 1Kor 15,3b-5 gipfelt in Mark 16,6-7 das ganze Evangelium[19]. Und da sie in 1Kor 15,1 als εὐαγγέλιον bezeichnet wird, ist sehr wahrscheinlich, daß mit dem "Anfang des Evangeliums" im ersten Vers des Markusevangeliums die ganze Schrift als Anfang (im Sinne der notwendigen Vorgeschichte) des Evangeliums (im Sinne des Auferstehungskerygmas)[20] oder als Evangelium im erweiterten, von dem Evangelium als Osterkerygma abgeleiteten Sinn bezeichnet ist[21]. Da Paulus in 1Kor 15,5-8 (vgl.V.11) eine relativ breite ökumenische Gemeinschaft nennt, welche die Pistisformel als den Ausdruck ihres Glaubens anerkannt hat, ist es klar, daß das umfassende Gestaltungselement des Markusevangeliums kein nur paulinischer "Mythus" über Tod und Auferstehung Jesu ist, wie Mack behauptet[22], sondern eine Formel, die schon vor Paulus für mehrere Gruppen der "Jesusleute" vor- und nachösterlicher Ursprungs bezeichnend war.

Schon im Jahre 1964 hat Philipp Vielhauer nachgewiesen, daß auch der vorpaulinische Jesus-Titel Sohn Gottes eine bedeutende Rolle in der theologisch literarischen Gestaltung des Markusevangeliums spielt (siehe Mark 1,11; 9,7; 15,39, ev. auch 1,1 nach B,D,L,W u.a.)[23]. Seine These, wonach das Markusevangelium als Thronbesteigung des Gottessohnes gestaltet ist, läßt sich zwar nicht halten, aber die

[19] Pokorný 1985, 1985ff.
[20] Pesch 1976, 62; Pokorný 1977, 126f.; ders. 1985, 1994; Baarlink 1977, 291ff.; Rau 1985, 2064; Schenke 1988, 148-53 u.a.
[21] Dormeyer (– Frankenmölle) 1984, 1582f.
[22] Mack 1988, 98ff.
[23] Vielhauer 1965.

Schlüsselrolle des Titels Sohn Gottes, wie er vor allem in der Sohnesformel aus Röm 1,3f. vorkommt, wurde als ein bedeutendes Kompositionselement des Markusevangeliums allgemein anerkannt: das, was zunächst nur Jesus und der Leser (Hörer) des Markusevangeliums weiß (1,11), wird zuletzt von dem Hauptmann am Kreuz als dem Modell eines Heidenchristen erkannt und bekannt (ἀναγνώρισις). Und die Tatsache, daß die Christologie der Sohnesformel, die das Kreuz Jesu überhaupt nicht erwähnt, der paulinischen Christologie und Soteriologie nicht entspricht, bestätigt nur unsere Behauptung, (1) daß Paulus mit seiner Theologie die älteren christlichen liturgischen Formeln zwar neu interpretiert hat, aber keinen neuen Mythus konstruierte und (2) daß Markus mit seinem Buch die christlichen Traditionen zwar neu gestaltete, aber sein theologisches Grundanliegen in vorpaulinischen christlichen Bekenntnissen verwurzelt sein muß.

Das, was wir jetzt über das Verhältnis des Markusevangeliums zu den älteren christlichen Formeln gesagt haben, schließt u.a. auch die Deutung des Markusevangeliums als eines Dokuments der radikalen Parusieerwartung aus, wie es E. Lohmeyer, W. Marxsen, N. Perrin und andere mit Hinweis auf Mark 16,7 (ὄψεσθε) vorausgesetzt haben. Der Hinweis auf das Sehen des Auferstandenen bezieht sich offensichtlich auf die Ostererscheinungen Jesu und die eben erwähnten christologischen Formeln widerspiegeln schon das Bewußtsein, daß die apokalyptische Naherwartung nicht die entscheidende Folge der Osterereignisse ist. Wenn Markus die Jesus-Traditionen mit den christlichen nachösterlichen Bekenntnissen verbunden hat, war es also keine Begründung eines neuen Christus-Mythus, sondern es war ein aus christlicher Sicht erfolgreicher Versuch, die damals schon in mehreren christlichen Gruppen verbreiteten christologischen Formeln und Titel zu literarischer Gestaltung und theologischer Deutung der parallel laufenden Traditionen über die Worte und Taten Jesu zu benutzen. Es war eine wirklich bedeutende neue Entscheidung, denn z.B. Paulus hat zwar sowohl die christologischen Formeln und Titel gekannt und anerkannt, aber ihre Verbindung in ein literarisches Ganzes noch nicht beabsichtigt. Was die Tradition über die Wundertaten Jesu betrifft, hat sie Paulus offensichtlich wenig nützlich für die Förderung des Glaubens gehalten: die Juden (nicht die wahren Christen) fordern Zeichen (1Kor 1,22). In seiner Courage zu literarischer Synthese und in seiner Fähigkeit, die Synthese theologisch zu gestalten, ist Markus wirklich eine bahnbrechende Gestalt.

## 5. Markus und die Passionsgeschichte

Die Passionsgeschichte hat man schon seit K. L. Schmidt als den Grundstein markinischer Erzählung betrachtet und Rudolf Pesch hat zu der vorausgesetzten vormarkinischen Leidensgeschichte Jesu einen wesentlichen Teil der zweiten Hälfte

des Markusevangeliums gerechnet[24]. Seit den sechziger Jahren hört man in der exegetischen Debatte jedoch auch Stimmen, wonach es vor Markus nur verstreute
kurze Erzählungen gab, die erst Markus in eine zusammenhängende Erzählung verbunden hat. Außer der möglichen Dekomposition der Passionsgeschichte wird diese These durch die Beobachtung unterstützt, wonach in ihr mehrere Themen des
Markusevangeliums ihren Höhepunkt und Abschluß finden. Diese Spur hat schon
W. Kelber verfolgt und sie gipfelt in dem Werk von B. L. Mack[25], der die Passionsgeschichte als Ganzes dem Evangelisten zuschreibt. Der Tod Jesu hat danach in den
narrativen Traditionen vor Markus keine entscheidende Rolle gespielt. Es ist wohl
wahr, daß die stellvertretende Deutung des Todes Jesu der eigentlichen Passionsgeschichte (Verhaftung, Verhör und Kreuzigung) fremd ist. Das Leiden Jesu ist dort
eher als die *passio iusti* interpretiert, der sich darüber hinaus zum Menschensohn
berufen kann und von ihm beim jüngsten Gericht seine Rehabilitierung erwarten
kann (Mark 14,62). Dies letzte Motiv hat den Christen schon vor Markus ermöglicht, sich mit dem Leiden Jesu positiv auseinanderzusetzen und die Passionsgeschichte als einen Teil des endzeitlichen Geschehens aufzufassen, das in der
Ankunft des Menschensohnes als des Richters der Richter Jesu gipfeln wird. Mit
der markinischen Christologie, die nach der Pistis- sowie der Sohnesformel mit der
Auferstehung Jesu noch vor der Endzeit rechnet, ist dies nicht identisch. Markus
mußte mit Hilfe von Sprüchen wie Mark 10,45 und den Leidensankündigungen
Jesu die Passionsgeschichte seinem Konzept anpassen, aber das gerade ist schon ein
Argument gegen die Hypothese, wonach Markus die Passionsgeschichte geschaffen hat. Eine solche Hypothese setzt übrigens voraus, daß die spezifischen Züge der
lukanischen und johanneischen Fassung der Passionsgeschichte eine redaktionelle
Bildung der Evangelisten sind und daß man sie von keiner von Markus unabhängi-
gen Erzählung über das Leiden Jesu ableiten kann. Und das ist auch sehr unwahrscheinlich. Schwer ist jene Hypothese auch mit der Tatsache zu vereinigen, daß
schon vor Paulus die Geschichte von der Verhaftung (und dem Prozeß und Kreuzigung?) Jesu mit der Erzählung über die Einsetzung des Herrenmahls verbunden
war, wie es Paulus vor den Worten der Einsetzung ausdrücklich bemerkt: "Der Herr
Jesus, in der Nacht, als er verraten wurde, nahm das Brot..." (1Kor 11,23b). Eine
Vorform der Passionsgeschichte war also schon zur Zeit des Paulus bekannt.

Was Markus neu gemacht hat, war also (1) das biographische Arrangement des
gesammelten Stoffes als Vorgeschichte der Passion und (2) die Deutung der Passionsgeschichte im Sinne des Evangeliums als Auferstehungsbotschaft.

---

[24] Pesch 1977, 1-27.
[25] Mack 1988, 262f.

## 6. Das Messiasgeheimnis und die Gleichnisse bei Markus

Die Gleichnisse Jesu, besonders die Gleichnisse des Wachstums aus Mark 4, sind offensichtlich ein Teil der anschaulichen Darstellung des Reiches Gottes. Jesus hat mehrere Gleichnisse erzählt, um den durch eine Metapher (βασιλεία τοῦ θεοῦ) ausgedrückten eschatologischen Zielwert durch weitere Aussagen in analogischer Rede zu vergegenwärtigen und seinen aktuellen Anspruch zu signalisieren[26]. Die Gleichnisse Jesu stehen in der Tradition der jüdischen *meshalim*, aber sie transzendieren die Grenzen dieser rhetorischen Untergattung. Schon Amos Wilder hat auf ihren säkularen Charakter und ihre schockierenden Züge aufmerksam gemacht, die den Hörer in eine aktive Mitarbeit hineinreißen[27]. Mehrere Bereiche, denen der Stoff der Gleichnisse entnommen wird, wie gerade auch das Wachstum des Samens, gehörten damals zu den Topoi geistiger Unterweisung überhaupt. Man kann fast sagen, daß das Judentum dadurch aus seinen besten Voraussetzungen den Bereich der universalen hellenistischen *paideia* betrat. Burton Mack hat es zur Interpretation der Gleichnisse Jesu in den Kategorien kynischer Unterweisung inspiriert[28].

Umso störender scheint die in Mark 4,10-12 ausgedrückte Parabeltheorie des Markus zu sein, welche die allegorische Deutung des Gleichnisses von Sämann einleitet. Die Gleichnisse scheinen dort ein Mittel zur Geheimhaltung der Wahrheit vor den Nichteingeweihten zu sein. William Wrede hat dies zur Formulierung seiner Theorie des Messiasgeheimnisses Anlaß gegeben, mit deren Hilfe Markus den Widerspruch zwischen dem nachösterlichen Dogma mit dem unmessianischen Leben Jesu versöhnen wollte[29]. Die formgeschichtlichen und redaktionsgeschichtlichen Untersuchungen haben jedoch überzeugend nachgewiesen, daß diejenigen Züge in der Komposition des Markusevangeliums, nach welchen Jesus seine in Wort und Tat ausgedrückte wahre Identität bis zu seiner Passion und Auferstehung geheimhalten wollte, eher die schon durch den Osterglauben geprägte Jesus-Tradition entchristologisieren sollte. Dadurch hat Markus erreicht, daß die Geschichte Jesu erst in Ostern gipfelt und aus der Sicht von Ostern und Auferstehung her gelesen wird[30].

Die Analyse der Geheimnistheorie als eines markinischen Gesamtkonzepts unterstreicht die Tatsache, daß Markus in seiner Darstellung Kreuz und Auferstehung als tragende Faktoren hervorhebt und zu diesem Zweck auch einige andere Elemente als Kompositionsmittel benutzt. Z.B. einige Schweigegebote, die in der mündlichen Tradition nur die Unaufhaltsamkeit der Wirkung Jesu unterstreichen sollten

---

[26] Perrin 1976, 89ff.
[27] Wilder 1971, 71ff.
[28] Mack (– Robbins) 1989, 143ff.
[29] Wrede 1963, 66ff.
[30] Strecker 1979.

(z.B. 7,36), gewinnen bei Markus eine neue Funktion: sie zeigen, daß die Popularität Jesu als eines Wundertäters und Thaumaturgen nicht die von Jesus gewollte und von der Kirche hervorgehobene ist[31]. Die markinische Parabeltheorie ist im Grunde ein Ausdruck der negativen Erfahrung der ersten Christen mit ihrer jüdischen Umwelt (οἱ ἔξω – 4,11), die sowohl die Botschaft Jesu als auch die nachösterliche Jesusverkündigung abgelehnt hat. Nicht weil sie es intellektuell nicht verstanden hätte, sondern weil sie es existenziell nicht bejahen konnte[32]. Markus hat es als *vaticinium ex eventu* mit den Parabeln Jesu verbunden[33], um zu zeigen, daß die Ablehnung der Umwelt keinen Strich durch die Pläne Gottes bedeutet, daß sie vorgesehen war. Mack hat es nur soziologisch interpretiert – als Ausdruck des Bewußtseins einer Gruppe, die sich von der Umwelt schon abgegrenzt hat[34].

## 7. Die erste Zwischenbilanz

In der markinischen Bearbeitung der älteren Stoffe sehen wir also eine doppelte Tendenz. Auf der einen Seite wird Jesus mit seinen Worten und Taten aus der nachösterlichen Sicht gesehen, auf der anderen Seite ist gerade das, was als Ostergeschehen bezeugt wird, der tiefste Grund für das Interesse an dem irdischen Jesus. Aus der Sicht des christlichen Glaubensbekenntnisses gewinnen seine irdischen Worte und Taten ein neues Gewicht. Die Deutung, die Mack anbietet, nämlich daß Jesus durch den Mythus von dem inkarnierten Unschuldigen verschlungen wurde, ist einseitig. Besser hat die Funktion des Mythischen in dieser ersten christlichen Schrift narrativer Art J. M. Robinson definiert: Die kosmisch-mythische Kulisse hebt in Wirklichkeit die Bedeutung des Geschehens hervor, das sich innerhalb der Geschichte abspielt. Es bedeutet, "daß das Ringen zwischen Geist und Satan auf der Ebene der Geschichte und nicht des Mythos ausgetragen wird"[35]. Die gnostische Weiterentwicklung der präsentischen Christologie, welche an den Auferstehungsglauben anknüpft, und welche J. M. Robinson in ihren gnostischen Auswirkungen verfolgt hat, kann also aus ihren inneren Voraussetzungen auch die Rückkoppelung mit dem irdischen Jesus hervorheben. Das hat Markus zur Gestaltung seines Jesusbuches benutzt. Die Gleichnisse Jesu können da als Modell dienen: Was "jetzt", d.h. in der Zeit des irdischen Jesus, geschieht (z.B. das Säen) hat eschatologische Folgen (Ernte) und der Leser (Hörer) muß darauf achten, weil es für die ganze Orientierung in seinem "Leser-Jetzt" von entscheidender Bedeutung ist. Das Evangelium als Ost-

---

[31] Luz 1965, 23f.; Theißen 1974, 153.
[32] Rau 1985, 2109.
[33] Haufe 1972, 421.
[34] Mack 1989, 164.
[35] Robinson 1989a, 36.

erbotschaft (vgl. Mark 16,6f.) hat die Bindung des eschatologischen Heils an die Person von Jesus aus Nazareth noch deutlicher hervorgehoben.

## 8. Markus und die Logienquelle (Q)

Nach der Zweiquellentheorie war die Sammlung der Sprüche Jesu (Q) neben dem Markusevangelium die zweite gemeinsame Quelle des Matthäus- und Lukasevangeliums. Wie wir schon gezeigt haben, ist das Markusevangelium eine Schrift, die sich mit Erfolg um eine Synthese des mündlichen Evangeliums und der Jesus-Tradition bemüht hat. Umso verwunderlicher ist es, daß Markus so viele bedeutende Sprüche Jesu in sein Buch nicht aufgenommen hat. Die Lösung dieses Problems kann man, grob gesagt, in drei Richtungen suchen[36].

Die einfachste Erklärung wäre, daß Markus die Logienquelle (Q) nicht gekannt hat. Dies ist jedoch unwahrscheinlich, denn die Logienquelle – soweit wir sie rekonstruieren können – scheint als Ganzes von den nachösterlichen Bekenntnissen weniger beeinflußt zu sein als andere Bereiche und Schichten der uns bekannten urchristlichen Literatur. Gegen eine solche Erklärung spricht auch die Tatsache, daß sowohl Matthäus als auch Lukas in ihrer christlichen Gemeinden sowohl das Markusevangelium als auch die Logienquelle kennengelernt haben. Es muß nicht bedeuten, daß diese beiden Texte in ihren Gemeinden liturgisch gleichrangig waren, aber es bedeutet jedenfalls, daß sie beide hohe Autorität besaßen. Wenn Markus und Logienquelle etwa in den achtziger Jahren in zwei verschiedenen Bereichen der Urkirche liturgisch koexistierten, ist es sehr wahrscheinlich, daß auch Markus die Logienquelle gekannt hat.

Die zweite Möglichkeit ist also, daß Markus die Logienquelle zwar gekannt hat, aber nicht aufnehmen wollte, weil sie für ihn theologisch nicht annehmbar war. Diese Vermutung haben mehrere Exegeten geäußert[37]. Die Aufforderung zur Feindesliebe, die in der Logienquelle eine bedeutende Position hat (Q /Lk/ 6,27-28 vgl. *Pap. Oxyrh.* 1224, p.176), hat man in der Kirche wirklich etwas schockierend empfunden und manchmal in einer mehr behutsamen Formulierung weitergegeben, wie es z.B. bei Paulus in Röm 12, 17-21 der Fall ist. Die Verlegenheit, in welche ein Spruch Jesu einige Christen gebracht hat, konnte jedoch nicht zur Ablehnung einer ganzen Sammlung der Herrenworte führen, die sich inhaltlich sogar mit einem Teil seiner Überlieferung deckt. Ernster muß man erwägen, daß vielleicht der Spruch "Warum sagt ihr zu mir Herr, Herr (κύριε, κύριε) und tut nicht, was ich euch sage" (Q 6,46) für Markus unannehmbar war, falls er unter dem Einfluß von Paulus stand.

---

[36] Boring 1977, 373ff.
[37] Als Möglichkeit führt es auch Schweizer 1967, 3 an, s. Boring 1977, 374.

Es widerspricht nämlich der Maxime, die Paulus geprägt hat, wonach das Bekenntnis zu Jesus als dem Herrn (und der Glaube) selbst zum Heil führt (Röm 10,9).

Jedenfalls waren die Sammlungen der Worte Jesu, die man ohne den narrativen Rahmen überliefert hat, der Gefahr einer Mißdeutung und verzerrenden Neuinterpretation ausgesetzt, wie das Thomasevangelium zeigt. Solche Worte haben offensichtlich die christlichen Propheten überliefert, die sie als Aussagen des im Geist gegenwärtigen Herrn auf konkrete Probleme appliziert haben[38]. Sie besaßen als Propheten ohne zweifel eine beträchtliche Autorität, aber wenig wahrscheinlich ist, daß sich die Warnung vor den falschen Propheten, die "Ich bin es" (Mark 13,6) sagen, auf die Tradenten von Q bezieht, denn die Autorität jener Worte ist nur von Jesus als dem Herrn abgeleitet. Die paulinische Ablehnung der nur die Weisheit (σοφία) Suchenden (1Kor 1,18f. 22) ist jedoch offensichtlich gegen eine Denkweise gerichtet, die in der Kirche mit der Überlieferung der Worte Jesu verbunden sein konnte, aber nichts spricht dafür, daß sie eine soziale Gruppe – eine profilierte Gruppe der Jesus-Anhänger repräsentieren. Möglichen Neuinterpretationen waren übrigens auch die Sammlungen der Gleichnisse Jesu ausgesetzt, die Markus in sein Werk aufgenommen hat. Wir sehen zwar, daß bei Markus außer der allgemeinen Aufforderung "Tut Buße!" in 1,15b nur wenig Aufforderungen zu innerer Umkehr, also nur wenig Aussagen in der "conversionist rhetoric" zu finden sind[39], aber auf der anderen Seite kann gerade dies ein Indiz für eine andere Erklärung der Abwesenheit von Q im Markusevangelium sein: Es ist möglich, daß Markus die Spruchsammlung, die eine andere Funktion als sein Buch in der Kirche hatte, bei aller möglichen Distanz zu einigen Sprüchen in seinem "Sitz in Leben" respektierte und weder in sein Werk integrieren noch herausdrängen wollte.

Die letzte Möglichkeit ist also, daß es sich im Verhältnis von Markusevangelium zur Logienquelle weder um Unkenntnis, noch um Ablehnung, sondern um parallele Koexistenz handelt. Für diese Lösung sprechen einige gewichtige Gründe. Markus hat offensichtlich das Vaterunser gekannt (vgl. Mark 14,36 mit Gal 4,6; Röm 8,15) und doch zitiert er dies Gebet in seinem Evangelium nicht. Er hat damit gerechnet, daß die Autorität dieses Gebets durch seinen Sitz in dem liturgischen Leben der Kirche garantiert ist. Ähnlich kann er sich auf die feste Rolle der Logienquelle im Leben der Kirche verlassen haben. Wir haben gesehen, wie verschieden und doch in ihren Funktionen komplementär die Rollen des (mündlichen) Evangeliums und der Worte des Herrn beim Apostel Paulus waren. Das Evangelium als Auferstehungsbotschaft war die Voraussetzung zur Weiterüberlieferung jener Sprüche. Die Logienquelle hat die Auferstehungsbotschaft konkretisiert und ihren ethischen Gehalt verkörpert. Die gegenseitige Beziehung hat die Koexistenz beider Formen der

---

[38] Sato 1988, 99f.
[39] Robbins 1993.

Überlieferung als autosemantischer Einheiten ermöglicht.

## 9. Die zweite Zwischenbilanz

Das von J. M. Robinson und noch viel radikaler von B. L. Mack entworfene Bild
der Rolle von Markus in der urchristlichen Theologie- und Literaturgeschichte wi-
derspiegelt zweifellos einige geistige Tendenzen, die innerhalb der Urkirche gewirkt haben. Als Ganzes wird jedoch ihr kritisches Bild durch folgende Feststellungen relativiert:

Erstens haben wir Belege, daß die alternativen christologischen Konzepte schon
in den ältesten uns erreichbaren Schichten der urchristlichen Literatur mit der Auf-
erstehungs- bzw. Erhöhungschristologie koexistiert haben, die auf dem mündlichen
Evangelium gegründet war: Paulus, der seine ganze Theologie als Deutung des
(Oster)Evangeliums begreift, zitiert die Worte des Herrn und hält sich für einen
christlichen Propheten und Geistträger (1Kor 7,25. 40), ähnlich wie die Träger der
Worte-Jesu-Tradition. Auch in der vormarkinischen Passionsgeschichte sind mehrere christologische Konzepte miteinander verbunden (leidende Gerechte, apokalyptischer Menschensohn, Auferstehung) und sogar schon in der vorpaulinischen
Pistisformel aus 1Kor 15 ist die Auferstehungs-Christologie mit der Aussage über
den stellvertretenden Tod kombiniert. Das mündliche Evangelium hat also sehr früh
zur Integration oder mindestens Koexistenz mehrerer christologischer Konzepte
beigetragen.

Zweitens ist es bisher nicht gelungen, die rekonstruierten alternativen Christologien mit den Berichten und Indizien zu harmonisieren, welche die historischen urchristlichen Gruppen betreffen, wie die "Hellenisten" um Stephanus, Petrus, den
Herrenbruder Jakobus, Paulus und die Gruppen seiner Schüler, die Christen aus
Alexandrien (Apollos), die Gruppe in Antiochien, den Johanneischen Kreis usw.[40].
Dies ist zwar noch kein Argument gegen die Existenz solcher Gruppen, aber es bedeutet jedenfalls, daß sie als selbständige Strömungen weniger einflußreich waren,
als die Vertreter der These über viele vormarkinische alternative Christologien voraussetzen.

Dies bedeutet nicht, daß das Markusevangelium eine logische Entwicklungspha-
se der urchristlichen Literatur war. Es bedeutet nur, daß mit der Entstehung des
Markusevangeliums keine bedeutende alternative Christologie herausgedrängt
wurde. Die Weise, auf welche Markus seine Synthese mehrerer (nicht aller) Formen
und Tendenzen christlicher Überlieferung durchgeführt hat, war jedoch neu und
schöpferisch.

---

[40] Holtz 1991, 35f.

## 10. Der narrative Rahmen und seine theologische Bedeutung

Es ist allgemein bekannt, daß K. L. Schmidt schon kurz nach dem Ende des ersten Weltkrieges (1919) entdeckt hat, daß der narrative Rahmen des Markusevangeliums, der seine ganze Komposition bestimmt, von Markus selbst stammt. Seine theologische Leistung, die mit der Bildung eines solchen umfassenden Rahmens verbunden war, hat er jedoch unterschätzt, ähnlich wie später Rudolf Pesch in seinem großen Kommentar. Wir haben schon gesagt, daß dieser Rahmen nicht nur ein literarisches Skelett ist, sondern daß er mit Hilfe des Titels Sohn Gottes und der inneren Struktur des mündlichen Evangeliums das ganze Werk auch theologisch akzentuiert. In einem wichtigen Punkt fallen die literarische und theologische Funktion des Rahmens ineins: Jesus mit seinen Worten und Taten ist hier der vorösterliche Jesus. Er hat zwar die wahre Autorität erst durch seinen Tod und seine Auferstehung erreicht und sein Anspruch ist erst von Ostern her verständlich (erst nach Ostern ist er kein μυστήριον mehr), aber was die konkrete Orientierung in der Geschichte und im persönlichen Leben betrifft, muß man von dem irdischen Jesus, seinen Worten und seinem Verhalten ausgehen. Im Unterschied zu dem Glauben, der sich nur auf die Auferstehung, bzw. Erhöhung Jesu konzentriert, tritt hier stark die Rückkoppelung zum irdischen Jesus hervor. Im Vergleich mit der Funktion und literarischer Gestalt der Spruchsammlungen (Logienquelle, die Sammlung der Sprüche Jesu, die Paulus zitiert, das Thomasevangeliums usw.) ist dies eine bedeutende Weichenstellung.

Keineswegs kann es jedoch als ein Schritt zurück, in die Verhältnisse vor Ostern betrachtet werden. Wir haben schon gesehen, daß Markus die Autorität des irdischen Jesus von seiner Passion und Auferstehung ableitet, wie es die ganze Struktur seines Werkes verrät. Sein Weg zurück in das irdische Leben Jesu ist durch die Notwendigkeit gegeben, die unkontrolliert weiterlaufende Tradition über das Leben Jesu (1) aufzubewahren und (2) zu interpretieren, d.h. vor allem auch eine kritische Auswahl zu treffen. Als ein Weg in die Vergangenheit ist seine Auffassung des Jesus-Buches eigentlich schon in der Grundstruktur der Osterverkündigung impliziert, wonach Gott Jesus erweckt hat. Jesus wurde danach erweckt, aber es ist Jesus von Nazareth, der gekreuzigte Jesus, zu dem sich Gott auf diese Weise bekannt hat. In der zweiten Generation und außerhalb Palästina mußte man fragen, wer dieser Jesus war, zu welchem sich Gott auf eine so einmalige Weise bekannt hat. Die kombinierten Formeln, die Jesus auch als den Gekreuzigten oder als Sohn David vorstellen sind schon fähig, ein solches *feedback* des christlichen Bekenntnisses ausdrücklich zu motivieren. Man kann es auch als eine Art Erdung betrachten, welche zum besseren Hören der Stimme des irdischen Jesus dient. Wir können nicht genau sagen, gegen welche Gefahr sich Markus durch die ganze Gestaltung seines

Buches gewandt hat. Ob es der apokalyptische Enthusiasmus war, wie es W. Schmithals behauptete, die ersten Zeichen des Doketismus (so W. Schenk) oder das Bild von Jesus als dem Wundertäter (L. Schenke, Th. J. Weeden)[41]. Der Hauptgrund war jedenfalls die Tendenz zur Synthese, die Polemik hat offensichtlich nicht die entscheidende Rolle gespielt. Erst in der späteren Phase der theologischen Reflexion hat die Orientierung am irdischen Jesus deutlich als eine antidoketische Sicherung fungiert, welche die Inkarnation hervorhebt, wie es in 1Joh 4,2f. und 2Joh 7 (vgl. 1Kor 12,2f.; Eph 4,20f.) ausdrücklich gefordert wird.

Der Weg zurück, in die Zeit der Offenbarung, ist also an sich keine Relativierung des Osterkerygmas, keine triumphalistische Zurückversetzung des hermeneutischen Wendepunktes von Ostern zur Zeit nach dem Bekenntnis des Petrus, wie J. M. Robinson anhand des Vergleichs zwischen dem Wort über die verdeckte Rede Jesu in 4,34, das wir in dem Abschnitt über die Parabeln besprochen haben, und der Erklärung in 8,32 behauptet, wonach Jesus begonnen hat, das Wort "offen" (παρρησία) zu reden[42]. Das "offen" in 8,32 bezieht sich nämlich auf die Rede im Kreis der Jünger, was in 4,34 auch schon vorausgesetzt wird. Es stimmt zwar, daß die Tradition von dem irdischen Jesus nach Ostern seine Worte und Taten immer aktualisierte. Seine innergeschichtlichen Wunderheilungen werden gleichzeitig als Bilder des eschatologischen Heils präsentiert, Jesu Worte sollen manchmal direkt auch die Leser anreden und z.B. zur Aufnahme christlicher Missionare auffordern (9,37), Jesus wird als das wahre Brot des Lebens präsentiert (8,14-31) und z.B. dient die Geschichte von der Syrophönizierin (7,24-30) als Modell zur Lösung des Problems der Interkommunion der beschnittenen und unbeschnittenen Christen, wie es in dem dritten Viertel des ersten Jahrhunderts aktuell war. Das alles geschieht jedoch im Rahmen der Erzählung, welche die Bindung der Geschichten und der Sprüche an die Zeit und den Raum des irdischen Jesus nicht leugnet. Das Markusevangelium versteht sich als Darstellung einer vergangenen, von der Gegenwart grundsätzlich abgehobenen Geschichte, wie Jürgen Roloff nachgewiesen hat[43]. Die Geschichte Jesu von seiner Taufe bis zur Passion und zum leeren Grab ist dadurch konserviert. Im Unterschied zu der direkten prophetischen Applikation der Worte Jesu als der Worte des Erhöhten, wie wir es in der Logienquelle oder bei Paulus gesehen haben, gehören hier die Worte Jesu und seine ganze Geschichte zum "Anfang" und dürfen als Ganzes nicht auf eine synchrone Weise aktualisiert werden[44]. Es handelt sich um ein Zeugnis, das auch seine referierende Dimension hat.

---

[41] Über die einzelnen Vorschläge s. Pokorný 1985, 1981-1986, 2007f., 2013 u.a.

[42] Robinson 1989b, 125.

[43] Roloff 1969, 92f.; vgl. Strecker 1979, 50f.

[44] Dormeyer 1989, 126f.

## 11. Die Folgen für die Entstehung der Idee eines christlichen Kanons

Die Pharisäer, die nach dem Jüdischen Krieg zur führenden Kraft des Judentums geworden sind, haben mit einer schriftlichen Fortsetzung der Schrift (des Gesetzes, der Propheten und der Psalmen /Luk 24,44/, bzw. der Schriften) nicht gerechnet. Der prophetische Geist war nach ihrer Meinung in Israel schon nicht mehr präsent (Ps 74,9) und die mündliche Tradition ist an seine Stelle getreten. Die erwartete neue Gabe des Geistes hat man als ein eschatologisches Ereignis erwartet (Joel 2,28-32), das die Ankunft des Tages des Herrn signalisiert (Joel 2,30f.). Die endgültige Offenbarung Gottes wurde schon als eine Theophanie erwartet, von der es nicht nötig sein wird, ein schriftliches Zeugnis abzugeben. Von der Überzeugung, daß alle Verheißungen auf die Endzeit hin gerichtet sind, wurde schon die Tradition der prophetischen Stoffe bezeichnet und dieselbe Überzeugung hat später im Talmud ihren Niederschlag gefunden (b.Ber 34b)[45]. Wenn Markus gewagt hat, von Jesus als dem Sohn Gottes ein Buch zu schreiben, war es also etwas Neues. Die mit Tinte auf Papyrus geschilderte Ankunft des Messias, war eine *contradictio in adiecto.* Ein umso größerer Einschnitt muß es in den Augen der pharisäischer Kreise gewesen sein mit ihrem Schriftverbot, wonach es nicht erlaubt war, die Deutung der Schrift aufzuschreiben. Die älteste Gestalt christlicher Überlieferung war die des eschatologischen und endgültigen mündlichen Kommentars zur Schrift – zur jüdischen Bibel. Die jüdische Bibel war in christlichen Gottesdiensten auch noch in der Zeit von Markus der "Text". Das christliche Zeugnis in narrativer, kerygmatischer oder paränetischer Form hat als authentische Predigt fungiert, nicht als der Text.

Was Markus, der offensichtlich als hellenistischer Jude erzogen war, mit der Sammlung, der narrativen Strukturierung und schriftlichen Konservierung der christlichen Tradition gemacht hat, war der erste Schritt zur Entstehung der Idee eines zweiteiligen christlichen Kanons. In seiner Zeit ist es schon klar geworden, daß die christliche eschatologische Erwartung zweipolig[46] oder "teleskopisch" ist: Das neue Zeitalter ist noch nicht da, aber der Messias ist schon bekannt, es ist schon klar, wer und was die Zukunft Gottes hat. Die Sünde und das Leiden der Welt sind noch nicht beseitigt, aber der Böse hat schon keine absolute Macht, seine Tage sind gezählt. Dies für die Juden unannehmbare Bewußtsein, das im Grunde schon in dem vorpaulinischen Evangelium impliziert ist, hat Markus durch seine Schrift für das liturgische Leben der Kirche literarisch ausgedrückt.

Sobald man diesen Schritt getan hat, ist es deutlich geworden, daß die konservierte Norm, auf welche die lebendige Verkündigung ständig hinweisen muß, einer Interpretation, eines Kommentars bedarf. Matthäus und Lukas (so nenne ich tradi-

---

[45] Pokorný 1993, 90f.
[46] Das Problem hat J. B. Souček analysiert, s. Pokorný 1972.

tionell die Autoren der anderen synoptischen Evangelien) haben die synthetische Tendenz weiter ausgezogen und auch die Kindheitslegenden, Logienquelle und die narrativen Schilderungen des eigentlichen Evangeliums – die Begegnungen mit dem Auferstandenen – in ihre Jesus-Bücher aufgenommen. Sie wollten beide das Markusevangelium ersetzen, ähnlich wie Johannes später ihre Schriften. Er wußte schon, daß die christlichen Schriften solcher Art in der Kirche praktisch die Rolle einer neuen Thora spielen und hat sein Buch mit den Worten eröffnet, mit welchen auch das Buch Genesis eröffnet wird: ἐν ἀρχῇ... (Joh 1,1). Es ist wahrscheinlich, daß sich dieser gewagten Analogie auch Matthäus (βίβλος γενέσεως Matth 1,1) und vielleicht sogar schon Markus (ἀρχή – Mark 1,1) bewußt waren. Im Matthäus-evangelium lesen wir zum Schluß, daß die Lehre des Auferstandenen durch die Jünger, also vermittelt, weitergegeben werden soll (Matth 28,19f.). Und Lukas hat den ganzen zweiten Band seines Werkes, die Apostelgeschichte, als Modell des neuen Anfangs – der Predigten und der existentiellen Antwort auf die im ersten Band ko-difizierte Geschichte und Verkündigung Jesu – konzipiert.

Die allmählich sich durchsetzende Sitte der aktualisierenden Predigt, deren Grundlage die Texte aus Evangelien geworden sind, war eine bedeutende indirekte Wirkung des Markusevangeliums – seiner Konservierung der Norm im Rahmen der irdischen Geschichte Jesu. Die Idee des christlichen zweiteiligen Kanons wurde da-durch schon unmittelbar gefördert.

## Bibliographie

Baarlink, Heinrich 1977: *Anfängliches Evangelium*, Kampen: J. H. Kok 1977.

Barrett, Charles K. 1990: *Das Evangelium des Johannes* (KEK – Sonderband; übersetzt v. Hans Bald), Göttingen: Vandenhoeck & Ruprecht 1990.

Bauer, Walter 1934: *Rechtgläubigkeit und Ketzerei* (BHTh 10), Tübingen: Mohr (Siebeck) 1934.

Borg, Marcus J. 1987: *A New Vision*, San Francisco: Harper & Row 1987.

— 1991: "Portraits of Jesus in Contemporary North American Scholarship", in: *HThR* 84 (1991) 1-22.

Boring, M. Eugene 1977: "The Paucity of Sayings in Mark: A Hypothesis", in: *SBL.SP* 11 (1977) 371-77.

Brown, Raymond E. 1985: *The Gospel According to John I-XII* (AncB 29), Garden City, NY: Doubleday [2]1985.

Cancik, Hubert (Hg.) 1984: *Markus-Philologie*. Historische, literargeschichtliche und stilistische Untersuchungen zum zweiten Evangelium (WUNT 33), Tübingen: Mohr (Siebeck) 1984.

Dodd, Charles H. 1931-32: "The Framework of the Gospel Narrative", in: *ET* 43 (1931-32) 396-400.

Dormeyer, Detlev (– H.Frankenmölle) 1984: "Evangelium als literarische Gattung und als theologischer Begriff", in: *ANRW* II,25,2, Berlin/New York: de Gruyter 1984, 1543-1704.

— 1989: *Evangelium als literarische und theologische Gattung* (EdF 263), Darmstadt: Wissenschaftliche Buchgesellschaft 1989.

Dupont, Jacques (Hg.) 1975: *Jésus aux origines de la christologie* (BEThL 40), Leuven – Gembloux: Leuven University Press – Duculot 1975.

Hartman, Lars 1966: *Prophecy Interpreted* (CB.NT 1), Lund: Gleerup 1966.

Haufe, Günther 1972: "Erwägungen zum Ursprung der sog. Parabeltheorie Markus 4,11-12", in: *EvTh* 32 (1972) 413-21.

Hengel, Martin 1983: "Probleme des Markusevangeliums", in: Peter Stuhlmacher (Hg.) 1983, 221-65.

Holtz, Traugott 1991: "Überlegungen zur Geschichte des Urchristentums", in: idem, *Geschichte und Theologie des Urchristentums*, Tübingen: Mohr (Siebeck) 1991, 31-44.

Kloppenborg, John S. 1987: *The Formation of Q*, Philadelphia, PA: Fortress 1987.

Lampe, Peter (mit U.Luz) 1983: "Diskussionsüberblick", in: Peter Stuhlmacher (Hg.) 1983, 413-31.

Luz, Ulrich 1965: "Das Geheimnismotiv und die markinische Christologie", in: *ZNW* 56 (1965) 9-30.

— 1983: see Lampe 1983.

Mack, Burton L. 1988: *A Myth of Innocence. Mark and Christian Origins*, Philadelphia, PA: Fortress 1988.

— 1989: (mit V. K. Robbins): *Patterns of Persuasion in the Gospels*, Sonoma, CA: Polebridge Press 1989.

Neirynck, Frans 1977: "John and the Synoptics", in: M. de Jonge (Hg.), *L'Évangile de Jean* (BEThL 44), Leuven – Gembloux: Leuven University Press – Duculot 1977, 73-106.

Nineham, D. E. 1955: "The Order of Events in St.Mark's Gospel – An Examination of Dr. Dodd's Hypothesis", in: D. E. Nineham (Hg.), *Studies in the Gospels* (FS R. H. Lightfoot), Oxford: Blackwell 1955, 223-39.

Perrin, Norman 1967: *Rediscovering the Teaching of Jesus*, London: SCM 1967.

— 1976: *Jesus and the Language of Kingdom. Symbol and Metaphor in the New Testament Interpretation*, Philadelphia, PA: Fortress 1976.

Pesch, Rudolf 1976-77: *Das Markusevangelium I-II* (HThK II/1-2), Freiburg i Br. u.a.: Herder 1976-77.

— (Hg.) 1979: *Das Markus-Evangelium* (WdF 411), Darmstadt: Wissenschaftliche Buchgesellschaft 1979.

Pokorný, Petr 1972: "Der Theologe Josef B. Souček", in: *EvTh* 32 (1972) 241-51.

— 1977: "Der Anfang des Evangeliums", in: R. Schnackenburg – J. Ernst – J. Wanke (Hgg.), *Die Kirche des Anfangs* (FS H. Schürmann), Leipzig: St.Benno 1977, 115-29.

— 1985: "Das Markusevangelium. Literarische und theologische Einleitung", in: *ANRW* II,25,3, Berlin/New York: de Gruyter 1985, 1969-2035.

— 1993: "The Problem of Biblical Theology", in: *Horizons in Biblical Theology*, 15 (1993) 83-94.

Rau, Gottfried 1985: "Das Markusevangelium. Komposition und Intention der ersten Darstellung christlicher Mission", in: *ANRW* II,25,3, Berlin/New York: de Gruyter 1985, 2036-2257.

Robbins, Vernon K. 1989: see Mack 1989.

— 1993: "Interpreting Miracle Culture and Parable Culture in Mark 4-11": Vorlesung an der Karlsuniversität zu Prag 5.10.1993 [Now published in: *SEÅ* 59 (1994) 59-81].

Robinson, James M. 1971 "LOGOI SOPHON: Zur Gattung der Spruchquelle Q", in: Helmut Köster – James M. Robinson, *Entwicklungslinien durch die Welt des frühen Christentums*, Tübingen: Mohr (Siebeck) 1971, 67-106.

— 1982: "Jesus: From Easter to Valentinus (or to the Apostles' Creed)", in: *JBL* 101 (1982) 5-37.

— 1989a: *Messiasgeheimnis und Geschichtsverständnis* (TB 81), München: Kaiser (z.T. 2. Aufl.) 1989.

— 1989b: "Gnosis und Neues Testament", in: Robinson 1989a, 115-25.

— 1993: "Die Logienquelle: Weisheit oder Prophetie?", in: *EvTh* 53 (1993) 367-89.

Roloff, Jürgen 1969: "Das Markusevangelium als Geschichtsdarstellung", in: *EvTh* 29 (1969) 73-93.

Sato, Migaku 1988: *Q und Prophetie* (WUNT 2/29), Tübingen: Mohr (Siebeck) 1988.

— 1993 "Q: Prophetie oder Weisheit?", in: *EvTh* 53 (1993) 389-404.

Schenke, Ludger 1988: *Das Markusevangelium* (UB 405), Stuttgart: Kohlhammer 1988.

Schmidt, Karl Ludwig 1919: *Der Rahmen der Geschichte Jesu* (Berlin 1919; Nachdruck Darmstadt: Wissenschaftliche Buchgesellschaft 1964). Zuletzt Teilabdruck in: Pesch (Hg.) 1979, 48-67.

Schnackenburg, Rudolf 1965: *Das Johannesevangelium I* (HThK VI/1), Freiburg u.a.: Herder 1965.

Schürmann, Heinz 1983: "Beobachtungen zum Menschensohn-Titel in der Redequelle", in: R. Pesch u.a. (Hgg.), *Jesus und der Menschensohn, FS A. Vögtle*, Freiburg i. Br.: Herder 1975, 124-47; Zitiert nach idem, *Gottes Reich – Jesu Geschick*, Freiburg i. Br. u.a.: Herder 1983, 153-82.

Schweizer, Eduard 1967: *Das Evangelium nach Markus* (NTD 1), Göttingen: Vandenhoeck & Ruprecht 1967.

Souček, Josef B. 1972: see Pokorný 1972.

Strecker, Georg 1979: "Zur Messiasgeheimnistheorie des Markusevangeliums", in: F. L. Cross (Hg.), *Studia Evangelica* III (TU 88), Berlin: Akademie Verlag 1964, 87-104; Zitiert nach idem, *Eschaton und Historie*, Göttingen: Vandenhoeck & Ruprecht 1979, 33-51.

Stuhlmacher, Peter (Hg.) 1983: *Das Evangelium und die Evangelien* (WUNT 28), Tübingen: Mohr (Siebeck) 1983.

Theißen, Gerd 1974: *Urchristliche Wundergeschichten* (StNT 8), Gütersloh: G. Mohn 1974.

Vielhauer, Philipp 1965: "Erwägungen zur Christologie des Markusevangeliums", in: idem, *Aufsätze zum Neuen Testament* (TB 31), München: Kaiser 1965, 199-215.

Wanke, Joachim 1981: *"Bezugs- und Kommentarworte" in den synoptischen Evangelien* (EThS 44), Leipzig: St. Benno 1981.

Wilder, Amos 1971: *Early Christian Rhetoric*, Cambridge, MA: University Press [2]1971.

Wrede, Wiliam 1963: *Das Messiasgeheimnis in den Evangelien* (1901), Göttingen: Vandenhoeck & Ruprecht [3]1963.

# A Context for Interpreting Paul

Hendrikus W. Boers

## 1. Introduction

Günther Bornkamm expresses a widely held view when he states: "[Die] ganze Verkündigung [des Paulus], auch dort, wo seine Rechtfertigungslehre nicht ausdrücklich zur Sprache kommt, ist nur dann richtig verstanden, wenn sie im engsten Zusammenhang mit dieser verstanden und auf sie bezogen wird."[1] With rare exceptions over a long period of time some form or other of this view has functioned as the fundamental hermeneutical principle for the interpretation of Paul. In terms of contextual interpretation, one of the many methodological issues that have concerned Lars Hartman, Galatians and Romans with their central issue, justification by faith, is considered by Bornkamm as the context for the interpretation of the rest of Paul's letters. The basis for this paper is the recognition gained in my study of Galatians and Romans[2] that Paul's "doctrine of justification" was not an enduring part of his thinking, but developed as a contingent teaching, a "polemical teaching" to use William Wrede's phrase,[3] in his letter to the Galatians in response to the Galatians' desire to become circumcised as the means of becoming children of Abraham, which Paul interpreted as a turn to Judaism as the means of justification. He developed this teaching further in Romans, formulating it more clearly at a number of points.

## 2. The Problem of the Center of Paul's Thought

Paul provides his clearest formulation of the teaching in Rom 4:10-12 by arguing that Abraham was a gentile when he was justified. Accordingly, both gentiles and Jews become inheritors of the promise to Abraham, not through circumcision and a

---

[1] Bornkamm 1969, 128.
[2] Boers 1993.
[3] Wrede 1904, 72; 1964, 67. ET 1907, 123.

Jewish heritage, but by emulating his faith as a gentile, that is, before he became a Jew by being circumcised. Rom 4:10-12 clarifies the meaning of this teaching which Paul expressed in its most succinct form in Gal 2:15-16, ἡμεῖς φύσει Ἰουδαῖοι καὶ οὐκ ἐξ ἐθνῶν ἁμαρτωλοί· εἰδότες [δὲ] ὅτι οὐ δικαιοῦται ἄνθρωπος ἐξ ἔργων νόμου ἐὰν μὴ διὰ πίστεως Ἰησοῦ Χριστοῦ, καὶ ἡμεῖς εἰς Χριστὸν Ἰησοῦν ἐπιστεύσαμεν, ἵνα δικαιωθῶμεν ἐκ πίστεως Χριστοῦ καὶ οὐκ ἐξ ἔργων νόμου, ὅτι ἐξ ἔργων νόμου οὐ δικαιωθήσεται πᾶσα σάρξ, which can be translated to bring out its meaning as follows: "We who are by heritage Jews, and not from the gentiles, sinners, knowing that no-one is justified by virtue of (ἐκ) being a Jew[4] unless[5] it is through the faith of Jesus Christ, we too have believed in Christ Jesus in order to be justified by virtue of the faith of Christ and not by virtue of being Jews, for no-one will be justified by virtue of being a Jew." It had become clear that what had here-to-fore been one of the most fundamental hermeneutical principles in the interpretation of Paul, justification by faith, had been completely misunderstood. Justification by faith is indeed an important principle in Paul's thinking, but its meaning is purely functional as the means of expressing his conviction that being a Jew was not a condition for salvation. *Justification by faith for Paul means specifically justification of the gentile.* As such it cannot function as a hermeneutical principle for his thought in general.

The more fundamental conviction that being a Jew was not a condition for salvation may come closer to being, not *the* hermeneutical principle for the interpretation of Paul, but an important component of such a principle. It appears to be only one way of formulating a more deep-rooted conviction which Paul expresses in other ways as well, for example, in the statement in 1 Cor 12:13, καὶ γὰρ ἐν ἑνὶ πνεύματι ἡμεῖς πάντες εἰς ἓν σῶμα ἐβαπτίσθημεν, εἴτε Ἰουδαῖοι εἴτε Ἕλληνες εἴτε δοῦλοι εἴτε ἐλεύθεροι, καὶ πάντες ἓν πνεῦμα ἐποτίσθημεν, in which negation of the distinction between Jews and gentiles (Hellenes) is only one component. What is not clarified in Galatians and Romans is the meaning of that faith through which one is justified. That meaning is presupposed. It had become clear that although we previously thought we knew, we did not know the meaning of faith, the concept that had been crucial for our understanding not only of Galatians and Romans but of all of Paul's thought.

I had come to a dead-end in my interpretation of Paul, similar to the zero point I

---

[4] ἔργα νόμου is of course literally, "works of the Law," but to translate like that would leave Paul's meaning ambiguous. He does not mean works that are done in obedience to the Law, as, for example, in Rom 2:13, "the doers of the Law will be justified," but to the Law as the means of establishing Jewish privileges over against the gentiles.

[5] As this translation shows, Paul meant "if not, unless" when he wrote ἐὰν μὴ, and not "but" ("sondern" in German) as the phrase is typically (mis)translated for purely dogmatic reasons.

had arrived at earlier in my understanding of Romans when it became clear that 3:21-24 and the doctrine of justification by faith were not the keys to the meaning of the letter. Taking 3:21-24 as the context for interpreting Romans works for better or for worse with regard to chapters 1-4, but leaves the rest of the letter contextually incomprehensible, especially, but not exclusively chapters 9-11. The realization that 3:21-24 did not provide the hermeneutical key to Romans did not prevent me from interpreting individual parts of the letter, but I had no clue as to what Paul was trying to say.

Starting with that realization in my further investigation of Romans, which ultimately led me to Galatians as well, I was able to establish that the point of Paul's reasoning in these letters was that it was not necessary for salvation to be circumcised, that is, to be a Jew. That provided me with a new hermeneutical center for the interpretation of Galatians and Romans, but it made clear at the same time that what I had thought was the key to Paul's thinking, justification by faith, could no longer function as such because justification by faith functioned purely as a way of addressing a contingent issue which arose when Paul learned that the Galatians, or at least some of them, wanted to become circumcised. I had arrived at a new zero point. Negation of the necessity to be circumcised clarified what Paul was trying to say in Galatians and Romans, but it did not provide a key to an understanding of Paul's thinking; it was not what could be considered the central core of his thought. What I present here is a methodological study, intended to lay the groundwork for moving beyond the recognition that justification by faith does not constitute the central core of Paul's thought, in an attempt to determine what then may be such a central core. Key to this endeavor will be the way in which context contributes to the meaning of a text.

## 3. Context in the Interpretation of Texts

I will use the term context in this paper in an expanded sense to refer to those factors that contribute to the meaning of a text other than what is concretely present in it. I will distinguish three kinds of context. First, the *interpretative* context. Bornkamm takes Paul's doctrine of justification as the context for interpreting all of his writings. The doctrine of justification is the "engste Zusammenhang," the closest environment, that is, the interpretive context for understanding Paul. It is the context provided by the interpreter to make sense of a text, which could be conscious, intentional, as in the case of Bornkamm, but it may also be sub-conscious. It is what Teun van Dijk calls the macro-structure with which an interpreter approaches a text.[6] In its most elementary form it is the expectation with which we approach a written text, an oral discourse, or even a stage production or film. Once we become involved in any of these, the macro-structure with which we began begins to change, in the sense of the hermeneutical circle made famous by Rudolf Bultmann in New Testament interpretation.

A second kind of context is in the form of another text, probably the most widely understood meaning of the term. In a text-linguistic sense I would like to refer to it as a *co-text*. Such a co-text can be illustrated with reference to the series of texts Paul quotes from the Hebrew Scriptures (in Greek of course) in Rom 3:10-18, to establish Jewish guilt before the Law, and in 15:9-12, to praise the unity in Christ of Jews and gentiles. There are two ways of approaching such quoted texts co-textually: One could try to determine whether the original co-textual context in the Hebrew Scriptures contributes to the meaning of a quoted text. This form of co-textuality can be referred to as *inter*-textual, external co-textuality in which the present text is drawn co-textually into the textual framework of another text.[7] There are cases where this is true, but in both of the above-mentioned cases the co-textual contribution to Paul's meaning is the other texts he quotes, creating anew co-textual context. This form of co-textuality can be referred to as *intra*-textual, internal co-textuality. The present text draws the other texts into its own textual framework. Paul's texts have to be read in the new context in which he has placed them, that is, their co-textual environment is no longer their original co-textual settings, but their current setting as part of the series of quotations.

A third kind of context is the original *communicative setting* of a text. It can be illustrated very well by what is called shared meaning in linguistics. This kind of context is the key to the transition between Gal 3:6 and 7. The conclusion which Paul draws in verse 7 from his quotation of Gen 15:6 in verse 6 is understandable only in the context of knowledge which he shared with the Galatians, that is, their understanding that one became a child of Abraham by becoming circumcised. The only way Paul could draw the conclusion that it is through faith that one becomes a child of Abraham from Gen 15:6 is as a counter argument to the view that one becomes a child of Abraham through circumcision. This is what provides the missing link between Paul's quotation of Gen 15:6 and the conclusion he draws from it. This kind of context does not have to be as complex as the transition from Gal 5:6 to verse 7. A large part of what is communicated, especially in oral discourse, is un-

---

[6] van Dijk 1972, 160. He defines it as follows: "… semantic macro-structures are necessary to explain in sufficiently simple terms how it is possible that throughout a text the selection of lexical items and underlying formation of semantic representations is heavily restricted by some global constraint." He adds an observation that is very relevant for us here: "… everybody will construct the macro-structure of a text which is relevant for him, personally, and the macro-structures will be different for the same text."

[7] See, e.g., H. F. Plett (ed.) 1991.

derstandable only because of the context, the setting in which it takes place. An excellent case in point is the parables of Jesus. When they became removed from their original contexts in Jesus' teaching—or in other situations in which many of them may have originated—they became incomprehensible to New Testament Christianity, until allegorical interpretations were discovered to adapt them to the new setting of the christologically oriented New Testament Christianity.

## 4. The Problem with Justification by Faith as the Center for Understanding Paul

My primary concern is the interpretive context for understanding Paul. It is important here to distinguish between context and co-text. In the case of the series of quotations in Rom 3:10-18 and 15:9-12, the relationship between context and co-text is indistinguishable. The co-textual environment of the series of quotations functions as the interpretive context for each of the individual quotations. That is not always the case. So, for example, in the case of Rom 3:21-4:25 the question is whether a part of the text provides the theme for the entire section, and so can function as its co-textual interpretive context. Two subsections come into consideration, Rom 3:29-30 and 3:21-24. The question is which one can function to clarify what is involved in the meaning of the passage. It could be 3:21-24, with its emphasis on justification by faith, or 3:29-30, which affirms that God is not of the Jews only, but also of the gentiles. In each case what is considered central or thematic determines the meaning of the entire passage, including the alternatively possible thematic section. Pointedly, should Rom 3:29-30 be read in the light of 3:21-24, or, inversely, 3:21-24 in the light of 3:29-30, that is, should God belonging to the Jews as well as the gentiles be interpreted in the context of justification by faith, or justification by faith in the context of the affirmation that God belongs to the Jews as well as the gentiles. To put it differently, is Paul's proposition that God is not of the Jews only but also of the gentiles an expression of the doctrine of justification by faith, or does justification by faith function as an argument in support of his conviction that God is not of the Jews only, but also of the gentiles. Formulated differently, is justification of the gentiles an instance of justification by faith, or is justification by faith an argument in support of the justification of the gentiles.

Moving beyond Galatians and Romans, the problem with taking the doctrine of justification by faith as the interpretive context, the hermeneutical center for interpreting Paul's thought in the sense of Bornkamm is that the expression occurs for the first time in verse 9 of the letter fragment in Phil 3:2-14,[8] καὶ εὑρεθῶ ἐν αὐτῷ, μὴ ἔχων ἐμὴν δικαιοσύνην τὴν ἐκ νόμου ἀλλὰ τὴν διὰ πίστεως Χριστοῦ, τὴν ἐκ θεοῦ δικαιοσύνην ἐπὶ τῇ πίστει. It is one of the latest of Paul's writings, as the following considerations make clear. The thematic closeness of the Philippians fragment to Galatians and Romans suggests chronological proximity. Recent studies have placed Galatians chronologically much later than has traditionally been assumed.[9] This agrees with the finding in my study of Galatians and Romans in which I concluded that Romans, particularly 1:18-4:25, is a product of Paul's further reflection on the fundamental issue of Galatians, rejection of circumcision and the Law as the means to salvation, revealing the chronological proximity of the two letters. The fact that the Philippians fragment does not make use of the figure of Abraham to argue that justification is by faith and not through works of the Law, poses a special problem with regard to its relationship to Galatians and Romans. One would have to assume that the fragment is earlier than Galatians; it is unimaginable that Paul could have written it between Galatians and Romans without leaving traces of the issue of the faith of Abraham. A date after Romans is also improbable, for similar reasons. The crucial role played by Abraham in Paul's reasoning in Galatians and Romans thus reveals a closer relationship between these two letters than their shared relationship to the Philippians fragment.

This contrast in the relationship between Galatians and Romans, on the one hand, and their common relationship to the Philippians fragment, on the other, is also indicated by the uncontroversial way in which Paul attaches positive value to circumcision in a metaphoric sense in Phil 3:3, ἡμεῖς γάρ ἐσμεν ἡ περιτομή, but especially to his own circumcision, περιτομῇ ὀκταήμερος in verse 5, similar to his positive evaluation of being of the seed of Abraham as a sign of his Jewish heritage in 2 Cor 11:22. His devaluing of his Jewish virtues in verses 7-8 is not absolute, but relative to what he had found in Christ. This is in stark contrast to his harsh negation of the value of being a Jew in the allegory of Sarah and Hagar in Gal 4:21-30, culminating in verse 30 with the harsh condemnation of the Jewish line represented by Hagar, Sinai and the present Jerusalem, ἀλλὰ τί λέγει ἡ γραφή; ἔκβαλε τὴν παιδίσκην καὶ τὸν υἱὸν αὐτῆς· οὐ γὰρ μὴ κληρονομήσει ὁ υἱὸς τῆς παιδίσκης μετὰ τοῦ υἱοῦ τῆς ἐλευθέρας. In Rom 3:1 Paul addresses the value of circumcision and being a Jew as a controversial issue, and affirms it in verse 2, taking up the issue as a separate topic in chapters 9-11. The Philippians fragment does not presuppose the reasoning concerning the value of circumcision and being a Jew in Romans, but af-

---

[8] By fragment I do not mean that Phil 3:2-14 could not have been an integral part of the letter, although it might not be; the connection with what follows is more fluid than the abrupt beginning. By fragment I indicate that it is structurally unrelated to its textual environment, which is what makes it virtually impossible to locate it chronologically in relationship to the rest of Paul's letters, and so also materially its place in the development of his thought.

[9] So, for example, Lüdemann places Galatians, 2 Corinthians 1-9, and 2 Corinthians 10-13 during the same Summer of 50 or 53 (1980, 273).

firms these Jewish values without a sense of controversy. Nevertheless, the common issue of the value of circumcision and being a Jew reveals a certain closeness between these three writings, notwithstanding their differences. As a group they appear to belong among the latest of Paul's letters.

My investigation revealed that what is at issue in Galatians and Romans is not works righteousness, but the Jewish claim of a privileged relationship with God through circumcision and the Law.[10] More important, the subject matter shared by these letters, justification by faith and not through works of the Law, cannot be considered as fundamental to Paul's thinking, but a contingent issue that arose when Paul rejected what he perceived as a willingness on the part of the Galatians to submit to circumcision, becoming Jews, as the means of salvation. At issue here is not to what degree Paul may have misunderstood the Galatians, but that justification by faith, a contingent issue that arose in Galatians, cannot be considered as the center of his teaching, as the interpretive context for understanding him. With the loss of justification by faith as the interpretive center of Paul's thinking it became clear to me that I no longer had access to his thought. It was not a problem of interpreting individual parts of his letters, but that did not contribute to an understanding of what Paul was trying to say. Interpreting the individual parts, verses or even longer stretches of discourse, was like using a dictionary to find the meaning of words in order to interpret the meaning of a sentence. The dictionary does not reveal how the choice of the possible meanings is determined by the way they are restrained by the syntax of the sentence. For that purpose one needs a grammar which clarifies the syntax.

Thus, in order to understand Paul's earlier letters we cannot take the issues or teaching of Galatians and Romans as the context for their interpretation, but will have to take them within their own contexts, without relying on Galatians and Romans. That does not exclude Galatians and Romans from co-textual considerations with regard to the Pauline corpus, but it places them on an equal basis with the rest of the letters. They have to be given a place among the other letters, and not allowed to become the dominant co-textual center, which applies in particular to Romans, and there specifically to Rom 3:21-24. Indeed, one should take Galatians and Romans as dependent on the earlier letters for their context. With regard to Paul's understanding of faith—not the doctrine of justification by faith—we will probably have to rely almost exclusively on the earlier letters because Paul's use of the concept in Galatians and Romans is so heavily determined by its applied sense of justification by faith.

---

[10] A similar conclusion was reached independently of each other, and with completely different methods of inquiry, by Sanders 1983, and Heiligenthal 1983.

## 5. The Question of a Structure of Convictions as the Foundation of Paul's Thought

The recognition that Galatians and Romans, and with them justification by faith, cannot be considered the contextual basis for interpreting Paul relieves Pauline interpreters of one of the most important, but mistaken factors providing what must be considered an erroneous coherence to Paul's thought. This insight makes clear that for the most part we do not know what was at the center, at the heart of Paul's thinking. Salutary about this loss is that it requires, and makes possible, a fresh start in trying to determine what, if anything, gives coherence to Paul's thought. An indispensable principle for progress in the interpretation of Paul is that the subject-matter of Galatians and Romans is contingent, and that these letters therefore cannot function as the co-textual interpretive context for such an interpretation. The main exceptions may be Romans 5-8 and 12-15 which may also not be as closely tied to the contingency of these letters.

It is not necessary to assume that everything Paul wrote manifests deeper level convictions. Indeed, one should consider it probable that his deepest convictions became manifest to varying degrees in his thinking, depending on the situations he addressed. In some cases other considerations, sometimes purely practical ones, may have been determinative. A case in which a conflict of convictions occurs is the discussion of the veiling of women in 1 Cor 11:3-16 where he tries to give theological reasons for his view that women should be veiled when they worship (vv. 3-10), but is unable to sustain his reasoning against a deeper conviction that "in the Lord" the distinctions he makes between the dignity of men and women cannot be sustained (vv. 11-12), and finally, when he appeals to his readers' sense of assumed social values, he reveals that his point was not motivated by theological convictions, but by the values of the social class to which he belonged. He ends the discussion by effectively throwing in the towel as far as proving his point is concerned in his *ad hominem* remark about people who are quarrelsome (v. 16). The conflict between two systems of values in this passage—the values of the social class to which he belonged and those which emerged from being in the Lord—reveals a deeper level of Paul's thinking in which conflicts occur of which he appears to have been at the most vaguely aware. The task of interpretation is to determine such and other, sometimes more subtle, distinctions. I will return to 1 Cor 11:3-16 below, showing its relationship to a network of texts expressing the same value of negating discriminating social distinctions in a variety of ways, illustrating how texts can be read not only syntactically but also paradigmatically.

One way of approaching the central core underlying Paul's thinking is to develop a theory of what motivated him, a macro-structure in the sense of van Dijk referred to above,[11] which makes it possible to discover crucial aspects of his thought. An excellent example is Karl Barth's theory of the infinite qualitative difference between time and eternity, which he derived from Kierkegaard and applied with such rigor in his interpretation of Romans that one might be able to say that his famous commentary is almost more Kierkegaard than Paul. And yet there are many enduring insights in that commentary, recognizable as true through precise exegetical investigation without relying on Barth's central theory, for example, his view that Paul's critique of Judaism becomes best understandable when applied directly to the contemporary church which suffers from the same kind of errors which Paul criticizes in Judaism. In making this assertion Barth skips a considerable number of steps from the text of Romans to his interpretive application, but precise exegesis will show that he had good reason to do so.

My intention in the further investigation of Paul is to make a new beginning, without a theory of what motivated his thinking, and to develop a method by means of which it would become possible to allow a structure of ideas, a configuration of values which gives coherence to his thought to emerge from the writings themselves. I am not interested in seeing what I can make of Paul, but would like to see if his writings can impose on the interpreter recognition of a central core which provides coherence to his thinking in the variety of its expressions, allowing for greater or lesser dependence on that central core in individual instances.

## 6. Methodological Background

The method I propose continues procedures I followed in my books on Jesus,[12] on John 4,[13] and on Galatians and Romans.[14] Since this is a methodological study—I wish I was farther along—I will clarify those procedures in so far as they are relevant for the task that lies ahead. In *Who Was Jesus?* I proceeded with complete skepticism that one could know anything historically reliable about Jesus. Even the two teachers from whom I had learned so much about critical theological research, Rudolf Bultmann[15] and Herbert Braun,[16] would not have found what they did if they did not have an idea what they were looking for in their books on Jesus. In each case the decisive importance of an existentialist interpretation provided the interpretive context for their investigations, determining the questions that were asked and what

---

[11] See footnote 6.
[12] Boers 1989.
[13] Boers 1988.
[14] Boers 1993.
[15] Bultmann 1926; ET 1958.
[16] Braun 1969. ET 1979.

answers might be relevant. There should be no question that in this way valuable results were obtained, similar to those that emerged from Barth's interpretation of Romans. It reminds one of Socrates' (Plato's) query: How can we look for something if we do not know what we are looking for, but why do we look for something if we already know what it is?

The interpretive context providing the macro-structure for my own investigation of the synoptic gospels was purely historical-critical principles without any idea of what may have emerged.[17] The results were so meager that one reviewer complained that there is not much about Jesus in the book. My answer is that the meager results are not due to a lack of effort, but to the lack of historically reliable information in the gospels, documents that were not written with a view to providing such information. Luke, who did undertake such an endeavor, was no longer able to uncover much either. The conclusion should be that unless one investigates the synoptic tradition knowing what it is one is looking for, these writings produce very little information about the Jesus behind them. I did not know what I was looking for, but wanted the material itself to provide the questions as well as the answers in accordance with the principles of historical inquiry.[18]

In my study of Paul it had become clear that it was not possible to systematize his thinking because he could use the same concept to express opposed and even contradictory meanings. The most obvious example is the apparent contraction between Rom 2:13, οὐ γὰρ οἱ ἀκροαταὶ νόμου δίκαιοι παρὰ [τῷ] θεῷ, ἀλλ' οἱ ποιηταὶ νόμου δικαιωθήσονται, and 3:20, ἐξ ἔργων νόμου οὐ δικαιωθήσεται πᾶσα σὰρξ ἐνώπιον αὐτοῦ, διὰ γὰρ νόμου ἐπίγνωσις ἁμαρτίας. I had no doubt that Paul meant both statements, that on the basis of Paul's own words one had to conclude that he affirmed both justification by faith and divine reward for the doing of good works, as he states explicitly in the conclusion of his reasoning in Romans 2:29, ... οὗ ὁ ἔπαινος οὐκ ἐξ ἀνθρώπων ἀλλ' ἐκ τοῦ θεοῦ. The problem was that I could not understand how he could do so. It is a problem which Pauline scholarship also cannot solve. Indeed, Pauline scholarship in general does not recognize the existence of a contradiction, preferring instead to deny that Paul affirms justifi-

---

[17] Let me state emphatically that I do not assume that my research was unbiased; it was biased by the historical-critical method which determined what questions should be asked and what would be relevant answers, with a heavy load of historical skepticism concerning the subject matter. The results do not disclose what happened in the life of Jesus, but only what a historian can make of the evidence. My skepticism included a willingness to accept miracles, but only if the evidence pointed in that way as the most probable historical explanation. Not surprisingly, nothing pointed in that direction.

[18] In my dissertation (Boers 1962), I did know what I had been looking for. What I wanted to know was whether the christological pronouncements in the gospels applied historically to Jesus. I found only negative answers.

cation for the doing of good works.

This dead end at which I had arrived is what prompted my engagement in text-linguistics and semiotics. I had come to the realization that methodologically I no longer knew the appropriate questions for an interpretation of Paul, not to mention possible answers. Prior to that I thought I knew, but I had come to a zero point in my understanding, not in principle but as the concrete results of my research. The slate had been wiped clean, at least in so far as it is possible to wipe a slate clean, literally and figuratively. A new beginning had become necessary. I was convinced that if progress were to be made the questions as well as their possible answers had to emerge from the Pauline texts themselves, not from some proposed theory because it was precisely theories of what Paul must have intended that brought me to this dead end. What I needed was something beyond conflicting theories about Paul, something more akin to the relative security of a grammar. Such a grammar could contribute significantly to an understanding of *how* Paul thought, and if we know that we might also be able to understand *what* he thought. At the same time, I was keenly aware that I did not have a method with which to engage in this endeavor.

In *Neither on this Mountain, nor in Jerusalem*, I developed a grammar by means of which it was possible to uncover the inner functioning of the text of John 4. I chose John 4 because it was an interesting example, but also because I did not want to begin with a Pauline text, which remained my primary objective. Many readers have complained in different terms about the high degree of abstraction in the first two-thirds of the study. When I engaged in linguistic-semiotic study as the possible means of understanding the inner workings of texts, both syntactically and semantically, it had become clear to me that unless I could move to the highest levels of abstraction where the actual, concrete meanings of the text were no longer in view, the results would remain tied to personal preferences. It was necessary to follow the logic, the syntax of an author's thought without considering what he or she was trying to say, before considering the latter, that is, the author's "Sache," to use Bultmann's insightful concept in his controversy with Barth on the interpretation of Paul. I do not deny that when one returns to the concrete text such preferences of necessity once more enter into the picture.

## 7. Justification of the Gentiles as the Interpretive Center of Galatians and Romans

What I learned from the study of John 4 prepared me to address the unsolved problems I had encountered in the interpretation of Paul, in particular of Romans. That did not mean simply applying the method I developed in the earlier study, but taking note of the way in which meaning is generated in a text. Building on the methodology developed in the study of John 4 with a continued attention to the text itself, I was led to the realization that what motivated Paul's thought in Galatians and Romans, prompted by the situation in Galatia, was that God was not of the Jews only, but also of the gentiles (Rom 3:29-30). It is a conception that was not new to Paul's thinking; he already brought the basic idea to expression in a different formulation in 1 Cor 7:19, repeating the same formulation with slight variations in Gal 5:6 and 6:15. These formulations repeat the same basic theme with different emphases: ἡ περιτομὴ οὐδέν ἐστιν καὶ ἡ ἀκροβυστία οὐδέν ἐστιν, ἀλλὰ τήρησις ἐντολῶν θεοῦ (1 Cor 7:19), ἐν γὰρ Χριστῷ Ἰησοῦ οὔτε περιτομή τι ἰσχύει οὔτε ἀκροβυστία ἀλλὰ πίστις δι᾿ ἀγάπης ἐνεργουμένη (Gal 5:6), and οὔτε γὰρ περιτομή τί ἐστιν οὔτε ἀκροβυστία ἀλλὰ καινὴ κτίσις (Gal 6:15). All three formulations are transformations at a concrete, surface level, adapted to different contextual and co-textual settings, of a single deeper level conviction in Paul's thought. In 1 Corinthians he uses this underlying theme as the basis for another conviction which he brought over from his Jewish heritage, the importance of keeping the commandments of God. In Gal 5:6 he interprets doing the commandments of God in terms of love, as he subsequently does thematically in Rom 13:8-10, and in Gal 6:15 he uses the same theme to emphasize the nature of the new being in Christ, in both cases applying it directly to what was at issue in Galatia as he understood it, namely, the Galatians in effect reaffirming the value of circumcision and the Law, and so the division between Jews and gentiles. That Paul himself did not completely devalue circumcision and being a Jew becomes clear in Rom 3:1 when he raises the question and replies positively to it in verse 2, τί οὖν τὸ περισσὸν τοῦ Ἰουδαίου ἢ τίς ἡ ὠφέλεια τῆς περιτομῆς; πολὺ κατὰ πάντα τρόπον. πρῶτον μὲν [γὰρ] ὅτι ἐπιστεύθησαν τὰ λόγια τοῦ θεοῦ.

It is tempting to consider negation of the separation of Jews and gentiles as what is at the deepest core of Paul's thought, and it certainly must be at least part of what is involved. He was after all a Jew who had considered the privilege of being a Jew of such supreme value to cause him to persecute the new religion emerging from Judaism for demeaning this value. His conversion meant the abandonment of this conviction, which finds appropriate expression in the texts referred to above, including Rom 3:29-30, ἢ Ἰουδαίων ὁ θεὸς μόνον; οὐχὶ καὶ ἐθνῶν; ναὶ καὶ ἐθνῶν, εἴπερ εἷς ὁ θεός ὃς δικαιώσει περιτομὴν ἐκ πίστεως καὶ ἀκροβυστίαν διὰ τῆς πίστεως. Reading Paul's letters, however, reveals that more is involved. The principle that neither being circumcised counts for anything nor not being circumcised, important as it is, by itself does not function as the central core of his thinking. The pervasiveness of the derivatives from the stem πιστ–, for example, and the ways he uses them in his writings, including the all important πίστις Ἰησοῦ Χριστοῦ, reveals that what these terms represent also plays an important part.[19] The way in which faith comes to play in Paul's reasoning in Gal 3:6-7 confirms this.

The transition between Gal 3:6 and 7 presupposes knowledge shared by Paul and his readers, namely, the Galatians' argument that one had to be circumcised to be a child of Abraham, for which they could have relied on Gen 17 as their most important source. It is important to note that Abraham is introduced here for the first time in the role he plays in Galatians and Romans, even though Paul referred to him once before. In 2 Cor 11:22 he referred to being of the seed of Abraham to underscore the validity of his Jewish heritage, whereas in Gal 3:6-7, contrary to such a view, he argues that it is through faith that one becomes a child of Abraham, concluding that part of his reasoning in 3:29 with a statement which makes it clear that it is being of the "seed of Abraham" that is at issue, εἰ δὲ ὑμεῖς Χριστοῦ, ἄρα τοῦ Ἀβραὰμ σπέρμα ἐστέ, κατ᾽ ἐπαγγελίαν κληρονόμοι. In Rom 4:9-12 he reinforces this view by proving that Abraham was justified while still a gentile.

In 2 Cor 11:22 "seed of Abraham" functions to reinforce Paul's Jewish heritage as a positive value, whereas in Galatians and Romans it functions to negate that very same value. The Galatians could have been willing to submit to circumcision as the means of becoming children of Abraham in order that they too could say as Paul does, "we are of the seed of Abraham" in the sense of 2 Cor 11:22. What this makes clear with regard to Gal 3:6-7 is that Paul did not introduce Abraham into the argument as part of his earlier thinking, but reacted to the way in which those whom he opposed in Galatia used him as an argument. For them "seed of Abraham" represented Jewish heritage as a positive value, similar to Paul's understanding in 2 Cor 11:22, but now he used the same concept to negate the value of that heritage.

Faith too is not introduced, but presupposed by Paul in his reasoning in Gal 3:6-7. But in this case it is not something which he took over from those whom he opposed in Galatia, nor from Gen 15:6 which he uses as the premise of his argument, but something he presupposed from his earlier teaching. Together these two concepts, the seed of Abraham which he picks up from the Galatians, and faith which he presupposes from his earlier teaching, lead him to Gen 15:6 in which Abraham as well as faith are present. These deliberations reveal that faith was fundamental in Paul's thinking, something he did not find necessary to introduce, but assumed.

The meaning of justification is also not clarified, but assumed. Like faith it functions as the means of establishing the believer's relationship to Abraham, because it was through faith that Abraham was justified (Gen 15:6). The meanings of these terms are not at issue in Galatians; what counts is the way they function to negate the value of circumcision and being a Jew for salvation. Paul's reasoning on this

---

[19] I would like to emphasize that what the terms derived from the stem πιστ– represent plays *an important part* in the central core of Paul's thought; I do not believe that it in itself constitutes that central core.

point differs in the two letters, with a more christological interpretation in Gal 3:8-18—Abraham's faith was a response to the fulfillment of the promise which Scripture foresaw in Christ—while in Rom 4:9-12 (cf. verses 23-24) believers are justified by emulating Abraham's trust in God. That faith could function differently in the two letters confirms that it is not what is at issue; in each case Paul presupposes its meaning and uses it to suit his reasoning. Its meaning as he uses it *is* its function.[20]

Even though the arguments in the two letters are different, they function with the same purpose in mind, that is, to negate the value which Paul assumed the Galatians attributed to circumcision and being a Jew. Faith as Paul developed the concept in Galatians and Romans, that is, in the circumscribed sense of justification by faith and not by being a Jew, does not reveal how he understood the concept before this particular application of it. In order to understand its meaning in Paul we have to turn our attention to the earlier letters with the understanding that we cannot rely on the way faith is used in Paul's conception of justification by faith in Galatians and Romans. Our point of departure should be the recognition that we do not know what faith meant for Paul in a sense that is more fundamental than its applied use in Galatians and Romans as an expression of the justification of the gentiles.

## 8. In Search of an Interpretive Context for Paul

The problem is that when one moves from Galatians and Romans to Paul's earlier letters there is not a single contextual center for Paul's thinking, such as we found in the issue of circumcision and being a Jew as the means of salvation in the Philippians fragment, Galatians and Romans. A variety of contexts are provided in the earlier letters by the variety of situations addressed by Paul. In many cases the context for his reasoning may have been determined largely by practical considerations relating to the situations he addressed. Looking for a deeper point of reference in such cases may prove unnecessary. There are however other cases in which the context determining Paul's meaning lies deeper, in convictions that are fundamental to his thinking. It is that context that interests me in this investigation. I still think in terms of a coherent center which determines the way Paul addressed contingent situations in his letters,[21] even though what was fundamental does not necessarily surface in all of what he wrote. Such a center does not have to be a single doctrine, such

---

[20] For a not too technical, well-written discussion of a functional approach to meaning, see de Beaugrande and Dressler 1981; also Halliday 1973.

[21] The distinction between the contingency of Paul's expressions and the coherent center of his thought is the major contribution of Beker 1980, although he has in the meantime expressed reservations about the formulation of this distinction.

as the doctrine of justification proposed by Bornkamm, or God's apocalyptic triumph proposed by J. Christiaan Beker,[22] but could be a configuration of fundamental convictions, such as proposed by Daniel Patte.[23] The solution I would like to propose is a grammatical structure, syntactic as well as semantic, in which the meanings of the parts are not established individually, but by the way in which they interrelate.

What is called for is a configuration of thought which makes it possible to understand how Paul reasons, sometimes making statements that appear contradictory. In the sense of van Dijk, it is necessary to find a coherent center to Paul's thinking as expressed in his letters by means of which is becomes possible to explain his choice of words, phrases and larger syntactic sequences as well as the ideas expressed in them.[24] For this purpose it will not be sufficient to propose a theory which functions as the interpretive context for Paul's writings, and then to show how well the theory functions to reveal important features of his thought. The danger of such a theory is that it becomes co-determinative of the proposed meaning of the text. Bultmann's existentialist interpretation proves that even the hermeneutical circle does not prevent the theory from remaining a factor in the interpretation of a text. The test of a theory is whether it succeeds in not becoming part of the meaning it helps to disclose. Such a test would be whether the meaning, once it has been established by means of the theory, is also evident without the theory. The theory should be considered as scaffolding which has to be removed to reveal the beauty of what it has served to realize. In whatever way one proceeds, inductively or deductively, the final test must be whether such an interpretive context makes it possible to understand why Paul wrote what he did throughout his entire corpus. The problem is not with abstraction—all thought is abstraction—but whether the abstraction can function to clarify the text. Beker's triumph of God is an abstraction, but that is not the problem. The problem is that he does not provide a means of reading the Pauline corpus, but makes a demand on the reader to recognize that his abstraction is present in the texts, some of the texts. In that regard Patte's procedure, notwithstanding its limitations, is more fruitful because it does address the relationship between Paul's convictions and his "arguments" better than Beker's theory of the apocalyptic triumph of God as the central core of Paul's thought, notwithstanding the promise of Beker's methodological distinction between coherent center and contingent expressions. I am not able to provide a solution to the problem of the coherent center of Paul's thought; all I would like to do here is reflect on ways in which we may proceed to find answers.

---

[22] Beker 1980.

[23] Patte 1983.

[24] See above, footnote 6.

### 9. Proposed Method

The method I would like to propose was developed by Claude Lévi-Strauss[25] for uncovering the meaning expressed in religious (mythical), that is, non-systematic texts[26] by reading them not only syntagmatically, i.e., with the flow of the stories, but also paradigmatically, by tabulating the recurrence of similar story elements or mythemes in a myth or a series of myths. He compares it with the reading of a musical score, not only horizontally with regard to its melody, but also vertically with regard to the harmony of the various voices of the instruments or singers. In that way it becomes possible for a series of recurring themes throughout a text or texts to form the context of interpretation, rather than a single significant one. Such a series of recurring themes becomes even more useful when they are recognized in structural relationships to other themes. The examination of a sufficient number enables the interpreter to discern structural patterns of oppositions between groups of mythemes. Lévi-Strauss illustrates this method, first with an analysis of the Oedipus myth,[27] and then the North American Zuni myth of origin and emergence.[28] The details of those analyses do not need to concern us here.

The following are two ways of gathering the material for such an interpretation from the Pauline corpus: 1. Reading through the entire corpus with a view to finding recurring themes, and 2. Collecting texts in which key terms recur. In the latter case a concordance could be a useful first step to identify such texts, but then a way must be found to read them together in a new co-textual context provided by them as a group, similar to Paul's series of texts in Rom 3:10-18 and 15:9-12. It will be necessary to print these texts out together, not mere phrases but entire verses, and in some cases even longer sections, in order to allow a new co-textual context for their reading to emerge.[29] It will soon become clear that not all texts in which a key term occurs are related thematically, but there will be enough texts to allow recurrent thematic material to emerge.

### 10. A Structure which Comes to Expression as the Negation of Human Distinctions in Christ

An illustration of the first procedure can begin with Paul's discussion of the veiling of women in 1 Cor 11:3-16 where he tries to give theological reasons for arguing

---

[25] Lévi-Strauss 1955, 1958; ET 1963, 208.

[26] Lévi-Strauss makes the distinction between texts with a mythical logic in contrast to the positive logic of philosophy/theology.

[27] Lévi-Strauss 1963, 209-14.

[28] Lévi-Strauss 1963, 215-26.

that women should be veiled when they worship (vv. 3-10), but is unable to sustain his reasoning against a deeper conviction that "in the Lord" the distinctions he makes between the dignity of men and women cannot be sustained (vv.11-12), and finally reveals that his point was motivated by social values of the class to which he belonged when he appeals to his readers' sense of those values. He ends the discussion by effectively throwing in the towel as far as proving his point is concerned in his *ad hominem* remark about people who are quarrelsome (v. 16). The task of interpretation is to determine such and other more subtle distinctions.

That the argument which impinges on Paul's reasoning in 1 Cor 11:3-10, πλὴν οὔτε γυνὴ χωρὶς ἀνδρὸς οὔτε ἀνὴρ χωρὶς γυναικὸς ἐν κυρίῳ (v. 11) is not new, but the coming to surface of a value that lies deeper in the structure of his thought, is revealed by its recurrence in his writings. The same value recurs in Gal 3:27-28 ὅσοι γὰρ εἰς Χριστὸν ἐβαπτίσθητε, Χριστὸν ἐνεδύσασθε. οὐκ ἔνι Ἰουδαῖος οὐδὲ Ἕλλην, οὐκ ἔνι δοῦλος οὐδὲ ἐλεύθερος, οὐκ ἔνι ἄρσεν καὶ θῆλυ· πάντες γὰρ ὑμεῖς εἷς ἐστε ἐν Χριστῷ Ἰησοῦ. The point of that passage appeared in a different formulation in 1 Cor 12:13 καὶ γὰρ ἐν ἑνὶ πνεύματι ἡμεῖς πάντες εἰς ἓν σῶμα ἐβαπτίσθημεν, εἴτε Ἰουδαῖοι εἴτε Ἕλληνες εἴτε δοῦλοι εἴτε ἐλεύθεροι, καὶ πάντες ἓν πνεῦμα ἐποτίσθημεν, and from there we are led to a fuller formulation in 2 Cor 5:14-17 ἡ γὰρ ἀγάπη τοῦ Χριστοῦ συνέχει ἡμᾶς, κρίναντας τοῦτο, ὅτι εἷς ὑπὲρ πάντων ἀπέθανεν, ἄρα οἱ πάντες ἀπέθανον· καὶ ὑπὲρ πάντων ἀπέθανεν, ἵνα οἱ ζῶντες μηκέτι ἑαυτοῖς ζῶσιν ἀλλὰ τῷ ὑπὲρ αὐτῶν ἀποθανόντι καὶ ἐγερθέντι. ὥστε ἡμεῖς ἀπὸ τοῦ νῦν οὐδένα οἴδαμεν κατὰ σάρκα· εἰ καὶ ἐγνώκαμεν κατὰ σάρκα Χριστόν, ἀλλὰ νῦν οὐκέτι γινώσκομεν. ὥστε εἴ τις ἐν Χριστῷ,

---

[29] A simple way of achieving this goal is with Gramcord, the Greek grammar and concordance program of the Gramcord Institute at Trinity Evangelical Divinity School with which concordance searches can be made. It is possible to instruct the program to retrieve entire verses. Gramcord is designed to work with Nota Bene Special Languages (version 3) and Lingua (version 4), WordPerfect, Chi-Writer and Bible-Word in DOS, and with all Mac programs. Greek screen and print fonts are provided by Nota Bene. For WordPerfect, Paul Miller of the Gramcord Institute recommends the Scripture Fonts add-on from Zondervan Electronics with which the Gramcord program in its Word Perfect version is integrated. The Scripture Fonts add-on can be obtained directly from Zondervan Electronics or as part of the Gramcord program from the Gramcord Institute. New Testament texts can be imported with minimal key strokes into files from within any of the word processors. Gramcord's most flawless operation is with Nota Bene.

Bible Windows is another program which makes such a concordance procedure easy and efficient. It has the advantage of a handy search menu which includes combined word searches, allowing the user to specify how far apart the words should be. An additional advantage is that Bible Windows provides much of the same capabilities for the Hebrew Bible, LXX, Vulgate, RSV and the King James version as well. Bible Windows requires Microsoft Windows 3.1 for its operation, but can import information into DOS programs as well. Texts are imported via a Windows clipboard. As with Gramcord, Bible Windows operates most flawlessly with Nota Bene Lingua.

καινὴ κτίσις· τὰ ἀρχαῖα παρῆλθεν, ἰδοὺ γέγονεν καινά. Participation in the death of Christ comes to expression in a different formulation in Rom 6:3-5 ἢ ἀγνοεῖτε ὅτι, ὅσοι ἐβαπτίσθημεν εἰς Χριστὸν Ἰησοῦν, εἰς τὸν θάνατον αὐτοῦ ἐβαπτίσθημεν; συνετάφημεν οὖν αὐτῷ διὰ τοῦ βαπτίσματος εἰς τὸν θάνατον, ἵνα ὥσπερ ἠγέρθη Χριστὸς ἐκ νεκρῶν διὰ τῆς δόξης τοῦ πατρός, οὕτως καὶ ἡμεῖς ἐν καινότητι ζωῆς περιπατήσωμεν. εἰ γὰρ σύμφυτοι γεγόναμεν τῷ ὁμοιώματι τοῦ θανάτου αὐτοῦ, ἀλλὰ καὶ τῆς ἀναστάσεως ἐσόμεθα. And καινὴ κτίσις in 2 Cor 5:17 links up with Gal 6:15 οὔτε γὰρ περιτομή τί ἐστιν οὔτε ἀκροβυστία ἀλλὰ καινὴ κτίσις, from where we are led once more by οὔτε γὰρ περιτομή τί ἐστιν οὔτε ἀκροβυστία to 1 Cor 7:19, ἡ περιτομὴ οὐδέν ἐστιν καὶ ἡ ἀκροβυστία οὐδέν ἐστιν, ἀλλὰ τήρησις ἐντολῶν θεοῦ, and Gal 5:6, ἐν γὰρ Χριστῷ Ἰησοῦ οὔτε περιτομή τι ἰσχύει οὔτε ἀκροβυστία ἀλλὰ πίστις δι᾽ ἀγάπης ἐνεργουμένη. Beginning with 1 Cor 11:11 we were led by Paul's own formulations to read vertically, paradigmatically, as well as horizontally, syntactically, uncovering a system of values that comes to the surface in different ways depending on the context. We do not need to stop at any one of these texts, but for the moment it is sufficient to show how one might proceed to read Paul in such a vertical, paradigmatic way.

We find the following images in this configuration:

*Affirming:*

ἐν ἑνὶ πνεύματι ἡμεῖς πάντες εἰς ἓν σῶμα ἐβαπτίσθημεν (1 Cor 12:13)
πάντες ἓν πνεῦμα ἐποτίσθημεν (1 Cor 12:13)
εἷς ὑπὲρ πάντων ἀπέθανεν, ἄρα οἱ πάντες ἀπέθανον (2 Cor 5:14)
ὑπὲρ πάντων ἀπέθανεν, ἵνα οἱ ζῶντες μηκέτι ἑαυτοῖς ζῶσιν ἀλλὰ τῷ ὑπὲρ αὐτῶν ἀποθανόντι καὶ ἐγερθέντι (2 Cor 5:15)
εἴ τις ἐν Χριστῷ, καινὴ κτίσις· τὰ ἀρχαῖα παρῆλθεν, ἰδοὺ γέγονεν καινὰ (2 Cor 5:17)
ὅσοι γὰρ εἰς Χριστὸν ἐβαπτίσθητε, Χριστὸν ἐνεδύσασθε (Gal 3:27)
[οὔτε γὰρ περιτομή τί ἐστιν οὔτε ἀκροβυστία] ἀλλὰ καινὴ κτίσις (Gal 6:15)
ὅσοι ἐβαπτίσθημεν εἰς Χριστὸν Ἰησοῦν, εἰς τὸν θάνατον αὐτοῦ ἐβαπτίσθημεν (Rom 6:3)
οὕτως καὶ ἡμεῖς ἐν καινότητι ζωῆς περιπατήσωμεν (Rom 6:4)
[ἡ περιτομὴ οὐδέν ἐστιν καὶ ἡ ἀκροβυστία οὐδέν ἐστιν,] ἀλλὰ τήρησις ἐντολῶν θεοῦ (1 Cor 7:19)
πάντες γὰρ ὑμεῖς εἷς ἐστε ἐν Χριστῷ Ἰησοῦ (Gal 3:28)
[ἐν γὰρ Χριστῷ Ἰησοῦ οὔτε περιτομή τι ἰσχύει οὔτε ἀκροβυστία ἀλλὰ πίστις δι᾽ ἀγάπης ἐνεργουμένη (Gal 5:6)

*Negating:*

οὔτε γυνὴ χωρὶς ἀνδρὸς οὔτε ἀνὴρ χωρὶς γυναικὸς ἐν κυρίῳ (1 Cor 11:11)
εἴτε Ἰουδαῖοι εἴτε Ἕλληνες εἴτε δοῦλοι εἴτε ἐλεύθεροι (1 Cor 12:13)
οὐκ ἔνι Ἰουδαῖος οὐδὲ Ἕλλην, οὐκ ἔνι δοῦλος οὐδὲ ἐλεύθερος, οὐκ ἔνι ἄρσεν καὶ θῆλυ (Gal 3:28)

οὔτε γὰρ περιτομή τί ἐστιν οὔτε ἀκροβυστία (Gal 6:15)
ἡ περιτομὴ οὐδέν ἐστιν καὶ ἡ ἀκροβυστία οὐδέν ἐστιν (1 Cor 7:19)
ἐν γὰρ Χριστῷ Ἰησοῦ οὔτε περιτομή τι ἰσχύει οὔτε ἀκροβυστία (Gal 5:6)

The problem which remains is what the relationship is between what I have formulated here as positive figures and negative figures. Gal 3:27 comes closest to expressing that relationship explicitly. The reason for οὐκ ἔνι Ἰουδαῖος οὐδὲ ῞Ελλην, οὐκ ἔνι δοῦλος οὐδὲ ἐλεύθερος, οὐκ ἔνι ἄρσεν καὶ θῆλυ is that πάντες γὰρ ὑμεῖς εἷς ἐστε ἐν Χριστῷ Ἰησοῦ (3:28). That still does not solve the problem. I will identify the first part as "negation of human distinctions" and the second as "unity in Christ." At first glance Paul's statement seems to suggest that the negation of human distinctions implies unity in Christ, negating human distinctions implies that one is united with Christ. The following analysis will show that the inverse is true, namely, that unity in Christ implies the negation of human distinctions. The following logical square reveals what is involved.

To remind you, the top horizontal arrow indicates contraries, the bottom one subcontraries. Both contraries cannot be true at the same time, but neither may be true; both subcontraries can be true. The vertical lines indicate implication, that is, if the top statement is true it implies that the bottom is true as well, which means the top cannot be true if the bottom is not true. The inverse is not true: If the bottom statement is true, that does not imply that the top is true as well. This will be very important when we look at the semiotic square which indicates what is actually the case; the logical square merely indicates what is true in principle. The diagonal arrows signify contradiction: If one statement is true, its contradictory is not true. There is no third alternative as in the case of the contraries.

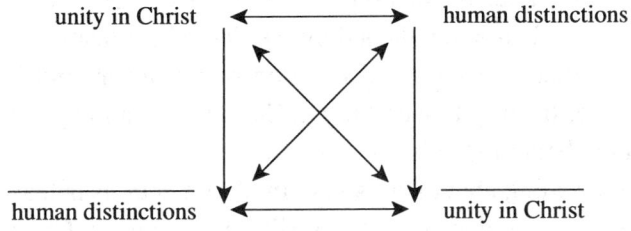

The contraries on this square reveal that in Paul's mind unity in Christ and maintaining human distinctions cannot both be true at the same time. The same is indicated by the line of implication: Unity in Christ implies the negation of human distinctions. The problem is that both subcontraries could be true, that is, human distinctions could be negated without a unity in Christ. The question is whether that is true for Paul. We may make progress in understanding Paul if we change over to a semiotic square which indicates not merely the logical possibilities in Paul's thought, but what he considered real.

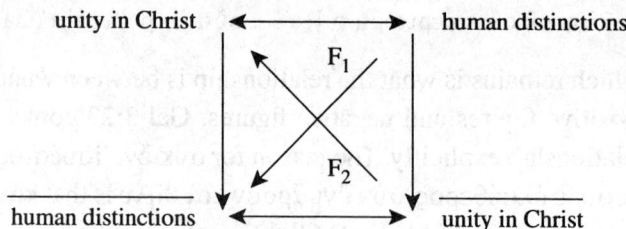

What the semiotic square clarifies is that the affirmation of human distinctions had to be transformed into their negation ($F_1$) before Paul could be united with Christ ($F_2$). His affirmation of human distinctions, particularly between Jews and gentiles had to be surrendered before he could accept being united with Christ. It was not possible for him to be united in Christ as long as he maintained the Jewish distinction between Jews and gentiles because in Christ there was no place for such distinctions. We would thus have to assume the possibility that there could have been Jews who did not respect the distinction between Jews and gentiles without being united in Christ. For Paul himself though, the negation of human distinctions was brought about by Christ's appearance to him.

That does not mean that Paul went through this sequence consciously. He may very well have been aware only of being overwhelmed by the appearance and his acceptance of Christ, but when he came back to his senses he would have realized that through his acceptance of Christ he had by implication betrayed his sense of Jewish privilege.

With that all the elements of the logical square are confirmed. Unity in Christ implies the negation of human distinctions, because unity in Christ and human distinction are contraries. This is strengthened by the line of implication at the right hand of the square: To maintain human distinction of whatever kind is irreconcilable with, that is, implies the negation of unity in Christ; maintaining human distinctions has no place in the being in Christ.

What is also revealing about Paul's system of convictions is that the mere negation of human distinction does not necessarily mean unity in Christ: both subcontraries can be true. Paul's negation of human distinctions, however, is not a product of general human tolerance, but of Christ's appearance to him, resulting in his being united with Christ. With that we have taken a first step in establishing at least one structural element in Paul's system of values. The recurrence of the figures that give expression to this structure reveals its pervasiveness in his thinking. The task is now to determine what other convictional structures we may establish in Paul's thinking, and then to see whether and in what way such structures may be related, to form a more complex unified structure.

## 11. The Function of Words from the Stem πιστ- in Paul's Thought

We may take a further step towards the objective of determining other convictional structures in Paul by following my second proposed methodological procedure, collecting texts in which a common term occurs, printing them out and reading them in the new co-textual context provided in this way. I propose for such a reading texts that are related by their common use of terms derived from the root πιστ-.[30] It is not possible here to provide a list of all the 137 verses in which the terms occur.

Characteristic of Paul's usage of words from the root πιστ- is that he assumes that their meanings are understood, and then uses them in a variety of ways, making ample use of the multivalence in their meanings. One of his most representative uses is of πίστις in an almost absolute sense as the characteristic feature of the emerging new religion—36 times in its verbal and nominal forms—in statements such as, ὥστε γενέσθαι ὑμᾶς τύπον πᾶσιν τοῖς πιστεύουσιν ἐν τῇ Μακεδονίᾳ καὶ ἐν τῇ Ἀχαΐα (1 Thess 1:7), and πρῶτον μὲν εὐχαριστῶ τῷ θεῷ μου διὰ Ἰησοῦ Χριστοῦ περὶ πάντων ὑμῶν ὅτι ἡ πίστις ὑμῶν καταγγέλλεται ἐν ὅλῳ τῷ κόσμῳ (Rom 1:8). This appears to be the most basic use of the term, which makes it possible for him to link its meaning to other uses. Closely related to faith in the above-mentioned sense is believing the gospel/the promise (17 times). Furthermore, a life of faith (7), to trust (5 times), the attitude of trusting (11), to be entrusted with an obligation (4 times), faith in opposition to the Law (8 times), justification by faith as the means of arguing for the justification of the gentiles (24), believing in Christ (1 time), and finally πίστις Ἰησοῦ Χριστοῦ (9 times). To these one may add the adjective πιστός (9 times). These meanings are not distinct in Paul's use of them, but flow into each other, a feature of which he makes extensive use.

The pervasiveness of terms derived from the root πιστ- in Paul's letters suggests that they represent a fundamental value for him. This understanding is strengthened by his use of πίστις in its nominal and verbal forms in a close to absolute sense, as discussed above. A further indication of faith's fundamental significance for Paul's thinking is that he rarely clarifies, but presupposes its meaning, also discussed above. Faith in its almost absolute sense remains part of the fundamental framework of his thought to such a degree that he does not find it necessary to clarify precisely, or even generally, what it means.

---

[30] I could have used almost any meaningful term: νόμος, πνεῦμα, χάρις, καύχημα, κ.τ.λ. All of these and many more terms will have to be investigated before the outlines of a grammar of Paul's thought can be expected to emerge from the kind of investigation I propose. The reason I chose the terms derived from the stem πιστ- is simply because I thought it would be interesting to see what might emerge now that it has become clear that justification by faith is not a fundamental concept in Paul.

Faith as part of the fundamental framework of Paul's thought can be illustrated by considering his reasoning in Rom 3:21-4:25. The specific point he wants to make is that God is not of the Jews only, but also of the gentiles (3:29-30), and his most important argument in this reasoning is that Abraham was a gentile when he was justified. The underlying framework of his reasoning, however, is the revelation of God's justice in Christ, as he states in 3:21-22, Νυνὶ δὲ χωρὶς νόμου δικαιοσύνη θεοῦ πεφανέρωται μαρτυρουμένη ὑπὸ τοῦ νόμου καὶ τῶν προφητῶν, δικαιοσύνη δὲ θεοῦ διὰ πίστεως Ἰησοῦ Χριστοῦ εἰς πάντας τοὺς πιστεύοντας, an understanding to which he returns at the end of the reasoning when he reframes all he said about Abraham christologically, οὐκ ἐγράφη δὲ δι' αὐτὸν μόνον ὅτι ἐλογίσθη αὐτῷ ἀλλὰ καὶ δι' ἡμᾶς, οἷς μέλλει λογίζεσθαι, τοῖς πιστεύουσιν ἐπὶ τὸν ἐγείραντα Ἰησοῦν τὸν κύριον ἡμῶν ἐκ νεκρῶν, ὃς παρεδόθη διὰ τὰ παραπτώματα ἡμῶν καὶ ἠγέρθη διὰ τὴν δικαίωσιν ἡμῶν (4:23-25), thus linking the beginning and ending of the section.[31]

The specific issue in Galatians and Romans is not faith, but whether it is necessary to be a Jew in order to be saved, but at a deeper level it is a question of the integrity of what it means to be in Christ, which Paul makes clear by framing the entire argument christologically. In this sense Paul repeats what he said in 1 Cor 7:19, ἡ περιτομὴ οὐδέν ἐστιν καὶ ἡ ἀκροβυστία οὐδέν ἐστιν, in Galatians (5:6 and 6:15) where he discusses the same issue as in Rom 1:18-4:25. At the deepest level of his thought the Jew/gentile issue was not the most crucial, but what that issue meant to him in terms of his acceptance of Christ as his savior. His acceptance of Christ meant a willingness to surrender the Jewish heritage which he had previously valued as of primary significance.

Paul's not clarifying the meaning of faith, but taking it for granted, leaves his interpreters with very little indication of how he understood the term. Unlike the Law in Rom 7:7-8:17, faith never comes into focus as a specific topic of discussion. The only minor exception is Abraham's faith of which he gives what amounts to definitions in Rom 4:5, [πιστεύων] ἐπὶ τὸν δικαιοῦντα τὸν ἀσεβῆ, and in 4:17, ἐπίστευσεν θεοῦ τοῦ ζῳοποιοῦντος τοὺς νεκροὺς καὶ καλοῦντος τὰ μὴ ὄντα ὡς ὄντα.

A clue to Paul's understanding of faith may be found in the way in which he correlates believing ἐπὶ τὸν ἐγείραντα Ἰησοῦν τὸν κύριον ἡμῶν ἐκ νεκρῶν (Rom 4:24) with Abraham's faith in God who made alive the dead (v. 17), referring to his own and Sarah's condition of being dead to childbirth (v. 19). The shared component of meaning which makes it possible for Paul to establish the link between Abraham's trust in God and believing in God who raised Christ from the dead is not

---

[31] This is an insight I gained in my fall 1993 seminar on Galatians and Romans in a discussion with Todd Penner, who saw clearly that the discussion in 3:21-4:25 was framed christologically by the statements in 3:21-24 and 4:23-25.

provided by πιστεύω, but by the common element of God who makes alive what is dead. Paul obviously assumed that the linking was also provided by πιστεύω, but the term as he uses it in the two cases does not share a common meaning. In the case of Abraham it is a *trust* that God could perform a certain act, and in 4:24 *believing* that God had performed another. Paul correlates Abraham's trusting God and believing God who raised Jesus from the dead by making use of the multivalence of a term like πίστις to link diverse meanings. Whereas the focus in Abraham's faith was on his *confidence* that God would make it possible for him and Sarah to have a child, trusting God who raised Christ from the dead includes as an important component *believing* in the reality of that event.

Belief in the reality of the event of Christ's having been raised from the dead would appear to be a mere matter of evidence. That more is involved becomes clear in Paul's quotation of a confessional statement in verse 25, ὃς παρεδόθη διὰ τὰ παραπτώματα ἡμῶν καὶ ἠγέρθη διὰ τὴν δικαίωσιν ἡμῶν. Here again we have him making use of the multivalence in the meaning of πιστεύω to link various meanings. In verse 24 the meaning is believing that an action of God in Christ did take place, but verse 25 makes clear that more than belief is involved for Paul. Believing that God raised Jesus from the dead is not the mere affirmation that an action did take place; acceptance of what took place means participation in that action as the event of salvation.

The added meaning of believing that Christ was raised can be further clarified by considering another discussion of belief in the resurrection of Christ, that is, 1 Cor 15:12-17. The repeated conclusions in verses 14, εἰ δὲ Χριστὸς οὐκ ἐγήγερται, κενὸν ἄρα [καὶ] τὸ κήρυγμα ἡμῶν, κενὴ καὶ ἡ πίστις ὑμῶν, and 17, εἰ δὲ Χριστὸς οὐκ ἐγήγερται, ματαία ἡ πίστις ὑμῶν, ἔτι ἐστὲ ἐν ταῖς ἁμαρτίαις ὑμῶν, emphasize belief in the resurrection as an essential component of salvific faith. Paul must certainly have become aware that the Christ who appeared to him was the Christ crucified and resurrected, shattering his prior confidence in the supreme value of Jewish distinctiveness. He may initially not have been aware of what hit him. His statement in 1 Cor 2:2, οὐ γὰρ ἔκρινά τι εἰδέναι ἐν ὑμῖν εἰ μὴ Ἰησοῦν Χριστὸν καὶ τοῦτον ἐσταυρωμένον, does not tell the whole story. He may have been able to claim that he proclaimed only Christ crucified, but 1 Cor 15:12-17 and Rom 4:23-25 make clear that he assumed that the Christ he proclaimed had been raised from the dead without which his proclamation of Christ crucified would have had no meaning, as he states explicitly in 1 Cor 15:12-17.

The link of 1 Cor 15:12-17 to Rom 4:24-25 is obvious—both correlate belief in Christ's resurrection to a salvific faith—but not to Abraham's trust in God who makes alive the dead in Rom 4:17, except through the correlation established via verse 24, expanded by means of the confessional statement in verse 25. In Paul's thinking all the meanings of faith are interrelated, including Abraham's trust in God, believing in the resurrection of Christ, and salvific faith. That he had more in mind with his appeal to Abraham than just trust in God, significant as that may be in itself, is shown clearly by the way he linked Abraham's trust in God directly to the Christ event in Gal 3:8, προϊδοῦσα δὲ ἡ γραφὴ ὅτι ἐκ πίστεως δικαιοῖ τὰ ἔθνη ὁ θεὸς, προευηγγελίσατο τῷ Ἀβραὰμ ὅτι ἐνευλογηθήσονται ἐν σοὶ πάντα τὰ ἔθνη, making the fulfillment in Christ the basis for the promise to Abraham. In Romans, Paul makes the same point, linking Abraham's trust in God (4:17) with the Christ event (4:25) via belief in God who raised Christ from the dead (4:23-24), revealing how he could express the same meaning in very different ways.

What I have presented here is only a first step towards uncovering an underlying structure in Paul's thinking that could function as the context for interpreting him. On the one hand, it was possible to see how a number of passages expressing the negation in Christ of human distinctions, between Jews and gentiles, males and females, etc., can be read co-textually to deepen our understanding of Paul's meaning, and to recognize that when he comes up with a new formulation it is an affirmation of a deeply rooted conviction. In the case of the texts related by the common occurrence of words derived from the root πιστ–, on the other hand, Paul's meanings have not been clarified because these terms express a meaning that is so fundamental to his thought that he takes it for granted. In this case we did not learn *what* the terms meant, but *how* Paul uses them, how he *means* them, contributing not so much to his thought, as to his thinking.

An indication that this first step in the investigation of Paul's thought can be fruitful is that it has shown that although the specific issue addressed in Galatians and Romans was the justification of the gentiles, the framework in which Paul placed the discussion of that issue revealed that circumcision or not being circumcised is not what matters ultimately, but the new being in Christ, as Paul himself formulates it as the culmination of his reasoning in Galatians, οὔτε γὰρ περιτομή τί ἐστιν οὔτε ἀκροβυστία ἀλλὰ καινὴ κτίσις (6:15).

## Bibliography

de Beaugrande, R.-A. and Dressler, W. 1981: *Introduction to Text Linguistics,* London and New York: Longman 1981.

Beker, J. Ch. 1980: *Paul the Apostle*, Philadelphia, PA: Fortress Press 1980.

Boers, H. W. 1962: *The Diversity of New Testament Christological Concepts and the Confession of Faith* (Bonn: [self-published] 1962).

— 1988: *"Neither on this Mountain, nor in Jerusalem." A Study of John 4* (SBL.MS 34), Atlanta, GA: Scholars Press 1988.

—1989: *Who was Jesus? An Interpretation of the Christological Passages in the Synoptic Gospels*, San Francisco, CA: Harper & Row 1989.

— 1993: *Justification of the Gentiles: Paul's Letters to the Galatians and to the Romans*, Peabody, MA: Hendrickson Press 1993.

Bornkamm, G. 1969: *Paulus*, Stuttgart/Berlin/Köln/Mainz: W. Kohlhammer 1969; [ET: *Saint Paul, the Apostle*, New Work: Harper & Row 1971].

Braun, H. 1969: *Jesus: Der Mann aus Nazareth und seine Zeit*, Stuttgart/Berlin: Kreuz-Verlag 1969; [ET: *Jesus of Nazareth: The Man and his Time* (translated by E. R. Kalin), Philadelphia, PN: Fortress Press 1979].

Bultmann, R. 1926: *Jesus*, Tübingen: J. C. B. Mohr (Paul Siebeck) 1926; [ET: *Jesus and the Word* (translated by Louise Pettibone Smith and Erminie Huntress Lantero), New York: Scribners 1958].

van Dijk, T. 1972: *Some Aspects of Text Grammars: A Study in Theoretical Linguistics and Poetics* (Janua Linguarum, Series Maior 63), The Hague/Paris: Mouton 1972.

Halliday, M. A. K. 1973: *Explorations in the Functions of Language*, London: Edward Arnold 1973.

Heiligenthal, R. 1983, *Werke als Zeichen. Untersuchungen zur Bedeutung der menschlichen Taten im Frühjudentum, Neues Testament und Frühchristentum* (WUNT 2. Reihe 9), Tübingen: J. C. B. Mohr (Paul Siebeck) 1983.

Lévi-Strauss, Cl. 1963: "The Structural Study of Myth," in: *Myth, A Symposium, Journal of American Folklore* 78 (1955) 428-44. [Translated with some additions and modifications as "La Structure des mythes," in: *Anthropologie Structurale*, Vol. I, Paris: Plon 1958, 225-55; [ET: *Structural Anthropology* (by Cl. Jacobson and B. Grundfest Schoeps), New York: Basic Books, Inc. 1963; paperback: New York: Doubleday 1967, 202-28].

Lüdemann, G. 1980: *Paulus, der Heidenapostel. Band I: Studien zur Chronologie* (FRLANT 123), Göttingen: Vandenhoeck & Ruprecht 1980.

Patte, D. 1983: *Paul's Faith and the Power of the Gospel*, Philadelphia, PA: Fortress Press 1983.

Plett, H. F. (ed.) 1991: *Intertextuality* (Research in Text Theory 15), Berlin/New York: de Gruyter 1991.

Sanders, E. P. 1983: *Paul, the Law, and the Jewish People*, Philadelphia, PA: Fortress 1983.

Wrede, W. 1964: *Paulus* (Religionsgeschichtliche Volksbücher I 5-6), Halle: Gebauer-Schwetschke 1904. Reprinted in: K. H. Rengstorf (ed.), *Das Paulusbild in der neueren deutschen Forschung* (WdF 24), Darmstadt: Wissenschaftliche Buchgesellschaft 1964, 1-97; [ET *Paul*, London: Philip Green 1907].

# Was Paul Against the Law?
## The Law in Galatians and Romans: A Test-Case of Text in Context[1]

James D. G. Dunn

## 1. Introduction

It would hardly be surprising if someone brought up in Protestant Christianity thought of Judaism as the antithesis of Christianity. The impression is rooted deeply in the basic gospel/law dialectic of Lutheran theology, where gospel, not unnaturally, is identified with Christianity, and law, also not unnaturally, is identified with Judaism. Even in the period following the second world war, when Christian conscience had been sensitised by the horror of the Holocaust, Christian scholarship still spoke of pre-Christian Judaism as Spätjudentum, of Jesus as having marked the end of Judaism, of Paul as having been converted from Judaism to Christianity.[2] The inconsistency of talking about first century Judaism as "late" hardly seems to have dawned on those who so spoke: if *first* century Judaism is *late*, what do we call the last nineteen centuries of Judaism? The double-think was occasioned, of course, by the idea that Judaism's only role was as precursor to Christianity; now that Christianity had come, Judaism no longer counted for anything.

In the last quarter-century, however, the picture has begun to change rapidly. The

---

[1] This study is dedicated to Lars Hartman, who I recall first meeting on a railway station many years ago as we both sought to make our way to the annual SNTS meeting. The pleasure of subsequent annual meetings has always been enhanced by his presence. I would have liked to make a contribution more directly related to his own work at points where our various writings have overlapped, but unfortunately I have not yet seen his book on Baptism, nor do I have enough Swedish to do justice to his commentary on Colossians, though I have greatly valued his articles on Colossians. But the theme "Paul and the Law" was in fact the subject of my lecture at the Exegetical Day at Uppsala in 1985 (full of pleasant memories), to which Lars kindly invited me, and the paper itself was delivered from notes as one of two lectures to the Menighetsfakultetet in Oslo in April 1993, so I hope he will find it sufficiently close, as we might say, theologically as well as geographically, to his own interests. To Lars: *ad multos annos*.

[2] See e.g. the critiques of C. Klein 1978, and J. T. Pawlikowski 1982, chap. 3.

term "late Judaism" no longer appears in scholarly circles; now the same period is usually, and more appropriately called "early Judaism". The Jewish reclamation of Jesus has gone apace and many NT specialists now talk of a "third quest of the historical Jesus", where the quest's distinctive new angle has been to focus on Jesus within the context of his own people, Jesus the Jew.[3] In both these cases the old language has been completely abandoned, its inappropriateness widely recognized.

With Paul, on the other hand, while the same process of reassessment is under way, its outcome is far from clear. It is true that the few lone voices who maintained that Paul's Damascus road experience should be seen as a call rather than a conversion,[4] have been joined by many others. But the idea that Paul had to abandon Judaism in order to become a Christian is still deeply entrenched. And nothing like the Jewish reclamation of Jesus has taken place in the case of Paul; for most Jews, he is still Paul the apostate.[5] Yet, should the tide of reassessment stop short at Paul? Has the relationship between Christianity and Judaism as summed up in the person of Paul been re-examined with sufficient thoroughness? The subject matter is sufficiently important to warrant further investigation.

The issue comes to sharpest focus in the question of the law. The prevailing impression within NT scholarship is still that Paul broke with or abandoned the law when he became a Christian. The text which best sums up what is again a particularly Lutheran perspective is Rom 10:4—"Christ is the end of the law...".[6] Typical also is the judgment that Paul had persecuted the Hellenists for their breach with the law—an inference drawn largely from a combination of Acts 6:13, Gal 3:13 and Phil 3:6—and was thus converted to what he had persecuted.[7] Particularly vehement is Hans Hübner in his thesis that Paul was uniformly hostile to the law in Galatians, though Hübner also maintains that Paul modified his position somewhat in writing the later Romans.[8] Others prominent in recent discussion are content to find Paul inconsistent in his written views of the law.[9]

Here then is a topic, Paul and the law, where the problem of relating text and context is nicely posed in its complexity. Is the context within which the issue should be weighed that of traditional Lutheran, Gospel/law dialectic? Or should it be the historical context within which Paul himself operated, so far as that may be recovered? Should the issue be handled "in front of" the text (a hermeneutical exercise),

---

[3] See e.g. D. Hagner 1984; S. Neill & T. Wright 1988, 379-403; J. H. Charlesworth (ed.) 1991; G. Vermes 1993.

[4] Notably K. Stendahl 1963.

[5] The issue is sympathetically handled by A. Segal 1990.

[6] See e.g. P. Stuhlmacher 1981, 166-91.

[7] E.g. S. Kim 1981; C. Dietzfelbinger 1985.

[8] H. Hübner 1985.

[9] E. P. Sanders 1985; H. Räisänen 1984/6.

or "behind" the text (an exegetical exercise)? Again, where two texts seem to be somewhat at odds with each other, should the questions raised be handled inter-tex-tually, or inter-contextually, or inter-text-within-contextually? And should a coher-ence be sought between two texts (Galatians and Romans) by the same author (Paul), or should we moderns be content to make as much sense as we can of each text on its own, lest any linking pattern be of our own devising?

In order to keep the discussion within the confines of a single paper I will limit it to the question posed in the title, Was Paul against the law?, and to the two letters of Paul in which the question of the law is treated most fully (Galatians and Ro-mans). We proceed by examining the way the law is treated in each of the two letters in turn before asking whether and if so how the two treatments hang together coher-ently.

## 2. The Law in Galatians

### 2.1. The Law as an Angelic Power

It is easy to draw a very negative picture of the law from Galatians. The impression is strongest in the section Gal 3:19-4:11. Paul has been speaking of the promise to Abraham, recalling particularly the promises to Abraham in Gen 12:3 and 7 (Gal 3:8, 16). The law came 430 years later (at Sinai), but it does not make the earlier promise void. "For if the inheritance is from law, it is no longer from promise; but to Abraham God gave it freely through promise" (3:18). Since the earlier references to the law had been consistently refutational (2:16, 19, 21; 3:2, 5, 10-13—"not from works of the law", "died to the law", "by the law no one is justified"), it can be plau-sibly argued that this further oppositional juxtaposition of law with promise pre-pares the reader for a thoroughly negative assessment of the law in the verses which follow.

3:19—"Why then the law?" To which the answer is given, τῶν παραβάσεων χά-ριν προσετέθη—"it was added because of transgressions". The force of the χάριν is not immediately clear, but a cross (intertextual) reference to Romans (context of Paul's thought) may be said to strengthen the negative tone of the immediately pre-ceding context. The parallel with Rom 3:20 suggests the sense, "in order to bring about a knowledge of transgressions", to make sin a conscious act.[10] While the clos-er parallel with Rom 5:20 ("the law came in to increase the trespass") suggests the

---

[10] So M. J. Lagrange 1925, 82; E. de W. Burton 1921, 188; F. Mußner 1977, 245-46; R. N. Longenecker 1990, 138; "to make wrong-doing a legal offence" (NEB/REB).

more negative force, "in order to bring about transgressions".[11]

3:19—"it was ordered through angels by the hand of an intermediary". The reference is most obviously to Moses, as most agree.[12] Once again the text sounds fairly innocuous, but the next verse ("Now an intermediary means that there is not just one party; but God is one") indicates clearly enough that the contrast between the law and the promise is being maintained: the promise was given directly by God to Abraham, whereas the law came to Israel at one remove. However, the allusion to "angels" adds a further complication: does it imply that the law was still more remote from God, with not only Moses but also angels intervening? Or is it, indeed, an attempt to remove the law completely from the domain of God? So some would argue: the clause is "a categorical denial of the divine origin of the Torah";[13] the law "is the product of demonic angelic powers".[14] Here the exegetical rationale is once again the negative tone of the preceding context. And though the sudden sharpness of antagonism and degree of hostility is unexpected, a Christian interpretation of the law as the product of fallen angels can be shown to go back to at least within two generations of Galatians (*Barn.* 9:4—"they erred because an evil angel was misleading them").

After a further contrast between the law and the promise (3:21-22), the more sharply negative tone seems to be resumed. 3:23 — "before the coming of this faith we were held in custody under the law, confined (ὑπὸ νόμον ἐφρουρούμεθα συγκλειόμενοι)…". Here the negative features come thick and fast. The law is treated as though it were a cosmic power, like sin—the ὑπὸ νόμον of 3:23 paralleling the ὑπὸ ἁμαρτίαν of 3:22. In other words, the law itself seems now to be identified with the (evil) angels of 3:19. Moreover, the first verb (ἐφρουρούμεθα) could have a very negative sense, "held in subjection", and the second (συγκλειόμενοι) strikes the same note, "confined" or "imprisoned". Hence, for example, NIV—"held prisoners by the law, locked up".[15]

With this picture in mind it is hardly surprising if the next one stirs up a similar picture of a rule tyrannous and harsh in character. 3:24 – "so that the law became our custodian (παιδαγωγός) to Christ". The image is the familiar one of the slave who conducted a boy to and from school. In such a case, where the word (παιδαγωγός) appears in only one other passage within Paul's letters (and the NT—1 Cor

---

[11] So e.g. BAGD 1979, s.v. χάριν 1; H. Schlier 1965, 152-54; H. D. Betz 1979, 163—the phrase "is to be taken in a wholly negative way".

[12] Betz, 1979, 170 notes that "by the hand of Moses" became almost a formula in the LXX. See further Longenecker 1990, 140-3.

[13] J. W. Drane 1975, 34, 113; similarly T. Zahn 1905, 171; Lagrange 1925, 83; R. Bring 1968, 144-46; R. B. Hays 1983, 227.

[14] Hübner 1985, 24-36.

[15] So also R. Y. K. Fung 1988, 168.

4:15), and where it clearly alludes to a familiar figure within ancient society, the exegete has little choice but to refer to the context of the times for illumination. In this case what has generally made most impression is the fact that in the literature of the time the παιδαγωγός is a figure often criticised for his abuse of power or is treated as a figure of fun.[16] In consequence, it has been natural to regard the reference here in a strongly negative light,[17] an impression if anything strengthened by the repetition of the phrase, ὑπὸ παιδαγωγόν, in 3:25.

The climax comes in 4:8-10, where Paul seems once again to liken the law to a spiritual power, but now to identify it still more clearly with the gods that are "no gods" and the "beggarly elemental forces". For the Galatians to "observe days and months and special times and years" was to put themselves back into slavery to such non- or radically inferior beings. To grasp the full train of thought it is again important for the exegete to be aware of such contextual factors as the Jewish attitude to other gods and the widespread belief within the ancient world that human life was influenced by the primal and cosmic forces which shaped and regulated the world as a whole.[18] Also of the fact that "days, months, special times and years" almost certainly refer to Jewish feasts and festivals.[19] For a Jew to disown the law to such an extent, to lump it together with non-gods and the basic stuff of the cosmos, was an extraordinary turnabout, which alone would seem to make unavoidable an affirmative answer to the question posed in the title. It looks very much as though Paul was turning wholly against the traditional Jewish belief that God had appointed angels to rule the other nations, but had kept Israel for himself (Deut 32:15; Sir 17:17). No! says Paul, in effect, the law has been Israel's angel, and, as in the hostile variation on the older tradition in *Jub.* 15:32-33, the purpose of this angelic power, of the law, was to lead astray the people over which it ruled. Jewish disdain of the nations has been turned against itself using the law for leverage.

This then is the heart of the case for reading the text of Galatians as a hostile polemic against the law. But is the justification sufficient? Has the context within which the text has been read been too selective and restrictive? In fact an equally, and indeed more persuasive case can be made for reading the same key passages in a much more positive way.

In the case of 3:19a the issue centres on the meaning of χάριν. Here we need to recall that the word is the accusative form of χάρις, "grace, favour", and that its usu-

---

[16] Betz 1979, 177.

[17] See e.g. Schlier 1965, 168-70; A. Oepke 1973, 121-22; Betz 1979, 177-78: "the pedagogue ... an ugly figure", "the radical devaluation of the law".

[18] See further the main commentaries on Galatians, all of which wrestle with the precise reference of these terms, particularly τὰ στοιχεῖα τοῦ κόσμου in 4:3 and 9.

[19] See Dunn 1993, 227-29.

al meaning as attested elsewhere in usage of the time is "for the sake of, on behalf of, on account of".[20] This suggests a much more immediately gracious objective for the law than simply "to make conscious of transgressions", and certainly than "to provoke transgressions". It suggests, in fact, the purpose of the law as it was generally recognized within the (OT) scriptures and the Judaism of Paul's time: that is, as a means of dealing with transgressions. In other words, what was probably in mind here was the whole sacrificial cult at whose centre was the provision of means for covering sin and removing guilt, means of atonement. The fact that the law has been set in contrast with promise up to this point in Galatians naturally gives rise to the question, "Why then the law?" But the flow of thought is equally well served if the answer to the question begins to explain the positive function of the law. Here we might say, then, is a battle of contexts: does it make more sense to read Gal 3:19a in the light of Rom 5:20, where the thought is rather different and the key term χά-ρις has a quite different function, or in the light of the positive, indeed gracious function which the law actually did serve for Israel from Sinai onwards?

As for the angels of 3:19b, it is certainly the case, as already noted, that the phrase strengthens the contrast with the promise, the double phrase, "through angels" and "by the hand of an intermediary", heightening the contrast with the immediacy of God's promise given to Abraham. But that said, it has also to be said that the reference itself does not imply that the angels in question were hostile or evil. On the contrary, anyone familiar with Jewish tradition would think most naturally of the well established Jewish belief that angels were indeed associated in the giving of the law (Deut 33:2 LXX—"angels from his right hand were with him [the Lord]"; *Jub.* 1:29-2:1; Philo, *Som.* 1:143; Josephus, *Ant.* 15:36; *Apoc. Mos.* preface).[21] And since the motif was also familiar elsewhere in Greek speaking Christianity (Acts 7:38, 53; Heb 2:2), the most natural inference is that Paul intended the same allusion. In other words, the allusion, while marking a contrast with the promise, certainly did not deny the law was given from God—even if at one or two removes. Here too, we may say, an awareness of the broader context of the time undermines an interpretation dependent on a rather narrow reading of the text.

Similarly with 3:23 and 24. In the former we do well to note that the principal sense of φρουρέω is "guard, watch over", as in the case of a city garrison (2 Cor 11:32), or "to protect, keep", as in the only two other NT uses (Phil 4:7; 1 Pet 1:5). That is to say, what Paul had in mind was probably a *protective* custody.[22] Which fits well with the image of the παιδαγωγός in 3:24. For here too the image was essentially positive—the slave given the responsible task of protecting his young

---

[20] LSJ 1966: χάρις VI.1.

[21] See further Str-B 1926, 3:554-56; T. Callan 1980.

[22] So Oepke 1973, 120; P. Bonnard 1953, 75; D. Guthrie 1969, 108; U. Borse 1984, 137.

charge and of instructing him in good manners. Of course the figure of the pedagogue became a butt for many a joke, as has the child's governess and school teacher in subsequent generations. But the essentially positive role is hardly to be thus
gainsaid, as recent studies have confirmed.[23] Here again we have to conclude that
an awareness of broader usage of language and metaphor, such as Paul could assume on the part of his more literate readers, prevents a reading which can be justified only by ignoring that wider usage and by pushing for a constricted reading of
the text.

In short, if indeed Paul was linking the law with angels and thinking of the law
itself as a kind of angelic power, it begins to look as though it was the law as a kind
of *guardian* angel which Paul had in mind. This provisional conclusion requires further analysis.

## 2.2. The Temporary Role of the Law as Guardian Angel

As already noted, there seems to be a predominantly negative thrust in all Paul's
early references to the law in Galatians. To be precise, specific reference to the law
as such is delayed until 2:16, but then between 2:16 and 3:18 "law" is mentioned
fourteen times. The initial references are all to "works of the law", all in the negative
formulation, "by works of the law" (ἐξ ἔργων νόμου), a phrase which recurs six
times in the sequence (2:16; 3:2, 5, 10). The others talk of dying to the law, deny
that righteousness and the inheritance comes through the law, set the law and faith
in antithesis, and speak of the curse of the law (2:19, 21; 3:11-13, 18). But it is only
with 3:19 that the question of the law's actual purpose is addressed. If it is so clear
what it was not for, why then was it given? In the flow of Paul's argument the question was inevitable and unavoidable.

Of course, the answer Paul gives in reference to the *function* of the law is contested, as we have seen (§2.1). But there can be little dispute that Paul regarded this
function as *temporary*. The law was given well after the promise (430 years), and
therefore cannot be confused with or understood as part of the promise or render the
promise null and void (3:17-18). And it was "added ... until the coming of the seed
to whom the promise was made" (3:19), until faith could be directed to the seed,
Jesus Christ.

> Before the coming of this faith we were held in custody (ἐφρουρούμεθα) under the
> law, confined till the faith which was to come should be revealed, so that the law be-
> came our custodian (παιδαγωγός) to Christ, in order that we might be justified from
> faith. But with faith having come, we are no longer under the custodian (3:23-25).

---

[23] See particularly D. J. Lull 1986; N. H. Young 1987.

Notable is the use of the first person plural, which most obviously betrays the perspective of one who thought of himself as a member of Israel, as a Jew.[24] To be sure, it is the perspective of one who recalls an earlier period as one of confinement from which he has now been delivered, the perspective of one who saw himself as having previously been under a custodian slave but who had now reached an age of maturity when the παιδαγωγός was no longer necessary. Whatever debate there may be over the fine print, therefore, the main thrust of this paragraph is surely clear enough: the role of the law as custodian (for Israel) was limited in time; it was a role which had extended from Sinai to the coming of the promised seed and to the proclamation of faith in him.

What this means within the sweep of God's saving purpose is elaborated with a correlated metaphor in 4:1-7. Children of Abraham are heirs of the promise to Abraham (of seed and blessing). But so long as they are under age they are under guardians and stewards, appointed by their father. Only when they reach the appropriate age of maturity do they begin to enter into their inheritance—something achieved (for Gentiles as well) by the coming of Christ and of the Spirit. Since 4:1-7 in effect constitutes a recapitulation of the argument of 3:23-29,[25] the point is clear enough so far as the law is concerned. To be under the law is to be under a custodian (παιδαγωγός), is to be under guardians and stewards (4:2). The law, in other words, has a temporary role for Israel because the coming of Messiah and his Spirit marks the point in time/history at which Israel's transition from childhood to (young) adulthood takes place—the implication being that for the (young) adult the inspiration and monitor of life is now more the Spirit than simply the law (see §2.3).

It should be noted that in this central metaphor, Israel under the law is again not an essentially negative status. On the contrary, Israel under the law is still heir of the promises to Abraham. The difference is relative—the difference between a son before, including just before reaching his majority, and the brother who has already reached, including just reached his majority. Paul may press the difference here, and more strongly later (4:28-31), but 4:19 shows that he was also conscious of just how relative was the difference: far from having already entered fully into the age of majority as children of Abraham, Gentile believers are still in the womb (4:19)! They too have yet to enter fully into that inheritance (5:21).[26] The contrast between unbelieving Jews (under the law) and believing Jews and Gentiles is not at all so sharp

---

[24] So W. M. Ramsay 1900, 381; T. L. Donaldson 1986, 98; Dunn 1993, 197-98; against the majority.

[25] See Dunn 1993, 210.

[26] Characteristic of this formulaic usage in the NT epistles is the understanding that the inheritance of the kingdom is still future (Gal 5:21; 1 Cor 6:9-10; 15:50; Eph 5:5; Jas 2:5); see further Dunn 1993, 306-7.

as some of the other passages taken alone might suggest.

The conclusion is hard to avoid, then, that for Paul during this interim period the role of the law in relation to Israel was essentially protective. In fact, the picture Paul draws here is very close to that asserted positively in the *Letter of Aristeas:*

> In his wisdom the legislator (Moses) ... surrounded us with unbroken palisades and iron walls to prevent our mixing with any of the other peoples in any matter, being thus kept pure in body and soul ... So, to prevent our being perverted by contact with others or by mixing with bad influences, he hedged us in on all sides with strict observances connected with meat and drink and touch and hearing and sight, after the manner of the Law (139, 142).

Indeed, in their different ways, all the main expressions of Judaism at the time of Paul would no doubt have seen themselves as protected by the law, whether from divine wrath on sin or from contamination by impure others or both. At this point, we may say, Paul's understanding of the law was quintessentially Jewish.

More controversial is my own view that one of the key phrases in the letter, "works of the law", should be understood within the same context. Still dominant in NT studies is the characteristically Lutheran interpretation of the phrase to mean in effect "good works achieved by human effort and expressive of human self-assertion".[27] But in the context of Galatians it is the function of "works of the law" as distinguishing Jew from Gentile which was probably closest to the top of Paul's mind. Certainly in the first rush of usage (2:16) the context indicates precisely that function, the clear implication of 2:11-18 being that Peter a "Jew by nature" had "separated himself" from the Gentile believers at Antioch ("Gentile sinners") on the basis of a theology of "works of the law". And this fits with the protective role of the law outlined later in the second half of chap. 3—"works of the law" maintaining both Israel's standing within the covenant,[28] and Israel's distinctiveness from others.[29]

Whatever the precise function of this last phrase, however, it is clear that for Paul this function of the law was no longer necessary. Now that the promise that Abraham's blessing would be shared by the nations was achieving eschatological fulfilment, the law in its role of protecting and distinguishing Israel from the nations was at an end. The distinctive marks of the eschatological children of Abraham are no longer "works of the law" but the inclusive markers of Abraham's faith, Christ and his Spirit (3:1-14, 3:22-4:7).

Here again, then, we can see that by setting the text within the context of Jewish

---

[27] See e.g. those cited in Dunn 1993, 135 n. 1.

[28] The attitude described by E. P. Sanders' phrase "covenantal nomism" (1977, 75, 180).

[29] See further Dunn 1990, 219-25, 237-41; also idem 1992.

thinking of the time, as illuminated by other texts from the period, an exegesis emerges which does fuller justice to the nuances of Paul's argument than a reading of the text as unyieldingly hostile to the law, and which thus focuses the controversial character of Paul's argument more sharply than the straight gospel/law antithesis.

## 2.3. *Otherwise the Law Still Has a Positive Function*

Two important conclusions have thus emerged. The first is that the contrast in Gal 3 between the promise and the law does not imply a wholly negative attitude to the law. On the contrary, the function of the law outlined in answer to the question, "Why then the law?" (3:19), is quite positive—the law as given by God as a kind of guardian angel for Israel. The second conclusion is that that role for the law was temporary, to fill the gap between the giving of the promise to Abraham and its fulfilment in the coming of Christ. That is to say, prior to the extension of Abraham's blessing to the nations through his seed, the law had a role to maintain Israel's distinctiveness as heir of the promise, to protect Israel in a hostile world—not to give life (3:21) but to mark out the pattern and way of life for the covenant people (3:12).[30]

It is this twofold conclusion which provides the key to the otherwise puzzling mix of negative and positive comments in Galatians regarding the law. On the negative front it now becomes clear that what Paul was worried about was the possibility of his Gentile converts treating the law as though its role in regard to Israel was permanent, of continuing eschatological validity as well as for the period prior to the coming of Christ. By undertaking "works of the law" such as the Jewish festivals (4:10) these Gentiles were in effect treating the law as if it were one of their old gods, a power interposed between them and God (4:8-10). By so doing they were failing to appreciate that the time of majority had come, the time of fulfilment (4:1-7). They were longing for the security of the child, always being told by another what to do, whereas they should be rejoicing in the freedom of the greater maturity which the gift of the Spirit brought as Abraham's blessing (3:2-3, 14). To re-erect the law as a bulwark which continued to distinguish and divide (believing) Jews from the (believing) nations was to subordinate the promise to the law and to render Christ's death pointless (2:17-21).[31]

On the positive side, the point is even clearer. For the temporary function of the law as a protection and bulwark for Israel was evidently not its complete function. And the negative thrust of Paul's argument is directed only against its being too

---

[30] On the meaning of and distinction between 3:12 and 3:21 see Dunn 1993, 175-76, 192-93.

[31] On the correlation between 2:21 and 3:13-14 see Dunn 1993, 147-49 and 176-80.

tightly related to Israel as exclusively Israel's. Once that role has been set aside, eschatologically discounted, there is yet more to be said. The law can still be spoken
of as having a positive function in the direction of life. This is clearly indicated in
5:14: for Paul "the whole law" was still an obligation for the believer, Gentile as
well as Jew. The difference is that "the whole law" is not fulfilled by "works of the
law", as in the time before Christ, but in the one word, the well-known, "You shall
love your neighbour as yourself" (Lev 19:18), a love which is also the fruit of the
eschatological Spirit (5:22).[32]

Under the same heading we should also include the reference to "the law of
Christ" (6:2). Presumably in Paul's mind was the loving concern for the other which
the Jesus tradition both documented for Jesus' own ministry and also summed up
in the love command (as the parallel with Rom 15:1-8 strongly suggests). But as in
5:14 Paul does not hesitate to describe this attitude and ethos by the same term
"law". The implication, as in 5:14, is that it is in fact the same law which Paul had
in view—the law as lived out and summed up in the life and teaching of Jesus,
hence "the law of Christ".[33] Perhaps we may further guess that Paul had in mind in
particular the Jesus-tradition's emphasis on Jesus eating with "sinners" (Mark 2:16-
17; Matt. 11:19/Luke 7:34), understood by Paul both as an example of Jesus' living
out the love command ("the law of Christ"), and as justification for his own stand
on "works of the law" in this letter (2:14-16). If so the inter-contextual links at this
point are exceedingly rich. But since they help explain the balance between the negative and positive treatment of the law in Galatians itself they cannot be dismissed
as merely speculative.

In short, once the negative thrust of Paul's treatment of the law is clarified and
set in the context both of the letter itself and of Judaism at the time of Paul, a coherent theology of the law in Galatians becomes evident. The more negative features
of the law relate to its temporary role as a kind of guardian angel for Israel in the
period before the coming of Christ. But that role, summed up in the phrase "works
of the law", is complete. What remains is the law understood in the light of the
Jesus-tradition, summed up in the love command, and fulfilled by the enabling of
the Spirit.

## *3. The Law in Romans*

In Romans the treatment of the law is fuller. Indeed, the theology of the law is ac-

---

[32] Drane 1975, 112-13 and Hübner 1985, 36-40 are quite unable to make sense of 5:14 in the light
of their earlier, too narrowly drawn conclusion that in Galatians Paul rejected the law entirely; see
further Dunn 1993, 288-92.

[33] See particularly H. Schürmann 1974.

tually the subplot of the letter: it features in every chapter from 2 to 10 inclusive; it forms the main theme in chaps. 2 and 7; and the way it is introduced throughout shows that it is the chief counterpoint to the central message of the gospel. Here we have space to draw attention only to the most significant features for a comparison with Galatians.

### 3.1. *The Law as Yardstick*

The most consistently emphasised function of the law in the early chapters is that of a yardstick—making aware of and measuring sin. In each case the reference is in an explanatory clause alluding to a function which was either so familiar or so obvious that it did not require further explanation or justification but could be taken wholly for granted:

> ... for through the law comes the knowledge of sin (3:20);
> (for) where there is no law there is also no transgression (4:15);
> For until the law, sin was in the world, but sin is not accounted in the
>     absence of the law (5:13);
> sin, that it might appear as sin ... in order that sin through the
>     commandment might become utterly sinful (7:13).

The point is obvious and is not disputed in modern discussion either, so it needs little further exposition: one of the chief functions of the law, according to Romans, is to define sin as sin, that is, to indicate the lines and limits of conduct appropriate for an Israelite, as laid down by God, and therefore to make the Israelite aware of what conduct is unacceptable to God and inappropriate within Israel. The Israelite instructed in the law thus knew what conduct should be avoided (3:19), knew the consequences of such conduct (4:15) and knew also how it was to be expunged (3:21). This theology of the law is at the heart of the two lengthier treatments of the law in Romans: it comes to fuller expression in 2:12-16 (the law as the measure of final judgment), and is also the starting point for the trial of the law which begins in 7:7 (see below).

Interestingly enough, this function of the law did not feature in Galatians. This fact presumably helps confirm that it was not the ordinary or basic function of the law which was at issue there, but almost exclusively its function of setting Jew apart from Gentile. In contrast, in Romans, though the Galatians' issue is not absent, what is essayed is a much fuller and more rounded exposition of the law and its functions. Which also strengthens the view that the situation addressed in Rome was of nothing like the same crisis proportions as that which confronted Paul in the churches of Galatia, so that a more measured response was both desirable and possible.[34]

## 3.2. The Law on Trial

Despite the theses of Drane and Hübner,[35] it is in Romans rather than Galatians that the more strongly negative note is sounded. Whatever Gal 3:19 might mean, it is hard to dispute the negative role attributed to the law in Rom 5:20: "The law came in to increase the trespass". The choice of verb (παρεισῆλθεν, "slipped in, interposed") and the use of the active voice (the law as subject) seems to increase the negative overtone and makes the law appear as a traitorous ally of the oppressive powers, sin and death—a guardian angel (Gal 3:19), one might say, subverted by the powers of evil.

This is all the more surprising in Romans, since, again in contrast to Galatians, the early treatment of the law in Romans has been on the whole fairly matter of fact and even positive (2:13-15, 25, 27; 3:21, 27b, 31; 4:16). Apart from some indications of an unsatisfactory relation with the law on the part of the Jewish interlocutor in 2:17-29 (but the law is not blamed), the only negative notes are struck by, once again, the repeated phrase "works of the law" (3:20, 27a, 28) and the contrast with the promise to Abraham (4:13-15). So the more fiercely negative note of 5:20 comes as something of a surprise.

Why Paul introduced such a negative note at this point is only partially clear. It must have been intended at least to heighten the contrast between the two ages of humankind's history outlined in 5:12-21. The age of Adam (Adam to Christ) is pictured as set under the powers of sin and death. Into this grim situation the law was introduced, not as a way of ameliorating the human condition (as in Gal 3:19), but as an ally of sin and death. Presumably the purpose was at least partly rhetorical: on the one hand to disturb any easy assumption on the part of the earlier Jewish interlocutor that the law protected Israel from the worst effects of sin and death (as implied in Rom 2:12ff. and Gal 3:23-24);[36] and on the other to increase the dramatic contrast with the effect of divine grace in and through Christ (5:20-21; 6:14-15). But the effect is still unnerving and leaves a question dangling about the relation of the law to sin and death. No doubt Paul felt able to do this because within a few paragraphs he was going to address this precise question.

Rom 7 (or more precisely 7:7-8:4) thus functions in many ways as a climax to the disturbing questions regarding the law raised by Paul in the preceding chapters. In 7:7-13 the question is posed explicitly: "Is the law sin?" Does the link between sin and law put forward in 5:20 amount to an equation of the two? Paul's answer is

---

[34] On the debates as to the purpose of Romans see particularly K. P. Donfried (ed.) 1991; A. J. M. Wedderburn 1988.

[35] See nn. 8 and 13 above.

[36] See also Dunn 1988, 286.

immediate: No! And he goes on to explain how it is that sin has made use of the law's commandment in order to incite transgression and achieve transgression's consequence of death (7:7-13). Here the blame is clearly transferred to the power of personified sin; the law is not the ally of sin (as 5:20 might have implied) but its dupe.

A further reason for sin's power, implicit but undeveloped in 7:7-13, is the weakness of the human condition, the weakness, that is, of the flesh, or to be more precise, the weakness of the "I" as flesh. Thus even sin's use of the law to demonstrate the utter sinfulness of sin (7:13) should not be taken as a criticism of the law itself: "we know that the law is spiritual; but I am fleshly, sold under sin" (7:14). The blame, once again, has to be wholly placed on sin (7:14-17).

With all the actors now introduced (sin, death, law, "I") the analysis of the human condition and the role of the law in relation to sin can be clarified and defended. The key is first of all to recognize that the "I" itself is divided (7:18-20): the "I" as flesh does evil, or to be precise, sin indwelling the "I" as flesh does evil; while at the same time the "I" wishes what is good. This inner division and contradiction of the "I" is matched, secondly, by an equivalent division and contradiction in the law (7:21-23): the law as used by sin, and the law as indicating the will of God. And the match is close: the "I" as willing what is good is the "I" instructed by the law of God, "I" as "inner man" (7:22), "I" as mind (7:25); while the "I" as flesh remains under the sway of sin, captive to the law as used by sin (in the way explained earlier) (7:23, 25), the law of sin and death (8:2-3).[37]

We need not attempt any further resolution of the much disputed issue regarding the identity of the "I".[38] It will suffice to observe that since the argument of 7:7-8:4 is a defence of the law against the indictment initially posed in 5:20, the most obvious explanation is to link the split in the "I" with the division of the ages outlined in 5:12-21—the "I" as flesh, under the power of sin and death as belonging to the age of Adam, and the "I" as "inner man" and mind standing for the human being as intended by God, delighting in the will of God indicated by the law, though in the event dependent on the enabling of the Spirit to overcome the weakness of the flesh and to fulfil the requirement of the law (8:4). But whatever the precise reference of the "I" it should be clear enough that the defence of the law ends with a very positive emphasis on fulfilment of the law's requirements.

---

[37] This recognition of the split in the law matching the split in the "I" seems to me to make much better sense of the sequence of law references in 7:21-8:4 than the alternative, still dominant view which understands the νόμος references in 7:21, 23 and 8:2a in the sense "principle"; in recent scholarship see J. Ziesler 1989, 197-98, 202; D. Moo 1991, 490-92, 504-8; J. A. Fitzmyer 1993, 131; but see also Dunn 1988, 392-95, 416-18, with further bibliography.

[38] The most recent full-scale review is by J. Lambrecht 1992.

The importance of 7:7-8:4 within the sub-theme of Romans' theology of the law should therefore not be underestimated. It is this passage which above all else shows that Paul was not against the law as such. For it is a skilful defence of the law which "lets it off the hook". The charge that law was sin and functioned as a quasi-heavenly power (like sin and death) was legitimate and indeed invited by the provocative climax to 5:12-21. But now it is clear that for Paul any indictment is against the law only as abused by sin; and in this indictment the weakness of human flesh is equally if not more culpable. But the real culprit is sin. Apart from that, however, the law continues to function as yardstick and measure of God's will; and it is still God's will that its requirements should be fulfilled; he sent his Son and gave his Spirit precisely for that purpose (8:3-4).

The hermeneutical corollary which follows from this is the danger of an atomistic exegesis.[39] In this case Rom 5:20 taken on its own, or only in the immediate context of 5:12-21, can easily lead to the conclusion that Paul's attitude to the law was thoroughly hostile, as hostile as his attitude to sin and death. But in a letter as well crafted as Romans it is important to take particular texts in the context of the developing argument and rhetoric of the letter as a whole. And elsewhere it is very obvious that part of Paul's technique was to state a radical criticism early on, *not* as his finished conclusion, but as an issue to be dealt with later (particularly 3:1-8). So with 5:20: since it poses an issue which is dealt with only in 7:7-8:4, it cannot be adequately understood except by reference to 7:7-8:4.

## 3.3. The Continuing Positive Role of the Law

No one who has grasped the point of 7:7-8:4, therefore, should be surprised at the repeatedly positive role attributed to the law elsewhere, and indeed throughout Romans. Indeed, it is only when the real thrust of Rom 7, that is as a defence of the law, has been thus grasped, that it becomes possible to make sense of this repeated positive emphasis on the law in Romans. Without the key provided by 7:7-8:4 Paul's theology of the law would remain a riddle, and the argument that that theology was incoherent and contradictory would be hard to counter.

The continuing positive role attributed to the law in Romans can be indicated briefly, without further exposition, since the nub of the argument has already been dealt with:

the doers of the law will be counted righteous (2:13);
circumcision is of benefit if you practise the law (2:25);
... the righteousness of God has been revealed, as attested by the law

---

[39] Räisänen's method of treating *Paul and the Law* (1984/6) illustrates the danger well and thus undermines much of his own exegesis.

and the prophets (3:21);

boasting has been excluded (not by the law of works but) by the law
of faith (3:27);

we establish the law (through faith) (3:31);

I rejoice in the law of God, so far as the inner man is concerned (7:22);

the law of the Spirit of life in Christ Jesus has set me free … (8:2);

God sent his Son … in order that the requirement of the law might
be fulfilled in us who walk not in accordance with the flesh but in
accordance with the Spirit (8:3-4);

theirs is … the law (9:4);

Israel pursuing the law of righteousness has not reached the law.
Why so? Because they did so not from faith but as if it was from
works (9:31-32);

Owe nothing to anyone except to love one another; for he who loves
the other has fulfilled the law. For the commandment(s are) …
summed up in this word, in the command, 'You shall love your
neighbour as yourself'. Love does no wrong to the neighbour;
therefore the fulfilment of the law is love (13:8-10).

It is difficult to see how anyone can conclude after such a catena of passages that
Paul had abandoned the law and denied it any continuing role in instructing those
who had believed in Christ. The key is to recognize that Paul's more negative thrust
against the law was not directed against the law as such but against the law as manipulated by sin, against the law regarded as sufficient in itself to overcome the
weakness of the flesh, against the law of works. Once the law had been freed from
that role, and the commandments which served that role and the way they served
that role clearly recognized, then the continuing requirement of the law as expressing the will of God could be re-emphasized. All requirements could be thus manipulated by sin, could become "works of the law". But so long as it was appreciated
that all the law's requirements were to be fulfilled through faith and the enabling of
the Spirit, and along the lines of the love command, then the weakness of the flesh
could continue to be overcome and the devices of sin defeated.

The contrast with Galatians is also marked at this point. For in Galatians the positive emphasis on the continuing role of the law is present, but only briefly, and the
more negative thrust (contrasted with promise, only temporary) predominates.
Whereas here the emphasis is, if anything, the reverse. We may presume that it was
the particular challenge of the other missionaries in Galatia, seeking to draw the Galatian Gentile believers (back) "under the law", which made Paul sound so critical
of the law in Galatians. If so, the equally logical deduction here is that in the more
reflective mood of Romans Paul was able to stand back and outline the role of the
law within his theology in larger terms of principle. In that less threatened situation
the continuing positive role of the law for believers (Gentile as well as Jew) could

be laid out more dispassionately and effectively.

In short, due regard for the complete sweep of the argument shows Romans to express a wholly coherent understanding of the law, and due regard for the different circumstances with a view to which Galatians and Romans were penned is quite sufficient to explain the different emphases between the letters. The hermeneutical tensions and problems on this theme which have resurfaced in recent debate have arisen primarily because the necessary tasks of setting text within context have been neglected or important historical contextual information has been ignored.

## *4. Conclusion*

Can we then integrate the treatments of the law in Galatians and Romans into a single coherent theology? I think so. It is possible to speak of "Paul's theology of the law" on the basis of these two letters—and not as an incoherent theology, with many loose ends and unresolved issues; nor as one which shifted on any point of major significance between the two letters.

Each has its own distinctive features, of course, and it is on these that we have mainly concentrated—Galatians' emphasis on the law's temporary role vis-à-vis Israel as Israel's guardian angel, and Romans' repeated mention of the yardstick function of the law and subtle defence of the law in Rom 7-8. The other emphasis on the continuing positive role of the law is given different weight in the two letters, but it is present in both. More important for us is the fact that the more distinctive emphases of each letter cohere with each other without any real difficulty. A coherent theology of the law as expressed in the different language and circumstances of the two letters is therefore fairly easy to draw out.

A first common feature is *the God-given character and function of the law.* This is most explicit in Rom 7's insistence on the law as holy and just and good. But it is evident also in the role of the law as Israel's protector and custodian, a role naturally appointed by God, albeit providing a less immediate relation with God than the promise (Galatians). It is evident also in Romans' stress on the continuing yardstick function of the law and on the law as the measure of final judgment. Paul evidently continued to think of the law as having been given by God to be obeyed, and failure to obey it as provoking serious consequences.

Second, the critique of the law in each letter can now be seen to be more specifically targeted. In Galatians it is against the law's protective function for Israel being maintained as a means to exclude Gentiles as Gentiles from participation in the blessing of Abraham, despite the eschatological fulfilment in Christ and the Spirit. Since Gentiles as Gentiles have also received the Spirit, the law is no longer needed as guardian to protect Jews from them as though they were still "sinners", still a source of defilement. In Romans it is against the law as used by sin to batten on the weakness of the flesh, to maintain the rule of sin and death as over the age of Adam.

The two critiques are in fact closely related. For in both letters, attempts by other (Christian) Jews to maintain their distinctive privileged standing before God was seen by Paul as a pandering to the flesh, quite as much as "works of the flesh" (Gal 3:2-3; 5:19; 6:12-13; Rom 2:28). And in both letters the criticised attitude is summed up in the phrase "works of the law" (Gal 2:16; 3:2, 5, 10; Rom 3:20, 27-28; 9:32). In Romans the same appreciation of the law is characterised as γράμμα —in effect a focusing of the law on the visible and fleshly, that is, on the ethnic distinction between Jew and Gentile which circumcision in particular indicated (Rom 2:27-29).

Romans also brings out an aspect of the temporary role of the law not explored in Galatians. For in Galatians the time before and apart from Christ is described not only as the period of Israel from Moses to Christ, but also as "the present evil age" (Gal 1:4) and, by implication, the "old creation" (Gal 6:15). In Romans this is elaborated as the age of Adam, under the rule of sin and death (Rom 5:12-21). But whereas in Galatians the role of the law during that period seems to be characterised as something essentially positive (protector, custodian, guardian), in Romans the role of the law in the age of Adam is portrayed as essentially sin's dupe. What we may say, then, is that in Romans Paul shows how the protective role of the law (Galatians) has been perverted by sin and the weakness of the flesh into a negative force preventing the full outworking of the gospel to all who believe. To that extent the "I" of Romans 7 is Israel,[40] caught between the conflicting roles of the law, the one manipulated by sin to tie Israel in effect more tightly to essentially fleshly concerns, the other awaiting the liberation of the Spirit for its role to be fulfilled. Moreover, since Rom 10:4 concludes a section criticising Israel for continuing to think of the law of righteousness in terms of works (9:32) and for continuing zealously to defend its special relationship with God (10:2-3), we may further deduce that what Christ marks the end of (10:4) is the temporary role of the law as Israel's protector weakened by the flesh and perverted by sin.

Thirdly, once the danger of the law caught in the nexus of sin and flesh has been fully appreciated, then the continuing positive role of the law can be expressed in its fullness. It still indicates the will of God. God still wants its requirements to be fulfilled. Only those who do the law will be justified. But these requirements are understood now in terms of faith and Spirit and love rather than works of the law— that is, the law fulfilled by trusting in God('s Christ), in walking by the Spirit, in loving the neighbour.

---

[40] Cf. particularly D. J. Moo 1986.

In formulating a coherent theology of the law as expressed in Galatians and Romans, therefore, it is important, finally, to maintain the proper Pauline dialectic. Not simply between the gospel and the law; that we can now see to be too crude. But between the law as a yardstick of what is good, and the law as the cat's-paw of evil; between the law (as the expression) of faith and the law as summed up in works of the law; between the law (as the expression) of the Spirit of life and the law as the tool of sin and death; between the law as showing how the life of faith should be lived through love of the other, and the law always in danger of becoming γράμμα, emphasising the visible marks which distinguish Jew from Gentile. In each case it is the same law—the law, caught like the willing but still fleshly "I" between the ages, between the competing claims of sin and grace, like the rest of creation awaiting the liberation of the children of God (Rom 8:19-23).

As a test-case for the most appropriate context(s) within which and in reference to which a Pauline text should be expounded, this study has reaffirmed the importance of reading particular texts within the context of the larger document of which they are part, of illuminating that context from the wider context of the time, and of correlating different texts from the same author inter-text-within-contextually. There are of course other contexts within which and in relation to which Pauline texts dealing with the law will be read, but if we are to speak of Paul's own theology of the law, the former must take precedence. The fact that by doing so we have been able to draw out a coherent theology of the law, which can be attributed to Paul as such, is simply a ratification of the appropriateness of the procedure.

## *Bibliography*

Bauer, W./Arndt, W. F./Gingrich, F. W./Danker, F. W. [= BAGD] 1979: *A Greek-English Lexicon of the New Testament and Other Early Christian Literature*, Chicago, IL & London: Chicago University Press [2]1979.

Betz, H. D. 1979: *Galatians* (Hermeneia), Philadelphia, PA: Fortress 1979.

Bonnard, P. 1953: *Galates* (CNT(N) 9), Neuchâtel: Delachaux & Niestlé 1953.

Borse, U. 1984: *Galater* (RNT), Regensburg: Pustet 1984.

Bring, R. 1968: *Galater*, Berlin: Lutherisches 1968.

Burton, E. de W. 1921: *Galatians* (ICC), Edinburgh: T. & T. Clark 1921.

Callan, T. 1980: "Pauline Midrash: The Exegetical Background of Gal 3:19b", in: *JBL* 99 (1980) 549-67.

Charlesworth J. H. (ed.) 1991: *Jesus' Jewishness. Exploring the Place of Jesus in Early Judaism*, New York: Crossroad 1991.

Dietzfelbinger, C. 1985: *Die Berufung des Paulus als Ursprung seiner Theologie* (WMANT 58), Neukirchen-Vluyn: Neukirchener Verlag 1985.

Donaldson, T. L. 1986: "The 'Curse of the Law' and the Inclusion of the Gentiles: Galatians 3.13-14", in: *NTS* 32 (1986) 94-112.

Donfried, K. P. (ed.), 1991: *The Romans Debate. Revised and Expanded,* Peabody, MA: Hendrickson 1991.

Drane, J. W. 1975: *Paul: Libertine or Legalist?,* London: SPCK 1975.

Dunn, J. D. G. 1988: *Romans* (Word Biblical Commentary 38), Dallas: Word 1988.

— 1990: "Works of the Law and the Curse of the Law (Gal. 3.10-14)", in: idem *Jesus, Paul and the Law,* London: SPCK/Louisville, KY: Westminster 1990, 215-41

— 1992: "Yet Once More—'The Works of the Law': A Response", in: *JSNT* 46 (1992) 99-117.

— 1993: *Galatians* (BNTC), London: A. & C. Black 1993.

Fitzmyer, J. A. 1993: *Romans* (AncB 33), New York: Doubleday 1993.

Fung, R. Y. K. 1988: *Galatians* (NIC), Grand Rapids, MI: Eerdmans 1988.

Guthrie, D. 1969: *Galatians* (NCeB), London: Oliphants 1969.

Hagner, D. 1984: *The Jewish Reclamation of Jesus,* Grand Rapids, MI: Zondervan 1984.

Hays, R. B. 1983: *The Faith of Jesus Christ,* Chico, CA: Scholars Press 1983.

Hübner, H. 1985: *Law in Paul's Thought,* Edinburgh: T. & T. Clark 1985.

Kim, S. 1981: *The Origin of Paul's Gospel* (WUNT II.4), Tübingen: Mohr (Siebeck) 1981.

Klein, C. 1978: *Anti-Judaism in Christian Theology,* London: SPCK 1978.

Lagrange, M. J. 1925: *Galates* (EtB), Paris: Gabalda ²1925.

Lambrecht, J. 1992: *The Wretched "I" and its Liberation. Paul in Romans 7 and 8,* Louvain: Peeters 1992.

Liddell, H. G./Scott, R./Jones, H. S. [= LSJ] 1966: *A Greek-English Lexicon,* Oxford: Clarendon 1966.

Longenecker, R. N. 1990: *Galatians* (Word Biblical Commentary 41), Dallas, TX: Word 1990.

Lull, D. J. 1986: "'The Law was our Pedagogue': A Study in Galatians 3:19-25", in: *JBL* 105 (1986) 481-98.

Moo, D. J. 1986: "Israel and Paul in Romans 7:7-12", in: *NTS* 32 (1986) 122-35.

— 1991: *Romans 1-8* (Wycliffe Exegetical Commentary), Chicago, IL: Moody 1991.

Mußner, F. 1977: *Galaterbrief* (HThK 9), Freiburg: Herder ³1977.

Neill, S. & Wright, T. 1988: *The Interpretation of the New Testament 1861-1986,* Oxford: Oxford University Press 1988.

Oepke, A. 1973: *Galater* (ThHK 9), Berlin: Evangelische Verlagsanstalt ³1973.

Pawlikowski, J. T. 1982: *Christ in the Light of the Christian-Jewish Dialogue,* New York: Paulist 1982.

Räisänen, H. 1984/6: *Paul and the Law* (WUNT 29); Tübingen: Mohr (Siebeck) 1984/Philadelphia, PA: Fortress 1986.

Ramsay, W. M. 1900: *Galatians*, London: Hodder 1900.

Sanders, E. P. 1977: *Paul and Palestinian Judaism*, London: SCM 1977.

— 1984/5: *Paul, the Law and the Jewish People*, Philadelphia, PA: Fortress 1984/London: SCM Press 1985.

Schlier, H. 1965: *Galater* (KEK 7); Göttingen: Vandenhoeck & Ruprecht [4]1965.

Schürmann, H. 1974: "'Das Gesetz des Christus' (Gal 6.2): Jesu Verhalten und Wort als letztgültige sittliche Norm nach Paulus", in: J. Gnilka (ed.), *Neues Testament und Kirche*. FS R. Schnackenburg, Freiburg: Herder 1974, 282-300.

Segal, A. 1990: *Paul the Convert. The Apostolate and Apostasy of Saul the Pharisee,* New Haven, CT: Yale University Press 1990.

Stendahl, K. 1963: "The Apostle Paul and the Introspective Conscience of the West", in: *HThR* 56 (1963) 199-215 (reprinted in his *Paul Among Jews and Gentiles*, London: SCM/Philadelphia, PN: Fortress 1977, 78-96).

Strack, H. L./Billerbeck, P. [= Str-B] 1926: *Kommentar zum Neuen Testament aus Talmud und Midrasch.* Vol. 3: Die Briefe des Neuen Testaments und die Offenbarung Johannis, Munich: Beck 1926.

Stuhlmacher, P. 1981: "'Das Ende des Gesetzes'. Über Ursprung und Ansatz der paulinischen Theologie", in: idem, *Versöhnung, Gesetz und Gerechtigkeit*, Göttingen: Vandenhoeck & Ruprecht 1981, 166-91.

Vermes, G. 1993: *The Religion of Jesus the Jew*, London: SCM Press 1993.

Wedderburn, A. J. M. 1988: *The Reasons for Romans*, Edinburgh: T. & T. Clark 1988.

Young, N. H. 1987: "Παιδαγωγός: The Social Setting of a Pauline Metaphor", in: *NT* 29 (1987) 150-76.

Zahn, T. 1905: *Galater*, Leipzig: Deichert 1905.

Ziesler, J. 1989: *Romans*, London: SCM/Philadelphia, PN: Trinity Press International 1989.

# Galatians in Romans 5-8 and Paul's Construction of the Identity of Christ Believers

Troels Engberg-Pedersen

## 1. Two Issues

I propose to discuss two issues that may initially appear unrelated, the question of the relationship between "theology" and "ethics" in Paul and that of the literary structure and function of Romans 5-8. I begin from an independent exploration of the two issues and only gradually move towards bringing them together.

## 2. Theology and Ethics

The relationship between "theology" and "ethics" in Paul is an issue that should continue to engage readers of his letters. Let us define Paul's "theology" here to stand for those sections of his writings in which he is speaking of the will, character and actions of God and Christ. Correspondingly, let his "ethics" stand for sections in which he is speaking of the behaviour of human beings towards one another and of the corresponding mental attitudes.

With these definitions it is already clear that the distinction between Paul's "theology" and his "ethics" raises more questions than it answers. For one thing, the crucially important notion of the human response to God's will, character and actions must be brought in too. Human faith somehow bridges the gap between "theology" and "ethics". In addition, even in those passages in his letters in which Paul turns explicitly to what we are used to calling moral exhortation, he explicitly grounds his recommendations in references to God's will or the like (e.g. Rom 12:1-2). Still, precisely in order to see the exact logic of the connectedness of Paul's "theology" and his "ethics", it is necessary first to keep the two notions analytically distinct.

Throughout much of this century the common understanding of "theology" and "ethics" in Paul has been defined in the terms set out in Rudolf Bultmann's famous

1924 essay, "Das Problem der Ethik bei Paulus".[1] There is the "indicative" of God's salvation and justification of humankind (albeit through faith) and there is God's "imperative" that human beings make their actions correspond to the indicative of justification.

Bultmann's proposal was a ruthlessly theological, God-centred, one. (i) The δικαιοσύνη of which Paul's letter to the Romans makes so much is God's and God's alone, his eschatological *Gabe*. Bultmann explicitly denied that a human, ethical δικαιοσύνη (justice) was also involved.[2] (ii) Even more starkly, the Pauline imperatives are expressly stated to represent the command of God, his *Gebot*.[3] To the extent that any human willing is at all involved, it takes the form of obedience, *Gehorsam*.[4] (iii) Thus neither the indicative nor the imperative has anything to do with ethics: *in Wahrheit handelt es sich in den Aussagen des Paulus über die Sünd-losigkeit des Gerechtfertigten gar nicht um eine Ethik.*[5]

Not many will agree with this extreme position, but Bultmann's essay is a classic and there are far more relics of it around than might initially appear. In any case, Bultmann's proposal has the virtue of clarity, which may help us sharpen our perception of what we would ourselves wish to say.

Here I shall argue that a passage like Romans 5-8 shows Paul to be centrally concerned with constructing an identity for his Christ-believing addressees. His primary focus in the passage is on how they should understand themselves: who they are, what their world looks like, where they belong. (i) As part of this we shall see that

---

[1] Bultmann 1924.

[2] E.g. Bultmann 1924, 127-28, where he states that the (already) "realisierte Seinsweise des Gerechtfertigten" has an "eschatologischen, wunderbaren Charakter" and so has nothing to do with "die im antiken wie im modernen Rationalismus und Idealismus herrschende Auffassung vom Menschen und seinem Vermögen … das Gute zu verwirklichen" (127). In fact, man stands "schlechthin als Sünder vor Gott" and his justification is not a matter of his "Gesinnung", his "sittliches Wollen": "Damit wäre der eschatologische Charakter der Rechtfertigung verkannt, wäre verkannt, daß die Rechtfertigung Gottes wunderbares Tun bzw. Gottes unbegreifliches Urteil ist" (128).

[3] E.g. Bultmann 1924, 140: "die im Imperativ sich aussprechende sittliche Forderung" is, for the believer, "Gottes Gebot".

[4] Bultmann 1924, 137. Note the almost wilful eccentricity of Bultmann's claim that while the ethical imperative in no way disappears (with the fact of justification), it, that is, the imperative, only acquires a new sense—of "*Gehorsam* unter Gott" (Bultmann's own emphasis). Not only is it *God's* command, but when Bultmann feels forced to speak of the human side he maintains his ruthlessly God-centred perspective by saying that the imperative, God's imperative, also *is* human obedience! Later (140) he speaks more correctly of human obedience as being, not the imperative itself, but "die der Forderung entsprechende Haltung des Gehorsams"—but only to insist that just as "die im Imperativ sich aussprechende sittliche Forderung" is "Gottes Gebot", so this "Haltung" is "Gabe Gottes".

[5] Bultmann 1924, 126.

Paul is very far from construing God's δικαιοσύνη as a matter of God's gracious gift alone. God's δικαιοσύνη also brings in human, ethical justice. (ii) Nor is the Pauline imperative in fact to be construed as God's or at all to be taken as a command that demands obedience. It is Paul's imperative, and it is not a command, but an appeal. (iii) And while Bultmann was right in saying that Paul's statements about the sinlessness of the justified person have nothing to do with ethics in the way Bultmann himself used the term (as something intrinsically opposed to a theological perspective),[6] we shall see that they are very much about human understanding and willing, and in areas too that fall under the "ethical" as defined above. (iv) Finally, we shall see that with respect to this passage, at least, the best account of the relationship between Paul's indicative statements (his "theology") and his imperatival statements (his "ethics") holds that they *converge* on the issue of human identity, of the human construction of the self. Paul's "theological" statements about God's will, character and actions and his "ethical" statements about the attitudes and behaviour of human beings towards one another *come together* in the notion of the construction of the identity of Christ believers.

## 3. Romans 5-8 — The Structure

The issue of the literary shape and function of Romans 5-8 raises a number of problems, which fall into two main groups.[7] The first concerns the structural delimitation of the passage, both at its beginning and at various points within it. The second concerns the basic theme or themes that Paul is addressing. These are hackneyed issues but I need to address them before I can present my reading of the overall point of the passage.

Scholars are divided on whether to take chap. 5 together with the preceding four chapters or with the following three ones.[8] On the one hand it is claimed that the chapter provides a fitting conclusion to the development right from 1:18: Paul is still speaking the language of justification, which he leaves behind in chaps. 6ff.; he is drawing the direct consequences for his readers of the change announced in 3:21

---

[6] Cf. Bultmann 1924, 127 (quoted above in n. 2), where Bultmann opposes the way in which Paul saw man with "die im antiken wie im modernen Rationalismus und Idealismus herrschende Auffassung vom Menschen und seinem Vermögen ..., nämlich dem Vermögen, das Gute zu verwirklichen".

[7] The best discussions of the literary structure of Romans (in particular chaps. 1-8) are Dupont 1955 and Luz 1969. See also Wilckens 1974. Beker 1980, 65-69, places these discussions within the wider framework of the German "two-crater theory" concerning Romans 1-8 (justification and Christ-mysticism) that was launched at the beginning of this century (A. Schweitzer and others).

[8] Beker 1980, 377 n. 43, catalogues scholars who are in favour of making a break either at 4:25/5:1; 5:11/5:12; or 5:21/6:1.

and spelling it out by contrasting the period of Adam with the new period of Christ; the fact that 5:1-11, in particular, employs a great deal of material that comes up again in the second half of chap. 8 only shows that Paul wished to conclude each major section of the letter in a similar way. Against this it is argued that while 5:1-11 does state the direct consequences of what comes before, it also brings in important new material which points clearly forward: the various motifs that are later taken up again in chap. 8 and also the motif of death and life (5:10), which is spelled out in full in 5:12-21 and plays a central role in chaps. 6-7 and well into chap. 8.[9]

There is no genuine issue here. Long ago Nils Dahl stated: "The problem of whether a main line of division should be drawn between chapters 4 and 5 or between 5 and 6 or, possibly, between 5:11 and 5:12 becomes acute only if we ask for some systematic outline and fail to follow Paul's vivid argumentation."[10] Indeed, a careful analysis of Paul's style of writing would reveal that he often, but not always, employs the technique of making one or more statements which at the same time serve to conclude what comes before and to introduce what comes after. Let us call this a *Pauline bridge*.[11] An example earlier in Romans is 2:11, which at the same time sums up the preceding verses and also introduces those that follow. 5:1-11, or indeed the whole of chap. 5, is just another such example.[12]

There is also a question concerning the division of chap. 6. Is it 6:1-11 plus 6:12-23 or 6:1-14 plus 6:15-23? Surely the latter. It is true that Paul leaves explicit reflection on baptism behind in 6:12, but the point of 6:12-13 is to spell out the consequences (already stated in 6:11) of that reflection for the question raised at 6:1. It is only with the marked restatement of that question in 6:15 that a new section begins.[13] Even typographically the Nestle-Aland 26th and 27th editions should therefore have had 6:12 follow directly upon 6:11 and have begun a new paragraph only

---

[9] There is a comprehensive rehearsal of the various arguments and individual views of scholars in Wolter 1978, 203-16.

[10] Dahl 1977, 91. Dahl had changed his mind since Dahl 1951, 39, in which he spoke in favour of a main break between 4:25 and 5:1. See Dahl 1969, 17 n. 15: "Today I would not argue so strongly that Romans 1-8 should be divided into 1-4 + 5-8 rather than into 1-5 + 6-8. The sections 5:1-11 and 5:12-21 function *both as conclusions of what precedes and as introductions to what follows*." (My italics.) This is precisely the notion of a Pauline "bridge" that I go on to introduce.

[11] After I had coined this phrase, I noticed that Kaye 1979, 8, 10, 13, 29, uses the same metaphor. I emphasize this notion because it shows how hundreds of pages of scholarly discussion may become obsolete as soon as one asks whether a genuine issue is being discussed.

[12] Wolter 1978, 209 and 211, rightly complains about the totally subjective and idiosyncratic character of scholarly decisions for and against 4:25/5:1; 5:11/5:12; 5:21/6:1. His methodological strictures on previous scholarly discussion are entirely justified. Unfortunately, he goes directly on to argue for his own solution, which (as it happens) is 5:11(21)/6:1. Instead, the logical conclusion to Wolter's methodological observations is the notion of a Pauline bridge.

[13] Good arguments in Wilckens 1980, 7-8.

with 6:15.

A further question concerns the allocation of 7:1-6. Here again we may speak of a Pauline bridge. On the one hand, the passage is clearly parallel to 6:15-23, speaking as it does of a slavery (chap. 6: to sin, chap. 7: to the law) from which Paul's addressees have been freed.[14] On the other hand, the fact that Paul now speaks of the law (and so very explicitly: 7:1) clearly points forward to 7:7ff. Indeed, 7:5-6 constitutes a brief pre-summary of the rest of chap. 7 (7:5) and the first part of chap. 8 (7:6). Again, therefore, there is no genuine structural issue between those who connect 7:1-6 with chap. 6 and those who see something new happening at 7:1. They are both right. 7:1-6 is a Pauline bridge.

As 7:5-6 already makes clear, there is no doubt that the section that begins at 7:7 goes well into chap. 8, but how far? In a perceptive discussion of 8:1ff., Ulrich Wilckens first noted the case for taking at least 8:12-13 closely with the preceding verses. After Paul's general contrast in 8:5-8 of "being and walking" (*Sein und Wandel*) according to the flesh or the spirit, 8:9-11 is a personal address that emphasizes the fact of the Romans' *being* in the spirit and 8:12-13 the corresponding personal address emphasizing their need to *act* too in accordance with the spirit. That consideration, so Wilckens, would count strongly for extending the passage until 8:17. However, since 8:14-17 brings in new motifs that lead into 8:18ff. and since the same passage gives a reason for 8:12-13 (cf. γάρ in 8:14), Wilckens finally decided to make the cut already after 8:11.[15]

Wilckens was of course right that 8:14ff. does bring in new motifs, most importantly the notion of being a son of God (8:14). If he was also right that 8:14ff. provides a reason for 8:12-13, the correct solution would be to see 8:14-17 as yet another Pauline bridge. In that case 8:12-13 should follow directly on 8:11, even typographically (against the Nestle-Aland 26th and 27th editions; cf. above on 6:12), and a new paragraph might begin at 8:14 in order to mark off 8:14-17 as a Pauline bridge.[16]

However, Wilckens may not be right on 8:14ff. In what way does 8:14 provide a reason for 8:13? Much hangs on how one construes 8:12-13. There can be little doubt that 8:12 constitutes an anacoluthon. Paul is not saying: "So then, brothers, we are under no obligation to the flesh to live in accordance with the flesh,"[17] which

---

[14] Compare Dupont 1955, 384, who perceptively notes that in 6:1-7:6 the theme of "l'obligation de ne plus pécher" is developed through an "argument dogmatique" (6:3-14), an "argument tiré de la vie sociale" (6:15-23), and an "argument juridique, emprunté à la législation du mariage" (7:1-6). Luz 1969, 170 and 176-77, is also helpful here.

[15] Wilckens 1980, 120.

[16] One of the few scholars who have seen and taken seriously the break at 8:13/14 is von der Osten-Sacken 1975, 61.

[17] This is James Dunn's translation, Dunn 1988, 446. Dunn does not discuss the question.

in any case would be a very odd understatement. That would have required the following in the Greek: Ἄρα οὖν, ἀδελφοί, <οὐκ> ὀφειλέται ἐσμέν—or ὀφειλέται <οὐκ> ἐσμέν—[οὐ] τῇ σαρκὶ τοῦ κατὰ σάρκα ζῆν. Instead he says: "So then, brothers, we are under an obligation, not to the flesh to live in accordance with the flesh"—meaning: *but* to the spirit to live in accordance with the spirit.[18] However, he breaks off the sentence he has begun by giving a reason why we do not owe it to the flesh to live in accordance with that (8:13a). This reason is then followed by another *reason* why we do owe it to the spirit to live in accordance with that—*as if* Paul had already made the former claim. What is supported by 8:14 is therefore not the basic paraenetic point that underlies 8:13, but at most the reason given for it in 8:13b.

Wilckens would probably agree. But then, if 8:14 does not directly support the paraenesis, which is surely the basic point of 8:12-13 (as Wilckens agrees and cf. the emphatic ἄρα οὖν), does it in any precise sense support the idea of "living" (ζήσεσθαι) that Paul brings in as his *reason* for the paraenetic point? No. Whereas in the preceding chapters, and as recently as 8:10-11, the life-talk has played a crucial role, it fades out, completely from 8:14 onwards. This is not to say that one could not devise an important link between "living" and being a son of God. Only Paul is not interested in doing so right here.

We should conclude that the γάρ of 8:14 is a "γάρ of continuation", of which there are of course plenty in Paul.[19] That only makes it even more obvious that a new typographical paragraph should begin at 8:14. In other words, the passage that begins at 7:7 goes as far as 8:13.

## *4. Romans 5-8 — The Theme*

The second group of problems that has been raised about Romans 5-8 concerns the overall theme or themes of these chapters. Three basic positions deserve to be mentioned.

The first is the traditional view that these chapters, or at least chaps. 6-8, are about sanctification, corresponding to the discussion of justification in the previous chapters. Taken generally, this is true enough but it needs precision. A second view

---

[18] Wilckens 1980, 118, *translates* correctly, but does not discuss the question. Cranfield 1975, 394, got it exactly right. I quote in order to settle the question: "The position of the negative strongly suggests that Paul intended to continue with something like ἀλλὰ τῷ πνεύματι τοῦ κατὰ πνεῦμα ζῆν, but broke off in order to insert the warning of v. 13a, and then, after adding a natural complement to v. 13a, failed to complete the sentence begun in v. 12."

[19] Bauer-Aland speak of a use of γάρ that is "anknüpfend u. fortführend" and almost equals a δέ. Among examples from Romans, 1:18 and 12:3 prove the point.

is that Paul is basically answering certain objections that follow from his earlier account. This position again concentrates on chaps. 6-8 and like the earlier one it has certain difficulties with fitting in the latter half of chap. 8 (from 8:14 onwards, as we should say). With respect to 6:1-8:13 it has much to recommend it, since Paul does start out from a number of supposed objections at various points, 6:1; 6:15; 7:7. Also, the idea that Paul is answering objections, or at least attempting to solve problems internal to his own earlier account, is supported by noting the way in which the issue raised in 6:1 has been hinted at already in 3:8, and the one raised in 7:7 introduced in 3:20 and kept alive through 4:15; 5:13-14, 20; and 6:14.

The main difficulty with this view is that it does not account sufficiently for the actual character, and indeed the strong urgency, of Paul's writing throughout chaps. 5-8. This urgency takes several forms. In 5:1-11 and 8:14-39 it takes the form of exploring in great detail and from a number of perspectives the state in which Christ believers *now stand* (in relation to God and in relation to the world)—*after* the Christ event and after their incorporation into it. In 6:1-8:13 it takes the form of an exceedingly strong elaboration of a *set of contrasts* within which Paul urges his Christ-believing addressees to see themselves: "dying" and being "buried" with Christ (in baptism) in order that they may lead a new life (6:1-14), being set free from slavery to sin by having come to be instead under grace and justification (6:15-23), being set free from the law so that they may instead serve in a new life of the spirit (7:1-6 and 7:7-8:13). In addition, 6:1-8:13 is marked by Paul's addressing himself directly to his listeners in the second person plural (6:3, 11, 12-13, 14, 16, 17-18, 19, 20-22; 7:1, 4; 8:9-13), often with the "Do you not know that ...?" of moral exhortation (6:3, 16; 7:1) and often directly *with* moral exhortation (6:11, 12-13, 19; 8:12-13).

The last point is of great importance. If we ask why Paul brought in baptism in chap. 6, the correct answer is not that he wished to show that Christ-believers *could* not "stay with sin" (6:1) because of what had happened to them in baptism. Rather, his aim is to bring out that just because Christ-believers cannot do that, they *must* not do it.[20] Thus 6:11 and 12-13 are of crucial importance for understanding the overall direction of Paul's thought. Similarly, his (indicative) statements throughout 6:15-23 about the change in allegiance they have undergone serve to underscore his imperative in 6:19 that they do undergo that change. On this background, although Paul does not in 7:1-6 actually employ any form of direct moral exhortation, there can be little doubt that his emphatic statement about what *has* happened to his addressees (cf. 7:4) has the same function of providing a background to moral exhortation. Only, here the exhortation is not actually made—or rather, it is kept in

---

[20] Compare Dupont 1955, 386: "A travers toutes les considérations de VI-VII, 6, Paul poursuit un même dessein: montrer au chrétien qu'il n'a plus le droit de pécher."

reserve to be brought in with full force in 8:9-13.

Finally, as regards 7:7-8:8 it will suffice once more to quote Nils Dahl, who stated: "Paul does not in Rom. 7 use the 'I' form in order to give biographical information, to set forth anthropological doctrines, or to give an abstract interpretation of pre-Christian existence under the Law. *He wants to engage his readers, so that they concur* both in the conclusion that the Law is good and in the thanksgiving for the liberation in Christ *and, thus, let the Spirit, not the flesh direct their lives.*"[21]

We should conclude that 6:1-8:13 is basically paraenetic.[22] This is not to say that Paul is not also concerned in this passage, for instance, to give an interpretation of the relationship between sin and the law and so to ward off the objection that according to the Pauline position "the law *is* sin" (7:7). The fact that he has prepared 7:7ff. so carefully earlier in the letter shows that he does have this concern. But basically, 7:7-25 serves as a foil to the description given in 8:1-4 of the new state in Christ and that description in turn gives the indicative basis (together with 8:9-11) for the exhortation of 8:12-13.

We should also conclude that the paraenetic section 6:1-8:13 is surrounded by two sections, 5:1-11 and 8:14-39, which are not paraenetic, but share with 6:1-8:13 a concern to elaborate the new "state in which we now stand".

The third position in regard to the overall theme or themes of the four chapters is that of Ulrich Wilckens. Actually Wilckens was speaking only of chaps. 6-8, since he had decided that chap. 5 belongs unilaterally with chaps. 1-4.[23] Correspondingly, he had real difficulties with fitting the latter half of chap. 8 into his understanding of Paul's concern in the three chapters. Still, his view is worth quoting for a number of reasons. It is *almost* on target. It brings into view the theme of God's δικαιοσύνη. And it shows how even a German reading of Paul that has its roots in dialectical theology may come very close to hitting the mark. (It also shows, rather amusingly, how difficult it was to overcome all the obstacles to making the correct point: the italics are Wilckens' own.)[24]

> Alles hängt daran, daß die Rechtfertigung des Sünders nicht zur Auflösung der Sittlichkeit, sondern vielmehr zu einem nun erst real möglichen, radikalen sittlichen Engagement führt, daß die geschenkte Gerechtigkeit des aus Glauben Gerechtigten *wirkliche Gerechtigkeit* ist. Denn alles hängt daran, daß die zur Gnade gewordene

---

[21] Dahl 1977, 94. (My italics.)

[22] I have not been able to find a single scholar who states this unequivocally and in the strong form in which I intend it to be understood: Rom 6:1-8:13 is basically paraenetic in exactly the same way in which, for instance, Gal 5:13-26 is it. Fortunately, I believe I am able also to explain why it has not been seen, see below.

[23] See Wilckens 1978, 181-82 and 286-88.

[24] Wilckens, 1980, 4.

Gerechtigkeit *Gottes* wirklich *Gerechtigkeit* ist, das heißt aber: Gerechtigkeit *Gottes*, die in der Gerechtigkeit der ihr zugehörigen *Menschen* ihre Tat-Entsprechung findet, so daß sie wirklich Heil schafft in einer durch Gerechtigkeit bestimmten Gemeinde.

So, God's δικαιοσύνη is after all also a matter of human, social justice. What Wilckens is saying here is virtually identical with what I have just said about 6:1-8:13, though he does not work out the *overall, paraenetic* character of the whole passage. In addition, Wilckens' statement very usefully raises, in relation to the present passage, some of the questions from which I began, concerning the relationship between the "theology" and the "ethics". What is the exact relationship between the δικαιοσύνη of God and that of "die ihr zugehörigen *Menschen*"? And what is the logical form of Pauline paraenesis?

Before I turn to these questions, I shall harden the above interpretation of the literary and thematic form of our passage by making one more proposal about how it should be read.

## 5. Paul's Writing of Romans

We do not quite know the precise reason why Paul wrote his long letter to the Roman Christ believers. During the last decades a large number of proposals have been made. They usually emphasize one particular element in the text as providing the key to the answer while to some extent neglecting others. As a result, the general consensus now seems to be that Paul may have had several purposes in mind when writing his letter.[25] That is both something of a counsel of despair vis-à-vis the ability of scholarship to answer its own questions and also quite likely true as it stands. What is required is some attempt to sort out different *types* of "purpose" or "reason" that may lie behind the writing of the letter.

This is not the place to go into this whole issue in any detail. Let us just note that there seems to be a valid distinction between whatever purposes Paul may have had with writing in this or the other way once he had made the initial decision to write to the Romans—and his reasons for making that decision in the first place. Let us also note that once we look for reasons why Paul decided to send the Romans a letter at all, it is *a priori* more likely, and in fact supported by the letter itself, that there should have been some specific occasion for doing so, something Paul wanted to bring about instead of merely providing general entertainment, no matter how serious, to his addressees. Finally, let us note that if indeed there was such a specific

---

[25] The following remarks are only meant to sharpen the issue and to present the "minimal" solution that I presuppose in this essay. A good overview of scholarly positions is given in Donfried 1991.

occasion, it must also have been of such a kind that it will explain at least the general shape of the actual letter, no matter what other purposes may have become apparent to Paul once he had decided to write it. One thing one may be looking for in discussing the purposes with and reasons for the letter is therefore this: (1) a specific occasion that triggered off Paul's writing a letter (2) with the overall, very comprehensive shape of the present one.

A careful reading of Rom 1:1-15 and 15:14-33 will show that there is in fact a single answer which satisfies these conditions and also has the virtue of being a "minimal" answer in the sense that while it is sufficient in itself to account for Paul's writing a letter (and a letter of that kind), it also allows for almost any other purpose that has been found to lie behind the letter. Since we have no access to Paul's own mind, such an answer is the furthest we can go, and any more elaborate speculation should be avoided.

The answer is this: Paul wished to prepare the way for a visit of his own to Rome, a visit that might cause some problems since (i) the Roman congregations had not been founded by Paul and were personally unknown to him, (ii) Paul had a principle of not preaching where Christ had already been mentioned, and (iii) Paul intended to stay some time in the city and indeed to create the kind of relationship between himself and the Romans which he had with the congregations he had himself established. His aim with this was very likely to make Rome his base of support for further mission in the western half of the Mediterranean, in the way Ephesus had served him in the East.[26] On this background, Romans is to be understood as a letter of self-recommendation.[27] Paul is saying: This is who I am—by stating in fairly comprehensive form "his gospel", what he stood for.[28] We may dignify this suggestion by calling the letter an ἐπιστολὴ συστατική, but mainly because Paul himself uses that term elsewhere (2 Cor 3:1). There is hardly much to be gained from comparing Romans with other specimens of the genre of letters of (self-)recommendation.

Suppose Paul is basically wanting to introduce himself to the Romans in preparation for an extended visit with them—but also, quite likely, *takes* the occasion to

---

[26] In 1963, Bornkamm admitted that these are the "few well-known facts" concerning Paul's writing of Romans (see Bornkamm 1963 in Donfried 1991, 17). Unfortunately, he also felt that "behind" those facts "the real questions" appeared—which led him to his own more speculative view concerning the occasion and purpose of the letter (focusing on 15:30-32 and Jerusalem), for which see also Bornkamm 1971. On these further questions scholars will never agree since we have no access to Paul's mind. Nor is any answer required in order to understand the letter as we have it.

[27] Compare Köster 1980, 575: "Es ist ein Empfehlungsschreiben des Paulus für sich selbst."

[28] Compare Kümmel 1980, 273, who speaks of Paul's "Wunsch, sich bei den Christen in Rom einzuführen, ihnen zu sagen, wer er ist und was er predigt".

comment on whatever issues he may have heard were at stake in Rome.[29] In that case, being rhetorically trained, as Paul undoubtedly was,[30] he will have done some "invention", consciously or unconsciously, before beginning to dictate the letter. Near the start of the pseudo-Ciceronian *Rhetorica ad Herennium*, the rhetorical category of *inventio* is defined as a "thinking out of material that is true or plausible and that may render the case convincing" (*excogitatio rerum verarum aut veri similium quae causam probabilem reddant*, 1.2.3). If the writing of Romans was triggered by the set of considerations just mentioned, Paul's *causa* will have been the presentation of himself as an apostle "called and set off to proclaim the gospel of God ... among all gentiles" (Rom 1:1 and 5). Where, then, would he find the material to make that *causa* convincing?

The obvious answer is: in his previous letters. The suggestion is of course not that Paul merely copied out what he had written earlier, or even that he looked it up again if he had copies of those letters. The suggestion is only that it is overwhelmingly likely that Paul would use whole *lines of thought* that he had worked out previously—and precisely in his letters, which some, at least, had felt to be weightier than his personal presence and speech (2 Cor 10:10). It has long been realized that to some extent Paul does do just that.[31] Thus Romans 4 relies on Gal 3; Rom 5:12-21 presupposes 1 Cor 15:21-22 and 45-49; Rom 12:4-7 uses ideas from 1 Cor 12; and Rom 14:1-15:6 is a generalized reworking of themes in 1 Corinthians 8 and 10. If the picture I have just sketched of the writing of Romans is correct, one would expect Paul to have made use of earlier material also in such an extended section of the letter as Romans 5-8. Is that in fact the case?

## 6. Galatians in Romans 6:1-8:13

Let us think back. I have already argued that Rom 6:1-8:13 is through and through paraenetic. We also know that there are three concepts that govern Paul's thought in these chapters, sin (chap. 6), the law (chap. 7) and the spirit (8:1-13). Moreover, we know that Paul combines the two first of these, at first more implicitly and by suggestion (6:14 and 7:5) and then in such a way as to make their combination his very theme (7:7-25). Finally, we know that the spirit is brought in (8:1ff.) to provide the resolution to the deadly entanglement of sin and the law, and here we may even note that Paul hints at a kind of reinterpretation of the law in the light of the spirit of the

---

[29] At least the following passages in the letter appear to be "directly topical": 11:13-24 and 14:1-15:13. 13:1-7 too seems to reflect Paul's awareness that he was writing to the political capital of the empire.

[30] Compare Hellholm 1994 for an extensive proof of this with regard to Romans 6.

[31] Compare, for instance, Bornkamm 1971, 130-33.

life in Christ Jesus (8:2). Have we met all this anywhere else in Paul's letters?

The obvious answer is: Yes, in Gal 5:13-26. (i) Here we find the basic opposition between spirit and flesh (5:22 against 16-17 and 19-21). Paul does not in the Galatians passage speak of "sin" (ἁμαρτία), but of flesh (σάρξ). But his use of the term "desire" (ἐπιθυμία; Gal 5:16-17, 24), combined with Rom 7:7, where ἐπιθυμία and ἁμαρτία are mentioned together, shows that thematically the issue is the same. Similarly, the list of fleshly acts given in Gal 5:19-21 corresponds closely with the one given in Rom 1:29-31, which instantiates gentile ἁμαρτία (cf. Rom 3:9). Finally, of course, in Romans too the contrast ends up being between spirit and flesh (8:3-13).

(ii) In the Galatians passage we also find the suggestion of an unholy alliance between the law and sin (flesh). Thus in 5:19-21 Paul lists a number of "acts" (ἔργα!) of the flesh which are apparently connected with being "under the law" (5:18). By contrast, if one is led by the spirit, one is outside the realm of the law (5:18 and 23). However, the exact connection between the law and flesh is not spelt out in any detail. That is only done in Rom 7:7ff. It is noteworthy, however, that Gal 5:17, in particular its final clause, contains the essence of the idea that Paul will later write out in Rom 7:15-23: that the law, in combination with sin, leads to the kind of stalemate of the will which in Greek philosophical vocabulary since Aristotle was termed ἀκρασία (weakness of will).

(iii) The Galatians passage is also quite clear that the spirit provides the solution to the unfortunate alliance of flesh and the law (5:16 and 22-24).

(iv) Finally, the kind of reinterpretation of the law that Rom 8:2 hints at has a correspondence in Paul's claim in Galatians that those who serve one another in love fulfil the whole law (5:13-14; cf. also 6:1-2 with its talk of "Christ's law").

There can be no doubt, therefore, that the basic idea underlying Gal 5:13-26 lies behind Rom 6:1-8:13 too: insisting that the law and sin go together and that sin has disappeared once a person is no longer under the law but filled with the spirit—and exhorting the addressees to see and realize this (Gal 5:16 and 25; Rom 8:12-13). Indeed, once this has become clear, one can hardly fail to see (v) that the theme of freedom, which plays an important role in Rom 6:15-23 and 7:1-6 but has not been prepared for earlier in that letter, is actually derived from the Galatians passage (5:13), where it has of course been carefully prepared for (4:3-9, 21-31).

Again, the suggestion is not that Paul consciously "thought of" the Galatians passage (how could we know?) or even looked it up, only that the very same basic idea underlies the two passages. Indeed, since the letter to the Romans was not written by an automaton, we may also say that the basic idea of Galatians 5:13-26 will have been present *somewhere*, in a way we cannot further specify, "in Paul's mind" when he conceived and wrote or dictated Rom 6:1-8:13.

Note that the above argument only partly presupposes my earlier argument that Rom 6:1-8:13 is through and through paraenetic. Rather, the argument turns primarily on the extensive and fairly detailed similarity of the two passages in the thematic development of the relationship between sin, the law and the spirit. To that extent, therefore, the similarity may also be employed to argue that the Romans passage is in fact basically paraenetic. We had reasons that were independent of the Galatians passage to argue that the Romans passage is basically paraenetic. We had a thematic argument to indicate that the Galatians passage, which is itself overtly paraenetic, is built upon the same idea as the Romans passage. When we bring the two things together, we have ample reason to claim that the two passages are basically identical not only in overall theme but also in literary function—and hence also additional support for claiming the Romans passage to be basically paraenetic.

Noting the overall thematic agreement of Rom 6:1-8:13 with Gal 5:13-26 is the first step in recovering the meaning of Romans 5-8.

## 7. Galatians in Romans 5:1-11 and 8:14-39

The two thematically connected passages in Romans that surround 6:1-8:13 contain much material to which a correspondence is not to be found in Galatians. There are some considerations to suggest, however, that Galatians may still be relevant.

(i) We saw that in one of its functions as a Pauline bridge, Rom 5:1-11 constitutes the conclusion to Paul's argument since 1:18, a conclusion that develops the new state in which Christ believers find themselves, partly through the use of new terminology (peace, hope, reconciliation), but also through a summary of how that state contains what was previously lacking (the proper καύχησις and salvation from God's wrath—at least as something securely hoped for on the basis of God's present justification of Christ believers through faith). The same structural idea of summarizing the previous argument in terms of what the situation looks like *now* for Christ believers is found in Galatians just before the paraenesis of 5:13ff., namely, in 5:2-6. Admittedly, the final summary as given in 5:6 is not at all thematically connected with that of Rom 5:1-11, but the basic *structural* idea is the same, of a summary leading into the paraenesis (in fact quite explicitly, witness the end of 5:6, which is a Pauline "title" for 5:13ff.).[32] In itself this is far from enough to posit a closer connection between the two passages. But there is more.

(ii) If we continue to think about the structure of Galatians, it is noteworthy that after the paraenesis (5:13-26 plus 6:1-10) Paul returns in 6:11ff. to the summarizing type of writing that he had employed in 5:2-6. And here we find a formulation of

---

[32] I take the notion of a Pauline *title* from Luz 1969, 166-67.

the new state which is almost verbally identical with the one given in 5:6: neither circumcision nor uncircumcision is anything, only a new creation (6:15). If we put this together with the uncontroverted fact that in Rom 8:14-39 Paul takes up again many themes from 5:1-11,[33] we may begin to see a certain pattern.

| Summary: *the new state* | Paraenesis | Summarizing conclusion: *the new state* |
|---|---|---|
| Gal 5:2-6 | 5:13-6:10 | 6:11-18 |
| Rom 5:1-11 | 6:1-8:13 | 8:14-39 |

*Apparently, in both letters Paul wished to bring out as strongly as possible certain characteristics of the new state and to fit in a paraenetic section within such a frame.* Again, this is not quite enough to posit a closer connection between the two passages. But again there is more.

(iii) For note now that immediately before Paul's first summarizing statement in Galatians (5:6), he says the following (5:5): "For in the spirit on the basis of faith we hope for and expect justification." This single Galatian verse expresses what is neither more nor less than the basic idea that underlies both Romans 5:1-11 and 8:14-39, the eschatological expectation based on possession of the spirit. We may surmise, therefore, that when Paul speaks, in his second summarizing statement in Galatians, of a "new creation" (6:15), he is being just as eschatological as he is in the two Romans passages, only here, in the later letter, he is being far more explicit about it. Indeed the "new creation" of Gal 6:15 may very well be seen to underlie Rom 5:*12-21* (together with the obvious loans from 1 Corinthians 15). We may schematize our findings as follows:

| Summary: *the new state* | Paraenesis | Summarizing conclusion: *the new state* |
|---|---|---|
| Gal 5:2-6 | 5:13-6:10 | 6:11-18 |
| Rom 5:1-11 | 6:1-8:13 | 8:14-39 |
| *Hope based on spirit* | | *Hope based on spirit* |
| Gal 5:5 | | 6:15 |
| Rom 5:5 | | 8:14-25 |

Now the picture begins to become rather more solid. But there is more.

(iv) Paul's mention in Gal 5:5 of the spirit in connection with a forward-looking expectation recalls an earlier passage in that letter in which he also speaks of the spirit and is also, though slightly more implicitly, looking towards the future: 4:6-7. Here the theme is the reception of the spirit in the hearts of Christ believers, their resulting cry of "Abba, Father!", and their knowledge that they are not only sons of God but also heirs. That theme, of course, corresponds closely with Rom 8:14-17, with which Paul introduces his second account of the new state in that letter. More-

---

[33] Established by Dahl 1951.

over, the idea of receiving the spirit "in our hearts" (Gal 4:6) closely resembles the statement in Rom 5:5 that God's love has been poured "into our hearts through the holy spirit that has been given us". In short, Gal 5:5 (recalling Gal 4:6-7) shows that already in Galatians Paul had all the material needed for writing an account of the new state that would rely heavily on the ideas of present spirit-reception and sonship and of future full inheritance. Again, we may schematize our findings as follows:

| Summary: *the new state* | Paraenesis | Summarizing conclusion: *the new state* |
|---|---|---|
| Gal 5:2-6 | 5:13-6:10 | 6:11-18 |
| Rom 5:1-11 | 6:1-8:13 | 8:14-39 |
| *Hope based on spirit* | | *Hope based on spirit* |
| Gal 5:5 | | 6:15 |
| Rom 5:5 | | 8:14-25 |
| *Reception of the spirit* | | *Reception of the spirit* |
| Gal 5:5 recalling 4:6-7 | | |
| Rom 5:5 | | 8:14-17 |

But there is more.

(v) Scholars generally agree, rightly, that passages like Gal 4:6-7; Rom 8:14-17; and also Rom 5:5 trade on the early Christian ritual of baptism. Note then the following corollary. If, by the argument just given, the idea of baptism does lie behind Gal 5:5 too, then it is hardly just coincidental that Paul begins his *paraenetic* section in Romans (6:1ff.) precisely from baptism. To put it differently, Paul *could* have brought in a reference to baptism in his Galatian paraenesis too if that had suited his other purposes. In Romans he does it. Thus what we have is actually this:

| Summary: *the new state* | Paraenesis | Summarizing conclusion: *the new state* |
|---|---|---|
| Gal 5:2-6 | 5:13-6:10 | 6:11-18 |
| Rom 5:1-11 | 6:1-8:13 | 8:14-39 |
| *Hope based on spirit* | | *Hope based on spirit* |
| Gal 5:5 | | 6:15 |
| Rom 5:5 | | 8:14-25 |
| *Reception of the spirit* | | *Reception of the spirit* |
| Gal 5:5 through 4:6-7 | | |
| Rom 5:5 | | 8:14-17 |
| *Baptism* | | *Baptism* |
| Gal 5:5 through 4:6-7 | | |
| Rom 5:5 | [6:1ff.] | 8:14-17 |

Note how we have been working back, in a kind of logical "regression" or analysis, to what appears to be the basic phenomenon that Paul is drawing on: from the new state to the notion of hope, from there to spirit-reception, and from there to baptism.

Seeing that in both Gal 5:2-6 and 6:11-18 and Rom 5:1-11 and 8:14-39 Paul describes the new state of eschatological hope (a) by activating the notion of spirit-reception in baptism and (b) as an entry into and conclusion to paraenesis is the second step in recovering the meaning of Romans 5-8.

## 8. Galatians in Romans 5-8 — The Baptism Cluster

From these observations concerning Rom 6:1-8:13 and 5:1-11/8:14-39 we should conclude that Galatians 5-6 and Romans 5-8 are built over the very same cluster of ideas. This cluster is focused on describing the new situation of Christ believers after the Christ event and after their initiation into it through baptism. One element in that situation is the new state of Christ believers in relation to God and to the world (Rom 5:1-11 and 8:14-39). In describing this Paul draws extensively on the idea that they possess the spirit through baptism. The Abba-cry from the heart, the idea of sonship, possibly also of being heirs are all parts of this.[34] In his interpretation of this material Paul claims that the new state is characterized by a quite special tension between something present and something future. In Romans he writes this out fully in what he says about living under the mode of hope, but the crucial ideas were present already in Galatians (5:5).[35] A second central element in the new situation is the issue of how Christ believers should live in the highly tensed period between their entry into the new state through baptism and the day of fulfilment. Paul addresses this issue in the emphatic piece of paraenesis (Gal 5:13-6:10; Rom 6:1-8:13) which in both letters he has placed *within* the framework of his account of the new state. In both cases the paraenesis focuses on the spirit and in Romans it even begins from baptism. Because of the crucial role played in all this—both the ideas and the literary structure—by baptism, we may speak of the *baptism cluster*. This reinforces the suggestion, argued strongly for on independent grounds by Wayne A. Meeks in *The First Urban Christians*, that there is a very close connection in Paul between (i) concrete ritual practice, (ii) ethical practice, and (iii) general understanding of the world (world-view).[36] In its forward-looking urgency, Romans 5-8 is also a meditation on baptism.

On the basis of these observations we may reasonably suggest that when scholars have generally found the overall structure of Romans 5-8 less cogent than that of

---

[34] If the idea of being heirs is not an intrinsic part of the baptism cluster, it is still common to Galatians and Romans.

[35] There are also certain differences. For instance, whereas in Galatians (5:5) Christ believers are only hoping for justification, in Romans they are already justified (5:1-2, 11), but still hoping for salvation (5:2-5, 10).

[36] Meeks 1983 chap. 5. On baptism see especially 154-57.

chaps. 1-4 (or -5), they have been wrong.[37] What Paul did in the four chapters was to write out fully the ideas that go into the baptism cluster, ideas that he had already used in Galatians 5-6, though not nearly with the degree of explicitness that they acquired in Romans.

However, one can also understand why the existence of this single structure in Romans 5-8 has not been immediately recognized. For as we shall see in a moment, Paul loads his *amplificatio* of the Galatians structure almost to breaking point.

## 9. Romans 5-8 Within the Letter as a Whole

There are two basic features of chaps. 5-8 which explain the immediate lack of structural transparency of these chapters.

The first is that Paul has decided, for whatever reasons, to provide a complete sketch of the whole world and its history in terms which in connection with this particular letter it is appropriate to christen "salvation history". It is for this reason that he spells out in great detail in 5:1-11 and 8:14-39 the tension between now and then. And it is for this reason too that he *inserts* (with all the difficulties it gives him, see below) 5:12-21 on Adam and Christ. Where did he get this whole idea from? Two facts suggest that the correct answer is again: Galatians. First, as already noted, the Galatian idea of a new creation points very clearly in the direction of the conception in Romans, and it makes a great deal of sense to say that Paul has taken up the notion of κτίσις ("creation") from Gal 6:15 only to extend it in Romans to encompass the whole world, human as well as non-human (8:20-22). Secondly, even if the letter to the Galatians does not itself contain a fully worked out sketch of the history of salvation, it is fair to say that seen in retrospect it does contain important germs for such a sketch, especially in Gal 3:15-4:7. But then the fact that Paul takes over in Romans 4 his Abraham analysis as given in Galatians 3 becomes a more than sufficient spring-board for Paul's more elaborate sketch in Romans.

The suggestion that in this respect too it is Galatians which lies behind Romans 5-8 (and now in fact including chap. 4) is corroborated by Paul's obvious difficulties with bringing the Adam–Christ contrast, which he drew from a *different* letter (1 Corinthians), into his general scheme in Romans. This accounts for the contortions of 5:12-14, which I shall leave on one side here.

---

[37] Compare, for instance, Beker 1980, 84: "The coherent clarity of Rom. 1:18-4:25 should not deceive us into thinking that 5:1-8:39 is equally coherent." I have not had access to two articles by A. Feuillet, 1982a and 1982b, which apparently both analyse Romans 1-8 in the light of Galatians and discover an overall scheme underlying those same chapters. To judge from the brief summaries in *NTAb* 26 (1982) no. 988 and 27 (1983) no. 210, as well as from Feuillet 1950, the proposal is both too complex and too heavily indebted to a traditional trinitarian dogmatics to be likely to be right.

The second complicating feature of Romans 5-8 is Paul's evident wish to find a place for the Mosaic law within his general scheme. Again he gets into difficulties, which may or may not be thought insoluble. Again too, as is universally recognized, the issue itself arises out of Galatians (chap. 3).

What we have, then, in Romans 5-8 is an extensive *amplificatio* of the themes contained *in nuce* in Galatians 5-6. This accounts for Rom 5:1-11; 6:1-8:13; and 8:14-39. But we also have a loading of the basic, underlying Galatians structure which from time to time is in danger of obliterating it altogether. This accounts for Rom 5:12-21, for the elaboration in 6:1ff. of the other basic contrasts in terms of the one between life and death introduced by 5:12-21, and for the extensive elaboration in chap. 7 of the issue of the relationship between sin and the law, which *almost* makes that issue and its resolution come out as a completely independent theme of its own. It is because Paul attempts in this way to weave a number of complex and only partly interlocking motifs into the basic, underlying structure that this structure has not been immediately clear to his readers. With the reintroduction of Galatians it again becomes clear.

We may add one observation on the connection between chaps. 5-8 and the following three chapters. Just as scholars have had difficulty with the structure of chaps. 5-8, so they have notoriously been at a loss to find a convincing way to fit chaps. 9-11 into the overall structure of the letter as a whole. In one way this is not at all strange. For if, with Romans 8, Paul had in effect come to the end of his Galatian master plan, there will necessarily be a break after that chapter. However, one can also easily see why Paul's salvation historical elaboration of his Galatians scheme leads almost inexorably into chaps. 9-11. If Paul is making a concentrated attempt in Romans 5-8 to sketch the history of the whole world, going back even to the first human being in the Jewish tradition, Adam, and also going into some detail about the role of the Jewish law, then the question of where and how to fit non-Christ-believing *Jews* into the scheme will have forcibly imposed itself on his mind—if he did not merely want to write them off altogether (as he clearly did not). So, the extension in Romans of the Galatian hints at a salvation historical scheme into a completely universal and all-embracing one virtually forced Paul to write chaps. 9-11.

## 10. Net Results

### 10.1. The Text Itself

What difference does it make to see Romans 5-8 in the way I have argued for: (i) an evocation of the completely new state in which Christ believers find themselves in the present but also looking forward to the future, final consummation, (ii) surrounding a section of paraenesis that is concerned with how to live concretely in the present? It makes a difference both to the understanding of the text itself and also to an understanding of the wider issue from which I began, the relationship between "theology" and "ethics" in Paul.

On the proposed reading, the primary aim of the whole passage is not to discuss issues that have somehow been left over from the previous discussion or to respond to objections that had either actually in fact been made or else, so Paul imagines, could be made to the picture he has drawn. Rather, the primary aim is a community-creating one. For the benefit of his addressees Paul constructs a universal story that tells of God's character as witnessed in his actions: the Christ event, which has already occurred, and the final salvation of Christ believers, which lies in the future but is also confidently hoped for in the present. He extends this story the whole way back to the first human being, Adam, in order to emphasize the radicality and revolutionary implications of the change that has already occurred with that other human being, Jesus Christ. But his basic point even with this is to make his addressees realize that through their own faith-response to the Christ event and in particular through their reception of the spirit in baptism, *they have themselves become partners* in this world-encompassing story. In fact, once they see themselves in the light of that story and understand their own identity as being defined by it, they all together become centrally important participants in the decisive event in that story represented by Christ.

Paul employs several means to develop the participatory aspect relating to his addressees. We may note the following features in the introductory section, 5:1-11, in which it is first brought in. (i) There is the warm emphasis throughout the section on the "we" who are in the new state, an emphasis that was in fact spelled out explicitly in the verses at the end of chap. 4 (23-25) that lead into the new section. (ii) There is the up-playing of the contrast between "our" *previous* relationship with God, in which "we" were both "ungodly" (ἀσεβεῖς; 5:6) and God's "enemies" (ἐχθροί; 5:10), and the *new* one, in which "we" have "peace" with God and "access" to him (5:1-2) and are "reconciled" with him (5:10-11). The immediate, emotional appeal of the language used to draw the contrast is obvious.

(iii) There is also the emphasis on the present tribulations and lack of fulfilment of what "we" hope for (5:3-5). (iv) But there is also the notion of "our" present, completely confident joy that "we" shall receive a share in God's glory (5:2, 11). These two themes play a central role in Paul's expansion of 5:1-11 in 8:14-39. Here the motif of tribulation, introduced in 8:17 together with that of the coming glory, constitutes the overall theme of 8:18-27 whereas that of the coming glory holds together 8:28-39 (cf. 30 and 37: ὑπερνικῶμεν). It is obvious that the idea of being already in the new state *in spite of* all the contravening factors will tend to reinforce the sense of a shared identity which has community-creating force. Similarly, the motifs that go with the "not yet" will tend in the same direction by formulating a goal for all to participate in. In fact, we may well speak here, with Wayne A. Meeks, of "an intensely corporate, sectarian vision".[38]

(v) Finally, we may mention the motif voiced in 5:5 of spirit reception resulting in God-love being poured into our hearts, a motif that again has a central role in 8:14-39 (e.g. 14-17, 26-27, 28, 31-39). Clearly, the idea of having God's love in "our" hearts (5:5) and of meeting it with a love of "our" own (8:28) is a very effective tool for bringing the addressees directly into the story that Paul is constructing.

What matters here is the very simple point, which far too rarely is given its full weight, that in 5:1-11 and 8:14-39 Paul is not merely *describing* a state, as if passing on some neutral piece of information that might or might not be useful to his addressees; instead, he is *evoking* a state and *inviting* his addressees to participate in it, he is speaking to their sense of their own identity, of who they are. Indeed, here as elsewhere we should pay attention to how, to borrow a phrase from the British philosopher J. L. Austin, Paul "does things with words", no less than to what he is directly and immediately saying.

The community-creating aim of the passage is strongly in evidence in the paraenetic section, 6:1-8:13, too. Again Paul attempts to reach his aim in a number of ways, among which the various features characteristic of paraenesis play an important role, the direct address in the second person plural, the appeal to knowledge they are supposed to have already, and the like. Here too one notices the strong emphasis on issues of identity, on who the Christ believers have become in baptism (6:2-6), on their quasi-identity with Christ in his death and resurrection (6:8, 11), on their relationship with sin and the law and again in identity-terms (of "being" slaves or free-persons in relation to them, 6:16-18), and on their "being" either in accordance with or "in" the flesh or the spirit (8:5, 9-11).

However, instead of going through all these various motifs, we should consider in what way a paraenetic section may generally play a role that is specifically community-creating. The most immediate answer would of course be: if the content of the given piece of paraenesis is behaviour that is itself either community-creating or community-maintaining. Interestingly, however, that is *not* quite the focus of Rom 6:1-8:13. That only comes in later, in 12:1-15:13, but then of course with full force. In fact, we should note that the paraenetic sections of Romans, 6:1-8:13 and 12:1-15:13, are divided in a way that corresponds closely with the similar division

---

[38] Meeks 1993, 60. Meeks is speaking of the Johannine writings, but his whole analysis of the ambivalence between "Loving and Hating the World" (52-65) is highly pertinent to Paul too. Compare also the section on "Evil and its Reversal" in Meeks 1983, 183-89.

in Galatians, between the more general paraenesis of 5:13-26 and the more specific one of 6:1-10. Seen in this light, Rom 6:1-8:13 (like Gal 5:13-26) appears to be more concerned with the basic issue of actually making Paul's addressees do, and see the need for doing, what should be done, more, that is, than discussing what those things actually are. How, then, will this particular focus serve a community-creating aim?

The answer is very simple. In 5:1-11; 5:12-21; and 8:14-39 Paul is concerned to construct what we may call the overall, completely universal frame of reference within which he wishes his addressees to see themselves. We have seen that even here Paul uses a number of rhetorical means to reach what appears to be a community-creating aim (speaking of "us", the shared new experience and the like). Still, such a universal frame of reference *could* be understood in a way which would not quite give it the community-creating force that Paul apparently intended it to have. It could be understood more superficially, as a universal framework of "ideas", a "world-view" that might be taken to be generally valid, but need not, perhaps, have any immediate relevance to one's own, concrete life. By bringing in his paraenesis Paul shows that these ideas are in fact to be taken completely seriously. For the paraenesis is about concrete practice, it is about doing, about actually "walking" *in accordance with* (8:4) that spirit the possession of which almost identifies the new *state* (5:1-11; 8:14-39; *and* the experience of baptism, 6:1-14, through which the spirit is given). The aim of the paraenesis is thus to spell out the concrete, practical content *of* the "world-view" in order to make that all-embracing shared understanding come home to each individual partner in it.

Of course, Paul himself does not for a moment distinguish between his salvation historical construction as a matter of "ideas" to be contrasted with his paraenesis as something that has to do with "practice". But that is precisely the point. In Romans 5-8 Paul wished to evoke a picture of the new state of Christ believers which *seamlessly* encompassed *everything*, from the most universal statements about the overall, objective shape of the world and God's actions in it, via accounts of the new, overall sense of their own identity that Christ believers have in response to those acts (rejoicing in God, loving him, and more), and down to the issue of individual human action that directly reflects the two other things. By situating his paraenesis *within* his construction of the overall shape of the world, Paul made it clear to his addressees that the new state, the contours of which he had been evoking, was a truly all-encompassing one, both horizontally, from Adam to the final day and including *all* human beings, and also vertically, from the actions and character of God to those of each individual human being. In terms of its content Paul's paraenesis in 6:1-8:13 is only indirectly community-creating. (Paraenesis with direct community-creating force only comes in later, in 12:1ff.). But in a different way it is very strongly community-creating since it makes totally clear to the individual addressee that the new state (which is *in fact* a community state) is also quite concretely a matter of *his* or *her* individual action.

By noticing the overall paraenetic purpose of 6:1-8:13 and the complementary evocative features of 5:1-11 and 8:14-39, we become able to see that the primary aim of this text as a whole is community-creation. This is not in the least to deny that Paul also had the subsidiary aims that we know so well, making sense in world-historical terms of the Christ event, developing the meaning import of baptism, and finding a satisfactory understanding of the role of the law as seen from the new perspective. Nor am I at all denying that he may be answering objections that had actually been made to him or which he thought *would* be made. But *the primary aim and overall point of the passage as a whole lies elsewhere*, in community-creation—or at least in a further forming of the already existing Roman congregations. It should be immediately clear that such an aim would also serve Paul's own purpose in writing. If *his* construction of the Christ belief were to succeed in generating a genuine community of Christ believers in Rome, then he would himself also become a part of that community.

## 10.2. Δικαιοσύνη *and the Logical Form of Pauline Paraenesis*

If Rom 6:1-8:13 is basically paraenetic, and if Paul is here engaged in paraenesis with the specific aim that I have just identified, we may ask the following question: As Paul describes Christ believers in 5:1-11, they are justified in the present through faith, but will only (hopefully) be saved in the future. How then do they stand with regard to sinning? Obviously they are no longer "under" sin or "under" the law, but "under" grace. Does that mean that they no longer actually sin—or is being "under" sin, the law and grace rather distinctly theological categories, which do not immediately speak of human willing and doing? Again, if Christ believers are "justified", are they themselves actually just—or is being "just" again a distinctly theological category that only pertains to the way Christ believers are reckoned by God?

We know that Bultmann denied that justification had anything to do with ethics. It was all seen from the perspective of God. God reckoned human beings just through faith and God issued his commands which human beings must follow. However, as a reading of Paul's paraenesis, the latter will not do. It is Paul who uses imperatives, not God. (Indeed, in Bultmann's prize exhibit, Gal 5:25, there is actually no imperative involved at all. Instead, Paul uses the subjunctive of shared exhortation!) Moreover, the way Paul argues for these imperatives, for instance in 6:1-11, shows that he is straightforwardly speaking of *human* justice, namely, the extent to which the new understanding of one's own identity that is symbolized or realized in baptism has done away with the "old human being" and the "body of sin" (6:6).

To the extent that this has happened, a person will no longer "obey the desires" (6:12) of his or her mortal body, but will instead turn his or her limbs into tools of justice (6:13). Since Paul here speaks of desires (ἐπιθυμίαι; 6:12) and further elaborates on this in 6:19 in terminology that recalls the description given in chap. 1 of straightforwardly immoral people (ἀκαθαρσία; cf. 1:24), it is beyond doubt that he is speaking of human, ethical justice and injustice.

So, Paul is not just speaking "theologically" in the above sense. He also means to be understood, as we would say, "ethically", that is, as speaking about the actual character and actions of human beings in the human sphere. But then the question again arises: Does Paul mean to say that Christ believers in the new state are actually, morally just and actually, morally sinless?

One's immediate reaction is to say no. For where, on such a view, would paraenesis fit in? If Christ believers are genuinely and actually outside of sin in a straightforwardly ethical sense, then why exhort them to become it? This, of course, is the very problem that furnished the starting point for Bultmann's quite different, wholly theocentric construal of the Pauline indicatives and imperatives. If that reading will not do, the best way to avoid the dilemma appears to be to deny that Paul was envisaging actual, ethical sinlessness. He will still be talking of justice and injustice that is human and ethical, but he will not be saying that Christ faith entails actual sinlessness. Rather, the purpose of his imperatives will precisely be to bring it into existence as far as that is at all possible.

Unfortunately, that will not do either. Paul's description in Romans 6 of the implications of baptism quite clearly shows that he does mean to say that the person who has been baptized has also left behind completely his or her own self and will therefore no longer sin (6:6). It is *because* the baptized person will no longer actually sin that Paul turns to baptism in support of his exhortation that the Romans should *stop* sinning. But again, why should one stop sinning, if one does not sin at all?

However, there is a solution to this dilemma. Consider the logical form of Paul's paraenesis. In spite of Paul's use of imperatives, his paraenesis does not in fact follow the logic of a command. In a command, a person, A, tells another person, B, to do something that A wishes to be done, but B does *not* wish to do for its own sake. B may wish to do it as a means to something else, paradigmatically in order to *avoid* something that it is in A's power to activate if the command is not followed. But B does not wish to do the thing for its own sake. On such an understanding of commands, Paul's paraenetic imperatives are not commands. Instead, they have the form of pointing something out to a person, B, that he or she *already* wishes to do, at least to some extent, and wishes to do for its own sake. That is the reason why Paul constantly uses commemorative *appeals* in his exhortation. Rom 6:1-11 exemplifies this. In 6:3; 6:6; and again in 6:9 Paul appeals to an understanding that he takes for granted in his addressees. Whether they did have it or not is immaterial. What matters is that for the purpose of his paraenesis Paul presupposes that they did. Clearly, the imperatives with which he ends (6:11-13) have their meaning *within* such a commemorative appeal to something the addressees are presumed *already* to know. In other words, they in a sense already are in the place that Paul wishes to bring them to, they already wish to act in the way he enjoins—only perhaps not quite!

The same central feature of Paul's paraenetic logic can be seen if one reflects for a moment on another aspect of Paul's interpretation of baptism, the idea that the baptized person is an altogether new being with a completely new identity that is tied in with that of Christ. Again the implication for the logic of paraenesis is that the baptized person now *is* such that he or she in fact already wishes to behave in the way enjoined by Paul. That type of behaviour is *beforehand* a part of the new identity that the baptized person has already acquired.

On such a construal of Pauline paraenesis there is no insoluble dilemma in having Paul claim that baptism implies actual, ethical sinlessness and also having him engage in paraenesis directed to baptized Christ believers in order to bring such sinlessness into existence. Baptized Christ believers, so Paul will have thought, empirically *are* outside of sin; they empirically do not sin; rather, as Paul says a little later (8:4), they fulfil the demands of the law. Still, there may be *some* need to remind them that that is what their new state consists in. There is no longer any genuine dilemma here, only a recognition of the frailty of human beings in spite of the tremendous impact of the Christ event.

Two ideas are presupposed in this reconstruction of the logic of Paul's paraenesis, (i) the distinction between a genuine imperative, which has the form of a real command, and Paul's weaker, "commemorative imperatives", (ii) and the idea of a kind of human frailty which is merely a matter of falling short of what one genuinely wants to do, in such a way that no actual change in the person is required to make him or her come over on the right side. It is highly noteworthy that Paul himself brings in something resembling these two ideas in Romans 5-8.

(i) In 8:15 Paul justifies his claim that those who are being led by God's spirit are his sons, by contrasting the spirit of sonship, which finds expression in crying "Abba, Father!", with a supposed "spirit of servitude leading back to fear". The contrast is clearly between feeling oneself to be brought up to the level of another person (the father) and responding out of one's own wish and will to whatever claims follow from that position—and on the other hand being pushed down into a state of servitude in which one will only comply with any demands that are made from above out of fear of the consequences of not complying. In this contrast, if the "father" should issue an imperative, it would be construed by the person not as a command in the above sense, but as part of a relationship in which the person him- or herself willingly participates. In the other case, by contrast, an imperative would be construed precisely as a command.

(ii) The connotations implied in Paul's talk of servitude in 8:15 underlie the other relevant passage, in which he introduces the notion of human frailty (ἀσθένεια), 6:19. In the preceding verses Paul has thanked God that his addressees have left behind their previous state of servitude to sin. Instead, they "obeyed (ὑπηκούσατε)" the new teaching "from the heart" (6:17). However, having in this way been freed from sin, they also became "enslaved to justice (δικαιοσύνη)" (6:18). In the light of Paul's later talk of sonship, his use of the term enslavement here in conjunction with justice is surprising. But note then how he proceeds: "I use human terms, because of the weakness (ἀσθένεια) of your flesh ... make your limbs slaves to justice (δικαιοσύνη) for your sanctification" (6:19). Clearly, Paul is here *apologizing for his use of the terminology of slavery* to describe the new state of his Christ-believing addressees. That is revealing. First, it supports the reading given above of 8:15. Paul did not in fact think of the relationship of Christ believers with God as one of servitude. Christ believers *will* what God wants them to do. Secondly, the fact that Paul feels the need to fall back on such language is to be explained by the ἀσθένεια of the flesh. As the context shows, Paul does not deny that his addressees are Christ believers. On the contrary, he has just thanked God that they did "obey from the heart". Still, there *may* be a need not only to engage in paraenesis of them, as Paul has already done and is again about to do, but also to make use of the language of master and slave in order to make them come round *fully* to the position they have *already* reached.

We should conclude that Pauline paraenesis presupposes that those being addressed already are where the paraenesis intends to bring them. It does not have the logical form of a genuine command. Instead, it trades on reminding people of their real identity, who they (already) are. It presupposes that people already wish to do what is enjoined and that their possibly not doing it will be a minor slip, a case of ἀσθένεια.

We should also conclude that Paul did not think of God's δικαιοσύνη as a "theological" phenomenon only. The person who is justified, through the Christ event and the proper faith response to that event, is also one who is outside of sin, one who is ethically, empirically just.

## 10.3. The Convergence of Paul's "Theology" and "Ethics" on a Construction of Identity

The literary analysis I gave of Romans 5-8 revealed that the passage has a firm, coherent structure and a single primary aim of community-creation. Structurally, the passage was made up of two sections, chap. 5 and 8:14-39, surrounding a paraenetic section. In the framing sections Paul was concerned to develop as comprehensive a picture as possible of the whole world and its history in salvation-historical terms, with (i) Adam and the law, (ii) Christ, and (iii) the final day as its fixed points. Many statements that go into these chapters are distinctly "theological", both in the sense that they are about God's actions and also that they are intended as objective statements about the basic features of the world. We saw, however, that even where Paul is developing an objective, "theological" picture of this kind, he goes out of his way to make it immediately relevant to his addressees. It is *their* story, which serves to identify their identity as Christ believers by stating where they belong in a universal scheme that encompasses the whole world.

In connection with the intervening paraenetic section, we noted a similar concern on Paul's part to construct an identity for his addressees. Thus we saw that corresponding to the "theological" and objective picture of God's δικαιοσύνη (in the sense of his δικαίωσις, 4:25, of human beings through the Christ event and the resulting faith), Paul also explicitly stated in his account of baptism that there is a human, "ethical" and subjective side to this, namely, a state of actual, ethical sinlessness. But this too was conceptualized by Paul, in his account of baptism, in identity terms, of being dead and risen, of having given up the old human being, and more.

Finally, we saw in connection with the same section that Paul's paraenesis too should be construed as presupposing an idea of self-understanding on the part of the person who is being exhorted. Paraenesis is directed towards making a person do what he or she already wishes to do since it reflects that person's self-understanding. Thus here too, where Paul is clearly speaking of the "ethical" dimension of the whole matter, there is a recurrence to the notion of identity, of who and what a baptized Christ believer *is* and how *this* should translate into action.

All through, then, Paul is either engaged in constructing an identity for his addressees or else appealing to an identity which they are already supposed to have. So far, therefore, the objective and distinctly "theological" statements and the subjective and distinctly "ethical" ones all seem to converge on the issue of human identity and human self-understanding.

We may strengthen this conclusion by noting a further feature about those sections in which Paul is at his most objective (chap. 5 and 8:14-39). We just recalled how Paul is here constantly attempting to relate his objective picture to his immediate addressees, by speaking of a "we", by emphasizing the contrast between then and now, and so on. But in fact, all through these sections (albeit less strongly in 5:12-21) he even provides his objective sketch of the new situation *through* the (presumed) experience of his addressees. Thus, for instance, instead of saying that God has been reconciled with human beings (or even with "us"), he says that *"we"* have been reconciled with *God* (5:1, 11). Clearly, what concerns Paul is the way his Christ-believing *addressees* will construe *their own* identity. He does not merely stay with objective language but bends it in the direction of human self-understanding. The point is of course not that Paul did not take his objective picture seriously as, literally, an objective one, only that he *uses* it in such a way that it converges on the very same concerns that animate passages where he is speaking about "ethical" matters. These concerns are about the construction of human identity. It is here, in this area of overlap between Paul's "theology" and his "ethics", that one will find the real connection between them, not in the ruthlessly theocentric perspective that was Bultmann's bid.

We may add one more observation that goes in the same direction and shows particularly clearly how closely Rom 5:1-11 and 8:14-39 are connected with what comes in between. I am referring to the role Paul gives to the spirit in 8:14-39 (and already in 5:5) as a mediator between God and "us". The spirit is God's (8:16 and 26-27), but it is also "ours" (8:16). It is given to "us" through God's love for "us" (5:5), and "we" respond with love for God (8:28). Clearly, Paul aims to suggest that there is a very extensive convergence between what God has done and what "we" do. Equally clearly, the convergence is on a point about human identity. After all, "those who let themselves be led by God's spirit, *these are*—sons of God" (8:14). But then we are back with baptism. "For ... you received the spirit of sonship, through whom we cry, Abba, Father!" (8:15). And baptism, as Paul has shown in chap. 6, *is* about a new identity.

The focus of Romans 5-8 is to use the experience of baptism in order to make Paul's Roman addressees grasp and experience a wholly new identity as their own, an identity which at one and the same time places them at the centre of an all-encompassing, objective picture of the world and its history and also reaches down to each ethical act to be performed by each individual. If together they all manage to grasp this, they will constitute a true community, and so also be at one with Paul.

## *Bibliography*

Beker, J. Christiaan 1980: *Paul the Apostle. The Triumph of God in Life and Thought*, Philadelphia, PA: Fortress 1980.

Bornkamm, Günther 1963: "The Letter to the Romans as Paul's Last Will and Testament", in: Donfried 1991, 16-28. Originally in *ABR* 11 (1963) 2-14.

— 1971: "Der Römerbrief als Testament des Paulus", in: idem, *Geschichte und Glaube, Zweiter Teil*, Gesammelte Aufsätze Band IV (BEvTh 53), München: Chr. Kaiser 1971, 120-39.

Bultmann, Rudolf 1924: "Das Problem der Ethik bei Paulus", in: *ZNW* 23 (1924) 123-40.

Cranfield, C. E. B. 1975: *The Epistle to the Romans* I (ICC), Edinburgh: T. &T. Clark 1975.

Dahl, Nils A. 1951: "Two notes on Romans 5", in: *StTh* 5 (1951) 37-48.

— 1969: "The Atonement—an adequate Reward for the Akedah? (Rom 8:32)", in: Ellis and Wilcox 1969, 15-29. (Also in: Dahl 1991, 137-52.)

— 1977: "The Missionary Theology in the Epistle to the Romans", in: idem, *Studies in Paul. Theology for the Early Christian Mission*, Minneapolis, MN: Augsburg 1977, 70-94.

— 1991: *Jesus the Christ. The Historical Origins of Christological Doctrine* (ed. Donald H. Juel), Minneapolis, MN: Fortress 1991.

Donfried, Karl P. (ed.) 1991: *The Romans Debate. Revised and Expanded Edition*, Peabody, MA: Hendrickson 1991.

Dunn, James D. G. 1988: *Romans 1-8* (Word Biblical Commentary 38A), Dallas, TX: Word Books 1988.

Dupont, Jacques 1955: "Le problème de la structure littéraire de l'Épître aux Romains", in: *RB* 62 (1955) 365-97.

Ellis, E. E. and Wilcox, M. (eds.) 1969: *Neotestamentica et semitica. Studies in Honour of Matthew Black*, Edinburgh: T. & T. Clark 1969.

Engberg-Pedersen, Troels (ed.) 1994: *Paul in his Hellenistic Context*, Minneapolis, MN: Fortress and Edinburgh: T. & T. Clark 1994.

Feuillet, A. 1950: "Le plan salvifique de Dieu d'après l'Épître aux Romains: Essai sur la structure littéraire de l'Épître et sa signification théologique", in: *RB* 57 (1950) 336-87, 489-529.

— 1982a: "Ressemblances structurales et doctrinales entre Ga 3,1-6,10 et Rm 1-8: La triple référence de l'Épître aux Romains aux origines de l'histoire humaine," *NV* 57 (1982) 30-64.

— 1982b: "L'Histoire du salut dans les lettres aux Galates et aux Romains: La progression des idées dans la première partie de l'Épître aux Romains," *EeV* 92 (1982) 257-67.

Hellholm, David 1994: "Enthymemic Argumentation in Paul: The Case of Romans 6", in: Engberg-Pedersen 1994, 119-79.

Kaye, Bruce N. 1979: *The Thought Structure of Romans with Special Reference to Chapter 6*, Austin, TX: Schola 1979.

Kümmel, Werner Georg 1980: *Einleitung in das Neue Testament*, 20th ed., Heidelberg: Quelle und Meyer 1980.

Köster, Helmut 1980: *Einführung in das Neue Testament*, Berlin/New York: Walter de Gruyter 1980.

Luz, Ulrich 1969: "Zum Aufbau von Röm. 1-8", in: *ThZ* 25 (1969) 161-81.

Meeks, Wayne A. 1983: *The First Urban Christians. The Social World of the Apostle Paul*, New Haven/London: Yale University Press 1983.

— 1993: *The Origins of Christian Morality. The First Two Centuries*, New Haven/London: Yale University Press 1993.

von der Osten-Sacken, Peter 1975: *Römer 8 als Beispiel paulinischer Soteriologie* (FRLANT 112), Göttingen: Vandenhoeck & Ruprecht 1975.

Wilckens, Ulrich 1974: "Über Abfassungszweck und Aufbau des Römerbriefs", in: idem, *Rechtfertigung als Freiheit: Paulusstudien*, Neukirchen-Vluyn: Neukirchener Verlag 1974, 110-70.

— 1978: *Der Brief an die Römer, 1. Teilband, Röm 1-5* (EKK VI/1), Zürich, Einsiedeln, Köln: Benziger; Neukirchen-Vluyn: Neukirchener Verlag 1978.

— 1980: *Der Brief an die Römer, 2. Teilband, Röm 6-11* (EKK VI/2), Zürich, Einsiedeln, Köln: Benziger; Neukirchen-Vluyn: Neukirchener Verlag 1980.

Wolter, Michael 1978: *Rechtfertigung und zukünftiges Heil. Untersuchungen zu Röm 5,1-11* (BZNW 43), Berlin/New York: Walter de Gruyter 1978.

# Paul's "Second Presence" in Colossians

## Hans Dieter Betz

### 1. Introduction

As Lars Hartman has shown in one of his insightful articles, to us reading other people's letters is generally reprehensible; in particular, the idea raises complicated hermeneutical questions when applied to Paul's letters.[1] More problems, morally and even legally, are raised by *writing* other people's letters. In the New Testament, this practice pertains to the so-called Pauline pseudepigrapha, that is to Colossians, Ephesians, 2 Thessalonians, and the Pastoral Epistles.[2] It is an anachronism, however, to approach ancient pseudepigraphy by way of the ethical problems it raises today. As is well known, in antiquity writing letters under the name of other authors was an acceptable literary convention. Especially in philosophical circles this literary convention served to pass on school traditions.

What was the significance of this literary convention of writing other persons' letters? In our age, which so much enjoys the "deconstruction" of authority, a common explanation for such pseudepigraphy is that it is a ploy equally popular today, namely that of fabricating authenticity and hence authority. Taking the high-ground of moral rectitude, this modern explanation exposes as fraud what in fact was a rather common literary device practiced by ancient writers.[3]

For a more adequate explanation of pseudepigraphy, therefore, we do well to examine what ancient writers themselves had to say about it.[4] In general, for the people living before the invention of telephone and television making absent persons

---

[1] See the title of his 1986 article "On Reading Others' Letters."

[2] On the Pastoral Epistles see, especially, Donelson 1986, 7-66; on 2 Thess see Holland 1988, 57-58, 62-63, 84-90, 91, 153-54; on 2 Peter see Fornberg 1977, 15-19.

[3] The same is true of painters. Rembrandt's self-portrait as the apostle Paul, now in the Rijksmuseum in Amsterdam, for instance, was neither a case of fraud nor done for the purpose of falsely legitimating authority or attracting more buyers for Rembrandt's paintings.

[4] In the following, translations of Greek and German citations are by the author, unless otherwise indicated.

present was not an unknown possibility. For antiquity, however, this possibility was confined mainly to writing letters, including pseudepigraphical letters.

## 2. Goethe's Concept of "Second Presence"

In our view, no one has given as good an explanation for the literary process as Goethe in a small but highly significant essay called "Wiederholte Spiegelungen" ("Repeated Mirror Images"). The essay, a little longer than a page in the Hamburg edition,[5] was written probably on January 29, 1823.[6] In the autumn of 1822 a Professor Näke of Bonn had visited Sesenheim and written an account of the visit, the manuscript of which was sent by a friend to Goethe. Goethe thanked this friend by his essay, in which he describes the impressions Näke's account made on him, using the image of "mirroring" known from his studies of repeating color reflections (*Entoptik*).

Goethe begins by speaking of the original impact the encounter with Friederike Brion had made on the young man, creating in him a youthfully happy ecstasy ("Ein jugendlich-seliges Wahnleben spiegelt sich unbewußt-eindrücklich in dem Jüngling ab"). For a long time afterward the remembered and even renewed image of Friederike flows back and forth inwardly ("Das lange Zeit fortgehegte, auch wohl erneuerte Bild wogt immer lieblich und freundlich hin und her, viele Jahre im Innern"). It is remembrance which then causes external expression, and thus another mirroring ("Das liebevoll früh Gewonnene, lang Erhaltene, wird endlich in lebhafter Erinnerung nach außen ausgesprochen und abermals abgespiegelt"). This secondary image, an appearance hardly distinguishable from the primary reality, inspires and impresses susceptible minds ("Dieses Nachbild strahlt nach allen Seiten in die Welt aus, und ein schönes, edles Gemüt mag an dieser Erscheinung, als wäre sie Wirklichkeit, sich entzücken und empfängt davon einen tiefen Eindruck"). This excitement sets in motion an urge to recall, in an almost magical sense, what can be recovered from the past ("Hieraus entfaltet sich ein Trieb, alles, was von Vergangenheit noch herauszuzaubern wäre, zu verwirklichen"). The longing increases, until it reaches the point, where someone actually visits the place of the first encounter, at least to become familiar with the location ("Die Sehnsucht wächst, und um sie zu befriedigen, wird es unumgänglich nötig, an Ort und Stelle zu gelangen, um sich die Örtlichkeit wenigstens anzueignen"). Luckily, Professor Näke turns out to be an appreciative and informed person, in whom the image had impressed itself as well

---

[5] Johann Wolfgang von Goethe, "Wiederholte Spiegelungen," *Goethes Werke,* Hamburger Ausgabe, vol. 12, 1981, 322-23.

[6] So according to the note, ibid., 710.

("Hier trifft sich der glückliche Fall, daß an der gefeierten Stelle ein teilnehmender, unterrichteter Mann gefunden wird, in welchem das Bild sich gleichfalls einge-drückt hat"). Goethe then sums up the sequence of interrelated mirror images: At the said locality, now in a sense deserted, arises the possibility to recover the event in a real sense, to create for oneself from the material fragments and from tradition a second presence, and again to encounter Friederike in all her loveliness ("Hier entsteht nun in der gewissermaßen verödeten Lokalität die Möglichkeit, ein Wahr-haftes wiederherzustellen, aus Trümmern von Dasein und Überlieferung sich eine zweite Gegenwart zu verschaffen und F r i e d e r i k e n  v o n  e h m a l s in ihrer ganzen Liebenswürdigkeit zu lieben"). For Goethe himself, this "second presence" has the effect that regardless of all events in the meantime she shows herself again in the soul of her old lover as in a mirror picture and renews in him her lovely pres-ence ("So kann sie nun, ungeachtet alles irdischen Dazwischentretens, sich auch wieder in der Seele des alten Liebhabers nochmals abspiegeln und demselben eine holde, werte, belebende Gegenwart lieblich erneuen").

In his conclusion, Goethe considers the wider implications of this phenomenon of repetitive mirroring. He refers to his scientific experiments with color reflections, which have shown him that not a decline, but an ascension occurs in the sequence of such mirror images. Rather than gradually fading away, such pictures increase in intensity. Applied to mental mirroring, such interplay not only keeps the past alive, but it moves past experiences to a higher level of excitement. Remarkably, Goethe ends by suggesting this to be a symbol of what happens daily and repeatedly in the history of art and scholarship, in the church, and even in the political realm ("Be-denkt man nun, daß wiederholte sittliche Spiegelungen das Vergangene nicht allein lebendig erhalten, sondern sogar zu einem höheren Leben emporsteigern, so wird man der entoptischen Erscheinungen gedenken, welche gleichfalls von Spiegel zu Spiegel nicht etwa verbleichen, sondern sich erst recht entzünden, und man wird ein Symbol gewinnen dessen, was in der Geschichte der Künste und Wissenschaften, der Kirche, auch wohl der politischen Welt sich mehrmals wiederholt hat und noch täglich wiederholt").

Basically, Goethe's essay sums up assumptions known to antiquity as well, in particular in regard to letter-writing. Especially his idea of a "second presence" ("zweite Gegenwart") was part of ancient statements concerning letter-writing. Ac-cording to ancient epistolary theory, the "first presence" was of course the face-to-face encounter, preferable to writing a letter. Isocrates' first letter, addressed to Di-onysius, provides a good example:

> If I were younger, I should not be sending you a letter, but should myself take ship and converse with you there; but inasmuch as it so happens that the fruitful period of my life and that of your own affairs have not coincided—since I am already spent

with years, and with you it is the high time for action—I shall try to disclose to you my views about the situation as well as I can in the circumstances.[7]

Isocrates then cites what is common assumption:

> I know, to be sure, that when men essay to give advice, it is far preferable that they should come in person rather than send a letter (μὴ διὰ γραμμάτων ποιεῖσθαι τὴν συνουσίαν, ἀλλ᾽ αὐτοὺς πλησιάσαντας), not only because it is easier to discuss the same matters face to face (παρὼν πρὸς παρόντα) than to give their views by letter (δι᾽ ἐπιστολῆς), nor yet because all men give greater credence to the spoken rather than to the written word, since they listen to the former as to practical advice and to the latter as to an artistic composition; but also, in addition to these reasons, in personal converse, if anything that is said is either not understood or not believed, the one who is presenting the arguments, being present (παρών), can come to the rescue in either case; but when written missives are used and any such misconception arises, there is no one to correct it, for since the writer is not at hand (ἀπόντος), the defender is lacking.[8]

## 3. Epistolary Formulae in Paul's Letters

Being the next best means of communication,[9] the letter, nonetheless, makes possible a "second presence" by literary features indicated by epistolary formulae. These formulae bring us closer to Paul's letters, where they are also found. It should be noted that, while the apostle makes use of the convention, his adaptation and interpretation make the formulae conform to the different contexts of the letters in which they occur.

When in 1 Cor 5:3 Paul uses the conventional formula concerning absence and presence,[10] his presence is said to be in no way weakened by his bodily absence: "absent in body, but present in spirit" (ἀπὼν τῷ σώματι παρὼν δὲ τῷ πνεύματι). In dealing with the transgressor charged in 1 Cor 5:1, the presence of Paul's spirit is all that matters. Conveying his judgment by letter he can act ὡς παρών. When the congregation assembles "in the name of our Lord Jesus" (ἐν τῷ ὀνόματι τοῦ κυρίου [ἡμῶν] Ἰησοῦ) Paul's own spirit (τοῦ ἐμοῦ πνεύματος) unites "with the power of our Lord Jesus" (σὺν τῇ δυνάμει τοῦ κυρίου ἡμῶν Ἰησοῦ) in the handing over of

---

[7] Isocrates, *Ep.* 1.1, trans. by Larue van Hook, LCL edition of *Isocrates*, vol. 3, p. 373.

[8] Idem, *Ep.* 1.2-3; see also 3.4; 6.4.

[9] For Paul, the best way to communicate is "face to face" (κατὰ πρόσωπον); see 2 Cor 10:1; Gal 2:11; cf. 2 Cor 8:24; 10:7; Gal 1:22; 2:11; 1 Thess 2:17-18; 3:10; Rom 1:9-13, etc.

[10] On this formula and its versions see Koskenniemi 1956, passim; Karlsson 1956; 1962, 40-45; Cancik 1967, 51-52; Constable 1976, 14; Thraede 1970, 39, 93-106 (on 1 Thess 2:17; 1 Cor 5:3-4; Col 2:5), 113-15, 146-57, 162-79, and passim; Malherbe 1988, 12. For the later periods see Müller 1980, 140-42; Krautter 1982.

the perpetrator to Satan. When the letter is being read to the congregation, the procedures are automatically set in motion. The letter thus has the effect of a "magical" letter, similar to Galatians.[11]

In 2 Corinthians 10:1-13:10, rightly called according to 2 Cor 2:4 the "letter of tears," Paul employs the formula again, although quite differently. The letter fragment does not carry a curse, but at most a threat. He emphasizes that he is absent and thus forced to resort to the sending of his word by letter (10:1, 11; 13:2, 10). Apparently, his adversaries in Corinth argued that Paul is able to write strongly-worded letters, but that he does not amount to much when he is present in person. Taking up their words, Paul ironically describes himself: "I who am unimpressive when face to face among you, but talking big to you when I am absent" (ὃς κατὰ πρόσωπον μὲν ταπεινὸς ἐν ὑμῖν, ἀπὼν δὲ θαρρῶ εἰς ὑμᾶς).[12] The apostle sheepishly concedes that he is a "layman in rhetoric" (ἰδιώτης τῷ λόγῳ [11:6; see also 10:10]), but he warns the Corinthians against making a mistake. When he comes to them and is "present" (παρόντες), they will see that he is strong "in action" (τῷ ἔργῳ [10:11]) and fully capable of punishing his adversaries (10:6; 13:2, 10). These threats are, however, to be understood as those of a teacher, coming with a rod to enforce discipline and order (cf. 1 Cor 4:21). Until now, the apostle indicates somewhat ironically, he has acted, "through the meekness and gentleness of Christ" (διὰ τῆς πραΰτητος καὶ ἐπιεικείας τοῦ Χριστοῦ [2 Cor 10:1, *RSV* trans.; cf. 1 Cor 4:21]). If necessary, this approach might change, but fortunately, as we know from his later evaluation in 2 Cor 2:1-11,[13] the Corinthians took Paul's words to heart. The weakness in communicating by letter is in part compensated for by self-ironically admitting that weakness and by threatening to pay a personal visit of severity (2 Cor 10:4; 13:10; cf. 2:1, 3).

Different again is the use of the formula in Phil 1:27, a letter written from prison (Phil 1:7, 13, 14, 17). It appears that the imprisonment has driven Paul to the point where he is ready to accept life or death (Phil 1:20). His famous dictum is stated in the next sentence: "For to me to live is Christ, and to die is gain" (Ἐμοὶ γὰρ τὸ ζῆν Χριστὸς καὶ τὸ ἀποθανεῖν κέρδος [Phil 1:21, *RSV* trans.]),[14] with his explanations in the following sentences (1:22-26).[15] Paul has been at the point of despair before in Asia (see 2 Cor 1:8-11); often before he has been as good as dead, "in death situations often" (ἐν θανάτοις πολλάκις [2 Cor 11:23]). In fact, risking one's life is what all his collaborators and "comrades in arms" (συστρατιῶται) must face (see Phil 2:25, 30; Phlm 2; Rom 16:4). Moreover, the apostle can speak of sacrificing his

---

[11] See Betz 1979, 25, 32-33.

[12] On this topic see Betz 1972, 57-69.

[13] In our view, the so-called "letter of reconciliation" (2 Cor 1:1-2:13; 7:2-16; 13:11-13) was written later than the "letter of tears" (2 Cor 10:1-13:10) and is the earliest commentary on it.

own eternal salvation for the sake of his fellow-Jews (Rom 9:3).

Peculiar to his later letters, Philippians as well as Romans (see Rom 15:30-32), is that Paul can look back on his life as though he were already dead. By implication, the letter to the Romans is intended as a kind of testament just in case the prayers for salvation from his enemies go unanswered. In Phil 1:27-30, he admonishes his most faithful congregation to get along without him. Whether "coming and seeing you or not" (εἴτε ἐλθὼν καὶ ἰδὼν ὑμᾶς εἴτε ἀπὼν ... [1:27]) is irrelevant. The Philippians must "now" (νῦν)[16] fight their own "fight" (ἀγών) which is the same as Paul's (1:30), and they must "conduct their own affairs (πολιτεύεσθαι) worthilyy of the gospel of Christ" (1:27).[17] Saying farewell is hard for the apostle, for he knows the Philippians' struggle will be tough. As they have been obedient "in my presence" (ἐν τῇ παρουσίᾳ μοῦ), even "much more so now in my absence" (νῦν πολλῷ μᾶλλον ἐν τῇ ἀπουσίᾳ μου) "you must work out your own salvation with fear and trembling" (μετὰ φόβου καὶ τρόμου τὴν ἑαυτῶν σωτηρίαν κατεργάζεσθε [2:12]). They now have to rely on no one but on God who is at work among them (2:13), but, as "I say with tears" (κλαίων λέγω), many are the enemies of Christ's cross against whom a firm stand has to be made (3:18).

## 4. A Pauline Formula in Colossians

The recurrence of the formula concerning Paul's absence and presence in the deutero-Pauline letter to the Colossians (2:5) is astonishing and calls for special explanation. What did the author of this letter, whom we take to be one of Paul's former close collaborators,[18] have in mind when he adapted this formula? The explanation can be given in terms of epistolographical features.

---

[14] For the interpretation see Droge 1988, 278-86; Droge and Tabor 1992. More clarity in the use of the terminology is needed, however. Self-determined suicide is clearly to be distinguished from acceptance of externally imposed martyrdom, and from voluntary self-sacrifice on behalf of others. As elsewhere in his letters, so also in Philippians Paul expresses his readiness to face death by the enemies of Christ as a consequence of preaching the gospel. Such a death implies a sharing of Christ's suffering on the cross as well as his resurrection, a sharing that unites the apostle and his congregation as well (Phil 3:8-11, 21; 4:14). Paul's statements in Phil 1:21-26, Stoic as some of them look, must be interpreted in this larger context.

[15] Cf. also Ignatius, *Smyrn.* 9:2; *Rom.* 7:2.

[16] The adverb νῦν has special significance in Philippians (see Phil 1:5, 20, 30; 2:12; 3:18).

[17] For the implications of this interpretation of the terms πολιτεύεσθαι and πολίτευμα, occurring only in Philippians (1:27; 3:20), I am indebted to the Chicago dissertation by Virginia Wiles 1993, 38-45, where she expands on suggestions made earlier by A. Schlatter and E. Lohmeyer.

[18] Regarding the author of Colossians, I agree with the position taken by Lars Hartman (1986, 140-41).

Clearly, the author of Colossians chose to let Paul speak by imitating the form of his letters from prison. According to Col 4:3-4, 18 the apostle is presumed to be in prison; in this respect, his suffering seems to be that of a prisoner (1:24, 29; 2:1; 4:12). Behind this literary screen, however, a different explanation for Paul's absence can be recognized. As the author indicates in 1:24, a passage extremely difficult to interpret, Paul is dead:

> Now I rejoice in my sufferings for your sake, and in my flesh I complete what is lacking in Christ's afflictions for the sake of his body, that is, the church (*RSV*).

> (Νῦν χαίρω ἐν τοῖς παθήμασιν ὑπὲρ ὑμῶν καὶ ἀνταναπληρῶ τὰ ὑστερήματα τῶν θλίψεων τοῦ Χριστοῦ ἐν τῇ σαρκί μου ὑπὲρ τοῦ σώματος αὐτοῦ, ὅ ἐστιν ἡ ἐκκλησία.)

The statement, made in the present, is a matter of the past from the standpoint of the author of Colossians. This is the reason why the churches of Colossae and Laodicea have not personally seen him face to face; in fact, "all those who have not seen my face in the flesh" (2:1) will never see him in that manner. The words καὶ ὅσοι οὐχ ἑόρακαν τὸ πρόσωπόν μου ἐν σαρκί sound an ominous tone of finality. Tychicus and Onesimus, his faithful colleagues, know the circumstances in detail (4:7-9), but the author does not reveal them.[19]

At any rate, the fact of Paul's death means that the formula in 2:5 must be interpreted differently from its previous occurrences: "for even though I am absent in the flesh, yet I am with you in the spirit" (εἰ γὰρ καὶ τῇ σαρκὶ ἄπειμι, ἀλλὰ τῷ πνεύματι σὺν ὑμῖν εἰμι). Some changes in terminology are noteworthy. Paul's absence is now one of his σάρξ,[20] not one of his σῶμα, as in Paul's authentic letters.[21] The reason is that the σάρξ passes away at death,[22] while the σῶμα is transformed.[23] Yet, despite his death, Paul is present with the Colossians "in the spirit." Also this part of the formula now appears in a different light.

Where, according to the author, is Paul now, and how is his "second presence" evident? Indeed, Paul is able to "hear" (ἀκούειν) of the Colossians' faith and love (1:4), having been informed by Epaphras (1:7-8; 4:12), most likely through prayer

---

[19] This silence appears to be strange, but there are parallels for it in other deutero-Pauline letters and the Acts of the Apostles (20:22-25).

[20] For Colossians, σάρξ refers to the physical side of human existence, which is subject to death; see Col 1:22, 24; 2:1, 5, 11, 13, 18, 23; 3:22.

[21] See 1 Cor 5:3; cf. 2 Cor 10:2, 10, 11; 11:9; 13:2, 10; Gal 4:18; Phil 1:26.

[22] See Col 1:24; 2:1, 5, 11, 13; cf. 1 Cor 15:50; 2 Cor 4:7-12.

[23] See 1 Cor 15:35-57; 2 Cor 3:18; Phil 3:21; Rom 12:1-2.

(1:8: ἐν πνεύματι).[24] The apostle is also able to "see" (βλέπειν)[25] "your [congregation's] good order and firmness of your faith in Christ" (τὴν τάξιν καὶ τὸ στερέωμα τῆς εἰς Χριστὸν πίστεως ὑμῶν),[26] a view that makes him rejoice (2:5). He knows of the "hope" (ἐλπίς) stored up for the Colossians in heaven (1:5), but because of the threats and temptations endangering their salvation he continues his "struggle" (ἀγών), working on their behalf (2:1-2) through continuous intercessional (1:3, 9; cf. 4:3) and thanksgiving prayers (1:12; cf. 2:7; 3:15-17; 4:2).

It should be evident that for the author Paul is in heaven; for him the promise of the gospel (1:5, 23) has come true: "He [sc. God the Father] has delivered us from the dominion of darkness and transferred us to the kingdom of his beloved Son, in whom we have redemption, the forgiveness of sins" (ὃς ἐρρύσατο ἡμᾶς ἐκ τῆς ἐξουσίας τοῦ σκότους καὶ μετέστησεν εἰς τὴν βασιλείαν τοῦ υἱοῦ τῆς ἀγάπης αὐτοῦ, ἐν ᾧ ἔχομεν τὴν ἀπολύτρωσιν, τὴν ἄφεσιν τῶν ἁμαρτιῶν [1:13-14]). It is from heaven, "in the spirit," through his collaborators (1:7-8; 4:7-17), and of course through the letter (1:1-2; 4:16, 18) that he continues to instruct and exhort his church.[27]

Interpreted in this way, the formula of 2:5 turns out to be an epistolary device for creating a "second presence" for Paul. The literary *topos* of "presence in absence" allows the author of Colossians to create what a letter should be, a conversation between friends when separated,[28] a being together (2:2-7) on a higher level ("in the spirit") and despite distances. This fulfills what Seneca, no doubt drawing on common opinion, states regarding the separation of friends:

> Just let your thoughts travel … You may hold converse with your friends when they are absent, and indeed as often as you wish and for as long as you wish. For we enjoy this, the greatest of pleasures, all the more when we are absent from one another … A friend should be retained in the spirit; such a friend can never be absent. He can see every day whomsoever he desires to see. I would therefore have you share your studies with me, your meals, and your walks. We should be living within too narrow limits if anything were barred to our thoughts. I see you, my dear Lucilius, and at this very moment I hear you; I am with you to such an extent that I hesitate whether I should not begin to write you notes instead of letters.[29]

---

[24] The expression ἐν πνεύματι, occurring only here and 2:5 (cf. πνευματικός), should first be interpreted in the context of Colossians, where it is related to worship, especially prayer (1:9; 3:16). Therefore, a connection with δηλώσας in 1:8 seems most likely. For a similar context see also Eph 1:3; 2:18, 22; 3:5; 5:18-19; 6:18. For the epistolary *topos* see Thraede 1970, 55-61, 146-57.

[25] For the epistolary *topos* of "seeing in spirit" see Thraede 1970, 44, 46, 56, 60, 80, 104-5, 112, 146-57.

[26] *RSV* trans., with my addition pointing to the institutional meaning of the term τάξις. See also Thraede 1970, 102-6.

[27] In this respect Colossians belongs to the genre of "heavenly letters."

[28] See on this point Cancik 1967, 51-52 (with references).

It is to be understood, of course, that in the case of Colossians the continuing exchange between Paul and his churches takes place in the context of worship. It is in the worship service that the apostle's letters are read (4:16); it is here that the congregation hears about Paul's prayers, teaching and concern on their behalf as well as his pleas for their prayers and remembrance (4:3, 18). Also their reply occurs in the context of their worship, teaching, and communal life in general (3:5-4:6).

## 5. Paul's Literary Portrait

Another distinctive feature of Colossians is the author's portrait of Paul, taking the form of a literary "self-portrait" (1:24-29). Self-portraits of this kind are not found in Paul's authentic letters, but Ephesians (3:1-19) and the Pastoral Epistles have them as well (1 Tim 1:12-17; 2 Tim 1:8-14). The portrait of Paul in Col 1:24-29 is carefully thought out:

> Now I rejoice in my sufferings for your sake, and in my flesh I complete what is lacking in Christ's afflictions for the sake of his body, that is, the church, of which I became a minister according to the divine office which was given to me for you, to make the word of God fully known, the mystery hidden for ages and generations but now made manifest to his saints. To them God chose to make known how great among the Gentiles are the riches of the glory of this mystery, which is Christ in you, the hope of glory. Him we proclaim, warning everyone and teaching everyone in all wisdom, that we may present everyone mature in Christ. For this I toil, striving with all the energy which he mightily inspires within me. (*RSV*, with some changes in vs. 28.)

This portrait in Col 1:24-29 shows Paul to be the faithful minister (διάκονος) of the church (1:23, 25), who rejoices in his sufferings. This means that through his martyrdom "in the flesh" (σάρξ) Paul is "completing" the continuing afflictions which Christ suffers through his body (σῶμα), identical with the church (1:24). Whereas, as is well known, details of the portrait are difficult to interpret, it is evident that the passage as a whole, meticulously formulated as it is, reflects a post-Pauline perspective of the author of Colossians.

What did the author have in mind inserting this portrait of Paul? The answer to

---

[29] Seneca, *Ep.* 55:9-11, cited according to the LCL ed. and trans. by R. M. Gummere 1967, 1.370-73. I am giving the Latin as well, since it is rather close to Colossians in terminology: *Huc usque cogitationes tuas mitte. Conversari cum amicis absentibus licet, et quidem quotiens velis, quamdiu velis. Magis hac voluptate, quae maxima est, fruimur, dum absumus ... Amicus animo possidendus est; hic autem numquam abest. Quemcumque vult, cotidie videt. Itaque mecum stude, mecum cena, mecum ambula. In angusto vivebamus, si quicquam esset cogitationibus clusum. Video te, mi Lucili; cum maxime audio. Adeo tecum sum, ut dubitem, an incipiam non epistulas, sed codicellos tibi scribere.*

this question can be given with the literary perspective in mind.

First, there is the general expectation that a letter should contain the author's "image of his soul" (εἰκὼν τῆς ψυχῆς). For this *topos* we can simply cite the famous passage in Ps.-Demetrius, *De eloc.* 4.227:

> The letter, like the dialogue, should abound in glimpses of character. It may be said that everybody reveals his own soul in his letters. In every other form of composition it is possible to discern the writer's character, but in none so clearly as in the epistolary.[30]

Second, while for a writer of his own letters these letters themselves will be his *imago* and *speculum animi*,[31] the writer of a pseudepigraphical letter cannot make such an assumption. To be sure, the author of Colossians cannot have been interested in communicating to his readers his own image; since he writes under the name of Paul, it is the image of Paul that must be presented. We can therefore conclude that this was the reason why he inserted a portrait of the apostle.

What was the origin of this portrait? Without being able to discuss the difficult issues involved, it is not likely that the portrait is simply derived from one or more of the authentic letters of Paul. While there are some allusions to Pauline phrases and concepts, the portrait as a whole is a new creation by the author.

How did he create the portrait? It is fascinating to see that it seems to be generated by interrelated mirror-images. If the author of Colossians was, as we assume, a close associate of the apostle during his lifetime, we can conclude that the portrait reflects the personal memory of his beloved mentor. Thus, the portrait he presents is the one that had first imprinted itself on his mind. Furthermore, this portrait is a mirror-image of the portrait of Christ, shown in the Christ-hymn (1:15-20); Christ, in turn, is the "image of God" (εἰκὼν τοῦ θεοῦ [1:15; cf. 3:10]). Finally, this portrait of Paul is the one the author wishes his addressees to remember (4:18).

Still another important aspect should be considered. If Paul's portrait is a reflection of Christ, the Colossian Christians are not simply thought of as other mirror-reflections. Rather, as a result of baptism, the Colossian Christians have already become united with Christ through the baptismal experience of death and resurrection (2:11-15, 20; 3:1-3; 1:21-23). In describing their Christian life, the author of Colossians does not conceive of it as a reflection of Paul's image. Instead, the baptismal terminology of "putting off the old" and "putting on the new humanity," that is

---

[30] Cited according to the LCL ed. and trans. by W. R. Roberts 1932, 440-41. The Greek reads: Πλεῖστον δὲ ἐχέτω τὸ ἠθικὸν ἡ ἐπιστολή, ὥσπερ καὶ ὁ διάλογος· σχεδὸν γὰρ εἰκόνα ἕκαστος τῆς ἑαυτοῦ ψυχῆς γράφει τὴν ἐπιστολήν. καὶ ἔστι μὲν καὶ ἐξ ἄλλου λόγου παντὸς ἰδεῖν τὸ ἦθος τοῦ γράφοντος, ἐξ οὐδενὸς δὲ οὕτως, ὡς ἐπιστολῆς.

[31] See for example Koskenniemi 1956, 178ff.; Cancik 1967, 52, 68ff. ; Thraede 1970, 146-57, 157-61, and passim; Malherbe 1988, 12.

Christ himself (3:9-11, 12-17), is used.

At this point, the differences between deutero-Pauline Colossians and Paul's own letters become apparent. While in his own letters the apostle calls for becoming "imitators" (μιμηταί) of him, just as he is an imitator of Christ (1 Thess 1:6; 2:14; 1 Cor 4:16; 11:1; Phil 3:17), Paul's death prevents the Colossians from such imitation of Paul.[32] A certain parallel with Romans should not be overlooked at this point. Since the Roman Christians are not personally acquainted with Paul (Rom 1:10-13; 15:22-32), they cannot imitate him. Instead of calling for imitation of him, he bases the Christian existence on the doctrine of baptism (Rom 6:1-11).[33]

## 6. Conclusion

Making good use of literary devices known to ancient epistolography allows the author of Colossians to create a "second presence" for his beloved teacher here on earth. Instead of bemoaning Paul's death as a martyr, the author of the letter shows the apostle to be permanently present "in the spirit." In other words, Paul's "second presence" is not confined to the paper on which the letter is written. Rather, as the letter is being read in the worship services, the apostle continuously and in various ways interacts "in the spirit" with the congregation. Far from calling on its addressees merely to remember a dead martyr, the letter to the Colossians points beyond itself by facilitating the living interaction between the apostle and his future readers and listeners.

## Bibliography

Betz, H. D. 1972: *Der Apostel Paulus und die sokratische Tradition: Eine exegetische Untersuchung zu seiner "Apologie" 2 Korinther 10-13* (BHTh 45), Tübingen: Mohr (Siebeck) 1972.

— 1979: *Galatians: A Commentary on Paul's Letter to the Churches in Galatia* (Hermeneia), Philadelphia, PA: Fortress 1979.

— 1994: "Transferring a Ritual: Paul's Interpretation of Baptism in Romans 6," in: T. Engberg-Pedersen (ed.), *Paul in His Hellenistic Context,* Minneapolis, MN: Fortress and Edinburgh: T. & T. Clark 1994, 84-118 [reprinted in: H. D. Betz, *Paulinische Studien. Gesammelte Aufsätze III,* Tübingen: Mohr (Siebeck) 1994, 240-271].

Cancik, H. 1967: *Untersuchungen zu Senecas Epistulae morales* (Spudasmata 18), Hildesheim: Olms 1967.

---

[32] Cf. also Eph 5:1-2, where the Pauline concept has been changed to "imitation of God."

[33] See Betz 1994.

Constable, G. 1976: "Letter and Letter-Collections," in: *Typologie des sources du moyen âge occidental,2:17*, Turnhout: Brepols 1976.

*Demetrius, On Style*, ed. and trans. by W. Rhys Roberts (LCL), London: Heinemann and Cambridge, MA: Harvard University Press 1932.

Donelson, L. R. 1986: *Pseudepigraphy and Ethical Argument in the Pastoral Epistles* (HUTh 22), Tübingen: Mohr (Siebeck) 1986.

Droge, A. J. 1988: "*Mori lucrum:* Paul and Ancient Theories of Suicide," in: *NT* 30 (1988) 263-86.

Droge, A. J./ Tabor, J. D. 1992: *A Noble Death: Suicide and Martyrdom among Christians and Jews in Antiquity*, San Francisco, CA: Harper Collins 1992.

Fornberg, T. 1977: *An Early Church in a Pluralistic Society* (CB.NT 9), Lund: Gleerup 1977.

Goethe, J. W. von 1981: "Wiederholte Spiegelungen," in: *Goethes Werke* (Hamburger Ausgabe, vol. 12), Munich: Beck 1981, 322-23.

Hartman, L. 1986: "On Reading Others' Letters," in: G. W. E. Nickelsburg with G. W. MacRae (eds.), *Christians among Jews and Gentiles: Essays in Honor of Krister Stendahl on His Sixty-fifth Birthday*, Philadelphia, PA: Fortress 1986, 137-46.

Holland, G. S. 1988: *The Tradition that You Received from Us: 2 Thessalonians in the Pauline Tradition* (HUTh 24); Tübingen: Mohr (Siebeck) 1988.

*Isocrates*, vol. 3, ed. and trans. by L. van Hook (LCL), Cambridge, MA: Harvard University Press; London: Heinemann 1945.

Karlsson, G. 1956: "Formelhaftes in Paulusbriefen?," in: *Eranos: Acta Philologica Suecana* 54 (1956) 138-41.

— 1962: *Idéologie et cérémonial dans l'épistolographie byzantine: Textes du Xe siècle analysés et commentés* (AUU. Studia Graeca Upsaliensia 3), 2nd ed., Uppsala: Almqvist & Wiksell 1962.

Koskenniemi, H. 1956: *Studien zur Ideologie und Phraseologie des griechischen Briefes bis 400 n. Chr.* (AASF. series B, vol. 102.2), Helsinki: Suomalainen Tiedeakatemia 1956.

Krautter, K. 1982: "Acsi ore ad os...: Eine mittelalterliche Theorie des Briefes und ihr antiker Hintergrund," in: *AuA* 28 (1982) 155-68.

Malherbe, A. J. 1988: *Ancient Epistolary Theorists* (SBL. Sources for Biblical Study 19), Atlanta, GA: Scholars Press 1988.

Müller, W. G. 1980: "Der Brief als Spiegel der Seele: Zur Geschichte eines Topos der Epistolartheorie von der Antike bis zu Samuel Richardson," in: *AuA* 26 (1980) 138-57.

*Seneca, Ad Lucilium Epistulae Morales*, ed. and trans. by R. M. Gummere, 3 vols., London: Heinemann and Cambridge, MA: Harvard University Press 1917-1925.

Thraede, K. 1970: *Grundzüge griechisch-römischer Brieftopik* (Zetemata 48), Munich: Beck 1970.

Wiles, V. 1993: *From Apostolic Presence to Selfgovernment in Christ: Paul's Preparing of the Philippian Church for Life in His Absence* (Ph.D. Dissertation, University of Chicago 1993).

# 1 Thessalonians 2:15-16:
## Prophetic Woe-Oracle
## with ἔφθασεν as Proleptic Aorist

### Bruce C. Johanson

## 1. Introductory

The difficulty of interpreting 1 Thess 2:15-16, and in particular the aorist verb ἔφθασεν at the end of the passage, has played an important role in various arguments regarding the authenticity or the integrity of 1 Thessalonians ever since the work of F. C. Baur.[1] Baur questioned the authenticity of the letter, not its literary integrity. He saw (1) the positive relation to the Judean churches reflected in 2:14 as uncharacteristic of Paul, (2) the use of the well-known Gentile charge of *odium generis humani* against the Jews and the vagueness of this polemic as unnatural for Paul, and (3) 2:16c (ἔφθασεν) as reflecting the destruction of Jerusalem in 70 A.D.[2] His radical position found little if any following, but his observations led others to question the literary integrity of the letter. Numerous interpolation theories developed which ranged from viewing only 2:16c on up to the whole of 2:15-16 as being later interpolation.[3]

Prior to my text-linguistic[4] and rhetorical analysis of 1 Thessalonians I was persuaded that 2:15-16 was probably a later interpolation. In particular, I had found Birger Pearson's able canvassing of this solution to be especially attractive.[5] However, after analysing the letter as a whole I found that there was intercorroborating evidence from the letter's text-pragmatic, text-semantic and text-syntactic dimensions that supported the text's coherence to such a degree that the probability of an

---

[1] Baur 1875, 87-88.

[2] Ibid.

[3] See the survey by Collins 1979, 68-85.

[4] On the field of text-linguistics see, e.g., Plett 1979; Gülich/Raible 1977; de Beaugrande/Dressler 1981.

[5] Pearson 1971, 79-94.

interpolation became highly dubious.[6] D. Schmidt endeavored to support Pearson's position by what he called "linguistic evidence" for 2:13-16 as an interpolation.[7] He argued that the longer chains of successively dependent clauses and the greater number of such embedments in 2:13-16 relative to the rest of 1:2-3:10 may be taken to indicate an aberration in Pauline style that supports the theory of interpolation. This evidence, however, is taken only from the syntactic dimension of the text. Furthermore, it only works with sentences rather than on the level of text. A multi-dimensional text-linguistic analysis shows that such aberrations in the syntactic dimension find a most adequate explanation in the text-pragmatic dimension as a rhetorical digression typically used for the strategy of praise or blame.[8]

In view of these findings there remains the need to make adequate sense of 2:15-16 as it stands. Frank D. Gilliard has moved in this direction by convincingly arguing that the comma at the end of 1 Thess 2:14 should be removed with the result that τῶν Ἰουδαίων begins a restrictive clause rather than a non-restrictive clause.[9] More recently Rainer Kampling has made an important contribution, especially with regard to understanding πᾶσιν ἀνθρώποις ἐναντίων.[10] He has demonstrated that this does not reflect anti-Semitism, as expressed in the well known pagan slogan mentioned above. Rather, in view of the context in 2:16 he has shown from the interpretations of 1 Thess 2:14-16 made by the early church fathers on down to Theodoret that it was and should be understood as polemic directed at Jewish hindrance to mission. In other words, it reflects an internal Jewish struggle and has nothing to do with political, ethnic defamation.[11] The present study, for its part, will concentrate on breaking some new ground regarding the difficulty presented by ἔφθασεν in 2:16c. In the process a new contribution will also be made to Pauline form criticism.

---

[6] See Johanson 1987, 169-173, esp. 170-172, (also 99, 109, 144, 149-151). By way of a brief explanation of these text-dimensions, H. F. Plett 1979, 52 observes these three text-dimensions as making up the complete semiotic capacity of text as such: "(1) Pragmatics concerns the relations between signs, designata and sign-users, (2) semantics concerns the relations between signs and designata, and (3) syntactics concerns the relations between signs and signs. These three dimensions stand in a hierarchical relationship with pragmatics inclusive of semantics and syntactics and with semantics as inclusive of syntactics. Furthermore these three dimensions interact intimately in texts so that whenever we focus on one of them in particular in a textual analysis, the other two dimensions can never be entirely excluded." (The translation of Plett is my own. See Johanson 1987, 7-8. See also Hellholm 1980, 22-27, for a fuller theoretical discussion.) The explicit use of these categories not only encourages a more complete description of textual features but also facilitates intersubjectivity.

[7] Schmidt 1983, 269-79.

[8] See Johanson 1987, 97; Lausberg 1973, 187, 542, 544; Wuellner 1979, 179-81.

[9] Gilliard 1989, 481-502.

[10] Kampling 1993, 185-91, 211-13.

[11] Kampling's study (1993, 211) also shows that polemic against Jews in the New Testament actually played a relatively small role in anti-Semitic arguments that developed later.

## 2. Summary and Critique of Some Important Options of Interpretation Regarding ἔφθασεν

To begin with, a few remarks are in order on some of the more attractive options for understanding ἔφθασεν which I reject. These generally focus on the semantics of the word.

E. Best finds that the possible meanings of φθάνειν ("to arrive") can include the semantic element of exclusion of participation in whatever experience lies at the destination in some instances of usage, while in other instances participation is included.[12] According to the former, the "wrath" would be seen as hanging over them and just about to fall on them. According to the latter, the "wrath" would be seen as actually having been manifested in a concrete event or series of events.

Best prefers the former meaning for our passage and supports it by referring to Dan Th 4:24f.: τοῦτο ἡ σύγκρισις αὐτοῦ, βασιλεῦ, καὶ σύγκριμα ὑψίστου ἐστίν, ὃ ἔφθασεν ἐπὶ τὸν κύριόν μου τὸν βασιλέα, καὶ σὲ ἐκδιώξουσιν ἀπὸ τῶν ἀνθρώπων, κτλ. ("This is the interpretation of it, O King, and it is the decree of the Most High, which came upon my lord the king, and they shall drive you out from men," etc.). Here he sees the decree as having been pronounced without having yet taken effect. On closer scrutiny, however, the focus is on σύγκριμα as God's "decision" or "decree" as such that had "reached" or "come upon" Nebuchadnezzar. There is no semantic feature of excluded participation in the "punishment" subsequently described in 4:28 where ἔφθασεν is used again, only this time with reference to the actualization of the punishment: ταῦτα πάντα ἔφθασεν ἐπὶ Ναβουχοδονοσορ τὸν βασιλέα ("All these things came upon king Nebuchadnezzar"). Thus, it is questionable whether one has any decisive evidence here for taking non-participation in the experience of what has "arrived" to be a semantic feature of the meaning of φθάνω.

As for the latter position where the "wrath" is seen as actually having been manifested in a concrete event or series of events, there is the difficulty of finding an event other than the eschatological "day of the Lord" (1 Thess 5:2) that would be of sufficiently universal significance for Paul's readers to make the connection.[13] Although one cannot take it for granted, one would expect Paul to uphold what text-linguists refer to as the communicative constraint of informativity, i.e. the extent to which the contents and structures of a particular text are commensurate with the recipient's knowledge level and expectations.[14] Apart from Baur's suggestion of the

---

[12] Best 1972, 119. For the former position, Clark 1940, 367-83 is referred to, and Kümmel 1957, 106-07 for the latter position.

[13] For a summary of events possibly referred to, see Best 1972, 119-20 and his refutation of such interpretations.

destruction of the temple in A.D. 70, such events as the expulsion of the Jews from Rome in A.D. 49, the famine of A.D. 46-47, etc., do not appear to qualify for such universal significance as to allow the addressees to inference these events without more indications than the single reference to the "wrath."[15]

Another solution is that of M. Dibelius who sees the aorist as indicating the inauguration of the end ("den schon eingetretenen Anfang vom Ende") and appeals to Matt 12:28.[16] This, however, does not do justice to the reception-process of the text. As I have shown elsewhere, there is a return in 2:13-16 to a cluster of expressions that were prominent in 1:2-10, i.e. εὐχαριστοῦμεν τῷ θεῷ (1:2; 2:13), μιμηταὶ ἐγενήθητε (1:6; 2:14), δεξάμενοι τὸν λόγον/ἐδέξασθε ... λόγον (1:6; 2:13) and ὀργῆς/ὀργή (1:10; 2:16).[17] Given the linear process of reading or hearing, and given the absence of any other specifying or modifying semantic feature other than ἔφθασεν in relation to ὀργή, the reader/hearer would naturally allow the eschatological reference to the future "wrath" in 1:10 to inform his or her understanding of "wrath" in 2:16. Dibelius' solution also influences him to propose the unlikely rendition of εἰς τέλος as "unto the end" in connection with the "wrath" ("der Zorn, der zum Ende führt").[18]

### 3. Preliminary Motivations for Investigating ἔφθασεν as a Proleptic Aorist

On the other hand, Dibelius described 1 Thess 2:15-16 as a whole as being "prophetic" in character.[19] It was basically this prophetic cast to the language that prompted such commentators as E. von Dobschütz and B. Rigaux to hold to a proleptic interpretation of ἔφθασεν.[20] This solution is drawn from the pragmatic dimension, i.e. the rhetorical, reader-impacting dimension of textual strategies. The representation of a future event by means of a past tense dramatically emphasizes the certainty that it indeed will take place. Although this dramatic use of the aorist is rare, it is not entirely foreign to Paul's usage elsewhere: κατηργήθητε ἀπὸ Χριστοῦ ὅτινες ἐν νόμῳ δικαιοῦσθε ("You were severed from Christ, you who would

---

[14] See de Beaugrande/Dressler 1981, 8-9, 139ff.

[15] See, e.g., Best 1972, 120 and Bruce 1982, 49.

[16] Dibelius 1937, 12.

[17] Johanson 1987, 149.

[18] Dibelius 1937, 12.

[19] Dibelius 1937, 13.

[20] Dobschütz 1909, 117; Rigaux 1956, 452. Some others supporting this view are, e.g., Frame 1912, 114 and Fuller 1954, 26. More recent commentators are for the most part not inclined to this view. See, e.g., Best 1972, 120; Okeke 1980-81, 130; Marshall 1983, 80; Donfried 1984, 151-52; Holtz 1986, 108.

be justified by law"—Gal 5:4).[21]

My thesis in this study is as follows: Firstly, the position that Paul makes use of prophetic language and style in 1 Thess 2:15-16 will be particularly enhanced if the use of a specific form or gattung of prophetic speech can be established for the passage. In this regard, I have in view the prophetic woe-oracle. Secondly, if it can be shown that the proleptic aorist is also used frequently, or even occasionally, in this particular gattung in the Septuagint, the case for interpreting ἔφθασεν as a proleptic aorist with a dramatic function will be significantly enhanced. Finally, the conclusions drawn will also have a bearing on the troublesome expression εἰς τέλος so as to prefer the meaning "utterly"[22] or the combination "fully and finally."[23]

The initial motivation for seeing 2:15-16 as possibly having a significant number of features in common with the prophetic woe-oracle comes from the topical and lexical correspondences between this passage and the woe-oracle in Matt 23:29-36 (see also Luke 11:47-51). There is

(1) the striking cluster of lexical parallels, i.e., ἀποκτείνω, προφῆται, (ἐκ)διώκω and (ἀνα)πληρόω,

(2) the similarity of Paul's "driving us out" to "you shall drive (them) from city to city" (Matt 23:34),

(3) the similarity of Paul's "so as to fill up their sins always" to "you shall fill up the measure of your fathers" (Matt 23:32),

(4) the similarity of Paul's "Jews who killed the Lord Jesus and the prophets" to "the prophets ... some of whom you will kill" (Matt 23:34), and

---

[21] Regarding such instances the grammars point out that this use is usually tied to a conditional clause: ἐὰν δὲ καὶ γαμήσῃς, οὐχ ἥμαρτες· καὶ ἐὰν γήμῃ ἡ παρθένος, οὐχ ἥμαρτεν ("But if you should marry, you did not sin, and if a young woman should marry, she did not sin", 1 Cor 7:28). See Blass/Debrunner/Funk 1961, 171; Moulton/Turner 1963, 74; Zerwick 1963, 84-85.

Another possible instance of this sort of dramatic usage for the aorist tense is found in the difficult reference ὅτι ἐπιστεύθη τὸ μαρτύριον ἡμῶν ἐφ᾽ ὑμᾶς in 2 Thess 1:10 in the context of the last judgment. In support of this G. S. Holland (1988, 40-41) observes that the author describes "future certainties as past events," something that "is certainly not a novelty within apocalyptic literature" (p. 40). He refers to Dan 7-12 and Rev 14-21. While I am attracted to Holland's interpretation of ἐπιστεύθη, I find the aorist in the mentioned apocalyptic literature to indicate more the perspective of the writers in relation to their visions than to have the kind of dramatic feature seen in 1:10. The dramatic effect is derived from the contrast with the surrounding tense usage, i.e., a departure from what one would normally expect.

[22] Other possibilities are "at last," "finally" (see, e.g., Frame 1912, 114-16; Rigaux 1956, 453; Best 1972, 121; RSV and NIV), or "for ever," (see, e.g., Stählin 1967, 434, and NEB) or "to the end" (see, e.g., Dibelius 1937, 12, "der Zorn, der zum Ende führt"). For a good overview see Marshall 1983, 81, who also rightly notes that an almost identical occurrence of the clause in *T. Levi* 6:11 is not of any help because the actual use of the clause in both texts is so different.

[23] Thus Marshall 1983, 81, following Ackroyd 1968-69, 126.

(5)  the correspondence of Paul's "the wrath came upon them utterly" to "all these things will come upon this generation" (Matt 23:36).

On the basis of such similarities J. B. Orchard took the view that Paul was dependent upon a primitive source in common with Matthew.[24] In particular, ἐκδιώκω and ἐναντίος are not used by Paul elsewhere, which indicates his likely use of some source or tradition. More recently, this position was given further support by R. Schippers.[25] B. Rigaux seems to have taken Orchard to be positing a direct dependence between the two texts.[26] While I did not read Orchard that way, I find Rigaux's position less plausible where he sees 1 Kgs 19:10, 14 as giving rise to both texts independently. As shown by H. J. Schoeps, the motif of the murder of the prophets by the Jews was traditional and informed Acts 7:52 and Heb 11:36-37, besides the texts just mentioned.[27] In fact the traditional character of this motif led R. Bultmann to propose that the woes in Matt 23:34-36, 37-39 may have been originally Jewish prophetic sayings either adopted by Jesus himself or ascribed to him later with various adaptations.[28] More recently D. E. Garland has investigated the woes in Matt 23 and found that they qualify as woe-oracles in the light of the findings of OT form-criticism.[29]

Given the shared traditional motifs together with the woe-oracular features in 1 Thess 2:15-16 to be explored below, there is the possibility of some shared tradition in which the motifs were already formulated by way of the woe-oracle. I do not argue this here, but merely note that these observed similarities pointed me in the direction of seeing woe-oracular contours in 1 Thess 2:15-16. The differences in wording and relative difference in formulation, however, show that Paul was no slave to this shared tradition, but freely renders his own version of it to suit his own purposes.

This last observation opens up the larger background of the literary influence of the Septuagint. As Paul's sacred text, it was read, re-read and no doubt committed extensively to memory. With this in view I shall subsequently attempt to draw from previous analyses of the woe-oracle as a form in the OT in order to see what light this can throw on 1 Thess 2:15-16. Since there is obviously no explicit "woe" expression in this passage, the objection may be raised that without the main characteristic of the woe-oracle form one would hardly expect to be able to establish the presence of such a form here. However, R. Knierim, among others, has shown us

---

[24] Orchard 1938, 20-23.

[25] Schippers 1966, 223-34, esp. 231.

[26] Rigaux 1956, 445.

[27] Schoeps 1950, 138ff.

[28] Bultmann 1968, 114.

[29] Garland 1979, 72-81.

that not only are there no pure forms, but that characteristic features of a form may be found not merely in the morphological, formulaic dimension of texts, but also in the dimensions of "content," "setting," "function," "intention," and "occupation of mind."[30] Taking all these dimensions into consideration, a sufficient constellation should be present so as to be able to establish a dominancy of features that help to distinguish a particular form as it occurs in a particular text. Such a significant constellation of features typical of the woe-oracle will be shown to be present in the passage under study.

Finally, in conjunction with the foregoing observations, given Paul's mixed Jewish and Hellenistic heritages, it is fair to see him as being influenced by such prophetic language and style when expressing judgment in a rhetorical *vituperatio*.

## 4. The Woe-Oracle as a Prophetic Form Mediated by Sacred Text

An attempt is not being made here to enter the form-critical discussion of the woe-oracle in its original setting in terms of its origin, etc.[31] Instead, I am proceeding from the perspective of Paul as reader of sacred text, and consequently my purpose is to deliniate it as a form mediated not only by sacred text but also by the Koine Greek.

To begin with, both i הוֹי and i אִוֹי are rendered most frequently by οὐαί (with some instances by ὦ) in the LXX. Οἴμμοι also occurs in a few instances. Consequently, the distinction between הוֹי and אִוֹי, so important for OT form-critics is lost for LXX readers.[32] OT form-critics have shown that אִוֹי is usually followed by the preposition לְ, whereas in fifty-one instances of הוֹי twenty-three instances have a participle and fourteen have a noun where both noun and participle express or introduce one or more accusations regarding the misbehavior or offences of the one to whom the "woe" is applied. Among the remaining instances four occur with prepositions, six belong directly to funerary lamentation and four have turned into a general exhortation.[33] A quick perusal of Hatch and Redpath's Concordance to the Septuagint shows that where the preposition לְ occurs, it is rendered in the Septuagint by the dative, and when Hebrew participles or nouns occur directly after the woe cry they are fairly consistently rendered in the Greek with corresponding participles or nouns.

---

[30] Knierim 1973, 449ff. See also, Buss 1974, 48ff. For work that casts light on form-criticism from the perspective of text-linguistics and semiotics see Hellholm 1980, 72-74 and Hartman's discussion of genre 1983, 329-43.

[31] Wolff 1977, 242-45, gives an able summary of this in his commentary on Amos and Joel.

[32] Wank 1966, 217.

[33] See Wolff's summary, 1977, 242.

E. Gerstenberger has observed that subsequent to the indictments introduced by the woe cry a wide variety of expressions may occur.[34] The initial indictment frequently leads to a threat or threats (e.g., Isa 5:9, 13 f, 24; 28:2-4; Hab 2:16), a lament (Isa 1:5f.), a series of ironical questions (Isa 10:3, 4a), a proverbial saying (Isa 29:16), a new accusation, some occurring with a renewed threat (Isa 45:11; Jer 22:15ff.), or a rhetorical question (Amos 6:2-3; Hab 2:7, 13), etc. On first sight such a diversity of expressions would appear to mitigate against seeing the presence of a recognizable form. As mentioned above, however, features that define a gattung are not limited to the morphological elements, but also include text-semantic and text-pragmatic elements. What Gerstenberger does not bring out is the fact that while the forms of expression may differ, in the vast majority of instances some kind of judgment is either expressed or implied. Thus, I find his observations useful when they are seen as establishing not only morphological features of expression and sequential organization, but also common text-semantic and text-pragmatic functions discernable in a variety of expressions.

For other characteristic features relating to content, intention, context, etc., I turn to W. Janzen who isolated features that are specific to what he calls the "hôy-pericopes" introduced by the "hôy-formula."[35] In using this terminology he is concerned to make it clear that he was not discovering a pre-prophetic hôy-genre. He arrived at what he called three essential "contextual" features:

(1) A characterization of the addressee, either from within Israel or representing a foreign nation, as one who acts in self-reliant independence of the sovereignty of Yahweh. This may manifest itself simply in false security, or in behavior defiant of covenant obligations towards the poor and needy, or in acts of national-political disloyalty to Yahweh.

(2) A "Day of the Lord" context within which the self-styled sovereignty will be confronted by the greater sovereignty of Yahweh in a terrifying visitation.

(3) This confrontation is often expressed in a manner approximating the *Talionsstil*, the style of declaration of revenge, frequently to the point of "reversal of imagery" which, in its most pointed form, takes on the pattern: "You have done X; therefore X will be done to you."[36]

With these features Janzen finds that he is able to specify this unit of prophetic speech with greater exactness than the general category of prophetic Gerichtsrede. He notes that these characteristics are also found in prophetic contexts other than those of the hôy-formula, but argues as follows: "we contend that the immediate

---

[34] Gerstenberger 1962, 249-63.

[35] Janzen 1972, 81-82.

[36] Janzen 1972, 81-82.

hôy-context shows the contrast between the pinnacles of haughty self-reliance and the depths of humiliation on Yahweh's Day, often a contrast that extends into the very vocabulary, with a sharpness and concentration that—though present in other passages—does not characterize prophecy throughout and therefore attracts attention to its frequent presence in the hôy-pericope."[37]

For the purpose of establishing typicalities of a form mediated by sacred text through a Greek translation, I find it defensible to combine some of the observations of Gerstenberger (as outlined above) with those of Janzen. As already mentioned, my focus is not on the origin of the woe cry and how it came to be used in prophetic speech, but rather on how Paul would have met this as a form in the Greek OT. I shall attempt to locate the features identified above in the three text-dimensions previously explained.[38] In that they are the most universal and exhaustive dimensions of text these categories provide for a more adequate description and organization of the formal features. The features observed by Gerstenberger fall for the most part in the text-syntactic dimension, while those that Janzen has located fall for the most part in the text-semantic and text-pragmatic dimensions.

A. *Predominantly text-syntactic features:* (1) The common succession of a woe cry, (2) followed by one or more indictments formulated either as, e.g., οὐαὶ οἱ ἰσχύον-τες, κτλ. (Isa 5:22), or as, e.g., οὐαὶ αὐτοῖς ὅτι, κτλ. (Hos 7:13), and (3) followed by some expression of judgment, which may be explicit or implicit in the varied expressions such as threat, lament, ironical question, proverbial saying, rhetorical question, etc.

B. *Predominantly text-semantic features:* (1) One or more indictments which are generally a characterization of someone or some group as acting in self-reliant independence of the sovereignty of God, and (2) a judgment generally involving a reversal of imagery in expressing the confrontation, namely some idea of "you have done X; therefore X will be done to you."

C. *Predominantly text-pragmatic features:* (1) A "Day of the Lord" context when this self-reliant independence will be confronted by the greater sovereignty of God. (2) A concentration of intensity in the presentation of the themes mentioned under the text-semantic features.

---

[37] Janzen 1972, 82.
[38] See Johanson 1987, 7-8; Plett 1979, 52; Hellholm 1980, 22-27.

Hab 2:15-17 is presented here for the sake of illustration:

WOE CRY:

| (2:15-17) Ω | Woe |
|---|---|
| **INDICTMENTS (v. 15):** | |
| v. 15: ᾧ ὁ ποτίζων τὸν πλησίον αὐτοῦ ἀνατροπῇ θολερᾷ καὶ μεθύσκων, ὅπως ἐπιβλέπῃ ἐπὶ τὰ σπήλαια αὐτῶν. | (to) him who gives his neighbour to drink the foul dregs (of wine), and intoxicates (him) that he may look upon his private parts. |
| **JUDGMENT (vv. 16-17):** | |
| (v.16) πλησμονὴν ἀτιμίας ἐκ δόξης πίε καὶ σὺ καὶ διασαλεύθητι καὶ σείσθητι· ἐκύκλωσεν ἐπὶ σὲ ποτήριον δεξιᾶς κυρίου, καὶ συνήχθη ἀτιμία ἐπὶ τὴν δό-ξαν σου. (v. 17) διότι ἀσέβεια τοῦ Λι-βάνου καλύψει σε, καὶ ταλαιπωρία θηρίων πτοήσει σε διὰ αἵματα ἀνθρώπων καὶ ἀσεβείας γῆς καὶ πόλεως καὶ πάντων τῶν κατοικούντων αὐτήν. | Drink your fill of disgrace instead of glory. Shake, heart, and quake! The cup of the Lord's right hand came (aorist!) around upon you, and dishonor gathered (aorist!) on your glory. For the impiety of Libanus will cover you, and distress from wild beasts will terrify you on account of the blood of men and of the impiety of land and city and of all who dwell in it. |

## 5. The Woe-Oracular Character of 1 Thessalonians 2:15-16

Turning to 1 Thess 2:15-16 we must ask if there is sufficient evidence of the above-mentioned features to posit a typicality that fits with the woe-oracle in spite of the absent woe cry.

| INDICTMENTS (2:14c-16b): | |
|---|---|
| (v. 14c) τῶν Ἰουδαίων, (v. 15) τῶν καὶ τὸν κύριον ἀποκτεινάντων Ἰησοῦν καὶ τοὺς προφήτας καὶ ἡμᾶς ἐκδιωξάντων καὶ θεῷ μὴ ἀρεσκόντων καὶ πᾶσιν ἀνθρώποις ἐναντίων, (v. 16) κωλυόντων ἡμᾶς τοῖς ἔθνεσιν λαλῆσαι ἵνα σωθῶσιν, εἰς τὸ ἀναπληρῶσαι αὐτῶν τὰς ἁμαρτίας πάν-τοτε. | the Jews, who killed both the Lord Jesus and the prophets, and drove us out, and do not please God, and are contrary to all men; forbidding us to speak to the Gentiles that they may be saved; so as to fill up their sins always. |

| JUDGMENT (2:16c): | |
|---|---|
| (v. 16c) ἔφθασεν δὲ ἐπ᾿ αὐτοὺς ἡ ὀργὴ εἰς τέλος. | But the wrath came upon them utterly. |

Regarding the features in the text-semantic and text-pragmatic dimensions, the indictments clearly characterize the offending "Jews" as acting in self-reliant independance over against God. This is even made explicit in the clause "and do not please God." The feature of reversal is also present, although not explicitly expressed in the imagery. The death they had meted out to Jesus and the prophets and their obstruction of the gospel of salvation to the Gentiles finds a reversal in the "wrath" they should themselves suffer. Furthermore, although it has now obtained Christian dimensions, the "Day of the Lord" context (see 1 Thess 5:2) is also obviously present in the reference to "wrath". Finally, also present is the sharpness and intensity of the contrast between the height of human self-reliance and the depths of humiliation before God which Janzen has observed. This is underlined by the succession of participial clauses expressing the indictments and the independent sentence at the end that climactically gives the judgment.

Regarding structural traits in the text-syntactic dimension, there is, of course, no οὐαί, but there is an identifying expression together with indictments that are expressed in a sustained series of participial clauses followed by an expression of judgment. The absence of οὐαί could possibly find a plausible explanation in view of the rhetorical strategy involved. As mentioned above, in 2:15-16 Paul is using what Greco-Roman rhetoricians would understand as a vituperative digression.[39] Consequently, the main point he was trying to make does not lie in the digression. To have ended the sentence at 2:14 with Ἰουδαίων and started 2:15 with οὐαὶ αὐτοῖς, ὅτι, κτλ. would have given the digressive material the kind of prominence it was not meant to have.

The participial form of the indictments would appear to be primarily due to the grammatical strategy Paul uses to realize the digression. On first sight this would seem to deter seeing any formal evidence here for a typical woe-oracle feature. On the other hand, the exceptional concentration of the participial clauses is not without weight in favour of such a connection.

## 6. Ἔφθασεν *as a Proleptic Aorist*

The upshot of the preceding observations is that they make a plausible case for a very concerted use of prophetic language and style in 1 Thess 2:15-16. This of

---

[39] See note 8 above.

course does not prove that Paul is using the aorist ἔφθασεν proleptically, but it certainly increases the probability of such a usage. A look at a number of woe-oracles in the OT where explicit threats express the judgment element shows that the threats may be expressed either by the imperfect or perfect verb in the Hebrew and, for the most part, either by a future or an aorist verb in the Greek.

| Isa 5:9 | imperfect יִהְיוּ | as future ἔσονται. |
| Isa 5:24 | imperfect יִהְיֶה | as future ἔσται. |
| Isa 5:24 | imperfect יַעֲלֶה | as future ἀναβήσεται. |
| Isa 28:3 | imperfect תֵּרָמַסְנָה | as future καταπατηθήσεται. |
| Isa 31:3 | imperfect יַטֶּה | as future ἐπάξει. |
| Zeph 3:5 | imperfect יִתֵּן | as future δώσει. |
| Hab 2:16 | imperfect תִּסּוֹב | as aorist ἐκύκλωσεν followed by συνήχθη. |
| Isa 31:2 | imperfect וַיָּבֵא | as aorist ἦγεν. |
| Isa 28:2 | perfect הִנִּיחַ | as future ποιήσει. |
| Isa 28:4 | perfect וְהָיְתָה | as future ἔσται. |
| Isa 30:5 | perfect הֹבִאישׁ | as future κοπιάσουσιν. |
| Isa 31:2 | perfect וְקָם | as future ἐπαναστήσεται. |
| Isa 5:13 | perfect גָּלָה | as aorist αἰχμάλωτος ... ἐγενήθη. |
| Isa 5:13 | perfect רָעֵב | as aorist ἐγενήθη νεκρῶν. |
| Isa 30:4 | perfect הָיוּ | as present εἰσιν. |

The general interchangability of these future and aorist tenses is interpreted as supporting a proleptic use of the aorists. This is particularly underlined by the observation that in some of the threats both the aorist and the future can stand side by side: Isa 5:13-15; 31:2 and Hab 2:16-17. In fact, a close parallel in sentiment and formulation to ἔφθασεν δὲ ἐπ᾿ αὐτοὺς ἡ ὀργὴ εἰς τέλος may be seen in Hab 2:16 presented above: ἐκύκλωσεν ἐπὶ σὲ ποτήριον δεξιᾶς κυρίου ("the cup of the right hand of the Lord came round upon you"). In the following verse (2:17) the remainder of the judgment is then expressed in the future tense: "For the impiety of Libanus will cover (καλύψει) you, and distress from wild beasts will terrify (πτοήσει) you," etc.[40]

In addition to these observations there is one instance of what may be a proleptic

---

[40] Since we are viewing the OT here from the perspective of Paul as reader and hearer of the LXX, the debate over whether or not there is a Hebrew prophetic perfect need not be addressed. See, e.g., Kautzsch 1910, 312-13 who argues for a use of this kind of perfect, pointing to Isa 5:13; 9:1ff.; 10:28; 11:9; 19:7; Job 5:20 and 2 Chr 20:37. Nyberg 1952, 280 says it does not exist.

aorist in a woe-oracle in the NT. This is found in Jude 11: οὐαὶ αὐτοῖς, ὅτι τῇ ὁδῷ τοῦ Κάιν ἐπορεύθησαν καὶ τῇ πλάνῃ τοῦ Βαλαὰμ μισθοῦ ἐξεχύθησαν καὶ τῇ ἀντιλογίᾳ τοῦ Κόρε ἀπώλοντο ("Woe to them, for they have walked in the way of Cain, and have plunged into Balaam's error for gain, and have perished in Korah's rebellion"). The reference is clearly being made to contemporary people who were seen by the author as perverting both the faith and the life of the community. The first two aorists may quite naturally be taken as perfective aorists, since the contents clearly indicate that indictments are being expressed. The third element, however, "they have perished in Korah's rebellion," due to the sense of the verb, should be seen as the concluding judgment in spite of the three-fold formal parallelism. As such, the aorist ἀπώλοντο naturally acquires a proleptic sense. The message is that "they will perish just as in Korah's rebellion."

## 7. Summary and Conclusion

In summary, there appears to be evidence for seeing 1 Thess 2:15-16 as reflecting the form of the OT woe-oracle. A significant constellation of common features was shown to be present so as to be able to establish a dominancy of features that typically distinguish this form. Also, parallels of a significant cluster of vocabulary and motifs in common with the woe-oracle in Matt 23:29-36 and Luke 11:47-51 suggest a connection via a common tradition and provide an additional incentive for seeing the passage as shaped by woe-oracular contours. Given this strong presence of prophetic language and style, the suitability and probability of taking ἔφθασεν as a proleptic aorist in ἔφθασεν δὲ ἐπ᾽ αὐτοὺς ἡ ὀργὴ εἰς τέλος is significantly enhanced. For, as indicated above, the "judgment" part of the woe-oracle in the Septuagint was expressed with either an aorist or a future tense. In fact, in some oracles the aorist and future are used side by side. While the proleptic aorist is rare in the NT, there is evidence of its use in a woe-oracle in Jude 11 and it shares the same dramatic quality of the aorist Paul uses in Gal 5:4.

The dramatic quality of this usage would tip the scales of probability in favour of taking εἰς τέλος in the sense of "utterly" or "fully and finally." There are a number of instances in the Septuagint of εἰς τέλος with this sense, including a couple in contexts where "anger" or "wrath" is expressed in terms of judgment.[41] The clause, then, would be literally rendered as "The wrath came upon them fully and finally." Such a translation, of course, is awkward in English. It would be better to allow εἰς τέλος, taken in the sense of "utterly" or "fully and finally" to express the dramatic quality and simply translate ἔφθασεν with the future: "The wrath will come upon

---

[41] See, e.g., 2 Chr 12:12 and Ps 73:1. See also Ackroyd 1968-69, 126.

them fully and finally."

Finally, granted the authenticity of 2:15-16 and the use of woe-oracular features in it to realize a persuasive strategy of *vituperatio*,[42] we are provided with another glimpse into the literary and rhetorical complexity of Paul in whom the Greco-Roman and Jewish worlds came together in a remarkable way.

## *Bibliography*

Ackroyd, P.R. 1968-69: "נצדה—εἰς τέλος", *ET* 80 (1968-69) 126.

Baur, F.C. 1875: *Paul the Apostle of Jesus Christ. His Life and Works, His Epistles and His Doctrine* (Trans. by A. Menzies), Vol. II., London: Williams and Norgate 1875.

de Beaugrande, R.-A., and W. U. Dressler 1981: *Introduction to Text Linguistics* (Longman Linguistic Library, 26), London and New York: Longman 1981.

Best, E. 1972: *A Commentary on the First and Second Epistles to the Thessalonians* (BNTC), 2nd ed. (1st ed., 1972), London: Adam and Charles Black 1972.

Blass, F. and A. Debrunner 1961: *A Greek Grammar of the New Testament and Other Early Christian Literature* (Trans. and rev. from the 9th-10th German ed. by R.W. Funk), Chicago: University of Chicago Press 1961.

Bruce, F. F. 1982: *1 & 2 Thessalonians* (Word Biblical Commentary 45), Waco: Word Books 1982.

Buss, M. J. 1974: "The Study of Forms", in: J. Hayes (ed.), *Old Testament Form Criticism*, San Antonio: Trinity University Press 1974, 1-56.

Clark, K. W. 1940: "Realised Eschatology", in: *JBL* 59 (1940) 367-83.

Clifford, R. J. 1966: "The Use of Hôy in the Prophets", in: *CBQ* 28 (1966) 458-64.

Collins, R. F. 1979: "A propos the Integrity of 1 Thess", in: *EThL* 55 (1979) 67-106.

Dibelius, M.. 1937: *An die Thessalonicher I II. An die Philipper* (HNT 11), 3rd ed., Tübingen: Mohr (Paul Siebeck) 1937.

von Dobschütz, D. E. 1909: *Die Thessalonicher-Briefe* (KEK 10), 7th ed.[= repr. 1974], Göttingen: Vandenhoeck & Ruprecht 1909.

Donfried, K. P. 1984: "Paul and Judaism. 1 Thessalonians 2:13-16 as a Test Case", in: *Interp.* 38 (1984) 242-53.

Frame, J. E. 1912: *A Critical and Exegetical Commentary on the Epistles of St. Paul to the Thessalonians* (ICC), Edinburgh: T. & T. Clark 1912.

Fuller, R. H. 1954: *The Mission and Achievement of Jesus*. An Examination of the Presuppositions of New Testament Theology (SBT 12), London: SCM Press 1954.

Garland, D. E. 1979: *The Intention of Matthew 23* (NT.S 52), Leiden: Brill 1979.

Gerstenberger, E. 1962: "The Woe Oracles of the Prophets", in: *JBL* 81 (1962) 249-63.

---

[42] Johanson 1987, 81-99, 145-53.

Gilliard, F. D. 1989: "The Problem of the Antisemitic Comma Between 1 Thessalonians 2.14 and 15", in: *NTS* 35 (1989) 481-502.

Gülich, E. and W. Raible 1977: *Linguistische Textmodelle*. Grundlagen und Möglichkeiten (UTB 130) Munich: Fink 1977.

Hartman, L. 1983: "Survey of the Problem of Apocalyptic Genre", in: D. Hellholm (ed.), *Apocalypticism in the Mediterranean World and the Near East*. Proceedings of the International Colloquium on Apocalypticism, Uppsala, Aug. 12-17, 1979, Tübingen: Mohr (Siebeck) 1983, 329-43.

Hellholm, D. 1980: *Das Visionenbuch des Hermas als Apokalypse*. Formgeschichtliche und texttheoretische Studien zu einer literarischen Gattung (CB.NT 13:1) Lund: CWK Gleerup 1980.

Holland, G. S. 1988: *The Tradition that You Received from Us: 2 Thessalonians in the Pauline Tradition* (HUTh 24), Tübingen: Mohr (Paul Siebeck) 1988.

Holtz, T. 1986: *Der Erste Brief an die Thessalonicher* (EKK 13) Zürich/Neukirchen-Vluyn: Benziger/Neukirchener Verlag 1986.

Janzen, W. 1972: *Mourning Cry and Woe Oracle* (BZAW 125), Berlin: de Gruyter 1972.

Johanson, B. C. 1987: *To All the Brethren*. A Text-Linguistic and Rhetorical Approach to I Thessalonians (CB.NT 16), Stockholm: Almqvist & Wiksell International 1987.

Kampling, R. 1993: "Eine auslegungsgeschichtliche Skizze zu 1 Thess 2,14-16", in: D.-A. Koch and H. Lichtenberger (eds.), *Begegnungen zwischen Christentum und Judentum in Antike und Mittelalter. Festschrift für Heinz Schreckenberg* (Schriften des Institutum Judaicum Delitzschianum 1), Göttingen: Vandenhoeck & Ruprecht 1993, 183-213.

Kautzsch, E. 1910: *Gesenius' Hebrew Grammar* (2nd ed. rev. in accordance with the 28th German ed. by A.E. Cowley), Oxford: Clarendon Press 1910.

Knierim, R. 1973: "Old Testament Form Criticism Reconsidered", in: *Interp.* 27 (1973) 435-68.

Kümmel, W. G. 1957: *Promise and Fulfilment*. The Eschatological Message of Jesus (SBT 23), London: SCM Press 1957.

Lausberg, H. 1973: *Handbuch der literarischen Rhetorik*. Eine Grundlegung der Literaturwissenschaft, 2nd ed. (1st ed. 1960) Munich: Hueber 1973.

Marshall, I. H. 1983: *1 and 2 Thessalonians* (NCeB), Grand Rapids, MI: Eerdmans 1983.

Moulton, J. H. and N. Turner 1963: *A Grammar of New Testament Greek*, Vol. III. Syntax, Edinburgh: T. & T. Clark 1963.

Nyberg, H. S. 1952: *Hebreisk Grammatik*, Stockholm: Almqvist & Wiksell 1952.

Orchard, J. B. 1938: "Thessalonians and the Synoptic Gospels", in: *Bib.* 19 (1938) 19-42.

Okeke, G. E. 1980-81: "I Thess ii. 13-16. The Fate of the Unbelieving Jews", in: *NTS* 27 (1980-81) 127-36.

Pearson, B. A. 1971: "1 Thessalonians 2:13-16: A Deutero-Pauline Interpolation", in: *HThR* 64 (1971) 79-94.

Plett, H. F. 1979: *Textwissenschaft und Textanalyse*. Semiotik, Linguistik, Rhetorik (UTB 328), 2nd ed. (1st ed. 1975), Heidelberg: Quelle & Meyer 1979.

Rigaux, B. 1956: *Saint Paul: Les Épîtres aux Thessaloniciens* (EtB), Paris: Librairie Lecoffre 1956.

Schoeps, H. J. 1950: "Die jüdischen Prophetenmorde", in: idem, *Aus früchristlicher Zeit*. Religionsgeschichtliche Untersuchungen, Tübingen: Mohr (Siebeck) 1950, 126-43.

Schippers, R. 1966: "The Pre-Synoptic Tradition in I Thessalonians II 13-16", in: *NT* 8 (1966) 223-34.

Schmidt, D. 1983: "1 Thess 2:13-16: Linguistic Evidence for an Interpolation", in: *JBL* 102 (1983) 269-79.

Stählin, G. 1967: "ὀργή", in: *TDNT*, Vol. 5., Grand Rapids, MI: Eerdmans 1967, 419-47.

Wank, G. 1966: "אוֹי" und "הוֹי", in: *ZAW* 78 (1966) 215-18.

Williams, J. G. 1967: "The Alas-Oracles of the Eighth Century Prophets", in: *HUCA* 38 (1967) 75-91.

Wolff, H. W. 1977: *Joel and Amos: A Commentary on the Books of the Prophets Joel and Amos*, Philadelphia, PN: Fortress Press 1977.

Wuellner, W. H. 1979: "Greek Rhetoric and Pauline Argumentation", in: W. R. Schoedel and R. L. Wilken (eds.): *Early Christian Literature and the Classical Intellectual Tradition*, FS for R. M. Grant (Théologie Historique 53) Paris 1979, 177-88.

Zerwick, M. 1963: *Biblical Greek* (SPIB 114), 8th edition adapted from the 4th Latin ed. by J. Smith, Rome: E Vicariatu Urbis 1963.

# James and Paraenesis, Reconsidered

## Wiard Popkes

## 1. The Heritage of Martin Dibelius

1.1. The combination of the terms "James" (i.e. the New Testament Epistle) and "paraenesis" invokes, at least traditionally in NT investigations, Martin Dibelius' heritage of classifying this writing.[1] In that tradition Jas is form-critically defined as a document of paraenetic teaching.[2] The approach implies primarily: (a) The text is incoherent; it is needless and useless to look for a compositional unity, since there is none. There are short disconnected units only, sometimes combined with brief elaborations. (b) The statements are of a general character, with no relation to a specific situation. Rather, the statements can be applied to varying situations, as anyone liked to serve him/herself. (c) The material is largely unoriginal, drawn from "international" sources. Dibelius added that Jas is a result of the need among early Christians to teach the (Gentile) converts appropriate Christian conduct. As Christianity was expecting the near return of the Lord, it was neither prepared to, nor interested in developing much of a daily life ethics of its own and hence relied largely upon Jewish (-Hellenistic) instruction of neophytes, which in itself had adopted quite a bit of Hellenistic material.

Jas became the example par excellence for New Testament paraenesis.[3] This approach presupposed, of course, a specific definition of paraenesis, achieved on form-critical grounds. For Dibelius[4] paraenesis is a form-critical category with typical features which can be demonstrated in the interpretation of Jas, as shown above. The prescriptive character of paraenesis is reflected in the many imperatives in Jas,

---

[1] Dibelius 1984, 13-23; cf. also Kürzdörfer 1966; von Lips 1990, 409f.; Thomas 1992, 258ff.; Blank 1981.

[2] As e.g. Kümmel 1983, 360; Vielhauer 1975, 571-573; Conzelmann/Lindemann 1989, §12,3; Strecker, 1991 and 1992; Küchler 1979, 569; Schnackenburg 1963, 80-82; Nieder 1956.

[3] Cf. Schnackenburg 1986/89 II 202f.; von Lips 1990, 28. Berger 1984a, 147, on the other hand, e.g. denies that Jas is a paraenesis throughout.

[4] Dibelius 1971, 238ff.; 1931, 207-242; 1975, 140ff.

the wisdom-tradition in the listing of proverbial statements.

1.2. There have been, of course, quite a few different approaches to the Epistle of James, in particular with regard to the structure and anteceding patterns[5], as well as to the placement of the document in early church history and to its authorship.[6] Questions of methodology have been raised, promoting the application of rhetorics[7], epistolography,[8] theories of communication, and the like as paradigmata of interpretation.[9] However, in all these approaches "paraenesis" does not nearly play the role as in Dibelius' and his successors' work. Does this mean that there can be no other combination of "James" and "paraenesis" than the one of this tradition? Does the application of paraenesis to Jas more or less stand or fall with Dibelius' position?

The purpose of this investigation is threefold: (a) To help clarifying the category "paraenesis", (b) to demonstrate the obstacles to Dibelius' treatment of Jas, and (c) to develop a different relation between Jas and a different concept of paraenesis. The character and intent of the Epistle will hopefully receive greater illumination along this way.

---

[5] Cf. Popkes 1986, 9ff.; Baasland 1988; Davids 1988; Church 1990; Pearson 1989; Via 1969; Jones 1969; Marshall 1968. Some presuppose a Jewish pattern, usually midrashic: Beck 1973; Blenker 1967; Gertner 1964; Jacob 1975; Meyer 1930; Obermüller 1972; Prockter 1989; Spitta 1896; cf. also Hanson 1978/79. Forbes 1972 finds thirteen "convenient little sections" to be read aloud; Crotty 1992 regards Jas as a halakha on πειρασμός (cf. Sigal 1981); Schille 1977 as a tract; Kürzdörfer 1966 as a παράκλησις in worship; Lohse 1957 as an *enchiridion*. Numerous other attempts in finding a sensible structure have been made, as is demonstrated in the sections given in the commentaries (cf. Popkes 1986, 19). Some proceed form-critically (as Baasland 1982), some distinguish between main and subordinate sections (as Fry 1978; cf. Terry 1992), some look for a "unifying theme" (Hiebert 1978 and 1984; cf. Schille 1977), some regard Jas 1:2-12 (or a similar portion) as a kind of inclusive prelude to the rest of the epistle (as von Lips 1990, 412ff.). Cf. also Hartmann 1942; Rustler 1952; Songer 1969 and 1986; Sato 1991.

[6] The dating in the lifetime of the Lord's brother James has been maintained by Mußner 1981; Hengel 1987; Adamson 1984 and 1989; Hartin 1991, and many others. — A "two-layered stage in the production of the letter" is favoured e.g. by Martin 1988 (quotation: lxxvii).

[7] E.g. Baasland 1982; Watson 1993a and 1993b. Cf. also Übelacker 1989.

[8] Francis 1970; cf. Stowers 1986, 94ff.; Klauck 1991, 73f. Burge 1977 refers to poetry. On the style: Westhuizen 1991; Wifstrand 1948. The function of certain images is discussed by Spencer 1989.

[9] Cf. Wuellner 1978; Baasland 1988.

## 2. Research on Paraenesis

2.1. Terminology is defined by history, i.e. by life and its usage of language. In the case of the history of the term "paraenesis" the result is diverging: on the one hand we observe a rather loose and general meaning, viz. "(moral) exhortation"[10]; on the other hand we have at least two more specific definitions, which are the form-critical one by Dibelius and, more recently, a sociological one according to the model of Victor Turner.[11]

There is no unanimity or agreement as to what the term "paraenesis" exactly stands for; hence it is necessary to indicate one's interpretation. The time may be gone to work towards a general re-definition of the term[12]; but if we use it, we must be aware of the semantic tools we apply. The very use of an "ancient", Greek word, applied to a text of the same time and culture (i.e. the New Testament), requires at least some attention to the background of our terminology. Even if a term has developed its own meaning in the course of history, it is still appropriate to rethink it time and again; this becomes imperative if, as in the case of "paraenesis", the very choice of a term indicates a deliberate reference to a specific background (viz. the ancient Greek) and, even more so, if different meanings emerged from history. In NT interpretation the use of "paraenesis" as a heuristic and defining term has received widespread acceptance. It is true that the Greek word παραίνεσις (verb: παραινέω) hardly occurs in the New Testament itself.[13] But this fact does not preclude the application of a term for discerning and describing certain events or facts.[14] Even more important than using a terminology which should not deviate too much from its origins is the awareness of what a term does *not*, or at least not necessarily, imply, lest we cast our terminology in too firm a mould. We must not be bound by strings which are more arbitrary than their authors think they are. This exactly is the problem with Dibelius' definition of paraenesis.[15]

---

[10] As indicated e.g. in the title of Malherbe 1986. Von Lips 1990, 394: "any kind of exhortation (Ermahnung)".

[11] Turner 1967a/b; 1972, applied in particular in the conference volume Semeia 50: Perdue/Gammie 1990.

[12] This is the opinion of Thomas 1992, 270 n.78.

[13] Only in Acts 27:9.22. The same is true for the Septuagint: Wis 8:9; 2 Macc 7:24-26; 3 Macc 5:17; 7:12.

[14] A similar case could be made with the terms "theology" or "ethics".

[15] Kürzdörfer 1966, 121; Baasland 1982, 119: Dibelius' definition of Jas as paraenesis "hat sich im Lauf der Zeit als allzu vieldeutig und ideologisch belastet erwiesen, um fruchtbar sein zu können". (Baasland himself perfers "hortatio").

2.2. For centuries "paraenesis" was used in a non-technical way, even far into modern times.[16] Ancient Greek lexicographers of a later period subsumed παραίνεσις/ παραινέω under "advice".[17] PsPlato *Defin.* 413C formulates: "An advice (συμβούλευσις) is a παραίνεσις to someone concerning a practice how to act". Ammonios 132 (= no. 455 Nickau) specifies: παραίνεσις is a kind of advice (συμβουλή) which does not have to expect opposition because it urges something evident, good, logic, and necessary.[18] The same opinion is found in PsLibanios' (p. 15 Weichert) defintion of a "paraenetic letter".[19] Apart from such a general direction παραίνεσις "is practically without formal definition".[20] Its usage and semantic field provide enough clarity, though, for describing its character.[21] Παραίνεσις, derived from the root αἰνέω (to praise, approve, recommend), signals positive, constructive, friendly, helpful connotations; παραίνεσις is benevolent advice. At the same time it implies authority, be it in the moral or logical evidence of the message or in the quality, competence and expertise of the speaker. As a rule parainesis is given from someone experienced (teacher, old person, sage, strategist, king, religious leader) to the

---

[16] Cf. Thomas 1992, 239ff.; Burgess 1902, 230; Hartlich 1889. —Surprisingly enough the traditional theological, historical and philosophical dictionaries do not contain an entry "paraenesis"; this is the case in all the editions of RE (1854-68, 1877-88, 1896-1913) and RGG (1909-13; 1927-31; 1956-65), in PW (1894-1963) and Encyclopedia of Religion and Ethics (1908-26); equally in the first editions of LThK (1930-38) and EKL (1956-61), then changing (Schnackenburg 1963; Paulsen 1992). Brief contributions are found in Lexikon der alten Welt (Gigon 1965a) and Historisches Wörterbuch der Philosophie (Bartsch 1989). —Cf. also the rather general use of the term by Kooy 1926; Gaiser 1959; Latacz 1977; Reinmuth 1985; Schmidt 1986; Bowe 1988.

[17] This is rightly taken up by Hartlich 1889; Berger 1984a, 36ff.; Stowers 1986, 91ff.

[18] Cf. Quinn 1990 and his emphasis on "irrefutability".

[19] PsLibanios distinguishes altogether 41 types of letters. Demetrios (pp.1-12 Weichert) has 21, no paraenetic one among them; however, no. 11 (symbouleutic) is very much the same in terms of content.

[20] Burgess 1902, 230 n. 2.

[21] παραίνεσις/παραινέω is used particularly by Greek historians, philosophers and poets. It is found rather seldom in papyri, more often in inscriptions (cf. on this Quinn 1990, 192 and 203, who rightly infers the "solemn, literary character of the terminology" which belongs to the vocabulary "of public charges and recommendations"). —The semantic field encompasses terms of advice, exhortation and challenge (as παράκλησις, συμβουλή, προτρεπτικός, νουθεσία, παρακέλευσις), education and teaching (παιδεία, ὑπόθεσις), request (δέησις), understanding and consent (σωφροσύνη, ὁμολογία), advantage (συμφέρον), benevolence (εὔνοια), difference of age (νεότεροι), and action (πρᾶξις—in all these references the verbs, adjectives and other derivates are included by implication). Cf. Fiore 1986 and my forthcoming study of "Paraenesis and New Testament" (to appear in Stuttgarter Bibelstudien).

inexperienced (student, young person, beginner etc.).[22] It is handed on to those who need to receive it. Parainesis conveys courage, guidance, and protection; it prepares the way, exhorts, admonishes, warns; it aims at thoughtful acceptance.[23] Examples serve that very purpose.[24] Typical situations are all kinds of important steps to be taken, as in government, war, conversion, growing up to maturity, both individually and collectively.[25]

Παραίνεσις did not become a special topic in rhetorics.[26] It was used in philosophical ethics.[27] It did not become, however, a term denoting a literary genre.[28] Its application in epistolography (cf. above about PsLibanios' paraenetic letter) clearly points in a functional, not a literary direction. In this regard παραίνεσις differs from its neighbour προτρεπτικός which indeed could mean a literary genre and was used even as a book-title.[29] Προτρεπτικός was also more widely used, often as a techni-

---

[22] Hence e.g. the frequent references by the historians to competent advice in war, in ruling a state, or the like: Thucydides II 45.88; IV 59; VII 63.69; Herodot I 80; Josephus *Bellum* 1,135. 246.259.434; 5,87.375; 6,240; Antiquities 5,243; 10,117, et al. Acts 27:9.22 follow this very direction (advice in a situation of need from a competent person, which better should not be disregarded).

[23] Much of this is reflected in the tradition of the Hellenistic moralists: Malherbe 1986 and 1992; Perdue 1981b and 1990a; Meeks 1986. Cf. also the material in Philo *Agr.* 84; *Virt.* 47.163ff.; *Fug.* 142.170; *Spec. Leg.* I 299; IV 131 (Quinn 1990, 192f.; Thomas 1992, 248) and ClemAlex *Paidagogos* I 1-2 (this text should not be overestimated, though, as Thomas 1992, 248f., and Stachowiak 1983, 178 n. 5, tend to do, in my regard).

[24] Cf. especially Fiore 1986; Perdue 1981b; also Boer 1962; Larsson 1962; Price 1975; Wolbert 1981; Haufe 1992.

[25] This is a special emphasis by various authors in Semeia 50: Perdue, Quinn, Levine, Williams, Attridge, Camp, Robbins (all 1990). Such situations may arise between e.g. teacher and student(s), patriarch (who is about to pass away) and descendants (fare-well discourse, testimonium, legacy), religious leader and neophytes, not unfrequently accompanied by *rites de passage*. Cf. furthermore Perdue 1981a; Karris 1971 and 1973.

[26] Burgess 1902, 231; Berger 1984b, 1075; Thomas 1992, 257; von Heintze 1965, 2220. Quintilian IX 103 has an occasional reference to "*exhortatio*, παραινετικός". Opera like Aristotle's "Rhetoric" can do without using the stem παραιν-, according to the indices in Kassel, 1976, 237, and E. M. Cope/J. E. Sandys 1877.

[27] This is usually documented by Seneca *ep.* 95,1 (cf. Thomas 1992, 246). His *ep.* 89,13 on the history of this philosophical topos contains a critical (!) remark on Ariston of Chios, which is largely identical with that in Sextus Empiricus (Ariston of Chios *frgm.* 356=SVF I 80): Ariston banned exhortation from philosophy and referred it to education.

[28] The list of writings in Xenocrates Platonicus (Diogenes Laertius IV 2,11) mentions συγγράμματα καὶ ἔπη καὶ παραινέσεις, i.e. treatises, poems and exhortations, but the latter may just mean hortative proverbs or the like. There is no other reference to parainesis denoting the form of a written document. On PsIsocrates *Demonicea* 3-5, which cannot bear the burden of proof either, see below.

[29] Diogenes Laertius has a whole list, beginning with Antisthenes and Aristotle. The list is not even complete (as e.g. on Isocrates). Cf. Burgess 1902, 229ff., especially 234; Hartlich 1889, 209.

cal term; cf. the discussion by the encyclopedians.[30] Sometimes a distinction between προτρεπτικός and παραίνεσις is made by philosophers and others in the direction that προτρεπτικός calls to a new way of life, parainesis admonishes to continue in that life.[31] Such a difference of emphasis can be obversed indeed, though not persistently; it should not be disregarded that the similarity between the two terms is greater than the difference.

2.3. A new development began around 1900. Dibelius was primarily influenced by Paul Wendland's investigation of PsIsocrates' *Speech to Demonikos*.[32] He also mentions[33] A. von Harnack[34] and A. Seeberg[35] as his predecessors; later R. Vetschera[36] provided additional material. Dibelius developed the programme in his commentaries and monographs on 1 Thess 4-5 (1911), Col 3-4 (1912), the Pastoral Epistles (1913), Q (1919)[37] and James (1921). The essential point of departure and key text was, as mentioned above, PsIsocrates *Demonicea*, usually correlated to Seneca *epistulae* 89 and 95.[38] PsIsocrates writes about his intention to compose a παραίνεσις, not "protreptic words", not a παράκλησις. He asserts that he wants to educate the young generation, not to "call (παρακαλέω) to λόγος". This is clearly polemical against the sophists or even against Aristotle's *Protreptikos*. The formulation should not be over-interpreted. Neither was the terminological distinction continued[39], nor did παραίνεσις become a literary category. We must not, therefore, deduce from the actual shape of *Demonicea*, which is indeed a collection of educational and sapiental maxims for select usage, that this is *the* form of paraenesis. The argument that *Demonicea* become widely used is not conclusive.[40] *Demonicea* simply does not provide a strong enough basis to build a whole theory upon. The mere fact that there are a number of wisdom collections etc. in various

---

[30] Hesychios discusses προτρεπτικός, not παραινετικός: Burgess 1902, 231.

[31] Stowers 1986, 91ff., cf. Gigon 1965a/b. Perdue 1990a, 23, relates προτρεπτικός to conversion, παραίνεσις to confirmation.

[32] Wendland 1905.

[33] Dibelius 1931, 212f.

[34] In a short note: von Harnack, 1909, I 173 n.2, in connection with *Did.* and related writings. Cf. also Grafe 1904, 47f.

[35] Seeberg 1906, 1908 and 1966 (originally 1903).

[36] Vetschera 1910/12.

[37] Dibelius 1971.

[38] Cf. Cancik 1967; Cecchi 1961; Rosenkranz 1966; Wefelmeier 1962.

[39] Cf. Thomas 1992, 257.

[40] Contra Thomas 1992, 252.

ancient cultures cannot prove Dibelius' case either.[41] This does not mean to deny that such collections could be used for paraenetic purposes; what is in question is the far-reaching equation of the two. A functional interpretation of *Demonicea* 3-5 is more in line with the general ancient understanding of παραίνεσις than a form-critical one.

2.4. In the course of time a number of modifications and corrections have been raised to Dibelius' position. Some prefer to abandon the term paraenesis altogether in NT interpretation, replacing it by παράκλησις.[42] Some started with Dibelius' concept, had to expand it along the way, however.[43] Some suggest much more caution in applying the term to the NT texts[44]; Rudolf Schnackenburg e.g. reduces the applicability virtually (and remarkably) to Jas only.[45] Some criticized Dibelius' crude restriction of paraenesis to general ("usuell") matters, which would exclude "actual" references to the situation.[46] Positive attention has been paid increasingly to conversion, baptism and neophyte instruction ("catechism") as the pivotal "Sitz im Leben" of NT paraenesis.[47] Over against Dibelius' opinion of a rather loose and superficial "christification" of "international" material the authentic Christian origin and character of the bulk of the NT tradition as well as of its "motives and motifs"[48] has been emphasized.[49]

---

[41] The range of the usually quoted literary products, their forms, styles, times and cultural backgrounds, is extremely wide. It includes inter alia Hesiod *Erga* (cf. Schmidt 1986); Theognis; Isocrates *or.* 2-3; Epictetus *diss*; PsPhocylides (cf. van der Horst 1978a/b; Thomas 1992); Prov; Wis; Tob 4.12; parts of *Test XII* (cf. de Jonge 1989), *Ethiopic and Slavonic Enoch*; 1QS 3-4; *Abot*. Cf. Zeller 1983; Küchler 1979; von Lips 1990; Perdue 1990b; Wilson 1991; Lincke 1911. Much of this is wisdom tradition. The desire to collect life experiences in proverbial and other clear-cut forms, easy to remember, is a universal cultural phenomenon and should not be equated with paraenesis tradition as such; paraenesis *may* adopt such a form, but not always nor necessarily.

[42] A number of scholars prefer παράκλησις rather than παραίνεσις as a leading term in NT interpretation: Schniewind 1946/47; Schlink 1956; Schlier 1972 and 1987; Grabner-Haider 1967; Stuhlmacher 1989; Schnackenburg 1986/89 II 8; cf. Mußner 1988. Παρακαλεῖν/παράκλησις is indeed much more frequent in the NT, but at the same time much more differentiated as well. Cf. Bjerkelund 1967; Thomas 1983b.

[43] E.g. Thyen 1955. Cf. Schrage 1961.

[44] Schnackenburg 1963; Berger 1984a, 36ff.; 1984b.

[45] Schnackenburg 1986/89 II 202.

[46] Ortkemper 1980, 11ff.; Schrage 1961, 42ff.

[47] Which was promoted by Dibelius himself (1971, 239ff.), but was observed by many others from various vantage points, as Seeberg 1966, 1906 and 1908; Carrington 1940; Selwyn 1961; Dodd 1968a/b; Schnackenburg 1986/89 I - 14 and II 61.77.202.227.

[48] Rigaux 1956, 184-194; Nieder 1956; Haufe 1964; Merk 1968; Romaniuk 1968; Cruz 1990.

[49] Schnackenburg 1963 and 1986/89; Hahn 1981; Schrage 1961 and 1989.

2.5. Two elements in Klaus Berger's investigations[50] deserve particular attention. First, he subsumes paraenesis under "symbouleutische Gattungen", which links the term more closely to its original Greek setting. Second, he underlines—among several other forms[51]—the "postconversional speech of exhortation."[52] Berger does not really distinguish between form and function; but at least the functional element of paraenesis receives greater weight.

Johannes Thomas, too, highlights the functional aspect.[53] The process of communication is what is really essential. Paraenesis intends to win a person or a group, on the basis of shared convictions, by exhortations and rules, to an appropriate conduct of practical life; usually the process turns out to be supportive for the underlying conviction.[54]

The functional essence (not just aspect) of paraenesis has been moved to the fore by several American scholars as well: Leo Perdue, Abraham Malherbe, Kent Stowers, John Gammie, Harold Attridge, Vernon Robbins *et al.*[55] The first point of approach is "Hellenistic moralism",[56] the elements being: reference to something known and accepted; personal relationship, especially between teacher and student; importance of personal examples[57]. The second point is the distinction between προτρεπτικός and παραίνεσις in the sense that the latter confirms what has been accepted and established already, thus placing paraenesis in a post-conversion situation.[58] Most influential became a third element, viz. the sociological model of Victor Turner; it is prevalent throughout the conference volume "Semeia 50".[59] The model depicts the transition from one group, conviction and position to another, thus a conversion, passing through the stages of separation (marginal), "on the threshold" (liminal), and re-integration (post-liminal or -conversional). Usually the transition occurs from a larger group (*societas*) to a smaller, more specific one (*communitas*). Paraenesis accompanies the whole process by advice, admonition and comfort, supported by *rites de passage*. Paraenesis can have different functional directions, both subversive towards the former context, and constructive towards

---

[50] Berger 1984a, 36ff.; 1984b.

[51] Actually too many, diversifying paraenesis into a number of bits and pieces; cf. von Lips 1990, 360.

[52] Berger 1984a, 40, starting with 1 Thess 4:2, concentrating on 1 John.

[53] Thomas 1992, 269ff.; in some degree he still leans on Dibelius, however (272).

[54] Thomas 1992, 271f.

[55] Perdue 1981a/b; 1990a/b; Malherbe 1986 and 1992; Stowers 1986; the others in Perdue/Gammie 1990.

[56] Cf. note 23.

[57] Cf. note 24.

[58] Cf. note 31.

[59] Cf. note 11.

the new. Paraenesis then renders guidance, stability and continuity. The model can be easily applied to subsequent new situations of transition, such as the testamental fare-well discourse before death or the passing through doctrinal, physical and other difficulties.[60] The model has, of course, immediate relations to conversion, the inception of faith, baptism etc.

2.6. K.-W. Niebuhr pursued "the form of concrete paraenesis" in Judaism.[61] He does not unfold his concept of parenesis; his interest is, rather, the form, contents and usage of "catechetic" texts in Judaism. Such texts were needed for instructing both the Jewish less educated people and the converts.[62] A flexible form was developed, starting from key texts (such as the decalogue), applied differently in changing situations, in order to provide a handy summary of what it means to be a Jew. Niebuhr deliberately does not extend his investigation into the NT; but the material connection is evident.

## 3. Characteristics of Paraenesis

Which is the situation then with regard to the understanding of paraenesis, and to which results does it lead us? In which sense can we adequately relate the term to Jas? The following aspects should serve as guiding principles, as I would evaluate the process of research.

3.1. Paraenesis, being "moral exhortation" of various kinds, is first of all a functional term. Paraenesis has the function of securing a steady and desired development, providing guidance in situations of transition and decision where clear and reliable advice is needed.

3.2. Paraenesis is not a term for a literary genre. A form-critical approach cannot adequately serve as a key to define paraenesis. The term cannot, therefore, be attached to certain texts only, which would fit the marks of a disconnected series of independent sapiental insights of a general character. The verdict that paraenetic texts are incoherent and non-situational *per se* can no longer be maintained.

---

[60] These latter aspects go beyond the scope of Semeia 50. The whole range of testamental literature thus becomes relevant for paraenesis, in the NT e.g. John 13-17 or Matt 24-25; likewise Acts 20, the Pastoral Epistles (especially 2 Tim), et al.

[61] Niebuhr 1987, the quotation p.1.

[62] Niebuhr 1987, 65, with reference to Delling 1974, 133-176 (143).

3.3. Paraenesis relates to "conversion" in more than one respect. Conversion as a process of decision and new direction requires trustworthy accompaniment. Paraenesis itself does not effect conversion[63]; it presupposes some kind of an encounter with people and what they stand for, which results in at least some significant change in the lives of the recipients.[64] Paraenesis is directive, path-leading, future-oriented, and in this sense an essential element of the whole process, both during and after the initial stage of conversion. Paraenesis intends to bring its addressees into the continuity of the experiences of its author, letting them share in what the speaker or writer regards as central for a successful life.[65] The semantic capacity of the term lent itself to such an application at several instances. The model of V. Turner[66] fits very well to this usage; it helps to further understand the social implications of guiding through conversion. It is no wonder that there is great unanimity among NT scholars about the "Sitz im Leben" of early Christian paraenesis, viz. "baptism", implying conversion, faith, new life, new communal relationships, ethics etc.

3.4. Paraenesis in the early church is documented first of all in texts which contain basic instructions to the neophytes.[67] With regard to the materials a certain tradition can be discerned at several instances. Several topoi[68] re-occur in a flexible fashion. This resembles the Jewish practice of developing comprehensive instruction in connection with key passages from Scripture.[69] Texts reflecting baptismal instruction (as Rom 6; Col 3; 1 Thess 4; Heb 5 and 1 Pet), or texts easily connected to that purpose (as Matt 5-7; Rom 12-15), demonstrate the variety of themes and scriptural references (especially decalogue[70], commandment of love[71]). We must not, however, confine the textual evidence to the so-called "latter parts of the epistles"; the sit-

---

[63] Cf. the distinction between παραίνεσις and προτρεπτικός, as mentioned in note 31.

[64] In such a description "conversion" would retain a fairly wide meaning, applicable even to non-religious experiences.

[65] The "speaker" being a leader, teacher, counsellor, testamentum or the like. Hence also the importance of the personal example (cf. note 23).

[66] As outlined in section II 5.

[67] With good reasons 1 Thess 4:1ff. has been the traditional starting point. —The neophyte tradition has been my major concern in connection both with paraenesis and Jas; cf. Popkes 1986, 136ff; 1989; 1990; 1992a/b.

[68] Cf. Bradley 1953. But the topoi are not collected at random in the NT! Baeumer 1973; Johnson 1983.

[69] Cf. Niebuhr 1987; Berger 1972.

[70] Berger 1972; Müller 1982; Vokes 1968.

[71] Lev 19 is one of the great chapters used for catechetical purposes, after all. Cf. Burchard 1990; Johnson 1982; Felder 1982; Grant 1947.

uation is much more manifold.[72] We must allow for greater variety in the epistolary devices, as can be demonstrated e.g. from 1 Cor, where Paul brings paraenesis along the way answering the Corinthian questions.[73] Various forms can be used to communicate paraenetic concerns; quite often Paul and others use prayers and blessings to indicate the very direction of their advice (e.g. 1 Thess 1:3ff.; 5:23f.). Furthermore texts like 1 John gain importance as "post-conversional exhortation". And even more, testamental passages like John 13-17; Acts 20:18ff. and 2 Tim add to the content and horizon of NT paraenesis.[74] On the other hand, traditional "major" forms as "Haustafel" and the catalogues of virtues and vices receive a more limited importance.[75]

---

[72] This can be well demonstrated by the discussion whether "the" paraenetical part of Gal begins in 5:1 or 5:13 or even later in 6:1. Cf. the commentaries and Merk 1969; Harnisch 1987; Nauck 1958. Recent rhetorical approaches have not completely changed the situation (cf. Harnisch 1987). —It seems to me that a review of methodology is required, both with regard to the structure of Gal and —even more so—to the theory that the (Pauline) letters have a latter, paraenetical part. The theory is usually documented by Rom and Gal; what about the other epistles? Even for Gal and Rom (note the parallel in 6:4.11ff. and chaps. 12-15, "newness of life") it does not really hold true.

[73] Cf. Probst 1991. — The review will have to include 1-2 Cor, Phil, Phlm as well as Col/Eph with their particular sections of baptismal paraenesis (Col 3 par.; cf. Luz 1989), the Pastoral Epistles with their testamental concern, 1 Pet with its references to the new birth, Heb with its mixture between dogmatic and paraenetical sections, and also 1 John (cf. Berger 1984a, 40).

[74] Cf. note 60.

[75] They have been presented as "the" forms of NT paraenesis (e.g. Conzelmann/Lindemann 1989, 136f.). —We should not overlook that there is just one extant Haustafel in the clear sense, viz. the one in Col 3-4! Eph 5 is an elaboration dependent on Col. It is true that there is a long and wide history behind the Haustafel, rooted in Greek philosophical teaching on social duties, oiconomics, Stoic ideas about *ordo* etc., adapted by Hellenistic Judaism (cf. Strecker 1989 and 1992; Fiedler 1986; Lührmann 1980/81; Yates 1991; Gielen 1990; Müller 1983; Thraede 1980; Schweizer 1976 and 1979; Schrage 1974/75; Goppelt 1973; Crouch 1972; Weidinger 1928). Indeed, all the components existed: triadic and pair structure, reciprocity, apodictic form, and the situation of the οἶκος— but "die charakteristische Kurzform der neutestamentlichen Haustafeln (ist) so nicht bezeugt" (Strecker 1989, 357). In Col/Eph all the addressees of the household code are Christians; this is at least partly different in 1 Pet 2-3 (cf. 1 Cor 7:10-17). Furthermore, here as in 1 Tim and Tit (cf. also 1 Pet 5; 1 John 2) some groups are missing, others are added, in particular the people of age and of public status (state, cf. Rom 13). The recent investigation by von Lips 1994 starts from 1 Pet and Tit, comparing then the observations with Col/Eph; the result is: Common to all the four epistles' material is an underlying scheme of post-baptismal paraenesis, encompassing several regions of life (church, house, society), the household code being a paraenetical topos of its own but not a "Gattung". — The adoption of catalogues of virtues and vices, especially in connection with baptismal instruction, creates much fewer problems (cf. Kamlah 1964; Wibbing 1959; Vögtle 1936). We should not disregard other lists, however, such as catalogues like Gal 3:28 (Rom 10:12; 1 Cor 9:19-21; Col 3:11; Gal 6:15) and the catalogues of hardships (cf. Fitzgerald 1988; M. Schiefer Ferrari 1991).

## *4. Observations in James*

4.1. Turning to the Epistle of James, several observations stand in conflict with Dibelius' coordination of this document and paraenesis, as the development of research has demonstrated.[76] First of all, for many scholars Jas purports a correction of a tradition which claims to be Pauline but in fact has run to an extreme position. Probably this is reflected not only in Jas 2:14-26 (the debate about faith and works)[77], but also in other parts, notably 2:1-13 (on faith and love).[78] "Pauline" problems are reflected in 3:13-18 (wisdom and peace) as well.[79]

Furthermore, investigations into the social, economic and ecclesial world of the addressees reveal a situation which is very much like the late- and post-apostolic situation of the Pastorals, Acts and other documents.[80] This is true also for the ecclesial structure (offices, "church of the words") of these churches.[81] The situation of the addressees is well in line with the kind of "Paulinism" Jas is confronted with.

The corollary then is that Jas is not a "general" writing "to whom it may concern"; rather, Jas interferes in church politics and theological development. Jas is a corrective writing with the pragmatic intention of accomplishing a change in those churches.[82]

4.2. The problem of how to discover and reconstruct Jas' composition and blueprint, as it were, is an old, many-sided and thornful story.[83] Various vantage-points resulted in all kinds of patterns. The question is indeed difficult to tackle. Whether an approach from rhetorics could basically change the picture, remains doubtful in

---

[76] Cf. Popkes 1986, 9-52.

[77] This section is certainly the crucial one; cf. the numerous studies in monographs, articles and commentaries: Burchard 1980b; Bieder 1949; Burge 1977; Cantinat 1973; Cranfield 1965; Davids 1982; Eichholz 1961; Frankemölle 1986; Hauck 1926; Karrer 1989; Lautenschlager 1990; Laws 1980; Lohse 1957 and 1988; Mitton 1966; Mußner 1981; Reicke 1964; Ross 1954; Schawe 1979; Schlatter 1984; Schnider 1987; Schrage 1980 and 1989; Tasker 1983; Vouga 1984; Walker 1964; Watson 1993a; Windisch 1951.

[78] Cf. Popkes 1994.

[79] Cf. Wilckens 1964, 526; Vouga 1984, 104.

[80] Noack 1964; Soucek 1958; Trocmé 1964; Boggan 1982; Popkes 1986; cf. Ahrens 1993. Different approaches are followed e.g. by Ward 1966; Laws 1980; Hengel 1987; Martin 1988.

[81] Popkes 1986.

[82] Cf. Frankemölle 1985, 1989 and 1994; Wuellner 1978. — On the ethical intentions of Jas in general cf. Adamson 1989; Bieder 1949; Blondel 1979 and 1980; Braumann 1962; Burchard 1980a; Cranfield 1965; Felder 1982; Frankemölle 1985; Johnson 1990; Karrer 1989; Laws 1982; Lohse 1988; Mußner 1989; Schawe 1979; Schille 1977; Schnackenburg 1986/89 II; Schrage 1989; Soucek 1958; Towner 1989; Weiß 1976; Zmijewski 1986.

[83] Cf. the material and literature listed in notes 5-9.

my estimation.[84] More successful seems to be the attempt of Hubert Frankemölle "to verify the textual coherence of the *entire* letter in terms both of form and contents."[85] A great deal of a sensible reconstruction of the composition will also depend on the correlation between the major tributaries and the redaction.

4.3. The various, conspicuous parallels to NT sections as Matt 5-7 and 1 Pet[86] make it plausible that Jas had access to an early Christian tradition of neophyte instruction.[87] Jas does not himself mention baptism[88]; in this respect he differs from 1 Pet. But he refers to this tradition, particularly in the beginning and closing passages of his writing. It is insufficient to deduce Jas' material only and directly from wisdom tradition, especially Sirach.[89] The question is not whether there are any resemblances to wisdom tradition, but rather how and for which purpose the material was assembled and used in early Christian instruction of converts, and how it got to Jas.[90] By alluding to this instructory tradition Jas reminds his addressees of where they started, under which conditions and with what a perspective. This look back serves to find again the correct course in the present situation and for the future.

## 5. Consequences

As a conclusion we may summarize the consequences for "James and paraenesis" as follows.

5.1. A functional approach to "paraenesis" is more adequate to the meaning and history of the term than the form-critical definition by Dibelius, which confines paraenesis to a limited portion of texts. In the light of such a revised concept of paraenesis the time has come to sever the traditional linkage between James and what has been understood by paraenesis, including the consequences for a textual coherence and

---

[84] Cf. Classen 1991.

[85] Frankemölle 1990, 164; cf. 1994, 71ff., 135ff., 153ff.

[86] Eleder 1964; Ferris 1939; Hartin 1991; Shepherd 1956; Vowinckel 1899; Schlatter 1984, 73-77; Francis 1970.

[87] On other NT traditions cf. e.g. Nauck 1955; Thomas 1968.

[88] Mußner 1972; Braumann 1962; cf. also Boismard 1957.

[89] Much on wisdom tradition draw: Kirk 1969; von Lips 1990; Luck 1967, 1971 and 1984; Hoppe 1977; Baasland 1982; Küchler 1979; Zeller 1977; Hartin 1991; Frankemölle 1994, 80ff; cf. also Johnson 1990. There is a special relation to Sir: cf. Frankemölle 1989; von Lips 1990.

[90] This is my criticism of Luck (cf. Popkes 1986, 24-27) and, in a different way, of von Lips (1990, 417ff.) who sees the background of Jas 1:2-12 much more fully in Sir 1-2 than I did. My replication is: Sir 1-2 may indeed provide most of the parts of Jas 1:2-12; but this does not yet explain the present textual structure in Jas 1.

references to an actual situation. Jas then should no longer be regarded as the classical example of NT "paraenesis", because this does not do justice to the terminology nor to the epistle itself. Strictly spoken, Jas "*is*" not a paraenesis in an undifferentiated, onesided meaning of the term; any application of the term to Jas has to be more distinctive.

5.2. Taking into consideration the affinity between paraenesis and conversion, and the existence of an early Christian tradition of a neophytes' instruction, which was in itself quite flexible, a number of traces of such a neophytic, (post)conversional heritage become visible in Jas. This becomes evident by comparing similar material in other NT documents (as Matt 5-7 and 1 Pet). The consequence of this observation is to say that Jas *presupposes* paraenesis, since the epistle seems to deliberately remind the readers of this tradition, right from the very outset in 1:2ff.

5.3. The reference to early Christian paraenetic tradition is instrumental for Jas' argumentation and pragmatic intention. By reminding the recipients of the very basis of Christian conduct, as they received it in connection with their conversion, Jas utilizes the tradition as a corrective in order to lead the addressees, who have run astray, back to the path of truth and virtue.

5.4. The corrective character of the epistle finds expression in a number of admonitions, warnings, prohibitive comments, advisory remarks etc. This accounts for the frequency of imperative clauses, which has often been noted. There is, of course, a linguistic and stylistic proximity between imperative and paraenesis. In this sense Jas shares certain characteristics of any "moral exhortation". From this view-point the epistle as a whole then may be regarded as a post-liminal paraenesis in a secondary stage, i.e. as a calling-back to the original direction.[91] Expressions like "this ought not to be so" (3:10) or "do not be deceived" (1:16) characterize Jas' style and intention. The recipients have lost the right track and even orientation, since they assert that they are running well. Jas has to counter-argue such an attitude and conviction.

5.5. Jas is an act and product of concerned pastoral counselling. The platform, from which the author asserts to write, is that of unquestionable expertise and authority.

---

[91] It should be noted though that most of the traditional terminology of paraenetic language is missing in Jas. Just once each occur ἀναστροφή and ἐλέγχω. The motif of (personal) example is found briefly in 3:1f., more often in the concluding part 5:7ff., which is of a more positive nature anyway (farmer, prophets, Job, Elijah); other persons (Abraham, Hagar: 2:21-25) are introduced as cases of argumentation, similar to the anonymoi in 2:2ff. and 2:15f.

It is partly grounded in what his name stands for. At the same time the irrefutability is related to his being a teacher who is well aware of his duties and responsibilities (3:1ff.). The teacher/recipient relation, as well as the difference between the experienced and the one needing advice, are typical of many paraenetic situations. In this sense Jas has a paraenetic character indeed.

5.6. Jas' intention to win back those who are in danger of running astray (cf. 5:19f.) is in itself a part of the early Christian paraenetic tradition.[92] The responsibility to take care of the weak, small, stumbling, and lapsing fellow believers is a motif found in a number of texts, often towards their end, as also in Jas: 1 Thess 5:14; Rom 14:1-15:7; Gal 6:1f.; 1 John 5:16f.; furthermore Matt 18:6-14; 1 Cor 8:7ff.; 10:23ff.; Col 3:16; 1 Pet 4:8; Heb 4:1. Jas' present paraenesis then is the consequence and implementation of what he himself inherited from traditional early Christian paraenesis.[93]

## Bibliography

Adamson, James B. 1984: *The Epistle of James* (NIC), Grand Rapids, MI: Eerdmans 1984 (reprint of 1976).

— 1989: *James. The Man and His Message*, Grand Rapids, MI: Eerdmans 1989.

Ahrens, Matthias 1993: *Arm und Reich im Jakobusbrief*, Diss. Hamburg 1993.

Attridge, Harold W. 1990: "Paraenesis in a Homily (λόγος παρακλήσεως): The Possible Location of, and Socialization in, the 'Epistle to the Hebrews'", in: *Semeia* 50 (1990) 211-26.

Aune, David E. 1987: *The New Testament in Its Literary Environment* (Library of Early Christianity 8), Philadelphia, PA: Westminster 1987.

— 1988: *Greco-Roman Literature and the New Testament. Selected Forms and Genres* (SBL. Sources for Biblical Study 21), Atlanta, GA: Scholars Press 1988.

Baasland, Ernst 1982: "Der Jakobusbrief als neutestamentliche Weisheitsschrift", in: *StTh* 36 (1982) 119-39.

— 1988: "Literarische Form, Thematik und geschichtliche Einordnung des Jakobusbriefes", in: *ANRW* II 25.5 (1988) 3646-84.

Baeumer, Max 1973: *Toposforschung* (WdF 395), Darmstadt: Wissenschaftliche Buchgesellschaft 1973.

Bartsch, Hans-Werner 1989: Art. "Paränese", in: *HWP* 7 (1989) 115f.

Beck, D.L. 1973: *The Composition of the Epistle of James*, Diss. Princeton, NJ 1973.

---

[92] Early Christians took this up from OT tradition: Jas 5:19f. quotes Prov 10:12, after all.

[93] There is some truth in the statements of Braumann (1962, 404) and Kürzdörfer (1966, 104-106) that 5:19f. is something like the inner aim of the epistle.

Berger, Klaus 1972: *Die Gesetzesauslegung Jesu I*, Neukirchen-Vluyn: Neukirchener Verlag 1972.

— 1984a: *Formgeschichte des Neuen Testaments*, Heidelberg: Quelle & Meyer 1984.

— 1984b: "Hellenistische Gattungen im Neuen Testament", in: *ANRW* II 25.2 (1984) 1031-32, 1831-85.

Bieder, Werner 1949: "Christliche Existenz nach dem Zeugnis des Jakobusbriefes", in: *ThZ* 5 (1949) 93-113.

Bjerkelund, Carl J. 1967: *Parakalô. Form, Funktion und Sinn der parakalô-Sätze in den paulinischen Briefen* (BTN 1), Oslo: Universitetsforlaget 1967.

Blank, Reiner 1981: *Analyse und Kritik der formgeschichtlichen Arbeit von Martin Dibelius und Rudolf Bultmann* (ThDiss 16), Basel 1981.

Blenker, Alfred 1967: "Jakobs brevs sammenhæng", in: *DTT* 30 (1967) 193-202.

Blondel, Jean-Luc 1979: "Le fondement théologique de la parénèse dans l'épitre de Jacques", in: *RThPh* 111/29 (1979) 141-52.

— 1980: "Theology and Paraenesis in James", in: *ThD* 28 (1980) 253-56.

Boer, Willis P. 1962: *The Imitation of Paul. An Exegetical Study,* Kampen: Kok 1962.

Boggan, Charlie W. 1982: *Wealth in the Epistle of James*, PhD Diss, Louisville, KY 1982.

Boismard, M.E. 1957: "Une liturgie baptismale dans la Prima Petri II. – Son influence sur l'épitre de Jacques", in: *RB* 64 (1957) 161-83.

Bottini, Giovanni Claudio 1986: "Sentenze di Pseudo-Focilide alla luce della lettera di Giacomo", in: *SBFLA* 36 (1986) 171-81.

Bowe, Barbara Ellen 1988: *A Church in Crisis. Ecclesiology and Paraenesis in Clement of Rome* (HDR 23), Minneapolis, MN: Fortress 1988.

Bradley, David G. 1953: "The *TOPOS* as a Form in Pauline Paraenesis", in: *JBL* 72 (1953) 238-46.

Braumann, Georg 1962: "Der theologische Hintergrund des Jakobusbriefes", in: *ThZ* 18 (1962) 401-10.

Burchard, Christoph 1980a: "Gemeinde in der strohernen Epistel. Mutmaßungen über Jakobus", in: Lührmann, Dieter/Strecker, Georg (eds.), *Kirche. FS Günter Bornkamm,* Tübingen: Mohr (Siebeck) 1980, 315-28.

— 1980b: "Zu Jakobus 2,14-26", in: *ZNW* 71 (1980) 27-45.

— 1990: "Nächstenliebegebot, Dekalog und Gesetz in Jak 2,8-11", in: Blum, Erhard et al. (eds.), *Die Hebräische Bibel und ihre zweifache Nachgeschichte. FS Rolf Rendtorff,* Neukirchen-Vluyn: Neukirchener Verlag 1990, 517-33.

Burge, Gary M. 1977: "'And Threw them thus on Paper': Recovering the Poetic Form of James 2:14-26", in: *SBTh* 7 (1977) 31-45.

Burgess, Theodore Chalon 1902: "Epideictic Literature", in: *Studies in Classical Philology III*, Chicago, IL: The University of Chicago Press 1902, 89-261.

Camp, Claudia V. 1990: "Paraenesis: A Feminist Response", in: *Semeia* 50 (1990) 243-60.

Cancik, Hildegard 1967: *Untersuchungen zu Senecas Epistulae Morales* (Spudasmata 18), Hildesheim: Olms 1967.

Cantinat, J. 1973: *Les Epitres de Saint Jacques et de Saint Jude* (SBi), Paris: Gabalda 1973.

Carrington, Philip 1940: *The Primitive Christian Catechism*, Cambridge: University Press 1940.

Cecchi, Sergio 1961: *La paideia ateniese dalle orazioni di Isocrate*, Turin: Lœscher 1961.

Church, Christopher Lee 1990: *A Forschungsgeschichte on the Literary Character of the Epistle of James*, PhD Diss, Louisville, KY 1990.

Classen, Carl Joachim 1991: "Paulus und die antike Rhetorik", in: *ZNW* 82 (1991) 1-33.

Conzelmann, Hans/Lindemann, Andreas 1989: *Arbeitsbuch zum Neuen Testament* (UTB 52), Tübingen: Mohr (Siebeck) [9]1989.

Cope, Edward Meredith/Sandys, John Edwyn 1877: *The Rhetoric of Aristotle*, Vol. I-III, Cambridge: University Press 1877.

Cranfield, C.E.B. 1965: "The Message of James", in: *SJTh* 18 (1965) 182-93 and 338-45.

Crotty, R.B. 1992: "The Literary Structure of the Letter of James" in: *ABR* 40 (1992) 45-57.

Crouch, James E. 1972: *The Origin and Intention of the Colossian Haustafel* (FRLANT 109), Göttingen: Vandenhoeck & Ruprecht 1972.

Cruz, Hieronymus 1990: *Christological Motives and Motivated Actions in Pauline Paraenesis*, Frankfurt/Bern/New York/Paris: Lang 1990.

Davids, Peter H. 1982: *The Epistle of James. A Commentary on the Greek Text* (NIGTC), Exeter: Paternoster 1982.

— 1988: "The Epistle of James in Modern Discussion", in: *ANRW* II 25.5 (1988) 3621-45.

Delling, Gerhard 1974: "Perspektiven der Erforschung des hellenistischen Judentums", in: *HUCA* 45 (1974) 133-76.

Dibelius, Martin 1912: *Die Briefe des Apostels Paulus an die Kolosser Epheser an Philemon* (HNT 12), Tübingen: Mohr (Siebeck) 1912.

— 1913: *Die Briefe des Apostels Paulus an Timotheus I II an Titus* (HNT 13), Tübingen: Mohr (Siebeck) 1913.

— 1931: "Zur Formgeschichte des Neuen Testaments (außerhalb der Evangelien)", in: *ThR* 3 (1931) 207-42.

— 1937: *Die Briefe des Apostels Paulus an die Thessalonicher I, II an die Philipper* (HNT 11), Tübingen: Mohr (Siebeck) [1]1911, [3]1937.

— 1971: *Die Formgeschichte des Evangeliums*,Tübingen: Mohr (Siebeck) [6]1971.

— 1975: *Geschichte der urchristlichen Literatur* (TB 58), reprint München: Kaiser 1975.

— 1984: *Der Brief des Jakobus* (KEK 15), Göttingen: Vandenhoeck & Ruprecht [6]1984 ([1]1921).

Dodd, Charles Harold 1968a: "ΕΝΝΟΜΟΣ ΧΡΙΣΤΟΥ" in: idem, *More New Testament Studies*, Manchester: Manchester University Press/Grand Rapids: Eerdmans 1968, 134-48.

— 1968b: "The Primitive Catechism and the Sayings of Jesus", in: *More New Testament Studies*, Manchester: Manchester University Press/Grand Rapids: Eerdmans 1968, 11-29.

Easton, Burton Scott 1932: "New Testament Ethical Lists", in: *JBL* 51 (1932) 1-12.

Eichholz, Georg 1961: *Glaube und Werke bei Paulus und Jakobus* (TEH 88), München: Kaiser 1961.

Eleder, Felix 1964: *Jakobusbrief und Bergpredigt,* Diss. Wien 1964.

Fabris, Rinaldo 1977: *Legge della libertà in Giacomo* (RevBib, Suppl. 8), Brescia: Paideia 1977.

Felder, Cain H. 1982: "Partiality and God's Law: An Exegesis of James 2:1-13" in: *JRT* 39 (1982) 51-69.

Ferris, T. E. S. 1939: "The Epistle of James in Relation to I Peter", in: *CQR* 128 (1939) 303-08.

Fiedler, Peter 1986: Art. "Haustafel", in: *RAC* 13 (1986) 1063-73.

Fiore, Benjamin 1986: *The Function of Personal Example in the Socratic and Pastoral Epistles* (An Bib 105), Rome: Biblical Institute Press 1986.

Fitzgerald, John T. 1988: *Cracks in an Earthen Vessel: An Examination of the Catalogues of Hardships in the Corinthian Correspondence* (SBL.DS 99), Atlanta, GA: Scholars Press 1988.

Forbes, P.B.R. 1972: "The Structure of the Epistle of James", in: *EvQ* 44 (1972) 147-53.

Francis, Fred O. 1970: "The Form and Function of the Opening and Closing Paragraphs of James and I John", in: *ZNW* 61 (1970) 110-26.

Frankemölle, Hubert 1985: "Gespalten oder ganz. Zur Pragmatik der theologischen Anthropologie des Jakobusbriefes", in: Brachel, H.-U. von/Mette, N. (eds.), *Kommunikation und Solidarität,* Fribourg/Münster: Edition Exodus 1985, 160-78.

— 1986: "Gesetz im Jakobusbrief. Zur Tradition, kontextuellen Verwendung und Rezeption eines belasteten Begriffes", in: Karl Kertelge (ed.), *Das Gesetz im Neuen Testament* (QD 108), Freiburg–Basel–Wien: Herder l986, 175-221.

— 1989: "Zum Thema des Jakobusbriefes im Kontext der Rezeption von Sir 2,1-18 und 15,11-20", in: *BN* 48 (1989) 21-49.

— 1990: "Das semantische Netz des Jakobusbriefes. Zur Einheit eines umstrittenen Briefes", in: *BZ* 34 (1990) 161-97.

— 1994: *Der Brief des Jakobus* (ÖTKB 17/1-2), Gütersloh: Gütersloher Verlag/Würzburg: Echter 1994.

Fry, Euan 1978: "The Testing of Faith. A Study of the Structure of the Book of James", in: *BiTr* 29 (1978) 427-35.

Gaiser, Konrad 1959: *Protreptik und Paränese bei Platon. Untersuchungen zur Form des platonischen Dialogs* (TBAW 40), Stuttgart: Kohlhammer 1959.

Gertner, M. 1964: "Midrashic Terms and Techniques in the New Testament: the Epistle of James, a Midrash on a Psalm", in: *StEv* 3 (1964) 463.

Gielen, Marlis 1990: *Tradition und Theologie neutestamentlicher Haustafelethik. Ein Beitrag zur Frage einer christlichen Auseinandersetzung mit gesellschaftlichen Normen,* Frankfurt/ Main: Hain 1990.

Gigon, Olof 1965a: Art. "Paränese (1)", in: *LAW* (1965) 2220.

— 1965b: Art. "Protreptik (1)", in: *LAW* (1965) 2459.

Goppelt, Leonhard 1973: "Jesus und die "Haustafel"-Tradition", in: Hoffmann, P. et al. (eds.), *Orientierungen an Jesus. Zur Theologie der Synoptiker. FS Josef Schmid,* Regensburg: Pustet 1973, 93-106.

— 1978: *Der Erste Petrusbrief* (KEK XII/1), Göttingen: Vandenhoeck & Ruprecht 1978, 163-79, Exkurs: Die Ständetafeltradition.

Grabner-Haider, Anton 1967: *Paraklese und Eschatologie bei Paulus. Mensch und Welt im Anspruch der Zukunft Gottes,* Münster: Aschendorff 1967.

Grafe, Eduard 1904: *Die Bedeutung und Stellung des Jakobusbriefes in der Entwicklung des Urchristentums,* Tübingen und Leipzig: Mohr (Siebeck) 1904.

Grant, Robert M. 1947: "The Decalogue in Early Christianity", in: *HThR* 40 (1947) 1-17.

Grundmann, Walter 1958/59: "Die *nepioi* in der urchristlichen Paränese", in: *NTS* 5 (1958/59) 188-205.

Hahn, Ferdinand 1981: "Die christologische Begründung urchristlicher Paränese", in: *ZNW* 72 (1981) 88-99.

Halson, B. R. 1968: "The Epistle of James: 'Christian Wisdom?'", in: *StEv* IV (1968) 308-14.

Hanson, A. 1978/79: "Seminar Report (Report on Working Group on 'The Use of the Old Testament in the Epistle of James'...)", in: *NTS* 25 (1978/79) 626f.

von Harnack, Adolf 1909: *Lehrbuch der Dogmengeschichte,* Tübingen: Mohr (Siebeck) [4]1909 (reprint: Darmstadt: Wissenschaftliche Buchgesellschaft 1964).

Harnisch, Wolfgang 1987: "Einübung des neuen Seins. Paulinische Paränese am Beispiel des Galaterbriefs", in: *ZThK* 84 (1987) 279-96.

Hartin, Patrick J. 1991: *James and the Q Sayings of Jesus* (JSNT.S 47), Sheffield: JSOT Press 1991.

Hartlich, Paulus 1889: "De exhortationum a Graecis Romanisque scriptarum historia et indole", in: *Leipziger Studien zur classischen Philologie* XI/2 (1889) 207-335.

Hartmann, Gerhard 1942: "Der Aufbau des Jakobusbriefes", in: *ZThK* 66 (1942) 63-70.

Hauck, Friedrich 1926: *Der Brief des Jakobus* (KNT XVI), Leipzig: Deichert (Scholl) 1926.

Haufe, Günter 1964: *Motive und Motivwandel in der frühchristlichen Paränese,* Habil.-Schr. Leipzig 1964.

— 1992: "Christus als Vorbild in der frühchristlichen Paränese", in: *Theol.Gespräch* 1 (1992) 15-24.

Heintze, H. von 1965: Art. "Paränese (2)", in: *LAW* (1965) 2220.

Hengel, Martin 1987: "Der Jakobusbrief als antipaulinische Polemik", in: Hawthorne, G. F. (ed.), *Tradition and Interpretation in the New Testament. FS E. Earle Ellis,* Grand Rapids–Tübingen: Eerdmans–Mohr (Siebeck) 1987, 248-78.

Hiebert, D. Edmond 1978: "The Unifying Theme of the Epistle of James", in: *BS* 135/539 (1978) 221-31.

— 1984: *The Epistle of James. Tests of a Living Faith,* Chicago, IL: Moody 1984 (= 1979).

Hoppe, Rudolf 1977: *Der theologische Hintergrund des Jakobusbriefes* (FzB 28), Würzburg: Echter 1977.

Horst, Pieter Willem van der 1978a: "Pseudo-Phocylides and the New Testament", in: *ZNW* 69 (1978) 187-202.

— 1978b: *The Sentences of Pseudo-Phocylides* (SVTP 4), Leiden: Brill 1978.

Jacob, I. 1975: "The Midrashic Background for James II,21-23", in: *NTS* 22 (1975) 457-64.

Johnson, Luke Timothy 1982: "The Use of Leviticus 19 in the Letter of James", in: *JBL* 101 (1982) 391-401.

— 1983: "James 3:13-4:20 and the TOPOS PERI PHTHONOY", in: *NT* 25 (1983) 327-47.

— 1990: "Taciturnity and True Religion. James 1:26-27", in: Balch, David L. et al. (eds.), *Greeks, Romans, and Christians. FS Abraham J. Malherbe*, Minneapolis, MN: Augsburg-Fortress 1990, 329-39.

Jones, Peter Rhea 1969: "Approaches to the Study of the Book of James", in: *RExp* 66 (1969) 425-34.

Jonge, Marinus de 1989: "Die Paränese in den Schriften des Neuen Testaments und in den Testamenten der Zwölf Patriarchen. Einige Überlegungen", in: Merklein, H. (ed.), *Neues Testament und Ethik. FS Rudolf Schnackenburg*, Freiburg: Herder 1989, 538-50.

Kamlah, Ehrhard 1964: *Die Form der katalogischen Paränese im Neuen Testament* (WUNT 7), Tübingen: Mohr (Siebeck) 1964.

Karrer, Martin 1989: "Christus der Herr und die Welt als Stätte der Prüfung. Zur Theologie des Jakobusbriefs", in: *KuD* 35 (1989) 166-88.

Karris, Robert A. 1971: *The Function and Sitz–im–Leben of the Paraenetic Elements in the Pastoral Epistles*, Diss. Harvard Univ. 1971.

— 1973: "The Background and Significance of the Polemic of the Pastoral Epistles", in: *JBL* 92 (1973) 549-64.

Kassel, Rudolf. 1976: *Aristotelis Ars Rhetorica*, Berlin/New York: de Gruyter 1976.

Kirk, J. A. 1969: "The Meaning of Wisdom in James: Examination of a Hypothesis", in: *NTS* 16 (1969) 24-38.

Klauck, Hans-Josef 1991: *Die Johannesbriefe* (EdF 276), Darmstadt: Wissenschaftliche Buchgesellschaft 1991.

Kooy, J. 1926: *De Paraenese van den Apostel Paulus*, Amsterdam: B. van der Land 1926.

Küchler, Max 1979: *Frühjüdische Weisheitstraditionen. Zum Fortgang weisheitlichen Denkens im Bereich des frühjüdischen Jahweglaubens* (OBO 26), Fribourg–Göttingen: Universitätsverlag–Vandenhoeck & Ruprecht 1979.

Kümmel, Werner Georg 1983: *Einleitung in das Neue Testament*, Heidelberg: Quelle & Meyer ²¹1983.

Kürzdörfer, Klaus 1966: *Der Charakter des Jakobusbriefes. Eine Auseinandersetzung mit den Thesen von A. Meyer und M. Dibelius*, Diss. Tübingen 1966.

Larsson, Edvin 1962: *Christus als Vorbild. Eine Untersuchung zu den paulinischen Tauf- und Eikontexten*, (ASNU 23), Lund–Kopenhagen: Gleerup–Munksgaard 1962.

Latacz, Joachim 1977: *Kampfparänese, Kampfdarstellung und Kampfwirklichkeit in der Ilias, bei Kallinos und Tyrtaios* (Zetemata 66), München: C. H. Beck 1977.

Lautenschlager, Markus 1990: "Der Gegenstand des Glaubens im Jakobusbrief", in: *ZThK* 87 (1990) 163-84.

Laws, Sophie 1980: *A Commentary on the Epistle of James* (BNTC), London: Black 1980.

— 1982: "The Doctrinal Basis for the Ethics of James", in: *StEv* VII, Berlin: Akademie Verlag 1982, 299-305.

Levine, Amy-Jill 1990: "Who's Catering the Q Affair? Feminist Observations on Q Paraenesis", in: *Semeia* 50 (1990) 145-61.

Lincke, K. F. A. 1911: "Phokylides, Isokrates und der Dekalog", in: *Philologus* 70 (1911) 438-42.

Lips, Hermann von 1990: *Weisheitliche Traditionen im Neuen Testament* (WMANT 64), Neukirchen-Vluyn: Neukirchener Verlag 1990.

— 1994: "Die Haustafel als 'Topos' im Rahmen der urchristlichen Paränese. Beobachtungen anhand des 1. Petrusbriefes und des Titusbriefes", in: *NTS* 40 (1994) 261-80.

Lohse, Eduard 1957: "Glaube und Werke – zur Theologie des Jakobusbriefes", in: *ZNW* 48 (1957) 1-22.

— 1988: *Theologische Ethik des Neuen Testaments* (ThW V 2), Stuttgart: Kohlhammer 1988.

Luck, Ulrich 1967: "Weisheit und Leiden. Zum Problem Paulus und Jakobus", in: *ThLZ* 92 (1967) 253-58.

— 1971: "Der Jakobusbrief und die Theologie des Paulus", in: *ThGl* 61 (1971) 161-79.

— 1984: "Die Theologie des Jakobusbriefes", in: *ZThK* 81 (1984) 1-30.

Lührmann, Dieter 1980/81: "Neutestamentliche Haustafeln und antike Ökonomie", in: *NTS* 27 (1980/81) 83-97.

Luz, Ulrich 1989: "Überlegungen zum Epheserbrief und seiner Paränese", in: Merklein, H. (ed.), *Neues Testament und Ethik. FS Rudolf Schnackenburg,* Freiburg: Herder 1989, 376-96.

Malherbe, Abraham J. 1986: *Moral Exhortation, A Greco–Roman Sourcebook* (Library of Early Christianity 4), Philadelphia, PA 1986.

— 1992: "Hellenistic Moralists and the New Testament", in: *ANRW* II 26.1 (1992) 267-333.

Marshall, S. S. S. C. 1968: *The Character, Setting, and Purpose of the Epistle of St. James*, BL–Thesis Oxford 1968.

Martin, Ralph P. 1988: *James* (Word Biblical Commentary 48), Waco, TX: Word 1988.

Mayor, Joseph B. 1954: *The Epistle of St. James,* London: MacMillan, 2nd ed. 1897, reprint: Grand Rapids, MI: Eerdmans 1954.

Meeks, Wayne A. 1986: *The Moral World of the First Christians* (Library of Early Christianity), Philadelphia, PA: Westminster 1986.

Merk, Otto 1968: *Handeln aus Glauben. Die Motivierungen der paulinischen Ethik,* Marburg: Elwer 1968.

— 1969: "Der Beginn der Paränese im Galaterbrief", in: *ZNW* 60 (1969) 83-104.

Meyer, Arnold 1930: *Das Rätsel des Jakobusbriefes* (BZNW 10), Gießen: Töpelmann 1930.

Mitton, C. Leslie 1966: *The Epistle of James*, London: Marshall, Morgan, Scott/Grand Rapids: Eerdmans 1966.

Müller, Gotthold 1982: "Der Dekalog im Neuen Testament. Vor-Erwägungen zu einer unerledigten Aufgabe", in: *ThZ* 38 (1982) 79-97.

Müller, Karlheinz 1983: "Die Haustafel des Kolosserbriefes und das antike Frauenthema. Eine kritische Rückschau auf alte Ergebnisse", in: Kertelge, Karl (ed.), *Die Frau im Urchristentum* (QD 95), Freiburg: Herder 1983, 263-319.

Mußner, Franz 1972: "Die Tauflehre des Jakobusbriefes", in: Auf der Maur, H./Kleinheyer, B. (eds.), *Zeichen des Glaubens. FS B. Fischer,* Einsiedeln–Freiburg: Johannes Verlag 1972, 61-67.

— 1981: *Der Jakobusbrief* (HThK XIII/1), Freiburg–Basel–Wien: Herder [4]1981.

— 1988: *Der Galaterbrief* (HThK IX), Freiburg–Basel–Wien: Herder [5]1988, 281-88: Evangelium und Paraklese (Paränese).

— 1989: "Die ethische Motivation im Jakobusbrief", in: Merklein, H. (ed.), *Neues Testament und Ethik. FS Rudolf Schnackenburg,* Freiburg: Herder 1989, 416-23.

Nauck, Wolfgang 1955: "Freude im Leiden", in: *ZNW* 46 (1955) 68-80.

— 1958: "Das οὖν-paraeneticum", in: *ZNW* 49 (1958) 134-35.

Niebuhr, Karl-Wilhelm 1987: *Gesetz und Paränese. Katechismusartige Weisungsreihen in der frühjüdischen Literatur* (WUNT II 28), Tübingen: Mohr (Siebeck) 1987.

Nieder, Lorenz 1956: *Die Motive der religiös-sittlichen Paränese in den paulinischen Gemeinde- briefen. Ein Beitrag zur paulinischen Ethik* (MThSt I 12) München: Zink 1956.

Noack, Bent 1964: "Jakobus wider die Reichen", in: *StTh* 18 (1964) 10-25.

Obermüller, Rudolf 1972: "Hermeneutische Themen im Jakobusbrief", in: *Bib.* 53 (1972) 234-44.

Ortkemper, Franz-Josef 1980: *Leben aus dem Glauben. Christliche Grundhaltungen nach Römer 12-13* (NTA NF 14), Münster: Aschendorff 1980.

Paulsen, Henning 1992: Art. "Paränese", in: *EKL*[3] III (1992), 1046-47.

Pearson, Birger A. 1989: "James, 1-2 Peter, Jude", in: Epp, Eldon Jay/MacRae, George W. (eds.), *The New Testament and Its Modern Interpreters,* Atlanta, GA: Scholars Press 1989, 371- 406.

Perdue, Leo G./Gammie, John G. (eds.) 1990: *Semeia 50. Paraenesis: Act and Form,* Atlanta, GA: Scholars Press 1990.

Perdue, Leo G. 1981a: "Liminality as the Social Setting of Wisdom Instructions", in: *ZAW* 93 (1981) 114-26.

— 1981b: "Paraenesis and the Epistle of James", in: *ZNW* 72 (1981) 241-56.

— 1990a: "The Social Character of Paraenesis and Paraenetic Literature", in: *Semeia* 50 (1990) 5- 39.

— 1990b: "The Death of the Sage and Moral Exhortation: From Ancient Near Eastern Instructions to Graeco-Roman Paraenesis", in: *Semeia* 50 (1990) 81-109.

Popkes, Wiard 1986: *Adressaten, Situation und Form des Jakobusbriefes* (SBS 125/26), Stuttgart: Katholisches Bibelwerk 1986.

— 1989: "Die Gerechtigkeitstradition im Matthäus-Evangelium", in: *ZNW* 80 (1989) 1-23.

— 1990: "Die letzte Bitte des Vater-Unser. Formgeschichtliche Beobachtungen zum Gebet Jesu", in: *ZNW* 81 (1990) 1-20.

— 1992a: "New Testament Principles of Wholeness", in: *EvQ* 64 (1992) 319-32.

— 1992b: "Zum Charakter von Galater 6,1-10", in: *Theologisches Gespräch* 1/1992, 8-15.

— 1994: "The Law of Liberty (James 1:25; 2:12)", in: Faculty of Baptist Theological Seminary (ed.): *Festschrift G. Wagner* (International Theological Studies: Contributions of Baptist Scholars 1), Bern: Lang 1994, 131-42.

Price, Bennet J. 1975: *Paradeigma amd Exemplum in Ancient Rhetorical Theory*, Diss. Berkley 1975.

Probst, Hermann 1991: *Paulus und der Brief. Die Rhetorik des antiken Briefes als Form der paulinischen Korintherkorrespondenz (1 Kor 8-10)* (WUNT II 45), Tübingen: Mohr (Siebeck) 1991.

Prockter, Lewis J. 1989: "James 4.4-6: Midrash on Noah", in: *NTS* 35 (1989) 625-27.

Quinn, Jerome D. 1981: "Parenesis and the Pastoral Epistles", in: J. Dore et al. (eds.), *De la Torah au Messie. FS Henri Cazelles*, Paris: Desclée 1981, 495-501.

— 1990: "Paraenesis and the Pastoral Epistles: Lexical Observations Bearing on the Nature of the Sub-genre and Soundings on its Role in Socialization and Liturgies", in: *Semeia* 50 (1990) 189-210.

Reicke, Bo 1964: *The Epistles of James, Peter, and Jude* (AncB 37), Garden City, NY: Doubleday 1964.

Reinmuth, Eckart 1985: *Geist und Gesetz. Studien zu Voraussetzungen und Inhalt der paulinischen Paränese* (ThA 44), Berlin: Evangelische Verlagsanstalt 1985.

Rigaux, Béda 1956: *Les Épitres aux Théssaloniciens*, Paris–Gembloux: Gabalda–Duculot 1956, 183-94.

Robbins, Vernon K. 1984: *Jesus the Teacher. A Socio-rhetorical Interpretation of Mark*, Philiadelphia, PA: Fortress 1984.

— 1990: "A Socio-Rhetorical Response: Contexts of Interaction and Forms of Exhortation", in: *Semeia* 50 (1990) 261-71.

Romaniuk, Kasimir 1968: "Les motifs parénétiques dans les écrits pauliniens", in: *NT* 10 (1968) 191-207.

Rosenkranz, Bernhard 1966: "Die Struktur der Ps-Isokrateischen Demonicea", in: *Emerita* 34 (1966) 95-129.

Ross, Alexander 1954: *The Epistles of James and John* (NIC), Grand Rapids, MI: Eerdmans 1954.

Rustler, Michael Kurt 1952: *Thema und Disposition des Jakobusbriefes,* Diss. Wien 1952.

Sato, M. 1991: "Wozu wurde der Jakobusbrief geschrieben? Eine mutmassliche Rekonstruktion", in: *AJBI* 17 (1991) 55-76.

Schammberger, Hermann 1936: *Die Einheitlichkeit des Jacobusbriefes im antignostischen Kampf,* Gotha: Klotz 1936.

Schawe, E. 1979: "Die Ethik des Jakobusbriefes", in: *WuA* 20 (1979) 132-38.

Schiefer Ferrari, M. 1991: *Die Sprache des Leids in den paulinischen Peristasenkatalogen* (SBB 23), Stuttgart: Katholisches Bibelwerk 1991.

Schille, Gottfried 1977: "Wider die Gespaltenheit des Glaubens – Beobachtungen am Jakobusbrief", in: *ThV* IX (1977) 71-89.

Schlatter, Adolf 1984: *Der Brief des Jakobus,* Stuttgart: Calwer [3]1984.

Schlier, Heinrich 1972: "Vom Wesen der apostolischen Ermahnung. Nach Römerbrief 12,1-2", in: idem, *Die Zeit der Kirche*, Freiburg: Herder [5]1972, 74-89.

— 1987: "Die Eigenart der christlichen Mahnung nach dem Apostel Paulus", in: idem, *Besinnung auf das Neue Testament*, Freiburg: Herder [2]1987, 340-57.

Schlink, Edmund 1956: "Gesetz und Paraklese", in: *FS Karl Barth*, Zollikon: Evangelischer Verlag 1956, 323-35.

Schmidt, Jens-Uwe 1986: *Adressat und Paraineseform. Zur Intention von Hesiods 'Werken und Tagen'* (Hypomnemata 86), Göttingen: Vandenhoeck & Ruprecht 1986.

Schnackenburg, Rudolf 1963: Art. "Paränese", in: *LThK*[2] 8 (1963) 80-82.

— 1986/89: *Die sittliche Botschaft des Neuen Testaments* (HThK Suppl.), Freiburg: Herder I 1986, II 1989.

Schnider, Franz 1987: *Der Jakobusbrief* (RNT), Regensburg: Pustet 1987.

Schniewind, Julius 1946/47: "Theologie und Seelsorge", in: *EvTh* 6 (1946/47) 363-67.

Schrage, Wolfgang 1961: *Die konkreten Einzelgebote in der paulinischen Paränese. Ein Beitrag zur neutestamentlichen Ethik*, Gütersloh: Mohn 1961.

— 1974/75: "Zur Ethik der neutestamentlichen Haustafeln", in: *NTS* 21 (1974/75) 1-22.

— 1980: "Der Jakobusbrief", in: Balz, Horst/Schrage, Wolfgang, *Die "Katholischen" Briefe* (NTD 10), Göttingen: Vandenhoeck & Ruprecht [12]1980.

— 1989: *Ethik des Neuen Testaments* (NTD ErgR. 4), Göttingen: Vandenhoeck & Ruprecht [5]1989.

Schweizer, Eduard 1976: *Der Brief an die Kolosser* (EKK XII), Zürich–Neukirchen: Benziger–Neukirchener Verlag 1976, 159-164: Exkurs: Die Haustafeln.

— 1979: "Traditional ethical patterns in the Pauline and post-Pauline letters and their development (lists of vices and house-tables)", in: Best, E./ Wilson, R.McL. (eds.), *Text and Interpretation. FS Matthew Black*, Cambridge: Cambridge University Press 1979, 195-209.

Seeberg, Alfred 1906: *Die beiden Wege und das Aposteldekret*, Leipzig: A. Deichert 1906.

— 1908: *Die Didache des Judentums und der Urchristenheit*, Leipzig: A. Deichert 1908.

— 1966: *Der Katechismus der Urchristenheit*. Mit einer Einführung von Ferdinand Hahn (TB 26), München: Kaiser 1966 (1st ed. 1903).

Selwyn, Edward Gordon 1961: *The First Epistle of St. Peter*, London: MacMillan [2]1961, Essay II, 363-488: On the Interrelation of I Peter and other N.T. Epistles. Appended Note by David Daube: Participle and Imperative in I Peter.

Shepherd, Massey H. 1956: "The Epistle of James and the Gospel of Matthew", in: *JBL* 75 (1956) 40-51.

Sigal, Phillip 1981: "The Halakhah of James", in: Hadidian, Dikran Y. (ed.), *Intergerini Parietis Septvm. FS Markus Barth*, Pittsburgh, PA: Pickwick Press 1981, 337-53.

Songer, Harold S. 1969: "The Literary Character of the Book of James", in: *RExp* 66 (1969) 379-89.

Songer, Harold S. et al. 1986: "James", in: *RExp* 83/3 (1986) 355-438.

Souček, J.B. 1958: "Zu den Problemen des Jakobusbriefes", in: *EvTh* 18 (1958) 460-68.

Spencer, A.B. 1989: "The Function of the Miserific and Beatific Images in the Letter of James", in: *Evangelical Journal* 7 (1989) 3-14.

Spitta, Friedrich 1896: *Zur Geschichte und Litteratur des Urchristentums. Vol. II: Der Brief des Jakobus; Studien zum Hirten des Hermas,* Göttingen: Vandenhoeck & Ruprecht 1896.

Stachowiak, Lech R. 1983: "Die Erforschung der paulinischen Paränesen im 20. Jahrhundert", in: *CoTh* 53 (1983) fasc.spec. 177-94.

Stowers, Stanley Kent 1986: *Letter Writing in Greco-Roman Antiquity* (Library of Early Christianity 5) Philadelphia, PA: Westminster 1986.

Strecker, Georg 1989: "Die neutestamentlichen Haustafeln (Kol 3,18-4,1 und Eph 5,22-6,9)", in: Merklein, H. (ed.), *Neues Testament und Ethik. FS Rudolf Schnackenburg,* Freiburg: Herder 1989, 349-75.

— 1991: Art. "Literaturgeschichte, Biblische II. Neues Testament, 2.4 Paränetische Texte", in: *TRE* 21 (1991) 342f.

— 1992: *Literaturgeschichte des Neuen Testaments* (UTB 1682), Göttingen: Vandenhoeck & Ruprecht 1992.

Stuhlmacher, Peter 1989: *Der Brief an die Römer* (NTD 6), Göttingen: Vandenhoeck & Ruprecht 1989, Exkurs XIV: Zur paulinischen Gemeindeermahnung (Paraklese), 191-94.

Tasker, R.V.G. 1983: *The General Epistle of James* (TNTC), Leicester: Inter-Varsity/Grand Rapids, MI: Eerdmans 1983 (=1956).

Terry, R.B. 1992: "Some Aspects of the Discourse Structure of the Book of James": *Journal of Translation and Textlinguistics* 5 (1992) 106-25.

Thomas, Johannes 1968: "Anfechtung und Vorfreude", in: *KuD* 14 (1968) 183-206.

— 1983a: Art. "παραινέω", in: *EWNT* 3 (1983) 52-53.

— 1983b: Art. "παρακαλέω, παράκλησις", in: *EWNT* 3 (1983) 54-64.

— 1992: *Der jüdische Phokylides. Formgeschichtliche Zugänge zu Pseudo-Phokylides und Vergleich mit der neutestamentlichen Paränese* (NTOA 23), Fribourg–Göttingen: Universitätsverlag–Vandenhoeck & Ruprecht 1992.

Thraede, Klaus 1980: "Zum historischen Hintergrund der 'Haustafeln' des Neuen Testaments", in: Dassmann, E. et al. (eds.), *Pietas. FS Bernhard Kötting* (JAC Erg.-Bd 8), Münster: Aschendorff 1980, 359-68.

Thyen, Hartwig 1955: *Der Stil der Jüdisch-Hellenistischen Homilie* (FRLANT 65), Göttingen: Vandenhoeck & Ruprecht 1955.

Towner, Philip H. 1989: *The Goal of Our Instruction: The Structure of Theology and Ethics in the Pastoral Epistles* (JSNT.S 34), Sheffield: JSOT Press 1989.

Townsend, Michael J. 1981: "Christ, Community and Salvation in the Epistle of James", in: *EvQ* 53 (1981) 114-23.

Trocmé, Etienne 1964: "Les Eglises pauliniennes vues du dehors: Jacques 2,1 à 3,23", in: *StEv* 2 (1964) 660-69.

Turner, Victor 1967a: *The Forest of Symbols,* Ithaca, NY: Cornell University 1967.

— 1967b: *The Ritual Process*, Ithaca, NY: Cornell University 1967.

— 1972: "Passages, Margins, and Poverty: Religious Symbols of Communitas", in: *Worship* 46 (1972) 390-425.

Übelacker, Walter G. 1989: *Der Hebräerbrief als Appell. I. Untersuchungen zu exordium, narratio und postscriptum (Hebr 1-2 und 13,22-25)* (CB.NT 21), Lund: Gleerup 1989.

Unnik, Willem Cornelis van 1960: "Die Rücksicht auf die Reaktion der Nicht-Christen als Motiv in der altchristlichen Paränese", in: W. Eltester (ed.), *Judentum, Urchristentum, Kirche. FS Joachim Jeremias* (BZNW 26), Berlin: de Gruyter 1960, [2]1964, 221-34.

Vetschera, Rudolf 1910/12: "Zur griechischen Paränese", in: *Jahresberichte des k.k. deutschen Staatsgymnasiums zu Smichow* 37 (Smichow 1910/11) 3-15; 38 (1911/12) 3-21.

Via, Dan Otto 1969: "The Right Strawy Epistle Reconsidered: A Study in Biblical Ethics and Hermeneutic", in: *JR* 49 (1969) 253-67.

Vielhauer, Philipp 1975: *Geschichte der urchristlichen Literatur,* Berlin: de Gruyter 1975, 49-57.

Vögtle, Anton 1936: *Die Tugend- und Lasterkataloge im Neuen Testament exegetisch, religions- und formgeschichtlich untersucht* (NTA 16, 4/5) Münster: Aschendorff 1936.

Vokes, F. E. 1968: "The Ten Commandments in the New Testament and in First Century Judaism", in: *StEv* 5 (1968) 146-54.

Vouga, François 1984: *L'Épitre de Saint Jacques* (CNT(N) XIIIa), Geneva: Labor et Fides 1984.

Vowinckel, Ernst 1899: *Die Grundgedanken des Jakobusbriefes verglichen mit den ersten Briefen des Petrus und Johannes* (BFChTh 1898/6), Gütersloh: Bertelsmann 1899.

Walker, Rolf 1964: "Allein aus Werken. Zur Auslegung von Jakobus 2,14-26", in: *ZThK* 61 (1964) 155-92.

Wanke, Joachim 1978: "Die urchristlichen Lehrer nach dem Zeugnis des Jakobusbriefes", in: Schnackenburg, Rudolf et al. (eds.), *Kirche des Anfangs. FS Heinz Schürmann,* Freiburg: Herder 1978, 489-511.

Ward, Roy Bowen 1966: *The Communal Concern of the Epistle of James,* ThD Diss. Cambridge, MA 1966.

— 1976: Art. "James, Letter of", in: *IDB Suppl.* (1976) 469-70.

Watson, D.F. 1993a: "James 2 in Light of Greco-Roman Schemes of Argumentation", in: *NTS* 39 (1993) 94-121.

—1993b: "The Rhetoric of James 3:1-12 and a Classical Pattern of Argumentation", in: *NT* 35 (1993) 48-64.

Wefelmeier, Carl 1962: *Die Sentenzensammlung der Demonicea,* Athen: J. Rossolatos 1962.

Weidinger, Karl 1928: *Die Haustafeln. Ein Stück urchristlicher Paränese* (UNT 14), Leipzig: Hinrichs 1928.

Weiß, Konrad 1976: "Motiv und Ziel der Frömmigkeit des Jakobusbriefes", in: *ThV* VII (1976) 107-14.

Wendland, Paul 1905: *Anaximenes von Lampsakos. Studien zur ältesten Geschichte der Rhetorik,* Berlin: Weidmann 1905.

Westhuizen, J. D. N. van der 1991: "Stylistic techniques and their functions in James 2:14-26", in: *Neotest.* 25 (1991) 89-107.

Wibbing, Siegfried 1959: *Die Tugend- und Lasterkataloge im Neuen Testament und ihre Traditions-geschichte unter besonderer Berücksichtigung der Qumran-Texte* (BZNW 25), Berlin: de Gruyter 1959.

Wifstrand, Albert 1948: "Stylistic Problems in the Epistle of James and Peter", in: *StTh* 1 (1948) 170-82.

Wilckens, Ulrich 1964: Art. "σοφία", in: *ThWNT* 7 (1964) 497-529.

Williams, James G. 1990: "Paraenesis, Excess, and Ethics: Matthew's Rhetoric in the Sermon on the Mount", in: *Semeia* 50 (1990) 163-87.

Wilson, Walter T. 1991: *Love without Pretense. Romans 12.9-21 and Hellenistic-Jewish Wisdom Literature* (WUNT II 46), Tübingen: Mohr (Siebeck) 1991.

Windisch, Hans 1951: *Die katholischen Briefe* (HNT 15), stark umgearbeitete Aufl. von H. Preisker, Tübingen: Mohr (Siebeck) 1951.

Wolbert, Werner 1981: "Vorbild und paränetische Autorität. Zum Problem der 'Nachahmung' des Paulus", in: *MThZ* 32 (1981) 249-70.

Wuellner, Wilhelm H. 1978: "Der Jakobusbrief im Licht der Rhetorik und Textpragmatik", in: *Ling Bibl* 43 (1978) 5-66.

Yates, R., "The Christian Way of Life 1991: The Paraenetic Material in Colossians 3:1-4:6", in: *EvQ* 63 (1991) 241-51.

Zeller, Dieter 1983: *Die weisheitlichen Mahnsprüche bei den Synoptikern* (fzb 17), Würzburg: Echter ²1983.

Zmijewski, Josef 1980: "Christliche 'Vollkommenheit'. Erwägungen zur Theologie des Jakobus-briefes", in: idem, *Das Neue Testament — Quelle christlicher Theologie und Glaubens-praxis.* Aufsätze zum Neuen Testament und seiner Auslegung, Stuttgart: Katholisches Bi-belwerk 1986, 293-323.

# PART II

## BIBLICAL TEXTS IN THEIR SITUATIONAL CONTEXTS

# Section C

## Biblical Texts and
## Their Historical Background

# The Palestinian Background of "Son of God" as a Title for Jesus

Joseph A. Fitzmyer, S.J.

## 1. The Problem

The designation of Jesus in the New Testament as "the Son of God" is widespread, and no other title of his can claim as much significance for later theological development than it. If the title ὁ υἱὸς τοῦ ἀνθρώπου outstrips it in enigma, it certainly does not in implication. Whether the title is used in the anarthrous form, υἱὸς θεοῦ, or the arthrous form, ὁ υἱὸς τοῦ θεοῦ, or uttered by a heavenly voice as υἱός μου, or used as a description of Jesus by some New Testament writer as υἱὸς αὐτοῦ or υἱὸς ἑαυτοῦ, its meaning is clear. It expresses the distinctive relationship of Jesus to Yahweh, who is his heavenly Father.

This title is not restricted to the Synoptics: Mark 1:1, 11; 3:11; 5:7; 15:39; Matt 2:15; 3:17; 4:3, 6; 8:29; 14:33; 16:16; 17:5; 26:63; 27:40, 43, 54; Luke 1:32, 35; 3:22; 4:3, 9, 41; 8:28; 9:35; 22:70. It is also found in the Johannine Gospel: 1:18, 34, 49; 3:18; 5:25; (9:35);[1] 10:36; 11:4, 27; 19:7; 20:31. Further, in Acts: 8:37; 9:20; 13:33; in uncontested Pauline letters: Rom 1:3-4, 9; 5:10; 8:3, 29, 32; 1 Cor 1:9; 2 Cor 1:19; Gal 1:16; 2:20; 4:4, 6; 1 Thess 1:10; in Deutero-Pauline writings: Eph 4:13; in the Epistle to the Hebrews: 1:5; 4:14; 5:5; 6:6; 7:3; 10:29; in the Johannine Epistles: 1 John 1:3, 7, 8; 3:23; 4:9, 10, 15; 5:5, 9, 10, 11, 12, 13, 20; 2 John 3; in the Book of Revelation: 2:18; and in 2 Peter: 1:17. Moreover, it not only occurs in some Pauline passages that are often regarded as fragments of the primitive kerygma (1 Thess 1:10; Rom 1:3-4), but it even develops within the New Testament itself so that it becomes an absolute title, "the Son," either on the lips of Jesus himself (Mark 13:32; Matt 24:36), or so used by Paul (1 Cor 15:28).

This usage suggests a certain parallelism with the title Κύριος, which is also used in an absolute form along with modified expressions.[2] But New Testament in-

---

[1] See the *apparatus criticus* on this passage.

[2] Compare the uses gathered in Fitzmyer 1979a.

terpreters, aware of the various nuances of the use of בּן or υἱός in the Old Testament to designate a special relationship of someone to God, have often noted that it is "a long way" from such simple usage in the Old Testament to the solemn and lofty title, "the Son of God," such as one finds in the New Testament, especially for Jesus. Years ago, W. Bousset posed the question:

> May we, without further ado, assume that the first community of Jesus' disciples had already taken the daring step and had creatively formed the title 'the Son of God,' which the Old Testament and the messianic faith of late Judaism did not know, out of Old Testament beginnings (Ps 2:7) and the tradition about Jesus' baptism and transfiguration? Or did this title ultimately develop first on Greek soil, in the Greek language?[3]

Although Bousset expressed a hesitation about the connection of the New Testament title with what he called "Jewish messianology"[4] and thought that it came to undisputed dominance in "the area of popular conceptions in the Gentile Christian church and in that of the Pauline-Johannine Christology,"[5] he did not go so far as A. Deissmann had, who saw a close "connection with the imperial cult and the well-known formula *Divi Filius* (θεοῦ υἱός)."[6] Thus, for Bousset, the New Testament title ὁ υἱὸς τοῦ θεοῦ was not so clearly of Hellenistic and pagan origin as Κύριος was alleged to be. As is well known, several writers sought blatantly to relate Κύριος as a title for Jesus to such an origin.[7] And a number of writers have related ὁ υἱὸς τοῦ θεοῦ to a similar Hellenistic origin; so with varying nuances G. P. Wetter,[8] W. G. Kümmel.[9] The opinion of R. Bultmann was more complicated. Although he thought that "Hellenistic-Jewish Christians had brought along the *title* 'Son of God' embedded in their missionary message, for the earliest Church had already called Jesus so,"[10] he also maintained that the connotation of the title as indicative of "divine origin" or of being "filled with divine 'power'" (and not merely messiahship) was related to a Gentile setting.[11] For him the title was associated with the role of Jesus as θεῖος ἀνήρ,[12] and its real content-element was thus of Hellenistic imprint.

Now it would be foolhardy to deny that such Hellenistic notions as demigods or heroes born of gods and goddesses, or θεῖοι ἄνδρες, to whom the title θεοῦ υἱοί

---

[3] Bousset 1970, 95-96.

[4] Ibid., 207.

[5] Ibid., 97.

[6] Deissmann 1909, 166-67. Cf. Deissmann 1927, 346-47.

[7] Cf. Fitzmyer 1979a.

[8] Wetter 1916.

[9] Kümmel 1973, 76.

[10] Bultmann 1952, 1:128.

[11] Ibid.

[12] Ibid., 130.

was at times given in the contemporary Greek world, had somewhat influenced early Christians in their use of the title for Jesus. This might be especially true of its use in the writings of Paul or John, which stem from settings in the Hellenistic world of the eastern Mediterranean area. But the problem really is to trace that "long way" from the Old Testament data, which many New Testament interpreters still think were at the root of the title, to the solemn title itself. No little part of the problem is the fact that the title as such (in the singular) occurs only rarely in late Old Testament writings despite the numerous allusions to figures in the Old Testament who are called "son(s)," yet scarcely with the connotation that the title has or may have in the New Testament.

So the problem is posed. Some new light has been shed on the Palestinian Jewish background of the title from the recent publication in full of the Qumran "Son of God" text. In order to understand the importance of this text and the place that it holds in the debate on the New Testament problem, I propose to group my further observations under three headings: (1) a survey of the Old Testament data bearing on the title; (2) the new Palestinian Jewish material; and (3) the implications of the new material for various New Testament passages.

## 2. Old Testament Data Bearing on the Title "Son of God"

The plural expressions in Hebrew בני (ה)אלהים (Gen 6:2,4; Job 1:6; 2:1; 38:7), בני אלים (Ps 29:1; 89:6), and בני עליון (Ps 82:6), are found in the Old Testament as names for angelic beings in the heavenly court of Yahweh.[13] Again, the plural expression, either as בני אל חי (Hos 2:1) or simply some form of בנים (Deut 14:1; Isa 1:2; 30:1; Jer 3:22), is sometimes put on God's lips and used of the Israelites. Moreover, on occasion collective Israel is spoken of in the singular as בני, "my son" (Exod 4:22; Hos 11:1). The closest one comes to the singular usage, resembling the New Testament title, is found not in Hebrew, but in Aramaic and Greek. Thus the figure who appears with Shadrach, Meshach, and Abednego walking about freely in the fiery furnace is described as דמה לבר אלהין, "(one) resembling a son of (the) gods" (Dan 3:25). Again, Israel itself is referred to in the singular as θεοῦ υἱόν (Wis 18:13). Yet neither of these expressions implies a physical father-son relationship between Yahweh and the person so designated. Obviously, neither the descriptive title for the angel in Daniel nor the collective title for the people of Israel in Wisdom provides the intelligible background to the New Testament title for Jesus of Nazareth. For this reason Bousset rightly spoke of the "long way" from one to the other.

The title "son" is also used at times of individuals in the Old Testament tradition.

---

[13] In Ps 82:6 the phrase may refer to "judges," according to some commentators.

Though he is never formally or explicitly called "Son of God," the king who sits on the Davidic throne is three times related to Yahweh as "son": 2 Sam 7:14; Ps 2:7; 89:26-27. These texts, however, call for further scrutiny.

Even though Ps 2:7 uses of the Davidic king the graphic expression יְלִדְתִּיךָ, "I have begotten you," commentators are usually hesitant to assert that this implies a physical divine sonship for the king, such as might be the connotation of similar expressions in the ancient eastern Mediterranean world.[14] Rather, the father-son relationship so expressed guarantees divine sponsorship, support, and assistance for the Davidic king, and by implication for his dynasty. This too is the implication of Nathan's oracle in 2 Sam 7:14, and the legitimation of the dynastic rule is further described in the poetic language of Ps 89:3-4, 19-37. Indeed, it may have been played out in the coronation ritual.[15]

In the deuterocanonical writings of Ben Sira and Wisdom, however, one finds "son" used also of the righteous or upright individual Israelite: "Be like a father to the fatherless and help a widow as a husband would; and God will call you 'son,' show you his favor, and save you from the pit" (Sir 4:10).[16] Again, "If the righteous man is God's son (υἱὸς θεοῦ), he will help him" (Wis 2:19).

Thus in a few instances in Old Testament writings we find a background for the expression "son of God": in the dynastic sayings about the Davidic king and in four instances even the formal singular expression itself, once of an angel, once of collective Israel, and twice of a righteous individual Israelite. The connotations may vary, but they are all figurative usages.

Psalm 2 is the source of the tendency of some biblical interpreters to regard the title "son of God" as messianic. Since this adjective is properly understood of such Old Testament figures as were "anointed," the title "son of God" does not express that idea either precisely or *per se*. And yet, the question whether the title "son of God" was used of the Messiah or of an Anointed One in pre-Christian Palestinian Judaism is constantly asserted and debated. The root of the problem is Ps 2:2, where the king on the Davidic throne is called "his (i.e., the Lord's) anointed" (מְשִׁיחוֹ), and its v. 7 says, "You are my son; today I have begotten you" (בְּנִי אַתָּה אֲנִי הַיּוֹם יְלִדְתִּיךָ). In v. 2, however, the phrase "his anointed" is used of a historical king, one who was sitting upon the Davidic throne and at whose enthronement was regarded as "anointed," and even called "my son." But it is not used there of a future, ideal David who is awaited, of which Jer 30:9 once spoke: "they shall serve the Lord their God and David their king, whom I will raise up for them."[17] Hence despite the ten-

---

[14] Gadd 1948, 45-50.

[15] von Rad 1947; Rengstorf 1962.

[16] In Hebrew ואל יקראך בן ויתנך ויצילך משחת. The Septuagint reads: καὶ ἔσῃ ὡς υἱὸς ὑψίστου.

[17] Fitzmyer 1971, 113-26, esp. 115-16.

uous connection of "anointed one" and "son" in Psalm 2, where they occur together, but several verses apart, it must be remembered that neither in pre-Christian Palestinian Judaism nor in that of the Diaspora have we any clear indication that that psalm was being understood "messianically," i.e. of an expected or coming anointed figure, a Messiah in the strict sense. Nor have we a clearly attested instance of the title "son of God" being applied to an expected "Messiah" in pre-Christian Jewish literature.

## 3. The New Palestinian Jewish Material

Now over against such an Old Testament background one has to consider the new Palestinian Aramaic text that has at length been made public in full form. The Qumran text that bears on the problem under discussion is 4Q246, which E. Puech recently published in full.[18] The Aramaic text runs thus in translation:

*Column 1*

1  [        when great fear] settled [u]pon him, he fell down before the throne.
2  [Then he said to the king, "Live], O King, forever! You are vexed, and changed
3  [is the complexion of your face; de]pressed is your gaze. (But) [you will rule over] everything forever!
4  [And your deeds will be g]reat. (Yet) distress will come upon the earth;
5  [there will be war among the peoples] and great carnage in the provinces,
6  [which the bands of] the king of Assyria [will cause]. [And E]gypt
7  [will be with them. But your son] will also be great upon the earth,
8  [and all peoples wi]ll make [peace with him], and they will all serve
9  [him, (for) he will be called [son of] the [gr]eat [God], and by his name will he be named.

*Column 2*

1  He will be hailed (as) son of God, and they will call him son of the Most High. Like comets
2  that one sees, so will their rule be. For (some) years they may rule upon
3  the earth and trample everything (under foot); people will trample upon people, province upon [pro]vince,
4  (*vacat*) until there arises the people of God, and everyone rests from the sword.
5  (Then) his kingdom (shall be) an everlasting kingdom, and all his ways (shall be) in truth. He shall jud[ge]
6  the land with truth; everyone shall make peace. The sword shall cease from the land,
7  and all the provinces shall pay him homage. The great God is himself his might;

---

[18] Puech 1992. Cf. Fitzmyer 1993, 153-74; Fitzmyer 1994.

8 He shall make war for him. Peoples He shall put in his power, and all of them
9 He shall cast before him. His dominion (shall be) an everlasting dominion, and
none of the abysses of [the earth shall prevail against it].

This fragmentary text has been dated palaeographically by J. T. Milik, who originally was supposed to publish it,[19] to the last third of the first century B.C. It is written in a fine Herodian script, easily decipherable. The person, however, to whom the
titles ברה די אל, "son of God," בר עליון, "son of the Most High," are attributed is unfortunately unknown because of the fragmentary nature of the document. For this
reason, his identity will be long discussed.

Six opinions have already been proposed to identify him: (1) The Seleucid king,
Alexander Balas, whose reign would be followed by the eschatological rule of the
people of God. So J. T. Milik in his Harvard lecture.[20] (2) An Antichrist, an idea
which is said to be "surely Jewish and pre-Christian," as in 2 Thess 1:1-12 and the
*Ascension of Isaiah* 4:2-16, which speaks of the incarnation of Beliar, in whom all
peoples will believe. So D. Flusser.[21] (3) An eschatological savior "of angelic nature," who "can be identified with Melchizedek, Michael, the Prince of Light" mentioned in other Qumran texts. So F. García Martínez.[22] (4) The Jewish people
collectively, "like the Son of Man in Dan. 7,13." So M. Hengel.[23] (5) The Messiah,
who is expected. So E. Puech, J. J. Collins.[24] (6) A coming Jewish ruler, but one
who is not regarded as a Messiah (in the strict sense of an expected *anointed* figure,
such as the future David of Jer 30:9). So I have argued.[25] The issue will long be debated and probably never resolved because of the broken condition of the text.

Yet no matter what interpretation may eventually win out and become commonly
accepted, the titles ברה די אל and בר עליון are clearly being attributed to a human being, apparently to some Jewish ruler in a Palestinian context, perhaps someone of
the Hasmonean dynasty. Since the text is written in Aramaic and this language was
also in common use in Syria at the time, as well as in Palestine, it might seem to be
of Syrian, even of Seleucid provenience. But it seems hardly likely that a Jew in Pal-

---

[19] Milik lectured on the fragment at Harvard University in December 1992 and was supposed to
publish it in *HThR*, but he never did. Two copies of the text were received in the mail shortly after
his lecture, and graduate students at Harvard were discussing the fragment in a seminar. It was then
judged to be in the public domain, and I published a few lines of the text. See Fitzmyer 1973-74,
391-94; reprinted in Fitzmyer 1979, 85-113, esp. 90-94.

[20] See now Milik 1991-92, 383-84.

[21] Flusser 1980; reprinted in Flusser 1988, 207-13.

[22] García Martínez 1983, 235; cf. García Martínez 1992, 169.

[23] Hengel 1976, 45.

[24] Puech 1992, 127-30. There Puech also toys with the interpretation of Milik, but he clearly prefers the messianic interpretation, as does Collins 1993.

[25] Fitzmyer 1993, 166-74. There one will find a critique of the foregoing five opinions.

estine would have copied such a non-Jewish writing, or that it would have been used among them, especially among the Essenes of Qumran. Since the Seleucid dynasty was fundamentally pagan and hellenistic, it is hardly likely that such titles would have emerged in such a context. Hence, it is unlikely that the person is a Seleucid king or a pagan usurper vaunting himself as "son of God,"[26] since he is understood in the text as one ruling over "the people of God." The tone of the text suggests that it at least fed the aspirations of the Qumran community, if it was not actually composed by someone in that community. Its presence in Qumran Cave 4 is, consequently, significant.

## 4. The Implications of the New Material for Various New Testament Passages

First, the titles ברה די אל and בר עליון are clearly related to an *apocalyptic* setting in this document of Palestinian Judaism. The apocalyptic character of the text is clear in its reference to occupying forces, which in God's good time will be overcome with his aid and assistance. This is part of the message that is being revealed and passed on to the enthroned king, and other apocalyptic stage-props are used.

Second, ברה די אל and בר עליון are used in this text in a *titular* sense in pre-Christian Palestine. This is shown by the Aramaic verbs that accompany them: יתאמר, "he shall be hailed," and יקונה, "they shall call him." In the given context there are also other verbs of "calling" or "naming" that leave no doubt about the appellative sense in which the phrases are being used.

Third, these titles are not applied to anyone who is directly called "messiah" (מְשִׁיחָא or מְשִׁיחָא); at least this term is not found in any part of the extant text. Thus, even this text bears out the contention that Bousset once maintained, that there is still no direct connection between the title "son of God" and "Jewish messianology."[27] But another of Bousset's comments can now be modified. He wrote, "The whole of later Jewish apocalypticism was unacquainted with the messianic title 'Son of God.'"[28] Yet Jewish apocalypticism was clearly not unacquainted with the title "son of God," even if it apparently still did not apply it to a messianic figure or use it with a messianic nuance. Since the titles are associated in this Aramaic text with someone who rules or will rule, possibly the son of a king, this makes unlikely the suggestion of W. Grundmann that "son of God" was the title for the *priestly* messiahship of Jesus.[29]

---

[26] Milik preferred the view that it refers to Alexander Balas, because his coins bore the title θεοπάτωρ. But would a Jewish writer acknowledge such an ascription?

[27] Bousset 1970, 207. Some scholars who had only heard about the text, but had not seen it, gave it a messianic interpretation.

[28] Ibid., 93.

Fourth, if there is no connection with the messianic expectation of Palestinian Jews or even with the messianism of the Qumran community, there is even less connection of the title "son of God" with miracles or with a θεῖος ἀνήρ setting, not to mention the association of it with gnostic redeemer myths.[30] The context of the Qumran text is one of political strife, and the "son of God" figure is hailed apocalyptically as a harbinger of peace and everlasting dominion, as a bearer of those things that could be associated with the restoration of Davidic kingship.

Fifth, the parallelism of the Qumran Aramaic text with a number of phrases in the Lucan infancy narrative is especially striking:

| | |
|---|---|
| οὗτος ἔσται μέγας (1:32) | (1:7) [ו]רב להוה על ארעא |
| υἱὸς ὑψίστου κληθήσεται (1:32) | (2:1) ובר עליון יקרונה |
| κληθήσεται υἱὸς θεοῦ (1:35) | (2:1) ברה די אל יתאמר |
| βασιλεύσει … εἰς τοὺς αἰῶνας (1:33) | (2:5) מלכותה מלכות עלם |
| ἐπελεύσεται ἐπὶ σέ (1:35) | (1:1) [ע]לוהי שרת |

Since this is not the first time that an Aramaic parallel to an expression in the Lucan infancy narrative has turned up in Qumran literature,[31] it raises a question about the long-standing debate about the sources that Luke used in that part of his Gospel. Because it is written in a more semitized Greek than the rest of the Gospel, the suspicion has been that the evangelist may have been depending on some sort of Semitic source. But in reality that Semitic character of the infancy narrative is largely owing to Lucan use of Septuagintisms. Attempts to relate the infancy narrative to Semitic sources have more often related them to Hebrew rather than Aramaic.[32] In my opinion, the parallels listed above scarcely show that Luke was dependent on the Aramaic text that we have now recovered from Qumran Cave 4. But was he aware of an Aramaic tradition that made use of such phrases? That is not impossible. For if I am right in agreeing with the ecclesiastical tradition that the author of the Third Gospel was Luke, a Syrian, possibly from Antioch, then he would have been a native Aramaic speaker as an *incola* of that area, who also enjoyed a good Greek, Hellenistic education, such as would have been usual in his day in such an area.[33]

Sixth, the title בר עליון along with ברה די אל shows how traditional Old Testament titles of God were being adapted for this title of filiation. The compound divine title אל עליון appears in the Genesis Apocryphon from Qumran Cave 1 (12:17; 20:12, 16; 21:2,20; 22:15, 16bis, 21).[34] Now the form אל appears here alone in an Aramaic text and may explain why the Aramaic form of Ps 22:2 appears in the Greek of Matt

---

[29] Grundmann 1956.

[30] Contrast Bultmann 1952, 1:130.

[31] See Fitzmyer 1958; reprinted in Fitzmyer 1971, 101-04.

[32] E.g. Box 1905; Gunkel 1903; Laurentin 1956; Winter 1953. Cf. Fitzmyer 1981-85, 312.

[33] Fitzmyer 1981-85, 41-47; Fitzmyer 1989, 3.

27:46 as ἠλὶ ἠλὶ λεμὰ σαβαχθάνι. In other words, the form ἠλί is not necessarily Hebraic, as has been claimed at times. Although we do not yet have a suffixal form of this name in an Aramaic text, this occurrence of אל in an Aramaic text reveals that it would not have been impossible for someone to have said אֵלִי. The title בר עליון also supplies a Palestinian Jewish background for that used by the demoniac of Gerasa in Mark 5:7; Luke 8:28: υἱὲ τοῦ θεοῦ ὑψίστου, "son of God Most High."

Seventh, the attestation of the title "son of God" in this pre-Christian Qumran text makes it possible at least that this title as used of Jesus of Nazareth was already part of the primitive kerygma as formulated by Jewish Christians in Palestine. In other words, the use of such a title for him was not necessarily the product of missionary activity among Gentiles in the eastern Mediterranean world.

Lastly, though in Psalm 2 the term "son" is related to "begetting," the titles in this Aramaic text do not directly express such a relation. The divine begetting of the person regarded as son is not mentioned in 4Q246. Hence, when this notion eventually enters the Christian tradition about Jesus, it may be dependent on the formulation of Ps 2:7, but also implied in a tradition that goes beyond such titles. The connotations, with which the New Testament title for Jesus is fraught, remain unmentioned in this Aramaic text, such as the implication of preexistence or miraculous conception. Moreover, it is scarcely to be expected that a Palestinian Jewish text mentioning a "son of God" or a "son of the Most High" would carry all the nuances that came to be associated with such titles for Jesus of Nazareth in the New Testament.

This use of such Palestinian titles is admittedly isolated. How much more frequently would they have been in use, and with what specific nuance is hard to say. One can raise such questions about them, but until the titles turn up again in some future discovery there is no answer to such queries. But we now see at least that there is evidence of a Palestinian background of the "son of God" title for Jesus in the New Testament.

## Bibliography

Bousset, W. 1970: *Kyrios Christos: A History of the Belief in Christ from the Beginnings of Christianity to Irenaeus*, Nashville, TN: Abingdon 1970.

Box, G. H. 1905: "The Gospel Narratives of the Nativity and the Alleged Influence of Heathen Ideas", in: *ZNW* 6 (1905) 80-101.

Bultmann, R. 1952: *Theology of the New Testament*, 2 vols., London: SCM 1952.

---

[34] It occurs in Hebrew texts of Qumran: 1QH 4:31; 6:33. And אל stands in parallelism with עליון in 1QS 10:11-12; 11:15.

Burrows, E. 1940: *The Gospel of the Infancy and Other Biblical Essays* (Bellarmine Series 6), London: Burns, Oates and Washbourne 1940.

Collins, J. J. 1993: "The *Son of God* Text from Qumran", in: M. C. de Boer (ed.), *From Jesus to John: Essays on Jesus and New Testament Christology in Honour of Marinus de Jonge* (JSNT.S 84), Sheffield, UK: Academic 1993, 65-82.

Deissmann, A. 1909: *Bible Studies*, 2nd ed., Edinburgh: T. & T. Clark 1909.

— 1927: *Light from the Ancient East: The New Testament Illustrated by Recently Discovered Texts of the Graeco-Roman World*, New York: Doran 1927.

Fitzmyer, J. A. 1958: "'Peace upon Earth among Men of His Good Will' (Luke 2:14)", in: *TS* 19 (1958) 225-27.

— 1971: *Essays on the Semitic Background of the New Testament*, London: Chapman 1971; repr., Missoula: Scholars 1974.

— 1973-74: "The Contribution of Qumran Aramaic to the Study of the New Testament", in: *NTS* 20 (1973-74) 382-407.

—1979: *A Wandering Aramean: Collected Aramaic Essays* (SBL.MS 25), Missoula, MT: Scholars 1979.

— 1979a: "The Semitic Background of the New Testament *Kyrios*-Title", in: Fitzmyer 1979, 115-42.

— 1981-85: *The Gospel according to Luke* (AncB 28, 28A), Garden City, NY: Doubleday, 1981, 1985.

— 1989: *Luke the Theologian: Aspects of His Teaching*. New York: Paulist, 1989.

— 1993: "4Q246: The 'Son of God' Document from Qumran", in: *Bib.* 74 (1993) 153-74.

— 1994: "The Aramaic 'Son of God' Text from Qumran Cave 4", in: M. O. Wise et al. (eds.), *Methods of Investigation of the Dead Sea Scrolls and the Khirbet Qumran Site: Present Realities and Future Prospects* (Annals of the New York Academy of Sciences 722), New York: New York Academy of Sciences 1994, 163-78.

Flusser, D. 1980: "The Hubris of the Antichrist in a Fragment from Qumran", in: *Immanuel* 10 (1980) 31-37.

— 1988: *Judaism and the Origins of Christianity*. Jerusalem: Magnes 1988.

Gadd, C. J. 1948: *Ideas of Divine Rule in the Ancient East* (Schweich Lectures of the British Academy 1945), London: G. Cumberlege/Oxford University 1948.

García Martínez, F. 1983: "4Q246: ¿Tipo del Anticristo o Libertador escatológico?", in: V. Collado y E. Zurro (eds.), *El misterio de la Palabra: Homenaje ... al profesor D. Luis Alonso Schökel ...*, Madrid: Cristiandad 1983, 229-44.

— 1992: "The Eschatological Figure of 4Q246", in: *Qumran and Apocalyptic: Studies on the Aramaic Texts from Qumran* (Studies on the Texts of the Desert of Judah 9), Leiden: Brill 1992 162-79.

Grundmann, W. 1956: "Sohn Gottes", in: *ZNW* 47 (1956) 113-33.

Gunkel, H. 1903: *Zum religionsgeschichtlichen Verständnis des Neuen Testaments* (FRLANT 1), Göttingen: Vandenhoeck & Ruprecht 1903.

Hengel, M. 1976: *The Son of God: The Origin of Christology and the History of Jewish Hellenistic Religion*, Philadelphia, PA: Fortress 1976.

Kümmel, W. G. 1973: *The Theology of the New Testament according to Its Major Witnesses: Jesus —Paul—John*, Nashville, TN: Abingdon 1973.

Laurentin, R. 1956: "Traces d'allusions étymologiques en Luc 1-2", in: *Bib.* 37 (1956) 435-456; 38 (1957) 1-23.

Milik, J. T. 1991-92: "Les modèles araméens du livre d'Esther dans la Grotte 4 de Qumrân", in: *RdQ* 15 (1991-92) 321-408.

Puech, E. 1992: "Fragment d'une apocalypse en araméen (4Q246 = pseudo-Dan[d]) et le 'royaume de Dieu'", in: *RB* 99 (1992) 98-131.

Rad, G. von 1947: "Das judäische Krönungsritual", in: *ThLZ* 72 (1947) 211-16.

Rengstorf, K.-H. 1962: "Old and New Testament Traces of a Formula of the Judaean Royal Ritual", in: *NT* 5 (1962) 229-44.

Wetter, G. P. 1916: *Der Sohn Gottes* (FRLANT 26), Göttingen: Vandenhoeck & Ruprecht 1916.

Winter, P. 1953: "Two Notes on Luke I, II with Regard to the Theory of 'Imitation Hebraisms'", in: *StTh* 7 (1953) 158-65.

# Asking for the Meaning of a Fragmentary Qumran Text
## The Referential Background of 4QAaron A

John J. Collins

## 1. Introduction

In his monograph, *Asking for a Meaning. A Study of 1 Enoch 1-5,* Lars Hartman outlined the notion of the "referential background" of a text:

> By 'referential background' I mean the general setup of institutions, customs, conventions, philosophies, ideas, etc. which, without necessarily being explicitly referred to in a text, nonetheless form a background of that to which the text refers, and this in such a way that one should know about this background in order to catch the full implication of the text.[1]

The recognition of this background is an essential step in the interpretation of any text. It is especially important in deciphering fragmentary texts, where much of the immediate literary context is missing. In the case of many of the newly available fragmentary texts from Qumran, recognition of the referential background is the indispensable key to interpretation.

The problem may be illustrated by a very interesting but very fragmentary Aramaic text recently published by Emile Puech.[2] This text, 4Q540-541, also known as 4QAaron A, was first brought to public attention by Jean Starcky in 1963. Starcky acknowledged that only a few of the fragments were intelligible, but claimed "but their interest is great, for they seem to us to evoke a suffering messiah, in the perspective opened up by the Servant poems."[3] Puech concurs in Starcky's understanding of the referential background: the figure in question "ne peut pas ne pas évoquer la figure du Serviteur du Deutéro-Isaïe."[4] He in turn is closely followed by George

---

[1] Hartman 1979, 123. He argues that the cultic celebration of the covenant provides the referential background of 1 Enoch 1-5.

[2] Puech 1992, 449-501.

[3] Starcky 1963, 492.

[4] Puech 1992, 496.

Brooke.[5] The possibility that the text refers to a suffering messiah has also been noted by Martin Hengel.[6] The figure in question in the Aramaic text is a priest, and it is not suggested that he is identified directly with the servant of the Isaianic passages. Rather, in the words of Brooke, "All in all, this priest's activities are not only referred to with some of the phraseology associated with the servant of Isaiah, but his career seems to mirror that of the servant—a universal mission, light against darkness, vilification, violent suffering, sacrifice, benefits for others."[7] On this view, the servant passages constitute the referential background of the text. While it is not explicitly cited, it allegedly forms the background of that to which the text refers.

The claim that we have here a suffering messianic figure is noteworthy indeed. One of the great anomalies of early Christianity in its Jewish context is the claim that a man who endured a humiliating death by crucifixion is nonetheless God's messiah. The Jew, Trypho, in Justin's *Dialogue*, protests: "for we know that he should suffer and be led as a sheep. But prove to us whether he must be crucified and die so disgracefully and so dishonourably the death cursed in the law. For we cannot bring ourselves even to think of this."[8] Many scholars feel that Trypho concedes too much, and that a real Jew (as opposed to a literary fiction) would not have granted that the messiah should suffer at all.[9] The argument turns on the interpretation of Isa 52:13-53:12, which portrays a "servant of the Lord" who "has borne our infirmities and carried our diseases ... was wounded for our transgressions, crushed for our iniquities" and was led like a lamb to the slaughter. The late Joachim Jeremias argued that Isaiah's suffering servant was interpreted as a suffering messiah by some Jews before the rise of Christianity.[10] More recent scholarship, however, has moved away from this position, and admits that it is difficult to demonstrate either the notion of a suffering servant in Judaism or the influence of Isaiah 52-53 in the New Testament.[11] Marinus de Jonge recently summed up the evidence as follows: "Notwithstanding J. Jeremias's careful listing of all possible references and allusions to the texts, words, phrases and ideas found in Isa 52.13-53.12 in the writings of the New Testament, the evidence for the use of this passage in early Christianity

---

[5] Brooke 1993, 83-100.

[6] Hengel 1992, 164. He refers to "ein aramäischer Text aus 4Q über eine sühnende, von Jes. 53 geprägte Offenbarergestalt."

[7] Brooke 1993, 93.

[8] Justin *Dialogue* 90:1; cf. 36:1; 39:7.

[9] Higgins 1979, 189: "The messianic ideas expressed by Trypho bristle with inconsistencies which no amount of ingenuity can resolve into a harmonious picture. This is due to the ill-matched combination of genuinely Jewish beliefs and of Christian doctrines which Justin has put into Trypho's mouth for apologetic purposes."

[10] J. Jeremias 1968, 686-700.

[11] Hooker 1959; Williams 1975, 111-20, 222-29.

is slight."[12] The fragmentary text from Qumran, then, is potentially important as a rare witness to the notion of a suffering servant in pre-Christian Judaism.

## 2. The Suffering Servant in Isaiah

It is important at the outset to clarify just what the notion of a suffering servant entails. The view that the Servant Songs (Isa 42:1-4; 49:1-7; 50:4-9 and 52:13-53:12) stand out from their context and are to be understood as an independent cluster, was introduced by Bernhard Duhm in the late nineteenth century,[13] and has become commonplace in modern scholarship.[14] Whether they really constitute a distinct unit is very questionable. These are not the only passages that speak of a servant—Jacob or Israel is explicitly addressed as servant in several passages (Isa 44:1, 21, 45:4, etc.). The notion of suffering is not conspicuous in 42:1-4 or 49:1-7. 50:4-9 speaks of a figure who endures blows, insults and spitting. The notion of a *suffering* servant, however, derives primarily from Isa 52:13-53:12. Only the fourth song is a clear literary unit in itself. It is unclear where the first song ends. There is a new oracular formula at v. 5, but vv. 5-7 are linked to other servant passages thematically (e.g. "I have made you ... a light to the nations"). Richard Clifford has argued persuasively that the first three songs constitute parts of longer poetic units, 41:1-42:9, 49:1-26, and 50:1-51:8.[15] But regardless of the literary judgment of modern critics, no one in antiquity distinguished four "servant songs" or assumed that these four passages constituted a distinct unit. This point was noted by Joachim Jeremias, the great proponent of the messianic interpretation of the servant.[16] He also noted that "one has to realise that in view of the atomistic character of the exegesis of the period a uniform interpretation of the Ebed cannot be presupposed." It is therefore not legitimate to assume that a phrase borrowed from Isa 42:1-7 or 49:1-7 (e.g. "a light to the nations") entails an allusion to a "suffering servant" as that figure is portrayed in Isaiah 53. Only in Isa 53 do we find the idea of vicarious suffering, where the servant "makes his life an offering for sin" (53:10) and bears the iniquities of others.

---

[12] de Jonge 1991, 49.

[13] Duhm 1892.

[14] Rowley 1965; North 1956.

[15] Clifford 1984, 84-93, 146-55, 156-64.

[16] J. Jeremias 1968, 682: "First it should be noted that the modern isolation of the Servant Songs, like the division of the book into Proto-, Deutero- and Trito-Isaiah, was completely unknown in that day."

## 3. The Servant in Pre-Christian Judaism

The view that some Jews in the pre-Christian period understood the servant of Isaiah 53 to refer to a suffering messiah is associated above all with Joachim Jeremias. His evidence, however, is very weak.[17] The Son of Man in the *Similitudes of Enoch,* who is called "messiah" at *1 Enoch* 48:10 and 52:4, is also repeatedly called "Elect" or "Chosen," and occasionally "Righteous One." The servant is called "chosen" in Isa 42:1, and "righteous" at Isa 53:11. In *1 Enoch* 48:4 the Son of Man is called the "light of the nations" (cf. Isa 42:6; 49:6). Even Jeremias admits, however, that the parallels are restricted to traits which exalt the servant's glory.[18] There is no suggestion in the *Similitudes of Enoch* that the Son of Man is a suffering messiah. The Targum on Isaiah takes some of the servant passages (42:1; 43:10; 52:13) in a messianic sense. In the case of Isaiah 52-53, however, the Targum systematically subverts the references to the suffering of the servant. So the "man of sorrows" is taken to refer to the Gentile kingdoms (53:3); it is the sanctuary that was desecrated because of our transgressions, delivered up because of our sins, but the messiah will rebuild it, (v. 5) and he will lay on the Gentiles the transgressions of which Israel was guilty (v. 8). Only a couple of traces of the suffering servant remain ("He will be despised," Isa 53:3; "he gave up his soul to death," 53:12). In short, where the servant is understood as the messiah, he is not believed to suffer. In the words of Jeremias, "step by step, Tg. Is. 52:13-53:12 depicts the glorious establishment of the Messianic rule over Israel. By consistent artificial reinterpretation the statements about the sufferings of the servant of God are so radically eliminated that only at two points do weak traces remain."[19] Nonetheless, Jeremias concluded that the messianic interpretation of the "passion sayings" in Isa 53:1-12 can be traced back with a high degree of probability to the pre-Christian period.[20] His evidence for this assertion lies in the translations of the Peshitta, Aquila and Theodotion, and rabbinic texts. The argument from the translations is highly inferential, but in any case none of this material is a reliable witness to the pre-Christian period. Jeremias further posited anti-Christian polemic in the Targum,[21] but even if this is correct we have no reason to infer that the Targum envisaged a suffering messiah at an earlier stage. There is simply no good evidence in pre-Christian Judaism for the notion of

---

[17] J. Jeremias 1968, 686-95. He cites Sir 48:10 ("to restore the tribes of Jacob," cf. Isa 49:6) but admits that "only a free allusion is made to Is. 49:6" and that "we cannot with full certainty infer a Messianic interpretation." He also finds evidence of a messianic interpretation in the translations of Aquila and Theodotion.

[18] J. Jeremias 1968, 688.

[19] Ibid., 695.

[20] Ibid., 699.

[21] Ibid., 682.

a suffering messiah.

## 4. The Text from Qumran

The text adduced by Starcky as evidence of a suffering messiah consists of 25 fragments, two of which have been joined, reducing the number to 24. There is also a second copy of which three fragments survive. The text is dated to the late second century, or about 100 BCE on palaeographic grounds.[22] Several of the fragments are so brief that they are virtually unintelligible. The claim about a suffering messiah rests on two passages, fragments 9 and 24. Fragment 9 reads:

> He will atone for all the children of his generation, and he will be sent to all the children of his [pe]oples. His word is like a word of heaven and his teaching is in accordance with the will of God. His eternal sun will shine, and his light will be kindled in all the corners of the earth, and it will shine on the darkness. Then the darkness will pass away [fro]m the earth, and thick darkness from the dry land.
>
> They will speak many words against him, and they will invent many [lie]s and fictions against him and speak shameful things about him. Evil will overthrow his generation ... His situation will be one of lying and violence [and] the people will go astray in his days, and be confounded.[23]

Fragment 24 is more fragmentary and obscure:

> Do [not] grieve for [him] ... God will set many thing[s] right ... many revealed things ... Examine and seek and know what the dove (or: Jonah?) sought (?) and do not afflict the weak by wasting or hanging ... [Let] not the nail approach him. So you will establish for your father a name of joy, and for your brothers a proven foundation ... You will see and rejoice in the eternal light, and you will not be an enemy.[24]

Puech relates this text to another fragmentary piece, 4QAJacob, which reports a vision of the tablets of heaven, and contains some instructions for sacrifices.[25] He suggests that all these fragments belong to an Aramaic *Testament of Levi,* since the subject matter is concerned with priesthood, and is similar to what we find in the Greek *Testament of Levi.* The opening part of fragment 9, cited above, is strikingly similar to *Testament of Levi* 18, which describes a "new priest" whom the Lord will raise up:

---

[22] Puech 1992, 452.

[23] For the text and a French translation, se Puech 1992, 466-67. There is an English translation in Eisenman and Wise 1992, 145.

[24] Puech 1992, 475; Eisenman and Wise 1992, 145.

[25] Puech 1992, 489, 495.

And his star will arise in heaven, as a king, lighting up the light of knowledge as by the sun of the day ... He will shine as the sun on the earth and will remove all darkness from under heaven, and there will be peace on all the earth.

Fragments of a Levi Apocryphon have been found in the Cairo Geniza and at Qumran[26] and some scholars had suggested that this Apocryphon concluded with a passage similar to *T. Levi* 18, long before 4QAaron A was published.[27] Unfortunately, however, the end of the Levi Apocryphon has not come to light. Since the other fragments of 4QAaron A show no clear parallels to the Levi Apocryphon, however, it is is unlikely that both are part of the same composition.[28] It is clear that 4QAaron A bears some general generic resemblance to the *Testament of Levi,* but their precise relationship is unclear.

The controversial aspect of 4QAaron A, however, does not lie in its affinity with the *Testament of Levi,* but in the claim that the referential background of this text is to be found in the Servant Songs of Second Isaiah. Puech characterizes the figure of whom the text speaks as a sage, a priest and "a servant despised and rejected."[29] The first two characterizations are beyond dispute. The wisdom of this figure is clearly emphasized in fragment 9, and the motif of wisdom also appears in other fragments of 4QAaron A.[30] The statement that "he will atone for all the children of his generation" shows that he is a priest: compare the role of the "messiah of Aaron and Israel" in CD 14:19.[31] Presumably, he will make atonement by offering sacrifices in the temple, as prescribed in the Torah. The eschatological priest in *Testament of Levi* 18 is also characterized by wisdom, "lighting up the light of knowledge as by the sun of the day."

Problems arise, however, when the figure described in 4QAaron A is said to be "a servant despised and rejected" and so to anticipate the Christian view of Jesus as a suffering messiah. Fundamental to this view is the claim that the Aramaic text has its referential background in the Servant Songs of Second Isaiah. Some basis for this claim is found in the motif of light. Fragment 9 says of the one who will atone for his generation that "his eternal sun will shine and his light will be kindled in all the

---

[26] Greenfield and Stone 1985, 457-69.

[27] Nickelsburg and Stone 1983, 199 n.3: "Correlations between Levi's prayer ... the description of his call (chap. 4), and chap. 18 suggest that this last passage in some form was the climax of the Aramaic text."

[28] Brooke 1993, 88 suggests that a reference to "seven" in the Aramaic fragment may correspond to the seven men in *T. Levi* 8:2 and the Bodleian fragment from the Geniza, col. a, line 9, but this is quite uncertain in view of the fragmentary nature of the text.

[29] Puech 1992, 492-99.

[30] Brooke 1993, 89.

[31] The phrase "messiah of Aaron and Israel" refers to two messiahs rather than one. See Cross 1992, 14. The atonement is presumably performed by the priestly messiah.

corners of the earth." The servant is described as "a light to the nations" in Isaiah 42 and 49. The Targum of Isaiah emphasizes that the Servant is a teacher who leads people to justice by his instruction and prays for their sins.[32] The correspondences here, however, are not very specific, and they do not involve the motif of suffering at all. There is, in fact, no question of vicarious suffering or death in 4QAaron A, and no parallel to Isaiah 53 where the classic description of the suffering of the Servant is found. Puech argues for some terminological parallels with the Targum of Isaiah 53, but as we have seen the Targum disassociates the suffering from the messianic Servant, and even Puech does not find parallels here to the biblical text of Isaiah.[33] There are, however, two passages that deal with suffering of some sort, and which seem to have given rise to the view that the author had the suffering servant in mind.

At the end of fragment 9 we are told that the eschatological priest will endure lies and calumnies:

> They will speak many words against him, and they will invent many [lie]s and fictions against him and speak shameful things about him. Evil will overthrow his generation ... His situation will be one of lying and violence [and] the people will go astray in his days, and be confounded.

The trials described here, however, hardly constitute suffering as it is envisaged in Isaiah 53, where the servant is bruised and ultimately killed.

The second passage is more obscure. Fragment 24, which we have quoted above, contains intriguing allusions to hanging (or crucifixion) and "the nail." The word translated "nail" (אצצ) is unknown in Western Aramaic, and is translated on the basis of its Syriac usage.[34] It is not certain that there is any reference to a nail here at all. If we assume, however, that the text does refer to crucifixion, there is still no question of a messianic figure being crucified. Rather, the person addressed in the text is told not to afflict the weak by crucifixion. Puech asks, nonetheless, whether there might not be a "negative reference" to the violent death of a "Priest-Servant" ("Faudrait-il voir dans les recommandations du patriarche au fr. 24 ii 4-5 des allusions, en négatif, à une mise à mort violente du 'Prêtre-Serviteur'? Ce ne serait pas impensable").[35] Presumably he means that the Suffering Servant constitutes the referential background of the passage, even though the person addressed is not identified as the Servant, but rather that person is told not to treat the weak as the Servant

---

[32] Puech 1992, 497.

[33] Puech 1992, 497-99; Brooke 1993, 92. The word *mk'wbykh*, sorrows, cf. Isa 53:3-4, occurs in fragment 6 in a context too fragmentary to be helpful.

[34] Puech 1992, 477-78.

[35] Ibid., 499.

is treated in the Isaianic prophecy. The Aramaic words for "afflict" and "weak," that are used in 4QAaron A fragment 24 also occur in the Targum on Isaiah with reference to the Servant,[36] but there are no direct allusions to the vocabulary of Isaiah. A "negative reference" is very hard to prove, and it does not seem to me that there is any reference whatever to the Servant Songs in fragment 24. There is certainly no prediction here of a figure who will be subjected to suffering, only an admonition against afflicting the weak.

There is, then, no reason to read 4QAaronA in the perspective opened up by the Servant poems of Second Isaiah. Fragment 9 refers to an eschatological priest who will encounter opposition, but there is no suggestion of vicarious suffering. Fragment 24 is extremely obscure, but while it may refer to crucifixion, it does not refer to the death of a "Priest-Servant" or of any particular individual. The Servant poems of Isaiah do not provide the referential background of 4QAaronA.

## 5. A Sectarian Background

A more plausible referential background for this text can be found in the sectarian writings of the Dead Sea Scrolls. Starcky, it is true, explicitly rejected any allusion to the Teacher of Righteousness, and further denied that the Teacher is ever assimilated to the eschatological priest in the Dead Sea Scrolls.[37] The opposition encountered by the eschatological priest in fragment 9, however, brings to mind precisely the trials of the Teacher of Righteousness in his struggle with the "Man of the Lie." In the Aramaic text:

> They will speak many words against him, and they will invent many [lie]s and fictions against him and speak shameful things about him. Evil will overthrow his generation ... His situation will be one of lying and violence [and] the people will go astray in his days, and be confounded.

According to CD 1:14-15: "The Scoffer arose who shed over Israel the waters of lies. He caused them to wander in a pathless wilderness ..." (trans. Vermes). A hymn which is usually thought to be the work of the Teacher[38] complains: "Teachers of lies [have smoothed] Thy people [with words], and [false prophets] have led them astray" and again "they, teachers of lies and seers of falsehood, have schemed against me a devilish scheme" (1QH 4:7, 9-10, trans. Vermes). The Teacher of Righteousness was, of course, a priest (see the *pesher* on Psalm 37, 3:18). Both the Teacher and the figure in 4QAaron A, then, are priests who endure the lies of their

---

[36] Ibid.

[37] Starcky 1963, 492.

[38] G. Jeremias 1963, 204-17.

opponents, which lead people astray. I do not suggest that the eschatological priest of 4QAaron A should be identified as the historical Teacher, but the Scrolls also envisage a Teacher who was yet to come. The Damascus Document, which clearly refers to the Teacher as a figure of the past, also envisages another one "who will teach righteousness at the end of days" (CD 6:11). Similarly we read of an Interpreter of the Law who was active in the early history of the community (CD 6:7), and another Interpreter of the Law who will arise with the Branch of David at the end of days (4QFlor 1:11, cf. CD 7:18-19).[39] It is highly probable that this figure should be identified with the Messiah of Aaron, or eschatological priest, who is linked with the Messiah of Israel in 1QS 9:11. Priests were also teachers. In the blessing of Moses, Levi is said to "teach Jacob your ordinances and Israel your law" (Deut 33:10). It is said of the priest in 4QAaron A that "His word is like a word of heaven and his teaching is in accordance with the will of God." This figure is clearly a figure for the end of days, and is both priest and teacher. The experiences of the historical Teacher, however, provided the referential background for the depiction of the eschatological priest. The future priest is imagined by analogy with the historical career of the Teacher, except that he has a more glorious finale. The parallel holds regardless of whether the Damascus Document and Hodayot are deemed to be reliable sources for the historical Teacher. In any case they present the account of his career, no doubt stylized, which was current in the Dead Sea sect. It is this stylized account, rather than raw historical occurrences, that provides the basis for the picture of the eschatological Priest/Teacher.

Several scholars have argued that the Teacher of Righteousness was himself modelled on the Suffering Servant of Isaiah.[40] The primary evidence for this view lies in the so-called Teacher hymns, in which the hymnist often complains of his sufferings (e.g. 1QH 7:10; 8:26-7; 8:35-6). The argument, however, cannot be sustained. In no case are the sufferings described in the Hodayot vicarious, nor do they make atonement for anyone else. The fact that the author occasionally refers to himself as a "servant" (עבד) is not significant; the word has a wide range of reference apart from the servant songs of Isaiah. There are allusions to Isa 50:4 ("the Lord has given me a disciples' tongue") in 1QH 7:10 and 8:35, but this is not a sufficient basis for identifying the Teacher with the Suffering Servant.[41] The Isaianic Servant does not provide the referential background for the Teacher any more than he does for the eschatological priest.

4QAaronA fragment 24 is more difficult to decipher. In so far as it yields any

---

[39] Brooke 1985, 197-205.

[40] Black 1953, 4-6; 1961, 143-44; Brownlee 1956/57, 18-20; 26-27; Dupont-Sommer 1959, 372-79.

[41] G. Jeremias 1963, 200-307.

sense, it would seem to warn the descendant of Levi not to afflict the poor and defenceless. It does not appear to suggest, even negatively, that the descendant of Levi might be subjected to suffering and death. The possible, but very uncertain, reference to crucifixion inevitably brings Jesus to mind, but as Puech quite properly points out, crucifixion was widely used as a means of punishment in the Roman era.[42] The Hasmonean priest-king Alexander Jannaeus is said to have crucified 800 of his Jewish opponents (probably Pharisees) "while he feasted with his concubines in a conspicuous place, and slaughtered their children and wives before the eyes of the still living wretches" (Josephus, *Ant* 13.14.2 §380). There is a well-known reference to him in the *Pesher on Nahum* from Qumran, as "the lion of wrath" who "who would hang men up alive."[43] It has generally been assumed that the Dead Sea sect disapproved of this action, although the fragmentary text of the *pesher* does not clearly condemn it.[44] 4QAaron A frag. 24 can be read as a condemnation of, or warning against such behavior: a descendant of Levi should not do such things.

It is not necessary to see here a direct reference to Alexander Jannaeus. That king's action merely serves as part of the referential background of our text, illustrating the kind of practices which are in view. Puech suggested a date about 100 BCE on the basis of the paleography, adding that the writing was of the same type as 1QS, 1QSa and 4Q175.[45] The typological comparison is more reliable than the absolute date, which must allow for a margin of error of at least plus or minus twenty five years. The paleography, then, is compatible with a view that the text dates to the time of Alexander Jannaeus and belongs to the general orbit of the Dead Sea sect. The sectarian interest in an eschatological Teacher/Priest and concern about the cruel punishments inflicted by Hasmonean kings provides a more reliable referential background to this text than the Servant poems of Second Isaiah.

## 6. Conclusion

The fragmentary Aramaic text 4QAaron A is undoubtedly one of the more interesting texts recently made available from the Dead Sea Scrolls. It expands the limited documentation available on the eschatological priest, and so bears directly on the

---

[42] Puech 1992, 499; Hengel 1977; Fitzmyer 1978.

[43] Horgan 1979, 163.

[44] Yadin 1971, 3-12, argued that crucifixion is prescribed as a punishment in the Temple Scroll (64:6-13) and that the sect looked on the Lion of Wrath as God's instrument in punishing the "Seekers after Smooth Things." This possibility deserves renewed attention in light of the recently published "Prayer for King Jonathan" (4Q 448, see Eshel and Yardeni 1992), which is apparently favorable to Alexander Jannaeus.

[45] Puech 1992, 452.

subject of messianism. Since the Scrolls often witness to aspects of ancient Judaism that were picked up in early Christianity but not in the Mishnah and Talmud, it is tempting to look for analogies to Christian beliefs in these fragmentary texts. In fact, some stunning parallels to the New Testament have come to light, such as the "Son of God" text, 4Q 246,[46] and the resurrection text, 4Q521.[47] I have argued, however, that the attempt to find in 4QAaron A a Jewish precedent for the use of the Servant Songs in a messianic context is mistaken. Fascinating though this figure who will atone for the children of his generation may be, he provides no analogy for the crucified messiah of Christianity.

## *Bibliography*

Black, Matthew 1953: "Servant of the Lord and Son of Man," in: *SJTh* 6 (1953) 1-11.

— 1961: *The Scrolls and Christian Origins,* New York: Scribners 1961.

Brownlee, William H. 1956/57: "Messianic Motifs of Qumran and the New Testament," in: *NTS* 3 (1956/57) 12-30, 195-210.

Brooke, George J. 1985: *Exegesis at Qumran. 4QFlorilegium in its Jewish Context,* Sheffield: JSOT 1985.

— 1993: "4QTestament of Levi^d(?) and the Messianic Servant High Priest," in: Martinus C. De Boer (ed.), *From Jesus to John. Essays on Jesus and New Testament Christology in Honour of Marinus de Jonge,* Sheffield: JSOT 1993, 83-100.

Clifford, Richard J. 1984: *Fair Spoken and Persuading. An Interpretation of Second Isaiah,* New York: Paulist 1984.

Collins, John J. 1993: "The *Son of God* Text from Qumran," in: Martinus C. De Boer (ed.), *From Jesus to John. Essays on Jesus and New Testament Christology in Honour of Marinus de Jonge,* Sheffield: JSOT 1993, 65-82.

— 1994: "The Works of the Messiah," in: *Dead Sea Discoveries* 1 (1994) forthcoming.

Cross, Frank Moore 1992: "Some Notes on a Generation of Qumran Studies," in: J. Trebolle Barrera and L. Vegas Montaner (eds.), *The Madrid Qumran Congress. Proceedings of the International Congress on the Dead Sea Scrolls, Madrid 18-21 March 1991,* Leiden: Brill 1991, 1-14.

Duhm, Bernhard 1892: *Das Buch Jesaja,* Göttingen: Vandenhoeck & Ruprecht 1892.

Dupont-Sommer, André 1959: *Les Écrits esséniens découverts près de la Mer Morte,* Paris: Payot 1959.

Eisenman, Robert and Michael Wise 1992: *The Dead Sea Scrolls Uncovered,* Rockport, MA: Element 1992.

---

[46] Puech 1992a, 98-131; Collins 1993, 65-82.

[47] Puech 1993, 475-519; Collins 1994.

Eshel, Esther and Hanan, and Ada Yardeni 1992: "A Scroll from Qumran Which Includes Part of Psalm 154 and a Prayer for King Jonathan and His Kingdom," in: *IEJ* 42 (1992) 199-229.

Fitzmyer, Joseph A. 1978: "Crucifixion in Ancient Palestine, Qumran Literature and the New Testament," in: *CBQ* 40 (1978) 493-513.

Greenfield, Jonas C. and Michael E. Stone 1985: "The Aramaic and Greek Levi Fragments," in: H. W. Hollander and M. de Jonge (eds.), *The Testaments of the Twelve Patriarchs*, Leiden: Brill 1985, 457-69.

Hartman, Lars 1979: *Asking for a Meaning. A Study of 1 Enoch 1-5* (CB.NT 12), Lund: Gleerup 1979.

Hengel, Martin 1977: *Crucifixion*, Philadelphia, PA: Fortress 1977.

— 1992: "Jesus der Messias Israels. Zum Streit über das 'messianische Sendungsbewusstsein' Jesu," in: Ithamar Gruenwald, Shaul Shaked and Gedaliahu Stroumsa (eds.), *Messiah and Christos: Studies in the Jewish Origins of Christianity*, Tübingen: Mohr 1992, 155-76.

Higgins, A. J. B. 1979: "Jewish Messianic Belief in Justin Martyr's Dialogue with Trypho," in: Leo Landman (ed.), *Messianism in the Talmudic Era*, New York: Ktav 1979, 182-89.

Horgan, Maurya P. 1979: *Pesharim: Qumran Interpretations of Biblical Books*, Washington, D.C.: Catholic Biblical Association of America 1979.

Hooker, Morna D. 1959: *Jesus and the Servant: The Influence of the Servant Concept of Deutero-Isaiah in the New Testament*, London: SPCK 1959.

Jeremias, Gert 1963: *Der Lehrer der Gerechtigkeit*, Göttingen: Vandenhoeck & Ruprecht 1963.

Jeremias, Joachim 1968: "*Pais Theou* in Later Judaism in the Period after the LXX," in: *TDNT* 5, Grand Rapids, MI: Eerdmans 1968, 677-700.

de Jonge, Marinus 1991: *Jesus. The Servant-Messiah*, New Haven, CT: Yale 1991.

Nickelsburg, George W. E. and Michael E. Stone 1983: *Faith and Piety in Early Judaism. Texts and Documents*, Philadelphia, PA: Fortress 1983.

North, C. R. 1956: *The Suffering Servant in Second Isaiah*, Oxford: Oxford University Press 1956.

Puech, Emile 1992: "Fragments d'un apocryphe de Lévi et le personnage eschatologique. 4QTest Levi^{c-d}(?) et 4QAJa," in: J. Trebolle Barrera and L. Vegas Montaner (eds.), *The Madrid Qumran Congress. Proceedings of the International Congress on the Dead Sea Scrolls, Madrid 18-21 March 1991*, Leiden: Brill 1992, 449-501.

— 1992a: "Fragment d'une apocalypse en Araméen (4Q246 = ps Dan^d) et le 'Royaume de Dieu'," in: *RB* 99 (1992) 98-131.

— 1993: "Une Apocalypse Messianique (4Q521)," in: *RdQ* 15 (1992) 475-519.

Rowley, H. H. 1965: *The Servant of the Lord and Other Essays on the Old Testament*, Oxford: Blackwell 1965.

Starcky, Jean 1963: "Les quatre étapes du messianisme à Qumrân," in: *RB* 70 (1963) 481-505.

Vermes, Geza 1987: *The Dead Sea Scrolls in English* (3rd ed.), Harmondsworth: Penguin 1987.

Williams, Sam K. 1975: *Jesus' Death as Saving Event. The Background and Origin of a Concept*, Missoula, MT: Scholars Press 1975.

Yadin, Yigal 1971: "Pesher Nahum (4Q pNahum) Reconsidered," in: *IEJ* 21 (1971) 1-12.

# ΕΥΣΕΒΕΙΑΝ ΕΔΕΙΞΕΝ ΤΟΙΣ ΑΝΘΡΩΠΟΙΣ

## The Significance of the Bilingual Asoka Inscription for New Testament Philology and for Research into the Notion of Hellenism

### Lars Rydbeck

## 1. Introductory Remarks

In 1957 and 1964 respectively two Greek Asoka texts were found in the neighbour-hood of Alexandria in Arachosia, the so-called Old Kandahar of today.

I will not go into the text from 1964 because I have become interested in the first text, which was found connected to a version in Standard Aramaic and which is usually known as the "bilingual Asoka inscription". The 1964 inscription which exists only in Greek follows fairly closely (as I have learnt from a Danish colleague of mine, Dr. Benedicte Mygind[1]) the Middle Indian Asoka originals, to be exact the end of edict number XII and the portion that has been preserved of edict number XIII.

Both Greek texts can be dated to approximately 250 BC, when King Asoka of Northern India—in the Greek text he is called Piodasses, Prakrit for "with a friendly look"—has experienced a conversion to Buddhism. He calls attention to his conversion through a series of inscriptions; some were drawn up in Middle Indian but others which were posted in Hellenistic Arachosia, roughly the south-eastern part of present-day Afghanistan which also fell under his jurisdiction, were in Greek and Aramaic.

The Greek texts have been commented upon by Louis Robert.[2] Much of what I have to say relies heavily on his competent discussion. I have now a few things to add to Robert's treatment of the 1958 Greek text.

When I first happened to read the Greek text of the bilingual inscription in the

---

[1] At a seminar in Côpenhagen on April 23rd 1994 on "Languages in contact during the Hellenistic period", at which occasion Dr. Mygind read a paper on the interrelationship between the Indian Asoka originals and the Greek version contained in the 1964 inscription.

[2] Robert 1958, 7-18 and idem 1964, 134–40.

late sixties, my thoughts went immediately to the Greek of the gospels: short clauses containing little more than a subject and predicate, an occasional participle, καί ("and") between the short pregnant clauses. In our text six instances are found of καί joining short small clauses to each other; yet the text as a whole seemed to be authentically Greek. This impression of mine is confirmed by Louis Robert.[3]

But if these 14 Asoka lines had been found in any of the Gospels, scholars would have alleged them to be a translation of an Aramaic original with its "w^e, w^e, w^e" between every nominal clause. As a matter of fact this "and-and-and" style is much less prominent in the Aramaic version than in the Greek: I have counted three instances of "w^e" or "u" answering to only three of the six καί connecting clauses.

The Greek portion of the Asoka bilingual text is the easternmost of all Greek inscriptions ever found.

## 2. The Greek-Aramaic Inscription of Asoka from Kandahar (Afghanistan).

Photo: Délégation Archéologique Française en Afghanistan. Paris.

---

[3] Idem 1958, 12.

## 3. The Greek Portion of the Inscription of Asoka.

The text is that of the original publication by D. Schlumberger[4] (with correction of a minor misprint). The translation is by F. Millar:[5]

>      Δέκα ἐτῶν πληρη[θέντ]ων βασιλεὺς
>      Πιοδάσσης εὐσέβεια[ν] ἔδειξεν τοῖς ἀν-
>      θρώποις, καὶ ἀπὸ τούτου εὐσεβεστέρους
> 4    τοὺς ἀνθρώπους ἐποίησεν καὶ πάντα
>      εὐθηνεῖ κατὰ πᾶσαν γῆν, καὶ ἀπέχεται
>      βασιλεὺς τῶν ἐμψύχων καὶ οἱ λοιποὶ δὲ
>      ἄνθρωποι καὶ ὅσοι θηρευταὶ ἢ ἁλιεῖς
> 8    βασιλέως πέπαυνται θηρεύοντες, καὶ
>      εἴ τινες ἀκρατεῖς, πέπαυνται τῆς ἀκρα-
>      σίας κατὰ δύναμιν, καὶ ἐνήκοοι πατρὶ
>      καὶ μητρὶ καὶ τῶν πρεσβυτέρων παρὰ
> 12   τὰ πρότερον, καὶ τοῦ λοιποῦ λῷον
>      καὶ ἄμεινον κατὰ πάντα ταῦτα
>      ποιοῦντες διάξουσιν.

When ten years had been fulfilled, Piodasses demonstrated piety before men, and from that time on has made men more pious, and all has prospered throughout the land. For the king abstains from (eating) living things, and other men—even such as are the king's hunters or fishermen—have abandoned the chase. And if any are lacking in self-control, they have left off their excesses so far as they can. Moreover they are obedient each to their father and mother, and to the elders, to an extent greater than previously. For the future, acting according to all these principles, they will live more agreeably and better.

---

[4] D. Schlumberger 1958, 2–3.
[5] F. Millar 1993, 20.

## 4. Commentary on the Inscription

The form of the letters locates the inscription in the period 275 to 225 BC. Comparable letter forms are to be found in inscriptions from Asia Minor, Rhodes and Egypt.[6] The Hellenism of Arachosia and the style of the lettering is part of the general phenomenon of Hellenism. Neither the editor of the text nor the carver of the lettering (I think they are different persons) live isolated from the common culture.

In his proclamation King Asoka addresses the Yona, that is the Ionians, the Greek inhabitants of his Arachosian kingdom. These Yona formed a community of Greek language and culture in the region bordering on India.

The Aramaic portion of the bilingual document addresses the so-called Cambojas, ancestors of the present-day Iranians. The local Old Iranian (Persian) was apparently not used as a written language and so the text was drafted in Standard Aramaic which was the 'lingua franca' of the Achaemenid empire. According to specialists in Semitic and Iranian languages we are dealing with a type of administrative official Aramaic which no longer functioned for daily use.

This is certainly not the case with the Greek version written as it is in a language supported by its environment, the Greek colony of Arachosian Alexandria.

The καί-style of the inscription goes very well with the religious proclamation of Asoka. According to Robert[7] this is not an Indian original which has been translated into Greek. It is almost the other way round: the editors of the Greek and Aramaic versions have drawn up their texts in conventional language for such a theme. The Greek version was at any rate written in good Greek for the Greek colony.

But now back again to the καί-style and the New Testament gospel atmosphere of the text. A Belgian scholar, Sophie Trenkner, has done research into characteristic stylistic features of early Greek sacred texts. In her opinion[8] the καί-style is well suited to eulogies of gods, aretalogies and all sorts of miracle tales. It is of course well suited to every genre which aims at solemnity but wishes to remain easily comprehensible. This is how I look upon the gospels, particularly the gospel of Mark, but in the case of Mark we have never seen anything in the way of a Semitic original. As to the Asoka text there exists a parallel version in Aramaic about which we can state with confidence that it did not trigger off the six καί between clauses in the Greek version.[9] Furthermore there are in fact two or three things in the Aramaic version which we would never have understood, if we had only had an Aramaic text

---

[6] Robert 1958, 9.

[7] Idem 1958, 12.

[8] Trenkner 1948, 54–55.

[9] How far a presumably paratactic alleged Prakrit original (with clause-connecting "ca") might have influenced our Greek text editor is not easy to tell.

unsupported by an easily comprehensible parallel version in Greek. This means that the editor of the Greek text has indeed produced an efficient presentation of Asoka's message *à la grecque*.

Another point we should consider is κατὰ δύναμιν ("as far as they can") in line 10. As far as vegetarianism is concerned the rational and relativistic Greek author appreciates human limitations. This qualifying phrase, "as far as they can", is not found in the Aramaic version. The Semite apparently did not feel the need to press this point. Obedience to "mother and father" in the Aramaic version is phrased in reverse order, "father and mother", in the Greek, with the qualification that you should obey "to an extent greater than previously" (lines 10–12). The Aramaic version substitutes this phrase with something abstruse and obscure which perhaps could be translated "in accordance with what Fate has assigned to each one".

Louis Robert argues strongly that the language and style of the document are authentically Greek. I am prepared to agree with him with the additional remark that there are extremely few representatives of this particular form of Greek in Hellenistic times. The other larger Greek Asoka inscription should not be compared linguistically to our bilingual document, since it was drafted in a more traditionally classical Greek style. This larger document further demonstrates how competent those Arachosian Greek text editors were, as the situation required, in producing linguistic and stylistic variation.

The Greek portion of our bilingual document surprises us with a glimpse of a Greek Arachosian Alexandria, where we could expect to find a gymnasium, attractive ephebes and places to meet for dinner-parties and conversation. Robert reminds us[10] that the Greeks who participated in the Alexander expedition were not only soldiers, craftsmen and farmers but were also what we in our modern journalese would call intellectuals. They included elementary school teachers, rhetoricians, poets able to produce from stock epigrams to the gods or the dead, ordinary actors, actors of pantomime (who would surely make contact with their Indian colleagues), philosophers, doctors, teachers of gymnastics, painters and sculptors, marble cutters, stone carvers, inscription editors, interpreters and translators. They were a multicoloured collection of well-educated people familiar with popular philosophy. This Hellenistic milieu stretched from Mauretania to India.

King Asoka of Northern India now turns to the Greeks of Alexandria in Arachosia: he demonstrates piety (εὐσέβειαν ἔδειξεν) before his Greek subjects and exhorts them to live as vegetarians (ἀπέχεσθαι τῶν ἐμψύχων) and lead lives of self-sacrifice and tolerance (πεπαῦσθαι τῆς ἀκρασίας κτλ.). We can only hope that those Greeks κατὰ δύναμιν—according to their ability—did not put King Piodass-

---

[10] The description of people involved in the Alexander enterprise is taken from Robert 1958, 13 and idem 1964, 139–40.

es *alias* Asoka to shame.

## Bibliography

Millar, F., 1993: "Taking the Measure of the Ancient World", in: *Proceedings of the Classical Association*, Vol. XC (1993) 11–33.

Robert, L. 1948: "Observation sur l'inscription Grecque", in: *Journal Asiatique* 146 (1958) 7-18.

— 1964: Communication in: *Académie des Inscriptions et Belles-Lettres. Comptes Rendus*, Paris: Librarie C. Klincksieck 1964, 134–40.

Schlumberger, D./Robert, L./Dupont-Sommer, A./Benveniste, E. 1958: "Une bilingue Gréco-Araméenne d'Asoka", in: *Journal Asiatique* 146 (1958) 1–48.

Schlumberger, D. 1964: "Une nouvelle inscription greque d'Asoka", in: *Académie des Inscriptions et Belles-Lettres. Comptes Rendus,* Paris: Librarie C. Klincksieck 1964, 126–140 (including a communication by L. Robert on pp. 134-40).

Trenkner, S. 1948: *Le style καί dans le récit attique oral* (Cahiers de l'Institut d'études polonaises en Belgique, I), Brussels: Institut d'études polonaises en Belgique 1948.

# Jesus and the Urban Culture of Galilee

Seán Freyne

## 1. Introduction

The past 20 years have witnessed an unprecedented interest in Galilee in antiquity for several reasons, not all of which have to do with the fact that Jesus was from Nazareth in Galilee. A number of academic disciplines which previously had operated quite independently of each other have of late begun to show a convergence of interests that makes it possible to achieve a more comprehensive picture of Galilean life than heretofore. Foremost among these is the archaeological work that is being done by a number of different teams, interested in situating the results of their work at individual sites within the framework of the wider social and cultural context of the region as a whole, an area that should not be confined to political Galilee as known to Josephus (Jos., *J.W.* 3,35). More detailed scientific analysis of the pottery has also achieved a much clearer impression of trading patterns on both an intra- and inter-regional basis. Social scientific models, especially those that deal with pre-industrial cities, are increasingly being employed as an aid to a better understanding of the scattered pieces of evidence that are available, by situating these within a coherent theoretical framework for ancient societies. Textual studies too have contributed to the discussion. The impact of his Galilean sojourn on the writings of Josephus has been clearly exposed, and redactional studies of both the gospels (especially Mark and Q) and the rabbinical corpus have sought to relate the various strata of these writings to specific historical moments and social contexts of Galilee.

All of these developments understandably have played a role in the most recent wave of interest in the historical Jesus. However, the marriage of Galilean studies and historical Jesus research is fraught with its own difficulties which have not always been successfully negotiated. Some latter-day Schweitzer will, no doubt critically evaluate the current crop of Jesus books, even if none of them can match the romantic idealisation of Galilee of an Ernest Renan. What concerns us here is the way in which the Galilean social world can so easily be manipulated to suit the particular Jesus figure that is being presented. The problem is exacerbated by the fact that the gospels, the very documents that provide us with access to Jesus, are also quite important literary evidence for reconstructing the larger picture. When it comes to dealing with Galilee it is difficult, even for critical scholars not to put Jesus at the centre and paint the picture of the region accordingly.

The explosion of specialised information on so many different fronts, even when dealing with a limited area such as Galilee, as well as the demand for methodological awareness in several disciplines, make it increasingly difficult for any one scholar to keep all aspects in focus. As one trained to deal with literary texts it has been my experience that the on-going dialogue with archaeology, especially socio-archaeology, can be both fruitful and challenging. I am not thereby suggesting that archaeology provides the "hard" facts which prove the gospels were right (or wrong). Rather, the dialogue between text and spade is highly complex, each with its own methodological constraints. It needs also to be recognised that, if it is true that "our texts are tellings rather than showings", it is equally true that archaeology is a showing that requires a telling, that is an interpretation, to which texts have a very real contribution to make. Insofar as is possible each should be allowed to tell its different story before any attempt is made to generate a single converging account.

These methodological observations are prompted by a reading of two of the most imposing of the recent crop of books on Jesus, those of J. D. Crossan and J. Meier.[1] The description "Mediterranean" and "marginal" as applied to Jesus in the titles of the two works seemed promising from a Galilean perspective, yet in this regard at least both disappointed in different ways. We shall have to await further volumes of Meier's projected study before it becomes clear what particular importance he gives to the Galilean setting of the ministry, something that is acknowledged more than once in this first volume, but without, it must be said, any real engagement with the recent archaeological evidence. Crossan's methodology is a deliberate attempt to keep literary, historical and social scientific procedures in critical dialogue, without giving precedence to any of them. Irrespective of what one might think about the possibilities of such an hermeneutical stance, what I found lacking here was an engagement with the specific Galilean contours of Jesus' career in favour of the more generalised category of Mediterranean, due in part to the fact that again archaeological evidence plays no part in the historical reconstruction in part two of the work where the social and political world of first century Palestine was being canvassed. "Mediterranean" enters the picture not primarily as an historical but as an anthropological category, which consequently can be used to make plausible the appear-

---

[1] Crossan 1991 and Meier 1991.

ance in Galilee of those most pervasive of Mediterranean counter-culturalists, the Cynics.

In effect Crossan has repeated, in a highly nuanced and sophisticated manner to be sure, the History of Religions approach to Galilee of such scholars as W. Bauer, W. Bertram and W. Grundmann,[2] namely, that the epithet, "Galilee of the gentiles" (Isa 8:23; 1 Macc 5:15) should be regarded as an accurate cultural and ethnographic description of the region in the first century. Bauer, for example, writing in a manner that scarcely disguises the then prevalent views of Pharisaic Judaism, states: "Der Galiläer Jesus vertrat das Judentum in einer dem allgemein Menschlichen zugewandeten oder, wenn man so will, in einer synkretistisch erweichten Form".[3] Such claims provided the scholarly (sic!) basis for W. Grundmann's claim that because "Galiläa heidnisch war", "Jesus kein Jude war".[4] To be fair to Crossan he is at pains to retain a Jewish element to the picture; his Jesus is a Mediterranean *Jewish* peasant, but when one analyses the data base on which this picture of Jesus is constructed very little of the distinctively Jewish concerns of the Jesus tradition as a whole is considered to be relevant.

It is indeed useful to see Galilee, or any other region for that matter, within the larger context—cultural, social and economic. The categories of honour/shame e.g. which Crossan regards as pivotal Mediterranean values, are applicable to Galilean life also, and have been used with excellent results by a number of scholars in elucidating the Jesus tradition. My contention, however, is that within such a general perspective more immediate geographical, historical and socio-cultural factors which apply to particular regions need also to be articulated in order to present a balanced picture that has the best chance of approximating to the real lives of actual people in that region at any given period. This must surely be the goal of all historical research, however much we need interpretative models that by their nature are general in order to make sense of the data. It is for this reason that I choose to start with the actual gospel narratives rather than with any reconstructed data base either of deeds or words, since the narratives, in their different ways to be sure, all anchor the ministry of Jesus within a coherent social world in Galilee. It is to an actual Galilee as "the world behind the text" that these accounts point, and at the risk of being unfashionable, I want to look at those narratives about Jesus, particularly as they apply to Galilee and re-present the ethos there. My aim is to test the ways in which these narratives situate the ministry of Jesus in that context with a view to judging how their tellings do or do not approximate to that world as we *today* can reconstruct it, and to judge how the actual Jesus might have related to it on the basis of a

---

[2] Bauer 1967; Bertram 1935; Grundmann 1941.
[3] Bauer 1967, 104.
[4] Grundmann 1941, 166-75.

critical use of the traditions about him that have been received.

## 2. Galilean Regional Geography and Jesus

By taking the gospel narratives as the starting point one is immediately confronted with the geography of Jesus' ministry, especially the Galilean geography. Much has been made of the symbolic intentions of the different evangelists in terms of their geographic references, especially in the wake of Lohmeyer's study of Mark and Conzelmann's treatment of Luke. Such symbolism need not, however, obliterate all actual reference, especially in a context in which the land and its different regions had always had definite religious associations from the Israelite experience and history (See e.g. Isa 8,23). Yet when one compares the gospel geography with the accounts of Palestine that pagan writers such as Strabo, Pliny and Tacitus provide us with, not to speak of Josephus and the Rabbinical writings, there is a stark contrast. Despite various inaccuracies and confusions that are easily attributable to the absence of maps or any other technical helps, there is a far greater sense of place in the pagan writers and a keener awareness of the natural resources. Josephus also has a very clear sense of boundaries, distances between various places and the length of time required for journeys between different destinations, as well as the topography of certain key sights—all matters we would expect somebody who had been active in the field as a military and political commander to be well-informed about. In the Rabbinical writings, on the other hand, geographical interests are directly related to halachic ordinances to do with the observance of tithing laws and the settling of disputed cases with regard to the place of provenance of various products. That these discussions were not purely academic emerges from such notices as that of Josephus concerning John of Gischala's exploitation of his co-religionists' desire to obtain native oil (Jos., *Life* 74), as well as from the mosaic floor in the synagogue at Rehov in the Bethshean valley, a section of which reproduces a text also found in several rabbinical writings, which describes the borders of *Eretz Israel*. It may well be no accident that the list of places is most detailed for the borders between Tyre and Galilee. The concern apparently was to define precisely the area within which tithes and other offerings would have to be set aside, and for this purpose the rabbis sought to temper strict observance with leniency in their description, especially in view of the economic hardships of the third century C.E.[5]

By comparison, the gospels show relatively little interest in these matters, even though there is a general awareness of such aspects as the regional divisions of the land (Galilee, Samaria and Judea), the surrounding territories and cities as well as

---

[5] Sussman 1981, 146-53.

other aspects of the physical geography, such as the lake and the activities associated with it. While there is no concentrated attention on these details within the narratives, the apparent distance, even vagueness, should not lull us into dismissing the geographical notices of the gospels as mere window-dressing, devoid of any intention of actual reference, however imprecise. Rather they summon us to discern more fully the intentions of these notices against their immediate historical background. For example, does the fact that Jesus is depicted as moving freely from Galilee to its environs, though never entering any of the cities, but only "the *territory* of the Gerasenes", "the *borders* of Tyre" or "the *villages* of Caesarea Philippi" (Mark 5:1; 7:24; 8:27), reflect the situation in Mark's own day in relation to Christian communities in the region? Or does it tell us anything about Jesus' attitudes as these were remembered as significant? And how might one go about answering such a question in historical terms? Even more intriguing still is the question of why there is no mention of either Sepphoris or Tiberias, the former refurbished and the latter founded during Jesus' life-time, and both playing such a significant role in the commercial and administrative life of Galilee, as Josephus makes abundantly clear?

The excursions of Jesus to outside territories in Mark (7:31) are generally believed to fit into the evangelist's gentile and missionary perspective.[6] There are, however, certain problems with that position from a purely historical perspective. On the assumption that Mark was written during or immediately after the Jewish war easy movement between Galilee and the surrounding non-Jewish territories would be highly improbable. Episodes like the insistence of the inhabitants of Taricheae that the refugee noblemen from Trachonitis should be circumcised (Jos., *Life* 113) show just how fraught relations were in that period. This is not surprising in the aftermath of the Jew/Gentile hostilities that had broken out in the territories of the Greek cities of Palestine immediately prior to the revolt (Jos., *J.W.* 2,457-465). In such a climate would Mark have presented a Jesus figure who seemed so indifferent to such tensions? Perhaps so. One can think of several reasons why such a presentation might have been significant at that juncture, especially if the gospel was directed to Christian communities in the Galilee or southern Syria, as has been suggested. On the other hand such a cavalier attitude to religious and social boundaries could only have been extremely provocative to Jews in the region, and made Christian communities there more vulnerable to attacks from Jewish neighbours.

What if we were to think of such inter-regional movements some thirty years earlier, informed by the evidence from the archaeological data? How well do they fit the situation then? Palestine, like other regions of the Mediterranean world seems to have enjoyed the relative peace of Tiberius' reign. In Galilee Antipas had politi-

---

[6] Lang 1978, 145-60; Schmeller 1994, 44-65.

cal quarrels with the Nabateans only. The Phoenician city territories, the territory of
Herod Philip and the Dekapolis would all have been accessible to Jewish traders
and craftsmen, and the Herodian cities of lower Galilee were certainly no less likely
to be unfriendly to gentiles then than later. The archaeological data mentioned earlier are highly relevant here, in that recent neutron activation analysis of common
household pottery in the Roman period shows that there was a thriving export industry of Kefar Hanania wares to the surrounding cities, especially in the Golan, at
both Jewish and non-Jewish sites, but also to Ptolemais and Caesarea Philippi. In
other words, the trade was both inter-regional and inter-ethnic, in all probability.[7]
Significantly, however, no wares emanating in Galilee are found in sites south of the
Nazareth ridge, e.g. at Bethshean or Samaria, or farther south in Judea, equally supporting the notices of Luke 9:52; John 4:10, that Jews and Samaritans do not have
any intercourse. The preponderance of Tyrian coinage not only at most of the upper
Galilean sites, but also at those in lower Galilee (including a number of hordes) supports the existence of such trade across religious and cultural boundaries in the
north, however.[8]

In other words, both the political realities and the material remains make the kind
of free movement between Jews and gentiles in the north more plausible for the period of Jesus than for that of the proposed dating of Mark. The material remains
show that such movement was a fact of everyday life, and was interrupted only by
concern for halachic observances at periods of heightened tension. When the political and religious climate was right Jews had long since learned how to live their
traditional way of life among gentiles and to deal with them commercially on a daily basis. The hostility that operated between Jew and non-Jew in the Hellenistic city
territories prior to the Great Revolt was, therefore, exceptional. The differences
with the Samaritans ran deeper, presumably because of the shared religious heritage
that was disputed, thereby precluding any possibility of normal everyday relations.

These observations are not intended as an uncritical vindication of the gospel
narratives with regard to the historical Jesus in the Galilean setting, nor should they
be read as providing further evidence for Bauer's and more recent claims for a syn-
cretised ethos in Galilee. Such generalised accounts ignore the fact that despite the
everyday contacts which the material culture can illustrate, real differences on religious and ethnic grounds could and did surface when Jewish self-identity in the region was under threat. Gerd Theißen's analysis of the story of the Syro-Phoenician
woman has shown that despite its being made to serve Mark's gentile purposes now,
he does not remove the Jewish bias of the pre-Markan account when viewed from
the perspective of its local colouring.[9] This suggests a much stronger ethno-centric

---

[7] Adan-Bayewitz 1993.

[8] Hanson 1980; Raynor and Meshorer 1985.

focus to Jesus' ministry than some of the recent accounts want to claim. We would also have to ask whether his other excursions to so-called "gentile territory" did not have a similar purpose: Jesus' interest in visiting such places was not to "go to the gentiles", but rather to "the lost sheep of the house of Israel", particularly in view of the fact, again on the basis of the material evidence, that it is possible to speak of a "cultural continuum" between upper Galilee and the Golan, the precise district that would have to be traversed in order to get to the region of the Dekapolis from the borders of Tyre.[10] Nor should it be overlooked that the restoration of Israel included the gentiles in messianic blessings also, according to varied strands of Second Temple literature (Isa 2:2-4; 45:2; Zeph 3:9; Zech 8:20-22; Tob 13:11; Sir 36:11-17; *Sib. Or.* 3:616). Thus a concern for the restoration of Israel, inspired by the prophetic tradition would not have been xenophobic as far as Jesus was concerned. Mark's careful presentation of his visiting the territories and villages of the surrounding cities, but not the cities themselves, would fit easily into such a pattern. Yet Mark also intimates that Jesus, despite his healing powers, was not welcomed by the people of Gerasa, who on hearing of his successful exorcism of the legion of demons asked him to depart their territory (Mark 5:17). In other words, the Markan narrative does not totally dilute the Jew/Gentile divide in cultural as well as religious terms in its handling of Jesus' movements, as Theißen notes, even when we might assume that it was in its own theological interests to do so.

Such a conclusion only makes the complete silence concerning Sepphoris and Tiberias all the more baffling. If the reasons for the omission is the lack of success that Jesus had in such centres then we might have expected a series of woes against them similar to those expressed against Corazin, Bethsaida and Capernaum. On the other hand if Jesus was prepared to visit gentile territories to address Jews living there, why exclude these cities from the ambit of his ministry, since they both were thoroughly Jewish in character in the first century, despite some minority gentile presence? Reading the gospels with the more complete picture of Galilee, both geographical and historical, as the subtext, one suspects that the silence is not just an omission, but was quite deliberate. It seems impossible for anyone to have conducted the kind of ministry attributed to Jesus in lower Galilee without having to encounter in some way these two Herodian cities and their spheres of influence. Perhaps a consideration of the political and economic roles of these centres will help to explain the enigma that our geographic considerations have thrown up with regard to the intention of Jesus' ministry.

---

[9] Theißen 1992, 61-81.

[10] Schmeller 1994; Meyers 1976, 95-01; idem 1985, 115-31.

## 3. The Role of Sepphoris and Tiberias

Our discussion of the geographic realities of Jesus' ministry as these are reflected in the gospel narratives raises the question of the Herodian cities of lower Galilee in a particularly acute manner. The usual ways of raising the issue of Jesus and Sepphoris are in my view too simplistic, focusing as they do on the psychological or personal impact that growing up beside such a centre, or even possibly plying one's trade there as a *tekton*, might have had on him. To pose the question in this way is to run the risk of psychologising Jesus after the manner of the nineteenth century liberal lives.[11] What should not be forgotten is that both centres were new foundations, and as such they symbolised and embodied rapid social change in Galilee as a whole under Antipas. Such a claim might appear to be unwarranted in view of the rather phlegmatic character that comes across in the gospel portraits, especially Luke's, and because Josephus does not give the same detailed account of his reign as he does of Herod the Great. Antipas had hoped to succeed his father, and foiled in that hope, he was all the more likely to have thrown himself into the task of proving himself to the Romans, never relinquishing the hope of kingship to the very end. Indeed the name *autokrator* as applied to Sepphoris and the calling of Tiberias after the Emperor shows how much he kept Roman imperial patronage in his sights. Rome allowed him a personal income of 200 talents, in the collecting of which he had need of a well disciplined, loyal and efficient administrative bureaucracy—tax-collectors, notaries, judges, military personnel, store and market managers—in short, a whole range of retainers, who could insure that he and his court would reap the full benefits of a relatively fertile region within an agrarian economy. Antipas' reign, therefore, marked the rapid development of the Galilean economy along lines that were directly opposed to the Jewish patrimonial ideal, as this had been enshrined in the Pentateuch, upheld by the prophets and re-enacted by reformers such as Nehemiah (Neh 5:1-11).

The archaeological evidence has a particular contribution to make towards a discussion of the import of these developments on Galilean life generally. While surveys have shown a cultural continuum between upper Galilee and the Golan in terms of linguistic habits and architectural styles, lower Galilee presents a somewhat different profile in that Greek inscriptions occur more frequently here than Aramaic or Hebrew ones, giving rise to the general assumption that lower Galilee is more "open" to the prevailing wider atmosphere, largely, but not entirely attributable to the presence of the two Herodian centres.[12] The detailed archaeological work

---

[11] Batey 1991, while attractively presenting some of the recent archaeological material from Sepphoris, in my opinion too easily assumes without adequate proof that proximity to a place means sharing the dominant values and ethos of that place.

now being conducted at Sepphoris suggests a profile for the city in the first century that is very different from nearby Beth Bethshean/Scythopolis for instance. No statues, temples or other public signs of pagan cult (apart from a few domestic figurines) have so far come to light. The numbers of *mikwaoth* especially in the residential area near the acropolis where presumably the more affluent residents dwelt, strongly suggest an observant Jewish ethos, even despite the presence of the theatre, one of the trappings of Greek culture, possibly from the first century already. The rightly acclaimed Dionysiac and Nile mosaics point in a different direction, but these are to be dated to a much later period when, as Diocaesarea, the city's character had changed considerably, while still not precluding an affluent and influential Jewish presence there as we know from rabbinical sources. Thus, archaeology has not provided the kind of evidence that might be considered necessary to support the case that Sepphoris was a hostile centre for Jewish peasants, at least as far as its religious affiliation.

In fact the ceramic evidence examined by D. Adan-Bayewitz, already referred to, would appear to preclude such a possibility. Following NAA analysis of the Sepphoris pottery remains, it is his conclusion that Kefar Hanania, known from the Mishnah as being situated on the dividing line between upper and lower Galilee as a pottery-making centre, has produced all the household wares for Sepphoris (and indeed all Galilee). In addition stone storage jars for the city were produced at another village, Shikhin, which has been identified with a site close to Sepphoris.[13] These findings suggest a pattern of co-operation between the city and the villages in the hinterland that would appear to rule out any idea of tension between them, however we are to interpret the literary evidence. Sepphoris, on the basis of this evidence could not be seen as a typical "consumer" city parasitically related to its hinterland, since it provided a market outlet for the village wares, and may have acted as a collection centre for grain and other produce from the fertile Bet Netofa valley, something that the many underground storage chambers strongly suggests. In addition the evidence of local villages specialising in different kinds of pottery production dispels the notion of the Galileans as boorish peasants, a representation that one sometimes encounters in various authors, ancient and modern.

Nevertheless, this evidence must not be allowed to tilt the picture so far in the opposite direction that all distinctions between city and hinterland are entirely obliterated. At this point a more general model of urban-rural relations can help in sorting out and interpreting the data, rather than simply juxtaposing discrete pieces of evidence either from archaeology or literary sources and making generalised claims from these. There is general agreement today among historians of antiquity,

---

[12] Overman 1993.

[13] Adan-Bayewitz and Perlman 1990.

that ancient, as distinct from medieval cities were symbiotically related to their immediate countryside, a shift in perspective which has been brought about by archaeological surveys at many different locations throughout the Mediterranean world, and which is, of course implied in the term *polis*.[14] Yet this does not answer the question of whether the relationship was balanced or not. Certainly, insofar as urban centres had administrative and military roles they were perceived as mediators of distant power and control on a region, and were often not experienced as benevolent by the non-elite regionals. It was Roman policy generally to encourage concentration of resources at certain centres, leading to the evolution of local elites who would vie with each other in expending their resources at the urban centre, only to be eventually assimilated with the Roman provincial ruling class. Thus the peasantry were deprived of an independent local leadership, who might be more sensitive to their needs.

The Herodians can be thought to fit this category rather well for first century Galilee. The building projects at Sepphoris and Tiberias presumably created a certain demand for local labour, yet if the system of *angaria*, or forced labour was employed, as seems to have happened in the founding of Tiberias (Jos., *Ant*. 18, 37), then these projects did little to improve the lot of the peasants. As Martin Goodman has persuasively argued, the problem of debt was one of the factors that lead to the Jewish revolt, and it was the direct result of the elites drawing off the resources of the countryside, but without any productive reinvestment.[15] Thus the political rebellion against Rome quickly degenerated into a social revolution, in which impoverished Jews from the countryside turned on their own aristocracy, replacing the reigning high priest with one elected on egalitarian lines. While these developments were associated in particular with Jerusalem and Judea, nevertheless the attacks of the Galilean peasants on both Sepphoris and Tiberias (Jos., *Life* 66. 376) should be seen as expressions of the same feelings. In these actions we are surely seeing symptoms of a peasantry frustrated with centres which were not prepared to offer the kind of solidarity between town and country that might have been expected but which was not in fact forthcoming. Thus the archaeological evidence which suggests close ties between Sepphoris, in particular, and its hinterland, in no way precludes resentment of the elites which comprised the bulk of the influential population in both centres.

What then was the real character of such places? The appellation *polis*, as applied to them needs to be carefully evaluated, since undoubtedly they were not "free and autonomous" as this description was understood within the Roman administrative system and as it applied to such places as Beth Bethshean/Scythopolis or the

---

[14] Rich and Wallace-Hadrill 1991; Freyne 1992.
[15] Goodman 1982.

Phoenician cities of the coast, who were empowered to mint their own coins as well as Roman imperial ones from the first century C.E. Rather, under Antipas, as distinct from later times, they were both eparchic, or administrative centres within the framework of a client kingdom. Thus they shared a common ethos as administrative centres whose population was that of the retainer class for the most part, without excluding wealthy landowners as a native aristocracy also. Josephus paints a picture of the mixed character of the population of Tiberias at its foundation—people from every quarter and background being brought together either by force or with blandishments of gifts of land in return for loyalty to Antipas (Jos., *Ant.*18,36-38), thus presumably violating Jewish law not merely in terms of building the city on a burial ground, but also in forcibly appropriating the land of others. This picture was maintained subsequently as we see in the account of the citizenry when Josephus himself arrived in the region in 66 C.E.—a combination of Herodian land-owning residents with estates across the lake, various officials at the Herodian court such as Justus of Tiberias, a man well-educated in the Greek ways, and the service classes —"sailors and destitutes" as the aristocratic Jerusalemite describes them (Jos., *Life* 32-38). The fact that in 66 C.E. Tiberias has the trappings of a Greek *polis* with its *boule* should not disguise the fact that it had a subordinate position within the Herodian administrative framework from the outset, and even that role had been diminished when Nero transferred it to the territory of Agrippa II in 54/5, thus ceding primacy in banking, market and other administrative functions to its rival Sepphoris, something that Justus bemoans. It was only in 66 that Sepphoris struck its first coins and Tiberias had to wait until 100 C.E., i.e. after the end of the Herodian dynasty, before it enjoyed the same privilege by favour of Trajan.[16]

Since land was the primary resource in antiquity generally and in Galilee in particular, the issue of Herodian land policy is crucial to the case being argued here, namely, an intensification of agrarian values in Antipas' Galilee as demonstrated by the emergence of the two centres. In debate is whether or not there was an appreciable move away from small family-run holdings in which reciprocity was still the basic mode of exchange, towards a situation of land used as a revenue-generating resource. In previous studies I have maintained that on the basis of the literary evidence (Josephus, the gospels, the Jewish writings and the Zenon papyri) land-ownership patterns in Galilee were mixed—large estates such as Beth Anath and small, family-run holdings that were part of the Jewish ideal (1 Macc 14:10; cf. Neh 5:1-11). Undoubtedly the pressure had come on these latter since the Hellenistic age, as increased taxation and narrow margins in terms of yields left the small land-owner increasingly vulnerable. Once a person was caught in the situation of having to bor-

---

[16] Meshorer 1985, 33 and 36.

row money for whatever reason, thus mortgaging their holding, it was extremely difficult for them to recover.[17]

The Similitudes of Enoch, which most commentators date to the Herodian period, reflect this situation with their repeated condemnation of "the kings, the governors, the high officials and the landlords" (*1 Enoch* 38:4; 46:3-5; 48:8; 53:5; 62), whereas the holy and just ones will "possess the earth", thus echoing the beatitude of Jesus (Matt 5:5). Clearly, whatever about the ideal the reality was that pressures on peasant ownership had increased considerably. The bequests of land that went with the foundation of Tiberias were at somebody's expense, yet when it and Taricheae were transferred to the kingdom of Agrippa II by Nero, significantly these places are not said to have a χώρα but rather they are given σὺν ταῖς τοπαρχίαις, that is, they were toparchic capitals rather than πόλεις in any strict sense (Jos., *J.W.* 2,252; cf. *Ant.* 20,159). Equally Josephus assumes that Sepphoris had villages associated with it which could have provided it with sufficient resources to resist Rome, had it so wished (Jos., *Life* 346). In neither case can there be any question of a city territory in the strict sense, and hence these references must point to a situation of wealthy citizens owning land in the countryside around, but residing in the city itself, as in the case of Crispus, the prefect under Agrippa I, who resided in Tiberias and was part of the elite of the city, but who was absent at his estates across the Jordan when Josephus arrived in Galilee in 66 C.E. (Jos., *Life* 33f.). Recently David Fiensy has produced the most up-to-date study of the topic of land-ownership in Herodian times in which he challenges my views about the persistence of the small landowning class, on the basis that the evidence does not allow us to decide between ownership of land and leasing. Yet later in the same work he acknowledges that the small landowners bore the brunt of the tax burden, which was considerable.[18] To some extent the issue is academic in this context as on either reading of the evidence the tension between two very different systems was real and growing all the time.

The intensification of the market that is represented in the emergence of Sepphoris and Tiberias as administrative centres within an agrarian economy brought about considerable changes in the lives of Galilean peasants. In such a climate it is the small land-owner that is most vulnerable since there is no protection built into the system against the failure of a bad harvest, illness or some other catastrophe. By

---

[17] Isaac 1992, especially p. 72, who notes that in the village of Engedi there were both crown property and privately owned land side by side. Document 11 from the cache relates how a centurion stationed in the town had made a loan of sixty denarii of Tyrian silver to a local Jewish resident who pledged his courtyard should he be unable to repay the loan. Fortunately, according to documents 19 and 20 the local was able to do so, suggesting somebody engaged in commercial rather than farming activity.

[18] Freyne 1980, 156-80; Fiensey 1991, 55-57 and 92f.

contrast leaseholders may be fortunate enough to be protected by a benign landlord in a culture where magnanimity could be seen as worthy of honour within a patron-client relationship. Archaeological evidence suggests that the single holdings were not large—an average of 6 to 9 acres has been estimated—and hence there was little possibility of increased output through more intense labour or specialised production. In all probability many engaged in mixed farming in an effort to meet the family's basic dietary requirements—vines, olives and grain. The demands of the tribute, other taxes and the religious dues had first to be met and in the case of grain crops the following year's seed requirements had to be set aside. This meant scarcity for domestic use with low nutrition resulting in a high incidence of illness and infant mortality.[19] In such conditions the reciprocal system of exchange with its in-built concerns for all members of the extended household or clan is more favourable to the poor than is the market economy which functions in favour of the ruling elite and their administrative retainers. The tensions between these two types of economic system and the increasing dominance of the latter in Herodian Galilee generated the social situation that many gospel parables depict—day labourers, debt, resentment of absentee landlords, wealthy estate owners with little concern for tenants needs, exploitative stewards of estates, family feuds over inheritance etc. In these vignettes we can catch glimpses of both systems in operation and the clash of values that are inherent, a topic we shall presently address.

The picture emerging from this discussion is one in which considerable tensions can be presupposed between Sepphoris and Tiberias on the one hand, and the Galilean rural hinterland on the other, essentially because they represented two very different value systems which could not easily co-exist, since the success of the one was dependent on the destruction of the other. The situation was complicated by the fact that the new Herodian elite represented by the two centres in question, continued to maintain allegiance to a Jewish way of life, while being imbued with the values of the Roman agrarian economy. A shared religious belief system with its stress on temple offerings based on ownership of land was difficult to maintain in such an atmosphere of social inequality. Only in distant Jerusalem, and then occasionally was it possible to bridge the gap between symbolic universe and social experience. Is it this religio-social vacuum within the region that Jesus sought to fill, with his message of the advent of the kingdom of God, and the implications of such a proclamation for the social life of those who accepted his word? As mentioned already there are several possible explanations for the absence of any mention of Sepphoris and Tiberias in the gospels—a strategic avoidance in view of the fate of his mentor the Baptist; a failed visit that went unrecorded unlike similar ones to Caphernaum,

---

[19] Hamel 1990, 94-141; Oakman 1986, 57-72.

Chorazin and Bethsaida or a principled avoidance as an act of solidarity with the victims in order to generate a prophetic critique of their oppressors. It is this latter suggestion that I wish to pursue in the final section of this paper.

## 4. Jesus in Galilee

Crossan and others with varying shades of nuance view the ministry of Jesus in Galilee in the light of Cynic ideals for coping with life's problems, which, it is claimed, were widely diffused in the early empire. This claim is based on a number of different assumptions: (1) the similarity of Jesus' life-style and that enjoined on his followers with the Cynic counter-cultural attitudes towards home, family and possessions; (2) the proximity of Galilee to the Dekapolis where it is believed Cynic ideas had widespread currency in view of the fact that Meleager of Gadara is known for his espousal of these ideas at Tyre in the second century B.C.E. already; (3) as urban centres in lower Galilee, Sepphoris and Tiberias would have mediated these ideas to the country people who visited for market or for other reasons. Thus Crossan believes that the most natural understanding of Jesus' talk about the kingdom of God among his peasant audience was not that of apocalyptic but rather the Cynic belief that the wise person is king, while Burton Mack (another influential proponent of the Cynic Jesus) believes that Jesus did for Jewish belief at a popular level what Philo had achieved on a more intellectual plane, namely to open it out to a broader understanding of life that was synonymous with the Hellenistic world-view.[20] To these opinions can be added the views of F. G. Downing, based on an intimate knowledge of the Cynic sources. According to his latest statement of the case the presence of Cynic elements in such a wide variety of early Christian writings, ranging from Q and Mark through Paul to James, is more readily explained if these ideas emanated with Jesus himself, rather than that his ideas were later subjected to a process of "Cynicisation". Thus, despite his acknowledgement of "the Jewish palette" in the earliest strata of the Jesus tradition and the presence of "older, native Jewish influences on Jesus", Downing also claims that a pervasive Cynic influence on Galilee at a popular level provides the most appropriate communicational context for Jesus' sayings, including those to do with the kingdom of God.[21]

It is beyond the scope of this paper to deal with these arguments in detail. The most significant aspect for the case being argued here is the assumption that close proximity to an urban culture meant assimilation of the ideas prevalent among the urban elites by the peasants. All the archaeological evidence from both upper and

---

[20] Crossan 1991, 72-88; Mack 1988, 72-74.
[21] Downing 1992; cf. Hengel 1973, 155-57.

lower Galilee shows clear signs of a distinctive Jewish presence in certain areas of both sub-regions, many of the sites dating to the early Roman period, (i.e. first century C.E.) if not earlier.[22] They had been able to maintain a religious and cultural identity, even when a case can be made for Greek being the *lingua franca*, at least in lower Galilee, especially along the lake shore. Are we to suppose that these people abandoned their inherited beliefs and values for those emanating from outside and mediated by centres that were treated with suspicion if not hostility? I remain unconvinced by such a scenario, preferring to see Jesus espousing a prophetic critique of the dominant prevailing ethos, based on covenantal ideals for a restored Israel, within an apocalyptic framework that made it possible to imagine and propose a radically different lifestyle and values. Such an understanding of the kingdom of God was much more likely to be familiar to Jewish peasants from synagogal prayers and scriptural readings than those touted by Cynic teachers in urban contexts, even if we were to suppose that they found expression in the urban centres of Galilee also.

Most treatments of Jesus' ministry begin by discussing the opposition which it generated among Jewish religious circles over issues of torah observance. In a Galilean context, however, that may be the wrong starting point, especially in the light of E. P. Sander's discussion within the context of what he describes as "common" Jewish practice among the ordinary people who would have regarded themselves as Jewish throughout the Galilean villages.[23] In suggesting that his most immediate target was the rapidly developing Herodian economy of Galilee, one should not go to the opposite extreme of turning him into a social revolutionary devoid of any religious intentions with regard to the renewal of Israel. In order to keep both aspects in proper focus it is important to recall the collusion between Herodian rule and an increasingly venal Jerusalem aristocracy, among whom were the upper echelons of the priesthood itself (Jos., *Ant.* 20,181. 206f.). It was in their interest to maintain the fiction of the theocratic ideal of the temple-state, while themselves being thoroughly imbued with the values of the elite rich of the Graeco-Roman world, as can be seen graphically from the discovery of luxury items in the Jewish quarter in Jerusalem. With this backdrop in view we shall approach the Jesus tradition in search of a critique of both Herodian political power and the values of the market economy which were shared by provincial Herodian and Jerusalem aristocracy alike.

## 4.1. Jesus and Herodian Kingship

Three items from the sayings tradition suggest themselves for consideration in

---

[22] Aviam 1993.
[23] Sanders 1990.

terms of a possible critique of the values of Herodian kingship: (a) the saying which contrasts the standards of human rulers with those which should operate in the community of Jesus (Mark 10:42-45 and parallels); (b) the reference to divided kingdoms and houses in the Beelzebul controversy (Mark 3:24; Q Matt 12:25 = Q Luke 11:17); (c) the disparaging reference to those who dwell in royal palaces in the encomium on the Baptist (Q Matt 11:9; Q Luke 7:25 = *Gos. Thom.* 78). While various redactional aspects of all three items can be readily recognised, there is still a very good case to be made for hearing in these sayings echoes at least of Jesus' voice, which warrants considering their impact in terms of the situation in Antipas' Galilee, irrespective of their use in later gospel settings.

(a) A dispute among the disciples over places of honour in the kingdom is the immediate context for Jesus' contrast between his standards and those of the world with regard to leadership. Luke has transferred the saying to the context of the last supper (Luke 22:25), where it forms part of a more general farewell discourse about attitudes in the community, thus reflecting later discussions about authority. Luke has also softened the implied criticism of secular kingship by acknowledging that kings can also be benefactors (εὐεργέται). The context of early Christian leadership may also be operative in Mark's setting already, but in contrast to Luke both he and Matt employ rare compound verbs by use of the preposition κατά together with κυριεῖν and ἐξουσιάζειν, suggesting a repressive, downward force or total dominion. Finally, whereas Matt and Luke speak directly of βασιλεῖς, kings of the gentiles, Mark is decidedly more ironic, speaking of "those who supposedly rule over gentiles" (οἱ δοκοῦντες ἄρχειν; cf. Gal 2:6,9). There is nothing in the allusion that would automatically refer it to Herodian kingship, and it could, arguably, be seen as a piece of generalised comment. Indeed the reference to ἐθνῶν/gentiles, might appear positively to exclude such an implied reference. At Acts 4:26, however, the Ps text which refers to "the kings of the earth" (τῆς γῆς) is applied both to Herod Antipas and Pilate, the representative of Roman rule. From a pious Jewish perspective the Herodians could, it would seem, be regarded as analogous to gentile rulers, despite their continued interest in, and in some instances, observance of their subjects' religious practices.

What then if we were to read the reference to earthly kings as directly inspired by conditions in Antipas' Galilee? Could it be said to agree with Theißen's category of "local colouring" for that period, even though he himself considers the present saying only in the context of the immediate post-70 situation, when Christian disciples as well as Jews in the region had to come to terms with the might of Rome?[24] As is well known, though Antipas aspired to kingship, he never actually obtained it,

---

[24] Theißen 1992, 286.

losing out in the end to his nephew, Agrippa I. He sought to play a role in international affairs, as his father had done, by arranging for a treaty between the Roman legate of Syria, Vitellius, and the Persian king, Artapanus, (Jos., *Ant.* 18,101-105). Josephus, as distinct from the gospel writers (especially Luke), has little doubt about his ruthless character in lording over his subjects, since his account of the peremptory justice for John the Baptist, as well as those compelled to inhabit Tiberias, is set in immediate contrast with the attitude of his brother Philip, who conducted sittings of his court at various places in order to facilitate his subjects (Jos., *Ant.* 18,106-108. 116-119). Here then is somebody who regards himself more highly than his status as ethnarch within Roman imperial administration warranted and behaved accordingly. Against such a background perhaps the critique in Mark's remark about kingship, especially with the implied put-down of the verb δοκεῖν, should not after all be understood as a generalisation. It could, with some justification, be heard as a fairly direct hit at Antipas, and to have originated within the circumstances of his rule as they are known to us from other sources.

(b) In both the Q and Markan versions Jesus counters the charge of being in league with Beelzebul by the image of a kingdom (βασιλεία) or house (οἶκος) divided against itself not being able to stand (Mark), or being left desolate (Q). The Q version as represented by both Matt and Luke agree with the more generalised form of the saying—every kingdom/πᾶσα βασιλεία—suggesting again ordinary wisdom based on everyday experience. Mark's use of the singular, but with a conditional "if", of itself would scarcely warrant seeing here a more direct reference to the immediate circumstances. However, in both versions, the overall context of the passage is the contrast between the kingdom of Satan and that of God. Within the classic apocalyptic framework of seeing earthly kingdoms, especially repressive ones, as representative of the present evil age which will be replaced by the kingdom of "the saints of the most high", as in the Danielic version of the mythic pattern, it would be natural for hearers to identify the image with the most immediate source of repression, either Herodian or Roman. While the context of Vespasian's ascent to imperial power in 69 C.E., the year of the three emperors, is suggestive as far as Mark's readership is concerned, Q's dating is earlier, even if we were to assign this passage with Kloppenborg to Q 2, as part of the judgement/apocalyptic strand of that document as he understands it.[25]

Again, therefore, we are justified in seeking a "Sitz im Leben" Jesu in terms of Herodian politics. The internecine struggle between the sons of Herod the Great over the terms of his will, leading eventually to Augustus' decision not to appoint any of them as king, immediately come to mind. Neither was the kingship restored

---

[25] Kloppenborg 1987, 121-27.

on the deposition of Archelaus in 6 C.E., nor subsequently in 37 C.E. on the death of Philip. Apart from the brief reign of Agrippa I (41-44 C.E.) Herod's kingdom was never reconstituted, falling foul of the Roman principle *divide et impera*. While some of these events are later than the career of Jesus, the fact that the dispute over Herod's will has left its traces in the Jesus-traditions in the Lukan reference to the "king who went into a far country to obtain kingship and then return" but whose subjects "did not want him to rule over them" (Luke 19:11-15), shows how the memory of those events continued to be current. Antipas too had his ambitions, as we have seen. If kingship was denied to him he seems to have received the dynastic title "Herod" on the deposition of Archelaus, thereby maintaining the semblance of a single house.[26] Yet the difficulties generated by his marriage to Herodias, his brother's wife, shows just how tenuous such unity really was. Again, our conclusion can only be tentative. Yet it must be admitted that if this saying was uttered by Jesus, his audience would have had little enough difficulty in hearing here a prophecy of the demise of Herodian rule, especially in view of all the circumstances surrounding Herod the Great's succession.

(c) The third possible reference to the Herodian presence in the sayings of Jesus occurs in the Q passage dealing with John the Baptist. Recent discussion of this encomium tends to see it having a composite tradition-history, though there is fairly general agreement that some elements do go back to Jesus, including the double section of immediate concern in this context, which has a parallel saying in the *Gospel of Thomas* (78:1-3).[27] The form of the section is that of three questions, the first two expecting the answer "no", followed by one which calls for a "Yes, indeed, John was a prophet!" The negative contrast of the first two questions insists that John is neither a reed shaken by the wind nor someone dressed in fine garments; and to this latter statement is added "those who wear luxurious clothes" (those who are gorgeously apparelled and live in luxury, Luke) "are in the houses of kings" (royal palaces, Luke). If Gerd Theißen's identification of "the reed shaken by the wind" is to be accepted as a veiled reference to Antipas on the basis of the emblem on his coins, then the mention of "houses of kings" or "royal palaces" would inevitably also refer to the Herodian court.[28] While the Matthean and Lukan wordings vary slightly, they both agree in the more general plural reference. This brings the comparison into line with the two previous passages discussed, but in this case also it does not thereby preclude a specific allusion to an actual situation, from the point of view of both speaker and hearer. The plurals οἴκοις/βασιλείοις are quite natural with reference to an Herodian royal residence, as is clear from Josephus also (Jos.,

---

[26] Hoehner 1972, 105-09.

[27] Kloppenborg 1987, 108-10; Catchpole 1993, 43-45; Funk and Hoover 1993, 178-82.

[28] Theißen 1992, 26-39; cf. however, the critique in Burnett and Phillips 1992, 296-99.

*Life* 66).

Confirmation of this implied criticism of the luxurious life-style of the court, at least as viewed from the world of the peasant (cf. *Gos. Thom.* 78, "Why have you come out to the countryside?"), may be seen in the account of Antipas' birthday, when John was beheaded in a wanton act (Mark 6:14-29). Josephus also reports that on the occasion of Augustus' deliberations over Herod's will a Jewish delegation appeared before him complaining about the bribery and corruption of those sent to collect the tribute, and bemoaning the corruption of their wives and daughters in drunken orgies (Jos., *Ant.* 17,304-309; *J.W.* 1,511). The mention of those sent out to collect the tribute in association with such conduct is all the more intriguing in view of the frequent allusions to Jesus' table-fellowship with tax-collectors that occur in the tradition, more especially in the immediate context in Q of the passage being discussed here (Matt 11:16-19; Luke 7:31-35). The parable of the children in the market place, refusing to rejoice or mourn, is applied by the Q redactor to the different stances of John and Jesus. John's is an ascetic life-style, whereas Jesus' celebratory attitude earns for him the sobriquet of "glutton and wine-drinker" and "the friend of tax-collectors and sinners". Thus, Jesus' behaviour and association with tax-collectors gains for him the same criticism as that levelled against the Herodian officials in Josephus, a criticism which is even more pointed still if, as has been recently claimed, "sinners" should be identified with women whose presence at public meals gave them a doubtful reputation.[29] Jesus rejects the charge, having aligned himself with John against "this generation", whose stance, like that of the children in the parable, is regarded as petty and childish.[30] Yet the implications of his actions and associations were double edged. On the one hand he ran the risk of being rejected by the pious circles who deplored the life-style of the court, while at the same time he was engaging in a subtle act of subverting the Herodian officials, probably of lower rank in the villages, by summoning them to listen to his and John's prophetic word to Israel.

This attempt to read the three sayings against the sharpened focus of the Herodian court, especially that of Antipas, may not be wholly conclusive. Nevertheless, enough has emerged from the exercise to suggest that Jesus was remembered among other things for his outspoken criticism of the standards of royal power and privilege as these were exercised in that world. The very use of such comparisons with their implied negative comment can only be described as daring, even provocative. There is here no idealisation of kingship in terms of the philosopher-king of the Cynic-Stoic world view. Rather the inspiration for the sayings is much more that associated with the apocalyptic world-view as this had received expression in vari-

---

[29] Corley 1993, 103-08; Herrenbruck 1981.
[30] Cotter 1987.

ous Jewish writings of the Second Temple period and which viewed the foreign rulers as belonging to the present evil age which was soon to be replaced by God's just
rule on behalf of the oppressed. The situation of rapid change postulated for the period of the ministry of Jesus as this was developed in the second part of this paper
might be considered sufficiently traumatic to have elicited such a prophetic response as that to be found in the words and deeds of Jesus, not least in his critique
of the prevailing value-system.

## 4.2. Jesus and the Values of the Market Economy

The argument in the second section of this paper was that co-incidentally with the
arrival of the adult Jesus in Galilee from the Jordan, there were obvious signs
present of the intensification of a very different value-system to that which was enshrined in the Jewish theocratic ideal of all Israel sharing in the fruits of the land.
This ideal still continued to appeal to many, especially the Galilean Jewish peasants,
despite the erosion of the vision and its basic values among its ruling, priestly elite,
as distinct from the ordinary priests. Josephus, who himself came from that background makes no attempt to hide this stark reality (Jos., *Ant.* 20,181. 206f.). As mentioned earlier it could well be that there were already in Galilee those who were
critical of the Jerusalem cult-centre and its priesthood. But if that were the case they
certainly do not appear as an organised circle or network within the region in the
way that the Essenes or Zealots had functioned in Judea, at least not in the Jewish
sources. It is only in the Jesus movement that we find such a critique. If the argument to this point is at all sustainable, the task now is to show that it was with an
essentially Jewish understanding of history and from a decidedly Jewish hope of
restoration and renewal that Jesus and his movement mounted their critique of both
value-systems, Herodian and theocratic alike. I do not believe that what began as a
set of insights for coping with life, which is what Cynicism of a popular kind essentially was, pace Crossan's best efforts to make it capable of generating an organised
counter-cultural life-style[31]—I do not believe that such a set of ideas could have
been transformed into the kind of apocalyptically inspired renewal movement with
a radical social agenda in such a short space of time, and with only the memory of
a discredited teacher of aphorisms to inspire it. At least I find that scenario historically less probable and logically less plausible than the one which I am proposing.
Here I can only sketch the briefest outline of the case to be argued.

The social setting I am now proposing as the most immediate and significant for
the earthly Jesus' ministry of deed and word, namely, the need to resist the changing
values and attitudes represented by the rise of Sepphoris and Tiberias, requires, it

---

[31] Crossan 1991, e.g., 128.

seems to me, something other than a strategy for coping with life, though of course in many instances in the ancient as well as in the modern world, that is all that is possible, and there are traces of a popular wisdom akin to that of Proverbs and Sirach to be found in the earliest stratum of the Jesus tradition also. If material as well as cultural factors are to be used in our attempt to explain as distinct from merely describe the Jesus movement and its emergence in this particular place (Galilee, not Judea or Idumea) and at this particular time (the reign of Antipas rather than 66 C.E., for instance), then we must attempt to show how its strategy and approach fit into the totality of life in that society at that particular time, and how precisely it was aimed at alleviating the perceived condition of alienation that was threatening as a result of the new developments under Antipas. Which of the following alternatives was likely to be better news for Galilean peasants threatened with loss of land and the kinship values associated with it, without any redress: to hear that if they honoured what was best they would be like kings, and would have the freedom "to dare to be different", or to be reassured that the advent of God's reign which was occurring now in their midst (ἐντὸς ὑμῶν of Luke 17:21) would mean the reversal of all the dominant values which were currently destroying their lives at every level? The former merely accepts the *status quo* and hopes to alleviate its most painful effects; the latter calls for envisaging the world differently. It is the dramatic suddenness of the changes which were occurring in their midst that in my opinion called forth the latter rather than the former understanding as the more adequate way of addressing the situation.

According to T. Carney rapid economic change can occur when not only are markets and money available, but also a change of values is present which supports exploitation of resources for profit rather than simply for providing subsistence.[32] This calls for very different attitudes towards nature itself, other people within the kinship network and the purpose and goal of life itself. Jesus' attitude towards possessions, money and the family, when read against the backdrop of the situation we have suggested, merits the description which Theißen has proposed in another context, namely, "a values revolution",[33] thereby attempting to counter the new dominant value system on which the Herodian economic policy rested.

The very founding of Tiberias and the allotment of land to the inhabitants must have meant some displacement. Similarly, the pressure on the private landowner meant the break-up or diminution of the small holdings, leading to intra-family feuding about property and inheritance rights that are echoed in the parables of Jesus. For those who were exposed in this way to the harsh realities of life and who had the will to resist there were few enough options open—from landowning to

---

[32] Carney 1975, 139-52.
[33] Theißen 1989.

leasing to day-labouring, to slavery or banditry. All of these possibilities remained within the existing structures and not even banditry which was the most violent response to the unequal situation had any alternative to put in its place, but was simply reactive. By contrast, Jesus' vision of shared goods and rejection of the normal securities, including money (Q Matt 6:19-21. 24; Luke 12:33-34; 16:13; *Gos. Thom.* 47:1-2; 76:3), which apart from land was the most important commodity in the market economy, though utopian in its intention did provide an alternative vision. This vision viewed the world of human relations, based on status maintenance, in a very critical light and instead allowed for oppressors and oppressed to relate as equals. In proposing such an ideal Jesus was not seeking to revert to a *status quo ante* for Israel as stated in the Pentateuch, but was operating within a genuinely prophetic framework of adapting the received tradition to the demands of a new situation, and doing so in the name of God's final prophetic word to Israel.

A similarly radical stance can be discerned in his dealing with the crisis that the family was faced with within the new situation. Again, Carney has remarked that the family unit bonded by factors other than economic ones is singularly ill-equipped for the market-economy which calls for specialised skills and the maximisation of resources. Under such pressures kinship values can easily be eroded. Josephus, relying as he was on his status as a Jerusalem priest to win the support of the Galilean country people, repeatedly appeals to ὁμοφυλία, that is, kinship, in order to appease their hostility towards the Jewish retainer class in Sepphoris and Tiberias, with, it must be said, only limited success (Jos., *Life* 55, 100, 171). Jesus, by contrast, challenges the absolute nature of kinship values which can of course legitimate situations of great inequality, proposing instead an ideal of community based on love, forgiveness and shared reciprocity (Q Luke 6:27-35; Matt 5:38-44). In these sayings one can detect a subtle, yet firm critique of the prevailing patriarchal family structure, which was one of the cornerstones, not just of the Herodian, but also of the theocratic systems that were competing with each other in Galilee as elsewhere in Palestine (Q Luke 9:57-61; Matt 8:20-22; Mark 1:16-20; 10:29-31). Family imagery and values are appropriated to the new social configurations that were emerging around Jesus and in his name, even as he refuses to endorse certain aspects of the existing family reality, recognising instead that adherence to his way would be disruptive of those set patterns, with their economic and social rootedness (Mark 3:33-35; Q Matt 10:37 Luke 14:26; *Gos. Thom.* 55:1; 101:1-3).

Not everybody in Jesus' putative audiences or who benefited from his charismatic healing ministry was ready for such a message. The threat to landownership was real and the signs of rapid change were now very tangible in terms of the new foundations. Yet as long as a tenuous link could be maintained with the old, many were uncertain about the new, at least such a radically new vision. The Galilean peasantry who in 66 C.E. were still prepared to bring their tithes to Josephus and his colleagues and support as leader one of Jerusalem priestly stock rather than any native person, shows how powerfully the old symbol system of temple and land still functioned. An idealisation of the destitute and a declaration that in the new economy theirs was the kingdom of heaven was only likely to resonate with those who were in reality destitute. On the other hand many of the sayings attributed to Jesus were not addressed to these but to people who did in fact own land or had other possessions. The relative failure of the Jesus movement as an inner-Galilean Jewish renewal movement must be judged not only in terms of the absence of clear evidence, archaeological or literary, of a Christian presence there in the first century, but also by the extent to which the Herodian and the theocratic system, each vying with the other for control of the resources, were still in place in 66 C.E.

## 5. Conclusion

In this paper I have attempted to perform a critical reading of certain aspects of the Jesus tradition against the backdrop of the larger picture of Galilean social life as this can be reconstructed from both archaeological and literary sources, without, I hope, engaging in a too easy conflation of the two pictures. The attempt to keep both in focus, or better, the exercise of bringing both into focus by critically juxtaposing them seems to be the best methodology for understanding how the Jesus tradition could have directly addressed certain pressing issues within that original setting, even when these traditions may have been used subsequently in other settings, both historical and geographical.

The question is particularly complex in view of the fact that recent studies of the sayings tradition, generally designated Q have attempted to highlight the geographical and social location of the so-called Q community, and Galilee has featured prominently in those discussions also.[34] The fact that greater precision has been introduced into the study of Q as a literary document in its own right means that, unlike the 19th century, no easy bridge can be built from Q to Jesus.[35] Kloppenborg's study on the formation of Q has been particularly influential with its separation of an earlier sapiential layer from a later apocalyptic/judgement one, which can then be related to two different stages of the Q community's history of mission and rejection in Galilee throughout the second half of the first century C.E.[36] Kloppenborg himself stresses that this literary analysis of Q does not prejudge the issue of

---

[34] Theißen 1992, 203f.; Kloppenborg 1993.
[35] Cf. Kosch 1991 for a good discussion of the issue.
[36] Kloppenborg 1991.

whether or not elements from the apocalyptic stratum originate with Jesus. Others who have found his analysis congenial to their own positions have used it to that effect, thereby postulating a sapiential (i.e. popular Cynic) rather than apocalyptic understanding of the kingdom as the primary inspiration of Jesus' own strategy.[37]

In this paper I have argued that if a co-relation between social situation and an apocalyptically inspired response is to be postulated, then the period of Jesus' ministry in Galilee in the reign of Antipas can be construed in such a way as to provoke that kind of response. In fact, that precise period with its rapidly changing ethos exemplified in the two Herodian foundations in lower Galilee is perhaps, more suited to such a response than any other time in the first century, at least until the immediate outbreak of hostilities with Rome in 66 C.E. Then, however, as Theißen and others have convincingly argued, it is in Mark rather than Q that we can sense the rumblings of those particular events in the background as far as Galilee is concerned.

## Bibliography

Adan-Bayewitz, D. 1993: *Common Pottery in Roman Galilee. A Study of Local Trade*, Ramat Gan: Bar-Ilan University Press 1993.

Adan-Bayewitz, D. and Perlman, I. 1990: "The Local Trade of Sepphoris in the Roman Period", in: *IEJ* 42 (1990) 153-72.

Adan-Bayewitz, D. and Wieder, M. 1992: "Ceramics from Roman Galilee", in: *Journal of Field Archeology* 19 (1992) 189-205.

Aviam, M. 1993: "Galilee: the Hellenistic to Byzantine Periods", in E. Stern (ed.), *The New Encyclopedia of Archeological Excavations in the Holy Land*, 4 Vols., Jerusalem: The Israel Exploration Society, Vol. 2, 1993, 452-58.

Batey, R. 1991: *Jesus and the Forgotten City. New Light on Sepphoris and the Urban World of Jesus*, Grand Rapids, MI: Baker Books 1991.

Bauer, W. 1967: "Jesus der Galiläer", in: idem, *Aufsätze und Kleine Schriften*, Tübingen: J. C. B. Mohr (Paul Siebeck) 1967, 91-108.

Bertram, W. 1935: "Der Hellenismus in der Urheimat des Evangeliums", in: *ARW* 32 (1935) 265-81.

Burnett, F. W. and Phillips, G. A. 1992: "Palm Re(a)ding and the Big Bang: Origins and Development of Jesus Traditions", in: *RStR* 18 (1992) 296-99.

Carney, T. F. 1975: *The Shape of the Past. Models in Antiquity*, Lawrence, KS: Coronado Press 1975.

Catchpole, D. 1993: *The Search for Q*, Edinburgh: T. & T. Clark 1993.

Corley, K. 1993: *Jesus, Women and Meals in the Synoptic Gospels*, Peabody, MA: Hendrickson

---

[37] Mack 1993.

1993.

Cotter, W. 1987: "The Parable of the Children in the Market Place, Q (Lk) 7,31-35", in: *NT* 29 (1987) 289-304.

Crossan, J. D. 1991: *The Historical Jesus. The Life of a Mediterranean Jewish Peasant*, San Francisco, CA: Harper & Row 1991.

Downing, G. 1992: *Cynics and Christian Origins*, Edinburgh: T. & T. Clark 1992.

Fiensy, D. 1991: *The Social History of Palestine in the Herodian Period*, Lewiston, NY: The Edward Mellen Press 1991.

Freyne, S. 1980: *Galilee from Alexander the Great to Hadrian. A Study in Second Temple Judaism*, Wilmington, DE: Glazier/Notre Dame University Press 1980.

— 1992: "Urban-Rural Relations in First Century Galilee. Some Suggestions from the Literary Sources", in: L. Levine (ed.) 1992, 75-94.

Funk, R. and Hoover, R. 1993: *The Search for the Authentic Words of Jesus. The Five Gospels*, New York: Macmillan/Polebridge Press 1993.

Goodman, M. 1982: "The First Jewish Revolt: Social Conflict and the Problem of Debt", in: *JJS* 33 (1982) 417-27.

Grundmann, W. 1941: *Jesus der Galiläer und das Judentum*, Leipzig: Wigand 1941.

Hamel, G. 1990: *Poverty and Charity in Roman Palestine, First Three Centuries C.E.*, Berkley, CA: University of California Press 1990.

Hanson, R. 1980: *Tyrian Influences in Upper Galilee*, Cambridge, MA: ASOR Publications 1980.

Hengel, M. 1973: *Judentum und Hellenismus*, 2nd ed., Tübingen: J. C. B. Mohr (Paul Siebeck) 1973.

Herrenbruck, F. 1981: "Wer waren die Zöllner", in: *ZNW* 72 (1981) 178-84.

Hoehner, H. 1972: *Herod Antipas*, Cambridge: Cambridge University Press 1972.

Isaac, B. 1992: "The Babatha Archive. A Review Article", in: *IEJ* 42 (1992) 62-75.

Kloppenborg, J. 1987: *The Formation of Q*, Philadelphia, PA: Fortress Press 1987.

— 1991: "Literary Convention, Self-Evidence and the Social History of the Q People", in: *Semeia* 55 (1991) 77-102.

— 1993: "The Sayings Gospel Q: Recent Opinion on the People behind the Document", in: *Currents in Research. Biblical Studies* 1 (1993) 9-34.

Kosch, D. 1992: "Q und Jesus", in: *BZ* 36 (1992) 31-58.

Lang, F. 1978: "'Uber Sidon mitten ins Gebiet der Dekapolis'. Geographie und Theologie in Markus 7,31", in: *ZDPV* 94 (1978) 145-60.

Levine, L. (ed.) 1981: *Ancient Synagogues Revealed*, Jerusalem: The Israel Exploration Society 1981.

— (ed.) 1992: *The Galilee in Late Antiquity*, New York and Jerusalem: The Jewish Theological Seminary 1992.

Mack, B. 1988: *A Myth of Innocence. Mark and Christian Origins*, Philadephia, PA: Fortress Press 1988.

— 1993: *The Lost Gospel. The Book of Q and Christian Origins*, San Francisco, CA: Harper 1993.

Meier, J. 1991: *A Marginal Jew. Rethinking the Historical Jesus*, New York: Doubleday 1991.

Meyers, E. 1976: "Galilean Regionalism as a Factor in Historical Reconstruction", in: *BASOR* 22 (1976) 95-101.

— 1985: "Galilean Regionalism: A Reappraisal", in: W. Scott Green (ed.), *Approaches to Ancient Judaism and its Greco-Roman Context*, Atlanta, GA: Scholars Press 1985, 115-31.

Meshorer, Y. 1985: *City Coins of Eretz Israel and the Dekapolis in the Roman Period*, Jerusalem: the Israel Museum 1985.

Oakman, D. 1986: *Jesus and the Economic Questions of his Day*, Lewiston, NY: The Edwin Mellen Press 1986.

Overman, A. 1993: "Recent Advances in the Archaeology of the Galilee in the Roman Period", in: *Currents in Research. Biblical Studies* 1 (1993) 35-58.

Raynor, J. and Meshorer, Y. 1985: *The Coins of Ancient Meiron*, Winona Lake, IN: Eisenbrauns 1985.

Rich, J. and Wallace-Hadrill, A. 1991: *City and Country in the Ancient World*, London and New York: Routledge 1991.

Sanders, E. P. 1990: *Jewish Law from Jesus to the Mishnah*, London: SCM Press 1990.

Schmeller, T. 1994: "Jesus im Umland Galiläas", in: *BZ* 38 (1994) 44-65.

Sussman, J. 1981: "The Inscription in the Synagogue at Rehob", in: L. Levine (ed.) 1981, 146-153.

Theißen, G. 1989: "Jesusbewegung als charismatische Werterevolution", in: *NTS* 35 (1989) 343-60.

— 1992: *The Gospels in Context. Social and Political History in the Synoptic Tradition*, Edinburgh:, T. & T. Clark 1992.

# The Resurrection of Jesus and the Rise of Christology

Edvin Larsson

In this article, dedicated to my friend and colleague Lars Hartman, I am trying to illuminate some moments in the rise of Christology in the early church. The main topic to be dealt with is the relation between Jesus and primitive Christological conceptions. In this regard the article forms a certain continuation of a paper I delivered in honour of Hartman's predecessor, Harald Riesenfeld, at the celebration of his 80th anniversary.

## 1. Jesus and Christology: Continuity or Discontinuity?

The exegetical discussion concerning Jesus and early Christology has to a great extent been dominated by the question, whether the relation is to be labelled as one of continuity or discontinuity.[1] The debate has divided scholars into two groups (not entirely separated, though). The traditional view was that there existed a firm connection between Jesus of Nazareth and the Christology of the primitive church. Historical criticism complicated the whole question. This did not necessarily mean, that the relation as such was questioned. As a rule scholars assumed some kind of connection between Jesus and the subsequent Christology. In our century this was a rather common conviction for instance in Catholic scholarship as well as in British and Scandinavian exegesis. The continuity between the "messianic" claims of Jesus and the Christology of the church was emphasised.[2] This positive attitude was by no means based on an uncritical approach to the New Testament texts. The critical investigations were numerous and of a diversified character. The outcomes displayed a rich variety of opinions. In spite of this the existence of some kind of con-

---

[1] For an introductory orientation of the problem, see E. Larsson 1993, 61ff.; idem 1994, 193ff. —for an overview of modern Jesusresearch, see W. G. Kümmel 1985; idem 1988-1991. Cf. B. Holmberg 1993, 69-76.

[2] Representative examples are A. Fridrichsen 1942, 26-45; A. Nygren 1942, 13-25. See also E. Hoskyns & N. Davey 1952, 12.

tinuity was taken for granted. Several scholars even maintained that the Christology to a considerable extent originated with Jesus himself. This view was strongly advocated among others by Harald Riesenfeld. In an article from 1956, reprinted 1967, he declared: "The centre of all Christology is Jesus Christ, not only because he is the object of theological and dogmatic thinking of the primitive church, but above all because he himself has created Christology in its very kernel".[3]

The other line of interpretation is followed by scholars, who are sceptical about the relation between Jesus and the church's Christology. They are inclined to think in terms of discontinuity. This view is of long standing, especially in German scholarship. If we just concentrate on our own century, one can remind oneself of Julius Wellhausen's famous statement from 1905: "Jesus war kein Christ, sondern Jude".[4] Correct as this saying may be, it is of little consequence for the discussion of Jesus and the rise of Christology. The debate had, after all, dealt with the possible messianic aspirations of the Jew Jesus and their subsequent transformation into Christology. A decisive step towards a strong sceptical view was taken by Rudolf Bultmann: Jesus was no theologian. He was an eschatological preacher of repentance. In this capacity he had no part in the formation of Christology. He was, however, the necessary condition for its development.[5]

This idea of the secondary character of the Christology had been self-evident to the liberal "Leben-Jesu-Forschung". The same view was predominant within the "History of Religion-School" (*Religionsgeschichtliche Schule*) and formed the starting point for its reconstruction and description of the rise of Christology, brilliantly manifested in Wilhelm Bousset's *Kyrios Christos*.[6] Bultmann, who originally came from this school, contributed to the picture with his consequent form-critical approach.[7] The birthplace of the gospel tradition was the early church, he maintained. The Jesus-material was collected, and to an important extent created, there. Consequently the history of Jesus appeared to be inaccessible to further investigation. Exegetical scholarship was restricted to the Jesus-picture given by the primitive church. This meant that Biblical scholars were bound to think in terms of discontinuity as regards Jesus of Nazareth and the *kyrios* of the *kerygma*.

Bultmann himself was not affected by this discontinuity. In his opinion the Christological reflection—in the early church as well as in our own time—has to be content with the very fact of the historical existence of Jesus. Further knowledge of his history is of no consequence. In Bultmann's conception the importance was

---

[3] H. Riesenfeld 1970, 42.
[4] J. Wellhausen 1905, 113.
[5] R. Bultmann 1984, 1.
[6] W. Bousset 1921.
[7] R. Bultmann 1931.

solely attached to the message (κήρυγμα) of God's act in Christ.

Some disciples of Bultmann could not stand this historical asceticism. They maintained that the Christ of the *kerygma* was bound to have some provable connections with the historical Jesus. If this relation was neglected, the Christian message was in danger of being mythologised. Out of these considerations a new "Leben-Jesu-Forschung" arose in the 1950's, often designated as "The new quest"[8] a name used in order to distinguish this approach from the old, liberal Jesus-research. The distinction between the "old" and the "new" quest turned out to be that the latter was concerned about the theological connection: Was the preaching of Jesus in any sense the basis of the Church's message of him as *kyrios Christos?*[9] Could the Christology of the church be derived from the historical Jesus?

The "new quest" represented an important effort. Its influence has, however, been limited. The results stand out as rather modest against the background of initial expectations. The reason for this outcome is easily found. Many participants in the discussion are dependant on a rather radical form-critical view, which prevents them from ascertaining with certainty anything about the historical Jesus.[10] The discontinuity thus has been lasting.

The dissatisfaction with this state of affairs has during the last decade lead to a certain reorientation within the field of Jesus-studies. Many scholars have deserted the theological approach and turned to historical problems in the life of Jesus and the early church.[11] This is no return to the liberal "Leben-Jesu-Forschung", it is maintained. The new element is the social perspective. It is emphasised that Jesus has to be seen in his social context, an aspect which was neglected by liberal scholarship with its individualistic orientation. With the aid of social sciences scholars try to depict the situation in the contemporary Jewish society and to illuminate the structures of the early church. These investigations are done in the hope of getting richer knowledge also of the originator of the Christian movement.

The new approach is interesting in its emphasising of the social aspects. The results are, however, so far hardly convincing. They often are contradictory. It is therefore an open question if investigations of this kind can successfully contribute

---

[8] Important introductory contributions were E. Käsemann 1954, 125-53; N. A. Dahl 1974a, 10-36 (= German idem 1960) and 1974b,48-89 (= German idem 1955); reprinted in idem 1991a, 27-47 and idem 1991b, 81-111 respectively. The article on "The Problem of the Historical Jesus" "goes back to a paper read in Uppsala in 1952" (idem 1991a, 45 note 2) and "originally appeared in a collection of lectures entitled *Rett lære og kjetterske meninger* (Oslo, 1953)" (idem 1991b, 109 note 1).

[9] J. M. Robinson 1959 was one of the first scholars, who very clearly pointed out the difference between the old and new quest.

[10] This becomes obvious from the rather confused discussion regarding criteria for delimiting the *ipsissima verba* Jesu. See J. P. Meier 1991, 167-95. Cf. Holmberg 1993.

[11] Holmberg 1993, 72ff.

to illuminating the relation between Jesus and early Christology.[12] The designation of this approach as the "third quest" might turn out to be premature.

Interesting is the fact that these new studies come close to Jewish investigations in this field. Jewish scholarship has been concerned with Jesus-studies during the whole of this century. When Gösta Lindeskog published his dissertation "Die Jesus-frage im neuzeitlichen Judentum" in 1938,[13] he indicated in the subtitle, that he was presenting the Jewish contribution to the "Leben-Jesu-Forschung". From Linde-skog's work it becomes clear, that these Jewish studies were strongly reminiscent of works, produced by contemporary liberal scholars. To both groups of exegetes Jesus appeared as a great religious personages but without supernatural traits. The results of these studies were rather similar on both sides. One difference was, however, that Jewish scholars depicted Jesus in all his Jewishness, while Christian exe-getes, eager to emphasise his universal relevance, often toned down the Jewish traits. With regard to the Christology in the New Testament, Jewish as well as Chris-tian scholars were of the same opinion: it was a creation of the early church. The thesis of Bousset that the Christology had emerged within Hellenism and from Hel-lenistic premises was gladly accepted by Jewish scholarship.

After World War II the situation has changed.[14] This concerns both Jewish and Christian Jesus-studies. The terrible experiences of the Jews during the Nazi-period has lead to an intensified reflection on the Jewish religion and its traditions. In this connection a remarkable reorientation has taken place. Jesus, who for centuries has been rejected by the Jews as the very symbol of "Christian" hatred and anti-Semit-ism, is now by some Jewish scholars understood as a brother in sufferings. He is even by some regarded as a symbol of the suffering Jewish people. In this connec-tion one has actualised anew the idea of the "Heimholung Jesu",[15] or of the "repa-triation of Jesus to the Jewish people", i.e. an including of him in the Jewish religious tradition.

---

[12] There are, however, some possibilities. If a connection can be detected (or indicated) socio-logically between the pre-Easter followers of Jesus and the Jesus-movement in the early church, then it is reasonable to presuppose some kind of continuity also as regards tradition-history. Opinions dif-fer among scholars at this point. Positive to the idea of a connection is M. J. Borg 1984. More reluc-tant is G. Theißen 1977, cf. idem 1987. If such a connection exists the task remains to clarify in what sense it eventually contributes to the illumination of the relation between Jesus and early Christolo-gy.

[13] G. Lindeskog 1938.

[14] Regarding the academic dialogue, see K.- J. Illman 1986, 13-36. O. Skarsaune 1986, 37-51 delivers an account of the ecumenical dialogue.

[15] The idea of "Heimholung Jesu" was launched already by H. A. Wolfson, L. Beck, M. Buber and others. It is taken up anew after World War II by several scholars for instance by S. Ben Chorin 1972; D. Flusser 1968; G. Vermes 1976; S. Sandmel 1965. For an overview see the interesting study by D. A. Hagner 1984.

What then has happened to Christology? It is still unacceptable to Jewish thought. But it is not Hellenistic any more. It does not seem alien to the same extent as before. Building-material and structure are of Jewish character, David Flusser maintains.[16] In this regard he gets support from Geza Vermes,[17] Samuel Ben Chorin[18] and others. Many of these scholars are ready to demonstrate the connection between the Jew Jesus and the Christology of the church, in spite of their own rejection of the latter phenomenon.

The situation thus appears as rather contradictory, marked by mild irony. Jewish scholars assume a real connection between the Jew Jesus and the church's Christology. They thus are advocates of the continuity. This possibility exists because of their having a greater confidence in the Jesustradition than their Christian colleagues. As regards the latter they are, as we have noted, willing to establish some kind of connection between the historical Jesus and the kerygmatic Christ. They are, however, to a considerable extent prevented from doing so because of their scepticism to the Jesustradition. Geza Vermes expresses a certain surprise about these Christian scholars, who are displaying "an agnostic tendency in regard to the authenticity of most of these words (Jesus-*logia*). Indeed, they even go so far as to reject the possibility of knowing anything historical about Jesus himself".[19]

The discussion about the historical Jesus and the Christology of the primitive church thus has been carried on along two lines of interpretation: one where the continuity has been emphasised, one where the discontinuity has been brought to the fore. These two models of interpretation are, however, insufficient as attempts to explain the development of Christology. Another factor has to be taken into account. Decisive is the mysterious event, which is designated as the resurrection of Jesus. In the light of this the tension between the two interpretations comes in its true perspective. To advocates of the discontinuity the resurrection appears as the starting-point of Christology. The knowledge of Jesus, which eventually existed before, was entirely overshadowed by the Christology, now developing. In reality it seems to be a new creation on the basis of the resurrection. To defenders of the continuity the resurrection does not mean a new creation of Christological elements. It is rather understood as giving rise to a radical transformation of the "messianism" of Jesus into Christology.

On this point of the exposition it is necessary to deal in brevity with the resurrection of Jesus as depicted in the New Testament. This short account is intended to present different kinds of material concerning the resurrection; further to clarify

---

[16] Flusser 1975.

[17] Vermes 1976.

[18] Ben Chorin 1972.

[19] Vermes 1976, 225.

how it is related to Christology; lastly to give a few indications of the discussion of the resurrection, which has been carried on during the last decades.

## 2. The Resurrection of Jesus

The New Testament as a whole is permeated by the conviction that Jesus is risen from the dead. This belief has been the driving force in the development of the New Testament itself. It has rightly been maintained, that no one would have cared to hand down the fiasco of this Jewish preacher, if nothing had occurred after his death. The rise of the New Testament thus can be understood as a consequence of an occurrence, the resurrection of Jesus, regardless of how one conceives of this event.

To begin with I am going to give a brief sketch of the different types of texts, dealing with the resurrection of Jesus. The resurrection-texts can be divided—mainly as regards form—in two groups: (a) Formula-material and (b) Narrative-material.

(a) *The formula-tradition*. This designation refers to confessional statements, kerygmatic formulas, exclamations of praise etc. It concerns materials which obviously is older than the writings into which it has been included and used. Clauses of this kind are mainly to be found in *corpus paulinum*, Acts, Hebrews and other New Testament epistles. They have already a fixed form and are supposedly derived from the liturgy of the early church. Examples are among others 1 Cor 15:3ff.; Rom 4:25; 10:9; Gal 1:1; Phil 2:6-11; Acts 3:15; Hebr 1:3c.

If we take a look at the content of these formula-sayings, we find that they usually proclaim that God has raised Jesus from the dead, or alternatively that he has exalted him. Both modes of expression refer to the same event: the resurrection of Jesus. In spite of this a certain difference is discernible. The motive of exaltation seems to have offered superior possibilities of depicting the universal lordship of the risen Jesus Christ.

The resurrection and exaltation of Jesus are in these formulas proclaimed without an attempt to verify the sayings. The appearance-traditions contain, however, references to witnesses, who are supposed to confirm the revelations of the risen Lord, the most obvious examples are to be found in 1 Cor 15:3ff.; cf. Luke 24:54. To these texts one can count also the μαρτυρία of Paul himself about the Lord's appearances to him, although these sayings are not taken from the tradition, see 1 Cor 9:1; 15:8; Gal 1:1b.

(b) *The narrative-tradition*. A brief glance at the resurrection-texts in the gospels shows that they are manifold and even contradictory. In this variety there are, however, two dominating factors: (1) Jesus has appeared to his adherents as living and thus convinced them of his resurrection from the dead (the gospel of Mark forming an exception). (2) The adherents of Jesus have found his tomb empty. This discovery was then connected with an *angelophany* by which their finding is interpreted as a sign of the resurrection of Jesus.

After this presentation of the material I will make some few remarks to its character. The first question to be dealt with is the interrelation between the two groups of texts. This theme has been intensely debated.

The most widely accepted view goes back to Martin Dibelius.[20] According to this opinion the formula-tradition is older and more reliable than the narratives in the gospels. These are regarded as illustrations to the message announced in the *kerygma* of the formula-tradition. The gospel-narratives thus are understood as representing a secondary development of the *kerygma*. Two comments are needed to that thesis.

*Firstly.* The formula-tradition is, to be sure, of fundamental importance for our understanding of the rise of Christology. These theologically pregnant clauses offer very valuable information about early Christological thought, prior to individual authors' including of the ideas in their own works and giving them their own profile. The early formulas thus are very fitting as basis for our attempt to illuminate the development of Christology.

*Secondly.* It is a questionable assumption to maintain that the narrative material forms a mere illustration of the resurrection-*kerygma* in the formula-tradition. Narrative-material has probably been needed from the very beginning for missionary purposes. It is hardly imaginable that the early church, not even for a short period, carried out missionary work solely with the aid of kerygmatic formulas. This means that formula-material *and* narratives of necessity have existed side by side. The theory of a simple development from *kerygma* to gospel-narrative is very vulnerable. A reverse order of development is quite thinkable: a concentration of narrative-material into kerygmatic formulations. In any case: the dominating theory is wide-open to criticism. This has been demonstrated in many history-of-tradition studies, for instance by John E. Alsup.[21]

The discussion of relevant material concerning the resurrection unavoidably leads to the question how these texts are to be understood. What exactly is meant by the message of the resurrection of Jesus?

Such a questioning brings us close to the *quaestio facti*. As is well known this problem cannot be discussed fruitfully in philosophical terms. From an immanent, philosophical perspective the resurrection of Jesus is an inconceivable or even im-

---

[20] M. Dibelius 1961 (1919). The problem is discussed in an instructive manner by L. Goppelt 1975, 278-99.

[21] J. E. Alsup 1975, 24 and 266-74. Alsup rejects the arguments for the usual assumption that the appearance stories of the gospels are dependent on the kerygma.

possible event. The message of the church is a challenge to this immanent world-view. It pretends that an entirely new event has occurred, an eschatological event without analogies. A discussion of the *quaestio facti* between these two systems of thought can hardly be expected to lead to mutual understanding.[22]

The *quaestio facti* can, however, be dealt with in another way: texts and traditions about the resurrection of Jesus can be scrutinized by the aid of literary criticism, form criticism, history-of-tradition criticism etc. The material as a whole can be tested in this way with regard to its reliability. Such investigations do not prove anything about the inaccessible event itself, the resurrection of Jesus. Still they are useful in their clarification of the historical situation and in pointing out the decisive moments, which might be of importance for personal decisions. In principle the exegetical examination of a passage could even result in a falsification of its content (for instance by demonstrating its legendary character).[23]

The resurrection of Jesus is mainly discussed on exegetical—non-philosophical—presuppositions. Two alternatives of interpretation are discernible in the debate. According to one line of understanding the texts bear witness to external events, experienced by the disciples (appearances of Jesus, finding of the empty tomb).[24] These occurrences gave rise to their belief in the resurrection. In the alternative interpretation it is maintained that the rise of the faith in the resurrection was an internal act by the adherents of Jesus. The process was a reaction to an external event, however, the death of Jesus. Bultmann claims that the disciples after the death of Jesus were brought up against a new decision (*Entscheidung*).[25] They had to overcome the offence of the cross. Their existential considerations brought them to the

---

[22] W. Pannenberg 1967, 233-49 makes an attempt to such a discussion. See also Hans Fr. von Campenhausen 1967, 191-206. According to v. Campenhausen the resurrection of Jesus is an event, which in principle cannot be grasped by the aid of historical methods. The resurrection, nevertheless, has taken place in history. This means that it has a side facing on to historical realities, which are accessible to historical investigations —R. Schwager 1993, 445ff. emphasises—contrary to the majority of scholars—the importance of the empty tomb. See also P. Stuhlmacher's well balanced discussion 1992, 175ff

[23] Matt 28:2-4 can be taken as an example. Some traits of the passage are most likely results of haggadic "legend-making".

[24] Stuhlmacher 1992, 162ff.; Goppelt 1975, 277-99. See the instructive orientation by A. Vögtle – R. Pesch 1975, 27ff. For a general introduction, see P. Hoffmann 1979, 478-513.

[25] Bultmann 1984, 47: "Die Entscheidung für Jesu Sendung, die seine 'Jünger' einst durch ihre 'Nachfolge' gefällt hatten, mußte von neuem und radikal gefällt werden infolge der Kreuzigung Jesu. *Das Kreuz* stellte gewissermaßen die Entscheidungsfrage noch einmal." According to this interpretation the adherents of Jesus had made no new and inexplicable experiences, evoking their belief In the resurrection of Jesus. The rise of this faith is to be explained solely out from the internal and external status of the disciples after the crucifixion of Jesus. See the account by Vögtle 1975, 28f.

insight that the crucified Jesus was God's decisive word to mankind. According to Willy Marxsen[26] the decisive factor was not the death of Jesus. The faith of the disciples was provoked by his *kerygma*. Bultmann as well as Marxsen take it as self-evident that the adherents of Jesus had to express their experiences and reflections in contemporary terms. This is the reason for the whole legend-making: appearance-stories and narratives of the empty tomb. The entire material has to be regarded as produced for the sake of concretion.

These solutions seem to be lying on such a high hypothetical level that they have become inaccessible to rational criticism.

More accessible is another interpretation, which regards the rise of the resurrection-belief as an internal process by the disciples of Jesus. One maintains that Jesus and his disciples were dependent on Jewish ideas of prophetic-messianic figures, who after their (martyr)death were exalted into heaven. Jesus, it is claimed, had instructed his disciples about his coming exaltation. At the crucifixion of Jesus his adherents thus were prepared to understand his death as an immediate exaltation, as an assumption of him into heaven. To them he was resurrected from the moment of his death. The narratives of the appearances and the empty tomb are just illustrations and explanations of this faith, founded already during the lifetime of Jesus.[27]

The weakness of this hypothesis—which occasionally enjoys support from radical as well as conservative scholars—clearly appears as soon as it is confronted with the texts. Our sources unanimously bear evidence of the frustration and sorrow of the disciples. Nothing indicates that they were believing that Jesus already was exalted into heaven. Everything points to the conclusion that they regarded the end of his life as a failure.[28]

The attempt to understand the belief in the resurrection as caused by an internal process by the adherents of Jesus can hardly be upheld. The most reasonable way of interpreting the texts seems to be an acceptance of their own reference to external events as the cause of their resurrection-belief. These external factors creating faith are the appearances of Jesus and the empty tomb. By this argumentation the resurrection of Jesus is by no means demonstrated. Still we have got an explanation of the firm belief in the resurrection of Jesus which is so easily found in the New Testament. At the same time we have reached a point in our expositions where it makes sense to deal with the question of the rise and development of Christology in the

---

[26] W. Marxsen 1958. The view of Marxsen which sometimes turns out to be a bit obscure, is admirably related by Vögtle 1975, 28f. Cf. G. Lüdemann 1994.

[27] See especially R. Pesch 1973, 201-28. Since the belief of the disciples in the resurrection of Jesus was founded already during his life-time, there is no need for Pesch to use hypotheses of their inner considerations and decisions after the death of Jesus (contrary to Bultmann and Marxsen).

[28] Cf. Vögtle 1975, 73f.

early church.

## 3. The Resurrection of Jesus and the Rise of Christology

### 3.1. Jesus as the Crucified and Resurrected Messiah/Christ

Biblical scholars, radicals and conservatives alike, agree in thinking that the early church first of all had to overcome the offence of the cross.[29] This is often emphasised, and rightly so. The death of Jesus on the cross was probably an even more disastrous catastrophe to his followers than we are able to imagine. Jesus, to whom they had attached their hope, had been sentenced to death. He had been found guilty of blasphemy by the Sanhedrin. He was judged in accordance to the law of God. The death-sentence was—on political premises—recognised by the Roman procurator. Roman soldiers had handled the execution. The case of Jesus could be put aside, at least as far as his adversaries were concerned.

His adherents had in addition to wrestle with another problem. It concerned the manner of his death. Jesus had been crucified. He was "hanged on the tree". In the light of Deut 21:23 this could be taken as a sign of his being cursed by God. His messianic claims (or the claims on his behalf) turned out to be false. For if he really had been the Messiah, he certainly would have been able to avoid this humiliating situation. Nor had any divine intervention rescued him from this disgraceful death. Such an interpretation of the events was probably close at hand in the Jewish environment, among adversaries as well as adherents. The cross of Jesus was a sign, indicating that the curse of God was placed upon him.[30]

The decisive turning point came, the resurrection of Jesus. To his disciples and other adherents this event was a powerful sign, that the God of the fathers had intervened and raised him from the dead. In kerygmatic formulas, for instance in Acts, this is clearly expressed.[31] The act of God negatively meant a non-approval of the adversaries of Jesus. With the law of God as means the Sanhedrin had condemned

---

[29] Bultmann 1984, 47: "Die Gemeinde mußte das Ärgernis des Kreuzes überwinden und hat es getan im Osterglauben". Goppelt 1975, 276-99.

[30] The curse placed on Jesus is referred to by Paul not only in Gal 3:13, where Deut 21:23 is quoted. The motive is discernible also in 2 Cor 5:21, where the apostle states about Christ that "God made him one with the sinfulness of men". For a broad discussion of the concept of curse, see K. A. Morland 1991.

[31] Acts 2:36; 3:15b; 4:10f.; 13:30ff. The missionary speeches in Acts are much debated, not least as far as date and authenticity are concerned. There is, however, reason to maintain that they are reflecting an early pattern of speeches, including traditional *topoi*, which were actualised in addressing a Jewish audience. For discussion and references of literature, see E. Larsson 1990, 59-62 and idem 1989, 153-55. For a comprehensive account of literature, see for instance F. Bovon 1978.

and killed a guiltless man, the only innocent man in the opinion of the disciples and the early church. Positively the intervention of God indicated, that the death of this guiltless man was a sacrifice. Jesus had been given up to death by God, but he was also raised from the dead by him. This designated him as an expiatory sacrifice, his cross as a sign of salvation. The resurrection at the same time identified Jesus as the saviour, the Messiah of whom scriptures had spoken. He was the fulfilment of Old Testament prophecies. This insight offered new and far-reaching possibilities of interpreting Jesus in the light of scriptures. This was especially needed with regard to his death on the cross. The cross of Jesus really was an offence. No salvific meaning could be attached to it before the resurrection. It could even be maintained, that the cross without the resurrection should have been nothing else than an instrument for execution.

I know from experience that a declaration of this kind easily provokes contradiction. In the homiletic tradition of the church we have been taught that the cross of Jesus is to be regarded as our only hope for salvation.[32] To many Christian movements Good Friday seems to be the decisive day, the day of Atonement. Easter Sunday with its message of the resurrection seems, on the other hand, to be understood basically as a happy end.

It has been objected that the cross of Jesus rightly has got this position. Paul designates, after all, his teaching activity as a preaching of the cross. Within contemporary Judaism one can find motives of expiation, which might have been used by the interpretation of the death of Jesus, entirely independent of the resurrection. In this connection one refers to ideas of atonement attached to *Ebed-Yahweh*, to the Jewish conceptions of blessings, emerging from the sufferings of the righteous ones and to the belief that the blood of Jewish martyrs could be of an expiatory character.[33] The question then arises: Why should not the sufferings and death of Jesus be regarded as an atoning acts apart from the resurrection?

To these objections some remarks have to be made. Paul's characterizing of his message as a preaching of the cross mainly comes to the fore, when the offensive foolishness of the saving gospel is emphasised.[34] In his preaching as a whole the resurrection of Jesus is of fundamental importance. Regarding the blood of Jewish martyrs and the sufferings of the righteous ones some special features are to be taken into account. Jewish martyrs were suffering because of their fidelity to the law

---

[32] A well-known example of the impact of this traditional view is the inscription on the memorial cross of A. Strindberg: "*Ave crux, spes unica*" (quotation from Venantius Fortunatus' cross-hymn, 6th century).

[33] 1 Macc 2:29ff.; 2 Macc 6:10f.; 6:17-7:42. To the theme of the sufferings of martyrdom, see Th. Baumeister 1980; D. R. Schwartz 1993. Cf. W. D. Davies 1955, 291ff.

[34] Examples 1 Cor 1:18-2:5; 2 Cor 4:1-15; Gal 4:12ff.; 6:14ff.; Phil 3:7ff.

of God. Jesus was condemned as violator of the same law. The persecutors of Jewish religious heroes were usually godless foreign rulers. The adversaries of Jesus belonged to the religious elite of Israel. His death on the cross could under these circumstances hardly be understood as an expiatory sacrifice. On the contrary: his cross was a means of execution. It appeared as a sign of curse.

The resurrection of Jesus offered the key for a true solution of the riddle. God's raising of Jesus from the dead bestowed a radical new significance on his cross. It now appeared as a means of salvation. This is not to say that the resurrection just revealed the saving character of the cross. Resurrection and cross form an organic unity with regard to salvation. This is apparent in the oldest layer of the formula-tradition in 1 Cor 15. There it is stated that "Christ died for our sins in accordance with the scriptures ... that he was raised to life on the third day according to the scriptures" (vv. 3-4). Here the death and resurrection are paralleled and interpreted in the light of scriptures. The organic unity of these moments is pointed out even more clearly in Paul's own comments on the resurrection-tradition in v. 17. There he proclaims that, if Christ is "not raised, your faith has nothing in it and you are still in your old state of sin". Paul thus states that the death of Jesus alone does not bring about salvation. God's raising of Jesus from the dead, his decisive intervention, qualified the death on the cross as a salvific act. A lot of formula-material could be brought forward, which confirms that the death and resurrection of Jesus were regarded as one saving act from the very beginning.[35] According to the formula in Rom 4:25 Jesus was "given up to death for our misdeeds and raised to life to justify us"; cf. 2 Cor 5:15b; 1 Thess 4:14; 5:10.

If we leave aside the formula-material and turn to individual authors in the New Testament, it becomes clear that they are presupposing and transmitting this view of the unity of cross and resurrection. This is apparent by Paul, Luke (Acts), John and the author of Hebrews.

The early church thus was confronted with a crucified and resurrected Messiah (Christ). It was a radically new and alien situation. In the light of the resurrection one tried to interpret the situation out from scriptures. This is, as we have seen, apparent already in the oldest resurrection-account (1 Cor 15:1-4). We have to abstain from dealing with the hermeneutical rules followed in this connection.[36] It just has to be stated, that the resurrection of Jesus gave rise to a far-reaching *interpretatio Christiana* of the Old Testament. This topic will be dealt with anew below.

Let us for a moment return to our main question: the problem about the relation between Jesus of Nazareth and the crucified and resurrected Messiah/Christ. How about the continuity?

---

[35] Goppelt 1975, 280ff. Cf. J. Iwand 1967, 291.

[36] An informative overview is Goppelt 1976, 375-388.

Just a few comments can be given here. There are traits in the history and teaching of Jesus, which indicate that he understood his life, mission and death in the light of scriptures. This impression is lasting even after a critical testing of the evidence.[37] In some sense he has regarded himself as the fulfilment of scriptures. If this is a sound conclusion, the Christological interpretation emanates from Jesus himself, although the decisive impulse to a further development obviously was caused by the resurrection. A certain continuity thus can be suggested with regard to the understanding of scriptures as pointing forwards to the Christ-event. Concerning the cross of Jesus Old Testament texts of affliction and sufferings are actualised, among others *Ebed-Yahweh* passages.[38] The synoptic accounts of the last supper reveal the sacrifice-motive connected with the death of Jesus, a tradition included already in 1 Cor 11: 23-26. The wording in the different passages is varying. Still they all express the view, that Jesus sacrificed himself for the sins of others. Mark 10:45 contains a Jesus-*logion* of the same content: "For even the Son of Man did not come to be served but to serve, and to give up his life as a ransom for many".[39] There seems to exist a kind of essential or "material" continuity between these synoptic sayings of Jesus and the formulations of the early church with regard to his death and its significance.

In the perspective of the resurrection and with the aid of scriptures and certain moments from the Jesustradition the early church interpreted the death of Jesus as an atonement for sins. Jesus was understood as the crucified and resurrected Messiah/Christ. This overcoming of the offence of the cross was evidently of fundamental importance for the further development of Christology. Other aspects of the Christ-event now could be brought to the fore. We are going to deal briefly with some of these interpretations of the life and achievement of Jesus.

## 3.2. Jesus as the Crucified and Exalted Kyrios/Messiah

In my presentation of the formula-material I pointed to a certain difference between resurrection and exaltation. The distinction is basically formal. Different verbs are used. They point, nevertheless, at the same event, the resurrection. Still it seems to have been more fitting to use the exaltation-category in depicting the universal reign of the resurrected Christ. The designation of the exalted one is usually κύριος, Lord.

The term *kyrios* means owner, lord. Objects of this ownership or lordship are human beings, animals, things. Κύριος is used in both profane and religious connec-

---

[37] M. de Jonge 1991. For discussion and critique H. J. de Jonge 1993, 21-37. Goppelt 1975, 207-53.

[38] Goppelt 1975, 243ff.

[39] Goppelt 1975, 241.

tions. In a profane setting κύριος in vocative form functions as a polite title. In a religious context it is used in addressing a divine being. As regards The Old Testament usage (LXX) the term usually signifies God in religious connections. In the New Testament κύριος is a designation for God as well as for Christ. The exaltation has occasioned that the risen Christ has been brought near God, seemingly being almost equal to him. In Acts 2:14-41, in Peter's Pentecostal speech, we find an interesting example illuminating the new situation. In v. 34 he applies the words of Ps 110:1 to Jesus: "The Lord (God) said to my lord (Jesus): sit at my right hand until I make your enemies your footstool".[40] The speaker then summarises his Christ-*kerygma* (v. 36) in words reminiscent of a confessional formula: Let all Israel then accept as certain "that God has made this Jesus whom you crucified, both Lord and Messiah". This proclamation means first of all that the messianic expectations of Israel have been fulfilled in Jesus. He is the Anointed One, God's Messiah. The term κύριος then gives this Messiah-designation a further qualification, which in reality transcends the traditional messianic conceptions. According to Ps 110:1, interpreted in the light of the resurrection, Jesus is now exalted and enthroned as κύριος in heaven, not in the nation of Israel. He is addressed as κύριος in his capacity of being God's co-regent over the world as a whole. By that the contemporary messianic hope in its manifold expressions has been transformed. Its new content makes it incommensurable to traditional messianic conceptions.

The title κύριος brings the risen Christ near to God without leading to identification. The most obvious example in the formula-tradition is Phil 2:6-11. In this carefully formulated passage, usually defined as a hymn, there is given an account of the preexistence of Christ, his incarnation, death on the cross and exaltation. We shall deal with the cross and the exaltation.

"He was obedient unto death, the death on the cross", it is stated in v. 8b. This concentrated pronouncement indicates, that Jesus submitted to the will of God and sacrificed himself on the cross. The expiatory-aspect is not mentioned but is most probably implied.[41] The main interest is directed towards the exaltation. It is described in a manner, which points to a qualified high-Christology. Because of

---

[40] M. Hengel 1993, 127f. Hengel delivers a very comprehensive interpretation of all exaltation-texts in the New Testament including Acts 2:33f.; 5:31; 7:55f. The exaltation-passages in the New Testament are belonging to an early conception of the enthronement of Christ, a pattern based on Ps 110:1. — L. Hartman 1993 treats the *kyrios*-issue in another way. To him the relation between baptism and Christology is important. He finds reason to assume that the title κύριος was actualized in the rite of baptism "to" or "in" the name of Jesus. As designation for a "cult-deity" the title easily could get transcendent connotations.

[41] E. Larsson 1962, 250ff.

Christ's sacrificing of himself on the cross God has exalted him (v. 9). He is raised above all powers in heaven, on earth and beneath the earth. These representatives for the entire universe shall therefore do homage to him as κύριος.[42] A lot of interesting traits are interwoven into this description of the exaltation. Let us point at just one: the declaration that God has bestowed on him "the name above all names". This statement indicates a name superseding the *kyrios*-designation. By the circumscription "name above all names" the author expresses the view, that God has given Christ his own name.[43] This means that he participates in God's rule over the world. Here a nearness to God is presupposed which has few equivalents in the New Testament. Possible parallels are John 1:18 and passages in Hebrews, where Old Testament sayings about God, and by God, without hesitation are applied to Christ.[44]

The History of Religion-School maintained that the title κύριος as designation for Jesus had emerged in Hellenistic-Christian churches (above all in Antioch). A *kyrios*-Christology, it was maintained, could be developed only in a Hellenistic environment, where people were used to regard the gods of the mysteries as κύριοι. The conclusion thus was that the *kyrios*-Christology was a late stage in the reflection on the Christ-event. Today's scholarship has strongly modified and to a considerable extent rejected this view. Jewish scholars as Geza Vermes and Christian exegetes like Joseph A. Fitzmyer have convincingly demonstrated that conditions for a *kyrios*-Christology existed already on Palestinian soil.[45] Long before that many scholars, among them Oscar Cullmann,[46] had advocated the view, that the cult-exclamation *marana tha* was an indication of the existence of a *kyrios*-Christology already in the Aramaic-speaking church of Palestine. Jesus as the crucified and exalted κύριος/Messiah thus seems to be a Christological conception of an early date.

## 3.3. Jesus, the Son of God, Exalted to Heaven

In his book "Christology in the making" James D. G. Dunn says the following: "The understanding of Jesus as the Son of God apparently did not provide the starting

---

[42] In spite of the grammatical forms the statements of the cosmic powers and their surrendering to Christ are best understood as pointing to a future event, the parousia.

[43] Larsson 1962, 255ff.

[44] Among commentaries to Hebrews, see H.-Fr. Weiß 1991, 171-81. Cf. also J. C. McCullough 1979/80, 363-79.

[45] Vermes 1976, 103-122; J. A. Fitzmyer 1979, 115-42.

[46] O. Cullmann 1963, 195-237.

point for a Christology of preexistence or incarnation".[47] The observation is entirely correct. The designation Son of God in the New Testament does not have a connotation, which beyond doubt points to a high-Christology. The Johannine writings, however, form an exception. It has been claimed, not unreasonably, that the Christology of our symbolas might have got another character, if the Johannine writings had been missing in the Canon.

The reason for this reluctance in using the title Son of God probably is that its content is wide and hard to define. On Hellenistic soil it stands for divine beings, royal persons, miracle-makers.[48] In Jewish context it designates for instance the people of Israel, the messianic king but also pious individuals, who are supposed to have an especially intimate relation to God. This last category has been brought to the fore by Geza Vermes and others.[49]

In the formula-material we find just a couple of statements where Jesus is mentioned as Son of God in reference to the resurrection. In 1 Thess 1:10 Paul gives an account of traditions, dealing with the Thessalonians themselves. According to these narratives they had learnt "to wait expectantly for the appearance from heaven of his Son Jesus, whom he raised from the dead, Jesus our deliverer from the terrors of judgement to come". There is no sign that Jesus is understood as having become the Son of God by the exaltation. It is just stated that he now holds a powerful position in heaven. He is further expected to save the addressees from the terrors of the last judgement. The Son of God, Jesus, raised from the dead and exalted to heaven, thus has an eschatological mission to fulfil.[50]

The task of the Son of God is not so clearly defined in the formula-fragment, which is discernible in Rom 1:3. The statement seems to have bearing not so much on the mission of Christ, but rather on his nature. Paul is dedicated to the gospel of God, which is about his Son. As regards this Son it is stated: "on the human level he was born of David's stock, but on the level of the spirit—the Holy Spirit—he was declared Son of God by a mighty act in that he rose from the dead". Many difficul-

---

[47] J. D. G. Dunn 1980. D. A. Hagner 1991, 20f. accuses Dunn for an unduly emphasis of the aspect "Jesus as God's agent". In Hagner's opinion this results in a rejection (or neglection) of such elements as preexistence and incarnation.

[48] According to Hengel 1975, 39ff. the evidences are few and scanty on Hellenistic soil. Cf. W. von Martitz 1972, 334-40.

[49] Vermes 1976, 192-213; Hengel 1975, 67-89. J. J. Collins 1993, 65-82 discusses the fragment from Qumran designated as 4Q246, often referred to as the "Son of God" text. Collins finds in the text a combination of the "son of man"-figure in Daniel and the traditional hope for a Davidic Messiah. The combination thus is no Christian innovation. It is to be found already in pre-Christian, sectarian Judaism, (p. 82).

[50] As regards the "terrors of judgement to come", see O. Linton 1964, 280.

ties are attached to the understanding of this clause.[51] The point, however, seems rather clear. Since the resurrection Jesus, the Son of God, occupies a position as Lord by God. This means among other things that he has made Paul an apostle with the mission to bring the gentiles under the obedience of the faith, i.e. to bring them under the universal lordship of the Son of God (cf. Acts 13:35).

## 4. Christ as Preexistent Co-creator

We have already dealt with a hymn, where Jesus is depicted as preexistent, Phil 2:6ff. Right through the New Testament there are, however, other passages of for-mula-character, where Christ is described as preexistent and in addition as the me-dium of creation. The texts are 1 Cor 8:6; Col 1:16f.; Hebr 1:3; Joh 1:3, 10; Rev 3:14. We have no possibilities of dealing in detail with the individual passages here. It is necessary, though, to concentrate on a few general viewpoints.[52]

The motive of Christ's role as God's agent at the creation belongs exclusively to the formula-tradition. The conception thus is of an early date, expressed in fixed forms already in 1 Cor. In 1 Cor 8:6, as well as in other passages, the activity of Christ at the creation is just mentioned. No information is given as to how his ac-tivity is understood. His position and function as God's co-creator are just pro-claimed. This proclamation, however, serves different purposes. In 1 Cor 8:6 Paul uses the motive of Christ as creator in order to convince the Corinthians that their *kyrios Christos* is superior to all divine beings in the syncretistic environment.[53] The co-creator-motive gets a similar function in Col 1:15-20. Christ, the agent of creation, is exalted above all powers in the universe, it is asserted. This consequent-ly means that the Colossians are free from paying any attention of cultic character to angels and other semi-divine beings (Col 2:18).[54] In Hebr 1:3 the conception of Christ as creator serves the purpose to underlay the thesis that the revelation through the Son is final and superior to the Old Testament revelation, which was mediated by angels.[55] *Logos*/Christ is the creator of all things according to John 1:5, 10. The emphasising of this seems to serve the end of asserting the a-dualistic character of

---

[51] See the profound and illuminating discussion by Hengel 1975, 93ff.

[52] E. Larsson 1982, 181-95; L. Hartman 1985, 40ff.

[53] In 1 Cor 8:5 Christ is depicted as creator in a cosmological as well as in a soteriological/ec-clesiological sense. I.e.: Both as creator and re-creator (redeemer). This twofold function demon-strates his total superiority to "competing" powers.

[54] In Col 1:15ff. the creation-motive is combined with the redeemer-conception, 1:18ff. (cf. 1 Cor 8:6). The combination of these two motives makes Christ a sovereign ruler over cosmos. The inclination of the Colossians to do homage to angelic beings thus is entirely out of place; cf. the warning against θρησκεία τῶν ἀγγέλλων (2:18).

[55] E. Larsson 1979, 91-108 discusses the "overbidding" of the Old Testament revelation.

the world.[56] Unlike Gnostic redeemers Christ comes to a world not alien to him. He came to his own, even though his own did not receive him. In Rev 3:14 the creation-motive obviously has the function to enforce the immense power of the heavenly judge.

The motive of Christ as co-creator of the world thus is used in a rather varying way in the different writings. The authors quote the formula-material regarding this topic for different purposes. What function these sayings might have served from the very beginning is hard to decide. They are seemingly derived from a cultic "Sitz im Leben". Perhaps their original and only task was to express the community's praises of Jesus as the Lord of the universe.

After this account of the relevant texts it is time to ask for the origin of this motive. No Jesus-*logion* is preserved, which could have served as basis for these reflections of his agency at the creation.[57] In spite of that the idea is discernible on an early stage in the primitive church. This remarkable fact is to be understood only in the light of the resurrection. We have already stated that this event led to a far-reaching *interpretatio Christiana* of the Old Testament. The risen Christ was understood as prefigured in scriptures and as the fulfilment of them. The holy tradition was in one way or another applied to him. This was the case also with the statements about the divine Wisdom. In the light of the resurrection Christ was identified with the personified Wisdom, depicted in the Old Testament and Jewish writings. The sayings about her were transferred to Christ. Consequently he inherited the role as God's co-creator. In this Wisdom-tradition the early church could find materials for hymns and confessions to Christ,[58] among them also those, that proclaimed him as the agent of God at the creation. The starting-point of this development into a Christology of creation thus is the resurrection of Jesus.

The resurrection has inspired the idea of Christ's preexistence and his activity at the creation. The preexistence in its turn forms the necessary condition for a genuine theology of the incarnation. The incarnation, however, is not to be dealt with in this article. It is a topic which needs a separate treatment.

## 5. Some Concluding Remarks

In this article I have dealt with some aspects of the relation between Jesus and Christological conceptions developed in the primitive church. In conclusion I want to stress the following points.

---

[56] R. E. Brown 1966, 25f. Cf. R. Kieffer 1987, 22f.
[57] Larsson 1982, 194ff.
[58] An excellent exposition of the theme is given by R. Deichgräber 1967.

(1) The problem of the relation between Jesus and early Christology is not to be solved simply by emphasising the continuity. A demonstration, for instances, of a firm connection between the "messianic" claims of Jesus and Christological ideas in the early church does not bring about a real solution, Such a one-sided accentuation of the continuity, fails to observe the revolutionary, transforming character of the resurrection of Jesus.

(2) It is no acceptable solution either to undo the knot in Gordian manner by cutting off the connection between Jesus and the subsequent thought of him, thus making the resurrection of Jesus the starting-point of Christological reflection. With such a discontinuity-solution one neglects the importance of the Jesus-traditions available in the early church.[59]

(3) The resurrection of Jesus is the decisive event in the development of Christology. In the perspective of the resurrection the primitive church transformed "messianic" ideas emanating from Jesus himself, as well as expectations by his adherents, into Christological conceptions. At the same time the resurrection gave a mighty impulse to further reflections on the person and achievement of Jesus.

(4) The resurrection-material in the New Testament can be divided in a formula-tradition and a narrative-tradition. Both groups of texts are of importance for a reconstruction of the development of New Testament Christology. The formula-tradition, discernible on different parts of the New Testament, is permeated by Christological ideas of an early date and thus especially valuable for an understanding of the rise of Christology.

(5) In the New Testament the resurrection of Jesus is understood as a real event. New Testament scholars as a rule regard the relevant texts as witnessing to an "event" of some kind. Concerning the character of this "event" opinions differ sharply among New Testament exegetes. In the view of some scholars the resurrection-texts testify to external experiences made by the adherents of Jesus. According to others they are witnesses of an internal act by the disciples. In spite of these differences among scholars the resurrection of Jesus preserves its "event"-character in the discussions regardless of how it is understood. It is interpreted by most exegetes as the decisive factor in the rise of New Testament Christology.

(6) It is generally acknowledged that the early church had to over-come the offence of the cross. The resurrection of Jesus became the very turning-point. The resurrection of Jesus from the dead was interpreted as God's mighty act on his behalf. This meant that Jesus, his life and work, in some sense was designated by God as the fulfilment of scriptures. He was the "Messiah" foretold by the prophets. His death and resurrection were prefigured in scriptures. The death on the cross became,

---

[59] See B. Gerhardsson 1961 and 1991; cf. idem 1979 and 1987.

in the light of the resurrection, a sacrifice for the sins of the world. Jesus was understood as the crucified and resurrected Messiah/Christ. This interpretation of the Christ-event was not only a post-resurrection-understanding. It was not built up only with the aid of Old Testament material. There are traits in the Jesus tradition, which indicate that he himself understood his mission, his life and coming death, in the light of scriptures. In the perspective of scriptures he regarded it as his mission to sacrifice himself for others. If this is a correct observation, there exists a continuity between Jesus' view of himself and the church's preaching of him and his death as an atonement for sins. By this way of interpreting the Christ-event the offence of the cross was overcome.

(7) The solving of the riddle of the cross was of fundamental importance for the development of other aspects of the Christ-event. By raising Jesus from the dead God had designated him as the Messiah. But the exaltation of him at the same time made him *kyrios*. This title, used in the context of the early church, indicates a position transcending traditional messianic expectations. It brings the exalted Christ near to God, although not leading to identification. The question, whether there exists a continuity between Jesus and the *kyrios*-Christology of the church is difficult to handle. In any case, however, it can be maintained that conditions for a *kyrios*-Christology existed already in the Palestinian surroundings of Jesus.

(8) In the formula-material there are just a couple of statements, where Jesus is labelled Son of God with reference to the resurrection. The Risen Christ is designated Son of God in his eschatological role as deliverer of the faithful at the last Judgement (1 Thess 1:10). The heavenly position of the resurrected Christ, the Son of God, enables him also to use the apostle Paul for bringing the Gentiles under the obedience of the faith (Rom 1:3). Already in the formula-tradition the risen Christ thus is proclaimed as Son of God. The fewness of examples is an indication, however, that the Son of God-Christology in a fuller sense belongs to a later stage in the development. This does not necessarily exclude the possibility of a continuity between Jesus and this Christological conception. The Jesus-tradition contains a lot of sayings and narratives, where the intimate relation between Jesus and his Heavenly Father is emphasised, material which might have stimulated the development of a Son of God-Christology.

(9) The resurrection of Jesus gave rise to a far-reaching *interpretatio Christiana* of the Old Testament, including "non-canonical" apocrypha and pseudepigrapha. This attitude to the holy tradition offered a considerable amount of possibilities for a rich development of Christological ideas. The Wisdom-conception of the Old Testament and Jewish tradition thus was interpreted as pointing to the pre-existent Christ as God's co-creator, his agent, at the creation of the world. This motive belongs exclusively to the formula-tradition. Consequently it is of an early date. Al-

though the co-creator motive is used for several purposes by the different authors, they all deliver a picture of Christ as a cosmic figure. The question of the continuity between Jesus and this Christological conception then becomes delicate. No Jesus-saying is preserved, which could have formed the basis for these ideas of Jesus, his cosmological status and agency. The development of this Christology is to be understood only in the light of the resurrection. It caused that the statements about the divine Wisdom in the holy tradition were transferred to Christ. He inherited the role as the pre-existent co-creator of God. The starting-point of this Christology of creation thus is the resurrection of Jesus. This offers us a valuable idea of the daring creativity, to which this event inspired the primitive church already at an early date.

## Bibliography

Alsup, J. E. 1975: *The Post-Resurrection Appearance Stories of the Gospel-Tradition. A History-of-Tradition Analysis*, Stuttgart: Calwer Verlag 1975.

Baumeister, Th. 1980: *Die Anfänge der Theologie des Martyriums* (Münsterische Beiträge zur Theologie 45), Münster: Aschendorff 1980.

Ben Chorin, S. 1972: *Bruder Jesus*, München: Schalom 1972.

Borg, M. J. 1984: *Conflict, Holiness and Politics in the Teaching of Jesus*, Lewiston, NY: Edwin Mellen 1984.

Bousset, W. 1921: *Kyrios Christos. Geschichte des Christusglaubens von den Anfängen bis Irenaeus* (FRLANT 21), Göttingen: Vandenhoeck & Ruprecht [2]1921.

Bovon, F. 1978: *Luc, le théologien. Vingt-cent ans de recherches 1950-1975*, Neuchâtel: Delachaux & Niestlé 1978.

Brown, R. E. 1966: *The Gospel according to John I-XII* (AncB 29), New York: Doubleday 1966.

Bultmann, R. 1931: *Geschichte der synoptischen Tradition* (FRLANT. NF 12), Göttingen: Vandenhoeck & Ruprecht 2. Aufl. 1931.

— 1984: *Theologie des Neuen Testaments*, Tübingen: J. C. B. Mohr (Paul Siebeck) 9. Auflage, durchgesehen und ergänzt von Otto Merk 1984.

von Campenhausen, H. Frh. 1967: "Der Ablauf der Osterereignisse und das leere Grab", in: B. Klappert (ed.), *Diskussion um Kreuz und Auferstehung*, Wuppertal: Aussaat Verlag 1967, 191-206.

Collins, J. J. 1993: "The Son of God Text from Qumran", in: M. C. De Boer (ed.), *From Jesus to John. Essays on Jesus and New Testament Christology. FS M. de Jonge*, Sheffield: JSOT Press 1993, 65-82.

Cullmann, O. 1963: *The Christology of the New Testament*, London: SCM Press [2]1963.

Dahl, N. A. 1955: "Der historische Jesus als geschichtswissenschaftliches und theologisches Problem", in: *KuD* 1 (1955) 104-132.

— 1960: "Der gekreuzigte Messias", in: H. Ristow/K. Matthiae (eds.), *Der historische Jesus und der kerygmatische Christus*, Berlin: Evangelische Verlagsanstalt 1960, 146-169.

— 1974a: "The Crucified Messiah", in: idem, *The Crucified Messiah and other Essays*, Minneapolis, MN: Augsburg Press 1974, 10-36.

— 1974b: "The Problem of the Historical Jesus", in: idem, *The Crucified Messiah and other Essays*, Minneapolis, MN: Augsburg Press 1974, 48-89.

— 1991a: "The Crucified Messiah", in: idem, *Jesus the Christ. The Historical Origins of Christological Doctrine*. Ed. by D. H. Juel, Minneapolis, MN: Fortress 1991, 27-47.

— 1991b: "The Problem of the Historical Jesus", in: idem, *Jesus the Christ. The Historical Origins of Christological Doctrine*. Ed. by D. H. Juel, Minneapolis, MN: Fortress 1991, 81-111.

Davies, W. D. 1955: *Paul and Rabbinic Judaism*, London: SPCK [2]1955.

Deichgräber, R. 1967: *Gotteshymnus und Christushymnus in der frühen Christenheit* (StUNT 5), Göttingen: Vandenhoeck & Ruprecht 1967.

Dibelius, M. 1961: *Die Formgeschichte des Evangeliums*, Tübingen: J. C. B. Mohr (Paul Siebeck) [4]1961 (first published 1919).

Dunn, J. D. G. 1980: *Christology in the Making*, London: SCM Press 1980.

Fitzmyer, J. A. 1979: "The Semitic Background of the New Testament Kyrios-Title", in: idem, *A Wandering Aramean: Collected Aramaic Essays* (SBL.MS 25), Chico, CA: Scholars Press 1979, 83-113.

Flusser, D. 1968: *Jesus in Selbstzeugnissen und Bilddokumenten*, Reinbek bei Hamburg: Rowolt 1968.

— 1975: "Thesen zur Entstehung des Christentums aus dem Judentum", in: *FrRu* 27 (1975).

Fridrichsen, A. 1942: "Messias och Kyrkan", in: G. Aulén (ed.), *En bok om kyrkan*, Stockholm: Diakonistyrelsens Bokförlag 1942, 26-45.

Gerhardsson, B. 1961: *Memory and Manuscript. Oral Tradition and Written Transmission in Rabbinic Judaism and Early Christianity* (ASNU 21), Uppsala: Almqvist & Wiksell 1961.

— 1979: *'Med hela ditt hjärta'. Om Bibelns ethos*, Lund: Liber 1979.

— 1987: "Agape and imitation of Christ", in: E. P. Sanders (ed.), *Jesus, the Gospel and the Church. FS W. R. Farmer*, Macon, GA: Mercer University Press 1987, 163-76.

— 1991: *Evangeliernas förhistoria*, Lund: Novapress 1991.

Goppelt, L. 1975: *Theologie des Neuen Testaments 1. Jesu Wirken in seiner theologischen Bedeutung*, Göttingen: Vandenhoeck & Ruprecht 1975.

— 1976: *Theologie des Neuen Testaments 2. Vielfalt und Einheit des apostolischen Christuszeugnisses*, Göttingen: Vandenhoeck & Ruprecht 1976.

Hagner, D. A. 1984: *The Jewish Reclammation of Jesus. An Analysis & Critique of the Modern Study of Jesus*, Grand Rapids, MI: Eerdmans 1984.

— 1991: "Paul's Christology and Jewish Monotheism", in: R. Müller/M. Shuster (eds.), *Perspectives on Christology. FS P. K. Jewett*, Grand Rapids, MI: Zondervan 1991, 19-38.

Hartman, L. 1985: *Kolosserbrevet* (Kommentar till Nya Testamentet 12), Uppsala: EFS-förlaget 1985.

— 1993: "Early Baptism—Early Christology", in: A. J. Malherbe/W. A. Meeks (eds.), *The Future of Christology. FS L. E. Keck*, Minneapolis, MN: Fortress Press 1993, 191-201.

Hengel, M. 1975: *Der Sohn Gottes. Die Entstehung der Christologie und die jüdisch-hellenistische Religionsgeschichte*, Tübingen: J. C. B. Mohr (Paul Siebeck) 1975.

— 1993: "Setze dich zu meiner Rechten". Die Inthronisation Christi zur Rechten Gottes und Psalm 110,1", in: M. Philonenko (ed.), *Le Trone de Dieu* (WUNT 69), Tübingen: J. C. B. Mohr (Paul Siebeck) 1993, 108-94.

Hoffmann, P. 1979: "Auferstehung", in: *TRE* 4, Berlin: de Gruyter 1979, 478-513.

Holmberg, B. 1993: "En historisk vändning i forskningen om Jesus", in: *SvTK* 69 (1993) 69-76.

Hoskyns, E./Davey, N. 1952: *The Riddle of the New Testament*, London: Faber and Faber [3]1952.

Hyldahl, N. 1993: *Den ældste kristendoms historie*, København: Museum Tusculums Forlag 1993.

Illmann, K.-J. 1986: "Judisk-kristen dialog på det akademiska området", in: T. Kronholm et. al. (eds.), *Judendom och kristendom under de första århundradena*. Nordiskt patristiker-projekt 1982-1985, Stavanger–Oslo–Bergen–Tromsø: Universitetsforlaget 1986, 13-36.

Iwand, J. J. 1967: "Kreuz und Auferstehung Jesu Christi:, in: B. Klappert (ed.), *Diskussion um Kreuz und Auferstehung*, Wuppertal: Aussaat Verlag 1967, 273-97.

de Jonge, H. J. 1993: "The historical Jesus' view of himself and of his mission", in: M. C. De Boer (ed.), *From Jesus to John. Essays on Jesus and New Testament Christology. FS M. de Jonge*, Sheffield: JSOT Press 1993, 21-47.

de Jonge, M. 1991: *Jesus, the Servant-Messiah*, New Haven, CT: Yale University Press 1991.

Käsemann, E. 1954: "Das Probem des historischen Jesus", in: *ZThK* 51 (1954) 125-53 (= idem, *Exegetische Versuche und Besinnungen* I, Göttingen: Vandenhoeck & Ruprecht 1960, 187-214).

Kieffer, R. 1979: *Nytestamentlig teologi*, Lund: Håkan Ohlsson 1979.

— 1987: *Johannesevangeliet 1-10* (Kommentar till Nya Testamentet 4A), Uppsala: EFS-förlaget 1987.

Kümmel, W. G. 1985: *Dreißig Jahre Jesusforschung (1950-1980)*, Bonn: Hanstein 1985.

— 1988-91: "Jesusforschung seit 1981", in: *ThR* 53 (1988) 229-49; 54 (1989) 1-53; 55 (1990) 21-45; 56 (1991) 27-53, 391-420.

Larsson, E. 1962: *Christus als Vorbild. Eine Untersuchung zu den paulinischen Tauf- und Eikontexten* (ASNU 23), Lund: Gleerup/Kopenhagen: Munksgaard 1962.

— 1979: "Sonen och änglarna i Hebr 1-2", in: I. Asheim et al. (eds.), *Israel – Kristus – Kirken. FS Sv. Aalen*, Oslo – Bergen – Tromsø: Universitetsforlaget 1979, 91-108.

— 1982: *Människan inför bibeln*, Arlöv: Skeab/Verbum 1982.

— 1989: "Apostlagärningarnas historiska värde", in: *SvTK* 65 (1989) 145-55.

— 1990: "Från Acta-forskningens fält", in: *TTK* 61 (1990) 49-66.

— 1993: "Kristologiska spörsmål hos Harald Riesenfeld", in: *SEÅ* 58 (1993) 59-69.

— 1994: "The Jewish-Christian Dialogue and its Impact on Christian Theology", in: A. Tångberg (ed.), *Text and Theology. FS M. Sæbø*, Oslo: Verbum 1994, 193-212.

Lindeskog, G. 1938: *Die Jesusfrage im neuzeitlichen Judentum. Ein Beitrag zur Leben-Jesu-For-schung* (AMNSU 8), Uppsala: Lundequistska Bokhandeln 1938 [Reprinted with a "Nach-wort", Darmstadt: Wissenschaftliche Buchgesellschaft 1973].

— 1986: *Das jüdisch-christliche Problem. Randglossen zu einer Forschungsepoche* (Historia Reli-gionum 9), Uppsala: Almqvist & Wiksell International 1986.

Linton, O. 1964: *Pauli mindre brev* (Tolkning av Nya Testamentet 9), Stockholm: Diakonistyrelsens Bokförlag 1964.

Lüdemann, G. 1994: *Die Auferstehung Jesu. Historie, Erfahrung, Theologie*, Göttingen: Vanden-hoeck & Ruprecht 1994.

von Martitz, W. 1972: "υἱός", "υἱοθεσία", in: *TDNT* 8, Grand Rapids, MI: Eerdmans 1972, 334-40.

Marxsen, W. 1968: *Die Auferstehung Jesu von Nazareth*, Gütersloh: Gerd Mohn 1968.

McCullough, J. C. 1979/80: "The Old Testament Quotations in Hebrews", in: *NTS* 26 (1979/80) 363-79.

Meier, J. P. 1991: *A Marginal Jew: Rethinking the Historical Jesus*, Vol. 1, New York: Doubleday 1991.

Morland, K. A. 1991: *The Galatian choice. Galatians 1:6-12 and 3:8-14 in the Light of Jewish Curse-texts and Antique Rhetoric*, Diss. Trondheim 1991.

Nygren, A. 1942: "Corpus Christi", in: G. Aulén (ed.), *En bok om kyrkan*, Stockholm: Diakonisty-relsens Bokförlag 1942, 13-25.

Pannenberg, W. 1967: "Die historische Problematik der Auferweckung Jesu", in: B. Klappert (ed.), *Diskussion um Kreuz und Auferstehung*, Wuppertal: Aussaat Verlag 1967, 233-49.

Pesch, R. 1973, "Zur Entstehung des Glaubens an die Auferstehung Jesu", in: *ThQ* 153 (1973) 201-228, 270-283.

Riesenfeld, H. 1957: *The Gospel Tradition and its Beginnings. A Study in the Limits of 'Formge-schichte'*, London: A. R. Mowbray & Co. Ltd. 1957.

— 1970: *The Gospel Tradition. Essays by Harald Riesenfeld*, Philadelphia: PA: Fortress Press 1970.

Robinson, J. M. 1959: *A New Quest of the Historical Jesus*, London: SCM Press 1959 [2nd revised and enlarged German edition: *Kerygma und historischer Jesus*, Zürich/Stuttgart: Zwingli Verlag 1967].

Sandmel, S. 1965: *We Jews and Jesus*, Oxford: Oxford University Press 1977.

Schwager, R. 1993: "Die heutige Theologie und das leere Grab Jesu", in: *ZKTh* 115 (1993) 435-50.

Schwartz, D. R. 1993: *Leben durch Jesus versus Leben durch die Thorah* (Franz-Delitzsch-Vorle-sung 1991), Münster: Institutum Judaicum Delitzschianum 1993.

Skarsaune, O. 1986: "Jødisk-kristen dialog på økumenisk område – en orientering", in: T. Kronholm et. al. (eds.), *Judendom och kristendom under de första århundradena*. Nordiskt patris-tikerprojekt 1982-1985, Stavanger–Oslo–Bergen–Tromsø: Universitetsforlaget 1986, 37-51.

Stuhlmacher, P. 1992: *Biblische Theologie des Neuen Testaments*, Göttingen: Vandenhoeck & Rup-recht 1992.

Theißen, G. 1977: *Soziologie der Jesusbewegung*, München: Chr. Kaiser 1977.

— 1987: *The Shadow of the Galilean: The Quest of the Historical Jesus in Narrative Form*, London: SCM Press 1987 [First published as *Der Schatten des Galiläers. Historische Jesusforschung in erzählender Form*, München: Chr. Kaiser 1986].

Weiß, H.-Fr. 1991: *Der Brief an die Hebräer* (KEK 13), Göttingen: Vandenhoeck & Ruprecht 1991.

Wellhausen, J. 1905: *Einleitung in die drei ersten Evangelien*, Berlin: Reimer 1905.

Vermes, G. 1976, *Jesus the Jew. A Historian's Reading of the Gospels*, London: Collins 1976.

Vögtle, A./Pesch, R. 1975: *Wie kam es zum Osterglauben?*, Düsseldorf: Patmos 1975.

# The Hidden Context
## Some Observations to the Concept of the
## New Covenant in the New Testament

Mogens Müller

## 1. "The Unparallelled Discovery"

Like all text interpretation New Testament exegesis is determined by its preconceived understanding. And the tricky thing is that this preconceived understanding
sometimes easily finds its confirmation in the texts. It, so to say, calls forward its
own reflected image and establishes connections on the strength of its own way of
presenting problems. The texts live their only life through their readers, and the
reader cannot therefore be eliminated so as to let the text speak for itself alone. It
has to borrow mouth and voice to be able to articulate itself. But it is an unending
enterprise to adjust the preconceived understanding from the text.

The New Testament texts are in constant danger of being interpreted isolated,
that is, without attention being given to the forces which created them or to their determinative context. All too easily this leads to a more or less conscious identification with the revelation which they testify to. Principally, then, exegesis considers
the New Testament and the traditions leading up to it as if it all began with a book.

In this context my famous compatriot, the clergyman, theologian and hymn writer Nikolaj Frederik Severin Grundtvig (1783-1872), in 1825 made a "discovery",
which has not always been given the attention it deserves in New Testament exegesis. This is all the more remarkable because, once made, it conveys a truism. The
"discovery" was first expressed in a highly polemical pamphlet, *The Church's Retort (Kirkens Gienmæle)*, directed at the young, albeit influential professor of theology, H. N. Clausen (1793-1877) on the occasion of his magisterial treatise *The
Church Constitution, Teaching and Rituals of Catholicism and Protestantism (Om
Katholicismens og Protestantismens Kirkeforfatning, Lære og Ritus)* from the same
year.[1] Here professor Clausen maintained that, in contradistinction to the historical

---

[1] See Pontoppidan Thyssen 1983, 40ff. Cf. Jørgensen 1993, 46-66.

and hierarchical institution of Catholicism, Protestantism rested directly on Scripture where, according to the unprejudiced research, it might discover Jesus' spirit and teaching. Against this insistence on what he defined as "exegetical papacy" Grundtvig maintained his "unparalleled discovery", as he himself named it. Briefly told, this meant that the Church was there from the beginning with its creed and sacraments, and that the New Testament did not come into being until later.

Grundtvig was fully aware that this meant a corrective to the way the Reformers viewed Christianity. An important passage in The Church's Retort runs:[2]

> We are forced to admit that the Reformers were mistaken with regard to the original shape of the Christian Church. Thereby they, more or less notoriously, laid the foundation of the new *exegetical papacy* under the rule of which the entire Christian congregation now sighs, and against which all Christian book-learned must unite themselves so as to destroy it. For it has now gone so far that the youngest professor of our university, as *summus Theologus*, wants to be the exegetical pope of the congregation, commanding that the historical Christian Church be demolished and a new one built on nothing but theological trash: that is, mutually conflicting exegetical note-books. In this self-effacing fantasy the Christian congregation has to confess that it *believes in the same thing, though what this is it knows not*. But when we, in honour of the truth, have admitted our mistake, which was most excusable when we exited from the darkness of papacy, the spiritual Egypt, then we may, by the light of history which is held in contempt by the children of darkness, distinguish *Martin Luther* from those who did not want to be united with him; and we may declare that to him and to those who followed him truthfully, this mistake was basically insignificant and to be compared to a formality. Thus, when our congregation founded itself on the gospel history and on the creed which the apostles themselves, as members of the congregation, confess to in their writings, then it must undeniably have relied upon the apostolic creed and interpreted the word of Scripture according to it; the failure was alone that the *authenticity* of the New Testament does not prove itself, but can only be proved by the evident testimony of the Church which for the same reason is the only true defensible foundation.

As it appears, Grundtvig is anxious to evade the equation, so often prevalent in Protestantism, of the living word of God with the dead letters of the book that carries the title of the New Testament. For Grundtvig the real New Testament was not a book, but the covenant of baptism.

---

[2] Grundtvig 1825, 340f. The full text of this pamphlet has never been translated into English, and the translation here is my own.

## 2. The Congregation as the Omnipresent Context

From Grundtvig's so-called "view of the Church" (den kirkelige Anskuelse) we may learn that the Church came before Scripture (= the New Testament). In other words, the New Testament writings are composed in a Church which already had a history. The constituent elements of the life of this Church therefore form the context in which these writings are to be understood. The way to a full acknowledgment of this has been long and arduous. The first major obstacle was the 'Life-of-Jesus'-theology which consciously tried to eliminate everything that might be classified as "congregational theology." Only with William Wrede's *The Messianic Secret in the Gospels* (1901) did it become obvious that to such a degree were the sources, i.e. the gospels, stamped by "congregational theology" that the 'Life-of-Jesus'-theology was made hopeless. As it was later stressed by dialectical theology it was impossible, historico-critically, to verify the foundation of faith.[3]

The form-critical work with the New Testament accentuated the influence of "congregational theology." Following the words of Martin Dibelius: "In the beginning was the preaching," the point of departure for the gospel transmission can be seen in the use of the Jesus-tradition in preaching and instruction. The fact, however, that this anonymous process of tradition has an independent profile in the gospels, was emphasized by the redaction criticism, which—rooted in the tendency-criticism of the Tübingen-school as it was—became dominant from about the middle of the fifties.

Among other things this meant that the New Testament authors were increasingly understood as theologians, i.e. people who at a certain time and in a certain context formulated a theology or formed the tradition according to their own theological opinion. In other words: The fact that we must always take our point of departure in the texts does not mean that these actually represent the point of departure. On the contrary, they are testimonies of different stages of a history which reaches at least decades behind their genesis.

This means that New Testament exegesis cannot be content with confining itself to what the texts handed down to us actually say. It must also be attentive to all that is presupposed because of the church context in which they have been created. Grundtvig's "unparalleled discovery" should be applied to the effect that the fully established church or concrete congregation, which the different writings were directed at, becomes visible.

---

[3] This was seen clearly already by Grundtvig. See for instance Grundtvig 1825/1941, 329ff. Cf. to this also Müller 1976, esp., 281ff. In this article I have given an account of the "solutions" of both Grundtvig and Søren Kierkegaard to Lessing's problem, how faith can build on accidental historical events.

It is of course impossible in this matter to avoid circular conclusions altogether. Also in respect of the ecclesiastical presuppositions, on which the New Testament author write, is it necessary to exercise caution when it comes to explicating what is implied by the texts. *Vestigia terrent* if one looks at the number of more or less breakneck attempts in the history of research to reconstruct the "religionsgeschicht-liche" and/or polemical context for individual New Testament writings. Examples of this are the alleged gnostic horizon of the Gospel of John or Paul's encounter with opponents whom he did not understand.

Maybe the most striking example of how the silence of the texts has been misin-terpreted as either ignorance or disinterestedness by its author, is Rudolf Bult-mann's handling of the question of Paul's relation to "the historical Jesus" and the Jesus-tradition. It was of course significant that Bultmann was deeply rooted in a dialectical theology, in which, theologically, historical matters were only allowed significance as a "thatness" ("das Dass") whereas the question "how" ("das Was") in this context was thought to be irrelevant—if not theologically illegitimate. Maybe we have here the very reason for Bultmann's artificial understanding of 2 Cor 5:16, leading him to attach the prepositional group κατὰ σάρκα to Χριστόν rather than to the verb ἐγνώκαμεν.[4]

The interpretation of the texts will be distorted or worse if the interpreter is una-ble to see what is presupposed as a matter of course by those who heard or read them. One such obvious presupposition is knowledge of the Bible, which was of course at that time the Jewish Bible. Generally speaking, the attitude in this case was without any reservation, which set the first Christians the hermeneutical task of reading the Holy Writ in an *interpretatio Christiana*. This means that the Christian congregations have been familiar with the Old Testament, first and foremost in the shape of the Septuagint, and it was certainly not perceived as expressing another "religion" than the Christian.

Another presupposition, and, indeed, the most central one, has been the Christian baptism and the concepts connected with it. We hear remarkably little about bap-tism in the New Testament writings. But this is only remarkable so long as we ex-pect these writings to be expositions of the entire preaching and teaching of Christianity, directed at outsiders. But all New Testament writings address them-selves to Christian congregations (or, in one single case, to one Christian) with a more or less prolonged Christian experience behind them, i.e. people who have heard the preaching and taken part in the teaching, and who are all baptized. This is simply the hidden context of everything written.

This was among the first things (ἐν πρώτοις) Paul transmitted to the Corinthians

---

[4] Bultmann 1976, 155.

(1 Cor 15:3). Thereafter he only needed to refer to it by catchword summaries. It was also this elaboration of the teaching (τύπος διδαχῆς) which the apostle presupposed in Romans 6:17, in connection with his elucidation of the meaning of baptism, and which he transmitted to the Roman Christians whose congregation he had not himself founded.

## 3. The Impact of the New Covenant

If we now ask for the concepts connected with Christian baptism[5], we have good reason to involve the Old Testament preaching of a new covenant which God will make with his people in the last days[6]. The main passage is, of course, Jer 31:31-34, where we find the expression "new covenant", but a long list of passages belong to this connection (see esp. Jer 32:38-40; Ezek 11:19-20; 36:26-27; furthermore Isa 42:6-7; 49:8; 54:10.13; 55:3; 59:20-21; 61:8; Ezek 16:59-63; 34:25; 37:24-28; Joel 3:1-2 and Mal 3:1).[7] According to this covenant God will not only write his law in the hearts of men, but he will also give them a new spirit within them. So, in reality, it is like a new creation.

Inquiring into some of the classic expositions of New Testament theology, the covenant idea cannot be said to prevail. Normally it only turns up in connection with the treatment of the words of institution of the Eucharist. This is no longer the case, as evident from two recent expositions of the biblical theology of the New Testament by Hans Hübner[8] and Peter Stuhlmacher[9]. Although equipped with the same title, these works are otherwise quite unlike each other. However, already a couple of years ago, in 1978, Lars Hartman, in a lecture entitled *Bundesideologie in und hinter einigen paulinischen Texten*[10], proved that the use of the concepts connected with a new covenant in the Old Testament was fruitful as a key to understand Paul.[11]

There is adequate reason for proceeding in this direction. For, in my opinion, probably no other Old Testament conception has had such a conclusive impact on New Testament theology as this preaching of God concluding a new covenant with his people in the last days. If one accepts the thought that the historical Jesus under-

---

[5] It is but natural here to refer to Hartman 1993.

[6] This only happens sporadically in Hartman 1993, see 34 and 71 (under the heading of "Urmotiven" (= primordial-motifs).

[7] In non-canonical literature one may refer to *Jub.* 1:21-25 and to the reference to a new covenant in the Damascus Rule VI,19; VIII,21; XIX,33-34; XX,12 and in 1QHab II,3.

[8] See Hübner 1990, esp. 90ff.

[9] See Stuhlmacher 1991, s.v. Bund.

[10] See Hartman 1980.

[11] An attempt at this, especially concerning the epistle to the Romans, is found in Müller 1989.

stood his relation to John the Baptist within the frames of the old Jewish conception of both a priestly and a kingly Messiah,[12] one may wonder whether the bond between them was the very assurance that now it was time for the conclusion of a new covenant. From the scanty information transmitted about the content of the baptism of John the Baptist (including the description in Josephus, *Antiquitates Judaicae* XVIII, 109-126) it may be concluded, that "it was a once-and-for-all baptism and as such denoted an initiation into a 'new' society, substantially different from the usual Jewish ... When Jews in particular were invited to submit to his baptism, this indicated that in a certain sense Judaism was not in itself 'sufficient'."[13]

In other words: through his baptism, John the Baptist founded a congregation that was constituted by another righteousness than that obtained through the ceremonial law, including the cult. As expressed in Josephus (*Ant.* XVIII, 117), John[14]

> had exhorted the Jews to lead righteous lives, to practise justice towards their fellows and piety towards God, and so doing to join in baptism. In his view it was a necessary preliminary if baptism was to be acceptable to God. They must not employ it to gain pardon for whatever sin they committed, but as a consecration of the body implying that the soul was already thoroughly cleansed by right behaviour.

This is to be compared with the picture of John the Baptist in the synoptic gospels proclaiming that the decisive difference between him and Jesus was that John baptised with water where Jesus would baptise with the Holy Spirit (Mark 1:8; Matt 3:11; Luke 3:16). So it is only with respect to means that the two differ from each other. According to the synoptic tradition Jesus brought the Spirit which was not yet present in the deeds of John and thus he fulfilled the mission which both of them were devoted to. This is finally connected with the motif of the preparing of the way (Isa 40:3), the reference to John as the rejected Elijah (Mark 9:11-13; Matt 17:10-13), the proclamation of John as more than a prophet and the greatest among the sons of women (Matt 11:9,11; Luke 7:26,28), as the one whose baptism came from heaven (Mark 11:30; Matt 21:25; Luke 20:4) and who also taught the way leading to righteousness (Matt 21:32). The picture is especially elucidated in Matt 26:28, where the forgiveness of sins—in contrast to Mark and Luke—is reserved for the deeds of Jesus which were completed with his death (compare Matt 3:2 with Mark 1:4 and Luke 3:3).

Thus I dare to put forward the hypothesis that the baptism of John the Baptist was undertaken with respect to the conclusion of the new covenant which in parts of the Old Testament prophetical literature is the eschatological event that makes the new

---

[12] Cf. Hyldahl 1993, 103ff.

[13] Hyldahl 1993, 101. My translation.

[14] The translation according to Louis H. Feldman in *LCL*.

righteousness accessible. But according to the faith and preaching of the first congregation, this decisive event of salvation was only achieved by Jesus. However, tradition maintained that both figures belonged to the Messianic era, the result being that the priestly Messianic achievement by John the Baptist was subordinated to Jesus' kingly Messianic achievement (in contrast to the old Jewish concept according to which the priestly Messiah was superior to the kingly Messiah).

This understanding being correct, it throws light on how Jesus perceived himself as the Messiah. Here it is not enough merely to lift the taboo which a leading trend in New Testament scholarship has laid on every attempt to answer the question how Jesus understood himself as Messiah. A minimal solution was offered by Nils Alstrup Dahl in his influential article *The Crucified Messiah* (originally 1960). Mainly on the basis of the inscription on the cross, Dahl concluded that Jesus was executed as Messiah. However, he did not proclaim himself as the Messiah during his public preaching and teaching, but, "before the accusation made in the face of impending death, he did not deny he was the Messiah."[15] Ragnar Leivestad, in his *Jesus in His Own Perspective* (originally 1982), went a step further and asserted that very likely Jesus, believing that he belonged to the house of David, was convinced that he was the Messiah; Isaiah 53 made it possible for him to connect this conviction with the way of suffering. Thus Jesus was a *messias designatus*. "This did not involve the necessity to proclaim himself as the Messiah. A true Messiah does not proclaim himself. He could only try to realize his secret destiny, live up to his call, do what God ordered him to do, speak with the insight bestowed on him by the Spirit, carry out those tasks which he had the power and right to perform. In this way his deeds would testify on his behalf."[16]

Only prejudices regarding the content of the Messianic belief and confession of it by the earliest congregation prevent us from accepting that there was a fundamental agreement between this and Jesus' understanding of the significance of his achievement. According to the descriptions of the synoptic gospels this achievement did in fact culminate in the institution of the new covenant in which Jesus anticipated and interpreted his death. In other words, Jesus understood his Messianic achievement as the completion of the institution of this covenant.[17] And the earliest congregation understood this and preached it, thus applying the concepts connected with this event in the Old Testament: The Coming of the Spirit as the condition of the possibility of a new life in obedience to the commandments of God.

Therefore, it is of no use to try to understand the Messiahship of Jesus from his various christological titles. In this connection it is significant that the "title" which

---

[15] Dahl 1991, 42.

[16] Leivestad 1987, 176f.

[17] Cf. also the discussion in Allison 1987, 65ff.

has without comparison played the greatest role, i.e. the expression "Son of man", has been substantiated not just as a title but as a circumlocution for the person speaking in certain delicate statements; in the gospels it occurs in sayings concerning Jesus' role as the Messiah.[18] The earliest congregation confessed to Jesus as the Messiah because of his introducing the Messianic era which, in accordance with Jewish apocalypticism, was imagined as a temporary period to be succeeded by the kingdom of the Father (see 1 Cor 15:23-28; Mark 12:35-37 par; Matt 13:37-43; Rev 20-21).

In this intervening time, the kingdom of the Son, the congregation of the new covenant exists. And the entrance into it is mediated through the baptism in which the baptized becomes liberated from the dominion of sin and death, receives the Spirit and is enabled to live his new life in true obedience to the commandments of God. The new covenant is a covenant of a clear conscience before God (cf. 1 Pet 3:21)[19] because the fulfilment of the law is not a condition for obtaining salvation but its consequence. This covenant is concluded in the heart as the seat of man's relation to God.

In 2 Cor 3:6 Paul expressly declares that God has made him a διάκονος τῆς καινῆς διαθήκης—1 Cor 11:25 is the only other passage in Corpus Paulinum containing the expression ἡ καινὴ διαθήκη. In this chapter the relationship between the old and the new covenant is described by means of nine "antitheses":

μέλαν — πνεῦμα θεοῦ ζῶντος (v. 3)
πλάκες λιθίναι — πλάκες καρδίαι σαρκίναι (v. 3)
ἀφ' ἑαυτῶν ἱκανοί — ἱκανότης ἐκ τοῦ θεοῦ (v. 5)
γράμμα ἀποκτεννοῦσα — πνεῦμα ζωοποιοῦσα (v. 6)
ἐν γράμμασιν ἐντετυπωμένη λίθοις — ἐν δόξῃ (vv. 7-8)
διακονία τοῦ θανάτου — διακονία τοῦ πνεύματος (vv. 7-8)
δόξα καταργουμένη — δόξα περισσεύουσα (vv. 7.9)
διακονία τῆς κατακρίσεως — διακονία τῆς δικαιοσύνης (v. 9)
τὸ καταργούμενον διὰ δόξης — τὸ μένον ἐν δόξῃ (v. 11)

---

[18] Considering the growing *consensus* concerning this understanding, at least as regards the meaning of the expression in the mouth of Jesus, it is pathetic that Stuhlmacher consequently omits any reference to it. Instead he carries on with the old idea of balancing the Messiah title by the Son of man expectation. See for instance Stuhlmacher 1991, 114 and 117.

[19] The rendering of ἐπερώτημα by "covenant" is peculiar to the Danish Bible translation tradition. It is also maintained in the 1992-translation, although, as before, provided with a footnote saying that the translation "prayer" is also possible. It developed into a particular Grundtvigian concern. The persistent defence for the rendering "covenant", found in a pamphlet by N. Clausen-Bagge 1942, is, curiously enough, still included in the bibliography in Bauer-Aland 1988, col. 578. Hartman 1993, 98 and 101 comes close to this understanding when he renders ἐπερώτημα by "förpliktelse" (= obligation).

When gospel tradition (pace John 3:22; cf. 4:1f.) omits to mention that it was Jesus who instituted baptism, this may be for purely historical reasons, but it may also be that the new covenant, according to the gospels, was not concluded until the death of Jesus. On the other hand, it seems obvious that the description of the baptism of Jesus anticipates the Christian baptism, including both the Father, the Son and the Spirit (cf. also Matt 28:19, where baptism is combined with the new life in accordance with all that Jesus had commanded).

Theology of baptism is accordingly theology of covenant. The infrequent allusions to the new covenant in the New Testament writings are not due to this concept lacking in importance. By contrast, it is the presupposition for most of what is said. And it can also be rendered probable that it had its origin in Jesus' own understanding of his achievement. However, it is only seen properly as the decisive substructure when the texts are considered in connection with the congregation in which they originated, i.e. the hidden albeit omnipresent context. It was no idle label when the addition which the Church later-on added to its Bible was named τὰ τῆς καινῆς διαθήκης βιβλία.

## Bibliography

Allison, D. C. 1987: "Jesus and the Covenant: A Response to E.P. Sanders", in: *JSNT* 29 (1987) 57-78.

Bauer, W. 1988: *Wörterbuch zum Neuen Testament*. 6., völlig neu bearbeitete Auflage von Kurt und Barbara Aland, Berlin/New York: de Gruyter 1988.

Bultmann, R.1976: *Der zweite Brief an die Korinther* (Hgg. von Erich Dinkler. KEK Sonderband), Göttingen: Vandenhoeck & Ruprecht 1976.

Clausen-Bagge, N. 1942: *"Eperotæma" (1. Pet. 3,21)*, Odense: Andelsbogtrykkeriet 1942.

Dahl, N. A.1991: "The Crucified Messiah", in: idem, *Jesus the Christ. The Historical Origins of Christological Doctrine*. Ed. by Donald H. Juel, Minneapolis, MN: Fortress Press 1991, 27-47 (German original: "Der gekreuzigte Messias", in: H. Ristow/K. Matthiae (eds.), *Der historische Jesus und der kerygmatische Christus. Beiträge zum Christusverständnis in Forschung und Verkündigung*, Berlin: Evangelische Verlagsanstalt 1960, 146-69).

Grundtvig, N. F. S. 1825/1941: *Kirkens Gienmæle* (1825). Here according to the edition in N. F. S. Grundtvig: *Værker i Udvalg* udgivet ved Georg Christensen og Hal Koch, Vol. 2, Copenhagen: Gyldendal. Nordisk Forlag 1941, 317-49.

Hartman, L. 1980: "Bundesideologie in und hinter einigen paulinischen Texten", in: S. Pedersen (ed.), *Die Paulinische Literatur und Theologie*. Anläßlich der 50. jährigen Gründungs-Feier der Universität von Aarhus (Teologiske Studier 7), Århus: Aros and Göttingen: Vandenhoeck & Ruprecht 1980, 103-18.

— 1993: *Till Herrens Jesu namn* (Tro & Tanke 1993:4), Uppsala: Svenska Kyrkans Forskningsråd 1993.

Hübner, H. 1990: *Biblische Theologie des Neuen Testaments*, Band 1: *Prolegomena*, Göttingen: Vandenhoeck & Ruprecht 1990.

Hyldahl, N. 1993: *Den ældste kristendoms historie*, København: Museum Tusculanums Forlag 1993.

Jørgensen, Th.1993: "Grundtvig's *The Church's Retort*—in a Modern Perspective", in: A. M. Allchin, D. Jasper, J. H. Schjørring, and K. Stevenson (eds.), *Heritage and Prophecy. Grundtvig and the English-Speaking World*, Århus: Aarhus University Press 1993, 171-90.

Leivestad, R. 1987: *Jesus in His Own Perspective*, Minneapolis, MN: Augsburg Publishing House 1987; (Norwegian original: *Hvem ville Jesus være?*, Oslo: Land og Kirke. Gyldendal Norsk Forlag 1982).

Müller, M. 1976: "Der Jesus der Historiker, der historische Jesus und die Christusverkündigung der Kirche", in: *KuD* 22 (1976) 277-98.

— 1989: "Ånden og Loven. Pagtsteologi i Romerbrevet", in: *DTT* 52 (1989) 251-67.

Pontoppidan Thyssen, A. 1983: "Grundtvig's Ideas on the Church and the People 1825-47", in: Ch. Thodberg and A. Pontoppidan Thyssen (eds.), *N. F. S. Grundtvig. Tradition and Renewal*, Copenhagen: The Danish Institute 1983, 226-92.

Stuhlmacher, P. 1991: *Biblische Theologie des Neuen Testaments*, Band 1: *Von Jesus zu Paulus*, Göttingen: Vandenhoeck & Ruprecht 1991.

# Liturgy and Literature:
## The Liturgical Factor in Matthew's Literary and Communicative Art

### Arland J. Hultgren

## 1. Introductory Remarks

In one of his writings Lars Hartman has suggested that the gospel tradition may well have been recited in a liturgical context in the early church, and that it would have been in such a context that at least some of the gospel traditions received their form and special features prior to being written down by the evangelists.[1] Such a perspective may apply above all to the traditions that have been formed and given their special features prior to and during the composition of the Gospel of Matthew. It is that gospel that has been recognized as having a "liturgical background" and "liturgical character" in the work of G. D. Kilpatrick.[2] Similarly, Michael D. Goulder has maintained "that the Gospel [of Matthew] was developed liturgically, and was intended to be used liturgically."[3]

The purpose of this essay is to explore Matthew's use of gospel traditions that have obviously been given a liturgical character, and were taken over into the gospel in that form, and then to ask what this usage does to the impact of the Gospel of Matthew as a whole, both as literature and as communication. We shall begin with a cursory review of those traditions that have a rather obvious liturgical character. Then we shall go on to ask how the use of such materials functions as a medium between the author and his readers.[4]

---

[1] Hartman 1963, 56.

[2] The terms in quotation marks are found in the titles of two chapters in the study of Kilpatrick 1946, 59 and 72, respectively.

[3] Goulder 1974, 172.

[4] Such is the question posed concerning Matthew's use of formula quotations in his gospel by Hartman 1970, 33; idem 1972, 133.

## 2. Liturgically Formed Materials

In his own day Kilpatrick argued what is taken for granted today, viz., that source theories do not account for all that is distinctive to the Gospel of Matthew. He maintained that there are three elements that have gone into its composition. These are written sources (and here he included not only Mark and Q but M as well), the editorial work of the evangelist, and "liturgical practices," the context in which the gospel came into being.[5] That context gave shape to a number of features which Kilpatrick surveys. Among the features that he claims to have been created for liturgical use are (1) a tendency to abbreviate narratives taken from the Gospel of Mark (for the sake of lucidity in oral public reading); (2) the addition of materials to make certain narratives easier to follow; (3) the alteration of materials (e.g., by use of direct discourse, antithesis, parallelism, repetition, and the improvement of style over that found in sources) to make them easier to follow or recall; and (4) the presence of characteristics that point to an anticipated homiletical use of the gospel (e.g., the use of the formula quotations, which can be paired with Old Testament readings, and the addition of hortatory endings to parables).[6] These features, says Kilpatrick, suggest that the Gospel of Matthew "was compiled out of materials which had already been read and expounded in services of the church and that the evangelist composed [the Gospel of Matthew] to serve this purpose more fully in the future."[7]

The features which Kilpatrick has underscored do not speak unequivocally in favor of his thesis. For example, the alteration of indirect discourse in a source to direct discourse in the Gospel of Matthew may be for a literary, rather than a liturgical, purpose. Nevertheless, this and the other features that Kilpatrick reviews are certainly compatible with a liturgical purpose. A liturgical purpose, such as the oral reading of gospel traditions in a gathered congregation, requires literary considerations suitable for such a setting.

What is even more promising than the approach taken by Kilpatrick is a review of materials in the Gospel of Matthew that are unmistakably liturgical. These are well known, and they include the following materials.

2.1. The Matthean Baptismal Formula. Baptismal allusions, metaphors, and formulas abound in the New Testament.[8] Within the Gospel of Matthew there is, besides the account of John's ministry of baptism (3:1-17) and Jesus' saying concerning it later (21:25), the explicit formula of 28:19, in which Christians are to

---

[5] Kilpatrick 1946, 69-70.

[6] Ibid., 72-100.

[7] Ibid., 100.

[8] A survey of these can be found in Moule 1961, 47.

be baptized "into the name of the Father, and of the Son, and of the Holy Spirit." This is the only instance in the gospel traditions of the first century where baptism is commanded by Christ,[9] and it is the only instance in the entire New Testament where a fully developed trinitarian formula is used in connection with baptism.[10] Undoubtedly the verse reflects the formula used in connection with baptisms in the Matthean community.

2.2. The Matthean Lord's Prayer. Two versions of the Lord's Prayer appear in the gospels. These are at Matthew 6:9-13 and Luke 11:2-4. Critical judgment on the sources or traditions from which the two evangelists derived their respective versions of the Lord's Prayer are notoriously diverse. Some have concluded that Matthew and Luke derived their respective versions from Q, and that the differences between them are due to the redactional work of one or both of the evangelists (at least Matthew).[11] Others have decided that each evangelist derived his version from his own special traditions, behind which there may or may not have been a more primitive form.[12] The matter need not be decided here. Generally, however, it is held that Matthew's version appears to have been developed for liturgical use either in the Matthean community or in an even earlier one.[13] In any case, it can be said with a high degree of probability that when the first evangelist wrote his gospel, he recorded that version of the Lord's Prayer that he knew—the version which he and his contemporaries actually prayed in the Matthean community.[14]

2.3. Eucharistic Texts. The Gospel of Matthew contains an account of the Lord's Supper (26:26-29), which the evangelist has taken over in the main from the Gospel of Mark (14:22-25). Matthew makes three important alterations, however. First, while Mark simply narrates that the disciples drank from the cup (14:23), Matthew substitutes a command: "Drink from it, all of you" (26:27). This brings the cup saying into parallel with the bread saying of 26:26 (also a command: "Take, eat; this is my body"), but it also lends itself more readily for eucharistic practice. Those assembled for the eucharist are thereby directed to partake of the cup, rather than simply hear that the disciples drank of it at the Last Supper. Here the transition from

---

[9] We set aside here, on the basis of textual criticism, the baptismal command in the "long ending" of the Gospel of Mark at 16:16.

[10] This remains true even in light of the claim that in Eph 4:4 there is evidence of the development of a "tripartite" formula, as maintained by Cullmann 1949, 43.

[11] Creed 1930, 155; Kilpatrick 1946, 20-21; Polag 1979, 24 and 48 (with reconstruction of the Q text); Fitzmyer 1981-85, 1.78 and 2.897; Kloppenborg 1987, 203-206; Taussig 1988, 25-26; and Stanton 1992, 334.

[12] Streeter 1930, 277-78; Manson 1955/56, 104; Lohmeyer 1965, 291-96; and Jeremias 1978, 87-89.

[13] Cf. Beare 1981, 171; Luz 1989, 369-72; and Fornberg 1989, 107.

[14] Cf. Koester 1990, 142.

Last Supper to Lord's Supper is marked in the gospel tradition itself, and the wording no doubt reflects the actual liturgical formula in use in Matthew's community. Second, while Mark's bread saying has simply "Take" (14:22), Matthew's has "Take, eat" (26:26); the insertion of the command to eat allows for a more precise liturgical parallel to the command to drink (26:27). Third, Matthew has added to the cup saying that the blood poured out for many is "for the forgiveness of sins" (26:28). By adding this phrase Matthew has secured for the account, more clearly than the other evangelists, its reading in a liturgical, sacramental setting. Again, the marks of transition from Last Supper to Lord's Supper, in which the participants receive forgiveness of sins through sacramental practice, is marked in the text. Although the account has been drawn from the Gospel of Mark, the Matthean version thrice altered has been made to mirror what was actually spoken in the eucharistic gatherings of the Matthean community.

Besides this specific text, there are indications in at least two others that Matthew has revised material derived from his source in such a way that liturgical features are evident. These are the Feeding of the Five Thousand and the Feeding of the Four Thousand (14:13-21; 15:32-39), which Matthew took and adapted from the Gospel of Mark (6:35-44; 8:1-10). In the first of these, although Matthew has mentioned the two fish (14:17, 19), he eliminates the narration of the distribution of the fish in 14:19 and the picking up of left-over fish in 14:20, even though both of these acts are narrated in his source (Mark 6:41, 43). His interest is focused on the bread—the blessing of God for it, the breaking of the loaves, and Jesus' giving them to the disciples, who assist him in the distribution. Matthew eliminates other items narrated in Mark's account as well, such as the disciples' reluctance to go out and buy bread (6:37) and the details about seating the crowd in groups (6:39-40). All these elements are trimmed away to highlight more clearly the eucharistic symbolism of the passage, adjusting it for reading during eucharistic gatherings.

The story of the Feeding of the Four Thousand also undergoes transformation at the hand of Matthew. Drawing from his source (Mark 8:5), Matthew writes that the disciples had seven loaves in their possession (15:34), but he adds "and a few small fish." The latter comes from the more elaborate Marcan text in which, after the blessing, breaking, and distribution of the bread (8:6), Mark has an entirely separate narrated action: "They had also a few small fish; and after blessing them, [Jesus] ordered that these too should be distributed" (8:7). For Matthew, however, there is only one action, in which Jesus takes up the seven loaves and the fish, gives thanks, breaks the loaves, and gives them to the disciples, and the disciples give to the crowds.

It goes without saying that ancient eucharistic symbolism sometimes contains fish as well as loaves of bread.[15] That may be reflected already in the New Testament at John 21:9-13[16] and perhaps in the accounts of Jesus' feeding the multitudes as well.[17] Yet the parallelism of language between the two feeding stories in the Gospel of Matthew and the eucharistic text of 26:26 has shifted the focus to the bread alone in the narration of the story. Interest in the fish is significantly diminished.

2.4. Worship of Jesus. Several times over in the Gospel of Matthew there are narrative indicators that those around Jesus actually worship him. In these instances the liturgical estimate of Jesus within the post-resurrection Matthean church is retrojected into the story of Jesus. The term προσκυνέω (to worship/do obeisance to) is used ten times in Matthew in reference to Jesus.[18] Twice the term appears in the post-resurrection narrative (28:9, 17); and three times it appears in the infancy narrative (2:2, 8, 11). But the remaining five uses of the term are set within encounters between Jesus and others during his earthly ministry. In each case Matthew has taken material from the Gospel of Mark which may or may not contain an indication of reverence when the other party approaches Jesus. But Matthew either adds a form of the verb προσκυνέω or transforms a phrase from Mark to imply it. Those who worship/do obeisance to Jesus include a leper who petitions Jesus for healing (8:2, προσκύνει αὐτῷ, replacing the textually uncertain γονυπετῶν of Mark 1:40), a leader of a synagogue who makes intercession to Jesus for his daughter (9:18, προσκύνει αὐτῷ, replacing πίπτει πρὸς τοὺς πόδας αὐτοῦ in Mark 5:22), Jesus' disciples after his walking on the sea (14:33, προσεκύνησαν αὐτῷ, replacing ἐξίσταντο of Mark 6:51), a Canaanite woman who asks Jesus to drive a demon out of her daughter (15:25, προσκύνει αὐτῷ, replacing προσέπεσεν πρὸς τοὺς πόδας αὐτοῦ in Mark 7:25), and the mother of the sons of Zebedee as she asks a favor of Jesus for her sons (20:20, προσκυνοῦσα, having no parallel at Mark 10:35).

To be sure, the Gospel of Mark contains language which speaks of the prostration of supplicants who fall down at Jesus' feet (5:22; 7:25), indicating devotion to him. But while falling at the feet of someone can be an appropriate gesture in the presence of high ranking persons or divine beings,[19] it is less fitting in connection with the worship of Israel's God (who has no feet!) either in the cultus of Israel or in early

---

[15] Cf. Gray 1921/22, 690-700.

[16] Cf. Brown 1966-70, 2.1098-1100.

[17] Besides the texts cited in regard to Matthew and Mark, the Feeding of the Five Thousand appears also in Luke 9:10-17 and John 6:30-44. The Feeding of the Four Thousand is only in the Gospels of Matthew and Mark.

[18] The term is also used at 4:9 regarding worship of the devil; at 4:10 in a quotation from Deut 6:13, regarding the worship of God; and at 18:26 in a parable.

[19] Cf. Bauer 1979, 659 (πίπτω, 1,b).

Christian worship. In these contexts the appropriate term is προσκυνέω,[20] which appears frequently in the Septuagint and other Hellenistic Jewish sources for the worship of God.[21] Matthew has employed this familiar word to speak of persons who encounter Jesus: the magi worship the infant Jesus (2:11; cf. 2:2); the disciples worship him in their post-resurrection encounter with him (28:9, 17); and various persons who come to him for aid, either for themselves or for others, worship him in his earthly ministry, as shown above. The attitude and gestures for the worship of God are, to Matthew, already present in the story of persons around the earthly Jesus, beginning with his birth and unfolding in his ministry, and then around the risen Lord.

2.5. Liturgical Phrases. In addition to the liturgical phrases found within the larger units, such as in the Lord's Prayer, there are additional expressions which most certainly reflect liturgical usages. In his celebrated essay on the Stilling of the Storm, Günther Bornkamm has shown how Matthew has transformed the story in such a way that the cry of the disciples for help in Mark's account (4:38, "Teacher, do you not care that we perish?") takes on the language of prayer in Matthew's story: κύριε, σῶσον, ἀπολλύμεθα (8:25, "Lord, save; we are perishing").[22] Heinz J. Held has carried the discussion further, suggesting that Matthew uses the language of prayer in the narration of various miracle stories in order to encourage his own community to have faith in the miracle-working Lord who is present.[23] That may or may not be Matthew's purpose (see below), but clearly Matthew has transformed sayings in the Gospel of Mark into petitions of prayer. Matthew has also included κύριε, σῶσόν με (14:30, "Lord, save me") as a petition of Peter to Jesus as he begins to sink while approaching Jesus on the Sea of Galilee, which has no parallel in the corresponding account within Mark's Gospel (6:45-52).

2.6. Kyrie Eleison. There is at least one instance, and perhaps as many as three, of the use of the liturgical phrase κύριε ἐλέησον ("Lord, have mercy") in the Gospel of Matthew. The use of this phrase by Matthew calls for special treatment. The Gospel of Matthew is the only gospel to contain this phrase. In fact, it is the only book in the New Testament to use it.

At 17:15 a man with an epileptic son cries out to Jesus, κύριε, ἐλέησόν μου τὸν υἱόν ("Lord, have mercy on my son"), whereas in the Gospel of Mark the father merely says, "Teacher, I brought you my son" and complains that Jesus' disciples had not been able to do anything for him (9:17-18).

---

[20] However, Matthew writes that on the Mount of Transfiguration the disciples "fell (ἔπεσεν) upon their faces" (17:6) in response to the voice from heaven.

[21] Gen 22:5; Deut 26:10; 32:43; Pss 5:8; 28:2; Josephus, *Ant.* 6.55; 8.119; 9.267; and 20.164.

[22] Bornkamm 1963, 55.

[23] Held 1963, 265-66.

Within the account of the Healing of Two Blind Men (20:29-34), based on the Blind Bartimaeus story of Mark 10:46-52, there may be one or two additional instances of the phrase κύριε ἐλέησον in 20:30-31. The text-critical problems with these two verses, however, call for caution. Each needs to be treated separately.

The basis for Matthew 20:30 is Mark 10:47 where Bartimaeus calls out, υἱὲ Δαυὶδ Ἰησοῦ, ἐλέησόν με, a reading that is all but absolutely firm. But at Matthew 20:30 there are three possible readings concerning the cry of the two blind men. A possible reading is κύριε, ἐλέησον ἡμᾶς, υἱὸς Δαυίδ, based on Vaticanus (B) and other Alexandrian majuscules (L, eighth century; Z, sixth century), certain Old Latin witnesses, the Vulgate, and Coptic texts. That was the reading adopted by Westcott-Hort (1881) and by Nestle-Aland in their 25th edition (1963). But other readings are possible, as the 26th edition of Nestle-Aland (1979) demonstrates.[24] A decision on the Matthean wording at this point remains inconclusive.

The basis for Matthew 20:31 is Mark 10:48 where Bartimaeus calls out, υἱὲ Δαυὶδ, ἐλέησόν με, a reading that is also firm. At Matthew 20:31 there are three possible readings concerning the cry of the two blind men. This time the reading κύριε, ἐλέησον ἡμᾶς, υἱὸς Δαυίδ is even better attested; it is the wording of both Vaticanus (B) and Sinaiticus (א), other Alexandrian majuscules (L and Z again), certain Old Latin witnesses, the Vulgate, and Coptic texts. Westcott-Hort and the 25th edition of Nestle-Aland adopted that reading. Again there are other possibilities, however, as the 26th edition of Nestle-Aland demonstrates.[25] While one must remain tentative, there is strong evidence here for the reading just given, which includes the phrase κύριε ἐλέησον.

The phrase κύριε ἐλέησον appears then in the Gospel of Matthew at least once for certain (17:15), probably twice (17:15; 20:31), and perhaps three times (17:15; 20:30; 20:31), depending upon text-critical judgments. It is also echoed in the cry of the Canaanite woman, ἐλέησόν με, κύριε (15:22), which has no parallel in Mark 7:25.

The phrase discussed here has a background in the worship life of Israel. It appears explicitly in the form κύριε ἐλέησον four times in the Septuagint (Pss 40:5, 11; 122:3; Isa 33:2) and with slight variations many other times (e.g., ἐλέησόν με, κύριε, Pss 6:3; 9:14; 85:3; cf. still other variations in phraseology at Sir 36:1; Bar

---

[24] The wording adopted in the 26th edition is ἐλέησον ἡμᾶς, [κύριε,] υἱὸς Δαυίδ. An alternative is the omission of κύριε, and that omission is very well attested, but then the wording comes under suspicion of being conformed to its doublet at 9:27.

[25] The reading adopted in the 26th edition is ἐλέησον ἡμᾶς, κύριε, υἱὸς Δαυίδ. The editors agreed that the support for this reading on external grounds is not as great as that for the alternative printed above (=Nestle-Aland 25th ed.), but they selected it anyway, since "it is the non-liturgical order of words"! See Metzger 1971, 54.

3:2). It appears also in the Greek Apocalypse of Ezra (5.6), whose date and provenance remain a puzzle, although it most likely comes from the Christian era.[26] Surprisingly the phrase appears once in the writings of Epictetus.[27] How to account for
the appearance of the phrase in his writings remains a mystery. It is not likely due
to his familiarity with either the Scriptures of Israel or the writings of the New Testament.[28] The fact that the phrase has a liturgical function even in his writings provides further form-critical evidence for its *Sitz im Leben* within liturgical contexts;
i.e., it has been liturgically formed.

What is one to make of the appearance of the phrase in the Gospel of Matthew?
As is well known, various forms of the "Kyrie eleison" came to be used in virtually
all historic liturgies of the Christian church—Greek, Roman, Coptic, Ethiopian, and
Syriac—and remained in Greek, regardless of the primary language of the rite in
which it was used.[29] Evidence for the simple form, "Kyrie eleison," in liturgies goes
back at least to fourth century Syria and Palestine,[30] and it was introduced into the
Roman rite in the fifth century in its three-fold form ("Kyrie eleison, Christe eleison, Kyrie eleison").[31] It can be concluded that κύριε ἐλέησον, originating in the
worship of Israel and used in the liturgies of the East (Syria and Palestine), was a
liturgical phrase indigenous to the world of Matthew and his community, and the
Gospel of Matthew can be taken as evidence for its use among Christians already in
the first century.

## 3. Literary and Communicative Functions

3.0. In light of the foregoing survey, the question remains: What does the inclusion
of liturgical material do for the Gospel of Matthew as literature and as a medium of
communication that would engage its readers? Admittedly that is a very broad ques-

---

[26] A date "sometime between A.D. 150 and 850 is probable," according to Stone 1983-85, 1.563.

[27] Epictetus, *Discourses* 2.7.12.

[28] Cf. Bonhöffer 1911, 39-41; and Sharp 1914, 4.

[29] Jungmann 1951, 333.

[30] According to the *Apostolic Constitutions* 8.6.3-9 (fourth century), the congregation responds
with "Kyrie eleison" to the petitions of the deacon in the Liturgy of the Catechumens; according to
Chrysostom (writing in Antioch, ca. A.D. 370-398), the congregation responds with "Kyrie eleison"
to the petitions for catechumens in the Liturgy of Antioch; and according to Egeria, *Diary of a Pilgrimage* 24 (her journey to Palestine and her literary work both dated variously from the late fourth
to the early fifth century), the phrase "Kyrie eleison" was used at Vespers in the church at Jerusalem. Already in the third century Origen, *On Prayer* 14.6 (ca. A.D. 233-34), cites "Kyrie eleison" as
a proper expression for use in intercessory prayer. Texts for Chrysostom, Egeria, and Origen are
printed in Brightman 1896, 470-81; Gingras 1970, 90; and O'Meara 1954, 57, respectively.

[31] Jungmann 1951, 333.

tion. It does not allow for a single approach that can be named—as in literary, rhetorical, or narrative criticism—even though it is related to each of them. Perhaps the best way to put the matter is to divide the question. First, what does the use of liturgical materials do to the Gospel of Matthew as literature? And, second, what does that use, apparently, do to readers of the gospel? The latter question is related to questions raised in rhetorical criticism. Northrop Frye, in one of his essays, speaks of the rhetoric of 'non-literary prose,' by which he means works that were not "designed with a primarily literary intention." Here he includes such things as the Bible and the dialogues of Plato. These works, according to Frye, often emphasize emotion and an appeal to action, and one of their functions is social persuasion.[32] Insofar as the Gospel of Matthew was written to inform and give shape to community life, its use of liturgical materials must have been to serve those ends.

3.1. In terms of literary matters alone, the use of liturgical materials in the composition of the Gospel of Matthew has a marked effect on the mood of the work. According to handbooks on literary criticism, the distinction between the "mood" or "tone" of a literary work is vague.[33] For our purposes, the term "mood" will be used, signifying the "emotive attitude conveyed by a literary work."[34]

Language is used not only to convey information but also to create a mood or an effect. That is certainly the case when an author makes use of liturgical materials in a composition. Literary and form critical studies have shown that liturgical materials abound in the writings of the New Testament, such as in the letters of Paul and the Revelation to John.[35] These materials enrich the various texts in profound ways. They elicit emotions from readers, awaken their memories of songs and prayers remembered, and by their familiarity bring the texts into the company of those addressed. Insofar as the materials are already known to the readers of the texts, they render the texts in which they appear a privileged authority. The texts are 'at home' among the readers.

In the case of the Gospel of Matthew, the use of liturgical materials by the evangelist gives to the composition *an elevated and solemn mood*. We have the advantage of having other gospels—both canonical and extra-canonical—with which to make comparisons, and none truly compares with the Gospel of Matthew in this respect. Undoubtedly that accounts, at least in part, for its favored use in historic lectionaries.

The Gospel of Matthew narrates the story of Jesus. But as our survey has shown, it portrays Jesus as the "Lord" upon whom people within that story—like those who

---

[32] Frye 1957, 326-27.

[33] Cf. Frye, Baker, and Perkins 1985, 296 and 463; and Baldick 1990, 225-26.

[34] Frye, Baker, and Perkins 1985, 296.

[35] Deichgräber 1967; Sanders 1971; and Jörns 1971.

hear it read aloud—call for help, as a teacher of the church's most solemn prayer, as the one whom persons worship as they supplicate him, as the one who commissions his disciples to baptize and to teach, and—more than in the other gospels—as the one who, in hosting his Last Supper, instituted the Lord's Supper of the church.

3.2. Kilpatrick was undoubtedly correct in maintaining that the Gospel of Matthew was composed for reading at worship services, even if that was not its only purpose. Certainly the inclusion of liturgical materials suggests that as a purpose, as a comparison with other books of the New Testament demonstrates. We know that Paul and other letter writers intended that their letters be read at services of worship (cf. 1 Thess 5:27; Col 4:16; Rev 1:3; 22:18), and that accounts in part for their inclusion of liturgical materials in what they wrote. As David Aune has written, the liturgical materials, derived from Christian worship, "enabled letters to fit comfortably into liturgical settings."[36] The liturgical materials within the Gospel of Matthew would likewise have served to fit this gospel comfortably into a liturgical setting; their use gives to this gospel *a liturgical ambiance*. As the Gospel of Matthew would have been read aloud, those gathered for worship would hear lines that have a familiarity, based on their similarity to liturgical forms, just as is the case today.

3.3. Perhaps the most obvious effect of the incorporation of liturgical materials into the Gospel of Matthew upon its readers would be that the gospel then takes on *an aetiological function*. It provides for its readers a foundation for the liturgical materials in the ministry of Jesus of Nazareth or, in the case of the baptismal formula, in the first appearance of the risen Lord, when he commissioned his remaining disciples. That means that the most solemn liturgical materials in use—those for baptism and the Lord's Supper, as well as the Lord's Prayer—are now seen to have been taught by Jesus to his disciples. That is particularly evident in the case of Matthew's transformation of Mark's account of the Last Supper. The liturgical text known to Matthew and his community, and used in celebrations of the Lord's Supper, now corresponds exactly to the account of events on the night of betrayal, including the words spoken by Jesus. In this way Jesus remains the authoritative teacher for the Matthean community. The church is to observe what Jesus has commanded his disciples (28:20). Or to turn matters around, the risen Lord who is present in and for the community (1:23; 18:20; 28:20) has himself provided for that community its liturgical forms—either in his earthly ministry or in his post-Easter commission—through his disciples.

3.4. Closely related to the aetiological function, the inclusion of liturgically formed materials *provides normative texts* for the community as part of "every-

---

[36] Aune 1987, 192.

thing" that Jesus has "commanded" (28:20). As persons are incorporated into the community, they are to be baptized with the trinitarian formula. The Lord's Supper is to be celebrated with the dominically given words. The Lord's Prayer is to be used, and used as given ("Pray then in this way," 6:9). The literary phenomenon in which a narrator quotes sub-texts, as here, has been called "narrative embedding" by Mieke Bal. Typically, she says, the sub-texts embedded in larger literary works remain coherent and maintain relative independence apart from the larger literary works that carry them.[37] It can be said that the Gospel of Matthew as story, powerful as it is, does not obliterate liturgical sub-texts within it. In fact, as shown above, the evangelist—or a predecessor within the community in which he lives—has actually enhanced the liturgical character of the gospel tradition at decisive points. These materials have a coherence and independence apart from the gospel narrative and can therefore serve as normative texts for liturgical use.

3.5. Similarly, the inclusion of liturgically formed materials, which are normative for the community's worship life, *provides catechetical materials* for the community. The catechetical interest of the evangelist has been highlighted in the works of various scholars, particularly Ernst von Dobschütz.[38] Von Dobschütz pointed to the 'catchword compilations' of the evangelist (such as on prayer, cares, and judging in 6:5-15, 6:19-34, and 7:1-5, respectively), the evangelist's 'stereotyped repetitions' of phrases, various forms of expression, doublets, and the assimilation of materials from his sources into easily memorable units as evidence of a catechetical interest. The case he presented can be augmented and strengthened by notice of the evangelist's use of liturgical materials. These texts are to become familiar to those who enter the community and are catechized in everything that Jesus has commanded.

3.6. The inclusion of liturgical materials in the Gospel of Matthew provides for it the power to *create a confessional ethos* within the community that reads it. Jesus is portrayed as a regal, numinous figure, teaching with authority and displaying divine power, and receiving worship and titles of majesty. As this gospel is read, those who hear and ponder its words and images are drawn to make a confession of who Jesus is, both as individuals, and also as a community.

3.7. Finally, the inclusion of liturgical materials in the Gospel of Matthew creates a *contemporaneity* between the story read and those who hear it in the very act of reading. The sense of temporal distance between the hearer and the risen and reigning Jesus of the hearer's faith is lessened, even overcome to a large degree, as one hears familiar liturgical words uttered in the story of Jesus. The sense of the church

---

[37] Bal 1981, 48.

[38] Von Dobschütz 1983, 19-29. The catechetical character of the Gospel of Matthew is also advocated on the basis of form and contents considerations by Schille 1957/58, 101-14.

as being founded by Jesus (16:18)—with its dominically given liturgical forms for baptism, eucharist, and its most solemn prayer—and the sense of Jesus' on-going presence with his own as they gather for worship (18:20)—both of these are kindled in the imagination of the heart.

## 4. Closing Remarks

The reading of the Gospel of Matthew in public worship continues to have an appeal for its presentation of Jesus in majesty and as authoritative teacher for his church. This gospel has features that lend themselves to a recollection of Jesus and, at the same time, a recollection of those liturgical lines that are foundational to and familiar in worship. Christian worship, although set in time and during seasons of the year, prompts a sense of the on-going, not-bound-by-time presence of Christ among his people. That sense is illustrated, for example, in a lovely Swedish hymn composed by Olov Hartman (1906-1982), the father of Lars Hartman:

> Vi tror på Gud som kom i världen,
> Marias son,
> ty Jesus hjälpte alla och bar vårt kors;
> han dog—men se han lever och bor bland oss.[39]

The lines can be translated literally as follows:

> We believe in God who came into the world,
> Mary's son,
> For Jesus helped all and bore our cross;
> He died—but lo he lives and dwells among us.

Among the achievements of the evangelist Matthew was the composition of a gospel concerning the one who "helped all and bore our cross," and who lives and dwells with his own until the end of the age. Both the remembrance of the traditions of Jesus and the sense of his presence are brought to mind and heart in the reading and hearing of this gospel.

---

[39] Hymn 335, stanza 2, in: *Den Svenska Psalmboken* (Stockholm: Verbum 1986) 412. The hymn was first published in 1970.

# Bibliography

Aune, David E. 1987: *The New Testament in Its Literary Environment*, Philadelphia, PA: Westminster Press 1987.

Bal, Mieke 1981: "Notes on Narrative Embedding", in: *Poetics Today* 2/2 (1981) 41-59.

Baldick, Chris 1990: *The Concise Oxford Dictionary of Literary Terms*, Oxford and New York: Oxford University Press 1990.

Bauer, Walter 1979: *A Greek-English Lexicon of the New Testament and Other Early Christian Literature*, 2nd ed., trans. and adapted by William F. Arndt, F. Wilbur Gingrich, and Frederick W. Danker, Chicago, IL: University of Chicago Press 1979.

Beare, Frances W. 1981: *The Gospel according to Matthew*, San Francisco, CA: Harper & Row 1981.

Bonhöffer, Adolf 1911: *Epiktet und das Neue Testament* (RVV 10), Giessen: Verlag von Alfred Töpelmann 1911.

Bornkamm, Günther 1963: "The Stilling of the Storm in Matthew", in: G. Bornkamm et al., *Tradition and Interpretation in Matthew*, Philadelphia, PA: Westminster Press 1963, 52-57.

Brightman, F. E. 1896: *Liturgies Eastern and Western:* Vol. I. *Eastern Liturgies*, Oxford: Clarendon Press 1896.

Brown, Raymond E. 1966-70: *The Gospel according to John* (AncB 29-29A), 2 vols., Garden City, NY: Doubleday & Company 1966-70.

Creed, John M. 1930: *The Gospel according to Saint Luke*, London: Macmillan 1930.

Cullmann, Oscar 1949: *The Earliest Christian Confessions*, London: Lutterworth Press 1949.

Deichgräber, Reinhard 1967: *Gotteshymnus und Christushymnus in der frühen Christenheit: Untersuchungen zu Form, Sprache und Stil der frühchristlichen Hymnen* (StUNT 5), Göttingen: Vandenhoeck & Ruprecht 1967.

Dobschütz, Ernst von 1983: "Matthew as Rabbi and Catechist", in: Graham Stanton (ed.), *The Interpretation of Matthew* (Issues in Religion and Theology 3), Philadelphia, PA: Fortress Press 1983, 19-29. [Original: "Matthäus als Rabbi und Katechet", in: *ZNW* 27 (1928) 338-48.]

Fitzmyer, Joseph A. 1981-85: *The Gospel according to Luke* (AncB 28-28A), 2 vols., Garden City, NY: Doubleday & Company 1981-85.

Fornberg, Tord 1989: *Matteusevangeliet 1:1-13:52* (Kommentar till Nya Testamentet 1A), Uppsala: EFS-förlaget 1989.

Frye, Northrop 1957: *Anatomy of Criticism: Four Essays*, Princeton, NJ: Princeton University Press 1957.

Frye, Northrop, Sheridan Baker, and George Perkins 1985: *The Harper Handbook to Literature*, New York: Harper & Row 1985.

Gingras, George E. 1970: *Egeria: Diary of a Pilgrimage*, trans. George E. Gingras (ACW 38), New York: Newman Press 1970.

Goulder, Michael D. 1974: *Midrash and Lection in Matthew*, London: SPCK 1974.

Gray, Arthur 1921/22: "The Last Chapter of St John's Gospel as Interpreted by Early Christian Art", in: *HibJ* 20 (1921/22) 690-700.

Hartman, Lars 1963: *Testimonium Linguae* (CNT 19), Lund: C. W. K. Gleerup 1963.

— 1970: "'Såsom det är skrivet': Några reflexioner över citat som kommunikationsmedel i Matteus-evangeliet", in: *SEÅ* 25 (1970) 33-43.

— 1972: "Scriptural Exegesis in the Gospel of Matthew and the Problem of Communication", in: M. Didier (ed.), *L'Évangile selon Matthieu: Rédaction et théologie* (BEThL 29), Gembloux: Études J. Duculot 1972, 131-52.

Held, Heinz J. 1963: "Matthew as Interpreter of the Miracle Stories", in: G. Bornkamm et al., *Tradition and Interpretation in Matthew*, Philadelphia, PA: Westminster Press 1963, 165-299.

Jeremias, Joachim 1978: *The Prayers of Jesus*, Philadelphia, PA: Fortress Press 1978.

Jörns, Klaus P. 1971: *Das hymnische Evangelium: Untersuchung zu Aufbau, Funktion und Herkunft der hymnischen Stücke in der Johannesoffenbarung* (StNT 5), Gütersloh: Gerd Mohn 1971.

Jungmann, Joseph A. 1951: *The Mass of the Roman Rite: Its Origins and Development*, New York: Benziger Brothers 1951.

Kilpatrick G. D. 1946: *The Origins of the Gospel according to St. Matthew*, Oxford: Clarendon Press 1946.

Kloppenborg, John S. 1987: *The Formation of Q: Trajectories in Ancient Wisdom*, Philadelphia, PA: Fortress Press 1987.

Koester, Helmut 1990: *Ancient Christian Gospels: Their History and Development*, Philadelphia, PA: Trinity Press International 1990.

Lohmeyer, Ernst 1956: *"Our Father": An Introduction to the Lord's Prayer*, New York: Harper & Row 1965.

Luz, Ulrich 1989: *Matthew 1-7: A Commentary*, Minneapolis, MN: Augsburg Publishing House 1989.

Manson, T. W. 1955/56: "The Lord's Prayer", in: *BJRL* 38 (1955/56) 99-113, 436-48.

Metzger, Bruce M. 1971: *A Textual Commentary on the Greek New Testament*, New York: United Bible Societies 1971.

Moule, C. F. D. 1961: *Worship in the New Testament*, Richmond, VA: John Knox Press 1961.

O'Meara, John J. 1954: *Origen: Prayer/Exhortation to Martyrdom*, trans. John J. O'Meara (ACW 19), Westminster, MD: Newman Press 1954.

Polag, Athanasius 1979: *Fragmenta Q: Textheft zur Logienquelle*, Neukirchen-Vluyn: Neukirchener Verlag 1979.

Sanders, Jack T. 1971: *The New Testament Christological Hymns: Their Historical Religious Background* (MSSNTS 15), Cambridge: Cambridge University Press 1971.

Schille, Gottfried 1957: "Bemerkungen zur Formgeschichte des Evangeliums: II. Das Evangelium des Matthäus als Katechismus", in: *NTS* 4 (1957/58) 101-114.

Sharp, Douglas S. 1914: *Epictetus and the New Testament*, London: Charles H. Kelly 1914.

Stanton, Graham 1992: *A Gospel for a New People: Studies in Matthew*, Edinburgh: T. & T. Clark 1992.

Stone, M. E. 1983: "[Introduction to the] Greek Apocalypse of Ezra", in: James H. Charlesworth (ed.), *The Old Testament Pseudepigrapha*, 2 vols., Garden City, NY: Doubleday & Company 1983-85, 1:561-70.

Streeter, Burnett H. 1930: *The Four Gospels: A Study of Origins*, rev. ed., New York: St. Martin's Press 1930.

Taussig, Hal 1988: "The Lord's Prayer", in: *Foundations & Facets Forum* 4/4 (1988) 25-41.

# Traditions juives selon Mc 7,1-23

René Kieffer

## 1. Introduction

L'article suivant, que nous dédions à notre cher collègue et ami Lars Hartman, veut engager une réflexion sur la possibilité de situer historiquement les traditions juives que transmet Marc en 7,1-23. Dans ce but nous présentons d'abord l'état synoptique de notre texte, pour ensuite l'éclairer en deux étapes: la dispute en 7,1-13, le *mashal* et son explication en 7,14-23. Quelques réflexions herméneutiques amorcent une discussion sur les limites de notre analyse, somme toute traditionnelle.

## 2. L'état synoptique de notre texte

Les récits qui précèdent Mc 7,1-23 et le texte correspondant de Mt 15,1-20, n'introduisent guère la discussion avec les Pharisiens et les scribes sur les traditions. De loin cependant, le lecteur est préparé à une confrontation à ce sujet, par l'autorité avec laquelle Jésus exerce son ministère, malgré l'opposition des scribes (Mc 2,6; 3,22; Mt 9,3) ou des Pharisiens (Mc 2,16.24; Mt 9,11; 12,2.24). On devine aussi que cette discussion prépare chez Marc et Matthieu d'autres polémiques, qui concernent plus spécifiquement l'autorité de Jésus (Mc 11,27-33; Mt 21,23-27; voir aussi les disputes, *Streitgespräche*, et les enseignements, *Schulgespräche*, en Mc 12,13-40 et Mt 22,15-23.36)[1]. La relativisation des lois de pureté prépare aussi la visite de Jésus en terre païenne (Mc 7,24-30; Mt 15,21-28). On devine que Marc a considéré l'ensemble de la discussion sur le pur et l'impur comme un enseignement adressé à l'Eglise, où règne la parole de Dieu et non les traditions des Anciens. Par son comportement Jésus a légitimé la mission de l'Eglise en terre païenne[2].

Signalons que Lc 11,37-54 a une version parallèle de la discussion entre Jésus et les Pharisiens, en provenance probablement de la source Q (voir aussi Mt 23,1-36)[3].

---

[1] Bultmann 1921.
[2] Voir Boismard 1972, 231 et Pesch 1976, I, 384.

Un jugement défavorable sur les scribes se trouve aussi dans un court texte commun aux trois évangiles synoptiques (Mc 12,38-40; Lc 20,45-47; remanié fortement en Mt 23,1-12).

Chez Marc et Matthieu la discussion sur la tradition des Anciens s'adresse directement aux Pharisiens et aux scribes de Jérusalem (Mc 7,1-13; Mt 15,1-9), alors que l'enseignement sur le pur et l'impur a comme auditoire d'abord la foule appelée spécialement par Jésus (Mc 7,14; Mt 15,10), puis les disciples qui interrogent Jésus (Mc 7,17; Mt 15,12). Comme ces deux péricopes sont associées par leur contenu, le thème de la pureté (voir le mot clef κοινόω et κοινός en Mc 7,3.5.15.18.20), on peut supposer que les disciples et les adversaires de Jésus sont présents aussi à l'enseignement adressé à la foule[4].

Selon les catégories élaborées par R. Bultmann[5], notre texte, grâce à sa première partie (Mc 7,1-13; Mt 15,1-9), constitue un apophtegme du genre *Streitgespräch*, c'est-à-dire des paroles de Jésus sont rapportées à l'intérieur d'un récit de dispute. Celle-ci ne surgit pas comme en Mc 2,1-12 (parr. Mt et Lc) ou Mc 3,1-6.22-30 (parr. Mt et Lc) à propos d'une guérison, mais comme en Mc 2,15-17.23-28 (parr. Mt et Lc) à cause du comportement des disciples (ou de Jésus). Comme dans d'autres *Streitgespräche*, les questions sont posées par les adversaires (voir Mc 10,2-12, par. Mt; Mc 12,13-27, parr. Mt et Lc), mais contrairement aux autres textes de Marc et de Matthieu, la réponse de Jésus est une critique explicite d'un exemple de casuistique. En y rattachant les explications sur le pur et l'impur (Mc 7,14-23; Mt 15,10-20), Marc et Matthieu semblent vouloir résumer la doctrine de Jésus face aux traditions juives.

Par l'association de deux traditions sur l'enseignement de Jésus, surgit un conflit dans la présentation de la doctrine de Jésus. D'abord celui-ci souligne la valeur de la Loi de Dieu en face des traditions (Mc 7,6-13; Mt 15,3-9), pour ensuite mettre en question les lois de pureté de la Loi elle-même (Mc 7,14-23; Mt 15,10-20)[6].

Dans la discussion avec les scribes et les Pharisiens, Jésus ne répond pas à leur question, mais les attaque à son tour en élevant le débat au niveau des principes: la tradition des hommes ne doit pas annuler le commandement de Dieu (Mc 7,8s.; cf. Mt 15,3). Dans la seconde partie, par contre, Jésus répond plus directement à la question posée. Il défend devant la foule la conduite de ses disciples à l'aide d'un *mashal* (en Mc 7,17 et Mt 15,15 παραβολή, un équivalent grec imparfait), qu'il ex-

---

[3] Boismard 1972, 229.

[4] Mt 15,12 semble supposer cela, en rapportant d'abord l'explication en parabole que Jésus donne à la foule, et ensuite la remarque des disciples sur les Pharisiens qui ont été choqués en entendant cette parole. Ceux-ci semblent avoir quitté la scène quand les disciples font leur remarque.

[5] Bultmann 1921.

[6] Lambrecht 1977 et Hooker 1991, 173s.

plique ensuite à ses disciples. Ici Jésus affirme sa propre autorité qui le place au-dessus des préceptes de pureté de la Loi. On peut donc dire que les deux parties du texte ont été intégrées pour former un tout cohérent, même si l'on devine des tensions dues à ce que les traditions antérieures ont été indépendantes[7].

Chez Marc nous constatons les maladresses usuelles: après avoir aux vv. 1s. introduit les observations que font les Pharisiens et les scribes, Marc se sent aux vv. 3s. obligé d'expliquer les coutumes juives, pour en venir au v. 5 à la question posée. Jésus y répond aux vv. 6-8 en citant Esaïe et en opposant le commandement de Dieu à la tradition des hommes. Mais au v. 9 Marc réintroduit la réponse de Jésus par "il leur dit", et réitère le contenu du verset 8. L'introduction de la foule au v. 14 est artificielle ("puis, appelant de nouveau la foule"). La remarque au v. 19 b, "il déclarait ainsi que tous les aliments sont purs", interrompt la réponse de Jésus, ce qui oblige le rédacteur à la réintroduire au v. 20 par "il disait".

Chez Matthieu qui, à l'exception de Matt 15,12-14, suit probablement le texte de Marc[8], la rédaction est sensiblement raccourcie et améliorée. Les Pharisiens et les scribes semblent tous venir de Jérusalem et avoir été informés à l'avance par d'autres sur ce que font les disciples. Jésus répond à la question des Pharisiens et des scribes par une autre question, ce qui permet à Matthieu de présenter la réponse de Jésus sans aucune interruption. Dans ce but il supprime aussi les explications de Marc sur les coutumes juives. En plaçant l'exemple du *qorban* avant la citation d'Es 29,13, l'évangéliste concrétise immédiatement ce que Jésus veut dire par sa contre-attaque en Mt 15,3. Nous obtenons ainsi un contraste avec la doctrine du Sermon sur la montagne, comme le souligne M.-E. Boismard: "Tandis que Jésus est venu 'accomplir la Loi' (5,17) en 'renchérissant' sur chacun des préceptes du Décalogue (5,21 ss), les Pharisiens au contraire, par leurs 'traditions', en sont venus à 'annuler' la parole de Dieu (15,6b), la vidant de son esprit et de sa rigueur contraignante"[9].

Dans la seconde partie sur le pur et l'impur, Matthieu développe de façon habile le dialogue entre Jésus et les disciples. Après la première question, il introduit aux versets 13s. deux *logia*, empruntés probablement à la source Q: le premier sur toute plante qui sera déracinée a son équivalent en l'évangile de Thomas 40 (d'ailleurs avec la mention des Pharisiens et des scribes au § 39), et le second sur l'aveugle qui guide un aveugle se trouve aussi en Lc 6,39 et en Thomas 34. Pour amorcer la seconde question adressée à Jésus, Matthieu introduit Pierre. En supprimant la note explicative de Mc 7,19b, l'évangéliste peut présenter la réponse de Jésus sans aucu-

---

[7] Boismard 1972, 232; Lambrecht 1977.

[8] Voir Westerholm 1978, 71 et 145, note 54. Matthieu semble suivre Marc en écrivant en 15,1 "Pharisiens et scribes", alors que partout ailleurs il écrit "scribes et Pharisiens" (au moins sept fois et cela surtout au chapitre 23, où la rédaction matthéenne est évidente).

[9] Boismard 1972, 230.

ne interruption inutile[10]. Matthieu a cependant banalisé la parabole de Marc en y ajoutant "la bouche" (15,11), ce qui supprime son caractère énigmatique. D'ailleurs Jésus est obligé de passer de la bouche au coeur (15,18), pour expliquer d'où viennent les vices[11].

Matthieu renforce la polémique par l'insertion des vv 13s. Si Jésus avait prononcé ces paroles véhémentes contre les Pharisiens et les scribes, il leur aurait dénié toute autorité quand ils invoquaient leur tradition. Mais on peut se demander, si le contexte tardif dans lequel Matthieu écrit n'a pas contribué à son attitude négative envers les scribes. Au chapitre 23 il attaque durement les scribes et Pharisiens (23, 13.15.23.26s.29) et les nomme des "guides aveugles" (23,16.24), "des insensés et aveugles" (23,17; cf. 23,19). Il est certain que Matthieu y a accentué la critique des Pharisiens et des scribes qu'il trouvait en Q (voir par comparaison Lc 11,39-52). L'explication la plus probable de ce phénomène est, à notre avis, que la communauté judéo-chrétienne de Matthieu a coupé les liens avec la synagogue juive[12]. Pour cette communauté il n'y a plus qu'un seul maître, Jésus (Mt 23,8), et les disciples qui le suivent sont les nouveaux scribes (cf. Mt 23,34), supérieurs aux Pharisiens et à tous les scribes juifs. La polémique matthéenne concerne donc en partie une époque postérieure à Jésus. Mais qu'en est-il du texte de Marc?

### 3. Le texte de Marc

### 3.1. La dispute en Mc 7,1-13

Nous avons la structure normale d'un *Streitgespräch* en trois parties: la description de la situation concrète qui fait scandale (vv. 1-4); l'objection des adversaires (introduits au v. 1, avec leurs observations personnelles au v. 2 et leur critique explicite au v. 5); la réponse de Jésus en deux étapes (vv. 6-8; 9-13)[13].

Les Pharisiens et les scribes de Jérusalem ont l'initiative dans le *Streitgespräch* qui s'engage avec Jésus: ils voient que les disciples prennent leur repas avec des mains impures, c'est-à-dire "non lavées", explique Marc, et reprochent cela implicitement au Maître qui en doit porter la responsabilité[14].

---

[10] Matthieu améliore aussi le style qu'il trouve chez Marc, en remplaçant, selon son usage, certains καί par τότε (aux vv. 1 et 12), en supprimant le πάλιν de Mc 7,14b au début de 15,10, et en remplaçant συνάγομαι πρός de Mc 7,1 par προσέρχομαι en 15,1. Voir Westerholm 1978, 145 (note 55).

[11] Voir Haenchen 1968, 269.

[12] Voir surtout Schweizer 1974, 11s. et 36s.; Luz 1985; Kingsbury 1991. Nous avons pu consulter un article non publié de R. Aguirre, "La communauté de Matthieu et le judaïsme. Etat de la question".

[13] Voir Pesch 1976, 369.

A l'adresse de ses lecteurs, l'évangéliste donne une plus ample information au sujet des Pharisiens et de tous les Juifs: il signale d'abord que selon la tradition des Anciens, ils se lavent les mains avec une poignée d'eau (7,3)[15], et, précise-t-il, ils s'aspergent d'eau avant de manger quand ils viennent de la place publique[16]. Ensuite Marc abandonne le contexte concret, quand il indique que les Pharisiens et tous les Juifs ont reçu d'autres choses auxquelles ils sont attachés: le lavage de coupes, de cruches et de plats d'airain (7,4)[17]. S. Zeitlin a souligné qu'avant la destruction du Temple, les écoles de Shammai et de Hillel adoptèrent les "Dix-huit mesures" qui rendaient tout Juif rituellement impur, s'il ne se soumettait pas à un bain. Mais pour des raisons pratiques, les rabbins avaient déclaré qu'un lavement des mains était suffisant[18]. Même si cette vue n'a pas été acceptée par d'autres savants, elle garde une certaine valeur[19].

Nous constatons immédiatement que Marc est imprécis quand il écrit "les Pharisiens et *tous* les Juifs" (7,2), puisque le mot technique qu'il emploie, "la tradition des Anciens", est du temps de Jésus typique pour les Pharisiens et non pas pour *tous* les Juifs. Après l'an 70, quand les traditions des Pharisiens commencèrent à l'emporter, on peut dire que *tous* les Juifs se sentaient obligés de suivre leurs traditions. Mais du temps de Jésus il ne s'agissait que d'un effort de la part des Pharisiens pour imposer leur interprétation de la Loi.

Le mot "tradition des Anciens" (7,3) montre que Marc est du moins partiellement informé sur le monde juif. Josèphe nous signale à propos des Pharisiens: "Ils ont transmis au peuple, héritées de la doctrine des Pères, de nombreuses prescriptions qui ne se trouvent pas écrites dans les lois de Moïse"[20]. Ni Josèphe ni Philon

---

[14] Voir Daube 1972-73, 8s.

[15] L'expression πυγμῇ a été interprétée de façon différente: "soigneusement"; "jusqu'au coude"; "avec une poignée d'eau" (cf. le latin *pugillo*) ou "avec la main à moitié fermée"; voir Pesch 1976, 371 et Hooke 1991, 175. Le sens de "avec une poignée d'eau" est de ne pas gaspiller l'eau; cf. dans la Mishna, Yad. 1,1.

[16] Il s'agit probablement d'une aspersion des mains ou de la nourriture devenues "impures" au marché; cf. Brandt 1910, 34-36.

[17] On peut comparer Mt 23,25s.; Lc 11,39-41 et Thomas 89. Ici on peut trouver des textes parallèles déjà dans l'Ancien Testament, où des ustensiles rendues impures devaient être purifiés; voir Lv 11,32 ss; 15,12; Nb 19,15.18. Il n'est donc pas étonnant que l'on puisse trouver chez des Pharisiens un intérêt spécial pour purifier différents ustensiles. Cela sera développé plus tard dans le traîté de la Mishna intitulé "Kelim"; cf. Neusner 1973a.

[18] Zeitlin, 1915.

[19] Voir Finkelstein 1940, 277ss; voir aussi Carlston 1968-69 et Neusner 1973. Lachs 1987, 246 commente l'explication de Zeitlin: "This is the best explanation of this passage".

[20] Ant. 13, 297. L'expression "traditions des Anciens" correspond aux *divrê zeqenim* ou les *mitzvot zeqenim*, c'est-à-dire "les paroles des Anciens" ou "les commandements des Anciens", peut-être même aux *divrê soferim*, "les paroles des scribes"; voir Lachs 1987, 245.

ne connaissent explicitement la doctrine des rabbins sur les deux Lois, l'une écrite, l'autre orale[21]. D'après Josèphe les Pharisiens considéraient les traditions venant des Pères comme liant les consciences, tout en n'étant pas attribuables à Moïse[22]. Paul, au passé pharisien, fait aussi allusion à ces traditions qui étaient transmises oralement dans les écoles rabbiniques (Ga 1,14; cf. Ac 22,3; 28,17), et seront fixées par écrit dans la Mishna au second siècle. Depuis le temps des Maccabées, aux luttes intenses contre les cultes étrangers, tout ce qui concernait les Anciens était préservé avec soin. Les Pharisiens qui soulignaient l'importance de ces traditions pouvaient certainement compter sur la faveur du peuple[23]. Que ces traditions ont joué historiquement un rôle important dans les disputes entre Jésus et les Pharisiens, paraît donc bien établi.

Quelle autorité avaient les traditions orales par lesquelles les Pharisiens interprétaient la Loi de Moïse? Jésus n'a pas voulu l'accepter dans les cas où les interprétations casuistiques semblaient annuler l'intention même de la Loi. C'est ce qu'il répond immédiatement à leur question: "Vous violez le commandement de Dieu afin de garder votre tradition". Comme exemple, Jésus ne prend pas une loi concernant les purifications rituelles, mais une tradition d'"offrande", qui annule le commandement d'honorer son père et sa mère (Ex 20,12 et Dt 5,16). L'exemple suppose que le fils, peut-être irrité par ses parents, consacre comme *qorban* ou offrande au Temple tout ce que ses parents auraient pu toucher de ses biens (7,11). Cela ne signifiait pas que l'offrande était due au Temple, mais qu'elle était soustraite à ses parents[24]. La doctrine pharisienne semble avoir été que, même dans le cas où le fils se repentait de son voeu, il était lié par lui; ainsi au sens propre: "vous ne lui permettez plus de rien faire pour son père ou sa mère" (7,12)[25]. La citation de Ex 21,17 au v. 10 ("celui qui maudit père ou mère, qu'il soit puni de mort") veut peut-être souligner le mépris envers les parents que la casuistique pharisienne reflète.

Que cette tradition a pu exister, est confirmé indépendamment par deux documents[26]: Un ossuaire daté du premier siècle apr. J.-C., trouvé près de Jérusalem, a une formule analogue pour prévenir tout vol: "Tout ce qu'un homme trouverait à son profit dans cet ossuaire est *qorban* (c'est-à-dire offrande) à Dieu de la part de celui qui est dedans"[27]. De façon plus explicite, le *Document de Damas* attaque,

---

[21] Voir Westerholm 1978, 16 et Belkin 1940, 29.

[22] Voir Josèphe, Ant. 13, 297: "Les Pharisiens ont transmis au peuple, de la succession de leurs Pères, de nombreuses observances qui ne sont pas écrites dans la loi de Moïse".

[23] Westerholm 1978, 16.

[24] On peut comparer dans la Mishna Ned. 1,3s. et Naz. 2,1-3. Sur la notion de *qorban*, voir surtout Rengstorf 1938, Hommel 1954, Buchanan 1965.

[25] La traduction de la TOB est moins précise: "vous lui permettez de ne plus rien faire pour son père ou sa mère". Les Pharisiens ne permettent pas au fils de se repentir de son voeu.

[26] Boismard 1972, 230.

comme Jésus, celui qui "sanctifie pour Dieu (c'est-à-dire déclare *qorban*, 'offran-de') la nourriture de sa bouche"; il encourt le reproche de Mi 7,2: "Ils se traquent l'un l'autre au filet" (CD 15,14s.). Mais ces deux exemples ne prouvent pas néces-sairement que la remarque ironique de Jésus sur le *qorban* reflète directement une situation historique.

Jésus prend la défense du commandement de la Loi contre l'interprétation qui en est donnée par les Pharisiens. Il a aussi recours à un autre texte scripturaire, Esaïe (29,13), pour critiquer ceux qui honorent Dieu des lèvres mais dont le coeur est éloi-gné de Lui. D'après le texte hébreu leur obéissance est seulement une apparence: ils pèchent en secret. Marc utilise cependant le texte des Septante qu'il abrège, et qui a un sens différent de l'hébreu massorétique[28]. Il accentue l'opposition entre com-mandements de Dieu et tradition humaine, et démasque ainsi les interprétations des scribes comme des "préceptes d'hommes" et un "culte vain envers Dieu". Jésus ré-tablit selon Marc l'autorité de Dieu et de sa Loi, s'en prenant ainsi aux interpréta-tions qui détournent les hommes d'un véritable culte de Dieu. Cet aspect a des chances de reproduire une polémique historique que Jésus a soutenu contre les Pha-risiens, mais la citation d'Esaïe semble ajoutée par Marc.

Les "scribes de Jérusalem" sont d'un point de vue historique probablement des Pharisiens, puisque la tradition rapportée est typique pour eux[29]. Mais il se peut que Marc ne l'ait pas entendu de cette façon: son texte fait penser à un interrogatoire of-ficiel, organisé par le Sanhédrin dont les Pharisiens faisaient partie. On peut cepen-dant objecter à cette hypothèse que cela n'est pas dit explicitement, ni ici, ni dans la querelle à propos des exorcismes de Jésus en Mc 3,22[30]. On peut tout au plus dire, que l'attitude des scribes pharisiens de Jérusalem correspond bien à leur trait caractéristique au temps de Jésus: ils essaient d'exercer leur influence dans toute la Palestine et sont très critiques à l'égard du vulgaire peuple (*'am ha-'aretz*) de Gali-lée, qui néglige les prescriptions de pureté.

On a soulevé trois questions à propos de cette première partie du texte[31]: 1. On a dénié que le lavement des mains fût requis à cette époque, même par les Phari-siens, pour ceux qui n'étaient pas prêtres. 2. Comme les versets 6-13 concernent la validité de la tradition des Anciens et non plus la question de la pureté amorcée aux versets 1-5, on a voulu considérer l'accusation contre Jésus et les disciples comme une ajoute secondaire pour introduire la critique de la tradition pharisienne. 3. On a

---

[27] Fitzmyer 1959.

[28] Voir Haenchen 1968, 262.

[29] Westerholm 1972, 72.

[30] Nous acceptons le raisonnement de Westerholm 1978, 72, contre l'opinion de Lohmeyer 1962, 244.

[31] Voir Westerholm 1978, 72-80.

mis en doute que les Pharisiens du temps de Jésus liaient les personnes dans leur voeu; au contraire, leur tradition était de les en délier[32].

La première question a été soulevée surtout par A. Büchler[33]. Après avoir d'abord soutenu que les prescriptions de pureté pour les repas furent introduites tardivement, au second siècle, il concéda que cette coutume était plus ancienne mais maintint qu'elle ne fut acceptée par les écoles rabbiniques qu'après l'an 70. Avec S. Westerholm, on peut y répondre que les *chaberim* du premier siècle essayaient déjà de manger dans un état de pureté[34]. Nous avons des documents qui soulignent le lavement des mains avant un acte religieux[35], mais nous avons aussi des indices que, du moins chez les Pharisiens, on se lavait aussi les mains avant les repas[36]. On devine que l'extension aux laïcs des règles de pureté concernant les prêtres, pouvait être due au principe que toute nourriture devait être considérée comme offerte au Temple[37].

A la seconde question on peut répondre que la tradition de se laver les mains avant le repas ne pouvait pas être directement prouvée par l'Ecriture[38]. Il est donc naturel que Jésus, pour contre-attaquer l'autorité des Pharisiens, doive invoquer un autre point de leur tradition où ils ont l'air d'interpréter l'Ecriture. En démolissant leurs arguments à ce sujet, il peut montrer que leur fameuse "tradition des Anciens" n'a pas toute l'autorité qu'ils lui attribuent.

A la troisième question, il faut répondre par de plus amples considérations. Comme le souligne Westerholm, l'Ecriture avait une attitude rigoureuse à l'égard des voeux; elle a été longtemps retenue par la tradition, pour faire progressivement place à une attitude plus compréhensive dans certaines parties de la Mishna[39]. Analysant un texte de la Mishna, Ned. 9,1 cité par H. Montefiore, J. Neusner souligne

---

[32] C'est ce que prétend Montefiore, 1927, vol. I, 149, en citant la Mishna, Ned. 9,1.

[33] Büchler 1906, 130 ss et 1909-10.

[34] Westerholm 1978, 14 et 73; voir aussi Hooker, 1991, 175, qui souligne que les *chaberim* étaient probablement des Pharisiens, mais que tous les Pharisiens n'étaient pas des *chaberim*. On peut donc dire qu'au moins une partie des Pharisiens propageaient ces règles au temps de Jésus.

[35] Voir p. ex. Aristée 305s. (avant la prière); Josèphe, Ant. 12,106 (avant d'interpréter la loi); cf. aussi Nb 18,8-13 l'obligation pour les prêtres d'être en état de pureté pour manger la nourriture qui avait été offerte en sacrifice.

[36] Voir dans la Mishna, en Ber. 8,2 et 8,4, les discussions déjà anciennes entre les écoles de Shammai et de Hillel sur le lavement des mains avant ou après de mélanger la coupe ou de nettoyer la chambre; voir aussi les discussions analogues entre disciples des deux écoles en Mik. 1,5s.

[37] Voir Talmud de Babylone, Chul. 105a; 106a-b; Shab. 13b-14b; cf. Hooker 1991, 175.

[38] Les rabbins postérieurs savaient que le commandement de se laver les mains était une "parole de scribes" et non directement une parole de Dieu; voir Talmud de Babylone Er. 21b et Chul. 106a.

[39] Westerholm 1978, 77-80. Il cite les quatre cas où un voeu peut être rompu, selon la Mishna, Ned. 3,1. Soulignons d'ailleurs, avec Lachs 1987, 246, que les rabbins interprétaient "honorer ses parents" comme signifiant: "subvenir à leurs nécessités physiques".

qu'Eliezer innove quand il permet d'annuler le voeu pour honorer ses parents, alors qu'avant lui, la tradition ne permettait pas d'en libérer[40]. On pourrait donc en conclure que le texte de Marc 7,9-13 reflète une connaissance réelle d'une pratique pharisienne antérieure. Nous pensons cependant que Westerholm exagère, quand il veut attribuer le texte directement à Jésus[41]: il suffit que Marc par ses sources soit suffisamment informé sur la pratique pharisienne. Il pourrait en effet devoir sa connaissance à un milieu juif postérieur à Jésus.

## 3.2. Le mashal et son explication en Mc 7,14-23

Avec raison, Pesch considère Mc 7,14-23 comme une nouvelle façon d'envisager la question du pur et de l'impur: il ne s'agit plus ici de la tradition *halachique* du lavement des mains, mais des commandements de la Tora elle-même au sujet des nourritures pures ou impures[42]. Jésus avait répondu à la question des Pharisiens par une attaque contre les traditions des Anciens; maintenant il y répond plus directement, d'abord à la foule par un *mashal* (7,15), ensuite aux disciples par l'explication du *mashal* (7,17-23)[43]. Marc suit ici le procédé qu'il a développé plus haut au chapitre 4 sur les paraboles: leur caractère énigmatique doit être expliqué aux disciples, qui "sont sans intelligence" (voir 7,18, à comparer avec 4,13).

L'enseignement de Jésus devrait cependant être facile à comprendre, si les disciples, comme ailleurs chez Marc, n'étaient pas si inintelligents: l'impureté et la pureté ne doivent pas être identifiées avec des choses extérieures à l'homme, mais à ce qui sort de son coeur[44]. Ici Jésus s'écarte non seulement de la tradition des Anciens, mais encore implicitement de la Loi elle-même.

La plupart des exégètes considèrent que le *mashal* du v. 15 remonte à Jésus luimême, en fonction du critère de dissimilarité: on ne voit pas bien comment il aurait pu naître de la tradition juive ou des intérêts de la première communauté chrétienne[45]. Il convient cependant d'ancrer le *logion* dans la vie de Jésus à partir aussi d'autres critères[46]: le *mashal* est cohérent avec ce que nous savons par ailleurs de l'enseignement de Jésus, à savoir son intérêt pour ce qui se passe à l'intérieur du

---

[40] Neusner 1973, vol. II, 110.

[41] Westerholm 1978, 78-80.

[42] Pesch 1976, I, 377. Boismard 1972, 232 ne semble pas avoir vu ce déplacement de la question.

[43] Entre les deux parties, de nombreux manuscrits ajoutent: "Si quelqu'un a des oreilles pour entendre, qu'il entende", une interpolation évidente à partir de Mt 11,15.

[44] Voir Boismard 1972, 232.

[45] Voir la présentation de l'histoire de l'interprétation du verset chez Merkel 1968 et comparer la remarque de Haenchen 1968, 265: "Die Keimzelle des ganzen Abschnitts ist der Spruch V. 15. Gegen seine Zurückführung auf Jesus selbst lässt sich nichts einwenden". Voir aussi Pesch 1976, I, 379s. et 383s.

[46] Pour ce qui suit, voir Westerholm 1978, 81ss.

coeur de l'homme[47]. Le style du *mashal* est antithétique et prégnant, il contient un jeu de mots et est paradoxal, comme dans d'autres *meshalim* de Jésus. La forme que lui donne Matthieu (et à sa suite Thomas 14) est cependant simplifiée, en comparaison du *mashal* énigmatique de Marc[48]. L'explication que Marc ajoute en 7,19 semble montrer que le *logion* de Jésus a été une source de législation dans de nouvelles situations, en l'occurence le contexte de la communauté de table entre chrétiens d'origine juive et chrétiens d'origine païenne (cf. Ac 10,1-11.18; Ga 2,12). C'est ce qui est du moins suggéré par la section des pains qui suit en 7,24-30[49].

On doit cependant souligner que le *mashal* de Jésus en lui-même demeure ambigu et ouvert. La première partie (15a) contredit la Loi qui connaît des objets impurs et des aliments impurs (Lv 11-15; Dt 14, 3-21); la seconde partie (15b) peut, selon le v. 19b, être interprétée en conformité avec la Loi et faire allusion aux excréments (cf. Dt 23,13-15)[50].

A la différence de l'attaque contre l'autorité des Pharisiens en 7,9-13, la mise en question de la Loi de Moïse n'est qu'implicite. On pourrait donc considérer le *logion* comme une formulation typiquement "sémitique" à propos de ce qui importe: les questions de pureté extérieure importent moins que celles concernant la pureté du coeur. Dans ce cas, Jésus, comme dans le Sermon sur la Montagne, réaffirmerait la volonté de Dieu comme l'ultime critère des prescriptions de la Loi. Marc aurait clarifié le discours énigmatique de Jésus en reformulant l'explication à l'adresse des disciples. Le *mashal* de Jésus révèlerait ainsi la richesse de son contenu à une époque plus tardive, où les chrétiens ont su l'appliquer à leurs discussions sur l'admission des païens à des repas communs. Une telle explication permettrait de mieux comprendre, pourquoi les discussions sur le pur et l'impur ne trouvèrent dans la communauté chrétienne qu'une solution progressive.

Dans l'explication en 7,18s., Jésus donne le sens de la première partie du *mashal:* la nourriture qui pénètre de l'extérieur dans l'homme passe dans le ventre et est éliminée. En précisant que la nourriture ne pénètre pas dans le coeur, Jésus prépare l'explication de la seconde partie du *mashal* en 7,20-23: c'est ce qui sort du coeur qui peut rendre l'homme impur. Il y a une parfaite correspondance entre le *mashal* et sa double explication. On pourrait donc penser que Jésus a bel et bien expliqué l'énigmatique *mashal* au groupe restreint des disciples.

---

[47] Cf. Montefiore 1927, I, 132s.: "There is no reason whatever why he should *not* have said it, and much reason why he should".

[48] Haenchen 1968, 269.

[49] Nous nous inspirons ici d'une note de la TOB 1972, 152 sur Mc 7,19. On peut même penser avec la TOB, p. 484, que ce que Paul écrit aux Romains: "Je le sais, j'en suis convaincu par le Seigneur Jésus: rien n'est impur en soi", s'appuie sur Marc 7,15-23 (et donc, ajouterions-nous volontiers, en particulier le *mashal* de Jésus).

[50] Voir Pesch 1976, I, 379 et 383s.

Cependant le catalogue des vices aux versets 21s. est si habilement disposé qu'on y devine une systématisation faite dans la communauté chrétienne postérieu-re[51]. Nous avons en effet d'abord la notion générale de "mauvais desseins", qui est précisée par deux groupes de six vices, l'un au pluriel ("débauches, vols, meurtres, adultères, cupidités, méchancetés"), l'autre au singulier ("ruse, impudicité, envie, diffamation, orgueil, déraison")[52]. Un *mashal* de Jésus a plus de chances de remonter à lui qu'une explication privée à l'adresse de quelques disciples[53]. On peut tout au plus dire que l'importance attribuée au coeur est en accord profond avec la doctrine générale de Jésus qui, comme les prophètes de l'Ancien Testament (Ez 11,19; 36,26; Jr 32,29), insiste sur les dispositions du coeur et de l'esprit (Mt 5,8; 6,22; Lc 21,14; cf. Mc 3,5; 3,29s. et parr.).

En même temps il ne faut pas oublier que certains pharisiens du temps de Jésus soulignaient comme lui la pureté du coeur. La polémique peut donc être adressée à ceux parmi eux qui, en augmentant l'importance des prescriptions extérieures, risquent de faire oublier l'essentiel.

## 4. Quelques réflexions herméneutiques

L'analyse précédente a été commandée par les méthodes historico-critiques que de nombreux commentateurs continuent à utiliser aujourd'hui. Comme on le voit, le propos dominant y est d'arriver à cerner dans un texte synoptique ce qui remonte à un milieu juif du temps de Jésus, ce qui est attribuable à des traditions chrétiennes postérieures, et ce qui relève des intérêts spéciaux du rédacteur. Nous avons pu constater qu'un minimum de faits peuvent éventuellement remonter à Jésus lui-même et au contexte historique qui était le sien: le *mashal* en Mc 7,15; la dispute avec les Pharisiens sur les traditions des Anciens et sur leur intérêt pour les purifications. Nous avons aussi vu que Marc peut avoir emprunté certains éléments à ses sources, sans être lui-même directement informé sur les institutions antérieures, p. ex. sur le *qorban* qu'il traite en 7,9-13. Nous avons finalement vu comment Marc peut avoir retravaillé sa documentation à partir des conflits de la première communauté sur l'admission des païens "impurs" à une communauté de table (voir sa remarque en 7,19b), ou encore avoir amplifié l'explication de Jésus par une énumération détaillée de vices (7, 21s.).

Toute méthode suit son propre "jeu"[54] et part de ses propres centres d'intérêt. La

---

[51] Voir Dibelius (1919) 1961, 222; Lohmeyer 1937, 142; Merkel 1968, 352.

[52] Voir Pesch 1976, 381s.; Haenchen 1968, 265s., qui cependant exagère le contraste entre l'explication "moralisante" de Marc, et le *mashal* de Jésus qui serait une attaque radicale de la Loi. Haenchen projette sur Jésus la polémique paulinienne contre la Loi.

[53] Voir Westerholm 1978, 84s.

méthode historico-critique est intéressée aux distinctions des niveaux d'information dans les textes synoptiques. Avec la *Formgeschichte* elle isole des "formes" (dans notre texte p. ex. le *Streitgespräch* et le *mashal*), ou encore, avec la *Redaktionsgeschichte*, elle considère les ajouts rédactionnels et la perspective spéciale des différents auteurs. Ce qui demeure problématique dans cette recherche, ce sont les différentes propositions de probabilité qu'on élabore: sur les sources de Marc, sur son travail rédactionnel, sur sa connaissance directe ou indirecte du milieu juif etc. Il s'agit toujours d'une reconstruction hypothétique, où les arguments demeurent fragiles.

Si nous avions suivi une méthode linguistique ou sémiotique, nous aurions pris comme point de départ la composition finale, sans nous soucier d'où proviennent les matériaux. Si par exemple nous lisions notre texte à partir de la situation de *communication* qu'il exprime entre l'auteur et son auditoire[55], nous insisterions sur l'aspect de critique globale des purifications juives que Marc veut transmettre. Certains lecteurs sont déjà assez éloignés du monde juif, pour qu'il se sente obligé de leur expliquer les coutumes qu'il rapporte. La technicité de son langage confère à la polémique un caractère historicisant. Marc a bien l'intention de rapporter quelque chose qui s'est passé autrefois et respecte en conséquence la distance entre son auditoire et le monde juif de Jésus. Mais les niveaux auxquels se situe le caractère historique des détails rapportés n'a pas d'importance, ni pour l'auteur ni pour ses lecteurs. C'est notre intérêt d'historiens qui essaie de déterminer les niveaux d'information contenue dans le texte.

L'effet de sens que Marc veut produire sur ses lecteurs est simplement de les confirmer dans leur sentiment de supériorité par rapport à des Juifs qu'ils risquent de fréquenter. Les motifs qu'ils ont de négliger les règles de pureté juives trouvent leur sanction en la polémique que déjà Jésus a soutenue contre les Pharisiens. On devine que dans le monde qui entoure l'auteur, les Pharisiens jouent encore un rôle assez important, du moins chez les Juifs. Les chrétiens, d'origine païenne ou juive, peuvent avec bonne conscience négliger toutes les règles de pureté juive, puisque leur religion s'occupe de choses plus sérieuses, de l'attitude morale et des dispositions du coeur.

Ces réflexions succinctes veulent simplement situer la valeur d'une enquête historique telle que nous l'avons faite ci-dessus. Notre travail a de l'intérêt dans la mesure où une communauté savante aujourd'hui encore veut surmonter le fossé qui existe entre nos textes et les événements rapportés. Pour Marc lui-même, notre étu-

---

[54] Voir notre article sur les méthodes 1979, 467s.

[55] Un point de vue cher à Lars Hartman dans différents travaux; voir p. ex. son article suédois "Att förstå en nytestamentlig text", son article anglais "The Eschatology of 2 Thessalonians" ou son commentaire suédois sur Colossiens.

de serait probablement dénuée de sens, puisque pour lui le portrait de Jésus qu'il dessine devait simplement confirmer les lecteurs dans leur adhésion à la doctrine qui leur avait été transmise par leurs prédicateurs.

## *Bibliographie*

Belkin, S. 1940: *Philo and the Oral Law*, Cambridge (Mass.): Harvard University Press 1940.

Boismard, M.-E. (avec P. Benoit) 1972: *Synopse des quatre évangiles,* tome II, Paris: Cerf 1972.

Brandt, W. 1910: *Jüdische Reinheitslehre und ihre Beschreibung in den Evangelien* (BZAW 19), Giessen: Töpelmann 1910.

Buchanan, G. W. 1965: "Some Vow and Oath Formulas in the New Testament", dans *HThR* 58 (1965) 319-326.

Büchler, A. 1906: *Der galiläische 'Am ha-'Aretz des zweiten Jahrhunderts*, Wien 1906.

— 1909-10: "The Law of Purification in Mark VII.1-23", dans *ET* 21 (1909-1910) 34-40.

Bultmann, R. 1921: *Die Geschichte der synoptischen Tradition* (FRLANT 29), Göttingen: Vandenhoeck & Ruprecht 1921.

Carlston, C. E. 1968-69: "'The Things that Defile' (Mark 7,14) and the Law in Matthew and Mark", dans *NTS* 15 (1968-1969) 75-96.

Daube, D. 1972-73: "Responsabilities of Master and Disciples in the Gospels", dans *NTS* 19 (1972-1973) 1-15.

Dibelius, M. (1919) 1961: *Die Formgeschichte des Evangeliums*, Tübingen: Mohr 1919; 1961 (4e éd.).

Finkelstein, L. 1940: *The Pharisees*, Philadelphia: The Jewish Publication Society of America 1940.

Fitzmyer, J. A. 1959: "The Aramaic *Qorban* Inscription from Jebel Hallet Eth-Thuri and Marc 7,11/ Matt. 15,5", dans *JBL* 78 (1959) 60-65.

Haenchen, E. (1966) 1968: *Der Weg Jesu. Eine Erklärung des Markus-Evangeliums und der kanonischen Parallelen*, Berlin: de Gruyter 1968 (2e éd.).

Hartman, L. 1976: "Att förstå en nytestamentlig text", dans *SvTK* 52 (1976) 115-121.

— 1985: *Kolosserbrevet* (Kommentar till Nya Testamentet 12), Uppsala: EFS-förlaget 1985.

— 1990: "The Eschatology of 2 Thessalonians", dans R. F. Collins (ed.), *The Thessalonian Correspondence* (BEThL 87), Leuven: University Press – Peeters 1990, 470-485.

Hommel, H. 1954: "Das Wort *korban* und seine Verwandten", dans *Philologus* 98 (1954) 9.

Hooker, M. D. 1991: *The Gospel According to St Mark* (BNTC), London: Black 1991.

Kieffer, R. 1979: "Analyse sémiotique et commentaire. Quelques réflexions à propos d'études de Luc 10.25-27", dans *NTS* 25 (1979) 454-468.

Kingsbury, J. D. 1991: "Conclusion: Analysis of a Conversation", dans D. L. Balch, (ed.), *Social History of the Matthean Community*, Minneapolis, MN: Fortress 1991, 259-269.

Lachs, S. T. 1987: *A Rabbinical Commentary on the New Testament*, New York: Ktav 1987.

Lambrecht, J. 1977: "Jesus and the Law. An Investigation of Mk 7,1-23", dans *EThL* 53 (1977) 24-79.

Lohmeyer, E. 1937: *Das Evangelium nach Markus* (KEK 1/2), Göttingen: Vandenhoeck & Ruprecht 1937.

— 1962: *Das Evangelium des Matthäus* (KEK: Sonderband), Göttingen: Vandenhoeck & Ruprecht 1962 (3e éd.).

Luz, U. 1985: *Das Evangelium nach Matthäus*, Band I (EKK I/1), Zürich et Neukirchen-Vluyn: Benziger et Neukirchener 1985.

Merkel, H. 1968: "Markus 7,15 – das Jesuswort über die innere Verunreinigung", dans *ZRGG* 20 (1968) 340-363.

Montefiore, C. G. 1927: *The Synoptic Gospels*, I-II, London: Macmillan 1927 (2e éd.).

Neusner, J. 1973: *Eliezer ben Hyrcanus. The Tradition and the Man*, I-II, Leiden: Brill 1973.

— 1973a: *The Idea of Purity in Ancient Judaism*, Leiden: Brill 1973.

Pesch, R.1976: *Das Markusevangelium,* vol. I (HThK II/1), Freiburg-Basel-Wien: Herder 1976.

Rengstorf, K. H. 1938: *"korban"*, dans *ThWNT*, vol. 3, Stuttgart: Kohlhammer 1938, 860-866.

Schweizer, E. 1974: *Matthäus und seine Gemeinde* (SBS 71), Stuttgart: Katholisches Bibelwerk 1974.

TOB 1972: *Traduction oecuménique de la Bible,* Edition Intégrale, Nouveau Testament, Paris: Cerf et Bergers 1972.

Westerholm, S. 1978: *Jesus and Scribal Authority* (CB.NT 10), Lund: Gleerups 1978.

Zeitlin, S. 1915: "Les dix-huit mesures", dans *REJ* 67 (1915) 22-36.

# Urchristlicher Liebeskommunismus
## Zum 'Sitz im Leben' des Topos ἅπαντα κοινά in Apg 2,44 und 4,32

### Gerd Theißen

## 1. Der Stand der Diskussion

So sehr die Formel "Kirche im Sozialismus" nach 1989 in Mißkredit geriet, so unbestreitbar ist, daß die Apostelgeschichte einen "Sozialismus in der Kirche" kennt:
die Gütergemeinschaft der Urgemeinde. Ihre Beurteilung in der Forschung fiel positiv aus, wo sozialistische Ideen positive Resonanz fanden. Ihre Ablehnung war oft
mit historischer Kritik an der Geschichtlichkeit der Überlieferung verbunden. Nun
ist historisch-kritische Forschung spröde gegenüber aktuellen Anliegen. Ergebnisse, die ihnen entsprechen, sind nicht falsch; Ergebnisse, die ihnen widersprechen,
nicht wahrer als andere. Entscheidend ist für sie die Fähigkeit, mit Hilfe methodisch
disziplinierter Forschung eine Unabhängigkeit gegenüber der eigenen Zeit zu gewinnen. Angesichts des rapiden Plausibilitätsverlusts, den alle sozialistischen Ideen
seit 1989 erfahren haben, muß es daher einen historisch-kritischen Exegeten reizen,
zu überprüfen, was es mit dem "urchristlichen Liebeskommunismus" historisch auf
sich hat.

Die Forschungsgeschichte kann hier nur kurz skizziert werden[1]: Im 19. und am Anfang des 20. Jhdts. war die Auseinandersetzung um die Gütergemeinschaft Teil eines
Legitimationskampfes um die rechte Gestalt der Gesellschaft. Sozialistische Autoren
beriefen sich auf sie, um den bestehenden Besitzverhältnissen ihre Legitimation zu
entziehen. Der religiöse Sozialist W. Weitling sah 1843 in ihr sein Ideal einer Gesellschaft verwirklicht[2], der marxistische Theoretiker K. Kautsky arbeitete dagegen
1908 ihre Grenze als ein reiner "Kommunismus des Genusses" heraus, der ohne Ver-
gesellschaftung der Produktivmittel blieb[3]. Ganz anders bewertete R. v. Pöhlmann
das Urchristentum: Während sozialistische Ideen in der Antike sonst nur in Staats-

---

[1] Für die Einordnung der folgenden Forschungspositionen in ihren forschungs- und sozialgeschichtlichen Kontext verweise ich auf R. Hochschild 1993. Vgl. ferner U. Wilckens 1969, 129-144.

[2] W. Weitling 1971. Die erste Auflage erschien 1843, wurde aber von der Züricher Polizei kon-
fisziert, die zweite konnte dann 1846 erscheinen.

utopien lebendig waren und an der Realität scheiterten, verbanden sie sich im Urchristentum mit einem religiösen Glauben an das Reich Gottes, der "größte(n) Massenillusion der Weltgeschichte"[4]. Und eben das habe die sozialistische Idee immun gegen die vielen Enttäuschungen gemacht, denen diese Idee sonst ausgesetzt war.

Theologische Forschung entfaltete sich in diesem Spannungsfeld von sozialistischer Utopie und antisozialistischem Affekt. Sie brachte in die Debatte ihre historisch-kritische Methodik ein und überwand mit ihrer Hilfe die bis dahin geltende Alternative, die Aussagen über die Gütergemeinschaft seien entweder hyperbolische Aussagen über gegenseitige Hilfsbereitschaft[5] oder in dem Sinne wörtlich zu verstehen, daß es in der Urgemeinde eine Gütergemeinschaft wie bei den Essenern gegeben habe[6]. Beide Auffassungen hielten den Text noch immer für einen historischen Bericht, stritten nur über seinen Sinn. Erst die historische Kritik rechnete mit einer Diskrepanz zwischen Textsinn und Realität. Ihre radikalere Variante bei F. Chr. Baur (1845), E. Zeller (1854), F. Overbeck (1870) und H. J. Holtzmann (1882/4) vertrat die These, die Aussagen seien wörtlich zu verstehen, aber ungeschichtlich. Sie entsprächen dem idealisierten Bild einer späteren Zeit von den Anfängen der Kirche[7]. Dies ungeschichtliche Wunschbild konnte H. J. Holtzmann unbefangen als Niederschlag einer allgemeinen "sozialistischen Zeitströmung" in der Antike interpretieren[8]. Die moderate Variante historischer Kritik, vertreten z.B. durch H. A. W. Meyer (1854) und E. Troeltsch (1912), rechnete dagegen mit einem historischen Kern der Überlieferung. Eine Gütergemeinschaft habe jedoch nur in Jerusalem als Fortset-

---

[3] K. Kautsky 1908. Vgl. schon derselbe 1895, dort S.16-39: "Der urchristliche Kommunismus". Wenn Kautsky die Grenzen eines reinen Konsumkommunismus betont, so sind das für ihn nicht Grenzen des Urchristentums, sondern der antiken Wirtschaft überhaupt, die auf Genuß-, nicht auf Gewinnmaximierung ausgerichtet war. Andererseits wird bei ihm auch das Besondere des urchristlichen Kommunismus deutlich: Es ist ein Kommunismus der kleinen Leute, keine Oberschichtutopie wie z.B. bei Plato.

[4] R. v. Pöhlmann 1925, Zitat dort S. 508. Die erste Auflage erschien unter dem Titel "Geschichte des antiken Kommunismus und Sozialismus" 1893 und 1901. R. v. Pöhlmann war ein Gegner aller sozialistischen Programme.

[5] So z.B. W. M. L. de Wette 1838, z.St.; der die Gütergemeinschaft als "die herrschende Bereitwilligkeit, das Privatvermögen zur Verfügung der Gemeinde zu stellen" deutet. Diese Ansicht wird in der exegetischen Literatur immer wieder auf Lorenz von Mosheim, *Dissertationes ad historiam ecclesiasticam pertinentes,* 1743, S.36f. und 1767, S.1f. zurückgeführt (non vidi!). Sie findet sich in allgemeinen Darstellungen jener Zeit, z.B. bei E. Chastel 1853, 47-51.

[6] In der damaligen exegetischen Literatur wird diese Ansicht auf H. Grotius zurückgeführt, vgl. z.B. W. M. L. de Wette/F. Overbeck 1870, 47.

[7] Vgl. F. Chr. Baur [2]1866/7, 31ff. E. Zeller 1854, 123: "Wir haben also nicht bloß einen hyperbolischen Ausdruck …, sondern eine unhistorische Angabe …." Zugrunde liege "die hohe Vorstellung einer späteren Zeit vom Zustand der ursprünglichen apostolischen Gemeinde". F. Overbeck in: de Wette/Overbeck 1870, 46-48: Die "Sage" habe "der weltentsagenden 'Gesinnung' der Urgemeinde den Körper der That gegeben" (S.48). Ähnlich H. J. Holtzmann 1882. In diesen allgemein verständlichen Vorträgen tritt die Auseinandersetzung mit dem damaligen Sozialismus etwas deutlicher zutage als in deren wissenschaftlicher Ausarbeitung in Holtzmann 1884, 29-60.

[8] Holtzmann 1897, 389.

zung der Gemeinschaft zwischen Jesus und seinen Jüngern (nicht als Nachahmung der Essener) existiert, sie sei freiwillig gewesen; die von ihr bewirkte Verarmung erkläre, warum sie außerhalb Jerusalems keine Nachahmung fand[9]. Diesen als geschichtlich angesehenen Sachverhalt grenzte man gegen andere sozialistische Ideen ab: Die Gütergemeinschaft sei kein Programm für das ganze Volk, sondern nur für die Gemeinde gewesen. Man müsse sie "im Unterschied zu allem anderen Kommunismus den religiösen Liebeskommunismus nennen" (E. Troeltsch)[10]. Man merkt in dieser Zeit des theologischen Liberalismus eine apologetische Haltung gegenüber zeitgenössischen sozialistischen Bewegungen, aber gleichzeitig eine Unbefangenheit, im Urchristentum eine Art "Sozialismus" oder "Kommunismus" anzuerkennen – sei es als Wunschbild, sei es als Realität.

Mit dem 1. Weltkrieg ändert sich das. J. Behm konstatierte in einem – auf Oktoberrevolution und Spartakusaufstand reagierenden – Aufsatz 1920[11] eine Alternative zwischen "Kommunismus oder Urchristentum"[12]. Der Begriff Liebeskommunismus sei ein "geistreiches Spiel mit Worten, das den tatsächlichen Kontrast verwischt"[13]. Das Urchristentum wollte keine sozialen Ideen verwirklichen, sondern mit dem transzendenten Gott konfrontieren. Dieser Relativierung der Idee des urchristlichen Liebeskommunismus kam die literarkritische Erkenntnis entgegen, daß die Summarien der Apg weithin Schöpfungen des dritten Evangelisten seien (M. Dibelius)[14]. Die redaktionsgeschichtliche Erforschung seines Doppelwerks fügte dem die Erkenntnis hinzu, daß schon Lk selbst historisierend auf die idealen Anfänge der Kirche zurückblicke (H. Conzelmann)[15]. Wenn das 'Ideal' der Gütergemeinschaft schon im Urchristentum kein handlungsrelevantes Leitbild war – so durfte sich erst recht die gegenwärtige Verkündigung von ihm lösen.

In der Gegenwart gibt es zwar eine Reihe von Stimmen, die für einen geschichtlichen Kern in den Überlieferungen von einem 'Liebeskommunismus' eintreten[16]. Meist aber wird er als unhistorisches Wunschbild betrachtet.

---

[9] So H. A. W. Meyer 1854, 67f.

[10] E. Troeltsch 1912, 49. Troeltsch gesteht der Überlieferung von der Gütergemeinschaft historisch "alle innere Wahrscheinlichkeit zu" (S. 50), aber er entfernt alle für das Bürgertum anstößigen Züge aus ihr: die Ablehnung des Erwerbs, der Ungleichheit, der Familie (vgl. S. 49f.). Zu Troeltsch vgl. W. Stegemann 1993, 51-79.

[11] J. Behm 1920, 275-297. Über Bolschewiki, Spartakusbund u.ä. heißt es dort: "Aus den Verbrechergesichtern so mancher Terroristen ... grinst uns die Bestie Mensch an, von Idee und Ideal keine Spur" (S. 276).

[12] J. Behm 1920, 297.

[13] J. Behm 1920, 286.

[14] M. Dibelius 1951a, 9-28, bes. S. 15f.; ders. 1951b, 108-119, bes. S. 111-113: "Lukas ... hat die Einzelfälle, von denen er wußte, benutzt, um ein Idealbild zu zeichnen ..." (S. 112). Grundsätzlich gelte, "daß die Einzelüberlieferung ... ältere Tradition, also zuverlässiger ist als das, was der Autor hinzugetan hat, der verallgemeinernde Sammelbericht" (S. 112f.).

[15] H. Conzelmann 1963, 31/²1972, 37: Die in den Summarien dargestellte Lebensform werde von Lk "nicht als Norm für die Gestaltung der Kirche in der Gegenwart dargestellt", sie solle nur "die Einmaligkeit der idealen Urzeit vor Augen führen".

Der kritische Konsens der gegenwärtigen Forschung[17] läßt sich in vier Punkten zusammenfassen:

1. Der Autor des lk Doppelwerkes zeichnet aufgrund eines in der ganzen Antike weit verbreiteten Topos, daß "Freunde alles gemeinsam haben", ein Idealbild der Urgemeinde: In ihr gehe dieses antike Wunschbild in Erfüllung, wobei es durch die alttestamentliche Verheißung, im Gottesvolke werde es keinen Bedürftigen geben (Deut 15,4 LXX), modifiziert und erweitert wurde[18].

2. Er stellt dies Ideal in der Form von zwei Summarien[19] dar, die weitgehend sein Werk sind (Apg 2,42-47; 4,32-35). Als redaktionelle Schöpfungen haben sie wenig Anspruch auf Historizität, sie haben vielmehr die literarische Funktion, aus wenigen Einzelüberlieferungen ein geschlossenes und historisierendes Bild von der Urgemeinde der Anfänge zu entwerfen, auf die man als eine vergangene Epoche zurückblicke.

3. Dies Bild ist in sich widersprüchlich. Das Idealbild zeigt Risse, durch welche die historische Realität hindurchscheint: Die Geschichte von Ananias und Saphira setzt voraus, daß keineswegs erwartet wurde, "allen solle alles gemeinsam" sein (Apg 5,1ff). Im Grunde kann der Autor nur ein einziges Beispiel anführen, auf das er sein Bild stützen kann: das des Barnabas. Der verkauft einen Acker. Er prägte sich der Erinnerung aber nur deshalb ein, weil er die große Ausnahme war, die Lk vorschnell verallgemeinert habe.

4. Geschichtlich läßt sich die Existenz einer Gütergemeinschaft in der Jerusalemer Urgemeinde weder durch Analogien in der Umwelt noch durch Nachwirkungen im Urchristentum wahrscheinlich machen. Die Gütergemeinschaft in Qumran war eine wirtschaftlich existenzfähige Produktionsgemeinschaft einer von der Gesellschaft isolierten Gemeinde unverheirateter Männer mit straffer Organisation. In der Urgemeinde dagegen handle es sich um einen wirtschaftsfernen Kommunismus des Konsums. Er wäre nach Verbrauch der verkauften Güter auf Dauer nicht lebensfähig gewesen. Es fehlt eine straffe Organisation sowie die Trennung von der Gesellschaft. Dazu komme, daß die Urgemeinde keine Nachahmung gefunden hat: Paulus setzt in der ersten Generation in seinen Gemeinden ganz selbstverständlich Privatbesitz voraus[20].

---

[16] Es ist kein Zufall, daß eine positive Anknüpfung an die urchristliche Gütergemeinschaft und ein positiveres Urteil über ihre Geschichtlichkeit von Theologen stammen, die aus der "Dritten Welt" stammen: G. Brakemeier 1988. Brakemeier war Dozent an der Theologischen Hochschule in Sao Leopoldo und wurde 1985 Präsident der Ev.-luth. Kirche Brasiliens.

[17] Dieser kritische Konsens wird gut dargestellt durch B. H. Mönning 1978.

[18] Einen guten Überblick über die antiken Belege gibt M. Wacht 1986, 1-59; H. J. Klauck 1982, 47-79.

[19] Vgl. H. Zimmermann 1961, 71-82.

[20] All diese Argumente finden sich schon in vorbildlicher Klarheit bei Holtzmann 1884, 28-36.

Trotz dieses kritischen Konsenses gibt es immer wieder eine Skepsis gegen die Skepsis. Sie wird oft von konservativen Exegeten geäußert, die zu bedenken geben: Gewiß sei der Topos der Freundeskommunität in der Darstellung des Lk wirksam; aber er färbe nur dessen Darstellung, habe sie aber nicht hervorgebracht. Die Summarien enthielten traditionelle Elemente, wie die vielen Spannungen und Widersprüche im Text erkennen ließen. Barnabas sei nur überlieferungsgeschichtlich eine Ausnahme gewesen: In den Gemeinden, aus denen Lk seine Informationen bezog (etwa aus Antiochien?), war nur sein Beispiel bekannt; daher erführen wir nur von ihm. Gewiß sei ein Liebeskommunismus weltfremd. Aber seine "wirtschaftsferne" Lebensweise sei angesichts der urchristlichen Naherwartung vorstellbar. Für eine kurze Zeit habe die Urgemeinde mit einer abweichenden Lebensform experimentiert[21].

Die Debatte ist m.E. offen. Da Abneigung oder Zuneigung zu sozialistischen Ideen keine historischen Argumente sind, sei ein neuer Versuch gewagt. Zunächst ist das lk "Bild" in sich selbst zu untersuchen. Danach werden die oben genannten vier skeptischen Argumente neu diskutiert. Am Ende soll eine neue Lösung des Problems skizziert werden. Die Alternative, entweder handelt es sich um Rückprojektion eines Wunschbildes in die Anfänge des Urchristentums oder um eine historische Realität, erfaßt m.E. nicht alle Möglichkeiten.

## 2. Das Bild der Apostelgeschichte

Das Idealbild des Lk zeigt zweifellos Risse. Aber es wird oft übersehen, daß diese Risse der Absicht des Lk entsprechen. Lk schildert nämlich das Gemeinschaftsleben der Urgemeinde nicht als einen statischen Zustand, sondern als eine Entwicklung. Das reine Ideal steht am Anfang. Jeweils neu auftauchende Probleme führen zu einer realistischen Abänderung dieses Ideals[22].

Das Ideal wird im ersten Summarium (Apg 2,42-46) entworfen. Die Apostel spielen hier nur eine einzige Rolle: Sie vertreten die Lehre. Verkauf und Verteilung der Güter wird von allen vorgenommen. Es heißt: "Sie verkauften Güter und Habe

---

[21] Für einen geschichtlichen Kern hinter den Berichten vom Liebeskommunismus plädieren u.a. M. Hengel 1973, 39-49; J. Roloff 1981, 89-91; R. Pesch 1986, 128-133, 179-194.

[22] Für die Gegenwart des Lk ist das Ideal der Urgemeinde nicht mehr direkt verbindlich, sondern das "korrigierte Ideal", in dem die Gemeinschaftsbindung des Besitzes mit einer Verpflichtung zur Unterstützung aller Bedürftigen erhalten blieb. Conzelmann 1963, 32/²1972, 37 hat insofern Recht: Die in den Summarien dargestellte Lebensform solle "die Einmaligkeit der idealen Urzeit vor Augen führen". Eine Urzeit wäre aber nicht "ideal", wenn in ihr nicht Leitbilder für die Gegenwart enthalten wären. Wertvorstellungen als allgemeine Leitbilder und konkrete Normen können in Spannung zueinander treten!

und teilten sie unter alle aus, je nachdem es einer nötig hatte" (2,45). Das Subjekt in "verkauften" (ἐπίπρασκον) und "verteilten" (διεμέριζον) ist dasselbe.

Im zweiten Summarium (Apg 4,32-35) wird eine erste Differenzierung vorgenommen. Wohl ist "allen Gläubigen alles gemeinsam", aber erst jetzt werden diejenigen erwähnt, die "Äcker und Häuser" besaßen und verkauften. Nicht alle gehören also zu den Spendern, wie Apg 2,42-46 nahelegen könnte. Die Begüterten spielen eine besondere Rolle. Erst jetzt übernehmen die Apostel eine spezifische Rolle innerhalb der "Besitzgemeinschaft": Der Erlös (der verkauften Güter) wird zu ihren Füßen niedergelegt (4,34f.). Das Bild "jemandem etwas zu Füßen hinlegen" ist ein Bild für die Übergabe von Verfügungsgewalt (vgl. Ps 8,7; 110,1)[23]. Entscheidend ist: Das bedürftige Gemeindeglied erhält seine Unterstützung nicht direkt vom Spender, sondern von der Gesamtgemeinde, die durch die Apostel repräsentiert wird. Jede unmittelbare Abhängigkeit der Hilfsempfänger von den Hilfeleistenden wird eingeschränkt, indem die Apostel in ihrer Funktion als Verwalter der Spenden eingeführt werden. Und auch die erst jetzt erfolgende Erwähnung der wohlhabenden Spender ist kein Zufall: Sie geschieht im Hinblick auf die folgenden Beispielgeschichten, in denen zwei Typen von Spendern kontrastiert werden. Barnabas als positives Beispiel; er hat einen Acker verkauft und den Erlös den Aposteln "vor die Füße gelegt" (Apg 4,36-37), Ananias und Saphira als negatives Gegenbeispiel: Sie unterschlagen einen Teil ihrer Spende (Apg 5,1ff.).

In dieser Geschichte von Ananias und Saphira übernehmen die Apostel noch eine weitere Funktion: Sie kontrollieren die Gemeinschaftsnormen für Spender. Die Geschichte gehört zu den wenigen Strafwundern im Neuen Testament. Während Strafwunder meist dazu dienen, Normen einzuschärfen[24], zielen sie hier auf Relativierung. Lukas, der noch kurz zuvor das Ideal einer uneingeschränkten Besitzgemeinschaft beschworen hatte, zeigt nun: Die Gemeinde ist mit einer eingeschränkten Besitzgemeinschaft zufrieden. Das wird an Ananias demonstriert. Bei ihm zielt der Vorwurf darauf, daß er einen Teil des Erlöses aus seinem Acker der Gemeinde vorenthalten hat. Er wird belehrt, daß er nicht alles verkaufen oder für die Gemeinde hätte spenden müssen. Anders der Vorwurf gegen Saphira. Petrus fragt sie nicht: Habt ihr den ganzen Acker verkauft?, sondern: Habt ihr ihn für den angegebenen Betrag verkauft? Die Bedingung für eine eingeschränkte Besitzgemeinschaft ist: Wenn man etwas spendet, gleichgültig wieviel, dann sollen Angaben über die Her-

---

[23] Interessant ist eine entfernte Parallele bei Cicero, *Flacc.* 68: "In Apamea wurden knapp hundert Pfund Gold, die man vor aller Augen beschlagnahmt hatte, auf dem Markt, zu Füßen des Prätors (*ante pedes praetoris*) … abgewogen". Der Kontext zeigt: Es geht darum, jeden Verdacht einer Unterschlagung zurückzuweisen. Wie Apg 5,1ff. zeigt, haben auch die Apostel die Funktion, über die Einhaltung der Normen zu wachen.

[24] Vgl. die bei A. Weiser 1981, 139-142 zusammengestellten Beispiele von Strafwundern.

kunft der Spenden stimmen. Die Geschichte zeigt: Auch gegenüber Großspendern werden die Gruppennormen geltend gemacht. Die Begüterten haben nicht von vornherein das höhere Sozialprestige. Vielmehr stehen sie im Verdacht, bei ihren Zuwendungen hinter ihren Möglichkeiten zurückzubleiben und dies zu verschleiern. Entscheidend für die Gemeinde ist Aufrichtigkeit, und darin sind ärmere und reichere Spender gleich. Spendenehrlichkeit ist unabhängig von Spendenhöhe.

Während Apg 4,32-5,11 Probleme darstellen, die beim Einsammeln der Spenden auftreten, werden in Apg 6,1-7 Probleme der Verteilung behandelt. Die "Hellenisten", d.h. die griechisch sprechenden Teile der Gemeinde, kritisieren, daß ihre Witwen bei der täglichen Versorgung "übersehen werden". Der Konflikt wird durch eine Arbeitsteilung zwischen den Aposteln und sieben "Diakonen" bewältigt. Die Apostel sollen sich ganz auf den "Dienst des Wortes" (6,4) konzentrieren können. Dafür übernehmen die "Diakone" den "Dienst an den Tischen" (6,2). Lk spricht zwar nicht ausdrücklich von "Diakonen", aber wahrscheinlich hat er bei dieser ersten Aufgliederung urchristlicher Ämter das Verhältnis von "Bischöfen" und "Diakonen" vor Augen, das in seiner Zeit schon verbreitet war.

Einen letzten Schritt auf die ihm vertrauten gegenwärtigen Verhältnisse zu findet sich im "Testament des Paulus" (Apg 20,18-35). Paulus verpflichtet in ihm die Gemeindeleiter von Ephesus, hart zu arbeiten, damit sie die Schwachen unterstützen könnten. Er selbst stellt sich als Vorbild solcher sozial-asketischen Lebensweise hin. Damit hat Lk klargemacht: Er erwartet einen innergemeindlichen Bedarfsausgleich nicht (allein) durch Spenden wohlhabender Gemeindeglieder. Er erwartet ihn als Ergebnis menschlichen Fleißes: Jeder, der arbeiten kann, soll von seinem Überschuß abgeben. Was den Gemeindeleitern zur Verpflichtung gemacht wird, gilt als Ideal für alle – auch für die kleinen Leute, die von ihrer Hände Arbeit leben. Die Gemeinde wird dadurch unabhängig von reichen Spendern (Apg 20,32-35)[25].

Aus der idealen Besitzgemeinschaft ist im lk Bild der Geschichte also schrittweise eine praktikable Solidargemeinschaft geworden: Eine Gemeinschaft von "klei-

---

[25] Anders das Ergebnis von F. W. Horn 1983, bes. 119-120: Die lk "Paränese ist Reichenparänese, welche auf eine privatisierte Einstellung vermögender Christen zu Besitz und auf ein dadurch bestimmtes Selbstverständnis zielt" (S. 119). Das alles soll freilich im "ekklesialen Raum" stattfinden. Daher die Kurzformel: "Lk bietet 'Almosenethik' im ekklesialen Raum" (S. 120). Dazu ist zu sagen: (1) Lk wendet sich nicht nur an Reiche, sondern gerade in seinem letzten Wort zum Thema Apg 20,32-35 an Bedürftige, die Barmherzigkeit nur durch ihre Handarbeit ausüben können – so wie die Jüngerin Tabita, die "viel Gutes tat und reichlich Almosen gab" (Apg 9,36), indem sie in eigener Arbeit Röcke und Mäntel herstellte (Apg 9,39). (2) Lk denkt nicht nur an individuelle Almosen, die einzelnen Bedürftigen zugewendet werden, sondern an einen von der Gemeinde organisierten Bedarfsausgleich, zu dem die Gemeinde sich verpflichtet weiß. Durch seine Institutionalisierung überschreitet er die Grenzen einer "privatisierten" Einstellung zum Besitz. Insofern enthält er Elemente einer Sozialethik, und zwar in Gestalt einer Gemeindeethik.

nen Leuten", die hart arbeiten müssen, um notleidende Gemeindeglieder unterstützen zu können. Einsammeln und Verteilen der Spenden ist institutionell geregelt. Der Aufruf zum Spenden geht von der "Lehre" der Gemeindeleiter aus; die Verteilung übernehmen "Diakone". Beide Funktionen liegen in verschiedener Hand – was ein Schutz gegen die Veruntreuung von Spenden ist. In diesen Gemeinden gibt es Tendenzen, sich der Solidarität zu entziehen – besonders deutlich bei den Begüterten. In drastischen Geschichten vergewissern sie sich jedoch der gemeinsamen Überzeugung: Unaufrichtigkeit bei Spenden ist todbringende Sünde gegen den Heiligen Geist.

Lk vollzieht also in narrativer Weise den Weg vom Ideal zur Realität[26]. Sein Bild von realen und realisierbaren Gemeindeverhältnissen stammt aus den ihm vertrauten Gemeinden. Umstritten ist, woher sein Idealbild stammt, das er in der Urgemeinde verwirklicht sieht. Hat Lk den antiken Freundschaftstopos in die Frühzeit der Urgemeinde zurückprojiziert?

## 3. Vier Argumente historischer Skepsis

Um eine Antwort auf diese Frage geben zu können, diskutieren wir noch einmal die vier Argumente historischer Skepsis gegen die lk Darstellung des urchristlichen Liebeskommunismus.

### 3.1. Der antike Freundschaftstopos und seine redaktionelle Verwendung in Apg 2,44 und 4,32

Der antike Freundschaftstopos war weit verbreitet[27]. Er wird ausdrücklich als "Sprichwort" zitiert. So bei Aristoteles: "Richtig ist das Sprichwort 'Freunden ist Besitz gemeinsam' (κοινὰ τὰ φίλων), denn in Gemeinschaft (ἐν κοινωνίᾳ) besteht Freundschaft" (Arist., *NE* VIII,11 1159b 31-33; vgl. *NE* IX,8 1168b 6-8)[28]. Dies Sprichwort wird für den lateinischen Bereich durch Cicero bezeugt: ... *ut in Graecorum proverbio est: amicorum esse communia omnia* (*off.* 1,16,51). Für das hellenistische Judentum findet sich ein Beleg bei Philo: Die gastfreundliche Aufnahme des Abraham durch Melchisedek zeige, daß Melchisedek dessen Glück als sein ei-

---

[26] Eine ganz andere Deutung der Besitzaussagen im lk Doppelwerk findet sich bei L. T. Johnson 1977. Die Besitzaussagen hätten metaphorischen Charakter. Sie sollen z.B. die Einheit des Gottesvolks und die Autorität der Apostel darstellen.

[27] Vgl. Klauck 1982, bes. 51f.; Wacht 1986; Mönning 1978, 74-86.

[28] Weitere Belege für den griechischen Bereich: Plato, *rep.* IV 424; V 449c; *leg.* V 739 b-d (dort bezeichnet er die Aussage ausdrücklich als alten Spruch); Eur., *Andr.* 376; *Or.* 733; *Phoin.* 250; Plut., *Praec. Coniug.* 34; Lukian, *Merc. cond.* 20.

genes betrachtet habe: "Und es war wirklich sein eigenes, denn 'gemeinsam ist' nach dem Sprichwort, 'der Besitz der Freunde' (κοινὰ τὰ φίλων), ganz besonders der der Guten, die das Ziel haben, Gott wohlgefällig zu sein" (Philo, *Abr.* 235).

Dies Sprichwort konnte mannigfaltig abgewandelt werden. Die Stoiker übertrugen es auf die Ehe. Die Ehe führe dazu, daß alles gemeinsam sei, lehrte Antipater aus Tarsos (Stob. IV,22,25). Ihr Zweck sei, daß die Ehepartner "zusammen miteinander leben und zusammen Kinder erzeugen und alle Dinge gemeinsam haben und nichts für sich (κοινὰ δὲ ἡγεῖσθαι πάντα καὶ μηδὲν ἴδιον), auch nicht ihren Körper" (Musonius 13A).

In den kynischen Briefen wird der Topos auf das Verhältnis von Bettelphilosoph und Spender angewandt. Wenn Gott Besitzer von allem sei, so gelte: "Der Besitz ist Freunden gemeinsam (κοινὰ δ' εἶναι τὰ τῶν φίλων), der Weise aber sei Freund Gottes. Deshalb wirst du nur um das bitten, was dein ist (τὰ ἴδια)" (Ps-Diogenes 10). Verwandt ist seine Verwendung im hellenistischen Judentum, wo der Topos nicht nur auf Gastfreundschaft angewandt wurde (s.o. Philo, *Abr.* 235), sondern auch auf Armenunterstützung: "Bist du reich, dann strecke deine Hand den Armen hin; an dem, was Gott dir gab, gewähre Bedürftigen Anteil. Aller Lebensunterhalt soll (allen) gemeinsam (zugute kommen) (ἔστω κοινὸς ἅπας ὁ βίος), und alles geschehe in Eintracht" (Ps.-Phok. 28-30).

Auch die Übertragung des Sprichwortes auf bestimmte Sondergruppen ist in der Antike belegbar. Pythagoras soll als erster gesagt haben, "daß Besitz Freunden gemeinsam sei (κοινὰ τὰ φίλων εἶναι) und daß Freundschaft in Gleichheit bestehe (καὶ φιλίαν ἰσότητα)". Seine Schüler hätten deshalb ihren Besitz zusammengelegt (Diog. Laert. 8,10). Epikur soll dagegen diese Besitzgemeinschaft als Zeichen von Mißtrauen unter Freunden verworfen haben (Diog. Laert. 10,11). In spätantiker Zeit wird die Gemeinschaft der Pythagoräer dann in ebenso idealisierenden Farben geschildert wie die Urgemeinde. So bei Porphyrius (*vit. Pyth.* 20) und Jamblichus (im 4. Jhdt. n.Chr.):

> Ursprung der Gerechtigkeit ist nun Gemeinschaft, gleiches Recht und eine Verbundenheit, in der alle ganz wie ein einziger Leib und eine einzige Seele dasselbe empfinden und mein und dein gleich bezeichnen ... Gemeinsam gehörte allen alles ohne Unterschied, privat besaß keiner etwas. Fand einer an der Gemeinschaft Gefallen, so gebrauchte er die gemeinsamen Güter aufs Gerechteste; andernfalls nahm er seine eigene Habe und mehr als er zum gemeinsamen Besitz beigesteuert hatte und ging von dannen.
> (Iamblichus, *vit. Pyth.* 167f.)

Für uns sind solche Überlieferungen über die Pythagoräer wichtig, weil Josephus die Essener mit den Pythagoräern vergleicht (*ant.* 15,371) und ihre Besitzgemeinschaft so beschreibt, daß der antike Topos der Freundschaftskommunität anklingt:

"Besitz aber ist ihnen gemeinsam" (τὰ χρήματά τε κοινά ἐστιν αὐτοῖς) (*ant.* 18,20).

Wir können hier darauf verzichten, den Gedanken der Freundschaftskommunität auch in Staatsutopien, sei es in theoretischen Entwürfen[29], geographischen Utopien[30] oder mythischen Urzeitträumen[31], nachzuweisen. Entscheidend ist ein erstes Ergebnis: Der Topos gewinnt seinen konkreten Sinn immer erst in bestimmten Kontexten. In der Apg ist eindeutig an Gemeinschaftsbesitz gedacht. Die Besitzenden verkaufen ihre Güter (von *allen* Gütern ist nicht direkt die Rede). Sie schaffen so einen Gemeinschaftsbesitz, über den die Apostel zugunsten der Bedürftigen verfügen. Wenn Lk später von diesem Ideal eines umfassenden Gemeinschaftsbesitzes (mit Tendenz, allen Besitz für die Gemeinschaft zu beanspruchen) abrückt, so ist das kein Argument gegen den klaren Sinn seiner Aussagen in den Summarien. Die narrative Abwandlung einer ursprünglichen Vorstellung gehört zu seiner Darstellungsart.

Ein zweites Ergebnis ist: Der Topos war so verbreitet, daß er überall denkbar ist, wo hellenistischer Einfluß wirksam war. Und dieser beginnt nicht erst mit dem Verfasser des lk Doppelwerks. Er beginnt schon mit den "Hellenisten" in der Urgemeinde (Apg 6,1). Könnten nicht schon sie diesen Topos auf die christliche Gemeinschaft angewandt haben? Zumal der Topos für das hellenistische Judentum nachweisbar ist und die in Apg 6,1ff. auftretenden "Hellenisten" aus dem hellenistischen Judentum stammen[32]. Könnte es also sein, daß Lk diesen Topos von den "Hellenisten" empfangen hat? Oder hat er ihn selbst erst ins Urchristentum eingeführt?

Für die letzte Möglichkeit spräche, daß Lk auch sonst Bildungsreminiszenzen in sein Werk einfügt. Die Anlehnung an die allgemeine literarische Kultur ist schon im

---

[29] Im platonischen Staatsideal wird der Gedanke der Freundschaftskommunität für die beiden oberen Stände, die Wächter und Philosophen, verpflichtend gemacht (vgl. Plato, *rep.* III 416de; V 457; V 462; V 464b-e). Auch in den Nomoi, wo ein gewisser Realismus zum Entwurf eines zweitbesten Staates führte, hält er für den besten Staat am Ideal der Gütergemeinschaft fest – als Erfüllung des Topos "Freunden ist Besitz gemeinsam" (*leg.* V 739c). Aristoteles lehnte dagegen die platonische Frauen-, Kinder- und Gütergemeinschaft ab.

[30] Was Plato für die Zukunft erträumte, schilderten andere als utopische Realität in einem fiktiven Land. Diodor Siculus hat ein Romanfragment des Euhemeros von Messene erhalten, in dem eine Insel "Panchaia" geschildert wird, wo alles Gemeinbesitz ist (Diod. 5,45). Ebenfalls durch Diodor erhalten ist die Utopie des 'Sonnenstaates' von Jambulos (Diod. 2,55-60), die einen radikalen Kommunismus auf fernen Äquatorinseln verwirklicht sieht.

[31] Als mythische Urzeit schildert Plato sein Bild von der Gütergemeinschaft der Krieger im ursprünglichen Athen (*Crit.* 110 cd). Seneca entwirft im 90. Brief ein farbiges Bild vom paradiesischen Urzustand: "Was war glücklicher als jenes Menschengeschlecht? Gemeinsam genoß man die Natur: Sie sorgte wie eine Mutter für den Schutz aller, sie war Gewähr für den sorgenfreien Besitz der gemeinsamen Güter ..." (Sen., *epist.* 90,38).

Prooemium spürbar (Lk 1,1-4). Sie zeigt sich in der Übernahme des sokratischen Topos, man müsse Gott mehr gehorchen als Menschen (Apg 4,19; 5,19 vgl. Plato, *Ap.* 29d) und in der Parallelisierung des Paulus mit Sokrates durch den Vorwurf, er wolle fremde "Dämonen" in Athen einführen (Apg 17,18 vgl. Xen., *Mem.* 1,1,1; Plato, *Ap.* 29d). Bildungsreminiszenzen sind das Aratoszitat in Apg 17,28 (vgl. Arat. 5) sowie die geläufigen Redewendungen "Geben ist seliger als Nehmen" (Apg 20,35) und "gegen den Stachel löcken" (Apg 26,14).

Insgesamt aber spricht die urchristliche Rezeptions- und Traditionsgeschichte des Topos "Freunden ist alles gemeinsam" gegen die Annahme, erst Lk habe ihn eingeführt. Er begegnet bei ihm schon in abgewandelter Weise: Lk redet nicht von "Freunden", sondern von "Gläubigen"; und er fügt die alttestamentliche Verheißung hinzu: "Es wird kein Bedürftiger (ἐνδεής) unter ihnen sein" (LXX Deut 15,4). Beide Variationen sind nicht spezifisch lk Abänderungen. Denn nur die lk (und die johanneischen) Schriften nennen im Neuen Testament die Christen gelegentlich "Freunde" (Lk 12,4; Apg 27,3). Nur Lk läßt in seinen Gleichnissen "Freunde" auftreten.[33] Lk hätte den Topos ohne Abänderung auf die Urgemeinde anwenden können. Auch seine Verschmelzung mit den Traditionen biblischen Glaubens ist nicht unbedingt lk Redaktion: Deut 15,4 wird nur an dieser Stelle im NT direkt oder indirekt aufgegriffen, und der von dort stammende Begriff "Bedürftiger" (ἐνδεής) findet sich im NT nur in Apg 4,34.

Nicht nur die Abänderungen des Topos, auch der Topos selbst steht innerhalb des lk Doppelwerks relativ isoliert da. Wenn der Topos wirklich das von Lk geschaffene Idealbild urchristlicher Gemeinden enthielte, – warum hat er ihn dann nicht Jesus in den Mund gelegt, etwa in Form eines Logions: "Habt alles gemeinsam und nennt nichts euer eigen!"? Warum hat er die Darstellung vom Verkauf von Gütern nicht stärker an die entsprechenden Aufforderungen Jesu angeglichen: "Alles, was du

---

[32] Die Herkunft der "Hellenisten" aus der Diaspora ergibt sich aus 1. der Herkunft des Nikolaos aus Antiochien (Apg 6,5), 2. den Kontakten des Stephanus zu den in Jerusalem lebenden Diasporajuden aus der Kyrenaika, Alexandrien, Kilikien und Asien (Apg 6,9), 3. der Notiz in Apg 11,20, daß unter den vertriebenen Christen einige aus Zypern und der Kyrenaika stammten und unter Heiden für den christlichen Glauben geworben hätten. Für eine spezielle Beziehung des Gedankens "Gläubigen ist alles gemeinsam" zu den Hellenisten in der Urgemeinde spricht u.a. die lk Komposition: Erst nach dem Pfingstwunder (und als Folge der Ausgießung des Heiligen Geistes) lebt die Urgemeinde nach dieser "Devise". Das Pfingstwunder aber bestand ja gerade darin, daß Menschen aus der ganzen Diaspora von der Botschaft angesprochen wurden (vgl. Apg 2,9-11). Noch Lk bringt so den Beitritt von "Hellenisten" zur Jerusalemer Urgemeinde in Verbindung mit Besitzgemeinschaft.

[33] Vgl. Lk 11,5-8; 14,7-11; 15,3-7. 8-10. 11-32. Sonst begegnet der Begriff "Freunde" nur in Mt 11,19 und im Joh-Ev (Joh 3,29; 11,11; 15,13ff.).

hast, verkaufe und verteile es an die Armen!" (Lk 18,22 vgl. 19,8)[34]? Aber von "Armen" ist im Zusammenhang mit der Urgemeinde (und in der ganzen Apg) nie die Rede, trotz der großen Bedeutung dieses Begriffs im Lk-Evangelium[35].

Während somit der Freundschaftstopos innerhalb des lk Doppelwerks wenig integriert ist, begegnet er im urchristlichen Schrifttum unabhängig von Lk in *Did.* 4,8: "Du sollst dich vom Bedürftigen nicht abwenden, vielmehr alles mit deinem Bruder teilen und nicht sagen, daß es dein Eigentum sei! Wenn ihr nämlich Genossen im Unsterblichen seid, um wieviel mehr im Sterblichen!" (vgl. *Barn.* 19,8)[36]. Auch Justin wendet den Topos in *Ap.* 1,14,2 unabhängig von Lk auf die christliche Gemeinschaft an: "Wir, die wir Reichtum und Besitz über alles liebten, machen jetzt auch das, was wir bereits haben, zum Gemeingut und teilen es mit jedem, der bedürftig ist." Er denkt dabei genauso wenig wie *Did.* 4,8 an eine konsequente Besitzgemeinschaft. Unter den Sentenzen des Sextus finden wir die Maxime: "Die, die Gott, und zwar als Vater, gemeinsam haben, ihren Besitz aber nicht, handeln unfromm" (Sextus 228). Selbst Außenstehenden fiel die Gemeinschaftsbindung des Besitzes bei den Christen auf. Lukian von Samosata verspottete die Christen, weil sie alles "als gemeinsam betrachten" (κοινὰ ἡγοῦνται) (*peregr.* 13). Wenn der Freundschaftstopos unabhängig von Lk im Urchristentum begegnet, aber bei Lk selbst relativ isoliert auftaucht, so spricht das für die Annahme, Lk gebe hier eine Tradition wieder, d.h. ein Bild von der Urgemeinde, das er nicht geschaffen, sondern von anderen empfangen hat.

---

[34] Lk hat bei der Bearbeitung der Perikope vom reichen Jüngling in Lk 18,22 zwei kleine Zusätze vorgenommen, die im folgenden gesperrt gedruckt sind: π ά ν τ α ὅσα ἔχεις πώλησον καὶ δ ι ά δος πτωχοῖς. Ph. Esler 1987, 186, will aus der zweiten Änderung den bewußten Versuch erschließen, "to bring Jesus' command into line with the language used of the distribution of alms in Acts 4,35". Dort steht ebenfalls διεδίδετο. Aber warum findet sich keine entsprechende Anpassung bei dem entscheidenden πάντα? Lk sagt in beiden Summarien wohl, daß die Urgemeinde alles (ἅπαντα!) gemeinsam hatten. Aber er sagt nicht ausdrücklich, daß die (begüterten) Christen *alles* verkauften. In 2,45 heißt es nur: "Sie verkauften die Güter und Besitztümer", in 4,34 liest man: "Diejenigen, die Besitzer von Grundstücken und Häusern waren, verkauften (sie) und brachten den Erlös der verkauften (Habe) und …". Vor allem fehlen in den Summarien die "Armen"!

[35] Natürlich setzt Lk auch in der Apg "Arme" in der Gemeinde voraus, wenn er z.B. von "Schwachen" (Apg 20,35) spricht. Möglicherweise aber kann er sich in der Gemeinde gar keine "Armen" vorstellen – weil in ihr Deut 15,4 in Erfüllung gehen soll. Ob er das Jesuswort "Die Armen habt ihr immer bei euch" (Mk 14,7) bewußt weggelassen hat, ist nicht sicher; denn er hat die ganze Perikope Mk 14,3-9 ausgelassen bzw. durch Lk 7,36-50 ersetzt.

[36] In *Did.* 4,8 begegnen drei Anklänge an Apg 4,32-34: Die Rede vom "Bedürftigen" (ἐνδεόμενος) erinnert an den "Bedürftigen" (ἐνδεής) in Apg 4,34. Der Gemeinschaftsgedanke klingt in συγκοινωνήσεις δὲ πάντα an. Die Wendung "sagen, es ist mein eigen" begegnet sowohl in *Did.* 4,8 wie Apg 4,32. Die Wortwahl ist jedoch immer so verschieden, daß eine wörtliche Bezugnahme auf Apg 4,32-34 m.E. ausgeschlossen ist – zumal die Gattung verschieden ist: Hier eine Mahnung, dort ein schilderndes Summarium.

## 3.2. Die Summarien und ihr historischer Quellenwert

Ein naheliegender Einwand ist: Das lk Bild einer urchristlichen Besitzgemeinschaft ist in redaktionell gestalteten Summarien erhalten. Aber spricht das gegen den traditionellen Charakter dieses Bildes oder einen historischen Kern in ihm? Die vom Mk-Evangelisten geschaffenen Wundersummarien erzählen z.B. nur von jenen Wundern Jesu, die als historisch gelten: von Exorzismen und Heilungen; von Naturwundern schweigen sie (Mk 1,32-34; 3,7-12; 6,53-56). Das redaktionelle Summarium der Verkündigung Jesu in Mk 1,14-15 ist eine zutreffende Zusammenfassung der Verkündigung des historischen Jesus; nur der Begriff εὐαγγέλιον weist auf nachösterlichen Sprachgebrauch. Redaktionell geschaffene Summarien können also einen historischen Kern haben. Das könnte auch für die Summarien der Apg gelten – selbst wenn Lk sie geschaffen haben sollte[37].

Aber ist das so sicher? Man fragt sich, warum er größere Summarien nur in den ersten fünf Kapiteln der Apg bringt[38]. Die Auskunft, er wolle aus allzu spärlichen Nachrichten ein geschlosseneres Bild der Urgemeinde entwerfen, erklärt nicht viel. Auch von der Gemeinde in Korinth oder in Ephesus hatte er nur wenige Einzelnachrichten. Wie nahe hätte es gelegen, das Bild der Tätigkeit des Paulus in diesen beiden Gemeinden durch Summarien abzurunden! Unbestreitbar ist ferner, daß Lk seine Überlieferungen von verschiedenen Gemeinden und Städten mit zutreffendem "Lokalkolorit" färbt: In Thessaloniki weiß er von "Politarchen" (Apg 17,6.8), Athen wird als Stadt der Philosophen geschildert (Apg 17,18ff.), Korinth stellt er als Sitz eines Prokonsuls dar (Apg 18,12). In Ephesus zeichnet er ein für die damaligen Verhältnisse realistisches Bild von den Machtverhältnissen (Apg 19,32ff.)[39]. Für jede dieser Städte und Gemeinden verarbeitet er spezifisches ihm zugetragenes oder von ihm selbst erworbenes Wissen. Sollte das bei Jerusalem und der Jerusalemer Urgemeinde anders sein?

Auch die Sprache der Summarien spricht für Tradition: Die "summarische Form" gab Lk mehr schriftstellerische Freiheit als die Wiedergabe konkreter Ein-

---

[37] Ein Unterschied ist freilich zwischen den Summarien der Evangelien und der Apostelgeschichte zu beachten: Die ersteren weisen auf Wundertaten Jesu hin, die in vielen Einzelüberlieferungen bekannt waren. Sie reduzieren das Außergewöhnliche, indem sie nur von Heilungen und Exorzismen berichten. Die Summarien der Apg steigern dagegen das Außergewöhnliche einzelner Überlieferungen zu einem diese überbietenden Ideal einer allgemeinen Besitzgemeinschaft.

[38] Neben den größeren Summarien (Apg 2,42-47; 4,32-35; 5,12-16), die sich alle auf das Leben der Urgemeinde in Jerusalem beziehen, kennt Lk noch kurze summarische Notizen über das Wachsen des Wortes, die sich auf Jerusalem (Apg 6,7), die Gemeinden in Palästina (9,31), Kleinasien (16,5) und Ephesus (19,20) beziehen; vgl. ferner 12,24. Zur Unterscheidung beider Formen von Summarien H. A. Brehm 1990, 29-40.

[39] Vgl. zu den griechischen Städten W. Elliger 1987.

zelüberlieferungen. Abweichungen von seinem sonstigen Sprachgebrauch weisen hier noch mehr auf Traditionsbindung als anderswo. Nun finden wir Singuläres gerade in den Formulierungen, welche die Gütergemeinschaft betreffen: Das Wort κοινωνία (Apg 2,42) ist ein lk Hapaxlegomenon[40]. Auch κοινός ist bemerkenswert, denn dies Adjektiv hat außerhalb der Summarien den Sinn von "unrein" (vgl. Apg 10,14.28; 11,8). Auffallend ist die Wendung "Güter und Habe" (κτήματα καὶ ὑπάρξεις), die ohne Analogie ist. Ihre zweite Hälfte weicht vom lk Sprachgebrauch ab: Normalerweise spricht Lk von den ὑπάρχοντα (achtmal in seinem Evangelium); nur in Apg 2,45 begegnet das Substantiv ὑπάρξεις[41]. Das Verb διαμερίζειν begegnet in der Bedeutung "verteilen" im LkEv nur, wo es Tradition ist: in den Einsetzungsworten (Lk 22,17)[42] und in einem AT-Zitat (Lk 23,31); sonst bedeutet es "spalten" (Lk 11,17.18 und Lk 12,52f.). Im zweiten Summarium ist die Wendung "ein Herz und eine Seele" singulär (Apg 4,32). Daß im AT Herz und Seele häufig nebeneinander stehen – auch in so vertrauten Texten wie dem Sch$^e$ma ("... von ganzem Herzen und von ganzer Seele" Deut 6,5) – weist nicht unbedingt auf lk Formulierung; schon vor ihm kann diese Formulierung im Christentum geläufig gewesen sein. Das spezifisch lk Wort zur Bezeichnung von Einmütigkeit wäre ὁμοθυμαδόν (Apg 1,14; 2,46; 4,24; 5,12 u.ö.). Singulär sind schließlich die Wörter ἐνδεής und κτήτορες (Apg 4,34). Nimmt man hinzu, daß die Summarien Spannungen und Inkohärenzen im Aufbau zeigen, die immer wieder eine Trennung von Tradition und Redaktion nahegelegt haben[43], so verdichtet sich der Eindruck: Lk betätigt sich bei

---

[40] Das Wort κοινωνία ist dagegen bei Paulus dreimal mit der Jerusalemer Gemeinde verbunden, dreimal mit der Kollekte (Röm 15,25; 2 Kor 8,4; 9,13), einmal mit den Abmachungen des Apostelkonzils (Gal 2,9). Das könnte auf eine durch die Tradition vorgegebene Bindung dieses Begriffs an die Jerusalemer Gemeinde auch bei Lk deuten!

[41] Im NT sonst nur noch Heb 10,34. E. Haenchen 1968, 157, erklärt die Abweichung vom lk Sprachgebrauch so: "τὰ ὑπάρχοντα bezeichnet im lukanischen Sondergut jeweils den gesamten Besitz. Neben dem Substantiv τὰ κτήματα war es demnach hier nicht am Platze, wo von einzelnen besonderen Besitztümern gesprochen werden soll." Leider stimmt die Prämisse nicht. Wenn Lk emphatisch den ganzen Besitz bezeichnen will, spricht er von "allen Besitztümern" (πάντα τὰ ὑπάρχοντα) (vgl. Lk 12,44; 14,33). Umgekehrt wird vom ungerechten Verwalter gesagt, er verschlendere die Besitztümer seines Herrn (τὰ ὑπάρχοντα αὐτοῦ), ohne daß damit alle Besitztümer gemeint sind.

[42] Ich nehme an, daß Lk hier in Übereinstimmung mit den ihm vertrauten Abendmahlsworten seiner Gemeinde(n) formuliert.

[43] Einen Überblick über die Forschung geben Haenchen 1968, 155-157; Zimmermann 1961, 71-73. Ausführlich B. H. Mönning 1978, 120-147, dort mit Übersichtstabellen zu den verschiedenen Quellenscheidungen S. 147 und 260f. Bei den verschiedenen Versuchen gibt es immer wieder zwei Möglichkeiten: Entweder wird angenommen, Lk habe ein ihm vorgegebenes Traditionsstück erweitert. So J. Jeremias 1937, 205-221 [= 1966, 238-255, dort S. 240f.].: In Apg 2,41-47 und 5,11-16 sei jeweils ein älterer Bestandteil 2,41f. und 5,11-14 durch Nachträge erweitert worden. Oder man nimmt eine sekundäre Einfügung in der Mitte der Summarien an. So für alle drei Summarien P. Benoit 1950, 1-10.

den Summarien der Apg genauso wenig als "frei schaffender Künstler" wie bei den Summarien in seinem Evangelium. Gewiß setzt er dort eigene Akzente, aber im großen und ganzen bearbeitet er die mk Tradition (vgl. Mk 1,32ff. mit Lk 4,40f.; Mk 3,7ff. mit Lk 6,17ff.).

## 3.3. Die Widersprüche in der Darstellung der Gütergemeinschaft

Das lk Bild des urchristlichen Liebeskommunismus enthält zweifellos Widersprüche – aber auch die historische Skepsis gegen sie ist von Widersprüchen nicht frei: Man kann nicht auf der einen Seite Einzelbeispiele gegen die Summarien ausspielen, auf der anderen Seite aber die Summarien aus den Einzeltraditionen (als deren unzulässige Verallgemeinerung) ableiten.

Unverkennbar ist: Die Summarien gehen über das hinaus, was die Beispiele sagen. Das Beispiel von Ananias und Saphira würde nur die Verallgemeinerung erlauben, daß man seine Habe ganz oder teilweise verkaufte, je nach Willen und Vermögen. Gerade das sagen die Summarien nicht. Das Beispiel des Barnabas handelt vom Verkauf eines "Ackers" (Apg 4,36f.). Aber im vorhergehenden Summarium wird von "Landstücken *und* Häusern" gesprochen. Für den Verkauf von "Häusern" hatte Lk keinen Beleg in den Einzeltraditionen der Apg[44]. Das allgemeine Bild, das Lk von der Urgemeinde überliefert bekommen hatte, war "idealer" als die Einzeltraditionen, so daß er dieses Bild sekundär an seine Einzeltraditionen anpassen mußte. Die einleitende Feststellung in 4,32: "Keiner nannte etwas von dem, was er hatte, sein Eigentum, sondern sie hatten alles gemeinsam" steht z.B. in Spannung zu dem später erwähnten Verkauf von "Ländern und Häusern" durch einzelne (4,34). Wenn allen alles gemeinsam war, hatte keiner ein Verkaufsrecht. Das individuelle Verkaufsrecht ist aber notwendig, um die folgenden Beispiele (Barnabas, Ananias und Saphira) vorzubereiten. Das zweite Summarium wurde hier an die folgenden Einzelgeschichten angeglichen.

Richtig ist auch, daß Lk nicht viele Beispielgeschichten gekannt haben wird. Aber Barnabas muß deshalb kein Sonderfall in Jerusalem gewesen sein, sondern verdankt seine Erwähnung möglicherweise der Tatsache, daß er der bekannteste Fall außerhalb Jerusalems war[45]. Er hatte in weiten Gebieten Syriens, Zyperns und Kleinasiens missioniert und gehörte in Antiochien zu den einflußreichsten Gestalten (vgl. Apg 13,1f.; Gal 2,11-14). Wenn Lk seine Überlieferung über die Urgemeinde aus Traditionen der aus Jerusalem geflohenen "Hellenisten" bezogen hat,

---

[44] Lk könnte von Häuserverkäufen unabhängig von Einzeltraditionen erfahren haben. Bei Christen, die Wandercharismatiker wurden, könnte es vereinzelt zum Verkauf von Häusern gekommen sein – und nicht nur dazu, daß sie diese "verließen" (Mk 10,28-30).

[45] So Hengel 1973, 41.

wäre verständlich, daß diese den Barnabas besonders hervorhoben.

Auch die anderen Widersprüche in der Darstellung der "Besitzgemeinschaft" der ersten Christen sind kein entscheidendes Argument gegen einen historischen Kern der Überlieferung. Die Aussagen schwanken zwischen: Besitzgemeinschaft ohne Privatbesitz (Apg 4,32), Gemeinschaftsbesitz, der auf privaten Zuwendungen basiert (Apg 4,34f.) und weiter existierendem Privatbesitz mit sozialer Verpflichtung (Apg 5,1ff.). Ähnliche Widersprüche begegnen auch in der Darstellung der Essener bei Philo. Zunächst stellt er fest, daß die Essener "mit Absicht weder Geld noch Land besitzen" (*prob.* 77). Das klingt nach völliger Ablehnung des Geldes. Aber dann wird ihnen dennoch Geldbesitz zugeschrieben: Einerseits in Form einer Gemeinschaftskasse, die allen gehört: "Sodann haben sie alle nur eine Vorratskammer und allen gemeinsam gehörendes Geld zum Ausgeben; allen gemeinsam gehören auch die Kleider sowie die Speisen" (*prob.* 86). Andererseits in Form von privaten Einkünften mit sozialer Bindung: "Denn was sie als Lohn für ihre tägliche Arbeit erhalten, das bewahren sie nicht als ihr persönliches Eigentum, sondern stellen es der Gemeinschaft zur Verfügung und lassen den daraus sich ergebenden Nutzen allen zukommen, die von ihm Gebrauch machen wollen" (*prob.* 86). Ähnlich äußert sich Philo über Häuser, die wohl den einzelnen gehören, aber allen zugänglich sind: "Niemand besitzt ein Haus so zu eigen, daß es nicht auch allen gemeinsam gehörte" (*prob.* 85). Früher schloß man aus solchen Widersprüchen, daß die essenische Gütergemeinschaft eine Fiktion sei[46]. Seit der Entdeckung der Qumrantexte wissen wir jedoch, daß hinter den idealisierenden und widersprüchlichen Aussagen des Philo (und des Josephus) eine historische Realität steht.

## 3.4. Die historische Wahrscheinlichkeit einer urchristlichen Gütergemeinschaft

Historisch wahrscheinlich wird eine umstrittene Überlieferung, wenn wir sie aus zeitlich vorhergehenden Voraussetzungen ableiten, durch Analogien erhellen und ihre geschichtlichen Wirkungen verständlich machen können.

Die historische Voraussetzung der "Gütergemeinschaft" ist die Verkündigung des historischen Jesus. Sie enthält reichtumskritische Motive. Solange Jesus mit seinen Jüngern heimat- und besitzlos im Lande umherzog, stimmten Existenz und Verkündigung überein. Mit der Gründung einer christlichen Ortsgemeinde in Jerusalem stellte sich das Problem, wie man die besitzkritischen Überlieferungen der Jesustradition in der veränderten Situation einer seßhaften Ortsgemeinde praktizieren konnte. Der Gedanke einer Besitzgemeinschaft (oder eines großen Gemeinschaftsbesitzes), der jedes Gemeindeglied vor Not schützen sollte, lag nahe. Eine

---

[46] So bes. W. Bauer 1924, 386-430.

Analogie finden wir nicht weit entfernt von Jerusalem: Die Qumrangemeinde praktizierte eine Art Gütergemeinschaft. Verbindungen zwischen Qumran und Jerusalem sind gut bezeugt. Es gab in Jerusalem ein Essenertor (*bell.* 5,145). Die Essener lehnten zwar den Tempelkult als unrein ab, sandten aber Weihegaben in den Tempel (*ant.* 18,19). Die Idee einer Gütergemeinschaft war in Jerusalem bekannt. Das belegt der Jerusalemer Josephus, der die Gütergemeinschaft der Essener mit großer Sympathie darstellt (*bell.* 2,122). Nichts spricht dagegen, daß auch andere Jerusalemer von ihr fasziniert waren. Warum nicht auch einige Christen in Jerusalem?

Wie ist es aber mit den Auswirkungen? Spricht nicht die fehlende historische Ausstrahlungskraft des urchristlichen Liebeskommunismus gegen deren Geschichtlichkeit? Wo wir von anderen Gemeinden in Palästina hören, wird nichts Vergleichbares vorausgesetzt (vgl. Apg 9,32ff.; 9,36ff.). Vor allem finden wir in den paulinischen Gemeinden – trotz des in ihnen lebendigen Enthusiasmus – keine Bemühung, eine konsequentere Gütergemeinschaft zu realisieren. Im Gegenteil, als in Korinth Konflikte zwischen Reichen und Armen beim Abendmahl sichtbar werden, wird dieser nicht auf der Grundlage des Gleichheitsgedankens gelöst; vielmehr empfiehlt Paulus den Bessergestellten, sich zu Hause satt zu essen (1 Kor 11,17ff.)! Je isolierter aber die Urgemeinde mit ihrer Gütergemeinschaft im ganzen Urchristentum erscheint, um so weniger wahrscheinlich wird die Gütergemeinschaft selbst: War die Urgemeinde nicht das große Vorbild für alle Gemeinden? Warum wurde sie nicht nachgeahmt[47]?

Gerade an diesem Punkt ist aber die Analogie der Essener aufschlußreich. Auch die Gütergemeinschaft der Essener wurde nur in ihrem Zentrum, in Qumran, praktiziert. Die im Lande verstreut lebenden Essener hatten Privatbesitz (vgl. CD 13,14-16; 12,9-11; 14,12-16). Die Sonderstellung Qumrans erklärt sich daraus, daß die dort ansässige Gemeinde konsequent jene priesterliche Reinheit und Heiligkeit praktizieren wollte, die sie im Jerusalemer Tempel vermißte. Die Gemeinde war ein Ersatz für den Tempel. Wieviel mehr konnte die Jerusalemer Urgemeinde, die in der heiligen Stadt selbst lebte, für sich eine Sonderstellung beanspruchen! Für diese Sonderstellung gibt es immerhin einen Beleg: die Kollekte des Paulus. Um für sie zu werben, greift Paulus auf den Gedanken eines konsequenten Besitzausgleichs zurück. So stellt er in 2 Kor 8 die armen Gemeinden in Makedonien der reicheren korinthischen Gemeinde als Vorbild für die Kollekte hin. Es kommt ihm aber nicht der Gedanke, daß der Besitzunterschied zwischen Makedonien und Achaia einen Ausgleich erfordere – genausowenig wie der Besitzunterschied in der korinthischen Gemeinde selbst. Vielmehr wendet er den 'Gleichheitsgedanken' nur auf die Jerusalemer Gemeinde in ihrem Verhältnis zu den heidenchristlichen Gemeinden an.

---

[47] So Holtzmann 1884, 35.

Nicht daß die anderen (d.h. die Jerusalemer) gute Tage haben sollen und ihr Not lei-
det, sondern daß es zur Gleichheit kommt (ἀλλ' ἐξ ἰσότητος). Jetzt helfe euer Überfluß ihrem Mangel ab, damit danach auch ihr Überfluß eurem Mangel abhelfe und
so Gleichheit verwirklicht werde, wie geschrieben steht: 'Wer viel sammelte, hatte
keinen Überfluß, und wer wenig sammelte, hatte keinen Mangel'.
(2 Kor 8,13-15)

Warum aktiviert er solche Gleichheitsgedanken nur im Hinblick auf Jerusalem?
Warum nicht bei anderen Gemeinden? Ist Paulus dem Gleichheitsgedanken in Jerusalem begegnet? War er die Legitimationsgrundlage seiner Kollekte? Zu erklären
wäre dann nur noch, warum aus einer Gleichheit innerhalb der Urgemeinde das Postulat einer Gleichheit zwischen ihr und den hellenistischen Gemeinden in der
Diaspora entstehen konnte (dazu s.u.).

Abschließend ist das Argument zu bedenken, der Jerusalemer Liebeskommunismus sei eine in sich widersprüchliche Idee gewesen, die nicht praktizierbar war:
Wie sollte er über längere Zeit Bestand haben, wenn Besitz nur verteilt, nicht aber
neuer Besitz geschaffen wurde? Dies Argument bewegt sich auf einer anderen Ebene als die bisherigen Argumente. Liefen jene darauf hinaus, daß Lk ein Idealbild in
die Anfänge zurückprojiziert habe, so ist das letzte Argument nur ein Einwand gegen den dauernden Erfolg des urchristlichen Liebeskommunismus, nicht aber gegen dessen Geschichtlichkeit überhaupt, im Gegenteil: Es setzt einen geschichtlichen Kern in den Überlieferungen voraus[48].

## 4. Versuch einer neuen Lösung

Mit all diesen Argumenten ist die Geschichtlichkeit des urchristlichen Liebeskommunismus nicht bewiesen. Die Beobachtungen zu den formalen Aspekten der Überlieferung (zu Topik und Summarienform) zeigen ja nur, daß nicht erst Lk den Traum
einer Gütergemeinschaft in die Anfänge des Urchristentums zurückprojiziert hat.
Die historischen Überlegungen zum Inhalt der Überlieferung (zu ihren Widersprüchen, geschichtlichen Voraussetzungen, Analogien und Auswirkungen) lassen nur
die Möglichkeit zu, daß die Überlieferung einen Anhalt in der Urgemeinde selbst

---

[48] Die Vertreter der Historizität des Liebeskommunismus weisen in der Regel auf die Situation
einer Gemeinde mit akuter Parusieerwartung hin, die eine so wirtschaftsfremde Lebensform wie die
in Apg 2,42ff. und 4,32ff. geschilderte ermöglicht haben könnte. Sachlich mit Recht, jedoch ohne
direkten Anhalt in den Quellen. In den Summarien der Apg finden wir nichts, was auf die eschatologische Erwartung einer bald sich wunderbar verändernden Welt hinweist, angesichts derer das Experiment des urchristlichen Liebeskommunismus nur ein schwaches Vorspiel gewesen wäre.
Allenfalls könnte man im "Jubel" (ἀγαλλίασις) der Urgemeinde einen Niederschlag der hochge-
spannten eschatologischen Erwartung vermuten (Apg 2,46). Man darf diese Erwartung für die Urgemeinde zwar voraussetzen. Lk hat sie wie auch sonst zurückgedrängt.

hat. Die Alternative, sie sei entweder historisch oder ein späterer Wunschtraum, ist jedoch zu einseitig. Möglicherweise wurde dieser Wunschtraum nicht erst von Lk, sondern von der Urgemeinde selbst geträumt. Anders gesagt: Der "urchristliche Liebeskommunismus" könnte eine Reformidee der Jerusalemer Urgemeinde selbst gewesen sein. Die Idee wäre in diesem Falle nicht der immer hinter ihr zurückbleibenden Realität erst gefolgt (so die übliche Sicht), sondern sie könnte ihr vorausgegangen sein. Der Topos: "Allen Gläubigen ist alles gemeinsam" könnte in den Anfängen des Urchristentums als Schlagwort lebendig gewesen sein. Die Hypothese kann hier nur kurz skizziert werden, ohne daß alle Voraussetzungen und Konsequenzen entfaltet werden können.

Ausgangspunkt dieser Hypothese ist die Tatsache, daß es sich bei dem Motiv des πάντα κοινά um einen hellenistischen Topos handelt, der mit biblischen Traditionen verschmolzen wurde. Als Trägergruppe eines solchen Topos kommen vor allem die Hellenisten innerhalb der Urgemeinde in Frage. Diese Hellenisten begegnen uns in Apg 6,1ff. im Streit um die Versorgung der Witwen in einer Weise, die den Gedanken nahe legt: Damals könnte der Topos "allen Gläubigen ist alles gemeinsam" von der ganzen Gemeinde lebendig gewesen sein, um das Problem der Versorgung bedürftiger Gemeindeglieder – allen voran der Witwen – zu lösen[49].

Wir können nicht alle Probleme von Apg 6,1ff. diskutieren[50]. Ein Problem aber

---

[49] Daß bei Lk sachlich zusammengehörende Überlieferungen und Aussagen auf verschiedene 'Abschnitte' der Apg verteilt werden, läßt sich auch an anderen Stellen belegen: Die beiden Reisen des Paulus nach Jerusalem (Apg 11,30 und 15,1ff.) gehören sachlich zusammen. Die drei Berichte von der Bekehrung des Paulus verteilen auf eine kunstvolle Weise verschiedene Sachaspekte auf drei Berichte (Apg 9,1-19; 22,3-21; 26,9-20). Ebenso könnte Lk bewußt drei Mal die "soziale Frage" in der Urgemeinde thematisiert – und dabei sachlich Zusammengehörendes auf drei Textpassagen verteilt haben (Apg 2,42-47; 4,32-37; 6,1-6).

[50] Zur Forschungsgeschichte vgl. H. Neudorfer 1983 und C. C. Hill 1992, 5-17. Gegenwärtig konkurrieren drei Erklärungsansätze für den Streit zwischen Hellenisten und Hebräern:

1. Seit F. C. Baur nimmt man eine tiefere theologische Spaltung der Urgemeinde an: Die Hellenisten repräsentieren einen radikaleren, thora- und tempelkritischen Flügel der Urgemeinde, der sich auch organisatorisch verselbständigt. Vgl. z.B. Haenchen 1968, 213-222. Gegen diese Annahme eines tiefen theologischen Gegensatzes wendet sich das o.g. Buch von Hill 1992.

2. Sprachliche Ursachen macht Hengel 1975, 151-206 für die Spaltung verantwortlich: Die griechischsprachigen und die aramäischsprachigen Christen begannen, eigene Gottesdienste in ihrer Muttersprache zu feiern. Später erst wurde auch ihre Diakonie getrennt.

3. Soziale Gründe betonen dagegen N. Hyldahl 1974, und N. Walter 1983, 370-393: Die christliche Gemeinde organisierte eine Unterstützung für Witwen von hellenistischen Juden, weil diese von der allgemeinen Witwenversorgung der jüdischen Gemeinde ausgeschlossen waren. Ich hoffe, meine eigene Sicht an anderer Stelle entfalten zu können. Für die Lokalisierung des Topos "Allen Gläubigen ist alles gemeinsam" in den Debatten der Urgemeinde ist nur die von allen anerkannte Tatsache eines Konflikts wichtig, bei dem das soziale Problem der Witwenversorgung eine Rolle spielte.

sei herausgehoben; die Asymmetrie zwischen dem in Apg 6,1ff. dargestellten Streit und dessen Lösung. Als Konfliktparteien treten auf: Hebräer und Hellenisten, d.h. aramäisch und griechisch sprechende Mitglieder der Jerusalemer Urgemeinde. Die Lösung des Konflikts aber wird einer Gruppe von sieben Männern anvertraut, die alle hellenistische Namen tragen – also Vertretern nur einer der beiden Konfliktparteien. Eine "normale" Konfliktlösung würde ein paritätisch besetztes Gremium vorsehen. Denkbar wäre diese einseitige Konfliktlösung jedoch, wenn die Hellenisten ein Programm hatten, dem alle zustimmen konnten – z.B. wenn in ihren Reihen die Utopie lebendig war, daß in der Gemeinde allen alles gemeinsam sein sollte, so daß keiner Not leiden mußte.

Man kann noch einen Schritt weiter gehen. Dies Programm war möglicherweise die tiefere Ursache des Streits und nicht erst eine Antwort auf ihn. So könnte eine weitere Merkwürdigkeit der Überlieferung erklärt werden. Nach Apg 6,1 protestieren nicht die "Witwen" gegen ihre Vernachlässigung, sondern die Hellenisten sind unzufrieden damit, daß "ihre Witwen" übersehen wurden, d.h. die Anführer im Streit sind nicht die Betroffenen selbst, sondern andere. Sind für sie die Witwen nur ein Anlaß, um ihre Vorstellungen durchzusetzen?

Was aber war dieser "Anlaß"? Wieder ist eine genaue Lektüre des Textes aufschlußreich. Er sagt: Es erhob sich ein Murren unter den Hellenisten, "weil ihre Witwen bei der täglichen Versorgung übersehen wurden (παρεθεωροῦντο)" (Apg 6,1). Das entscheidende Verb "übersehen" steht im Imperfekt, nicht im Aorist, d.h. es wird nicht an einen plötzlich einsetzenden neuen Zustand gedacht, sondern an einen wiederkehrenden oder längere Zeit andauernden Zustand. Die Witwen "pflegten" übersehen zu werden. Sie waren bisher in die allgemeine Versorgung nicht integriert – möglicherweise weil sie gar nicht als arm galten. Als aber immer mehr Witwen aus der aramäisch sprechenden Bevölkerung durch die Gemeinde versorgt werden sollten – denn die Gemeinde wurde immer größer (Apg 6,1) –, da verlangten die Hellenisten, daß konsequenterweise auch ihre Witwen in die gemeinschaftliche Versorgung einbezogen würden. Denn "alles sollte allen gemeinsam sein". Mit diesem Programm konnte sich die ganze Gemeinde einverstanden erklären.

Aber nicht nur von ihrem Programm her, sondern auch aufgrund ihres sozialen Status kamen vor allem die Hellenisten für eine 'Organisation' eines konsequenten Bedarfsausgleichs in Frage. Viele Indizien sprechen dafür, daß die Hellenisten in der Urgemeinde wohlhabender waren als die aus Galiläa nach Jerusalem übergesiedelten Fischer und Bauern[51]. Wahrscheinlich hat einer von ihnen, Barnabas, durch eine große Spende die materielle Grundlage für das Experiment einer Gütergemeinschaft gelegt (Apg 4,36f.). Bei den "Hebräern" wurde das Programm dieser Gütergemeinschaft dagegen u.U. viel zurückhaltender aufgenommen. Ananias und Saphira könnten – wegen ihrer Namen – zu den Hebräern gehört haben. Aber das ist nicht sicher.

Wenn die "Hellenisten" die Verfechter des Programms "Allen ist alles gemeinsam" waren, so wird die Wirkungsgeschichte dieses "Programms" verständlich. Nach der Flucht der Hellenisten aus Jerusalem und der Gründung "hellenistischer" Gemeinden in Syrien (Apg 11,19ff.) wurde aus einem Programm für einen Besitzausgleich innerhalb der Jerusalemer Gemeinde eine Idee zum Besitzausgleich zwischen den neugegründeten Diasporagemeinden und Jerusalem (Gal 2,10; 2 Kor 8,13-15). Barnabas, der durch seine große Spende das Experiment des Liebeskommunismus in Jerusalem (mit-)ermöglicht hatte, wird jetzt zum Verfechter eines solchen überregionalen Besitzausgleichs (Gal 2,10). Als *exemplum* für die Kollekte der Diasporagemeinden für Jerusalem ging die große Spende des Diasporajuden Barnabas für Jerusalem in die Überlieferung ein (Apg 5,36f.).

Die hier vorgeschlagene Hypothese läuft also darauf hinaus, daß der urchristliche Liebeskommunismus eine Reformidee innerhalb der Jerusalemer Urgemeinde war, die von den Hellenisten ideell und materiell getragen wurde[52]. Zur Verwirklichung dieser Reformidee sind wahrscheinlich ernsthafte Bemühungen gemacht worden.

Nicht zuletzt dank des hellenistischen Programms "πάντα κοινά" erlebte die Gemeinde einen Aufschwung. Sie wurde in der Öffentlichkeit bekannt. Ihre abweichende Lebensweise und ihre Ideen wurden diskutiert. Kein Wunder, daß konservative Kreise in Jerusalem die neue Bewegung unterdrücken wollten. Stephanus, die

---

[51] Argumente für den relativ gehobenen Status der "hellenistischen (d.h. griechischsprachigen) Juden" in Jerusalem im Vergleich zu den "Hebräern" in der Urgemeinde sind: Die aus Galiläa übergesiedelten Anhänger Jesu hatten dort die Grundlagen ihrer wirtschaftlichen Existenz zurückgelassen. Die "Hellenisten", die sich der Gemeinde anschlossen, waren dagegen schon länger in Jerusalem ansässig – oft schon seit Generationen, wie die Theodotos-Inschrift zeigt (*CIJ* 2 Nr. 1404). Die Ossuarien-Inschriften in Jerusalem sind zu 55% aramäisch, 36% griechisch und 8% bilingual (nach J.N. Sevenster 1968, 146). Ossuarien gehören zu Bestattungen in Felsengräbern. Diese waren ein Luxus. Die armen Leute wurden in Erdgräbern bestattet, wie man sie in Qumran gefunden hat. In der Oberschicht Jerusalems waren also mindestens 44% zweisprachig. Hellenisten waren in ihr überrepräsentiert. Nimmt man das in der Apg (vgl. 4,13 mit 6,3) angedeutete Bildungsgefälle zwischen den "Aposteln" und den "Sieben" hinzu, so ist der Schluß erlaubt: Die Hellenisten in der Urgemeinde gehörten zu den bessergestellten Kreisen. L. Schottroff/W. Stegemann 1978, 152 haben recht, wenn sie die hellenistischen Witwen zu einer Gruppe von Menschen zählen, "die durchaus nicht – grundsätzlich – zu den bedürftigen zu rechnen sind".

[52] Die Verbindung des Topos "Allen ist alles gemeinsam" mit den Hellenisten hat Lk aufgelöst. Das ist verständlich. Denn er wurde gewiß in der ganzen Gemeinde gerne rezipiert. Die Verbindung mit den Hellenisten geht aber nicht nur aus den vielen hellenistischen Parallelen zu diesem Topos hervor. Das erste Summarium, das in seinem Lichte das Leben der Urgemeinde schildert, folgt unmittelbar nach dem Pfingstereignis. Mit ihm aber ist eine Aufnahme vieler Diasporajuden in die urchristliche Gemeinde verbunden.

leitende Gestalt der Hellenisten, wurde hingerichtet, sein Kreis mußte Jerusalem verlassen. Das Experiment eines urchristlichen Liebeskommunismus fand ein rasches Ende, ehe es auf seine Praktikabilität getestet werden konnte. Seine Idee aber hat nachgewirkt.

Im Kern sagt die hier vorgelegte Hypothese: Nicht erst Lk träumte von einem gemeinschaftlichen Leben der Urgemeinde mit sozialem Bedarfsausgleich, sondern schon in der Urgemeinde war dieser Traum lebendig – mehr als Programm und Lösungsansatz denn als eine organisierte Lebensform. Der Topos πάντα κοινά war in der Antike so offen und wurde in so verschiedenen Kontexten verwandt, daß man aus ihm keine konkreten Organisationsformen ableiten konnte. Und doch hat er zum Handeln motiviert. Er wurde vielleicht nie auf Dauer realisiert. Aber der in ihm enthaltene Traum wurde wirklich geträumt – und nicht erst sehr viel später zurückdatiert. Sein Kern ist einfach und klar: Niemand soll in der Gemeinde Not leiden. Unter diesem Aspekt ist jeder Privatbesitz Gemeinschaftsgut. Lk weiß sehr wohl, daß es dabei mit einem Appell an die Reichen zum Besitzverzicht nicht getan ist. Im Testament des Paulus Apg 20,32-35 stellt er klar: Was man für Bedürftige und Schwache gibt, muß zunächst durch Arbeit erwirtschaftet werden. Und dabei sind alle gefordert – auch die Ärmeren, die wie Paulus selbst nur die Arbeit ihrer eigenen Hände in den Bedarfsausgleich einbringen können.

## Bibliographie

Bauer, W. 1924: Art. "Essener", in: *RE Suppl.* IV (1924) 386-430.

Baur, F. Chr. 1845: *Paulus, der Apostel Jesu Christi,* Leipzig: Fues [2]1866/7.

Behm, J. 1920: "Kommunismus und Urchristentum", in: *NKZ* 31 (1920) 275-297.

Benoit, P. 1950: "Remarques sur les 'sommaires' des Actes 2,42 à 5", in: *Aux sources de la tradition chrétienne, FS M. Goguel,* Neuchâtel/Paris: Delachaux/Niestlé 1950, 1-10.

Brakemeier, G. 1988: *Der "Sozialismus" der Urchristenheit. Experiment und neue Herausforderung* (KVR 1535), Göttingen: Vandenhoeck & Ruprecht 1988.

Brehm, H. A. 1990: "The Significance of the Summaries for Interpreting Acts", in: *SWJT* 33 (1990) 29-40.

Dibelius, M. 1951a: "Stilkritisches zur Apostelgeschichte" (1923), in: idem, *Aufsätze zur Apostelgeschichte* (FRLANT 42), Göttingen: Vandenhoeck & Ruprecht 1951, 9-28.

— 1951b: "Der erste christliche Historiker" (1948), in: idem, *Aufsätze zur Apostelgeschichte,* 108-119.

Chastel, E. 1853: *Études historiques sur l'influence de la charité durant les premiers siècles chrétiens,* Paris: Capelle 1853.

Conzelmann, H. 1963/²1972: *Die Apostelgeschichte* (HNT 7), Tübingen: Mohr (Siebeck) 1963/ ²1972.

Elliger, W. 1987: *Paulus in Griechenland* (SBS 92/93), Stuttgart: Katholisches Bibelwerk 1987.

Esler, Ph. 1987: *Community and Gospel in Luke-Acts. The Social and Political Motivation of Lucan Theology* (MSSNTS 57), Cambridge: Cambridge University Press 1987.

Haenchen, E. 1968: *Die Apostelgeschichte* (KEK 3), Göttingen: Vandenhoeck & Ruprecht ⁶1968.

Hengel, M. 1973: *Eigentum und Reichtum in der frühen Kirche. Aspekte einer frühchristlichen Sozialgeschichte,* Stuttgart: Calwer 1973.

— 1975: "Zwischen Jesus und Paulus. Die 'Hellenisten', die 'Sieben' und Stephanus (Apg 6,1-15; 7,54-8,3)", in: *ZThK* 72 (1975) 151-206.

Hill, C. C. 1992: *Hellenists and Hebrews. Reappraising Division within the Earliest Church,* Minneapolis, MN: Fortress 1992.

Hochschild, R. 1993: *Sozialgeschichtliche Exegese. Entstehungsgeschichte und Ergebnisse einer neutestamentlichen Forschungsrichtung,* Diss. theol. Heidelberg 1993.

Holtzmann, H. J. 1882: *Die ersten Christen und die soziale Frage* (Wissenschaftliche Vorträge über religiöse Fragen 5), Frankfurt/Main: Diesterweg 1882.

— 1884: "Die Gütergemeinschaft der Apostelgeschichte", in: Festschrift für E. Zeller (Straßburger Abhandlungen zur Philosophie), Freiburg/Tübingen: Mohr 1884, 29-60.

— 1897: *Lehrbuch der neutestamentlichen Theologie,* Bd 1, Freiburg/Leipzig: Mohr 1897.

Horn, F. W. 1983: *Glaube und Handeln in der Theologie des Lukas* (GTA 26), Göttingen: Vandenhoeck & Ruprecht 1983.

Hyldahl, N. 1974: *Udenfor og indenfor,* Kopenhagen: Gad 1974.

Jeremias, J. 1937/66: "Untersuchungen zum Quellenproblem der Apg", in: *ZNW* 36 (1937) 205-221 [= *Abba. Studien zur neutestamentlichen Theologie und Zeitgeschichte,* Göttingen: Vandenhoeck & Ruprecht 1966, 238-255].

Johnson, L. T. 1977: *The Literary Function of Possessions in Luke-Acts* (SBL.DS 39), Missoula, MT: Scholars Press 1977.

Kautsky, K. 1895: *Die Vorläufer des Neueren Sozialismus. Bd.1,1. Von Plato bis zu den Wiedertäufern,* Stuttgart 1895 (= Berlin: Dietz 1991).

— 1908: *Der Ursprung des Christentums. Eine historische Untersuchung,* Stuttgart 1908 (= Berlin: Dietz ¹⁶1977).

Klauck, H. J. 1982: "Gütergemeinschaft in der klassischen Antike, in Qumran und im Neuen Testament", in: *RdQ* 41 (1982) 47-79.

Meyer, H. A. W. 1854: *Kritisch exegetisches Handbuch über die Apostelgeschichte,* Göttingen: Vandenhoeck & Ruprecht ²1854.

Mönning, B. H. 1978: *Die Darstellung des urchristlichen Kommunismus nach der Apostelgeschichte des Lukas,* Diss. theol. Göttingen 1978.

von Mosheim, L. 1743: *Dissertationes ad historiam ecclesiasticam pertinentes,* Altona: Iversen 1743.

Neudorfer, H. 1983: *Der Stephanuskreis in der Forschungsgeschichte seit F. C. Baur*, Gießen/Basel: Brunnen 1983.

Pesch, R. 1986: *Die Apostelgeschichte* (EKK V,1), Zürich/Neukirchen: Benziger/Neukirchener 1986.

von Pöhlmann, R.1925: *Geschichte der sozialen Frage und des Sozialismus in der antiken Welt*, 2 Bde, München: Beck [3]1925 (= Darmstadt: Wissenschaftliche Buchgesellschaft 1984).

Roloff, J. 1981: *Die Apostelgeschichte* (NTD 5), Göttingen: Vandenhoeck & Ruprecht 1981.

Schottroff, L./Stegemann, W. 1978: Jesus von Nazareth – Hoffnung der Armen (UTB 639), Stuttgart: Kohlhammer 1978.

Sevenster, J. N. 1968: *Do You Know Greek?* (NT.S 19), Leiden: Brill 1968.

Stegemann, W. 1993: "Zur Deutung des Urchristentums in den 'Soziallehren'", in: F. W. Graf/T. Rendtorff (Hgg.), *Ernst Troeltschs Soziallehren. Studien zu ihrer Interpretation*, Gütersloh: Gerd Mohn 1993, 51-79.

Troeltsch, E. 1912: *Die Soziallehren der christlichen Kirchen und Gruppen*, Tübingen: Mohr 1912.

Wacht, M. 1986: "Gütergemeinschaft", in: *RAC* 13 (1986) 1-59.

Walter, N. 1983: "Apostelgeschichte 6,1 und die Anfänge der Urgemeinde in Jerusalem", in: *NTS* 29 (1983) 370-393.

Weiser, A. 1981: *Die Apostelgeschichte* (ÖTBK 5,1), Gütersloh/Würzburg: Gerd Mohn/Echter 1981.

Weitling, W. 1971: *Das Evangelium des armen Sünders – Die Menschheit wie sie ist und wie sie sein sollte*, W. Schäfer (Hg.), Reinbek: Rowohlt 1971.

de Wette, W. M. L. 1838: *Kurze Erklärung der Apostelgeschichte*, Leipzig: Weidmann 1838.

de Wette, W. M. L./Overbeck, F. 1870: *Kurze Erklärung der Apostelgeschichte*, Leipzig: Hirzel [4]1870.

Wilckens, U. 1969: "Urchristlicher Kommunismus", in: W. Lohft/B. Lohse (Hgg.), *Christentum und Gesellschaft. Ringvorlesung der Ev.-Theol. Fakultät der Universität Hamburg*, Göttingen: Vandenhoeck & Ruprecht 1969, 129-144.

Zeller, E. 1854: *Die Apostelgeschichte nach ihrem Inhalt und Ursprung kritisch untersucht*, Stuttgart: Carl Mäcken 1854.

Zimmermann, H. 1961: "Die Sammelberichte der Apostelgeschichte", in: *BZ* 5 (1961) 71-82.

# Der vorchristliche Paulus
## Überlegungen zum biographischen Kontext biblischer Überlieferung — zugleich eine Antwort an Martin Hengel

Georg Strecker †
im Zusammenarbeit mit Torsten Nolting

## 1. Einleitung

In der Geschichte der Forschung findet sich eine große Verschiedenartigkeit der Paulusauslegungen und damit auch des Bildes des Apostels. Hier wird Paulus einmal als Rabbi, ein anderes Mal als Hellenist oder als hellenistischer Judenchrist dargestellt. Es werden auf ihn die Bezeichnungen Chiliast, Mystiker, Gnostiker und Mysterienadapt angewendet. Die verschiedenen Urteile zeigen nicht nur die Disparatheit auf, welche die gegenwärtige Forschung kennzeichnet, sie haben vielmehr jeweils Anhaltspunkte in der paulinischen Theologie selbst.

Das paulinische Denken ist religionsgeschichtlich gesehen wie das Urchristentum allgemein ein synkretistisches Phänomen. In ihm stoßen religiöse Strömungen verschiedener Herkunft aufeinander. Im Kontext der Frage nach den religionsgeschichtlichen Voraussetzungen paulinischer Theologie ist besonders auf das Verhältnis des Paulus zum Judentum einzugehen. Nach verbreiteter Anschauung hat die Kontinuität zwischen dem Judentum und dem paulinischen Denken eine für das Verständnis der Theologie des Paulus ausschlaggebende Bedeutung. Demnach ist Paulus auch als Christ ein Jude geblieben. Dem steht jedoch gegenüber, daß Paulus sich als Apostel an die Heiden verstanden hat und durch seine Berufung zum Heidenapostel, die zugleich seine Bekehrung einschließt, nach eigenem Verständnis fundamental vom Judentum geschieden wußte[1].

Freilich lebte der Apostel auch nach seiner Bekehrung in einer jüdischen Vorstellungswelt und machte von ihr in seiner Verkündigung wie auch in seinem theologischen Denken umfassend Gebrauch. Die Grundlagen jüdischer Vorstellungen, die sich in den paulinischen Briefen finden, reichen bis in die Zeit vor der Bekehrung

---

[1] Vgl. Gal 1,13ff.; Phil 3,7.

des Paulus zurück. Diese vorchristliche Zeit in der paulinischen Biographie näher zu betrachten, ist somit eine Aufgabe, die bei der Behandlung des historischen Kontextes paulinischer Literatur nicht außer acht gelassen werden darf.

## 2. Die Position Martin Hengels

Die Frage nach dem vorchristlichen Paulus kann nur auf der Grundlage der Selbstzeugnisse in den echten Paulinen beantwortet werden. Die Apostelgeschichte wird die paulinischen Aussagen ergänzen, der Auctor ad Theophilum muß seine eigenen Nachrichten über Paulus jedoch einer kritischen Prüfung unterziehen lassen. Hinsichtlich des Quellenwertes stehen die paulinischen Briefe grundsätzlich über der Apostelgeschichte, so daß von hier aus deren Aussagen entweder bestätigt oder widerlegt werden können. Einen grundlegend anderen Weg beschreitet *Martin Hengel* in seinem Aufsatz *Der vorchristliche Paulus* (Hengel 1991).

2.1. Hengel versucht, ein umfassendes Bild des jungen Juden Saulus zu zeichnen. Die Apostelgeschichte erscheint dabei als wertvolle Ergänzung[2] der autobiographischen Quellen und der "indirekten Schlüsse"[3] aus der Theologie des Paulus, die einen "latent 'jüdischen' Charakter"[4] aufweisen soll, wobei sich Hengel von einer skeptischeren Einschätzung des historischen Wertes der lukanischen Berichte abgrenzt[5].

Dem Zeugnis der Apostelgeschichte könne in größerem Umfang Vertrauen entgegengebracht werden als dies in der kritischen Forschung in der Regel der Fall ist. Schließlich lägen den lukanischen Berichten genaue Beobachtungen zugrunde, wenn der Verfasser z. B. in Apg 22,3d andeutungsweise die Art und Weise des Unterrichts im "pharisäischen Lehrhaus" zu Jerusalem behandelt und die ἀκρίβεια als

---

[2] Vgl. Hengel 1991, 179.

[3] Ebd., 178.

[4] Ebd., im Original hervorgehoben. Vgl. dazu auch die epigonale Arbeit von *Karl-Wilhelm Niebuhr* "Heidenapostel aus Israel" (1992), der Hengels Ergebnisse zum Werdegang des vorchristlichen Paulus voraussetzt, zum Teil nur noch einmal zusammenfaßt, ohne neue Argumente anzuführen, und daher hier weitgehend unberücksichtigt bleiben kann. Er kommt (a. a. O., 110) zu dem Urteil: "Stellt Paulus damit auch seinen Wandel vom exemplarischen Vertreter jüdischen Lebens zum Apostel Jesu Christi als radikale Kehrtwendung dar, so beurteilt er diese Wende doch nicht als Abkehr von den Inhalten jüdischen Gottesglaubens und Heilsverständnisses".

[5] Ebd. 179 Anm. 6.

besonderes Merkmal der Pharisäer herausstellt[6]. Die kritische Forschung treffe in ihrem Gebrauch der Apostelgeschichte als Quelle eine Tendenzauswahl[7]. Dabei seien viele historische Tatsachen heute doch nur aufgrund des lukanischen Zeugnisses bekannt[8].

Als beispielhaften Repräsentanten einer nach Hengel richtigeren Einschätzung des Quellenwertes der Apostelgeschichte wird der Althistoriker *E. Meyer* angeführt. Meyer sieht zwar die Tendenz, die dem Werk zugrunde liegt, meint aber: "Ein Mißgriff war es, daraus zu folgern, daß sie ein spätes, das ursprüngliche Material verfälschendes und daher geschichtlich kaum verwendbares Buch sei. Vielmehr ist es die Auffassung eines mithandelnden Zeitgenossen selbst, die uns hier entgegentritt: wir sehn, wie Lukas, der Schüler und Begleiter des Paulus, ( ... ) sich das große Problem, das die werdende Kirche bewegt ( ... ), unter dem Einfluß der Lehren seines Meisters zurechtgelegt hat. Das führt mit Notwendigkeit zu einer Verschiebung in der Auffassung der Einzelereignisse und zu dem Versuch einer Überbrückung der Gegensätze. Aber die Grundlinien der Entwicklung sind trotzdem richtig gezeichnet"[9].

Die für ihn maßgebliche Grundhaltung bei der Benutzung der Apostelgeschichte als Quelle kann Hengel von daher wie folgt formulieren: "Paulus ist gewiß selbst die Hauptquelle, aber wir können Lukas heranziehen, solange keine wirklich schwerwiegenden Gründe gegen ihn sprechen, denn die ahistorische Tendenz, die ihm ständig vorgeworfen wird, er verfälsche die wahren geschichtlichen Sachverhalte bewußt und erfinde statt dessen neue Fakten, erweist sich als sachlich fragwürdig"[10]. Damit ist der eingeschlagene Weg vorgezeichnet. Die Rede von der sach-

---

[6] Vgl. ebd., 239: "Lukas scheint die Art und Weise des Unterrichts im Lehrhaus zu kennen: Der angesehene Lehrer sitzt auf einem Stuhl, die Schüler 'zu seinen Füßen' auf dem Fußboden: ... Auch seine Formel κατὰ ἀκρίβειαν τοῦ πατρῴου νόμου zeigt, daß Lukas mit pharisäisch-schriftgelehrtem Milieu vertraut war. Es ist doch erstaunlich, daß der viel geschmähte Lukas diese Tatbestände so exakt auszudrücken vermag".

[7] Vgl. ebd., 197: "Es ist eigenartig, daß dort, wo den antiken Quellen wegen ihrer 'Tendenz' radikal mißtraut wird, die Möglichkeiten der eigenen tendenziösen Phantasie sich um so mehr ausbreiten, weil alle Grenzpflöcke fallen". Vgl. auch ebd., 183, 200 und 214.

[8] Vgl. ebd., 182 und 214.

[9] Meyer 1923, 64, zitiert bei Hengel 1991, 179 Anm. 7. Es braucht kaum noch ausdrücklich gesagt zu werden, daß es sich durch die redaktionsgeschichtlich geprägten Kommentare zur Apostelgeschichte von Ernst Haenchen und Hans Conzelmann zu Recht durchgesetzt hat, den historischen Quellenwert des lukanischen Doppelwerkes skeptischer zu beurteilen. Der Vorwurf, Lukas verfälsche die wahren geschichtlichen Sachverhalte, kann weder in seiner Bejahung, noch hinsichtlich seiner eindeutigen Verneinung dem historischen und theologischen Anliegen der Geschichtsschreibung des Lukas gerecht werden, auch wenn man dem heilsgeschichtlichen Interesse des Auctor ad Theophilum nicht ohne weiteres "romanhafte" Ergebnisse zuzuschreiben braucht.

[10] Hengel 1991, 214.

lichen Fragwürdigkeit fordert nun aber gerade dazu heraus, sich die Sache, die auf diesem Weg von Hengel eruierten Einzelergebnisse, einmal genauer zu betrachten.

2.2. In einem ersten Abschnitt behandelt Hengel die Herkunft des Apostels aus Tarsus, die nur in Apg 9,11;21,39; 22,3[11] erwähnt wird. Paulus soll – wohl als Abkömmling von Freigelassenen – von Geburt an das römische Bürgerrecht, vielleicht auch das tarsische, besessen haben. Hengel betont dabei vor allem den für einen Diasporajuden ungewöhnlichen jüdischen Namen Saul(os)[12], die prinzipielle Vereinbarkeit des römischen Bürgerrechts mit einem Leben als strenggläubiger Jude[13] und die Existenz von jüdischen Freigelassenen, die nach Judäa zurückwanderten und dort als römische Bürger lebten[14]. Dies ermöglicht die Hypothese, Paulus habe einen größeren Teil seiner vorchristlichen Zeit in Jerusalem verbracht, die im folgenden näher ausgeführt wird. Tarsus, das in Strabos Schilderung (geogr. 14.5.13) als Stadt dargestellt wird, in der griechische Bildung hervorragend vermittelt wurde, muß nicht die Stadt gewesen sein, in der Paulus seine Bildung erworben hat. An einem hellenistischen Rhetorikunterricht hat er wahrscheinlich ohnehin nicht teilgenommen. Seine Handwerksausbildung kann im Zusammenhang mit einem jüdischen Gelehrtenstudium stehen, das ebenfalls nicht in Tarsus lokalisiert werden muß[15].

Hengel stellt die Hypothese auf, daß Paulus noch in Tarsus eine griechische Elementarschule besucht hat, in der jüdische Literatur gelesen wurde. Er beherrschte auch Hebräisch und Aramäisch und kehrte noch als Heranwachsender mit seiner Familie nach Jerusalem zurück[16]. Darin werden die Texte Phil 3,4-6; II Kor 11,21b-22; Röm 11,1; Röm 9,3b-5a als im Grunde mit den Angaben in Apg 22,3; 26,4f.; 23,6 übereinstimmend gesehen, und von hier aus sei palästinischer Hintergrund naheliegend. Trotz entgegengesetzter Intention in ihrer Darstellung sollen hier beide Autoren "inhaltlich sehr nahe beieinander stehen"[17].

Die Angaben in Gal 1,13ff. sollen ebenfalls nicht gegen einen Aufenthalt des

---

[11] Die Textstellen Apg 9,30 und 11,25 sind nicht gerade ein Beleg für die Herkunft des Apostels aus Tarsus! Vgl. Hengel 1991, 182 Anm. 14.

[12] Vgl. ebd., 199.

[13] Vgl. ebd., 204f. Vgl. Lüdemann 1987, 249f. Lüdemann begründet die Annahme, daß Paulus römischer Bürger gewesen sei, indem er auf den römischen Namen des Paulus verweist. Ebenso erkläre sich die Überstellung an das Kaisergericht in Rom am einfachsten aus einer Berufung an den Kaiser, wie sie nur römischen Bürgern möglich war. Als weiterer Hinweis könne die Konzentration der paulinischen Missionsaktivitäten auf römisch kolonisierte Gebiete gelten.

[14] Vgl. Hengel 1991, 205.

[15] Vgl. ebd., 210.

[16] Vgl. zusammenfassend ebd., 237ff.

[17] Ebd., 216.

vorchristlichen Paulus in Jerusalem sprechen: Die Wendung ἐν τῷ γένει μου in Gal 1,14 meint nicht "in meiner Heimat", also in Tarsus, sondern "in meinem Volk"[18]; die Reise des Paulus nach Arabien (Gal 1,17) soll von Jerusalem ausgegangen sein, weil Hengel eine hypothetische Reise von Tarsus nach Arabien, ohne daß Paulus dabei in Jerusalem Station gemacht habe, für unbegründet hält. Ferner schließt Gal 1,22 die Möglichkeit nicht aus, daß Paulus in Jerusalem lebte und dennoch den judäischen Gemeinden unbekannt war, zumal Jerusalem nach Hengel mehr als die von J. Jeremias geschätzten 25 000 Einwohner gehabt haben soll[19].

Außerdem nennen Apg 22,3 und Röm 15,19b Jerusalem als Ausgangsort der paulinischen Mission[20]. Die Selbstbezeichnung Ἑβραῖος (Phil 3,5; II Kor 11,22) zeigt die enge Bindung des Paulus an das palästinische Mutterland ebenso wie die Beschneidung am 8. Tag und sein Eifer für das Gesetz. Er war Pharisäer, der Pharisäismus aber ist genuin-palästinisch und auf den palästinischen Raum beschränkt. Sein Torastudium kann nirgendwo anders als in Jerusalem stattgefunden haben. In der griechischen Sprache aufgewachsen, betreibt er nach seiner Übersiedlung nach Jerusalem eigene schriftgelehrte Studien anhand des hebräischen Urtextes.

2.3. Ist für die Lokalisierung des Studiums des Paulus Jerusalem im folgenden vorausgesetzt, so ermöglicht dies, Paulus und seine Theologie in der Nähe eines liberalen, palästinischen Pharisäismus einerseits und verschiedener apokalyptischer und essenischer Einflüsse im kosmopolitischen Klima Jerusalems andererseits zu sehen. Hengel versucht dabei, insbesondere den Pharisäismus anhand von späteren, rabbinischen Quellen inhaltlich näher zu bestimmen. Paulus erhielt danach im Anschluß an sein Studium eine auf den mündlichen Synagogenvortrag ausgerichtete rhetorische Grundausbildung. Als qualifiziertes Mitglied einer Jerusalemer hellenistischen, griechischsprachigen Synagoge tritt er als Verfolger des griechischsprechenden Teils der judenchristlichen Gemeinde Jerusalems auf. Eine Reminiszenz an diese Verfolgung stelle der Stephanusbericht dar. Nach Damaskus entsandt, erlebe Paulus dort seine Lebenswende, die eine radikale Umkehrung der früheren Werte und Ziele des jüdischen Lehrers Paulus mit sich gebracht habe. Darauf beruhe seine Theologie. Bausteine und Denkstruktur derselben seien aber weiter fast ausschließlich auf das Judentum zurückzuführen.

---

[18] Vgl. ebd. 218, gegen Mommsen 1901, 85f.

[19] Erwähnt werden (Hengel 1991, 219) die Schätzungen von M. Broshi/J. Wilkinson (zwischen 32 000 und 80 000). Vgl. Wilkinson, 1974, 33-51; Broshi 1975,5-14. Die Einwohnerzahl von Jerusalem und Umgebung bestimmt Hengel später (258) tendenziös auf ca. 100 000. Vgl. Jeremias 1969a, 97f.

[20] Vgl. Hengel 1991, 219.

### 3. *Die neutestamentlichen Notizen über den vorchristlichen Paulus.*
### *Tarsos oder Jerusalem*

"Ein Glück, daß der letztere [= Simon bar Gamaliel] (und damit auch sein Vater) bei
Josephus erwähnt wird, sonst würde die 'kritische Forschung' in dem ersten Gamaliel lediglich einen lukanischen Anachronismus bzw. eine Rückprojektion seines
sehr viel besser bekannten Enkels Gamaliel II. aus der Zeit um 90/100 in das Jerusalem vor der Tempelzerstörung sehen"[21]. – Solche Kritik an der historisch-kritischen Forschung kann hier nicht übergangen werden. Auch wenn man die Freude
des Autors über die Quellenlage hinsichtlich Gamaliels I. teilt, muß doch bedacht
werden, ob der hier kritisierte Gebrauch der Quellen wirklich so unangemessen ist,
wie er dargestellt wird. Die Existenz Gamaliels I. dürfte nach dem Zeugnis der
Quellen niemand bestreiten. Daß die Möglichkeit eines lukanischen Anachronismus zu bedenken wäre, wenn Gamaliel I. bei Josephus nicht erwähnt wäre, dürfte
aber ebenso unstrittig sein; vielmehr wäre dies die einzig sachgemäße, methodologische Fragestellung, unabhängig von dem Ergebnis, das sie auch bei Anwendung
von anderen, z. B. sprachlichen Kriterien nahelegen könnte. Ist nun die Person Gamaliel I. keine historische Fiktion, so ist damit noch keine Beziehung des jungen
Paulus zu ihm bewiesen. Die Herkunft der Notiz darüber wird genau und unvoreingenommen zu untersuchen sein.

Historisch-kritisches Arbeiten heißt immer auch Hypothesen unterschiedlicher
Wahrscheinlichkeit gegeneinander abwägen zu müssen. Eventuell wird dabei auch
festgestellt werden müssen, daß die Informationen zu bestimmten Sachverhalten
nicht für eine Hypothese ausreichen. Es ist das Ziel zu verfolgen, Aussagen von
möglichst hoher Wahrscheinlichkeit zu gewinnen, aber eine kritische Betrachtung
der Quellen abzulehnen hieße, sich in einer falschen Sicherheit zu wiegen, die dann
auch falsche Ergebnisse hervorbringt. Es wird streng unterschieden werden müssen
zwischen wahrscheinlichen und weniger wahrscheinlichen, möglichen und unmöglichen Sachverhalten, wie dies exemplarisch bereits W. Heitmüller zum Thema vor-
geführt hat[22], der folgerichtig auch zu ganz anderen Ergebnissen als Hengel kommt.

3.1. Wenden wir uns also einer kritischen Betrachtung der Texte zu, in denen über
den vorchristlichen Paulus berichtet wird, und beginnen wir mit dem, was Paulus
selbst über seine jüdische Vergangenheit schreibt. Die genaueste Auskunft gibt der
Abschnitt Phil 3,4b-6:

---

[21] Ebd., 244.
[22] Vgl. Heitmüller 1912, 326ff.

(4b)  Εἴ τις δοκεῖ ἄλλος πεποιθέναι ἐν σαρκί, ἐγὼ μᾶλλον·
(5)  περιτομῇ ὀκταήμερος,
    ἐκ γένους Ἰσραήλ, φυλῆς Βενιαμίν, Ἑβραῖος ἐξ Ἑβραίων,
    κατὰ νόμον Φαρισαῖος,
(6)  κατὰ ζῆλος διώκων τὴν ἐκκλησίαν,
    κατὰ δικαιοσύνην τὴν ἐν νόμῳ γενόμενος ἄμεμπτος.

Der Kontext reflektiert eine Auseinandersetzung mit judenchristlichen oder wahrscheinlicher jüdischen Gegnern. Diese rühmen sich jüdischer Errungenschaften, insbesondere des Besitzes des Gesetzes, das den Juden gegenüber den Heiden eine Vorrangstellung verleiht. Dem entgegnet der Apostel: Als Christ hält er solchen Vorzug für "Dreck" (V. 8 σκύβαλα), in seiner vorchristlichen Zeit aber, und zwar von Geburt an, war er dem Gesetz unterstellt, das nicht nur Anspruch, sondern zugleich Vorzug bedeutet.

Die Beschneidung am achten Tage entspricht der alttestamentlichen Weisung in Gen 17,12 und Lev 12,3. Paulus gehört von seiner Geburt an — verdeutlicht und religiös überhöht durch die Beschneidung — zum alttestamentlichen Gottesvolk, ist also kein Proselyt. So ist die Angabe ὀκταήμερος in erster Linie zu verstehen. Für die Eltern des Paulus heißt das, daß sie gesetzesstrenge Juden gewesen sein müssen[23]. Eine besondere Auszeichnung, die über das Judesein von Geburt hinausreicht, ist hier nicht zu erkennen. Paulus betont sein eigenes Beschnittensein im Hinblick auf seine Gegner, kann für sich selbst aber die Beschneidung als κατατομή (V. 2) kritisieren und zurückweisen.

Die Zugehörigkeit zum Volk Israel hat einen religiösen Beiklang. "Israel" ist eine das jüdische Volk auszeichnende Benennung, ein Würdename des von Gott erwählten Volkes[24]. Die Zugehörigkeit zum Stamm Benjamin trifft einen bevorzugten Teil dieses Volkes, ist doch Benjamin als der Jüngste der Jakobssöhne im jüdischen Ursprungsland geboren. Eine ähnliche Herkunftsbezeichnung gibt Paulus im Römerbrief (Röm 11,1b) an:

καὶ γὰρ ἐγὼ Ἰσραηλίτης εἰμί, ἐκ σπέρματος Ἀβραάμ, φυλῆς Βενιαμίν.

Die Angabe "Israelit aus dem Stamm Benjamin" erscheint hier erweitert, die Erwähnung der Abrahamskindschaft greift auf Röm 9,7 zurück und ist dem Kontext angepaßt. Deutlich ist jedoch daß für Paulus beide Elemente der Wendung, Volks-

---

[23] Die bei Strack/Billerbeck 1956 (IV/1, 23-27) genannten rabbinischen Texte belegen die strenge Handhabung der Beschneidung am 8. Tage auch noch in späterer Zeit.

[24] Vgl. II Kor 3,7; 11,22; Röm 9,6.31; 10,19; 11,1f.25f. u. ö. Paulus kann diesen Ehrentitel auch auf die christliche Gemeinde übertragen. (Vgl. Gal 6,16, wo mit Ἰσραὴλ τοῦ θεοῦ sicher nicht nur die Judenchristen, sondern Juden- und Heidenchristen gleichermaßen gemeint sind. Das vorangehende καὶ verdeutlicht den universalen Charakter der Aussage. Die galatische Gemeinde, von der zuvor die Rede ist, wird in den umfassenden Kontext der Christenheit insgesamt gestellt.)

und Stammeszugehörigkeit, wenn es um seine jüdische Identität geht, zusammengehören. Daß Paulus seine Herkunft genealogisch auf einen der altisraelitischen Stämme zurückführen kann, zeugt vom Traditionsbewußtsein seiner Familie. Sein nur von der Apostelgeschichte überlieferter jüdischer Name Saulos, der Name des wohl berühmtesten Benjaminiten, deutet ebenfalls darauf hin, daß die Vorfahren des Paulus als strenggläubige Juden zu gelten haben, Vertreter eines Geschlechts, das stolz auf seine Herkunft zurückblicken konnte.

In die gleiche Richtung weist die vierte im Philipperbrief genannte Herkunftsbezeichnung: Ἑβραῖος ἐξ Ἑβραίων[25]. Der Terminus Ἑβραῖος läßt gelegentlich eine Beziehung auf die hebräische Sprache zu: so vermutlich Apg 6,1 in Gegenüberstellung zu den "Hellenisten". Weder für Paulus, noch für seine Gegner in Philippi und in Rom ist daraus aber eine palästinische Herkunft oder Kenntnis des Hebräischen zu erschließen[26]. Vielmehr ist "Hebräer" im hellenistischen Judentum wie auch im paganen Griechentum weithin eine Bezeichnung für das jüdische Volk in alter Zeit, so daß dem Ausdruck eine archaisierende Färbung eigen ist[27]. In solcher Weise kann Ἑβραῖος auch als Ehrenname gebraucht werden, etwa in der sekundären Überschrift des neutestamentlichen Hebräerbriefes, der sich ja auch nicht an palästinische oder hebräisch sprechende Juden wendet, sondern an Christen. Paulus benutzt "Hebräer" als ehrenvolle jüdische Selbstbezeichnung im Unterschied zum Begriff "Juden" als einem vorwiegend von Außenstehenden gebrauchten Terminus[28]. Der Schwerpunkt der Wendung Ἑβραῖος ἐξ Ἑβραίων liegt sicherlich in ihrem zweiten Teil: Paulus ist nicht nur selbst Hebräer, sondern auch Abkömmling von Hebräern. Bedenkt man z. B. die Kritik an Mischehen, wie sie in Esra 9 formuliert wird, so beansprucht Paulus eine kaum noch zu überbietende Vollkommenheit hinsichtlich seiner Abstammung.

Die Ausrichtung all dieser Selbstprädikationen hat bereits *H. Lietzmann* richtig bestimmt: Es ist wahrscheinlich, daß sich Paulus hier vornehmlich als 'Vollblutjude' bekennen will, der den väterlichen Gebräuchen und Sitten treu geblieben ist[29].

Auf die Aufzählung derjenigen Vorzüge, die Paulus von Geburt an aufweisen konnte, folgen drei Angaben, die sprachlich und inhaltlich eng zusammengehören und die Vorzüge betreffen, die sich Paulus aktiv erwerben mußte. Den Beginn der

---

[25] Auch diese Bezeichnung erscheint ein weiteres Mal in den Paulusbriefen, nämlich in II Kor 11,22, auch dort wieder verknüpft mit anderen Termini: Ἑβραῖοί εἰσιν; κἀγώ. Ἰσραηλῖταί εἰσιν; κἀγώ. σπέρμα Ἀβραάμ εἰσιν; κἀγώ.

[26] Gegen Hengel 1991, 221f.; auch Gnilka 1976, 190, und Dibelius 1925, 67f., beziehen den Begriff auf die hebräische Sprache, allerdings mit sehr viel vorsichtigeren Schlußfolgerungen.

[27] Vgl. Gutbrod 1957, 374-376; Wanke 1992, 894.

[28] Ἰουδαῖοι wird sogar von Paulus in distanzierender Weise gebraucht, so etwa in der Parallelisierung zu den "Heiden" (ἔθνη): I Kor 1,23f.; 10,32; II Kor 11,24; Röm 1,16; 2,9f.; 3,9 u. ö.

[29] Vgl. Lietzmann/Kümmel 1969, 150.

Reihe, deren einzelne Glieder jeweils durch κατά eingeleitet werden, markiert die Selbstbezeichnung "nach dem Gesetz ein Pharisäer". Schon auf der sprachlichen Ebene ist es deutlich, daß Φαρισαῖος von den vorhergehenden Bestimmungen geschieden ist. Keinesfalls kann in V. 5 eine Anordnung vom Weiteren zum Spezielleren ausgemacht werden, die auch die Nachricht vom "Pharisäer nach dem Gesetz" einschließt[30]. Allenfalls für den Beginn des fünften Verses könnte mit *J. B. Lightfoot*[31] eine solche Anordnung vermutet werden, die aber auch hier nicht wahrscheinlich ist: Wie gezeigt, reiht Paulus zwar keine Synonyma aneinander, jedoch gehören die Mitteilungen über seine Abstammung eng zusammen; sie wird lediglich unter verschiedenen Blickwinkeln betrachtet.

Als Pharisäer gehörte Paulus einer einflußreichen religiösen Gruppe an, die besonderen Wert auf eine streng jüdische Lebenshaltung, insbesondere auf genaue Toraobservanz, legte. "Pharisäer nach dem Gesetz" hat darüber hinaus den Beiklang eines religiösen Würdetitels, der den Träger als Menschen von herausragender Frömmigkeit auszeichnet. In der Darstellung des Josephus (Ant. VII. XV. XVII. XVIII; Bell I und II; Vita 38) repräsentieren die Pharisäer in Leben und Lehre das jüdische Volk nach seinen besten Seiten. Kennzeichnend für sie ist die Verbindung von Frömmigkeit und politischem Engagement.

Solches Engagement muß sich nicht nur gegen die römische Besatzungsmacht gerichtet haben, sondern kann auch innerjüdische Strömungen betreffen, als die Paulus das Urchristentum ansehen mußte. So ist es nicht erstaunlich, wenn im zweiten Glied der κατά-Reihe von einer Verfolgung der Kirche die Rede ist. Die Wendung κατὰ ζῆλος fällt aus dem Rahmen: Sie bezeichnet anders als die beiden anderen nicht ein Kriterium, an dem die Haltung des Paulus gemessen werden kann, sondern eine Erläuterung zu dieser Haltung. Sein Eifer um das Gesetz war derart, daß er die christliche Gemeinde verfolgte. Das Faktum der Verfolgung ist gut bezeugt: Paulus erwähnt sie in I Kor 15,9 nochmals, wo er sich als den geringsten der Apostel (ὁ ἐλάχιστος τῶν ἀποστόλων) bezeichnet, διότι ἐδίωξα τὴν ἐκκλησίαν τοῦ θεοῦ, ferner in Gal 1,13.23, worauf noch einzugehen sein wird. Der Auctor ad Theophilum zeichnet (Apg 8,3; 9,1f.; 26,10f.) das Bild von einer gewalttätigen Verfolgertätigkeit des Paulus gegenüber der Jerusalemer Gemeinde; der Apostel selbst berichtet dagegen nichts Näheres über den Ort oder die Art und Weise seiner Verfolgertätigkeit.

---

[30] Gegen Hengel 1991, 220f.Völlig unangemessen vermutet Hengel wegen der Stellung von Ἑβραῖος unmittelbar vor Φαρισαῖος, daß Ἑβραῖος ein für den Pharisäer Paulus wichtiger Ehrentitel sei, der die Herkunft aus dem aramäisch sprechenden Mutterland bezeichne.

[31] Vgl. Lightfoot 1868, 144.

Das Verbum διώκειν bezeichnet hier wie auch andernorts im NT die Verfolgung aus religiösen Gründen[32]. Die Verfolgertätigkeit dient hier der Demonstration der Überzeugung des Apostels, daß er der im Gesetz geforderten Gerechtigkeit nach untadelig war. Dies wird kein sarkastischer Seitenhieb auf seine Gegner sein, vielmehr spiegelt sich hier die Überzeugung des Pharisäers Paulus, der nicht nur anstrebte, das Gesetz zu erfüllen, sondern darin auch von seinen Möglichkeiten, es konkret zu praktizieren, weitestgehenden Gebrauch machte. So wird er sich durch eine strengere Lebensführung ausgezeichnet haben als allgemein üblich, ganz wie es der pharisäischen Lehre entsprach.

Ähnliche Aussagen wie in Phil 3,4b-6 finden sich Gal 1,13f.:

(13) Ἠκούσατε γὰρ τὴν ἐμὴν ἀναστροφήν ποτε ἐν τῷ Ἰουδαϊσμῷ,
ὅτι καθ᾽ ὑπερβολὴν ἐδίωκον τὴν ἐκκλησίαν τοῦ θεοῦ καὶ ἐπόρθουν αὐτήν,

(14) καὶ προέκοπτον ἐν τῷ Ἰουδαϊσμῷ ὑπὲρ πολλοὺς συνηλικιώτας ἐν τῷ γένει μου, περισσοτέρως ζηλωτὴς ὑπάρχων τῶν πατρικῶν μου παραδόσεων.

Mit diesen Versen leitet Paulus eine Erörterung ein, die dazu dient, die in 1,11f. formulierte These, das paulinische Evangelium sei kein menschliches Evangelium und beruhe auf einer Offenbarung Jesu Christi, zu beweisen. Paulus erläutert zunächst anhand seiner Biographie, wie er aufgrund einer göttlichen Offenbarung vom strenggläubigen Juden zum christlichen Heidenapostel wurde und daß er seit seiner Lebenswende von menschlicher Weisung unabhängig sei. Prinzipiell erlaubt diese Argumentation die Abwehr von zwei Vorwürfen:

(A) Paulus kann vorgeworfen worden sein, sein Evangelium sei nicht eschatologisch legitimiert; er sei kein von Gott eingesetzter Apostel. Dem hielte er dann entgegen, daß er das Evangelium von keinem Menschen empfangen habe, daß seine Lebenswende allein durch Gott bewirkt wurde.

(B) Seine Gegner kritisieren seine mangelnde Autorisation durch die Jerusalemer Gemeindeleitung, in Judäa sei Paulus noch nicht einmal bekannt (1,22). Dagegen setzt Paulus, daß er keine menschliche Autorisation seiner Verkündigung brauche, sein Evangelium komme von Gott, nicht von Menschen. Außerdem sei sein Evangelium wie auch sein Apostolat von den Jerusalemern nachträglich anerkannt worden (2,1-10). Beide Vorwürfe könnten auch zusammengefallen sein.

Die jüdische Vergangenheit des Heidenapostels war den Gemeinden in Galatien bekannt, sei es durch seine Gegner, sei es – wahrscheinlicher –, daß er selbst die Galater davon in Kenntnis gesetzt hat. Der "Wandel ἐν τῷ Ἰουδαϊσμῷ" meint nicht nur eine allgemeine jüdische Religion, sondern bezieht sich, besonders im Hinblick auf Phil 3,5f. auf eine streng jüdische Lebensführung. Zu dieser gehörte für Paulus

---

[32] Vgl. z. B. Mt 10,23; 23,34; Lk 21,12; Joh 5,16; 15,20.

die Feindschaft gegen die ἐκκλησία τοῦ θεοῦ, die auch die in Phil 3,6 erwähnte Verfolgertätigkeit einschließt. So wird es hier verschärfend mit dem Verbum πορθεῖν (vernichten) beschrieben: Paulus versuchte[33] die Gemeinde Gottes zu vernichten[34]. Zwar besteht die *Möglichkeit* daß mit πορθεῖν auch gewalttätige Maßnahmen bezeichnet werden, es dürfte sich jedoch als schwierig, wenn nicht gar unmöglich erweisen, darüber etwas mit hinreichender Wahrscheinlichkeit auszusagen. Ob freilich *A. Schlatter*[35] recht zu geben ist, wenn er diese Aussage auf der Grundlage von Apg 26,10f.[36] interpretiert wissen will, ist denn doch mehr als problematisch. Die von den Oberpriestern bevollmächtigte Verfolgertätigkeit des Paulus würde danach eine richterliche Funktion einschließen. Funktionen eines Richters aber, so wird weiter gefolgert, durfte nur ein ordinierter Rabbi ausüben. Danach wäre Paulus ein ordinierter Rabbi gewesen[37]. Jedoch ist fraglich, ob zur Zeit des Apostels eine rabbinische Ordination überhaupt praktiziert wurde[38].

In jedem Fall erfahren wir aus den Selbstzeugnissen nichts über Einzelheiten der Verfolgung der christlichen Gemeinde(n) durch den vorchristlichen Paulus[39]. Er bestätigt in Gal 1,13 nur die Tatsache, die nun aber in V. 14 interpretiert wird: Der durch die Verfolgertätigkeit näher klassifizierte Wandel im Judentum ist motiviert durch großen Eifer für die väterlichen Überlieferungen. Diese Äußerung ist vor dem Hintergrund von Phil 3,5f. zu sehen; der Eifer für das Gesetz und die väterlichen Überlieferungen entsprechen pharisäischer Lebensweise. Darin brauchte Paulus auch nicht den Vergleich mit seinen Altersgenossen im jüdischen Volk zu scheuen; er machte in seiner Lebensführung Fortschritte, die die anderer übertrafen und ihn selbst der Gesetzesgerechtigkeit nach untadelig erscheinen ließen. Daß sich solche Fortschritte hier auf ein Gesetzesstudium pharisäischer Prägung beziehen, ist reine Spekulation, die auch nicht durch die Apostelgeschichte als externe Quelle

---

[33] Das Imperfekt ist sicher als *imperfectum de conatu* zu übersetzen. Vgl. etwa Lk 1,59; 5,6; 9,49; Apg 7,26; 26,11a; Heb 11,17 u.ö.

[34] Vgl. Gal 1,23; Apg 9,21.

[35] Vgl. Schlatter 1983, 112-129; vgl. Oepke 1964, 412f.

[36] Apg 26, 9-11: (9) ἐγὼ μὲν οὖν ἔδοξα ἐμαυτῷ πρὸς τὸ ὄνομα Ἰησοῦ τοῦ Ναζωραίου δεῖν πολλὰ ἐναντία πρᾶξαι, (10) ὃ καὶ ἐποίησα ἐν Ἱεροσολύμοις, καὶ πολλούς τε τῶν ἁγίων ἐγὼ ἐν φυλακαῖς κατέκλεισα τὴν παρὰ τῶν ἀρχιερέων ἐξουσίαν λαβὼν ἀναιρουμένων τε αὐτῶν κατήνεγκα ψῆφον. (11) καὶ κατὰ πάσας τὰς συναγωγὰς πολλάκις τιμωρῶν αὐτοὺς ἠνάγκαζον βλασφημεῖν περισσῶς τε ἐμμαινόμενος αὐτοῖς ἐδίωκον ἕως καὶ εἰς τὰς ἔξω πόλεις.

[37] Zu diesem Ergebnis kommt auch Jeremias 1926, 310-312; ders. 1929, 321-323.

[38] Vgl. Riesner 1988, 266-274.

[39] Gänzlich unwahrscheinlich ist auch, daß in I Thess 2,14 eine Reminiszenz an eine paulinische Verfolgung in Judäa zu finden sein soll (vgl. Hengel 1991, 276). Natürlich werden solche Hypothesen niemals mit absoluter Sicherheit auszuschließen sein; es handelt sich aber um eine bloße Möglichkeit, die anzuführen sich allenfalls dazu eignet, einem unkritischen Leser die Plausibilität bestimmter unhaltbarer Thesen zu suggerieren.

gestützt werden kann[40].

3.2. Ausführlicher weiß der Auctor ad Theophilum über den vorchristlichen Paulus zu berichten. "Lukas" legt in Apg 22,3-5 Paulus eine Zusammenfassung fast aller Informationen, die er über den vorchristlichen Paulus weitergibt in den Mund. Dort heißt es:

(3) ἐγώ εἰμι ἀνὴρ Ἰουδαῖος, γεγεννημένος ἐν Ταρσῷ τῆς Κιλικίας,
ἀνατεθραμμένος δὲ ἐν τῇ πόλει ταύτῃ,
παρὰ τοὺς πόδας Γαμαλιὴλ πεπαιδευμένος κατὰ ἀκρίβειαν τοῦ πατρῴου
νόμου, ζηλωτὴς ὑπάρχων τοῦ θεοῦ καθὼς πάντες ὑμεῖς ἐστε σήμερον·

(4) ὃς ταύτην τὴν ὁδὸν ἐδίωξα ἄχρι θανάτου δεσμεύων καὶ παραδιδοὺς εἰς
φυλακὰς ἄνδρας τε καὶ γυναῖκας,

(5) ὡς καὶ ὁ ἀρχιερεὺς μαρτυρεῖ μοι καὶ πᾶν τὸ πρεσβυτέριον,
παρ᾽ ὧν καὶ ἐπιστολὰς δεξάμενος πρὸς τοὺς ἀδελφοὺς εἰς Δαμασκὸν
ἐπορευόμην,
ἄξων καὶ τοὺς ἐκεῖσε ὄντας δεδεμένους εἰς Ἰερουσαλὴμ ἵνα τιμωρηθῶσιν.

Mit einem autobiographischen Rückblick verteidigt sich Paulus gegenüber dem Volk in Jerusalem. Weil er sich in diesem Kontext als Jude darstellen muß, ist seine vorchristliche Zeit besonders wichtig.

V. 3 folgt einem biographischen Schema (γεγεννημένος – ἀνατεθραμμένος – πεπαιδευμένος)[41] und hebt sich darin von den folgenden beiden Versen ab. Daß Paulus ein ἀνὴρ Ἰουδαῖος war, ist bereits aus seinen Selbstzeugnissen bekannt, auch wenn er den Terminus Ἰουδαῖος auf sich selbst nicht anwendet[42]. Die Notiz über seinen Geburtsort taucht auch in Apg 9,11; 21,39 auf. Apg 21,39 bezeichnet Tarsus als οὐκ ἄσημος, was den außerbiblischen Nachrichten entspricht[43]. Aus Apg 16,37ff.; 22,25ff.; 23,27 ist bekannt, daß Paulus das römische Bürgerrecht besessen haben soll, nach 21,29 ist er auch πολίτης der Stadt Tarsus, was sich auf das Bürgerrecht beziehen, aber auch einfach die Herkunft bezeichnen kann. Weitergehende Spekulationen sind hier nicht angebracht. Die Nachricht von der Herkunft des Apostels aus Tarsus dürfte jedenfalls auf älterer Tradition beruhen, da sie dem Bemühen des Verfassers der Apostelgeschichte entgegenläuft, Paulus schon früh mit der heiligen Stadt in Verbindung zu bringen, wie wir noch sehen werden.

In der Darstellung der Apostelgeschichte beschränkt sich der Aufenthalt des jun-

---

[40] Gegen Hengel 1991, 240.

[41] Vgl. Apg 7,20; Ovid, Tristia IV, 10,3ff.; Procopius v. Caesarea, Anecdota X,1; Platon, Kriton 50e, 51c; Philo,VitMos II 1, Flacc 158.

[42] S.o., § 3.1. Anm. 28. Vgl. besonders Apg 21,39. Der distanzierende Ausdruck ist ein ausgesprochenes Vorzugswort der Apg. Die Juden treten in der Apg besonders als Gegner der christlichen Mission in Erscheinung, so auch hier der Apostel.

[43] S. o., § 2.2.

gen Paulus in Tarsus denn auch auf die allererste Lebenszeit. Darauf läßt die Bestimmung schließen, Paulus sei in Jerusalem erzogen worden. Dabei wird offenbleiben müssen, ob hier ein Vorgang im Elternhaus, also bereits das Nähren des Kleinkindes und die allererste Erziehung[44], oder eine weitergehende schulische Erziehung, mithin eine Erläuterung des Folgenden, gemeint ist. Nach Jerusalem übergesiedelt, nimmt Paulus ein Gesetzesstudium auf; er wird zu den Füßen Gamaliels ausgebildet.

Ein Γαμαλίηλας wird von Josephus (Ant. XX 213.223; Vit 190.309; Bell IV 159) als Vater der Jerusalemer Priester Jesus und Simon erwähnt. Er wird, so darf vermutet werden, in den Jahren nach Jesu Tod in Jerusalem gelebt und bereits Beziehungen zu den führenden Kreisen in der Stadt gehabt haben. Mehr wissen nur die rabbinischen Quellen von Gamaliel zu berichten: Gamaliel, ein Enkel Hillels, soll als Präsident des Jerusalemer Synedriums gewirkt haben. Der Talmud führt drei Briefe an, die Gamaliel in dieser Funktion diktiert haben soll (babylonischer Talmud, San 11b; Tosefta, San 2,6; Jerusalemer Talmud, San 1,2.18d), einzelne Lehrsätze werden ihm zugeschrieben (Git 4,2f.; Yev 16,7), Schüler werden genannt (Pea 2,6; Orl 2,12; Yev 16,7). Seine rechtgläubige Gesetzesstrenge wird erwähnt (Sot 9,15), ebenso soll er Beziehungen zum Königshaus gehabt haben (Pes 88b). Die Apostelgeschichte entwirft ein Bild Gamaliels, das ihn als bekanntes Mitglied des Hohen Rates (Apg 5,34) und als schriftgelehrten Lehrer (Apg 22,3) zeigt. Er wirkt besonnen und gottesfürchtig (Apg 5,34ff.).

Unabhängig davon, ob die außerbiblischen Notizen über Gamaliel historisch Zutreffendes berichten, konstituieren sie somit ein Bild Gamaliels, das dem lukanischen nahekommt und dem Auctor ad Theophilum und seinen Lesern bekannt war. Dieses Bild kann ferner durch die Person Gamaliels II., des Enkels Gamaliels I., geprägt worden sein, der als Leiter des Lehrhauses zu Jabne zur Zeit der Abfassung der Apostelgeschichte wohl einen deutlich höheren Bekanntheitsgrad als sein Großvater gehabt hat. Zeichnet Apg also ein historisch mögliches Bild, so ist doch die Funktion wichtiger, die Gamaliel im lukanischen Werk erhalten hat. In der Vorstellung des Lukas ist der Name Gamaliel die Bezeichnung für einen bekannten jüdischen Gesetzeslehrer schlechthin.

Die Herkunft der Notiz über Paulus' Beziehung zu Gamaliel ist unbekannt. Es besteht die Möglichkeit, daß Lukas sie bereits in der legendarischen Paulustradition

---

[44] So z. B. van Unnik 1962, 285ff. Die Unterscheidung von Erziehung in leiblicher (ἀνατρέφειν) und intellektueller Hinsicht (παιδεύειν) lehnt van Unnik aber ab (gegen Grosheide 1948, II 284 Anm. 1). Er nimmt darüber hinaus an, daß Apg hier historisch gesicherte Fakten aus dem Leben des Paulus berichtet, was unwahrscheinlich ist. Paulus sei somit in Tarsus geboren, aber schon in frühester Kindheit mit seinen Eltern nach Jerusalem gekommen, wo er seine weitere Erziehung und Ausbildung erhalten habe (van Unnik 1962, 301f.).

vorfand, die er bei seinen Nachforschungen sammelte. Allerdings qualifiziert die Erwähnung Gamaliels in Apg 22,3 nicht nur die Ausbildung des Paulus, sondern ist auch ein kompositorisch äußerst geschickter Rückgriff auf die fiktive Rede Gamaliels vor dem Hohen Rat in Apg 5,34ff. Abgesehen von der historischen Person wird auch dort der Name Gamaliel funktional benutzt. In Apg 5,34ff. soll ausgesagt werden, daß sich am Missionserfolg der Christen zeigt, daß ihr Vorhaben von Gott stammt. Lukas legt diese Aussage, die erst angesichts des christlichen Missionserfolgs formuliert wurde, Gamaliel in den Mund – ein Kunstgriff, der der Aussage nicht nur eine höhere Dignität verleiht, sondern sie auch für einen polemischen oder apologetischen Gebrauch geeignet erscheinen läßt. Daß nun Paulus von Gamaliel ausgebildet wurde, der die Möglichkeit erwogen hat, die christliche Sache habe eine göttliche Legitimation, läßt die paulinische Verfolgertätigkeit in einem um so dunkleren Licht erscheinen. Vermutlich will darüber hinaus die Erwähnung der Ausbildung des Paulus mit dem konkreten Bezug auf Gamaliel in Apg 22,3 die Aussage von 5,39 in Erinnerung rufen, wonach es Gamaliel war, der indirekt die christliche Sache als von Gott ins Leben gerufen beurteilte. Dies geschieht nunmehr im Rückblick auf den zuvor geschilderten Erfolg der christlichen Mission und läßt nachträglich Gamaliels Urteil als begründet erscheinen. So entspricht es auch dem apologetischen Kontext von Apg 22,3. Die Erwähnung Gamaliels stammt demnach wahrscheinlich aus der Feder des Lukas.

Die ἀκρίβεια gegenüber dem Gesetz, der Eifer für die Überlieferungen, all das erinnert an den vorchristlichen Paulus, wie er in Phil 3 und Gal 1 dargestellt ist. Auch in der lukanischen Schilderung zeichnet sich der Pharisäer Paulus[45] durch strengen Lebenswandel[46] und peinlich genaue Gesetzestreue aus. Wie in Gal 1,13 und Phil 3,6 wird darin das Motiv für die paulinische Verfolgung gesehen. Diese wird in Apg 22,4 und 5 näher charakterisiert. Die Verse liefern den Grundstock für die Saulus-Notizen in Apg 7-9 und stellen eine Parallele zum oben angeführten Abschnitt Apg 26,9-11 dar[47]. Die Verfolgertätigkeit wird durch gewaltsame, durch das Synedrium legitimierte Maßnahmen des Paulus bestimmt. Der Auctor ad Theophilum will als Ort dieser Verfolgung Jerusalem gesehen wissen[48]. Die Lebenswende des Paulus ist aber in Übereinstimmung mit Gal 1,17 mit der Stadt Damaskus verbunden[49].

In der Darstellung des Damaskuserlebnisses folgt Lukas einer älteren Tradition,

---

[45] Vgl. Apg 23,6b; 26,5. Nach Apg 23,6b soll Paulus darüberhinaus aus pharisäischer Familie stammen.

[46] Vgl. Apg 26,4f.

[47] S. o., § 3.1. Anm. 36.

[48] Vgl. Apg 26,10; 9,21.

[49] Vgl. Apg 9,1ff; 26,12.

in der Paulus zum Idealtyp des Konvertiten geworden ist. Der Verfasser schließt sich einer idealisierenden, zum Zweck der Erbauung tradierten Erzählung an, die eine unhistorische, legendarische Ausrichtung aufweist. Die hier verarbeitete, vorlukanische Paulusüberlieferung steht mit der historischen Wirklichkeit schwerlich im Einklang, zumal der Einfluß nichtchristlicher, hellenistisch-jüdischer Vorstellungsschemata, wie sie z. B., wenn auch nicht ausschließlich, in der Heliodor-Legende wiedergegeben sind (4 Makk 4), deutlich spürbar ist. Mit ähnlicher Vorsicht wird der historische Wert der Berichte über die paulinische Verfolgung in Jerusalem zu beurteilen sein. Es wurde schon oft beobachtet, daß der lukanische Autor die Paulustradition nur sehr oberflächlich mit der Verfolgung in Jerusalem verknüpft[50].

Saulus-Paulus erscheint in Apg 7,58 recht unvermittelt am Rande des Berichtes über das Stephanusmartyrium: Die Zeugen der Steinigung legten ihre Kleider zu seinen Füßen ab[51]. Als Gegner des Stephanus treten besonders hellenistische Juden auf[52], die in Jerusalem ansässig waren, Paulus spielt dabei in der Vorstellung des Lukas kaum eine Rolle[53]. Die Versuche, die lukanische Überlieferung dahingehend zu korrigieren, daß Paulus zumindest bei der Steinigung des Stephanus aktiv mitwirkte[54], überzeugen wohl kaum. In 8,1 zeigt sich Paulus mit der Ermordung einverstanden, eine große Verfolgung der Jerusalemer Gemeinde wird erwähnt, ohne daß sie ursächlich auf Paulus zurückgeführt wird.

In 8,3 taucht wieder Paulus auf, diesmal in gänzlich anderer Weise als in 7,58 und 8,1: Er dringt in die Häuser ein, verhaftet Christen und bringt sie ins Gefängnis; er ist der Organisator der Verfolgung. Später wird er mit φόνος und ἀπειλῆ (9,1) in Verbindung gebracht. Das Bild des gewalttätigen, mörderischen Verfolgers Saulus ist sicher ebenso übertrieben gezeichnet wie auch die spätere Notiz, Paulus sei vom Synedrium zur Verfolgung nach Damaskus entsandt. Paulus wird weder die rechtliche Handhabe zu einer derartigen Verfolgung gehabt haben, noch konnte das Synedrium über derartige Maßnahmen verfügen. Von den Gegnern des Stephanus ist nicht mehr die Rede. Wie auch in 7,58 und 8,1a erscheint die Notiz in 8,3 redaktionell in einen durch die Verfolgungssituation bestimmten traditionellen Rahmen eingefügt. Grundlage ist das Faktum einer Verfolgung durch den jungen Paulus; bei der Ortsbestimmung und der Verbindung mit dem Stephanuskomplex ist nicht anzunehmen, daß der Redaktor sie in der Tradition bereits vorgefunden hat. Insbeson-

---

[50] So z. B. Harnack 1908, 139; Wendt 1913, 150 Anm. 1 u. a.

[51] (Apg 7,58b) καὶ οἱ μάρτυρες ἀπέθεντο τὰ ἱμάτια αὐτῶν παρὰ τοὺς πόδας νεανίου καλουμένου Σαύλου, ... (8,1a) Σαῦλος δὲ ἦν συνευδοκῶν τῇ ἀναιρέσει αὐτοῦ. (8,3) Σαῦλος δὲ ἐλυμαίνετο τὴν ἐκκλησίαν κατὰ τοὺς οἴκους εἰσπορευόμενος, σύρων τε ἄνδρας καὶ γυναῖκας παρεδίδου εἰς φυλακήν.

[52] Apg 6,9ff.

[53] Vgl. auch die Parallelstelle Apg 22,20.

[54] Vgl. Zahn 1922, 264.

dere die Verortung der paulinischen Verfolgung in Jerusalem erklärt sich aus dem Gesamtbild, das der Auctor ad Theophilum von der Ausbreitung des Christentums zeichnet.

Die Richtung der Darstellung wird schon zu Beginn der Apostelgeschichte vorgegeben: Lukas läßt den auferstandenen Jesus in 1,8 sagen, daß die Jünger seine Zeugen sein werden ἔν τε Ἰερουσαλὴμ καὶ ἐν πάσῃ τῇ Ἰουδαίᾳ καὶ Σαμαρείᾳ καὶ ἕως ἐσχάτου τῆς γῆς. Damit ist ein geographisches Ordnungsprinzip vorgegeben, nach dem die Apostelgeschichte aufgebaut ist[55]. Hinzu kommt, daß Lukas die Absicht hat, Paulus als denjenigen darzustellen, der eine breit angelegte Mission betreibt und auch beginnt. Seine Mission ist besonders qualifiziert, da die Erzählung vor seiner Bekehrung den syrisch-palästinischen Raum nicht überschreitet. Dann allerdings kann die Verfolgung durch ihn, die ja ebenfalls vor seiner Bekehrung stattgefunden haben muß, in der Vorstellung des Lukas nur in Jerusalem lokalisiert werden. Erst in Apg 8,4 wird ja berichtet, daß eine weitere Gemeinde als Konsequenz dieser Verfolgung in Samarien entsteht, *die* christliche Gemeinde ist in Apg 7 die in Jerusalem, und Paulus, der *die* Gemeinde verfolgt, verfolgt folgerichtig die Jerusalemer. Verfolgt Paulus nun aber die Gemeinde in Jerusalem, wie Lukas konstruiert, so muß er sich dort vorher nicht nur aufgehalten, sondern bereits eine gewisse Machtposition aufgebaut haben. Lukas versucht dies damit zu erklären, daß er Paulus in Jerusalem aufwachsen läßt und ihn mit schriftgelehrten Kreisen, ja mit dem Synedrium in Verbindung bringt.

Dem Schema "Jerusalem – Judäa und Samaria – Ende der Erde" scheint die Notiz Röm 15,19b zu entsprechen, Paulus habe von Jerusalem und ringsumher bis nach Illyrien das Evangelium von Christus verkündigt[56]. Hengel versucht daraus zu schließen, das lukanische Schema entspreche der historischen Wirklichkeit auch im Detail[57]. Dies ist aber schwerlich zutreffend. Auch wenn man nicht mit *U. Wilckens* annehmen will, daß Paulus hier in erster Linie von der Gesamtbewegung des Evangeliums spricht[58], sondern schon seine eigene Missionstätigkeit im Blick hat, wird man nicht umhin können, die Notiz als Ausdruck theologischer Reflexion zu verstehen. Paulus ordnet seine Missionstätigkeit in ein Schema ein, daß dem der Apostelgeschichte ähnelt: Die Ausbreitung des Evangeliums vollzog sich von Jerusalem bis nach Illyrien. Die Notiz setzt die in Gal 1,18 und 2,1ff. beschriebenen Jerusalembesuche des Paulus voraus, Jerusalem und Illyrien geben zwei Punkte an, zwischen denen sich die paulinische Mission bewegt haben wird. Für einen Aufenthalt des

---

[55] Vgl. Conzelmann 1972, 27; Weiser 1981, 27f.; Schille 1984, 72; Pesch 1986, 69f., u. a.

[56] Röm 15,19b: ...ὥστε με ἀπὸ Ἰερουσαλὴμ καὶ κύκλῳ μέχρι τοῦ Ἰλλυρικοῦ πεπληρωκέναι τὸ εὐαγγέλιον τοῦ Χριστοῦ.

[57] Vgl. Hengel 1991, 219f.

[58] Vgl. Wilckens 1982, 120.

Paulus in Illyrien, also in Dalmatien oder Pannonien, fehlen jegliche Anhaltspunkte. Nicht nur wird ein solcher Aufenthalt nicht in Apg erwähnt, auch über christliche Gemeinden in Illyrien sind bis ins zweite Jahrhundert hinein keine Nachrichten erhalten. Von II Tim 4,10 ausgehend könnte vermutet werden, daß die Wirkung der paulinischen Mission bis nach Illyrien ausgestrahlt habe, auch dies ist aber sehr unsicher. Möglicherweise bedeutet Illyrien nicht mehr als eine Richtungsangabe: Paulus missioniert in Richtung Italien, in Richtung Rom.

Die Abfolge ist theologisch motiviert, auch die historische Gesamtbewegung der paulinischen Mission von Jerusalem in Richtung Rom ließ sich in dieser Weise betrachten, was wegen des lukanischen Entwurfs als gesichert gelten dürfte. Falsch ist es jedoch, daraus Schlüsse für bestimmte Einzelereignisse zu ziehen, weder ist ein Aufenthalt des Paulus in Illyrien noch der tatsächliche Beginn seines missionarischen Lebensweges in Jerusalem hierdurch zu belegen. Röm 15,19b bezieht sich *nur* auf den — theologischen wie geographischen — Gesamtrahmen.

Zeichnet die Apg ein redaktionell gestaltetes, wenn auch doch historisch denkbares Bild des Verfolgers und jungen Juden Saulus in Jerusalem, so ist damit das Problem noch nicht geklärt, ob der spätere Apostel in Jerusalem seine vorchristliche Zeit verbrachte oder nicht. Es ist ja nicht zu bestreiten, daß Lukas für seine Darstellung und seine Antwort auf die Fragen, die die Überlieferung offenließ, Anhaltspunkte in der Paulustradition hatte, zumal wenn Jerusalem für Paulus keine unbedeutende Rolle spielt[59].

3.3. Es ist nun aber so, daß Hinweise dafür vorliegen, daß die paulinische Verfolgung nicht in Jerusalem stattgefunden haben kann. Paulus schreibt in Gal 1,22f. im Hinblick auf seine judenchristlichen Gegner:

(22) ἤμην δὲ ἀγνοούμενος τῷ προσώπῳ ταῖς ἐκκλησίαις τῆς Ἰουδαίας ταῖς ἐν Χριστῷ.
(23) μόνον δὲ ἀκούοντες ἦσαν
ὅτι ὁ διώκων ἡμᾶς ποτε νῦν εὐαγγελίζεται τὴν πίστιν ἥν ποτε ἐπόρθει.

Diese Angabe steht in krassem Gegensatz zur Darstellung der Apostelgeschichte. "War Paulus damals in Jerusalem und hat er die dortige Gemeinde [Apg] 8,3 verfolgt, so konnte er Gal 1,22 nicht sagen, er sei den 'Gemeinden Judäas' nicht persönlich bekannt gewesen. Das sind einander ausschließende Angaben"[60]. Wenn Paulus die Gemeinde in Jerusalem verfolgte, ja sogar gewalttätig vorging, dann sollte er seinen Opfern doch wohl auch persönlich bekannt gewesen sein. Dies gilt umso mehr, wenn Paulus tatsächlich von seinen Gegnern in Galatien vorgeworfen

---

[59] Ἰερουσαλήμ kommt siebenmal in den Paulusbriefen vor, Ἰεροσόλυμα dreimal.
[60] Heitmüller 1912, 327.

wurde, er sei in Judäa unbekannt[61]. In jedem Fall könnte diese Notiz seiner Argumentation nicht dienlich sein, wenn sie nicht der Wahrheit entspräche. Dann hätten seine anscheinend gut informierten Gegner ein leichtes Spiel mit ihm gehabt. V. 23 gibt seinerseits eine Nachricht aus der wirklich von Paulus verfolgten Gemeinde wieder, ohne zu sagen, wo sich diese befand. Den Christen in Judäa wurde lediglich mündlich zugetragen, daß Paulus ein Verfolger war; ἡμᾶς bezieht sich auf die christlichen Gemeinden, die den Christen in Judäa die Mitteilung von der paulinischen Lebenswende überbrachten.

Wo Paulus also den christlichen Glauben kennengelernt und die Gemeinde zunächst verfolgt hat, ist unsicher. Es käme zuerst Damaskus in Frage, die Stadt, die im Kontext der Lebenswende von Bedeutung ist und die in Gal 1,17 erwähnt wird. Mögliche, wenn auch aus chronologischen Gründen weniger wahrscheinliche Lokalisierungen wären Tarsus und Antiochia am Orontes — möglich vor allem, weil eine schnellere Ausbreitung der christlichen Sekte als in der Apostelgeschichte dargestellt ohnehin angenommen werden muß. Ein reger Austausch zwischen dem heiligen Land und der hellenistischen Diaspora, z. B. durch die alljährlichen Pilgerströme zu den großen jüdischen Festen, sollte in Erwägung gezogen werden. Wie dem auch sei: "Sicher und wertvoll ist zunächst die negative Erkenntnis, daß Paulus das Christentum nicht in Jerusalem kennen gelernt und nicht durch die jerusalemische Urgemeinde die ersten entscheidenden Eindrücke vom Christentum erhalten hat"[62].

Dagegen hat Hengel mehrere Einwände erhoben. Gegen die Lokalisierung der paulinischen Verfolgung in Tarsus spreche die Verbindung des Apostels mit Damaskus (Gal 1,17). Es sei ferner besonders fragwürdig, wie denn Paulus von Tarsus nach Arabien gekommen sein soll, ohne Jerusalem zu besuchen[63]. Hier irrt Hengel jedoch: Eine Reise von Tarsus direkt nach Arabien ist hier gar nicht im Blick, wenn Paulus schreibt, daß er nach Arabien zog und dann nach *Damaskus* zurückkehrte. Das kann nur heißen, daß er auch von Damaskus aufgebrochen ist. Somit stehen Tarsus, Damaskus und Arabien als Stationen seiner Reise fest. Eine Reise von Tarsus nach Damaskus und später von Damaskus nach Arabien und zurück ist aber sehr wohl unter Umgehung Jerusalems nicht nur möglich, sondern auch die wahrscheinlichere. Bei einem fluchtartigen Aufbruch aus Damaskus legt es sich darüber hinaus dringend nahe, nicht den Umweg über die heilige Stadt zu machen; eingeschlossen war darin auch ein Aufstieg von ca. 1000 m – man sehe sich das einmal auf der Karte an!

---

[61] S. o., § 3.1.
[62] Heitmüller 1912, 328.
[63] S. o., § 2.2.

Um an Jerusalem als Ort der Verfolgung festhalten zu können, führt Hengel die Möglichkeit an, Paulus habe den Stephanuskreis verfolgt, also den hellenistischen, griechischsprachigen Teil der Jerusalemer Christenheit[64]. Die Äußerung in Gal 1,23 bezöge sich dann auf die aramäischen Gemeinden Judäas um den Apostel Petrus[65]. Dem Petruskreis sei die Verfolgung zwar zu Ohren gekommen, diese Gemeinde kenne Paulus aber nicht. Dies setzt voraus, daß die unterschiedlichen christlichen Gemeinden Jerusalems keinen engeren Kontakt pflegten, ferner, daß in Jerusalem "große" Verhältnisse vorlagen[66]. Es ist erforderlich, dann auch anzunehmen, Paulus habe mit seiner Verfolgung die hellenistische Gemeinde Jerusalems erfolgreich zerstört und ihre Mitglieder verjagt, sonst gäbe es ja eine judäische Gemeinde, die ihn kennen müßte[67]. Das setzt aber wieder voraus, daß die hellenistische Gemeinde Jerusalems sehr klein gewesen sein mußte, wenn sie durch die Anstrengung eines einzelnen vernichtet werden konnte[68]. Und unbedingt erforderlich ist es dann auch, die redaktionelle Verknüpfung von Paulus und Stephanus in der Apostelgeschichte als historische Reminiszenz zu bestimmen[69]. Jedoch ist in der kritischen Forschung unbestritten, daß die Apostelgeschichte in ihrer Charakterisierung der Jerusalemer Urgemeinde eine höchst unsichere historische Grundlage darstellt. Welche Quelle berichtet aber dann vom sogenannten Stephanuskreis? — Mag dies nun vielleicht nur entfernt wie eine Tendenzauswahl erscheinen, so ist doch sicher, daß es sich um eine Aneinanderreihung von Vermutungen handelt, die sämtlich eine Möglichkeit konstruieren, wie der Verfolger Paulus mit der Stadt Jerusalem verbunden werden kann. Denn über die bloße Möglichkeit kommt eine Aneinanderreihung von Hypothesen nicht hinaus. Es ist nicht nur nicht sicher, sondern äußerst unwahrscheinlich, daß die historische Wirklichkeit dem Konstrukt Hengels entspricht. Dies belegt vor allem die Beobachtung, daß Lukas ganz offensichtlich seinen Helden Paulus nicht im Rahmen der Stephanustradition vorgefunden hat, sondern ihn nachträglich einführen mußte. Viel plausibler und aufgrund von Gal 1,22f. auch wahrscheinlicher ist es, daß Paulus zur Zeit des Stephanusmartyriums und auch sonst in seinem Leben nicht in Jerusalem ansässig war.

---

[64] Vgl. Hengel 1991, 279f.

[65] Vgl. ebd., 281.

[66] Zur Schätzung der Einwohnerzahl Jerusalems, s. o., 2.2. Anm. 19.

[67] Vgl. Hengel 1991, 279.

[68] Vgl. ebd.

[69] Vgl. ebd., 272ff.

## *4. Diasporapharisäer und Gelehrtenschüler*

Hat der Verfolger Paulus nicht in Jerusalem gewirkt, so muß auch bezweifelt werden, daß die Notizen der Apostelgeschichte, durch die Paulus im Vorfeld der Verfolgungsberichte mit Jerusalem in Verbindung gebracht werden soll und die Erziehung und Ausbildung betreffen, einen historisch zutreffenden Sachverhalt wiedergeben. Es legt sich nahe, daß Paulus zumindest nicht primär als palästinischer Jude anzusehen ist. Seine religionsgeschichtlichen Voraussetzungen sind nicht primär im Land der Väter, in Palästina, zu suchen. Gegen diese Ansicht werden besonders zwei Argumente ins Feld geführt: Zum einen bezeichnet Paulus sich selbst als Pharisäer; der Pharisäismus aber sei genuin-palästinisch und auf den palästinischen Raum beschränkt. Zum anderen habe Paulus eine pharisäisch-schriftgelehrte Bildung erworben; dies sei in der Diaspora nicht möglich gewesen. Dazu im einzelnen:

4.1. Die religiöse und politisch orientierte Bewegung der Pharisäer ist zwar nahezu ausschließlich für den palästinischen Raum nachzuweisen. Jedoch muß angenommen werden, daß Pharisäer auch über die Grenzen Palästinas hinaus gewirkt haben. Mt 23,15 setzt dies voraus, wenn den Pharisäern und Schriftgelehrten vorgeworfen wird, daß sie Meer und Land befahren, nur um einen Proselyten zu gewinnen[70]. Es ist offen, ob dies vom palästinischen Standpunkt aus gesagt wurde[71], bezieht sich aber jedenfalls auf die Wirksamkeit der Pharisäer in der Diaspora. Die Bedeutung der jüdischen Diaspora kann auch für die Zeit des zweiten Tempels nicht hoch genug eingeschätzt werden. Das Vorhandensein zahlreicher jüdischer Gemeinden von z. T. beachtlicher Größe außerhalb des heiligen Landes ist ein Grunddatum für die Zeit, in der Paulus gelebt hat. Nicht nur Vertreibung und Verschleppung waren die Gründe für eine Ansiedlung außerhalb Palästinas, auch wirtschaftliche Faktoren werden eine Rolle gespielt haben. Auch in Kilikien, der Heimat des Paulus, können jüdische Gemeinden nachgewiesen werden[72].

Die Wirksamkeit der Pharisäer in der Diaspora wird sich sicher nicht auf den Gewinn von Proselyten beschränkt haben, höchstwahrscheinlich brachten sie den dort ansässigen jüdischen Gemeinden auch ihre eigenen Vorstellungen und Ideale nahe;

---

[70] Mt 23,15a: Οὐαὶ ὑμῖν, γραμματεῖς καὶ Φαρισαῖοι ὑποκριταί, ὅτι περιάγετε τὴν θάλασσαν καὶ τὴν ξηρὰν ποιῆσαι ἕνα προσήλυτον.

[71] Mt 23,15 ist selbstverständlich primär vom Standpunkt des Matthäus aus zu sehen, der vermutlich im griechischsprechenden Syrien geschrieben hat, so daß die Äußerung keineswegs notwendig den palästinischen Standpunkt voraussetzt, sondern vom Autor aus gesehen ein Beleg für die außerpalästinische Wirksamkeit der Pharisäer gewesen ist.

[72] Vgl. Philo, LegGai 281, CIJ Nr. 925, OGIS Nr. 573; ferner in Josephus Ant XX, 145 den Bericht von der Konversion des Königs Polemon II. von Pontos und Kilikien zum Judentum, die mit der Intention vollzogen wurde, Berenike, die Tochter Agrippas zu heiraten.

denn eine von den jüdischen Diasporagemeinden losgelöste pharisäische Mission ist nicht vorstellbar. Ohne eine entsprechende Infrastruktur hätten Pharisäer im Ausland nicht leben können, denn es wäre nicht möglich gewesen, die Vorschriften der Tora genau einzuhalten, wenn man in heidnischer Umgebung auf sich allein gestellt war. "Da für Juden alles heidnische Gebiet mit Totenunreinheit behaftet, und jeder Heide *eo ipso* unrein war, und dies auch für die von Heiden erworbenen Speisen galt, die darüber hinaus stets der Verbindung mit dem Götzendienst verdächtig waren, wurde eine wirkliche Einhaltung der Vorschriften der Tora auf heidnischem Gebiet unmöglich"[73]. Hier wird aus richtigen Beobachtungen ein falscher Schluß gezogen. Gerade das religiöse Defizit, das die heidnische Umwelt mit sich bringt, kann der Auslöser für einen engeren Zusammenschluß der Juden in der Diaspora sein. Der Wunsch nach der Heiligung des täglichen Lebens muß gerade in der Anfechtung ein optimaler Nährboden für eine Gemeinschaft, wie sie die Pharisäer darstellten, gewesen sein. Es war notwendig, auch im heidnischen Gebiet bestimmte Bereiche von ritueller Unreinheit freizuhalten; es war notwendig, über die rechte Lehre zu wachen; es war notwendig, Nahrungsmittel und Rohstoffe zu erwerben, die nicht von Heiden stammten, und zwar nicht nur aus Gründen der Reinheit, sondern auch aus wirtschaftlichen Erwägungen: Man denke nur einmal daran, was es z. B. bedeuten würde, wenn bei der Verzehntung nicht nur das Endprodukt, sondern auch alle Rohstoffe und Zwischenprodukte verzehntet werden, was im Zweifel zu geschehen hätte. Diesen Zweifel auszuschalten ist dann das Ziel pharisäischer Gemeinschaften.

Die Einhaltung der Vorschriften der Tora ist auf heidnischem Gebiet also zwar erschwert, nicht aber unmöglich gewesen. Die Vorstellung, daß man nur im heiligen Land richtig Jude sein kann, tritt erst in späteren, rabbinischen Schriften zutage[74]. Bei ihrer Interpretation ist größte Vorsicht geboten. Ein kontinuierlicher Zusammenhang zwischen dem Pharisäismus vor 70 n. Chr. und dem Rabbinismus nach 70 n. Chr. kann nur sehr schwer rekonstruiert und sollte zumindest nicht einfach vorausgesetzt werden[75]. Tatsache ist, daß die Heiligkeit des Landes Israel bei allem theologischen Rigorismus stets eine Fiktion war und es unter römischem Joch und vielfältigen heidnisch-hellenistischen Einflüssen auch bleiben mußte.

Es ist also ganz und gar nicht ersichtlich, warum Paulus nicht in der Diaspora Anschluß an den Pharisäismus gefunden und dort auch als Pharisäer gelebt haben kann. Eine in Palästina so einflußreiche religiöse Gruppe wird auch auf die Juden in der Diaspora, die ja durchaus Bindungen an das Mutterland hatten, eine nicht unerhebliche Wirkung gehabt haben. Die Vorbildlichkeit des religiösen Wandels des

---

[73] Hengel 1991, 228.
[74] Vgl. Ohal II,3; Ohal XVIII, 6.
[75] Vgl. Schäfer 1991, 170.

jungen Paulus hat auch damit zu tun, daß er seine Frömmigkeit unter erschwerten Bedingungen zu leben hatte. Darin aber war er untadelig und ging weiter als seine Altersgenossen.

4.2. Die Bildung des Apostels Paulus ist geprägt vom jüdisch-hellenistischen Umfeld, in dem er aufgewachsen ist. Selbstverständlich ist er dort nicht zu einem herausragenden Exponenten griechischer Gelehrsamkeit geworden; aber seine geistige und theologische Bildung ist doch von der palästinisch-jüdischen zu unterscheiden. Das, was oftmals als rabbinische Denkweise des Paulus in Anspruch genommen wird, ist den Einflüssen des Diasporajudentums zu verdanken, wie Paulus es in seiner Heimatstadt durch jüdische Lehrer kennenlernte. Die rhetorische Fertigkeit, die in den echten Paulusbriefen zutage tritt, deutet darauf hin, daß Paulus nicht nur eine hellenistische Elementarschule besucht, sondern das hellenistische Schulsystem in allen Stufen durchlaufen hat. Insbesondere wird Paulus eine rhetorische Grundausbildung absolviert haben, die auf den praktischen Gebrauch – in erster Linie den mündlichen – ausgerichtet war[76]. Das Griechische ist die Muttersprache des Paulus; so besteht z. B. nicht der geringste Zweifel, daß er (bzw. seine Mitarbeiter, soweit diese als Mitglieder der "Schule des Paulus" an den Vorarbeiten und der Abfassung der Paulusbriefe mitbeteiligt waren) die griechische Übersetzung des AT benutzt hat. Er zitiert den Septuaginta-Text selbst dort, wo dieser gegenüber dem masoretischen Text Fehler aufweist, und er folgt auch dann der Septuaginta, wenn der masoretische Text für ihn einen passenderen Wortlaut bereitgestellt hätte[77].

Soweit Abweichungen von dem Septuagintatext in den paulinischen Zitaten vorliegen, sind diese unterschiedlich zu erklären. Zunächst ist damit zu rechnen, daß Paulus selbst dort, wo er einen schriftlichen Text vor sich hat, diesen nicht Wort für Wort zitiert. Vielmehr können Änderungen des Textes bewußt vorgenommen worden sein, um den gemeinten und hineingedeuteten Sinn herauszustellen[78]. Darüber hinaus ist mit der Möglichkeit zu rechnen, daß Paulus frühe Septuagintarezensionen verwendet, die mit dem überlieferten Septuagintatext nicht immer identisch sind.

---

[76] Vgl. zur hellenistischen Ausbildung des Apostels v. a. Hellholm 1992.

[77] Z. B. I Kor 2,16: Zitiert ist Jes 40,13 LXX (νοῦς κυρίου); das masoretische *ruach jhwh* = πνεῦμα κυρίου hätte dem Kontext entsprechend näher gelegen.

[78] Vgl. Röm 1,17 (Hab 2,4) und weitere derartige Textverkürzungen in II Kor 3,16 (Ex 34,34); Gal 3,13 (Dtn 21,23c); Röm 10,15 (Jes 52,7). Die Auslassung Gal 3,12 (Lev 18,5; diese Stelle vollständig zitiert in Röm 10,5) ist eine bewußte Angleichung an die im Text benachbarten Zitate. Eine Hinzufügung liegt Röm 10,11 (Jes 28, 16c) vor; dasselbe Zitat findet sich unverändert Röm 9,33. Der genaue Wortlaut des Jesaja-Zitates ist Paulus somit bekannt, die Hinzufügung geschieht bewußt. Vgl. auch Röm 4,3; Gal 3,6 (Gen 15,6).

Ein Beispiel: Das Zitat in I Kor 15,54 κατεπόθη ὁ θάνατος εἰς νῖκος weicht vom masoretischen Text (Jes 25,8) ab, aber auch von der Septuagintaüberlieferung (so im Passiv κατεπόθη und in der Lesart εἰς νῖκος für das hebräische לָנֶצַח). Dagegen finden sich wörtliche Übereinstimmungen bei den jüdischen Übersetzern Theodotion und Aquila, Parallelen auch bei Symmachus[79]. Umstritten ist, ob die Übereinstimmung mit Theodotion ein Beweis für die Abhängigkeit des Paulus von einem "Ur-Theodotion" ist[80], auch, ob hieraus auf ein höheres Alter des Theodotion geschlossen werden kann[81]. Jedenfalls ist davon auszugehen, daß die Septuagintavorlage des Paulus mit unseren Septuagintatexten nicht immer gleichgesetzt werden kann; es dürfte in I Kor 15,54 eine vorchristliche jüdische Vorlage zugrundeliegen, welche dem Septuagintatext entsprechend der Zwölfprophetenbuchrolle von Murabaʾat (Mitte des 1. Jh. n. Chr.) nach dem hebräischen Text korrigiert.Solche frühen Rezensionen haben vermutlich Einfluß auf die späteren Übersetzer Theodotion, Aquila und Symmachus gehabt[82].

Dies kann auch die beiden Stellen erklären, in denen Paulus andernfalls auf den hebräischen Text zurückgegriffen haben würde[83]: Röm 11,35 (Hi 41,2) und I Kor 3,18 (Hi 5,12f.). Da sich trotz Anzeichen von sprachlichen Verbesserungen kein paulinischer Übersetzungsstil feststellen läßt, liegt auch hier eine griechische AT-Übersetzung zugrunde, die als Überarbeitung des Septuagintatextes anzusehen ist[84]. Daher steht bei Beachtung der genannten Variationen die Septuagintagrundlage fest, und es ist ausgeschlossen, daß Paulus jemals den hebräischen Urtext benutzte. Insofern ist der Apostel in seinem Schriftgebrauch ein Repräsentant des hellenistischen Judentums.

Die jüdischen Voraussetzungen der paulinischen Theologie zeigen sich auch an der Art und Weise, wie Paulus den Text des AT benutzt. Hier sind vor allem Schlußverfahren zu nennen, die teilweise im rabbinischen Judentum belegt sind, aber auch

---

[79] Während der LXX-Text zu Jes 25,8 κατέπιεν ὁ θάνατος ἰσχύσας lautet, existieren für Theodotion zwei unterschiedliche Übersetzungen, die לָנֶצַח mit εἰς νῖκος wiedergeben. Aquila übersetzt καταποντίσει τὸν θάνατον εἰς νῖκος und der etwas spätere Symmachus καταποθῆναι ποιήσει τὸν θάνατον εἰς τέλος.

[80] Dagegen z. B. Rahlfs 1921.

[81] Die Möglichkeit, daß Theodotion nicht um 180 n. Chr. gewirkt hat, wie es die Erwähnung bei Epiphanius (de mensuribus et ponderibus, PL XLIII, 264f.) darstellt, und daß die Notiz des Irenäus (haer III, 24) glaubhafter sei, wird von Brock 1980 vermutet. Danach wäre die Übersetzung Theodotions in die Mitte des 1. Jh. n. Chr. zu datieren – was aber eine Abhängigkeit des Paulus von Theodotion nicht wahrscheinlicher macht.

[82] Vgl. hierzu Hanhart 1981, 293-303, ders.1988, 179-196. Ähnlich Koch 1986, 57-81, der von hebraisierenden Überarbeitungen der Septuaginta spricht, die Paulus z. T. in schriftlicher Form vorgelegen haben.

[83] So Ellis 1957, 144 Anm. 3.

[84] Vgl. Koch 1986,78f. Gegen Hengel 1991, 233ff.

schon im griechischsprachigen Judentum des 1. Jh. v. Chr. bekannt waren[85]:

(a) Häufig gebraucht wird der Schluß *a minori ad maius*, "vom Geringeren auf das Größere". Dieses Schlußverfahren ist an der griechischen Steigerungsform πολλῷ μᾶλλον bzw. πόσῳ μᾶλλον erkennbar. Es findet sich in der Adam-Christus-Typologie (Röm 5,15.17), in der Darstellung der Bedeutung des Todes Christi "für uns" (Röm 5,9f.), des heilsgeschichtlichen Problems Israels (Röm 11,12: Ps 68,23 LXX in 11,9; auch 11,24), ferner in der Gegenüberstellung des Dienstes Moses zum Dienst des Geistes (II Kor 3,7-9.11: Ex 34,30). Dieses Auslegungsverfahren wird in der rabbinischen Überlieferung mit קַל וָחֹמֶר ("Leichtes und Schweres") bezeichnet. Andererseits ist auch das umgekehrte Schlußverfahren belegt, nämlich der Schluß vom "Größeren auf das Geringere" *(a maiori ad minus*; vgl. Röm 8,32; I Kor 6,2f.).

(b) Der *Analogie*schluß (in der rabbinischen Überlieferung גְּזֵרָה שָׁוָה = "gleiche Entscheidung"). Hier werden zwei Bibelstellen, die gleiche Begriffe verwenden, aufeinander bezogen und die eine durch die andere erläutert (so Röm 4,3-8: Gen 15,6 und Ps 31,1f. LXX; beide Male erscheint das Wort λογίζεσθαι in verschiedener Weise; Paulus verbindet beide Stellen miteinander, so daß λογίζεσθαι sowohl "den Glauben zur Gerechtigkeit anrechnen" als auch "die Sünde nicht anrechnen" bedeutet).

Die beiden eben genannten Auslegungsverfahren zählen zu den sieben Regeln ("*Middot*") des Rabbi Hillel, die eine "Zusammenstellung von damals üblichen Hauptarten des Beweisverfahrens" waren[86]. Jedoch ergibt sich daraus nicht die Folgerung, Paulus habe die Regeln Hillels gekannt oder er sei ein Hillelit gewesen[87]; denn Hillel verwendete noch weitere Beweisverfahren und die eben genannten waren nicht nur in der jüdischen Lehre üblich, sondern haben Entsprechungen in der hellenistischen Rhetorik, so daß auch für das rabbinische Schlußverfahren eine Beeinflussung aus dem hellenistischen Bereich anzunehmen ist.

Das weitgehende Fehlen von Hinweisen dafür, daß Paulus die klassische griechische Literatur genauer kannte[88], mag damit zusammenhängen, daß er als frommer Jude heidnischen Schriftstellern gegenüber Vorbehalte hegen mußte. Mögen auch seine rhetorischen Fähigkeiten anhand heidnischer Autoren geschärft worden sein, so tritt inhaltlich die intime Kenntnis der griechischen Bibel an ihre Stelle. Die hel-

---

[85] Siehe dazu Michel 1929, 91ff.; Koch 1986, 199ff.

[86] Strack /Stemberger 1982, 27.

[87] Anders Jeremias 1969b; hier werden weitere Parallelen zu Hillel genannt: J. Jeremias zählt drei weitere hillelitische Regeln auf, die er bei Paulus ausmachen zu können glaubt: Die fünfte Regel (Generelles und Spezielles) läßt umfassende und spezielle Gebote sich gegenseitig bestimmen. Paulus wende diese Regel Röm 3,9; Gal 5,14 an. Die sechste Regel (Näherbestimmung einer Bibelstelle mit Hilfe einer verwandten Stelle) sieht Jeremias Gal 3,16 verwendet und die Benutzung der siebten Regel (die Folgerung aus dem Zusammenhang) in Röm 4,10-11a; Gal 3,17.

[88] Vgl. aber I Kor 15,33 die Anspielung auf Menander, Thais, Frgm 218 (Kock).

lenistische Ausbildung ist eine hellenistisch-jüdische: Paulus wird seine Jugend
nicht ohne Bindung an eine Synagoge und ihr Erziehungssystem verbracht haben.
Selbst wenn die Ausbildung, an die hier zu denken ist, nicht spezifisch pharisäisch
zu sein braucht, ist ein pharisäischer Einfluß, wie er für das Diasporajudentum als
möglich vorausgesetzt werden muß, mit einzuschließen. Jedenfalls wird auch ein
Torastudium im Jerusalemer *bet midrash* bei Paulus nicht erwähnt. Jerusalem war
zwar die angesehenste und größte Lehrstätte für ein Gesetzesstudium, aber ein Studium der Tora ist ebenfalls denkbar an einer anderen Lehrstätte oder im synagogalen und privaten Rahmen, also außerhalb eines *bet midrash*. Ein Studium in
Jerusalem für Paulus anzunehmen, ist vom lukanischen Geschichtsbild inspiriert.

Wenn zur Erläuterung eines solchen Studiums rabbinische Quellen herangezogen werden, so verkennt das den großen Stellenwert, der dort dem Torastudium, das
nicht an ein *bet midrash* gebunden ist, beigemessen wird[89]. Schriftgelehrte Beschäftigung ist zur Zeit des zweiten Tempels im heiligen Land wie in der Diaspora
ein wichtiger Teil allen frommen Lebens. Es ist nicht nur möglich, sondern auch
wahrscheinlich, daß der Diasporapharisäer Paulus unbeschadet seiner hellenistischen Ausbildung das Torastudium in der Synagoge und im Kreis seiner pharisäischen Genossen fortsetzte[90], womit auch eine weitere mögliche Funktion pharisäischer Gemeinschaften in der Diaspora gegeben ist.

## 5. Folgerungen: Der vorchristliche Paulus.

5.1. Damit scheint es möglich, sich in Umrissen einem Gesamtbild des vorchristlichen Paulus anzunähern, das zwar hier und da gewisse Lücken aufweist, die aber
dadurch bedingt sind, daß die vorchristliche Zeit für den Heidenapostel Paulus eine
nur noch untergeordnete Rolle spielte.

Der junge Paulus wurde in Tarsus geboren und wuchs wahrscheinlich auch dort
auf. Er erhielt eine fundierte hellenistische Schulbildung, lernte aber auch die griechische Bibel und die jüdische zwischentestamentarische Literatur gut kennen,
wohl im Rahmen einer Diasporasynagoge. Ob er bereits von Geburt Pharisäer war
oder erst später an diese Gemeinschaft Anschluß fand, ist unklar, möglich, ja wahrscheinlich ist, daß dies in der Diaspora geschah. Außer, daß Paulus sich als Pharisäer um ein gesetzesstrenges Leben mit einigem Erfolg bemühte, irgendwann mit
dem christlichen Glauben in Berührung kam und die Christen aus im einzelnen un-

---

[89] Vgl. Av 1,6; ARN A,8 (p.36); Av 3,3; Er 18b; 54a.

[90] Vgl. Safrai 1974, 968: "The Torah was studied at all possible times, even if only a little at a
time, one or two halakoth or a haggadic story during attendance at the synagogue for the morning or
evening prayer, or at home in the evening. Some people formed groups of varying sizes and studied
together on weekday nights or on the sabbath".

bekannten Gründen verfolgte, wissen wir nichts über ihn bis zu dem Datum, das durch die Lebenswende bestimmt ist und das er selbst mit Damaskus verbindet. Die Verfolgung zuvor fand vielleicht in oder in der Gegend von Damaskus statt, sicher aber nicht in Jerusalem. Seine Lebenswende ist charakterisiert durch eine Umwertung aller Werte, die bis dahin sein Leben bestimmt haben müssen.

5.2. Für die religionsgeschichtliche Einordnung des Apostels Paulus sollte bedacht werden, daß seine spätere Position nicht nur aus einer Umwertung aller Werte, die seine vorchristliche Zeit bestimmt haben, zu erklären ist. Zu einem gewissen Teil wird er Elemente seiner Theologie auch aus den verschiedensten Zusammenhängen seiner vorchristlichen Zeit positiv übernommen haben, es ist ferner mit einer Beeinflussung durch christliche Gemeinden und das pagane Umfeld zu rechnen[91]. Diese Überlegung sollte vor einseitigen Urteilen über den religionsgeschichtlichen Hintergrund des Paulus bewahren. Er war weder in seiner vorchristlichen Zeit nur ein jüdischer Schriftgelehrter, noch in seiner christlichen ausschließlich der hellenistische Heidenmissionar. Als Wanderer zwischen zwei Welten ist Paulus eine viel kompliziertere Figur als es derartig vereinfachende Thesen erfassen können. Von daher sollten auch die Fragen nach seiner vorchristlichen Zeit nicht überbewertet werden. Eine Alternative "Tarsus oder Jerusalem" ist zwar für die Anfänge nicht zu umgehen, sie ist aber für das Auftreten des Paulus insgesamt nicht nahegelegt; denn der Apostel war gerade während seiner Tätigkeit als Heidenmissionar bemüht, bei aller historischen Diskontinuität und theologischen Diskrepanz zur Jerusalemer Urgemeinde die Verbindung zu Jerusalem nicht abbrechen zu lassen und die kirchliche Einheit den sich ergebenden Schwierigkeiten zum Trotz zu erhalten. Dies jedoch nicht in Entsprechung zum harmonistischen lukanischen Geschichtsbild, das — konsequent verfolgt — zur historisch und theologisch abwegigen Behauptung der persönlichen Bekanntschaft des Heidenapostels mit dem historischen Jesus und damit zur historischen Kontinuität "Jesus – Paulus" führen würde[92].

---

[91] Es hilft nicht weiter, außerjüdische Hintergründe von vornherein auszublenden und ein Bild des Heidenapostels Paulus nur aufgrund seiner jüdischen Identität zeichnen zu wollen, wie es etwa Niebuhr versucht. Das Bild eines Paulus als "Heidenapostel um Israels willen" (1992, 184) entspringt einer unzulässigen Minimalisierung.

[92] Hengel zieht diese letzte Konsequenz nicht; eine Begegnung zwischen Paulus und Jesus wird bei ihm aber immerhin erwogen und für möglich gehalten (266).

# Bibliographie

Bammel, E. 1968: "Gal 1,23", in: *ZNW* 59 (1968) 108-112.

Barth, G. 1979: *Der Brief an die Philipper* (ZBK NT 9), Zürich: Theologischer Verlag 1979.

Bauernfeind, O. 1939: *Die Apostelgeschichte* (ThHK 5), Leipzig: Deichert 1939.

Becker, J. 1989: *Paulus: der Apostel der Völker*, Tübingen: Mohr (Siebeck) 1989.

Brock, S. P. 1980: Art. "Bibelübersetzungen I", in: *TRE* 6, Berlin/New York: de Gruyter 1980, 163-172.

Broshi, M. 1975: "La Population de l'ancienne Jerusalem", in: *RB* 82 (1975) 5-14.

Conzelmann, H. 1972: *Die Apostelgeschichte* (HNT 7), Tübingen: Mohr (Siebeck) 1963; [2]1972.

Dibelius, M. 1925: *An die Thessalonicher I, II, an die Philipper* (HNT 11), Tübingen: Mohr (Siebeck) 1925.

Ellis, E. E. 1957: *Paul's use of the Old Testament*, Edinburgh: Oliver and Boyd 1957.

Gnilka, J. 1976: *Der Philipperbrief* (HThK X/3), Freiburg/Basel/Wien: Herder 1976.

Grosheide, F. W. 1948: *De Handelingen der Apostelen*, Amsterdam: Bottenburg 1948.

Gutbrod, W. 1957: Art. "Ἰσραήλ κτλ. C., D.", in: *ThWNT* III, Stuttgart: Kohlhammer [2]1957, 370-394.

Haenchen, E. 1977: *Die Apostelgeschichte*. Neu Übersetzt und erklärt (KEK III), Göttingen: Vandenhoeck & Ruprecht [16]1977.

Hanhart, R. 1981: *Das Neue Testament und die griechische Überlieferung des Judentums* (TU 125), Göttingen: Vandenhoeck & Ruprecht 1981.

— 1988: "Septuaginta", in: W. H. Schmidt/W. Thiel/R. Hanhart, *Altes Testament* (GKT 1), Göttingen 1988, 179-196.

Harnack, A. 1908: *Beiträge zur Einleitung in das NT III: Die Apostelgeschichte*, Leipzig: Hinrichs 1908.

Heitmüller W. 1912: "Zum Problem Paulus und Jesus", in: *ZNW* 13 (1912) 320-337.

Hellholm, D. 1992: "Paulus von Tarsos – Zum Problem der hellenistischen Ausbildung", Manuskript, 1992 (Deutsche Faßung bisher unveröffentlicht; norwegisch in: T. Eide & T. Hägg [Hgg.], *Dionysos og Apollon. Religion og samfunn i antikkens Hellas* [Skrifter utgitt av det norske institutt i Athen 1], Bergen: Universitetet i Bergen, Klassisk Institutt 1989, 259-282).

Hengel, M. 1975: "Zwischen Jesus und Paulus. Die 'Hellenisten', die 'Sieben' und Stephanus (Apg 6,1-15; 7,54-8,3)", in: *ZThK* 72 (1975) 151-206.

— 1991: "Der vorchristliche Paulus", in: M. Hengel/U. Heckel (Hgg.), *Paulus und das antike Judentum*. Tübingen-Durham-Symposium im Gedenken an den 50. Todestag Adolf Schlatters (WUNT 58), Tübingen: Mohr (Siebeck) 1991, 177-293.

Hübner, H. 1973: "Gal 3,10 und die Herkunft des Paulus", in: *KuD* 19 (1973) 215-231.

Jeremias, J. 1926: "War Paulus ein Witwer?", in: *ZNW* 25 (1926) 310-312.

— 1929: "Nochmals: War Paulus Witwer?", in: *ZNW* 28 (1929) 321-323.

— 1969a: *Jerusalem zur Zeit Jesu. Kulturgeschichtliche Untersuchung zur neutestamentlichen Zeitgeschichte,* Göttingen: Vandenhoeck & Ruprecht ³1969.

— 1969b: "Paulus als Hillelit", in: E. E. Ellis/M. Wilcox (Hgg.), *Neotestamentica et Semitica,* FS M. Black, Edinburgh: T. & T. Clark 1969, 88-94.

Koch, D. A. 1986: *Die Schrift als Zeuge* (BHTh 69), Tübingen: Mohr (Siebeck) 1986.

Lietzmann, H. 1932: *An die Galater* (HNT 5), Tübingen: Mohr (Siebeck) 1932.

Lietzmann, H./ Kümmel, W. G. 1969: *An die Korinther I, II* (HNT 9), Tübingen: Mohr (Siebeck) ⁵1969.

Lightfoot, J. B. 1868: *St. Paul's Epistle to the Philippians,* London/Cambridge: MacMillan 1868 [neudruck der zweiten Aufl. von 1913: Grand Rapids, MI: Zondervan 1953, ¹⁶1978].

Lüdemann, G. 1980: *Paulus der Heidenapostel I: Studien zur Chronologie* (FRLANT 123), Göttingen: Vandenhoeck & Ruprecht 1980.

— 1983: *Paulus und das Judentum* (Theologische Existenz heute 215), München: Kaiser 1983.

— 1987: *Das frühe Christentum nach den Traditionen der Apostelgeschichte,* Göttingen: Vandenhoeck & Ruprecht 1987.

Lührmann, D. 1978: *Der Brief an die Galater* (ZBK NT 7), Zürich: Theologischer Verlag 1978.

Meyer, E. 1923: *Ursprung und Anfänge des Christentums* III, Stuttgart/Berlin: Cottasche Buchhandlung Nachf. 1923.

Michel, O. 1929: *Paulus und seine Bibel,* Gütersloh: Bertelsmann 1929.

Mommsen, Th. 1901: "Die Rechtsverhältnisse des Apostels Paulus", in: *ZNW* 2 (1901) 81-96.

Niebuhr, K. W. 1992: *Heidenapostel aus Israel* (WUNT 62), Tübingen: Mohr (Siebeck) 1992.

Oepke, A. 1969: "Probleme der vorchristlichen Zeit des Paulus", in: K. H. Rengstorff (Hg.), *Das Paulusbild in der neuerern deutschen Forschung* (WdF 24), Darmstadt: Wissenschaftliche Buchgesellschaft 1969, 410-446.

Pesch, R. 1986: *Die Apostelgeschichte,* 2 Bde. (EKK V), Zürich/Einsiedeln/Köln/Neukirchen-Vluyn: Benziger/Neukirchener Verlag 1986.

Rahlfs, A. 1921: "Über Theodotion-Lesarten bei Justin", in: *ZNW* 20 (1921) 182-199.

Riesner, R. 1988: *Jesus als Lehrer* (WUNT II 7), Tübingen: Mohr (Siebeck) ³1988.

Rohde, J. 1989: *Der Brief des Paulus an die Galater* (ThHK IX), Berlin: Evangelische Verlagsanstalt 1989.

Safrai, S. 1974: "Education and Study of the Torah", in: *The Jewish People in the First Century* (CRI I/2), Assen: van Gorcum 1974, 945-970.

Sanders, E. P. 1977: *Paul and Palestinian Judaism,* London: SCM Press 1977.

Schäfer, P. 1991: "Der vorrabbinische Pharisäismus", in: M. Hengel/U. Heckel (Hgg.), *Paulus und das antike Judentum* (WUNT 58), Tübingen: Mohr (Siebeck) 1991, 125-172.

Schille, G. 1984: *Die Apostelgeschichte des Lukas* (ThHK V), Berlin: Evangelische Verlagsanstalt ²1984.

Schlatter, A. 1962: *Die Apostelgeschichte* (Erläuterungen zum Neuen Testament 4), Stuttgart: Calwer 1962.

— 1983: *Die Geschichte der ersten Christenheit*, Stuttgart: Calwer [6]1983.

Schlier, H. 1971: *Der Brief an die Galater* (KEK VII), Göttingen: Vandenhoeck & Ruprecht [5]1971.

Strack, H. L./Billerbeck, P. 1956: *Kommentar zum Neuen Testament aus Talmud und Midrasch*, Bd. IV, Exkurse zu einzelnen Stellen des Neuen Testaments, 1. Teil, München: Beck [2]1956.

Strack, H. L./Stemberger G. 1982: *Einleitung in Talmud und Midrasch*, München: Beck [7]1982.

Strecker, G. 1976: "Befreiung und Rechtfertigung. Zur Stellung der Rechtfertigungslehre in der Theologie des Paulus", in: J. Friedrich/W. Pöhlmann/P. Stuhlmacher (Hgg.), *Rechtfertigung*, FS E. Käsemann, Tübingen/Göttingen: Mohr (Siebeck)/Vandenhoeck & Ruprecht 1976, 479-508 [neu abgedruckt in: idem, 1979a, 229-259].

— 1979: "Paulus in nachpaulinischer Zeit", in: idem, 1979a, 311-319.

— 1979a: *Eschaton und Historie. Aufsätze*, Göttingen: Vandenhoeck& Ruprecht 1979.

van Unnik, W. C. 1954: "Once again: Tarsus or Jerusalem" (1954), in: idem, *Sparsa Collecta* (NT.S 29), Leiden: Brill 1972, 321-327.

— 1962: "Tarsus or Jerusalem, The City of Paul's Youth" (1962), in: idem, *Sparsa Collecta* (NT.S 29), Leiden: Brill 1972, 259-320.

— 1993: *Das Selbstverständnis der jüdischen Diaspora in der hellenistisch-römischen Zeit* (AGJU 17), Leiden: Brill 1993.

Wanke, J. 1992: Art. "Ἑβραῖος, ου, ὁ", in: *EWNT* I, Stuttgart: Kohlhammer [2]1992, 892-894.

Weiser, A. 1981: *Die Apostelgeschichte, Kapitel 1-12* (ÖTBK 5/1), Gütersloh/Würzburg: Mohn/ Echter 1981.

— 1985: *Die Apostelgeschichte, Kapitel 13-28* (ÖTBK 5/2), Gütersloh/Würzburg: Mohn/Echter 1985.

Wendt, H. H. 1913: *Die Apostelgeschichte* (KEK III), Göttingen: Vandenhoeck & Ruprecht [9]1913.

Wikenhauser, A. 1961: *Die Apostelgeschichte* (RNT 5), Regensburg: Pustet [5]1961.

Wilckens U. 1982: *Der Brief an die Römer*, 3. Teil (EKK VI/3), Zürich/Neukirchen-Vluyn: Benziger/Neukirchener Verlag 1982.

Wilkinson, J. 1974: "Ancient Jerusalem: Its Water Supply and Population", in: *PEQ* 106 (1974) 33-51.

— 1978: *Jerusalem als Jesus knew it*, London: Thames and Hudson 1978.

Zahn, Th. 1922: *Die Apostelgeschichte. Erste Hälfte Kapitel 1-12*, Leipzig/Erlangen: Deichert/ Scholl 1922.

# Romans 9-11 and the
# "History of Early Christian Religion"[1]

Heikki Räisänen

## 1. Introduction

The quotation marks in my title refer to the name of a disputed discipline. Almost a century ago William Wrede stated programmatically that the traditional title "New Testament theology" was misleading and should be replaced with "history of early Christian religion" or "history of early Christian religion and theology".[2] I think that he was right and that the goal of New Testament scholars writing syntheses should be an account of early Christian thought rather than a New Testament theology proper.

I have pleaded for a revival of Wrede's view elsewhere.[3] I find it crucial to separate historical understanding from theological contemporization. Such a two-stage programme of "biblical theology" was suggested by Gabler in the eighteenth century.[4] After Wrede it was elaborated by Krister Stendahl in our century.[5] Strangely enough, the programme has never been put into practice.[6] It is, of course, quite usual to distinguish between "what it meant" and "what it means" (Stendahl) in everyday exegetical work, and I understand that Lars Hartman belongs to those who find the distinction sound.[7] But in the extant syntheses the two are entangled.[8] Here I shall discuss Romans 9-11 in the light of this shift from "New Testament theology"

---

[1] A plenary address in the series "Interpreting Classic Texts" at the Society of Biblical Literature Annual Meeting in San Francisco, November 1992. The text has been slightly revised.

[2] A translation of Wrede's address (delivered in 1897) is found in Morgan 1973, 68-116.

[3] Räisänen 1990.

[4] Sandys-Wunsch/Eldredge 1980.

[5] Stendahl 1984, 11-44.

[6] See now, however, Teeple 1992. Without referring to Wrede this work goes quite some way toward for the first time realizing his programme.

[7] Cf. e.g. Hartman 1979, 115.

[8] See Räisänen 1990.

to "history of early Christian religion" which has been proposed in programmatic statements but not realized in actual overall works. How has this particular text been treated in "New Testament theologies"? We shall see that it has as a rule received a less than adequate treatment. This must have something to do with the fact that the historical task is blended with theological concerns. What difference, then, will a change of perspective make?

* * *

Romans 9-11 is regarded as "the *locus classicus* for the relation of young Christianity to the people of Israel".[9] This is an accurate shorthand description of the focus of the chapters.[10] What is less clear is their "classic" status; such a perception is of recent origin,[11] and classics, if anything, should have a history. Romans 9-11 rarely crops up as a connected whole in pre-modern Christian thought; one has spoken of a history of its *suppression*.[12] Used piecemeal, the chapters yielded two or three well-known lines. Romans 9 provided the classic support for the doctrine of double predestination. Chapter 11 predicted the conversion of the Jews. Romans 10 was the source for the statement that Christ is the τέλος of the law, whatever that was taken to mean.[13]

## 2. On the Early Reception of Romans 9-11

From the beginning, Romans 9 was treated in connection with the problems of "Grace and Faith".[14] Chrysostom, typical of Greek theology, found an "overemphasis upon the grace of God" here. He insisted that Paul nevertheless did "justice also to the human side of the divine-human relationship", resorting to the idea of God's foreknowledge of how people will behave.[15] For on the whole, Scripture gives "a

---

[9] Küng 1991, 610.

[10] Provided that "Christianity" is not taken to refer, at this point, to a new religion, distinct from Judaism, but rather to "the most important Messianic sect of Judaism" (thus the sub-title of Rowland 1987).

[11] Dating, perhaps, from the statement *Nostra Aetate* (1965) by the Second Vatican Council in which Rom 9:4f. and 11:28f. are central.

[12] Theobald 1987, 1.

[13] For the sake of simplicity I shall call the section Romans 9:6-29 "Romans 9" and Romans 9:30-10:21 "Romans 10".

[14] See Wiles 1967, 94-110.

[15] Wiles 1967, 94f.; Gorday 1983, 122f.

proper place both to the elective will of God and also to human free-will".[16] Romans 9 was treated as a problem to be explained away; it was not allowed to make any independent contribution.

Western interpreters rejected the appeal to foreknowledge. God's election, they held, is based solely on his will, but his will is always characterized by justice, even if this justice is inscrutable.[17] Augustine's interpretation came to be "absolutely determinative for Western Christian exegesis"; "the issue of double predestination" was seen as the theme of Romans 9. "The discussion with Judaism is completely gone"; Paul was taken to deal abstractly with the salvation of individuals.[18]

The notion of Israel's eschatological salvation (Romans 11) plays a very minor role in patristic exegesis. Yet it was not quite lost, and Augustine rescued it for posterity as an individual eschatological *topos*.[19]

Such classic uses of parts of Romans 9-11 have deeply influenced the ways in which the section is handled in modern "New Testament theologies".

## 3. The Place of Romans 9-11 in Modern "New Testament Theologies"

In *Rudolf Bultmann's* unsurpassed work, Romans 9-11 is definitely not a classic text; it hardly exists.[20] Romans 9 is briefly discussed under "Faith" as posing a problem. Paul's "downright predestinarian" talk cannot be taken literally, for otherwise an insoluble contradiction results in his theology. The point is simply that the *decision* of faith does not go back to this-worldly motives.[21] Like the Greek fathers, Bultmann explains away Paul's strong language by appealing to his other statements[22] so that the character of faith as decision too is preserved.

Romans 11 fares worse. My main complaint is *not* with Bultmann's notorious doing away with Paul's vision of Israel's salvation as "speculative fantasy". The real problem is that he does not discuss Paul's speculation under "The Theology of Paul" at all; he only mentions it later in "The Development Toward The Old Church".[23]

Bultmann is keen on building into his presentation his modern application of the

---

[16] Wiles 1967, 99.

[17] Ibid., 102.

[18] Gorday 1983, 232f., 243f.

[19] Schelkle 1958, 400f.

[20] The "selection of the more important" passages in Bultmann's index includes some 300-400 items. The only verse from our section is Rom 11:36, being of interest to Bultmann because "Paul is using a formula of Stoic pantheism": Bultmann 1951, 229.

[21] Ibid., 329f.

[22] Such as "let reconcile yourselves with God ..." (2 Cor 5:20).

[23] Bultmann 1955, 132.

New Testament message. The fact that this enterprise leads him to separate Paul's supposedly existentialist theology so drastically from his salvation-historical fantasies illustrates the need to go beyond his work in contemplating how a synthesis of early Christian thought should be constructed.

*Hans Conzelmann* does devote several pages to Romans 9-11 in his synthesis.[24] He notes some tensions and problems. The section is discussed in connection with Christian *preaching*. Basically, Paul wants to show that "faith cannot be derivative", but "only arises from preaching".[25] In accordance with a long line of interpreters,[26] Conzelmann thinks that Israel is treated as an example of something else: it "is kept in view in so far as the nature of the preaching is made clear by it (salvation through the stumbling block of the cross)."[27] Because of his contemporizing concern Conzelmann, too, has missed the real point of the chapters.

Bultmann and Conzelmann, though stamped by dialectical theology, also stand in the tradition of liberal and history-of-religion exegesis which had a sharp eye for internal tensions and problems in the texts.[28] Recent syntheses are less critical.[29] On the other hand, many of them have the merit of treating the chapters in a more

---

[24] Conzelmann 1969, 248ff.

[25] Ibid., 251.

[26] Barth applied Romans 9-11 wholly to the problem of how (not Israel but) "the Church confronts the gospel" (Barth 1968, 332). Conzelmann goes a long way in the same direction. Cf. also Goppelt 1978, 461f.

[27] Ibid., 250. Cf. 252: "These remarks will perhaps become clearer if we illustrate them from our own position in the church. It is analogous to Paul's position in Israel to the extent that the church is our past ... We already find ourselves in a historical relationship to it ... We inherit our membership of the church, but not faith. So the concept of the church, if the church is understood in the light of the proclamation, contains the constant distinction between the true church and the empirical church."

[28] Baur 1864, 184ff. noted the tension between Rom 9 and Rom 10, dissolving it with the explanation that chap. 9 only serves to abrogate the justification of "Jewish particularism"; no attention, however, was paid by him to chap. 11. See further Holtzmann 1911, 182ff.; Weinel 1928, 312ff. Kaftan 1927, 145ff. found a hard contradiction between chaps. 9 and 11: Paul teaches both double predestination and the ἀποκατάστασις πάντων; "such contradictions belong to the essence of Paul's proclamation" (147f.). Teeple 1992, 382 does note that Paul "arrives at several solutions" when he tackles the problem of Jewish disbelief; yet in his synthesis Romans 9-11 fades out of sight altogether.

[29] Lohse 1974 (see following note) fails to mention any internal tensions within Romans 9-11. Kümmel 1969, 207 comments on Romans 9-11 in a section on "divine predestination", using Rom 11 only (!) to refute the idea of double predestination. Ibid., 217 he raises (in view of 11:25ff.) the question whether Paul teaches the salvation of all humanity, answering in the negative. Kümmel's approach is purely doctrinal.

There is very little on Romans 9-11 in Guthrie 1981 (see 624f., 808f.), and almost nothing in Morris 1986 (see 87). Stuhlmacher 1992, 307 (cf. 339, 357) underlines the eschatological salvation of all Israel (Rom 11:25-32), but wholly ignores the section 9:6-29.

fitting context: the issue of the continuity of the church with Israel.[30]

The most adequate account in a "New Testament theology" is found, of all places, in *Ethelbert Stauffer's* work, originally of 1941, which generally presents a harmonizing system. The treatment of Romans 9-11 is a fine exception. To be sure, Stauffer starts with the old dogmatic questions and even brings the doctrinal approach to a head: discussing "Creation and Fall" (!) he claims that "the N(ew) T(estament) teaches the supralapsarian *praedestinatio gemina*" about which "Paul is quite clear".[31]

Yet Stauffer later discusses Romans 9-11 in the chapter "Church and Synagogue".[32] He finds a total change in Paul's views. In 1 Thessalonians, Paul "appears as a sworn enemy to everything Jewish" and "does not hesitate to take over the formulae of the anti-Semitic propaganda of his time".[33] According to Galatians, God's promises to Israel have been directed from the beginning to the church alone. Yet in Romans "there is an astonishing *volte face.*"[34] "The polemical thesis" is abandoned.[35] To be sure, first Paul still tries to spiritualize the "children of Abraham" in Romans 9; but in chapter 11 the "realism" of his "theology of history" triumphs over such "first attempts".[36] Stauffer is sensitive to the intense struggle conveyed by Romans 9-11. He also notes that after Paul "anti-Jewish forces very quickly got the upper hand" in the church; Romans 11 became incomprehensible.[37]

Since 1941 much progress has been made in the study of Romans 9-11. Unfortunately, very little of this is to be seen in the recent syntheses, which remain far below Stauffer's level in their treatment of these chapters. An adequate treatment ought to do justice to two insights: the modern perception that Israel is in focus in

---

[30] Lohse 1974, 87, 101f. discusses them in a paragraph on "God's Righteousness" as well as in that on "The Church". For somewhat similar approaches (a fitting context for the section, but little sensitivity to its immanent problems) cf. Richardson 1958, 271ff.; Ladd 1991, 537ff. (the idea of Israel's divine hardening is not even mentioned); Rowland 1987, 224ff.; Gnilka 1989, 91; Schelkle 1976, 173ff. Schelkle does hint at important questions (does Paul adopt reproaches from ancient anti-Semitism? did his attitude change?), but he does not try to answer them.

[31] Stauffer 1955, 54.

[32] Ibid., 188ff. In this context he fails to mention predestination at all.

[33] Ibid., 189f.

[34] Ibid., 190.

[35] Ibid., 191.

[36] Ibid., 192. In the discussion that followed this paper, Professor Gerd Lüdemann expressed surprise over my appreciation of Stauffer who, he pointed out, was a Nazi. I have carefully reread the relevant section in Stauffer's work, but I am now as before unable to find any anti-Semitic overtones in it. On the contrary, Stauffer notes that "in Paul's attitude to the Jewish question" (in Romans 11) "the Spirit of Jesus triumphed over the spirit of anti-Semitism and the polemics of the oppressed (I Thess. 2)" (ibid., 192).

[37] Stauffer 1955, 309 n. 644.

Romans 9-11, and the liberal idea that Paul is involved in logical problems as well. With the partial exception of *Hans Hübner's* recent volume, I know of no contemporary "New Testament theology" which combines both these notions.[38]

Hübner expounds the chapters at length, first in his rhetorical analysis of Romans[39] and then in a large section "Romans 9-11: Israel and the Justification by Faith".[40] He does note tensions between the various parts, but allows for no real contradictions; instead, Paul follows an intentional strategy, keen on taking the reader by surprise.[41] Nonetheless Paul is correcting earlier statements on Israel which he had made in 1 Thessalonians and Galatians. A re-reading of Isaiah after the writing of Galatians had led him to new spiritual insights concerning the "mystery" of Israel's destiny. On the whole, Hübner's treatment leaves an intellectualistic impression: Paul is developing a theological argument concerning *sola gratia* and *sola fide* rather than struggling with a personal problem.[42]

## 4. A Brief Analysis of Romans 9-11

### 4.1. Introductory remarks

Recent interpreters agree: Paul is concerned with the problem of Israel which is also the problem of the trustworthiness of God's promises.[43] There is also a growing awareness that earlier research focused excessively on Paul's theological *ideas* (this is very clear in Bultmann and Conzelmann).[44] The *social* context and function of Paul's writing has to be taken seriously. Paul's social experience is reflected throughout the section.

---

[38] See, however, the brief but adequate treatment in the context of a history of the "beginning of Christianity" by Craig 1943, 255f. (in a chapter entitled "The Fight with Legalism"): Paul's missionary experience "forced on him a heartbreaking problem, the unbelief of the Jews". "Had God cast off his people? Through three chapters he wrestled with the problem as one who at heart had never ceased to be a Jew, trying different answers."

[39] Hübner 1993, 252-58.

[40] Ibid., 306-20.

[41] Hübner has interpreted Romans 9-11 in detail in his earlier monograph of 1984. For a critique see Räisänen 1987b, esp. 2931f.; and 1988, 193.

[42] Hübner focuses on the New Testament authors' use of the Greek Old Testament. Paradoxically, this concern tends to give his voluminous work the appearance of a monograph rather than a real synthesis, though his basic goal is a pan-biblical theology of both testaments. As his third volume has not appeared yet, it remains to be seen how Romans 9-11 will be related to New Testament passages outside the Pauline corpus.

[43] For a summary of recent scholarship see Räisänen 1987b and 1988.

[44] Bultmann 1951, 209 could still hold that Romans "develops in purely theoretical fashion the principle of Christian faith in antithesis to the principle of the Jewish Torah-religion".

It is also agreed that the chapters are "as full of problems as a hedgehog is of prickles"[45], but the solutions go in quite different directions. Here I can only sketch my own reading of the text and my understanding of the social dynamics behind it.[46] I shall limit my remarks mainly to chapters 9 and 11, which directly address the question of Israel's election.

To me, the internal tensions provide a key to the section.[47] There has been a debate on Paul's theological consistency.[48] Unlike some of my critics[49], I do not think that inconsistency is a wicked thing; it is simply human. Raymond Brown notes that "it is curious that sometimes a radical scholarship that has been insistent on the humanity of Jesus balks at any real indication of the fallible humanity of Paul!"[50]

The amount of exegetical ingenuity needed by those who plead for consistency is noteworthy. In order to get a consistent Paul, interpreters often put forward a whole series of strained interpretations.[51] The price for blameless logic is, then, that the apostle proves a rather bad communicator, as *all* previous interpreters have got him wrong, in passage after passage. In a recent book the statement "all *Israel* will be saved" is taken to mean that *Gentiles* will join Abraham's family; for the author thereby "the case for finding fundamental contradiction within Romans 9-11 falls to the ground."[52] To me, it is a weighty argument *against* consistency that so artificial interpretations are needed to rescue it.

Inconsistency should not be reduced to a problem of Paul's psychology[53]; "conflicting convictions" about the relation of the new to the old are found in early Christianity at large. To Paul goes the credit for really wrestling with the problems.

---

[45] Wright 1991, 231.

[46] I have dealt extensively with this text and with its interpretations in Räisänen 1987b; cf. also Räisänen 1988.

[47] Cf. recently Fiedler 1990, 75-81; Segal 1990, 276ff.; more cautiously Ziesler 1989, 237.

[48] Largely in connection with Räisänen 1987a. For a fair overall discussion of the problems see Westerholm 1988 and my review in *Bib.* 1990, 269-272.

[49] See esp. Wright 1991, 4ff., 143 etc. Cf. my forthcoming review of Wright's book in *SJTh.*

[50] R. E. Brown 1983, 114. Cf. Goodenough 1986, 40f.: "the idea that Jesus, Paul, and John … presented us with a consistent way of thinking is the modern survival of the fallacy of scholasticism".

[51] Cf. e.g. the very different reconstructions of Gaston 1987 (see my review in *ThLZ* 1989, 191f.) and Wright 1991. For some earlier attempts cf. Räisänen 1987a, 4 n. 29.

[52] Wright 1991, 251. Wright (250) wishes to take "all Israel" in Rom 11:26 "as a typically Pauline polemical redefinition" of Israel, overlooking however that "all" in v. 26 contrasts with ἀπὸ μέρους in v. 25.

[53] The first edition of my *Paul and the Law* was somewhat one-sided on this score. See the preface to the second edition: Räisänen 1987a, xxv.

## 4.2. Romans 9

Paul's concern for the fact that most Jews have rejected his message leads him to raise the worrisome question of the dependability of God's word (9:1ff.). What sort of God does not see to it that his promises to Israel come true? What gain will Israel have for all the advantages Paul lists in verses 4f. (sonship, glory, promises ...) if they remain outside the salvation in Christ? Has God's word failed, if Israel stays outside? Paul answers by redefining "Israel": all those who are "of Israel" (the empirical people) do *not* really belong to "Israel" (v. 6). Who belongs and who does not is freely decreed by God. He has always freely called some, like Jacob, and not others, like Esau, without any regard to their character or ancestry (9:7-13).

Therefore, the initial question is falsely put. The gospel is *not* being rejected by the *elect* of God, for the majority of ethnic Israel never belonged to the elect![54] The gospel is being rejected by the non-elect and accepted by the *true* "Israel". Everything is as God meant it to be.

Paul goes to great lengths in undergirding the thesis of God's free election. That God can show unexpected mercy is in line with the surprising experience that he has lately called Gentiles to enter his people. But this point alone does *not* account for the emphasis on the *negative* side of God's action (9:14-18).[55] God "hardens whom he wills", too.[56] The Great Potter has the right to create what he wants, even "vessels of wrath" prepared for destruction (9:22). This would logically imply double predestination.

Paul then shows from Scripture that God always intended to also call Gentiles to be his sons (9:24ff.). He further argues from Scripture that not all Israel will be saved, but only such seed as God has *left* in it (9:27ff.). This idea of a remnant does not entirely agree with the one just presented that all Israel was never elected. Yet Romans 9 gives a clear answer to the question, Has God's word failed? No, it has not, for God never promised anything for *ethnic* Israel. It seems clear that the majority of the Jews will remain outside of salvation.

---

[54] It is quite inadequate to summarize the point of Rom 9:6ff. as Dunn 1991, 148 does: "Those who are Israelites, but who *fail to recognize* the covenant character of their status as Israelites, have to that extent sold their own birthright ..." (my italics); cf. Dunn 1988, 540: "Paul's argument concerns the character and mode rather than the fact of election". No, it concerns precisely the "fact"! It is not a question of "a schism within Israel" (*contra* Theobald 1987, 8).

[55] It is hard to see why Gentile faith should be a problem for Paul (*contra* Johnson 1989, 143ff.). Israel's unbelief is the problem (9:3) which calls forth the statements concerning God's "negative" acts in Romans 9.

[56] This is not taken seriously enough by Johnson 1989, 148ff. (who focuses one-sidedly on "God's creative mercy") nor by Wright 1991, 238f.

## 4.3. Romans 10

Romans 10 introduces a different point of view. Paul explains why Israel, now seen as an ethnic entity after all, has failed to attain righteousness, whereas Gentiles have found it (9:30ff.). We now hear nothing about sovereign divine hardening. On the contrary, God has held out his hands toward Israel all day long, patiently inviting her to salvation, but Israel remains stubborn (10:21).[57] Clinging to works, she has refused to obey God and accept his action in Christ with faith. Thus she has stumbled over the stumbling stone, Christ (9:32f.).

## 4.4. Romans 11

In Romans 11 Paul continues to talk of Israel in the ethnic sense. He now asserts that God *cannot* have rejected his people (11:1f.). This is rather surprising after chapter 9, but it continues the argument about the remnant. Ethnic Israel has split into the elect remnant and the hardened rest (11:7). This is in keeping with chapter 9 insofar as the contrast between divine election and divine hardening seems definitive. There will always be a remnant, but no happy end is envisaged for the people.

Paul goes on to suggest that the hardening of Israel has a positive purpose in God's plans: it serves to bring salvation to the Gentiles (11:11f.). He then presents the parable of the olive tree, from which some branches have been broken off, and onto which some branches of a wild tree have been grafted (11:17ff.). He says in effect that Israel remains God's people; apostates have been excluded and believing Gentiles accepted as proselytes. This is basically in keeping with the notion of the remnant, though the image of a tree and branches suggests—contrary to reality— that only a small minority has fallen away. The present state of things is caused by the unbelief of "some" (11:17, 20): by human failure, not by a divine decree. Gentiles are admonished to remain in faith so that they will not be "broken off" as well (v. 22). Here the idea of divine hardening would be out of place. But God has the power to graft anew those Israelites who have fallen, if only they will give up their unbelief (v. 23).

And indeed they will! This is Paul's message in the final section. He discloses a "mystery": the hardening will not be final. When the full number of the Gentiles has "come in", *all* Israel—not just a remnant—will be saved, for God's call is irrevocable (11:25ff.). Paul implies that he has received this knowledge as a revelation, probably through a spirit-guided exegesis of Scripture.

The suggestion that Paul here envisages two different roads to salvation, one for Christians and another for Jews, has been much debated. The proposal that for Paul

---

[57] It is unjustified simply to identify "disobedient" with "hardened by God" (thus Johnson 1989, 140).

Jesus was not the Messiah of Israel, but only the Saviour of the Gentiles,[58] is admirable in its ecumenical scope, but there is very little evidence for it.[59] The "mystery" of Romans 11 is a tenuous basis for an assertion which would nullify everything that Paul writes elsewhere (including Romans 10) about the significance of Jesus for all humanity[60], to the Jew first (!) and also to the Greek. Still in the olive tree parable Paul stated that the broken-off branches would be "grafted back in precisely when they no longer persisted in their lack of belief, i.e. when they too came to faith in Jesus Christ".[61] In v. 26 he must mean: all Israel will be saved, for all Israel will—somehow or other—embrace faith in Christ.

It is more difficult to decide whether this conversion will take place as a response to apostolic preaching[62] or as a divine miracle independent of it. Paul may even have deliberately expressed himself vaguely.[63] It is not clear that he is referring to the parousia in his quotation from Isaiah (Isa 59:20f.; 27:9): "the Deliverer will come from Zion, he will banish ungodliness from Jacob ..." (Rom 11:26f.) After all, the returning Christ should come from Heaven, not Zion. Paul may simply be referring to Jesus' "first" coming; then the future tense only indicates that this was a future event for *Isaiah*, not for Paul.[64] But this issue can be left undecided.

God cannot, according to this passage, reject his chosen people. Instead, Paul has rejected the thrust of his earlier argument. Ethnic Israel, or at least its majority, will be saved.

### 5. Paul's Theological and Social Problems
### as the Background of Romans 9-11

Romans 9-11 contains two main intellectual problems: the discrepancy between predestination and human freedom, and the election or non-election of ethnic Israel. Both problems are rooted in Paul's social experience in his mission fields; this seems to colour the section stronger than the situation in Rome. The latter plays some part but does not seem crucial.

The problem of predestination versus free will is no Pauline peculiarity. It is par-

---

[58] Thus Gaston 1987; Gager 1983.

[59] Cf. Räisänen 1988, 189ff.; Johnson 1989, 176ff.

[60] The same applies to the older attempts to find Paul teaching a doctrine of ἀποκατάστασις πάντων on the basis of Rom 11:25ff.; thus Beyschlag 1892, 274f.; Weinel 1928, 315. In itself, the logic of 11:25ff. would undoubtedly lead precisely to this conclusion.

[61] Ziesler 1989, 285.

[62] Becker 1989, 499ff.

[63] Cf. Segal 1990, 280f.

[64] Becker 1989, 500f.

alleled in the Old Testament (Pharaoh, Isaiah's task Isa 6:9f.), in Qumran, in the gospels (Mark's parable theory Mk 4:11f., God's concealing things from the wise and revealing them to the "babes" in Q, Matthew and Luke, Lk 10:21f. par) and in the Qur'an.[65] The talk of negative predestination has a social function. The idea crops up in settings where the religious majority does not accept the message preached by a minority. It consoles the minority when they fail to convert others, and justifies the situation for them. The tension between divine hardening and that human freedom which is presupposed in preaching is seldom felt.[66]

Elsewhere (2 Cor 4:3-4) Paul occasionally attributes the blinding of the unbelievers not to God, but to the "god of this aeon". This shows how far he is from possessing a "systematic" doctrine of hardening: the introduction of Satan into Romans 9 would have destroyed the argument based on God's sovereignty. The problem of unbelief remains the same; the solutions vary.

The problem of different views on Israel is more distinctly Pauline. Romans 11 differs sharply from the harsh judgment in 1 Thessalonians (2:14-16)[67] and from the writing off of Israel in Galatians, but it differs equally sharply from the notion that ethnic Israel was never elected, put forward in Romans 9.

The parable of the olive tree differs from Paul's way of seeing the new community in his other letters. Galatians suggests that, like Gentiles, Jews too must take a new step to find righteousness with God (Gal 2:15ff.); they too must become "a new creation" (Gal 6:15). In 1 Corinthians 10:32 Paul speaks of "God's church" as a third entity alongside Jews and Greeks. If we were to invent an image for Paul's usual "ecclesiology", we might devise a third tree onto which both Christ-believing Jews and Gentiles, taken from two other trees, are "grafted". That would correspond to Paul's missionary practice.

Paul's practice implies that Jews ought to accept Jesus as the Christ and undergo a new initiation rite, baptism. In effect, then, clinging to God's ancient covenant with Israel is *not* enough. Even a Jew has to join a new group, distinct from the synagogue (though he need therefore not yet leave the synagogue). He must also be prepared to sacrifice some of his Torah observance; Paul speaks of his accommodation to it among Jews "as if" he were a Jew! Although Paul holds that God gave the Torah as a guide to life, in practice it has come to an end: parts of the divine com-

---

[65] See Räisänen 1976.

[66] Even according to Calvin, "ministers and elders must proceed as if there were no predestination; must proceed indeed as if everyone had a free choice whether to accept or reject the offer of salvation in the Word". Höpfl 1985, 229.

[67] The text can hardly be excised as post-Pauline. Becker 1989, 489f. argues for a pre-Pauline (probably Antiochian) origin.

mands no longer need to be observed, at least not when Jews and Gentiles come together in Paul's communities.[68]

No matter how conservative were the utterances which Paul was, at times, able
to make (e.g. in Rom 3:31), this attitude of assimilation was bound to make his loyalty to the covenant doubtful in the eyes of most Jews. He certainly did perceive
himself as a loyal Jew, but he could not move many others to share this perception.[69] For the average Jewish perception, selectivity regarding the Torah meant
apostasy.[70]

Paul thus finds himself in a difficult situation. He is committed both to his old
tradition and to his new experience, trying to do justice to both. God has acted decisively at the Exodus and at Sinai, establishing his covenant and giving the Torah;
but he has also acted decisively in Jesus, making salvation available to all, but also
conditional on faith in Jesus. Paul tries to have the best of both worlds.[71] In Romans
9 he presupposes that salvation is to be found in Christ alone, views unbelieving Israel as condemned and non-elect and resorts to an extreme theology of predestination to account for this situation. But in Romans 11 he verbally pleads for classic
covenantal theology, although he tacitly lets this melt with his conviction of salvation in Christ.

From the viewpoint of a non-Christian Jew, Paul's statement of the salvation of
all Israel is not so generous as many Christians think. In effect he is saying that you
will be saved, since eventually you will become like us. This "mystery" assures, as
Rosemary Ruether saw, "the ultimate vindication of the church". Jews "must admit
finally that it is not through Torah, but through faith in Jesus as the Christ, that they

---

[68] Cf. Räisänen 1992, 112ff., esp. 123ff.

[69] Cf. Casey 1991, 121f.: Paul's "dramatic redefinition" of the term "Jew" (as in Rom 2:28f.)
"shows how seriously assimilated St Paul himself was". "Observant Jews were bound to conclude
that Paul had abandoned Judaism." Casey rightly emphasizes that "there are cases where the identity
of individuals and of groups may be differently perceived" (ibid., 12). The obvious fact that Paul
himself perceived himself to be a Jew to the end of his life (to which e.g. Dunn 1991, 148f. refers)
therefore does not at all solve the problem of the amount of his continuity or discontinuity with average Judaism. Cf. already Riddle 1943, 244: "Always regarding himself as a faithful and loyal Jew,
his [Paul's] definitions of values were so different from those of his contemporaries that, notwithstanding his own position within Judaism, he was, from any point of view other than his own, at best
a poor Jew and at worst a renegade." See now the perceptive work of Segal 1990.

[70] The claim that the Torah is "paradoxically fulfilled whenever anyone confesses that Jesus is
the Lord" or that "when Christ is preached and believed, Torah is being paradoxically fulfilled"
(Wright 1991, 244f., formulating Paul's point in Rom 10:5-8) was (and is) bound to appear as nonsense to most non-assimilated Jews.

[71] Therefore, I do not find it a fair description of my position to claim that I argue that "Paul was
totally alienated from his ancestral faith, from Judaism" (Dunn 1991, 140). It should be clear that I
consider Paul's position to be more complex.

are intended to be saved."[72] It is *Paul's mission* that will be justified in the near future.

It is indeed a question of self-legitimation. It is the tension between a novel liberal practice and the pressure toward a more conservative ideology that gets Paul into difficulty. His practice, the abandonment of circumcision and food laws, amounts to a break with sacred tradition; but his legitimating theory in Romans stresses continuity, so that he can even assert that it is he who truly establishes the law. Comparable moves can be observed in Matthew[73] and in Luke-Acts.[74]

A somewhat similar tension is also found in Qumran. A member of the Qumran sect, too, had to take a new step to enter the community; he had to believe in the new things revealed to the Teacher.[75] On the other hand, the rest of the people had fallen away[76] while the sectarians had remained faithful. Does one then remain in the covenant from which others have turned away, or does one take a new step? In any case, despite the novelty, Qumran stuck strictly to the central visible symbols of the old covenant. The sect spiritualized circumcision (1QS 5:1-5), but it certainly did not stop exercising it, and no one thought of accepting Gentiles as members. Therefore, the Jewish identity of the sect was not in doubt. Paul's case was different.

Some Qumran passages (esp. 1 QSa 1:1-6)[77] suggest "that eschatological Israel would be formed by the conversion of the rest of Israel to the way of the sect".[78] If so, the sect expected its final vindication before the majority, much as Paul does in Romans 11.[79]

---

[72] Ruether 1974, 105f.

[73] Cf. Matthew's ambiguous use of πληροῦν (in 5:20 and elsewhere) and Suggs 1970, 112: "Matthew's presentation of Jesus' relation to the law makes jugglers of all of us".

[74] Cf. Esler 1987. Luke legitimates Jewish-Gentile table-fellowship by re-writing the history of early Christianity relating to this subject (ibid., 107). On Luke-Acts see also Räisänen 1991, esp. 106-11.

[75] Cf. Sanders 1977, 225ff.

[76] Cf. 1QpHab 8:8-13 (the wicked priest); CD 15:9f.

[77] "This is the rule for *all the congregation of Israel* in the *last days*, when they *shall join* [the Community to wa]lk according to ... when they come ..." (tr. G. Vermes). Less clear, but possible indications: 1 QH 6:7f.; 1 QpHab 5:3-6.

[78] Sanders 1977, 247f.

[79] Casey 1991, 121. Cf. also 4 Ezra 13:39-50: a great multitude will be saved (after all!): the ten tribes who have been obedient in a distant land. Jewish covenantalism has been disqualified by the author (as by Paul in Romans 9), but through this device, to some extent, he "hopes to keep his case within traditional lines", the appearance of the ten tribes being his "ace up the sleeve". Only here in 4 Ezra is it revealed that "the number of the saved constitute an innumerable multitude, rather than the paltry few over which Ezra and Uriel debate in the earlier episodes" (Thompson 1977, 237, followed by Longenecker 1991, 129f.). Thus the trustworthiness of God is maintained. The analogy to Paul's struggles is striking. On the analogies between Paul and 4 Ezra in general see Longenecker 1991, passim.

## *6. Romans 9-11 in a History of Early Christian Religion*

In a synthesis of "early Christian religion", Romans 9-11 would not primarily belong to a section on "soteriology". Its appropriate context would be a chapter on the *identity* of the new sect and the battles, external and internal, connected with it. The same chapter would deal with the Torah and Jewish "identity markers" as well as the Christian appropriation of Scripture by projecting new ideas into the old texts.[80]

No "doctrines" can be deduced from Romans 9-11, neither a doctrine of predestination nor one of Israel's salvation. In a sense, then, Bultmann and Conzelmann were right in neutralizing the section in their accounts of Pauline theology. Both Romans 9 and Romans 11 are singular passages in Paul's letters, though in opposite ways: Romans 9 is "too" negative and Romans 11 "too" positive about the situation of Israel. Neither passage can be taken as such as a summary of what Paul "really" thought when dictating Romans.

But Romans 9-11 should not disappear without a trace from a synthesis. Taken as a whole, the section vividly illustrates how central and how difficult the questions of identity and continuity were.[81] It shows a prominent member of the new sect in a struggle to legitimate his mission and to assert his and his group's identity in terms of the old values.[82] In the tree parable, Paul talks as if the church were a mainstream synagogue, with some new proselytes, from which a few apostates have been expelled. The social reality was quite different! Here a sectarian attempts to claim mainstream status for his group. An account of early Christian religion should convey a sense of the intensity of this struggle; there is a glimpse of this in Stauffer's work.

Paul's personal struggles are to be related to the range of options that existed in defining the relation to the old community.[83] Paul stands at a turning point when the Jesus movement, originally a Jewish revitalization movement, is distancing itself

---

[80] To this last category belongs Rom 10:5ff., a passage which I cannot discuss here. Meeks 1991, 110ff., esp. 117 attempts to rescue Paul from "atomistic and arbitrary" proof-texting by suggesting that, while suppressing the plain meaning of a text, "Paul requires that plain sense as the strong but unspoken counterweight to his christological confession". This seems quite unlikely, and indeed even Meeks has his doubts here (ibid., 112).

[81] Cf. Houlden 1986, 90: "Early Christian attitudes to their relationship with God's Israel (exemplified in Paul's agonized argument in Romans 9-11)" belong to "the ways in which those Christians ... sought identity and intelligibility for themselves". The "ideas about Israel" were "not 'hard' doctrine, but simply attempts to solve pressing problems in the only terms then available".

[82] On the issue of legitimation in general see Esler 1987. He notes that a particularly common characteristic of any symbolic universe erected to legitimate a new social order is "the claim that it is not novel, but is actually old and traditional" (ibid., 19).

[83] Cf. Räisänen 1987a, 203-28; id. 1992, 269-77.

from its Jewish roots. The gospels and Acts likewise witness to an effort to retain continuity—often a verbal one—amidst centrifugal tendencies.

Later we find at one end of the spectrum the conservative "Jewish Christian" groups which retained the old symbols, but were finally encapsulated, ceasing to influence the emerging Catholic Christianity. These include the group which produced the *Kerygmata Petrou*; the *Pseudo-Clementines* contain a remarkable "two-covenant" statement to the effect that God accepts the one who has believed either Moses or Jesus.[84] At the other end are those who denied continuity with Judaism, as Christian Gnostics, Marcion or *Barnabas* were to do in different ways. Catholic Christianity wrenched the Scripture from the Jews, reinterpreting it to fit its own experience. Covenantal symbols were appropriated by way of spiritualized and ethical interpretations: circumcision of the heart; observance of moral commands. In accordance with Paul's other letters, non-Christian Jews were mostly thought to be without hope. The hopeful note of Romans 11 remains rare, but not quite singular: the optimistic exceptions include the Christian interpolator of the *Testaments of the Twelve Patriarchs*,[85] Marcion, and possibly Justin Martyr.[86]

The case of Marcion invites special interest.[87] For all his contempt for the Old Testament, he did grant the Jews the right to expect their own Messiah who "would bring an earthly kingdom which would incorporate Jews and proselytes". Marcion held out for the Jews "a future described in their own terms—even though ... it could not compete with the eternal kingdom brought by Jesus". Marcion's condescending attitude notwithstanding, this seems closer than Romans 11 to a two-covenant theology. Paul redefined the Jewish symbols; his attitude to the Jewish people

---

[84] Ps.Clem. *Hom.* 8.6-7; cf. *Rec.* 4.5. My attention was drawn to these texts by Professor Stephen Wilson, who kindly made the text of his 1992 paper available to me. Wilson notes that the statements concerning the equality of Jews and Christians were preserved by those Gentile Christians who produced the Pseudo-Clementines in their final form. Moreover, he refers to those Christians—possibly Gentile Judaizers—who caused alarm to the author of the Epistle of Barnabas by saying that "our covenant remains theirs too" (*Barn.* 4:6).

[85] Jervell 1969; de Jonge 1986; Wilson 1992. See especially *T. Ben.* 10.11: "all Israel will be gathered unto the Lord" and the astonishingly universalist vision in *T. Sim.* 7.2: "For the Lord will raise up from Levi someone as a high priest and from Judah someone as a king, God and man. He will save all the Gentiles (!) and the tribe of Israel." Cf. *T. Asher* 7.3,7; *T. Jud.* 22.2; *T. Jos.* 19.6. Whether the basis for Israel's hope is, in the view of the Jewish Christian interpolator, a conversion to Christ or God's original promise remains unclear; apparently he does not sharply distinguish between the two.

[86] Wilson 1992 infers from such passages as *Dial.* 25.6-26.2, 45.2 and 134.3 that "Justin quite possibly did harbour a hope for the salvation of righteous, non-Christian Jews, even if it was to be effected by Christ in the End times"; like Paul, he might have "found himself torn in more than one direction in this matter".

[87] Wilson 1986, 53ff.

oscillated. Catholic Christianity took the symbols and attacked the people. Marcion "attacked the symbols but left the people alone". As Stephen Wilson also notes, it is worth a moment's reflection "whether the Marcionite position, had it prevailed, would have led to the same sad consequences as the view of its opponents".[88]

## 7. On the History of Influence

Although the problem of Romans 9-11 is the sect's relation to the synagogue, Romans 9 should also be mentioned in the chapter on soteriology (where it used to be located). It would have to be shown how the "doctrine" of double predestination arose by accident, as it were, as Paul once went to extremes in trying to distinguish the empirical from the true Israel. The consequences, when Paul's statements were taken at face value, are worth noting. For it is with some reason that Robert Wilken took New Testament scholars to task for believing that their work has been completed once one has shown what an idea means in the New Testament. "The placing of past phenomena into context" requires that we also look at "the things that happened after."[89]

For some, the abstract "doctrine" of predestination became a source of courage[90] but also "a fearful doctrine". It armed an Augustine "against feeling" in his relentless dealings with dissenters: he could let Donatists burn, predestined as they were for hellfire anyway.[91] For others, the haunting question "Am I predestined to hell?" presented itself.[92] The "peculiar existential importance" of the notion of a "calling" in Calvinism "was linked with anxieties occasioned by the Calvinist doctrine of predestination",[93] derived from Romans 9.[94] To overcome such anxiety, there was a "psychological pressure to demonstrate one's election" by exhibiting the signs of

---

[88] Ibid., 58.

[89] Wilken 1979, 154f.

[90] Cf. P. Brown 1967, 403ff.

[91] In 420, the Donatist bishop Gaudentius had retired to his basilica and had threatened to burn himself with his congregation. An imperial agent was worried. "Augustine will now find it only too easy to answer this worried man; the fearful doctrine of predestination had armed him against feeling: 'Seeing that God, by a hidden, though just disposition, has predestined some to the ultimate penalty (of Hellfire), it is doubtless better that [an overwhelming majority of the Donatists should have been collected and reabsorbed ... while] a few perish in their own flames: better, indeed than that all Donatists should burn in the flames of Hell for their sacrilegious dissension.'" P. Brown 1967, 335f.

[92] See Höpfl 1985, 231ff.; McGrath 1990, 240ff.

[93] McGrath 1990, 242.

election—including "active involvement in the affairs of the world".[95] The general later Protestant attitude towards work and secular activism may be taken as the residue of this anxiety over predestination.[96] Moreover, "the notion of predestination is easily secularized into that of 'fate' or 'destiny'"; the fact that "a secularized America was still able to think of itself as singled out among nations" is to be "traced to America's Puritan past"[97] and thus, in part at least, to Paul's occasional assertions in Romans 9.

The "suppression" of Romans 11 in Christianity has been much criticized of late. But is it not unrealistic to expect that an unrepeated and rather vague suggestion of a happy end should have undone all the negative comments about Israel made by Paul himself and others? Paul might have provided an important corrective for Jewish-Christian relations, if only he had stated clearly what many of his recent interpreters take him to mean: the ongoing validity of the Jewish covenant. If only he had written: "I have changed my mind, I am sorry for some of the things I have said!" It might have helped if he had asked Tertius to cancel a page or two Paul had just dictated (Romans 9). He did nothing of the sort, leaving the task of making sense of the whole to his interpreters. Small wonder that the optimistic vision was read in the light of the more common statements.

Anyway, Romans 11 did have some practical influence on Christian attitudes towards Jews and even on post-Constantinian legislation. Care had to be taken that the Jews were not *totally* destroyed, for then how could their predicted conversion and, consequently, the parousia take place?[98] Christians debated just how many Jews it was necessary to have left,[99] but Paul's mystery seems to have saved the lives of some. A few Christians even pleaded for clemency with regard to the Jews'

---

[94] It was because of his view of Scripture that Calvin was bound to teach double predestination. "Scripture teaches nothing but what is necessary and beneficial for us to know. Scripture teaches predestination." Höpfl 1985, 230, cf. 237. However, "the entire edifice of scriptural demonstration of reprobation rests on Romans 9.18-23, and Jacob and Esau, as interpreted by St Paul in the same chapter": ibid., 289 n. 34. Therefore, Calvin would not have taught *double* predestination (including reprobation), had it not been for Romans 9.

[95] McGrath 1990, 241.

[96] McGrath 1990, 243.

[97] McGrath 1990, 259f.

[98] Kötting 1968, 146.

[99] For a Duns Scotus it seemed enough that a handful were kept isolated on some island where they could observe their law; in them would the prediction of Isaiah, quoted by Paul in Rom 9:27, be fulfilled: Eckert 1968, 220. Here the salvation of "all Israel" is interpreted as the salvation of the *remnant*—an idea put forward by Paul a little earlier.

end-time salvation.[100]

The promise of Israel's salvation was interpreted by some as a stimulus for missionizing Jews. Others, like Spener, anticipated small missionary success, the conversion being a miracle of God. The founder of Pietism gave attention to Paul's parable of the olive tree and his warning of Gentile arrogance. Such thoughts were in their time a step toward religious tolerance,[101] though the main reason for a positive attitude to the Jews was still the assurance that one day they would convert.

These are some of the fruits, beneficial and harmful, that have grown from the seeds of Paul's message to Roman Christians. An assessment of the influence of texts on the life of people could provide the bridge from a historical account of early Christianity to theological or philosophical evaluation. Historical scholarship cannot produce normative results. There is no direct bridge from "what it meant" to "what it means". What Paul meant need not be what we have to say. What historical scholarship can do for today is to give incentives for constructive thinking in new situations.

## 8. Toward a Personal Appreciation

Alan Segal writes that, "as a believing Jew and a 20th century humanist", he could have hoped for a different outcome of Paul's meditations in Romans 9-11. "It is easy to see how a person with Paul's experience of metamorphosis and career of trying to represent the rights of Gentile Christianity—risking all to bring the communities together and failing—would have ended his meditation in this way."[102] Yet "the theology outlined by Stendahl, Gaston, and Gager[103] makes more sense for today than does Paul's actual conclusion. It would have been easier for today's Christianity had Paul embraced cultural pluralism more fully."[104]

Rather than taking any of Paul's statements as direct answers to our questions it

---

[100] E.g. Bernhard of Clairvaux and his pupils: Blumenkranz 1968, 122f., 131, 133. Bernhard also quoted Rom 9:4f. Cf. Friedrich's (1988, 52) assessment of 17th century Protestant theologians' attitude to Jews: the belief in their coming conversion "gestattete es nicht, die Juden ganz aufzugeben und ungebremster Verfolgung auszusetzen. Im weniger bibelfesten Volk konnte sich Judenfeindschaft daher viel einfacher ... äussern und sehr viel radikaler auswirken als bei den Theologen." Cf. ibid., 147.

[101] Schmidt 1970, 91ff. goes too far in thinking that Pietism anticipated the egalitarian ideas of the Enlightenment (92, cf. 122). For a more realistic assessment see Friedrich 1988, 124ff., 138ff., 148.

[102] I.e., ambiguously stating that Israel will embrace Christianity. Cf. above, n. 61.

[103] I.e. a two-covenant theology which views Judaism and Christianity as two parallel roads to salvation; cf. above n. 58.

[104] Segal 1990, 281.

might be better to see his *struggle* as a potential example in our situation as well, when embracing cultural pluralism is imperative. Paul is wrestling with his sacred tradition in the light of his new experience (positively, the living together of different ethnic groups in his church; negatively, the rejection of his message by most Jews). We, too, try to make sense of *our* traditions in the light of *our* experience which includes the necessity of a critical approach to all traditions, and an awareness of the terrible things that have happened and are happening in the world, partly due to some of our own traditions.

The man "was no plaster saint. Nor did he find lasting and real solutions to many of the problems he encountered. Possibly he did not even see the implications of some of them. He was a man of his time and place, with a particular ... religious background, facing a specific ... social situation. He was also deeply human ... and the roots of his attitudes and actions were deep and tangled, as are most people's. ... He hurt some, yet consoled and sustained many. He was caught in compromises inevitable in public life. But fundamentally he was a man of vision and action, who asked many of the profoundest questions that face humankind as it struggles to live in community. It was his confrontation out of a real humanity which marks his true stature and which makes his struggles and glimpses of truth of enduring significance. As a man of his time who asked the deepest questions, even though he could not answer them, he became a man for all times and places."

Originally, this was not said of Paul. It is the conclusion to an outstanding biography of Mahatma Gandhi by Judith Brown.[105] But with very little modification her words can be applied to Paul as well. In a new situation, Paul's work—like Gandhi's—in trying to unite different communities must be carried on critically. His views must be treated selectively; they must be adapted and enhanced. As a man of his time who asked some of the deepest questions, Paul, too, could be seen as a man for all times and places.

## Bibliography

Barth, K. 1968 (1933): *The Epistle to the Romans*, London: Oxford University 1968.

Baur, F. C. 1864 (1973): *Vorlesungen über neutestamentliche Theologie*, Darmstadt: Wissenschaftliche Buchgesellschaft 1973.

Becker, J. 1989: *Paulus*. Der Apostel der Völker, Tübingen: J. C. B. Mohr 1989.

Beyschlag, W. 1892: *Neutestamentliche Theologie 2*, Halle: Eugen Strien 1892.

Brown, J. M. 1990: *Gandhi*. Prisoner of Hope, Delhi: Oxford University 1990.

---

[105] J. M. Brown 1990, 394.

Brown, P. 1967: *Augustine of Hippo*. A Biography, Berkeley - Los Angeles, CA: University of California 1967.

Brown, R. E. 1983: "Rome", in: R. E. Brown - J. P. Meier, *Antioch and Rome:* New Testament Cradles of Catholic Christianity, London: Geoffrey Chapman 1983, 87-216.

Bultmann, R. 1951-1955: *Theology of the New Testament 1-2*, New York - London: Charles Scribner's Sons 1951-55.

Casey, P. M. 1991: *From Jewish Prophet to Gentile God*. The Origins and Development of New Testament Christology, Cambridge: James Clarke 1991.

Conzelmann, H. 1969: *An Outline of the Theology of the New Testament*, London: SCM 1969.

Craig, C. T. 1943: *The Beginning of Christianity*, New York - Nashville, TN: Abingdon - Cokesbury 1943.

Dunn, J. D. G. 1988: *Romans 9-16* (Word Biblical Commentary 38B), Dallas, TX: Word Books 1988.

— 1991: *The Partings of the Ways*. Between Christianity and Judaism and their Significance for the Character of Christianity, London: SCM 1991.

Eckert, W. 1968: "Hoch- und Spätmittelalter. Katholischer Humanismus", in: Rengstorf - v. Kortzfleisch (eds.) 1, 210-306.

Esler, P. F. 1987: *Community and Gospel in Luke-Acts*. The Social and Political Motivations of Lucan Theology (MSSNTS 57), Cambridge: Cambridge University 1987.

Fiedler, P. 1990: "'Das Israel Gottes' im Neuen Testament – die Kirche oder das jüdische Volk?", in: H. Frohnhofen (ed.), *Christlicher Antijudaismus und jüdischer Antipaganismus*. Ihre Motive und Hintergründe in den ersten drei Jahrhunderten (Hamburger Theologische Studien 3), Hamburg: Steinmann & Steinmann 1990, 64-87.

Friedrich, M. 1988: *Zwischen Abwehr und Bekehrung*. Die Stellung der deutschen evangelischen Theologie zum Judentum im 17. Jahrhundert (BHTh 72), Tübingen: J. C. B. Mohr 1988.

Gager, J. G. 1983: *The Origins of Anti-Semitism*. Attitudes Toward Judaism in Pagan and Christian Antiquity, New York - Oxford: Oxford University 1983.

Gaston, L. 1987: *Paul and the Torah*, Vancouver: University of British Columbia 1987.

Gnilka, J. 1989: *Neutestamentliche Theologie*. Ein Überblick, Würzburg: Echter 1989.

Goodenough, E. R. 1986: "The Bible as Product of the Ancient World", in: idem, *Goodenough on the History of Religion and on Judaism* (eds. E. S. Frerichs - J. Neusner; Brown Judaic Studies 121), Atlanta, GA: Scholars Press 1986, 33-46.

Goppelt, L. 1978: *Theologie des Neuen Testaments* (UTB 850), Göttingen: Vandenhoeck & Ruprecht ³1978.

Gorday, P. 1983: *Principles of Patristic Exegesis*. Romans 9-11 in Origen, John Chrysostom, and Augustine, New York - Toronto: Edwin Mellen 1983.

Guthrie, D. 1981: *New Testament Theology*, Leicester: Inter-Varsity 1981.

Hartman, L. 1979: "Att förstå en nytestamentlig text. Undersökningsmetoder och tolkningsresultat", in: *SEÅ* 44 (1979) 115-121.

Holtzmann, H. J. 1911: *Lehrbuch der neutestamentlichen Theologie 2,* Tübingen: J. C. B. Mohr ²1911.

Höpfl, H. 1985: *The Christian Polity of John Calvin*, Cambridge: Cambridge University 1985 (repr.; original 1982).

Houlden, J. L. 1986: *Connections*. The Integration of Theology and Faith, London: SCM 1986.

Hübner, H. 1984: *Gottes Ich und Israel*. Zum Schriftgebrauch des Paulus in Römer 9-11, Göttingen: Vandenhoeck & Ruprecht 1984.

— 1993: *Biblische Theologie des Neuen Testaments 2*. Die Theologie des Paulus und ihre neutestamentliche Wirkungsgeschichte, Göttingen: Vandenhoeck & Ruprecht 1993.

Jervell, J. 1969: "Ein Interpolator interpretiert. Zu der christlichen Bearbeitung der Testamente der zwölf Patriarchen", in: W. Eltester (ed.), *Studien zu den Testamenten der Zwölf Patriarchen* (BZNW 36), Berlin: Walter de Gruyter 1969.

Johnson, E. E. 1989: *The Function of Apocalyptic and Wisdom Traditions in Romans 9-11* (SBL.DS 109), Atlanta, GA: Scholars Press 1989.

de Jonge, M. 1986: "The Future of Israel in the Testaments of the Twelve Patriarchs", in: *JSJ* 17 (1986) 196-211.

Kaftan, J. 1927: *Neutestamentliche Theologie*, Berlin: Martin Warneck 1927.

Kötting, B. 1968: "Die Entwicklung im Osten bis Justinian", in: Rengstorf - v. Kortzfleisch (eds.) 1, 136-174.

Kümmel, W. G. 1969: *Die Theologie des Neuen Testaments nach seinen Hauptzeugen*, Göttingen: Vandenhoeck & Ruprecht 1969.

Küng, H. 1991: *Das Judentum 2*. Die religiöse Situation der Zeit, München-Zürich: Piper 1991.

Ladd, G. E. 1991: *A Theology of the New Testament*, Cambridge: Lutterworth 1991 (= 1974).

Lohse, E. 1974: *Grundriss der neutestamentlichen Theologie*, Stuttgart: Kohlhammer 1974.

Longenecker, B. W. 1991: *Eschatology and the Covenant*. A Comparison of 4 Ezra and Romans 1-11 (JSNT.S 57), Sheffield: Sheffield Academic Press 1991.

McGrath, A. E. 1990: *A Life of John Calvin*. A Study in the Shaping of Western Culture, Oxford: Oxford University 1990.

Meeks, W. A. 1991: "On Trusting an Unpredictable God: A Hermeneutical Meditation on Romans 9-11", in: J. T. Carroll, C. H. Cosgrove, E. E. Johnson (eds.), *Faith and History*, Essays in Honor of Paul W. Meyer, Atlanta, GA: Scholars Press 1991, 105-124.

Morgan, R. 1973: *The Nature of New Testament Theology*. The Contribution of William Wrede and Adolf Schlatter, (SBT Second Series 25.) London: SCM 1973.

Morris, L. 1986: *New Testament Theology*, Grand Rapids, MI: Academie Books 1986.

Räisänen, H. 1976: *The Idea of Divine Hardening*, Helsinki: Finnish Exegetical Society [2]1976.

— 1987a: *Paul and the Law* (WUNT 28), Tübingen: J. C. B. Mohr [2]1987.

— 1987b: "Römer 9-11: Analyse eines geistigen Ringens", in: *ANRW* II.25.4, Berlin/New York; de Gruyter 1987, 2891-2939.

— 1988: "Paul, God and History. Romans 9-11 in Recent Research", in: J. Neusner et al. (eds.), *The Social World of Formative Christianity and Judaism*, in Honor of H. C. Kee, Philadelphia, PA: Fortress 1988, 178-206.

— 1990: *Beyond New Testament Theology*. A Story and a Programme, London: SCM – Philadelphia, PA: Trinity 1990.

— 1991: "The Redemption of Israel. A Salvation-Historical Problem in Luke-Acts", in: P. Luomanen (ed.), *Luke-Acts*. Scandinavian Perspectives (Publications of the Finnish Exegetical Society 54), Helsinki: Finnish Exegetical Society – Göttingen: Vandenhoeck 1991, 94-114.

— 1992: *Jesus, Paul and Torah*. Collected Essays (JSNT.S 43), Sheffield: Sheffield Academic Press 1992.

Rengstorf, K. H. – von Kortzfleisch, S. (eds.) 1968-1970: *Kirche und Synagoge 1-2*. Handbuch zur Geschichte von Christen und Juden, Stuttgart: Ernst Klett 1968-70.

Richardson, A. 1958: *An Introduction to the Theology of the New Testament*, London: SCM 1958.

Riddle, D. W. 1943: "The Jewishness of Paul", in: *JR* 23 (1943) 240-244.

Rowland, C. 1987: *Christian Origins*. An Account of the Setting and Character of the most Important Messianic Sect of Judaism, London: SPCK [2]1987.

Ruether, R. R. 1974: *Faith and Fratricide*. The Theological Roots of Anti-Semitism, New York: Seabury 1974.

Sanders, E. P. 1977: *Paul and Palestinian Judaism*. A Comparison of Patterns of Religion, London: SCM 1977.

Sandys-Wunsch, J. – Eldredge, L. 1980: "J. P.Gabler and the Distinction Between Biblical and Dogmatic Theology: Translation, Commentary, and Discussion of His Originality", in: *SJTh* 33 (1980) 133-158.

Schelkle, K. H. 1958: *Paulus - Lehrer der Väter*. Die altkirchliche Auslegung von Römer 1-11, Düsseldorf: Patmos [2]1958.

— 1976: *Theologie des Neuen Testaments 4/2*, Düsseldorf: Patmos 1976.

Schmidt, M. 1970: "Protestantismus vom Aufkommen des Pietismus bis zur Mitte des 19. Jahrhunderts", in: Rengstorf - v. Kortzfleisch (eds.) 2, 87-128.

Segal, A. 1990: *Paul the Convert*. The Apostolate and Apostasy of Saul the Pharisee, New Haven, CT- London: Yale University 1990.

Stauffer, E. 1955: *New Testament Theology,* London: SCM 1955 (German original: *Die Theologie des Neuen Testaments,* Stuttgart -Berlin: Kohlhammer 1941.)

Stendahl, K. 1984: "Biblical Theology: A Program", in: idem, *Meanings*. The Bible as Document and as Guide, Philadelphia, PA: Fortress 1984, 11-44.

Stuhlmacher, P. 1992: *Biblische Theologie des Neuen Testaments 1*. Grundlegung. Von Jesus zu Paulus, Göttingen: Vandenhoeck & Ruprecht 1992.

Suggs, M. J. 1970: *Wisdom, Christology, and Law in Matthew's Gospel*, Cambridge, MA.: Harvard University 1970.

Teeple, H. M. 1992: *How Did Christianity Really Begin?* A Historical-Archaeological Approach, Evanston, IL: Religion and Ethics Institute 1992.

Theobald, M. 1987: "Kirche und Israel nach Röm 9-11", in: *Kairos* 29 (1987) 1-22.

Thompson, A. L. 1977: *Responsibility for Evil in the Theodicy of IV Ezra* (SBL.DS 29), Missoula, MT: Scholars Press 1977.

Weinel, H. 1928: *Biblische Theologie des Neuen Testaments.* Die Religion Jesu und des Urchristentums, Tübingen: J. C. B. Mohr [4]1928.

Westerholm, S. 1988: *Israel's Law and the Church's Faith.* Paul and His Recent Interpreters, Grand Rapids, MI: Eerdmans 1988.

Wiles, M. 1967: *The Divine Apostle.* The Interpretation of St. Paul's Epistles in the Early Church, Cambridge: Cambridge University 1967.

Wilken, R. L. 1979: *The Myth of Christian Beginnings*, London: SCM 1979.

Wilson, S. G. 1986: "Marcion and the Jews", in: idem (ed.), *Anti- Judaism in Early Christianity 2: Separation and Polemic*, Waterloo: Wilfrid Laurier University 1986, 45-58.

— 1992: "The Salvation of the Jews in Early Christian Literature" (Presidential address for the Canadian Society of Biblical Studies, June 1992. Manuscript).

Wright, N. T. 1991: *The Climax of the Covenant.* Christ and the Law in Pauline Theology, Edinburgh: T. & T. Clark 1991.

Ziesler, J. 1989: *Paul's Letter to the Romans.* (TPI New Testament Commentaries), London: SCM – Philadelphia, PA: Trinity 1989.

# Paul and Commensality

## Bengt Holmberg

## 1. Introduction

Commensality—eating together—is a very appropriate theme for an essay written to celebrate the gift of friendship with a distinguished and dear colleague like Lars Hartman. But as a matter of fact commensality is not always a pleasant and peaceful phenomenon, not even in the Bible. A look at the uses of the verb συνεσθίειν "to eat together" in the NT will confirm this:

Luke 15:2   Jesus is accused by Pharisees and scribes for receiving sinners (ἁμαρ-τωλούς) and eating with them.

Acts 10:41   Peter tells the Cornelius group that "we" ate and drank with Jesus after his resurrection from the dead.

Acts 11:3   Peter is accused by οἱ ἐκ περιτομῆς for having gone in to uncircumcised men and eaten with them.

1 Cor 5:11   Paul specifies his earlier instruction to the Christians in Corinth not to mingle with fornicators (μὴ συναναμίγνυσθαι πόρνοις): this concerns a "brother" (Christian) who sins grossly; the readers should not eat with such a one (τῷ τοιούτῳ μηδὲ συνεσθίειν).

Gal 2:12   Paul reproaches Peter for first having eaten with gentiles (μετὰ τῶν ἐθνῶν συνήσθιεν) and then withdrawing from table fellowship with them because of his fear of τοὺς ἐκ περιτομῆς.

What stands out from just these five cases is that συνεσθίειν entails an intimate fellowship or communion between people, a communion fraught with social and moral significance that is actually only once judged favourably (Acts 10:41). It appears that sharing one's intimate sphere with other people is a sensitive thing, which not seldom causes conflict. Both Jesus and Peter were accused of sharing their intimate sphere with people who ought to have been kept outside it: "sinners", or (what amounts to the same) uncircumcised non-Jews. We see Paul making commensality the ground for sharp reproach, both when it is denied and when it is upheld: on the one hand Paul scolds Peter for having excluded uncircumcised from table fellowship (his sphere of intimacy), but on the other hand Paul is sharply critical of the Corinthian Christians for not yet having excluded a gross sinner from their fellowship (1 Cor 5:2b). Commensality is obviously a phenomenon that arouses strong opinions—and very diverse ones too! Such an interesting phenomenon needs to be interpreted and understood more deeply.

## 2. Commensality Decoded

This heading suggests that meals are a kind of language, and that eating together conveys a message to participants and onlookers, although it may need some interpreting effort to be fully understood. This is in fact the common (and cross-cultural) perspective of cultural anthropology: food and meals are phenomena rich in meaning, and the very title of the famous essay "Deciphering a meal" by Mary Douglas tells the reader (in the words of another anthropologist) that "the apparent trivialities of the domestic table may be as significant as poetry or other exalted forms of communication in ordering thought and experience."[1] Douglas states:[2]

> If food is treated as a code, the message it encodes will be found in the pattern of social relations being expressed. The message is about different degrees of hierarchy, inclusion and exclusion, boundaries and transactions across the boundaries … Food categories encode social events.

Food is commonly one of the principal ways in which differences among social groups are marked, distinguishing men from women, children from adults, kin from others, gods from human beings.[3] More specifically:[4]

> In establishing precisely who eats what with whom, commensality is one of the most powerful ways of defining and differentiating social groups. It may be used to represent kinship or connubium. It may also be used to establish a community of interests, marking close relationship, among those who are neither kin nor affines.

It is important to remember that terms like "fellowship", "kinship", "connubium" signify, not just a feeling of togetherness and sympathy, but, more importantly, mutual social obligations. "Those who sit at meal together are *united for all social effects* [my italics], those who do not eat together are aliens to another, without

---

[1] Feeley-Harnik 1981, 14
[2] Douglas 1975, 249.
[3] Feeley-Harnik 1981, 10.
[4] Feeley-Harnik 1981, 11.

fellowship in religion and without reciprocal social duties."[5] Meals normally express and confirm existing social structure:[6]

> Meals are not *rituals,* rites of status change and transformation. Rather they are *ceremonies* ... [which] bolster the boundaries defining a group or institution, even as they confirm established roles and statuses within the group. Unlike rituals, which are concerned with the perimeter, ceremonies focus on the inside, the inward dimension of a social body and its structure. They attend, not to change, but to stability; they are concerned, not with newness, but with continuity. Meals-as-ceremonies replicate the group's basic social system, its values, lines, classifications, and its symbolic world.

Analysing meals and commensality means reading the map of social reality, because commensality is a language of social identity, telling us which people belong together and can be expected to share the obligations of accepting one another. And correspondingly, once established as an intended fact, commensality refused is a very clear negative boundary marker that helps define social structure and establish group identity. Using the biblical Passover meal as an example, the rules about participation (all Israel should, but no uncircumcised may, share in the Passover, Exod 12:47–48) make very clear the boundaries of God's holy people.

In an investigation of early Jewish and Christian attitudes to meals Gillian Feeley-Harnik has pointed out that this area became increasingly important in post-exilic Judaism:[7]

> The evidence suggests that food was one of the most important languages in which Jews expressed relations among human beings and between human beings and God. Food was identified with God's word as the foundation of the covenant relationship in scripture and in sectarianism. During the inter-Testamental period, when God's word became increasingly identified with the law, food law came to represent the whole law. The violation of dietary rules became equivalent to apostasy.

Commensality in first-century Jewish society was thus a social behaviour of paramount significance: it structured reality and kept persons in their proper places, at a deep level conforming to God's own holy order. This religious significance of commensality is also the reason why breaking its rules was so provocative and threatening.

### RECKLESS COMMENSALITY

Luke 15:2 is a reminder that Jesus was known for having practised a rather reckless

---

[5] Robertson Smith 1889, 251, quoted from Feeley-Harnik 1981,11.

[6] Neyrey 1991, 362–63.

[7] Feeley-Harnik 1981, 19; cf. 107 and 165.

commensality; reckless, that is, in the meaning that it transgressed the norms for decent behaviour of a teacher or prophet in Israel. The gospels have several stories
showing Jesus at meals, and a number of them concern the subject of Jesus eating
with sinners, and his habit of not keeping an appropriate distance between himself
and their impurity. In an important logion, Matt 11:19, Jesus himself quotes what is
being said about him:

λέγουσιν,
Ἰδοὺ ἄνθρωπος φάγος καὶ οἰνοπότης,
τελωνῶν φίλος καὶ ἁμαρτωλῶν.

They say:
What a glutton and wine-drinker,
a friend of tax collectors and sinners!

NOTE ON QUOTING INSULTS

The words φάγος καὶ οἰνοπότης are probably an allusion to the wording of Deut
21:20, where parents bring their hopelessly disobedient son to the elders in the gate,
*i.e.* to the local court, where they accuse him of (a) disobedience, and (b) being a glutton and winebibber (LXX: συμβολοκοπῶν οἰνοφλυγεῖ), and turn him over to be
stoned to death. The saying about Jesus is thus both an insult and a serious accusation, and the fact that he nonetheless quotes it throws an interesting light on his own
person. He is considered to be a profligate son (Matt 11:19), but knows himself to be
"the Son" (Matt 11:27)! He also knows himself to be sent to collect and save the lost
sheep of the house of Israel (15:24), but the effect of his ministry is—as pointed out
by himself—a division that tears families apart (10:34), which in Mic 7:6 is seen as
a symptom of the deep moral decay that God will punish Israel for! This juxtaposition of the claim to absolute centrality in Israel and the awareness of deviant status
in Jewish society (almost allowing that Scripture speaks against him!) represents a
stunning blend of supreme self-confidence and self-irony that betrays a truly remarkable personality—and I do not think it is the evangelist's.

John Dominic Crossan has pointed out that the really provocative element in Jesus'
behaviour is that he eats with just anyone. "It is that 'anyone' that negates the very
social function of table, namely, to establish a social ranking by what one eats, how
one eats, and with whom one eats. It is the random and open commensality of the
parable's meal that is its most startling element," and which constitutes its strongly
egalitarian challenge. "And the almost predictable counter accusation to such open
commensality is immediate: Jesus is a glutton, a drunkard, and a friend of tax collectors and sinners. He makes, in other words, no appropriate distinctions and dis-
criminations. He has no honor. He has no shame."[8] Crossan goes on to point out that
this was part of a calculated attack from Jesus on social distinctions in first-century

---

[8] Crossan 1991, 262.

Palestinian Judaism—or any society.[9] Jerome Neyrey, likewise, after having established how meals serve to uphold the existing social structures, points out that Jesus can also turn the commensality system upside down, effecting a revolution.[10] And this unseemly commensality of Jesus is, according to most scholars, very probably a historical fact, awful to his contemporaries and rather difficult to handle even for his adherents.

## 3. Commensality Delimited

Paul's attitude to commensality is far closer to the conventional and cautious than Jesus'. While Jesus seems (but probably was not) blissfully unaware of the danger of moral contamination from bad company, Paul is very much aware of it and demands that his fellow Christians in such cases refrain from "dangerous" commensality. There are parallels to this in contemporary Judaism; a good example is found in 1 QS 6:24–7:24, where rules are given concerning the partial or complete exclusion of offenders from the commensality ("purity") of the religious community.

### 3.1. Commensality Decried—1 Cor 5

In 1 Cor 5 Paul takes up (and decides and argues, in that order) a case which he considers very serious, not only because the sin is exceptionally heinous, but even more because the Christian community in Corinth has condoned or even defended it (5:2 πεφυσιωμένοι ἐστέ), rather than having expelled the sinner. Expulsion is necessary, however, and consequently follows in a forceful way (3–5). The apostle also explains why this has to be done: in order to save the sinner himself (5), and the community (6): do you not know that a little leaven (of malice and evil, v. 8) leavens the whole lump = even one person's sin will affect the whole community negatively. Condoning sin by living together with sinning fellow Christians as if nothing had happened will eventually contaminate the whole community and make it impure. In the final part (9–13) the apostle gives general rules about the need of non-association with (Christian) sinners, referring now also to previous written instructions.

#### PASSOVER PURITY IN CHRISTIAN MEALS

The imagery in the central section (6–8) with the theological motivation for the expulsion of the incestuous man, sounds surprisingly Jewish and ritualistic. Terms having to do with the Jewish Passover abound: ζύμη–"leaven" (old and new), ἐκκαθάρατε–"cleanse out", τὸ πάσχα–"the paschal lamb", ἐτύθη–"sacrificed",

---

[9] Crossan 1991, 263.
[10] Neyrey 1991, 362–63, 374–77, and 378–81, 384 respectively.

ἑορτάζωμεν–"celebrate the festival", ἄζυμα–"unleavened bread"; Forkman considers it possible that Paul here is using a well-known introduction to a Christian Passover celebration as basis for his theological-ethical instruction on the necessity of church discipline.[11] This reminds us of the observation by E. P. Sanders that Paul makes negative statements on the law only in the context of membership requirements, where faith is to be the criterion, while he can refer positively to the law when he discusses behaviour within the Christian community.[12] So Paul is not at all adverse to using the vocabulary of Jewish law when he wants to discuss questions of Christian communal ethics. Paul even uses the kind of language one would have thought furthest removed from everyday (Gentile) Christian life in Corinth, viz. the terms of Jewish cultic purity. He uses the image of the temple and its desecration in 1 Cor 3, of Passover purity in 1 Cor 5, of ordinary meals in purity in 1 Cor 5:11, of the body as God's pure and holy temple in 1 Cor 6, etc.[13]

This Pauline propensity gives an added meaning to the use of Passover terminology in 1 Cor 5. There *could* be a connection, then, between the fact that the Jewish Passover meal is the most nonaccessible of Jewish meals for persons not belonging to the people of God and the fact that Paul uses terminology having to do with Passover purity when he argues theologically for restricted commensality.[14] What is at stake in both cases is the identity of God's holy people, which is manifested and upheld by keeping outsiders away. The common element between the Jewish Passover and Christian commensality is that both are guarded by stringent demands for purity, although purity does not mean the same in Jewish and Christian contexts. The demands for purity are ethnic and cultic in the former case, and ethical and sacral in the latter.

### NO MIXING (= COMMENSALITY) WITH CHRISTIAN SINNERS

Something of a purity terminology appears also in the following section of Paul's argument (9–13), which he starts by referring to what he has already written to the Corinthians: μὴ συναναμίγνυσθαι πόρνοις. He carefully explains that πόρνοι here means πόρνοι οἱ ἔσω, not οἱ ἔξω (in the terminology of v. 12). The latter, the non-Christians "of this world" outside the community, will be judged by God, while it is the responsibility of the Christians as God's holy people to "drive out the wicked" from out of their own community (a half-quote from Deut 17:7). This means that here too the Christians in Corinth are invited to regard themselves as the holy peo-

---

[11] Forkman 1972, 147–49.

[12] Sanders 1983, 84, 113.

[13] Segal 1990, 169–70, referring to Newton 1985.

[14] I thank Dieter Mitternacht for suggesting the idea of an analogy between Exod 12:48 and 1 Cor 5:11.

ple of God, who must defend their holy character against inner rot. The remarkable thing is that it seems much more important to keep the boundaries clear between "pure and impure", or sin and holiness, *within* the Christian group, than avoiding contact with general pagans outside the community. The policy the apostle enjoins can thus be formulated as "strict discipline within the church; complete freedom of association outside it".[15]

The verb συναναμίγνυσθαι appears in LXX both in its ordinary sense of "mingling or associating with other people" and in a pejorative sense, denoting "intermingling with other nations in which the purity of the saved people is forfeited".[16] This negative sense is unmistakably there in the three NT occurrences of the verb (1 Cor 5:9 and 11, 2 Thess 3:14), where it denotes undesirable dealings with fellow Christians who are sinners (πόρνοι and ἄτακτοι). The verb did not function as a technical term for unrestricted communion or commensality in the Christian group; it is used only in prohibitions and seems to be a word with solely negative connotations, while the positive word for such communion is συνεσθίειν (as can be seen in Gal 2:12 and Acts 11:3).

> As was the case in Qumran, Paul's church discipline also included the cutting off of relationships which from the point of view of purity were particularly sensitive. The offender is to be noted down [here the author discusses 2 Thess 3] and isolated—not from every social contact, but from such relationships as can contaminate those that are pure.[17]

The grammatical construction of v. 11 (with two negated infinitives, μὴ συναναμίγνυσθαι ... μηδὲ συνεσθίειν) raises the question whether "associating, mingling with" is something different from and more demanding than "eating with". The μηδέ can be understood as equivalent to "not even", i.e. as indicating something in addition to what has been mentioned ("Steht οὐδέ [μηδέ] zu Anfang des Ganzen oder nach οὐ [μή] innerhalb desselben Satzstücks, so heißt es 'auch nicht, nicht einmal'"[18]). In such case, συναναμίγνυσθαι would denote a higher degree of intimacy than συνεσθίειν—a conclusion drawn by Johannes Weiß, who considers the "mixing" in v. 9 to denote a closer personal communion with possible moral contamination, while "eating with" in v. 11 would refer to more indifferent chance meetings at the same meal at the house of a third party, in a guild or suchlike—not the Agape-meals, from which such a notorious sinner would of course be excluded.[19]

This understanding is difficult to accept, as commensality certainly must belong

---

[15] Barrett 1973, 132.
[16] Greeven 1971, 853–54.
[17] Forkman 1972, 138; cf. 150 on 1 Cor 5:9–11.
[18] Blaß-Debrunner 1970, § 445, 2.
[19] Weiß 1925, 143.

to a more intimate social sphere than simply mixing with people, greeting them and talking with them.[20] It also introduces the idea that different forms of commensality among Christians also differed in character: communal eating in a worship context (Agape-meals and the Lord's Supper) with high holiness requirements on the one hand, and private, rather secular meals in Christian homes on the other.[21] There is no warrant in the text for such a distinction between communal and private table fellowship, and one also wonders whether such a distinction does not presuppose a too modern idea about the difference between sacred meals and other commensality within the Corinthian church. And would it really be in accordance with Paul's will for the Corinthians to invite that incestuous man to their homes, or to dine at his house? It seems more probable that *any* eating with such a sinner is prohibited by the apostle, and that the μηδέ should be understood, with Greeven, as an epexegetical conjunction (= "i.e.", "and therefore", "which means"), spelling out the meaning of the first infinitive in v. 9 by adding the second in v. 11, or in other words, that συναναμίγνυσθαι actually refers to commensality.[22]

As Greeven points out,[23] the intention of the apostle in 1 Cor 5 is that God's people should be kept pure and undefiled, not by refraining from contact with non-Christians (which is unnecessary and would be impossible, v. 10), but by removing evil from inside the community. As Forkman has shown, "mixing" refers in Paul's letters only to relationships which have to do with (endangered) purity in the Christian community.[24] The conclusion seems to be, then, that the mingling that defiles can occur only *within* this holy community. Eating in other contexts, e.g. with outsiders (1 Cor 10:27), is an act that does not in itself pollute a Christian, most likely because it does not involve deeper or more significant levels of intimacy, like personal and corporate holiness and moral responsibility for each other.

## 3.2. Commensality Deferred — 2 Thess 3:6–15

In this *paraenesis* the author starts by exhorting his addressees to withdraw from every brother (Christian) who lives disorderly (στέλλεσθαι ὑμᾶς ἀπὸ παντὸς ἀδελφοῦ ἀτάκτως περιπατοῦντος). What ἀτάκτως means can be gathered from the statement in v. 7–8 that "we", the author/s, did not live disorderly (οὐκ ἠτακτήσαμεν) and did not eat bread for free (οὐδὲ δωρεὰν ἄρτον ἐφάγομεν) when staying with the Thessalonians, but rather toiled so as not to burden others. In addition to giving this good example, "we" also explicitly taught (10b) that "if somebody

---

[20] So also Tomson 1990, 222, note 6.

[21] Fee 1987, 226.

[22] Greeven 1971, 855.

[23] Greeven 1971, 854.

[24] Forkman 1972, 138.

doesn't want to work neither shall he eat" (μηδὲ ἐσθιέτω). Verse 11 confirms that living disorderly means not working (μηδὲν ἐργαζομένους), and calls forth a weighty command to such persons (v. 12) that they should work and eat their own bread (ἐργαζόμενοι τὸν ἑαυτῶν ἄρτον ἐσθίωσιν). Finally (v. 14) comes an instruction how to treat fellow Christians who do not conform to these instructions: they should be "marked out" (noted down) and not mixed with (τοῦτον ση- μειοῦσθε, μὴ συναναμίγνυσθαι αὐτῷ). This does not mean excommunication for good, as the purpose given is that s/he should take warning and turn about, ἵνα ἐν- τραπῇ,[25] and v. 15 expressly states that such a person should not be viewed as an enemy, but as an erring fellow Christian to be admonished.

What we have here is clearly a case of church discipline, and, interestingly, it focuses on eating disorders: a minority of Christians in Thessalonike who burden others by sharing in the common meals without contributing anything to them, and who consequently should be excluded from commensality with the majority until they have mended their ways.[26] What strengthens the case for understanding the recommended measure as an exclusion of fellow Christians from the common meals of the Christian group is the use of the verb συναναμίγνυσθαι. Except here, it is used only in 1 Cor 5: 9 and 11, where commensality is clearly denoted and forbidden. Robert Jewett has presented a good case for the rule of 2 Thess 3:10b having grown out of a specific community situation in Thessalonike, not formulated *ad hoc* by Paul or by an author writing in his name. This was a social setting in which one shared one's meals regularly, and where the refusal to work affected the community so seriously that sanctions against this deviation were necessary—and where the sanction (μηδὲ ἐσθιέτω) was enforcable, i.e. where (the majority of) the community actually decided who participated in their communal meals. Jewett calls this community a "tenement church", i.e. a rather egalitarian group of Christians, who were so poor that it really mattered that everybody brought and shared their resources (cf. 1 Thess 4:9 and 11)—not a house-church, where an affluent patron could afford to feed also the non-contributors.[27]

It is hard to be absolutely sure that Paul did not write 2 Thess, especially the paraenetic section in 3:6–15, which seems to stand in a Pauline tradition. (1) As in Rom 16:17b this *paraenesis* advocates withdrawal from fellow Christians whose presence is harmful to the community, (2) like 1 Cor 5:11 it uses deprivation of commensality as a sanction against sinners, and (3) the punishment is temporary, given with a view to reforming the erring and then receive them back in the com-

---

[25] Engberg-Pedersen 1993, 130 note 44.

[26] For a different view on exclusion, see Rengstorf 1971b, 590, who is more undecided in Rengstorf 1971a, 266.

[27] Jewett 1993, 22–23.

munity, much as in 2 Cor 2:6–7. Forkman ingeniously suggested that the repetition of terms and ideas related to church discipline from 1 Thess in 2 Thess 3 should not be understood as the work of a pseudepigrapher who anxiously wanted to keep close to the original Paul, but rather as the apostle's conscious and intended repetition of earlier instructions. In Qumran (CD 9:16–23) reprovings from different occasions can be united so that a case can "be judged according to two or three witnesses" (Deut 19:15). Paul's writing down of the same instruction or warning in a second letter can be understood as following a similar understanding of the rule of more than one testimony in Deut 19, done in order to make it clear to the Thessalonians that they now have sufficient grounds to take formal measures against the ἄτακτοι.[28]

My case does not stand or fall with Pauline authorship of 2 Thess, however. If genuine, it serves as one more instance of Paul's policy of using restrictions in commensality as a means of social control within Christian groups for which he felt responsible; if not, the text shows that this policy was continued in the Pauline tradition. The difference between 1 Cor 5 and 2 Thess 3 lies mainly in the severity of the measure: in the former case we find an exclusion from commensality that seems to be irrevocable punishment, actually an excommunication, while the latter rather aims at a temporary, educative measure—commensality deferred.

## 3.3. Commensality Declined—1 Cor 10:14–22

I hope later to enter into a discussion of the many and complex questions concerning the discussion about food in 1 Cor 8–10, but it is enough for my purposes here to note that several scholars nowadays agree in understanding the whole argument of these chapters as a strong warning against eating idol meat, a warning delivered by several different lines of argument.[29] The section where the apostle explicitly speaks about Christians eating and drinking in a pagan temple is 1 Cor 10:14–22, esp. 20b–21:

οὐ θέλω δὲ ὑμᾶς κοινωνοὺς τῶν δαιμονίων γίνεσθαι.
οὐ δύνασθε ποτήριον κυρίου πίνειν καὶ ποτήριον δαιμονίων,
οὐ δύνασθε τραπέζης κυρίου μετέχειν καὶ τραπέζης δαιμονίων.

I do not want you to be partners with demons.
You cannot drink the cup of the Lord and the cup of demons.
You cannot partake of the table of the Lord and the table of demons.

---

[28] Forkman 1972, 132–34.

[29] Engberg-Pedersen 1993, 127–29, Fee 1987, 360 and throughout his commentary on 1 Cor 8–10, Gooch 1993, passim.

This is an unmistakable prohibition for Christians to take part in cultic meals in a temple precinct. Such meals were rather ordinary forms of social intercourse in Hellenistic cities, at least for people of some social standing.[30] But Paul leaves the possible ordinariness and low-key religious character of such meals aside, as well as the fact that most of the participants are other human beings. The decisive fact for him in such meals is the presence of and deep communion (κοινωνία) with demons—which is absolutely impermissible for a Christian. "The table of the Lord is the table or meal which the Lord provides (1 C. 10:4) and which claims those who receive it for Him (1 C. 10: 16). Similarly the table of demons is the table of the sacrificial meal, or the meal itself, which is dispensed by demons and which delivers up those who participate to them."[31] Goppelt adduces some interesting support from the (later) Jewish-Christian Pseudo-Clementines on table fellowship with demons:[32]

> He ... who has partaken of a sacrificial offering is not free of an unclean spirit. He has become a table companion of demons and has a part in the demon whose figure he has formed in his own spirit out of fear or love. (*Ps. Clem. Recogn.* II, 71.)

> Over none of you do the demons have power if you have not previously contracted life fellowship with their chiefs; for it was legally established by God ... for the two chiefs that neither has power over a man unless he is first his table companion (ὁμοτράπεζος) and has resolved to do good or evil. (*Ps. Clem. Hom.* 7, 3, 2f.)

The basic idea of Paul's reasoning about commensality here is κοινωνία, and his conviction that such deep communion with the power of the κύριος named in the dedication formula of the meal (whether it is κύριος Ἰησοῦς or some other "lord" or "god", cf. 1 Cor 8:5) cannot be avoided. For this reason one cannot alternate between the two meals ("tables"); the Lord does not allow any gods but Himself, 1 Cor 10:22.

This notion of κοινωνία also throws light on Paul's earlier reasoning about commensality in 1 Cor 5, and is the reason for my previous statement that the demands for purity in Christian commensality are ethical *and sacral*. The requirements for participating in Christian fellowship meals, centred around κύριος Ἰησοῦς as they are, are not simply ethical, i.e. demands of avoiding sin and practising virtue, but also concern previous cleansing from sin by baptism and being filled with Holy Spirit, which means incorporation into the Body (1 Cor 12:13). Every believer individually, and the whole church corporatively, is united with the Lord Jesus, and this belonging to the Lord raises claims on every participant in the Christian fellow-

---

[30] Gooch 1993.

[31] Goppelt 1972, 213.

[32] Goppelt 1972, 213 note 40.

ship meals—claims which can be summarized in one word: holiness (ἁγιασμός). Every Christian who shares in the κοινωνία with the Lord has to grow up into conformity with him, and be holy as He is holy.

## 4. Commensality Demanded

So far we have been looking at cases where Paul wants to delimit commensality, trying to find the rationale behind his instructions. I believe that the same basic convictions on the meaning of eating together and belonging to the Lord Jesus lie behind the cases where the apostle wants table fellowship restored: 1 Cor 11:17–34 and Gal 2:11–14. A few points will have to suffice to indicate how my understanding of Paul and commensality affects these texts.

In 1 Cor 11:17–34 Paul sees the Corinthian table fellowship as in some need of repair.[33] It is so obviously flawed by selfish practices that the apostle can state: "when you come together it is not for the better but for the worse" (v. 17b), and in v. 20: "when you assemble, it is not to eat the Lord's supper" (συνερχομένων οὖν ὑμῶν ἐπὶ τὸ αὐτὸ οὐκ ἔστιν κυριακὸν δεῖπνον φαγεῖν). That is no doubt what the Corinthians think they are doing, but the apostle crisply disabuses them of that idea, by pointing to the discrepancy between the meaning of that meal and the fake commensality they actually are engaging in. They (and "they" refers to "the haves", who make a private banquet of the celebration) seem to have forgotten, both the presence of the "have-nots" who sit hungry at the common meal, and the presence of the Lord himself, whose sacrificial death is proclaimed by the very act of having this meal together. They do not "discern the body" (διακρίνειν τὸ σῶμα, v. 29), or in other words they forget the κοινωνία they are sharing in, which should put the Lord Christ in centre and unite all present believers into one body. One might say that they have flaunted, both the demands of commensality generally by neglecting the consideration for the poor members of the congregation, and, more importantly, the real consequences of the Christian κοινωνία they are sharing in.

Looking at the conflict depicted in Gal 2:11–14 with Paul's eyes, I think one can say that what Cephas was asking for (without words),[34] is the reintroduction of purity requirements of the Jewish Passover type: only οἱ ἐκ περιτομῆς may eat with me/us Jewish Christians. Now, Paul is prepared to apply taxing demands—even (in a transferred sense) Passover purity requirements—on those who are to participate in Christian commensality, as we saw above on 1 Cor 5. But the difference between

---

[33] For two recent treatments of this text, see Engberg-Pedersen 1993, and Sandnes 1994, 154–161.

[34] See Holmberg 1990, 91.

him and Cephas is that the latter actually closes his commensality to other Christians, *simply on the ground that they are not Jews*. Those Gentile Christians who really wanted to belong—and who up to the new praxis of Cephas believed that they did—must have felt shut out, squarely placed outside the boundary of God's holy people, and more or less compelled to "judaize" all the way, or, in other words, compelled to become Jews in order to remain being Christians. Commensality is a language of identity, so Peter's acting amounts for Paul to substituting a Jewish identity in the Antiochian, mixed Jewish-Gentile church, for its *Christian* identity, which is clearly unacceptable. Paul's demand must have been that the Jewish Christians give up their Jewish identity markers and accept to reopen table fellowship with their Gentile fellow Christians. The truth of the gospel (2:14) demands open commensality within the whole Christian church.

## Bibliography

Barrett, C. K. 1973: *The First Epistle to the Corinthians* (BNTC), 2nd ed., London: A. and C. Black 1973.

Blaß, Friedrich – Debrunner, Albert 1970: *Grammatik des neutestamentlichen Griechisch*, 13th ed., Göttingen: Vandenhoeck & Ruprecht 1970.

Crossan, John Dominic 1991: *The Historical Jesus: The Life of a Mediterranean Jewish Peasant*, San Francisco: Harper 1991.

Douglas, Mary 1975: "Deciphering a meal", in: eadem, *Implicit Meanings*, London: Routledge & Kegan Paul 1975, 249–275.

Engberg-Pedersen, Troels 1993: "Proclaiming the Lord's Death: 1 Corinthians 11:17–34 and the Forms of Pauls' Theological Argument", in: David M. Hay (ed.), *Pauline Theology. Volume II: 1 & 2 Corinthians*, Minneapolis, MN: Fortress 1993, 103–132.

Fee, Gordon D. 1987: *The First Epistle to the Corinthians*, Grand Rapids, MI: Eerdmans 1987.

Feeley-Harnik, Gillian 1981: *The Lord's Table. Eucharist and Passover in Early Christianity*, Philadelphia, PA: University of Pennsylvania Press 1981.

Forkman, Göran 1972: *The Limits of the Religious Community: Expulsion from the Religious Community within the Qumran Sect, within Rabbinic Judaism, and within Primitive Christianity* (CB.NT 5), Lund: Gleerup 1972.

Gooch, Peter D. 1993: *Dangerous Food: 1 Corinthians 8–10 in Its Context*, Waterloo, Ont.: Wilfrid Laurier University Press 1993.

Goppelt, Leonhard 1972: Art. "τράπεζα", in: *TDNT* VIII, Grand Rapids, MI: Eerdmans 1972, 209–215.

Greeven, Heinrich 1971: Art. "συναναμείγνυμι", in: *TDNT* VII, Grand Rapids, MI: Eerdmans 1971, 852–855.

Holmberg, Bengt 1990: "Sociologiska perspektiv på Gal 2:11–14(21)", in: *SEÅ* 55 (1990) 71–92.

Jewett, Robert 1993: "Tenement Churches and Communal Meals in the Early Church: The Implications of a Form-Critical Analysis of 2 Thessalonians 3:10" (manuscript – August 1993 – for an article to be published in *Biblical Research*).

Newton, Michael 1985: *The Concept of Purity at Qumran and in the Letters of Paul*, Cambridge: Cambridge University Press 1985.

Neyrey, Jerome H. 1991: "Ceremonies in Luke-Acts: The Case of Meals and Table Fellowship", in: idem (ed.), *The Social World of Luke–Acts: Models for Interpretation*, Peabody, MA: Hendrickson 1991, 361–387.

Rengstorf, Karl Heinrich 1971a: Art. "σημειόω", in: *TDNT* VII, Grand Rapids, MI: Eerdmans 1971, 265–266.

— 1971b: Art. "στέλλω", in: *TDNT* VII, Grand Rapids, MI: Eerdmans 1971, 588–590.

Robertson Smith, William 1889: *Lectures on the religion of the Semites: First series, the fundamental institutions*, Edinburgh: A. and C. Black 1889.

Sanders, E. P. 1983: *Paul, the Law and the Jewish People*, Philadelphia, PA: Fortress 1983.

Sandnes, Karl Olav 1994: *A New Family: Conversion and Ecclesiology in the Early Church with Cross-Cultural Comparisons* (Studies in the Intercultural History of Christianity 91), Bern, Berlin etc.: Peter Lang 1994.

Segal, Alan F. 1990: *Paul the Convert: The Apostolate and Apostasy of Saul the Pharisee*, New Haven–London: Yale University Press 1990.

Tomson, Peter J. 1990: *Paul and the Jewish Law. Halakha in the Letters of the Apostle to the Gentiles*, Assen/Philadelphia: Van Gorcum/Fortress 1990.

Weiß, Johannes 1925: *Der erste Korintherbrief* (KEK 5), 10th ed., Göttingen: Vandenhoeck & Ruprecht 1925.

# Die Auferstehungsleugner in Korinth:
## Was meinten sie eigentlich?

Jarl Henning Ulrichsen

## 1. Das exegetische Problem

Nachdem Paulus die Korinther in 1 Kor 12–14 über die Geistesgaben belehrt hat, führt er in Kap. 15 ohne Überleitung ein neues Thema ein, das nicht durch ihre direkte Anfrage veranlaßt worden ist, sondern durch Gerüchte. Das Stück handelt von der Auferstehung der Toten. Dieses Thema kommt freilich erst in Vv. 12ff. deutlich zur Sprache. Auf den ersten Blick scheint die Einleitung (Vv. 1–11) auf etwas anderes hinzuzielen als auf die Auferstehung der Toten. Bei näherem Hinsehen erweist sie sich aber als angemessen. Im Blickfeld steht nämlich die entscheidende christliche Glaubensvorstellung, die Auferweckung Christi, die für Paulus die Grundlage der Hoffnung auf eine Auferstehung der Verstorbenen bildet. Rückblickend erkennt man, daß das Thema durch Vv. 1–11 vorbereitet wird. Den Ausgangspunkt der Ausführungen des Apostels bildet das gemeinchristliche Glaubensbekenntnis, das auch den Korinthern überliefert und von ihnen anerkannt ist: Christus starb für unsere Sünden, wurde begraben und auferweckt und erschien seinen Jüngern.

Der Anlaß dafür, daß Paulus dieses Thema behandelt, findet sich in der vielumstrittenen Aussage in V. 12: Εἰ δὲ Χριστὸς κηρύσσεται ὅτι ἐκ νεκρῶν ἐγήγερται, πῶς λέγουσιν ἐν ὑμῖν τινες ὅτι ἀνάστασις νεκρῶν οὐκ ἔστιν; In Korinth ist eine Debatte über die Auferstehung der Toten aufgekommen, und eine nicht näher definierte Gruppe, τινες genannt, bestreitet die Vorstellung einer Auferweckung der Toten.

Die hier bekämpfte Fraktion wird herkömmlich "die Auferstehungsleugner" genannt. Wer sie sind, wissen wir nicht. Das Textmaterial läßt in dieser Hinsicht keine Antwort zu. Dagegen glaubt man zu wissen, wie die Aussage ἀνάστασις νεκρῶν οὐκ ἔστιν zu verstehen ist. In der Literatur finden sich mindestens vier Deutungsalternativen[1]:

## A. *"Materialismus"*
Einige Exegeten sind der Ansicht, daß die Gegner des Paulus die Weiterexistenz des Individuums nach dem Tode verneinen[2]. Es handle sich, meint man, um eine Skepsis gegen ein Nachleben, die sowohl in jüdischem wie in griechischem Denken Parallelen aufweist.

## B. *"Realisierte Eschatologie"*
Andere Ausleger behaupten, die Auferstehungsleugner glaubten, die Auferstehung habe bereits (in der Taufe, mit dem Empfang des göttlichen Geistes) stattgefunden[3]. Des öfteren findet sich die Meinung, daß die Korinther die Auferstehungshoffnung spiritualisieren. Das Bestreiten der Auferstehung meint also die Leugnung einer künftigen, leiblichen Auferweckung der Toten.

## C. *"Ultra-konservative Eschatologie"*
Wieder andere Kommentatoren meinen, die Gegner seien der Überzeugung, daß das Heil nur gewinne, wer die Parusie noch erlebe[4]. Eine Auferweckung der Toten gebe es somit nicht. Im Gegensatz zur ersten Alternative setzt man hier eine Hoffnung voraus, die über die gegenwärtige Wirklichkeit hinausgeht – jedoch ausnahmslos für die Lebenden.

## D. *"Unsterblichkeit der Seele"*
Schließlich finden viele Exegeten in der Auferstehungsleugnung den Glauben an die Unsterblichkeit der Seele ausgesprochen[5]. Die von Paulus bekämpfte Gruppe lehre die griechische Vorstellung von der Weiterexistenz der Seele im Jenseits und lehne deshalb eine körperliche Auferstehung ab.

---

[1] Die Literatur zum Thema ist unüberschaubar. Die Bibliographie erhebt deshalb keinen Anspruch auf Vollständigkeit. Sie will lediglich eine (hoffentlich) repräsentative Auswahl bieten. Die nachfolgende Klassifizierung berücksichtigt nicht, daß die Exegeten oft verschieden argumentieren, auch wenn sie zu demselben Ergebnis kommen.

[2] Diese Position ist in der heutigen Forschung selten; vgl. z.B.: Doughty 1975, 74ff.

[3] Vgl. z.B.: Bartsch 1964, 265ff.; Becker 1976, 74ff.; Brandenburger 1962, 70f.; Klauck 1984, 112; Kümmel, in: Lietzmann 1969, 192 (zu S. 79 Z. 13); 194 (zu S. 83 Z. 39); Lang 1986, 218f.; Rissi 1962, 86; Wendland 1968, 144f.; Wilson 1968, 97ff.

[4] Vgl. z.B.: Orr/Walter 1976, 319; 340; Spörlein 1971, bes. 190ff.; Schweitzer 1930, 94; s. auch: Conzelmann 1969, 310f.

[5] Vgl. z.B.: Bruce 1971, 144 (mit Vorbehalt; oder möglicherweise Alternative B); Hoffmann 1966, 241; Lietzmann 1969, 79; Odeberg 1944, 280; 293; Sandelin 1976, 19f.; 130ff.; Schmithals 1965, 147ff.

Der vorliegende Aufsatz will eine kritische Beurteilung dieser Alternativen vornehmen. Um dieses Ziel zu erreichen, werde ich zunächst (in Abschnitt 2.) einige methodische Überlegungen anstellen. Dann folgt (in Abschnitt 3.) eine erste Übersicht über relevante Texte mit Bezug auf 1 Kor 15. An diese schließt sich ein skizzenhafter Überblick über jüdische und griechisch-hellenistische Jenseitsvorstellungen an, um den ideengeschichtlichen Hintergrund zu vergegenwärtigen. Im Hauptteil (Abschnitt 4.) werden die Alternativen der Reihe nach geprüft. Schließlich (in Abschnitt 5.) erfolgt eine Zusammenfassung der Ergebnisse.

## 2. Das methodische Problem

Aus 1 Kor 15 läßt sich ablesen, wie Paulus die Position seiner Gegner auffaßt. Die Aufgabe des Auslegers erschöpft sich aber nicht darin, das Verständnis des Paulus zu ermitteln. Die Frage lautet vielmehr: Wie ist die Aussage ἀνάστασις νεκρῶν οὐκ ἔστιν *im Sinne der Gegner* zu verstehen? Der Grund dafür, daß diese Problemstellungen auseinandergehalten werden müssen, ist quellenkritischer Art: Paulus ist kein Primärzeuge. Er hat nur eine mittelbare Kenntnis der Position seiner Gegner, kennt sie also nur indirekt. Ein sekundäres Zeugnis ist immer mit Problemen behaftet. Wir wissen z.B. nicht, woher seine Auskünfte stammen, obwohl sich die Leute der Chloë (1,11) als denkbare Informanten anbieten. Wir haben ferner keine Garantie dafür, daß seine Gewährsmänner ein zuverlässiges Bild gezeichnet haben oder daß Paulus sie korrekt wiedergibt. Es liegen somit mehrere Unsicherheitsfaktoren vor.

Der Exeget ist trotzdem auf den Text des 1 Kor verwiesen. Da die Aussage in 15,12 nur eine negative Bestimmung der Position der Gegner enthält, die sich offensichtlich verschieden auslegen läßt, bedarf es solcher Argumente, die eine positive Bestimmung erlauben. Ich setze (mit der Mehrzahl der Ausleger) voraus, daß die paulinische Argumentation andere Aussagen und Vorstellungen enthält, die sich auf die Gegner zurückführen lassen und uns einen Einblick in die Denkweise der Gegner vermitteln. Es spielt in diesem Zusammenhang keine Rolle, ob Paulus die Argumente seiner Gegner richtig oder falsch interpretiert. Wesentlich ist nur, ob seine Darstellung zu einer positiven Bestimmung beitragen kann. Wer diesen Ausgangspunkt nicht teilt, beraubt sich im voraus jeder Möglichkeit einer religionsgeschichtlichen Einordnung der Gegner. Glücklicherweise handelt es sich im vorliegenden Fall nicht um ein exegetisches Wagnis. Im Gegenteil: Die meisten Exegeten scheinen in diesen Bahnen zu denken. Der Wert einer These darf übrigens nur auf Grund des konkreten Resultats eingeschätzt werden. Ob sich die vorliegende Voraussetzung bewährt, bleibt abzuwarten.

Wilson[6] warnt mit Recht vor einer Parallelomanie, die dem Material außerhalb des 1 Kor zu viel Gewicht beimißt. 15,12 ist primär auf Grund von Kap. 15 und der sich aus 1 Kor ergebenden Gesamtlage der Korinthergemeinde zu beurteilen. Andere Texte dürfen herangezogen werden, sind aber nicht gleichwertig mit dem Zeugnis des 1 Kor. Die Auslegungsgeschichte zeigt leider, daß man nicht immer scharf genug zwischen primärem und sekundärem Stoff unterscheidet. Obwohl die paulinische Darstellung der Position seiner Gegner im quellenkritischen Sinn kein Primärzeugnis bietet, gebührt 1 Kor die Priorität vor anderen Quellenstücken. Der Text darf nicht durch anderen Stoff ersetzt werden. Anderes Material kann die Richtigkeit einer Exegese unterbauen oder in Frage stellen, niemals aber als Basis und Richtschnur der Auslegung dienen. Die Zahl der relevanten Angaben, die sich zunächst dem Kap. 15 und schließlich dem Brief als ganzem entnehmen lassen (s. 3.1.), ist gering, aber andere Quellen, die auf die Korinthergemeinde Bezug nehmen und zugleich 1 Kor zeitlich vorangehen, liegen bekanntlich nicht vor.

Lenken wir zunächst den Blick auf die wenigen Spuren, die uns nach der Ansicht vieler Ausleger ein weiteres Zeugnis der Position der Gegner bieten. Es handelt sich hier in erster Linie um eine Zusammenstellung der relevanten Indizien. Dabei wird die Auslegung auf ein notwendiges Minimum beschränkt, um voreilige Schlüsse zu vermeiden. Die exegetischen Implikationen für die Lösungsvorschläge werden bewußt aufgeschoben.

## 3. Das Material

### 3.1. Der erste Brief an die Korinther

Nach fast einhelliger Ansicht der Forscher ist die Aussage ἀνάστασις νεκρῶν οὐκ ἔστιν als Zitat anzusehen. Diese Annahme mutet auf den ersten Blick recht plausibel an, weil die Aussage einen prägnanten, formelhaften Charakter aufweist. Bei näherem Hinsehen kommen freilich Bedenken auf, weil Paulus in der Fortsetzung ähnliche, jedoch unwesentlich modifizierte Formulierungen benutzt; vgl. Vv. 13.15. 16.29.32. Es ist deshalb vorstellbar, daß die Aussage in V. 12 auf Paulus zurückgeht und als eine Zusammenfassung der ihn erreichten Gerüchte anzusehen ist. Wie dem auch sei: Die Formulierung reflektiert offenbar die Position der Gegner. Sie behaupten, daß es keine Auferstehung gebe. Für die vorliegende Untersuchung bleibt dabei ohne Belang, daß die Aussage – isoliert betrachtet – mehrdeutig ist und verschieden interpretiert wird. Es kommt vor allem darauf an, daß Paulus uns tatsächlich Zugang zur Auffassung seiner Gegner gewährt. Aus der Fortsetzung ergibt sich, daß

---

[6] Wilson 1968, 98.

Paulus die Formulierung ἀνάστασις νεκρῶν οὐκ ἔστιν als ein Synonym für νεκροὶ οὐκ ἐγείρονται gebraucht. Aus 15,22 läßt sich außerdem ablesen, daß Paulus sich diese Auferweckung als eine Wiederbelebung (ζωοποιηθῆναι) vorstellt.

Das Vorkommen einer Aussage, die sich – eventuell mit dem erwähnten Vorbehalt – auf die Auferstehungsleugner zurückführen läßt, ist bedeutend, weil sie die Annahme nahelegt, daß der Text vielleicht noch andere Verweise auf ihre Position enthält. Diese Vermutung ist um so natürlicher, weil schon die ersten elf Verse im Hinblick auf die Auferstehungsleugner formuliert sind.

Ein Stück, das in diese Richtung weist, findet sich in V. 29: Ἐπεὶ τί ποιήσουσιν οἱ βαπτιζόμενοι ὑπὲρ τῶν νεκρῶν; εἰ ὅλως νεκροὶ οὐκ ἐγείρονται, τί καὶ βαπτίζονται ὑπὲρ αὐτῶν;[7] Dieser rätselhafte und vieldebattierte Text[8] scheint eine Vikariatstaufe vorauszusetzen[9]. Dabei bleibt freilich der Sinn dieses Ritus im Dunkeln. Wesentlich ist, daß diejenigen, die sich für die Toten taufen lassen, mit der Gruppe der Auferstehungsleugner identisch sein müssen[10]. Sonst wäre der Hinweis ohne argumentative Kraft; denn Paulus hätte kaum die Auferstehungsleugner für die Praxis anderer Christen verantwortlich machen können.

In V. 35 führt Paulus offenbar noch einen gegnerischen Einwand ein: Ἀλλὰ ἐρεῖ τις, Πῶς ἐγείρονται οἱ νεκροί; ποίῳ δὲ σώματι ἔρχονται; Daß es sich hier um einen Verweis auf die Position der Gegner handelt[11], wird von einigen Auslegern bestritten[12]. Dagegen läßt sich aber anführen, daß Paulus es nicht nötig hat, auf diese

---

[7] Die großen Kommentare informieren über andere Interpunktionsvorschläge, die den Text kaum begreiflicher machen.

[8] Vgl. zur Geschichte der Auslegung: Rissi 1962, bes. 6ff.

[9] Vgl. z.B.: Bartsch 1964, 268; Bruce 1971, 148f. (oder = Raeder; s. unten); Bultmann 1968, 172; Conzelmann 1969, 328f.; Fee 1987, 763ff.; Hoffmann 1966, 240f.; Klauck 1984, 115f.; Lang 1986, 229; Lietzmann 1969, 82; Odeberg 1944, 290f.; Orr/Walter 1976, 335; 337; Rissi 1962, bes. 57ff.; Schmithals 1965, 146; 148; 244ff.; Wendland 1968, 150; Wolff 1982, 185ff. Nach Raeder 1955, 258ff. handelt es sich um Ungläubige, die sich um ihrer im Glauben entschlafenen, christlichen Angehörigen oder Freunde willen taufen ließen – im Sinne des Übertrittes zum Christentum –, um bei der Auferstehung mit ihnen vereinigt zu werden; vgl.: Jeremias 1966, 303f.

[10] So die meisten Exegeten. Anders z.B.: Doughty 1975, 76 Anm. 63; Spörlein, 1971, 82ff. Er argumentiert u.a. damit, daß die Auferstehungsleugner an keiner Stelle in Kap. 15 direkt angesprochen sind. Daß Paulus sich an die ganze Gemeinde richtet, ist korrekt. Die Mehrzahl der Gemeindeglieder hielt aber an dem Auferstehungsglauben fest, bedürfte also keiner Belehrung, sondern allenfalls des Beistands gegen die drohende Häresie. Die Ansicht Spörleins überrascht, weil er in 15,35–38 dazu neigt, eine Bezugnahme auf die Argumentation der Gegner zu sehen; vgl. a.a.O. 96ff. Klauck 1984, 115 will die Praxis dieser Sitte nicht auf die Auferstehungsleugner beschränken; vgl.: Orr/Walther 1976, 337. Becker 1976, 70 überlegt, ob es sich nur um ein den Korinthern bekanntes Beispiel handle.

[11] So z.B.: Bartsch 1964, 268; Brandenburger 1962, 73 mit Anm. 2; Fee 1987, 779; Héring 1949, 145; Hoffmann 1966, 240; Klauck 1984, 117; Lang 1986, 232; Lietzmann 1969, 83; Orr/Walter 1976, 342; Spörlein 1971, 27; Wendland 1968, 152; Wolff 1982, 195.

Frage einzugehen, wenn sie kein Problem darstellt. Der Diatribstil mit dem Singular τις deutet nicht darauf hin, daß keine konkrete Bezugnahme vorliegt. Eine scheinbar neutrale Formulierung findet sich ebenfalls in V. 29.

Es handelt sich nicht um zwei verschiedene Fragen[13]. Die zweite Frage präzisiert vielmehr die erste. Die Auferstehungsleugner fragen nach dem Leib der Auferweckten und veranlassen Paulus dadurch, eine umfangreiche Argumentation zu entfalten.

Damit ist das relevante Material in 1 Kor 15 erschöpft. Daß die Auslegung sich anderer Stellen des 1 Kor bedienen kann, sofern diese die Fragestellung berühren, muß nicht eingehend begründet werden[14]. Man darf nämlich vermuten, daß ein Zusammenhang zwischen der Leugnung der Auferstehung und vielen der Probleme besteht, die Paulus behandelt. Man kann sehr wahrscheinlich voraussetzen, daß die Gegner Enthusiasten sind, die dem Besitz des Geistes entscheidende Bedeutung beimessen. Das Bild, das der Brief vermittelt, ist also entweder typisch für die Gemeinde als ganze oder repräsentativ für die Auferstehungsleugner im besonderen. In mehreren Punkten liegt die letztere Annahme näher.

## 3.2. Andere neutestamentliche Texte

Von den übrigen paulinischen Texten scheint mir der zweite Brief an die Korinther einen natürlichen Vorzug zu haben, weil er an dieselbe Gemeinde gerichtet ist. In 2 Kor 5,1ff. findet sich ein interessanter Text, der m.E. einen Beitrag zur Aufklärung leistet. Paulus geht hier noch einmal auf das Problem ein, freilich in einem anderen Kontext und ohne seine alten Gegner ausdrücklich zu erwähnen. Trotzdem läßt der Text einen polemischen Unterton vermuten, gerade weil er Begriffe und Vorstellungen enthält, die unmittelbar auffallen. Es ist nicht zu leugnen, daß sich die Situation in Korinth bei der Abfassung des 2 Kor verändert hat und daß Paulus z.T. an anderen Fronten kämpft. Nichtsdestoweniger lassen einige Bemerkungen ahnen, daß er in der Zeit zwischen dem ersten und zweiten Brief weitere Informationen über seine Gegenspieler empfangen hat und daß ihm ihre Position begreiflicher geworden ist; vgl. dazu 4.4.

Andere paulinische und urchristliche Texte sind ebenfalls zu beachten, sofern sie Licht auf das Problem werfen. Gegenstand der Diskussion sind immer wieder zwei Stellen: 2 Tim 2,17f. und 1 Thess 4,13ff. Sie werden in 4.2. bzw. 4.3. behandelt.

---

[12] Vgl. z.B.: Schmithals 1965, 147.

[13] So: Jeremias 1966, 304.

[14] Ich setze mit der großen Mehrzahl der Forscher die Einheitlichkeit des 1 Kor voraus.

## 3.3. Jüdische und griechische Jenseitsvorstellungen

Da die Exegeten regelmäßig auf jüdische und griechisch-hellenistische Jenseitsvorstellung verweisen, ist es an dieser Stelle angebracht, an das relevante Material zu erinnern. Im Rahmen dieser Arbeit muß es notwendigerweise sehr skizzenhaft dargestellt werden.

In der altisraelitischen Religion herrscht die Vorstellung von einem schattenhaften Dasein nach dem Tod im Scheol (1 Sam 28,8ff.; Jes 8,19)[15]. In der nachexilischen Periode setzt sich die Hoffnung auf eine persönliche Weiterexistenz durch, die sich aber verschieden gestalten kann. Im Alten Testament finden sich zwei Stücke, die von einer Auferstehung, einer Rückkehr ins Leben, sprechen (Dan 12,2.13; Jes 26,19). In den Apokryphen und Pseudepigraphen liegen mehrere Vorstellungen vor[16]. Einige Texte rechnen mit einer Auferstehung (2 Makk 7,9; äthHen 51,1; 61,5; u.m.); andere setzen die Unsterblichkeit der Seele voraus (Weish 1–5; TestAbr passim; u.m.); wieder andere scheinen diese Vorstellungen zu kombinieren (äthHen 22; 4 Esr 7; u.m.). Zur Zeit Jesu ist der Auferstehungsglaube vorherrschend und einer der vielen Punkte, auf die sich das Urchristentum (Mk 12,18ff.) und der Pharisäismus (Act 23,6ff.; BerR 14,5; WaR 14,9; usw.[17]) einigen. Es gibt aber auch Kreise, die ein Nachleben verneinen. Kritische Stimmen finden sich bereits im Alten Testament (Hi 7,9f.; 14,1ff.; Koh 3,18ff.; 9,3ff.; Ps 6,6) und hinterlassen auch in den intertestamentarischen Schriften Spuren (äthHen 102,6ff.; Weish 2,1ff.[18]). Die bekanntesten Auferstehungsleugner um die Zeitenwende – und zugleich Leugner jedes Nachlebens – sind die Sadduzäer (Mk 12,18ff.; Act 4,2; 23,8; b.San 90b)[19].

Im griechischen Bereich begegnen ebenfalls verschiedene Auffassungen[20]. Das älteste Zeugnis, die sogenannte große und kleine Nekyia (Odyssee 11 und 24,1–204), erinnert an die altisraelitische Vorstellung. In den orphischen Kreisen, im Pythagoreismus und in den eleusinischen Mysterien ist der Unsterblichkeitsglaube ein zentraler Gedanke. Unter den Philosophen liefert vor allem Platon Argumente für die Unsterblichkeit der Seele (Phaidon; usw.). Die Vorstellung der Unsterblichkeit ist im orphischen, pythagoreischen und platonischen Denken mit der Lehre von der Seelenwanderung verbunden.

Diese Unsterblichkeitslehre ist nicht allgemein anerkannt; denn ein Materialis-

---

[15] Vgl. z.B.: Eichrodt 1961, 145ff.

[16] Gute Übersichten bieten: Cavallin 1974; Nickelsburg 1972; s. auch: Hoffmann 1966, 81ff.

[17] Vgl. zu den beiden letztgenannten Belegen Anm. 34.

[18] Es handelt sich in beiden Texten um Aussagen, die in den Mund der Sünder gelegt werden.

[19] Aus Josephus Bell., II,164ff.; Ant., XVIII,16 ergibt sich, daß die Sadduzäer nicht nur die leibliche Auferstehung verneinten, sondern jede Weiterexistenz nach dem Tode.

[20] Vgl. bes.: Nilsson 1955, 174ff.; 653ff.; 1950, 220ff.; 333ff.; 657ff.; Rohde 1910, I,1ff.; 68ff.; 278ff.; 301ff.; II,103ff.; 263ff.; 296ff. Eine kürzere Zusammenfassung bietet Hoffmann 1966, 26ff.

mus wird bereits unter den alten Naturphilosophen verfochten oder vorausgesetzt; vgl. z.B. Demokrit und Anaxagoras. Die Epikureer leugnen jede Form der Existenz nach dem Tod[21]. Eine ähnliche Auffassung geht aus mehreren Grabinschriften hervor[22]. Die stoische Philosophie ist weniger konsequent, rechnet aber mit einem Aufhören der individuellen Seelen zu irgendeiner Zeit nach dem Tod. Im griechischen Raum ist die Auferstehung der Toten keine Alternative.

Es erübrigt sich zu sagen, daß der Begriff 'Auferstehung' nicht eindeutig ist. Der von Paulus in 15,35 erwähnte Einwand ist höchst aktuell[23]. Aufersteht der tote Körper, bekommt die Seele des Gestorbenen einen neuen Leib, oder aufersteht vielmehr die Seele? Handelt es sich um eine Rückkehr in die alte Welt oder wird die Welt verwandelt? Ist die Auferstehung ein eschatologisches Ereignis oder auferstehen die Toten unmittelbar nach dem Tode zu einem neuen, himmlischen Leben? Diese und verwandte Fragen begegnet demjenigen, der eine vollständige Übersicht über den Hintergrund des paulinischen Auferstehungskapitels geben will. Es versteht sich von selbst, daß eine Behandlung dieser Probleme den Rahmen der vorliegenden Arbeit sprengen würde.

Wir wenden uns jetzt einer kritischen Beurteilung der verschiedenen Auslegungstypen zu. Dieser Durchgang ist synthetischer Art: Ich nehme eine Zusammenstellung verschiedener Argumente aus der Literatur vor, ohne auf das Vorliegen der Argumente bei jedem einzelnen Ausleger einzugehen.

### 4. Kritische Beurteilung der Lösungsvorschläge

### 4.1. A. "Materialismus"

Für diese Alternative spricht zunächst die oben erwähnte materialistische Auffassung der Sadduzäer bzw. der Epikureer. Dabei ist die griechische Parallele sicher wesentlicher als die jüdische, weil man in einem griechischen Kontext primär nach einheimischen Entsprechungen zu suchen hat. In dieselbe Richtung weist darüber hinaus die paulinische Argumentation; denn Paulus setzt voraus, daß seine Gegner die Weiterexistenz nach dem Tode verneinen.

---

[21] Vgl. z.B.: Nilsson, 1950, 239ff.; Rohde 1910, II,331ff. Beispiele und Literatur auch bei: Cavallin 1977, 51 mit Anm. 52–59.

[22] Cavallin 1977, 51f. liefert einige Beispiele und verweist a.a.O. 52 Anm. 65 auf relevante Sekundärliteratur.

[23] Das Problem ist im Judentum ebenfalls bekannt; vgl. syrBar 50,1ff.

Die Position der Gegner hält Paulus insofern für unlogisch, als sie offensichtlich die Auferstehung Christi anerkennen[24]. Die Auferstehung Christi ist aber nach Paulus kein isoliertes Phänomen, sondern ein Heilsgeschehen, das die zukünftige Auferstehung (der Christen) mit einschließt (15,20ff.)[25]. Hält man also an der Auferstehung Christi fest, ergibt sich die Auferstehung aller (Christen) von selbst. Paulus setzt in seiner Argumentation in 15,13ff. deutlich voraus, daß seine Gegner jede Art von Nachleben verwerfen. Die Aussage in V. 19 ist typisch: εἰ *ἐν τῇ ζωῇ ταύτῃ ἐν Χριστῷ ἠλπικότες ἐσμὲν μόνον, ἐλεεινότεροι πάντων ἀνθρώπων ἐσμέν*. Mit dem Argument in V. 29 will Paulus zeigen, daß die Taufpraxis der Auferstehungsleugner sinnlos ist. Warum lassen sie sich für Tote taufen, wenn sie die Auferstehung verneinen? Die Taufe zu Gunsten der Toten ist zwecklos, εἰ ὅλως νεκροὶ οὐκ ἐγείρονται, d.h. falls sie nicht mehr zum Leben zurückkehren. Man beachte, daß Paulus die Sitte der Vikariatstaufe weder tadelt noch billigt. Der Grund dafür ist einfach: Er will bewirken, daß die Auferstehungsleugner sich auf ihre eigene Handlungsweise besinnen und – so Paulus – auf ihren Mangel an Logik aufmerksam werden[26]. Die Argumente in Vv. 30–32a setzen ebenfalls voraus, daß die Gegner jede Art von Nachleben leugnen. Nach der Ansicht, die er seinen Gegenspielern zuschreibt, ist es sinnlos, sich täglich Gefahren auszusetzen; denn wenn mit dem Tode alles aus ist, kommt eine jenseitige Belohnung oder Strafe nicht in Frage. In V. 32b (εἰ νεκροὶ οὐκ ἐγείρονται, Φάγωμεν καὶ πίωμεν, αὔριον γὰρ ἀποθνήσκομεν) zieht er dann den Schluß, der nach seiner Meinung aus diesem Materialismus resultiert.

Gegen diesen Lösungsvorschlag wenden sich Bedenken. Ein konsequenter Materialismus wäre theoretisch denkbar, weil es sachliche Parallelen gibt. Man kann sich vorstellen, daß die Auferstehungsleugner die Wirkung der christlichen Riten als ausschließlich diesseitig denken könnten. Überzeugen kann diese Annahme jedoch nicht. Man vermißt eine Erklärung dafür, warum sich derartige Materialisten der christlichen Gemeinde hätten anschließen wollen. Vor allem läßt sich dieser Lösungsversuch kaum mit dem offenkundigen Enthusiasmus der Korinther vereinbaren; vgl. 4.2. Dieser scheint für die gesamte Gemeinde charakteristisch zu sein; die

---

[24] So die große Mehrzahl der Kommentatoren; vgl. aber: Lang 1986, 208; 219 ("… sie verstanden die traditionelle Wendung von der Auferstehung im Sinn einer Auferstehung Jesu Christi im Geist."); Sandelin 1976, 15ff.; Wolff 1982, 152; 195.

[25] Deshalb erwägt er nicht die Möglichkeit, die Auferstehung Christi als Ausnahme aufzufassen. Man vergleiche seine Argumentation in Vv. 13ff.

[26] Das Futurum des Ausdruckes τὶ ποιήσουσιν ist somit ganz logisch: Was werden die Auferstehungsleugner künftig tun, wenn sie sich auf ihren Mangel an Logik besinnen? Werden sie an ihrem Ritus festhalten – oder ihn aufgeben? Vgl.: Rissi 1962, 57; 91f.; Wolff 1982, 189. Fee 1987, 763 Anm. 10 paraphrasiert: "When they realize what they are doing and that there is no real future for the dead, how will it affect them?"

Auferstehungsleugner bilden keine Ausnahme. Man darf im Gegenteil vermuten, daß die Auferstehungsleugnung in ihrem Enthusiasmus begründet ist.

Der Gedanke an die Auferstehung ist für das Urchristentum und Paulus etwas Selbstverständliches. Deshalb legt sich die Annahme nahe, daß Paulus die Auferstehung in Korinth gepredigt hat. Dagegen erhebt sich jedoch der Einwand, daß Paulus in 1 Kor 15 nicht auf eine frühere Belehrung verweist. Gegen diese Annahme führen mehrere Ausleger auch den ersten Brief an die Thessalonicher an. Dort taucht bekanntlich die Frage nach dem Schicksal der Verstorbenen auf, und Paulus müsse, meint man, die Thessalonicher über die Auferstehung belehren; vgl. 1 Thess 4,13ff. Viele Exegeten folgern daraus, daß die Thessalonicher mit dieser Lehre nicht vertraut seien. Auf Grund der Parusieerwartung (1,10; 3,13; 5,23) habe Paulus das Thema der Auferstehung der Toten nicht behandelt. Dasselbe sei auch in Korinth der Fall.

Daß Paulus kein Wort von der Auferstehung geredet haben soll, mutet zunächst überraschend an, zumal dieser Glaube ein fester Bestandteil seines jüdischen Erbes ist. Für unser Verständnis des 1 Kor ist die erwähnte Auslegung des 1 Thess allerdings irrelevant. Sie scheitert an V. 12. Die Leugnung der Auferstehung zeigt nämlich, daß die Problemstellung bekannt ist. In der Tat handelt es sich ja nur um eine Gruppe der Korinther, die die Auferstehung leugnet.

Darum drängt sich die Folgerung auf, daß die Auferstehungsleugner nicht schroffe Materialisten sind. Daß sie wirklich an eine Form der Weiterexistenz nach dem Tode glauben, ergibt sich aus der paulinischen Argumentation; denn die Taufe für die Toten ist nicht Beweis einer unlogischen Praxis, sondern Zeugnis einer Jenseitshoffnung. Wie sich diese Jenseitsvorstellung gestaltet, bleibt noch zu fragen.

Aus diesen Erwägungen folgt, daß Paulus seine Gegner mißversteht[27].

---

[27] So z.B.: Bultmann 1967, 299; 1968, 172; Schmithals, 1965, 147; s. auch: Conzelmann 1969, 310; Wedderburn 1981, 240f. Die These eines Mißverständnisses bestreiten z.B.: Brandenburger 1962, 73 Anm. 2; Kümmel, in: Lietzmann 1969, 192f.; Lang 1976, 218; Wilson 1968, 92f.; Wolff 1982, 147f.; 175. Wolff meint, daß Paulus in V. 29 den Glauben an eine postmortale Existenz bei den Korinthern voraussetze. Vgl. dazu meinen Text. Hoffmann 1966, 245ff. meint, daß das Mißverständnis eher darin liege, daß Paulus sich keinen leiblosen Vollendungszustand vorstellen könne. Paulus ignoriere die gesamte in der griechischen Seelenvorstellung begründete Jenseitshoffnung. Hoffmann betont, daß die Voraussetzung in V. 32 nicht "wenn mit dem Tode alles aus ist", sondern "wenn die Toten nicht auferweckt" laute. Dabei unterschätzt er einerseits den griechischen Skeptizismus und übersieht andererseits, daß Paulus 'auferstehen' und 'lebendig gemacht werden' gleichsetzt. Man beachte übrigens, daß z.B. in Vv. 30ff. kein Wort von einer eventuellen Bestrafung im Jenseits verlautet. Das läßt sich am einfachsten mit der Voraussetzung einer totalen Annihilation beim Sterben vereinbaren, die Paulus m.E. den Auferstehungsleugnern zuschreibt.

## 4.2. B. "Realisierte Eschatologie"

Für diese Position verweist man im allgemeinen auf eine verwandte Aussage in 2 Tim 2,17f.: (καὶ ὁ λόγος αὐτῶν ὡς γάγγραινα νομὴν ἕξει.) ὧν ἐστιν Ὑμέναιος καὶ Φίλητος, οἵτινες περὶ τὴν ἀλήθειαν ἠστόχησαν, λέγοντες [τὴν] ἀνάστασιν ἤδη γεγονέναι … . Wegen der Knappheit der Aussage bleibt unklar, was Hymenäus und Philetus wirklich behaupten. Viele Exegeten vermuten, daß Hymenäus und Philetus eine besondere Auffassung der Taufe verfechten: In der Taufe auferstehe man mit Christus zur Unsterblichkeit. Man will dann eine entsprechende Auffassung in 1 Kor 15,12 wiederfinden. In dieselbe Richtung weise auch, meint man, die realisierte Eschatologie, die in 4,8 belegt sei. Diese Annahme ist problematisch.

Wegen seiner Unklarheit ist das Stück 2 Tim 2,17f. kaum zur Beleuchtung des Problems geeignet. In den geläufigen, deutschsprachigen Kommentaren zu 2 Tim wird des öfteren vorausgesetzt, daß Hymenäus und Philetus Gnostiker sind[28]. Mehrmals verweist man zur Beleuchtung des Textes auf Vorstellungen, die erst erheblich später belegt sind, z.B. in den Schriften des Justinus, Tertullianus und Irenäus[29]. 'Auferstanden' sei also derjenige, der durch die Gnosis erlöst sei. Unmittelbar wirkt die Aussage viel konkreter. Will man also überhaupt zu späten Parallelen greifen – vgl. dazu Abschnitt 2.! –, bietet sich m.E. die Lehre des Menander an. Nach Irenäus behauptet Menander, "daß seine Schüler die Auferstehung durch die Taufe auf ihn empfangen und fürder nicht sterben können, sondern fortdauern, nicht alternd und unsterblich"[30]. Eine derart konkrete Auffassung[31] ist aber in Korinth nicht denkbar; denn die Gemeinde hat schon zur Zeit des 1 Kor mehrere Todesfälle erfahren; vgl. 11,30. Die merkwürdige Tradition in Mt 27,52f., wonach die Leiber vieler der entschlafenen Heiligen auferweckt worden und nach der Auferstehung Jesu in Jerusalem erschienen sind, ist als Erklärungsmodell ebenfalls ungeeignet. Zum einen handelt es sich um einen Text, der im Urchristentum sonst keine Spuren hinterlassen hat, zum anderen läßt die Anwendung des perfektischen Aspekts in 2 Tim 2,18 gerade an ein Geschehnis denken, das fortdauernde und aktuelle Bedeutung hat.

Entscheidend ist aber, daß die Aussage in 2 Tim 2,17f. sich nicht mit dem Wort-

---

[28] Vgl. z.B.: Brox 1969, 36f.; 248f.; Dibelius/Conzelmann 1966, 52ff.; 83; Holtz 1965, 172f.; Jeremias 1981, 56f.; Merkel 1991, 67f.

[29] Vgl. z.B.: Brox 1969, 36f.; Dibelius/Conzelmann 1966, 81f.; Jeremias 1981, 57; Merkel 1991, 68.

[30] Adv Haer, I,23,5: … *resurrectionem enim per id, quod est in eum baptisma, accipere eius discipulos, et ultra non posse mori, sed perseverare non senescentes et immortales.* (Deutsche Übersetzung nach Brox 1969, 37.) Vgl. schon Justin Apol, I,26,4.

[31] Schmithals 1965, 150 meint freilich, daß Menander an die Unsterblichkeit des Pneuma-Selbst gedacht habe.

laut in 1 Kor 15,12 deckt. Während nämlich die Auferstehungsleugner behaupten, daß es keine Auferstehung gebe, sagen Hymenäus und Philetus, daß sie schon stattgefunden habe. Dieser signifikante Unterschied darf nicht übersehen werden.

2 Tim 2,17f. scheidet somit als Parallele aus. Die zugrundeliegende Hypothese, daß einige der Korinther eine Auferstehung in spiritualisierendem Sinn in der Taufe lehren, ist also unabhängig von 2 Tim zu behandeln. Man könnte in diesem Fall von einem Mißverstehen der paulinischen Tauflehre ausgehen. Paulus selbst stellt die Taufe bekanntlich als eine Analogie zum Tod Christi dar. Er verlegt aber die Auferstehung in die Zukunft (Röm 6,5; 1 Kor 15,22ff.; 1 Thess 4,16). Ein Mißverständnis auf Seiten der Gegner, das in ihrem Enthusiasmus begründet sein könnte, wäre freilich möglich; denn Kol 2,12 zeigt, daß man bald die Taufe als einen Tod- *und* Auferstehungsritus aufgefaßt hat. Als Schlüssel zur Auffassung der Auferstehungsleugner bietet sich gerade der Verweis auf ihren Enthusiasmus an. Dabei spielen Aussagen wie 4,8 (ἤδη κεκορεσμένοι ἐστέ, ἤδη ἐπλουτήσατε, χωρὶς ἡμῶν ἐβασιλεύσατε· … .), die vermutete magische Sakramentsauffassung der Korinther (vgl. Kap. 10–11) sowie ihre Betonung des Geistesbesitzes (Kap. 12–14) zentrale Rollen. Diese Überlegungen sind aber irrelevant. Die Leugner der Auferstehung behaupten ja nicht, daß die Auferstehung in der Taufe stattfinde, sondern, daß es *keine* Auferstehung gebe. Es bleibt deshalb unverständlich, daß einige Forscher einerseits den Korinthern eine realisierte Auferstehungslehre zuschreiben, andererseits aber ein Mißverständnis auf der Seite des Paulus verneinen. Die ganze paulinische Argumentation zeigt, daß Paulus die Leugnung der Auferstehung als die Verneinung einer künftigen, leiblichen Auferstehung versteht. Sein Mißverständnis ist also womöglich noch größer, falls die Korinther eine Auferstehung in der Taufe lehren.

## 4.3. C. "Ultra-konservative Eschatologie"

Die dritte Position verweist für gewöhnlich auf den schon erwähnten Text in 1 Thess 4,13ff. Die ersten Todesfälle der Christen in Thessalonich erzeugen teils Verwirrung, teils Verzweiflung. Einer brennenden Naherwartungsvorstellung zufolge glaubt man die Parusie des Herrn zu erleben, und die Frage nach der Rolle der Verstorbenen beim Kommen Jesu drängt sich deshalb auf. Aus der Antwort des Paulus versucht man die zugrundeliegende Problemstellung der Thessalonicher zu konkretisieren. Viele Exegeten vermuten, Paulus müsse die Annahme widerlegen, daß das Heil nur denjenigen gelte, die bei der Wiederkehr Christi noch am Leben seien.

Eine parallele Situation nimmt man auch für Korinth an. Paulus kämpfe hier gegen Leute, die nur an eine Verwandlung der Lebenden bei der Parusie glauben, nicht aber an eine Auferweckung der Toten.

Nun ist dieses Verständnis des 1 Thess 4,13ff. nicht unumstritten. Man unterscheidet mehrere Auslegungsvarianten[32]. Die erwähnte Auslegung ließe sich mit dem Hinweis auf eine fehlende Auferstehungsverkündigung vorzüglich begründen. Diese Möglichkeit hat sich aber als höchst zweifelhaft erwiesen und wäre jedenfalls, wie wir gesehen haben, für Korinth nicht zutreffend; vgl. 4.1. Gegen die These einer 'ultra-konservativen Eschatologie' erhebt sich der Einwand, daß 1 Kor 15 eine Naherwartung mit keinem Wort erwähnt[33] und keine Spur davon aufweist, daß diese Erwartung der Grund der Probleme sei. Dazu kommt, daß die Lehre einer Verwandlung der Lebenden nicht von den Gegnern des Paulus herrührt, sondern vielmehr ein wesentlicher Teil der paulinischen Argumentation ist. Sie wird in 15,51 als ein Geheimnis dargestellt, also als eine Vorstellung, die den Korinthern unbekannt ist. Wie die Gegner in Korinth über die Übriggebliebenen denken, wissen wir nicht. Dagegen läßt sich mit Sicherheit behaupten, daß sie das Heil nicht auf die Lebenden begrenzen. Die mehrmals zitierte Aussage in V. 29 zeigt, daß sie die Verstorbenen ebenfalls vor Augen haben.

## 4.4. D. "Unsterblichkeit der Seele"

Wir kommen jetzt auf die vierte Alternative zu sprechen, die m.E. die richtige ist. Sie läßt sich unschwer mit den Argumenten und Vorstellungen der Gegner in Kap. 15 vereinbaren und bietet sich von vornherein an, weil sie dem griechischen Geist entspricht. Wir haben mehrmals (15,29!) gesehen, daß die Auferstehungsleugner nicht das Nachleben an sich verwerfen, obwohl Paulus sie in dieser Weise versteht.

---

[32] Vgl.: Lüdemann 1980, 220ff. Neben der in 4.1. erwähnten Interpretation behandelt er drei andere Haupttypen: 1. eine gnostisch begründete Bestreitung der Auferstehung. Die jüdische Lehre von der Auferstehung der Toten sei der Gemeinde zweifelhaft geworden. 2. Eine Exegese, die von der Aussage οἱ ζῶντες οἱ περιλειπόμενοι εἰς τὴν παρουσίαν τοῦ κυρίου οὐ μὴ φθάσωμεν τοὺς κοιμηθέντας in 4,15b ausgeht. Es handle sich um die Befürchtung, daß die Toten gegenüber den Lebenden einen Nachteil hätten. Man gründe sich in Thessalonich auf die eschatologische Vorstellung, daß die Auferstehung erst nach der Parusie erfolgen solle. 3. eine Erklärung, die von irgendeinem Unvermögen der Thessalonicher bei der Bewältigung des Todes ausgeht. Dieses Unvermögen sei der Grund der Trauer.

Obwohl Lüdemanns Monographie mehr als zehn Jahre alt ist, ergänzen neuere Arbeiten zum Thema das Bild kaum durch weitere Deutungsalternativen. Vgl.: Becker 1976, 46f.

Ich halte die zweite Alternative für erwägenswert. Das Problem der Thessalonicher besteht demnach in Unsicherheit über die Teilnahme der Verstorbenen am messianischen Reich, das der allgemeinen Totenauferstehung vorausgehen würde. Dieselbe Problemstellung kennen wir aus 4 Esr 7,26ff. Die allgemeine Auferstehung findet dort erst nach dem messianischen Reich statt. Der Messias und die Übriggebliebenen verfallen am Ende des 400-jährigen messianischen Reiches dem Tode und stehen dann zusammen mit den schon vor dem messianischen Reich Verstorbenen auf.

[33] Die Naherwartung wird freilich andernorts vorausgesetzt; vgl. z.B.: 1,7–9; 3,10–15; 4,1–5; 10,11; 16,22.

Sie glauben an die Unsterblichkeit der Seele, doch die Vorstellung einer leiblichen Auferstehung ist ihnen fremd; vgl. Act 17,32. Das läßt sich aus 15,35 ablesen: Ἀλλὰ ἐρεῖ τις· πῶς ἐγείρονται οἱ νεκροί; ποίῳ δὲ σώματι ἔρχονται; Hier begegnet nochmals das Verb ἐγείρομαι, das Gewicht aber liegt auf dem Begriff σῶμα. Die Frage der Gegner ist natürlich darin begründet, daß sie sich eine Auferstehung des toten Körpers nicht vorstellen können. Der Körper ist ja nach griechischer Auffassung ein Gefängnis der Seele. Der Einwand, daß sich die Argumentation in 1 Kor nicht gegen die Annahme der Unsterblichkeit der Seele richtet, ist irrelevant, weil Paulus seine Gegner mißversteht und deshalb gegen die Position argumentiert, die er ihnen zuschreibt. In 15,35 kommt dieses Mißverständnis besonders deutlich zum Ausdruck. *Sie* weisen auf die Unmöglichkeit einer leiblichen Auferstehung hin, *er* faßt ihr Argument als eine Verneinung jeder Weiterexistenz auf.

Die Berechtigung dieser Exposition ergibt sich ebenfalls aus 2 Kor 5,1–10. Zunächst folgt eine kurze Darstellung der paulinischen Auferstehungshoffnung in 1 Kor 15, damit 2 Kor 5,1ff. verständlicher wird.

Die Auffassung des Paulus von der Auferstehung der Toten ist originell. Sie stellt eine Weiterentwicklung des jüdischen Glaubens dar, denn Paulus hält einerseits daran fest, daß die Toten wirklich leiblich auferweckt werden. Andererseits verneint er, daß der einst gestorbene Körper wiederbelebt wird[34]. Er nimmt vielmehr an, daß die Seele einen neuen Leib bekommt. Diesen Leib nennt er σῶμα πνευματικόν, den irdischen, vergänglichen Körper dagegen σῶμα ψυχικόν (15,44). In 15,36–41 versucht er durch verschiedene Analogien, die Realität dieses pneumatischen Leibes begreiflich zu machen. In 15,42–44a zieht er dann die Folgerung. An Hand von vier Antithesen stellt er heraus, daß der künftige Leib einen Gegensatz zum irdischen Leib bildet. Daß es wirklich einen überirdischen Leib neben dem irdischen gibt, läßt sich laut Paulus aus der Schrift ablesen; vgl. 15,44b–49. Hier herrscht die Antitypik. Auf Grund einer korporativen Vorstellung zeigt er, daß die Nachkommen Adams wie Adam geworden sind und sein Bild getragen haben. Deshalb sind sie gleich ihm sterblich geworden. Die Nachfahren Christi werden dagegen das Bild des Himmlischen tragen und unsterblich werden wie er (vgl. Vv. 22ff.). Aus Phil 3,20f. wissen wir, daß die Christen – so Paulus – ein σῶμα bekommen werden, das dem verherrlichten Leib des Herrn entspricht. In 15,50 faßt er das Gesagte zusammen: "Fleisch und Blut können das Reich Gottes nicht erben; das Vergängliche erbt nicht das Unvergängliche". Da seine Darstellung in 15,35ff. nur für die gestorbenen Christen Relevanz hat, fügt er in 15,51ff. einige Erwägungen hinzu, die auch für die zur Zeit der Parusie lebenden Christen Gültigkeit haben. Alle – sowohl Entschlafene als auch Lebende – werden verwandelt werden.

---

[34] Die Wiederherstellung der früheren Leiblichkeit ist in den pharisäischen Kreisen vorherrschend; vgl.: Strack/Billerbeck 1926, 473f.

2 Kor 5,1ff. gehört in diesen Zusammenhang hinein[35]. Der Abschnitt zählt zu den strittigsten Perikopen des Neuen Testaments[36]. Im Rahmen dieser Arbeit interessieren in erster Linie die Hoffnung auf einen Auferstehungsleib und die in V. 3 erwähnte 'Nacktheit'. Im einleitenden Satz (Οἴδαμεν γὰρ ὅτι ἐὰν ἡ ἐπίγειος ἡμῶν οἰκία τοῦ σκήνους καταλυθῇ, οἰκοδομὴν ἐκ θεοῦ ἔχομεν, οἰκίαν ἀχειροποίητον αἰώνιον ἐν τοῖς οὐρανοῖς.) häufen sich die Probleme. Hier stehen der irdische, vergängliche und der himmlische, ewige Leib einander gegenüber; vgl. 1 Kor 15,36ff. Der erstgenannte wird als ἡ ἐπίγειος ἡμῶν οἰκία τοῦ σκήνους charakterisiert. Der Genitiv τοῦ σκήνους ist epexegetisch, und σκῆνος bedeutet schlicht 'Leib'[37], also: 'unser irdisches Haus, d.h. der Leib'[38]. Dieser Leib ist zum Untergang (καταλυθῆναι) bestimmt. Dabei bleibt die Auslegung von ἐὰν ... καταλυθῇ umstritten. Der Aorist Konjunktiv läßt von einer Deutung auf das tägliche Leiden (des Apostels), den gegenwärtigen Zerstörungsprozeß[39] absehen. Näher legt sich die Annahme, daß die Auflösung des Körpers im Tod gemeint ist[40]. Mehreren Auslegern zufolge reflektiert Paulus jedoch nicht den Zeitpunkt der Auflösung. Er spricht vielmehr die Gewißheit aus, einen neuen Leib zu bekommen[41]. Ἐὰν ist jedenfalls nicht mit einem ὅταν zu verwechseln.

Aus V. 1b entsteht leicht der Eindruck, daß dieses neue Haus, also der Auferstehungsleib, im Himmel schon vorhanden ist; vgl. slHen 22,9f. Die Hauptpointe liegt darin, daß Paulus diesen Auferstehungsleib als etwas ganz und gar unirdisches darstellen will. In Vv. 2–4 steht freilich der Tod zentraler. Dort spricht Paulus von einer 'Überkleidung' (ἐπενδύσασθαι[42]) bzw. 'Entkleidung' (ἐκδύσασθαι), nämlich der

---

[35] Mein Verständnis von 2 Kor 5,1ff. gründet sich auf Bultmann 1967, 298ff.

[36] Umfangreiche bibliographische Auskünfte bzw. Forschungsübersichten finden sich z.B. in: Hoffmann 1966, 254ff.; Prümm 1967, 262ff.; 441ff.; 450ff.; Spörlein 1971, 135ff.; Wolff 1989, 101ff.; 106ff.

[37] Die übliche Übersetzung 'Zelt' versteht σκῆνος als eine jüngere Form von σκηνή. Das ist historisch-sprachlich richtig, doch σκῆνος wird durchweg in übertragenem Sinne als Bezeichnung für 'Leib' gebraucht. Vgl. zum richtigen Verständnis: Spörlein, 1971, 136f.

[38] Vgl.: Spörlein 1971, 136.

[39] So z.B.: Brun 1929, 207ff., bes. 216ff.

[40] So z.B.: Hoffmann 1966, 262f.; 269f. (Im Zentrum stehe freilich weder das 'Wie' noch das 'Wann' der Bekleidung mit dem himmlischen Leib, sondern die Zuversicht, einen neuen Leib zu besitzen.); Hughes 1962, 162; Lang 1986, 286; Lietzmann 1969, 117f.; u.a.

[41] Vgl. z.B.: Bultmann 1967, 303 (oder eventuell bei der Parusie; a.a.O. 304); Kümmel, in: Lietzmann 1969, 202; Prümm 1967, 264ff., bes. 268ff.; Wendland 1968, 194.

[42] Das Präfix (ἐπι-) hat vielleicht seine Kraft verloren – wie es oft im Koinegriechischen der Fall ist –, so daß das Verbum eventuell nur 'bekleidet werden', 'anziehen' bedeutet. Die Pointe liegt jedenfalls darin, daß die nackte Seele bekleidet bzw. überkleidet wird; vgl. den Text. Zur Vorstellung s. auch 1 Kor 15,51ff.

Seele[43]. Der Begriff 'Seele' kommt jedoch im ganzen Abschnitt nicht vor. In 4,16 dagegen spricht Paulus von ('dem äußeren Menschen' und) 'dem inneren Menschen', d.h. dem Ich oder der Seele[44]. Die Seele, die ihr Haus, das irdische σῶμα abgelegt hat, ist entkleidet und nackt (V. 3)[45]. Diese Entkleidung geschieht primär beim Sterben; denn für die zur Zeit der Parusie Lebenden erwartet Paulus eine Verwandlung. Die Seele, die ein neues, ewiges σῶμα bekommt, ist dagegen überkleidet. Solche Überkleidung findet bei der Wiederkehr des Herrn statt, die zugleich die Auferstehung mit sich bringt. Paulus kombiniert in diesem Abschnitt zwei Bilder – das des Hauses und das des Kleides –, die einander logisch ausschließen, aber leicht verständlich sind: Der Leib kann nämlich sowohl als ein Haus als auch als ein Kleid für die nackte Seele angesehen werden.

Für unsere Problemstellung ist dieser Text insofern interessant, als er offenbar davon zeugt, daß Paulus seine Gegner inzwischen besser versteht. Zur Zeit des 1 Kor glaubt er, daß sie jede Weiterexistenz verneinen. Die Auferstehungsleugner fassen die Vorstellung von einer Aufweckung der Toten in jüdischer Weise auf, d.h. als eine Wiederbelebung des toten Körpers. Da sich von der Verwesung des σῶμα nach dem Tod jeder überzeugen kann, stellen sie die naheliegende Frage: Πῶς ἐγείρονται οἱ νεκροί; ποίῳ δὲ σώματι ἔρχονται; Eine somatische Auferweckung lehnen sie also ab, wobei sie sich als wahre Griechen erweisen. Weil Paulus sich auf unpräzise Gerüchte stützen muß, hat er keine Möglichkeit, ihre Argumentation zu verstehen.

Zur Zeit des 2 Kor dagegen liegen ihm bessere Informationen vor. Er erkennt jetzt, daß seine Gegner keine Materialisten sind. Er weiß inzwischen, daß sie die Unsterblichkeit der Seele lehren. Paulus nimmt die frühere Diskussion nicht wieder auf. In 1 Kor 4–5 scheint er aber gerade im Blick auf die Korinther zu formulieren[46]. Das gilt besonders für 5,1–5; denn in diesen Versen steht nicht das apostolische Amt im Blickfeld[47]. Der Grundgedanke dieses Abschnitts ist nach Bultmann polemisch, nämlich gegen die korinthischen Gnostiker gerichtet, die das Zukunftsbild des Paulus verwerfen[48]. Die Auffassung des Apostels stimmt mit derjenigen seiner Gegner insofern überein, als auch er von der Weiterexistenz der Seele über-

---

[43] Die strittige Frage, ob in V. 3 ἐκδύσασθαι oder ἐνδύσασθαι den Vorzug verdient, kann hier nicht abgehandelt werden. Auf Grund meiner Gesamtauffassung ziehe ich die erste Alternative vor.

[44] Wegen dieser dualistischen Vorstellung kann Paulus in 5,8 von einer 'Auswanderung' (ἐκδημῆσαι) aus dem Leib sprechen.

[45] Vgl. zum richtigen Verständnis dieser Nacktheit: Bultmann 1967, 299f.; 1976, 137ff.; Hoffmann 1964, 276f.; Hughes 1962, 169ff.; Spörlein 1971, 144ff.

[46] So schon: Brun 1929, 227.

[47] Sie setzen freilich 4,16ff. fort.

[48] Bultmann 1976, 132. Vgl. zur Annahme einer polemischen Tendenz z.B.: Hoffmann 1966, 267; 269ff.; Schmithals 1965, 246ff.; Wolff 1989, 106.

zeugt ist. Sie sichert nach paulinischer Überzeugung die Kontinuität der Persönlichkeit. Im Gegensatz zur korinthischen Gruppe betont er aber, daß diese Seele nicht nackt bleiben, sondern von einem neuen, ewigen Leib überkleidet werden wird. Während seine Gegner sich nach der Befreiung der Seele vom Leib sehnen, hat Paulus keinen Sinn für diese Nacktheit.

Die Auferstehungsleugner glauben also an die Unsterblichkeit der Seele. Läßt sich ihre Jenseitsvorstellung noch weiter bestimmen? Man darf vermuten, daß sie an einen Aufstieg der Seele in die himmlische Welt unmittelbar nach dem Tode glauben[49]. Das ist ein weiteres Argument, eine leibliche Auferstehung für unmöglich zu halten.

## 5. Zusammenfassung

Die Auferstehungsleugner in Korinth sind nicht Materialisten, die jedes Nachleben verneinen. Sie meinen nicht, daß die Auferstehung schon in der Taufe stattfinde. Sie lehnen den Auferstehungsglauben nicht ab auf Grund der Vorstellung, nur die Übriggebliebenen gewännen das Heil. Sie sind vielmehr wahre Griechen, die an die Unsterblichkeit der Seele glauben. Eine leibliche Auferstehung halten sie deshalb für sinnlos, weil die Seele ihrem Verständnis gemäß sofort nach dem Tod in die himmlische Herrlichkeit eintritt. Paulus mißversteht die Lage und schreibt ihnen die erstgenannte Ansicht zu. Später, zur Zeit des 2 Kor, ist er zu besserer Einsicht gelangt.

## Bibliographie

Bartsch, H.-W. 1964: "Die Argumentation des Paulus in I Cor 15 3–11", in: *ZNW* 55 (1964) 261–74.

Becker, J. 1976: *Auferstehung der Toten im Urchristentum* (SBS 82), Stuttgart: Verlag Katholisches Bibelwerk 1976.

Brandenburger, E. 1962: *Adam und Christus*. Exegetisch-religionsgeschichtliche Untersuchung zu RÖM. 5 12–21 (1. KOR. 15) (WMANT 7), Neukirchen: Neukirchener Verlag 1962.

---

[49] Eine verwandte Ansicht bei: Becker 1976, 74 (Das Pneuma kehre im Tod zu Christus zurück; daneben die Alternative: Der Herr werde die pneumatischen Selbste bei seiner Parusie auferwecken. Diese letztere Annahme stimmt aber schwerlich mit der Leugnung der Auferstehung überein.); Bultmann 1968, 172 Anm. 1; 203; Fee 1987, 715; 744; Hoffmann 1966, 243; Klauck 1984, 112; Sandelin 1976, 134; Schmithals 1965, 254; Wedderburn 1981, 239; Wolff, 1980, 213f.; u.a. Justin Dial, 80 erwähnt bekanntlich eine Gruppe, die die Auferstehung leugnet und die Aufnahme der Seele in den Himmel sofort nach dem Tode lehrt. Wegen des Zeitabstandes ist der Wert dieser Aussage freilich begrenzt.

Brox, N. 1969: *Die Pastoralbriefe*. Übersetzt und erklärt (RNT 7/2), Regensburg: Friedrich Pustet [4]1969.

Bruce, F. F. 1971: *1 and 2 Corinthians* (NCeB), London: Marshall, Morgan & Scott 1971.

Brun, L. 1929: "Zur Auslegung von II Cor 5 1–10", in: *ZNW* 28 (1929) 207–29.

Bultmann, R. 1967: "Exegetische Probleme des zweiten Korintherbriefes", in: idem, *Exegetica*. Aufsätze zur Erforschung des Neuen Testaments ausgew., eingel. und hg.v. E. Dinkler, Tübingen: J. C. B. Mohr 1967, 298–322. [Ursprünglich in: *SyBU* 9 (1947) 3–31.]

— 1968: *Theologie des Neuen Testaments* (NTG), Tübingen: J. C. B. Mohr [6]1968.

— 1976: *Der zweite Brief an die Korinther*, hg. v. Erich Dinkler (KEK 6), Göttingen: Vandenhoeck & Ruprecht 1976.

Cavallin, H. C. C. 1974: *Life After Death*. Paul's Argument for the Resurrection of the Dead in I Cor 15. Part I: An Enquiry into the Jewish Background (CB.NT 7:1), Lund: Gleerup 1974.

— 1977: "Förnekelse av liv efter döden i urkristendomens omvärld" ("Leugnung eines Lebens nach dem Tode in der Umwelt des Urchristentums"), in: *RoB* 36 (1977) 45–56.

Conzelmann, H. 1969: *Der erste Brief an die Korinther*. Übersetzt und erklärt (KEK 5), Göttingen: Vandenhoeck & Ruprecht 1969.

Dibelius, M./Conzelmann, H. 1966: *Die Pastoralbriefe* (HNT 13), Tübingen: J. C. B. Mohr [4]1966.

Doughty, D. J. 1975: "The Presence and Future of Salvation in Corinth", in: *ZNW* 66 (1975) 61–90.

Eichrodt, W. 1961: *Theologie des Alten Testaments* II–III, Stuttgart/Göttingen: Ehrenfried Klotz Verlag/Vandenhoeck & Ruprecht [4]1961.

Fee, G. D. 1987: *The First Epistle to the Corinthians* (NIC), Grand Rapids, MI: Eerdmans 1987.

Héring, J. 1949: *La première épître de Saint Paul aux Corinthiens* (CNT(N) 7), Neuchâtel/Paris: Delachaux & Niestlé 1949.

Hoffmann, P. 1966: *Die Toten in Christus*. Eine religionsgeschichtliche und exegetische Untersuchung zur paulinischen Eschatologie (NTA, NF 2), Münster Westf.: Aschendorff, 1966.

Holtz, G. 1965: *Die Pastoralbriefe* (ThHK 13), Berlin: Evangelische Verlagsanstalt 1965.

Hughes, P. E. 1962: *Paul's Second Epistle to the Corinthians*. The English Text with Introduction, Exposition and Notes (NLC), London/Edinburgh: Marshall, Morgan & Scott 1962.

Jeremias, J. 1966: "'Flesh and Blood Cannot Inherit the Kingdom of God' (I Cor. XV. 50)", in: idem, *Abba*. Studien zur neutestamentlichen Theologie und Zeitgeschichte, Göttingen: Vandenhoeck & Ruprecht 1966, 298–307. [Ursprünglich in: *NTS* 2 (1955/56) 151–59.]

— 1981: *Die Briefe an Timotheus und Titus*. Übersetzt und erklärt (NTD 9), Göttingen: Vandenhoeck & Ruprecht [2]1981.

Klauck, H.-J. 1984: *1. Korintherbrief* (NEB 7), Würzburg: Echter 1984.

Lang, F. 1986: *Die Briefe an die Korinther*. Übersetzt und erklärt (NTD 7), Göttingen/Zürich: Vandenhoeck & Ruprecht 1986.

Lietzmann, H. 1969: *An die Korinther I.II*, erg. v. W. G. Kümmel (HNT 9), Tübingen: J. C. B. Mohr [5]1969.

Lüdemann, G. 1980: *Paulus, der Heidenapostel*. Bd. I. Studien zur Chronologie (FRLANT 123), Göttingen: Vandenhoeck & Ruprecht 1980.

Merkel, H. 1991: *Die Pastoralbriefe.* Übersetzt und erklärt (NTD 9/1), Göttingen: Vandenhoeck & Ruprecht 1991.

Nickelsburg, G. W. E. jr 1972: *Resurrection, Immortality, and Eternal Life in Intertestamental Judaism* (HThS 26), Cambridge, MA: Harvard University Press 1972.

Nilsson, M. P. 1955/1950: *Geschichte der griechischen Religion I–II* (Handwörterbuch der Altertumswissenschaft V.2.1/V.2.2), München: C. H. Beck'sche Verlagsbuchhandlung $^2$1955/1950.

Odeberg, H. 1944: *Pauli brev till Korintierna* (Tolkning av Nya Testamentet 7), Stockholm: Svenska Kyrkans Diakonistyrelses Bokförlag 1944.

Orr, W. F./Walther, J. A. 1976: *I Corinthians.* A New Translation. Introduction with a Study of the Life of Paul, Notes, and Commentary (AncB 32), New York: Doubleday 1976.

Prümm, K. 1967: *Diakonia Pneumatos.* Der zweite Korintherbrief als Zugang zur apostolischen Botschaft. Auslegung und Theologie. Bd. I. Theologische Auslegung des zweiten Korintherbriefes, Rom/Freiburg/Wien: Herder 1967.

Raeder, M. 1955: "Vikariatstaufe in I Cor 15,29?", in: *ZNW* 46 (1955) 258–60.

Rissi, M. 1962: *Die Taufe für die Toten.* Ein Beitrag zur paulinischen Tauflehre (AThANT 42), Zürich/Stuttgart: Zwingli Verlag 1962.

Rohde, E. 1910: *Psyche I–II.* Seelencult und Unsterblichkeitsglaube der Griechen, Tübingen: J. C. B. Mohr $^{5.6}$1910.

Sandelin, K.–G. 1976: *Die Auseinandersetzung mit der Weisheit in 1. Korinther 15* (Meddelanden från stiftelsens för Åbo akademi forskningsinstitut 12), Åbo: Åbo akademi 1976.

Schmithals, W. 1965: *Die Gnosis in Korinth.* Eine Untersuchung zu den Korintherbriefen (FRLANT 66), Göttingen: Vandenhoeck & Ruprecht $^2$1965.

Schweitzer, A. 1930: *Die Mystik des Apostels Paulus*, Tübingen: J. C. B. Mohr 1930.

Spörlein, B. 1971: *Die Leugnung der Auferstehung.* Eine historisch-kritische Untersuchung zu I Kor 15 (BU 7), Regensburg: Friedrich Pustet 1971.

Strack, H./Billerbeck, P. 1926: *Kommentar zum Neuen Testament aus Talmud und Midrasch.* III. Die Briefe des Neuen Testaments und die Offenbarung Johannis, München: C. H. Beck'sche Verlagsbuchhandlung 1926.

Wedderburn, A. J. M. 1981: "The Problem of the Denial of the Resurrection in I Corinthians XV", in: *NT* 23 (1981) 229–41.

Wendland, H. D. 1968: *Die Briefe an die Korinther.* Übersetzt und erklärt (NTD 7), Göttingen: Vandenhoeck & Ruprecht 1968.

Wilson, J. H. 1968: "The Corinthians Who Say There Is No Resurrection of the Dead", in: *ZNW* 59 (1968) 90–107.

Wolff, C. 1982: *Der erste Brief des Paulus an die Korinther.* Zweiter Teil: Auslegung der Kap. 8–16 (ThHK VII/2), Berlin: Evangelische Verlagsanstalt 1982.

— 1989: *Der zweite Brief des Paulus an die Korinther* (ThHK 8), Berlin: Evangelische Verlagsanstalt 1989.

# The Temporary Reign of the Son: 1 Cor 15:23-28

## Wayne A. Meeks

There is a vast literature on 1 Cor 15, but surprisingly little on the puzzling verses that speak of "the end" when Christ "hands over the kingdom to God the Father." Most of what has been written has been concerned to show that Paul cannot really have taught a "Subordinationism" or that these verses do not support an Origenist kind of Apokatastasis.[1] In recent decades, these traditional systematic concerns have receded; commentators have tried instead simply to understand why Paul should have interrupted his argument for the resurrection of the dead with this bit of eschatological lore that seems so extraneous to his purpose. Not infrequently, interpreters suggest that Paul, having once ventured into an apocalyptic scenario in order to refute an opposing position in Corinth, is simply carried along by the tradition he follows. The remarks of Conzelmann in his commentary are typical: "Der Abschnitt zeigt Paulus in der Tradition der Apokalyptik. Deren Grundgedanke, daß der Weltlauf einem vorbestimmten Plan folgt, und eine konkrete Vorstellung von diesem Plan, den Etappen des Ablaufes, ist gegeben".[2] A further assumption, often unexpressed, seems to be that the apocalyptic timetable includes a "messianisches Zwischenreich," into which Christ's reign must be fitted. However, Hans-Alwin Wilcke rather effectively demonstrated already in 1967 that no such notion can be found in the Pauline letters.[3]

More fundamentally, Lars Hartman has taught us that "apocalyptic timetables" do not work so mechanically in Jewish apocalypses. Indeed, I think it would not misrepresent Hartman's insight to say that these so-called timetables have less to do with a "preordained plan for the course of world history" than with a peculiar kind of intertextuality. The apocalypticists were usually engaged in an imaginativ ereinterpretation of scripture and tradition in order to construct a scenario that will provide consolation, admonition, warning, or correction for their particular communi-

---

[1] For a survey of the patristic discussion, see Schendel 1971.
[2] Conzelmann 1969, 319.
[3] Wilcke 1967.

ties facing particular situations. Hartman showed that only very rarely is the function of one of these scenarios simply to convey supposed information about the facts of the future. Rather, such timetables have a variety of functions, which must be determined from the rhetorical situation and context in each instance.[4] It would be uncharacteristic of Paul, who here and elsewhere often shows himself a radical revisionist of scripture and tradition, thoughtlessly to incorporate some preformulated scheme into his argument. If Hartman is right, it would also be quite untypical of other apocalyptic literature.

I propose to apply the Hartman rule to 1 Cor 15:23-28, to see whether we can understand why Paul's argument here may have taken this odd turn. The immediate argumentative context, of course, is Paul's attempt to refute those τινες who say there is no resurrection of the dead (v. 12). These are presumably the same τινες whom Paul accuses of being "ignorant of God" (v. 34). By speaking of them in the third person, Paul invites his audience to dissociate themselves from the notions of those unnamed others, for "bad company ruins good character" (v. 33, REB). Implicit in the way Paul thus brackets the part of the argument with which we are immediately concerned is that his primary purpose is practical rather than theoretical.

If we look to the beginning and end of the chapter, the practical intent of the whole is even clearer. Paul begins his summary of the gospel preached to the Corinthians with an implied warning, "unless you believed in vain [εἰκῇ]" (v. 2). He concludes with an exhortation to "be steadfast, immovable, always excelling in the work of the Lord," backed by the assurance, "because you know that in the Lord your labor is not in vain [κενός]" (v. 58, NRSV). In between, he has argued that, if the dead (including Christ) are not raised, then the faith of believers is indeed vain (κενή, ματαία) (vv. 14-19), and Paul's own labor has been pointless and empty (vv. 14, 30-32). We may say, then, that the purpose of this chapter is not so much to teach correct beliefs as to reassure and stabilize a community that has work to do in the world—even though the "form" of that world, as Paul said in 7:31, is "passing away."

This practical use of the resurrection kerygma is consistent with a pattern that we see elsewhere in this letter. First, Paul's rhetorical questions in vv. 30-32, which ask the reader to contemplate the futility of Paul's own endangerment and sufferings if there were no resurrection, remind us of his ironic use of a catalogue of difficulties in 4:8-13. There he sets the hardships and dishonor of the apostolic life in contrast to the exalted freedom of those whose "wisdom" has given them already kingship and satiety—claims that Paul attributes to the Corinthian audience. A generation ago many scholars shared a near-consensus that those claims were based upon a "re-

---

[4] Hartman 1975; see also his foundational work on apocalyptic interpretation of scripture, Hartman 1966.

alized eschatology" held by some of the Corinthians, who supposedly believed like Hymenaeus and Philetus that "the resurrection has already occurred" (2 Tim 2:18).[5] In light of more recent scholarship that explanation has seemed less and less convincing, though the possibility of some such set of beliefs cannot be absolutely excluded.[6] Certainly it is not necessary to posit a full-blown or even an incipient Gnosticism of the Valentinian type.[7] The language Paul uses to satirize the schismatic tendency of the Corinthians is borrowed from watchwords of the Stoa: "Only the wise man is rich"; "Only the wise man is king." Paul is lampooning the pretense (as he sees it) by some of his audience to superior wisdom, not by exposing flaws in their philosophical logic, but by pointing to their immaturity in practical wisdom, their foolishness in being "puffed up each on behalf of one and against the other [i.e., Paul and Apollos respectively]"(4:6).[8] Whether or not "realized eschatology" describes the point of view that Paul here chides, expectations of an end to come do play a large role in Paul's own argument. Relativizing all the differences between apostles and between their fans, he warns against invidious judgments "before the time, until the Lord comes, who will illuminate the things hidden in darkness and expose the counsels of hearts" (4:5; cf. 3:5-15).[9] While Paul does not mention the resurrection in these chapters, it is implicit in the "foolish" message of the crucifixion (1:18-25), and the hope of the resurrection enables the paradoxical life of the apostles described in 4:9-13, though Paul will not make that explicit until 15:30-32.

The paradoxicality of the crucifixion-and-resurrection kerygma is the hidden warrant also in chaps. 8-10, in which Paul twits the "knowing" sophisticates who scandalize the "weak" by their unconcern about eating "idol-sacrifices." Paul insists that the status-superior sophisticates ought to yield their privileges for the sake of the weak "brother for whom Christ died." In the middle of this complex argument Paul inserts his own personal example in chap. 9. He describes his radical lowering of himself, as a free person enslaving himself to all (9:19), in terms that would be quite understandable in Graeco-Roman rhetoric.[10] It is not until the conclusion of this whole topic in 11:1 that the underlying and controlling paradigm of Christ's self-humbling is expressly if tersely asserted.

The most direct use of the resurrection hope in Paul's moral argument in this let-

---

[5] This construction of the Corinthian error was first clearly enunciated by von Soden 1931. For a brief survey of development of this position later, see Kuck 1992, 16-25. Among the interpreters of 1 Cor 15:20-28 who presuppose some form of this consensus are Conzelmann 1969, Luz 1968, and Barth 1970.

[6] Kuck 1992, 25-37.

[7] See Pearson 1973; Lambrecht 1982, 515-16, as well as Kuck 1992.

[8] Fitzgerald 1988, 135-43; Stowers 1990.

[9] See Kuck 1992.

[10] Martin 1990; Malherbe 1994.

ter is also the most surprising. In 6:12 Paul imagines, in the diatribal style he uses frequently in this letter, an interlocutor responding to his previous argument with a slogan that suggests the same kind of royal freedom so dear to Stoics and Cynics that Paul has already satirized in 4:8. It was a commonplace of moral discourse that such freedom must accept self-limitation for the sake of the community,[11] and Paul's answers to the slogan remain at first within the common usage: not all things are beneficial; freedom that leads to being dominated by something defeats itself; not all things build up the community.[12] Then, however, he imagines his interlocutor saying something else: "Foods are for the stomach and the stomach for foods; God will after all destroy both" (v. 13a). Here is a specifically theological claim: choices about bodily functions are matters of indifference because God brings them to an end. "Yes," says Paul, "but *the body* is not for πορνεία but for the Lord, and the Lord for the body; God raised the Lord and he will also raise us through his power" (vv. 13b-14). This is a quite remarkable claim. Paul wants his audience to understand that God, by raising Jesus bodily from the dead and promising thereby the resurrection, at the end, of all our bodies (albeit in a transformed, "spiritual" state, as he will explain in chap. 15), lays claim on the body. Paul backs this claim with a direct, earthy example and two metaphors. One might entertain the notion that sin is essentially "outside the body" (v. 18), but at least in case of πορνεία in its strict sense, prostitution, that assertion is absurd. Union with the prostitute renders the body unfit, first, for its spiritual union with the Lord (v. 17) and, second, as a shrine of the Holy Spirit (v. 19). Finally Paul likens the Christian life, as he often does, to slavery, summing up: "You have been bought at a price; so glorify God *in [or, with] your bodies*" (v. 20).[13]

So far we have seen that Paul's pragmatic focus in his argument against denial of the resurrection echoes rhetorical moves that he makes at a number of other places in the letter. Before returning to the details of 15:23-28, we need accordingly to ask whether there is an overall rhetorical structure to the letter to which we can relate the discourse on the resurrection. The recent monograph by Margaret Mitchell has made a convincing case that there is such a structure, which in ancient rhetorical theory and practice would have been recognized as deliberative rather than forensic or epideictic. She concludes that "1 Corinthians is in fact a unified and coherent appeal for unity and cessation of factionalism." Along the way, she demolishes the arguments of those who would partition the letter; positively she sets forth persuasive arguments that the entire letter is a single composition according closely with the standards and common practice of ancient deliberative rhetoric, particularly in

---

[11] See, e.g., Dio Chrysostom *Or.* 3.10; 62.3.

[12] Cf. Stowers 1981.

[13] See further my discussion of this passage in Meeks 1993, 132-33.

speeches and letters urging concord (ὁμόνοια). Thus 1:10 sets forth the thesis statement (πρόθεσις) not merely for the first four chapters, but for the entire letter.[14] In her correct concern to show that the letter is not a disjointed collection—either fragments of several letters or loosely related paraenetic responses to various problems—Mitchell has perhaps underestimated the importance of the specific issues that have been brought to Paul's attention by letter and oral report and which he does treat seriatim. Nevertheless, she has effectively demonstrated that the particular topics are all fitted by Paul into an overarching attempt to persuade the Corinthian Christians to give up their factionalism and self-ambition in favor of "building up" the community.

There is something else to be noted about Paul's repeated and varied appeals for concord in the Corinthian community. Again and again these appeals focus, often with high irony, on concerns about rank, status, and distinction. Such concerns are most explicit at the beginning of the letter, especially in 1:26-31, but they are implicit in the whole discussion of chaps. 1-4, which turns, as we have seen, on the apparent rivalry between fans of Apollos and those of Paul. "Status-specific expectations," as Gerd Theißen calls them, may also underlie the debate over lawsuits in common courts (6:1-11), differing attitudes toward sacrificial meat and dinner invitations to pagan homes (chaps. 8-10), and the disorder at the Lord's Supper (11:17-34).[15] The concern over social level and zeal for the honor appropriate to one's station was, of course, pervasive in the urban society of the Roman empire.[16] To judge from monuments and inscriptions from Roman Corinth, such φιλοτιμία was particularly vigorous there, and it is particularly noteworthy how many of the inscriptions were erected by first-, second-, or third-generation descendants of slaves. It looks as if this Roman colony, less than a century old when Paul arrived there, afforded unusual opportunities for freedpersons to rise on the social ladder.[17] No wonder "status-specific expectations" remained alive in the new Christian household communities. At the same time, some novel signs of status seem to have been discovered by those communities themselves: distinctions having to do with possession of or by the Spirit, special "gifts" like glossolalia or prophecy, or unique wisdom imparted by a favored apostle.[18] In every case, Paul urges that those who possess relative power, status, and knowledge yield their prerogatives for the sake of the unity

---

[14] M. M. Mitchell 1992/93, quotation from p. 19.

[15] It was Gerd Theißen who first and most clearly identified the problem of social level behind 1 Corinthians: Theißen 1974a, 1974b, 1975 (reprinted in Theißen 1983). See also Meeks 1983, chap. 2. On 6:1-11, see A. Mitchell 1993.

[16] The stratified nature of Graeco-Roman society is well known; in recent scholarship the description in MacMullen 1974 has become a classic.

[17] See Meeks 1983, 47-49, and further references given there.

and order of the community. The rhetorical means of persuasion he employs are manifold, and almost all of them fall within the range of topics and strategies common in ancient speeches urging ὁμόνοια and opposing στάσις, as Mitchell has demonstrated. As a personal example of such relinquishing of advantage for the sake of the community, Paul usually cites his own actions as an apostle. Nevertheless, Paul expected his audience to recognize that the implicit model, only occasionally expressed, is the paradoxical story of the Christ's crucifixion and resurrection: "Become imitators of me as I am of Christ" (11:1).

If we keep in mind both the overall deliberative purpose of the letter and its most powerful christological paradigm, perhaps we can come closer to solving our initial puzzle: why has Paul interrupted his proofs of the resurrection with an account of the Son's eventual submission to the Father? Several commentators have supposed that Paul wants "to make it clear that the Son is not a revolutionary god in the style of the Greek gods who oust the ancient gods ... and as the unknown God of Marcion dispossesses the God of the Old Testament."[19] Yet there is nothing in the letter to suggest any such beliefs as a problem among Corinthian Christians. Perhaps more plausible is the intriguing suggestion that Mitchell gleans from John Chrysostom's commentary on the text. When all of the enemies lie at his feet, says Chrysostom, the Son, far from rebelling (στασιάζειν) against the One who begot him, is at pains to demonstrate his ὁμόνοια.[20] Can it be that Paul describes the ultimate submission of Christ's kingship to God as the supreme example of the sacrifice of one's own power and advantage for the sake of general concord? Certainly we see him a few years later, in the letter to the Philippians, using a different cosmic scenario of Christ's self-lowering for a closely parallel rhetorical purpose.[21] There, however, the focus of Paul's evocation of the famous "hymn" in Phil 2:6-11 is not the "end" when all enemies are defeated, but the ταπείνωσις of the Christ to the point of obedient death, followed by his exaltation and installation as κύριος. Nevertheless, there are strong hints in Phil 2:10-11 of the submission of chthonic, earthly, and heavenly powers to this Lord. And later in this letter, in a passage that clearly echoes the poem 2:6-11 (σχῆμα / μετασχηματίζειν; μορφή / σύμμορφον; ταπεινοῦν / ταπείνωσις), Paul does use language that is very close to that in 1 Cor 15: ὃς μετασχηματίσει τὸ σῶμα τῆς ταπεινώσεως ἡμῶν σύμμορφον τῷ σώματι τῆς δόξης αὐ-

---

[18] The status ambitions shared with the larger society may not have been entirely unrelated, of course, to those charismatic distinctions within. Martin 1991 warns against supposing that glossolalia, for example, would have occurred in antiquity characteristically among the lower classes as it so often does in modern societies.

[19] Héring 1964, 168.

[20] Chrys. *hom. in 1 Cor.* 39.5-6 (*PG* 61.340-42); M. M. Mitchell 1992/93, 289, nn. 280, 281.

[21] See Meeks 1991.

τοῦ κατὰ τὴν ἐνέργειαν τοῦ δύνασθαι αὐτὸν καὶ ὑποτάξαι αὐτῷ τὰ πάντα (3:21). Here both the subordination of "all things" to the Christ and the transformation of the believers' bodies (cf. 1 Cor 15:35-53) are emphasized. What is strikingly absent from this passage, when we compare it with 1 Cor 15:23-28, is any mention of the Christ's submission to God. Is it perhaps precisely the competition for status and distinction, which seems to have plagued the Corinthian household congregations, that led Paul to fill out his scenario of the "end," in 1 Cor 15:23-28 and nowhere else in the extant letters, with the vision of the Son's final "handing over" of his reign to the Father?

If Paul did construct this final scene as the ultimate example to reinforce his appeal in 1 Corinthians for mutual forbearance and communal harmony, the question remains, what suggested it to him? We must begin with the obvious. The explicit warrant Paul provides is his harmonizing paraphrase of the two scriptural texts, Ps 110:1 and 8:7. Paul's use of these texts here has been well analyzed;[22] for our purposes we need only emphasize a few details.

First, among the changes that Paul makes, in comparison with the LXX text we know, some are particularly significant. For the κάθου ἐκ δεξιῶν μου of Ps 109:1 LXX, Paul writes δεῖ γὰρ αὐτὸν βασιλεύειν. Maier suggests that Paul wants the reader to hold in reserve the thought of the heavenly enthronement, because the immediate focus is on the earthly consequence of the messianic reign.[23] The change, however, also provides a more direct warrant for the assertion in v. 24 that at "the end" the Christ will "hand over the reign to God the Father," resumed in v. 28 in different language to form an inclusio. In addition, Paul may well wish the audience to recall his ironic put-down of the Stoic-like boast in 4:8, [ἤδη] χωρὶς ἡμῶν ἐβασιλεύσατε. Paul does not use βασιλεία language very often; in 1 Corinthians, only in three other passages besides these two. In 4:20, continuing his earlier sarcasm against those who love rhetorical skill and "wisdom," Paul says that the reign of God is not ἐν λόγῳ but in power. In 6:9-10 he employs a formula that was apparently common in the Pauline groups (cf. Gal 5:21; Eph 5:5): those who are guilty of [various named vices] cannot inherit the kingdom of God. In our chapter, he rings a significant change on that formula: "flesh and blood cannot inherit the kingdom of God" (1 Cor 15:50). Again we see that Paul is not addressing theoretical questions so much as he is aiming to change attitudes and behavior. The reign of Christ, as a paradoxical exercise of power, is a paradigm that implicitly rebukes the status ambitions of many of the Corinthian Christians.

---

[22] Maier 1932; Hay 1973, esp. 36f., 60-62; Lambrecht 1982. See also Luz 1968, 343-52, though I am not persuaded by Luz's argument (accepted by Hay) that the combination of the two texts was part of a pre-Pauline tradition.

[23] Maier 1932, 150f.

Second, as most commentators note, Paul has imported the πάντα of Ps 8:7 into his paraphrase of Ps 110:1. Maier points out that this prepares the way for singling out one of the enemies, as well as for the rhetorical move of emphasizing the one exception in v. 28.[24] The πάντα in its context in Ps 8, of course, does not refer to "enemies" but to "the works of [God's] hands." Paul does not ignore this wider referent, which is implicit in v. 28. Nevertheless, this Psalm, too, speaks of God's enemies (v. 3), so it is not surprising that Paul reads Psalms 8 and 110 as "twins" (Maier) exhibiting the imagery of military triumph. Significantly the δεῖ γάρ in v. 25, which introduces the double paraphrase, recurs in v. 53, introducing another sketch of the defeat of the last enemy, also backed by a double scripture quotation (vv. 53-57). The keyword here is νῖκος.

These connections, however, do not completely account for Paul's emphasis on "all"—the word occurs ten times in vv. 23-28. The point, Gerhard Barth suggests, is the expectation of the *total* rule of Christ and, through it, the total rule of God.[25] Again, however, this emphasis is related to the admonitions that Paul has been making all through this letter. So, in the beginning of his dialectical discussion of the "knowing" and the "weak" confronting "meat offered to idols," he expands the monotheistic premiss of the sophisticates:

> But for us: one God, the Father
> from whom are τὰ πάντα and ourselves destined for him,
> and one Lord, Jesus Christ,
> through whom are τὰ πάντα and ourselves through him. (8:6)

More pointedly, as Paul approaches the climax of his attack on the incipient factionalism reported to him by Chloe's people, he emphasizes his admonition, "So no one ought to boast in human figures," with a tightly composed rhetorical climax: "For everything [πάντα] is yours, whether Paul or Apollo or Cephas or world or life or death or present or future: all is yours—but you are Christ's, and Christ is God's" (3:21-23).[26] Again, the emphasis is on concord and order, which God accomplishes both through Christ's "submission" and through his triumph over "all the enemies," and which must also manifest itself in God's community, "for God's proper attribute is not ἀκαταστασία but peace" (14:33).

Most of what we have seen so far Paul could have managed to read into Psalm 110; was it only for the word "all" or the emphasis of doubling that Paul made Psalm 8 its "twin"? Paul can hardly have ignored the fact that the object of the sub-

---

[24] Maier 1932, 148-53.

[25] Barth 1970, 524.

[26] Cf. Schweizer 1975, 312, who appropriately compares Phil 2:11, "to the glory of God the Father."

jection, in the verse he quoted, was the *human* (ἄνθρωπος ... ἢ υἱὸς ἀνθρώπου, Ps 8:5). And of course Paul's depiction of Christ as "the last Adam," the δεύτερος ἄνθρωπος, is a key element in his representation here of the final victory over death (1 Cor 15:21-22, 44-49). Is there reason to agree with David Hay that "behind 15.20-28 as a whole (as behind much of 15.42-50) there must lie a congeries of Adamic speculation of a quasi-gnostic type"?[27] Today one would be more chary of the vague term "quasi-gnostic," but there do seem to be echoes of traditional expansions of the Adam story, found in Jewish sources of various provenance and date. The history of those traditions is difficult to describe precisely; in any case space is wanting here to attempt anything like a detailed assessment of their pertinence to our passage. Nevertheless, a few preliminary observations may be suggestive.

In a letter that, as we have seen, urges concord to be achieved by submission to proper order, the Adam described in Genesis 1 and 2 is an obvious negative example. In Rom 5:12-21, where Paul is elaborating on some of the motifs he has used in 1 Cor 15:20-28, it is precisely Adam's "transgression" (παράπτωμα) that is set in contrast with Christ's "righteousness" (δικαίωμα, δικαιοσύνη). The later aggadic expansions of the story not only continue to depict the results of Adam's στάσις, however. They also often introduce a rivalry between the already-created angels and the upstart human.[28] It is not impossible that Paul alludes to such notions as well. The creation of the "first human" brought disorder not only by humanity's own rebellion, but also by the jealousy of the rival "powers." It is the "last Adam" who restores order both by his victory over all inimical powers and by his own obedient submission, "that God may be all in all." In Paul's vision of "the end," the last enemy, Death, is of course *our* final enemy, but the victory is not in the first instance *our* victory, but God's. As Paul would later write to the Romans, it is only "through the one who loved us" that we enjoy our "supertriumph" (Rom 8:37), for we have also been enemies who are now reconciled (Rom 5:10).

I hope this brief sketch has been enough to show the fruitfulness of the approach pioneered by Lars Hartman to passages like this peculiarly difficult one. If we may indeed call Paul's evocation of the sequence of end-time events in 1 Cor 15:23-28 "an apocalyptic timetable," then the way to understand it is to follow Hartman's model analysis that combines sensitivity to intertextual strategies, interpretive traditions, and rhetorical form and situation. That what results is the discovery of considerable complexity in Paul's argument is no surprise; at the same time, I believe we discover more consistency and deliberate argumentative pertinence in these verses than has usually been noticed.

---

[27] Hay 1973, 60.

[28] Schäfer 1975 provides a collection, in translation, and analysis of some of the most important rabbinic texts.

## Bibliography

Barth, Gerhard 1970: "Erwägungen zu 1. Korinther 15, 20-28", in: *EvTh* 30 (1970) 513-27.

Conzelmann, Hans 1969: *Der erste Brief an die Korinther* (KEK 5), Göttingen: Vandenhoeck & Ruprecht 1969.

Fitzgerald, John T. 1988: *Cracks in an earthen vessel: An examination of the catalogues of hardships in the Corinthian correspondence* (SBL.DS 99), Atlanta, GA: Scholars Press 1988.

Hartman, Lars 1966: *Prophecy interpreted: The formation of some Jewish apocalyptic texts and of the eschatological discourse, Mc 13 par.* (CB.NT 1), Lund: CWK Gleerup 1966.

— 1975: "The functions of some so-called apocalyptic timetables", in: *NTS* 22 (1975) 1-14.

Hay, David M. 1973: *Glory at the right hand: Psalm 110 in early Christianity* (SBL.MS), Nashville, TN: Abingdon 1973.

Héring, Jean 1964: *The first epistle of Saint Paul to the Corinthians*, London: Epworth Press 1964.

Kuck, David W. 1992: *Judgment and community conflict: Paul's use of apocalyptic judgment language in 1 Corinthians 3:5-4:5* (NT.S 66), Leiden: E. J. Brill 1992.

Lambrecht, Jan 1982: "Paul's christological use of scripture in 1 Cor. 15.20-28", in: *NTS* 28 (1982) 502-27.

Luz, Ulrich 1968: *Das Geschichtsverständnis des Paulus* (BEvTh 49), Munich: Chr. Kaiser Verlag 1968.

MacMullen, Ramsay 1974: *Roman social relations 50 B.C. to A.D. 284*, New Haven, CT: Yale University Press 1974.

Maier, Friedrich Wilhelm 1932: "Ps 110,1 (LXX 109,1) im Zusammenhang von 1 Kor 15,24-26", in: *BZ* 20 (1932) 139-56.

Malherbe, Abraham J. 1994: "Determinism and free will in Paul: The argument of 1 Corinthians 8 and 9", in: Troels Engberg-Pedersen (ed.), *Paul in his hellenistic context*, Minneapolis, MN: Fortress Press and Edinburgh: T. & T. Clark 1994, 231-55.

Martin, Dale B. 1990: *Slavery as salvation: The metaphor of slavery in Pauline Christianity*, New Haven, CT: Yale University Press 1990.

— 1991: "Tongues of angels and other status indicators", in: *JAAR* 59 (1991) 547-89.

Meeks, Wayne A. 1983: *The first urban Christians: The social world of the apostle Paul*, New Haven, CT: Yale University Press 1983.

— 1991: "The man from heaven in Paul's letter to the Philippians", in: B. A. Pearson (ed.), *The Future of early Christianity: Essays in honor of Helmut Koester*, Minneapolis, MN: Fortress Press 1991, 329-36.

— 1993: *The origins of Christian morality: The first two centuries*, New Haven, CT and London: Yale University Press 1993.

Mitchell, Alan C., SJ 1993: "Rich and poor in the courts of Corinth: Litigiousness and status in 1 Corinthians 6.1-11", in: *NTS* 39 (1993) 562-86.

Mitchell, Margaret Mary 1992/93: *Paul and the rhetoric of reconciliation: An exegetical investigation of the language and composition of 1 Corinthians* (HUTh 28), Tübingen: J. C. B. Mohr (Paul Siebeck) 1992 and Louisville, KY: Westminster/JohnKnox 1993.

Pearson, Birger A. 1973: *The pneumatikos-psychikos terminology in 1 Corinthians: A study in the theology of the Corinthian opponents of Paul and its relation to gnosticism* (SBL.DS 12), Missoula, MT: Scholars Press 1973.

Schäfer, Peter 1975: *Rivalität zwischen Engeln und Menschen: Untersuchungen zur rabbinischen Engelvorstellung* (SJ 8), Berlin and New York: de Gruyter 1975.

Schendel, Eckhard 1971: *Herrschaft und Unterwerfung Christi: 1 Korinther 15,24-28 in Exegese und Theologie der Väter bis zum Ausgang des 4. Jahrhunderts* (BGBE 12), Tübingen: J. C. B. Mohr (Paul Siebeck) 1971.

Schweizer, Eduard 1975: "1. Korinther 15,20-28 als Zeugnis paulinischer Eschatologie und ihrer Verwandtschaft mit der Verkündigung Jesu", in: E. Earle Ellis and Erich Gräßer (eds.), *Jesus und Paulus: Festschrift für Werner Georg Kümmel zum 70. Geburtstag*, Göttingen: Vandenhoeck & Ruprecht 1975, 301-14.

Soden, Hans Freiherr von 1931: "Sakrament und Ethik bei Paulus: Zur Frage der literarischen und theologischen Einheitlichkeit von 1 Kor. 8-10", in: Heinrich Frick (ed.), *Marburger Theologische Studien: Rudolf Otto-Festgruß*, Gotha: Leopold Klotz 1931, 1-40.

Stowers, Stanley K. 1981: "A 'debate' over freedom: 1 Corinthians 6:12-20", in: Everett Ferguson (ed.), *Christian teaching: Studies in honor of LeMoine G. Lewis*, Abilene, TX: Abilene Christian University 1981, 59-71.

— 1990: "Paul on the use and abuse of reason", in: D. L. Balch, E. Ferguson, W. A. Meeks (eds.), *Greeks, Romans, and Christians: Essays in honor of Abraham J. Malherbe*, Minneapolis, MN: Fortress Press 1990, 253-86.

Theißen, Gerd 1974a: "Soziale Integration und sakramentales Handeln: Eine Analyse von 1 Cor. XI 17-34", in: *NT* 16 (1974) 179-206.

— 1974b: "Soziale Schichtung in der korinthischen Gemeinde: Ein Beitrag zur Soziologie des hellenistischen Urchristentums", in: *ZNW* 65 (1974) 232-72.

— 1975: "Die Starken und Schwachen in Korinth: Soziologische Analyse eines theologischen Streites", in: *EvTh* 35 (1975) 155-72.

— 1983: *Studien zur Soziologie des Urchristentums* (WUNT 19), Tübingen J. C. B. Mohr (Paul Siebeck) [2]1983.

Wilcke, Hans-Alwin 1967: Das Problem eines messianischen Zwischenreiches bei Paulus (AThANT 51), Zürich and Stuttgart: Zwingli Verlag 1967.

# Paul's Self-Sufficiency (Philippians 4:11)

Abraham J. Malherbe

## 1. Introduction

This paper deals with Philippians 4:11, specifically, with Paul's statement that he was αὐτάρκης in all things. I wish to argue that the statement should be understood in the context of ancient discussions of friendship and not the technical Stoic idea of αὐτάρκεια. It is quite popular to say that αὐτάρκεια is a Stoic term, but there is considerable difference of opinion on the degree to which and the manner in which Paul is thought to appropriate the Stoic notion.

For example, E. N. O'Neill, in speaking of the term, says of the text in which it occurs in Philippians, "the whole passage (vss. 11-13) must be considered. These words of Paul could just as easily have been uttered by Antisthenes, Diogenes, Crates, or even Teles."[1] That, of course, is gross overstatement.

Rudolf Bultmann is more interesting. First, he portrays what he considers the Stoic view. According to Bultmann, the Stoic must free himself from his emotions. "For these seek to attach him to 'alien things'. He must strive for self-sufficiency (αὐτάρκεια), both within and without. He must cultivate renunciation and endurance. For then he will be free and happy, and nothing can assail him ... He withdraws into himself and with clarity of mind perceives the divine, universal law, which, when all is said and done, he cannot alter."[2] Bultmann then interprets Paul in light of this view of self-sufficiency. Paul's freedom is said to be his radical openness for the future. "Such a conception of freedom," says Bultmann, "seems to bring Paul very close to Stoicism. Indeed, the very fact that he defines genuine human existence in terms of freedom, a concept unknown to the Old Testament and Judaism, is itself to suggest an affinity between Paul and the Stoics, to say nothing of the actual vocabulary he uses. The Stoic wise man is, like Paul, free from all external necessities and claims from the outside world, its conventions, judgements

---

[1] O'Neil 1978, 312.
[2] Bultmann 1956, 139.

and values."[3]

In Bultmann's interpretation, then, Philippians 4:11 describes Paul's interior detachment. "Like Paul, the Stoic could say: 'I know both how to be abased, and I know how to abound'... But he would not continue: 'I can do all things through Christ who strengtheneth me' (Phil 4:12f.) This is just where the difference lies. The Stoic is free because of his reason. He concentrates on reason by turning his back on all encounters and claims from the outside world. This makes him free from the future. He is enabled to escape from the toils of life in time. Paul, on the other hand, is free because he has been made free by the grace of God, and has surrendered freely to his grace. He has been freed from all the claims which seek to bind him to all reality, present, transitory and already past. He has become free for the future, for encounters in which he will experience God's grace ever anew as a gift from the outside."[4]

Other commentators, without Bultmann's originality, have also drawn attention to the Stoic use of the term but have been careful to point out that Paul was quite un-Stoic in claiming that it was Christ who supplied the power by which Paul could live as he did. Yet others have recognized that, while the term was used by Stoics (and Cynics), it "had a wider currency than simply that of a technical expression in the Cynic-Stoic (sic) school," and that Paul transformed the term.[5] These interpretations generally focus on the word, rather than the larger context of the text in Philippians. And they almost never give serious attention to the fact that αὐτάρκεια frequently appeared as part of larger complexes of ideas, some of which are also present in Paul's discussion here. One of the commonplace discussions in which self-sufficiency was often taken up was that of friendship.

## 2. Friendship Language in Philippians

The importance of friendship in ancient society needs no extended discussion, and its importance has become increasingly clear to NT scholars in recent years. For instance, a group in the Society of Biblical Literature, recently organized by John Fitzgerald to study hellenistic moral philosophy and early Christianity, in its 1991 session devoted seven hours to the examination of friendship in a wide selection of ancient writers and documents, and in 1992 devoted three papers to Phil 4:10-20

---

[3] Bultmann 1956, 185.

[4] Bultmann 1956, 186.

[5] Martin 1976, 162, referring to Sevenster 1961, 113f., and Vincent 1897, 143; Michaelis 1935, 70; Beare 1959, 152-153.

from the perspective of ancient discussions of friendship.[6] I shall draw attention to the language of friendship in Phil 4:10-20, but before doing so, I briefly point to the occurrence of such language in other parts of the letter. Paul's use of this language is in fact at the heart of his strategy in dealing with the problems faced by his readers.[7]

Two short definitions of friendship, occurring already in Aristotle, are used by Paul in Philippians: friends are people of one soul (1:27; cf. 2:2), and they think the same thing (2:2; 4:2); a third one, that friends have all things in common, is reflected in Paul's repeated concern with sharing in the letter (1:5, 7; 2:1).[8] In addition, numerous clichés from the literature on friendship are scattered throughout the letter: friends rejoice together (1:4, 18, 25; 2:2, 28, 29; 3:1; 4:1, 4, 10),[9] have confidence in each other because of their constancy and loyalty (1:6, 14, 25; 2:24),[10] defer to each other (2:8, 17, 27, 30),[11] and engage in mutual enterprises (note the cognates with σύν: συνεργός, 2:25; 4:3; συναθλέω, 1:27; 4:2; συστρατιώτης, 2:25; σύζυγος, 4:3; συγκοινωνός, 2:8, 17, 27, 30). The point is that 4:10-20 is not unique in using friendship language, but is in fact the culmination of a letter that employs such language from its very beginning.

## 3. Friendship Language in Philippians 4:10-20

Modern scholarship has interpreted 4:10-20 as Paul's thank you note for a financial contribution he had received from the Philippians, but has then found it difficult to fit this text into the remainder of the canonical letter or the historical situation that the canonical letter may be taken to presuppose. The frustration caused by Paul's "danklose(r) Dank",[12] expressed so late in the letter, has contributed to a prepared-

---

[6] Berry 1992; Fitzgerald 1992b; Reumann 1992. I am particularly indebted to Berry, who deals with some of the same material I do.

[7] See also White 1990.

[8] Clichés describing friendship are conveniently collected by Bohnenblust 1905. μία ψυχή: Arist., *Eth. Nic.* 9.8 1168b6ff.; Diog. Laert. 5.20; Plut., *De amic. mult.* 96E; cf. Acts 4:36; τὸ αὐτὸ φρονεῖν: Cic., *De amic.* 15, 16, 21; Dio Chrys., *Or.* 34.20; Dion. Halic., *Ant. R.* 4.20.4,2; 7.59.7.5, 9; 8.15.1.6; κοινὰ τὰ φίλων: Plato, *Lysis* 207C; Cic., *De off.* 1.51; Diog. Laert. 8.10; cf. Acts 4:3.

[9] On this commonplace in letters, see Stowers 1986, 61, 65, 83, 99, who provides examples.

[10] Cic., *De amic.* 33-34, 64-65; Plut., *De amic. mult.* 95AB; *De adulat.* 52A-53B. See, further, Steinmetz 1967, 116-123.

[11] Cic., *De amic.* 34, 69-73.

[12] A description by Dibelius 1937, 95, often repeated, most recently by Schiefer Ferrari 1991, 271. Peterman 1991 has suggested that Paul follows a convention according to which one withheld verbal gratitude from social intimates. Stowers 1986, 61 refers to the commonplace that friends need not verbally express their thanks.

ness to view these verses as a thank you note written on an earlier occasion, which a later redactor combined with a number of other fragments to compose the letter in the form in which we now have it.[13] I do not wish here to address in detail the matter of the letter's integrity; suffice it to say that I think the letter in its present shape makes perfectly good sense. My interest is rather to point out that 4:10-20 contains a number of the clichés of friendship also found elsewhere in the letter, and that it is reasonable to attempt to understand the passage in light of Paul's playing on the theme of friendship. Let me just note a few of those themes which will assist us in gaining a firmer grasp on Paul's intention.

Basic to ancient friendship was the notion of sharing, including sharing the adversity encountered by a friend. Cicero says, "… friendship adds a brighter radiance to prosperity and lessens the burden of adversity by dividing and sharing it" (*De amic.* 22); one may have pride in aiding a friend and sharing his dangers (Lucian, *Toxaris* 7). So Paul speaks of the Philippians as sharing his affliction (4:14).

Friends also shared benefits, including those of a material sort, and this "mutual interchange is … inseparable from friendship" (Cic., *De amic.* 26). Commercial language, for example, that of credits and debits, taken from the terminology of accountancy, was used to describe this interchange (Cic., *De amic.* 26). The obligation to share could result in cold calculation, however, and Cicero warned against it: "It surely is calling friendship to a very close and petty accounting to require it to keep an exact balance of credits and debits (*ratio acceptorum et datorum*). I think that true friendship is richer and more abundant than that and does not narrowly scan the reckoning lest it pay out more than it has received" (*De amic.* 58). Paul uses exactly the same language when in 4:15 he writes of the Philippians who had shared with him in giving and receiving (λόγος δόσεως καὶ λήμψεως = *ratio acceptorum et datorum*).

Seneca reflects another concern about sharing one's friendship when he considers when one should return a benefit. There is a fine line to be drawn. One does not want to be gauche and return a benefit too promptly. "He who hastens at all odds to make a return shows the feeling, not of a person that is grateful, but of a debtor. And, to put it briefly, he who is too eager to pay his debt is unwilling to be indebted, and he who is unwilling to be indebted is ungrateful" (*De ben.* 4.40.5). That does not mean, however, that one should delay in returning a benefit. Seneca again: "No gratitude is felt for a benefit when it has lingered long in the hands of him who gives it … Even though some delay should intervene, let us avoid in every way the appearance of having deliberately delayed; hesitation is the next thing to refusing, and gains no gratitude" (*De ben.* 2.1.2). But it is otherwise when circumstances prevent

---

[13] For discussion, see Fitzgerald 1992a.

one from reciprocating: "I am not responsible for the delay if I lack either the opportunity or the means" (*De ben.* 4.40.3).

I suggest that it is in the context of such discussions of friendship that we should understand Phil 4:10. The understanding of vs. 10 reflected by the Revised Standard Version has led to the consternation about the verse. That translation reads, "I rejoice in the Lord greatly that now at length you have revived your concern for me; you were indeed concerned for me, but you had no opportunity." Ralph Martin illustrates the difficulties commentators have with the verse. He thinks vs. 10a is a "roundabout and oblique allusion to the church's gift" which has caused scholars to describe it as Paul's "thankless thanks".[14] Martin surmises that Paul wrote in this way because he "felt a certain embarrassment over money matters, and that his ambiguous way of writing reflects something of a conflict between his desire to express gratitude for the gift received both recently and earlier (v. 15) and a concern to show himself superior to questions of depending on others for financial support."[15]

I wish to argue that once one recognizes the conventions about friendship with which 4:10-20 is replete, Paul is not roundabout or oblique, nor does he write a thankless thanks, nor is he embarrassed about money matters. What he does, rather, is to draw out, with the aid of such conventions, the significance of the gift as an act by which he and his readers had been drawn more closely together.

To begin with, Paul affirms that the Philippians had been concerned for him, had shown that concern on more than one occasion, and done so concretely from the time of his earliest association with them (vss. 15-16). Furthermore, he interprets the delay in their most recent contribution as due to a lack of opportunity, thus letting them know that he does not think they had deliberately delayed or hesitated. Seneca had said that no gratitude was felt for a benefit when it was long delayed. Paul, on the other hand, presuming that there was good reason for the delay, rejoiced greatly for their expressed concern. So, delay there had been, but rather than chiding them for it, Paul interprets it as failing to thwart the friendly intentions of his readers.

The positive way in which Paul interprets the Philippians' action is further evident in his use of ἀναθάλλειν, translated "revive" in the RSV ("now at length you have revived your concern for me"). I choose to translate ἀνεθάλετε τὸ ὑπὲρ ἐμοῦ φρονεῖν as "you have bloomed again, so far as your care for me is concerned." Commentators and lexicographers agree that this rendering is possible, even if most of them prefer another. My translation is influenced by my perception of the language of friendship in this letter. It is not unusual in such language to use agricultural or horticultural metaphors in describing friendship and its benefits. So Cicero

---

[14] Martin 1976, 160.
[15] Martin 1976, 161.

says that friendship is "desirable, not because we are influenced by the hope of gain, but because its entire fruit is in the love itself" (*De amic.* 31). And the response to an unsought kindness, he says elsewhere, should be to "imitate the fields, which return more than they receive" (*De off.* 1.15.48). Such language describes the generosity and lack of calculation with which true friends render benefits to each other. If understood thus, Paul's use of ἀναθάλλειν is intended as a compliment of the spontaneity and good will with which the Philippians made the contribution rather than as chiding for finally having ceased their neglect of him. In other words, rather than continuing to draw attention to the timing of the gift, as he had with ἤδη ποτε ("now finally"), Paul prefers to drive to the disposition that led to the contribution. The same thing is seen in his affirmation in vs. 17 that rather than seek the gift, he seeks the fruit that accrues to their credit.[16] So, rather than beginning the discussion of the Philippians' gift in the awkward fashion often attributed to him, Paul in fact does so positively, in a complimentary manner indebted to the discussions of friendship. Such discussions also inform vss. 11-13, the immediate context for his claim in vs. 11 that he is αὐτάρκης.

## 4. A More General View of Αὐτάρκεια

Before examining Philippians 4 more closely, I wish to draw attention to the idea of self-sufficiency, particularly in its non-technical meaning. I confine myself to the Cynics and Pythagoreans, who are adequate for my argument.[17]

Audrey Rich summarizes the Cynic view as follows:

> To Diogenes the Cynic, αὐτάρκεια meant, broadly speaking, two things: on the physical plane, contentment with the bare necessities of life; and on the spiritual level, complete detachment from the world and worldly values. The αὐτάρκης was the man who had dispensed with the superfluous in every department of life and reduced his needs to a minimum. All that he required for his material well-being was food,

---

[16] Attention has already been drawn to this type of language by Ebner 1991, 349 n. 118, who also points (348 n. 102) to καρπός (sc. *fructus*) in Cic., *Ad fam.* 13.22.2; 50.2; 65.2; *De amic.* 31 (see also 22); Aristotle, *Ep.* 3.

[17] The literature on self-sufficiency is immense. Useful general discussions are Wilpert 1950; Rabe 1971; Vischer 1965; Ebner 1991, 338-343. For the Cynics, see Niehues-Pröbsting 1979, 148-206, esp. 155-158, 184-198. While it is always important to do justice to the differences between philosophical schools on a particular matter, there was nevertheless a tendency toward a vulgarization of philosophical ethics. On the phenomenon, see Malherbe 1992, 332. It may be that people were no longer interested in the philosophical foundations of such moral topics (thus Dihle 1966, 666, cf. 652ff.), yet their philosophical allegiances nevertheless provided distinct perspectives on the common coin of moral discourse. It is sufficient for my immediate purpose to draw attention to common elements in that discourse.

shelter and clothing of the meanest sort; his spiritual needs could be satisfied by virtue alone, the possession of which was sufficient to ensure happiness. The Cynic, then, had no desire for wealth, knowledge, pleasure or friendship. In his mind all these would be classed together as unnecessary luxuries. Nothing, in fact, that was to be derived from any source external to himself had any value for him or could affect him in any way. The Cynic aimed at αὐτάρκεια as it was exemplified in Diogenes, and his motive in doing so was obvious. Self-sufficiency alone, in the Cynic view, can give security and immunise man against the ills inflicted by Fortune.[18]

Self-sufficiency in its most uncompromising form continued to be the ideal of many Cynics. A few examples illustrate this attitude. The Cynic in the pseudo Lucianic *Cyniscus* (15) prays: "I pray that I may not need bedclothes any more than the lions, nor expensive fare than the dogs. But may I be αὐτάρκης in having for my bed the whole earth, may I consider the universe my house, and choose for food that which is easiest to procure. Gold and silver I do not need, neither I nor any of my friends. For from the desire of these grow up all men's ills-civic strife, wars, conspiracies and murders. All these have as their fountainhead the desire for more. But may this desire be far from us, and never may I reach out for more (πλεονεξία) than my share, but be able to put up with less than my share."

Another example is provided by the rigorous Cynic Demetrius, the friend of Seneca, and thus a contemporary of Paul. According to Seneca, Demetrius used to scorn theory and scientific speculation because they served no practical purpose. For example, Demetrius claimed that people given to gluttony and lust could not know true pleasure. True pleasure, he said, comes, not from the hedonistic life, but comes from on high and is "constant, serene, always unclouded, (and) is experienced by the man who is skilled in the laws of gods and men ... Such a man rejoices in the present, and puts no faith in the future; for he who leans upon uncertainties can have no sure support. Free, therefore, from the great anxieties that rack the mind, there is nothing that he hopes for or covets (*cupit*), and, content (*contentus*) with what he has, he does not plunge into what is doubtful. And do not suppose that he is content with a little, for all things are really his as a wise man."[19]

A reaction against the austere Cynicism represented by Demetrius had already set in two centuries earlier. Bion of Borysthenes represented this milder strain of Cynicism. The term αὐτάρκεια does not occur in the surviving fragments of his work; of greater significance is that he represents the attitude of this type of Cynicism toward the world which became widespread. For such Cynics, αὐτάρκεια was not so much a stern renunciation of the world as an attempt to adapt oneself to the

---

[18] Rich 1956, 23.

[19] Seneca, *De ben.* 7.2.4-5. For Demetrius' freedom from want, see Billerbeck 1979, 20-31, and further, on his philosophy, Kindstrand 1980.

world and changing circumstances just as an actor adapts himself to the varied roles he has to play.[20] Here self-sufficiency becomes synonymous with the widely used phrases ἀρκεῖσθαι τοῖς παροῦσιν, "to be satisfied with what is at hand," and χρᾶσθαι τοῖς παροῦσιν "to make do with what is at hand."[21]

How self-sufficiency was understood in this sense appears from the tractate Περὶ Αὐταρκείας by Teles, in which Teles is primarily concerned with the wise man's attitude toward poverty. Teles develops the theme that the wise man adapts himself to circumstances, and that he is not really in want of things since he has learned to be satisfied with what is at hand. As the good actor performs well whatever part the poet assigns him, so the good man acts well whatever role Fortune should lay upon him. The good man therefore does not fight poverty, for it does not really deprive him of the necessities of life. The hungry man, for instance, eats with greater relish than the man who habitually stuffs himself. The good man does not blame the circumstances in which he finds himself, nor does he attempt to change them, but prepares himself to adapt to them, just as sailors prepare themselves for the sea. They do not attempt to change the wind and sea, but prepare themselves to turn with them. In the same way, the good man uses what is at hand and so is self-sufficient. He lives with the circumstances allotted to him. If he deals with them in one way they will appear favorable and easy, but if in another, they will appear harsh. This αὐτάρκεια, then, is not a withdrawing into oneself, but an acceptance of one's circumstances and a concern to discover value in them.[22]

Characteristic of these Cynic attitudes is their individualism; only very seldom is the focus wide enough to include anyone else. Other philosophers, however, did take into consideration the social dimension. Note, for example, the way the ideal king, who is taken to be the paragon of self-sufficiency, is described in a tractate on kingship attributed to the Pythagorean Ecphantus:

> In so far as (the ideal king) has a sacred and divine mentality he will cause all good things, but nothing that is evil. And he will clearly be just, one who has κοινωνία with all. For κοινωνία consists in equality (ἰσότης), and while in the distribution of equality justice plays the most important part, yet κοινωνία has its share. For it is impossible to be unjust while giving a share of equality, or to give a share of equality and not be κοινωνός. And could anyone doubt that the self-sufficient man is self-controlled? For extravagance is the mother of self-indulgence, which in turn is the mother of insolence (ὕβρις), from which most human ills arise. But self-sufficiency does not beget extravagance or her brood. Rather, self-sufficiency, being a primal en-

---

[20] See the discussion in Kindstrand 1976, 64-67.

[21] For ἀρκεῖσθαι τοῖς παροῦσιν, see Xenophon, *Symp.* 4.42; Teles, *Fr.* IVA (38, 10-11; 41, 12 Hense); Epict., *Diss.* 1.1.27; cf. Heb 13:5; 1 Tim 6:8. For χρᾶσθαι τοῖς παροῦσιν, see Philo, *Quod omn. prob.* 122; Dio Chrys., *Or.* 30.33; Plut., *De exilio* 606D.

[22] *Fr.* IVB; text and translation in O'Neil 1977, 48-54.

tity, leads all things, but is itself led by nothing, and precisely this is a property alike of God and the king himself, to be the ruler, but to be ruled by no one … In ruling over men and in controlling his own life he uses one and the same virtue, not amassing acquisitions on account of any lack, for his personal service, but doing as one does in a life of action according to nature. For although κοινωνία exists, each man nevertheless lives sufficient unto himself. For in conducting his life the self-sufficient man needs nothing outside himself; and if he must live an active life, and take other factors into account, he nonetheless will keep his self-sufficiency. For as he will have his friends as a result of his own virtue, so in making use of them he acts in accordance with no other virtue than what he uses also in his own life.[23]

For our purpose, it is important to notice that αὐτάρκεια has become widely used, by people of many persuasions, most frequently without the intellectual or psychological baggage of Stoicism. It is also of interest that the non-Cynic self-sufficient man is concerned with κοινωνία, φιλία, and virtue, and that in his social relations his self-sufficiency consists in equality. As self-sufficient, he lacks nothing. He takes into consideration the circumstances under which he lives, but nevertheless remains self-sufficient.

## 5. Friendship and Self-Sufficiency

Below the surface of Ecphantus' text shimmers a problem that becomes overt in discussions of friendship: how could a friend claim self-sufficiency and still participate in the exchange of benefits, which, we have noted, was central to friendship? The problem was discussed with great regularity, particularly in connection with the motives or reasons for friendship. A variety of reasons were given, two of which concern us. The highest form of friendship, according to Aristotle, was that which arose between two people because of their similarity in character or virtue (*Eth. Nic.* 8.3.1-9). A less noble reason, advocated by Epicurus and roundly rejected by others, especially the Stoics, was utilitarian, namely, that friendship arises out of need or for the attainment of certain goals, such as happiness or tranquility.[24]

Cicero shows us how these two conflicting views had entered non-technical discussion by the first century B.C. Virtue, he says, "is the parent and preserver of friendship and without virtue friendship cannot exist at all. To proceed, then, let us interpret the word 'virtue' by the familiar usage of our everyday life and speech, and not in pompous phrase apply it to the precise standards which certain philosophers use; and let us include in the number of good men those who are so considered …

---

[23] This extract of Stobaeus (4.7.66 = 4.278, 23-279, 20 Hense) is printed in Thesleff 1965, 83,18-84, 8. For this and other Neopythagorean tractates on kingship, see Goodenough 1928.

[24] See Diog. Laert. 10.120; Mitsis 1988, 98-128, for the Epicureans. For rejection of their position, see Cicero, *De amic.* 27-28, 30; Seneca, *Ep.* 9.17.

who satisfy the ordinary standard of life" (*De amic.* 21; cf. 33, 100). "It is far from being true that friendship is cultivated because of need (*indigentiam*); rather it is cultivated by those who are most abundantly blessed with wealth and power and especially with virtue, which is man's best defence; by those least in need of another's help; and by those most generous and most given to acts of kindness ... It is not the case, therefore, that friendship attends upon advantage, but advantage (*utilitas*) attends upon friendship" (*De amic.* 51).

Friends show goodwill and affection for each other, rejoice with each other, and share the burdens of adversity. "... friends, though they be absent, are at hand; though in need, yet abound; though weak, are strong; and—harder saying still— though dead, are yet alive ..." (*De amic.* 23). All this being so, how can friends be said to be self-sufficient?

Cicero's answer is that "to the extent that a man relies upon himself and is so fortified by virtue and wisdom that he is dependent on no one and considers all his possessions to be within himself, in that degree is he most conspicuous for seeking out and cherishing friendships. Now what need did Africanus have of me? By Hercules! none at all. And I, assuredly, had no need of him either, but I loved him because of a certain admiration for his virtue, and he, in turn, loved me, because, it may be, of the fairly good opinion which he had of my character ..." (*De amic.* 30).

Yes, "the wise man is self-sufficient. Nevertheless, he desires friends, neighbors, and associates no matter how much he is sufficient unto himself ... In this sense the wise man is self-sufficient, that he can do without friends, not that he desires to do without them." (Seneca, *Ep.* 9.3, 5).

So, it is on the basis of virtue, understood in the ordinary, general sense, that a friendship is formed. One seeks out the person who is worthy of one's friendship, Plutarch says, and attaches oneself to him (*De amic. mult.* 94E). The more fully one understands this, the more fully one grasps the truth that one does not develop friendships because of need; indeed, true friendship does not proceed from need but virtue, the virtuous person seeking a friend who is like himself.

## 6. *Philippians 4*

Now, how does Philippians 4 read in light of all this? We begin with vs. 8, Paul's exhortation that his readers reflect on a list of moral qualities which constitutes the most Greek verse in all of Paul's letters. That ἀρετή, virtue, occurs in the climax of the list should not disconcert us; we remember that Cicero spoke of virtue in an ordinary sense, descriptive of a good person.[25] The qualities Paul enumerates are precisely those which would universally characterize such a person. Parallel to what the Philippians are to reflect on (λογίζεσθε) in vs. 8 is what they are to do (πράσσετε) in vs. 9, and that is what they have heard, received and heard from Paul. Paul, in other words, is to continue to be the paradigm for their moral conduct. While it is not explicitly stated that Paul embodies the virtues enumerated, the list functions to delineate the paradigm he presents. Cicero would say that the quality of character without which friendship could not exist was present in Paul and that the Philippians had accepted him as worthy of their friendship.

In vs. 10, I have argued, Paul compliments them for the friendly disposition with which they had recently shown their friendship to him. Then, in vss. 11-13, he is at great pains to make certain they understand that he did not consider their gift in a utilitarian manner: Paul had rejoiced over their gift, which should not, however, be taken to mean that he rejoiced because his need was met, for he was αὐτάρκης. Self-sufficiency is thus introduced in a discussion of friendly social relations. The circumstances in which Paul learned to be αὐτάρκης are illustrated by a series of six (resp. five) infinitives, which reveal an understanding of self-sufficiency very much like that of Teles: Whatever the circumstances one encounters, go with them. Paul can do so because Christ empowers him.[26]

There is no Stoic introspection present here despite the long exegetical tradition that has brought the Stoic notion into play. Paul is essentially concerned with personal relationships rather than introspection. His purpose, here in the conclusion of his letter, is to strengthen the tie of friendship that binds him and his readers by raising the matter of their gift to a higher plane, that of friendship. But, in denying that he viewed their gift in terms of need, Paul stresses his sufficiency to such a degree that the value of the gift could be put in question. Anticipating this, Paul qualifies (πλήν) his statement, once more with a cliché of friendship: they nevertheless did well in sharing in his affliction (vs. 14), thus acting in the way friends act.

To say that Paul describes his relations with the Philippians in the clichés of friendship and that he does not indulge in introspection is not to imply that there is no other dimension to that relationship. Vss. 10-20 opens with a thanksgiving to the Lord for the Philippians' concern for him (vs. 10), and the section closes with a doxology (vs. 20). Within this *inclusio* Paul expresses the conviction that as he was empowered to be αὐτάρκης in all circumstances, God out of his riches will supply the Philippians' every need (vs. 19). Indeed, what Paul had already received was a sacrificial gift acceptable to God (vs. 18). As he does elsewhere, then, Paul uses the moral philosophical language of his day, but places it within a larger framework

---

[25] Ἀρετή, understood in the Greek sense of moral achievement or excellence, appears contradictory to Paul's ethics. See Schrage 1988, 217-218, and the literature cited there. Wibbing 1959, 103 correctly thinks that Paul uses the word here in a general sense.

[26] The formal features of Paul's statement heightens the significance of ἐν τῷ ἐνδυναμοῦντί με: Schiefer Ferrari 1991, 273-277.

quite foreign to the philosophical tradition he uses.[27]

Paul's deft use of the language of friendship shows that he was fully aware of how the subject was being discussed and was able to use the language for his own purpose. What strikes one, however, is that he does not actually use φίλος or φιλία. This omission could only have been deliberate, but why did Paul avoid these words? He does so elsewhere, too, and various reasons have been suggested for the omission.

Paul may in general have avoided these words because of the anthropocentric connotations they carried, whereas in his view Christian relationships were determined by God.[28] There may, however, also have been local circumstances that contributed to his avoidance. He may have omitted them from 1 Thess 5:9-12 because he wanted his readers to avoid social attitudes like those associated with the Epicureans, which were tied up with φιλία.[29] Perhaps he did not use them in his correspondence with the Corinthians because he refused their offer of friendship with its attendant obligations.[30] Something similar may also have been behind his omission in Philippians; it is likely, I think, that Epaphroditus, with the Philippians' contribution had brought a letter from them in which they expressed their desire, as Paul's friends, to meet his needs.[31] Paul's denial that he is speaking καθ᾽ ὑστέρησιν could then mark a move to a yet higher level of discussion that even dispenses with φίλος and φιλία. But the matter deserves closer scrutiny.

## Bibliography

Beare, F. W. 1959: *The Epistle to the Philippians* (Harper's New Testament Ccommentary), New York: Harper & Brothers 1959.

Berry, Ken L. 1992: "The Function of Friendship Language in Philippians 4:10-20", Unpub. paper.

Billerbeck, Margarethe 1979: *Der Kyniker Demetrius. Ein Beitrag zur Geschichte der frühkaiserzeitlichen Popularphilosophie* (Philosophia Antiqua 36) Leiden: E. J. Brill 1979.

Bohnenblust, G. 1905: *Beiträge zum Topos Περὶ Φιλίας*, Inaug. Diss., Univ. Bonn, Berlin: Gustav Schade (Otto Francke) 1905.

Bultmann, Rudolf 1956: *Primitive Christianity in Its Contemporary Setting*, Cleveland, OH: Collins 1956.

---

[27] For numerous other examples where he does the same thing, see Malherbe 1989. See also Stowers 1991, 117-121 on friendship and theology in the letter.

[28] Sevenster 1954/55.

[29] Malherbe 1987, 104.

[30] Marshall 1987.

[31] Malherbe 1990, 254 and n. 44.

Dibelius, Martin 1937: *An die Thessalonicher I-II. An die Philipper* (HNT 11), Tübingen: J. C. B. Mohr (Paul Siebeck) 1937.

Dihle, Abrecht 1966: "Ethik", in: *RAC* 6, Stuttgart: Hiersemann 1966, 646-796.

Ebner, Martin 1991: *Leidenslisten und Apostelbrief: Untersuchungen zu Form, Motivik und Funktion der Peristasenkatalogen bei Paulus* (Forschung zur Bibel 66), Würzburg: Echter 1991.

Fitzgerald, John T. 1992a: "Philippians, Epistle to the', in: *Anchor Bible Dictionary*. New York: Doubleday 1992:5, 318-26.

— 1992b: "Philippians 4 in Light of Some Ancient Discussions of Friendship", Unpub. paper.

Goodenough, Erwin R. 1928: "The Political Philosophy of Hellenistic Kingship", in: *YCS* 1 (1928) 52-102.

Kindstrand, Jan Fredrik 1976: *Bion of Borysthenes* (AUU. Studia Graeca Upsaliensia 11) Uppsala: Almqvist & Wiksell 1976.

— 1980: "Demetrius the Cynic", in: *Philologus* 124 (1980) 83-98.

Malherbe, Abraham J. 1987: *Paul and the Thessalonians: The Philosophical Tradition of Pastoral Care*, Philadelphia, PA: Fortress 1987.

— 1989: *Paul and the Popular Philosophers*, Minneapolis, MN: Fortress 1989.

— 1990: "Did the Thessalonians Write to Paul?" in: R. T. Fortna & B. R. Gaventa (eds.), *The Conversation Continues: Studies in Paul and John in Honor of J. Louis Martyn*, Nashville, KY: Abingdon 1990, 246-57.

— 1992: "Hellenistic Moralists and the New Testament", in: *ANRW* 2.26.1, Berlin/New York: de Gruyter 1992, 267-333.

Marshall, Peter 1987: *Enmity in Corinth: Social Conventions in Paul's Relations with the Corinthians* (WUNT 2.23), Tübingen: J. C. B. Mohr (Paul Siebeck) 1987.

Martin, Ralph 1976: *Philippians* (NCeB), Grand Rapids, MI: Eerdmans 1976.

Michaelis, W. 1935: *Der Brief des Paulus an die Philipper* (ThHK 11), Leipzig: Deichert 1935.

Mitsis, P. 1988: *Epicurus' Ethical Theory: The Pleasures of Invulnerability*, Ithaca, NY: Cornell Univ. Press 1988.

Niehues-Pröbsting, Heinrich 1979: *Der Kynismus des Diogenes und der Begriff des Zynismus*, Munich: Wilhelm Fink 1979.

O'Neil, Edward N. 1977: *Teles (the Cynic Teacher)* (SBL.TT 11), Missoula, MT: Scholars Press 1977.

— 1978: "De cupiditate divitiarum (Moralia 523C-528B)", in: H. D. Betz (ed.), *Plutarch's Ethical Writings and Early Christianity* (SCHNT 1), Leiden: E. J. Brill 1978, 289-362.

Peterman, Gerald W. 1991: "'Thankless Thanks': The Epistolary Social Convention in Philippians 4:10-20", in: *TynB* 42 (1991) 261-70.

Rabe, H. 1971: "Autarkie, autark", in: J. Ritter et al. (eds.), *Historisches Wörterbuch der Philosophie*, Basel: Schwabe 1971, 685-91.

Reumann, John 1992: "Philippians, Especially Chapter 4, as a 'Letter of Friendship'", Unpub. paper.

Rich A. N. M. 1956: "The Cynic Conception of AUTARKEIA", in: *Mnemosyne* Ser. 4.9 (1956) 23-29.

Schiefer Ferrari, Markus 1991: *Die Sprache des Leids in den paulinischen Peristasenkatalogen* (SBB 23), Stuttgart: Katholisches Bibelwerk 1991.

Schrage, Wolfgang, 1988: *The Ethics of the New Testament*, Philadelphia, PA: Fortress 1988.

Sevenster, J. N. 1954/55: "Waarom spreekt Paulus nooit van vrienden en vriendschap?" in: *NedThT* 9 (1954/1955) 356-63.

— 1961: *Paul and Seneca* (NT.S 4), Leiden: E. J. Brill 1961.

Steinmetz, Fritz-Arthur 1967: *Die Freundschaftslehre des Panaitios: Nach einer Analyse von Ciceros 'Laelius de amicita'* (Palingenesia 3), Wiesbaden: Steiner 1967.

Stowers, Stanley K. 1986: *Letter Writing in Greco-Roman Antiquity,* Philadelphia, PA: Westminster 1986.

— 1991: "Friends and Enemies in the Politics of Heaven", in: Jouette M. Bassler (ed.), *Pauline Theology I: Thessalonians, Philippians, Galatians, Philemon,* Minneapolis, MN: Fortress 1991, 104-21.

Thesleff, Holger 1965: *The Pythagorean Texts of the Hellenistic Period* (AAAbo, Ser. A 30.1), Åbo: Åbo Akademi 1965.

Vincent, M. 1897: *The Epistles to the Philippians and to Philemon* (ICC), Edinburgh: T. & T. Clark 1897.

Vischer R. 1965: *Das Einfache Leben: Wort- und motivgeschichtliche Untersuchungen zu einem Wertbegriff der antiken Literatur,* Göttingen: Vandenhoeck & Ruprecht 1965, 60-87.

White, L. Michael 1990: "Morality Between Two Worlds: A Paradigm of Friendship in Philippians", in: David L. Balch et al. (eds.), *Greeks, Romans, and Christians: Essays in Honor of Abraham J. Malherbe,* Minneapolis, MN: Fortress 1990, 201-15.

Wibbing, Siegfried 1959: *Die Tugend- und Lasterkataloge im Neuen Testament und ihre Traditionsgeschichte unter besonderer Berücksichtigung der Qumran-Texte* (BZNW 25), Berlin: Töpelmann 1959.

Wilpert, P. 1950: "Autarkie", in: *RAC* 1, Stuttgart: Hiersemann 1950, 1039-50.

# A Social-Scientific Criticism of 1 Peter

Birger Olsson

## 1. Introductory Remarks

Some scientific monographs, also in the Biblical field, develop into new methods or schools. John H. Elliott's book *A Home for the Homeless* seems to belong to this category, which in the first edition of 1981 was subtitled "A Sociological Exegesis of 1 Peter", and in the paperback edition of 1990, "A Social-Scientific Criticism of 1 Peter". The change of the subtitle exposes the development towards another new approach among all the others in the New Testament exegesis of today. This method has now been introduced in the American Guides to Biblical Scholarship series in John H. Elliott's: "What is Social-Scientific Criticism?", published in 1993.[1]

Work on basic methodological questions was an important part of Lars Hartman's period as professor in Uppsala, especially as regards different kinds of text-oriented analyses. A quick look at his bibliography shows such an interest.[2] Lars Hartman is a very strong analyser, able to ask probing questions of everything. All of us who were members of the seminar in Uppsala are very much aware of that. Even when he had a very high appreciation of what was written he posed his questions. What follows is of the same style but not of the same critical depth. I genuinely appreciate J. H. Elliott's works, but there are still questions.

John H. Elliott's second book on 1 Peter is a very important contribution both to the interpretation of this "step-child" in modern New Testament scholarship—as Elliott has characterised the letter—and to the history of Early Christianity.[3] For a very long time 1 Peter has been read from a strongly Pauline perspective and in our century it has been primarily analysed as a conglomeration of different kinds of traditions. Now 1 Peter, which in many ways is a central letter from the early Christian

---

[1] Elliott 1981; idem 1990; idem 1993. References to pages in the text will refer to these books of Elliott.

[2] See also Olsson 1985.

[3] Elliott wrote his dissertation on 1 Peter 2:4–10. Se Elliott 1966. The characterisation of 1 Peter is found in idem 1976.

movement, is being released from its Pauline captivity and its one-sided historical-genetic approaches. We can easily see this change if we compare this new book by Elliott with his first one. There is now a very strong emphasis on the synchronic, social dimension of the letter. One first question is whether 1 Peter in its new freedom has been captivated again by some sociological theories, or whether these changes are only shifts of perspective. 1 Peter, interpreted by us, will never be "free".

It is easy to mention positive things about Elliott's work:

> • the many contributions in details to the exegesis of 1 Peter, not least concerning the receivers of the letter
> • the description of the early Christian movement and especially of the situation in Asia Minor in New Testament time
> • the new and fresh interdisciplinary approach
> • the focus on the socio-religious strategy of an ancient document
> • the interest for broadening the exegetical art, which has been bound for such a long time to historical and theological aspects alone.

I could make this list much longer but in this article I want to formulate some critical questions about his analysis, about his results and, even more, about his method, or methods.[4] I will comment on six aspects:

> (1) the analytical procedure in general
> (2) the summarising periphrastic outline at the end of the book
> (3) theory-bound observations and over-interpretations
> (4) the literary strategy and other strategies
> (5) the evaluation 1990, and
> (6) the new subdiscipline of exegesis 1993.

## 2. A Sociological Exegesis

> This study is an exercise in sociological exegesis … A more comprehensive description of the method would be a "literary-historical-sociological-theological analysis" (pp. 7,8).

There is a description of the method in the introduction but I am now more interested in what is done in the five chapters which in many ways can be read as separate essays. There are many repetitions, especially in chaps. 3 and 4, and it is perhaps not so easy to give a good answer to the question: What is he doing?

In *chap. 1* we find an analysis of a single Greek word. What is the meaning and

---

[4] I discussed the analysis of 1 Peter with John H. Elliott at the SBL Meeting in Dallas, Texas, and wrote a review in Swedish in *SEÅ*. See Olsson 1984.

use of πάροικος? We get an answer in the same way as we have, for example, in *Theologisches Wörterbuch zum Neuen Testament*. When 1 Peter is analysed some related words are added: παρεπίδημοι, διασπορά, Βαβυλών. There is only one example of πάροικος in 1 Peter and one of παροικία. As πάροικοι the addressees are identified as "displaced persons", characterized by "political, legal, social and religious limitation and estrangement", like rural people, relocated to cities, or immigrant artisans, craftsmen, traders, and so on. This result is the first step in Elliott's interpretation of 1 Peter.

*Chap. 2* continues to analyse the addressees, now regarding their social profile. What do we know about the geographical area, the topography, the population and the ethnic composition? The legal, economic and social condition of the addressees is described mainly from "their identification as πάροικοι" and the religious identity from "the sectarian character" of the intended recipients. A sect sociology from Bryan R. Wilson and others about sect types, sect conditions and sect developments is used in the interpretation of 1 Peter and we get a much more concrete picture of the addressees: as πάροικοι in a technical meaning they were attracted by the Christian message and fellowship and became Christians but as such they only experienced a continuous social polarization, combined with a threat to the internal cohesion.

*Chap. 3* reads 1 Peter as a response to the παροικία situation described in the two first chapters, or more precisely with Elliott's own words: as "a response to those problems with which conversionist sects in general must struggle" (p. 102). With this sociological, or sectarian screen Elliott sees two main aspects of the conflict of the addressees: the *distinctiveness* and the *solidarity* of the community. "The comparative use of a sect typology" gives us a still more concrete picture of the problems in Asia Minor and, in addition, of the response of 1 Peter. Elliott therefore can describe the socio-religious strategy of the letter as an attempt to counteract the demoralizing and disintegrating impact of social tension upon the Christian sect by reassuring them of their identity, reminding them of the cohesion *within* and the separation *without*, and providing them with a rationale for continuous commitment and faith.

*Chap. 4* clarifies the strategy a step further by focusing the role and function of the model of the household (οἶκος): the meaning of οἶκος in 1 Peter 4:17 and 2:5, οἶκος as a term and social reality in the Graeco-Roman world, in the Old Testament, in the New Testament and in Early Christianity, employing the same procedure as he did with πάροικοι but without any sociological theory as an analogue of the ancient οἶκος. At last 1 Peter is analysed with this background, and we get the following results:

The concept of the household thus serves an integrative literary, theological and sociological function. The identification and exhortation of the Christian communities as the household of God were a most direct, realistic and cogent way of correlating religious rationale and social reality. The most obvious and ingenious example of such correlation is the set of terms used to describe the social condition and divine vocation of the audience and the authors: *paroikoi* and *oikos tou theou* (p. 231).

*Chap.* 5 which treats the ideological implications of 1 Peter, its collective authorship and its role in the Christian movement in general is not clearly integrated to the previous chapters. I would like to concentrate my critique on the first four chapters.

First a few comments on some significant features in Elliott's analysis:

(1) The sociological exegesis begins with *a single word* (πάροικος), even commenting on syllables:

The composite substantive *par-oikos* derives its meaning from the denotations and connotations of the *oik*-root and such terms as *oikos, oikia, oikeo* and *oikeios*. ... As these and many related *oik*-terms refer to kith and kin, friend and brother, the familiar and familial, so, contrariwise, *paroikos* (*paroikein, paroikia,* etc.) denotes the strange, the alien, the foreign, the "other" (p. 24).

But words do not function in this way. Since this kind of "word-exegesis" depends on the sociological method, as I see it, I will discuss it later on. In this context we can notice the love of single words. How πάροικοι and related words are used *in combination with* other words is often not analysed adequately (1:1, 14; 2:11 etc.), the argumentation in a paragraph is frequently overlooked and the phenomenon *text* is noticeably absent from this interpretation of a "specific biblical *text*" (p. 7). The sociological model is very closely connected with lexical studies.

If the main purpose is to interpret a document (a text) we must have some kind of text model. Let us take this one:[5]

---

[5] Hellholm 1980, 16f. and Wiklander 1984, 40, who have taken this model from E. Gülich and W. Raible. I am not sure that Elliott will accept this model because he is emphasizing texts as social phenomena, Elliott 1993, 49–55. Different kinds of text models can explain the many criticisms we have today.

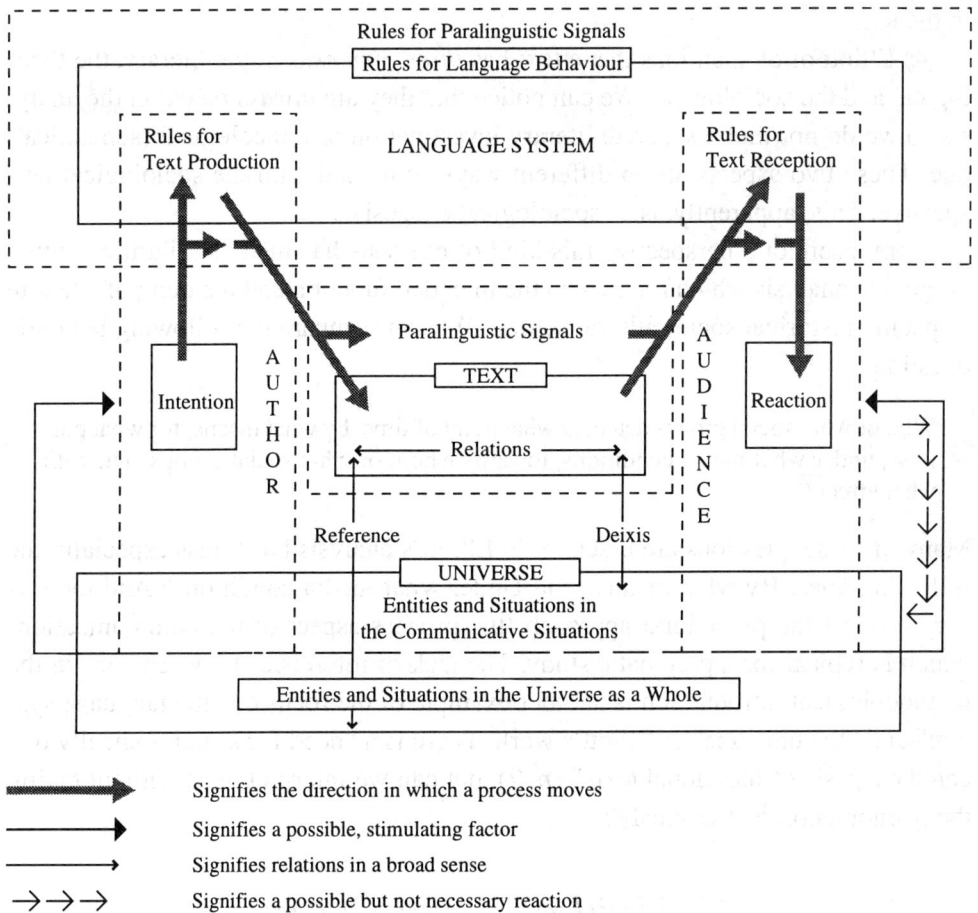

| | |
|---|---|
| ![arrow] | Signifies the direction in which a process moves |
| ![arrow] | Signifies a possible, stimulating factor |
| ![arrow] | Signifies relations in a broad sense |
| →→→ | Signifies a possible but not necessary reaction |

Elliott begins with "the language system" but has no interest for the rules of the text production or text reception. The first chapter is an ordinary lexical study of a few words (especially one word, πάροικος) referring to the audience in the text. There is no analysis of all the words in 1 Peter, which refer to the recipients.[6]

(2) There are no reflections about *the relation between a text and the historical reality*. Chap. 2 focuses on "the universe", but what is said about the real situation of the addressees is without comment transferred to the text level, not considering, for example, the sender(s) and his view of the addressees. Even here, "the text" is forgotten.

(3) *The audience and the author(s)* are symptomatically *separated* so that we meet the receivers mostly in the first chapters and the sender in the last chapter.

---

[6] This critique is also found in Feldmeier 1992, 203–10.

There is no dynamic process between these two main factors as they are manifested in the text.

(4) Elliott often mentions that a text has *three dimensions*: the literary, the theological and the sociological. We can notice that they are *always mixed* in the analysis so we do not find a separate literary investigation or a theological (semantical) one. These two aspects are in different ways combined with the sociological perspective. This, apparently, is a "sociological exegesis".

From a semiotic perspective this kind of exegesis has many similarities with a pragmatic analysis which focuses on the intended function and meaning of a text in a specific historical socio-cultural setting. We can compare the following heuristic question:

> Who or what social groups acted, at what point of time, by what means, for what purpose, under what media conditions, towards whom or what social groups, and with what effect?[7]

Many of these questions are essential in Elliott's analysis but I miss especially the following ones: By what means? and Under what media conditions? And there is very little of the procedural approach (the process aspect of the communication) which is typical for a pragmatic study. The lack of references to pragmatics in the methodological introduction is another example of the focus on "the language system" and "the universe" in Elliott's work. There is a "need for a sociologically oriented exegesis of individual texts" (p. 7), but can we interpret texts without taking the phenomenon *text* seriously?

## 3. A Periphrastic Outline of 1 Peter

> A periphrastic outline of 1 Peter which attempts to reflect the literary structure and composition of the text as closely as possible while also explicating its integrating theme and emphases ... (p. 234).

Elliott's exegesis of 1 Peter is in may ways summarized in an outline at the end of the book,[8] especially if we read it in the light of what is said in the previous chapters about the παροικία situation and the role and function of οἶκος. One way of react-

---

[7] Breuer 1977, 31.

[8] Elliott 1981, 234–36. This outline is not only a summary of the interpretation but also an attempt "to reflect the literary structure and composition of the text as closely as possible while also explicating its integrating theme and emphases" (p. 234). It is an important description of the strategy of the letter — including the rhetorical strategy—pace Elliott 1990, xxxi. Here the differences between "sectarian" strategy and literary strategy become obvious. My own interpretation of 1 Peter is found in Olsson 1982.

ing to Elliott's work is to read this summarizing display in comparison with the Greek text of 1 Peter, in a more ordinary exegetical manner. Such a reading raises a lot of questions, and I want to mention some of them. The division of the text, made explicit in this outline, is very traditional, and I will discuss it later on when I treat the literary strategy of the letter.

*Example 1*

1:3–2:10          By the mercy of God *you strangers in society* have become the elect and holy people of God, *the household of faith* (my emphases).

• Why are the addressees described as "strangers in society"? We find almost nothing about that in this section. They may have been πάροικοι in a technical meaning—or some of them—but they are not addressed as such here. Their new status is very much emphasized but not in comparison with other people of the time. The great division into two groups is introduced in 2:7–10 as a preparation to 2:11–4:11.

• Where do we find evidence that they all were πάροικοι before they become Christians? The only explicit phrase in this section, "during the time of your παροικία" (1:17) seems rather to imply that their time as Christians is a time of παροικία. Compare the temporal contrasts in 1:14 and 4:2–3.

• Why take the phrase "the household of faith" as the climactic description of the new and unique status of the addressees? The text is quite clear on this point:

But you are a chosen race, a royal priesthood, a holy nation, God's own people, that you may declare the wonderful deeds of him who called you out of darkness into his marvellous light. Once you were no people but now you are God's people; once you had not received mercy but now you have received mercy (2:9–10).

All these terms are honorific predicates of Israel now ascribed to the addressees. They are the people of God.[9] The author is using traditional terms about the people of God, not any οἶκος terminology.

*Example 2*

2:11–12          (Transition) As the elect and holy household of faith (1:3–2:10), *live as holy strangers* so that through *your distinctive style of behavior* even hostile outsiders ("Gentiles") might come to glorify God (my emphases).

• Are these two verses only a transition? You have, of course, transitional features in v. 11, as in every new beginning of a paragraph or section in 1 Peter. But these verses give us at the same time the main theme for the next two sections (2:11–3:12

---

[9] Elliott's separation of βασιλεῖον and ἱεράτευμα, partly motivated by a redactional analysis, has not convinced me; Elliott 1966; Olsson 1982, 79–81, 94–95.

and 3:13–4:11), expressed in positive form in v 12.

• Can you take "live as holy strangers" or "your distinctive style of behavior" as the theme or function of these verses? The main words are "maintain good conduct among the Gentiles" and "your good deeds". The first impression is something opposite to separation and distinctiveness. They have to live together with the Gentiles, and they have to live according to the Gentiles' standard, too. "Good deeds" in 1 Peter are not works of mercy, as exemplified in Matt 25:31–46, but socially accepted deeds, a behavior that could not be blamed with regard to what the society required.

## Example 3

3:7          Husbands, *live in household harmony* with your wives and respect them
             as coheirs of the grace of life (my emphases).

• Has the verb συνοικεῖν the meaning "to live in household harmony"? I seriously doubt it. What about κατὰ γνῶσιν? The whole phrase, read in its context, seems to mean "live with your wives according to (your new, Christian) insight", i.e., according to your new relation to God and Christ.

## Example 4

3:8–12       *All members of the household*, maintain *the unity of the community*; you
             have been called to avoid evil and do good (my emphases).

• Why take πάντες as "all members of the household"?—Perhaps all Christians in Asia Minor to the west of the Mountains of Tauros were members of οἶκοι, but, at any rate, they are not addressed as such here. Vv. 8–12 are not a part of a household code but the concluding remarks of 2:11–3:12, addressed to all recipients.

• Is the focus in these verses "the unity of the community"? You have this idea there but the emphasis is more on the relation between Christians and non-Christians. The most distinctive—and difficult—feature of this paragraph is the combination of relations of people *within* the community and relations to people *outside* it.

According to Elliott you have the same theme in 5:1–11: "maintain the unity of the brotherhood". Even if you find the word "brotherhood" as part of the argumentation, it is very difficult to follow Elliott here. The problem of suffering and glory, so dominant in 4:11ff., is taken up again with old and new arguments and with full assurance at the end that God will take care of his people and exult them in due time—if they humble themselves (within and outside the community).

*Example 5*

3:13–4:11     *Distinguish yourselves by the doing of good*, even in the face of outsiders'
          ("Gentiles'") hostility: God vindicates the righteous (my emphases).

• Is "distinctiveness" by "doing good" the theme or emphasis of this section? You
may find evidence for the idea of separation in 4:1–6, but not combined with "good
deeds". And the main part of the section has other themes: to reverence Christ as
Lord, to be prepared to make a defence, to follow the righteous one who preached
for the worst generation of all, died for the righteous and was exalted after that. The
temporal aspects are much more in the focus here than they were earlier in the argumentation about the suffering and the glory of the Christians (God's patience
waited, the rest of the time, the judgement, the end of all things).

The emphasis on distinctiveness returns as the theme of 4:12–19 in Elliott's display. Suffering is a distinguishing mark. Although the situation of the addressees
may be such, this is not the theme of 4:12–19.

Many of these questions can probably be answered by a reference to the main thesis
of Elliott's work:

> The correlation of *paroikia* and *oikos tou theou* and of the two disparate realities
> which they represented constitutes, in a nut-shell, the focus of the socioreligious
> strategy of 1 Peter, the heart of its evangelical message (p. 233).

This proposal implies two other theses:

1. The receivers and senders of the letter are πάροικοι in a technical meaning of
the word.

2. The community as οἶκος τοῦ θεοῦ is a sect of conversionist type with its problem of distinctiveness and solidarity.

A comparison with the text of 1 Peter seems in a first or a second reading not to give
sufficient evidence for these theses. You cannot explicitly or in a direct way see how
the text supports the given interpretation. The distance between text and exegesis
can, however, be rather wide. You may use a specific meta-language—for example,
psychological, sociological, or philosophical categories—in your analysis, or a specific language in order to convey the meaning to others. One problem in Elliott's
sociological exegesis, explicit in his periphrastic outline, is that he is using the terminology of the text, οἶκος, πάροικος, etc., but filling them with meaning either derived from sociological theories or dependent on such theories.

## 4. Theory-Bound Observations and Overinterpretations

A home for the homeless, an οἶκος for πάροικοι—how fitting such a description might be for Christian community as well! (p. 105).

Oh, yes! But how fitting is such a description for understanding 1 Peter? There are, as I see it, three basic premises behind Elliott's interpretation:

• The receivers (and the senders) are πάροικοι in the technical meaning of the word, and they were πάροικοι already before they became Christians.

> Living on the margin of political and social life, these *paroikoi* no doubt had seen in this new salvation movement new opportunity for social acceptance and improvement of their economic lot. Coming from the already suspect ranks of strangers, resident aliens and lower classes, however, these "Christlackeys" gained only further disdain for the exotic religion they embraced (p. 83).

• The communities addressed in 1 Peter has a sectarian composition. Bryan R. Wilson's "characterization of a 'conversionist response to the world' and its comprehension of evil and of salvation is that to which the community of 1 Peter most closely conforms" (p. 76).

• The problems of the addressees are "those problems with which conversionist sects in general must struggle" (p. 102), mainly the *distinctiveness* (status, identity) and the *solidarity* (group consciousness, internal cohesion) of the community.

These three premises undoubtedly depend on the application of a sociological theory to the exegesis of 1 Peter. It is "the comparative use of sect typology" that makes them necessary for the analysis of the text. In my view Elliott's interpretation presupposes that all three premises must be true. If they can be falsified, his interpretation must be dropped.

How, then, to prove these premises? We can, as Elliott does, refer to *external* and *internal* evidence. The first question is a very general one: What was the situation for Christian communities in Asia Minor? The second question is more restricted, limited to the analysed document: How can we find support for the premises (and the interpretation) in 1 Peter?

I would not like to discuss the external evidence here, only ask for some clarifications:

• Is 1 Peter addressed to *all* the Christians in the five provinces mentioned? If so, had all of them (including the senders in Rome) been πάροικοι before they became Christians? Were all the communities in this area of the same sectarian type? How were the senders acquainted with all of these people?

• Is 1 Peter addressed only to *certain παροικία communities* in this area, with members who had been πάροικοι before they became Christians?

• Is 1 Peter addressed to *some members* of the Christian communities in Asia Minor, to those who had been and still were πάροικοι? If so, how was the letter read in these mixed communities?

The letter as such seems to present itself as a message to all Christians in the congregation and to all communities in Asia Minor to the west of the Mountains of Tauros. Can Elliott's description of these Christians (formerly πάροικοι, predominantly rural, sectarian composition of a conversionist type etc.) be verified by material outside 1 Peter? That is an important question, and other more competent people can answer this question about "the reality". I would like to take up two aspects of the internal evidence given, the relation between the given exegesis and the text of 1 Peter. What kind of support can you get from 1 Peter itself?

## 4.1. Overinterpretations

The analogy of a conversionist sect functions best if the addressees were πάροικοι before they became Christians, and you find a lot of πάροικοι among country people. A part of Elliott's argumentation is that the addressees are "predominantly rural". We find the internal evidence for that on p. 63: *rural metaphors* (agrarian, 1:22–24, herding 2:25, 5:2–4, domestic, "the abundant recurrence of household imagery" and *allusions to a rural environment* (φρουρούμενος in 1:5, "recalling the many forts and strongholds (φρουρία) of the provincial interior", κλῆροι in 5:3, "reminiscent of the apportioned sections of land given to clients of the king or to Roman military veterans", and the ravenous lion in 5:8). None of these examples are convincing. Most of them are very traditional (biblical), and Paul, for example, has many rural metaphors although he writes to urban communities. I would call this exegesis an "overinterpretation", related to what was said about the "word-exegesis" of *par-oikos* above. Their value as evidence for the thesis that 1 Peter is addressed to predominantly rural people is very weak, or quite worthless.

We find such overinterpretations also on pp. 135–136, in an argumentation for a strong emphasis on solidarity in 1 Peter. Elliott refers to eight constructions with σύν, used to "reinforce the social distinctiveness as well as the unity of the Christian sect" (p. 136). An analysis of the different passages shows that these compose terms involve very different relations. How can, for example, the ordinary word συμβαίνοντες in 4:12 (rendered by the author "*con*tacting") be said to emphasize "the social cohesion"? This exegesis of single words reminds us of old allegorical interpretations.

There are more examples: in the argumentation for the household theme in 1 Peter on pp. 201–208 (συνοικεῖν in 3:7, the co-elect sister in 5:14, God as Father in a household perspective, etc.) and in the introductory emphasis on πάροικοι and οἶκος (τοῦ θεοῦ). These two last terms are said to recur "at key points in the structure of the document" (p. 23). I think that nobody can maintain that "the structural position" and "the rhetorical function of these *words*" (my emphasis) is especially significant in 1 Peter.[10] Many other words are more important, both structurally and rhetorically. The weight of these terms in Elliott's opinion depends on his reconstruction of the situation of the addressees, or, more precisely, on his use of sect sociology, and not on a structural or a rhetorical analysis of the letter. Theory-bound observations easily lead to overinterpretations, not only to a reading "between the lines", making implicit things explicit but also to a reading "into the text/words" (*eisegesis*).

## 4.2. Simplifications

The use of theories/terms in text analysis (sociological, psychological, structural, rhetorical, philosophical, etc.) has many advantages in comparison with an unconscious, intuitive reading. You know what you are doing. Elliott says on p. 102:

> By comparing the addressees and their situation as described in 1 Peter with the closest sociological analogue, that of a conversionist sect, I am attempting to "read between the lines" of the letter, so to speak, in order to gain a broader and yet more specifically social picture of the issues involved.

But there are many risks. I have just mentioned different kinds of overinterpretations. A too strong or too one-sided simplification is another risk. The "theoretical screens" make you one-eyed. When Elliott describes the meaning and use of πάροικος in 1 Peter, he has problems with the religious dimension of the word given by the usage in biblical and Jewish texts.[11] Πάροικος expresses in his opinion the actual social condition of the addressees, and I think he is right. The horizontal dimension of the word (the relation to other people) is given by both the general usage and the context in 1 Peter. But this does not exclude a religious, theological meaning. The παροικία situation of the Christians in Asia Minor depends on *both* their relation to the Gentiles *and* their relation to God through Jesus Christ. "Divine election granted and required exclusive social as well as religious 'otherness'" (p. 126). God's people had experienced that in many situations. This correlation, conveyed by the usage of πάροικος and exemplified by the social reality of God's peo-

---

[10] See also Feldmeier 1992, 206-10.
[11] Elliott 1981, 37–49, 129–32.

ple, explains the situation of the addressees in 1 Peter much better than a hypothesis that they all were πάροικοι before they became Christians. This first premise in Elliott's interpretation, suggested by the sect analogy, has no support in the text. As Christians the receivers and the senders of the letter—like their "brotherhood throughout the world" (5:9)—had gradually and probably in different degrees received the status of πάροικοι and had to live as such, independent of their previous status. Elliott's description of the addressees is confusing, because of the premise that they were "strangers in society long before their adherence to the Christian sect".[12] The relations involved, both vertical and horizontal ones, are in my view simplified by the applied sociological theory.

As a sect the addressees are involved in a conflict characterized by *distinctiveness* and *solidarity*. Elliott has given very good reasons explaining why these two themes are important in 1 Peter. Yet the text seems to imply a much more complicated argumentative situation. The receivers are and have to be distinctive, with their own identity and their own status. But at the same time they should live together with all people, even hostile Gentiles, and in some way be like them, like those whom the state can praise, or those whom the unbelieving husbands can admire, 2:11–3:12.

The internal cohesion is very important and necessary, but at the same time they should honor everybody. They have to be humble to everybody, 2:11–3:12; 5:1–11. The relations to Christians and to non-Christians are sometimes very much mixed in a disturbing way, 3:9–12. In this context we can quote the summary statement in 2:17:

> Honor all men. Love the brotherhood. Fear God. Honor the emperor.

The most distinctive feature in this verse is the *coordination* of the four sentences. They have to do all four things! Distinctive communal identity and status does not exclude a social life together with all men. Solidarity and internal cohesion include openness to others. They have their "home" both in the community and in God's world. Elliott summarizes 2:13–17 like this:

> Be subordinate to civil authority *but* love the brotherhood and fear *only* God (p. 235, my emphases).

This interpretation, depending on his understanding of the conflict in Asia Minor, is a one-sided simplification of the argumentation of 1 Peter. The application of different kinds of theories may lead to clarifying simplifications. Elliott's use of a comparative sect sociology has given us a much more concrete picture of *some* aspects

---

[12] Especially the argumentation on pp. 131–32.

of this ancient document from the early Christian movement but in my opinion he
has simplified the argumentation too much.

## 5. The Role of the Literary Dimension

> The literary text serves as the primary focus, starting point, and empirical control of
> sociological analysis (p. 8).

The general objective of Elliott's work includes the analyses, interpretation and correlation of "the *literary, sociological* and *theological* features and dimensions of the
text".[13] Throughout the whole book this threefold aspect of the text is stressed.[14]
We can quote from pp. 220f.:

> The deliberation with which *oikos* terminology, imagery and tradition have been se-
> lected, arranged and accentuated in 1 Peter indicates the major role which the con-
> cept of the household (of God) plays in the *literary and theological integration* of the
> letter. In 1 Peter, moreover, the ecclesiological image of the believing community as
> the family of God also has a key *social* significance, a *sociological as well as literary
> and theological function.*

And the literary text is said to serve "as the primary focus, starting point, and empirical control of sociological analysis" (p. 8). The literary dimension is a very important part of the study.

After these statements you look for a literary analysis, too, but you do not find
any. I do not know why. A communicative aspect, or let us say, a rhetorical aspect
of the literary dimension of 1 Peter must be very relevant and useful, analysing
"how and why that text was designed to function, and what its impact upon the life
and activity of its recipients and formulators was intended to be" (p. 8). But now
Elliott is much more interested in single words or parts of words than in the literary
design of the letter, in the rhetoric argumentation or in the type of letter (is it a circular letter, a kind of mass communication?). My earlier reactions on many details
depend very much on a reading of the text as a whole, taking into consideration the
many rhetorical features we have in 1 Peter.

There is not time to give the results of my own literary-rhetorical studies but I
will mention two aspects: the segmentation of the text into smaller functional units
and the central rhetorical strategy of the letter, analysed from a textual, literary approach.

---

[13] Elliott 1981, 8 (my emphases).
[14] Elliott 1981, 8, 21, 107, 220–21, 229, 284.

## 5.1. Functional Units of 1 Peter

A very conscious use of terminal and transitional features, of different kinds of repetition, of thematic words, thought-patterns, rhetorical figures etc. gives us the following display:[15]

```
1:1–2
        1:3–2:10
                1:3–12
                1:13–25
                2:1–10
        2:11–4:11
                2:11-25
                3:1–12
                3:13–24
                4:1–11
        4:12–5:11
                4:12–19
                5:1–11
        5:12–14
```

In the middle section 2:11–25 and 3:1–12 are strongly linked to each other. 3:13–24 and 4:1–11 are also linked but in a much weaker way. The last section, 4:12–5:11, functions like a *peroratio*: the most important things are repeated, the argumentation is strengthened, sender and receivers are bound together, a strong emotive attitude for right behavior is built up, etc. This literary design has implications for the exegesis given in Elliott's periphrastic outline. My results can be wrong, but a thorough literary analysis—a pragmatical, rhetorical one—is necessary, if the text truly serves as the empirical control.

## 5.2. A Rhetorical Strategy?

In Elliott's analysis, πάροικοι and οἶκος τοῦ θεοῦ have an important role in the literary dimension as well.[16] It is, however, very difficult to verify this from the text, read in a synchronic perspective. If you want terms for the literary, rhetorical strategy of 1 Peter I would suggest παθήματα, δόξαι and χάρις together with some related words. In a very cautious way the author mentions this theme for the first time in his introductory thanksgiving, 1:5–6 (with a lot of reservations!). The essence of the χάρις as παθήματα and δόξαι μετὰ ταῦτα is given in the same paragraph, 1:11, exemplified by Christ and explored already by the "exegetical" prophets. The con-

---

[15] Olsson 1982, 199–201.
[16] Elliott 1981, 23–24, 220–21, 229.

crete meaning of these sufferings is presented first in 2:11–3:12, but still in a very cautious way (see for example 2:19–20). The sufferings of Christ are painted in 2:21–24 and together with his glories in 3:18–22 as parts of the argumentation. The formulations in 3:13–4:11 are somewhat clearer but the author is quite explicit first in 4:12–5:11: παθήματα and δόξα. The deictic word ταύτην in the summary of the letter at the end, 5:12, refers to this theme of suffering and glory: "this is the true grace of God".

If this is the rhetorical strategy of the letter, how can it be combined with Elliott's sect analogy? Is the letter focusing more on the single individuals than on the groups in Asia Minor? At any rate, I agree with Elliott that a sociological exegesis of a document must be controlled by the literary text, including an analysis of the literary features in a communicative aspect.

## 6. The Evaluation of the Analysis 1990

Since the volume's initial appearance in 1981, the need for such an approach to the social moorings and functions of New Testament writings has impressed a growing number of scholars, particularly in the Americas. ... Not all reviewers or commentators on the work, of course, are convinced by all its arguments. The questions or objections registered, however, are neither numerous nor substantive enough to warrant a revision of the case as originally presented.[17]

The critical questions above were mentioned very early in a discussion with John H. Elliott at the SBL Meeting in Dallas, Texas, when the book was just published. Later on they were summarized in a Swedish review in 1984.[18] To these I added the basic question about the integration of the new approach with other methods, because Elliott takes the historical-critical method as something given and regards this new sociological analysis as an addition.

In the new publications in 1990 and 1993, mentioned at the beginning of this article, Elliott comments on his analysis and gives a full presentation of the new method. In this context, with reference to what has been said above, I only want to follow up three of my concerns: (1) The integration of the new subdiscipline into "the method of exegesis". (2) The place of a literary (text-oriented) analysis in the new method. (3) The interpretations of 1 Peter. As Elliott said in 1990, his study had a double aim to be an interpretation of 1 Peter and to be an exercise in a form of literary-historical criticism complemented by the theory, models and research of the social sciences.[19]

---

[17] Elliott 1990, xxvi.

[18] Olsson 1984.

[19] Elliott 1990, xix.

When Elliott describes the development of the new sociological approach during the 1970s he mentions the focus on the text as his specific contribution. He employed a self-consciously social-scientific method for analysing 1 Peter and provided "a model for examining an entire New Testament document from a social-scientific perspective" (p. xx). He now wants to use the word "social-scientific", because this label embraces not only sociology but also anthropology, economics, sociolinguistics, semiotics, and other related subdisciplines of the field of social science. The new edition has the subtitle "A Social-Scientific Criticism of 1 Peter, Its Situation and Strategy".

Elliott stated very clearly in 1990 that this new criticism is an expansion, not a replacement, of the conventional historical-critical method. "It complements the other subdisciplines of the exegetical enterprise (text criticism, literary criticism, form and genre criticism, historical criticism, tradition and redaction criticism, theological criticism, reception criticism) through its attention to the social dimensions of the text, its contexts of composition and reception, and their interrelationships" (p. xix). The textcritical and literary analysis is said to be presupposed in the work on 1 Peter. The question of how this new ingredient is to be integrated into "the exegetical method" is not mentioned, much less discussed in the new foreword. The impression is as before: it is only an addition.

When Elliott told his readers in 1990 how to use his method for analysing other biblical documents he is very much bound to his analysis from 1981. He refers to the different analyses in the chapters of the book and summarizes the procedure in four questions.[20] (1) Who are the explicated (or implied) readers and how is their situation portrayed (explicitly and implicitly) in the document? (2) What is the description of and response to the situation presented in the document? (3) What is the interpreter's analysis and explanation of the description, diagnosis, and evaluation of the situation given in the document and the response it seeks of its audience? What is the nature of the situation as seen from a social-scientific perspective? (4) Who are the producers (authors) of this document? These questions correspond very much to the composition of his book on 1 Peter, described above.

The reception of *A Home for the Homeless* has rightly been very positive. Elliott could see no reason in 1990 for a revision of his work. But he commented on some of the objections. He agrees with me that this method must be accompanied by more attention to text-oriented analysis but leaves it by referring to sociolinguistics and a 1986 dissertation by Jacques Rosseau. The interrelation between the social-scientific criticism and rhetorical criticism is recognized. "Here, too, I believe the time has come for methodological consolidation on these two fronts also" (p. xxxi).

---

[20] Elliott 1990, xxiv–xxvi.

The confession, however, does not lead to any new literary analysis of 1 Peter. The 1981 interpretation of the letter does not need any revision according to Elliott. Some specific passages can be discussed: πάροικοι and οἶκος may have both literal and metaphorical connotations, but the letter's general strategy is still to be combined with a conversionist sect strategy.[21]

In 1990 Elliott gives new information about the development of the new approach, makes the analysis procedure somewhat clearer, and comments on some objections, but on the whole he confirms his analysis from 1981. By the new subtitle and the given historical background Elliott's work of 1981 is elevated to the standard example of the social-scientific criticism.

## 7. The New Subdiscipline 1993

Social-scientific criticism of the Bible is that phase of the exegetical task which analyzes the social and cultural dimensions of the text and of its environmental context through the utilization of the perspectives, theory, and research of the social sciences. As a component of the historical-critical method of exegesis, social-scientific criticism investigates biblical texts as meaningful configurations of language intended to communicate between composers and audiences.[22]

With this definition Elliott begins his presentation in 1993 of the new method in a new volume of Guides to Biblical Scholarship. I welcome this summary of the new approach. There is no time for a general review here, aside from some notes on my earlier concerns: the integration of the new subdiscipline, the place of text-oriented analyses, and the interpretation of 1 Peter. Does Elliott offer any new insights in 1993 on these three areas I mentioned at the beginning of the 1980s?

The new criticism is emphatically described as "a subdiscipline of exegesis", inseparably related to the other operations of the exegetical enterprise. It complements, as said before, the other modes of critical analysis, all of which are designed to analyse specific features of the biblical texts. It "expands the historical-critical method by adding".[23]

We receive this information all through the book from 1993. At the same time there are serious comparisons between the new discipline and historical criticism, emphasizing the many differences.[24] How are these "oppositions" to be combined in the interpretation of a text? Is a combination possible? "I shall presume that the

---

[21] Against Balch in Talbert 1986. As I mentioned above the readings of Elliott and Balch can and are to be combined from a rhetorical perspective.

[22] Elliott 1993, 7.

[23] Elliott 1993, 7–8, 14, 55–56, 87.

[24] See Elliott 1993, 12, 33, 55–56, and especially Appendix 1 (pp. 107–09).

conventional exegetical operations have already taken place", Elliott says, when he wants to illustrate the method by his analysis of 1 Peter (p. 71). A simple additive operation? I still question this description of how to integrate—if always possible—the new subdiscipline to all the others in interpreting texts. Are there different types of interpretations, side by side, depending on different definitions of texts?

We have the same questions when we limit ourselves to the relationships between text-oriented analyses and the new discipline. Social-scientific criticism, as a subdiscipline of exegesis, focuses primarily on texts. It is specifically exegetical in nature "and directs primary attention to the interpretations of biblical texts. Here social-scientific criticism supplements the other methods of critical interpretation". "The theory and method of literary, semiotic, social, historical, theological and ideological analysis are combined to understand the text" (p. 23).

In what ways? It is said that literary, semiotic, linguistic, and rhetorical analyses "must be supplemented" by the new subdiscipline (p. 69), but can we also say the opposite, for example, that social-scientific criticism must be supplemented by a rhetorical analysis? Or does the new subdiscipline overrule all the others? There is no clear answer.

New in Elliott 1993 are some pages about text theory, but they are very much reduced to the social (pragmatic) dimension of language.[25] At the end we find the same confession as before: We have to analyse the relationships between social-scientific and modern text-oriented analyses (new literary criticism, narratology, structural criticism, and sociorhetorical criticism). "With the gradual maturation of these newer criticisms, it now seems an appropriate time to pursue this issue of methodological integration" (p. 100). But this is not taken as a critique of the new subdiscipline and its results, only as a desideratum.

In my opinion, the interpretation of 1 Peter Elliott offers in 1981, 1990 and 1993 has to be supplemented by a thorough rhetorical analysis. — I find it symptomatic that instead of a rhetorical strategy of the letter there is in 1993 "the sectarian strategy of 1 Peter". — Such a supplementation will also revise Elliott's interpretation of 1 Peter.

## Bibliography

Breuer, Dieter 1977: "Die Bedeutung der Rhetorik für die Textinterpretation", in: H. F. Plett (ed.), *Rhetorik*. Kritische Positionen zum Stand der Forschung, München: Fink 1977, 23-44.

Elliott, John H. 1966: *The Elect and the Holy*. An Exegetical Examination of 1 Peter 2:4–10 and the Phrase *Basileion Hierateuma* (NT.S 12), Leiden: E. J. Brill 1966.

---

[25] Elliott 1993, 49–55.

— 1976: "The Rehabilitation of an Exegetical Stepchild. 1 Peter in Recent Research", in: *JBL* 95 (1976) 243–54.

— 1981: *A Home for the Homeless*. A Sociological Exegesis of 1 Peter. Its Situation and Strategy, Philadelphia, PA: Fortress 1981.

— 1990: A *Home for the Homeless*. A Social-Scientific Criticism of 1 Peter, Its Situation and Strategy. Minneapolis, MN: Fortress 1990.

— 1993: *What is Social-Scientific Criticism?* Minneapolis, MN: Fortress 1993.

Feldmeier, Reinhard 1992: *Die Christen als Fremde*. Die Metapher der Fremde in der antiken Welt, im Urchristentum und im 1. Petrusbrief (WUNT 64), Tübingen: J. C. B. Mohr 1992

Hellholm, David 1980: *Das Visionenbuch des Hermas als Apokalypse. Formgeschichtliche und texttheoretische Studien zu einer literarischen Gattung*. I: Methodologische Vorüberlegungen und makrostrukturelle Textanalyse (CB.NT 13:1), Lund: CWK Gleerup 1980.

Olsson, Birger 1982: *Första Petrusbrevet* (Kommentar till Nya Testamentet 17), Stockholm: EFS-förlaget 1982.

— 1984: "Ett hem för hemlösa. Om sociologisk exeges av NT", in: *SEÅ* 49 (1984) 89–108.

— 1985: "A Decade of Text-Linguistic Analyses of Biblical Texts at Uppsala", in: *StTh* 39 (1985) 107–26.

Talbert, Charles H. (ed.): 1986: *Perspectives on First Peter* (NABPR.SS 9) Macon, GA: Mercer University Press 1986.

Wiklander, Bertil 1984: *Prophecy as Literature*. A Text-Linguistic and Rhetorical Approach to Isaiah 2–4 (CB.OT 22), Malmö: CWK Gleerup 1984.

# Λόγος ἀπὸ σιγῆς προελθών[1]
## (Ignatius, *Mag.* 8:2)

### Einar Thomassen

## 1. Introduction

In his letter to the Magnesians, chapters 8–10, Ignatius warns against Judaizers: For those who have received grace through Christ it is no longer possible to live κατὰ ἰουδαϊσμόν. And "the most divine prophets" lived even they according to Jesus Christ. For their message was that "there is one God, who revealed himself through Jesus Christ his Son, who is his Word which proceeded from silence, who in every way pleased him who sent him" (εἷς θεός ἐστιν ὁ φανερώσας ἑαυτὸν διὰ Ἰησοῦ Χριστοῦ τοῦ υἱοῦ αὐτοῦ, ὅς ἐστιν αὐτοῦ λόγος ἀπὸ σιγῆς προελθών, ὃς κατὰ πάντα εὐηρέστησεν τῷ πέμψαντι αὐτόν, 8:2).

1.1. What interests us here are the words λόγος ἀπὸ σιγῆς προελθών.[2] The imagery does not seem to be directly motivated by the ideas forwarded in the passage. Rather, the expression has the appearance of an already fixed and approved formula, which Ignatius cites parenthetically to give rhetorical support to his argument. We are dealing, it seems, with a *topos*.[3] And in that case we are entitled to try to identify its original background.

    1.2.1. The most frequently asked question concerning this text in the history of

---

[1] A previous version of this paper was presented in the New Testament seminar of the Theological Faculty at the University of Uppsala, on April 19, 1990. I wish to thank all the participants, and Professor Lars Hartman in particular, for the instructive comments offered on this occasion.

[2] The received Greek text of the middle recension (*Cod. Mediceo-Laurentianus* 57,7), followed by the Latin, has λόγος ἀΐδιος οὐκ ἀπὸ σιγῆς προελθών. The words ἀΐδιος οὐκ are absent from the Armenian and Arabic versions, as well as from the quotation of this passage by Severus of Antioch. Anti-heretical concerns presumably motivated this interpolation. Cf. Lightfoot 1989, II/2, 126–127; Schoedel 1985, 120 n. 12.

[3] Cf. Elze 1963, 57.

exegesis is without doubt this: is it Gnostic?[4] Σιγή is a term well known from gnostic texts. Most famous of all is its occurrence in Iren. *Haer.* I 1:1 as the name of the female "partner" of the supreme divine principle, Βυθός. Here, Σιγή is depicted as the womb from which go forth the aeons, including one called Logos, which make up the transcendent Pleroma. On this interpretation, Ignatius would be the witness of a gnostic theory of emanation. The significance of such an interpretation is not only that it admits the possibility of a gnostic influence on Ignatius, but, more importantly, that it would allow us to push the date of these gnostic theories further back, from Irenaeus (180–190) to the second decade of the second century.

1.2.2. Another approach (which has not always been clearly distinguished from the first) has been to construct a background in what may broadly be called Hellenistic mysticism; reference is here made to a series of Pagan texts which speak of silence as the proper way to worship the god.[5] On this interpretation, Ignatius would be influenced in the passage by this notion of a god who is essentially characterized by, and approached in, silence.

1.2.3. A third line of interpretation has been to concentrate more closely on Ignatius' own context, and to emphasize that the metaphor of the word proceeding from silence in this passage does not refer to protology, nor does Ignatius use "silence" simply as a name for God. Rather, Ignatius is speaking about the incarnation, as God's revelation of a mystery concealed during previous generations and known only to the prophets. The ideas are thus quite similar to Rom 16:25–26 ἀποκάλυψιν μυστηρίου χρόνοις αἰωνίοις σεσιγημένου, φανερωθέντος δὲ νῦν διά τε γραφῶν προφητικῶν.[6] W. R. Schoedel, who argues for this interpretation in his recent commentary, concludes: "The silence of God is invoked to account for the supposed inability of the Jews and Judaizers to understand Scripture. And Christ is thought of as emerging from a sphere of silence only in the sense that his appearance brings the hidden purpose of God to light".[7]

1.3. The alternatives thus seem to be: (1) a gnostic and protological, (2) a Hellenistic and mystical, and (3) a Biblical and salvation-historical interpretation. What I shall try to show in this article, however, is that these various approaches to the passage should not be considered as alternatives in such a way that one must be accepted to

---

[4] A note in *The Ante-Nicene Fathers,* I, 62 n. 5 informs us: "Some have argued that the Gnostic Σιγή, *silence,* is here referred to, and have consequently inferred that this epistle could not have been written by Ignatius". For more recent advocates of this view, see in particular Schlier 1929, 38–39; Barnard 1963, 201–203; Paulsen 1978, 110–122; Paulsen 1985, 52. Also cf. Bauer 1920, in loc.; Bartsch 1940, 57–61.

[5] See the references in Bauer 1988, s.v. σιγή.

[6] Cf. Lightfoot 1989, II/2, 127–128; Schoedel 1985, 120–122.

[7] Schoedel 1985, 122.

the exclusion of the others. Rather, they can be seen to complement one another in the sense that each of them points to historically preformed semantic elements which have been absorbed into the full range of meanings contained in Ignatius' passage. Moreover, viewed in the mutual relationship between them suggested by the passage, these elements can be made to cast an interesting light on some general developments of religious thought in late Hellenism.

1.4. A distinction must of course be made in principle between the formula itself and the use to which Ignatius puts it. Since Ignatius did not himself invent it, it is quite possible that the formula originated in a different ideological context from the one in which it serves in the present passage. Thus although alternative (3) may be preferable as an interpretation of Ignatius' intentions, alternatives (1) or (2) may still be valid as hypotheses about the original meaning of the expression. On the other hand, since Ignatius here seems to draw on an already established formula, it is reasonable to assume that the use he makes of it is not totally unrelated to its conventional associations. So while we still have to distinguish between original context and present use, we also need to see if we can uncover what hermeneutical relationship might exist between them.

## 2. Traditio-historical Elements

### 2.1. Jewish Ideas about Creation from Silence

The idea that speech goes forth from silence comes readily to mind, it may be assumed, once the notion of speech itself is reflected on. We do not need to postulate a single source of diffusion for it. In fact, the idea can be found, independently it seems, both in a Jewish and in a Hellenistic context. We shall deal later with some Hellenistic versions of it. First we shall draw attention to some early Jewish texts where this idea occurs as an expansion of the notion of the divine word. Thus Wis 18:14ff. describes the manifestation of God's power through the killing of Egypt's first-born in these terms: "For while peaceful silence enwrapped all things, and night in her swiftness was in mid course, thine all-powerful word leaped from heaven down from the royal throne, a stern warrior, into the midst of the doomed land, bearing as a sharp sword thine unfeigned commandment" (ἡσύχου γὰρ σιγῆς περιεχούσης τὰ πάντα ... ὁ παντοδύναμός σου λόγος ἀπ᾽ οὐρανῶν ... εἰς μέσον τῆς ὀλεθρίας ἥλατο γῆς ...). Here, the contrast of silence and word provides a dramatic effect, and serves to emphasize the powerfulness of the divine intervention. The notion of the word obviously has heavy theological connotations. That cannot, however, be said here about "silence", which seems to rest chiefly on the author's poetical imagination.[8]

It is more relevant, I think, to consider a couple of texts which use the pair silence/word in connection with the creation.[9] Thus in a psalm put into the mouth of David in the Pseudo-Philonic *Liber Antiquitatum Biblicarum,* it is said that *tenebre et silentium erant antequam fieret seculum, et locutum est silentium et apparuerunt tenebre* (LAB 60:2). Here a primeval silence is associated with the darkness of Gen 1:2. The silence is broken by speech, analogously to the way the darkness is dissipated by the first light of creation. These notions clearly derive from exegetical considerations on the order of creation in Gen 1:1–3. Since Gen 1:3 mentions not only the first light, but also God's speech, the inference is made that creation was preceded by silence as well as darkness. The same exegetical tradition is witnessed to by 4 Ezra 6:38–40:

> *O Domine, loquens locutus es ab initio creaturae, in primo die dicens: Fiat caelum et terra, et tuum verbum opus perfecit. Et erat tunc spiritus volans, et tenebrae circumferebantur et silentium, sonus vocis hominum nondum erat abs te. Tunc dixisti de thesauris tuis proferri lumen quod luminis, ut apparerent tunc opera tua.*

The primeval silence is also referred to in 4 Ezra 7:30, as well as in *2 Apoc. Bar.* 3:7. With these texts, unlike the one in Wisdom, we are dealing with a genuine traditional theological *topos,* and the likelihood is therefore greater that they should be seen as belonging in some way to the background of Ignatius' formula. The main obstacle is, of course, that the context in these texts is protological, whereas Ignatius' perspective is salvation-historical. This obstacle can, I think, be overcome. But we shall defer our conclusions in this regard until we have surveyed some of the other evidence.

## 2.2. The Gnostic Evidence

From gnostic texts we have the following:

(1) *Gos. Truth* 37:4–12: "Each one of his words are the work of his one will in the revelation of his Word. From being the depths of his thought, the Word (λογος) went forth and manifested them along with a mind that speaks the one Word (λογος) through silent grace".

(2) *Tri. Trac.* 63:17–64:4: "In order that the Father may be glorified by each one, and manifest himself, and because in his ineffability he is invisibly hidden, he is admired in mind. Because of that, the greatness of his exaltedness becomes manifest when they speak of him and see him, as they sing hymns to him in gratitude because

---

[8] Lightfoot 1989, 127, and Elze 1963, 58, see this passage as an important parallel to Ign. *Magn.* 8:2. That is probably to place too great a burden on the word "silence" here.

[9] Cf. Wilson 1958, 143–144 n. 122; Philonenko 1962, 49–50; Jeremias 1968, 82.

of his overflowing sweetness. < ... > and just as the marvels of the silences are eternal procreations—they are the offspring of mind—so also the faculties of the *logos* are spiritual emissions. The two, being as those of a *logos,* are [...] and they are thoughts born [of] him, and eternally living roots which have become manifest".

(3) From the "Revelation of Sige" by Marcus the Magician: (a) Iren. *Haer.* I 14:1: "When first the inconceivable and non-material Father ... willed to make utterable that of him which was ineffable and to give form to that which was invisible, he opened his mouth and sent forth a word (λόγον) which was similar to himself". (b) Ib. I 14:3: ("Man") "is the source of all speech, the beginning of every sound, the expression of all that is unspeakable, and the mouth of the silent Sige".

(4) *Gos. Eg.* NHC III (2): 43:21–24 = IV (2):53:20–26: (Domedon Doxomedon, the aeon of the aeons) "is the Word, the [lumin]ous Fa[ther] of the all, the one who [came] forth from silence, while he rests in silence".

(5) *Trim. Prot.* 46:11–17: "There is a light [that] dwells hidden in silence (cιгн), and it came forth. Whereas the Mother alone exists as silence, I alone am the word (λοгoc), ineffable, unpolluted, immeasurable, inconceivable. The word is a hidden light, bearing a fruit of life ...". (Also cf. 33:32–36:3, 42:4–5, 46:5ff.).

(6) *Thund.* 14:9–15: "I am the silence that is incomprehensible and the idea whose remembrance is frequent. I am the voice whose sound is manifold and the word whose appearance is multiple. I am the utterance of my name".

In all these examples, silence represents the ultimate source of being, and λόγος its manifestation. There are two aspects to this concept of manifestation. First, it is protological and explanatory: the metaphor of silence giving birth to speech describes the origin of differentiation and form from undifferentiated unity. Secondly, it is soteriological: the manifestation of λόγος is a revelatory gift, an act of grace, by which it is possible to know and partake of the essence of that which is manifested, the transcendent first principle. The soteriological and the protological are intimately and systematically linked in gnostic thought. At the same time, however, it is possible to make a relative distinction between these aspects, and to describe the gnostic perspective as a combination between them. Such a distinction is required in particular for a genetic reconstruction of gnostic thought, indispensable for an historical understanding of it. The present example offers a good illustration of how this gnostic process of synthesizing may be reconstructed. The notion of the word going forth from silence in these texts can in fact be seen as relating to at least two distinct *topoi,* one of which is protological, another soteriological, which they combine in novel and creative ways.

## 2.3. A Protological Application of a Linguistic Theory

Many gnostic systems are clearly inspired by contemporary theorizing about the relationship of language to thought. Among Christian theologians such interests are
not confined to Gnostics. Thus the application of notions akin to the Stoic distinction between the λόγος ἐνδιάθετος and the λόγος προφορικός can be found in authors such as Athenagoras,[10] Theophilus of Antioch,[11] and Tertullian,[12] as they
undertake to explain to a gentile audience the relationship between Father and Son.
In gnostic systems such notions often play a constitutive role, as they posit a
Thought (ἔννοια, ἐνθύμησις) at the beginning of the process of projection.[13] Representing the mental activity of the Father, the concept of the Thought serves to explain the origin of duality in oneness. At the same time it is the "mother" of the
aeons born from this duality. It is this original Thought which is sometimes called
Silence: "(this Thought) whom some have called Thought (ἔννοιαν), and others
Grace (χάριν), ... but those who speak truly have addressed her as Silence (σιγήν),
since Greatness completed all things through thinking without speech (δι' ἐνθυμή-
σεως χωρὶς λόγου)" (Epiph. *Pan.* XXXI 5:2). These various names for the Father's
"partner" is known from other Valentinian sources as well.[14]

According to Cyril of Jerusalem, *Catech.* 6:17, "Valentinus" said that βυθός ...
ἐγέννησε σιγὴν καὶ ἀπὸ τῆς σιγῆς ἐτεκνοποίει τὸν λόγον.[15] Cyril's testimony is
no doubt secondary and inaccurate. The actual systems that we possess generally
display much more elaborate versions of the projection process. On the other hand,
these versions can all be seen as variations on a basic theme, which Cyril seems to
convey quite well. In the primary ogdoad of Iren. *Haer.* I 1:1 we have:

1. Bythos-Sige
2. Nous (Monogenes)-Truth
3. Logos-Life
4. Man-Church

This appears to be a systematic elaboration of an underlying model Father-Thought/
Silence-Logos, by splitting the element Thought into two entities, Sige and Nous.

---

[10] *Suppl.* 10.

[11] *Ad Autol.* II 10.22.

[12] Esp. *Prax.* 5 and 7.

[13] "Projection" is to be preferred in this context to "emanation", as a more accurate rendering of
προβολή.

[14] Cf. Iren. *Haer.* I 1.1; *Tri. Trac.* 57:3–8; also cf. *Eugnostos* NHC III 88:7ff. parr. Silence also
appears in *Exc. Theod.* 29-30, and Grace-Silence plays a major role in Marcus the Magician, Iren.
*Haer.* I 13ff.

[15] Bauer 1920, 225; Schlier 1929, 38.

Other Valentinian systems can be shown to perform variant operations on this model, by distinguishing or identifying the terms Thought, Silence and Mind.[16] Sometimes, too, the scheme is expanded by the insertion of another mental faculty, that of Will.[17]

A basic source for these theories is clearly the linguistic commonplace of the internal and the external *logos*. In these terms, too, Irenaeus understands and criticizes the Valentinian doctrine: "It is impossible that Sige can exist in the presence of Logos, or again, that Logos can manifest itself in the presence of Sige. ... Where Sige is, there cannot be Logos; and where Logos is, there certainly cannot be Sige. But if they say that Logos exists internally (*endiatheton*), Sige also will exist internally, and will not the less be destroyed by the internal Logos" (*Haer.* II 12:5). The Gnostics certainly drew upon such ideas. But it is clear that this cannot be the whole answer. First, the prominence of Silence in the Gnostic systems cannot be fully explained by the linguistic paradigm. It is not entirely absent from it, as we can see from the argument of Irenaeus just quoted, as well as from Tertullian, *Prax.* 5: *nam etsi deus nondum sermonem suum miserat, proinde eum cum ipsa et in ipsa ratione intra semetipsum habebat tacite cogitando et disponendo secum quae per sermonem mox erat dicturus.* But clearly the emphasis placed on Silence in the gnostic texts far exceeds what is usual with this paradigm. Secondly, we have to account for the strongly revelatory and soteriological functions of the gnostic Silence. For these aspects we have to look in another direction.

## 2.4. "Mystical" Silence

Obviously, "silence" used in connection with notions of the divine serves to say something about the nature of deity. God is ineffable, according to a widespread belief in later Antiquity. To say that God "dwells in", or is characterized by, silence,[18] is thus a way of expressing the deity's transcendence of speech. But it is more than just a negative epithet. Silence is also a medium of communication between God and the human mind. Thus, silence is a way in which the ineffable god may be approached by the worshipper. It is a fairly common idea that the proper way to wor-

---

[16] Cf. Thomassen and Painchaud 1989, 282–283.

[17] Ibid. 278.

[18] Cf. Iren. *Haer.* I 1.1; *Tri. Trac.* 55:37; *Ap. John* BG 26:7–8 parr; *Soph. Jes. Chr.* BG 123:11–13; *Paraph. Shem* 13:7, 17:6; *Val. Exp.* 22:22; *Marsanes* 4:21, 7:3–25, 9:14–16, 15:1; *Allogenes* 61:20–22, 63:35; *Trim. Prot.* 37:29–30. Silence associated with the highest sphere of reality also appears repeatedly in *Gos. Eg.* Outside of gnosticism, later Neoplatonists also speak about the πατρικὴ σιγή; such language probably goes back to the *Chaldaean Oracles,* cf. Lewy 1978, 160 n. 353, Theiler 1933/66, 10.

ship God is in silence, or by means of silent hymns.[19] Conversely, the silence of the deity implies a capacity for, or even an instrument of, revelation.[20] In other words, the notion of silence expresses the idea of a god who is transcendent and at the same time capable of being manifested. Thus it also expresses the paradoxical nature of communication between god and man, designating a liminal interface between essentially separate planes of reality.

The person who enters into contact with this transcendent reality does not remain unchanged, but is transformed by being allowed to partake of it. In *Corp. Herm.* XIII, silence brings about a veritable rebirth: Asked about the details of rebirth, Hermes Trismegistos explains that the womb in which it takes place is "intelligent wisdom in silence" (σοφία νοερὰ ἐν σιγῇ), the seed is the ἀληθινὸν ἀγαθόν, and providing the seed is the will of God (XIII 2). When baptism, in the Valentinian *Tripartite Tractate* 128:30–32, is given the epithet "silence", this probably presupposes the same idea, that rebirth takes place from silence.[21] From this it is a small step to the personification of Σιγή as a divine mother figure and revealer, such as we can find in Marcus the Magician (Iren. *Haer.* I 13:6ff.).

The concept of silence as a source of revelation unites, then, the protological and the soteriological. The protological notions of first beginnings are modelled upon the soteriological notions of rebirth, and vice versa. In both contexts, silence is the source of true being, of a gnosis which conveys a substantial continuity with the Father as the ultimate ground of existence. At the same time as protological birth and soteriological rebirth mirror one another, however, each notion nevertheless retains a relative autonomy according to their different functions in the religious system. Thus protological Silence is joined with the notion of the primal Thought, and with the linguistic paradigm discussed above; this elaboration belongs primarily to the context of protological speculation, and does not apply to the gnostic-sacramental dimension of the mystical silence. On the other hand there are certain other aspects proper to the notion of the primal Thought which we must deal with next, in order to complete the picture.

---

[19] E.g. Jambl. *Myst.* VIII 3: διὰ σιγῆς μόνης θεραπεύεται. Similarly, Porph. *Abst.* II 34; *Sent. Sextus* 427, 578; *PGM* IV 558ff., 1782; *Corp. Herm.* I 31, X 5; *Disc.* 8–9 58:20ff., 59:13–15; *Steles Seth* 119:29–30; *Mart. Pet.* 10 (Lipsius-Bonnet I 96:16ff.); Philo *Plant.* 126; *Tri. Trac.* 63:20–23, 72:25–36; *Testim. Truth* 69:4; *Marsanes* 8:21–22, 9:22–24. Cf. Bauer 1988, s.v. σιγή; Paulsen 1978, 113–114. The classic study is Casel 1919. For Clement of Alexandria, see Mortley 1973.

[20] This aspect of silence is clearly demonstrated by the gnostic texts quoted above, as well as in the ones referred to in n. 14. Valentinian texts sometimes stress the concealing, at other times the revealing aspect of Silence, cf. Thomassen and Painchaud 1989, 280. The fertile, giving, aspect of Silence is also found in the *Chaldaean Oracles* 16 des Places: τῇ θεοθρέμμονι σιγῇ τῶν παρέρων.

[21] Thomassen and Painchaud 1989, 444.

## 2.5. The Primal Thought

Historically, the gnostic concept of the primal Thought can be said to have two major sources. On the one hand it is indebted to concepts of Intellect in the Greek metaphysical tradition. According to contemporary Platonism in particular, the realm of ideas is contained in the transcendent νοῦς, as the thoughts of God. Gnostic metaphysics frequently depart from this model, however, in two important respects. In the first place, there is a tendency to place the ultimate ground of being even above the Intellect of the philosophers. This explains, for instance, why, in the main Valentinian system reported by Irenaeus, the divine Thought is split in two: the supratranscendental Ἔννοια = Σιγή, and the Νοῦς = the Onlybegotten. Secondly, the gnostic systems are more dynamic and processual in character than traditional Platonist taxonomies. Entities are said to "go forth", or to be "projected" or "born" from the First Principle. Notions of latency and manifestation can be found in this context, so that not only are the aeons contained within the Thought of the Father in the same way that the ideas are contained in the Platonist Intellect,[22] but they can sometimes be said to exist there in a hidden and embryonic manner, in order to be subsequently revealed.[23]

These protological ideas about embryonic existence and birth are without doubt strongly motivated by the soteriological paradigm of rebirth, as we noted above. The birth of the aeons is modelled upon, and mythologically prefigures, conceptions about the process of salvation.[24] But there is still another traditio-historical factor which needs to be taken into account here—the second major source for the gnostic concept of the Thought. That is the role which the idea of *divine purpose* plays in the Judeo-Christian theological tradition.

In *Tri. Trac.,* the existence of the aeons within the Thought of the Father (60:1ff.) is connected with the idea that the Father has conceived a plan for them: He "wished to direct (and) to bring up [that] which was wanting, from the [..., to bring] forth those who [were] in him" (60:6–11). The projection of the aeons is thus associated with a plan for their education. "The Father had provided for them not only that they should exist for him, but that they should exist for themselves also; that they should, then, exist in his thought as thought-substance, but that they should exist for themselves also" (61:1–7). In *Gos. Truth* it is still clearer that the preexistence of the aeons within the deity's mind is connected with notions of pre-election and predes-

---

[22] Cf. ibid., 291.

[23] *Gos. Truth* 27:22–25, 27:34–28:4, 37:7–8; *Tri. Trac.* 60:1–5.17–37. Cf. Thomassen and Painchaud 1989, 292–296.

[24] Thomassen and Painchaud 1989, 295. This is not to deny that Neopythagorean notions about the Monad-Intellect containing potentially all numbers and ideas also contributed to making this theory plausible as a protological concept; cf. ibid.

tination according to a divine plan of salvation: When the Saviour appeared in this world, there was manifested together with him "the living book of the living", "written in the thought and mind [of the] Father, which from before the foundation (ⲕⲁⲧⲁⲃⲟⲗⲏ) of the totality was within his incomprehensibility" (19:36–20:3). Here, the "book" is clearly a metaphor for the preexistent community—the passage alludes of course to Apoc 13:8, 17:8, but it should also be compared with *Exc. Theod.* 41:2 πρὸ καταβολῆς κόσμου ... ἡ ἐκκλησία ἐκλέλεχθαι, and thus with Eph 1:4 ἐξελέξατο ἡμᾶς ἐν αὐτῷ πρὸ καταβολῆς κόσμου. In this context it is clear that the manifestation of that which was hidden within the Father's Thought is described as a salvation-historical event. It is no longer part of a protological theory, but takes place in time and history, as the fulfilment of a pre-conceived plan of the deity.

## 2.6. Myth and History

Now let us take a closer look at the passage in *Gos. Truth* where the terms λόγος and silence appear. We need now to quote a larger portion of the text:

> He is good. He knows his plantings, because it is he who planted them in his paradise. And his paradise is his place of rest. This is the perfection in the thought of the Father, and these are the words of his deliberation. Each one of his words are the work of his one will in the revelation of his Word. From being the depths of his thought, the Word went forth and manifested them along with a mind that speaks the one Word, through silent grace. It was called "thought", since they were in it before they were manifested. It came about then, that he came forth at the time when the will of him who willed desired it. (36:35–37:18)

The passage is difficult, and it is hardly possible to construe from the present Coptic version an exact interpretation of all the details of the text, which quite probably was characterized by ambiguity even in the lost Greek original. But it seems clear that there is a strong emphasis on divine providence in the passage. The salvation of the elect is contained within the mind of the Father, and is brought to pass by the Word, which goes forth[25] and manifests what was hidden there. There is some uncertainty as to the position of the complement "through silent grace" (ϩⲛ̄ⲛ ⲟⲩⲭⲁⲣⲓⲥ ⲉⲥⲕⲁⲣⲁⲉⲓⲧ). It can be taken to go with either of the verbs "speaks" (ⲉϥϣⲉⲭⲉ), "manifested" (ⲁϥⲟⲩⲱⲛϩ̄), or even "went forth" (ⲛ̄ⲧⲁϩⲣ̄ ϣⲁⲣⲡ̄ ⲛ̄ⲉⲓ ⲁⲃⲁⲗ). None of these interpretations can be definitely excluded. This uncertainty is not essential for our purposes, however, since the Valentinian material referred to above indicates that Thought, Grace and Silence are conventionally associated as equivalent names

---

[25] The translation of ⲣ̄ ϣⲟⲣⲡ̄ ⲛ̄ⲉⲓ ⲉⲃⲟⲗ as "to be first to come forth" (thus e.g. *The Nag Hammadi Library in English)* should be avoided. The Coptic expression simply renders the Greek προ-έρχεσθαι.

of the same reality, i.e. as the source from which the revealing Word goes forth through the action of the paternal will.

What is particularly interesting about this passage is that it demonstrates how the same set of notions may apply equally well to revelation in a salvation-historical and in a protological context. And this indicates something which may provide us with a very fruitful hermeneutical key to gnostic thinking in general (or at least the kind of gnosticism which is represented by *Gos. Truth*): Salvation-history and protology are essentially interchangeable. This means that salvation-historical events are mythicized, i.e. they are interpreted in a language which is also capable of expressing, in narrative form, the fundamental relations which are conceived to exist between God, man and the world. In other words, the historical events are rewritten as a myth of origins. Thereby these events become soteriologically significant and universally valid. Moreover, this myth acquires a ritual correlate, so that its soteriological import is instantiated through appropriate sacramental action. In this way it is possible to explain why "silence" as the source of revelation may appear in three diverse contexts: in connection with sacramental rebirth, with the protological birth of the Father's offspring, and the historical effectuation of the deity's hidden design. The revelation of the Saviour in history is an image of the original revelation at the beginning of all things, and the mythical paradigm which unites these two revelations is in turn re-enacted though ritual rebirth. And in each context the event can be depicted as the word coming forth from silence.

## 3. The Context of the Theme in Ignatius

### 3.1. The Theme of Revelation in Magnesians

In the preceding survey we have attempted to distinguish a number of different themes which might be relevant to the expression λόγος ἀπὸ σιγῆς προελθών. There is (1) a Jewish cosmogonical theme; (2) a linguistic metaphor of mind and speech; (3) the theme of mystical silence, where in turn a theological and a soteriological aspect may be distinguished; (4) the Platonist concept of the divine mind as the place of the ideas; (5) the Jewish and Christian theme of the hidden divine plan. We have also argued that gnostic theologians made creative use of these received themes by combining them associatively so as to establish links between soteriology and protology. Thus the mystical silence from which the neophyte is reborn is at the same time the ineffability surrounding the transcendent deity from which all things have come forth. This original and maternal silence is further associated with the mind of God, which makes it possible to exploit both Platonist metaphysics, Jewish and Christian notions about divine providence and the economy of salvation in history, and, finally, the linguistic metaphor of mind and speech. Thus at least the last four of the themes listed above have been adopted into the play of gnostic *mythopoiesis*. Whether the first, Jewish cosmological theme was another such source is hardly possible to determine on the basis of the available evidence.

The gnostic use of the silence/logos theme cannot, then, be reduced to one single meaning. We are dealing with a multivalent symbol which must be understood in its complexity if we are to employ it for purposes of traditio-historical reconstruction. If, with this insight, we go back to Ignatius, are we in a better position now to say something about the meaning of the words λόγος ἀπὸ σιγῆς προελθών in *Magn.* 8:2?

Let us first take a look at the context of the passage in *Magn.* The present passage is not the only one in this letter where Ignatius introduces a parenthetical reference to the manifestation of Christ in order to illustrate some general point. Earlier he did so in 6:1: "I exhort you: be eager to do all things in godly concord, with the bishop set over you in the place of God (εἰς τόπον θεοῦ), and the presbyters in the place of the council of the apostles, and the deacons, most sweet to me, entrusted with the service of Jesus Christ, who before the ages was with the Father and appeared at the end (ὃς πρὸ αἰώνων παρὰ πατρὶ ἦν καὶ ἐν τέλει ἐφάνη)". And likewise in 7:2: "All of you, hurry together as to one temple of God, as to one altar, to one Jesus Christ, who proceeded from the one Father and was with the one and returned (to him) (τὸν ἀφ᾽ ἑνὸς πατρὸς προελθόντα καὶ εἰς ἕνα ὄντα καὶ χωρήσαντα)". When we finally arrive at the words ὅς ἐστιν αὐτοῦ λόγος ἀπὸ σιγῆς προελθών, ὃς κατὰ πάντα εὐηρέστησεν τῷ πέμψαντι αὐτόν in 8:2, they seem, then, to refer back to these earlier two mentions of the revelation of Christ, rather like a refrain which is repeated and varied with each repetition.

The variations on the refrain are in each case determined by the theme provided by the various exhortations: In the first passage the theme is that of loyalty to one's commission: the community with its officials should be loyal to the bishop just as Christ fulfilled the will of the one who sent him. The words παρὰ πατρὶ ἦν apparently allude to his closeness to the Father, and ἐν τέλει ἐφάνη to the accomplishment of his mission which was the effect of this closeness. In the second passage the unity of the Son with the Father becomes a model for unity in the community. Finally, in the third passage the theme is the invalidity of Judaism. By describing Christ as the word which proceeded from silence, Ignatius is in fact saying that the commandments of the Jews are not the word of God. All along, God kept his silence to the Jews; only now was the word sent forth.

But there must be more to the expression than this. How were the prophets able to "live according to Jesus Christ" and "be inspired by his grace" if the word went forth only at the incarnation of Christ—assuming that the "going forth" of the second and third passages is equivalent to the ἐν τέλει ἐφάνη of the first passage? This problem suggests that the silence of God cannot have been purely negative. The words ὃς κατὰ πάντα εὐηρέστησεν τῷ πέμψαντι αὐτόν seem in fact to allude to an intention in God: God had designed a plan, and Christ carried it out to his full satisfaction. This was, we recall, also implied in the first of the three passages quoted above; reference may also be made on this point to the notion of the γνώμη θεοῦ, which occurs elsewhere in Ignatius.[26] In some form or another, this divine plan must have been divulged to the prophets, so that they were able to anticipate the coming of the Christ, though Ignatius does not offer any details about the theory about the inspiration of Scripture which he presupposes, apart from saying that the prophets were "disciples in spirit" (*Magn.* 9:2).

## 3.2. Mystical Silence in Ignatius

We find, then, that Ignatius does draw a connection between the silence of God and the hidden plan of salvation, a connection which is also made in such gnostic texts as the *Gospel of Truth.* What we still need to ask, however, is how this connection came to be made. Why does Ignatius use the metaphor of silence and word to express God's hidden will and purpose in history? It is not satisfactory to say that it merely indicates the absence of previous divine revelation to the Jews. As was pointed out at the beginning of this study, the expression gives the impression of having been preformed in another context and taken over by Ignatius for his own purposes. For the gnostic material we have suggested that the connection was made possible through the notion of mystical silence: because silence is the mother of the neophyte, and because generation and regeneration mirror one another, silence came to be associated with both protological and salvation-historical notions of the divine mind. The question now is: does a similar—or a different—chain of associations underlie Ignatius' usage?

Two avenues seem possible here. One is to try to assess whether the word-from-silence theme has resonances elsewhere in the Ignatian corpus where Ignatius attributes a religious significance to silence.[27] In *Eph.* 6:1 Ignatius exhorts the Ephesians to stand in awe of the bishop who keeps silent, because he is a representative of the Lord. However we may understand the relationship between God, Christ and the bishop which this passage implies,[28] it is clear at least that silence is here given high value as a sign of the presence of the divine. Again, in *Eph.* 15:1–2 the virtues of silence in a teacher, along with his words, are praised. A comparison is made in

---

[26] *Eph.* 3:2, *Smyrn.* 6:2; cf. Paulsen 1978, 116–117.

[27] The passages are listed in Paulsen 1978, 115.

[28] For the various interpretations which have been offered here cf. Schoedel 1985, 56–57.

this regard with the one teacher (Christ) "who 'spoke and it was so,' and also what he has effected in silence was worthy of the Father. He who truly possesses the word of Jesus is able also to hear his silence ... (εἷς οὖν διδάσκαλος, ὃς εἶπεν, καὶ ἐγένετο· καὶ ἃ σιγῶν δὲ πεποίηκεν, ἄξια τοῦ πατρός ἐστιν. ὁ λόγον Ἰησοῦ κεκτημένος ἀληθῶς δύναται καὶ τῆς ἡσυχίας αὐτοῦ ἀκουεῖν)". The point here is that God is manifested not only in words but also in silent deeds, so again silence is a way that divine presence may be felt.

In *Eph.* 19:1 we have "The virginity of Mary and her giving birth eluded the ruler of this age, likewise also the death of the Lord—three mysteries of a cry which were done in the stillness of God (τρία μυστήρια κραυγῆς, ἄτινα ἐν ἡσυχίᾳ θεοῦ ἐπράχθη)". Here there is an allusion to the hiddenness of God's plan of salvation, and thus another instance of the association of God's silence with his preconceived salvific design which we discerned in *Magn.* 8:2. But in addition to this, there is a mystery dimension to the topic. If we read this passage together with the other passages from *Eph.* which give prominence to the virtue of silence, it is clear that Ignatius recommends silence generally as a proper way for the Christian to relate to God. There is an unspeakability to God and his actions, in such a way that silent intuition is required for them to be understood and appropriated. The conclusion can hardly be avoided that the Hellenistic notion of mystical silence is operative in some form for Ignatius.

This insight provides us with some more light with regard to *Magn.* 8:2. A tension of silence and word can be observed in a couple of passages in the Ignatian corpus. We have already cited *Eph.* 15:1–2, where teaching by silence is portrayed as at least as meritorious as teaching by means of words. Another passage which may be cited in this context is *Rom.* 2:1, where the Romans are asked not to intervene in Ignatius' impending martyrdom: "For I shall never have such an opportunity to attain God, nor can you, if you remain silent be credited with a better deed; for if you remain silent and let me be, I shall be a word of God, but if you love my flesh, I shall again be a (mere) voice". Ignatius plays here, in rhetorical fashion, upon a series of opposites: σιωπᾶν–ἔργον–λόγος–φωνή. The λόγος which Ignatius wishes to be is not a mere voice, but a true witness to God, who is most authentically served in silence. This λόγος thus possesses an ambiguous status, being an outward manifestation of God's will which nevertheless does not compromise the unutterable mystery it witnesses to.

We do not have to assume that Ignatius is making "a bold connection between himself as the word of God and Christ the Word"[29] in order to think it likely that the imagery of silence and word in *Magn.* 8:2 possesses conceptual affinities with that

---

[29] Schoedel 1985, 171.

of these last two passages. The "word proceeding from silence" which is Christ may thus be interpreted as an authentic manifestation of the silence of God; a word which is not like ordinary speech, but is able to express truly the divine mystery not previously revealed to the world, and which makes it possible to grasp even the stillness of God (cf. *Eph.* 15:2: "He who truly possesses the word of Jesus is able also to hear his silence").

## 3.3. Protological Aspects

The other approach to determining the significance of the word-from-silence image in *Magn.* 8:2 is to take another look at the immediate context of the passage, and try to discern any protological motifs that it may contain. The sequel to the passage is interesting in this regard: "If, then, those who lived in old ways came to newness of hope, no longer keeping Sabbath, but living in accordance with the Lord's day, on which also our life arose through him and his death (which some deny), through which mystery we received faith ...". It seems quite likely that Ignatius is here alluding to notions about the Lord's day representing a new creation, in contrast to the Jewish view of creation as being fulfilled on the Sabbath.[30] In this perspective, the Sabbath, and Judaism in general, which Ignatius polemicizes against in this passage, come to represent a pre-creational state. This renders it quite plausible that the phrase about the word proceeding from silence should be taken as implying a reference to the word in its cosmogonic capacity as well, and that the silence which characterizes the absence of divine revelation to the Jews is also meant to be understood in terms of the pre-cosmic silence figuring in those Jewish exegetical traditions on Gen 1:1–3 which were referred to near the beginning of this article. Ignatius picks up this cosmogonic theme and applies it to the Christian interpretation of Christ as the Logos and to the idea that the resurrection represents a new creation. When Christ appeared, he implies, the world began anew; what was before has no more reality than the pre-cosmic situation before the maker sent forth his word.

This interpretation is supported by *Eph.* 15:1–2, where Ignatius also exploits the silence-word metaphor, as we saw above, and where the speaking and silent Christ is directly associated with the cosmogonic word (ὅς εἶπεν, καὶ ἐγένετο).[31] This passage indicates that the exegetical tradition on Gen 1:1–3 figuring silence and word is known to Ignatius and easily comes to his mind when he uses the metaphor. In traditio-historical terms, then, this exegesis stands out as the most plausible source of Ignatius' language here, as in *Magn.* 8:2.

---

[30] Cf. *Barn.* 15:8, Just. *Dial.* 138; Dahl 1964, 430. The commentators seem to ignore this aspect.
[31] Cf. Jeremias 1968, 82.

## 4. Ignatius and Gnosticism

In this study we have been asking questions, first, about the meaning and background of the expression λόγος ἀπὸ σιγῆς προελθών in Ignatius; secondly, about similar expressions in gnostic texts; and thirdly, about the relationship between Ignatius' and gnostic language on this point. We must now try to wind up the many threads that had to be pursued in trying to answer these questions, and reach out for some general conclusions.

4.1. First of all: Ignatius. Ignatius is, as some have suggested previously,[32] indebted to a Jewish exegetical tradition concerning Gen 1:1–3. The fact that he is using a protological theme to describe the salvation historical events of incarnation and resurrection is no great difficulty with this interpretation,[33] since such parallelism is current in early Christian theology.

On the other hand we have tried to show that silence also has positive religious value for Ignatius. It is not merely a negativity which is annulled with the appearance of the word; silence is a source of grace and insight, and Ignatius is influenced on this point by Hellenistic ideas on mystical silence.[34] Thus in the one case we are interpreting silence as lack of revelation, as ignorance in fact, whereas in the other it represents a medium of knowledge. Now we are not entitled to assume that a term always carries with it the same full range of connotations whenever it is used by an author. Nor would it be appropriate to treat Ignatius as a systematic thinker. On the other hand we ought not to be blind to the possibility that Ignatius' manner of expression may be ambiguous in itself. While it is generally true that metaphorical speech (and thus nearly all forms of language) cannot be reduced to simple meanings, it is particularly relevant here to recall that the reality which the silence-word metaphor expresses in Ignatius is in itself ambiguous. As we remarked above in connection with *Rom.* 2:1 and *Eph.* 15:1–2, Ignatius' thinking in relation to this metaphor is preoccupied with the notion of a word which authentically expresses the silence of God. It is a problematic inherent in the concept of revelation itself that the word breaks the divine silence, and at the same time makes it accessible and thus necessarily also in a sense preserves it.[35] Consequently, although we should interpret the silence of *Magn.* 8:2 as referring to the lack of revelation, this does not ex-

---

[32] See above, n. 9.

[33] Schoedel 1985, 78 and 120, fails to observe this.

[34] This objection is raised against the protological interpretation of the *topos* by Paulsen 1978, 116 n. 26. But we do not have to assume that an author can have only one thought in his mind at a time.

[35] It may be recalled that a similar ambiguity exists with the gnostic notion of Silence; see above, with n. 20.

clude that the term here also carries with it the connotations of mystical silence which are clearly present in the other passages where Ignatius speaks about God's σιγή, or ἡσυχία.

4.2. The expression λόγος ἀπὸ σιγῆς προελθών is, then, as far as Ignatius is concerned, a Jewish protological *topos* which Ignatius uses in a salvation-historical context, with additional connotations of mystical silence. With the similar expressions in gnostic texts the situation is a bit different. Here I would be inclined to see mystical silence as primary, and the use of expressions similar to that of Ignatius in protological and salvation-historical contexts as being genetically dependent on the notion of mystical silence applied in a regenerational-sacramental setting. The Jewish cosmogonical theme which inspired Ignatius cannot be discerned as a source for the gnostic mythologies.[36] Thus the nearly identical formulations in Ignatius and in the gnostic texts do not come from the same source. As far as their provenance is concerned, they represent different *topoi,* the one is Jewish, the other arises out of Hellenistic soteriology.

4.3. At least as important, though, as the different genealogies of the expression itself are the further layers of meaning which have been added to it, and which contribute creatively to the way it is being used. The pregnancy and evocativeness of the expression is such that it easily lends itself to be used with more than one meaning, and also to serve as a powerful multivalent and mythopoetic symbol by which connections between these meanings can be made. As a mythopoetic symbol it provides a formula for interpreting present experience in the light of foundational, and potentially protological events.[37] In this way, Ignatius creates a mythicizing effect by using the word-from-silence symbol to link salvation history with protology, and with notions of unfathomable mystery. The Logos which revealed itself in history is at the same time the primordial word by which God expresses his true will, and the word is also accessible by mystical intuition in the present. By interpreting the historical Christ as the primordial word, and as revelatory grace to those who now are attentive to the divine silence, Ignatius refashions historical events as myth,

---

[36] This may be the place to take exception to Philonenko's view (1962, 49), that the σκότος and σιγή in these Jewish texts are ancestors of the Valentinian syzygy βυθός–σιγή. σκότος never figures in the gnostic texts, and it is hardly conceivable how a term which negatively characterizes a precosmic lack of divine presence could have been turned into a designation of the ultimate reality. Besides, any pre-cosmic pair of concepts does not amount to a Valentinian syzygy, which is essentially a soteriological concept. The pair σκότος–σιγή in these texts can be satisfactorily explained as the result of exegetical filling in the gaps in Gen 1:1–3.

[37] I claim no originality for the theory underlying these statements, which are intended roughly in the sense of Eliade 1969.

whereby the present is symbolically integrated into a cosmogony. In a sense, then, those who have received grace are made to be present at the moment of creation, when God's authentic design is revealed.

From this point of view strong parallels can be drawn with the gnostic concept. Here, too, the word-from-silence metaphor acts as a mythopoetic symbol producing homologies between the salvation experience of the present (sacramental rebirth), protology, and salvation history. Here, too, the Saviour of history is at the same time the protological Logos manifesting the hidden mind of the deity, and an actual salvific mediator transmitting to each Christian neophyte the grace of a deity beyond speech. There thus exists an important structural affinity between Ignatius and the Gnostics. What makes us see similarities between them, then, is not only the superficial resemblance of language, but also the fact that this language is being used to express a soteriology involving a peculiar admixture of historical and mythical thought. Although it might perhaps be argued that Ignatius still is "more" historical and the Gnostics "more" mythical in their thinking about salvation, this nevertheless seems to amount more to a difference of degree than of substance. Along the lines indicated, Christian gnostic soteriology may be described as a more elaborated manifestation of patterns of thought which Ignatius shows can be found at an earlier stage as well in the history of Christian theology.

4.4. A simplistic view of the relationship of gnosticism to early Christianity is that gnostic thought was essentially mythical, ahistorical and Hellenistic, whereas "orthodox" theologians such as Ignatius maintain a historical perspective on salvation and represent a continuity with Judaism. As it happens, one of the conclusions we have drawn in this study on the word-from-silence expression is that Ignatius has taken it over from Jewish sources, whereas the Gnostics get it from a Hellenistic context. But this conclusion cannot be used to support the view about the difference in essence and background of Ignatius and the Gnostics. For the Jewish expression taken over by Ignatius does not belong to a context of historical soteriology, but to protology. Its function is precisely to mythicize salvation history, and, at the same time, to cut the bonds with Judaism by presenting Christianity as a new beginning. I shall try to elucidate this point by taking another look at the relationship between history, Judaism and myth in Ignatius.

By rejecting the relevance of Judaism, in *Magn.* 8–10, Ignatius at the same time evinces an ambiguous attitude to the role of history as the medium of salvation. Obviously Ignatius does not deny that the work of Christ took place at a particular moment in the continuum of historical time. On the other hand, however, not only are "the old fables" of Judaism "useless", but the time to which they belonged is not really time at all but rather like the pre-cosmic state which obtained before God sent forth his creative word and made a true beginning on the Lord's day. Thus while the appearance of Christ as the word takes place in time, it also annuls time, and even represents a beginning of time. Ignatius makes his point by using vocabulary and notions taken over from Judaism while at the same time denying the validity of Judaism; thus the ambiguity in his attitude to history is mirrored by the ambiguity in his attitude to the Jewish tradition. History, it might be said, *is* Judaism, both of which Ignatius denies, but nevertheless cannot do without: Just as both time and no time can be said to have existed before the going forth of Christ, the word, so there both was and was not a divine revelation to the Jews—though God on the one hand kept his silence to the Jews, on the other hand the word was nevertheless revealed to the prophets.

The notion of silence serves, it seems, as the major vehicle for expressing these sets of ambiguity. It refers, at one and the same time, to the pre-incarnational phase of history, a pre-creational condition, and a mystery whose revelation is accessible in the present. Correspondingly, the revelation of the word takes place in time, at the beginning of time, and regardless of time. All these meanings of the word-from-silence expression exist simultaneously, it cannot be reduced to any one of them in particular. This situation is able to offer an explanation for why Ignatius can say that the word was revealed to the prophets: From one point of view the prophets lived before the revelation of the word, but since revelation for Ignatius also has the sense of a revelation of divine mystery taking place regardless of chronological temporality, it is possible to think of the prophets as being contemporaneous, in a mythical warp zone, as it were, with the Christians of the present.

The form of thought we are witnessing here is one which mythicizes history, but nonetheless does not abandon a historical view of salvation. Rather, it seeks to integrate myth and history into a complex dialectic. Clearly, understanding this dialectic presents a theoretical challenge to the discipline of the history of religions, where history and myth are often regarded as mutually exclusive modes of thought. Moreover, it is a form of thought, I would contend, which characterizes Ignatius *as well as* the Christian Gnostics. The difference between them cannot be defined in terms of a distinction between history and myth. So just as the distinction of myth and history appears to need some rethinking on the theoretical level, so do we need, as historians, to reflect on the extent to which this distinction is implicitly or explicitly operative, and hence legitimate, whenever the labels "Christianity" and "gnosticism" are made to serve as distinctive categories.

# *Bibliography*

Barnard, L.W. 1963: "The Background of St. Ignatius of Antioch", in: *VigChr* 17 (1963) 193–206.

Bartsch, Hans-Werner 1940: *Gnostisches Gut und Gemeindetradition bei Ignatius von Antiochien*, Gütersloh: Bertelsmann 1940.

Bauer, Walter 1920: *Die Briefe des Ignatius von Antiochia und der Polykarpbrief* (HNT 18: Die Apostolischen Väter II), Tübingen: Mohr (Siebeck) 1920.

— 1988: *Wörterbuch zum Neuen Testament*, 6th ed., Kurt and Barbara Aland (eds.), Berlin and New York: de Gruyter 1988.

Casel, O. 1919: *De Philosophorum Graecorum Silentio Mystico* (RVV 16:2), Giessen: Töpelmann 1919.

Dahl, N. A. 1964: "Christ, Creation and the Church", in: W. D. Davies and D. Daube (eds.), *The Background of the New Testament and its Eschatology: In Honour of Charles Harold Dodd*, Cambridge: Cambridge University Press 1964, 422–443.

Eliade, Mircea 1969: "Methodological Remarks on the Study of Religious Symbolism", in: M. Eliade and J. M. Kitagawa (ed.), *The History of Religions: Essays in Methodology*, Chicago, IL and London: Chicago University Press 1969.

Elze, Martin 1963: *Überlieferungsgeschichtliche Untersuchungen zur Christologie der Ignatiusbriefe*, Diss., Tübingen 1963.

Jeremias, Joachim 1968: "Zum Logos-Problem", in: *ZNW* 59 (1968) 82–85.

Lewy, Hans 1978: *Chaldaean Oracles and Theurgy: Mysticism, Magic and Platonism in the Later Roman Empire* (1956), new ed. M. Tardieu, Paris: Études augustiniennes 1978.

Lightfoot, J. B. 1989: *The Apostolic Fathers,* 2 vols. in 5 parts (1889–1890), Peabody, MA: Hendrickson 1989.

Mortley, R. 1973: "The Theme of Silence in Clement of Alexandria", in: *JThS* 24 (1973) 197–202.

Paulsen, Henning 1978: *Studien zur Theologie des Ignatius von Antiochien* (FKDG 29), Göttingen: Vandenhoeck und Ruprecht 1978.

— 1985: *Die Briefe des Ignatius von Antiochia und der Brief des Polykarp von Smyrna*, zweite, neubearbeitete Auflage der Auslegung von Walter Bauer (HNT 18: Die Apostolischen Väter II), Tübingen: Mohr (Siebeck) 1985.

Philonenko, Marc 1962: "Remarques sur un hymne essénien de caractère gnostique", in: *Semitica* 11 (1962) 43–54.

Schoedel, William R. 1985: *Ignatius of Antioch: A Commentary on the Letters of Ignatius of Antioch* (Hermeneia), Philadelphia, PA: Fortress 1985.

Schlier, Heinrich 1929: *Religionsgeschichtliche Untersuchungen zu den Ignatiusbriefen* (BZNW 8), Giessen: Töpelmann 1929.

Theiler, Willy 1933/66: *Die Chaldäischen Orakel und die Hymnen des Synesios* (Schriften der Königsberger Gelehrten Gesellschaft: Geisteswissenschaftliche Klasse 10) 1933. [Reprinted in: *Forschungen zum Neuplatonismus* (Quellen und Studien zur Geschichte der Philosophie 10), Berlin: de Gruyter 1966.]

Thomassen, Einar and Louis Painchaud 1989: *Le Traité Tripartite* (Bibliothèque Copte de Nag Hammadi, Section «Textes» 19), Québec: Les presses de l'Université Laval 1989.

Wilson, R. McL. 1958: *The Gnostic Problem*, London: Mowbray 1958.

# SECTION D

## HISTORY OF INTERPRETATION

### AND

## PRESENT-DAY HERMENEUTICS

# Jesus' Missionary Speech as Interpreted in the Patristic Commentaries and the Apocryphal Narratives[1]

François Bovon

## 1. Introduction

The sending of the Apostles and Jesus' missionary speech (Matt 10//Mark 6//Luke 9 and 10) form the background and at the same time the centre of this paper. The usual treatment of this pericope is to make a comparison between the synoptic Gospels, to detect the oldest, traditional elements and to establish the missionary scheme of Jesus in the context of first century Jewish life, a backward direction in time. My intention here is the contrary, to inquire into the *subsequent* life of the Gospels, that is into the reception and interpretation of these texts in patristic times, not only to understand the historical effects of these canonical texts (Matt 10, Mark 6, Luke 9 and 10) but also to draw some conclusions about the time of Jesus and the early church by a retrospective deduction; this implies looking ahead, beyond the events.

During the same period, between the second and fifth centuries C.E., Christian theologians gave a full account of Jesus' missionary speech in their interpretations of the synoptic Gospels and, in a parallel development, Christian novelists tried to tell the stories of the Apostles' missions and martyrdoms. As a result of this twofold effort, we have on the one side the patristic commentaries of the Gospels, those of Origen, Jerome, Ambrose or Cyril of Alexandria; and on the other side, the so called Apocryphal Acts of the Apostles, those of Peter, John, or Philip.

It is my intention to compare these two contemporaneous productions, to inquire into their functions, and finally, to test the following hypothesis: are these two kinds of literature not two legitimate ways of interpreting the teaching of Jesus, the one

---

[1] These pages are dedicated to Professor Lars Hartman on the occasion of his sixty-fifth birthday. He has demonstrated his exegetic acumen and his theological wisdom for many years with modesty, brio and humor. I express my thanks to him for deepening contacts between exegetes of different cultural and religious spheres.

intellectual and theological, the other imaginative and narrative? I would even suggest that these two streams of Christian literature are two logical products of a first century reality, the simultaneous interpretation of the teaching of Jesus on a *reflective* level, as attested in the hermeneutics of the Pauline letters, and on a *narrative* level, by the telling of stories which give an interpretive fulfillment of the prophecies and prescriptions of Jesus, as attested in the Acts of the Apostles. Theological interpretation and narrative verification were probably two complementary ways of receiving the Christian legacy.

In the first section, I will characterize some patristic commentaries on Jesus' missionary speech; in the second I will focus on the noteworthy points in the apocryphal novels devoted to the apostles; and in the third, I will make a critical comparison between these two Christian strands in order to check my own hypothesis.

But before that, let us briefly recall the biblical situation: the sending of the disciples is told in such a similar way by Mark and by Q (the second synoptic source), that we may presume it was based on a single original literary unit. To quote Ferdinand Hahn: "Part of this primary redaction was first the sending, then the question of equipment, then the prescriptions about the stay in the houses, finally the behavior in the cities."[2] This primitive version was probably a Christian post-Easter construction with archaic, pre-Easter, independent elements. Both Mark and Q received and adapted this literary unit. Matthew then merged these two versions of Mark and Q in one single episode (Matt 10) whereas Luke reproduced them separately, making out of Mark the sending of the Twelve (Luke 9) and of Q the sending of the Seventy-two (Luke 10).

## 2. The Patristic Commentators

The reader of patristic commentaries—either Eastern or Western—is met with some surprises! Whereas the biblical pericope is in *our* eyes a missionary text, the Church Fathers treat it in the context of their ecclesiological concerns. In what can be considered as the first commentary of Luke's Gospel, the fourth book of the *Adversus Marcionem* by Tertullian, a passionate and polemical interpretation to be sure, the African writer says strangely little on the sending itself (in his pages on Luke 9).[3] Similarly, Ambrose, in *Homilies on Luke's Gospel*, understands the lambs and wolves metaphor not as the situation of Christian missionaries in the midst of pagans, but as the dramatic and actual tension between the Catholics and the heretics

---

[2] F. Hahn 1963, 34. A more recent study is D. J. Weaver 1990.

[3] Tertullian, *Adversus Marcionem* IV, 21.

(the Arians)[4]. Along the same line, the Venerable Bede in his commentary on Luke, makes a twofold ecclesiological equation: the twelve of Luke 9 are to be understood as the bishops whereas the seventy-two are to be seen as predecessors of the priests.[5]

There is a second surprise. The modern preacher is concerned to show the necessary implementation of Jesus' prescriptions in *real* life. An exegete of Antiquity has primarily a different preoccupation: he seeks to underline the harmony between Jesus' prescriptions and the Old Testament. This is particularly true for the strange obligation, present only in Luke, to refrain from greeting people on the road (Luke 10:4b). An explanation, which runs from Tertullian down to modern times (Calvin, for example), is to justify this rule by comparison with Elisha who ordered Gehazi, his servant, to give no greeting on his way (2 Kgs 4:29).[6]

This strong presence of the Old Testament is particularly manifest in the numerous homilies which Cyril of Alexandria dedicates to Jesus' sending of the disciples.[7] Cyril quotes Jer 23:16, 21 and 14:14 to distinguish the disciples sent by Christ from false prophets.[8] The condition of the Christian missionary does agree with some instructions or prophecies of the Old Testament. Cyril quotes Psalms 55:22 ("Cast your burden on the Lord and he will sustain you")[9] and Exod 12:11 ("This is how you shall eat it: your loins girded, your sandals on your feet, and your staff in your hand..."). The gesture of shaking the dust is connected by Cyril to the oil of anointment in Psalms 141:5 ("never let the oil of the wicked anoint my head").[10] The apostolic power over demonic forces is endorsed by two Old Testament scriptures; Isa 10:14 (according to the Septuagint, "I will hold the whole world in my hand as a nest...") and Hab 2:7 ("That suddenly they shall arise that bite thee...").[11]

Particularly interesting is the question of the remuneration of the missionaries. Like other Greek and Latin Fathers, Cyril operates through a chain of authorities: From Paul's opinion (1 Cor 9:11), he takes the solution he himself chooses for the salary of Christian priests and ecclesiastical workers. He feels it is faithful to the rule established by Jesus in his missionary speech, which in turn is nothing other than the Old Testament regulation of Deut 25:4.[12] Again and again the concern of the Christian commentators looks back in time to Moses and the Hebrew prophets.

---

[4] Ambrose of Milan, *Expositio in Lucam* VII, 44-53.

[5] Bede the Venerable, *In Lucam* III, 1871-74.

[6] Tertullian, *Adversus Marcionem* IV,24; J. Calvin, *Harmonie évangélique* ad Lc 10,1-12.

[7] Cyril of Alexandria, *Sermones in Lucam* 47 (on Luke 9:1-5) and 60-64 (on Luke 10:1-16).

[8] Ibid., 64.

[9] Ibid., 47. In the Septuagint, to which Cyril refers, Ps 54:23.

[10] Ibid. In the Septuagint, Ps 140:5.

[11] Idem.

[12] Ibid., 62.

Third surprise: When the sending of the disciples or apostles is not put in the light of the Old Testament, neither it is connected to any historical application in the life of the Apostles, *but rather to other teaching of Jesus himself.* Concerning the equipment of the apostles and their dedication to God, Cyril quotes two famous sayings of Jesus: "You cannot serve God and Mammon" (Luke 16:13) and "For where your treasure is, there your heart will be also" (Matt 6:21).[13]

From the patristic commentaries I have read, I know only a few firm connections with the canonical Acts of the Apostles, i.e. with the historical fulfillment of Jesus' promises: 1) explaining the poverty Jesus requires, Ambrose gives Acts 3:6 as proof of the obedience of the apostles, where Peter, accompanied by John, proclaims that he has no money, neither gold nor silver.[14] 2) Cyril, elaborating on apostolic strength and confidence, quotes once some words from Acts 4:33, showing the great power and authority of the Apostles.[15] 3) In another place,[16] the same Cyril wonders how the missionary openness to pagan unbelievers co-existed with the strict rule of Jesus "not to give holiness to dogs, nor again to cast pearls before swine" (Matt 7:6). He remembers the risk of expounding the Christian message to unbelievers, for example, the awkward position of Paul in Athens when the Greek philosophers laughed (Acts 17:32). (For Cyril, the laughter was not brought on by the message of the resurrection but by the presentation of a spiritual God who does not dwell in temples built by human hands.)

In his first *Homily on Matthew 10*, John Chrysostom is to my knowledge an exception, encouraging his audience to compare the starting point, namely the words of the Lord Jesus, with the following events, namely the application of these words to the life of the apostles.[17] Also exceptional is Cyril, when he dares to remember the fate of the apostles as the fulfillment of promises and prescriptions of the Lord:

> Let us see whether they [the pagans] too also were not at one time beasts of prey, and fiercer than wolves against the ministers of the Gospel message of salvation, but were transformed unto the gentleness and guilelessness which are by Christ's help. They too persecuted the holy apostles, not so much like men struggling with wolves, as like beasts of prey, raging savagely against sheep. And though they wronged them not, but rather called them to salvation, they stoned them, they imprisoned them, they persecuted them from city to city.[18]

That is all the reader learns; there is no concrete description of the Christian mis-

---

[13] Ibid., 47.

[14] Ambrose of Milan, *Expositio in Lucam* VII, 54.

[15] Cyril of Alexandria, *Sermones in Lucam* 64.

[16] Ibid., 62.

[17] John Chrysostom, *Homiliae in Matthaeum* 33.

[18] Cyril of Alexandria, *Sermones in Lucam* 61. Transl. R. Payne Smith.

sion, no single story of one apostolic martyrdom, no itinerary of an apostolic expedition. Even the canonical life of Peter or Paul is very poorly used as proof of the validity of Jesus' prophecy and prescriptions for mission. The only concrete notice I found in patristic commentaries not taken from canonical scriptures is an allusion by the Venerable Bede to the tragic death of apostates who abjure the Christian faith: the non-canonical tragic death of Simon the Magician is put side by side with the well known death of Judas.[19]

At the end of this first look at the field of Christian commentaries, let me draw some preliminary conclusions.

Although written for colleagues or for people of the congregation, commentaries and homilies are in fact the products of theologians, scholars preoccupied with the doctrinal unity of the two Testaments and the adequacy of their interpretation for the Christian creed, and prepared to use these interpretations in a polemical way. They do not feel the modern need to see the historical application of the text in the life of the apostle, nor do they dare to communicate the delight of telling the fate of the disciples in a narrative genre. It is also possible that in some places the "commentary" genre prevented them from following a narrative interpretation. Finally, the existence of heretical Acts of the apostles must surely have confirmed their reluctance.

## 3. The Apocryphal Narratives

The reader of the so-called Apocryphal Acts of the Apostles[20] also has cause for amazement. On the one hand, the reader notices an extreme affinity between these texts and Jesus' missionary speech, and on the other (the difference between the two kinds of documents is evident) the scarcity of explicit references to the canonical Gospels.

The motif of the sending of the apostles appears in some apocryphal texts: as a post-Easter appearance narrative, it develops texts like Matthew 28 in a very free fashion and actualizes the first pre-Easter sending of Matthew 10//Luke 9.[21] Attention is given to a single apostle. In the earliest Acts, the apostle travels alone, but in

---

[19] Bede the Venerable, *In Lucam* IV, 185-86. This may be in fact an allusion to the story of Simon, told in Acts 8:9-24, but in that passage the fate of Simon is not yet sealed.

[20] On these, cf. E. Plümacher 1978; F. Bovon (ed.) 1981; D. R. MacDonald (ed.) 1986; R. I. Pervo 1987. The recent *Clavis Apocryphorum Novi Testamenti* by M. Geerard 1992 provides the necessary indications for the study of the Apocryphal Acts of the Apostles (publications, monographs, etc.) and has attributed a reference number to each document.

[21] For example, *The Acts of Thomas* 1; see J.-D. Kaestli 1981.

the later compositions, like the *Acts of Andrew and Matthias*,[22] there are often two apostles and the canonical rule is observed. It is interesting to mention that orthodox re-writings of apocryphal literature give to a lonely apostle a strong companion— the person of Peter himself. In this case, the intention is twofold: to respect the rule of the two messengers, and to give doctrinal protection by the Prince of the apostles! In any case, the names of these apostles correspond to the list we have in our canonical Gospels and Acts: Peter, John, Thomas, and so on.

The possible situations that the missionary speech of Jesus envisages are all illustrated in the travel narratives of the apocryphal Acts. We read the apostolic peregrinations on sea and on land recounted in a very novelistic style, with dangers and adventures, shipwrecks and terrifying monsters. The entrance to cities and to houses, both situations examined in Matthew 10 and Luke 10, are illustrated with talent. In a still unpublished fragment,[23] one writer tells us the story of the arrival of Philip, Bartholomew and a third companion, a woman, Mariamne, the sister of Philip, in the city called Ophioryme. In a dramatic way, we are told that at the city gates, the guards wear cruel snakes on their shoulders. When the travellers are worshippers of the Adder, goddess of the city, the snakes let them enter without harm. But if the travellers, like Philip and his companions, worship other gods, their lives are in danger. Without any explicit quotation from Matthew or Luke, this narrative interprets the coming of the apostles and the descent of peace onto a town which is then liberated from the demonic oppression of the Adder goddess and the snakes.

The same is true of the prescribed entry into homes. In a charming, novelistic episode, the author of the Acts of Paul tells us how the apostle meets the young girl Thecla. On his way to Iconium, he is welcomed by a man who is very eager to invite him to his home. Answering the greetings of Onesiphorus, Paul salutes him with the words "Grace be with you and with your house". This house—following the Christian rule attested by the missionary speech—becomes the meeting place of the newly founded congregation. Prayers and liturgy take place here. In a neighboring house lives a young girl Thecla, who falls under the charm of Paul's voice (she has not seen him, only heard him). Several episodes bring her to faith and the apostle to prison, before they meet each other at last![24]

The question of financial remuneration (that is, in return for the gracious gift of the gospel, a minimum compensation in the form of daily food is accepted) plays a certain role in the apocryphal novels in discrete, implicit harmony with Christian usage and Gospel prescription (Matt 10:8: gratuity; Matt 10:9: "Provide neither gold, nor silver nor brass in your purses"). We already recalled the sentence of Peter

---

[22] Publication and study of these Acts in D. R. MacDonald 1990.

[23] *The Acts of Philip* XIII.

[24] *Acts of Paul and Thecla* 1-43.

in the canonical Acts of the Apostles ("Silver and gold have I none; but such as I have give I thee: In the name of Jesus Christ of Nazareth rise up and walk" Acts 3:6). We might also keep in mind some of the reactions of the apostles in the apocryphal acts: Philip for example, refuses to take a large provision of bread for the trip:[25] John pushes asceticism so far as to be nourished sufficiently by a single date for a full week![26] Often the Christian apostles do refuse gold and silver, pretentious banquets, luxurious furniture or expensive clothes.[27] All of these illustrations, easy to understand for the pagan reader, are didactic and delightful, free and faithful interpretations of the Gospel prescriptions.

Important also is the *power* of the apostle. We remember that, according to the canonical Gospels, Jesus gave power and authority to his twelve disciples (Matt 10:1//Luke 9:1//Mark 6:7). The speeches, the miracles, the sovereign knowledge, and many qualities of the heroes of the apocryphal Acts are like musical, narrative variations of this theme. Let us give ear to these words of the apostle Peter in his own legendary Acts:

> For this is not only to convince you with words that it is the Christ that I am preaching, but also by deeds and marvellous powers I urge you through the faith in Jesus Christ....[28]

The following passage from the *Acts of Andrew*[29] shows the prestige of this supernatural power bestowed upon the apostle. It is a servant of the Roman governor Aegeates who makes this revelation to his master:

> There is a foreigner who sojourns here and became famous not only in this city, but in all Achaea. He accomplishes great miracles and healings which are above human capacity, as I can partly testify because I was present when dead people were resurrected by him.[30]

If this assumption of divine forces empowering the disciples is perhaps the most constant motif throughout the apocryphal Acts, the suffering and martyrdom, which the canonical Jesus announced to his disciples, are also integral parts of the apocryphal scene. The dramatic death of the apostle is prepared by his ascetic way of life. Accustomed to the renouncement of pleasure, the apocryphal apostle is ready to freely (masterfully I would say), renounce his own life. In agreement with an aret-

---

[25] *Acts of Philip* VII, 7 (93).

[26] *Acts of John in Rome* 5-6. These Acts, to be distinguished from the early Acts, bear the number 216 in the *Clavis* of Geerard 1992.

[27] See, for example, *Acts of Philip* V, 14-22 (56-60).

[28] *Acts of Peter* 7. English transl. R. McL. Wilson; Hennecke/Schneemelcher (eds.) II 1965, 289.

[29] See the edition by J.-M. Prieur 1989.

[30] *Acts of Andrew* 25.

alogical tendency, the authors do embellish the dreadful tortures, but it is important to remark that at no place is martyrdom removed from the picture. The Christian necessity to testify not only by words, but also by deeds (by giving life through miracles and by giving one's own life in sacrifice) runs through the apocryphal Acts and its origin lies in the canonical Gospel, in the Beatitudes (Matt 5:1-12//Luke 6:20-23) and in the missionary teaching of Jesus (Matt 10:17-20//Mark 13:9-13//Luke 21:12-19).

It is not only the fate of the apostle, his successful mission and his accepted suffering which accomplish the promises of Christ. It is also the mood and the character of the apostle. There is a kind of *normative psychology* of the apostle, be he Peter or Thomas, Paul or John. The repetitious, sometimes tedious style of these works is explained, beyond the similarity of the narrative motifs, by this normative Christian behavior. The apostle is never too tired to preach; his fortitude is endless. He is never openly anxious, and if once he is, particularly at the moment of departure for mission, he is briskly chastised by the Lord. This absence of cowardice is particularly evident in the public scenes. Before the most impressive Roman legate, even the most ruthless Emperor (Nero in the *Acts of Paul*[31]), our apocryphal apostle fulfils the word of the canonical Jesus: "And ye shall be brought before governors and kings for my sake, for a testimony against them and the Gentiles. But when they deliver you up, take no thought how or what ye shall speak: for it shall be given you in that same hour what ye shall speak. For it is not ye that speak, but the spirit of your Father which speaketh in you" (Matt 10:18-20). Do we not read a narrative echo of this promise at the end of the *Acts of Paul*:

> And among the many Paul also was brought bound; to him all his fellow-prisoners gave heed, so that Caesar [i.e. the emperor Nero] observed that he was the man in command. And he said to him: "Man of the great king [the Lord Christ who just resurrected the friend of the emperor, Patroclus], but (now) my prisoner, why did it seem good to thee to come secretly into the empire of the Romans and enlist soldiers from my province?" But Paul, filled with the Holy Spirit, said before them all: "Caesar, not only from thy province do we enlist soldiers, but from the whole world."[32]

The apostle is always modest. According to the evangelical rule, he never asks in the Apocrypha for better equipment or more powerful means. An episode of the *Acts of Philip* is devoted to the evangelical rule not to return evil for evil. During his martyrdom, Philip, remembering the evangelical temptation to punish the Samaritans (Luke 9:54) vindicates himself and from the cross fustigates his oppressors and sends them into the swaling earth. The heavenly Lord rectifies the situation and

---

[31] *Acts of Paul, Martyrdom* 1-5.
[32] Ibid., 3. Transl. R. McL. Wilson; Hennecke-Schneemelcher (eds.) II 1965, 384.

promises to his boiling apostle a temporary punishment *post mortem*! A negative vision of an apostle who has still the time *ante mortem* to repent![33]

Even when he is a man of the lower class, the apostle is never ashamed if he is confronted with aristocratic ladies or political authorities. He is "wise as a serpent and harmless as a dove" (Matt 10:16). He is the narrative incarnation of the apodictic prescription. The apocryphal Acts are novelistic commentaries of the canonized Gospels.

And of course, the apostle is ready to die as a witness to his God. If he is powerful and sovereign because of the divine force which inhabits him, he is also obedient and submissive to his master (the difference between God the Father and the Lord Jesus Christ is not always clearly noticed by the apocryphal Acts). This bi-polarity of strength and weakness, of moral standing and existential defeat, which is unique in the literature of the antique world, connects strongly the apocryphal Acts to the canonical Gospels.

At the end of this second part, let me conclude with some formal observations. In my opinion, the apocryphal Acts constitute clear evidence for the *reception* of Jesus' missionary speech as attested in the canonical Gospels. They manifest a narrative (which does not mean popular) understanding of the teaching of Jesus. The intellectual levels of the various writers may differ strongly, from the philosophical author of the *Acts of Andrew* to the prosaic and uneducated Christian who wrote the *Acts of Peter*. Nevertheless, all of them—independently of their more or less ascetic and Encratite ideal—believe that the missionary will of Jesus has been empowered by the concrete commitment of his disciples. To remember with details and delight the ups and downs in the disciples' lives is for the writers a legitimate form of taking the canonical text into Christian consideration.

But like all commentators, the authors of the apocryphal Acts make certain choices and omissions and express their preferences. They simply "forget" the prescription of Jesus to restrict mission to the lost sheep of Israel and to avoid the road of the Samaritans and the Pagans (Matt 10:5-6). They also substitute their spiritual and personal belief in a generous (and a little narrow-minded) divinity for the eschatological and universal Kingdom of God (Matt 10:7//: "And as ye go, preach saying, The Kingdom of heaven is at hand" plays no role at all in this apocryphal literature).

The follow-up of the Gospel metaphors is also interesting to consider. On one side we observe a certain flexibility: as possible fulfillment of the sentence on the sheep and the wolves, we find in the *Acts of Philip* the reconciliation of a leopard and a kid.[34] In that case, the apocryphal narrative commentary is not the usual sort

---

[33] *Acts of Philip, Martyrdom* 23-48 (127-45).

[34] *Acts of Philip* VIII, 15-21 (96-101).

of meta-text,[35] i.e. the commentary, but an unusual—in any case a not sufficiently recognized—narrative extension. Through this new metaphor, ("new" compared with the old canonical Gospel), the author adds a supplementary metaphor to the Gospel metaphor of the sheep and the wolves: in this way he tells us more than does the Gospel: not only will the Christian mission be painful and dangerous (canonical metaphor) but it will emerge in an eschatological peace (apocryphal metaphor). Quoting explicitly neither the New nor the Old Testament, our subtle author is clearly alluding to the prophet Isaiah who, as we remember, expects paradisiac peace between lambs and wolves, leopards and kids in the eschatological future (Isa 11:6). So the *newer* apocryphal metaphor of the leopard and the kid proves to be as biblically old as the new, Gospel one.

Another aspect of the fate of the metaphors is their transformation from image to reality. If it is already visible by the story of the leopard and the kid, which are real animals and real converts in the *Acts of Philip*, it is even more evident in the *Acts of Peter and Andrew*, where the apostle Peter is strong enough to let a real camel go through a no less real needle.[36] This concretization of the metaphor coincides with a historization of the prescription of Jesus. What he *said* has become *deeds* through the work and lives of his apostles. Such is the apocryphal conviction, whereas the theological commentaries are eager to demonstrate rather that the sayings of Jesus are in harmony with other sayings, the written prescriptions of the Law.

## 4. The Comparability of the Patristic Interpretations and the Apocryphal Narratives

I shall limit my comparison of these two kinds of early Christian literature to three main topics: a) the endowment of divine power to the apostle; b) the strict limitation of means; and c) the readiness to face pain and death. These are the most relevant aspects forming the background of a general confrontation. Christology and the image of God may differ extensively. Ecclesiology and questions of ministry or ethics are often substantially distinct, as appears for example in the orthodox re-writing of our Apocrypha at a later date: the docetic Christology of apocryphal discourses is rectified in the later versions, and the condemnation of marriage and the proposing of encratic behavior softened. It was the theology of the Fathers which imposed these doctrinal improvements.

In contrast, the activity of the apostle was treated similarly by church fathers and

---

[35] In the terminology of G. Genette 1982, 10-11.
[36] *Acts of Peter and Andrew* 13-21. No. 237 in the *Clavis* of Geerard 1992.

apocryphal writers. Both *admired* the first disciples of Christ. Both were convinced that the mediation of the apostles was an indispensable benediction. Whereas the New Testament refuses any hagiographical interest in the disciples (their picture disappears behind their message) patristic and apocryphal literature both draw iconic images of the apostles. Through their deeds, their wisdom, and even their person, the power of Christ can reach the human world which expects and needs this beneficial influence.[37]

Cyril of Alexandria speaks again and again in his *Homily on Luke* 9[38] of the apostolic powers. Christ, he says, remunerates the believers, particularly the apostles, for their faith. He gives them the strength to overcome demonic powers. These specific gifts which the apostles receive are to be admired, for they are a parallel and a continuation of the divine force which God transmitted to Christ himself. It would have been useless to be appointed apostle only to be deprived of divine power. This thaumaturgic gift brings the skeptics to reason, which means for Cyril to the faith. The conclusion of the Bishop of Alexandria is that we must *venerate* the apostles, because through them we can venerate the *Christ* who sent them.

These patristic witnesses are in complete harmony with the picture drawn by the Apocrypha. Already in 1932 Rosa Söder distinguished what she called the "aretalogical element" (ἀρετή—Phil 4:8; 2 Pet 1:5; virtue as manifestation of divine power in current Greek) as the most important motif in the Apocryphal Acts of the Apostles.[39] Here are just a few examples of this manifestation of power: (1) in the Coptic fragment of the original *Acts of Peter*, the apostle performs a double miracle on his own daughter;[40] (2) the Latin *Acts of Peter* tell of a "fight" (ἀγών) between the apostle Peter and Simon the Magician, in which Peter establishes his superiority by being able to perform several resurrections;[41] (3) in the *Acts of Thomas*, the cupbearer of the king from Andrapolis must undergo dreadful punishment at the hands of the apostle because he laughed at him;[42] (4) in the *Acts of Andrew* preserved in the *Life* of this apostle by Gregory of Tours,[43] we find a typical repetitive sequence of persuasive miracles. Whereas the New Testament miracles of the apostles were limited and concentrated on the healing of human beings, the apocryphal miracles concern animals as well as humans, material objects (stones, plants etc.) as well as the living world.[44]

---

[37] Cf. Bovon 1981.

[38] Cyril of Alexandria, *Sermones in Lucam* 47.

[39] R. Söder 1932/69, 51-102.

[40] Cf. M. Tardieu 1984, 217-22, 403-10.

[41] *Acts of Peter* 23-29.

[42] *Acts of Thomas* 6-8; cf. A.-J. Festugière 1983, 47-49.

[43] Cf. Prieur 1989 II, 551-651.

[44] Cf. Söder1932/69, 60-65, 109-12.

In a world where belief in the irrational was strong,[45] the divine power of the apostle—either proclaimed as commentary of New Testament teaching or depicted as apocryphal illustration—had the same function: to validate the truth of the Christian message by miracles and healings, that is by the very activity of a victorious God. In the *Acts of John* the Ephesians proclaim: "We are converted, now that we have seen thy marvellous works!"[46] To this missionary function, we may add a double apologetical intention: a) to counter-balance the social weakness of the Church with a spiritual strength; and b) to prove the divine—and not the demonic—origin of the thaumaturgic success of the Christians. In so doing, both patristic exegesis and apocryphal narratives lost hold of an important element of the Gospel of Jesus and of Paul: the strength of God is no longer shown by the weakness of human reality; on the contrary, the theology of the cross is over-shadowed by the theology of glory and triumphalism. But this evolution did not start in the time after the New Testament: it is present from the beginning, traces of it being already visible in the canonical Acts of the Apostles and in the Gospel of John.[47]

As to the equipment of the apostles, to the poverty of means at their disposal, we find a similar understanding in the patristic interpretations and in the Apocrypha. Christ's rules are open to an admirative description or an admirative picture of apostolic behavior. Such a description could be tempered by a stoic tone, as in the idealized interpretation of Cyril who underlines the simplicity and the disinterestedness of the apostles. This infers an internal disposition to cast one's burdens on the Lord (Ps 55:22) and ends for the Church Father in a practical advantage.[48] Bede the Venerable follows the same line: to be confident in God and not to lose time with worldly affairs is an expression of human wisdom.[49] But in the Apocrypha, apostolic poverty or the apostolic limitation of means according to Jesus' missionary speech is *not* an emphasized element. The refusal of provisions or of money, when it is mentioned, is not connected with the prescriptions of Jesus, but with the encratic intention of the apostle himself.[50] The effect, however, is the same. Through little means the apostle will have much to show and to offer. The disciple of Christ needs the help of divine power, but scorns the usual human capacities and material means.

This observation becomes pertinent when we consider the apostolic martyrdoms. In the case of the apocryphal Andrew, for example, the crowd pleads: "He has hung

---

[45] Cf. E. R. Dodds 1959 and idem 1965.

[46] *Acts of John* 42. Cf. E. Junod and J.-D. Kaestli 1983.

[47] Cf. Acts 5:15; 13:9-12; 14:3, 8-10; 19:11-7; John 2:11; 5:19-47; 9:1-7; 11:4-16, 38-44.

[48] Cyril of Alexandria, *Sermones in Lucam* 47.

[49] Bede the Venerable *In Lucam* III, 1921-6.

[50] Cf. *Acts of John* 56-57; *Acts of John in Rome* 5-6; *Acts of Philip* VII, 7 (93); cf. Bovon 1988, 4492.

there for two days and he is still alive. He has eaten nothing but has nourished all of us with his words."[51]

As prophesied by the canonical Jesus, the disciple is persecuted by political authorities, in the case of Andrew, by Aegeates, the Roman governor of Achaea.[52] Even if Matthew 10 is not explicitly quoted, it is certainly the events prophesied in Matthew 10 which are taking place ("And ye shall be brought before governors and kings for my sake..." v. 18). Two narrative detours give a theological and ethical interpretation to the prophesied event: first, a demonic force is presupposed behind the decision of the governor. The author explains that the Devil inspires the prince, according to a Jewish and Christian belief.[53] Secondly, the pagan hostility arises out of frustration. It is not so much the conversion of the wife of Aegeates which gives reason for persecution, but the new sexual ethics of the converted Maximilla, her sudden chastity.[54]

As Jesus had foretold, "whoever does not take up the cross and follow me is not worthy of me" (Matt 10:38). In the apocryphal Acts, Andrew is logically condemned to this very torment. And as the canonical Jesus promised it, "when they hand you over, do not worry about how you are to speak or what you are to say; for what you are to say will be given to you at that time; for it is not you who speak, but the Spirit of your Father speaking through you" (Matt 10:19-20). It may be said—*cum grano salis*—that on that occasion the Holy Spirit was very loquacious, for the dying apostle speaks in long discourses, to the cross itself, to the converted people, to the crowd and so on.[55] There is, however, a strong difference between the canonical prophecy and the apocryphal fulfillment, a difference which is also perceptible in the theology of glory of the Church Fathers: whereas the New Testament does not eliminate the reality of suffering and agony, the apocryphal apostle is smiling on the cross, showing to everybody that the human punishment does not reach him in a painful way.[56] This docetic touch in the Apocrypha is confirmed by the content of the apostolic teaching: "In one word you left away every transitory thing: let yourselves now be taken away with me".[57]

The martyrdom of Andrew is a sublime trip, the passing away from material to spiritual reality. In a sense, for us in a very strange sense, this death is a narrative

---

[51] I quote the second Greek version of the *Passio sancti Andreae Apostoli*, also called *Epistle of the Presbyters and Deacons of Achaea* 12. On this, see Prieur 1989, 13-14; Geerard 1992, 138 (no. 226).

[52] *Acts of Andrew* 51-65.

[53] Ibid., 45.

[54] Ibid., 51.

[55] Ibid., 54-59 (note that the apostle addresses his eulogy to the cross before mounting it).

[56] Ibid., 55.

[57] Ibid., 57.

interpretation of the sentence of Jesus also preserved in the Matthean missionary speech: "Do not fear those who kill the body but cannot kill the soul; rather fear him who can destroy both soul and body in hell" (Matt 10:28). Indeed, Andrew has no fear of the governor, but he fears the God who holds body and soul at his disposal.[58]

This theological interpretation of martyrdom is not peculiar to the Apocrypha. We find it as well in several commentaries of Matt 10 and Luke 10. One example is the first homily John Chrysostom devotes to Jesus' missionary speech (Matt 10). Concerning Matt 10:22 ("You will be hated by all because of my name. But the one who endures to the end will be saved"), the famous preacher says that the Christian apostles outmatch pagan heroes by far; for finding their human adversaries like devils, they do not slay them. On the contrary, they transform them into companions (rivals in goodness) of angels. And all this, the apostles accomplish through their martyrdom.[59]

## 5. Conclusion

Just like neighbors who ignore each other yet share the same sunshine and water, the patristic interpretations and the apocryphal narratives have stood side by side down through the centuries. My hypothesis is that this strange phenomenon has biblical roots: the Pauline epistles and the synoptic tradition stand also side by side, ignoring each other. Both are nevertheless in our New Testament because both are legitimate witnesses and legitimate heirs of the Gospel. Patristic interpretation, like the canonical epistles, is a theological, intellectual and pastoral reception of the message of Jesus. The apocryphal novels, like the canonical Acts of the Apostles, are narrative implements and commentaries of the prescriptions and prophecies of Jesus. Both the patristic commentaries and the apocryphal novels are necessary because together they testify to the complementarity of words and deeds. To speak and to act—the words and the deeds of Jesus are the structural bi-polarity of the Good News. Without words, the deeds look like mute and unintelligible events; without narratives, the words sound like unreal and unbelievable promises. The Christian faith rests in these two pillars.

What I have defended so far is the legitimacy of two kinds of reception. My demonstration was made mainly within a formal framework. The content of the stories as well as the intrinsic quality of their interpretation must also be tested. However, I have not forgotten the danger of a theology of glory. One could also challenge in the patristic commentaries the use and abuse of allegorization, and condemn in the

---

[58] Ibid., 62.

[59] John Chrysostom, *Homiliae in Matthaeum* 33.

Apocrypha a gospel message which is based more on the apostle and his spiritual God than on the Christ and his historical life and death. But here let us limit ourselves to the content of the form (to use the terminology of some linguists), for in it we find the inspiring support for action and for meditation. Have we not had in our century an ecumenical confirmation of these two complementary elements, with the movement of "Life and Work" and the meetings of "Faith and Order"?[60]

## Bibliography

Bovon, F. (ed.) 1981: *Les Actes apocryphes des apôtres: Christianisme et monde païen* (Publications de la Faculté de théologie de l'Université de Genève 4), Geneva: Labor et Fides 1981.

Bovon, F. 1981: "La vie des apôtres: Traditions bibliques et narrations apocryphes", in: Bovon, F. (ed.) 1981, 141-58.

— 1988: "Les Actes de Philippe", in: Temporini, H. and Haase, W. (eds.), *Aufstieg und Niedergang der römischen Welt (ANRW)* II, 25,6, Berlin/New York: de Gruyter 1988, 4431-527.

Dodds, E. R. 1951: *The Greeks and the Irrational* (Sather Classical lectures 25), Berkeley, CA: University of California 1951.

— 1965: *Pagans and Christians in an Age of Anxiety: Some Aspects of Religious Experience from Marcus Aurelius to Constantine* (Wiles Lectures 1963), Cambridge, Eng.: Cambridge University Press 1965.

Festugière, A.-J. 1983: *Les Actes apocryphes de Jean et de Thomas: Traduction française et notes critiques* (Cahiers d'Orientalisme 6), Geneva: P. Cramer 1983.

Genette, G. 1982: *Palimpsestes: La littérature au second degré* (Collection poétique), Paris: Seuil 1982.

Geerard, M. 1992: *Clavis Apocryphorum Novi Testamenti* (Corpus Christianorum), Turnhout: Brepols 1992.

Hahn, F. 1963: *Das Verständnis der Mission im Neuen Testament* (WMANT 13), Neukirchen-Vluyn: Neukirchener Verlag 1963.

Hennecke, E. and Schneemelcher, W. (eds.) 1965: *New Testament Apocrypha,* 2 vols., translated by R. McL. Wilson et al., Philadelphia, PA: Westminster Press 1965.

Junod, E. and Kaestli, J.-D. 1983: *Acta Iohannis,* 2 vols. (Corpus Christianorum, Series Apocryphorum 1-2), Turnhout: Brepols 1983.

Kaestli, J.-D. 1981: "Les scènes d'attribution des champs de mission et de départ de l'apôtre dans les Actes apocryphes", in: Bovon, F. (ed.) 1981, 249-64.

---

[60] Other elements of the *Wirkungsgeschichte* of Jesus' missionary speech can be found in U. Luz 1990, II, 74-161 et passim. I would like to thank my assistants for their help, Ms. Isabelle Chappuis–Juillard and Ms. Eva Tobler. I would like also to express my gratitude to Ms. Jane Haapiseva–Hunter who applied her talents of translation in giving English form to these pages.

— 1983; see under Junod, E. and Kaestli, J.-D. 1983.

Luz, U. 1985/90: *Das Evangelium nach Matthäus,* 2 vols. (EKK 1), Neukirchen-Vluyn: Neukirchener Verlag; and Zürich: Benziger 1985-90.

MacDonald, D. R. (ed.) 1986: *The Apocryphal Acts of the Apostles* (*Semeia* 38), Atlanta, GA: Scholars Press 1986.

MacDonald, D. R. 1990: *The Acts of Andrew and the Acts of Andrew and Matthias in the City of the Cannibals* (SBL.TT 33, Christian Apocrypha Series 1), Atlanta, GA: Scholars Press 1990.

Pervo, R. I. 1987: *Profit with Delight: The Literary Genre of the Acts of the Apostles,* Philadelphia, PA: Fortress Press 1987.

Plümacher, E. 1978: "Apokryphe Apostelakten", in: *Pauly-Wissowa Realenzyclopädie,* Suppl. XV, Munich: A. Druckenmüller 1978, cols. 11-70.

Prieur, J.-M. 1989: *Acta Andreae,* 2 vols. (Corpus Christianorum, Series Apocryphorum 5-6), Turnhout: Brepols 1989.

Schneemelcher, W. 1965; see under Hennecke, E. and Schneemelcher, W. (eds.) 1965.

Söder, Rosa 1932/69: *Die apokryphen Apostelgeschichten und die romanhafte Literatur der Antike* (Würzburger Studien zur Altertumswissenschaft 3), Stuttgart: W. Kohlhammer 1932 [reprinted, Darmstadt: Wissenschaftliche Buchgesellschaft 1969].

Tardieu, M. 1984: *Écrits gnostiques: Codex de Berlin* (Sources Gnostiques et Manichéennes 1), Paris: Cerf 1984.

Weaver, Dorothy J. 1990: *Matthew's Missionary Discourse: A Literary Critical Analysis* (JSNT.S 38), Sheffield, Eng.: JSOT Press 1990.

# God, the Fathers, and the Prophets
## The Use of Heb 1:1 in Recent Theology of Religions

### Tord Fornberg

## 1. Introduction

Long ago (πάλαι) God spoke to our fathers (πατέρες) in many and various ways (πολυμερῶς καὶ πολυτρόπως) by the prophets (προφῆται); but in these last days he has spoken to us by a Son, whom he appointed heir of all things, through whom he also created the worlds.

With these well-known words (Heb 1:1-2) the unknown author of the Epistle to the Hebrews takes his starting point. His whole introductory paragraph (Heb 1:1-4)[1] is extremely well construed, comparable to Luke 1:1-4. Its basic meaning is clear; the author compares two ways through which God has revealed himself to the world, "by the prophets" and "by a Son," the revelation by the Son being infinitely more valuable. The author thus at once brings in the typology that he will pursue all through his writing. Christ, being God's own Son, who "reflects the glory of God" (Heb 1:3), became human and purified humanity from sins and finally was enthroned at the right hand of God (Heb 1:3-4). He is thus the climax of all divine revelation.

## 2. The History of Interpretation

But who are the fathers (πατέρες) and the prophets mentioned in 1:1? Through most of church history the answer has been self-evident: the author writes about the Israelite patriarchs, Abraham, Isaac and Jacob, and those who took up their inheritance, among them prophets like Isaiah,[2] to whom God revealed his sending of the Mes-

---

[1] See Gräßer 1990, 56-57 for a short discussion of how Heb 1:1-4 was used in early Christian theology.

[2] Cf. Sir 44:1 introducing chaps. 44-50 on the Jewish "fathers." See also Matt 23:30, 32, Rom 9:5, Acts 3:13 and *m. Abot* with statements ascribed to early Rabbinic authorities.

siah, fulfilled when the Virgin Mary said her yes to Gabriel (Luke 1:38).[3]

Some examples will be given to show this unanimity among theologians all through church history. Modern historical-critical scholarship takes for granted that the author of Hebrews wrote about the ancestors of the Jewish people, including not only the patriarchs Abraham, Isaac and Jacob but all the past generations of Jews, and that the prophets include not only Isaiah, Jeremiah, Ezechiel and the minor prophets but also Moses, sometimes called the greatest of all prophets, and other great men through whom God has revealed himself to the Israelites.

We may mention some of the most recent commentaries. Thus the evangelical W. Lane[4] finds no reason to specify the identity of the fathers but indicates that the prophets "may actually refer to the OT Scriptures."[5] It is of course not surprising that an author in the Word Biblical Commentary expresses a traditional evangelical position that revelation is limited to the biblical sphere. The fact that he does not find it necessary to argue his case vis-à-vis more liberal exegetes, however, mirrors the virtual unanimity among biblical scholars on this question.

These latter can be exemplified by two other authors of newly published commentaries. Harold Attridge, writing in the often radical Hermeneia series,[6] just takes for granted that οἱ πατέρες refer to "the fathers of the old covenant" and that οἱ προφῆται "encompass all those, from the patriarchs through Moses, Joshua, David, and the classical prophets, through whom God speaks." The German Protestant theologian Erich Gräßer, writing in the ecumenical series Evangelisch-katholischer Kommentar zum Neuen Testament, identifies the fathers of the old covenant with those of the new covenant;[7] the New Testament fathers listened to the proclamation of salvation in the Old Testament.

These examples could easily be multiplied.[8] This, however, would hardly serve any real purpose; the meaning of the two words πατέρες and προφῆται is beyond discussion for modern scholarship.

It is of course no wonder that the vast majority of pre-20th century scholars also expressed this view; it was an axiom that the only valid pre-Christian revelation was given through the great figures of the Old Testament.[9] These theologians were certainly faithful to the inheritance from the Reformers, especially Martin Luther and

---

[3] See de la Potterie 1987 for hermeneutical problems in this pericope, esp. in Luke 1:28.

[4] Lane 1991, 11; thus also Hagner 1990, 21.

[5] He makes this suggestion in spite of the parallelism between the two prepositional expressions ἐν τοῖς προφήταις and ἐν υἱῷ.

[6] Attridge 1989, 38-39.

[7] Gräßer 1990, 53.

[8] E.g., Weiß 1991, 137, Vanhoye 1969, 57-58, Bruce 1964, 2 and Héring 1970, 2.

[9] E.g., Starke 1741, 730, Bengel (1742) 1860, 858-59, Ebrard 1855, 12, Delitzsch 1857, 2-3 and, somewhat later, Westcott 1909, 6.

John Calvin, who, however, differed from each other in their view of the relationship between the Old Testament and the New Testament, Luther emphasizing the discontinuity and Calvin the continuity between the two covenants.[10]

In his lectures on Hebrews Luther comments upon 1:1-2[11] according to the rule *a minore ad maius* and thus points to the great difference between the two covenants. He writes next to nothing about the identity of the prophets but happens to exemplify them in passing by Isaiah or David, thus revealing—as could be expected—that he was thinking of the great men of the Old Testament. His emphasis on the vast chasm between the revelation through the prophets and through Christ may, however, open up the possibility for Lutheran theologians to include non-Israelite revelation as well, but this is not stated explicitly and hardly even implicitly.

John Calvin comments upon Heb 1:1-2[12] and finds a three-fold contrast in the text: formerly by the prophets *contra* now by the Son, formerly to the fathers *contra* now to us and formerly at various times *contra* now at the end of the times. But he immediately goes on to point out the agreement between the OT Law and the NT Gospel[13] and thus the continuity in the biblical revelation earlier emphasized by Thomas Aquinas. The very firm connection between the OT and the NT, pointed to by Calvin, however, serves the purpose to show a united Bible in contradistinction to later Church tradition as exemplified by "the whole system of Popery."

The Church fathers also took it for self-evident that the author of Hebrews thought of the biblical revelation. The earliest text is to be found in Clement of Alexandria in the late 2nd century AD. He had the phrase "in many and various ways" refer to "the prophets and the gospel and the blessed apostles."[14] The contrast between the OT and the revelation through Christ has disappeared and no distinction is made. The corollary is of course that the OT revelation is distinguished clearly from all non-biblical revelation. His successor in the Alexandrian tradition, Origen, used the same phrase in a letter to Africanus and had it refer to how Daniel prophesied in different manners, "by vision, by dreams, and by the appearance of an angel."[15]

Augustine may open up the possibility of a wider interpretation, which, however,

---

[10] Hagen 1974, 14-19 and 53-55. Luther followed Chrysostom and Erasmus, and Calvin followed Thomas Aquinas. See Caragounis 1990, 38-39 who finds an argument for a total continuity between the OT and the NT in Heb 1:1-2.

[11] Ed. Pelikan 1968, 109.

[12] Ed. Owen 1948, 31-33. On this text see also *Institutes* 2.10,1; ed. McNeil 1960, 424 and 2.15,1, pp. 494-95.

[13] See, e.g., Hagen 1981, 58-65, esp. pp. 64-65.

[14] *Stromateis* 7.16.

[15] *To Africanus* according to Greer 1973, 31. Other notes on Heb 1:1 can be found in John Chrysostom, *Homily* 15 on John 1:18 and possibly Paulinus of Nola, *Letter* 12.2.

does not leave the confines of the OT, even if it is partly pre-Israelite. After having quoted Heb 1:1 he goes on to mention those to whom God spoke: Adam, Cain and Noah followed by Abraham and others in the Israelite tradition.[16]

We can summarize the historical part of this paper by stating the total consensus that the fathers and the prophets mentioned in Heb 1:1 refer to those mentioned in the Old Testament. Both terms are used in a somewhat vague meaning, but nowhere do we find any hint that the author of Hebrews may think of a divine revelation outside the people of Israel. The revelation in the Old Testament stands out as the only possible *preparatio evangelica* according to the author of Hebrews. But the Augustinian text, mentioned above, follows the list of heroes of the faith in Hebrews 11 and lists pre-Israelite persons like Adam, Cain and Noah who receive revelations from God, and thus indicates the possibility that the perspective of some interpreters of Hebrews was wider than has normally been taken for granted.

In the mid 1960s—maybe under the influence of the Second Vatican Council—Heb 1:1 was used occasionally as a support of a more open theology of religions than the one expressed in what had been normative theology for many centuries. Thus the brilliant Swiss theologian Hans Urs von Balthasar quoted Heb 1:1 when he discussed how the sources of the Pentateuch expressed the polytheism of the patriarchal age, later on to be incorporated into a narrative framework which unequivocally expressed normative OT monotheism. Correct religion was on its way, and it became evident for the interpreters of the traditions embedded in Genesis that God had spoken in many and various ways to the ancestors.[17]

## 3. Heb 1:1 in Modern Indian Catholicism

At the same time Heb 1:1 was taken up by the adventurous Indian theologian Raymundo Panikkar in his speech at the important conference on the theology of religions which was held in Bombay in 1964 in connection with the visit of Pope Paul VI to that city. Panikkar mentions that "Christ did not come to found a religion, and much less a new religion, but to fulfil all justice (Matt. 3.15) and to bring to its fullness every religion of the world." A note refers the reader to Matt 5:7 ("Blessed are the merciful, for they will receive mercy") and Heb 1:1 without any further comments.[18] Of course, such a vague and tentative use of a biblical passage is commonplace in theology, and it is difficult, or rather dangerous, to draw firm conclusions. However, it may not be coincidental that this text emerged around the time of Vati-

---

[16] *Commentary on the Psalms* 62.11.

[17] von Balthasar 1967, 41, commented upon in Waldenfels 1969, 261.

[18] Panikkar 1967, 168-69.

can II both in Europe and in India as a support for a more open view of other religions. This prefigured what was to come, especially in the Indian sub-continent. Thus Panikkar himself became more outspoken in his introduction to the second edition of his epochal book *The Unknown Christ of Hinduism*. Here he takes his starting point in Heb 1:1-2 which is quoted and commented upon with the words: "From this we may surmise that the Son has inspired not only the prophets of Israel but also the sages of Hinduism, and that he has been present in all the endeavours of Man," which in its turn is supported by Heb 1:3.[19] Panikkar does not argue from the choice of tenses of the Greek verbs, but he could have done so: "he (God) sustains (pres. participle φέρων) all things" followed by a statement in aorist (καθαρισμὸν ... ποιησάμενος) on how Christ made purification for sins.

This way to understand Heb 1:1-3 as a scriptural basis for God's twofold action in the world, his constant presence in and support of humanity as a whole (present tense) as well as his salvific action in Christ once for all (aorist tense), paved the way for the use of this passage in later Indian theology. We may mention the *Guidelines for Inter-Religious Dialogue*, published by the Catholic Bishops' Conference of India in 1989. Here Heb 1:1 is mentioned together with 1 Tim 2:4 and Acts 14:17 on God's universal salvific will.[20] The document interprets Heb 1:1 in the light of the whole epistle and goes on to mention Heb 6:20-7:18 on Melchizedek and Heb 11:4-7 with references to Abel, Enoch and Noah as recipients of divine revelation outside (or rather before) Israel. It concludes that "the biblical faith itself offers us elements for a theology of pluralism." Heb 1:1 is quoted once again as support for the view that the different religions play a positive role in the economy of salvation, and thus they are neither rival nor parallel movements but rather "stepping stones in the growing revelation of God 'in many and various ways,' who 'in these last days has spoken to us by a son' (Heb 1:1)."[21]

We also find that Heb 1:1-3 was used as the introductory text from the Bible in the Inaugural session of the Meeting on the Reign of God at the National Biblical Catechetical and Liturgical Centre in Bangalore in 1989. It thus functioned as the interpretative key for the readings from four religions which followed, Buddhism, Hinduism and Islam in addition to Christianity.[22] The four texts were evidently considered of equal value as God's word, all four introduced by the prayer "Oh Lord, speak. Your servant is listening." The Christian text was Luke 4:40-44, and it may be important that v 41 has *demons* confess that Jesus is "the Son of God" and Jesus

---

[19] Panikkar 1982, 1-2, commented upon in Adappur 1982.

[20] Catholic Bishops' Conference of India 1989, 28.

[21] Catholic Bishops' Conference of India 1989, 55.

[22] Puthanangady 1990, 16-18. The four readings were taken from the Vimalakirti-nirdesa-sutra, Sura 114, the Atarva Veda and Luke 4:40-44.

rebuke them before he goes on to "proclaim the good news of the kingdom of God to the other cities also."

While the final statement[23] writes that history took a decisive turn in the person of Jesus because "God's reign of love made a definitive appearance" in the world, it goes on to talk about the great role played by the other religions "to the dawn of God's Reign" and mentions how Rama and Krishna liberated the people from Ravana and Kamsa among others. No difference is made between the basic historicity of the Jesus-event, a corollary of the doctrine of the Incarnation, and the mythological character of the stories about the Hindu avataras. Jesus is here considered equal with the great figures of the other religions, and he is said to witness about the same God (or non-theistic transcendental reality) as they do.

We have noted that Heb 1:1-3 was used as a programmatic text at the inaugural session. But it is only the words about God's past revelation "in many and various ways" in 1:1 which coloured the thoughts of the workshop; the very high Christological statements in 1:2-3 are expressly denied through the reading of Luke 4:41 where those confessing Jesus as the Son of God are demons who are then silenced by Jesus. One single phrase in Heb 1:1 thus was used as the biblical support for a pluralistic theology of religions which gives all the great religions the same role for the coming of the kingdom of God.

The well-known Indian NT scholar Joseph Pathrapankal, who teaches at the Dharmaram Vidya Kshetram in Bangalore and was a member of the Pontifical Biblical Commission in 1984-89, hints at the fact that our passage does not allow such a pluralistic theology putting all religions on a par with each other. But it opens up to the view, no doubt radical enough for many theologians, that the Christ event leads to the fulfilment of all religions, Christ being the definite and decisive revelation of God. Pathrapankal goes on to state that many theologians of today find this inclusive theology to be too negative toward other religions, these being equally valid and relevant as Christianity itself.[24] Pathrapankal himself sympathizes with this radical pluralism, but he is perfectly conscious of the fact that the biblical text itself does not support this radicalism[25], while it is quite possible to argue for an inclusivism which seriously counts with positive values in other religions.[26]

---

[23] Puthanangady 1990, 4-15.

[24] Pathrapankal 1986, 112, 126 and 1993, 67-68.

[25] See also Pathrapankal 1986, 136 where he describes Paul's attitude toward Gentiles and Gentile religions as a weakness. See also p. 129 where Pathrapankal explains this negative view by Paul's Jewish background.

[26] See also Ariarajah 1985, 19 who distinguishes between creation as general revelation and Christ as the special or unique revelation with the help of Heb 1:1 and then goes on to argue that the exclusivity which dominates the NT is at odds with "Jesus' own God-centred life," p. 21. See also Hirudayam 1979, 136 and Gispert-Sauch 1983, 21 on the use of Heb 1:1 in Indian theology.

## 4. The Use of Heb 1:1 by the Vatican

The traditional way to understand Heb 1:1 hardly allows other religions to play a positive role in God's economy of salvation. We may mention the quotation of 1:1 in the encyclical *Mortalium animos* by Pope Pius XI,[27] published in 1928 and arguing against cooperation between different churches as expressed in the Life and Work-conference in Stockholm three years earlier. God has certainly spoken to humanity ever since her beginning, but the final revelation through Christ is said to rule out not only the possibility that another religion than Christianity is valid but also the possibility to accept any other Christian churches than Roman Catholicism.

We find a later example of the use of Heb 1:1 in some speeches by Cardinal Jozef Tomko, Prefect of the Congregation for the Evangelization of Peoples. In a conference on missiology in Rome in 1988 the Cardinal quoted parts of 1:1-2 and distinguished between the human search for the Absolute, mentioned in a positive way, and God's revelation through the Son who reveals "the true face of God to humanity: Jesus Christ as the Incarnate Word is the best Revealer of God and so also the 'way' (Jn 14:6), as he himself indicated."[28] He goes on to argue against "one group of missionaries" who consider this theology to be unacceptable, "because it degrades non-Christian religions to an effort from below and exalts Christianity as the religion coming from above, whereas in truth all religions are equally inspired by God and constitute ways of salvation." While Cardinal Tomko puts the emphasis on the words about the Son in 1:2, these radical theologians—Indian Catholic scholars are intended—emphasize 1:1 and have it talk about divine revelation through Hindu sages and other great men and women in the different religions of humanity.

In his speech at the end of the conference the Cardinal returned to his use of Hebrews 1 and quoted 1:1-3 followed by a statement that the Christian faith does not negate what God has revealed to humanity during her "age-old search for him."[29] This quotation is used in a context that refers to several high Christological passages like John 1:1-4 and Matt 16:16. Tomko goes on to argue that the fact that there are good gentiles (Acts 11:17-18) did not prevent Peter from baptizing, e.g., the family of Cornelius. Tomko once again puts the emphasis on 1:2 with its Christological message, and it is only cautiously that he opens up to a positive view of other religions. No doubt he is conscious of the fact that 1:1, interpreted along the lines of

---

[27] Pius XI 1928.

[28] Tomko 1991, 14-15.

[29] Tomko 1991a, 245-46. See also Tomko 1990, 59.

Christian tradition or historical-critical exegesis, hardly supports such a conclusion.[30]

## 5. Additional Texts in Hebrews

However, we have found that the words in Heb 1:1 ("Long ago God spoke to our
fathers in many and various ways by the prophets") have been used as a biblical
support for the development of a pluralistic theology of religions. The epistle as a
whole provides us with two additional arguments for such a use of its opening statement. These are the role played by Melchizedek in Heb 4:14-7:19 and the list of heroes of faith in chapter 11. We will now turn to these arguments.

The mysterious priest Melchizedek is of basic importance in the central Christological part of Hebrews. As is well known, Melchizedek, to whom Abraham, the ancestor of the Israelite people, gave a tenth when they met near Jerusalem (Gen
14:18-20), later on became a Messianic figure, when the king on Zion was said to
be "a priest forever according to the order of Melchizedek" (Ps 110:4).[31] In Heb
4:14-7:19 he is a most significant *typos* for Christ, thus prefiguring him. It is important that Melchizedek, as we meet him in the Bible, did not belong to the Israelite
people but was a priest-king of Jerusalem at a time when there was still no connection between the God of Israel and that city. This fact has been taken up in the Indian
discussion about other religions as ways of salvation: Theologians have laid stress
upon the episode when Abraham accepted a Canaanite priest of "God Most High"
as his superior, and the question has been posed if this Canaanite priest who served
a religion with roots in the vegetation cycle and the fertility of nature was so different from the priests of Eastern religions like Hinduism.[32] Certainly Melchizedek
may be included among the "prophets" who spoke to ancestors like Abraham as is
mentioned in Heb 1:1. If so, there is a possibility that the un-known author of Hebrews reckons with an economy of salvation which is broader than the strictly Isra-

---

[30] The conviction that Heb 1:1 does not really support a pluralistic theology of religions but at
most an inclusivistic one may explain the fact that Pietro Rossano (e.g., Rossano 1980), the exegetical architect behind the Catholic opening up toward other religions, evidently did not use this text
but instead found most of the biblical support in the Ephesian corpus of the NT; see Fornberg 1995,
33-36.

[31] See Attridge 1989, 192-95 on the role of Melchizedek in the NT era.

[32] Abhishiktananda 1976, 35-36 writes: "who, after all, was Melchizedek if not a Canaanite priest
of the 'cosmic religion'? He exercised his priesthood independently of any mission received from
the *debar Yahweh* ... He was not so different from those contemporary Vedic priests—rather he
might be called their brother." We must go behind the Mosaic covenant and liturgy "to the priestly
cult of the cosmic religion, in order to find the first foreshadowing of the unique sacrifice of the Saviour and the liturgy of the New Covenant." See Fornberg 1995, 119-25 on Abhishiktananda.

elite one, Christ fulfilling not only Israelite *typoi* but also at least one Canaanite *typos*.

Recent theologians of religions have also referred to the list of examples of faith in Hebrews 11 and pointed out that the first three among these, Adam, Enoch and Noah, were pre-Israelite and thus were not members of God's own people. We must also think of later figures like Rahab and Jephthah. All these are considered true witnesses of God in the same way as Abraham and those who followed after him. This possibility to argue for a wider salvation history than the Israelite—Jewish—Christian one was widely used by the fathers of the early church.[33] It was revived after World War II by eminent European theologians like Jean Daniélou in his book *Les saints païens de l'Ancient Testament*[34] and Hans Urs von Balthasar[35] and thus helped to pave the way for a more open theology of religions in the decade leading up to Vatican II and its Declaration on the Relationship of the Church to Non-Christian Religions, *Nostra aetate* of 1965.

## 6. Evaluation and Conclusions

It is, however, doubtful whether a really pluralistic theology of religions can be argued from these texts in Hebrews. It is true that the role played by Melchizedek as well as by the first three, pre-Israelite heroes of faith seems to allow the conclusion that pre-Israelite revelation may have a real value as a pointer to Christ. But Heb 1:1 is more problematic: The combination of the words πατέρες and προφῆται, both of which normally refer to figures in the Israelite tradition as recorded in the OT and the Rabbinic literature, seems to rule out the possibility to view non-Israelite revelation from the time after Abraham was chosen by God as God's true word to humankind. The phrase "in many and various ways" (πολυμερῶς καὶ πολυτρόπως), as far as we know not used before our text, can hardly throw this view into doubt. We can conclude that historical-critical exegesis supports the conviction, dominating both the NT and later Christian tradition, that the church must point to Christ as the only saviour of humanity.

However, this need not necessarily be the last word. The famous Indian Catholic scholar Raimundo Panikkar points out that his attempt—certainly inspired by the fact that his mother was a Spanish Catholic and his father an Indian Hindu—to understand Christianity and Hinduism together and to find Christ hidden in the mes-

---

[33] Congar 1952 with the striking title "Ecclesia ab Abel."
[34] Daniélou 1956.
[35] von Balthasar 1967, 42.

sage of Hindu sages[36] really has parallels in normative Christian theology. Thus Thomas Aquinas and other Scholastic theologians made heavy use of the philosophy of ancient Greece and especially of Aristotle who provided High Scholasticism with the philosophical categories for its work with theology. The art of the Italian Renaissance, first in Florence and then in Rome and not least in the Vatican itself, provides ample examples of how Graeco-Roman philosophers were considered inspired by God together with OT prophets and NT apostles.[37] Panikkar points out that Hinduism as a religion really is closer to Christianity than was Hellenism, being basically a philosophy. It is certainly reasonable to argue that if the Christian faith can be expressed in categories from Graeco-Roman philosophy and if the heroes of that tradition can be considered as divinely inspired revealers, something similar can be said about the sages of Hinduism. The unique position of the Bible and of Christian tradition generally is unquestionably softened by the fact that the interpretative keys used to understand it sometimes have been found far outside classical Christianity.

It is of course widely known that biblical passages have been re-read in the light of history already in biblical times and that Vincent of Lerin's famous statement that the church teaches "what is believed everywhere, always and by everyone"[38] does not tell the whole truth. Thus the famous words about the young woman who will conceive and bear a child according to Isa 7:14 are reinterpreted in Matt 1:23 in the light of the Incarnation. Now it is a virgin who will conceive through the Spirit and thus give God's own Son to the world. This no doubt is at odds with what the prophet Isaiah intended to say some 700 years earlier. But reinterpretations like this one were caused by the Christ event which for all future changed the presuppositions for biblical hermeneutics. Other examples can be found in passages like Gen 3:15, a statement of punishment and curse following the fall, but ever since the late second century AD it has been understood as the first promise of salvation from evil, and Rev 12:1-6, 13-18 with its glorious vision of daughter Zion who became the church only to become the Virgin Mary after some centuries. These examples will suffice to show that biblical interpretation is not static but is radically changed by God's presence in the world through his incarnate Son. The centrality of the Incarnation and thus of the concept of history has as its corollary that biblical interpreta-

---

[36] Panikkar 1982, esp. pp. 163-69, and the comments in Adappur 1982. Panikkar points out that "the 'discovery' of a Sankara or a Ramanuja is just as important for Christian theology as the assimilation of Plato and Aristotle was in ages past," p. 167.

[37] See Fornberg 1995, 205-8 on the use of non-Christian sources in theology. We may mention how the Sibyl is referred to in the hymn *Dies irae* by Thomas of Celano and how Virgil acts as a guide in Dante's *Divina Commedia*.

[38] Quoted from Schoof 1970, 178 and 225.

tion must be influenced by the experiences of every new generation.

It has thus been pointed out that the delay of the parousia caused the Christians to reinterpret many of Jesus' words and parables. Statements like Mark 9:1 "there are some standing here who will not taste death until they see that the kingdom of God has come with power" became problematic around the turn of the century when the eye-witnesses of Jesus had died and nothing happened. Several parables as we find them in the canonical gospels show us that the Christians even earlier were anxious about this delay, which also forced Paul to rethink his individual eschatology as early as in 1 Thess 4:13-5:11, thus around the year AD 50.

The Incarnation stands out as the most important factor that caused these basic re-readings[39] of the biblical message. The delay of the parousia is another such factor, less important but important enough to bring about reinterpretations which became normative for the future. The last decades have been characterized by an ever increasing internationalism and pluralism in the field of religion.[40] It has been proposed that this will legitimize a new understanding of the biblical passages dealing with the claims of the church to represent the only divine revelation to the world.[41]

This, however, seems to be doubtful. The Mediterranean world of the first century AD was very much like our own time with regard to its pluralism in the field of religions, and it can be argued that an important Graeco-Roman city like Corinth shows considerable similarities with big cities of today like Hong Kong or Bombay to mention two examples. It is evident that the pluralistic situation of today with its meetings between adherents of different faiths is matched by that of Antiquity, and it seems reasonable to argue that the attitude of the New Testament authors must remain normative for the church of today as well.

We must mention an additional pericope that has been used in this discussion, the well-known text about the tower of Babel in Gen 11:1-9. Theologians arguing for a pluralistic theology of religions have emphasized that it was not their pride and haughtiness but rather the unity which the people of Babel searched for that was something evil. They have concluded that God did not confuse their language and scatter them over all the earth in order to punish them but in order to bless them with the riches of pluralism.[42] This interpretation can be doubted, but it shows a kind of "liberal biblicism" that dominates much of the discussion. Theologians who argue against a traditional exclusivism often try to base their opinions of other religions

---

[39] Neo-Thomism worked with Aristotelian categories and spoke about a *sensus plenior* which could be found in the light of the new development.

[40] See Fornberg 1995, 7-10.

[41] Cf. Ucko 1991a, 31-32.

[42] Thus Ucko 1991, 5 against Chung 1991, 41. Geffré 1991, 253 points to the ambiguity of the story of Babel.

on stray biblical texts. Gen 11:1-9 has been used that way; Heb 1:1 is another example.

These attempts are often open to doubt, and they may be difficult to uphold in the light of historical-critical scholarship. Still it may turn out that a text like Heb 1:1[43] with its context about Abel, Enoch, Noah and finally Melchizedek can help the church to open up cautiously to such a revelation and thus bring humans of all religions closer to each other.

## Bibliography

Abhishiktananda (Swami) 1976: *Hindu-Christian Meeting Point*, 2nd ed., Delhi: Indian SPCK 1976.

Adappur, A. 1982: "The Theology of Inter-Faith Dialogue," in: *Vidyajyoti* 46 (1982) 485-98.

Ariarajah, Wesley 1985: *The Bible and People of Other Faiths,* Geneva: WCC 1985.

Attridge, Harold 1989: *Hebrews* (Hermeneia), Philadelphia, PA: Fortress 1989.

von Balthasar, Hans Urs 1967: "Der Zugang zur Wirklichkeit Gottes," in: Johannes Feiner and Magnus Löhrer (eds.), *MySal* 2, Einsiedeln: Benziger 1967, 15-43.

Bengel, Albert 1742: *Gnomon Novi Testamenti* (original ed. 1742), Stuttgart: Steinkopf 1860.

Bruce, Frederick Fyvie 1964: *The Epistle to the Hebrews*, Grand Rapids, MI: Eerdmans 1964.

Caragounis, Chrys 1990: "L'universalisme moderne. Perspectives bibliques sur la révélation de Dieu," in: *Hokhma* 45 (1990) 17-45.

Catholic Bishops' Conference of India 1989: *Guidelines for Inter-Religious Dialogue*, 2nd ed., New Delhi: C.B.C.I. Centre 1989.

Chung Hyun Kyung 1991: "'Come, Holy Spirit' – Renew the Whole Creation," in: Michael Kinnamon (ed.), *Signs of the Spirit. Official Report Seventh Assembly*, Geneva: WCC, and Grand Rapids: Eerdmans 1991, 37-47.

Congar, Yves 1952: "*Ecclesia ab Abel*," in: Marcel Reding (ed.), *Abhandlungen über Theologie und Kirche*, FS Karl Adam, Düsseldorf: Patmos 1952, 79-108.

Daniélou, Jean 1956: *Les saints païens de l'Ancien Testament*, Paris: Seuil 1956.

Delitzsch, F. 1857: *Commentar zum Briefe an die Hebräer*, Leipzig: Dörffling & Franke 1857.

Ebrard, J. A. H. 1855: *Brefwet till de Hebreer* (original ed. 1850), Örebro: Lindh 1855.

Fornberg, Tord 1995: *The Bible in a World of Many Faiths*, Lewiston, NY: Mellen 1995.

Geffré, Claude 1991: "Toward a Hermeneutics of Interreligious Dialogue," in: Werner Jeanrond and Jennifer Rike (eds.), *Radical Pluralism and Truth*, New York: Crossroad 1991, 250-69.

Gispert-Sauch, George 1983: "Inspiration and Extra-Biblical Scriptures," in: *ITS* 20 (1983) 16-36.

---

[43] Other texts that may be relevant are, e.g., 2 Tim 1:9-10 and Tit 1:2.

Gräßer, Erich 1990: *An die Hebräer (Hebr 1-6)* (EKK 17:1), Zürich: Benziger and Neukirchen-Vluyn: Neukirchener 1990.

Greer, Rowan 1973: *The Captain of our Salvation* (BGBE 15), Tübingen: Mohr 1973.

Hagen, Kenneth 1974: *A Theology of Testament in the Young Luther. The Lectures on Hebrews* (SMRT 12), Leiden: Brill 1974.

— 1981: *Hebrews Commenting from Erasmus to Bèze 1516-1598* (BGBE 23), Tübingen: Mohr 1981.

Hagner, Donald 1990: *Hebrews* (New International Biblical Commentary 14), Peabody, MA: Hendrickson 1990.

Héring, Jean 1970: *The Epistle to the Hebrews*, London: Epworth 1970.

Hirudayam, Ignatius 1979: "Theology of Inculturation and Mission," in: Herbert Hoefer (ed.), *Debate on Mission. Issues from the Indian Context*, Madras: Gurukul 1979, 135-53.

Lane, William 1991: *Hebrews 1-8* (Word Biblical Commentary 47A), Dallas: Word Books 1991.

McNeil, J. (ed.) 1960: *Calvin* (LCC 20), Philadelphia, PA: Westminster 1960.

Owen, John (ed.) 1948: *John Calvin. Commentaries on the Epistle of Paul the Apostle to the Hebrews*, Grand Rapids, MI: Eerdmans 1948.

Panikkar, Raymundo 1967: "The Relation of Christians to their Non-Christian Surroundings," in: Joseph Neuner (ed.), *Christian Revelation and World Religions*, London: Burns & Oats 1967, 143-84.

— 1982: *The Unknown Christ of Hinduism*, 2nd ed., Bangalore: Asian Trading Corporation 1982.

Pathrapankal, Joseph 1986: *Critical and Creative. Studies in Bible and Theology*, Bangalore: Dharmaram 1986.

— 1993: *Text and Context in Biblical Interpretation*, Bangalore: Dharmaram 1993.

Pelikan, Jaroslav (ed.) 1968: *Luther's Works* 29, Saint Louis, MO: Concordia 1968.

Pius XI 1928: "*Mortalium animos,*" in: *AAS* 20 (1928) 5-16.

de la Potterie, Ignace 1987: "Κεχαριτωμένη en Lc 1,28. Étude philologique," in: *Bib.* 68 (1987) 357-82 and 480-508.

Puthanangady, Paul (ed.) 1990: *Reign of God. Report on the South Asian Workshop on Reign of God (10th-14th October 1989)*, Bangalore: National Biblical Catechetical and Liturgical Centre 1990.

Rossano, Pietro 1980: "Gospel and Culture at Ephesus and in the Province of Asia at the Time of St. Paul and St. John," in: *BSNC* 15 (1980) 282-96.

Schoof, Mark 1970: *Breakthrough. Beginnings of the New Catholic Theology*, Dublin: Gill and Macmillan 1970.

Starke, Christoph 1741: *Kurzgefasster Auszug Der gründlichsten und nutzbarsten Auslegungen über alle Bücher Neues Testaments* 2, Leipzig: Breitkopf 1741.

Tomko, Jozef 1990: "Christian Mission in Asia Today," in: *Catholic International* 1 (1990) 58-64.

— 1991: "Missionary Challenges to the Theology of Salvation," in: Paul Mojzes and Leonard Swidler (eds.), *Christian Mission and Inter-Religious Dialogue* (Religions in Dialogue 4), Lewiston, NY: Mellen 1991, 12-32.

— 1991a: "Christian Mission Today," in: Paul Mojzes and Leonard Swidler (eds.), *Christian Mission and Inter-Religious Dialogue* (Religions in Dialogue 4), Lewiston, NY: Mellen 1991, 236-62.

Ucko, Hans 1991: "The Assembly and People of Other Faiths," in: *Current Dialogue* 20 (1991) 2-6.

— 1991a: "Dialog och religionsteologi — ekumeniska perspektiv," in: Ingrid Holmberg Skäremo (ed.), *Kyrkan och det judiska folket*, Uppsala: Svenska Kyrkans Mission 1991, 31-40.

Vanhoye, Albert 1969: *Situation du Christ. Hébreux 1-2* (LeDiv 58), Paris: Cerf 1969.

Waldenfels, Hans 1969: "Zur Heilsbedeutung der nichtchristlichen Religionen in katholischer Sicht," in: *ZM* 53 (1969) 257-78.

Weiß, Hans-Friedrich 1991: *Der Brief an die Hebräer* (KEK 13), Göttingen: Vandenhoeck & Ruprecht 1991.

Westcott, Brooke Foss 1909: *The Epistle to the Hebrews*, London: Macmillan 1909.

# Eine hermeneutisch unverzichtbare Unterscheidung: Vetus Testamentum und Vetus Testamentum in Novo receptum

Hans Hübner

## 1. Die Trias "historisch – theologisch – hermeneutisch"

Für meinen Beitrag zu der Herrn Prof. Dr. Lars Hartman gewidmeten Festschrift habe ich eine hermeneutische Thematik gewählt. Zunächst eine grundsätzliche Feststellung: Der Exeget, der notwendig zunächst *historisch* vorgehen muß, darf sich aber nicht primär als Historiker verstehen, sondern muß, was er aufgrund seiner historisch-kritischen Methodik den Schritten des Neuen Testaments entnimmt, im *theologischen* Horizont verstehen und interpretieren. Damit rückt er aber in diesen Horizont die *hermeneutische* Grundproblematik ein. So ist der Neutestamentler, weil er als Historiker notwendig zugleich Theologe ist, in grundsätzlicher Weise gefordert, seine exegetisch-theologische Arbeit hermeneutisch zu reflektieren. Der hier zu ehrende Jubilar ist ein bedeutender, international anerkannter Exeget, der zugleich an der hermeneutischen Frage lebhaft interessiert ist. Also ist es sicherlich angebracht, daß in der ihm zu Ehren publizierten Festschrift auch ein Beitrag erscheint, der ganz der hermeneutischen Frage gewidmet ist.

Mehrfach habe ich in größeren und kleineren Publikationen auf die historische und theologische Differenz zwischen dem *Vetus Testamentum* – genauer: *Vetus Testamentum per se*, also dem Alten Testament nach seinem Literalsinn – und dem *Vetus Testamentum in Novo receptum* hingewiesen[1]. Zwar waren die meisten Reaktionen, entweder brieflich oder in Rezensionen, äußerst positiv, viele sogar mit geradezu emphatischer Zustimmung, mit der ich so nicht gerechnet hatte. Doch haben einige wenige Kollegen recht energisch widersprochen. Und da diese Einwände immerhin von solchen kamen, die ein sehr wichtiges Wort in der neutestamentlichen Wissenschaft und vor allem in der Frage der Biblischen Theologie, in der es ja um das historische und theologische Verhältnis von Altem und Neuem Testament

---

[1] H. Hübner 1988; idem 1990, vor allem 44-76; idem 1993.

zueinander geht, gesprochen haben, gebietet es die wissenschaftliche Pflicht, ihnen in der gebührenden Weise zu antworten. Dafür ist eine Festschrift ein hervorragender Ort. Natürlich, mancher Beitrag ist schon dadurch, daß er in irgendeiner Festschrift veröffentlicht wurde, der öffentlichen Wirkung entzogen worden. Aber viele Festschriften, nämlich die für bedeutende Wissenschaftler, wurden sehr aufmerksam beachtet. Und so gehe ich bei Lars Hartman davon aus, daß seine Festschrift gelesen wird.

## 2. Contra und pro: Die theologisch und historisch eigenständige Größe "Vetus Testamentum in Novo receptum"

Zu denen, die meine Unterscheidung von *Vetus Testamentum* und *Vetus Testamentum receptum* entschieden ablehnen, gehört der Tübinger Neutestamentler *Peter Stuhlmacher*. Mit ihm verbindet mich die theologisch unverzichtbare Aufgabe, über die Grenzen der eigenen theologischen Disziplin hinaus das Ganze der Theologie anzuvisieren. Und dazu gehört, *theologisch* das Verhältnis der beiden Testamente zueinander zu reflektieren. Das ist schon allein deshalb erforderlich, weil die Autoren beider Testamente für sich in Anspruch nehmen, daß in ihren Schriften Gottes Offenbarung zum Ausdruck komme. Die Frage nach dem theologischen Verhältnis beider Testamente zueinander kann also nicht dadurch von vornherein unter ein theologisches Verdikt gestellt und damit für theologisch illegitim erklärt werden, daß man unter Berufung auf *Johann Philip Gablers* Altdorfer Antrittsrede *De iusto discrimine theologiae biblicae et dogmaticae regundisque recte utriusque finibus* vom 30. März 1787, in der dieser den historischen Charakter der Biblischen Theologie im Gegensatz zum didaktischen Charakter der Dogmatischen Theologie herausstellte und zugleich die je gesonderte Behandlung der Theologien beider Testamente postulierte, eine Biblische Theologie untersagt. Denn der Begriff "Biblische Theologie" ist so lange eine Leerformel, wie nicht durch die genaue Untersuchung der durch die Autoren des Neuen Testaments vorgenommenen Rezeption alttestamentlicher Aussagen festgestellt ist, *wie* diese das Alte Testament und ihre jeweiligen alttestamentlichen Belegstellen verstanden. Denn das Ergebnis einer auf *diese Weise* konzipierten Biblischen Theologie könnte ja durchaus sein, daß ein starker Hiatus zwischen beiden Testamenten deutlich würde und somit allen Verfechtern einer betonten Kontinuität vom Alten zum Neuen Testament hin die Argumente aus der Hand geschlagen würden. Aber es könnte auch sein, daß denen, die die Diskontinuität so sehr betonen, um dem Neuen im Neuen Testament gerecht zu werden, eine herbe Enttäuschung bereitet würde. Der Begriff "Biblische Theologie" ist also lediglich Ausdruck einer *Fragestellung*, deren Antwort gerade nicht *a priori* festgelegt werden darf.

Fragen wir nach dem Verhältnis beider Testamente zueinander und haben wir erkannt, daß diese Frage nur beantwortet werden kann, wenn eine akribische Untersuchung gezeigt hat, auf welche Weise die neutestamentlichen Autoren sehr unterschiedlich auf das Alte Testament – das zu ihrer Zeit bekanntlich noch nicht Altes Testament hieß, weil es noch kein Neues Testament gab – zurückgegriffen haben, so beginnt eine solche Frage natürlich nicht beim Nullpunkt. Denn wer sich einer solchen Untersuchung unterzieht, weiß ja doch schon etwas davon, daß der Literalsinn der alttestamentlichen Zitate im Neuen Testament in vielen Fällen in einen anderen Sinn umgebogen ist. Und er weiß auch, daß in anderen Fällen durchaus eine inhaltliche Kontinuität des alttestamentlichen Literalsinns zur neutestamentlichen Aussageintention hin besteht. Daß *Vetus Testamentum* und *Vetus Testamentum in Novo receptum* in wichtigen Fällen divergieren, ist also zumindest ein *vages Vorverständnis*. Aber, wie gesagt, dieses Vorverständnis bedarf der Fundierung oder der Korrektur. Soviel also zunächst, um zu zeigen, wogegen Peter Stuhlmacher sich wendet. Ich greife hier nur auf seine Äußerungen im 1. Band seiner "Biblischen Theologie des Neuen Testaments"[2] zurück, die immerhin, im selben Verlag erschienen, denselben Titel wie mein dreibändiges Werk trägt. Was der Tübinger Exeget sagt, ist für mich z.T. nicht recht verständlich, z.T. kommen seine Argumente aus einer Richtung, die m.E. eine falsche Perspektive nicht nur auf meine Konzeption, sondern sogar auf die Aufgabe einer Biblischen Theologie bedeutet.

Peter Stuhlmacher begrüßt, daß ich bei meiner Unterscheidung nicht nur die Zitate berücksichtigen will, sondern auch die zweifelsohne schwieriger verifizierbaren Anspielungen. Und er betrachtet meine Intention "Es muß klar werden, was im Neuen Testament an alttestamentlichem Geist insgesamt offenbar wird – ungebrochen oder gebrochen, aufgegriffen oder negiert!"[3] als bedenkenswerten Ansatz. Freilich verstehe ich nicht, daß Stuhlmacher behauptet, ich ließe mir von der Forschung als logischen Ausgangspunkt meiner Arbeit die Unterscheidung von *Vetus Testamentum per se* und *Vetus Testamentum in Novo receptum* vorgeben[4], wenn mein Entwurf nicht einfach die theologische Kontinuität der beiden Testamente herausstellt, sondern von der betonten Reflexion des Verhältnisses von Kontinuität und Diskontinuität geprägt ist[5]. Von der *Forschung* habe ich mir diese Unterscheidung gerade nicht vorgeben lassen, sondern vom *biblischen Befund*! Aber es mag sein, daß ich Stuhlmacher hier falsch verstanden habe.

Weit gravierender ist, wenn er die genannte Unterscheidung als kanongeschichtlich und hermeneutisch gleich problematisch charakterisiert und in *diesem* Zusam-

---

[2] P. Stuhlmacher 1992.
[3] Hübner 1990, 64.
[4] Stuhlmacher 1992, 36.
[5] Hübner 1990, 64.

menhang meine Frage nach dem einen Gott in beiden Testamenten als sogar
theologisch fragwürdig bezeichnet. Wieso mache ich mich hier von der kritischen
Forschungslage "abhängig"? Was heißt überhaupt *kritische Forschung*? Es ist doch
wohl die Forschung, die mittels der Methode der *Geschichts*-Wissenschaft *geschichtliche* Texte der Heiligen Schrift untersucht. Hat sich der *ewige* Gott in Jesus
Christus als Gestalt der *Geschichte* ereignet, ist also Jesus Christus eine geschichtliche Gestalt, zu deren Wirkungsgeschichte sowohl das, was im Neuen Testament
gesagt ist, gehört als auch die frühe Kirchengeschichte, aus deren Schoß das Neue
Testament erwachsen ist, so stellt sich notwendig die Frage: Darf nach dem *Geschichte gewordenen Gott* nicht mit den Fragen der *Geschichte*, also mit den Fragen
der *Geschichtswissenschaft* gefragt werden? Ist ein solches Fragen deshalb verbo-
ten, weil es von der "Forschung" betrieben wird? Gehört zur Kondeszendenz Gottes
nicht auch, daß er sich in seiner geschichtlichen Existenz aller Zweideutigkeit aus-
setzt, die nun einmal – notwendig! – aller Geschichtsforschung eignet? Welches
Verständnis von Geschichte hat Peter Stuhlmacher, wenn er hier im Blick auf die
geschichtliche Existenz des ewigen Gottes eine solch negative Aussage im Blick
auf die Geschichtsforschung macht? Natürlich – ich mache mich in der Tat von der
Geschichtsforschung "abhängig". Ich muß es aber tun, weil ich als Fragender selbst
ein geschichtliches Wesen bin. *Wilhelm Dilthey* erklärt: "Die erste Bedingung für
die Möglichkeit der Geschichtswissenschaft liegt darin, daß ich selbst ein geschichtliches Wesen bin, daß der, welcher die Geschichte erforscht, derselbe ist, der
die Geschichte macht!"[6]. Dilthey hat recht, auch wenn man über die Einordnung
dieser Aussage in seinen geschichtsphilosophischen Entwurf durchaus kritisch denken kann[7]. Von der Geschichtsforschung und ihren Ergebnissen, die im Blick auf
das Alte und Neue Testament theologisch relevant sind, könnten wir uns nur dann
dispensieren, wenn wir schon jenseits der Geschichte existierten. Aber noch leben
wir auf dieser Erde! Peter Stuhlmacher spricht von der Gefahr der Abhängigkeit
von der kritischen Forschungsgeschichte. Ja, es ist zuzugeben, die Gefahr besteht!
Aber kein Exeget kann sich aus diesem Gefahrensraum *per modum theologiae* ab-
sentieren. Und jeder Exeget weiß, daß sein Horizont, sein historisches Erkenntnis-
vermögen begrenzt ist. Auch wer sich nicht von der Geschichtsforschung abhängig
machen möchte, bleibt innerhalb ihrer Grenzen. Schlimm ist es nur, wenn man diese Selbstverständlichkeit ignoriert oder, wie auch immer, zu überspielen versucht.
Peter Stuhlmacher selbst traut sogar, was die Vorgeschichte der paulinischen Theologie angeht, seiner Rekonstruktion weit mehr zu, als ich es vermag. Es liegt schon
ein klein wenig Ironie darin, daß er, der mich in Abhängigkeit von der rekonstruie-
renden Geschichtsforschung sieht, die Aufgabe einer Biblischen Theologie des

---

[6] W. Dilthey 1973, 278.
[7] So z.B. H.-G. Gadamer 1972, 205ff.

Neuen Testaments primär als Aufgabe der Rekonstruktion faßt, während mir mehr an der Interpretation liegt. Mit *Rudolf Bultmann* bin ich der Meinung, daß für eine Theologie des Neuen Testaments die Rekonstruktion im Dienste der Interpretation zu stehen hat[8]. M.E. ist Bultmann mit dieser an sich richtigen Devise noch gar nicht radikal genug gewesen. Er bleibt noch zu nahe bei der Rekonstruktion[9].

Peter Stuhlmacher bringt gegen meine Konzeption als das für ihn wahrscheinlich wichtigste Argument den Einwand, daß mit meiner Unterscheidung von *Vetus Testamentum per se* und *Vetus Testamentum in Novo receptum* eine Differenzierung praktiziert werde, die den neutestamentlichen Autoren noch ebenso fremd gewesen sei wie ihren jüdischen Adressaten und Kontrahenten. Mit ihrer Bezugnahme auf bestimmte alttestamentliche Bücher und die Hintanstellung anderer hätten die neu-testamentlichen Zeugen ebensowenig einen neuen Kanon heiliger Schriften aufstel-len wollen wie die Essener von Qumran oder Philo mit ihrem eklektischen Schriftgebrauch. Und er bringt als weiteres Argument, daß die Pointe der Ausein-andersetzung zwischen Juden und Christen über den Sinn der Heiligen Schriften ge-rade die gewesen sei, daß doch beide Seiten von denselben Heiligen Schriften ausgegangen seien und dieselben exegetischen Methoden auf sie angewendet hät-ten. Doch gerade diese Argumentation des Tübinger Exegeten verkennt einen ent-scheidenden Sachverhalt. Er hat mich hier auch essentiell mißverstanden. Ich bestreite doch gar nicht, daß meine Unterscheidung den neutestamentlichen Auto-ren fremd gewesen sei. Diese waren in der Tat weitesthin der Meinung, sie würden die Schrift so zitieren, wie sie *eigentlich* gemeint sei. (Über das "eigentlich" ist frei-lich gleich noch zu sprechen.) Und natürlich sei nicht bestritten, daß sie "dieselben" exegetischen Methoden wie die Juden praktiziert haben – obwohl auch dazu gleich noch einige klärende Bemerkungen vonnöten sind. Die Unterscheidung zwischen dem *Vetus Testamentum* in seinem Literalsinn und dem *Vetus Testamentum in Novo receptum* ist ja eine Unterscheidung, die zunächst einmal *wir* machen. Wir prakti-zieren sie, weil *uns* die *inhaltliche* Differenz sehr deutlich geworden ist. Ist uns aber einmal diese Differenz aufgefallen, haben wir sie als *factum* registriert, dann haben wir sie zunächst einmal auch festzuhalten. Und dann haben wir sie als festgehaltene zu *interpretieren*. Das muß natürlich auch auf dem Hintergrund der damaligen In-terpretationsgeschichte geschehen. Und so ist es Aufgabe der exegetischen und hi-storischen Forschung, den alttestamentlichen Literalsinn so genau wie irgend möglich herauszuarbeiten. Und es ist Aufgabe dieser Forschung, genau herauszuar-beiten, wie der jeweilige neutestamentliche Autor den jeweiligen alttestamentlichen

---

[8] R. Bultmann 1984, 600.

[9] In Hübner 1993 habe ich bei der Darstellung der paulinischen Theologie und ihrer neutesta-mentlichen Wirkungsgeschichte zu zeigen versucht, wie der Weg Bultmanns konsequent weiter be-schritten werden sollte.

Text verstanden und in seine eigene theologische Argumentation eingebracht hat. Die Differenz, von der ich gesprochen habe und die nur aufgegeben werden könnte, wenn sie nicht tatsächlich bestände, also die Differenz, die die Heilige Schrift selbst an den Tag legt, sie ist **Grunddatum** einer Biblischen Theologie des Neuen Testaments – es sei denn, man dürfte Differenzen, die *wir* als Differenzen erkennen, nicht mehr beim Wort nehmen. Was wir als Differenz ansehen und nicht mit dem uns nicht mehr zu Verfügung stehenden Instrumentarium der allegorischen Schriftauslegung rechtfertigen können, war für die neutestamentlichen Autoren eben keine theologische Differenz, und zwar deshalb nicht, weil sie den Literalsinn einer Stelle als verbalen Ausdruck eines tieferen Sinnes zu sehen meinten, während wir es in vielen Fällen bei der Konstatierung des Auseinanderfallens zwischen dem Literalsinn des Alten Testaments und dem bewußt pneumatischen Sinn des alttestamentlichen Zitats durch den neutestamentlichen Autor bewenden lassen müssen.

Aber gerade dadurch, daß sich die neutestamentlichen Autoren, allen vorab Paulus, bewußt waren, daß sie einen pneumatischen Sinn alttestamentlicher Aussagen postulierten, ist unsere oben getroffene Feststellung ein wenig zu relativieren, daß *wir* es sind, die die Differenz von *Vetus Testamentum per se* und *Vetus Testamentum in Novo receptum* erkennen und nicht die neutestamentlichen Autoren. Ihnen war jedenfalls *zum Teil* bewußt, daß der von ihnen "verstandene" pneumatische Sinn, also der Sinn unter christologischen Vorzeichen, nicht mit dem alttestamentlichen Literalsinn identisch war. Sie freilich sahen, wie gesagt, den Literalsinn als einen durch den geistigen Sinn zu vertiefenden Sinn an, während wir bei der Konstatierung der Differenz von beiden Sinnen bleiben müssen. Und es ist auch unbedingt zu bemerken, daß durch Stuhlmachers Bemerkung, auf beiden Seiten – von Juden und Christen – würden "dieselben" exegetischen Methoden praktiziert, diese Sache etwas zu formal gesehen wird. Denn es ist die *inhaltliche* Seite, die entscheidend ist. Es ist das *christologische Vorzeichen*, das entscheidet, wie die Schrift Israels nach neutestamentlicher Sicht wirklich zu verstehen ist.

### 3. Geschichtlicher Horizont und Wirklichkeitsverständnis

Und hier ist nun erneut anzusetzen. Aus Platzgründen muß ich es bei Andeutungen belassen und auf einen Vortrag verweisen, den ich vor kurzem vor der Guardini Stiftung gehalten habe[10]. Es gibt wichtige alttestamentliche Zitate im Neuen Testament, die in der Tat ein christologisches Vorzeichen tragen, die also in einem theologischen Zusammenhang stehen, der alttestamentlich nicht gegeben ist, die aber in der *Offenheit des Alten Testaments* interpretierbar sind. Denn das Alte Testa-

---

[10] H. Hübner 1994.

ment kennt zwar nicht überall, aber doch an wichtigen Stellen Aussagen, die christologisch *erweitert* werden können. Sie verlieren dadurch nicht ihren ursprünglichen Literalsinn. Aber dieser Literalsinn ist neutestamentlich in der Weise rezipierbar, daß von der alttestamentlichen Ausgangslage Wesentliches nicht verlorengeht. Als Beispiel sei hier nur ψ 142,2 (Ps 143,2) in Gal 2,16 genannt[11].

Mit dem, was soeben über die christologische Erweiterung des ursprünglichen Literalsinns einer alttestamentlichen Aussage gesagt wurde, ist aber ein weiterer hermeneutischer Sachverhalt von noch grundlegenderer Bedeutung und Bedeutsamkeit angesprochen. Es geht nämlich um nichts Geringeres als um die Frage, ob das, was einmal gedacht, gesagt und schriftlich formuliert und fixiert wurde, überhaupt von einem, der später lebt, *unmodifiziert* aufgegriffen werden kann. Ist es überhaupt möglich, in der Vergangenheit Ausgesprochenes genauso zu verstehen, wie der, der es ausgesprochen hat, auch verstanden hat? *Gibt es identisches Verstehen für Vergangenheit und Gegenwart?* Die Antwort kann nur eindeutig *nein* heißen. Jedenfalls gilt dieses Nein für alle geschichtlichen Texte, für alle Texte also, in denen Gehalte ausgesprochen sind, die in irgendeiner Weise bedeutsam für das Selbstverständnis sind. Verdeutlichen wir es an einem Beispiel, das für unsere Thematik relevant ist. Ich nehme als ein solches Beispiel den das Alte Testament, also die γραφή theologisch reflektierenden Paulus. Da liest dieser das Buch des Propheten Jesaja, liest jene Abschnitte, die wir in unserer exegetischen Fachsprache Deutero- und Tritojesaja nennen. Er liest wiederholt bei "Jesaja" Aussagen über die δικαιοσύνη Gottes. Der Horizont, in dem er dieses für "Jesaja" als auch für ihn selbst so bedeutsame Wort liest, ist für beide jeweils ein anderer. Der Horizont *muß* sogar jeweils ein anderer sein, weil beide ihr Selbstverständnis von einer anderen geschichtlichen und gerade darin theologischen *Wirklichkeit* her verstehen. Deutero- und Tritojesaja konnten nur in *ihrem* geschichtlichen Horizont die Gerechtigkeit Gottes verstehen. So haben die Verfasser dieser beiden Teile des Jesaja-Buches die exilische bzw. nachexilische Situation vor Augen. Gerechtigkeit Gottes ist demnach etwas, was Gott als der Gerechte im geschichtlichen Wirken am geschichtlichen Volke Israel wirkt. Die Wirklichkeit, *von der her* Paulus denkt, *in der* er denkt, die Wirklichkeit also, die sein Selbstverständnis bestimmt, ist das Christusereignis. Er weiß sich "in Christus". Christus ist *seine* Wirklichkeit. *Von ihr kann er nicht abstrahieren.* Einmal ganz davon abgesehen, daß Paulus niemals auf die Idee gekommen wäre, es zu tun: Er kann gar nicht eine Auslegung der Jes-Texte in der Weise vornehmen, daß diese Texte nicht auf Christus zu beziehen wären. Hat "Jesaja" seine Botschaft, weil sie ja in den Augen des Paulus eschatologische Botschaft im strengen Sinne des Wortes ist, im Blick auf Christus geschrieben, dann ist dieses

---

[11] Ausführlicher Nachweis bei Hübner 1993, 64ff.

Buch gar nicht anders lesbar denn als prophetische Ankündigung des eschatologischen Handelns Gottes in Jesus Christus. Natürlich, Paulus weiß, daß diejenigen Juden, die nicht an Jesus als den Messias glauben, die δικαιοσύνη Gottes nicht als die
in Jesus Christus erschienene Gerechtigkeit Gottes sehen. Aber zugleich ist ihm
klar, daß dies ein defizientes Verstehen des "Jesaja" ist. Halten wir fest: Paulus versteht das alttestamentlich prophetische Buch notwendig im Horizont eines anderen
Wirklichkeits-verständnisses als die Verfasser dieses Buches. Er versteht sie somit
notwendig im Horizont eines anderen Selbstverständnisses. Er kann als geschichtliche Gestalt seiner geschichtlichen Zeit nicht mehr hinter seine eigene Wirklichkeit
zurück.

Doch schon kommt der Einwand: Aber *wir* sind doch in der Lage, durch exegetisches Vorgehen das, was Deutero- und Tritojesaja verstanden haben, objektivierend darzustellen und in dieser Objektivation zu erfassen. Und gleiches gilt auch für
Paulus! Nun soll nicht bestritten werden, daß für die *objektivierende* Erkenntnis
dies zweifellos zutrifft. Kein vernünftig Denkender könnte das bestreiten. Aber Verstehen meint ja mehr als vorstellungsmäßiges und begriffliches Erfassen von Objektivation in irgendeiner Vergangenheit. Unser *wirkliches* Verstehen neutestamentlicher Texte ist ja kein primär begriffliches. Verstanden im Sinne des Neuen Testamentes haben wir dieses nur, wenn wir im Glauben das Evangelium als das uns geltende Wort Gottes verstanden haben. Verstehen im Sinne des Paulus und überhaupt
im Sinne des Neuen Testamentes ist, was der Apostel z.B. 1 Kor 2,6-16, vor allem
2,12 sagt: "Wir haben den Geist aus Gott empfangen, ἵνα εἰδῶμεν τὰ ὑπὸ τοῦ θεοῦ
χαρισθέντα ἡμῖν". Mit Paulus können wir also, wollen wir wirklich als christliche
Theologen Theologie betreiben, nicht hinter die verstehende Erkenntnis dessen,
was uns in Christus geschenkt ist, also hinter die χαρισθέντα zurück.

Wie aber steht es dann mit dem Abstand zwischen Paulus und uns? Gibt es da
keinen "garstigen, breiten Graben"? Insofern ist mit nein zu antworten, als es der
gleiche Glaube ist, der uns mit dem Apostel verbindet. Andererseits ist aber nun
doch die Existenz eines solchen Grabens insofern zuzugeben, als das Wirklichkeitsverständnis des Paulus in vieler Hinsicht ein anderes ist als das unsere. Es ist zunächst ein *weltanschaulicher* Graben, der ungeheuer breit ist. Da sind die
Determinanten seiner antiken Weltanschauung. Wir können sie objektivierend kon-
statieren, jedoch nicht existentiell nachvollziehen. Es wird uns nicht gelingen, uns
unverkrampft in seine Sicht von Dämonen und ihrer teuflischen Macht hineinzuver-
setzen. Es wäre schon ein recht verkrampftes Bemühen, uns mit einem antiken
Menschen vor den allgegenwärtigen Dämonen zu fürchten – ganz abgesehen davon, daß die modernen "Dämonen" fürchterlich genug sind! Wir sind also in der Lage, die weltanschaulichen Gebundenheiten des Paulus zu durchschauen und
dementsprechend das Eigentliche seiner theologischen Aussagen und zeitgebunde-

nen Vorstellungen zu sondern. *Insofern* läßt sich auch in der Tat sagen, daß wir Paulus besser verstehen, als er sich verstanden hat. Aber eben: *nur insofern!*

Aber auch der Gewinn, den wir durch philosophische Reflexion der letzten Jahrhunderte haben, muß hier einkalkuliert werden. Wir haben in dieser Epoche über Zeit und Raum nachgedacht. Wir haben in erkenntnistheoretischer Hinsicht neue Einsichten, die wir nicht einfach über Bord werfen können, gewonnen. Wir sind in der Lage, all das in einen Horizont hineinzubringen, in dem wir dann auch die theologischen Aussagen des Paulus in einem *neuen geistesgeschichtlichen Koordinatensystem* sehen und verstehen können, ohne daß seine Theologie durch dieses Eingeordnetwerden auch nur irgendetwas an Bedeutsamkeit verlöre. All dies ist inzwischen auch schon *fundamentaltheologisch* reflektiert worden, bedarf aber noch weiterer intensiver fundamentaltheologischer Reflexion. Die Theologie der biblischen Gehalte wird sich insofern immer wieder mit der Systematischen Theologie überlappen. Biblisch-exegetische und systematisch-theologische Arbeit greifen in vielen Punkten Hand in Hand. Ohne den Dialog mit der Philosophie und der Systematischen Theologie ist heute Biblische Theologie nicht mehr vollziehbar, es sei denn, man blieb in bloßer Begrifflichkeit stecken und würde nicht zum eigentlichen Verstehen durchschreiten.

Doch wieder zurück zu Paulus und zur Auslegung alttestamentlicher Texte durch seine Theologie! Wir sagten, daß es die teilweise Offenheit der alttestamentlichen Texte sei, die eine Linie in die Verkündigung und Theologie des Neuen Testamentes, speziell die Verkündigung und Theologie des Paulus hindurchzuziehen ermöglichte. Diese Offenheit impliziert freilich, daß auch eine Linie in eine andere, eben nicht christliche Richtung hätte führen können. Und eine solche Linie wurde ja immerhin von den Rabbinen durchgezogen. Es war das *kontingente*, also geschichtliche Wirken und Geschick Jesu, in dem sich das nichtkontingente, also göttlich initiierte Geschehen geschichtlich verwirklichte. Aber gerade diese spezielle Kontingenz ist im Alten Testament nicht ausgesagt. Gesteht der christliche Theologe, der christliche Exeget ein, daß die Offenheit des Alten Testaments in unterschiedliche Kontingenzen hineinmünden kann, so gibt er zugleich zu, daß der Literalsinn der in Frage kommenden Aussagen des Alten Testaments nicht das kontingente Christusgeschehen im Blick hat. Dann aber bedeutet die Unterscheidung von *Vetus Testamentum per se* und *Vetus Testamentum in Novo receptum*, daß dem Judentum nicht *seine*, nämlich nicht christlich ausgelegte Heilige Schrift genommen wird, sondern lediglich deren – nur teilweise! – Offenheit auf Christus hin. Der christliche Theologe gibt somit offen zu, daß das im Neuen Testament und dann durch zwei Jahrtausende hindurch christlich interpretierte Alte Testament nicht unbedingt ein *Altes* Testament ist, vielmehr daß das *Vetus Testamentum per se* ein jüdisches Buch ist und bleibt. Viel Verkrampfung im christlich-jüdischen "Gespräch" hätte vermieden werden können, wenn die genannte Unterscheidung schon früher dazu geführt hätte, Israel sein geistliches Eigentum zu belassen, nämlich seine dem Literalsinn nach ausgelegte Bibel! Um aber keine Mißverständnis aufkommen zu lassen: Vom christlichen Glauben aus ist die Offenheit alttestamentlicher Aussagen auf das kontingente und zugleich von Gott initiierte Christusereignis eine Offenheit, die durch eben dieses Christusereignis nun um sein Offensein gebracht ist. So bleibt für den Christen das *Vetus Testamentum* als ihn angehende Heilige Schrift nur als das *Vetus Testamentum in Novo receptum* verbindlich.

Das ist aber genau das, was z.B. *Origenes* im 4. Buch seiner Prinzipien auf den theologischen Punkt gebracht hat, wenn er die πνευματικὴ διήγησις (IV, 2, 13) herausstellt. Seine allegorische Methode ist sicherlich für uns heute keine theologische Möglichkeit mehr. Seine Unterscheidung von der Seele und vom Leib der Schrift (τὴν ψυχὴν καὶ τὸ πνεῦμα τῆς γραφῆς, IV, 2, 12) trägt natürlich Züge eines überholten Denkens aufgrund einer überholten antiken Weltanschauung. Hinter dieser Allegorie verbirgt sich aber, was mit unserer Unterscheidung von *Vetus Testamentum per se* und *Vetus Testamentum in Novo receptum* als theologische Grundforderung ausgesagt wurde.

## Bibliographie

Bultmann, R. 1984: *Theologie des Neuen Testaments*, 9. Auflage, durchgesehen und ergänzt von O. Merk, Tübingen: J. C. B. Mohr (Paul Siebeck) 1984.

Dilthey, W. 1973: *Gesammelte Schriften VII*, Stuttgart/Göttingen: B. G. Täubner/Vandenhoeck & Ruprecht [6]1973.

Gadamer, H.-G. 1972: *Wahrheit und Methode. Grundzüge einer philosophischen Hermeneutik*, Tübingen: J. C. B. Mohr (Paul Siebeck) [3]1972.

Hübner, H. 1988: "Vetus Testamentum und Vetus Testamentum in Novo receptum. Die Frage nach dem Kanon des Alten Testaments aus neutestamentlicher Sicht", in: *JBTh* 3 (1988) 147-162.

— 1990: *Biblische Theologie des Neuen Testaments I: Prolegomena*, Göttingen: Vandenhoeck & Ruprecht 1990.

— 1993: *Biblische Theologie des Neuen Testaments II: Die Theologie des Paulus und ihre neutestamentliche Wirkungsgeschichte*, Göttingen: Vandenhoeck & Ruprecht 1993.

— 1994: "Eine moderne Variante der mittelalterlichen Lehre vom vierfachen Schriftsinns: Vetus Testamentum und Vetus Testamentum in Novo receptum", in: Paolo Chiarini und Hans Peter Zimmermann (Hgg.), *Schrift Sinne. Exegese, Interpretation, Dekonstruktion* (Schriftenreihe des Forum Guardini 3), Berlin: Guardini Stiftung 1994, 54-64.

Stuhlmacher, P. 1992: *Biblische Theologie des Neuen Testaments I: Grundlegung. Von Jesus zu Paulus*, Göttingen: Vandenhoeck & Ruprecht 1992.

# A Basic Code in the New Testament

## Harald Riesenfeld

The centre of the Christian movement has, from its very beginning, been the apostolic preaching about Jesus Christ and his gospel. This means that there were—inseparable from one another—on one hand the witness about a person, Jesus the Messiah, and on the other the continued proclamation of the message, the good news, he had pronounced.

In his first letter to the Corinthians, Paul starts from the testimony to Christ, the Messiah; this testimony has been confirmed in the congregation he addresses (1:6). The decisive importance of the very person of him who is the object of the testimony is stressed by the terminology which Paul preferably uses when speaking of Jesus: our Lord Jesus Christ, Christ Jesus, Christ. It is worth while to pay special attention to the ways in which Paul speaks of Jesus the Christ.

This is apparent when the death of Jesus is called a stumbling stone and folly (1:23–25; 2:2). It was Christ, in the very sense of this word, who was crucified. Analogously Paul never speaks of the resurrection of Jesus; it was Christ who was raised from the dead. Referring to the tradition which the congregation in Corinth had received at their conversion, the apostle quotes: "that Christ died for our sins in accordance with the scriptures, that he was buried, that he was raised on the third day in accordance with the scriptures…" (15:3f.). It is significant that the name Jesus is not used in one of the oldest pieces of Christian tradition.

In the mind of Paul—and obviously also in the language of the congregation he addresses—Christ is more than the name or the designation of an ordinary human person. This is clear from the way in which the apostle compares Adam and Christ: "The first man Adam became a living being; the last Adam became a life-giving spirit … The first man was from the earth, a man of dust; the second man is from heaven" (1 Cor 15:45–47).

In the life of the early church the continuation of the good news about the kingdom of heaven drawing near can be traced in the proclamation of a newness of life awaiting all believers in the presence of God — beyond the trials of a life on earth, beyond suffering and death. Human life has got its destination, intended from the very beginning, past the limits of space and time.

As to their contents, the letters of the New Testament—and also the Book of Revelation—have a tripartite structure: references to the salvific achievement of Jesus the Messiah; instructions concerning life in this world and discipleship within the congregations, in the invisible presence of the exalted Lord; outlooks on the return of Christ at the end of time, the final judgment and the fulfilment of human life in a world without end.

It is, however, striking that no convincing traces can be found, in the writings of the Early Church, of a successive divinization of the historical figure of Jesus of Nazareth. The belief in his resurrection did not essentially change the impression he had made during his lifetime but corroborated it. Obviously this belief is traceable in the gospel material in its final shape, but there is no fundamental discrepancy. When Paul says, in one of his earlier letters and with reference to Jesus, that "the second man is from heaven" (1 Cor 15:47), he makes no attempt to explain this idea to his addressees. For them it must have been an obvious element, based on the instruction they had received at their conversion, of their belief in Jesus the Christ.

Here the idea of the pre-existence of Jesus the Messiah is not only clearly pronounced but—which is more important—taken for granted, obviously within the limits of Christian belief. The fact that the pre-existence of Christ is expressly mentioned in the context of 1 Cor 15, is important with regard to the way in which Paul's quotation from catechetical tradition in the beginning of the same chapter (vv. 3–8) has to be interpreted. Throught the ages the death of Jesus on a cross and his resurrection have been considered the decisive items of his salvific achievement. On second thoughts, however, the death and moreover the resurrection of a human person scarcely make sense in a wider context. When Paul writes that Christ died "for our sins" (v. 3) and that by his resurrection "death is swallowed up in victory" (v. 54), he must have been convinced of the pre-existence and the divinity of Jesus Christ, who during his earthly life was Jesus of Nazareth. This is evident also from a passage where the pre-existence of Christ has not expressly been mentioned but in view of the context is an inevitable supposition: "For you know the grace of our Lord Jesus Christ, that though he was rich, yet for our sake he became poor, so that by his poverty you might become rich" (2 Cor 8:9).

As a matter of course Paul's belief in the divinity and pre-existence of Christ does by no means imply a verified or verifiable factuality of the object of his belief. It is, however, worth noticing that these conceptions appear in a relatively early period of the primitive church.In accordance with his belief Paul describes the resurrection of Christ as source of a newness of life for human beings: "For as in Adam all die, so also in Christ shall all be made alive. But each in his own order: Christ the first fruits, then at his coming those who belong to Christ" (1 Cor 15:23f.). After his resurrection Christ has been lifted up to heaven; from there he will return at the parousia. This idea is explicitly dealt with in 1 Thess 4:13–17. The theme of the parousia is related to that of the judgment, which Paul focuses in 1 Cor 3:10–14; 4:1–5, as he does in 1 Thess 1:10; 5:2–10, in this latter passage in connection with the theme of vigilance. Finally Christ subjects himself to God (1 Cor 15:28).

From its beginning, Christological belief in the early church contains five characteristic elements as far as the person of Jesus being the Christ is concerned: (1) pre-existence as a divine being in close relation to God; (2) a human life in obedience and yet with authority; (3) an atoning death; (4) a resurrection which opens the way to a life beyond death; (5) the return from heaven of the exalted Christ, a general judgment and an unrestricted dominion of God.

This characteristic structure of Christology can be found, more or less explicitly developed, not only in the Pauline letters but in a majority of writings in the New Testament. Therefore it is appropriate to speak of a basic code.

The question arises: where did it originate? For more than a century the predominating answer in occidental biblical studies has been: in congregations belonging to the first and second generation of the Christian movement, as the result of a complicated process of interpretation and speculation. But one question has hardly been answered: how was it possible to unite a multitude of scattered interpretations and speculations into an impressive and convincing wholeness? An indisputable fact is the rapid and surprisingly homogeneous extension of the Christian faith.

Most striking is, however, the fact that what we have called the basic code is evident, more manifestly than in other contexts, in the sayings about the Son of man as they appear in all four gospels. Do we have to explain it as a mere coincidence that this genre of sayings, taken as a whole, is characterized by a consistent structure of thought?

In the opinion of the present writer many difficulties in explaining the ways in which early Christian ideology developed could be overcome by an appropriate use of Occam's razor. Instead of attributing the genesis of the synoptic and the Johannine sayings about the Son of man to hypothetical processes in anonymous congregations, it might be worth while to ask anew whether a bulk of these sayings—all of them attributed exclusively to Jesus in the gospel tradition—have in fact been pronounced, as it is described in our sources, by Jesus himself. This could explain not only the offence caused by his person as well as by his proclamation during his public ministry, but also the immediate rise of Christological reflection among his disciples after his resurrection. In this case, it is true, we should have to admit that Jesus had some kind of self-consciousness, the authenticity of which, however, cannot be proved in an objective way. But it might be easier to presuppose a conviction or an idea in the mind of Jesus than to assume a miraculous harmony of creative fantasy in a temporal and geographical diversity of thinkers who conceived each of them one or another of the sayings about a Son of man.

A short survey will show the way in which different sayings about the Son of man reflect the five elements of the basic code.

(1) Pre-existence. As far as I know, one peculiarity of wording in the sayings has not been sufficiently examined. This is the enigmatic "has come" which appears in a number of these sayings. From where has the Son of man come and why is it repeatedly said that he has come? The background is most likely the vision of Daniel as it stands in Dan 7:13–14. The Aramaic text as well as its Greek translation read: "…with the clouds of heaven there came one like a son of man, and he came to the Ancient of days". In the vision of Daniel the heavenly being comes to the throne of God (cf. v. 9). In the gospels the Son of man "has come"—obviously from heaven; that is why he is now present on earth. A Johannine saying reads: "No one has ascended into heaven but he who descended from heaven" (John 3:13).

(2) A human life in obedience and yet with authority. Most striking, not least because of the reference to Dan 7:13–14, is the following saying: "…even as the Son of man came not to be served but to serve…" (Matt 20:28 par.). To the Danielic figure was given dominion, so that all people should serve him. On earth "the Son of man has nowhere to lay his head" (Matt 8:20).

The contrast of the heavenly pre-existence to the humility of a human life in an exposed position is expressed here in a characteristic way. On the other hand the Son of man, as a human being, is bearer of qualities that surpass all limitations. This is evident from the narrative of the paralytic's healing: "But that you may know that the Son of man has authority on earth to forgive sins …" (Matt 9:6). In an analogous way the Son of man is lord of the Sabbath (Matt 12:8).

(3) An atoning death. During his human life as a servant the Son of man faces his heavy task "to give his life as a ransom for many" (Matt 20:28 par.). In this saying the Danielic symbol of the heavenly Son of man and that of the Suffering servant in Deutero-Isaiah (Isa 53:12) have been combined in an original way.

In some of these sayings attributed to Jesus our attention is attracted by glimpses which intimate a deeply rooted conviction and intention: "How is it written about the Son of man, that he should suffer many things and be treated with contempt?" (Mark 9:12); "The Son of man goes as it is written of him" (Matt 26:24; cf. Luke 22:22).

(4) A resurrection which anticipates the general resurrection of the dead. In the threefold synoptic prediction of the passion (Matt 16:21 parr.; 17:22–23 parr.; 20:18–19 parr.) the suffering and death of the Son of man are followed by his resurrection. The authenticity of the substance of this tradition is corroborated by reflections and echoes existing in the synoptic material. We are told that three of the

disciples were charged by Jesus not to tell anybody what they had seen when present at his transfiguration "until the Son of man should have risen from the dead" (Mark 9:9). This causes the disciples' mutual question what the rising from the dead meant (v. 10). Another echo, after the narrative about the crucifixion, is attributed to some representatives of the Jews: "We remember how that impostor said, while he was still alive: After three days I will rise again" (Matt 27:63). Standing at the empty tomb some women who had followed Jesus are said to have been reminded of words that Jesus had uttered before his death (Luke 24:6–7). In one saying attributed to Jesus the "sign of Jonah" has been combined with the death and resurrection of the Son of man (Matt 12:40).

Also the Fourth gospel contains a prediction of the "lifting up" of the Son of man (John 3:14; cf. 12:34). This is said to pave the way to eternal life (through a resurrection) for his believers. In Johannine reflection Jesus will raise up every one who believes in him (6:34); he calls himself "the resurrection and the life: he who believes in me, though he die, yet shall he live" (11:25).

The obvious connection of the resurrection of Christ and a general resurrection reflects an early topic in Christian belief. This is evident from the way in which Paul argues both in 1 Thess 4:13-18 and in 1 Cor 15:3-23. It is worth while observing that Paul in 1 Cor 15:3f. and 12 does not speak of Jesus but of Christ.

(5) The future return from heaven of the Son of man, judgment, the final kingdom. The motif of a future return from heaven of the Son of man appears in different strata of synoptic material and is related to that of a final judgment: "The Son of man is to come with his angels in the glory of his Father, and then he will repay every man for what he has done" (Matt 16:27; cf. Mark 8:38 par.); "Then will appear the sign of the Son of man in heaven … and they will see the Son of man coming on the clouds of heaven with power and great glory, and he will send out his angels … and they will gather his elects …" (Matt 24:30, 31 parrs.; cf. 25:31–46). The return happens when it is not expected, and therefore wakefulness is required (Matt 24:44 par.). The kingdom of heaven is finally realized when the Son of man is seated "at the right hand" of God (Matt 26:64 parrs.; cf. Matt 6:10; Luke 11:2).

The basic code inherent in the sayings about the Son of man in their entirety appears in a remarkable passage of Paul's letter to the Philippians. As the present writer has demonstrated in detail in the volume dedicated to the memory of the late Rafael Gyllenberg,[1] the so-called hymn, 2:6–11, shows not a single one of the distinctive features of a hymn, either Greek or Oriental. It is, on the contrary, a piece of pro-

---

[1] H. Riesenfeld, "Unpoetische Hymnen im Neuen Testament?", in: J. Kilunen/V Riekkinen/H. Räisänen (eds.), *Glaube und Gerechtigkeit. In Memoriam Rafael Gyllenberg* (Schriften der Finnischen Exegetischen Gesellschaft 38), Helsinki: Finnische Exegetische Gesellschaft 1983, 155-68.

found reflection, rhetorically stylized and beyond doubt due to the apostle himself.

In this passage as well as in other christological statements in the Pauline letters, the basic code underlying the sayings about the Son of man becomes apparent. That is why it seems reasonable to suppose that Paul was not unfamiliar with sayings about the Son of man, especially Matt 20:28 par. in the context of Matt 20:20–28, as the context of Phil 2:1–11 makes plausible.

# Death and Rebirth of Rhetoric
## in Late Twentieth Century Biblical Exegesis[1]

### Wilhelm Wuellner

## 1. Introduction

It was indeed a momentous occasion for the International Society for the History of Rhetoric (ISHR) to sponsor at its eighth biennial meeting for the first time in its relatively short history since the mid-1970's a special section devoted to the role the Bible played in the history of Western rhetoric. Its role has been so central to the developments of Western rhetoric that one is led to wonder about the reasons for the marginal role the Bible has played in the history of ISHR until this year. The purpose of this paper is threefold: (1) to outline and briefly comment on the causes for rhetoric's demise in the publications of professional biblical exegetes and in the scholarly activities of our learned societies; the causes for rhetoric becoming *so* marginalized in the history of biblical interpretation that it ceased to play any significant role—for the theological and ethical interpretations no less than even the linguistic, syntactical interpretations.

(2) I want to comment briefly on the extraordinary rebirth of rhetoric in both Jewish and Christian biblical studies in the last 15 years. Some of the revived interest is noticeable also in the study of non-Western religious literature.[2]

(3) I want to address myself to two assessments of this new situation by seeking answers to two questions: (a) what can we learn, indeed what have we learned, we biblical exegetes, from the history of rhetoric, mainly, but not exclusively, from the rhetoric in the Western tradition? And (b) what can we learn, we rhetoricians, from the history of biblical exegesis about the essence, or the motives, of rhetoric?

---

[1] This paper was first presented at the Eighth Biennial Conference of the International Society for the History of Rhetoric at Baltimore/Washington, DC, September 28, 1991. It has been revised and is now dedicated to Lars Hartman in appreciation for his sustained efforts and his contributions to bringing about a rebirth of rhetoric in Scandinavian biblical scholarship.

[2] See e.g. Issa J. Bollata 1988; D. Margoliouth 1897; James L. Fitzgerald 1983; the pioneering study of Robert T. Oliver 1971; Greory D. Alles 1986.

## 2. Rhetoric's Demise in Modern Biblical Interpretation

What are the causes of rhetoric's decline in its role in the interpretation of biblical literature in modern times (17th – 20th Centuries)? Let me select and comment on four causes:

One of the factors that disqualified rhetoric in the Western philosophical and theological traditions was "the idea of the unicity of truth."[3] Closely related to, but distinct from this factor, is the growing impact of modern scientism with its univocal dimension of scientific discourse,[4] which affected biblical scholarship and the rhetoric of its inquiry.[5]

Another factor that changed rhetoric in theory and practice was the emergence of a new rhetoric in the wake of the vernacular movements in the late Middle Ages. Simultaneously we witness, as a legacy of Renaissance humanism, a lingering conflict between Western rhetorics (whether Greek or Latin, or the vernacular versions) and non-Western rhetorics. This conflict was experienced in two ways: (a) the classical Ciceronian Greek or Latin view of rhetoric clashing with biblical Hebrew and Rabbinic (Mishnaic/Talmudic) rhetoric,[6] a conflict reflected also in the work of Christian Hebraists,[7] and (b) European cultures (including the Jewish diaspora in Europe) clashing with the spreading Moslem culture.[8] Colonial and missionary expansion led to the imposition of Western rhetorics on non-Western cultures, but also the first awareness of alternative theories and practices of rhetoric.[9]

A third factor was rhetoric's linkage with the educational system, i.e. the linkage with what Quintilian calls rhetoric's "public utility." This linkage dates back to late antiquity, and undergoes major reforms, from the Carolingian renaissance,[10]

---

[3] Chaim Perelman 1979, 12.

[4] See Renato Barilli 1989, 113-14.

[5] See Klaus Scholder 1990; Amos N. Wilder 1991, 101-82 on "Genres, Rhetorics and Meaning."

[6] For an assessment of "Talmudic study as culture critique" see Daniel Boyarin 1993, 227-45. On rhetoric as model of culture or as counter-culture's anti-rhetoric, see Renate Lachmann 1977 and eadem 1978/90.

[7] For an overview, see Rudolf Hallo 1983; and William McKane 1989.

For special historical periods, e.g. the Patristic period, see H. Bietenhard 1974; N. R. M. DeLange 1976; Günter Stemberger 1993.

For the medieval and modern periods, see Barouh Mevorah 1982; Ilana Zinguer (ed.) 1992; Eric Zimmer 1980; Olivier Fatio and Pierre Fraenkel (eds.) 1978; David Katz 1989; Peter T. van Rooden 1989.

[8] See Brian Vickers 1988, 473, n.44.

[9] See Robert T. Oliver 1971.

[10] See Klaus Dockhorn 1974. For the period prior to this, see H.-I. Marrou 1981; and Thomas M. Conley 1990, 29-32 on "Enkyklios paideia" and 82-86 on "The First Renaissance of Rhetoric in the Middle Ages."

throughout the Middle Ages and the rise of Humanism.[11] The reforms of rhetoric's linkage with the educational system reached a crucial phase in the 16th century, whether on the Reformation side (the Ramist reform),[12] or the Counter-Reformation side.[13] The educational reform advocated by Peter Ramus affected exegesis profoundly for centuries. Ramism influenced biblical exegesis at the very time that missionaries went world-wide to found Western centers of learning. Ramism's effect was the institutionalization of the separation of the study of rhetoric's *officium* from the study of rhetoric as τέχνη. In early modern times it became the separation of the study of thought or content from the study of form or feeling. Ever since we have remained preoccupied in the West with theology (or ethics) at the expense of religion or aesthetics or poetics.

Fourth, the decline and death of rhetoric in the 19th century was engendered by the linkage between romanticism and irrationalism on the one hand, and between romanticism and the Enlightenment on the other hand,[14] what Barilli called "the κοινή between romanticism and positivism, with its emphasis on feelings and common sense."[15]

In retrospect on this history it might be said that, whereas traditional rhetoric atrophied by being reduced to stylistics, modern rhetoric tends to get atrophied anew by being reduced either to communication studies, or to social studies, in the name of the desired, indeed demanded, "full-bodied encounter with the (Biblical) text."[16]

## 3. Rhetoric's Rebirth in Late 20th Century Biblical Interpretation.

This astonishing process can be seen as one of the results of what Bakhtin saw as the mandate of restoring rhetoric "to all its ancient rights".[17] Instead of rebirth or

---

[11] See e.g. G. R. Evans 1980, and J. Koch (ed.) 1976.

[12] Kees Meerhoff 1986. Thomas M. Conley 1990, chap. 5 "Rhetoric and Renaissance Humanism", and 124-33 "Revolutions in Rhetoric: Agricola and Peter Ramus [128-33]".

[13] See Wilfried Barner 1970, and Thomas M. Conley 1990, 151-87 "Rhetoric in the Seventeenth Century," especially 152-57 on "Jesuit Rhetorics," and 173-76 on rhetoric in the Oratorian Order, the chief rival of the Jesuits in education and theological disputation, e.g. Bernard Lamy's *Rhétorique, ou L'Art de Parler* (1675).

[14] Harold Bloom 1989, 115-41. For David Jasper 1993, 155 Bloom's approach is "a revived romanticism which cloaks a sinister gnosticism." Cf. also Klaus Dockhorn 1991.

[15] Barilli 1989, 110.

[16] Dale Patrick and Allen Scult 1990, 18; Gabriel Josipovici 1988. See also the motto chosen by Wilhelm Nestle for his *Novum Testamentum Graece*, taken from the Preface of a Greek NT text edition of 1734 by Johann A. Bengel, a member of the influential Piestist movement: *Te totum applica ad textum: rem totam applica ad te*. On the fateful separation between exegesis and application, see Klaus Berger 1988, 108-20.

revival, Eagleton prefers to speak of the reinvention of rhetoric.[18] Biblical exegetes are coming to focus on what Eagleton calls the "discursive practices" in the biblical text, and of "grasping (them) as forms of power and performance" or "as forms of *activity* inseparable from the wider social relations between writers and readers." While Harold Bloom holds that "psychology, rhetoric, and cosmology are three names for a single entity,"[19] one could also maintain that sociology, rhetoric, and literary anthropology are three names for a single entity. It is here that we perceive what Leff and Procario called "the nexus between rhetoric and ideology."[20]

What is the essence of this reborn, reinvented rhetoric of the late 20th century? The essence of rhetoric, like that of poetry, is seen not as communication, but as the creation of states of communion;[21] its essence, as traditionally defined, is to "move" and "please" the reader. But for Kenneth Burke, its essence is far more than that; for Burke it is the "goadings of mystery." This phrase takes on special meaning in the study of religious literature like the Bible with is own mystery, including "the terror of mysterious misconceptions,"[22] i.e. the misreadings of the mystery. Historically and culturally such misreadings are evident in the ever-present religious schisms and sectarian formations, not to speak of the "heresies."

The essence of sacred rhetoric has been identified as the rhetoric of the sublime, as literary mysticism in the languaging of the ineffable or the unspeakable.[23] The sublime of the Bible's sacred rhetoric is, indeed, a literary sublime, whose mystery rests not so much on "the beauty of holiness," but more on the katachretic or "monstrous" dimensions experienced in the paradoxes, ironies, or oxymorons,—whether in human history or in nature, whether in reality or in the act of reading. This "lit-

---

[17] M. M. Bakhtin 1981, 267. See also David S. Cunnigham 1991, 19-30 "The death and resurrection of rhetoric;" and Josef Kopperschmidt 1990a and idem 1991a.

[18] Terry Eagleton 1983, 205-6. See also Jasper 1993.

[19] Bloom1989, 123.

[20] Michael C. Leff and Margaret O. Procario 1985. See also Michael Cahn 1989-90; Hans Georg Gadamer 19(67)/88; and Renate Lachmann 1977, and eadem 1978/90. For a critique of Leff's view, see Celeste Condit 1990.

[21] Chaim Perelman and L. Olbrechts-Tyteca 1969, 163-67.

[22] Bloom 1989, 166. Jasper (1993, 155/56) speaks of the "well tested" rhetoric of the old heresies in his critique of Bloom.

[23] On the rhetorical sublime, see Jörg Villwock1989; and Lynn Poland 1990. Manuela Colombo 1987; Stephen A. Tyler 1987. See also the essays edited by Franco Bolgiani (ed.) 1977; and the studies by David B. Morris 1972; Theodore E. B. Wood 1972; Thomas Weiskel 1974; the whole issue of *New Literary History* 16 (1985) devoted to the sublime.

On the grotesque, the gruesome, dreadful, or weird as an integral part of the sublime of the holy, or of the apocalyptic, see Rudolf Otto 1925; also Morton D. Paley 1986.

On the role of the sublime in modern psychoanalysis, see Neil Hertz1985; Julia Kristeva 1982; and Jean-François Lyotard 1991, and idem 1988.

erary sublime" is defined by Bloom as "the reader's sublime." Bloom means by this that the reader is goaded "to defer pleasure, yielding up easier satisfactions in favor of a more delayed and difficult reward"[24]—in Kenneth Burke's term, in favor of "perfection." As the sublime and the monstrous or grotesque complement each other, so do the divine and humor in the tradition of the "divine comedy" going back to Scripture itself.[25]

The sublime in biblical literature as part of imaginative literature cannot be distinguished, on *literary* grounds, as a sacred sublime from a secular sublime, though efforts continue to be made along that fateful divide of the sacred and the secular. Every imaginative literature, of which biblical literature as religious literature is a part, has come to be seen, however, as inescapably culture-specific. Bloom sees as "peculiarly Judaic" the belief "that God's interventions are always primarily for the purpose of eliciting Israel's response; for the reader of the Bible it is God's interventions for the reader's response—as distinct from non-Jewish imaginative literature.[26]

It is this reinvented and expanded concept of rhetoric that distinguishes the new rhetoric from classical and modern rhetoric. The "new" rhetoric gives a completely new connotation to what Ong called "The Presence of the Word,"[27] and what Kennedy referred to as the power in, or of, the text. Whether "presence" or "power" (or other concepts), modern rhetorical theory includes here not only the reader as part of the text, but also the producer and reader of theories about this "power." Leff and Procario rightly warn that the expansion of the perception of the realm of rhetoric, of rhetoric's *officium*, threatens "to alienate us from each other as we identify with other scholarly areas and isolate our work in increasingly disparate content areas."[28] The biannual ISHR conferences illustrate the dilemma as well as do the annual conferences of the SBL, SNTS, etc.

A representative definition of modern rhetorical criticism, applied to biblical exegesis, is the one by Patrick and Scult as the study of "the means by which a text establishes and manages its relationship to its audience in order to achieve a particular effect."[29] Or take Booth's definition as "the study of use, of purpose pursued,

---

[24] Bloom 1989, 5.

[25] See Robert M. Polhemus 1980; and Umberto Eco 1990, 163-73. See also Jasper 1993, 136-49 on "The Christian Art of Missing the Joke."

[26] For a view similar to Bloom's, about the Hebraic way of reading texts as distinct from Greek and Christian ways, see José Faur 1986; and Meir Sternberg 1985.

For a critique of this position, see Philip S. Alexander 1990. Cf. also Geoffrey H. Hartman 1985.

[27] Walter J. Ong 1967.

[28] Leff and Procario 1985, 26.

[29] Dale Patrick and Allen Scult 1990, 12. For other attempts at defining rhetorical criticism, see Jan Lambrecht 1989; Burton L. Mack 1990; Dennis L. Stamps 1992.

targets hit or missed, practices illuminated for the sake not of pure knowledge, but of further (and improved) practice."[30] In both Western and non-Western cultures, rhetoric is recognized as inherent in the use of written or spoken, poetic or ordinary language, indeed in all use of signs, as forms and functions of living discourse—not just once when first uttered, but retaining in its textuality the text's power for future readers. That is the rhetorical dimension of the exegete's hermeneutical efforts, or what J. Hillis Miller calls the task of rhetorical reading.[31]

## 4. Assessment and Outlook

Two questions invite some concluding critical reflections about the position of the biblical interpreter at the cross-roads of rhetorical and biblical studies.

What have exegetes learned from the history of rhetoric—indeed, *have* they learned?

In its long and checkered history, in both Western and non-Western cultures, down to our times, the nature of rhetoric, and the scope of its critical practices and theories, reflect the wider social and cultural situations in which they were, and continue to be, cultivated. There is no monolithic, uniform tradition of rhetoric, and of rhetorical criticism, despite the appearance of rhetoric as a closed system based on the tradition of rhetorical handbooks (e.g. Lausberg)[32] which has blinded us far too long about "the enduring identity crisis [which is] characteristic" of rhetorical scholarship.[33]

We have learned, furthermore, that what modern rhetorical criticism discerns in Jewish and early Christian literature is something that *challenged* the prevailing dominance of norms of discourse in their respective societies. Rhetoric in Hellenistic-Roman culture could depend on "a common value set as criteria for selecting ... the ... means for resolving common problems" confronting society.[34] This was challenged, however, in the cultural conflict which classical and late antiquity cultures generated within themselves. The different theories and practices of rhetoric in classical and late antiquity times[35] are no less indicative of cultural conflicts than

---

[30] Wayne C. Booth 1983, 44.

[31] See J. Hillis Miller 1989.

[32] Heinrich Lausberg 1973. On the origin of the rhetorical textbooks, see George A. Kennedy 1959; for its broader cultural context, cf. Manfred Fuhrmann 1960.

[33] Leff-Procario 1985, 26.

[34] D. P. Cushman and P. K. Tompkins 1980, 51. Conley (1990, 46) noted that the Hellenistic rhetoric curriculum, as well as its Latin version in the tradition of Cicero, "...was intended to foster ... the cultural and social values [of the times]." See also Renate Lachmann 1977 and eadem 1978/90.

[35] See Conley 1990, 1-71.

the conflict between "Athens and Jerusalem." What can be said of the "influx of Athens into Jerusalem [having] saved Judaism, and the Jews, from being scattered into oblivion among the nations, by giving the Jews a central formulation of their own culture ..."[36]—which, of course, was the formation of Rabbinic Judaism—, that same influx saved nascent and fledgling Christianity. Clarke even ventured to call Christianity "a rhetorical religion" despite of, or better still because of, its conflict with rhetoric, especially in its virulent Ciceronian tradition in the age of the Second Sophistic.[37] This conflict arose not only between classical antiquity and Judaism or Christianity respectively. It was also generated by the clash of indigenous cultures resisting the homogenizing forces of cultural, political, racial, or gender ideologies—whether among Pagans, Jews, or Christians. A variation on this theme will reappear in the reform movements, and revolutionary movements, of medieval and modern Christian and Jewish traditions.

Thirdly, we are beginning to learn about and appreciate the rich sources "of alternative views to the Euro-American tradition" of rhetoric, both as to practice and theory of rhetorical criticism, which can be found, for instance, in Asian rhetorics, with its own diversity due to the social and cultural contexts which shape all rhetoric, as they do all religion. Similar claims are now also being made for rhetoric in the Jewish tradition.[38]

Finally, what can we rhetoricians learn from biblical interpretation about the essence or motives of rhetoric?

Booth spoke of "targets hit *or* missed" and of "*improved* practice," when it comes to today's practices of rhetorical criticism. The rhetorical enactment of a text's meaning, or text as practice, is perceived as taking place within a plurality of interpretive communities. Critics dedicated to feminist or womanist criticism and other forms of political or ideological criticism are examples of such interpretive communities. Each such community has its own institutional manifestations and representations, whether in religion, or in education and academia, or in politics and economics, or in ethnic and cultural communities struggling for justice and freedom, or devoting themselves to strengthening their respective identity or reaching for deeper levels of identification, which is Kenneth Burke's motive of perfection.[39]

In Palinkas' analysis of "Rhetoric and Religious Experience"[40] as evident

---

[36] Bloom 1989, 148; on Talmudic culture as culture critique, see Boyarin 1993.

[37] M. L. Clarke 1953, 149.

[38] See Mary Garrett 1991; and J. Vernon Jensen 1987.
On Jewish rhetorical traditions, see Isaac Rabinowitz 1985; and Wilhelm Wuellner 1994, forthcoming.

[39] Kenneth Burke 1950.

[40] Lawrence A. Palinkas 1989.

among immigrant Chinese churches and their uses of the Bible, we see the same problems today that prevailed in the dynamics between "orthodoxy and heresy in earliest Christianity" (Bauer, 1971) or in similar dynamics developing in Judaism. The dynamics of rhetoric and religious experience has been taken as a reflection of the "discontents"[41] generated by the biblical canon as literary or rhetorical unit. As such a sacred canon of literature, "the Bible is now [as it always has been] the most recalcitrant and difficult of all libraries."[42] For Bloom it was "the very power of [the Bible's] rhetoric [that] encouraged the rebellious Gnostic [or Kabbalistic] imagination."[43]

But in Bloom's own sweeping survey of poetry and belief from the Bible to the present, the *Jewish* cultural imagination, regardless whether secular or sacred, remains discernibly distinct from the nonJewish cultural imagination, whether Hellenistic or Roman, Christian or Pagan. The same cannot be said of the *Christian* cultural imagination, secular or sacred, because the *Jewish* cultural imagination keeps influencing it due to the normative role that the Hebrew Bible continues to play as integral part of the Christian Bible. The New Testament plays no such role for the Jewish cultural imagination. The *Moslem* cultural imagination is distinct from both: it is influenced by both Jewish and Christian cultural imagination, but includes neither the Old Testament, nor the New Testament in its normative canon, the Koran.

If "the goadings of mystery" or the motive of perfection is essential to every rhetoric, secular or sacred, as it certainly *is* essential for sacred rhetoric, then we rhetoricians can learn from the reinvention of rhetoric in modern biblical exegesis a common task facing us. This task is twofold: one is to account for the rhetoricity of the texts we analyze when we practice rhetorical criticism of texts like the Bible or the Koran. Secondly, we need to account for the rhetoricity of the *scientific* discourse generated and sustained by rhetorical theory, or theories, and the interpretive communities which this critical or theoretical discourse, cultivated and promoted e.g. in the Society of Biblical Literature, or the American Academy of Religion, is supposedly to serve.[44] If theology is coming back under the disguise of theory,[45]

---

[41] See Herbert N. Schneidau 1977. A similar point is made by Northrop Frye 1981.

[42] Bloom 1989, 156.

[43] Bloom 1989, 150.

[44] Representative of this emerging concern with the rhetoric of science are such works as Bruno Latour and Steve Woolgar 1979/86. Richard Harvey Brown 1987, and idem 1989; Alan G. Gross 1990, and idem 1991; J. E. McGuire and Trevor Melia 1989, and eidem 1991; Herbert W. Simons (ed.) 1990. See also the "Project on Rhetoric of Inquiry" (POROI) in Iowa City, IA: University of Iowa, operating since the late 1980's.

[45] Regina M. Schwartz (ed.) 1990, 1-15.

we need to be doubly leery and on guard against both: theology and theory, while critically appreciating both.[46]

## *Bibliography*

Alexander, Philip S. 1990: "Quid Athenis et Hierosolymis? Rabbinic Midrash and Hermeneutics in the Graeco-Roman World", in: P. R. Davies and R. T. White (eds.), *A Tribute to Geza Vermes. Essays on Jewish and Christian Literature and History* (JSOT.S 100), Sheffield: Academic Press 1990, 101-24.

Alles, Greory D. 1986: *Epic Persuasion: Religion and Rhetoric in the ILIAD and Valmiki's RAMAYANA* (Ph. D. Dissertation University of Chicago, March 1986).

Bakhtin, M. M. 1981: *The Dialogic Imagination. Four Essays* (ed. Michael Holquist), Austin, TX: University of Texas Press 1981.

Barilli, Renato 1989: *Rhetoric* (Theory and History of Literature 63; trans. Guiliana Menozzi), Minneapolis, MN: University of Minnesota Press 1989.

Barner, Wilfried 1970: *Barockrhetorik. Untersuchungen zu ihren geschichtlichen Grundlagen*, Tübingen: Niemeyer 1970.

Bauer, Walter 1971: *Orthodoxy and Heresy in Earliest Christianity*, Philadelphia, PA: Fortress 1971.

Berger, Klaus 1988: *Hermeneutik des Neuen Testaments*, Gütersloh: Mohn 1988.

Bietenhard, H. 1974: *Caesarea, Origenes und die Juden*, Stuttgart: Kohlhammer 1974.

Bloom, Harold 1989: *Ruin the Sacred Truths: Poetry and Belief from the Bible to the Present*, Cambridge, MA: Harvard University Press 1989.

Bolgiani, Franco (ed.) 1977: *Mistica e Retorica*, Florence: Olschki 1977.

Bollata, Issa J. 1988: "The rhetorical interpretation of the Qu'rân: *i'jâz* and related topics", in: A. Rippin (ed.), *Approaches to the History of the Interpretation of the Qu'rân*, Oxford: Clarendon 1988, 139-57.

Booth, Wayne C. 1983: *The Rhetoric of Fiction*, Chicago, IL/London: University of Chicago Press, 2nd edition 1983.

Boyarin, Daniel 1993: *Carnal Israel: Reading Sex in Talmudic Culture* (The New Historicism 25), Berkeley, CA/Los Angeles, CA/Oxford: University of California Press 1993.

Brown, Richard Harvey 1987: *Society as Text: Essays on Rhetoric, Reason, and Reality*, Chicago, IL: University of Chicago Press 1987.

---

[46] David Jasper (1993, 69) pleads for "an indirect, reflective, reflexive, creative adoption of [rhetoric]." Cf. the ambitious project in the SUNY Series in Rhetoric and Theology (Albany, NY: State University of New York Press, 1991), edited by David Tracy and his student S. H. Webb. Less critical is Cunnigham 1991, 204-58.

For the broader context for such critical reserve in the rehabilitation of rhetoric, see Stanley Fish 1989; C. Jan Swearingen 1991; Josef Kopperschmidt (ed.) 1990 and idem (ed.) 1991; and earlier Barbara Herrnstein Smith 1983.

— 1989: *Social Science as Civic Discourse: Essays on the Invention, Legitimation, and Uses of Social Theory,* Chicago, IL: University of Chicago Press 1989.

Burke, Kenneth 1950: *A Rhetoric of Motives,* Berkeley, CA/Los Angeles, CA/London: University of California Press 1950.

Cahn, Michael 1989-90: "L'Ideologia della Retorica", in: *Helikon* 29/30 (1989-1990) 25-42.

Clarke, M. L. 1953: *Rhetoric at Rome: A Historical Survey,* London: Cohen & West 1953.

Colombo, Manuela 1987: *Dai Mistici a Dante: il linguaggio dell'ineffabilita,* Florence: La Nuova Italia Editrice 1987.

Condit, Celeste 1990: "Rhetorical Criticism and Audiences: The Extremes of McGee and Leff", in: *Western Journal of Speech Communication* 54 (1990) 330-45.

Conley, Thomas M. 1990: *Rhetoric in the European Tradition,* New York/London: Longman 1990.

Cunnigham, David S. 1991: *Faithful Persuasion. In Aid of a Rhetoric of Christian Theology,* Notre Dame, IN/London: University of Notre Dame Press 1991.

Cushman, D. P. and Tompkins, P. K. 1980: "A Theory of Rhetoric for Contemporary Society", in: *Philosophy and Rhetoric* 13 (1980) 43-67.

DeLange, N. R. M. 1976: *Origen and the Jews* (University of Cambridge Oriental Publications 25), Cambridge: Cambridge University Press 1976.

Dockhorn, Klaus 1974: "Rhetorica movet: Protestantischer Humanismus und karolingische Renaissance", in: Helmut Schanze (ed.): *Rhetorik: Beiträge zu ihrer Geschichte in Deutschland vom 16.-20. Jahrhundert,* Frankfurt: Fischer 1974, 17-42.

— 1991: "Die Rhetorik als Quelle des vorromantischen Irrationalismus in der Literatur- und Geistesgeschichte", in: J. Kopperschmidt (ed.), *Rhetorik.* Vol. 2: *Wirkungsgeschichte der Rhetorik,* Darmstadt: Wissenschaftliche Buchgesellschaft 1991, 37-59 [excerpt from K. Dockhorn, *Macht und Wirkung der Rhetorik.* Vier Aufsätze zur Ideengeschichte der Vormoderne (Republica Literaria 2), Bad Homburg–Berlin–Zürich: Gehlen 1968, 46-95].

Eagleton, Terry 1983: *Literary Theory. An Introduction,* Minneapolis, MN: University of Minnesota Press 1983.

Eco, Umberto 1990: *The Limits of Interpretation,* Bloomington/Indianapolis, IN: Indiana University Press 1990.

Evans, G. R. 1980: *Old Arts and New Theology: The Beginnings of Theology as an Academic Discipline,* Oxford: Clarendon 1980.

Fatio, Olivier and Fraenkel, Pierre (eds.) 1978: *Histoire de l'Exégèse au XVIe Siecle: Textes du Colloque International, Genève 1976* (Études de Philologie et d'Histoire 34), Geneva: Librairie Droz 1978.

Faur, José 1986: *Golden Doves with Silver Dots: Semiotics and Textuality in Rabbinic Tradition,* Bloomington, IN: Indiana University Press 1986.

Fish, Stanley 1989: *Doing What Comes Naturally. Change, Rhetoric, and the Practice of Theory in Literary and Legal Studies,* Durham, NC: University of North Carolina Press 1989.

Fitzgerald, James L. 1983: "The great epic of India as religious rhetoric: a fresh look at the MAHABHARATA", in: *JAAR* 51 (1983) 611-30.

Frye, Northrop 1981: *The Great Code: The Bible and Literature*, New York/London: Harcourt Brace Jovanovich 1981.

Fuhrmann, Manfred 1960: *Das systematische Lehrbuch. Ein Beitrag zur Geschichte der Wissenschaften in der Antike*, Göttingen: Vandenhoeck & Ruprecht 1960.

Gadamer, Hans Georg 1967/88: "Rhetoric, Hermeneutics, and the Critique of Ideology: Metacritical Comments on TRUTH AND METHOD", (1967), reprinted in: Kurt Mueller-Vollmer (ed.), *The Hermeneutics Reader. Texts of the German Tradition from the Enlightenment to the Present*, New York: Continuum 1988, 274-92.

Garrett, Mary 1991: "Asian Challenge", in: S. K. Foss, K. A. Foss, and R. Trapp (eds.), *Contemporary Perspectives on Rhetoric*, Prospect Heights, IL: Waveland Press, 2nd edition 1991, 295-314.

Gross, Alan G. 1990: *The Rhetoric of Science,* Cambridge, MA: Harvard University Press 1990.

— 1991: "Rhetoric of Science without Constraints", in: *Rhetorica* 9 (1991) 283-99.

Hallo, Rudolf 1983: "Christian Hebraists", in: *Modern Judaism* 3 (1983) 95-116.

Hartman, Geoffrey H. 1985: "On the Jewish Imagination", in: *Prooftexts* 5 (1985) 201-20.

Herrnstein Smith, Barbara 1983: *Contingencies of Values: Alternative Perspectives for Critical Theory*, Cambridge, MA: Harvard University Press 1983.

Hertz, Neil 1985: *The End of the Line: Essays on Psychoanalysis and the Sublime*, New York: Columbia University Press 1985.

Jasper, David 1993: *Rhetoric, Power and Community: An Excercise in Reserve*, Louisville, KY: Westminster/J. Knox 1993.

Jensen, J. Vernon 1987: "Rhetoric of East Asia — A Bibliography", *Rhetoric Society Quarterly* 17 (1987) 213-31.

Josipovici, Gabriel 1988: *The Book of God: A Response to the Bible*, New Haven, CT/London: Yale University Press 1988.

Katz, David 1989: "The Abendana Brothers and the Christian Hebraists of Seventeenth-Century England", in: *JEH* 40 (1989) 28-52.

Kennedy, George A. 1959: "The Earliest Rhetorical Handbooks", in: *AJP* 80 (1959) 169-78.

Koch, J. (ed.) 1976: *Artes Liberales. Von der antiken Bildung zur Wissenschaft des Mittelalters* (reprint of 1959 edition in Studien und Texte zur Geistesgeschichte des Mittelalters 5), Leiden: Brill 1976.

Kopperschmidt, Josef (ed.) 1990: *Rhetorik.* Vol. 1: *Rhetorik als Texttheorie*, Darmstadt: Wissenschaftliche Buchgesellschaft 1990.

— 1991: *Rhetorik.* Vol. 2: *Wirkungsgeschichte der Rhetorik,* Darmstadt: Wissenschaftliche Buchgesellschaft 1991.

Kopperschmidt, Josef 1990a: "Rhetorik nach dem Ende der Rhetorik. Einleitende Anmerkungen zum heutigen Interesse an Rhetorik", in: idem (ed.) 1990, 1-31.

— 1991a: "Das Ende der Verleumdung. Einleitende Anmerkungen zur Wirkungsgeschichte der Rhetorik", in: idem (ed.) 1991, 1-33.

Kristeva, Julia 1982: *Powers of Horror: An Essay on Abjection* (trans. Leon S. Roudiez; European Perspectives), New York: Columbia University Press 1982.

Lachmann, Renate 1977: "Rhetorik und kultureller Kontext", in: H. F. Plett (ed.), *Rhetorik. Kritische Positionen zum Stand der Forschung* (Kritische Information 50), München: Fink 1977, 167-86.

— 1978/90: "Rhetorik und Kulturmodell", in: *Slavische Studien. Zum VIII. Internationalen Slavistenkongreß in Zagreb 1978*, Köln/Wien: Böhlau 1978, 279-98; reprinted in Josef Kopperschmidt (ed.), *Rhetorik*, 1: *Rhetorik als Texttheorie*, Darmstadt: Wissenschaftliche Buchgesellschaft 1990, 264-88.

Lambrecht, Jan 1989: "Rhetorical Criticism and the New Testament", in: *Bijdragen* 50 (1989) 239-53.

Latour, Bruno and Woolgar, Steve 1979/86: *Laboratory Life: The Social Construction of Scientific Facts*, Beverly Hills, CA: Sage, 1979; republished with the new subtitle *The Construction of Scientific Facts*, Princeton, NJ: Princeton University Press 1986.

Lausberg, Heinrich 1973: *Handbuch der literarischen Rhetorik. Eine Grundlegung der Literaturwissenschaft*, München: Hueber, 2 vols., 2nd edition 1973.

Leff, Michael C. and Procario, Margaret O. 1985: "Rhetorical Theory in Speech Communication", in: T. W. Benson (ed.), *Speech Communication in the 20th Century*, Carbondale/Edwardsville, IL: Southern Illinois University Press 1985, 3-27.

Lyotard, Jean-François 1988: "L'interêt du sublime", in: Jean-François Courtine et al. (eds.), *Du Sublime*, Paris: Belin 1988, 149-77.

— 1991: "The Sublime and the Avant-Garde", in: *The Inhuman: Reflections on Time* (trans. G. Bennington and R. Bowlby), Stanford, CA: Stanford University Press 1991, 89-107.

Mack, Burton L. 1990: *Rhetoric and the New Testament* (Guides to Biblical Scholarship, New Testament), Minneapolis, MN: Augsburg Fortress 1990.

Margoliouth, D. 1897: "On the Arabic Version of Aristotle's Rhetoric", in: G. A. Kohut (ed.), *Semitic Studies in Memory of Rev. Dr. Alexander Kohut*, Berlin: S. Calvary 1897, 376-87.

Marrou, H.-I. 1981: "Education and Rhetoric", in: Moses I. Finley (ed.), *The Legacy of Greece. A New Appraisal*, Oxford: Oxford University Press 1981, 185-201.

McGuire, J. E. and Melia, Trevor 1989: "Some Cautionary Strictures on the Writing of the Rhetoric of Science", in: *Rhetorica* 7 (1989) 87-99.

— 1991: "The Rhetoric of the Radical Rhetoric of Science", in: *Rhetorica* 9 (1991) 301-16.

McKane, William 1989: *Select Christian Hebraists*, Cambridge/New York: Cambridge University Press 1989.

Meerhoff, Kees 1986: *Rhétorique et Poétique aux XVIe Siècle en France: Du Bellay, Ramus et Les Autres* (Studies in Medieval and Reformation Thought 36), Leiden: Brill 1986.

Mevorah, Barouh 1982: "Christian Hebraists in the Post-Medieval Period", in: *Immanuel* 14 (1982) 114-23.

Miller, J. Hillis 1989: "Is There an Ethics of Reading?", in: James Phelan (ed.), *Reading Narrative: Form, Ethics, Ideology,* Columbus, OH: Ohio State University Press 1989, 79-101.

Morris, David B. 1972: *The Religious Sublime: Christian Poetry and Critical Tradition in 18th-Century England*, Lexington, KY: University Press of Kentucky 1972.

*New Literary History* 16 (1985).

Oliver, Robert T. 1971: *Communication and Culture in Ancient India and China*, Syracuse, NY: Syracuse University Press 1971.

Ong, Walter J. 1967: *The Presence of the Word*, New Haven, CT: Yale University Press 1967.

Otto, Rudolf 1925: *The Idea of the Holy. An Inquiry into the Non-Rational Factor in the Idea of the Divine and its Relation to the Rational* (trans. John W. Harvey), London/New York: Oxford University Press, revised edition 1925.

Paley, Morton D. 1986: *The Apocalyptic Sublime*, New Haven, CT: Yale University Press 1986.

Palinkas, Lawrence A. 1989: *Rhetoric and Religious Experience. The Discourse of Immigrant Chinese Churches*, Fairfax, VA: George Mason University Press 1989.

Patrick, Dale and Scult, Allen 1990: *Rhetoric and Biblical Interpretation* (Bible and Literature 26), Sheffield: Almond Press 1990.

Perelman, Chaim 1979: *The New Rhetoric and the Humanities. Essays on Rhetoric and Its Application* (Synthese Library 140), Dordrecht/Boston, MA/London: Reidel 1979.

Perelman, Chaim and Olbrechts-Tyteca, L. 1969: *The New Rhetoric. A Treatise on Argumentation* (trans. J. Wilkinson and P. Weaver), Notre Dame, IN/London: University of Notre Dame Press 1969.

Poland, Lynn 1990: "The Bible and the Rhetorical Sublime", in: Martin Werner (ed.), *The Bible as Rhetoric: Studies in Biblical Persuasion and Credibility*, London: Routledge 1990, 27-47.

Polhemus, Robert M. 1980: *Comic Faith. The Great Tradition from Austen to Joyce*, Chicago, IL/London: University of Chicago Press 1980.

Rabinowitz, Isaac 1985: "Pre-Modern Jewish Study of Rhetoric: An introductory bibliography", in: *Rhetorica* 3 (1985) 137-44.

Schneidau, Herbert N. 1977: *Sacred Discontent: The Bible and Western Tradition*, Berkeley, CA: University of California Press 1977.

Scholder, Klaus 1990: *The Birth of Modern Critical Theology: Origins and Problems of Biblical Criticism in the Seventeenth Century*, London: SCM/Philadelphia, PA: Trinity Press International 1990.

Schwartz, Regina M. (ed.) 1990: *The Book and the Text: The Bible and Literary Theory*, Cambridge/Oxford: Basil Blackwell 1990.

Simons, Herbert W. (ed.) 1990: *The Rhetorical Turn. Invention and Persuasion in the Conduct of Inquiry*, Chicago, IL: University of Chicago Press 1990.

Stamps, Dennis L. 1992: "Rhetorical Criticism and Rhetoric of New Testament Criticism", in: *Literature and Theology* 6 (1992) 268-79.

Stemberger, Günter 1993: "Hieronymus und die Juden seiner Zeit", in: D.-A. Koch and H. Lichtenberger (eds.): *Begegnungen zwischen Christentum und Judentum in Antike und Mittelalter. FS für Heinz Schreckenberg*, Göttingen: Vandenhoeck & Ruprecht 1993, 347-64.

Sternberg, Meir 1985: *The Poetics of Biblical Narrative. Ideological Literature and the Drama of Reading*, Bloomington, IN: Indiana University Press 1985.

Swearingen, C. Jan 1991: *Rhetoric and Irony: Western Literacy and Western Lies*, New York/Oxford: Oxford University Press 1991.

Tyler, Stephen A. 1987: *The Unspeakable: Discourse, Dialogue, and Rhetoric in the Postmodern World* (Rhetoric of the Human Sciences), Madison, WI: University of Wisconsin Press 1987.

van Rooden, Peter T. 1989: *Theology, Biblical Scholarship, and Rabbinical Studies in the Seventeenth Century: Constantijn L'Empereur (1591-1648), Professor of Hebrew and Theology at Leiden* (Studies in the History of Leiden University; trans. J. C. Grayson), Leiden/New York: Brill 1989.

Vickers, Brian 1988: *In Defense of Rhetoric*, Oxford: Clarendon 1988.

Villwock, Jörg 1989: "Sublime Rhetorik. Zu einigen noologischen Implikationen der Schrift *Vom Erhabenen*", in: Christine Pries (ed.), *Das Erhabene: Zwischen Grenzerfahrung und Grössenwahn* (Acta Humaniora), Weinheim: VCH 1989, 33-53.

Weiskel, Thomas 1974: *The Romantic Sublime: Studies in the Structure and Psychology of Transcendence*, Baltimore, MD/London: Johns Hopkins University Press 1974.

Wilder, Amos N. 1991: *The Bible and the Literary Critic*, Minneapolis, MN: Fortress 1991.

Wood, Theodore E. B. 1972: *The Word "Sublime" and Its Context, 1650-1760* (De Proprietatibus Litterarum, series maior 7), The Hague: Mouton 1972.

Wuellner, Wilhelm 1994: "Der Vorchristliche Paulus und die Rhetorik", in: Simon Lauer (ed.), *Tempelkult und Tempelzerstörung (70 n. Chr.). Festschrift Clemens Thoma* (JudChr 15), Bern/New York: Peter Lang 1994, forthcoming.

Zimmer, Eric 1980: "Jewish and Christian Hebraist Collaboration in Sixteenth Century Germany", in: *JQR* 71 (1980) 69-88.

Zinguer, Ilana (ed.) 1992: *L'Hébreu au temps de la Renaissance* (Brill's Series in Jewish Studies 4), Leiden: Brill 1992.

# Identification with Christ.
## A Psychological View of Pauline Theology[1]

Peter Lampe

## 1. Introduction

Crossing borders into other scholarly contexts—for New Testament scholarship, this motto has been increasingly important. In the last decades, a fair number of Biblical scholars, including our jubilee-celebrator, have been engaged in a dialogue with modern linguistics as well as with the social and psychological sciences. New Testament exegetes have shed new light on old texts by using theoretical tools devised in these neighboring fields. In this essay, I would like to dialogue with one of these disciplines—with that of psychoanalysis. This may be a red flag to some. Crossing borderlines and engaging in an interdisciplinary dialogue is risky, and I may rip my pants climbing over the fence into the yard of psychology. I am convinced, however, that psychology—and even psychoanalysis as only one, often disputed niche in the psychological yard—is able to comment on some of Paul's theological language, contributing to the understanding of this language without leading to a theologically fatal reductionism.

We will focus our attention on a central category in Pauline thinking—on that of identification. Paul's readers are expected to identify with Christ, from their baptism on (Rom 6) throughout their Christian lives. For this identification process, the two primary christological points of orientation—or hinges—are Jesus' cross and his resurrection. Christians are expected to identify with the crucified and risen Christ.

This paper proposes that the non-Pauline term "identification" depicts the common focal point of a variety of Pauline phrases, such as "being crucified and buried with Christ," "carrying the marks of Jesus branded on one's body," "sharing Jesus' sufferings by becoming like him in his death" or "clothing oneself with Christ." As we borrow the "identification" term from our contemporary everyday language, the

---

[1] Guest lecture at the Universities of Bergen and Oslo in October 1993. The lecture format is maintained.

dialogue with psychoanalysis will assist us in controlling our usage of the "identi-fication" term. This dialogue will help us to realize, for example, the difference be-tween mere imitation and identification.

I will start out with a well known exegetical insight. The fascinating thing about Pauline Christology is the persistence with which the apostle applies traditional christological statements to human life. Christology is interpreted for basic struc-tures of human existence, and therefore it is dressed in the gown of soteriology, as Bultmann noted. In Paul's writings, however, this fact is conveyed in a less abstract way than in Bultmann's perspective. For Paul, it is important to relate Christology to specific situations of persons and congregations and to the ethical problems in-volved in these concrete situations. In Paul, Christology is applied Christology, that is, practical Christology.

In Paul's thinking, the Christ-story is applied to human existence partly by means of identification which operates as hermeneutical transmission. According to Paul, several identification processes take place between Christ and the believers. These processes are verbalized in two chains of statements; one chain is oriented soteriologically and the other ethically.

## 2. Soteriologically Oriented Statements

In view of the enormous attention that the soteriological identification statements have enjoyed in the theological tradition, I will refrain from discussing them in de-tail. At the conclusion, I will return to the soteriological aspect of the Christians' identification with Christ.

At least two different invitations to identification are formulated by Paul. Ac-cording to the concept of sacrifice of atonement (Rom 3:25), the believer may iden-tify with the dying, sacrificial Christ, by perceiving *Christ's* blood offering as the offering of one's *own* culpable life from which the believer is redeemed.[2]

The concept of "corporate representation" is set forth in the frame of Adam-Christ-typology. Both Adam and Christ embody whole groups. Each one of them represents many people, and the act of each determines the destiny of the many (Rom 5:12-19). Christ's act of righteousness on the cross leads to justification of the many, provided that they accept the invitation to identify with Christ as their repre-sentative and make *Christ's* attribute of being righteous their *own*. Their righteous-ness then comes from Christ and not from their own achievements.

Whether we think in the category of atonement sacrifice or of corporate repre-sentation, in each case the formulation of 2 Cor 5:14 holds true: "One has died for

---

[2] Cf., e.g., Janowski 1982, 359.

all; therefore all have died." The death of Christ is the Christians' death.

## 3. The Ethically-Oriented Chain of Statements: Identification as Basis for a New Christian Life Style

This time not the categories of corporate representation and sacrifice of atonement are in the background but the idea of imitating Christ when following him—a widely spread idea in Early Christianity[3] that Paul picks up on and takes to greater depths. We need to distinguish several clusters of statements from one another.

3.1. At first we will look at a very simple pattern. The identification with Christ as model leads to imitating specific behavior that Christ exhibited. Two aspects of Christ's behavior are focused on by Paul.

3.1.1. The identification with Christ as model leads to interhuman love and up-building instead of selfishness (Rom 15:2-3,7; 1 Cor 10:33-11:1). It leads to altruism and self-denial (Phil 2:3-12), to love and generosity (2 Cor 8:7-9), to gentleness and meekness (2 Cor 10:1).[4]

In theological perspective this kind of identification with Christ is very elementary. Every child in Sunday school has heard about it. In a psychological view, however, this kind of identification process in the church is remarkable, compared to other groups in society. How is it possible that members of a social group develop loving behavior toward one another? This question already kept Sigmund Freud busy in his writing "Massenpsychologie und Ich-Analyse," in which he frequently used the church—and the army—as illustrating examples. Interestingly enough, in the body of this writing, Freud did not mention the Christ-identification of Christians as a decisive motor for loving behavior within the church. Only in an appendix did Freud take notice of it:

> Each Christian … is supposed to identify with Christ and to love the other Christians, as Christ loved them.[5]

Freud here uses the term "identification" in the same way as it is still defined in today's psychoanalysis, for example by Laplanche -Pontalis in their key work about psychoanalytical terminology:[6] An individual (in this case a church member)

---

[3] Cf., e.g., Matt 10:24-25,38-39; Mark 8:31-35; 10:39; 14:31; Luke 14:27; 9:23; 22:33; John 11:16; 15:27.

[4] 2 Cor 10:1: "I appeal to you in the meek and gentle way that Christ exhibited." *Διά* denotes manner, esp. with verbs of saying. Cf., e.g., Acts 15:27,32; 18:9; Eph 6:18.

[5] Freud 1921, 125 (my translation).

[6] J. Laplanche – J.-B. Pontalis 1992, 219.

adopts an attribute of another person (in this case Christ's love toward all Christians). By doing this, the individual transforms him- or herself according to this model.

Freud mentions this motor for loving behavior within the church only in an appendix, because this particular stimulus, according to him, is unusual for social groups. It distinguishes the church from other groups such as the army.

What *is* normal for social groups? We will follow very briefly some thoughts of this writing by Freud. In groups such as the army, the bonding between the group members generally is not based on love and affection but on identification processes. According to Freud[7] identification can happen whenever an individual realizes that he or she has something in common with another person. Often the aspect they have in common is of emotional nature, that is, often they realize, that they both are attached to one and the same leader. The vertical bonding or attachment to a leader is the aspect that they share; it leads to the identification among themselves on the horizontal level. Applied to the church, this means:[8] Each Christian loves Christ, and therefore feels bonded to the other Christians by means of identification. In the church, however, this is only one side of the coin, only one kind of identification, as Freud noted. The church requires more from the individual, more than other social groups do. The church member, in addition, is expected to identify *with Christ* and to *love* the other Christians as Christ did. In this way, in the vertical dimension, identification is added on to where there usually is only affection or love toward a leader. And on the horizontal level, love and affection toward fellow group members are added on to where there usually is only identification. This is what makes the church so outstanding. In the army it would be ridiculous if the common soldier *identified* with the general—like a whole bunch of little Napoleons running around. According to Freud, what seems funny in a military hierarchical context, is a serious "plus" of the church in comparison to other social groups. Freud suspects that this bonus, this further development of inner-group libido structure, is probably the reason why Christianity claims to have achieved a higher ethos than other social groups.[9]

So much for Freud's thoughts. The Pauline texts quoted earlier can be interpreted in this Freudian frame of reference. Christians not only have love and affection for Christ, some also *identify* with Christ and therefore start loving other people unselfishly like Christ himself did. Interhuman love is a consequence of the identification with Christ, as Freud construes it. However, I must add, this does not yet catch the depth of what Paul is saying. Yes, in Paul the vertical identification with Christ plays a role, but this identification is further qualified as identifying with a *crucified* Lord.

---

[7] Freud 1921, 100-101.
[8] See Freud 1921, 125.
[9] Freud 1921, 125-126.

The cross stands out as the climax of Christ's self-denial for the benefit of others (Phil 2:8) and is the hinge for the Christian identification process with Christ. At the cross, Christ loved by letting his human self-interests come to an end (cf. Phil 2:3-8). Whoever applies Christ's cross to his or her own existence is led to self-humiliation. One does not need to "look to one's own interests" (Phil 2:4), to count oneself better than others (verse 3), but a person is free to make the interests of others his or her own (verse 4). And this is nothing less than love (verses 1-2). If agape toward others is unpopularly defined in a way that it includes self-denial, then the possibility to identify with a crucified Christ, who emptied himself, is a decisive help to practice a similar love. Freud, thus, needs to be modified in this way if we want to understand Paul adequately: Identification with a Christ who loves all Christians equally is, for Paul, an identification with a Christ who gave himself up—who emptied himself. In this way, love is defined in a much more radical and uncomfortable way than Freud projects. Paul is not only talking about loving others as oneself, he is talking about loving others *more* than oneself. "Do not seek your own advantage, but that of the other" (1 Cor 10:24; cf. 10:33; 13:5; Phil 2:3ff; Rom 15:1-3). Identifying with the *crucified* Christ promotes a radicalized understanding of interhuman love in Pauline churches—whether we like it or not.

3.1.2. A second behavior is also tied to the Christ-identification. Paul propagates a patient and joyful enduring of troubles (1 Thess 1:6; 2 Cor 6:4; 1 Cor 4:12-13). How is this possible? The apostle identifies with the crucified Christ model in such a way that Christ's death is actually echoed in his own afflictions. The suffering and weak apostolic existence is interpreted as a mirror image, as a reflection of Christ's death. In this way present tribulations and weaknesses are interpreted positively. They become acceptable. The Pauline texts speak for themselves:

> I carry the marks of Jesus branded on my body (Gal 6:17). We suffer with him so that we may also be glorified with him (Rom 8:17). As the sufferings of Christ are abundant for us, so also our consolation is abundant through Christ (2 Cor 1:5; cf. 1:8-11). We are afflicted in every way, but not crushed ..., always carrying in the body the death of Jesus, so that the life of Jesus may also be made visible in our bodies. For while we live, we are always being given up to death for Jesus' sake, so that the life of Jesus may be made visible in our mortal flesh (2 Cor 4:8-11). I want to know Christ ... and the sharing of his sufferings by becoming like him in his death (Phil 3:10; cf., e.g., 2 Cor 13:4; Gal 2:19).

The suffering with Christ is joyfully endured because of its image or reflection character; and secondly because Paul invites the readers to identify also with Christ's *rising* from the dead. The afflictions do not have the last word, because resurrection with Christ is expected in the eschaton (2 Cor 4:14,17). Proleptically, the resurrection aspect is experienced even in the apostle's cross existence (2 Cor 4:7ff.). It is experienced where God's power is active in Paul's weaknesses. It is experienced where congregations are founded in spite of the apostle's troubles and shortcomings (2 Cor 4).

To summarize this point: The two-fold identification with Christ's suffering on the cross and his rising from the dead enables the apostle to interpret and to accept present afflictions as something positive and meaningful. It helps him to discover glimpses of the reality of resurrection already now in the presence of death. The two-fold invitation to identify with Christ creates a psychologically efficient dam against the floods of "despair" (2 Cor 4:8). Crucifixes hanging in catholic hospital rooms have exactly to do with this point.

When Paul gave his present weaknesses and pain a positive meaning by identifying with the crucified and risen Christ, already his ancient readers in Corinth shook their heads, because *they* focused on apostolic signs, wonders and power display and did not know how to handle apostolic weaknesses. In fact, they denied Paul his apostleship because of his human shortcomings. However, in a psychological perspective, the acceptance of one's own deficiencies and limits represents a step toward maturing and toward gaining identity.[10] Paul's energy and missionary activity are not impeded by the experiences of his own shortcomings and inescapable afflictions. By accepting his weaknesses, Paul is freed to surprisingly much vigor. And maybe our mainline churches today can learn from this when anxiously facing decreasing membership numbers, when facing the loss of societal territories which have been settled by Christian values in the past but which are being secularized today. The provocative apostle invites today's churches to accept the new limits, to quit licking their wounds and to concentrate on their mission joyfully.

Paul also has a message for society as a whole. After decades of living beyond our means and resources, it is time to realize and to respect our limits, to mature collectively by willingly scaling back our present exuberant life styles—which might be the only chance for future generations to survive. Paul invites us to identify with a God's son who, in human eyes, is weak and emptied himself for the benefit of others (Phil 2:7). Admittedly, the apostle's invitation is a fading voice in the choir of western cultural traditions, but it gains actuality today. The task of the churches will be to make this voice known a little better, not by holding a microphone and a loudspeaker in front of Paul's mouth, but by beginning to accept Paul's invitation to *live* in accordance with the crucified Christ who emptied himself. If Christians scale back their life styles because they learn to identify with *this* Christ, they for their part might be able to become models and identification objects for non-Christians. In this way also non-Christian sectors of society might be transformed. We are talk-

---

[10] Cf. Stollberg – Lührmann 1978, 217ff; Klessmann 1989, 156-72.

ing about two steps: The crucified Christ serves as identification object for Christians who therefore are transformed in their behavior (step 1). These transformed Christians for their parts become identification objects for non-Christians in society (step 2). Paul has a similar—not an identical but a similar—identification pyramid in mind when he calls himself imitator of Christ (1 Cor 11:1), an imitator who also serves as identification *object* for others. These others become imitators of Paul (1 Cor 11:1; Phil 3:17).

3.2. It is time to move on in our definition of identification as a psychoanalytical category. Two aspects need to be made more specific:

3.2.1. In their psychoanalytical definition of identification, Laplanche – Pontalis maintain that the individual "transforms" him- or herself according to the model of the identification object.[11] Several psychoanalytical studies describe more specifically this transformation, this restructuring of one's self. They clearly distinguish between mere imitation and authentic identification. What is the difference? The imitator only displays the behavior of the model person. The one who *identifies* with the model, on the other hand, also adopts the model's motivations. She or he assumes the model's role by taking over the goals and emotions that are expressed in the role. Acquiring the *motivations*, *goals* and *emotions* which are connected with a behavior—these are the key words that characterize genuine identification as opposed to imitation.[12]

We discussed two Pauline behavioral aspects: interhuman love on the one hand and acceptance of suffering on the other. We do not need to waste time on proving that these Pauline behavioral aspects were not only based on imitation but on identification with Christ. As the world was saved by means of Christ's love and death, the apostle's suffering and love serve the σωτηρία of others (1 Cor 1:18). Paul's motivation and goal, of course, concur with the Saviour's. And Paul's loving behavior certainly is accompanied by corresponding emotions when he, for example, talks about zeal, cheerfulness, longing and desire (2 Cor 8:8; 9:2,7,14) or repeatedly mentions joy (6:10; 13:9) in the context of his afflictions. We have no reason to diagnose empty rhetorics here.

3.2.2. The psychological definition of identification needs to be also specified at a second point. According to psychoanalytical theory, a genuine identification which differs from mere imitation can only take place if the identifying individual has a libido component in his or her attitude toward the model person. Without this *Id*-impulse, there are only pseudo-identifications, only imitations which lead to an "as if"-personality.[13]

---

[11] Laplance – Pontalis 1992, 219.
[12] Cf., e.g., Loch 1968, 271 and 281-82.

Can we find corresponding material in the Pauline texts? Is there affection, a libido impulse, in the Christians' relationship with Christ? Certainly there is. Several texts speak about mutual love between Christ and the Christians.[14] In 2 Cor 11:2, Paul uses the metaphors of bride and groom. This libido impulse was possible because Christ, the model, was not only a past and remote figure but a risen Lord who was perceived as being present in the congregations, especially in the sacraments. A *personal* relationship could be maintained with him. The Christians prayed to him and praised him. They perceived him as near in their pneumatic experiences. Thus, *the early Christian doctrine about Christ's resurrection and the early Christian pneumatology were a prerequisite for successful genuine identifications in the psychoanalytical sense of the word.* Without the belief in Christ's resurrection and pneumatic presence, a past impressive teacher would have been *imitated* but probably not *identified with* in a genuine way.

3.3. *New creation or radical restructuring of the Ego by means of identification with Christ.* How genuine the Pauline Christ-identification was, that is, as how strongly he perceived the restructuring of his own self, is made clear by statements like Gal 2:19-20. According to the apostle, there is hardly any continuity between his old and the new ego. The restructuring of his self is echoed in statements such as: baptized Christians "have clothed themselves with Christ" (Gal 3:27; cf. Rom 13:14) or "It is no longer I who live, but it is Christ who lives in me" (Gal 2:20). Christ, the identification object, is internalized or introjected, as psychological language words it. And the early Christian language of drinking, that is, of physically internalizing the Spirit, who is identical with Christ, represents a remarkable parallel (1 Cor 12:13; 10:4; 2 Cor 3:17; cf. 1 Cor 6:17).

Paul perceives the restructuring of his self as so strong and incisive that he describes going through death into a newly created existence. With this we have arrived at *Romans 6*. Rom 6:6 explains baptism as a ritual identification process with Christ: "Our old self was crucified *with him* so that the sinful body might be destroyed, and we might no longer be enslaved to sin." The parts of the ego that hinder a new life according to new ethical standards are construed as having died in baptism with Christ. They are buried with him. The way is free for a new ethical orientation of one's life (Rom 6:1-13; also Gal 5:24; 6:14).

On the one hand, the identification act in baptism refers to Christ's cross. Paul's key phrases are "buried with him," "crucified with him," "died with Christ," or "united with him in a death like his." On the other hand, the identification act refers to Christ's rising from the dead. "As Christ was raised from the dead, we too might

---

[13] Cf., e.g., Loch 1968, 279 and 282; Stork 1982, 166.

[14] Cf., e.g., Gal 2:20; Phil 1:8; 2 Cor 5:14-15; Röm 5:5-8; 8:35,37,39.

walk in newness of life" (Rom 6:4)—already now. This two-fold identification with the crucified and risen Lord is ritually acted out in baptism. And the participants in baptism perceive this identification act as so powerful that they can declare that a new existence, a new ego is being created in this sacrament. "Our *old* self was crucified with him" (Rom 6:6). There is "newness of life" (6:4) and new creation (2 Cor 5:17). This new existence, manifest in a new way of living and behaving, does not make the eschatological resurrection superfluous (Rom 6:5,8), but it partially anticipates the eschatological rising (6:4,11). Through baptism as ritual identification act, the early Christian is led to a new self-image, feeling revitalized and *capable* of a new moral behavior, feeling free from sin (cf. Rom 6:4,7).

With this, ethics are back on the table. However, this time they are touched upon in a more general way, comprising the entire new Christian life style and not only the two behavioral aspects of interhuman love and readiness for suffering. To put it in psychoanalytical language:[15] In his identification with Christ, Paul not only adopts the two Christ attributes of love and readiness for suffering, transforming himself according to the Christ model in these two respects. No, he also adopts Christ's attribute of going through death into new life. That is, Paul's Christ-identification not only leads to some kind of transformation in one or two respects (like all identifications do). Also, the very attribute of radical transformation itself (through death on the cross into new life) is adopted. In this way, the reorganization of the self is put into the center. Paul interprets the Christian's radical restructuring as a transformation of the sinful self into a person capable of a new way of living.[16]

At this point we need to pick up briefly the old question about the ontological character of the new creation that takes place within the human personality.[17] According to Peter Stuhlmacher Paul envisioned this new creation as a call from the creator, which truly overturned the old existence.[18] In pre-Pauline and Pauline Christianity, baptism was construed as a real transformation of existence through God's creating word and call. This describes the exegetical perspective from within, which tries to understand what Paul was thinking.

What about the perspective from without, looking from the outside through psychological lenses? Is a new moral ability really created in baptism? Do changes in the psychic structure really take place which make possible a new way of living?

---

[15] Cf. above at note 13.

[16] In spite of becoming "capable," the person, however, stays vulnerable to relapses into sin. For Paul, even the restructured baptized person, of course, remains within the realm of σάρξ, and the imperative therefore joins the indicative.

[17] We need to block out the debated question whether or not in Paul "new creation" also intends a cosmological along with the anthropological dimension. For the ethical aspects of καινὴ κτίσις, cf. 2 Cor 5:14-17; Gal 6:13-15; *Jub.* 19:25; *Tg. 1 Chr* 4:23.

[18] P. Stuhlmacher 1967.

Exegetes interested in the internal theological perspective strongly emphasize the word of *God* as the source of new creation within us. In the psychological perspective from without, however, we cannot talk like this. What we can do is analyze the role of human words in baptism. If a new self-image is conveyed in baptism, asserting, "Yes, you *are* a new creation and you *are capable* of new moral behavior, freed from impediments that prevent a new way of living," then one receives a decisive psychological boost to restructure one's life and behavior. From a psychological perspective, the early Christian talk about a newly created ego does not *describe*, mirror or represent an already *existing* reality. No, it *creates* this reality of a new ego, being information (*informatio*) in the original sense of the word—that is, a forming and creating word, performative language.

Does it make sense to speak about creating words within the perspective of modern sciences, about words that transform reality by assuring and reassuring?[19] The entire realm of social relationships is based on words and information that *create* reality. All social connections are based on cognitive and language processes that put the involved persons into social relationships. Apart from these informing, that is, creating mental and verbal processes, no social relationships exist. Apart from them, not even the bond between mother and child comes about, because biological birth itself is neither a sufficient nor a necessary prerequisite for a mother-child-relationship. It is not a sufficient prerequisite, because many biological mothers in world history have given up their newborn babies. And it is not a necessary prerequisite, because adoptions also can lead to mother-child-relationships. Adoption examplifies well a mental and verbal process that creates and transforms social reality.

Creating words, reality-transforming words, are also exercised in some of the new psychotherapeutical movements which exhibit a pseudo-religious character.[20] They use assuring statements, such as, "You are OK and somebody special! You have a right to yourself!" etc. Once the patient begins accepting these assurances, the effect can be transforming. Such therapy is often done in groups. In this way, the created reality gains a dimension beyond the individual, because others also hear the assurances, accept them and begin acting in accordance with them. This added dimension from the group also holds true for the reality created by the early Christian assurance that those who are baptized are new creations, because this assurance was conveyed publicly in ritual contexts in the presence of entire congregations.

What have I done with this psychological commentary on the early Christian baptismal event, focusing on the reality creating character of words? In a psychological perspective from without, by definition, the early Christian assurance of be-

---

[19] For performative language, cf., e.g., the excellent study by Austin 1980.
[20] Cf., e.g., Küenzlen 1985 and 1994.

ing a new creation can only be construed as a *human* language event. Does that force us to eliminate the theological perspective which focuses on *God's* word as the decisive language event? What do we do about this juxtaposition of perspectives from within and from without—should we just declare that one of them does not apply? I do not think so. The exegetical result from within has to be brought into a dialogue with the psychological perspective from without, if we want to communicate the gospel to people of the 20th and 21st centuries. This dialogue should not serve a reductionist purpose, with the discussion about God being abandoned and the theological-exegetical result being cut back to some statements that can be accounted for psychologically. One partner in the dialogue would be devoured by the other, and the dialogue obviously would be over. No, this dialogue first humbly should look for convergencies between both. In this way, it would be made obvious where people molded by modern sciences might possess some fertile ground for the seed of the theological message.

In this synthesis perspective, a creating *human* word, which is open to scrutiny by modern sciences, might be also interpreted as *God's* word by believers in the 20th century. Whereas *without* the scientific insight into the creating character of words, the traditional concept of God's creating word might decay as a dusty antique in the church attic.

The convergence between the perspectives from within and from without becomes even more dramatic once we recall the baptismal identification process. The assurance of a new existence is not only conveyed verbally. Also, it is made emotionally plausible by means of the act of identification with the dying and rising Christ. In this way the assurance of being new is significantly enhanced. And it is further enhanced by the fact that this identification act is reinforced by a *ritual*, by a baptismal ritual. Psychologically seen, this two-fold enhancement of the assurance of being new is a very effective set up.

Furthermore, psycho-analytically seen, the identification process inaugurates indeed a real change in the psyche of the baptized Christian. A restructuring of the self takes place in regard to behavioral, emotional and motivational aspects, as we have seen. Therefore also in the perspective from without, it can be stated that at least partially a transformed person emerges—and this is a remarkable convergence with the theological-exegetical insight about new creation in the perspective from within.

## 4. Conclusion

The Corinthian Christian culture oriented itself to the *risen* Lord, with his attributes of glorious resurrection and triumph. The Corinthians were therefore interested in triumphant apostolic signs and wonders. They misinterpreted human weaknesses as absence of God's power. Paul on the other hand, reminds them that God is visible in the face of the crucified Christ, and that both resurrection *and* cross are the hinges for any identification with Christ. I hinted at two areas where the Pauline category of identification might be relevant for both society and the mainline churches. I am aware, however, that the hermeneutical application of Paul's identification perspective also creates serious problems. One might object that his message was particularly tailored for macho men in Corinth and elsewhere who boasted about their spiritual strengths and whose triumphant pose needed to be deflated. Can abused women identify with a crucified man? Can suffering have a positive meaning? Is self-denial a healthy basis for love? These questions, just to choose a few, show where Paul and our own culture are about to collide. They show where we are criticized by Paul, by our own tradition—in as much as we might want to criticize this tradition in return. Obviously we are not going to solve the conflict of these questions in a short essay. I only want to hint at one area where Paul's message especially goes against the traffic of our hedonistic culture: at our almost addictive media dependency. Through the media we are flooded with an odd mix of all kinds of invitations to identification—from Rambo to Barney. Every culture needs identification objects, and the ones that are picked say almost everything about this culture. Subconscious identification processes take place within the media consumers' personalities, and the role models in the mass media increase their influence in as much as the direct personal contacts—with family, friends and colleagues—lose importance in the individuals' lives. Psychology can diagnose this, but what do we do about it? The Pauline invitation to identify with Christ offers a challenging alternative to the mass media's seduction to identify with the stronger—an alternative perspective in which God can be glorified as *God* again. Why? Because perceiving oneself as being crucified with Christ means acknowledging that one's own attempts at self redemption and self healing are powerless. At the cross an individual has ceased to be the director of his or her own history and becomes totally dependant on God—the Creator into whose hands Christians commend their spirits.

## Bibliography

Austin, J. L. 1980: *How To Do Things With Words* (eds. J. O. Urmson – M. Sbisà), 2nd ed., Oxford: Oxford University Press: 1980.

Freud, S. 1921: *Massenpsychologie und Ich-Analyse* (1921), Studienausgabe Vol. IX, Frankfurt a. M.: Fischer 1982.

Janowski, B. 1982: *Sühne als Heilsgeschehen. Studien zur Sühnetheologie der Priesterschrift und zur Wurzel KPR im Alten Orient und im Alten Testament* (WMANT 55), Neukirchen-Vluyn: Neukirchener Verlag 1982.

Klessmann, M. 1989: "Zum Problem der Identität des Paulus," in: *Wege zum Menschen* 41 (1989) 156-72.

Küenzlen, G. 1985: "Psychoboom und Weltanschauung. Der Glaube der humanistischen Psychologie," in: *Materialdienst der Evangelischen Zentralstelle für Weltanschauungsfragen* 3 (1985) 60-69.

— 1994: *Der Neue Mensch. Zur säkularen Religionsgeschichte der Moderne*, München: Fink 1994, 200-25.

Laplanche, J. – Pontalis, J.-B. 1992: *Das Vokabular der Psychoanalyse*, 11. Auflage, Frankfurt: Suhrkamp 1992.

Loch, W. 1968: "Identifikation – Introjektion. Definitionen und Determinanten," in: *Psyche* 22 (1968) 271ff.

Stollberg, D. – Lührmann, D. 1978: "Tiefenpsychologische oder historisch-kritische Exegese? Identität und der Tod des Ich (Gal 2,19-20)," in: Y. Spiegel (ed.), *Doppeldeutlich. Tiefendimensionen biblischer Texte*, München: Kaiser 1978, 217ff.

Stork, J. 1982: "Die seelische Entwicklung des Kleinkindes aus psychoanalytischer Sicht," in: D. Eicke (ed.), *Tiefenpsychologie. Band 2: Neue Wege der Psychoanalyse*, Weinheim – Basel: Beltz 1982, 131-95.

Stuhlmacher, P. 1967: "Erwägungen zum ontologischen Charakter der καινὴ κτίσις bei Paulus," in: *EvTh* 27 (1967) 1-35.

# The Function of Biblical Texts in a Modern Situational Context

Bernard Lategan

## 1. Introduction

The work of Lars Hartman as New Testament scholar is characterized by a respect for the original context in which this collection of documents came into being and a sensitivity for the contexts in which it is read by subsequent readers. His linguistic and literary expertise enables him to explore intra- and inter-textual relations, but this does not result in a one-sided analysis of the textual contexts only. True to his training in the historical tradition, he is equally interested in the *Sitz im Leben* of this material. At the same time, he is well aware that these documents cannot be confined to their original context, but that they were and are read in many different contexts by subsequent readers and that they were in fact intended to be read in this way.[1] This implies that the social location of the exegete also needs to be accounted for, as it has a definite influence on the way texts are approached and understood.[2]

The self-reflecting and inclusive approach exemplified by Hartman in his exegetical work and his refusal to be confined to one context, has prompted him to enter into dialogue with a variety of partners in the field of New Testament studies, but also further afield. By taking up the controversial challenge to work towards a New Testament theology,[3] he is responding in part to the need often expressed by colleagues in systematic theology that biblical exegetes should work not only in an analytical, but also in a synthetic mode.[4] His teaching at a state university has inevitably led him to consider the wider humanistic dimensions of theology in interaction with non-theologians.[5] His interest in and concern for the struggle of emerging and exploited societies, has made him a valued partner in the continuing

---

[1] Hartman 1986, 141 and idem 1993, 153.

[2] Hartman 1990, 187.

[3] Hartman 1990.

[4] Cf. Smit 1992.

[5] Cf. Hartman 1990, 187.

first/third world dialogue. Hartman has thus consistently broadened the scope of the discourse which results from his primary activity as an exegete and interpreter of the New Testament.

Once the study of these documents is placed in a wider context, the tension between past and present readers, between original and modern contexts becomes all the more evident. On the theoretical level, this tension is indicative of the pragmatic intention of these texts. In response to the request of the editors to focus on the importance of context and in order to continue the dialogue with Hartman, the aim of this contribution is to move to the extreme end of the pragmatic trajectory of the text and to focus on a present day context of interpretation. We propose to concentrate on a situation of social transition and more specifically, the transition from authoritarian and unrepresentative rule to an inclusive democratic dispensation. Several countries in Europe, Asia, Africa and Latin America are experiencing the throes of such a transition and find themselves at various stages of the process. What relevance does the study of the New Testament have in this context and what contribution—if any—can be expected from exegetes?

Basically, we are dealing with the relationship between religion (in this case as represented by the New Testament) and civil society. In terms of David Tracy's distinction[6] between the three different publics of theology (the academy, the church and general culture), the focus will be on the third public. Rather than discussing conceptual and substantive issues of special significance in the New Testament, we want to concentrate on the *way* in which theological discourse is conducted in the public sphere. The underlying hypothesis is that this discourse is ineffective for various reasons and that the impact of New Testament values and ethical precepts on civil society is consequently not of any great significance. It therefore becomes important to understand the reasons for this ineffectiveness and to propose possible alternatives.

First of all, it is important to realize that it is not sufficient to distinguish between different publics of theology. Other variables need to be taken into account. These include the *subject* or *subjects* responsible for what is called 'theology', as well as the different *modes* in which theology is done. The wrong choice of mode more often that not is the main reason for the ineffective operation of theology in this field. The interaction between theology and civil society will remain hamstrung as long as these matters do not receive the attention they merit.

Historically speaking, the relationship between religion and civil society has had a long and chequered history. As far as Christianity is concerned, the concept of a holy Roman empire was one of the earliest attempts to give expression to such a re-

---

[6] Tracy 1981.

lationship. A prominent feature of this history is the amazing variety of patterns in which both religious traditions and local circumstances shaped this uneasy relationship, ranging from close co-operation to active opposition. Each society and tradition has a different story. This is the case not only between the major traditions of Christianity, but also on the level of denominational variations. Furthermore, the kind of society and especially the prevailing conditions at a certain point in its history can be highly significant.

South Africa is one of the countries which finds itself in a critical stage of transition. Existing value systems are disintegrating or are under serious threat. A new public ethos is emerging or is bound to emerge—but the contours of such an ethos is all but clear. In the market place, opposing philosophies are vying with each other to form the basis of an economic system, of a development strategy, of an education policy, of a democratic culture and of all the critical elements which together make up a civil society.

Conspicuously lacking in this intense debate is a substantial contribution from the side of theology. There certainly is no dearth of pronouncements by synods or church bodies, but these are mostly done in isolation or in opposition. A sustained and constructive participation in the public arena and in terms of the public debate to develop a common value system and an ethos that will sustain a democratic dispensation, is still sorely missing. There are various reasons for this deficiency. Perhaps the most important is an inability to understand the *kairos* brought about by the transition and the urgent need for a new public ethos. For some churches, it is the result of an 'once bitten, twice shy' attitude. After being heavily involved in politics and having supported discriminatory policies and practices, there now is a tendency to withdraw from politics and to privatise religion. For others who for so long had to resist these very policies, it still is a question whether the attitude of resistance should now be changed to one of engagement and of constructive participation.[7]

But the problem might be even more fundamental than the change of ingrained attitudes and the inability to seize the opportunity. There is reason to suspect that we are dealing with a 'structural deficiency'—the apparent inability of theology to participate meaningfully and effectively in the public arena. Could it be that the very nature of doing theology up to this point has rendered it incapable of making such a contribution?

## 2. The Variables in Theological Discourse

In order to answer this question, it is necessary to take a closer look at the different

---

[7] Cf. Villa-Vicencio 1992; Pityana 1994; De Gruchy 1994; Cochrane 1994 and Du Plessis 1994.

variables involved in the complex process of what we call 'doing theology'. Reception theory has helped us to understand that audiences (or publics in Tracy's terms) are indeed important, but that many other factors influence the process of communication. After discussing the various audiences on the receiving end of theology, we also have to consider the subject or subjects involved and the different modes or forms in which theological discourse takes place.

## 2.1. Publics

David Tracy's distinction between the three major publics of theology (the academy, the church and society at large), has not only clarified the issue, but it also marks a new phase in the discussion of a complex problem.[8] Historically speaking, the position of theology at the university is a disputed one,[9] with variations in different contexts.[10] In this regard, it is interesting to see how Hartman describes his own social location as exegete—"a faculty of divinity at a state university, studying theology as *Religionswissenschaft*".[11]

Theology is exposed or 'public' in the critical environment of the university in a specific way. Due to the demand for rationality in this context, the emphasis is on cognitive criteria of coherence and the ideals of inter subjective validity.[12] In the United States of America, the constitutional separation between church and state, reinforced by a series of court cases,[13] made the teaching of theology at university, but especially in public schools, a bone of considerable contention. This contributed in a large measure to what is experienced as the marginalization of theology.[14] In other countries the situation may be different,[15] but there are also some marked similarities. This complex problem has lost none of its urgency. In the present South African transition, religion as a field of study at universities, but also in schools, once again has become an important issue. Because of prominence of African religions in this context, the debate has taken on new and very interesting dimensions, which unfortunately cannot be discussed here in further detail.

The second public, that of the church or the believing community, demands different ways of speaking and different ways in doing theology.[16] But, although this

---

[8] Tracy 1981, 1-46.

[9] Cf. Lategan 1993.

[10] Cf. Harvey 1989; Kaufmann 1991; Heckel 1986; Baumgartner 1991; Wirsching 1991; Meuleman 1991 and De Gruchy 1986.

[11] Hartman 1990, 176.

[12] Cf. Tracy 1990, 3-4.

[13] Cf. Clark 1990.

[14] Cf. Farley 1983 and idem 1988; Kitagawa 1992; Long 1990 and Harvey 1989.

[15] Cf. Kaufmann 1991 and Meuleman 1991.

seems to have the nature of an in-house conversation, there is a very specific and distinct 'public' dimension to this discourse. According to Tracy, the basis for this communality is some aspect of shared human experience. This is specifically inherent in the foundational documents of the church, which lend to them 'classical' status. Although rooted in a very particular context, these texts have a disclosive power, "speaking to a potentially universal audience, because it expresses, through its very intensified particularity, some aspect of a shared human experience".[17]

For the purposes of this contribution, our attention will be focused on the third public which theology addresses (or should address)—society at large. In context of a society in transition, this public is of critical importance. It is the acid test for the contribution many are expecting theology to make and which theology itself is claiming to be able to make. However important other tasks and challenges for theology might be, this is the terrain which to a large extent will determine its future and the role it is likely to play in a new and fundamentally different society.

Taking the third public seriously, makes a critical analysis of this public, but also of its social location, essential. Reception theory has made us aware of the important role which audiences play in making successful communication possible. Audiences are not passive receptors, but active participants in a process of interactive exchange. The typology of readers also apply to the third public. What readers make up this public? Informed readers like policy makers? 'Ordinary readers' who may be the marginalized and powerless part of the third public? Resistant readers who are deeply suspicious of theology and especially of its intrusion in the public sphere?

The typology and social location of the third public are therefore important issues which require the tools and insights of social analysis to prepare the way for successful theological discourse in this context. In order to do this, we first have to take notice of the other variables in the equation.

## 2.2. Subjects

Tracy's focus on the different audiences of theology therefore fits in very well with central concepts of reception theory and has indeed opened the way to apply these insights in a much more extensive way. But in order to do this, the differentiation in terms of audiences must also be extended to subjects. In the discussion of a public theology, 'theology' is used in a much too monolithic and undifferentiated way. Who are the exponents and formulators of this theology? Who do we expect to be the subject(s) of a public theology? Are we talking about the organised church in its

---

[16] Cf. Kelsey 1990; Farley 1982, 183-191.
[17] Conradie 1993, 34.

official capacity, which in concrete terms would mean that synodical decisions, policy statements or official documents form the substance of such a theology? Are we referring to the work of a prominent theologian or theologians like Niebuhr, Tracy, Kelsey or others who are specifically engaged in this debate? Or is the recently discovered 'ordinary believer' the real subject of a public theology? Empirical research would seem to indicate that ordinary believers do not believe the way they are supposed to believe. Church members hold views quite different and even contrary to quite basic elements of the official position. And yet, it is this 'ordinary believer' who more than anybody else finds him- or herself in the public arena and at the cutting edge where issues demanding a theological input or a value judgement are decided. It is an exposed position where the protection of the cloth and the advantage of the home turf in the form of the moral high ground is not available. It is in the cut and thrust of this environment where representatives of the official position are not present, that out of necessity a theology of sorts takes shape. The need is not only a reactive one, aimed at making sense and surviving in an often hostile environment, but also a challenge to pro-actively influence and shape life in the public sphere. To respond successfully to this challenge, the *mode* in which theology is done becomes a critical issue.

## 2.3. Modes of Doing Theology

The third variable is the mode or style in which theology is done by the various subjects in order to communicate with various publics. Variations in subject and public is accompanied with variations in mode. Burkhalter distinguishes between four modes of discourse. These modes formed part of a heuristic model developed to address the differentiation assumed in the praxis of religious studies. This was the result of an intense debate on the restructuring of religious education organised by the National Endowment for the Humanities in 1986. Although focused on the needs of religious education, the distinction is also useful for our purpose:[18]

1. *The discourse of the believer,* expressed in worship and practice. The mode is affirmative, articulated in ritual, myth and symbol. The style is spontaneous, emotive, uncritical or rather pre-critical.

2. *The discourse of second-order reflection* within the tradition itself. Remaining within the broader outlines of the tradition, the mode is one of discovering, interpreting, clarifying, redefining, and identifying. The form might be that of theological or philosophical reflection, credal statements or codes of order or conduct. Essentially, it is an in-house activity.

3. *The discourse of the academic and the university.* Employing the critical tools

---

[18] Cf. Burkhalter 1990, 150-51.

of the Enlightenment sciences, the mode is one of detached analysis, critical evaluation and the exploring of alternative possibilities.

4. *The discursive practice of the student.* This discourse cuts across the other modes and seeks to integrate them in a way that is personally meaningful and communally relevant.

The modes useful for religious education can be supplemented by yet further variations, for example:

5. *Apologetics*, where the mode is one of defending 'truth claims' in a wide variation of styles which could be persuasive, judgmental, confrontational, prescriptive or divisive.

6. *Proclamation*, in the style of propounding, positing, claiming and not very suitable for the purposes of engagement and dialogue.

7. *The prophetic mode*, usually in the form of witnessing and speaking out without fear or favour. Precisely because the prejudices and sensitivities of the audience are not taken into account, this is also a mode not congenial to dialogue.

Of considerable importance for our theme is the further distinction which Gustafson[19] adds to the prophetic, narrative and ethical modes of moral discourse. He calls this 'policy discourse', aimed at formulating a particular course of action about quite specific issues. Subject of this discourse is not so much the moralist or the theologian, but "accountable agents with certain powers and limits of power".[20] This is exactly the focus of this study and to which we shall return in the final section.

## 3. Addressing the Third Public in the South African Context

Against the background of the variables discussed in the previous section, we can now look at how the third public can and should be addressed in the South African context. However, the situation is not without difficulties, because of theology's past history in the public sphere.

### 3.1. Factors Rendering Public Discourse Ineffective

There are several factors impeding the development of an effective public theology in the South African context. First of all, we are dealing with a mixed legacy. On the one hand, there is the extremely negative and deeply disturbing experience of a previous attempt to shape public life according to theological principles—the disas-

---

[19] Gustafson 1988.
[20] Gustafson 1988, 50.

trous experiment in social engineering in the form of the apartheid state, stoutly
defended on theological grounds by some and presented as based on 'Christian-na-
tional' principles. For many, this has discredited all further attempts at developing
a public theology. Ironically, the reaction of some of the prominent exponents of an
apartheid theology was to withdraw from public life ("the church must never again
meddle in politics") and to retreat to the perceived safe haven of private religion.[21]

On the other hand, there is the tradition of resistance theology in various forms
of liberation theology, which for a long time was an important stronghold in the
struggle against apartheid. It participated very effectively in the public sphere in the
mode of resistance, protest and even confrontation. The genre of the *Kairos Document* is that of a prophetic witness against the (public) powers of the day. It exemplified a specific style in which the public debate was conducted—a style that has
lost none of its importance or relevancy. And yet, the question remains whether the
time has not come to consider other modes of doing theology in the public sphere
in order to remain effective in this debate. In his latest book, Villa-Vicencio[22] makes
a plea for the transformation of resistance theology into a theology of reconstruction
in order to restore the humanity of the post-apartheid era and to assist the process
of nation building. The question then becomes: What style or mode would suit this
way of doing theology best?

It is not only the local situation and the legacy of South Africa's past which frus-
trate the development of an effective public theology. The problem is more universal in nature, as illustrated by the so-called Chicago-Yale debate. It is not the
intention to go into the substance of this debate. For that purpose, the reader is referred to the excellent article by Conradie from 1993, of which I shall be making
extensive and grateful use. I only want to illustrate how an inappropriate mode of
doing theology can still inhibit serious and well-conceived attempts to develop an
alternative approach. The Chicago-Yale debate deals in essence with two approaches to a public way of doing theology. Tracy, as the most prominent exponent of the
Chicago school, is deeply concerned with the *public* nature of theology in all three
publics he distinguishes. Dialogue and persuasion are important in all spheres, and
therefore some form of rationality. However, the nature of publicness may differ
from public to public, requiring different strategies in each case. "The public defence of theological truth claims therefore requires, for Tracy, a particular form of
rationality and a particular set of criteria for rationality in each of the three publics
of theology".[23] In the case of the third public, the transformative potential of any
theological truth claim is critically assessed and the consequences of Christian ac-

---

[21] For similar tendencies elsewhere, cf. Conradie 1993, 27.

[22] Villa-Vicencio 1992.

[23] Conradie 1993, 35.

tion and beliefs are evaluated. In order to be convincing, truth claims cannot merely be described, but need some basis of agreement and some measure of universality with those outside the faith community.

It is exactly this attempt to be universal and convincing on the basis of common rationality that led the so-called Yale school to opt for an 'intra-textual' approach to a public way of doing theology. Whereas Tracy gives preference to the modes of explaining and justifying, they concentrate on *describing* the way in which Christian truth claims function within a particular faith community.[24] In terms of the Wittgensteinian concept of language games, the integrity of the language of the specific community is to be respected. The interests of such a community are best served by a sensitive and empathetic description of the rules of the language and how they function in that community.

Although there are clear differences between the more 'extrovert' approach of the Chicago school and the more 'introvert' attitude of their Yale colleagues, the preoccupation with the 'truth claims' of Christianity and their defence remains. The concern of the Yale school is that the attempt to render Christian beliefs universally and therefore publicly accessible by translating them into categories more familiar and congenial to the public sphere, can only lead to the loss of the specifically Christian or theological character of such discourse.[25] The implication is that Christian truth claims should rather be described within their own frame of reference if one is to serve their persuasive power and if they are to have any value for someone outside the community of faith.[26]

Tracy appreciates the value of such an intra-textual approach, but does not believe that it will produce the desired result in the public sphere. He therefore insists "that we should not only describe the truth claims of the Christian tradition accurately, but should also proceed to assess how what we believe through our religious tradition coheres or does not cohere with what we otherwise know, practice, and believe".[27]

What interests us here is not the respective merits of the two approaches, but to see how strongly the focus is still on preserving the integrity of the Christian faith, albeit by following different routes. This is directly linked to the mode chosen to preserve this integrity or vindicate the truth claims of theology. In essence, the third public is engaged in the mode of *apologetics*—be it apologetics proper or so-called '*ad hoc*-apologetics'. The form in which this apologetics is conducted may differ widely—from the purist position which states bluntly that the best form of apolo-

---

[24] Conradie 1993, 37.
[25] Conradie 1993, 38.
[26] Conradie 1993, 40.
[27] Conradie 1993, 41.

getics is good dogma[28] to much more subtle and accommodating forms of discourse. Accordingly, different modes are also employed, ranging from description, explanation and justification.[29] Even when Tracy insists that although Christianity has its own terms, rules and methods, these can be translated into the conceptual universe of any reasonable person who is genuinely open to the subject of conversation,[30] the presupposition remains that the task consists of the translation of a given entity in some public accessible form. However desirable this translation may be, a fundamental condition is that the integrity of the belief system is not violated in the process. Furthermore, the aim is to demonstrate the reasonableness of the truth claims of theology. This is an end in itself, not the first step in a further process.

### 3.2. The Supporting Role of Other Modes of Theological Discourse

In order to avoid any misunderstanding, it must be clearly stated that the intention of this proposal is *neither* the replacement of existing modes of discourse by a 'superior' form *nor* the devaluation of alternative modes. The argument is rather one of 'horses for courses'. The suitability and effectiveness of a particular discourse are in direct relation to the purpose for which it is employed. But more than that— the different modes of discourse play a *supporting* role in relation to each other. Intra-textual analysis, rediscovery of the own tradition, reformulation and re-affirmation of dogma, describing the world of the text in its own terms, narrating the story of Biblical texts for their own sake, explaining and defending the truth claims of theology, prophetic resistance and confrontation, uncompromising witnessing, apologetics of a more subtle or a more aggressive kind—all have their validity and function. The issue is to take into account which public one is dealing with and decide on which mode or modes would be suitable for that purpose. Furthermore, the more clarity that can be obtained in the context of the second public regarding the nature and content of faith propositions, the more effectively the discourse with the third public can be conducted. The different modes are complementary to each other and should be valued for their supportive contribution.

### 3.3. The Need for a Different Type of Discourse

Nonetheless, after all that has been said so far and returning to the introduction of this contribution, the need still exists for a different type of discourse to respond to the challenge and opportunity now presenting itself in the South African context. Alongside the modes of critical analysis and of prophetic witness and resistance,

---

[28] Cf. Conradie 1993, 40.

[29] Cf. Conradie 1993, 37.

[30] Cf. Conradie 1993, 41.

there is also the need to contribute to the establishment of a new public ethos in civil society—an ethos where theology and Christianity will not necessarily have a privileged position. This will require theology to move beyond its preoccupation with itself, beyond being concerned primarily with the validity of its own truth claims, beyond its defensive attitude, beyond its experience of marginalization and its resignation of not being able to influence civil society. But in order to be effective, this further step in the context of the third public will also require a change of style. It is important to spell out what the main characteristics of this style should be.

### 4. Proposal for an Interactive, Constructive Mode of Theological Discourse in the Public Arena

What is being proposed here, arises from the attempt, in various forms, to develop a value system in the context of civil society that will support the transition to an inclusive, democratic dispensation in South Africa. As already pointed out, it is critical that changes in political structures and constitutional arrangements are accompanied and informed by a change in value system in order to establish a new public ethos in the country. Various projects of the Centre for Contextual Hermeneutics at the University of Stellenbosch related to voter education and education for democracy have underlined the need for concentrated attention to the issue of values. Cooperation with participants from the public sector, and more specifically, the Stellenbosch Economic Project in collaboration with the Department of Economics, aimed at the investigation of aspects of a post-apartheid economy, has stimulated the discussion of values in a non-theological environment. The invitation to develop common values on a major gold mine in the Western Transvaal in a totally secular setting, provided a unique opportunity to participate in a discourse not from a privileged and protected theological position, but which nonetheless generated values compatible with basic theological concepts. The important point was that these values were not formulated in theological, but 'secular' language and illustrated the need for and possibility of a discourse of a completely different nature. The plea is therefore to move beyond what is conventionally understood as theological discourse and to explore the possibilities of a form of language that is not primarily interested in preserving the integrity of theology, but to serve a wider cause. The leading question for this purpose is not: How do we defend Christian truth claims?, but: What contribution can theology make to the process of developing and establishing a new public ethos?

What is proposed here, comes close to what Gustafson calls 'policy discourse'—a discourse "which seek to recommend or prescribe quite particular courses of action about quite specific issues".[32] As we have already seen above, it is a discourse conducted in the public arena with the focus on concrete issues, within the constraints of the possible. It has the added dimension of taking responsibility for what is proposed in this discourse and therefore demands accountability. Gustafson points out that it is a discourse not conducted "by external observers, but by the persons who have the responsibility to make choices and to carry out the actions that are required by the choices".[33]

For such a discourse to succeed, very specific characteristics are required. Firstly, it needs to be non-prescriptive. Theology and theologians tend to be judgmental in their approach— listening to different positions and then declaring what is good or bad—with clear instructions on what should be done. The attitude should rather be one of joint discovery, allowing parties in the public debate to participate on their own terms and articulate from their own experience and perspective—letting issues and formulations emerge before directing and confining the discourse.

This implies secondly that the style needs to be *inclusive*, that is, open to the flow of ideas, to the new and unexpected, but also concerned that all possible contributions are considered and included. In the South African context, it means the ability draw from the many and diverse traditions which form part of the public scene and to enrich the discourse in the process. A Western humanistic tradition stands to gain from an African understanding of humanity and vice versa, but that presupposes an inclusive approach to public discourse.

Thirdly, an *interactive, participatory* style of discourse, not developed in the artificial and protected environment of the own group, where stereotypes are neither exposed nor corrected. It implies the willingness to become vulnerable, to be challenged, and not to claim a privileged position for theology.

In order to be effective in a pluralistic public environment, it fourthly requires a discourse that gives evidence of *hermeneutical* competence. This not only implies bi- or multilingual skills,[34] that is, familiarity with different discourses, but also the ability to move between these discourses and to mediate and interpret the issues as they are expressed and experienced in different contexts.[35]

Theological discourse in the public sphere cannot succeed if it is conducted in a dominating of self-centred way, pre-occupied with its own concerns. It fifthly needs to adopt a *serving* mode, losing and transcending itself to become liberated in service to the other.

Without denying the importance of resistance and protest, public discourse sixthly needs to be *constructive* in the sense of a willingness to reach out, to build, to

---

[32] Gustafson 1988, 45.

[33] Gustafson 1988, 46.

[34] Bellah—cf. Conradie 1993, 44.

[35] Cf. Bauman 1987 for an extensive analysis of the issue.

take responsibility and to jointly map out a possible course of action.

Finally, theology needs to transcend itself in the sense that it becomes *anony-mous* or 'secular'—a discourse no longer formulated in recognisable theological language,[36] but effectively translating theological concepts in a public discourse accessible to participants from other discourses and in a form that is genuinely 'public'.

In this way, theology has much to learn from but also much to give to the development of a functional public ethos and a healthy civil society. If the pragmatic intention of New Testament texts are taken seriously, also in modern situational contexts, the study of these documents has indeed an important contribution to make in the process of social transformation.

## *Bibliography*

Bauman, Z. 1987: *Legislators and interpreters,* Cambridge: Polity Press 1987.

Baumgartner, H. M. 1991: "Von der Königin der Wissenschaften zu ihrem Narren?", in: *ThQ* 171 (1991) 278-99.

Burkhalter, S. L. 1990: "Four modes of discourse: Blurred genres in the study of religion", in: Reynolds & Burkhalter (eds.) 1990, 141-61.

Clark, W. R. 1990: "The legal status of Religious Studies programmes in public higher education", in: Reynolds & Burkhalter (eds.) 1990, 109-40.

Cochrane, J. R. 1994: "Participating in Power: Elections, the Church and a Democratic Citizenry", in: *JTSA* 86 (1994) 139-51.

Conradie, E. M. 1993: "How should a public way of doing theology be approached?", in: *Scriptura* 46 (1993) 24-49.

De Gruchy, J. W. 1986: *Doing Christian theology in the context of South Africa or God-talk under Devil's Peak*, Cape Town: University of Cape Town 1986.

— 1994: "Midwives of Democracy", in: *JTSA* 86 (1994) 14-25.

Du Plessis, L. M. 1994: "The Genesis of South Africa's first Bill of Rights", in: *JTSA* 86 (1994) 52-66.

Farley, E. 1982: *Ecclesial Reflection.* An Anatomy of the Theological Mind, Philadelphia, PA: Fortress Press 1982.

— 1983: *Theologia: The Fragmentation and Unity of Theological Knowledge*, Philadelphia, PA: Fortress Press 1983.

— 1988: *The Fragility of Knowledge*: Theological Education in the Church and the University, Philadelphia, PA: Fortress Press 1988.

---

[36] Cf. Tracy 1989, 198 on the issue of camouflaged language.

Gustafson, J. M. 1988: *Varieties of Moral Discourse*. Prophetic, Narrative, Ethic and Policy, Grand Rapids, MI: Calvin College and Seminary 1988.

Hartman, L. 1986: "On Reading Others' Letters", in: *HThR* (1986) 137-46.

— 1990: "Is the Crucified Christ the Center of a New Testament Theology?", in: Jennings, T. W. (ed.): *Text and Logos*. The Humanistic Interpretation of the New Testament. FS Hendrikus Boers (Scholars Press Homage Series), Atlanta, GA: Scholars Press 1990, 175-88.

— 1993: "Galatians 3:15-4:11 as Part of a Theological Argument on a Practical Issue", in: J. Lambrecht (ed.), *The Truth of the Gospel (Galatians 1:1 - 4:11)* (Monographic Series of «Benedictina» 12), Rome: «Benedictina» Publishing 1993.

Harvey, V. A. 1989: "On the intellectual marginalization of American theology", in: Lacey, M. J. (ed.): *Theology and twentieth-century American intellectual life*, Cambridge: Cambridge University Press 1989, 172-92.

Heckel, M. 1986: *Die theologischen Fakultäten im weltlichen Verfassungstaat*, Tübingen: J. C. B. Mohr (Paul Siebeck) 1986.

Kaufmann, F.-X. 1991: "Theologie zwischen Kirche und Universität", in: *ThQ* 171 (1991) 265-77.

Kelsey, D. H. 1990: "Church discourse and the public realm", in: Marshall, B. D. (ed.): *Theology and Dialogue*, Notre Dame: University of Notre Dame Press 1990, 7-33.

Kitagawa, J. M. (ed.) 1992: *Religious Studies, Theological Studies and the University-Divinity School*, Atlanta, GA: Scholars Press 1992.

Lategan, B. C. 1993: "Teaching Theology in the Context of the Humanities", in: *Scriptura* S 11 (1993) 28-35.

Long, C. H. 1990: "The University, the Liberal Arts, and the Teaching and Study of Religion", in: Reynolds, F. E. & Burkhalter, S. L. (eds.) 1990, 19-40.

Meuleman, G. E. 1991: "Theologie aan de universiteit", in: *GThT* 91 (1991) 1-27.

Pityana, N. B. 1994: "The Evolution of Democracy in Africa", in: *JTSA* 86 (1994) 4-13.

Reynolds, F. E. & Burkhalter, S.L. (eds.) 1990: *Beyond the Classics?* Essays in Religious Studies and Liberal Education, Atlanta, GA: Scholars Press 1990.

Smit, D. J. 1992: "Oor 'n 'Nuwe Testamentiese etiek', die Christelike lewe en Suid-Afrika vandag", in: *Scriptura* 9a (1992) 303-325.

Tracy, D. W. 1981: *The Analogical Imagination*. Christian Theology and the Culture of Pluralism, London: SCM Press 1981.

— 1989: "Afterword: Theology, Public Discourse and the American Tradition", in: Lacey, M. J. (ed.), *Religion and Twentieth-Century American Intellectual Life,* Cambridge: Cambridge University Press 1989, 193-203.

— 1990: *Dialogue with the Other*. The Interreligious Dialogue, Grand Rapids, MI: Eerdmans 1990.

Villa-Vicencio, C. 1992: *A Theology of Reconstruction*. Nation-building and Human Rights, Cambridge: Cambridge University Press 1992.

Wirsching, J. 1991: "Evangelische Theologie an der Universität", *ThQ* 171 (1991) 299-315.

# John 2:4 in a Chinese Cultural Context:
## Unnecessary Stumbling Block for Filial Piety?

### Thor Strandenæs

## 1. Necessary and Unnecessary Stumbling Blocks in the New Testament

1.1 When crossing cultural barriers in translation,[1] one of the aims is to eliminate unnecessary cultural obstacles for the readers.[2] This is not only the case when preparing strictly cultural reinterpretations[3] but in any rendering of texts which aims at intelligibility. Whether or not an obstacle is inherent in the text itself or only surfaces as an obstacle in the receptor culture, must be determined through a careful study of the total context of the original communication event as well as the receptor language and culture.[4] How this is reflected in the final version depends on the guidelines adopted by the translator.

For both translators and interpreters it is necessary to distinguish between different kinds of obstacles for understanding. And these obstacles, or stumbling blocks as I shall also refer to them in the following, may be characterized as necessary or unnecessary depending on whether they are inherent in the originals or are created by different cultural presuppositions in the receptor language.

1.2 Some stumbling blocks in the texts can only be resolved if the intended readers are willing to accept some presuppositions accepted by the texts themselves, e.g.,

---

[1] The cultural factor in bible translation is the topic of the monographs by Nida and Reyburn (1981) and Wendland (1987, see especially pp. 207-12 for some particularly relevant reference materials). See also Shorter 1973 and Taber 1979.

[2] Nida and Reyburn (1981, 14-17) have divided the cultural presuppositions of a society into five classes: the physical earth and living beings, history and destiny, supernatural beings, interpersonal relations, and intellectual activity.

[3] Although any translation involves some degree of interpretation, I agree with de Waard and Nida (1986, 41) who refer to cultural translations as *cultural reinterpretations*, thereby distinguishing between translation and reinterpretation, since the latter involves "transferring the cultural setting from one language-culture context to another".

[4] For a summary of the steps involved in this process, see Wendland 1987, 21-48.

the need of humankind for reconciliation and an atoning sacrifice (2 Cor 5:18ff.; Eph 2:13-16; Col 1:19f.) or the divinity of Christ.[5] Other features may be explained in footnotes or other supplementary aids in the printed version and thus be clarified to the reader.[6] If it is to read naturally in the receptor language, one must also rid the translation of awkwardness[7] and unnecessary foreignness in idiom and style. Furthermore, while leaving aside such matters that cannot be removed or altered without changing the meaning of the originals, one must remove also any *unnecessary stumbling blocks* caused by cultural presuppositions in the originals which are of an optional nature or even caused by traditional translation or interpretation. Often it is at times of revision, or when translating the Bible anew, that these problems are brought to the fore and identified clearly.

To the informed readers—including those who master the originals well—the problem addressed here may seem less important than to the uninformed. In apologetical work, however, and when introducing new readers to Christian faith, the foreignness or supposed countercultural character of the New Testament may appear quite overwhelming if the right steps have not been taken in exegesis and translation to remove unwanted obstacles for readers of any translation. It seems fair to recognize three main types of cultural elements in the NT texts, viz., such cultural features which may well agree with those found in some cultures but not in others; secondly, the transcultural features which constitute core elements of Christian faith and whose universal character must transcend any particular culture; thirdly, the countercultural features which challenge the culture(s) where a translation is used. In this essay I restrict myself to dealing with the countercultural elements.

I have made it my task in this presentation to ask whether John 2:4, after all, is an unnecessary stumbling block in a Chinese cultural context, and whether a different way of translating—and interpreting it—removes its character as a stumbling block among people for whom filial piety is highly cherished. In other words, are some of the cultural elements *only supposedly* countercultural? And, may these in fact turn out to agree perfectly well with a given culture, provided care is taken in the different stages of translation to ensure this?

1.3 Faced with various difficulties in translating texts into other languages, Bible translators tend to come across linguistic and translation problems which have ei-

---

[5] That Jesus Christ himself may become a stumbling block for people, is a possibility which is recognized in the New Testament, Matt 21:42-46; Rom 9:30-33; 1 Pet 2:8.

[6] Cf. Wendland 1987, 29f. and de Waard and Nida 1986, 201.

[7] How exegesis and translation can be assisted by pragmatics has been demonstrated by Hope (1988). The different aspects of pragmatics are all closely interrelated and complement each other. The pragmatic approach to a text assists the exegete and the translator in defining the intentions of the author, ibid., 126f.

ther not been solved or dealt with previously. Also, translation as a cross cultural exercise involves asking such questions regarding the biblical texts which may have direct exegetical bearings. As a result, exegetical discoveries are made, earlier theories modified and new solutions to exegetical, linguistic and translational problems are found. Thus, modern writers of exegetical commentaries and articles cannot afford to overlook the material accumulated in relevant publications such as *The Bible Translator* or *Helps for Translators*.[8]

One of the areas in life where Chinese readers feel challenged or offended is where New Testament texts offer (or seem to offer) alternative ethical codes to what is traditionally regarded as the normative social code of action. As code of action it is not only highly respected but belongs to the cultural presuppositions in society. This particularly goes for the area of expected behaviour in family relations,[9] both with regard to the family ties in general and filial piety in particular.[10] There are for instance several texts in the Gospels which puzzle filial Chinese readers, e.g., Matt 12:46-50 and Luke 14:26.[11] Yu Chi-Ping has pointed out the problem which is felt even among Chinese Christians when they read such texts:

> Many Chinese Christians, especially those from non-Christian families, often find themselves torn between loyalty to Christ and that to their beloved parents. And they often struggle over the incompatibility of being a Christian and a Chinese.[12]

Traditionally the statement which Jesus makes in his dialogue with Mary, John 2:4, τί ἐμοὶ καὶ σοί, γύναι; οὔπω ἥκει ἡ ὥρα μου, is rendered in such a way that many readers, let alone the Chinese, get the impression that Jesus is being impolite or even rude. When faced with this and some other rather challenging New Testament family-related texts they may argue as follows: if a person behaves in this manner vis-à-vis his parents, brothers and sisters, then it is not surprising at all that he teaches others to behave in an unfilial or disrespect way and even to alienate their rela-

---

[8] E.g., the handbooks (e.g., Newman & Nida 1980) and guides (e.g., Bratcher 1981) in the Helps For Translators Series of the United Bible Societies.

[9] It belongs to the class of underlying cultural presuppositions in any given society which Nida and Reyburn (1981, 14-17) refer to as *interpersonal relations*, cf. note 2 above.

[10] Yu (1984, 87) observes that the Chinese find the biblical teaching of filial piety "more congenial with the Jewish filial ethos than with the Christian one. A large part of this is due to some of Jesus' stern teachings on discipleship."

[11] Other examples from the gospels are Matt 10:34-37 and Luke 12:51-53. In his analysis of the New Testament perspective of filial piety, Yu (1984, 93-100) also gives several examples from the Pauline letters.

[12] Yu 1984, 87f.

tives![13] In a culture deeply penetrated by Confucian ethics[14] such behaviour is especially distasteful and does not invite confidence in the New Testament teaching.[15] Since religion by many Chinese is also considered basis for a good ethos, it may eventually lead to a general distrust in Christianity as such.

1.4 Stating it more precisely: one wonders whether the impression of rudeness in the statement of John 2:4 is caused by a problem inherent in the Greek text—and thus constitutes a stumbling block which cannot easily be eliminated or modified— or whether it is only a supposed countercultural obstacle caused by formal correspondence translation.[16] The restless activity of biblical commentators in search for a plausible explanation of the statement is in itself an indication that it may, perhaps, even be a combination of the two.[17] It may seem somewhat pretentious to choose this text and offer a possible solution to the problem in light of the work done by Birger Olsson in his excellent text-linguistic analysis of John 2:1-11.[18] The approach in the present essay is, however, prompted by the *cultural obstacles* which I have seen that the text has caused Chinese readers, either when struggling to translate the Greek originals or when reading one of the Chinese versions. And, while agreeing with Olsson in his definition of the text type of John 2:1-11 as "a symbolic narrative text with many allusive elements",[19] I find it necessary to qualify his definition further.

I agree that, as a narrative text in its present context, John 2:1-11 has a *predom-*

---

[13] The Chinese will allow for a certain foreignness to pertain to the NT texts, but when this limit is exceeded, the texts may, as a result, appear totally irrelevant and uninteresting to many of the possible readers.

[14] Even Chinese popular sayings demonstrate the degree to which filial piety is regarded a high value virtue in the Chinese society: "Filial piety moves Heaven" and "Of all the teachings in the Classics, filial piety comes first" (literally: "In 1000 scriptures and 10,000 scrolls, filial piety comes first").

[15] Instead of emphasizing the differences between the New Testament and filial piety, Chinese Christians are likely to emphasize the points of contact and similarities. This is done by Yu (1984, 101-03 and 162-76). Cf. Nkwoka's (1991) article as an example of how, in a Nigerian society, another aspect of family relations is harmonized with a New Testament picture of Jesus.

[16] Obviously de Waard and Nida (1986, 36) are right when they claim that the conflict between formal correspondence and functional equivalence often causes the crucial problems of translation. In this essay *formal correspondence* and *functional equivalence* are used in the same sense as in de Waard and Nida 1986, 36-40.

[17] Goodspeed (1952, 70f.), Buck (1956) and Brown (1966, 99f. and 110f.) give some of the alternatives which have been suggested. Schnackenburg (1951, 10ff.) and Smitmans (1966) offer surveys of how the text has been interpreted in the cause of history and also give valuable references to literature where the different solutions have been offered.

[18] Olsson 1974, 18-114.

[19] Olsson 1974, 114.

*inantly or mainly* symbolic function, a fact which Olsson's dissertation demonstrates beyond doubt. However, its predominantly symbolic function—also in the wider perspective of the gospel—does not deprive the text from its function as a narrative witness to what took place in the original event at Cana.[20] Olsson's classification also does not rule out that this passage—despite its brevity—relates the account of an event where the logic in the dialogue between Jesus and his mother on the one hand, and the coherence between the dialogue and the rest of the narrative on the other are both intact. Thus, the symbolic function of John 2:1-11 is not in contradiction to, but conditioned by and additional to, its value as an interpretative narrative of something which once took place. In the gospel of John the narrative in ch 2:1-11 both functions as an interpretative account which testifies to *what took place* in the Cana event—an event which v. 11 specifies as the first of the signs which Jesus made—and as a symbolic interpretation with many allusive elements to the wider context of John. A translation of the text should not obscure, but rather be open to this fact. Perhaps the text type could better be classified as *a predominantly symbolic narrative text with many allusive elements*. Irrespective of the wording of the definition it is important that *the translation* as far as possible reflects both the historical and symbolic features of the narrative.

In the following I therefore wish to identify firstly what problem the statement in John 2:4, τί ἐμοὶ καὶ σοί, γύναι; οὔπω ἥκει ἡ ὥρα μου, in the context of John 2:1-11 causes to Chinese readers and most likely also to readers in other cultures where filial piety is highly valued. Then I shall proceed to asking whether the problem is inherent in the originals, whether it may be overcome, and if so, how this can be done.

## 2. Τί ἐμοὶ καὶ σοί, γύναι; οὔπω ἥκει ἡ ὥρα μου
### — in Chinese and in Greek

2.1 The impression of rudeness in Jesus' statement in John 2:4 is created by a coincidence of several factors: firstly, a formal correspondence translation of γύναι *"nü ren"*[21] ("woman" / "womanfolk" / "wife") leaves one with the impression that Jesus is harsh or cold and keeps his mother at a distance.[22] Because of this, many Chi-

---

[20] The majority of scholars presently see some sort of deeper meaning in the miracle. I think they are right in doing so, but this view does not imply a total lack of interest in the miracle event itself, cf. Olsson 1974, 18-20.

[21] *The Studium Biblicum Sinense Chinese Bible Version* 1968.

[22] A formal correspondence translation is preferred in many NT versions, e.g., the English, cf. Buck 1956, 149.

nese versions have a functional equivalent translation, e.g., *"muqin"* ("mother")[23] and *"mama"* ("ma" / "mum" / "mummy" / "mother")[24].

Secondly, the expression τί ἐμοὶ καὶ σοι;, like in many non-Chinese versions,[25] is mainly interpreted as having a negative and restrictive sense:[26] *"wo yü ni you shemma xiānggan"*[27] ("What have I to do with you?"). It also corresponds to the tendency among exegetes to interpret this idiom in a purely restrictive sense, e.g., C. K. Barrett[28] and Morris.[29]

Thirdly, when οὔπω ἥκει ἡ ὥρα μου is added—making one think that Jesus rejects Mary's problem because he lacks time,[30] or that he is unwilling to do anything about it—it only adds to the impression created by the two first factors, viz. of Jesus as being standoffish and speaking disrespectfully. Thus, in a Chinese context, the second half of the statement only emphasizes the negative sense which is created by the first. But is this how the Greek statement is to be understood in its present context?[31]

2.2 If we look at the flow of the entire story (John 2:1-11) it is evident that no basic or principle conflict exists between Jesus and Mary with regard to solving the problem of want of wine. As the story runs, Mary notes the problem, notifies or reminds Jesus about it (v 4) and instructs the servants to obey him (v. 5), which they in turn do (v. 7f.).[32] As a result, the wedding is given a new supply of choice wine (v. 9f.). In v. 11 the miracle of turning water into wine is identified as the first of the signs which Jesus did. Thus, on the one hand Mary's approach is not necessarily a request for a miracle, and, on the other hand nothing seems to indicate that Mary was not expecting him to act *in some way or another* with regard to their want of wine. And

---

[23] *The Chinese Union Version of the Bible* 1919.

[24] Like in *The New Testament in Today's English Version* 1966, a colloquial alternative has been chosen in the *Today's Chinese Version of the New Testament* 1976. The catholic version by Jin Lu-xian has *"taitai"* ("madam" / "lady" / "missis").

[25] E.g., *The Holy Bible ... Revised Standard Version* 1971: "O woman, what have you to do with me?", *The Jerusalem Bible* 1966: "Woman, why turn to me?".

[26] Cf. Morris 1971, 180: "And if the form of address is tender, the rest of Jesus' words makes it clear that there was something of a barrier between them".

[27] *The Union Version* 1919. Similarly translated by *The New Chinese Bible Commission Version* 1976.

[28] Barrett 1955, 159.

[29] Morris 1971, 180f. Morris also there gives examples of translators with similar views.

[30] Thus, e.g., *The Chinese Union Version* 1919: *"wode shihou hai mei you dao"* ("my time has not yet come").

[31] Olsson (1974, 35), as well as Smitmans (1966, 16ff., 272ff.), having considered the multitude of suggested renderings, correctly observes the understanding of this statement reflects the scholars' total interpretation.

this is exactly what he does: the miracle takes place and the newlyweds and their guests once more have wine, both abundant in quantity and excellent in quality.

On this background, then, it is necessary *either* to explain why John 2:4 sounds so awkward *in contrast to* the entire account of John 2:1-11 *or* show that it is not so awkward at all. Most of the exegetical commentaries or essays dealing with John 2:4 presuppose or try to show that Jesus' statement is awkward,[33] or represents a reprimand of Mary, and must be dealt with accordingly. As a result, the attention of the exegetes is all too soon turned to theologizing.[34] I intend to show here that the statement is not so awkward as many exegetes and translators suppose it to be.

## 3. Γύναι

Starting with γύναι, then, it seems relevant first to ask how this form of address is used by Jesus elsewhere in John and the gospels.

In John γύναι, the vocative of γυνή, is used twice with reference to the mother of Jesus. In both contexts Mary is referred to as his mother, John 2:1,3,5; 19:25,26. Nothing is done in the narrative to play down this fact.[35] Rather, it is referred to quite naturally. Also, Mary does play an important role in both narratives *because of the need she represents*: in John 2:4 she presents to Jesus the want of wine—a problem and a public shame for the close as well as the extended family and certainly not an auspicious beginning of a matrimony. In John 19:25f., by the cross, she stands as the grieving mother, her son soon to be taken away from her.

Jesus never addresses Mary by name in John.[36] The only two times he addresses her directly he uses γύναι (John 2:4; 19:26), and both times the two of them are in a public place with eyewitnesses present (John 2:2,5,7; 19:25-27). Prior to the first

---

[32] As Buck (1956, 150) has correctly observed, "Mary does not react like one who has been rebuked. What follows is a direction to the servants made in full confidence." Many commentators try to explain why Mary was there (See Smitmans 1966, 11f.; cf. Olsson 1974, 29f.). Morris (1971, 178) suggests that it may be significant that Mary was already there and that this may mean that she had taken up residence. She was obviously well informed, although this does not necessarily mean that she was part of the family. On major festive occasions in the East both food and drink—including the abundance or lack of it—are on the lips of all guests.

[33] Thus Olsson 1974, 38.

[34] Thus e.g., Dillon 1962, 288-90.

[35] Cf. note 33. Brown (1966, 99) points out that the use of γύναι is "not an attempt to reject or devalue the mother-son relationship." Contrary to this Morris (1971, 180f.) holds that "the rest of Jesus' words make it clear that there was something of a barrier between them ... A new relationship was established. Mary must not presume."

[36] Buck (1972, 175) has pointed out that John uses the name *Mary* fifteen times, but never with reference to the mother of Jesus.

instance, John 2:4, Mary has presented Jesus with a problem.[37] Then again, by the cross (19:26), she faces a lonely and uncertain future without her son around to care for and provide for her through her remaining days. Thus it is the need which attracts the attention of Jesus.[38]

Γύναι is also used in the vocative elsewhere in John, as has been rightly observed[39]. However, *the significance of the individual context* in which it appears has not been given sufficient attention. A good exception here is, however, Haenchen's treatment of the narrative.[40] Whereas commentators generally agree that γύναι is not used in any derogatory sense or cannot be considered impolite, and some even refer to usage in Greek literature,[41] few attempts are made to find the semantic meaning of the word in John.[42] Commentators tend to be puzzled by the fact that Jesus uses it when addressing his mother, find this awkward and suggest that its appearance in John 2:4 has symbolic significance.[43] All too soon, however, the focus is then shifted to "woman" as a theological motif in John.[44]

If we look carefully at the instances in which Jesus uses γύναι when addressing a woman, bearing in mind the contexts in which they appear, we meet women who, when faced with a need or a problem, sought or found—directly or indirectly—the assistance of Jesus. His assistance was either given by means of a miracle John 2:1-11 (cf. Matt 15:28; Luke 13:12) or by some other providence of his.[45] Through his clever directions, the woman at the well of Sychar was given new insight with regard to her ethical behaviour as well as a new relation to her fellow Samaritan citizens (John 4:16-42). The adulteress (John 7:53-8:11)[46] was freed from her

---

[37] This corresponds to the alternative interpretation preferred by Olsson (1974, 43).

[38] Jesus' concern for the need of his disciple John is, of course, also implicit here. But it seems that the son's making provision for the care of his mother is in focus here, cf. Barrett 1955, 459.

[39] Buck 1972, 175.

[40] Haenchen 1984, 175f.

[41] Beasley-Murray (1987, 34) has drawn attention to the interesting example from Josephus' *Antiquitates Judaicae* 17:74, where Pheroras, when seriously ill, is quoted as having addressed his wife —whom he is known to have had great affection for—by "woman". Oedipus thus addresses his wife Jokaste (Sophocles, *Oedipus tyrannus* 642).

[42] Brown (1966, 99) merely states that it was Jesus' "normal, polite way of addressing women". He also lists five references in the Gospels where γύναι is used and adds that this sense is also attested in Greek writing.

[43] Thus Brown 1966, 99 and Kieffer 1987, 58.

[44] Thus Brown 1966, 99 and 107-09.

[45] This and the following correctly noted by Morris 1971, 180 note 18.

[46] Although John 7:53-8:11 is not likely to have been admitted to the Gospels until some time in the second century (cf. Metzger 1971, 219-22 and Aland and Aland 1987, 227) and cannot per se testify to *Johannine* usage, as a contribution to the gospel tradition it nevertheless serves as a witness to confirm this form of address being used publicly by Jesus.

persecutors and her own sin 8:10f. Mary Magdalene by the tomb was relieved of her sorrow and despair (John 20:15). Finally, the two women (Matt 15:21-28 and Luke 13:10-17) who are addressed by Jesus in Matt 15:28 (ὦ γύναι, μεγάλη σου ἡ πίστις) and Luke 13:12 (γύναι, ἀπολέλυσαι τῆς ἀσθενείας σου) either approached him with a need or, by their very presence represented an obvious need. And he, in turn, meets their needs by healing them.

Thus, in all instances in the Gospels where the vocative γύναι occurs, Jesus is the person who addresses the women. Also, in all instances where the vocative γύναι is used, Jesus is using it when addressing publicly a woman in need who directly or indirectly seeks his help. The use is not derogatory or implying a disrespectful attitude on behalf of Jesus. Rather, it is his normal, polite way of addressing women.[47] Furthermore, the two instances in which Jesus uses γύναι when addressing Mary in John (2:4; 19:26) are no exception to this.

This observation, in turn, indicates that the vocative γύναι, when used by Jesus in a public place to address a person, who may or may not belong to his (immediate) family, politely expresses respect, while still maintaining an affectionate tone. This is also the meaning of γύναι in the often cited examples from the Greek classics.[48] Although Brown observes that no precedent is found in Hebrew or Greek literature for a son using "woman" alone when addressing his mother,[49] it does not change this fact. That Jesus uses γύναι when addressing a woman *in public* is sufficient evidence to prove that this form of address is not awkward, even when used by the woman's son. As in many cultures, *in casu* the Chinese, the difference between form of address in private and in public is significant.[50] One should consider Jesus' use of γύναι to address his mother *in public* as an instance of such awareness.

With regard to the referential meaning of γύναι, then, the above evidence must have bearings on the direction one chooses. When Brown advocates a formal equivalent translation, "woman",[51] it corresponds to his understanding of the entire passage and his specific interest in the theological motifs in the narrative.[52] However, in light of the evidence, the direction of Newman and Nida,[53] implying that one should search for the closest functional equivalent in the receptor language, seems the only right one to choose. As already noted above, functional equivalence has

---

[47] Thus Brown (1966, 99) who states it as a matter-of-fact without demonstrating that it is so.

[48] Cf. note 39 above and Goodspeed 1952, 70f.

[49] Brown 1966, 99.

[50] Cf. Chao 1956.

[51] Brown 1966, 99: "To translate it as "Mother" would both obscure this possibility [i.e. the symbolic import in the title] and cloak the peculiarity of the address."

[52] One of the four theological motifs which Brown (1966, 103-10) finds in the narrative is the symbolism of the Mother of Jesus, the "woman", at Cana (ibid., 107-09). Cf. note 34 above.

[53] Newman and Nida 1980, 57.

been sought along two lines in the Chinese versions, like in the English: 1. either by omitting mention of "woman"[54] or 2. by an equivalent expression showing proper respect, such as "mother" / "my mother".[55] This, of course, does not prevent one from supplying in *notes* such information as opens the reader to the possible symbolic value of γύναι in the originals, as it is done in Jin Luxian's translation.[56]

In the same direction as *The Jerusalem Bible* and Buck's choice ("And Jesus said, 'Madam, why is that our concern?'")[57] goes Jin Luxian's translation. "*Yesu dui ta shuo: 'tai tai! Zhe huo ni wo you he guanxi?'*" ("Jesus said to her, madam / misses! What does this have to do with me and you?")

## 4. Τί ἐμοὶ καὶ σοί, γύναι;

It is possible that the translation τί ἐμοὶ καὶ σοί, γύναι; in John 2:4 of an underlying Aramaic statement was not the best functional equivalent possible at the time of translating. This might be the reason why it has puzzled so many translators and commentators before. However, before drawing this conclusion, it seems only fair that one examines the contexts in which the same phrase has been used in the Septuagint and also takes seriously the context of the phrase in John 2:4. It is quite possible that such an examination may give new input to how the passage may best be rendered. This is what I intend to do in the following.

If we study the idiom τί ἐμοὶ καὶ σοί; in the *Septuagint* and the New Testament, the observations of both Brown[58] and Olsson[59] are relevant and to the point. There

---

[54] Like in *The New Testament in Today's English Version* 1966, and *Today's Chinese Version of the New Testament* 1975. This alternative seems to echo Goodspeed's (1952, 70f.) suggestion.

[55] Thus *The Chinese Union Version of the Bible* 1919 and J. B. Phillips, *The New Testament in Modern English* 1972.

[56] The translation of Jin Luxian is accompanied by a note which both comments that it literally means "*funü*" ("woman") and that Jesus also used the same form of address to her while on the cross. The note goes on to say that this usage has a significance which becomes apparent when one reads Genesis: whereas the first woman—Eve—committed the original sin which brought along death, the second—the holy mother—brought life to humankind. As has been stated in the preface of the version, the translation is relying on *The Jerusalem Bible*, which is clear from the note up to this point. Jin Luxian goes on to state that for a Jewish reader this parallel would be obvious also in the Greek translation. Since, however, this would not be the case for Chinese readers, to whom "*funü*" ("woman") sounds inappropriate, Jin Luxian, unlike *The Jerusalem Bible*, has chosen a more functional equivalent rendering. Also the translation of John 2:1-11 in the *Studium Biblicum Sinense Version* 1968 is accompanied by an explanatory note which gives the reader some clues to possible symbolic meanings. See (Conclusion) 6.2 - 6.3 below.

[57] Buck 1956, 150.

[58] Brown (1966, 99) deals with these passages based on the Hebrew text of the OT.

[59] Olsson 1974, 36-40.

are, however, a few more points to be made.

Brown rightly points out that the expression is used in the OT with two shades of meaning, viz. (a) when one party is unjustly bothered by another and (b) when someone is asked to get involved in a matter which he feels is no business of his.[60] This observation must be coupled with another which is obvious if one looks at the entire narrative in which the question appears and has a view to the outcome of each story. It implies two more shades of meaning: (c) one party challenges another who, in turn, acts contrary to the wishes of the first, and (d) one party challenges another who, in turn, acts in accordance with the wishes of the first. Obviously different combinations of (a), (b), (c) and (d) also give differing shades of meaning. One must therefore seek a translation which most adequately catches the shade of meaning in each specific combination and context.

> It should be noted here that one can easily imagine how the phrase would have sounded in the oral dialogue or conversation, and that it is not only plausible but even likely that the stress and tone of the same phrase would vary. The listener would be able to tell from the stress and tone in the phrase whether a person was planning to act in accordance with or contrary to the will of the challenger. From the writing, however, one can only guess. But the wider context in which each phrase stands also gives sufficient signals to identify its meaning *in each respective place*, a fact which should not be forgotten here.

It is interesting to note that so far very few lexicographers have suggested that the sense of the interrogative τί in the idiom τί ἐμοὶ καὶ σοί, γύναι; is better translated by something else than the traditional *"what"*. I venture to suggest that an alternative rendering of τί, *"why / how come"* is to be preferred in the context of the idiom τί ἐμοὶ καὶ σοί, γύναι;. This suggestion coincides with the observation of Newman[61] and corresponds to the entry of Louw and Nida to John 2:4.[62] The use of *"why/how come"* instead of *"what"* in the idiom makes sense and is applicable also if one turns to texts which are contemporary to the New Testament, e.g., by Epictetus.[63] Taking τί in this sense, the whole idiom translates as follows: "why (is this a matter of concern both) for me and for you?", or "how come (this matter is of concern both) to me and to you?" Using this kind of translation one is better able to take

---

[60] Brown 1966, 99.

[61] Newman (1971, 182f.) has translated the idiom τί ἡμῖν (ἐμοι) καὶ σοί, by "what have you to do with us (me)?", but has in the entries listed in his lexicon indicated that the interrogative τί et alii may also be rendered as *"why? for what reason* or *purpose?*

[62] Louw and Nida (1989, entry 92.15, Vol. I, 815) suggest that John 2:4 is best rendered with *"why/for what reason are you saying or doing this to me?"*. They also suggest that in some languages it may be preferable to translate John 2:4 by *"why do you ask me this?"*. Cf. also the translation offered by Buck (1956, 150).

[63] *Dissertationes ab Arriano digestae* 1,16; 22,15; 27,13 and *Enchiridion* 19,16.

care of the shades in each of the different combinations of (a), (b), (c) and (d) as well as the special problem normally encountered in the translation of John 2:4.

Thus, when it is obvious from the context that the parties involved have conflicting intentions or wishes, and that the one party is asked to get involved in a matter which he feels is no business of his, the phrase sounds more offensive and harsh and expresses irritation. It may then be translated: "why are you bothering me?!" But, when both parties have corresponding or similar intentions or wishes and the one party feels unjustly bothered by the other, the phrase sounds milder and expresses surprise: "how come you make this *your* problem (as well)?"[64] This means that the entire context must assist the translator and interpreter in determining which direction the question is to be understood. It also means that a translation which is compatible with the context of each occurrence will be found somewhere on the line between the two extremes "why are you bothering me?!" and "how come you make this *your* problem also?".

In the following instances where the idiom occurs each story contains sufficient qualifying markers and signals to support the interpreter in judging which shade of meaning is justified in the story concerned. The main guide is the outcome or conclusion of the story. But additional information can be found in each story if the exact meaning of the idiom in each given context is to be determined. In each of the examples below I have indicated the main shades of meaning which the idiom has in its context by reference to the letters (a)-(d) above. Since a fuller study of each story is needed if the exact meaning of the idiom in each context is to be determined, I shall restrict myself to pointing out the main shades of meaning here:

*Judg 11:12* The challenged Jephtha (on behalf of the challenged) asks the question, gives proof to show that the Israelites are entitled to the land, and has his will: the land stays with Israel. [(a) + (c)]

*2 Sam 16:10 and 19:22*. King David is challenged (16:10 plotted upon 19:22) by Abishai, puts the question and has his will. [(a) + (c)]

*1 Kgs 17:18*. The widow in Zarephtah, obviously feeling offended by Elijah, challenges the prophet by this question and has her will: her son is given back to her. [(a) + (d)]

*2 Kgs 3:13*. The prophet Elisha, obviously feeling offended, asks king Joram the question. However, because of the presence of King Jehoshaphat, the challenger is in the end given what he asks for: help to keep the land under the dominion of Israel. [(b) + (d)]

---

[64] Olsson (1974, 36; cf. also Schnackenburg 1967, 333) is right when he states that the significance of the idiom is highly dependent on context and intonation and that we therefore must expect differing meanings and shades of meanings in different contexts.

*2 Kgs 9:18f.* The twice challenged Jehu twice asks the question τί σοι καὶ εἰρήνῃ and each time has his will. [(a) +(c)]

*2 Chr 35:21.* Pharaoh Necho is challenged by King Josiah, asks the question and has his will. [(a) + (c)]

*Josh 22:24.* Taking preventive measures *so as not to be challenged* by the western tribes of Israel with this question in the future, the tribes of Reuben, Gad, and East Manasseh have their will in the end. [(a) + (d)]

*Acts of Thomas V:45.* As Maynard correctly observes,[65] the usage here is heavily dependent upon Mark 5:7 (//Matt 8:29 and Luke 8:28) and Mark 1:24 (//Luke 4:34) where the demons are many. The demons challenge Jesus by asking the question, but Jesus has his will: he exorcises them. [(a) + (c)]

*Matt 8:29.* The demoniacs challenge Jesus with this question, but Jesus has his will: he exorcises them, v. 30-32. [(a) + (c)]

*Mark 1:24.* The man with an unclean spirit challenges Jesus with the question, but Jesus has his will by taking control, v. 25f. [(a) + (c)]

*Luke 4:34.* The man with the spirit of an unclean demon challenges Jesus with the question, but Jesus has his will by taking control, v. 35. [(a) + (c)]

*John 2:4.* Jesus is challenged, asks the question, has his will, but the outcome corresponds with the intentions or concerns of his mother, Mary. [(a) + (d)]

From the above occurrences in the Greek OT and NT it might look as if it all boils down to a question of *power or will* or of *conflicting interests*, i.e., *whose power or will wins or prevails*. But this is not so in the instances mentioned above where the challenged party acts in accordance with the wishes of the challenger (referred to under type (d) above). Here there is no obvious conflict of interest at all. Also, the focus in the contexts of these stories is not on *whose power or will wins or prevails*. Instead it is a question of *demonstrating power*.

This is the case in John 2:5-11, where the instructions of both Mary (v. 5) and Jesus (v. 7f.) prepare the reader for a demonstration of power, which, as a result turns the water into wine (v. 8f.). That it is a demonstration of power is further confirmed in v. 11, where the miracle is counted as the first of his signs.[66] In v. 11 the demonstration of power is also said to have manifested his glory and resulted in his

---

[65] Maynard 1985, 583.

[66] That *sign* here, like elsewhere in John, (cf. John 12:23; 17:24) is used as a manifestation of Jesus' divine origin. His bringing the Messianic times does not contradict the fact that it is equally used with reference to demonstrating his power through visible miracles, e.g., John 2:23; 3:2; 6:2,14; 20:30f.

disciples believing in him.[67] Thus, here the power is demonstrated *in accordance with the intentions of the challenger*. As already noted under 2.2, Mary's approach is not necessarily a request for a miracle, rather an indirect request for Jesus to act in some way or another to relieve the wedding party from the (possible) embarrassment. In a Chinese culture the husband or the oldest son is a most natural person of reference for a woman when a problem of causing embarrassment to the whole party arises. Also in a Jewish culture Mary's approach is natural, yes even to be expected.

Albeit that Mary here may seem as if she is interfering in something which Jesus already has taken responsibility for, the miracle itself proves that, with regard to the problem of the wedding hosts, the two of them have common interests. When translating the idiom in John 2:4, therefore, one must keep all the above observations in mind.

Before suggesting a translation of the idiom which gives the shade of meaning called for in the context of John 2:4, I wish to draw attention to an idiom in English which, with regard to its possible shades of meanings, is comparable to τί ἐμοὶ καὶ σοί; viz., "I beg your pardon". There are at least three shades of meaning in its usage which immediately comes to one's mind: 1. "Sir, I beg your pardon." 2. "I beg your pardon?" and 3. "I beg your pardon!" The first expresses an excuse / politeness, the second surprise and the third indignation. Now, with regard to John 2:4, several possible functional renderings seem possible based on the understanding that the interrogative τί here means "why / how come?". The idiom as a whole then renders "why is this a matter of concern both to me and to you?", or "how come this matter is of concern both to me and to you?". The entire event shows that Jesus already has made this a concern of his, a fact which he signals to his mother. He shows surprise that she approaches him. There is no reason to doubt that, at the same time, he is already engaged in finding a solution. Instead of rendering it "why should this (problem) bother both of us?" or "how come you make this *your* problem as well?", thus using a question which does not reveal adequately the role played by Jesus, one may simply avoid the question form and instead translate it by a statement: "leave it to me."

---

[67] As *the beginning of the signs* (thus Olsson 1974, 67-69), John 2:1ff. brings out the symbolic meaning without losing contact with the original communication event.

## 5. Οὔπω ἥκει ἡ ὥρα μου

The third and final problem concerns the translation of the latter half of Jesus' state-ment, οὔπω ἥκει ἡ ὥρα μου. I believe Brown[68] is right in distinguishing with re-gard to the use of ὥρα in John. According to his analysis, the instances where ὥρα is used with a definite article or a possessive pronominal adjective "clearly refer to a special period in Jesus' life, a period best defined in xiii 1—the hour of the return to the Father."[69] He goes on to note the parallelism with the absolute Synoptic use of "the hour" for the passion of Jesus, concluding that "here as elsewhere, the Fourth Gospel has made a major theme of something that appears only incidentally in the other Gospels."[70] This meaning of ὥρα would reinforce the parallelism be-tween John 2:4 and 19:26 as already suggested by the form of address used by Jesus.

However, with the frequent use in John of double-sense-expressions (e.g., the use of ἄνωθεν with reference both to "again" / "anew" and "from above" in δεῖ ὑμᾶς γεννηθῆναι ἄνωθεν, John 3:7, cf 3:3-6)[71] it is not only possible but also likely that the translation of the expression οὔπω ἥκει ἡ ὥρα μου has a double meaning.[72] The first focuses on the immediate problem—the lack of wine and the solution to that problem—the second focuses on Jesus' final "hour", his death on the cross. This leaves us with a twofold interpretation of its meaning: 1. "With regard to the want of wine it is not yet time for me to act, according to my plan of action (but it will be soon)." 2. "According to God's plan for me, death on the cross is still (some time) ahead of me." ἡ ὥρα μου does refer to a specific point in time, but in the orig-inal narrative setting its reference may be to both alternatives—whether this was obvious or not to the participants in the original event related by John.[73] Since both 1 and 2 refer to *a future point in time*—immediate and less immediate—neither of them must therefore be precluded. Although I otherwise follow the convincing ar-

---

[68] Brown 1966, 517.

[69] Ibid.

[70] Ibid., 518.

[71] Cf. Brown 1966, 130f. and 137-44.

[72] Thus Marsh (1968, 144f.) suggests that in typical Johannine fashion Jesus is combining more meanings than one: "The time has not yet come when he can assist the marriage festivities; it has not yet come for him to make a public manifestation of himself, in spite of his public appearance with his disciples; it has not yet come for him to offer himself as the Lamb of God for the sins of the world."

[73] This is supported by Olsson's (1974, 43) observation that the interpretations of this phrase tend to fall in two categories: "In the one the phrase is regarded as *a statement about the opportune mo-ment for Jesus to intervene* in the situation reported to him by his mother...while in the other it is *a statement about the "hour" of Jesus*, a technical expression in John, referring to the completion of Jesus' mission on earth, i.e. his death and glorification."

guments of Brown[74] and Olsson[75] for alternative 2, I cannot follow them when alternative 1 is said to be refuted (Brown) and ἡ ὥρα μου is said to be "understood primarily about the 'hour' of Jesus in the special Johannine sense" (Olsson). As I have already indicated under 2.1 above, οὔπω ἥκει ἡ ὥρα μου also has the function of emphasizing or qualifying the first half of the statement. I have already argued that τί ἐμοὶ καὶ σοί, γύναι; has a meaning which, rather than estranging Mary, relieves her of her burden of concerns.[76] It only follows as a natural consequence of this that οὔπω ἥκει ἡ ὥρα μου first and foremost has the function of expressing Jesus' affirmation to Mary that he is ready to act *when time is due*. And, with regard to Jesus' terms of reference for *when his final hour would be*, this is of course determined by the plan and will of his Father.[77] In a literary critical approach, one must pay due attention not only to the plot of the story of John, but also to each of the individual events or actions on which the plot rests.[78] It seems therefore only fair that, when regarding the plot of the story in John 2:1-11 in light of the preceding observations regarding τί ἐμοὶ καὶ σοί, γύναι;, it can only be justified that alternatives 1 and 2 are *both* given due attention in exegesis *as well as* in translation.

## 6. Conclusion

6.1 This essay started out with a question. Is John 2:4 an unnecessary stumbling block for filial piety in a Chinese cultural context? Our survey has led to the conclusion that the question may be answered in the affirmative. The statement in John 2:4 must be read in the total context of verses 2-11 and translated accordingly. In so doing it has become evident that none of the three problems caused by the translation of John 2:4 and listed in part two above are inherent in the originals. They are therefore also not of a countercultural nature. Rather, they are likely to occur if one uses formal correspondence translation instead of looking for functional equivalents. This means that the translation of John 2:4 into Chinese need not stand as an example of the unfilial nature of Christianity—or of Jesus himself. Rather, what may still turn out to be a possible stumbling block to non-Christian Chinese readers of John 2:1-11 is the miracle—or sign—which Jesus is told to have performed. But

---

[74] Brown 1966, 100 and 518.

[75] Olsson 1974, 45.

[76] This is well expressed in the Weymouth (1905) translation, cited by Buck (1956, 149).

[77] Haenchen 1984, 173.

[78] For a literary approach to the gospel genre, *in casu* to Matthew, see Kingsbury 1986, 1-40. In chapter four he deals with Jesus' journey to Jerusalem (pp. 78-94) and shows how Matthew secures the cohesion of events through two literary devices, one being the journey of Jesus, the other his passion prediction.

then it is belief or non-belief in Jesus' ability to perform miracles which is in focus and not the supposed unfilial behaviour of Jesus. As such the former stumbling block is of a countercultural or transcultural nature wherever people do not share the presuppositions of Christian faith. The latter need not represent a stumbling block, as far as exegesis and translation are concerned. Hence, when translating John 2:4 into Chinese hereafter (and for that sake into any language) one should therefore aim at some degree of functional equivalent translation along the following guidelines:

6.2 With regard to the translation of γύναι, two alternatives seem possible. Either: avoid the direct address and use instead simple statement which replaces or supplies γύναι with a polite word such as *"please"* (or even a polite expression). Or: use a functional equivalent translation of γύναι such as "mother" / "mum". In either case one should take care to let the translation reflect naturally the entire communication event and to indicate that it is a natural and polite address in a public place. This is also the case *if* one chooses a more formal rendering of γύναι, such as the one suggested by Buck.[79] Also, in either case a translator's note may be provided, giving the formal correspondence translation of γύναι.

6.3 When rendering the entire statement, the following seems to catch best the gist of the originals in its present context: *"Please (, mother,) leave it to me. The time for me to act has not yet come (is not yet here)."* The translators must, as far as possible, secure that the expression οὔπω ἥκει ἡ ὥρα μου is rendered in such a way that neither the imminent nor the less imminent future aspect are precluded as terms of reference. A translator's note may also be provided here, giving the formal correspondence translation of ἡ ὥρα μου. This note may also include references to other verses in John where the expression ἡ ὥρα μου occurs.[80]

## *Bibliography*

### I. ANCIENT TEXTS

Epictetus, *Dissertationes ab Arriano Digestae*, ed. H. Schenkl, *Epicteti dissertationes ab Arriano digestae*, Leipzig: Teubner 1916 (repr. Stuttgart: Teubner 1965).

Josephus, Flavius *Antiquitates Judaicae*, ed. B. Niese, *Flavii Iosephii opera*, vols. 1-4. Berlin: Weidmann 1885-1892 (repr. 1955).

---

[79] Buck (1956, 150) suggests "And Jesus said, 'Madam, why is that our concern?'".
[80] Cf. part five above and Brown 1966, 517f.

Sophocles, *Oedipus tyrannus*, ed. A. Dain and P. Mazon, *Sophocle*, vol. 2, Paris: Les Belles Lettre 1958; repr. 1968 (1st edn. rev.), 72-108.

## II. VERSIONS

*The Chinese Union Version of the Bible* (*Xin Jiu Yue Quan Shu: Guanhua hehe yiben*), Shanghai: British & Foreign Bible Society 1919.

*The Studium Biblicum Sinense Chinese Bible Version* (Sigau Shengjing Xuehui fanyi, *Shengjing*), Hong Kong: Sigau Shengjing Xuehui 1968.

*Today's Chinese Version of the New Testament* (*Xinyue quanshu, xiandai zhongwen yiben*), Hong Kong: Hong Kong Bible Society 1975.

*The New Chinese Bible Commission Version*, (*Xin Yue Quan Shu, Xin Yi Ben*), Hong Kong: The Lockman Foundation 1976.

*Jin Luxian's Chinese Version of the New Testament*, Part 1, The Four Gospels (*Hsinjing, Xiang, Si Fuyin*), Shanghai: Tianjujiao Shanghai Fiao Chuyin 1986.

*The Jerusalem Bible*, Garden City, NY: Doubleday 1966.

*The Holy Bible...Revised Standard Version*, New York: Division of Christian Education of the National Council of Churches of Christ in the United States of America, 2nd ed. 1971.

*The New Testament in Today's English Version,* New York: American Bible Society 1966.

Phillips, J. B., *The New Testament in Modern English*, Dorset: Collins, 2nd ed. 1972.

## III. PERIODICALS

*The Bible Translator*

## IV. BOOKS AND ARTICLES

Aland, Kurt and Aland, Barbara 1987: *The Text of the New Testament*, Grand Rapids, MI: Eerdmans and Leiden: Brill 1987.

Barrett, Charles Kingsley 1955: *The Gospel According to St. John*, London: S.P.C.K. 1955.

Beasley-Murray, George R. 1987: *John* (Word Biblical Commentary 36), Waco, TX: Word Books Publisher 1987.

Bratcher, Robert G. 1981: *A Translator's Guide to The Gospel of Matthew* (Helps For Translators), London, New York, Stuttgart: United Bible Societies 1981.

Brown, Raymond E. 1966: *The Gospel According to John, I-XII* (AncB 29), New York: Doubleday 1966.

Buck, Harry M. 1956: "On the Translation of John 2:4", in: *BiTr* 7 (1956)149-50.

— 1972: "Redactions of the Fourth Gospel and the Mother of Jesus", in: David Edward Aune (ed.), *Studies in New Testament and Early Christian Literature*. Essays in honour of Allen P. Wikgren (NT.S 33), Leiden: Brill 1972, 170-80.

Chao Yuen Ren 1956: "Chinese terms of address", in: *Language* 32 (1956) 217-41.

Dillon, R. J. 1962: "Wisdom Tradition and Sacramental Retrospect in the Cana Account (Jn 2,1-11)", in: *CBQ* 24 (1962) 268-96.

Goodspeed, Edgar J. 1952: "Problems of New Testament Translation", in: *BiTr* 3 (1952) 68-71.

Haenchen, Ernst 1984: *John 1* (Hermeneia), Philadelphia, PA: Fortress 1984.

Hope, E. R. 1988: "Pragmatics, Exegesis and Translation", in: Stine, Philip C. (ed.) 1988, 113-28.

Horstmann, A. 1983: "τίς, τί", in: Balz, Horst/ Schneider, Gerhard (eds.), *EWNT* III, Stuttgart etc.: Kohlhammer 1983, 863-66.

Kieffer, René 1987: *Johannesevangeliet 1-10* (Kommentar till Nya Testamentet 4A), Uppsala: EFS-förlaget 1987.

Kingsbury, Jack Dean 1986: *Matthew as Story*, Philadelphia, PA: Fortress Press 1986.

Louw, Johannes P. and Nida, Eugene A. 1989: *Greek-English Lexicon of the New Testament Based on Semantic Domains*, 2 Vols., 2nd ed., New York: United Bible Societies 1989.

Marsh, John 1968: *The Gospel of St. John* (PNTC), Harmondsworth: Penguin 1968.

Maynard, A. H. 1985: "ΤΙ ΕΜΟΙ ΚΑΙ ΣΟΙ", in: *NTS* 31 (1985) 582-86.

Metzger, Bruce M. 1971: *A Textual Commentary on the Greek New Testament*, London and New York: United Bible Societies 1971.

Morris, Leon 1971: *The Gospel according to John*, Grand Rapids, MI: Eerdmans 1971.

Newman, Barclay M. 1971: *A Concise Greek-English Dictionary of the New Testament*, Stuttgart: United Bible Societies 1971.

Newman, Barclay M. and Nida, Eugene A. 1980: *A Translator's Handbook on the Gospel of John* (Helps For Translators), London, New York: United Bible Societies 1980.

Nida, Eugene A. 1980: see: Newman, Barclay M and Nida, Eugene A. 1980.

Nida, Eugene A. and Reyburn, William D. 1981: *Meaning Across Cultures* (American Society of Missiology Series 4), New York: Orbis Books 1981.

Nida, Eugene A. 1986: see: de Waard, Jan and Nida, Eugene A. 1986.

— 1989: see: Louw, Johannes P. and Nida, Eugene A. 1989.

Nkwoka, A.O. 1991: "Jesus as eldest brother, (Okpara): An Igbo Paradigm for Christology in the African Context", in: *AJTh* 5 (1991) 87-103.

Olsson, Birger 1974: *Structure and Meaning in the Fourth Gospel*. A Text-Linguistic Analysis of John 2:1-11 and 4:1-42 (CB.NT 6), Lund: Gleerup 1974.

Reyburn, William D. 1981: see: Nida, Eugene A. and Reyburn, William D. 1981.

Schnackenburg, Rudolf 1951: *Das erste Wunder Jesu*, Freiburg i. Br.: Herder 1951.

— 1967: *Das Johannesevangelium I. Teil* (HThK IV:1), 2nd ed., Freiburg i. Br.: Herder 1967.

Shorter, Aylward 1973: *African Culture and the Christian Church*, London: Geoffrey Chapman 1973.

Smitmans, Adolf 1966: *Das Weinwunder von Kana*. Die Auslegung von Jo 2,1-11 bei den Vätern und heute (BGBE 6), Tübingen: Mohr (Siebeck) 1966.

Stine, Philip C. (ed.) 1988: *Issues in Bible Translation* (UBS.MS 3), London, New York, Stuttgart: United Bible Societies 1988.

Stott, John and Coote, Robert (eds.) 1979: *Gospel and Culture*, South Pasadena, CA: William Carey Library 1979.

Taber, Charles 1979: "Hermeneutics and Culture: An Anthropological Perspective", in: Stott, John and Coote, Robert (eds.) 1979, 109-131.

de Waard, Jan and Nida, Eugene A. 1986: *From One Language to Another*, Nashville, Camden, New York: Thomas Nelson 1986.

Wendland, Ernst R. 1986: *Language, Society, and Bible Translation,* Cape Town: Bible Society of South Africa 1986.

— 1987: *The Cultural Factor in Bible Translation* (UBS.MS 2), London, New York, Stuttgart: United Bible Societies 1987.

Yu Chi-Ping 1984: *Confucian and Biblical Concepts of Filial Piety: Implications for Pastoral Care in the Chinese Church in Taiwan* (Th.D. Dissertation, Boston University, School of Theology), Boston 1984.

# Römer 13, 'Obrigkeit' und 'Kirche im Sozialismus'

## Wolfgang Schenk

Der evangelische Landesbischof von Berlin-Brandenburg, Otto Dibelius, fragte 1959 im Blick auf Röm 13,1 und Luthers Übersetzung der 'übergeordneten Mächte' (ἐξουσίαις ὑπερεχούσαις) mit 'Obrigkeit' (im Singular!):

> Das ist die Frage, ob dies Wort dasjenige wirklich wiedergibt, was Paulus gemeint hat, oder ob es gar den Bibelleser zu einem falschen Verständnis einer wichtigen biblischen Weisung verführt? ... 'Obrigkeit' oder 'Oberkeit', 'Oeberkeit' oder 'Ubirkeit' sagt Martin Luther! Das ist er, der Reformator, wie er leibt und lebt! Die Engländer sagen, nüchtern wie immer: 'higher powers', die Franzosen sagen ähnlich: 'puissances superieures'. Luther aber sagt 'Obrigkeit'. Man bemerke den Singular! Von ihm haben es die Skandinavier übernommen. In der schwedischen Bibel [1917; ähnlich die neue Übersetzung von 1981] steht: 'Var och en vare underdånig den överhet som han har över sig' ... Obrigkeit – das ist ein schönes Wort. In dem Wort ist Seele und Gemüt. Es ist etwas von väterlicher Autorität darin – wie denn auch Martin Luther nicht müde geworden ist, die Parallele zu ziehen zwischen der väterlichen Autorität und der Obrigkeit ... 'Wilhelm von Gottes Gnaden, König von Preußen, Kurfürst von Brandenburg' – das ist Obrigkeit![1]

---

[1] Dibelius 1960, 25 (nach dem Privatdruck 1959). Diese Funktionalisierung der Vokabel im Singular zu einem Wertbegriff ist auszuschließen, wie schon die früheste Alternative in der Reformationszeit zeigt. "Daß der Staat von Gott eingesetzt ist, bedeutet für Zwingli und Calvin nicht einfach Sanktionierung jedweden Regiments und seiner Verfügungen ... Daß er von Gott eingesetzt ist, heißt vielmehr, daß er zu einer spezifischen Funktion eingesetzt ist. Bei Calvin kommt das schon sprachlich zum Ausdruck, indem er das Regiment nicht 'Obrigkeit', sondern 'Administration' nennt. Die Staatslehre Calvins in *Institutio* IV/20 ist betitelt *De politica administratione*', 'von der politischen Zudienung'; die Regierung bezeichnet er als 'Magistrat'. Es ist interessant, daß das deutsche Wort 'Obrigkeit' im Französischen und Englischen kein Äquivalent hat" (Busch 1992, 167 n. 37; vgl. n. 36: "Dienerin *Gottes* heißt für Zwingli, daß sie '*für etwas*' zu dienen hat: für ein Zusammenleben in Frieden und Gerechtigkeit" und für Calvin "*zu einem Zwecke* von Gott eingesetzt, nämlich zur Sorge für Gemeinwohl und Frieden [*Inst.* IV/20,10]; und entsprechend bedeutet das 'Untergeordnetsein' der Bürger unter den Magistrat, 'von seiner *Funktion* ehrerbietig denken' [*Inst.* IV/20,22])". Dieser Aspekt kommt in den neueren Kommentaren am stärksten bei Cranfield 1979, 651-73 zum Tragen (und monographisch bei Duchrow 1970, 137-80).

## 1. Die Christenheit im Deutschland des 'Dritten Reiches'

Thomas Mann hat als vom deutschen Staat bedingter, unfreiwilliger Gast im amerikanischen Exil am 29. 5.1945 seinen Gastgebern die berühmte Rede 'Deutschland und die Deutschen' gehalten[2]. Bei diesem Versuch seiner Analyse der politischen Gegenwart Deutschlands sieht er sowohl Luther als auch Röm 13 für maßgebend an[3]:

---

[2] Zur Entstehung vgl. die wiederholten Äußerungen in seinen Briefen seit Beginn jenes Jahres: Mann 1963, 439-60.

[3] Mann 1948, 19-20. Dabei fällt nicht nur auf, daß er Röm 13,1 (aus assoziativer Erinnerung zitierend) verstärkend in die direkte Anrede des Singular versetzt hat (bei Paulus erst und nur rhetorisch im Diatribe-Stil V.3b-4b), sondern auch, daß er für die Differenz zwischen Paulus und Luther ein psychologisches Motiv bei Paulus aus seiner Situation heraus als maßgebend veranschlagt. Doch diese "psychologisierende Vermutung, Röm 13,1-7 weise auf die positiven Erfahrungen hin, die Paulus mit dem römischen Staat gemacht habe (z.B. Spitta 1901, 91ff.; Weiß 1917, 461; Bauer 1967, 265f.), ist nicht nur in sich fragwürdig (vgl. nur 2 Kor 11,25f.), sondern könnte angesichts eines so traditionellen Textes, wie er in V. 1-7 vorliegt, nicht einmal für die paulinische Autorschaft dieses Abschnittes geschweige denn für die Integrität des Römerbriefes geltend gemacht werden" (Schmithals 1988, 460).

Dagegen ist dieser Auslegungsansatz im Anschluß an W. Bauer (und wesentlich von dessen Nachweis der positiven Rezeption bei frühchristlichen Apologeten im Kontrast zur auffallenden Nichtrezeption in Märtyrertexten her) nochmals repristiniert worden von R. Heiligenthal (1983, 60): "In einer spezifisch historisch-soziologischen Situation (missionierende Minderheitenkirche)" ist "nüchterne Einsicht in das Gegebene" gefordert: "Paulus richtet diese Mahnung an einer Ethik der Alltäglichkeit aus, an der Einsicht, daß das Überleben einer Minorität nur durch die Konformität gegenüber übermächtigen äußeren Machtstrukturen garantierbar bleibt" (ebd.58). Belege für die Anwendbarkeit dieses Modells für den konkret vorliegenden Fall werden nicht erbracht, da die Rezeptionen eines Textes keinesfalls als solche schon den gleichen semantischen Gehalt und die gleiche pragmatische Funktion garantieren. Nicht minder fatal ist die Vermutung einer aktuellen Situation einer neronischen Steuerverschärfung (die aber Tac. Ann. 13,50-51 später liegt!), die Friedrich *et al.* zu der Motivationsspekulation verleitete: "Es ist ratsam, die Steuerbelastung durchzustehen, weil Widerstand oder Steuerverweigerung die Gemeinde in ihrer Existenz bedrohen würde" (1976, 156-65. 165); das wird schon durch die indikativisch begründende Aussage Röm 13,6a ausgeschlossen, die darauf rekurriert, daß die römischen Christen (sehr im Unterschied zu außenstehenden Dritten, die V. 2 anvisiert waren) ja unbestritten Abgabenzahler sind (V. 6a wird dabei [entgegen seinem γάρ wie καί] zu Unrecht wie von Zahn und Schmithals z.St. als Imperativ aufgelöst, einem Vorgang, dem Stuhlmacher 1989, 178. 182 nicht mehr folgt, wiewohl er ebd. 175. 179-80. 181-2 die damalige Prämisse von der verschärften aktuellen Steuersituation weiter beibehält; dgg. Riekkinen 1980, 155; Wilckens 1982, 34. 40; Schottroff 1984, 20; Wengst 1986, 103f.; Schrage 1989, 244f.). Noch weniger trägt die Spekulation situationsgebundener Konformität, die mit der geplanten Spanienreise des Paulus motiviert wird: "Auseinandersetzungen mit der 'Obrigkeit' konnten sein Vorhaben nur verzögern, so ist ihm die unbedingte Gehorsamsforderung ein Gebot der Stunde" (so Riekkinen 1980, 219; dgg. m.R. Wengst 1986, 219 n. 77).

Das spezifisch und monumental Deutsche … stellt Luther dar, der musikalische Theolog. Er brachte es im Politischen nicht weiter, als daß er beiden Parteien, den Fürsten und den Bauern, unrecht gab, was nicht verfehlen konnte, ihn bald dahin zu führen, daß er nur noch und bis zur berserkerhaften Wut den Bauern unrecht gab. Seine Innerlichkeit hielt es ganz mit dem Paulinischen 'Sei untertan der Obrigkeit, die Gewalt über dich hat!' Aber das hatte sich ja auf die Autorität des römischen Weltreiches bezogen, das die Voraussetzung und der politische Raum war für die christliche Weltreligion, während es sich im Falle Luthers um die reaktionäre Winkelautorität der deutschen Fürsten handelte. Seine antipolitische Devotion, dies Produkt musikalischer deutscher Innerlichkeit und Unweltlichkeit, hat nicht nur für die Jahrhunderte die unterwürfige Haltung der Deutschen vor den Fürsten und aller staatlichen Obrigkeit geprägt; sie hat nicht nur den deutschen Dualismus von kühnster Spekulation und politischer Unmündigkeit teils begünstigt und teils geschaffen. Sie ist vor allem repräsentativ auf eine monumentale und trotzige Weise für das kerndeutsche Auseinanderfallen von nationalem Impuls und dem Ideal der politischen Freiheit[4].

Auch in der 'Evangelischen Kirche in Deutschland' ist das Problem im 'Dritten Reich' (und zwar schon am Anfang) verschärft gesehen und schon in der 5. These der 'Theologischen Erklärung der Bekenntnissynode von Barmen' (30.5.1934) formuliert worden[5]. Die neueren Kommentare zum Römerbrief erinnern daran. So schließt P. Stuhlmacher seine Erklärung des Abschnitts damit hermeneutisch ab[6]:

Wie Kirche und Staat nach moderner politischer Erfahrung aufeinander zu beziehen sind, lehrt deutlich noch die (5. These der vor allem von Karl Barth entworfenen) 'Theologische(n) Erklärung' von Barmen … Sie nimmt Röm 13,1-7 und 1Petr 2,13-17 direkt auf und lehrt:
  'Die Schrift sagt uns, daß der Staat nach göttlicher Anordnung die Aufgabe hat, in der noch nicht erlösten Welt, in der auch die Kirche steht, nach dem Maß menschlicher Einsicht und menschlichen Vermögens unter Androhung und Ausübung von Gewalt für Recht und Frieden zu sorgen. Die Kirche erkennt in Dank und Ehrfurcht gegen Gott die Wohltat dieser seiner Anordnung an. Sie erinnert an Gottes Reich, an Gottes Gebot und Gerechtigkeit und damit an die Verantwortung der Regierenden und Regierten. Sie vertraut und gehorcht der Kraft der Wortes, durch das Gott alle Dinge trägt ….'
  In dieser These ist die Quintessenz von Luthers Zwei-Regimente-Lehre berücksichtigt. Dies und die Nähe zu den genannten biblischen Texten läßt es theologisch ratsam erscheinen, sich in der Frage nach dem Verhalten der Christen gegenüber den (und in den) staatlichen Autoritäten heute vor allem an Barmen V zu orientieren.

Die sympathisch erscheinende Harmonisierung mit Röm 13, die Stuhlmacher hier vornimmt, mag nach seiner Auslegung exegetisch als berechtigt erscheinen. Historisch aber bleibt festzustellen, daß Röm 13 in 'Barmen' gerade nicht 'direkt aufgenommen' worden war:

Zu den Besonderheiten der 5. These gehört nicht nur die Tatsache, daß sich hier zwei

---

[4] Zur Rezeption Luthers vgl. zusammenfassend Wilckens 1982, 49-52 (und ebd. 57-64 zur Kontinuität im deutschen Luthertum). Mit dem Verweis auf die "Innerlichkeit" kommt bei T. Mann zur Geltung, daß Luthers Unterscheidung von 'zwei Reichen/Regimenten' wesentlich auf der fragwürdigen Anthropologie Augustins beruht, der zwischen Seele (*anima*, deren Heimat im Himmel ist) und Fleisch (*caro*) entsprechend differenzierte: "Der Staat hat seine Gewalt nur in diesem, keineswegs in jenem Bereich. Über die Seele verfügt der Staat nicht" (ebd. 46f.). Das führt "zum Grundgedanken der Sozialethik" Luthers, daß der Christ, der als solche 'Seele' "ein freier Herr über alle Dinge und niemanden untertan" sei, in der Liebe (als 'Fleisch') zu einem "dienstbaren Knecht aller Dinge und jedermann untertan" werde (*Von der Freiheit eines Christenmenschen*, 1520). So erstreckt sich das 'weltliche Regiment' nur "über Leib und Gut, und was äußerlich ist auf Erden. Denn über die Seele kann und will Gott niemanden regieren lassen denn sich selbst allein" (*Von weltlicher Obrigkeit, wie weit man ihr Gehorsam schuldig sei*, 1523; vgl. Wilckens 1982, 50). Von daher gesehen erscheint ihm dann der Fehler der revoltierenden Bauern darin zu bestehen, daß sie "alle Menschen gleich machen und aus dem geistlichen Reich Christi ein weltlich äußerlich Reich machen, welches unmöglich ist" (*Ermahnung zum Frieden auf die zwölf Artikel der Bauernschaft in Schwaben*, 1525). Genau dagegen richte sich die Gehorsamsforderung in Röm 13, die ohne jede Einschränkung den Christen gelte: "denn (!) die Taufe macht nicht Leib und Gut frei, sondern die Seelen" (ebd.; vgl. Wilckens 1982, 51). Zu diesem augustinisch konstruierten Modell, das anthropologisch ansetzt, hat sich allerdings schon in der Reformationszeit eine Alternative gefunden: "Luther konnte das Problem des Gehorsams gegenüber Gott und den Regenten im Sinne einer paradoxen Identität lösen, so daß etwa jemand im selben Akt (äußerlich) Henker sein und (innerlich) die Bergpredigt üben kann" (vgl. seine Schrift von 1523). "Die reformierten Väter lösten das Problem eher im Sinne einer Rangfolge, so daß die Christen immer zuerst Gott und nur sekundär irdischen Instanzen zu gehorchen haben. Der berühmte Satz, daß 'man Gott mehr als den Menschen zu gehorchen hat', bezeichnet nicht bloß eine *ultima ratio* im extremen Konfliktfall, sondern eine Grundregel christlicher Existenz (Calvin, *Inst.* IV/20,32 … als eine Zusammenfassung seiner Staatslehre und als Überleitung zum betonten Schlußsatz: 'Ehre sei Gott!')" (Busch 1992, 165). Damit wird dem präzisen Sinn von θεοῦ διαταγή als 'Anordnung' (Röm 13,2 = V. 1 ὑπὸ θεοῦ τεταγμέναι ['eingerichtet': Käsemann 1973, 337] = V. 4a.d θεοῦ διάκονος ['Werkzeug': Delling 1962, 58 n. 132; 1969, 38 n. 5]) besser Rechnung getragen, während die Fehlbestimmung als 'Ordnung' (als stünde das Resultandum διάταγμα da; Cranfield 1979, 663 n. 4) eine der exegetisch unhaltbaren Grundlagen einer staatsmetaphysischen Auswertung des Textes darstellt (Heiligenthal 1983, 60 n. 3). Schon die sekundäre Lesart (typischerweise in den griechisch-lateinischen [und so die Staatskirche im Ost- wie Westreich ansprechenden] Bilinguen D* F G - ferner 629 945 pc), die V.1c ἀπό statt ὑπό bietet, verschiebt den Gedanken auf einen direkten "göttlichen Ursprung irdischer Herrschaft" hin (Wilckens 1982, 33 n. 152; vgl. Schlier 1977, 388: Damit ersetzt wieder der heidnische Gedanke der "Herkunft" den der "Einsetzung", an dem Paulus liegt: "Die ἐξουσία, die Anordnungen erläßt, ist selbst eine 'Anordnung', eine 'Verfügung' Gottes"). Ein von dieser Lesart aus konstruierter Urtext ist darum (neben der fehlenden Rezeption im 2. Jahrhundert) ein wesentlicher Grund für die Behauptung "des nichtpaulinischen Ursprung(s) der absoluten Obrigkeitsbejahung in Röm 13,1-7" (Barnikol 1961, vgl. dgg. Michel 1966, 322-23; Käsemann 1973, 339; für unpaulinisch halten den Text auch: Pallis 1920, 14; Kallas 1965; O'Neill 1975, 207-10 ['absolute obedience']; Munro 1983, 18. 140; 1990, 434f. 437 Simonis 1989; und am umfassendsten Schmithals 1975, 185-87. 191-97; 1988, 456-76 (drei Schichten: Profaner Basistext V.1a. 3b. 4b, hellenistisch-jüdische Theologisierung V. 1b-2. 4a.c-5, christliche Redaktion V. 6-7).

Verwerfungen anschließen, und daß nur diese These mit der Formulierung beginnt: 'Die Schrift sagt uns...', sondern, daß ihr ein im Zusammenhang dieses Problems nicht gerade bekanntes biblisches Zitat vorangestellt wird. Man erwartet Röm 13, die klassische Stelle über das Verhältnis von Kirche und Staat. Statt dessen hören wir die kurze Formulierung aus 1 Petr 'Fürchtet Gott, ehret den König'. Es ist eine Bibelstelle, die aus einer sogenannten Haustafel des NTs mit noch weiteren Ermahnungen stammt. Schon das mag ein Hinweis darauf sein, daß das Problem des Verhältnisses von Kirche und Staat ein relatives Problem ist. Es ist nicht die Mitte des Glaubens; von seiner Lösung hängt die Existenz der Kirche nicht ab. Die Christen sollen Gott fürchten und den König ehren, die Brüder lieben und ein rechtschaffenes Leben unter den Heiden führen und mit guten Taten den unwissenden und törichten Menschen das Maul stopfen. Daß man diesen größeren Zusammenhang beachtet, ist eine Hilfe für jede nüchterne und klare Rede, die dann in der Formulierung der These folgt. Die 5. These, selbst nicht die Mitte der 'Barmer Theologischen Erklärung', argumentiert von den Grenzen des Staates, nicht von seinem Wesen her.

Die klare Rede ist darum besonders eindrücklich, weil sie nicht nur gegen eine grassierende Mystifizierung des Staates redet, die damals im Schwange war, sondern weil die evangelische Kirche und die evangelische Theologie sich damit von einer Geschichte trennte, in der bis dahin das Thema 'Staat' unter dem Oberthema 'Schöpfung' abgehandelt worden war. In 'Barmen' wird der Staat unter dem Oberthema 'Kirche' abgehandelt, nachdem diese Kirche zuvor ihre Existenz von Christus her bestimmt hat. Das war neu. Gegen ihre eigene Vergangenheit und gegen die düster qualmige politische Gegenwart, in der eine Partei den Staat für sich okkupierte, stellt diese These dann dem Staat klare Aufgaben vor: er soll für Recht und Frieden sorgen. Für diese Anordnung Gottes ist die Kirche dankbar. Sie erinnert an Gottes Reich.

Zwei Dinge sind vermieden: Einmal ist damit jeder billigen oder teuren Anpassung an die Verhältnisse ein Riegel vorgeschoben. So klar und deutlich wird gesagt, was der Staat tut und was die Kirche tut. Klar und deutlich wird so unterschieden, daß Anpassung nicht mehr stattfinden kann, es sei denn um den Preis des eigenen Selbstverständnisses. Zum anderen: Vermieden ist es, daß die Kirche die Gegenwelt macht oder wird, die Nische, in die man flüchten kann, wohin Politik nicht reicht. Vermieden ist es, daß die Kirche sich selbst aus 'der noch nicht erlösten Welt, in der

---

[5] Vgl. grundlegend historisch und sachlich Wolf 1957/70/84; zur Entstehungsgeschichte im einzelnen Nicolaisen 1985.

[6] Stuhlmacher 1989, 185; vgl. Schmithals 1988, 470: "Auch der Christ hat 'nach dem Maß menschlicher Einsicht und menschlichen Vermögens unter Androhung und Ausübung von Gewalt für Recht und Frieden zu sorgen' (5. Barmer These). Etwas distanzierter ist die Rezeption von 'Barmen' bei Wilckens 1982, 63: "Zwar wird in der 5. These der Barmer Bekenntnissynode 1934 eine klare Absage an den NS-Staat ausgesprochen, womit zugleich 'alle Theoreme neuprotestantischer Staatsideologie' als theologisch illegitim erklärt wurden [E. Wolf 1957/70/84, 877]. Aber eine Staatslehre als Alternative, in der sowohl das kritische Gegenüber zum Staat wie auch die Pflicht zu verantwortlicher Teilnahme anders und neu begründet wurde, stand nicht zur Verfügung. Das im Horizont reformierter Tradition von K. Barth entworfene Modell 'Christengemeinde und Bürgergemeinde' [K. Barth 1970, 20] war von den Lutheranern schwerlich übernehmbar. Aber einer ungebrochenen Übernahme der traditionell lutherischen Auswertung von Röm 13 stellten sich die Erfahrungen mit dem NS-Staat entgegen".

auch die Kirche steht', entfernt. Aber auch das in unseren Tagen aufgekommene Wort von der 'Partnerschaft' zwischen Kirche und Staat, das so gern gebraucht wird, wird der Bestimmung von 'Barmen' nicht gerecht[7].

## 2. Die Christenheit im Deutschland der 'Diktatur des Proletariats'

Unter der neuen Herausforderung einer spezifischen Situation der Christenheit in der 1949 gegründeten 'Deutschen Demokratischen Republik' (DDR) hat die Synode der 'Evangelischen Kirche der Union' (EKU) im Dezember 1957 'Ein Wort der Hilfe, wie wir Christen uns zu unserem Staat verhalten sollen', beschlossen:

> Viele Christen wissen heute nicht, wie sie sich als Menschen, die Gott gehorchen wollen, dem Staat der DDR gegenüber verhalten sollen. Der seelische Druck, unter dem sie stehen, bringt sie in Gefahr, in ihrem Glauben schwankend zu werden oder auch mit Haß zu antworten. Beides wäre ungehorsam gegen unseren Herrn, der uns in den Dienst seiner Liebe genommen hat".

Im direkten Anschluß an und unter Berufung auf Barmen V wird hier so beraten, indem nun auch Röm 13 (in Luthers Übersetzung) selbst unmittelbarer aufgenommen ist[8]:

> Die Heilige Schrift sagt uns: 'Es ist keine Obrigkeit ohne von Gott; wo aber Obrigkeit ist, die ist von Gott verordnet' (Röm 13,1-2). Dieses Wort läßt keine Ausnahme zu. Nicht die Staatsform, nicht die Art, wie der Staat entstanden ist, nicht einmal, wie er sich selbst versteht – ob er Gottes Willen anerkennt oder nicht –, ist der Grund dafür, wie wir Christen zu ihm stehen. Sondern Gottes Wort befiehlt uns, den Staat in seinem Auftrag als ein Werkzeug Gottes ernst zu nehmen. Gottes Wort befiehlt uns darum auch, vom Staat trotz aller Enttäuschungen immer wieder Handlungen zu erwarten, in denen wir Christen Gottes bewahrende Güte erkennen können … Ein Christ ist aus der Verantwortung für seinen Staat niemals entlassen. Er nimmt sie

---

[7] Hüffmeier 1986, 15-16 vgl. 50-51. Symptomatisch ist die Episode der Versammlung der lutherischen Synodalen am Vortage in Barmen, wo der Münchener Oberkirchenrat Breit den Wünschen der Lutherischen Landeskirche Bayerns entsprechend eine Modifikation versuchte: "So fügte er in These V das Schriftwort Röm 13,1b ein: 'Es ist keine Obrigkeit ohne von Gott; wo aber Obrigkeit ist, die ist von Gott verordnet'. In altlutherischer Weise redet er dann vom Schwertamt des Staates und vom Gehorsam der Kirche 'gegen die heilsam äußeren Ordnungen in Volk und Staat'. Ein Hauptinteresse der zeitgenössischen neulutherischen Theologie: die Nennung der 'Ordnung des Volkes und Staates', war damit berücksichtigt. Das Staatsverständnis der These V … erlitt eine grundlegende Änderung. Der Staat erschien nun in seiner *Gegebenheit* als Geschenk Gottes, nicht als eine Sache, welche Menschen im Gehorsam gegenüber Gottes Anordnung selbst zu finden und zu gestalten haben" (ebd. 39). Kennzeichnend für eine staatsmetaphysische Verwendung von Röm 13 ist außer den Fehlübersetzungen im einzelnen auch "die an der Textintention vorbeigehende Verlagerung des Aussageschwerpunktes auf die begründenden Verse 1b-3a" (Heiligenthal 1983 60 n. 3), die dann gewöhnlich verkürzt allein zitiert werden und an den Funktionsbestimmungen V.3b-4 vorübergehen.

auch dann wahr, wenn er im Gehorsam gegen Gottes Wort Widerspruch anzumelden hat.

Damit ist die exegetische Einsicht durchgehalten[9]:

> Die Loyalitätsforderung begründet Paulus an dieser Stelle mit dem (jüdischer Theologie enstammenden) Hinweis darauf, daß alle 'Mächte und Herrschergewalten', alle 'Obrigkeit', wie Luther mit einem entsprechend weiten Begriff richtig übersetzt, also der ganze imperiale, provinziale, kommunale Behördenapparat des römischen Staatswesens von Gott angeordnet und (mag er darum wissen oder nicht) unter Gottes Auftrag steht.

Hinter dem Ausdruck ἐξουσία stehen vielleicht noch spezifischer die lateinischen Äquivalente *potestas/magistratus* als Beschreibungen der 'niederen Amtsgewalt' (im Unterschied zu *imperium* als der höheren Befehlsgewalt der Palast- und Regierungspolitik, die hier nicht im Blick ist)[10]. Man wird unter textpragmatischem Aspekt noch stärker veranschlagen müssen, daß die Briefadressaten von Röm 13 ja nur die angeschriebenen stadtrömischen Christen speziell sind, aber nicht Bewohner der Provinzen im ganzen oder im einzelnen. Man darf nicht sofort von der uni-

---

[8] Vgl. den Text bei Hüffmeier 1986, 107-8. Zusammen mit Barmen V ist diese Grundlegung dann auch wörtlich zitierend wieder aufgenommen in der bleibend wegweisenden 'Handreichung' der EKU-Synode 1959 'Das Evangelium und das christliche Leben in der DDR' (ebd. 110f.), wo sie präzisierend entfaltet ist unter den konkreten Aspekten: "(a) Unter einer Diktatur" (ebd. 111f.), "(b) Im sozialistischen Weltanschauungsstaat" (ebd. 113-17), "(c) Unter einer deutschen Teilregierung" (ebd. 117-19: "Wir wollen auch durch unsere Mitverantwortung und Mithilfe versuchen, der Aufrichtung des Rechtes, der Eindämmung der Willkür, der Wahrung der Menschenwürde und also der Konsolidierung unseres Staates hinsichtlich seines legitimen Auftrags zu dienen").

Diese Linie gegen einen resignierenden Untertanengehorsam (vgl. auch schon Barth 1958) und damit verbundenen Rechtsnihilismus wahren auch die im Auftrag der 'Konferenz der Evangelischen Kirchenleitungen in der DDR' am 8.3.1963 veröffentlichten 'Zehn Artikel über Freiheit und Dienst der Kirche' (Text ebd. 119-26; vgl. Wilkens 1964 und die Rezension von Barth 1963), sofern Artikel 4-6 'Rechtfertigung und Recht', 'Versöhnung und Friede', 'Die Arbeit' noch dem Artikel 7 'Obrigkeit' vorangestellt sind: "Gottes Gerechtigkeit gebietet, daß alles irdische Recht die Würde des von Gott geschaffenen und erlösten Menschen achtet und die Gleichheit aller vor dem Gesetz wahrt, daß es den Schutz der Schwachen sichert … Wir handeln im Ungehorsam, wenn wir es nur schweigend hinnehmen, daß das Recht um politischer oder wirtschaftlicher Interessen willen mißbraucht oder zerstört wird, und wenn wir nicht für unsere entrechteten und in ihrem Menschsein bedrohten Nächsten eintreten und mit ihnen leiden" (ebd. 122). Und dann: "Die Träger staatlicher Macht bleiben in der Hand Gottes und unter seinem Auftrag, auch wenn sie diesen verfehlen, sich zu Herren der Gewissen machen und in das Amt der Kirche eingreifen. In dieser Gewißheit haben wir der Obrigkeit die Wahrheit zu bezeugen, auch wenn wir dafür leiden müssen … Wir handeln im Ungehorsam, wenn wir für die Wahrheit nicht einstehen, zum Mißbrauch der Macht schweigen und nicht bereit sind, Gott mehr zu gehorchen als den Menschen" (ebd. 124). Es ist bezeichnend für unsere damalige Situation, daß alle diese Verlautbarungen in der DDR selbst nicht publiziert, sondern 'nur für innerkirchlichen Dienstgebrauch' beschränkt vervielfältigt werden konnten.

versaleren Adresse des 1 Petr her diese auch in Röm 13 eintragen; noch weniger ist
der dort ausdrücklich genannte Caesar (1 Petr 2,13ff. wie auch Mk 12,13ff.) und seine Statthalter von da aus nach Röm 13 einzutragen, wo diese Größen offenkundig
noch keine Rolle spielen und nicht im Blick sind[11]:

> Gegen das traditionell vorherrschende Interesse an unserem Text (wird hier) über-
> haupt nicht vom Staat als solchem oder vom römischen Imperium gesprochen. Die
> personale Redeweise ist nicht zufällig. Dem Apostel stehen, wie seine Terminologie
> anzeigt, die verschiedenen lokalen und regionalen Behörden, und zwar weniger als
> Institution, mehr in ihren Organen und Funktionen vom Steuereintreiber über die Po-
> lizei zu den Magistratsangestellten und römischen Beamten hin, vor Augen. Es han-
> delt sich um jenen Kreis von Machtträgern, mit denen der kleine Mann in Berührung
> kommen kann und hinter denen er die regionale und zentrale Verwaltung sieht.

Was Käsemann so primär senderorientiert formuliert hat, wird im konsequenten
Ernstnehmen der empfängerorientierten Beschränkung auf die stadtrömischen
Adressaten noch zu verstärken sein.

## 2.1. 'Obrigkeit' – als bleibendes Leitwort

Bischof Dibelius schloß seine Streitschrift von 1959 mit dem Vorschlag, das Wort
'Obrigkeit' aus den Übersetzungen von Röm 13 zu streichen und zu ersetzen; "etwa

---

[9] E. Wolf, in: Mochalski/Werner 1960, 89. Daß Röm 13 im wesentlichen die Terminologie der
hellenistisch-römischen Administration zugrunde liegt, hat (in Wiederaufnahme des Ansatzes von T.
Mommsen) grundlegend Strobel 1956; 1964 gezeigt. Eine weiterführende Ergänzung zu der grundlegenden komplementären Funktion von "Lob und Strafe durch die Obrigkeit" (als seit Xenophon
gängigem Ideal) lieferte van Unnik 1975. Winter 1988 belegte schließlich verstärkend, daß solche
öffentlichen Ehrungen nicht nur eine Sache persönlichen Beliebens oder der Sitte, sondern feste
Rechtspflicht waren, wenn Bürger (auch Christen, wie hier vorausgesetzt ist) sich für die Verbesse-
rung der Alltagslage ihrer Mitbürger eingesetzt hatten. Käsemann hat richtig gesehen, daß es hier um
"einen ohne jedes 'vielleicht' verheißenen ἔπαινος" geht (1973, 345 – aber nach Winter 1988 nicht
etwa um eine "reichlich verwegene", sondern um eine durchaus normale und realistische Erwartung). Die Wahrnehmung öffentlicher und sozialer Verantwortung und nicht sektiererische Abge-
schlossenheit ist also im Horizont von Röm 13 und 1 Petr 2 auch das Kennzeichen einer christlichen
Gemeinde in der Minderheit. Dazu bedarf es nicht einer staatlichen Privilegierung der Kirchen als
"Körperschaften öffentlichen Rechts" (wie sie seit der DDR-Verfassung 1968 nicht mehr gegeben
war; theologisch ist sie von Barmen V her ohnehin ausgeschlossen: "Wir verwerfen die falsche Lehre als solle und könne sich die Kirche über ihren besonderen Auftrag hinaus staatliche Art, staatliche
Aufgaben und staatliche Würde aneignen und damit selbst zu einem Organ des Staates werden").

[10] Strobel 1956, 75-9; vgl. Delling 1962, 63-4: "Vielleicht könnte sogar … das Wort ἐξουσία
nicht zufällig gebraucht sein (es hätte ja z.B. das Wort ἀρχή verwendet werden können, sei es etwa
im Wechsel: vgl. Lk 12,11; Tit 3,1). Das geschähe … deshalb, weil das Wort die Größe 'Regierung',
'Staat' nach der Seite der 'Vollmacht', der 'Autorität' (nicht zunächst nach der Seite der 'Gewalt')
zu kennzeichnen imstande ist. Dem wäre es durchaus gemäß, daß ἐξουσία dem lateinischen *potestas*
entspricht".

so: 'Jeder füge sich in die Ordnungen ein, die von der rechtmäßigen Gewalt gesetzt sind!' Oder: 'Rechtmäßige Gewalt soll bei jedermann Gehorsam finden!' Oder so ähnlich"[12]. Mit dieser Verquickung wurde er weder Paulus noch Luthers Übersetzung gerecht. Man mußte ihm widersprechen[13]:

> Der Staat ist kein Gottesgnadentum: Während für Luther und die lutherischen Bekenntnisschriften 'Obrigkeit' ein sehr weiter Begriff ist, unter den auch die städtischen Behörden fallen, formal ganz entsprechend der paulinischen Rede von 'Mächten und Herrschgewalten', versteht Dibelius unter 'Obrigkeit' in deutscher Sprache die patriarchalisch-personhafte Autorität, das Gottesgnadentum des monarchischen Herrschers.

Man spricht im deutschen Sprachraum inzwischen klassifizierend vom 'Obrigkeitsstaat' (und 'obrigkeitsstaatlich' als Adjektiv), um einen monarchischen oder diktatorischen Typ von Staat vom demokratischen Verfassungsstaat (mit Gewaltenteilung) abzuheben.

Daß es O.Dibelius (der aber diese Aspekte nicht hinreichend deutlich genug unterschied) dabei auch um die Grundsatzfrage der Legitimität des Staates ging, um seine Unterordnung unter ein unabhängiges Recht und um eine Kontrolle staatlicher Macht, wurde dabei von den Kirchen in der DDR wohl zu wenig gesehen, wie es im Nachhinein scheint[14]:

---

[11] Käsemann 1973, 341f. Der Ausdruck "bezeichnet in Röm 13 kein Abstraktum, weder 'die' Obrigkeit noch 'den' Staat" (Delling 1969, 29 mit Käsemann 1959, 324; vgl. auch Broer 1981, 28). Das Gegenteil behauptete gleichzeitig völlig zu Unrecht O. Dibelius: "Paulus denkt offenbar auch nur an einen eng begrenzten Kreis von Machthabern, nämlich an die, die berechtigt sind, das Schwert zu führen, direkt oder indirekt. Er denkt also nicht an das Heer von Beamten … Diese alle sind nicht persönlich Obrigkeit. Sie sind nicht einmal, als Personen betrachtet, 'überragende Mächte'".

Dabei läßt das ominöse 'Schwertamt' immer an das *ius gladii*, die Kapitaljuristiktion (die Todesstrafe, aber nicht Krieg einschloß) denken (so die Ausleger im allgemeinen). Doch Paulus redet nicht vom Richtschwert ῥομφαία, sondern vom Kurzschwert μάχαιρα. Außerdem war jene *ius-gladii*-Gerichtsbarkeit eine Angelegenheit des Kaisers über das Heer, die er auch Provinz-Statthaltern übertrug. Dagegen wird man angesichts der stadtrömischen Adressaten dies hier als irrtümliche Anwendung (Cranfield 1979, 666f.: "confusing"; vgl. zur Sache Sherwin-White 1963, 8-11) ausschließen müssen: "Das 'Schwert', von dem Paulus in V. 4 spricht, meint vom (Fach-)Ausdruck her nicht das Richtschwert, sondern die staatliche Straf- und Polizeigewalt. Die Polizeisoldaten, die die römischen Steuereinnehmer (in Ägypten) begleiteten, wurden 'Schwertträger' genannt" (Stuhlmacher 1989, 178 mit Friedrich et al. 1976, 140-44; Plümacher 1981, 980; Wilckens 1982, 35 n. 167; Schrage 1989, 247; vgl. zum Ausdruck μαχαιροφόροι für bewaffnete Steuereintreiber Philo *Spec.Leg.* II 92-95; III 159-63).

[12] Dibelius 1960, 31a. Schon 1949 hatte er "die Grenzen des Staates" staatsmetaphysisch im Sinne der echten, alten Monarchie bestimmt in unverkennbarer Frontstellung gegen den 'atheistischen' Staat. Das rief den marxistischen Protest über einen solchen "Mißbrauch der Religion" gegen den 'Arbeiter-und-Bauern-Staat' auf den Plan (z.B. an der Leipziger Universität: Schwartze 1956).

Damit war aber faktisch akzeptiert, daß der Verzicht auf die dritte Gewalt und die Machtkontrolle grundsätzlich eine legitime Art staatlicher Machtausübung sei. Wenigstens die Frage jenes Streites von 1960 ist nie mehr ernstlich gestellt worden. Es war deshalb konsequent, daß fortan alle weiteren Fragen, die die Kirche an diesen Staat zu stellen hatte, zu Fragen des 'Arrangements' mit der Macht wurden. An die Stelle des Rechts traten sogenannte 'Gespräche'. Damit aber war genau jene Grauzone geschaffen, die als ein Feld kirchlicher Einflußnahme auf die Art und Weise der Ausübung der Macht erschien. Von daher lag es auch nicht ganz so fern, eben durch 'Gespräche' ins Dunkel der Macht hinein zugunsten der Kirche oder einzelner in der Kirche tätig zu werden. So gesehen sind jene kirchlichen Konspirationen nicht einfach ein der Imagination und Begabung einzelner zuzuschreibender Zufall. Sie sind die Folge eines Versäumnisses im Zentrum der theologischen Ethik, das sich die ganze Kirche zuzuschreiben hat.

---

[13] E. Wolf, in: Mochalski/Werner 1960, 89-90. Auch der verbreitet eingetragene Gedanke, daß der Staat 'Erhaltungsordnung' zu dem Zwecke sei, daß die Menschheit nicht im 'Chaos' versinke (vgl. zuletzt Stuhlmacher 1989, 181. 194), geht über die Rechtsmotivation in Röm 13,3f. hinaus und trägt ein staatsmetaphysisches Konzept von Plato her in den Text ein: "Platonisch ist es der Demiurg, der die ungeordnete sichtbare Welt aus der ἀταξία in die τάξις des Kosmos überführte (Plat *Tim.* 30a; bei Philo wird ganz ähnliches vom Schöpfergott gesagt *Plant.* 3, vgl. *Som.* I 241, aber auch Augustus *Leg.Gaj.* 112f. Nichts von alledem bei Paulus" (Delling 1969, 30f. n. 22; vgl. auch Balz 1973, 211 vgl. 190 hellenistische Belege zum Motiv 'Anarchie'-Verhinderung). Dennoch war selbst in die EKU-Handreichung von 1959 der Topos eingeflossen, daß "rechtliche und staatliche Ordnungsfunktionen ... im Sinne vom Röm 13 ein *bellum omnium contra omnes* verhindern" (zitiert nach Hüffmeier 1986, 115). Das hängt auch mit einem bestimmten theologischen Konzept des 'Gesetzes' zusammen: "'Gesetz' *ist*" für Luther "die Obrigkeit schon durch sich selbst und durch ihre möglichst große Autorität, kraft der sie das Volk im Zaum hält. Deshalb wird in dieser Sicht ein Staatswesen vor allem von unten, durch den Ungehorsam des Volkes, bedroht". Doch für Zwingli und Calvin "liegt die eigentliche Bedeutung des 'Gesetzes' nicht in deren *Funktion*, Sünder zu erschrecken oder abzuschrecken, sondern in seinem bestimmten *Inhalt*. Das hat die Konsequenz, daß die Regierung eines Volkes niemals das 'Gesetz' für das Volk sein kann, sondern daß zwischen ihr und dem Gesetz genau unterschieden werden muß, ... daß ein Staatswesen bestimmt sein muß nicht nur durch das Gegenüber von Regierenden und Regierten, sondern zugleich durch die dritte Größe der 'Gesetze', die von Regierten *und* Regierenden zu befolgen sind" (Busch 1992, 168. 169: "Das staatliche Recht ist mit dem Willen Gottes konform, wenn es für die Menschen primär und wesentlich einen heilsamen Charakter hat, ... je mehr er die positive Aufgabe wahrnimmt, menschlicher Staat zu sein in Obsorge für ein menschenwürdiges Zusammenleben in Gerechtigkeit und Frieden").

[14] Krötke 1992, 8, der damit in der Diskussion um die Rechtfertigung von konspirativen Kontakten kirchlicher Mitarbeiter mit der 'Staatssicherheit' (dem Geheimdienst) der DDR den entscheidenden Punkt eines falschen Umgangs mit der Macht dingfest macht: Die sogenannten 'Gespräche' mit dem sogenannten 'Partner' verschleiern schon im aufwertenden Wortgebrauch die semantische Tatsache, daß das hier maßgebende Antonym dazu im betreffenden Wortfeld eigentlich 'Recht' ist. Gerade angesichts der jüngsten 'Stasi'-Diskussion ist m.R. betont worden, daß die den Kirchen gebotene 'Umkehr' darin bestehen muß, daß "sie sich in ihrer Theologie – deutlicher als bisher – von dem autoritären Verständnis des Staates als einer bevorzugten Ordnungsmacht trennt, die per se als 'gute' Ordnung ('Schöpfungsordnung') gegen das 'Chaos' von Natur und Gesellschaft stünde" (Link 1992, 368).

Konkret heißt das, daß bei aller Lernbereitschaft in den Kirchen der DDR letztlich die alte Linie, die sich in einer auf die Anfangspassage verkürzenden Zitierung von Röm 13,1-2 immer wieder abzeichnet, bestimmend geblieben (oder wieder geworden) ist, während die reformierte Betonung der in Röm 13,3-4 gegebenen Bestimmungen der Rechtsfunktionen nicht in der gebührenden Weise zum Tragen gekommen ist und zu der notwendigen Sensibilisierung geführt hat.

Dokumente der Spitzeltätigkeit kirchlicher Funktionäre für den staatlichen Geheimdienst der DDR konnten darum unter dem Titel "Seid untertan der Obrigkeit" vorgestellt werden: Auch eine solche geheime 'Partnerschaft' und solche konspirativen 'Gespräche' rechtfertigten die so Agierenden damit, "Römer 13: ... immer bemüht im Sinne der Obrigkeit" – also "immer bemüht im Sinne der DDR" geltend zu machen[15]. Das Wortfeld der deutschen Ausdrücke 'Obrigkeit' – 'Untertan' steht heute mehr denn je für "vorauseilenden Gehorsam" und "freiwillige Selbst-Unterwerfung". Das wesentliche Versagen der Christen in der DDR lag in der Generationen lang eingeübten Bereitschaft, sich zu unterwerfen. Der Hallenser Psychologe H.-J. Maaz hat darum in der Diskussion um den ehemaligen Konsistorialrat M.

---

[15] Krone/Schult 1992, 9f. Schon die bloße Äquivokation eines Ministeriums für 'Staats'-Sicherheit bescherte also Anfälligkeiten. "Die 'Stasi' war" aber "ein nachgeordnetes Organ der herrschenden Partei, kein Staat im Staate. Wer sich mit Geheimdiensten einläßt, läßt sich auch auf ihre Spielregeln ein. Auch für Kirchendiplomaten wie M. Stolpe und andere mußte das verbotenes Terrain sein." Denn schließlich gab es "für alle kirchlichen Mitarbeiter den dringenden Rat, sich mit den Vertretern des Ministeriums für Staatssicherheit nicht einzulassen. Wenn aber mit ihnen dennoch gesprochen wurde, dann sollte das nur unter Zeugen stattfinden. Wenn das nicht möglich war, sollte Dekonspiration angekündigt werden" (Tschiche 1992, III). So haben wir jeden Studenten der Kirchlichen Hochschulen (und anderer kirchlicher Einrichtungen) verpflichtet. Daß diese Praxis auch erfolgreich möglich war, kann ich wie viele andere aus eigener Erfahrung bestätigen. Es war darum "ein eklatanter Vertrauensbruch, wenn Vertreter der Kirchenleitungen an Synoden vorbei sich auf Geheimdienste einlassen. Die Patriarchen hintergehen so die Demokraten. Es kommt in diesem ganzen Streit die hierarchische Grundstruktur der Kirche ans Licht. Es stellt sich die Frage, ob solch eine Grundstruktur nicht einfach zu einer ungerechtfertigten Staatsnähe verführen muß, die hinter verschlossenen Türen und dem gemeinen Kirchenvolk verborgen zelebriert wird ... Nach diesem Grundmuster verlief auch das Handeln kirchlicher Chefetagen über die Verwicklung in 'Stasi'-Kontakten hinaus. Es gab eine Tendenz zur Staatsnähe, die die Kritiker des 'real existierenden Sozialismus' benachteiligte. Die Geheimdiplomatie wurde als Realpolitik bezeichnet, die öffentliche Kritik wurde als Politikunfähigkeit, als Konfrontationskurs und als Martyriumssucht diffamiert" (ebd.). Der Ausdruck 'Obrigkeit' verleitet als solcher immer wieder dazu, auch von 'kirchlicher Obrigkeit' zu reden oder mindestens zu denken: So wurde Röm 13 explizit seit Pelagius und noch im neuzeitlichen Katholizismus auf 'beide Gewalten' bezogen "und zwar so, daß der Anspruch der Superiorität der kirchlichen über die staatliche Gewalt grundsätzlich immer aufrechterhalten worden ist" (Wilckens 1982, 46. 56-7) Obwohl Luther 1523 betont hatte, das 'Regiment der Bischöfe' sei "keine Obrigkeit oder Gewalt, sondern ein Dienst und Amt" (vgl. Zitat ebd. 50), ist ein tendenzieller Rückfall hier immer wieder insgeheim zu beobachten gewesen.

Stolpe und seine 'Gespräche' als konspirativer 'Partner' der geheimdienstlichen
Mitarbeiter des 'Ministeriums für Staatssicherheit der DDR' diesen Zusammenhang treffend analysiert[16]:

> Einer wie Stolpe mußte gar nicht erst ein IM werden, um ein IM zu sein. Seine und
> damit auch der Kirche machterhaltende Interessenlage entspricht haargenau dem
> Hauptinteresse der Staatssicherheit: Ruhe und Ordnung im Land, Disziplin und Ge-
> horsam, Anerkennung der Obrigkeit und schnelle Beruhigung von Spannungen und
> Konflikten.

## 2.2. Das Leitwort 'Kirche im Sozialismus' als Steigerung

Der Brief der evangelischen Bischöfe (vom 15.2.1968) zu dem Entwurf der neuen
DDR-Verfassung bestimmte die Aufgabenstellung für die Entscheidung der Christen noch normativ offen, "den Sozialismus als eine Gestalt gerechteren Zusammenlebens zu verwirklichen". Nach der Gründung des (von den Landeskirchen im
Westen Deutschlands separierten) 'Bundes der Evangelischen Kirchen in der DDR'
(10. Juni 1969 und dem erst am 24.4.1971 gewährten 'Antrittsbesuch' beim 'Staats-
ratsvorsitzenden') protestierten Staatsvertreter noch auf das heftigste, als Propst Dr.
H. Falcke (Erfurt) in seinem Vortrag vor der Bundessynode in Dresden 1972 in der
Auftragsbestimmung immer noch dieses dynamische Element eines "verbesserlichen Sozialismus" festhielt. Angesichts der westeuropäischen Marxismus-Rezep-
tion und dem 1968 niedergeschlagenen 'Prager Frühling' eines "'Sozialismus' mit
menschlichem Antlitz" wurde der *status quo* der herrschenden Partei- und Gesell-
schaftsordnung in der DDR mit der Abwehrformel vom "real existierenden Sozialismus" unmißverständlich festgeschrieben. Dessen 'Staatsorgane' definierten sich
als 'sozialistische Nation' und 'sozialistisches Vaterland'.

Im gleichen Jahr 1973, in dem der Staatsratsvorsitzende der DDR, Erich Honek-
ker, diese drohende Abwehrparole vom "real existierenden Sozialismus" geprägt
hatte, entstand im 'Bund der Evangelischen Kirchen in der DDR' die Formel von
der "Kirche im Sozialismus". Diese Synchronizität ist nicht zufällig und nicht unwichtig (also nicht nur 'im', sondern, de facto als 'im' sich als "real existierend" de-
finierenden!).

> Die Eisenacher Bundessynode 1971 hatte [noch] formuliert: 'Eine Zeugnis- und
> Dienstgemeinschaft von Kirchen in der DDR wird ihren Ort genau zu bedenken ha-
> ben: in dieser so geprägten Gesellschaft, nicht neben ihr, nicht gegen sie. Sie wird
> die Freiheit ihres Zeugnisses und Dienstes bewahren müssen'. Erst 1973 stand im
> Bericht über die Bundessynode von Schwerin beieinander, was zuvor noch getrennt

---

[16] Maaz 1992 ('IM' = 'Inoffizieller Mitarbeiter'), zustimmend zitiert bei Dieckmann 1993, 63;
vgl. außer dem Material bei Krone/Schult 1992 schon das bei Besier/Wolf, 1991 Vorgelegte (vgl. zur
Diskussion auch die Rezensionen).

war: 'Kirche im Sozialismus wäre die Kirche, die dem christlichen Bürger und der einzelnen Gemeinde hilft, daß sie einen Weg in der sozialistischen Gesellschaft in der Freiheit und Bindung des Glaubens finden und bemüht sind, das Beste für alle und für das Ganze zu suchen'. Hier sagte die Synode, was Kirche sein will. Die Abgrenzungen gegen Mißdeutungen fielen weg[17].

Das war mindestens ein Schritt zu weit in Richtung auf eine Akklamation hin.

Spätestens seit dem Gebrauch der Formel 'Kirche im Sozialismus' ist der 'real existierende Sozialismus' wieder und wieder als der im Grundsatz begrüßte und bejahte Ort interpretiert worden, der der Kirche, indem er sie von der Macht fernhält, ermöglicht, in rechter Weise Kirche zu sein. Es ist falsch, wenn heute gesagt wird, die Wendung 'im Sozialismus' sei bloß formal als Ortsangabe des Daseins der Kirche zu verstehen gewesen. Das läßt sich breit belegen. Es ist in unzähligen Varianten im Innern der DDR, im Westen und in der Ökumene verbreitet worden, daß der Sozialismus in seiner realen Form nicht eine Not, sondern eine Chance für die Kirche ist, die sich andere Kirchen sogar zum Exempel zu nehmen hätten[18].

Die Präposition 'im' (in diesem Zusammenhang von ihrem Urheber definiert als Mittleres zwischen "nicht für und nicht gegen den Sozialismus") mag ekklesiologisch auf den ersten Blick als eine bloße Angabe des Bereichs semantisch noch tolerabel erscheinen (analog zu einer Alternative von "Church of Christ in England" gegenüber "Church of England"). Doch der geschichtlich-semantische Kontext dieser Bestimmung sowohl in ihrer Synchronie (mit "real existierender Sozialismus") wie Diachronie (Abrücken vom "verbesserlichen Sozialismus" bzw. "gerechterer Gestalt des Zusammenlebens") machen sie fragwürdig. Der exemplarische Grenzfall der konspirativen Kontakte von Mitgliedern der kirchlichen Leitungsetagen signalisiert den vermessenen und von Anfang an theologisch gescheiterten Weg der Gratwanderung unter der Legitimationsformel "Kirche im Sozialismus". Damit war das Gefälle zu einer Art "DDR eigner" 'civil religion' im Sinne eines religiös-nationalen Einheitsbandes zum Zwecke der Legitimierung eines besonderen 'sozialistischen Staates deutscher Nation' unverkennbar geworden. Der marxistische Impetus, "die Welt verändern" (statt "nur interpretieren") zu wollen, war auf den *status quo* der je aktuellen Parteitagsbeschlüsse der führenden 'Arbeiterpartei' hin ausge-

---

[17] Onnasch 1992, 1. vgl. Falcke 1993, der unseren, gemeinsam seit Anbeginn dagegen vertretenen Widerstand sehr gut aus diesem situativen Kontext heraus verdeutlicht. Mit der historischen Analogie des theologischen Systematikers Abraham Kuyper (1837-1920) in den Niederlanden (1901-5 Ministerpräsident) habe ich immer argumentiert: "Kirche nicht in und nicht unter den Generalstaaten" – "mar bij de Generalstaaten". Schriftlich erschien ein Widerspruch in der DDR 1988 möglich bei Schröder (1990, 49-54. 149-59).

[18] Krötke 1992, 9 im Unterschied zur beschwichtigenden Interpretation der Kurzformel durch ihren maßgebenden episkopalen Vertreter (und wohl auch Erfinder), A. Schönherr 1992 (und die weitere Diskussion in EPD [Ev. Pressedienst] 11/1992).

richtet, statt wie in der Zeit vor dieser Formel noch eindeutiger auf die soziale Substanz solcher Veränderungen hin orientiert zu sein, so daß ihrer jeweiligen politischen Praxis gegenüber ein besseres Kriterium gegeben war.

### 3. Konsequenzen

Nicht nur O. Dibelius stellte 1959 eine weiterlaufende Rezeption des Ausdrucks 'Obrigkeit' infrage, sondern auch K. Barth stellte 1963 verwundert die erneute Rezeption dieses Leitwortes in den 'Zehn Artikeln über Freiheit und Dienst der Kirche' fest[19]:

> Wann wird das in seiner altväterlichen Kälte so unerfreuliche Wort 'Obrigkeit' endlich aus der christlichen Sprache verschwinden?

Der von Dibelius gemachte Vorschlag 'rechtmäßige Gewalt' entspricht zwar nicht einer isolierten Wortsemantik, kann aber übersetzungslinguistisch von der Textsemantik her gerechtfertigt werden, sofern primär der Gesamttext selbst der Bedeutungsträger ist und das Vorkommen der einzelnen Seme im Metatext einer Übersetzung durchaus an verschiedenen Stellen erscheinen kann, denn Röm 13,3b-4 "blickt Paulus zweifellos auf die Rechtsfunktion der Gewaltinhaber, wenn er von ihrem Strafen und Lohnen redet"[20]. Dibelius hat also *de facto* Röm 13,3-4 nach Röm 13,1 vorgezogen. Sofern man (wie so oft) den Abschnitt auf seine Anfangssätze verkürzend zitiert, so erscheint es als Markierung einer solchen Abkürzung in der Tat dem Gesamttext adäquater, dieses semantische Element schon mit einfließen zu lassen, statt es zu unterschlagen. Als eine zusammenfassende Überschrift wäre es semantisch verantwortbarer als die isolierte Zitierung des Eröffnungssatzes.

Daß Röm 13,1-7 als letzte Konkretion der Bereiche menschlichen Zusammenle-

---

[19] Barth 1963, 414. Von den jüngsten Kommentaren verwendet es immer noch durchgehend Schmithals 1988, 456. Sonst bevorzugt man 'Gewalt(en)' seit Käsemann (1964, 209): "Ich übersetze darum das griechische Wort ἐξουσία und seine Derivate durch 'Gewalt', 'Gewalten', 'Gewalthaber', um so auch Tyrannis und Despotie einzuschließen, die im Bereich des römischen Imperiums jedenfalls weithin herrschten". 'Gewalt' (indogermanisch *'val' vgl. lateinisch 'valere') = 'Verfügungsgewalt haben', "meint zunächst wertneutral jede freie Ausübung von 'Macht'. Ob die 'Gewalt' im Einzelfall Recht oder Unrecht bewirkt, läßt sich daher von der Struktur der Gewalt selbst nicht erkennen, sondern wird erst durch hinzutretende Eigenschaften bestimmt. Diese Ambivalenz des Begriffes 'Gewalt', der semantisch die Wiedergabe von lateinisch *'potestas'* und *'violentia'* deckt, bestimmt den deutschen Sprachgebrauch bis heute" (Haag 1983, 200 n. 25 mit Röttgen 1974, 562-70 s.v). Weil hier aber *violentia* nicht als solche im Blick ist, so wäre der anvisierte neutrale Aspekt unmißverständlicher durch 'Machthaben' auszudrücken: 'Macht' = 'Können'/'Vermögen', wie "ontologisch gesehen allem Sein von seinem Ursprung her eine 'Mächtigkeit' eignet, deren rechter Gebrauch sich in der Verantwortung vor Gott vollzieht" (ebd.; vgl. Kobusch 1980, 585-88).

bens (nach 12,3-8 innergemeindliche Funktionen, 12,9-13 personale Relation zwischen Christen, 12,14-21 personale Relation von Christen zu Nichtchristen) unter dem Vorzeichen der Überschrift von Röm 12,1-2 steht, macht es eigentlich erforderlich, daß dann, wenn Röm 13,1-7 als isoliertes Segment zitiert wird, immer auch Röm 12,1-2 mit verbalisiert werden müßte: Wozu Gott uns befähigt (Indikativ) und was er von uns zu sein und zu tun fordert (Imperativ), sofern er uns als der Vater Jesu Christi zur bezeugenden Partizipation an seiner Geschichte mit seiner Welt befreit hat. Auch Röm 13,1-7 ist das häufigste Autosemantikon (6mal) nicht etwa ἐξουσία oder ὑποτάσσεσθαι, sondern θεός (V. 1b.c. 2. 4a.d. 6); und dieser Signifikant ist nicht ein austauschbarer Allweltsausdruck eines religiösen Monotheismus, sondern semantisch konkret (wie überall bei Paulus) der Träger des spezifischen Signifikats: "der, der Jesus von den Toten erweckt hat". Das deutliche Nebeneinander von behördlichen Funktionsangaben und theologischen Verortungen hat darum nicht die Funktion einer "theologischen Überhöhung" oder "metaphysischen Begründung" einer "sakrosankten Staatsmacht"[21], sondern will der Christenheit zeigen, wie sie den vielfach auf sie eindringenden, geforderten Loyalitäten gegenüber im Interesse des Zusammenlebens aller so begegnen, daß sie den Gott bezeugt, der sie und alle Menschen in der Auferweckung Jesu zur Zukunft mit sich erwählt hat.

Eine Übersetzung sollte das ebenso bedenken wie die innere Kohärenz, die durchgehend (und nicht erst am Ende) auf öffentliche Gelder bezogen ist: Die Stellung des Christen zu den öffentlichen Abgaben, den Verwaltern öffentlicher Gelder

---

[20] Käsemann 1964, 210. Dabei versteht er auch (wie die meisten) das σοὶ εἰς τὸ ἀγαθόν in der theologischen Begründung V. 4a mit Luther als "dir zugute", "als das irdische Wohl ... als Schutz vor Übergriffen" (1974, 345). Die Präposition als Angabe des Ziels, einer Bestimmung "zum Nutzen" im nichtethischen Sinne (wie 8,28; 15,2) ist zwar möglich (Bauer/Aland 1988, 462 s.v. 4d), dürfte hier aber nur für die Lesart ohne den Artikel bei B pc vorliegen. Der anaphorische Artikel indessen ist zu deutlich ein Rückweiser auf das hier eben ethisch verwendete 'Gute' V. 3a.b und darum kaum im unethischen Sinne des 'Wohles/guten Geschicks' (und somit synonym mit ἔπαινον V. 3b) zu deuten (Delling 1962, 58-9). Dagegen spricht auch der Begründungscharakter von V. 4a (γάρ) in Relation zu V. 3b. Darum hat man die Präposition in seiner Bedeutung der Angabe der Absicht, des Zweckes genommen "zum Tun des Guten" (Wilckens 1982, 34-5 n. 166: "= ἵνα τὸ ἀγαθὸν ποιῇς [vgl. 16,19]" analog schon außer Delling auch Lietzmann 1933, 112; Michel 1966, 312. 318 n. 7; Wolbert 1981, 64: "Sie steht im Dienst Gottes und verlangt, daß du das Gute tust"). Aber auch gegen ein futurisch zu Tuendes (Absicht) spricht der Begründungscharakter des Satzes. Darum wird man die Präposition hier kontextgemäß am besten zur Bezeichnung der Beziehung auf etwas, also: 'hinsichtlich' der schon getanen Wohltätigkeit (nicht erst einer zu tuenden) verstehen müssen (Winter 1988, 94-5: "with respect to/on behalf of the benefaction"). Damit ist also nicht erst V. 6a das faktisch vorgegebene Tun der Adressaten im Blick, sondern schon V. 4a. Dies steht andererseits im Gegensatz zu dem V. 2b.c im Perfekt als schon vorgegeben angesprochenen, gegenteiligen Handelns Dritter, die offenkundig nur außerhalb der Adressaten auszumachen sind.

und ihrer Verwendungsentscheidung:

(1) Keine Gesinnung[22] entziehe sich der Entscheidungsbefugnis der Verwalter öffentlicher Geldmittel!
Denn auch diese stehen in jedem Falle unter dem, der Jesus von den Toten erweckte und haben ihre Aufgabenstellung von ihm.
(2) Folglich hat sich ein solcher Behörde Entziehender zugleich einer Anordnung dessen entzogen, der Jesus von den Toten erweckte, und diejenigen, die sich so entzogen haben, werden für sich ihre Verurteilung empfangen.
(3) Denn die Verwalter öffentlicher Geldmittel sind nicht eine Bedrohung für die Wohltätigkeit[23], sondern für das Zufügen von Schaden.
Willst du also keine Geldstrafe befürchten,
dann übe Wohltätigkeit,

---

[21] So Schmithals 1988, 465.467-8 als "sekundäre Theologisierung" der hellenistischen Synagoge gewertet, was aber textlinguistisch und rezeptionssemantisch dann nur für einen gemutmaßten Vorlagetext gelten kann und nicht automatisch auf den vorliegenden Text in seinem Kotext (und gegen dessen Semantik) übertragen werden darf. Röm 13 als einen essentiell christlichen Text zu verstehen war das Hauptanliegen der DDR-Exegeten Neugebauer und (seines Lehrers) Delling 1962 (12-20 – allerdings mit der zu bestreitenden Prämisse einer jesuanischen Voraussetzung in Mk 12,17), die beide gegen ihren Hallenser Kollegen Barnikol 1961 stehen. Typisch für die Spätphase der DDR (und dem, was dort publiziert werden konnte,) ist Bindemann 1981, wo der Text als exemplarisch für eine Paränese 'in nichtrevolutionärer Situation' (= 'materialistische Bibelinterpretation') steht, in der Zivilcourage erforderlich sei.

[22] ψυχή meint primär 'Gesinnung' (so daß die Zusammenfassung V. 5 nicht einen neuen Aspekt einbringt, sondern auf diese Formulierung in Ansatz der Eröffnungsthese zurückweist): Es ist Metonym für 'Mensch', sofern er aus 'Gesinnung' heraus handelt, griechisch (vgl. Passow 1983, II 2589b) wie auch lateinisch (Georges 1988, I 440 *animus = homo*) gebräuchlich – vor allem im Hinblick auf *beneficia* (vgl. Seneca, *Benef.* 3,18,2,4, weshalb selbst ein Sklave zu *beneficia* seinem Arbeitgeber gegenüber fähig ist!).

[23] Mit Winter 1988 ist davon auszugehen, daß es hier nicht nur um 'gute Taten' im allgemeinen geht, sondern die spezielle Rechtsinstitution angesprochen ist (definiert Seneca, *Benef.* 1,1,3): "In der Kaiserzeit war es vor allem ein System privater Sozialfürsorge und leistete das, wozu heute die Systeme staatlicher Existenzsicherung ('soziales Netz') dienen. Generell war der gesellschaftlich und wirtschaftlich Höherstehende dazu verpflichtet, den sozial und wirtschaftlich Schwächeren nicht nur materiell zu unterstützen, sondern ihm in vielfältiger Form bei der Bewältigung seiner Lebensprobleme behilflich zu sein. Alle diese Leistungen wurden als *beneficia* bezeichnet. Ihr Empfänger war seinerseits zu Gegenleistungen, *officia* verpflichtet" – in 'Dank/Dankbarkeit' (Rosenbach 1989, VII) vgl. IX: *beneficia reddere/referre* erklärt Seneca, *Benef.* 6,5,2 "nicht dasselbe wird 'zurückgegeben', sondern etwas Entsprechendes". 7,19,1f. diskutiert Neros Staatskanzler Seneca in seiner von 58-60 (also kurz nach dem Römerbrief) verfaßten Moralschrift die Semantik dieses Verbs im einzelnen. Da Paulus auch hier V. 7 dieses Verb als abschließendes Leitverb verwendet, so ist der rückwärtige Zusammenhang zu den *beneficia* von V. 3f. ein verbindendes Element der semantischen Isotopie des Textsegments: Diesem privaten Akt sozialer Umverteilung entspricht komplementär der staatliche Steuerzwang als gesellschaftlich-öffentlicher Akt der sozialen Umverteilung. Beiden gegenüber steht V. 3f. als Antonym κακόν als der schädigende Akt, der ja eine asoziale Umverteilung darstellt.

und du wirst von ihr belohnende Anerkennung empfangen!

(4) Denn sie ist die Beauftragte dessen, der Jesus von den Toten erweckte, hinsichtlich deiner Wohltätigkeit.

Solltest du aber Schaden anrichten, dann fürchte sie!

Denn sie trägt das Kurzschwert (das Zeichen institutionalisierter Rechtsmacht) nicht ohne Recht. Ja, sie ist als Werkzeug dessen, der Jesus von den Toten erweckte, ein Anwalt der Rechtsahndung für jeden, der Schaden anrichtet.

(5) Folglich ist es also notwendig, sich nicht zu entziehen, und zwar nicht nur aus Angst vor rechtmäßiger Strafe, sondern auch aus guten christlichen Überzeugungsgründen.

(6) Schließlich entrichtet ihr ja auch aus diesen Gründen eure Abgaben;

denn sie sind als Nehmer öffentlicher Abgaben vom Vater Jesu Christi betraut, wenn und sofern sie eben dazu beständig tätig sind[24].

(7) Fahrt also fort, jedem das zu entrichten, worauf er einen Anspruch hat:
• Abgaben dem, der auf Abgaben Anspruch hat,
• Gebühren dem, der auf Gebühren Anspruch hat,
• Strafgeld dem, der auf Strafgeld Anspruch hat.
• Honorar[25] dem, der auf Honorar Anspruch hat!

So ruft uns Röm 13,1-7 als 'Magna Charta' einer "nonkonformistischen Loyalität"[26] weiterhin als Christenheit in die Verantwortung, nach den vom Vater Jesu Christi gesetzten Aufträgen auch innerhalb der bestehenden gesellschaftlichen Machtverhältnisse zu suchen und handelnd zu gestalten.

---

[24] Mit der temporalen Codierung des Partizips "trägt er dem Umstand Rechnung, daß es nicht immer so sein muß" (Swartley 1984, 78 mit Yoder 1981, 184-86). "Auf den Münzen aus der Regierungszeit des Claudius (41-54) ist eine neue kaiserliche Tugend verewigt: *Constantia*, die Beharrlichkeit. Alle jene Vorgänger, die diese Eigenschaft hatten vermissen lassen, beanstandete er" (Grant 1978, 172. 33 vgl. 170-1: Ihm "war die Rechtsprechung eine Passion, die ihm fast jeden Tag einen guten Teil seiner Zeit kostete … Der Schutz der Schwachen lag ihm am Herzen, und er bemühte sich darum, einem jeden zu seinem Recht zu verhelfen"). Dieser konkrete Bezug auf eine durch Münzen weitverbreitete neue Losung ist naheliegender als der Vorschlag, den Satz syntaktisch mit dem Folgenden zu verbinden und vom Voranstehenden zu trennen: "Denn Amtsleute Gottes sind sie. Indem *ihr* eben das ständig im Auge behaltet, erfüllt ihr allen gegenüber, was ihr schuldig seid" (so Wengst 1986, 101 mit Riekkinen 1980, 35-6; dgg. Schmithals 1988, 469).

[25] Daß τιμή von 2,7. 10; 12,10 her im "Röm immer Ehre" bedeuten müsse (Hübner 1983, 857), ist nicht zwingend. Mindestens hat die Bedeutung 'Wert' immer noch eine nahe finanzielle Bedeutungskomponente (Frisk 1966, 901: neben 'Preis' auch 'Entschädigung, Buße, Strafe') Von 1 Kor 6,20; 7,23 her ist auch für Paulus eine finanzielle Semanalyse möglich, zumal in der Verbindung mit ἀποδιδόναι τινί "einen Preis bezahlen" (Plat *Leg*. 5,744a; Passow 1983, II 1901); seit Homer auch als rechtlicher Ausdruck 'Strafe, Ersatz-Leistung' bezeichnend (vgl. 'Summe' Mt 27,9; Apg 4,34; 5,2f.; 7,16; 19,1 und Sir 38,1 'Arzthonorar'; Bauer/Aland 1988, 1629f.). Sollte aber das vierte Glied der Aufzählung ebenso wie die beiden ersten finanzielle Fälle ansprechen, dann müßte man das auch für das dritte Glied annehmen: Also nicht etwa 'Ehrfurcht' (Strobel 1964; Bauer/Aland 1988, 1722) gerade in Differenz zu V. 3-4, sondern eher doch als anaphorische Renominalisierung der dort voranstehenden Verwendungen her als gefürchtetes 'Strafgeld' (metonymisch für ein solches gesetzt).

## Bibliographie

Balz, H. 1973: Art. "φοβέω", in: _ThWNT_ IX, Stuttgart: Kohlhammer 1973, 186-216.

Barnikol, E. 1961: "Römer 13: Der nichtpaulinische Ursprung der absoluten Obrigkeitsbejahung von Röm 13,1-7", in: _Studien zum NT und zur Patristik. FS E. Klostermann_ (TU 77), Berlin: Akademie Verlag 1961, 65-113.

Barth, K. 1958: _Brief an einen Pfarrer in der DDR_, Zollikon: Evangelischer Verlag 1958.

— 1963: "Theologisches Gutachten zu den 'Zehn Artikeln über Freiheit und Dienst der Kirche'", in: _KiZ_ 18 (1963) 414.

— 1970: _Rechtfertigung und Recht. Christengemeinde und Bürgergemeinde_ (ThSt (B) 104), Zürich: EVZ $^2$1970.

Bauer, W. 1967: "Jedermann sei untertan der Obrigkeit", in: idem, _Aufsätze und kleine Schriften_, Tübingen: Mohr 1967, 263-84.

Bauer, W./Aland, K./Aland, B. 1988: _Griechisch-deutsches Wörterbuch zu den Schriften des NT_, Berlin: de Gruyter $^6$1988.

Besier, G./Wolf, S. 1991: _Pfarrer, Christen, Katholiken_, Neukirchen-Vluyn: Neukirchener Verlag 1991; $^2$1992 (Rez.: D. Koch, in: _EvTh_ 52 [1992] 360-65; A. Kistenbrügge, in: _VF_ 38/2 [1993] 45-50).

Bindemann, W.1981: "Materialistische Bibelinterpretation am Beispiel von Röm 13,1-7", in: _Die Zeichen der Zeit_ 35 (1981) 136-45.

Broer, I. 1981: Art. "ἐξουσία", in: _EWNT_ II, Stuttgart: Kohlhammer 1981, 23-29.

Busch, E.1992: "Gott hat nicht auf sein Recht verzichtet: Die Erneuerung der Kirche im Verhältnis zum politischen Bereich nach dem Verständnis der reformierten Reformatoren", in: _EvTh_ 52 (1992) 160-76.

Cranfield, C. E. B. 1979: _The Epistle to the Romans_, Vol. II (ICC), Edinburgh: Clark 1979.

Delling, G. 1962: _Römer 13,1-7 innerhalb der Briefe des NT_, Berlin: Evangelische Verlagsanstalt 1962.

— 1969: Art. "τάσσω", in: _ThWNT_ VIII, Stuttgart: Kohlhammer 1969, 27-49

Dibelius, O. 1949: _Die Grenzen des Staates_, Berlin: Wichern 1949.

— 1963: _Obrigkeit_, Stuttgart/Berlin: Kreuz 1963 = Privatdruck, Berlin 1959 = in: Mochalski/Werner 1960, 21-31a.

Dieckmann, C. 1993: "Abendlicht: eine Predigt für und wider den Mythos DDR", in: _Die Zeit_ 48/9 (26.2.93) 8.

---

[26] Huber/Reuter 1990, 43 vgl. 217f. Wolbert 1981, 64: "Nur für diesen" (V. 4 angegebenen) "Fall kann die staatliche Gewalt Gehorsam fordern. Da sie im _Dienst_ Gottes steht, bestimmt sie nicht selber, was gut und böse ist, es ist ihr vorgegeben. Daraus folgt zwingend, auch wenn Paulus das nicht eigens betont, daß, falls sie das Böse fordern sollte, die staatliche Gewalt keinen Gehorsam beanspruchen kann, da sie in diesem Fall aus dem Dienst Gottes heraustreten würde; die Voraussetzung, unter der sie Gehorsam fordern kann, wäre nicht gegeben".

Duchrow, U. 1970: *Christenheit und Weltverantwortung: Traditionsgeschichte und systematische Struktur der Zweireichelehre* (FBESG 25), Stuttgart: Kohlhammer 1970.

Falcke, H.1993: "Die Kirche im Sozialismus", in: G. Heydemann/L. Kettenacker (eds.), *Kirchen in der Diktatur*, Göttingen: Vandenhoeck & Ruprecht 1993.

Friedrich, J./Pöhlmann, W./Stuhlmacher, P. 1979: "Zur historischen Situation und Intention von Röm 13,1-7", in: *ZThK* 73 (1979) 131-66.

Frisk, H. 1966: *Griechisch etymologisches Wörterbuch* II, Heidelberg: Quelle & Meyer 1966.

Georges, K. E. 1988: *Ausführliches lateinisch-deutsches Handwörterbuch*, Darmstadt: Wissenschaftliche Buchgesellschaft 1988 (= Hannover [8]1913).

Grant, M. 1978: *The Twelve Caesars*, London: Weidenfels 1975; dt.: *Roms Caesaren*, München: Beck 1978.

Haag, E.1983: "Die Botschaft vom Gottesknecht – ein Weg zur Überwindung der Gewalt", in: N. Lohfink (ed.), *Gewalt und Gewaltlosigkeit im AT* (QD 96), Freiburg: Herder 1983, 159-213.

Heiligenthal, R. 1983: "Strategien konformer Ethik im NT am Beispiel von Röm 13,1-7", in: *NTS* 29 (1983) 55-61.

Huber, W./Reuter, H. R. 1990: *Friedensethik*, Stuttgart: Kohlhammer 1990.

Hübner, H. 1983: Art. "τιμή", in: *EWNT* III, Stuttgart: Kohlhammer 1983, 856-60.

Hüffmeier, W. (ed.) 1986: *Für Recht und Frieden sorgen: Auftrag der Kirche und Aufgabe des Staates nach Barmen V*, Gütersloh: Mohn 1986.

Käsemann, E. 1959: "Röm 13,1-7 in unserer Generation", in: *ZThK* 56 (1959) 316-76.

— 1964: "Grundsätzliches zur Interpretation von Röm 13", in: idem, *Exegetische Versuche und Besinnungen II*, Göttingen: Vandenhoeck & Ruprecht 1964, 204-22.

— 1973: *An die Römer* (HNT 8a), Tübingen: Mohr 1973.

Kallas, J. 1965: "Romans 13.1-7: An Interpolation", in: *NTS* 11 (1965) 365-74.

Kobusch, T. 1980: Art. "Macht", in: *HWP* V, Darmstadt: Wissenschaftliche Buchgesellschaft 1980, 585-88.

Krötke, W. 1992: "Mußte die Kirche mit der Stasi reden?", in: *Die Zeit* 47/37 (4.9.92) 8-9.

Krone, T./Schult, R.1992: *Seid untertan der Obrigkeit: Originaldokumente der Stasi-Kirchenabteilung XX/4*, Berlin: Basis Druck 1992.

Lietzmann, H. 1933: *An die Römer* (HNT 8), Tübingen: Mohr [4]1933.

Link, C. 1992: "Über den Umgang mit der Schuld", in: *EvTh* 52 (1992) 365-68.

Maaz, H.-J. 1992: *Die Entrüstung*, Berlin: Argon 1992.

Mann, T. 1948: *Neue Studien*, Frankfurt: Fischer 1948, 8-34.

— 1963: *Briefe 1937-1947*, Frankfurt: Fischer 1963.

Michel, O. 1966: *Der Brief an die Römer* (KEK 4), Göttingen: Vandenhoeck & Ruprecht [4]1966.

Mochalski, H./Werner, H. (eds.) 1960: *Dokumente zur Frage der Obrigkeit: 'Violett-Buch' zur Obrigkeitsschrift von Bischof O. Dibelius*, Darmstadt: Stimme [2]1960.

Munro, W. 1983: *Authority in Paul and 1 Peter: The Identification of a Pastoral Stratum in the Pauline Corpus and 1 Peter* (MSSNTS 45), Cambridge: University Press 1983.

— 1990: "Interpolation in the Epistles: Weighing Probabality", in: *NTS* 36 (1990) 432-43.

Neugebauer, F. 1962: "Zur Auslegung von Röm 13,1-7", in: *KuD* 8 (1962) 151-72.

Nicolaisen, C. 1985: *Der Weg nach Barmen: Die Entstehungsgeschichte der Theologischen Erklärung von 1934*, Neukirchen-Vluyn: Neukirchener Verlag 1985.

Onnasch, M. 1992: "Am Anfang war der Argwohn", in: *Kirche im Sozialismus, Beilage zu Deutsches Allgemeines Sonntagsblatt* 32 (7.8.92) I.

O'Neill, J. C. 1975: *Paul's Letter to the Romans* (PNTC), Harmondsworth: Penguin 1975.

Pallis, A. 1920: *To the Romans*, Liverpool: Faber 1920.

Passow, F. 1983: *Handwörterbuch der Griechischen Sprache*, Darmstadt: Wissenschaftliche Buchgesellschaft 1983 (= Leipzig [5]1841).

Plümacher, E. 1981: Art. "μάχαιρα", in: *EWNT* II, Stuttgart: Kohlhammer 1981, 978-80.

Riekkinen, V. 1980: *Römer 13* (AASF 23), Helsinki: Universität 1980.

Röttgen, K. 1974: Art. "Gewalt", in: *HWP* III, Darmstadt: Wissenschaftliche Buchgesellschaft 1974, 562-70.

Rosenbach, M. 1989: *L. A. Seneca Philosophische Schriften* V, Darmstadt: Wissenschaftliche Buchgesellschaft 1989.

Schlier, H. 1977: *Der Römerbrief* (HThK 6), Freiburg: Herder 1977.

Schmithals, W. 1975: *Der Römerbrief als historisches Problem* (StNT 9), Gütersloh: Mohn 1975.

— 1988: *Der Römerbrief*, Gütersloh: Mohn 1988.

Schönherr, A. 1992: "Weder Opportunismus noch Opposition: Kirche im Sozialismus – der beschwerliche Weg der Protestanten in der DDR", in: *Die Zeit* 48/7 (7.2.1992), 4-5 = *EPD (Ev. Pressedienst)* 11/1992, 25-28.

Schottroff, L. 1984: "Gebt dem Kaiser, was den Kaiser gehört, und Gott, was Gott gehört", in: J. Moltmann (ed.), *Annahme und Widerstand* (Kaiser Traktate 79), München: Kaiser 1984, 15-58.

Schrage, W. 1971: *Die Christen und der Staat nach dem NT*, Gütersloh: Mohn 1971.

— 1989: *Ethik des NT* (GNT 4), Göttingen: Vandenhoeck & Ruprecht [5]1989.

Schröder, R. 1990: *Denken im Zwielicht*, Tübingen: Mohr 1990.

Schwartze, H. 1956: "Über den Mißbrauch der Religion zu irdischen Zwecken: Bischof D.Dr. Dibelius und das Verhältnis der Christen zum Staat der Arbeiter und Bauern", in: *Forum* 1.2.1956 (Wissenschaftliche Beilage 1), 1-16.

Sherwin-White, A. N. 1963: *Roman Society and Roman Law in the NT*, Oxford: Clarendon 1963.

Simonis, W. 1989: *Der gefangene Paulus: Die Entstehung des sogenannten Römerbriefs und anderer urchristlicher Schriften in Rom*, Bern/Frankfurt: Lang 1989.

Spitta, F. 1901: *Untersuchungen über den Brief des Paulus an die Römer*, Berlin: Reimer 1901.

Strobel, A. 1956: "Zum Verständnis von Röm 13", in: *ZNW* 47 (1956) 67-93.

— 1964: "Furcht, wem Furcht gebührt: Zum profan-griechischen Hintergrund von Röm 13,7", in: *ZNW* 55 (1964) 58-62.

Stuhlmacher, P. 1989: *Der Brief an die Römer* (NTD 6), Göttingen: Vandenhoeck & Ruprecht 1989.

Swartley, W. M. 1984: "Die Steuerfrage im NT", in: W. Krauß (ed.), *Was gehört dem Kaiser?*, Weisenheim: Agape 1984, 66-82.

Tschiche, H.-J. 1992: "Die Kirche hat gekungelt: Konflikte mit den Gruppen: Warum Distanz zum SED-Staat richtiger gewesen wäre", in: *Kirche im Sozialismus, Beilage zu Deutsches Allgemeines Sonntagsblatt* 32 (7.8.92) III.

van Unnik, W. C. 1975: "Lob und Strafe durch die Obrigkeit: Hellenistisches zu Röm 13,3-4", in: E. E. Ellis/E. Gräßer (eds.), *Jesus und Paulus. FS W. G. Kümmel*, Göttingen: Vandenhoeck & Ruprecht 1975, 334-43.

Weiß, J. 1917: *Das Urchristentum*, Göttingen: Vandenhoeck & Ruprecht 1917.

Wengst, K. 1986: *Pax Romana: Anspruch und Wirklichkeit*, München: Kaiser 1986.

Wilckens, U. 1982: *Der Brief an die Römer* (Röm 12-16) (EKK VI/3), Zürich/Neukirchen-Vluyn: Benziger/Neukirchener Verlag 1982.

Wilkens, E. 1964: *Die Zehn Artikel über Freiheit und Dienst der Kirche: Theologisch-politischer Kommentar*, Stuttgart: Kreuz 1964.

Winter, B.W. 1988: "The Public Honouring of Christian Benefactors: Romans 13.3-4 and 1 Peter 2.14-15", in: *JSNT* 34 (1988) 87-103.

Wolbert, W. 1981: *Ethische Argumentation und Paränese in 1 Kor 7* (MSS 8), Düsseldorf: Patmos 1981.

Wolf, E. 1957/70/84: *Barmen: Kirche zwischen Versuchung und Gnade*, München: Kaiser 1957, [2]1970, [3]1984.

Yoder, J. H. 1981: *Die Politik Jesu – der Weg des Kreuzes*, Maxdorf: Agape 1981.

Zahn, T. 1925: *Der Brief des Paulus an die Römer* (KNT 6), Erlangen: Deichert [3]1925.

# Apostolic Commitment and "Remembering the Poor"
## A Study in Gal 2:10

### Joseph Pathrapankal

## 1. Introduction

One of the striking phenomena of contemporary biblical exegesis and theological reflection is the increasing awareness and commitment of theologians and exegetes to underline the social dimensions of the Bible. Basic to this awareness is the encouraging fact that there is a better sense of realism and consequent openness to a more contextualised understanding of the Bible as the Word of God. In fact, the entire theology of liberation, which has its origin and development since the mid-1960s, owes much of its insights to the Bible and its concern for the poor and the oppressed. Exegetes and theologians vie with each other to bring out the social message of the Bible, such as the social stance of the prophets of the Old Testament, the social commitment of Jesus of Nazareth and of the early church presented in the Gospels and the Acts of the Apostles.[1] As a matter of fact, the revival of this awareness is a welcome sign for the ministry of the church in the world. With this existential and praxis-oriented hermeneutics in biblical and theological reflection the people of God are once again reminded that the power of the Word of God is something that can transform the human society in the same way as the rain and the snow make the earth fertile and fruitful (cf. Isa 55:10-11).

For the Roman Catholic church this awareness and concern about the dynamism of the Word of God is clearly spelt out in the document of Vatican II, *Gaudium et Spes* known as the Pastoral Constitution on the Church in the Modern World, which emphasizes the special responsibility the Christians all over the world have toward "those who are poor or in any way afflicted" and underlines the increasing gap between the 'haves' and 'have-nots' as well as the universal mandate "to count social necessities among the primary duties of modern world". Taking advantage of this favourable directives, the Roman Catholic exegetes and theologians in the so-called

---

[1] Cassidy 1978 and idem 1987.

Third World are now trying to bring to light some of the important insights the various books of the Bible offer regarding the social commitment of its various authors. Among others, Paul is also considered as an important New Testament author who laid emphasis on this social dimension, a concern which he reveals in his several letters, the main among them being a duplicate appeal he made to the Christians of Corinth to help the poor Christians of Judea, which he understood as a "ministry to the saints" (διακονία εἰς τοὺς ἀγίους) (2 Cor 8:4; 9:1).

Paul is often presented as having contributed very much to a theology of liberation, not only through his theological reflection understanding the work of Christ as a liberation from sin (Rom 5:12-21), from the tragedy of death (Rom 6:3-11) and from the slavery of the law (Rom 7:1-25) but also through his bold stance for establishing the equality of Jew and Greek, slave and free as well as male and female (Gal 3:28). It is true that Paul did not fight for the liberation of the slaves; what he did was to establish certain sound theological principles which were to serve as the basis for everyone to be free and equal persons. Thus Paul exhorted Philemon to accept his slave Onesimus not as a slave, but as a beloved brother both in the flesh and in the Lord (Phlm 16). So also, though Paul is said to have restricted the freedom of women in the Corinthian church through his instructions about women covering their head in liturgical gatherings (1 Cor 11:2-16) as well as they keeping silent in such assemblies (1 Cor 14:33b-36), it is in the same letter that we find him clearly establishing the equality of male and female in marital life (1 Cor 7:2-6). As a matter of fact, the Pauline authorship of 1 Cor 14:33b-36 is very much doubted as it disrupts the line of thinking in 1 Cor 14:33a continued in 1 Cor 14:37. For Paul, freedom was something precious radically rooted in the Christ event, and he wanted that all enjoy it in their own realm of life (Gal 5:1). This freedom meant a liberation from all oppressive and restrictive powers, and hence Paul's understanding of liberation and liberated existence has all-embracing and holistic dimensions.

It is in this perspective that we have to understand Paul's efforts to assist the economically poor Christians of Judea through his continuous appeal to the churches of Gentile regions to contribute to his project of raising funds for these poor members of the church. Though we do not know much about this collection made in the churches of Galatia, we have detailed information about his efforts in the churches of Macedonia and Achaia (cf. 1 Cor 16:1-4; 2 Cor 8:1-24; 9:1-15). In fact, Paul understood this work of assisting the poor Christians as something noble and sacred, as part of his very apostolic ministry, and hence we have his profuse use of theological concepts to describe this work, such as χάρις (2 Cor 8:6,7,19), διακονία (2 Cor 8:4; 9:1,12,13; Rom 15:25), ἁδρότης (2 Cor 8:20), εὐλογία (2 Cor 9:5), λειτουργία (2 Cor 9:12) and κοινωνία (2 Cor 9:13). Paul made use of his persuading language to encourage the Corinthians to assist the poor Christians not as an obligation but as a praiseworthy act of Christian solidarity. Hence he presented before them the self-emptying act of Christ who became poor, so that through his poverty the believers become rich (2 Cor 8:9). It was also a very encouraging fact that in this campaign for the poor Christians, Paul was assisted by Titus and several other Christians from Macedonia who made it their duty and privilege to help Paul in this endeavour. Writing to the Romans from Corinth, Paul was very much happy about the outcome of his efforts because the Christians of Macedonia and Achaia were pleased to contribute their resources to the poor Christians in Jerusalem (Rom 15:25-26). In fact, Paul had written to the Corinthians that the Christians of Macedonia had been so generous in their contributions and that they even gave beyond their means because they understood it as their privilege to help the poor (2 Cor 8:1-4). The basic rationale behind this apostolic ministry, as Paul understood it, seems to lie in a crucial passage, which is a concluding statement in the context of the leaders of the church of Jerusalem discussing the controversial issue of admitting Gentiles into the church (Gal 2:1-10). The purpose of this study is to analyse this passage and see its theological meaning and pastoral significance in the apostolic ministry of Paul as well as its message for our times.

There have been a number of studies related to Gal 2:10 which, however, do not seem to take much interest in analysing the theological and apostolic meaning of the passage. Two studies of L. E. Keck are exclusively concerned with demonstrating the theory of Karl Holl[2] about οἱ πτωχοί in Gal 2:10 as a designation of the whole church of Jerusalem as false and ill-founded.[3] A study of Klaus Berger is mainly concerned with the historical context of the collection made by Paul.[4] In a short comment on "St. Paul and Famine Relief: A study in Gal 2:10" David R. Hall, after trying to establish that Paul was concerned with a famine relief at the time of his visit to Jerusalem described in Gal 2:10, refers to the missionary task of the church as consisting not only of the preaching of the gospel but also of economically helping the churches in their needs; in other words, the relation between evangelistic preaching and social service.[5] This passing suggestion made by Hall seems to open a line of thinking the exegetes and theologians are very much in need of in our times. Whereas in some of the studies referred to above very much attention is given to analyse the meaning of ἐσπούδασα as related to Paul's response to the request made by the leaders of the church of Jerusalem, very little attention is paid to explain the theological meaning of μνημονεύωμεν, as related to the request made by the same leaders, which verb seems to contain a very important concept in the entire

---

[2] Holl 1921, 920-47.
[3] Keck 1965, 100-29; idem 1966, 57-78.
[4] Berger 1977, 180-204.
[5] Hall 1971, 309-11.

biblical thinking. The result is that Gal 2:10, which constitutes an important dimension in the holistic understanding of Pauline apostolate, is not given the significance it deserves. Hence this study purports to highlight these points and derive some theological and practical conclusions for the mission of the church in our times.

## 2. The Context of Gal 2:10

The question regarding the relationship between Gal 2:1-10 and Acts 15:1-29 seems to have been more or less answered with the majority view that Gal 2:1-10 is a Pauline version of what Luke gives in Acts 15:1-12, whereas Acts 15:13-29 deals with a later event in Jerusalem over which James presided, and the issue was all about the table fellowship of Jewish and Gentile Christians, an event which Paul probably came to know from James only when the former returned to Jerusalem after his third missionary journey (Acts 21:25). Whereas in Acts 15:1-12 the author focuses on the ecclesial dimension of the problem of the admission of the Gentiles into the church and its solution, as was the case in the problem of the widows in Acts 6:1-6, in Gal 2:1-9, as far as possible, Paul is preoccupied with establishing his apostolic authority and his independence from the Jerusalem church.

The conclusion of the dialogue between the 'pillars' and Paul was a compromise and an understanding on a division of labour between them, that the leaders of the Jerusalem church would concentrate their attention on the ministry among the Jews, and Paul and Barnabas would continue to work among the Gentiles. This implied that full agreement on principles was reached in the discussion between the two groups. Paul goes on to say: "The leaders asked us one thing, that we should continue to remember the poor, which was actually what I had been eager to do" (Gal 2:10). In this statement of Paul there are two issues: (i) the request made by the leaders and (ii) the reaction and response of Paul to this request. To understand the full significance of these two issues we have to analyse them separately.

## 3. The Request made by the 'Pillars' (Gal 2:10a)

The basic question to be answered here is whether by the term οἱ πτωχοί the whole community of the Jerusalem church is meant or only the economically poor members of this church. K. Holl's thesis was that Paul was using a technical term for the church as a whole, which it appropriated from Judaism's traditional regard for the poor, who thereby felt themselves especially close to God. This position has been vigorously attacked by L. E. Keck in his two studies, mentioned above. The general opinion of scholars is that here it was not a question of a designation for all Christians, rather it was all related to a group of Christians who were poor because of Judea's special geographical and economic conditions. In Acts 6:1-6 we read about the presence of widows in the Jerusalem church and the quarrel that arose when the Hellenistic widows were neglected in the daily distribution of food. The help the leaders of the church asked Paul for was for meeting the needs of the 'saints' (2 Cor 9:12) and they did not have another technical designation as 'the poor' which later on became the ebionite Christianity.

It must be equally maintained that the financial help proposed to Paul by the leaders of the Jerusalem church was not a stipulation in order to have his gospel approved by them, but a request and a friendly suggestion to him. The Greek word μόνον placed at the very beginning of this clause makes it clear that the help to the poor was not an obligatory test of Paul's loyalty to Jerusalem or of his subservience to its authority. Hence any attempt to understand this offering as a Christian version of the temple tax among the diaspora synagogues has to be rejected. In fact, several exegetes have been tempted to explain this request along these lines. This is an untenable interpretation as it contradicts the very meaning of the second part of v. 10. Hence what the leaders requested and what Paul readily agreed to was a gesture of Christian solidarity between Jewish and Gentile Christians, the proof of which was already given in the help sent to Jerusalem from Antioch (Acts 11:27-30), which probably Paul and Barnabas brought to Jerusalem during their visit described in Gal 2:1-10. This approach to the proposed help also better explains the designations Paul uses for the collection in 2 Corinthians, such as χάρις, διακονία, and κοινωνία, which we have mentioned above.

The fact that what the leaders proposed was a request and not a stipulation becomes even clearer when we analyse the meaning of the verb μνημονεύωμεν. Paul is asked to 'remember' the poor, and the meaning is that Paul is requested to think of the poor in such a way that he does something concrete to alleviate their hardships. Why exactly did Paul make use of this Greek verb? If we take into account the fact that the Greek verbs μνημονεύω with its derived substantive μνημόσυνον and ἀναμιμνήσκω with its derived substantive ἀνάμνησις have a profound theological meaning both in the Old Testament and the New Testament, we are closer to seeing the meaning of μνημονεύωμεν as the content of the request made by the leaders of the Jerusalem church. In the Bible 'remembering' is much more than a psychological exercise of calling to memory something of the past, but an act of the mind and the will, out of which a corresponding action follows for one's own or others' benefit or sometimes even a punishment.

Thus God is said to have "remembered Noah and all the domestic animals that were with him in the ark" (Gen 8:1), as a result of which God made a wind blow over the earth, and the waters subsided and the flood came to a halt. Hannah prayed to the Lord asking him to look on her misery and to 'remember' her by giving her a male child, whom she would dedicate to the Lord as a *nazirite* (1 Sam 1:11) and later it is said that the Lord 'remembered' her and gave her a son, Samuel (1 Sam 1:19). Whereas God remembering someone means immediate action and blessing, the humans are exhorted to remember because they lack the courage and commitment to do what they have to remember. Hence Tobit told his son, Tobias, about his mother; "Remember her, my son, because she faced many dangers for you while you were in her womb. And when she dies, bury her beside me in the same grave" (Tob 4:5). Jonathan, the High Priest, wrote to the Spartans: "We remember you constantly on every occasion, both at our festivals and on other appropriate days, at the sacrifices that we offer and in our prayers, as it is right and proper to remember brothers" (1 Macc 12:11).

The Book of Deuteronomy dwells on this remembrance motif as part of its persuasive language inviting Israel to live in their new home with a meaningful remembrance of their past: "Remember that you were a slave in the land of Egypt, and the Lord your God brought you out from there with a mighty hand and an outstretched arm" (Deut 5:15; 15:15; 16:12; 24:17,22). When Israel had to deal with their own slaves, when they were celebrating their festivals, and when they were harvesting, they were exhorted to remember their past and to be generous to their own people as well as to strangers, orphans and widows, and the main reason behind this generosity was that they themselves had undergone the hardships of slavery and poverty. They were exhorted to remember also the fact that God fed them when they were hungry, after letting them experience the pain of hunger, precisely to enable them to know that one does not live by bread alone, but by every word that comes from the mouth of the Lord (Deut 8:2-3). The Deuteronomist, through his retrospective reflection on history, knew very well that the Israelites were likely to forget their past when they had everything at their disposal and would lead an irresponsible life towards themselves and others. Hence he used a persuading language to warn the Israelites of the dangers associated with prosperity, a problem any nation and any people will have to face anywhere in the world. Consequently, the motif of remembrance occupies a very important place in Deuteronomy, and it is probable that Paul also had been influenced by this message of the Book of Deuteronomy when he used μνημονεύωμεν in Gal 2:10 as the content of the request made by the church leaders.

It is against the background of this remembrance motif in the Old Testament that we have to understand several passages in the New Testament related to remembrance. Thus Mary, in the context of her thanking God for being blessed with the promise of a child, recalls how God helped his servant Israel in remembrance of his mercy (μνησθῆναι ἐλέους) (Luke 1:54). So also in his hymn of joy and gratitude,

Zechariah refers to God as remembering his holy covenant (μνησθῆναι διαθήκης ἁγίας) with the result that he kept his promises made to Abraham and enabled his people to live in security and to serve him in holiness and righteousness (Luke 1:72-73). The loving act of the woman anointing Jesus and thus preparing him for his burial is presented by Mark as a meaningful act that will be remembered as part of the gospel preached throughout the world (Mark 14:9). Cornelius, a devout man of Caesarea, was given a share in the good news of salvation as a result of his prayers and alms (Acts 10:4), which ascended as a memorial (μνημόσυνον) before God, namely, God remembered the devout life and the good actions performed by him, and the result was that God gave him an opportunity to hear the gospel preached to him by Peter.

In the Farewell Discourse Jesus reminds his disciples about what would happen to them precisely because their master had to undergo persecution (John 15:20). The disciples are told about the hardships of discipleship so that, when they would happen to them, they could remember his words and squarely face the challenges. The author of the Acts of the Apostles presents Paul as having convened a meeting of the Elders of Ephesus at Miletus where Paul explained to them his hard work for the church of Ephesus and asked them to remember how earnestly he worked for them night and day. Paul was convinced that it was better to give than to receive, because he remembered the words of the Lord Jesus (Acts 20:34-35). The angel of the church of Ephesus reminded the believers of that church that they have to remember from what heights they have fallen and consequently they have to be ready for conversion (Rev 2:5).

An important question to be asked in this connection is whether the ἀνάμνησις passage in the institution of the Lord's Supper (1 Cor 11:24-25; Luke 22:19) deals with this same theme of remembrance or not. It is to be observed that this command and invitation to remember is found only in the Pauline-Lukan branch of the tradition. On linguistic and stylistic grounds it must be regarded as pre-Pauline. However, the command to repeat the rite is not necessarily a part of the liturgical formula, since the celebration itself was its fulfilment. It could be that here we are dealing with an early, special tradition which found a place only in the Antiochene branch of the tradition about the Lord's Supper. It is to be further noted that in Palestine also such memorial formulae are to be found in the liturgy and prayers. Already in the Old Testament the Passover was celebrated annually *lᵉzikkaron* (Exod 12:14). About prayers it is said that they were raised εἰς μνημόσυνον (*1 Enoch* 99:3), that they, together with alms, have ascended as a memorial before God (cf. Acts 10:4).

The crucial question in this context is this: who is the subject of this remembrance in the institution narrative? Is it the celebrating community or God? Does it mean: "Do this in order that you remember me", in which case it is the celebrating community that remembers what Jesus did, or does it mean: "Do this in order that God remembers me", in which case it is God who remembers Christ who instituted the Lord's Supper. The Old Testament has several cases which have the latter meaning of something done or brought before God as a memorial, something denoting a representation before God so that God may remember, a remembrance which was effective and creative. God's remembrance always means an action in mercy or judgement.

But how are we to understand the command of Christ: τοῦτο ποιεῖτε εἰς τὴν ἐμὴν ἀνάμνησιν? τοῦτο ποιεῖτε is a common expression for the repetition of a rite (Exod 29:35; Num 15:11-13; Deut 25:9). In our case it refers to the rite of "breaking the bread" and "blessing the cup". What is the purpose of doing it? Taking the whole context into consideration, the obvious answer seems to be this: To remember the one who does the act, namely, Jesus, who through the signs of bread and wine offers himself to the community which confirms his wilful offering of himself to God and to his people. This interpretation, obvious and sensible as it is, has been questioned by J. Jeremias,[6] who tries to see this as a case of God remembering Jesus: "Do this, that God may remember me". Grammatically and, probably also historically, such an interpretation is possible. However, taking the whole context of the institution of the Lord's Supper into consideration and also understanding the passage in the living context of the celebrating community, it seems more natural to understand this passage as a command given by Jesus to the community to celebrate the Lord's Supper in remembrance of the one who did it for them. The meaning of this remembrance is that the celebrating community must enter into a living and dynamic relationship with the one who did it for them.

In fact, we have to see this command to remembrance in relation to the foot washing ceremony in the Upper Room as narrated by John. The Gospel of John does not contain the story of the institution of the Lord's Supper, and it substitutes it with the episode of the washing of the feet, a gesture of service, love and brotherhood. John seems to see in this episode the profound meaning of the Lord's Supper by making the disciples understand the message of what Jesus did for them. Jesus asked: "Do you know what I have done to you? ... If I, your Lord and Teacher, have washed your feet, you also ought to wash one another's feet. For I have set you an example, that you also should do (ὑμεῖς ποιῆτε) as I have done to you" (John 13:12a-15). In the celebration of the Lord's Supper also the celebrating community is asked to remember the meaning and message of what Jesus did for them in such a way that they, in their turn do, as Jesus did, in their interpersonal relationship by making themselves available to others through

---

[6] Jeremias 1977, 252.

their altruism. Paul goes on to explain the relationship of this remembrance to the death of Christ in so far as the believers are thereby proclaiming (καταγγέλ- λετε) the death of the Lord until he comes (1 Cor 11:26). The ἀνάμνησις is at the same time a proclamation, by which the death of Christ as a past event becomes an event of the present and at the same time looks forward into the future till the parousia inviting the celebrating community to lead a life inspired by the Christ event.

It is in the light of these above considerations about remembrance that we have to understand the profound meaning of the request made by the leaders of the Jerusalem church that Paul should remember the poor, meaning thereby that this remembrance on the part of Paul would result in his genuine commitment to the cause of the poor. The auxiliary verb μνημονεύωμεν, being subjunctive, points to a desired ongoing activity, and so it is better translated: "we should continue to remember". What the leaders of the Jerusalem church seem to have asked for was that Paul, in exercising his freedom to carry on an independent strategy for preaching the gospel among the Gentiles, should continue to keep in mind also the welfare of poor Christians of Jerusalem. In other words, Paul's commitment to the Gentiles should not in any way distract him from his good relations to Jerusalem, a sign of which would be his efforts to help the poor Christians in that church.

## 4. Paul's Commitment to the Cause of the Poor (Gal 2:10b)

Paul welcomed the request made by the leaders as something dear to him and says that it was something which he had been eager to do (ἐσπούδασα). This statement of Paul makes it abundantly clear that the leaders did not attach any kind of obligation or condition to their proposal to Paul to remember the poor; rather it was all a question of Christian solidarity and mutual sharing of concerns. For Paul it was another opportunity to show that Jewish and Gentile Christians were equal before God and that their leaders have to share the blessings and the burdens of their apostolate even as they work in their respective areas agreed upon among themselves. Though in Rom 15:27 Paul writes about the reciprocity of the spiritual blessings received by the Gentiles and the material blessings given by them to their Jewish brethren, it is doubtful whether Paul wanted to see this monetary help given by the Gentile Christians as a compensation and an obligation on their part. In any case, through that statement Paul never wanted to mean that the Gentile Christians are only second class Christians who had received only the "crumbs that fell from their masters' table" (Matt 15:27). However, Paul was aware of the fact that the gospel was preached to the Gentiles in all earnestness because "the Jews had rejected it and judged themselves to be unworthy of eternal life" (Acts 13:46). The same approach is found in Paul's analysis of the problem of the infidelity of the Jews in relation to the faith of the Gentiles (Rom 9:1-11:36). Here Paul was referring to the historical sequence of events rather than to any theological principle of superiority.

A related question about Paul's enthusiasm and his extraordinary commitment to raising a fund for the Christians of Judea is whether or not it was a diplomatic move on his part to please the leaders of the Jerusalem church. As at many other levels of human relationship, the monetary aid programmes are a very attractive way of winning over the good will and gratitude of the beneficiaries, the more so when they are economically poor and consequently are dependent. To argue it that way in the case of Paul would be discrediting the very personality of Paul we know from his writings. It is true that Paul understood this aid programme as something "right not only in the Lord's sight but also in the sight of others" (2 Cor 8:21). But it would be absolutely wrong to understand the motivation of Paul behind this programme as something to please the leaders of the Jerusalem church. Paul writes: "If I were still pleasing people, I would not be a servant of Christ" (Gal 1:10). "This is our boast, the testimony of our conscience: we have behaved in the world with frankness and godly sincerity; not by earthly wisdom but by the grace of God and all the more toward you" (2 Cor 1:12), Paul wrote to the Corinthians about his relationship to that church. Both as a Jew and as a believer in Jesus Christ, Paul never did anything according to human standards. He lived by his convictions and was fully committed to them. If it were ever his plan to please the leaders of the Church of Jerusalem or, for that matter, anybody else, he would not have fought so strongly for the freedom of the Gentile Christians from the Jewish rite of circumcision and the observance of the Mosaic law. He never made his plans according to ordinary human standards of behaviour (2 Cor 1:17).

Basically, Paul's commitment to the poor Christians was an expression of his apostolic altruism and his readiness to be available to all (1 Cor 9:19-23). For Paul, the model for this altruism was the very person of Christ who became poor so that by his poverty all might become rich (cf. 2 Cor 8:9). Consequently, for Paul the collection of a material help for the poor Christians was a proof of the Christian solidarity the Corinthians had to demonstrate through their generosity. Paul explained to the Corinthians how the Macedonians generously helped the poor Christians in spite of their own poverty because, for them, it was a "ministry to the saints" through which they "gave themselves first to the Lord" and then to Paul (cf. 2 Cor 8:5). It is not that Paul wanted to relieve the Christians in Jerusalem at the costs of the hardships to the Corinthians; rather it was a question of equality. Hence Paul writes: "At the moment your surplus meets their need, but one day your need may be met from their surplus. The aim is equality" (2 Cor 8:13-14). The resources of this material world are meant for all and all have a right to use them and lead a dignified life. It happens that at one time some have these resources in abundance while others live in poverty and misery. But in course of time it could happen that those who were rich become poor and the poor become rich. This is a lesson of history, then and now.

That Paul was the least bound up with the honour and privilege of being a benefactor to the church of Jerusalem becomes clear from the way he directed the Corinthians to have their collections made and later on taken to Jerusalem (1 Cor 16:1-4). On the one hand, Paul did not want to supervise the collections in Corinth; rather he asked them to put aside and reserve what they could spare on every first day of the week when they came together for the celebration of the Lord's Supper. On the other hand, he asked them to have their own people approved by them to be sent to Jerusalem to deliver the gift. It was not only a question of making the Corinthians feel that it was their gift but also a delicate matter in which he wanted to keep his hands off, for fear that later on the Corinthians would complain that Paul had manipulated their gift for his own advantage. Paul worked hard to earn his own livelihood and he did not want to have his right for boasting that he did not depend on others to become an empty word (cf. 1 Cor 9:6-15). He worked hard night and day rather than become a burden to anyone as he preached the gospel (1 Thess 2:9). A person of such calibre and self-respect would be the last one to arrange a programme of helping the poor Christians of Jerusalem just for the sake of some cheap popularity among the church leaders in Jerusalem.

A last question regarding Paul's commitment to the programme of helping the poor Christians is related to the verbal expression ὃ καὶ ἐσπούδασα αὐτὸ τοῦτο ποιῆσαι, which is translated as "which is what I have always been eager to do". The neuter relative pronoun ὃ picks up the whole idea of its immediate antecedent "to continue to remember the poor". αὐτό is added to τοῦτο as an intensive pronoun which strengthens the latter demonstrative pronoun to make it read "this very thing". The verb ἐσπούδασα is particularly interesting because of its aorist tense as well as the first personal singular used. ἐσπούδασα has been translated in three ways: (i) NRSV: "which was actually what I was eager to do"; (ii) NEB: "which was the very thing I had made it my business to do"; (iii) JB "as indeed I was anxious to do in any case". Since the verb is in the aorist, it must have the meaning of a completed action and it corresponds to an English pluperfect.[7] The verb ἐσπούδασα therefore means: "I had made an effort to do this very thing in the past also." We have parallels of this grammatical construction in Matt 14:3; Mark 8:14 and Luke 8:27. The context of Gal 2:10 implies that here Paul was referring to what he had been doing so far and not to something he undertook at the suggestion of the

---

[7] Hall 1971, 310.

leaders in Jerusalem. The conclusion of the meeting in Jerusalem according to Gal 2:1-10 was that the leaders added nothing to the teaching of Paul (Gal 2:6); rather they gave to Paul and Barnabas full approval of the gospel they preached (Gal 2:9). The only request they made was that they should continue to take care of the poor, and this, Paul says, was the very thing he had been doing so far. The full approval given by the leaders to Paul was proved in nothing more clearly than in the fact that their only request was the very thing to which Paul had been committed in the past also, probably referring to the help from the church of Antioch (cf. Acts 11:27-30). Why then Paul did not use the first person plural because Barnabas was also involved in this specific famine relief? It may be noted that in Gal 2:1-10, even when speaking of events where Barnabas was also present, Paul primarily refers to himself (cf. Gal 2:1-3, 6-9a) because here Paul had to defend himself and his apostolic authority against his accusers, and also because things were often happening mainly through Paul's initiative and leadership.

## 5. Paul's Anxiety about the Destiny of the Relief Fund

Though Paul had made all efforts to persuade the Gentile Christians of Galatia, Macedonia and Achaia to give generously to his relief fund, making use of several theological and psychological arguments (cf. 2 Cor 8-9), when the right time came for him to deliver it to the Jerusalem church, he had his anxiety whether his gift would be acceptable to that church at all. Paul wrote to the Romans: "I appeal to you, brothers and sisters, by our Lord Jesus Christ and by the love of the Spirit, to join me in earnest prayer to God on my behalf, that I may be rescued from the unbelievers in Judea and that my ministry to Jerusalem may be acceptable to the saints, so that by God's will I may come to you with joy and be refreshed in your company" (Rom 15:30-32).

Why did Paul have this anxiety about the acceptance of the gift by the church of Jerusalem? Paul had worked hard to keep the promise he made to the leaders of that church and now he is afraid that his offer would be turned down! It seems that circumstances had changed very much from the time the meeting in Jerusalem between the leaders and Paul took place around AD 49 and Paul wrote the letter to the Romans around AD 58. Though the Jerusalem meeting had established clearly the principle that faith is the only requirement for being a follower of Christ, there were still efforts being made later on by many Judaizers to introduce the Jewish custom of circumcision among the Gentile Christians. It is possible that Paul gave up his programme of collecting help in the Galatian churches precisely because this problem was very strong in that territory. It is also possible that some leaders in Jerusalem did not like that Paul was preaching to the Jews in the synagogues in Asia Minor and Greece during his second and third missionary journeys (cf. Acts 17:1-3; 1 Cor 9:20). As a matter of fact, things had not improved very much after the Jerusalem council regarding the question of the admission of Gentiles into the Church. Many Jewish Christians still maintained that to be a Christian meant to be a Jew also at the same time. It is probable that Paul attempted at a systematic presentation of his gospel in the letter to the Romans precisely to convince his Jewish and Gentile Christian readers that divine acceptance, which Paul explains as *justification*, was exclusively a matter of God's mercy and love. In this letter Paul established at the very outset that he was not ashamed of the gospel, and that he was a debtor to both Greeks and barbarians, to both the wise and the foolish (cf. Rom 1:14-16). What he did in this letter was to establish the place of both Jews and Gentiles as partners in God's plan of salvation.

Even as Paul was realizing for himself the basic truth about the gospel that it is something available to all on the basis of their faith, things were getting worse in Jerusalem, and it seems that Paul had a prognosis of it while he was writing the letter to the Romans. That is why he wrote to the Romans to pray for him that he may be rescued from the unbelievers in Judea and that his bringing of a gift may be acceptable to the saints (cf. Rom 15:31). We can surmise the nature of the new problem that was brewing in Jerusalem from a close reading of the Acts of the Apostles. It seems that, when Paul reached Jerusalem, the whole question of the "alms for the nation" (Acts 24:17) which he had brought with him in the company of Sopater, Aristarchus, Secundus, Gajus, Timothy and Tychicus, had receded to the background. When Paul reached Jerusalem, a fresh accusation against him was ready, that he taught the Jews living among the Gentiles to forsake Moses and not to circumcise their children or observe their customs (Acts 21:21). The Acts presents it as an information given by James, who otherwise seems to be favourable to Paul's mission among the Gentiles. As such, the leaders in the Jerusalem church were happy about what Paul was doing among the Gentiles. We read that, when James and the elders heard about what God had done among the Gentiles through Paul, they praised God (cf. Acts 21:19-20). But the accusation that he taught the Jews to forsake Moses was derogatory not only for the Jews but also for the Jewish Christians. Hence he did not get any real support from the Jewish Christians in Jerusalem nor from the leaders of the church.

It seems that, as a result of this confusion created in Jerusalem, the whole issue of the relief fund brought by Paul and his associates did not create any impression on the Jerusalem church and its leaders. It is possible that the Roman governor, Felix, expected some money from Paul because he knew that Paul had brought the relief fund with him for Jerusalem. James is said to have tried to save Paul from this embarrassing situation by suggesting to him to undergo a Jewish rite, through which

Paul had to prove that he was still observing the Jewish law and customs and that he had nothing against them (Acts 21:23-24). But it did not work out. The Jews from Asia (Galatia?) accused him of bringing Greeks into the temple and defiling the holy place, which led to the story of the uproar against Paul and his consequent arrest by the Roman tribune of the cohort (Acts 21:27-33). The author of the Acts does not say anything about what happened to the relief fund because it was not a major issue for his theology of the Acts. Reflecting on what Paul must have felt about the whole outcome of his untiring labour to help the poor Christians of Jerusalem, we may conclude that, for Paul, it was another proof of how even a good cause can get thwarted through religious fanaticism. But what Paul did to help the poor Christians of Jerusalem in the midst of his demanding missionary activities stands out as a clear demonstration of how Paul was committed to the poor as part of his holistic concept of apostolic commitment.

## 6. The Message of Gal 2:10

Exegetes and theologians, as a rule, study the person and theology of Paul specifically along the lines of his contributions to anthropology and christology from an abstract soteriological perspective. They refer to what Paul did to help the poor Christians in Judea more as an academic piece of information without in the least concerned about its real apostolic objective. It is another proof of how existential and other vital concerns of theology and exegesis get neglected when the reins of theological and biblical disciplines are decided by theologians and exegetes of the affluent West. By certain paradoxes of history humankind has been unjustly divided into several groups of 'haves' and 'have-nots', the so-called First, Second and Third Worlds. Of late there is so much written and discussed about the Third World, either by theologians of the First World who keep on encouraging it to develop its own theology or by the theologians of the Third World itself who try to articulate their right to selfhood and self-determination in matters related to their culture and concrete concerns. There are also several international agencies in the First World involved in aid-programmes for helping the churches in the Third World in their religious, spiritual, theological, pastoral and social activities. In a certain sense, these aid-programmes are indirect ways of repaying the exploitation of the Third World during past centuries through military colonialism, during which the military and the missionary joined hands, and the latter preached a theology of salvation reserved for these exploited millions in the world that was to come! Fortunately, things have changed very much and there is a better sense of realism in the universal church regarding inter-church relationship and cooperation between the churches.

The important question is this: Do the churches and their organisations realize that through all these aid-programmes and missionary assistance they are continuing a 'ministry' and exercising a 'grace' as an expression of their *koinonia*, as Paul understood and practised it during his apostolate? It is this major task the community of theologians and exegetes are called upon to undertake as an integral part of their commitment to the Word of God and to the larger world of God. Unfortunately, theology and biblical scholarship have not fully become a reality which feed humanity at large. Hermeneutics and biblical scholarship are very much busy with abstract speculation and they render little service to the less fortunate sections of the humankind which constitute the majority of the world population. Hence it is high time for the theologians and exegetes to realize that God's world is larger than the Western world and that God's concerns are more radical and vital than abstract speculation on the dead text of the Bible. The Word of God in the Bible must become a liberating force, and it is the duty of the exegetes to help release its liberating and redeeming power for the total benefit of the humankind. There is much discussion today about contextuality and contextual principle in biblical interpretation. If this principle is to have any meaning and relevance, it must go hand in hand with the entire science of biblical hermeneutics. Any hermeneutics that pretends first to discover general, time-and-space transcending interpretations, which are then adapted and applied to particular and concrete situations, is not only deluding itself but is actually failing to fulfil the very task, to which it is, in fact, called, and cannot possibly lead to any kind of real contextuality. Consequently, the hermeneutic problem is to be shifted from theoretical and cognitive level to the existential and historical level of action and mission, marked by the church's task in history and in the world at large. As such, hermeneutics should become fundamentally a dialogue between the biblical text and the present-day socioeconomic and political reality of the historical process that is at work in our societies.[8] Theology and exegesis are not ends in themselves, carried out for the intellectual entertainment and for the satisfaction of the academic curiosity of the scholars; they are tools and models of radical Christian faithfulness and witness, within concrete time, space, and cultural situation.

This task is all the more imperative for the Indian theologians and exegetes. After centuries of Western colonialism followed by foreign missionaries looking after the theological formation as well as the theological thinking of this subcontinent, the time has come for the Indian theologians and exegetes to develop a theology in tune with the culture and social imperatives of this country. One of their major tasks is to become aware of the social thrust of the Word of God, a thrust through which the Word of God can transform the Indian society as a whole. Whereas for Paul it was

---

[8] Wink 1973, 6.

a question of conscientizing the Gentile Christians about their duty to assist the poor Christians in Jerusalem, the Indian theologians and exegetes have to develop a more broad and universal outlook, transcending the barriers of religion, region and language, by which they commit themselves to making the entire nation aware of its grave task to work for the poor, the oppressed and the underprivileged. It is a known fact that, whereas about 10% of the Indian population is affluent, more than 30% of it is below the poverty line and the entire Indian society is made up of a high complexity of social realities under the destructive influence of caste, colour and creed. It is precisely in this situation that Indian theologians and exegetes must pool together their energy to build up a theology of social involvement as part of their ecclesial commitment. It is this theology that has to become the motivating force for the church in India to commit itself to a radical transformation of the Indian society.

Gustavo Gutierrez, the pioneer of liberation theology in Latin America, before 30 years committed himself to the task of making theology relevant to his country and to his people. His task it was to determine and to interpret the situation of his country in the light of his religion and its Scriptures, which were supposed to define and interpret that religion for him and for the millions of his country. He strongly reacted to the established principles of interpreting religion and its relation to society, principles which were handed down through centuries without reference to time, culture and the real needs of the society. It was a reaction to theology traditionally understood as wisdom and rational knowledge. At the same time, it was also an attempt to establish theology as a critical reflection on historical praxis based on the gospel of Jesus Christ as well as the experiences of men and women committed to the process of liberation in the oppressed and exploited land of Latin America. The power as well as the challenge he released through his bold and inspiring interpretation of the gospel have made inroads in many countries of Latin America and is influencing many theologians of the Third World in their theological reflection, inviting them to commit themselves to a more radical, relevant and meaningful interpretation of their religion and its Scriptures.

It is to be further observed that Gutierrez had his major inspiration for his new theological thrust from the Bible itself. He saw in the Bible a God who was committed to a radical liberation of the humankind, the clearest example of which was the exodus of Israel from Egypt, which was basically a political action of breaking away from a situation of oppression and misery for the construction of a just and fraternal society through the mediation of Moses.[9] The paradox of the whole programme was that the Israelites, faced with the first difficulties, told Moses that they preferred the security of slavery in Egypt to the uncertainties of a liberation that was

---

[9] Gutierrez 1973, 155-60.

in process. A gradual process of success and failure would be necessary for them to become aware of the roots of their oppression in order to struggle against it and to perceive the profound sense of liberation, to which they were called. The same is, to some extent, true of our times. Theologians and exegetes in the Third World, instead of taking up the challenge of developing a theology that is relevant and meaningful to their land and culture, often take refuge in some thought patterns and theological traditions inherited during their studies in western universities.

As a trained Pharisee, Paul must have been influenced by the message of the Old Testament, which enabled him to understand his apostolic commitment as having also a social dimension, a dimension which included not only theological principles establishing the equality between Jews and Greeks, slaves and free, and between male and female (Gal 3:28), but also practical actions through which he wanted to assist the poor Christians in the church of Jerusalem. Paul must have understood it as a continuation of the message of the book of Deuteronomy, exhorting Israel to help the poor among them, recalling and remembering their own past history. Consequently, we have to understand that the leaders of the church of Jerusalem was not placing a demand on Paul or proposing a condition to him, when they requested him to remember the poor Christians in Jerusalem, nor did Paul understand this request as a necessary condition for his gospel to be approved by its leaders. Rather the entire issue was a sharing of Christian fellowship and solidarity, and its message stands out as a permanent reminder to the church of all times and her theologians to commit themselves to the task of liberating the people of God from all oppressive and dehumanizing structures in order to enable them to live a more human and dignified life. The missionary commitment of the church means much more than what has been understood and practised in the history of the church during past many centuries, and a looking back into the apostolic commitment of Paul enables us to recapture the holistic dimensions of the mission of the church in our times.

## Bibliography

Berger, Klaus 1977: "Almosen für Israel: Zum historischen Kontext der paulinischen Kollekte", in: *NTS* 23 (1977) 180-204.

Cassidy, Richard J. 1978: *Jesus. Politics and Society: A Study of Luke's Gospel,* Maryknoll, NY: Orbis Books 1978.

— 1987: *Society and Politics in the Acts of the Apostles*, Maryknoll, NY: Orbis Books 1987.

Gutierrez, Gustavo 1973: *A Theology of Liberation*, Maryknoll, NY: Orbis Books 1973.

Hall, David R. 1971: "St. Paul and Famine Relief: A Study in Galatians 2:10", in: *ET* 82 (1971) 309-11.

Holl, Karl 1921: "Der Kirchenbegriff des Paulus in seinem Verhältnis zu dem der Urgemeinde", in: *SPAW.PH* 1921, 920-47.

Jeremias, Joachim 1977: *The Eucharistic Words of Jesus,* London: SCM Press 1977.

Keck, Leander E. 1965: "The Poor among the Saints in the New Testament", in: *ZNW* 56 (1965) 100-29.

— 1966: "The Poor among the Saints in Jewish Christianity and Qumran" *ZNW* 57 (1966) 54-78.

Wink, Walter 1973: *The Bible in Human Transformation: Towards a New Paradigm for Biblical Study,* Philadelphia, PA: Fortress Press 1973.

# Selected Bibliography—Lars Hartman

Tord Fornberg

## 1963

*Testimonium linguae* (CNT 19), Lund: Gleerup, and Copenhagen: Munksgaard 1963.

"Davids son. Apropå Acta 13,16–41," in: *SEÅ* 28–29 (1963–64) 117–34.

Review of K. Aland, *Synopsis Quattuor Evangeliorum*, in: *SEÅ* 28–29 (1963–64) 156–57.

## 1964

Commentaries in *Kommentar till evangelieboken. Högmässotexterna* 1–3, Uppsala: Svensk Pastoraltidskrift 1964.

## 1966

*Prophecy Interpreted* (CB.NT 1), Lund: Gleerup 1966.

Commentaries in *Kommentar till evangelieboken. Aftonsångstexterna*, Uppsala: Svensk Pastoraltidskrift 1966.

Review of B. de Solages, *Synopse Grecque des évangiles* and P. Benoit and M.–E. Boismard, *La synopse des quatre évangiles en Français avec parallèles des apocryphes et des Pères* 1, in: *SEÅ* 31 (1966) 133–35.

## 1967

"Antikrists mirakler," in: *RoB* 26 (1967) 37–63.

Summary of L. Hartman, *Prophecy Interpreted*, in: *SEÅ* 32 (1967) 148–52.

Review of J. Jeremias, *Abba*, and E. Schweizer, *Das Evangelium nach Markus*, in: *SEÅ* 32 (1967) 152–54.

Review of P. Borgen, *Bread from Heaven*, in: *SEÅ* 32 (1967) 154–56.

## 1968

Review of J. Lambrecht, *Die Redaktion des Markus–Apokalypse*, in: *Bib.* 49 (1968) 130–33.

## 1969

Review of R. Pesch, *Naherwartungen. Tradition und Redaktion in Mk 13*, in: *Bib.* 50 (1969) 576–80.

"Nytestamentlig isagogik," in: B. Gerhardsson (ed.), *En bok om Nya Testamentet*, Lund: Gleerup 1969, 11–132. Later editions: 2nd ed. 1970, 3rd ed. 1976, 4th ed. 1982, 5th ed. 1989.

## 1970

(ed.), *Ur Nya Testamentet*, Lund: Gleerups 1970.

"'Såsom det är skrivet.' Några reflexioner över citat som kommunikationsmedel i Matteusevangeliet," in: *SEÅ* 35 (1970) 33–43.

## 1971

"Dopet 'till Jesu namn' och tidig kristologi," in: *SEÅ* 36 (1971)136–63.

Review of R. Walker, *Die Heilsgeschichte im ersten Evangelium*, in: *SEÅ* 36 (1971) 179–80.

Review of Chr. Burchard, *Der dreizehnte Zeuge*, in: *SEÅ* 36 (1971) 180–81.

Review of G. Delling, *Studien zum Neuen Testament und zum hellenistischen Judentum*, in: *SEÅ* 36 (1971) 182–83.

## 1972

"Dop, ande och barnaskap," in: *SEÅ* 37–38 (1972–73) 88–106.

"Scriptural Exegesis in the Gospel of Matthew and the Problem of Communication," in: M. Didier (ed.), *L'évangile selon Matthieu: Rédaction et théologie* (BEThL 29), Gembloux: Duculot 1972, 131–52.

## 1973

"Texten," in: B. Gerhardsson (ed.), *En bok om Nya Testamentet* (3rd ed.), Lund: Liber, and Oslo: Universitetsforlaget 1973, 107–27.

## 1974

"Some remarks on 1 Cor. 2:1–5," in: *SEÅ* 39 (1974) 109–20.

"'Into the Name of Jesus,'" in: *NTS* 20 (1974) 432–40.

"Baptism 'Into the Name of Jesus' and Early Christianity," in: *StTh* 28 (1974) 21–48.

Review of B. Mack, *Logos und Sophia*, in: *SEÅ* 39 (1974) 174–76.

Review of H.–W. Kuhn, *Ältere Sammlungen im Markus–evangelium*, in: *SEÅ* 39 (1974) 188–89.

Review of J. Jervell, *Luke and the People of God*, in: *SEÅ* 39 (1974) 190–91.

Review of W. Trilling, *Untersuchungen zum zweiten Thessalonicherbrief*, in: *SEÅ* 39 (1974) 199–200.

## 1975

"Bibelvetenskap" (with Helmer Ringgren), in: *Religionsvetenskap. En introduktion*, Uppsala: Teologiska institutionen 1975, 42-56. 2nd ed. 1978, 43-57.

"The Functions of Some So–Called Apocalyptic Timetables," in: *NTS* 22 (1975) 1–14 [To be reprinted in Hartman 1995a].

*Handikapp lidande skuld i ljuset av Nya Testamentet*, Diakoniaktuellt nr 4, 1975.

Review of M. Müller, *Messias og "menneskesøn" i Daniels Bog, Første Enoksbog og Fjerde Ezrabog*, in: *SEÅ* 40 (1975) 120–21.

## 1976

"'Comfort of the Scriptures' — an Early Jewish Interpretation of Noah's Salvation, 1 En 10:16–11:2," in: *SEÅ* 41–42 (1976–77) 87–96.

"New Testament Exegesis," in: *Faculty of Theology at Uppsala University. Uppsala University 500 years* 1 (AUU). Uppsala: University 1976, 51–65.

## 1978

"Enhet och mångfald i urkyrkan och dess förhållande till judendomen," in: *RoB* 37 (1978) 3–13.

"Till frågan om evangeliernas litterära genre," in: *AnASU* 21 (1978) 5–22 [To be translated and published as "Some Reflections on the Problem of the Literary Genre of the Gospels" in Hartman 1995a].

Review of H. Conzelmann and H. Lindemann, *Arbeitsbuch zum Neuen Testament*, in: *SEÅ* 43 (1978) 126–28.

Review of G. Strecker (ed.), *Das Problem der Theologie des Neuen Testaments*, in: *SEÅ* 43 (1978) 138–40.

Review of H. Kraft, *Die Offenbarung des Johannes*, in: *SEÅ* 43 (1978) 168–69.

## 1979

*Asking for a Meaning* (CB.NT 12), Lund: Gleerup 1979.

"Att förstå en nytestamentlig text. Undersökningsmetoder och tolkningsresultat," in: *SEÅ* 44 (1979) 115–21.

## 1980

"Bundesideologie in und hinter einigen paulinischen Texten," in: S. Pedersen (ed.), *Die paulinische Literatur und Theologie* (Teologiska studier 7), Århus: Aros, and Göttingen: Vandenhoeck & Ruprecht 1980, 103–18.

"Lär oss att bedja," in: *Bibeln — lär oss att bedja*, Stockholm: Svenska bibelsällskapet 1980, 19–30.

"*Hierosolyma / Ierousalem*," in: H. Balz and G. Schneider (eds.), *EWNT* 2 (1980) 432–39.

"Form and Message. A Preliminary Discussion of 'Partial Texts' in Rev 1–3 and 22,6ff.," in: J. Lambrecht (ed.), *L'Apocalypse johannique et l'Apocalyptique dans le Nouveau Testament* (BEThL 53), Gembloux: Duculot, and Leuven: University 1980, 129–49 [To be reprinted in Hartman 1995a].

Review of K. Aland, *Novum Testamentum Graece* (26th ed.), in: *SEÅ* 45 (1980) 143–45.

Review of W. O. Walker (ed.), *The Relationships among the Gospels*, in: *SEÅ* 45 (1980) 146–47.

## 1981

"Nya Testamentet i ny översättning," in: *Signum* 8 (1981) 232–35.

"*onoma, onomazo*," in: H. Balz and G. Schneider (eds.), *EWNT* 2 (1981) 1268–77.

Review of J. Jeremias, *Die Sprache des Lukasevangeliums*, in: *SEÅ* 46 (1981) 183–84.

Review of H. Köster, *Einführung in das Neue Testament*, in: *SEÅ* 46 (1981) 179–80.

## 1982

"Situationen inom den nytestamentliga exegetiken," in: *SvTK* 58 (1982) 109–16.

"Your Will be done on Earth as it is in Heaven," in: *ATJ* 11 (1982) 209–18.

## 1983

"1 Co 14,1–25: Argument and Some Problems," in: L. De Lorenzi (ed.), *Charisma und Agape (1 Ko 12–14)*, Rome: Benedictina 1983, 149–69 [To be reprinted in Hartman 1995a].

"Zur Hermeneutik neutestamentlicher eschatologischer Texte," in: H.–J. Zobel (ed.), *Hermeneutik eschatologischer biblischer Texte*, Greifswald: Ernst–Moritz–Arndt–Universität 1983, 30–48.

"Survey of the Problem of Apocalyptic Genre," in: D. Hellholm (ed.), *Apocalypticism in the Mediterranean World and the Near East*, Tübingen: Mohr 1983 (= 2nd ed. 1989), 329–43 [To be reprinted in Hartman 1995a].

"An early example of Jewish exegesis: 1 Enoch 10:10–11:2," in: *Neotest.* 17 (1983) 16–27.

"Att förstå en nytestamentlig text," in: R. Kieffer and B. Olsson (eds.), *Exegetik idag* (Religio 11), Lund: Teologiska institutionen 1983, 7–13.

"Den apokalyptiska genrens problem," in: R. Kieffer and B. Olsson (eds.), *Exegetik idag* (Religio 11), Lund: Teologiska institutionen 1983, 66–82.

## 1984

Review of J. Kiilunen et alii, (eds.), *Glaube und Gerechtigkeit*, in: *TAik* 3 (1984) 216–18.

"Hermeneutics of New Testament eschatological texts," in: *HTS* 40 (1984) 4–15.

"An Attempt at a Text–Centered Exegesis of John 21," in: *StTh* 38 (1984) 29–45 [To be reprinted in Hartman 1995a].

## 1985

*Kolosserbrevet* (Kommentar till Nya Testamentet 12), Uppsala: EFS–förlaget 1985.

"En framtid och ett hopp," in: *KISA–rapport* nr 25 (1985).

"La formule baptismale dans les Actes des apôtres: Quelques observations relatives au style de Luc," in: F. Refoulé (ed.), *A cause de l'évangile. Mélanges offerts à Dom Jacques Dupont* (LeDiv 123), Paris: Cerf 1985, 727–38.

"Universal Reconciliation (Col 1,20)," in: A. Fuchs (ed.), *Studien zum Neuen Testament und seiner Umwelt* 10, Linz: Plöchl 1985, 109–21.

**1986**

"'Kroppsligen', 'personligen' eller vad? Till Kol 2:9," in: *SEÅ* 51–52 (1986–87) 72–79.

"Theological Education in Sweden," in: *Canadian Theological Society Newsletter* 6:1 (1986) 7–8.

Review of Michel Quesnel, *Baptisés dans l'Esprit*, in: *ThLZ* 111 (1986) 431–32.

"On Reading Others' Letters," in: G. Nickelsburg and G. MacRae (eds.), *Christians Among Jews and Gentiles. Essays in Honor of Krister Stendahl*, Philadelphia, PA: Fortress 1986, 137–46; also in: *HThR* 79 (1986) 137–46 [To be reprinted in Hartman 1995a].

*'Att sammanföra de krafter som finnas ...' Uppsala Exegetiska Sällskap 1936–1986*, Uppsala: Uppsala Exegetiska Sällskap 1986.

**1987**

"Guds ord och människors förståelse," in: *Signum* 13 (1987) 130–32.

"I Faderns och Sonens och den Helige Andes namn...," in: *Kateket–nytt* 1987:1, 5–8.

Co–author of the report *Läroansvar i kyrkan — teologisk belysning*, Stockholm: Civildepartementet DsC 1987:13.

"Vad säger Sibyllan? Byggnad och budskap i de sibyllinska oraklens fjärde bok," in: P.W. Böckman and R.E. Kristiansen (eds.), *Context: Essays in Honour of Peder Johan Borgen*, Trondheim: Tapir 1987, 61–74 [To be translated and published as "'Teste Sibylla'. Construction and Message in the Fourth Book of the Sibylline Oracles" in Hartman 1995a].

"Johannine Jesus–Belief and Monotheism," in: L. Hartman and B. Olsson (eds.), *Aspects of the Johannine Literature* (CB.NT 18), Stockholm: Almqvist & Wiksell 1987, 85–99.

"Code and Context: A Few Reflections on the Parenesis of Col 3:6–4:1," in: G. Hawthorne and O. Betz (eds.), *Tradition and Interpretation in the New Testament. Essays in Honor of E. E. Ellis*, Grand Rapids, MI: Eerdmans, and Tübingen: Mohr 1987, 237–47.

**1988**

"Some Unorthodox Thoughts on the 'Household–Code Form,'" in: J. Neusner et alii (eds.), *The Social World of Formative Christianity and Judaism. Essays in Tribute to Howard Clark Kee*, Philadelphia, PA: Fortress 1988, 219–32 [To be reprinted in Hartman 1995a].

Review of H. Räisänen, *The Torah and Christ*, in: *TAik* 93 (1988) 149–50.

Review of J. Kremer, *Die Geschichte einer Auferstehung*, in: *SEÅ* 53 (1988) 127–29.

Review of H. Cancik (ed.), *Markus–Philologie*, in: *SEÅ* 53 (1988) 124–26.

Review of M. J. J. Menken, *Numerical Literary Techniques in John*, in: *SEÅ* 53 (1988) 126–27.

## 1989

"'He spoke of the Temple of His Body' (Jn 2:13–22)," in: *SEÅ* 54 (1989) 70–79.

"Varför i all världen? En judisk apokalyps för 2000 år sedan," in: E. Jansson (ed.), *Meningar om livets mening i asiatiska kulturer* (Skrifter utgivna av Sällskapet för asienstudier 4). Uppsala 1989, 78–87.

"Minikommentar till Kol," in: L. Hartman et alii, *Minikommentar till 1 Kor 1–4, 12–15, Fil 2, Kol*, Uppsala: Teologiska institutionen 1989, 27–37.

## 1990

"Tolkning och tillämpning av två bud" (with A. Jeffner), in: *KISA–Rapport* 1990:3, 35–45.

"The Eschatology of 2 Thessalonians as Included in a Communication," in: R. Collins (ed.), *The Thessalonian Correspondence* (BEThL 87), Leuven: University and Peeters 1990, 470–85 [To be reprinted in Hartman 1995a].

Review of G. Delling, *Die Bewältigung der Diasporasituation durch das hellenistische Judentum*, in: *SEÅ* 55 (1990) 119–20.

Review of J. Collins, *The Apocalyptic Imagination*, in: *SEÅ* 55 (1990) 120–21.

Review of E. Brandenburger, *Markus 13 und die Apokalyptik*, in: *SEÅ* 55 (1990) 140–42.

"En okänd filosof i urkristendomen," in: *Kungliga Vitterhets Historie och Antikvitets Akademiens Årsbok* 1990, Stockholm: Kungliga Vitterhets Historie och Antikvitets Akademien 1990, 141–48.

"Skepp, fårflock, byggnad ... Kyrkvisioner i Bibeln," *Kyrkligt Magasin* 1990:6, 39–48.

**1991**

"Is the Crucified Christ the Center of a New Testament Theology?" in: Th. W. Jennings, Jr. (ed.), *Text and Logos*. Essays in Honor of Hendrikus Boers (Scholars Press Homage Series), Atlanta, GA: Scholars 1991, 175–88.

**1992**

*Auf dem Namen des Herrn Jesus. Die Taufe in den neutestamentlichen Schriften* (SBS 148), Stuttgart: Katholisches Bibelwerk 1992.

"Reading Luke 17,20–37," in: F. van Segbroeck et alii (eds.), *The Four Gospels 1992. Festschrift Frans Neirynck* (BEThL 100), Leuven: University and Peeters 1992, 1663–75 [To be reprinted in Hartman 1995a].

"Baptism," in: *The Anchor Bible Dictionary* 1, New York: Doubleday 1992, 583–94.

"Scandinavian School, NT Studies," in: *The Anchor Bible Dictionary* 5, New York: Doubleday 1992, 1002–4.

**1993**

*Till Herrens Jesu namn* (Tro och Tanke 1993:4), Uppsala: Svenska Kyrkans forskningsråd 1993.

"Early Baptism—Early Christology," in: A. J. Malherbe and W. A. Meeks (eds.), *The Future of Christology. Essays in Honor of Leander E. Keck*, Minneapolis, MN: Augsburg Fortress 1993, 191–201.

"Från 'patternism' till bildspråk," in: *SEÅ* 58 (1993) 51–58.

"Frötallar och ropande eldtungor. Om bilder i predikan," in: *Tro och Tanke* 1993:8, Uppsala: Svenska Kyrkans forskningsråd 1993, 47–66.

Review of H.–Fr. Weiß, *Der Brief an die Hebräer*, in: *ThLZ* 118 (1993) 33–35.

"Galatians 3:15–4:11 as Part of a Theological Argument on a Practical Issue," in: J. Lambrecht (ed.), *The Truth of the Gospel (Galatians 1:1–4:11)* (Monographic Series of "Benedictina" Biblical–Ecumenical Section 12), Rome: Benedictina 1993, 127–58 [To be reprinted in Hartman 1995a].

**1994**

"Obligatory Baptism—but Why? On Baptism in the Didache and in the Shepherd of Hermas," in: *SEÅ* 59 (1994) 127-43.

"Tre läsningar av uttågsberättelsen. En nutida exeget, en alexandrinsk jude, en forn-kyrklig biskop," in: *Tro & Tanke* 1994:5, Uppsala: Svenska kyrkans forskningsråd 1994, 39-53.

Review of F. Neirynck et alii, The Gospel of Mark. A Cumulative Bibliography 1950-1990, in: *SEÅ* 59 (1994) 179-81.

## 1995

*On Reading Others' Letters. Collected Essays.* Ed. by David Hellholm (forth-coming 1995a) [Two essays have not been published earlier: "Doing Things with the Words of Colossians" and "A Sketch of the Argument of 2 Cor 10–13"].

"Humble and Confident. On the So-Called Philosophers in Colossians," in: *Studia Theologica* 49 (1995) (forthcoming 1995b).

"Dop och ande—nio frågor," in: R. Hvalvik/H. Kvalbein (eds.), *Ad Acta. Studier til Apostlenes gjerninger og urkristendommens historie. Tilegnet professor Edvin Larsson på 70-årsdagen*, Oslo: Verbum 1995, 89-108.

# Index of Passages
(Selective)

## I. ISRAELITE AND JEWISH TEXTS

### A. Old Testament

**Genesis**

| | | | |
|---|---|---|---|
| 1:1-3 | 850, 861-863 | 15:6 | 432, 441, 736 |
| 1:22 | 134 | 17 | 441 |
| 1:24-25 | 384 | 17:12 | 719 |
| 1:26-29 | 381 | 19 | 400 |
| 1:26-28 | 377 | 24:26-27 | 324 |
| 1:26 | 372-375, 382-383, 387 | 24:26 | 329 |
| | | 25:22 | 133 |
| 1:28 | 134, 371-375, 382-383, 387 | | |
| | | Exodus | |
| 2:4 | 60, 61 | 4:22 | 569 |
| 2:7 | 384 | 7-10 | 405 |
| 3:15 | 897 | 7:19 | 405 |
| 5:1 | 60, 61, 62 | 9:18 | 84 |
| 5:21-24 | 337 | 10:14 | 84 |
| 6:1-4 | 334-335, 350, 356 | 11:16 | 84 |
| 6:2 | 569 | 12:10 | 176-177 |
| 6:4 | 361, 569 | 12:14 | 1007 |
| 6:5-9:17 | 335 | 12:23 | 263 |
| 8:1 | 1005 | 12:47-48 | 769 |
| 9:1-3 | 387 | 13:21-22 | 262 |
| 9:1-2 | 381 | 14:19 | 262 |
| 9:2 | 376 | 14:21-22 | 262 |
| 9:26 | 324 | 14:24 | 262 |
| 11:1-9 | 897-898 | 16:4 | 262 |
| 12:2f. | 210 | 16:15 | 262 |
| 12:3 | 457 | 17:2-3 | 263 |
| 12:7 | 457 | 17:6 | 262 |
| 14:18-20 | 894 | 18:10-12 | 329 |
| 14:19-20 | 321 | 18:10-11 | 321 |

| | |
|---|---|
| 19-24 | 174 |
| 19:5 | 210 |
| 19:6 | 210 |
| 19:8 | 175 |
| 19:10f. | 174 |
| 19:16 | 174 |
| 20:12 | 680 |
| 21:17 | 680 |
| 29:35 | 1008 |
| 32 | 261, 266 |
| 32:6 | 263, 267, 271 |
| 34:30 | 736 |

**Leviticus**

| | |
|---|---|
| 11-15 | 684 |
| 12:3 | 719 |
| 17-18 | 217, 238 |
| 18:24-30 | 238 |
| 19 | 544 |
| 19:18 | 465 |
| 26 | 382 |
| 26:3-4 | 383 |
| 26:6 | 382 |
| 26:22 | 384 |
| 28 | 382 |

**Numbers**

| | |
|---|---|
| 11:4-6 | 263 |
| 11:6 | 262 |
| 12:6-8 | 293 |
| 14:14 | 262 |
| 14:16 | 264 |
| 14:28-39 | 264 |
| 15:11-13 | 1008 |
| 20:8-11 | 262 |
| 24:7 (LXX) | 386 |
| 25 | 266 |
| 33:8 | 262 |

**Deuteronomy**

| | |
|---|---|
| 4:29f. | 204 |
| 5:15 | 1006 |
| 5:16 | 680 |
| 6:4-5 | 95 |
| 6:5 | 702 |
| 7:6 | 210 |
| 8:2-3 | 1006 |
| 8:15 | 262 |
| 10:15 | 386 |
| 12:11 | 208 |
| 12:21 | 208 |
| 13 | 391 |
| 13:1f. | 400 |
| 13:2-3 | 270 |
| 14:1 | 569 |
| 14:2 | 210 |
| 14:3-21 | 684 |
| 15:4 (LXX) | 692, 699 |
| 15:15 | 1006 |
| 16:12 | 1006 |
| 17:7 | 772 |
| 19:15 | 178, 184, 196, 203-204, 776 |
| 21:5 | 204 |
| 21:20 | 770 |
| 21:23 | 632 |
| 23:13-15 | 684 |
| 24:17 | 1006 |
| 24:22 | 1006 |
| 25:9 | 1008 |
| 26:15 | 204, 209 |
| 28 | 382 |
| 28:1 (LXX) | 386 |
| 28:10 | 208 |
| 30:11-14 | 386 |
| 31-33 | 346 |
| 32:7-27 | 261, 266 |
| 32:15 | 459 |

| | |
|---|---|
| 33 | 338 |
| 33:1-2 | 343 |
| 33:2 (LXX) | 460 |
| 33:10 | 587 |
| | |
| Joshua | |
| 22:24 | 971 |
| | |
| Judges | |
| 2:18-3:6 | 270 |
| 11:12 | 970 |
| | |
| Ruth | |
| 4:14-15 | 324 |
| | |
| 1 Samuel | |
| 1:11 | 1006 |
| 1:19 | 1006 |
| 25 | 323 |
| 28:8ff. | 787 |
| | |
| 2 Samuel | |
| 5:20 | 6 |
| 7 | 209 |
| 7:14 | 570 |
| 16:10 | 970 |
| 18:28 | 322 |
| 19:22 | 970 |
| 22 | 321 |
| 23:1-7 | 325 |
| | |
| 1 Kings | |
| 1:48 | 322 |
| 2:31 | 5 |
| 5:7 | 322 |
| 5:8-9 | 322 |
| 8 | 321, 326, 329 |
| 8:14-15 | 322 |
| 8:16-21 | 322 |

| | |
|---|---|
| 8:22-53 | 322 |
| 10:6-9 | 322 |
| 17:1 | 405 |
| 17:7-24 | 174 |
| 17:18 | 970 |
| 19:10 | 524 |
| 19:14 | 524 |
| 21:8 | 61 |
| | |
| 2 Kings | |
| 1:10ff. | 405 |
| 3:13 | 970 |
| 4:29 | 873 |
| 6:21 (LXX) | 322 |
| 9:18f. | 971 |
| | |
| III Regnorum | |
| 19:19-21 | 103, 105-106 |
| | |
| 1 Chronicles | |
| 14:11 | 6 |
| 16 | 325-326 |
| 16:4f. | 133 |
| 16:25 | 326 |
| 29:10-19 | 325 |
| 29:10 | 327 |
| | |
| 2 Chronicles | |
| 2:11-16 | 322 |
| 9:8 | 322 |
| 35:21 | 971 |
| | |
| Ezra | |
| 7:27-28 | 325 |
| 9 | 720 |
| | |
| Nehemiah | |
| 5:1-11 | 604, 607 |
| 8:3ff. | 220 |

| | | | |
|---|---|---|---|
| 9:6-37 | 261, 266 | 66:10-12 | 327 |
| 13:19 | 8 | 66:13-20 | 326 |
| | | 68 | 326 |
| Job | | 69:22 | 175 |
| 1:6 | 569 | 74:9 | 423 |
| 1:21 | 324 | 78 | 261, 266 |
| 2:1 | 569 | 78:18 | 263 |
| 5:12f. | 735 | 82:6 | 569 |
| 7:9f. | 787 | 85:3 | 666 |
| 11:17 | 8 | 89:26-27 | 570 |
| 14:1ff. | 787 | 95:8-11 | 261, 266 |
| 38:7 | 569 | 96:4 | 326 |
| 41:2 | 735 | 106 | 261, 266, 326 |
| | | 106:14 | 263 |
| Psalms | | 106:25 | 263 |
| 2:2 | 570 | 109:1 (LXX) | 807 |
| 2:7 | 568, 570, 575 | 110:1 | 636, 694, 808 |
| 6:3 | 666 | 110:4 | 894 |
| 6:6 | 787 | 113:2 | 327 |
| 8:4 | 401 | 119:12 | 327 |
| 8:5 | 809 | 122:3 | 665 |
| 8:7 | 694, 808 | 124:6 | 327 |
| 9:14 | 666 | 143:2 | 907 |
| 18 | 321, 329 | 144 | 329 |
| 18:46-48 | 327 | | |
| 28:1-4 | 327 | Proverbs | |
| 28:6 | 327 | 1:1 | 122 |
| 29:1 | 569 | 26:2 | 5 |
| 31:1f. (LXX) | 736 | | |
| 34 | 326 | Ecclesiastes (Qohelet) | |
| 34:21 | 176-177 | 1:1 | 122 |
| 40:5 | 665 | 3:18ff. | 787 |
| 40:11 | 665 | 9:3ff. | 787 |
| 48:1 | 326 | | |
| 51 | 326 | Canticles | |
| 63:23 (LXX) | 736 | 1:1 | 122 |
| 66:1-3 | 327 | | |
| 66:1 | 133 | Isaiah | |
| 66:5-9 | 327 | 1:5f. | 526 |

| | | | |
|---|---|---|---|
| 2:2-4 | 603 | 47:8 | 398 |
| 5:9 | 526 | 47:10 | 398 |
| 5:13-15 | 530 | 49:1-7 | 581 |
| 5:13f. | 526 | 49:6 | 582 |
| 5:22 | 527 | 50:4-9 | 581 |
| 5:24 | 526 | 52-53 | 339 |
| 6:3 | 325 | 52:13-53:12 | 580-581 |
| 6:9f. | 107, 753 | 52:13 | 177 |
| 7:14 | 896 | 53 | 655 |
| 8:19 | 787 | 53:1-12 | 582 |
| 8:23 | 599-600 | 53:4ff. | 177 |
| 10:3 | 526 | 53:11 | 582 |
| 10:4 | 526 | 53:12 | 914 |
| 11 | 387 | 55:10-11 | 1001 |
| 11:4 | 396 | 59:20f. | 752 |
| 11:6-9 | 383 | 61:1ff. | 134 |
| 11:6 | 880 | 65-66 | 336 |
| 13:10 | 401 | 65:25 | 383 |
| 13:13 | 399 | | |
| 25:8 | 735 | Jeremiah | |
| 26:19 | 787 | 13:25-27 | 266 |
| 26:20-21 | 336 | 14:10 | 264 |
| 27:9 | 752 | 15:9 | 5 |
| 28:2-4 | 526 | 22:15ff. | 526 |
| 29:13 | 681 | 30:9 | 572 |
| 29:16 | 526 | 32:29 | 685 |
| 31:2 | 530 | 32:38-40 | 653 |
| 33:2 | 665 | 33:20 | 5 |
| 40:3 | 654 | 33:25 | 5 |
| 40:9ff. | 134 | | |
| 40:9 | 133 | Ezekiel | |
| 42:1-4 | 581 | 3:12 | 325 |
| 42:1 | 582 | 4 | 399 |
| 42:6 | 582 | 11:19-20 | 653 |
| 44:1 | 581 | 11:19 | 685 |
| 44:21 | 581 | 16:15-16 | 266 |
| 45:2 | 603 | 21:34 | 7 |
| 45:4 | 581 | 30:16 | 5-9 |
| 45:11 | 526 | 36:26-27 | 653 |

| | | | |
|---|---|---|---|
| 36:26 | 685 | 2 | 266 |
| | | 7:13 | 527 |
| Daniel | | 11:1 | 569 |
| | 391ff. | | |
| 2:20-23 | 325 | Joel | |
| 2:29 | 398 | 1:1 | 122 |
| 2:39 | 398 | 2 | 404 |
| 2:45 (Θ) | 398 | 2:28-32 | 423 |
| 3:25 | 569 | 2:31 | 395, 401 |
| 3:26-45 | 325 | 3:1f. | 140 |
| 3:28-29 | 325 | | |
| 3:52-90 | 325 | Amos | |
| 4:24f. (Θ) | 521 | 1:1 | 122 |
| 4:28 (Θ) | 521 | 6:2-3 | 526 |
| 7 | 339 | 9 | 211-212 |
| 7:10 | 401 | 9:11f. | 204, 213, 215 |
| 7:13-14 | 351, 914 | | |
| 7:13 | 394, 400-401, 572 | Micah | |
| 7:14 | 401 | 1 | 338 |
| 9:2-27 | 348 | 7 | 391 |
| 9:27 | 88 | 7:2 | 681 |
| 10 | 395 | 7:6 | 399, 770 |
| 11 | 396 | | |
| 11:31 | 88, 396, 399-400 | Nahum | |
| 11:36 | 399 | 1:1 | 122 |
| 11:45 | 396 | | |
| 12 | 396 | Habakkuk | |
| 12:1 | 84, 400 | 2:7 | 526 |
| 12:2 | 336, 787 | 2:13 | 526 |
| 12:3 | 350 | 2:15-17 | 528 |
| 12:6-7 | 79 | 2:16-17 | 530 |
| 12:7 (LXX) | 398 | 2:16 | 526 |
| 12:11 | 88, 400 | | |
| 12:12 (Θ) | 398 | Zephaniah | |
| 12:13 | 787 | 1:1 | 122 |
| | | 2-3 | 336 |
| Hosea | | 3:9 | 603 |
| 1:1 | 122 | | |
| 1:2 | 122 | | |

| Zechariah | | Malachi | |
|---|---|---|---|
| 2:15 (LXX) | 208 | 1:1 | 122 |
| 8:20-22 | 603 | 4:5 | 395 |
| 11:4-17 | 324 | 8:1-2 | 336 |
| 12:10 | 177 | | |
| 13:1 | 179 | | |

## B. Apocrypha, Pseudepigrapha, and Other Early Jewish Texts

| Aristeas to Philocrates | | 10:2-3 | 336 |
|---|---|---|---|
| 139 | 463 | 10:4-15 | 364 |
| 142 | 463 | 10:16-11:2 | 333 |
| | | 12-16 | 337-340, 359 |
| Baruch | | 12:4 | 350 |
| 2:11-15 | 261, 266 | 15-16 | 361 |
| 3:2 | 666 | 15:8-16:1 | 338 |
| | | 15:8-12 | 359 |
| 2 (syr) Baruch | | 16:3 | 363 |
| 3:7 | 850 | 22 | 787 |
| 14:17-19 | 379 | 22:5-7 | 336 |
| 15:7 | 379 | 26-27 | 336 |
| 21:24 | 379 | 32:6 | 336 |
| 73:6 | 383 | 37-71 | 339-340 |
| 87:1 | 38 | 38:4 | 608 |
| | | 46-47 | 339-340 |
| 1 (ethiopic) Enoch | | 46:3-5 | 608 |
| | 333-352, 355-365 | 48:2-5 | 339 |
| 1-5 | 333, 338, 579 | 48:4 | 582 |
| 5:8 | 350 | 48:8-49:4 | 339 |
| 6-11 | 334-336, 356-358 | 48:8 | 608 |
| 7:1 | 363 | 48:10 | 582 |
| 7:2-6 | 363 | 49:4 | 339 |
| 8:1 | 363 | 51:1 | 787 |
| 8:3 | 336 | 52:4 | 582 |
| 9:8 | 336 | 53:5 | 608 |
| 10-11 | 338 | 61:5 | 787 |

| | | | |
|---|---|---|---|
| 62-63 | 339 | 17:17 | 459 |
| 62 | 608 | 24:13-21 | 345 |
| 72-82 | 345 | 24:32-33 | 348-350 |
| 81:1-82:3 | 343 | 24:33 | 345 |
| 81:5-82:3 | 345 | 36:1 | 666 |
| 85-90 | 340-342 | 36:11-17 | 603 |
| 91:1-3 | 346 | 36:15-16 | 348 |
| 91:11-17 | 343-344 | 39:1 | 348 |
| 93:1-10 | 343-344 | 39:5-7 | 348 |
| 94-102 | 345 | 44:1 | 888 |
| 94:5 | 340 | 48:10 | 582 |
| 99:3 | 1007 | | |
| 102:6ff. | 787 | Josephus (Flavius) | |
| 104:9-105:2 | 344 | *Antiquitates Judaicae* | |
| 106-107 | 337 | 7 | 721 |
| | | 13:14,2 | 588 |
| 2 (slavonic) Enoch | | 13:297 | 680 |
| 22:9f. | 795 | 15 | 721 |
| | | 15:36 | 460 |
| | | 15:371 | 697 |
| 1 Esdras | | 17 | 721 |
| 4:40 | 325 | 17:74 | 966 |
| 4:58-60 | 325 | 17:304-309 | 615 |
| | | 18 | 721 |
| 4 Ezra | | 18:16 | 787 |
| 6:38-40 | 850 | 18:20 | 698 |
| 6:53 | 373 | 18:36-38 | 607 |
| 6:54-59 | 379 | 18:37 | 606 |
| 7 | 787 | 18:101-105 | 613 |
| 7:10f. | 379 | 18:106-108 | 613 |
| 7:30 | 850 | 18:109-126 | 654 |
| 9:13 | 379 | 18:116-119 | 613 |
| 13:39-50 | 755 | 18:117 | 654 |
| | | 20:145 | 732 |
| Ezra, Greek Apocalypse of | | 20:159 | 608 |
| 5:6 | 666 | 20:181 | 611, 616 |
| | | 20:206f. | 611, 616 |
| Jesus Sirah (Ben Sira) | | 20:213 | 725 |
| 1-2 | 547 | 20:233 | 725 |
| 4:10 | 570 | | |

*De bello Judaico*

| | |
|---|---|
| Proem. 4 | 84 |
| 1 | 721 |
| 1:511 | 615 |
| 2 | 721 |
| 2:122 | 705 |
| 2:164ff. | 787 |
| 2:252 | 608 |
| 2:457-465 | 601 |
| 3:35 | 597 |
| 4:159 | 725 |
| 5:145 | 705 |

*Vita Josephi*

| | |
|---|---|
| 32-38 | 607 |
| 33f. | 608 |
| 38 | 721 |
| 55 | 618 |
| 65 | 608 |
| 66 | 606 |
| 74 | 600 |
| 100 | 618 |
| 113 | 601 |
| 171 | 618 |
| 190 | 725 |
| 309 | 725 |
| 346 | 608 |
| 376 | 606 |

Jubilees

| | |
|---|---|
| | 347 |
| 1:21-25 | 653 |
| 1:29-2:1 | 460 |
| 4:15 | 363 |
| 4:17-19 | 344, 346 |
| 5:1-2 | 363 |
| 15:32-33 | 459 |
| 19:25 | 939 |
| 23:26-31 | 336 |

1 Maccabees

| | |
|---|---|
| 1:54 | 88 |
| 2:29ff. | 633 |
| 4:30-33 | 330 |
| 5:15 | 599 |
| 12:11 | 1006 |
| 14:10 | 607 |
| 14:41 | 349 |

2 Maccabees

| | |
|---|---|
| 1:17 | 330 |
| 6:10f. | 633 |
| 6:17-7:42 | 633 |
| 7:9 | 787 |
| 7:24-26 | 537 |
| 15:34 | 330 |

3 Maccabees

| | |
|---|---|
| 5:17 | 537 |
| 7:12 | 537 |

4 Maccabees

| | |
|---|---|
| 4 | 727 |
| 12:13 | 374 |

Martyrdom of Isaiah

| | |
|---|---|
| 4:1-18 | 403 |

Oracula Sibyllina (incl. Christ. Oracles)

| | |
|---|---|
| 3:616 | 603 |
| 3:788-795 | 383 |
| 4:1-23 | 59 |
| 4:48 | 59 |
| 4:117-139 | 403 |
| 4:119-130 | 403 |
| 4:130-139 | 404 |
| 4:138-160 | 403 |
| 5:36-40 | 406 |
| 5:155-161 | 403 |

## Philo and Pseudo-Philo

|                          |              |
| ------------------------ | ------------ |
|                          | 369-387      |

### De Abrahamo

|     |     |
| --- | --- |
| 235 | 697 |

### De animalibus

|        |     |
| ------ | --- |
|        | 387 |
| 77-100 | 376 |

### De decalogo

|       |          |
| ----- | -------- |
| 52-65 | 380      |
| 66-76 | 380      |
| 76-80 | 380-381  |
| 80    | 381      |

### In Flaccum

|     |     |
| --- | --- |
| 158 | 724 |

### Legatio ad Gaium

|     |     |
| --- | --- |
| 161 | 374 |
| 281 | 732 |

### Legum allegoriae

|       |     |
| ----- | --- |
| 3:161 | 385 |

### Liber Antiquitatum Biblicarum

|      |     |
| ---- | --- |
| 60:2 | 850 |

### De opificio mundi

|         |               |
| ------- | ------------- |
| 77-88   | 371-372, 385  |
| 77-86   | 382           |
| 77-78   | 378-379       |
| 79-81   | 379           |
| 79      | 379           |
| 82      | 384           |
| 83-84   | 372-375       |
| 84      | 371           |
| 88      | 374           |
| 142-144 | 384           |

### De praemiis et poenis

|         |          |
| ------- | -------- |
| 1-3     | 370-371  |
| 79-172  | 382      |
| 79-126  | 381      |
| 79-84   | 386      |
| 88      | 381      |
| 89-90   | 383      |
| 91-97   | 386      |
| 98-125  | 383      |
| 127-152 | 383      |

### Quod omnis probus liber sit

|    |     |
| -- | --- |
| 77 | 704 |
| 85 | 704 |
| 86 | 704 |

### De plantatione

|     |     |
| --- | --- |
| 126 | 854 |

### De providentia

|         |     |
| ------- | --- |
| 2:84    | 379 |
| 2:91-92 | 379 |
| 2:103   | 379 |

### Quaestiones in Genesin

|      |     |
| ---- | --- |
| 1:56 | 376 |
| 2:56 | 381 |

### De Somniis

|       |     |
| ----- | --- |
| 1:143 | 460 |

### De specialibus legibus

|           |     |
| --------- | --- |
| 1:13-14   | 385 |
| 1:19      | 375 |
| 1:303     | 386 |
| 2:166     | 386 |
| 4:119-121 | 379 |

*De vita Mosis*

| | |
|---|---|
| 1:60-62 | 379 |
| 2:1 | 724 |
| 2:45ff. | 371 |
| 2:45-46 | 370 |
| 2:52 | 386 |
| 2:271 | 261, 266 |

Pseudo-Phocylides
*Sententiae*

| | |
|---|---|
| 28-30 | 697 |

Psalms of Solomon

| | |
|---|---|
| 2:37 | 330 |
| 5:19 | 330 |
| 6:6 | 330 |
| 18:50 | 211 |

Testament (Assumption) of Moses

| | |
|---|---|
| | 347 |
| 1:12 | 379 |

Testament XII Patriarchs
*Testament of Reuben*

| | |
|---|---|
| 5 | 362 |

*Testament of Simon*

| | |
|---|---|
| 7:2 | 757 |

*Testament of Levi*

| | |
|---|---|
| 8:2 | 584 |
| 18 | 583-584 |

*Testament of Juda*

| | |
|---|---|
| 22:2 | 757 |

*Testament of Asser*

| | |
|---|---|
| 7:3 | 757 |

*Testament of Joseph*

| | |
|---|---|
| 19:6 | 757 |

*Testament of Benjamin*

| | |
|---|---|
| 10:11 | 757 |

Tobit

| | |
|---|---|
| 1:1 | 60 |
| 4:5 | 1006 |
| 4:12 | 541 |
| 7:13 | 61 |
| 11:14 | 330 |
| 13:1-2 | 330 |
| 13:5 | 330 |
| 13:11 | 603 |
| 13:18 | 330 |
| 14:4-5 | 348 |

Wisdom of Solomon

| | |
|---|---|
| 2:1ff. | 787 |
| 2:19 | 570 |
| 4:10-15 | 337 |
| 7:17 | 374 |
| 8:9 | 537 |
| 18:13 | 569 |
| 18:14ff. | 849 |
| 19:18-21 | 374 |

## C. Qumran and Related Texts

| | | |
|---|---|---|
| CD (Cairo [Genizah of the] Damascus [Document]) | 1:14-15 | 586 |
| | 7:14ff. | 211 |

| | | | | |
|---|---|---|---|---|
| 7:16 | 212 | | 8:8-13 | 755 |
| 6:7 | 587 | | | |
| 6:11 | 587 | | 1QapGen (Genesis Apocryphon) | |
| 7:18-19 | 587 | | | 574 |
| 9-12 | 348 | | | |
| 9:16-23 | 776 | | CAVE 4 | |
| 12:9-11 | 705 | | 4QFlor | |
| 13:14-16 | 705 | | | 214 |
| 14:12-16 | 705 | | 1:10ff. | 211 |
| 14:19 | 584 | | 1:11 | 587 |
| 15:9f. | 755 | | 1:12 | 213 |
| 15:14f. | 681 | | | |

| | | | | |
|---|---|---|---|---|
| | | | 4Q169 (Pesher Nahum) | |
| CAVE 1 | | | | 588 |
| 1QS (Manual of Disciplin) | | | | |
| 5:1-5 | 755 | | 4Q171 (Pesher Psalms[a]) | |
| 5:7-11 | 348 | | 3:18 (Ps 37) | 586 |
| 6:24-7:24 | 771 | | | |
| 9:11 | 587 | | 4Q246 (Aramaic Apocalypse) | |
| 11:15-22 | 330 | | | 571-575, 589, 638 |

| | | | | |
|---|---|---|---|---|
| 1QSa (Rule of the Congregation) | | | 4Q448 (Apocryphal Psalm and Prayer) | |
| 1:1-6 | 755 | | | 588 |

| | | | | |
|---|---|---|---|---|
| 1QH (Thanksgiving Hymns) | | | 4Q502 (Ritual of Marriage) | |
| 4:7 | 586 | | | 330 |
| 4:9-10 | 586 | | | |
| 7:10 | 587 | | 4Q503 (Daily Prayers[a]) | |
| 8:26f. | 587 | | | 330 |
| 8:35f. | 587 | | | |
| 13:20 | 330 | | 4Q504 (Words of the Luminaries) | |
| 18:14 | 330 | | | 330 |

| | | | | |
|---|---|---|---|---|
| 1QM (War Scroll) | | | 4Q507 (Festival Prayers[a]) | |
| 13:2-9 | 330 | | | 330 |
| 14:4-7 | 330 | | | |
| | | | 4Q509 (Festival Prayers[c]) | |
| | | | | 330 |
| 1QpHab (Pesher on Habakkuk) | | | | |
| 7:4-8 | 348 | | | |

4Q511 (Songs of the Sage[b])                              589
         330
                                        4Q537 (Apocryphon of Jacob)
4Q512 (Ritual of Purification)                           583
         330
                                        4Q 540-541 (Aaron A)
4Q521 (Messianic Apocalypse)                            579-589


**D. Rabbinic Texts**


1. Mishna-, Tosephta-, Talmudtractates      *ʾAbot*
*m. Berakot*                                  1:6          737
8:2              682                          3:3          737
8:4              682
                                             *ʿErubim*
*m. Nazir*                                    18b          737
2:1-3            680                          54a          737

*m. Nedarim*                                 *Gittin*
1:3f.            680                           4:2f.        725
9:1              682
                                             *ʿOrla*
*b. Berakot*                                  2:12         725
34b              423
                                             *Peʾa*
*b. Sanhedrin*                                2:6          725
11b              725
38a              378                          *Pesahim*
90b              787                           88b          725

*t. Sanhedrin*                               *Yebamot*
2:6              725                           16:7         725
8:7              377-378
8:9              377-378                      2. Midrashim, Targumim et al.

*y. Sanhedrin*                               *Apocalypse of Moses*
1:2              725                           Preface       460
1:18d            725
4:9              378                          *ʾAbot de Rabbi Natan*

| | | | |
|---|---|---|---|
| 8 | 737 | 11 | 375 |
| 37 | 385 | | |
| | | *Sipre Deuteronomium* | |
| *Bereshit Rabba* | | 48:85a | 379 |
| 14:5 | 787 | | |
| | | *Tanhuma Pequde* | |
| *Genesis Rabba* | | 3 | 374 |
| 8:6 | 379 | | |
| 34:12 | 376 | *Wayiqra Rabba* | |
| | | 14:9 | 787 |
| *Numeri Rabba* | | | |
| 14:12 | 374 | *Targum of 1 Chronicles* | |
| | | 4:23 | 939 |
| *Pesiqta Rabbati* | | | |
| Suppl. 21 | 373 | *Targum of Isaiah* | |
| | | 52-53 | 582 |
| *Pirqe Rabbi Eliezer* | | | |

## II. EARLY CHRISTIAN TEXTS

### A. New Testament

| | | | |
|---|---|---|---|
| Matthew | | 4:3 | 121, 567 |
| | 11-66, 77-90 | 4:6 | 121, 567 |
| 1:1 | 58-64, 424 | 4:12-13 | 46 |
| 1:2-4:16 | 60-65 | 4:12 | 49 |
| 1:2-2:23 | 60-65 | 4:17 | 14, 42-51, 49-51 |
| 1:2-25 | 60-65 | 4:19 | 81 |
| 1:2-17 | 59-64 | 4:23 | 14, 52-58 |
| 1:23 | 668, 896 | 5-7 | 544, 547-548 |
| 2:2 | 663-664 | 5:1-7:29 | 53 |
| 2:8 | 663 | 5:1-12 | 878 |
| 2:11 | 663-664 | 5:5 | 608 |
| 2:12 | 139 | 5:7 | 890 |
| 2:15 | 567 | 5:8 | 685 |
| 2:22 | 139 | 5:20 | 755 |
| 3:1-17 | 660 | 5:23-24 | 89 |
| 3:11 | 654 | 5:38-44 | 618 |
| 3:15 | 890 | 6:5-15 | 669 |
| 3:17 | 567 | 6:9-13 | 661 |

| | | | |
|---|---|---|---|
| 6:9 | 669 | 12:8 | 914 |
| 6:10 | 915 | 12:24 | 675 |
| 6:19-34 | 669 | 12:25 | 612 |
| 6:19-21 | 618 | 12:28 | 522 |
| 6:21 | 874 | 12:40 | 915 |
| 6:22 | 685 | 12:46-50 | 961 |
| 6:24 | 618 | 13:37-43 | 656 |
| 7:1-5 | 669 | 13:39 | 78 |
| 7:6 | 874 | 13:40 | 78 |
| 7:28 | 13, 33, 37 | 13:49 | 78 |
| 8:1-9:34 | 53 | 13:53 | 13, 33 |
| 8:2 | 663 | 14:3 | 1011 |
| 8:20-22 | 618 | 14:13-21 | 662 |
| 8:20 | 914 | 14:26ff. | 167 |
| 8:25 | 664 | 14:30 | 664 |
| 8:29 | 567, 971 | 14:33 | 121, 567, 663 |
| 9:3 | 675 | 15:1-20 | 675 |
| 9:6 | 914 | 15:21-28 | 675, 967 |
| 9:11 | 675 | 15:22 | 665 |
| 9:18 | 663 | 15:25 | 663 |
| 9:35 | 14, 52-58 | 15:27 | 1009 |
| 9:36-38 | 56 | 15:32-39 | 662 |
| 10 | 871-885 | 16:13 | 47 |
| 10:1-4 | 56 | 16:16ff. | 173 |
| 10:1 | 57 | 16:16 | 121, 567, 894 |
| 10:17-20 | 878 | 16:18f. | 81 |
| 10:22 | 884 | 16:18 | 670 |
| 10:23 | 79, 80 | 16:21 | 12, 14, 42-51, 914 |
| 10:28 | 884 | 16:27 | 915 |
| 10:34-37 | 961 | 16:28 | 79-80 |
| 10:37 | 618 | 17:6 | 664 |
| 10:38 | 883 | 17:10-13 | 654 |
| 11:1 | 13, 33, 37, 57 | 17:15 | 664-665 |
| 11:9 | 612, 654 | 17:22-23 | 914 |
| 11:11 | 654 | 17:24-27 | 89 |
| 11:16-19 | 615 | 18:6-14 | 549 |
| 11:19 | 465, 770 | 18:18 | 81 |
| 11:27 | 770 | 18:20 | 81, 668, 670 |
| 12:2 | 675 | 19:1 | 13, 33 |

| | | | |
|---|---|---|---|
| 19:28 | 80 | 24:48 | 82 |
| 20:18-19 | 914 | 24:50 | 81, 82 |
| 20:20 | 663 | 25:5 | 82 |
| 20:28 | 914, 916 | 25:13 | 81, 82 |
| 20:29-34 | 665 | 25:19 | 82 |
| 21:23-27 | 675 | 25:31-46 | 834, 915 |
| 21:25 | 654, 660 | 25:31ff. | 80, 82 |
| 21:32 | 654 | 26:1 | 13, 33, 35 |
| 21:42-46 | 960 | 26:13 | 85 |
| 22:7 | 88 | 26:24 | 914 |
| 22:15-23:36 | 675 | 26:26-29 | 661 |
| 22:40 | 236 | 26:28 | 654 |
| 23 | 678 | 26:63 | 121 |
| 23:1-38 | 36 | 26:64 | 915 |
| 23:1-36 | 675 | 27:40 | 567 |
| 23:15 | 732 | 27:43 | 567 |
| 23:16-22 | 89 | 27:46 | 575 |
| 23:29-36 | 523, 531 | 27:52f. | 791 |
| 23:30 | 888 | 27:54 | 567 |
| 23:32 | 888 | 27:63 | 915 |
| 23:34-36 | 524 | 28 | 875 |
| 23:36 | 79, 80 | 28:2-4 | 630 |
| 23:37-39 | 524 | 28:9 | 663-664 |
| 24:1-3 | 36 | 28:17 | 153, 663-664 |
| 24:2 | 80 | 28:19 | 81, 85, 424, 657, 660 |
| 24:3 | 78, 90 | 28:20 | 81, 424, 668-669 |
| 24:5 | 398 | | |
| 24:14 | 81, 85 | **Mark** | |
| 24:15ff. | 80, 83, 84, 86, 87 | | 594 |
| 24:16 | 84 | 1:1 | 99, 111-125, 424, 567 |
| 24:20 | 89 | 1:2f. | 107 |
| 24:21f. | 88 | 1:8 | 654 |
| 24:29 | 80, 82, 85, 86, 88, 89, 90 | 1:11 | 121, 413-414, 567 |
| | | 1:14f. | 49-51, 93, 98-99, 701 |
| 24:30f. | 915 | 1:15 | 94, 102, 106 |
| 24:34 | 79 | 1:16-20 | 105-106, 618 |
| 24:36 | 81, 90 | 1:18 | 103 |
| 24:42 | 81, 82 | 1:21f. | 95 |
| 24:44 | 81, 82 | 1:24 | 971 |

| | | | |
|---|---|---|---|
| 1:27 | 95 | 5:43 | 98 |
| 1:32-34 | 701 | 6 | 871-885 |
| 1:39 | 53 | 6:1-6 | 96 |
| 1:40 | 663 | 6:1 | 104 |
| 2:1-12 | 676 | 6:6 | 98 |
| 2:5 | 94, 95, 96, 98 | 6:7 | 97 |
| 2:6 | 675 | 6:14-29 | 615 |
| 2:10 | 95 | 6:14f. | 102 |
| 2:14 | 103 | 6:35-44 | 662 |
| 2:15-17 | 676 | 6:45-52 | 664 |
| 2:15 | 103, 104 | 6:51 | 663 |
| 2:16-17 | 465 | 6:53-56 | 701 |
| 2:16 | 675 | 7:1-23 | 675-687 |
| 2:23-28 | 676 | 7:1-13 | 678-683 |
| 2:24 | 675 | 7:14-23 | 683-685 |
| 3:1-6 | 676 | 7:24-30 | 422, 675 |
| 3:7-12 | 701 | 7:24 | 601 |
| 3:7 | 104 | 7:25 | 663, 665 |
| 3:11 | 121, 123 | 7:31 | 601 |
| 3:22-30 | 676 | 7:36 | 417 |
| 3:22 | 675, 681 | 8:1-10 | 662 |
| 3:24 | 612 | 8:11 | 102 |
| 3:33-35 | 618 | 8:14 | 1011 |
| 4 | 416 | 8:27 | 601 |
| 4:10-12 | 97, 107, 416 | 8:28 | 102 |
| 4:11f. | 753 | 8:31 | 100 |
| 4:11 | 94, 417 | 8:32 | 422 |
| 4:26 | 94 | 8:34-9:1 | 94, 104 |
| 4:30 | 94 | 8:34 | 104, 106 |
| 4:33f. | 97 | 8:35 | 99 |
| 4:34 | 422 | 8:38 | 121, 915 |
| 4:38 | 664 | 9:1 | 94, 106, 165, 397, 401, 897 |
| 4:40 | 96 | | |
| 5:1 | 601 | 9:7 | 121, 413 |
| 5:7 | 575 | 9:9 | 915 |
| 5:17 | 603 | 9:11-13 | 654 |
| 5:22 | 663 | 9:12 | 914 |
| 5:24 | 104 | 9:14-29 | 97 |
| 5:34 | 95, 96 | 9:17-18 | 665 |

| | | | |
|---|---|---|---|
| 9:19 | 94, 98 | 13:14ff. | 403 |
| 9:24 | 98, 133 | 13:14 | 399 |
| 9:29 | 94 | 13:19 | 400 |
| 9:37 | 422 | 13:20 | 400 |
| 9:38-50 | 98 | 13:21-23 | 100-101 |
| 9:47 | 94 | 13:24-27 | 94, 106, 397 |
| 10:18 | 95 | 13:26 | 351, 400 |
| 10:21 | 105 | 13:28-37 | 94 |
| 10:28 | 103 | 13:30 | 397 |
| 10:29-31 | 618 | 13:32 | 90, 121, 567 |
| 10:29 | 99 | 14:8 | 100 |
| 10:32 | 104 | 14:9 | 100, 1007 |
| 10:35-40 | 164 | 14:22-25 | 661 |
| 10:42-45 | 612 | 14:25 | 94 |
| 10:45 | 415, 635 | 14:28 | 94 |
| 10:46-53 | 105 | 14:36 | 121, 419 |
| 10:46-52 | 665 | 14:61 | 121 |
| 10:52 | 95, 96, 98, 105-106 | 14:62 | 351, 415 |
| 11:9 | 104 | 15:7 | 197 |
| 11:12-25 | 97 | 15:26 | 103 |
| 11:22-25 | 96, 97-98 | 15:32 | 99, 102 |
| 11:22 | 100, 102, 106 | 15:39 | 121, 123, 413, 567 |
| 11:23f. | 94 | 15:41 | 104 |
| 11:27-12:12 | 101 | 15:43 | 94 |
| 11:27-33 | 675 | 16:6-7 | 413, 418 |
| 11:30 | 102, 654 | 16:7f. | 166 |
| 12:6 | 121 | 16:7 | 94, 414 |
| 12:13-40 | 675 | 16:16 | 661 |
| 12:13ff. | 986 | | |
| 12:18ff. | 787 | Luke | |
| 12:29 | 95 | 1-2 | 129-144 |
| 12:34 | 94 | 1:1-4 | 887 |
| 12:35-37 | 656 | 1:2 | 171 |
| 12:38-40 | 676 | 1:6 | 143, 235 |
| 13 | 397-402 | 1:13 | 138 |
| 13:5-13 | 397 | 1:26-56 | 132-137 |
| 13:6 | 419 | 1:26-38 | 141 |
| 13:9-13 | 878 | 1:28-33 | 130 |
| 13:14-23 | 98, 397 | 1:28 | 888 |

| | | | |
|---|---|---|---|
| 1:32-35 | 574 | 7:1 | 33, 36 |
| 1:32 | 567 | 7:25 | 612 |
| 1:35 | 121, 142, 567 | 7:26 | 654 |
| 1:38 | 131, 143, 888 | 7:28 | 654 |
| 1:39-45 | 131 | 7:31-35 | 615 |
| 1:39 | 129-130, 141 | 7:34 | 465 |
| 1:41 | 133 | 7:36-50 | 140 |
| 1:42-45 | 133-134 | 8:27 | 1011 |
| 1:42 | 130 | 8:28 | 575 |
| 1:45 | 131 | 9-10 | 871-885 |
| 1:46-55 | 132, 134 | 9:52 | 602 |
| 1:48 | 131 | 9:54 | 878 |
| 1:52 | 143 | 9:57-61 | 618 |
| 1:54 | 1006 | 10:21f. | 133, 753 |
| 1:56 | 131 | 10:25 | 236 |
| 1:57-79 | 138 | 11:2-4 | 661 |
| 1:67-79 | 331 | 11:2 | 915 |
| 1:68-79 | 321 | 11:17 | 612 |
| 1:72-73 | 1007 | 11:27 | 134 |
| 2:16 | 130 | 11:37-54 | 675 |
| 2:36-38 | 139 | 11:47-51 | 523, 531 |
| 3:10-14 | 143 | 12:4 | 699 |
| 3:16 | 654 | 12:33-34 | 618 |
| 4:3 | 121 | 12:51-53 | 961 |
| 4:9 | 121 | 13:10-17 | 967 |
| 4:16-21 | 142 | 14:26 | 618, 961 |
| 4:25f. | 140 | 15:2 | 767, 769 |
| 4:25 | 405 | 15:11-32 | 138 |
| 4:34 | 971 | 16:13 | 618, 874 |
| 4:39 | 129 | 16:17 | 234 |
| 4:40-44 | 892 | 16:31 | 220 |
| 5:4-11 | 158 | 17:15 | 138 |
| 5:25f. | 137 | 17:18 | 138 |
| 5:25 | 129 | 17:21 | 617 |
| 6:20-23 | 878 | 17:31f. | 400 |
| 6:20ff. | 134 | 18:14 | 143 |
| 6:27-35 | 618 | 18:22 | 700 |
| 6:27-28 | 418 | 19:5f. | 130 |
| 6:46 | 418 | 19:8 | 143 |

| | | | |
|---|---|---|---|
| 19:11-15 | 614 | 3:7 | 973 |
| 20:4 | 654 | 3:11 | 180 |
| 20:45-47 | 676 | 3:13 | 914 |
| 21:8 | 398 | 3:14 | 915 |
| 21:12-19 | 878 | 3:22 | 657 |
| 21:14 | 685 | 3:30 | 172 |
| 22:19 | 1007 | 3:32f. | 180 |
| 22:22 | 914 | 4 | 439 |
| 22:25 | 612 | 4:10 | 602 |
| 22:70 | 121 | 4:16-42 | 966 |
| 24:6-7 | 915 | 4:22 | 175 |
| 24:44 | 423 | 4:42 | 152 |
| 24:49 | 133 | 5:31 | 170 |
| 24:54 | 628 | 6 | 167 |
| | | 6:16-25 | 151 |
| John | | 6:34 | 915 |
| 1:1 | 424 | 7:17 | 175 |
| 1:1-4 | 894 | 7:37-39 | 179 |
| 1:3 | 639 | 7:53-8:11 | 966 |
| 1:5 | 639 | 8:28 | 178 |
| 1:10 | 639 | 8:59 | 152 |
| 1:14 | 152, 162 | 9:27 | 102 |
| 1:18 | 168, 567, 637 | 10 | 160 |
| 1:19 | 184 | 10:41f. | 184 |
| 1:29-34 | 171 | 11:25 | 915 |
| 1:29 | 176, 184 | 11:47ff. | 161 |
| 1:34 | 180, 567 | 12:34 | 915 |
| 1:35-42 | 171, 182 | 12:41 | 152 |
| 1:35-39 | 172 | 13-17 | 545 |
| 1:35ff. | 158, 184 | 13:12a-15 | 1008 |
| 1:37 | 171 | 13:23 | 163, 168 |
| 1:38f. | 152 | 13:24 | 159 |
| 1:40-42 | 172 | 14:6 | 893 |
| 1:49 | 567 | 15:5 | 167 |
| 2:1-11 | 149-150, 174, 959-975 | 15:20 | 1007 |
| | | 15:27f. | 171 |
| 2:4 | 959-975 | 16:32 | 171 |
| 2:9 | 175 | 16:33 | 152 |
| 2:18-22 | 151 | 18:15-18 | 167, 171 |

| | | | |
|---|---|---|---|
| 18:15 | 159 | 2:42-46 | 693-710 |
| 18:25-27 | 167 | 2:44f. | 143 |
| 19:18 | 179 | 2:44 | 689-710 |
| 19:25-37 | 174 | 3-4 | 137 |
| 19:25-27 | 171 | 3:6 | 877 |
| 19:25 | 965-968 | 3:12-26 | 195 |
| 19:26 | 163, 965-968 | 3:13 | 888 |
| 19:28-35 | 175 | 3:15 | 628, 632 |
| 19:30 | 174 | 4:2 | 787 |
| 19:35 | 177, 180 | 4:7 | 198 |
| 20:2 | 163 | 4:8-12 | 195 |
| 20:3-8 | 160 | 4:8 | 399 |
| 20:15 | 967 | 4:10f. | 632 |
| 20:17f. | 165 | 4:12 | 209 |
| 20:30f. | 148-155 | 4:19-20 | 195 |
| 21 | 147-185 | 4:19 | 699 |
| 21:9-13 | 663 | 4:24 | 702 |
| 21:20 | 159 | 4:26 | 612 |
| 21:24 | 156 | 4:32-5:11 | 695 |
| | | 4:32-35 | 143, 694-710 |
| Acts | | 4:32 | 689-710 |
| 1:6 | 85 | 4:33 | 874 |
| 1:8 | 40, 44, 133, 728 | 5:1ff. | 692, 694 |
| 1:14 | 702 | 5:12 | 702 |
| 1:15 | 130 | 5:19 | 699 |
| 2 | 137, 194 | 5:29-32 | 195 |
| 2:14-41 | 636 | 5:31 | 636 |
| 2:14-36 | 195 | 5:32 | 399 |
| 2:17 | 140 | 5:34ff. | 198, 725-726 |
| 2:21 | 209 | 5:36f. | 709 |
| 2:22 | 194 | 6:1-7 | 695 |
| 2:25f. | 194 | 6:1-6 | 1004 |
| 2:27 | 194 | 6:1ff. | 698, 707-708 |
| 2:29 | 194 | 6:13f. | 234 |
| 2:33f. | 636 | 6:13 | 83, 235, 456 |
| 2:36 | 632 | 7 | 194 |
| 2:37-47 | 144 | 7:8ff. | 200 |
| 2:38 | 209 | 7:20 | 724 |
| 2:39 | 195 | 7:38ff. | 236 |

| | | | |
|---|---|---|---|
| 7:38 | 234, 235, 460 | 10:48 | 209 |
| 7:41-43 | 237 | 11:3 | 767, 773 |
| 7:44-50 | 234 | 11:5-9 | 233 |
| 7:44ff. | 212 | 11:8 | 702 |
| 7:52 | 524 | 11:9 | 230 |
| 7:53 | 235, 239, 460 | 11:17-18 | 894 |
| 7:55f. | 636 | 11:18 | 230, 233 |
| 7:58 | 727 | 11:19ff. | 709 |
| 8 | 136 | 11:27-30 | 1005, 1012 |
| 8:3 | 721, 727 | 11:27 | 130 |
| 8:4 | 728 | 12:2 | 164 |
| 8:16 | 209 | 13:1f. | 703 |
| 8:37 | 567 | 13:16-41 | 195 |
| 9 | 136 | 13:27ff. | 143 |
| 9:1f. | 721 | 13:30ff. | 632 |
| 9:11 | 716, 724 | 13:35 | 639 |
| 9:15 | 399 | 13:38 | 143 |
| 9:20 | 567 | 13:46 | 1009 |
| 9:32ff. | 705 | 14:15-17 | 195, 245 |
| 9:36ff. | 705 | 14:15f. | 237 |
| 9:36 | 240 | 14:17 | 891 |
| 10-11 | 136, 232-235 | 15 | 231, 232-235 |
| 10 | 137 | 15:1-29 | 1004 |
| 10:1-11 | 684 | 15:1-21 | 191-221 |
| 10:1 | 240 | 15:1-12 | 1004 |
| 10:2 | 143 | 15:1 | 230 |
| 10:4 | 240, 1007 | 15:2 | 197 |
| 10:10-16 | 233 | 15:5 | 230 |
| 10:14 | 702 | 15:10 | 236 |
| 10:18 | 684 | 15:13-29 | 1004 |
| 10:22 | 240 | 15:13-21 | 191-221 |
| 10:28 | 230, 233, 702 | 15:20 | 227-240 |
| 10:31 | 240 | 15:27 | 395 |
| 10:34-43 | 195 | 15:28 | 235, 236 |
| 10:34 | 230, 233 | 15:29 | 227-240 |
| 10:35 | 230, 233 | 15:32 | 395 |
| 10:36 | 409 | 15:36-41 | 230 |
| 10:38-40 | 409 | 16:4 | 227-240 |
| 10:41 | 767 | 16:17 | 234 |

| | | | |
|---|---|---|---|
| 16:20 | 234 | 23:8 | 787 |
| 16:37ff. | 724 | 23:27 | 724 |
| 17:1-3 | 1013 | 24:10-21 | 195 |
| 17:16-33 | 245-253 | 24:12ff. | 234 |
| 17:18 | 699 | 24:12f. | 199 |
| 17:22-31 | 195, 245-253 | 24:17f. | 234 |
| 17:22 | 237 | 24:17 | 1013 |
| 17:28 | 699 | 24:19 | 199 |
| 17:32 | 794, 874 | 25:10 | 198 |
| 18:1 | 252 | 26:2ff. | 195 |
| 18:10 | 210 | 26:4f. | 716 |
| 18:18 | 240 | 26:8 | 234 |
| 18:35ff. | 198 | 26:9-11 | 726 |
| 20:18-35 | 695 | 26:10f. | 721, 723 |
| 20:18ff. | 545 | 26:14 | 699 |
| 20:32-35 | 695, 710 | 26:30 | 399 |
| 20:34-35 | 1007 | 27:3 | 699 |
| 20:35 | 699 | 27:9 | 537 |
| 21:15-26 | 232 | 27:22 | 537 |
| 21:17ff. | 239 | 28:29 | 197 |
| 21:20 | 236 | | |
| 21:21 | 1013 | Romans | |
| 21:23-24 | 1014 | 1 | 203 |
| 21:25 | 227-240 | 1:1-15 | 486 |
| 21:27-33 | 1014 | 1:3f. | 414, 567 |
| 21:27ff. | 234 | 1:3 | 638, 642 |
| 21:28 | 83, 233 | 1:8 | 449 |
| 21:29 | 724 | 1:9 | 567 |
| 21:39 | 716, 724 | 1:10-13 | 517 |
| 22:1-21 | 195 | 1:14-16 | 1013 |
| 22:3-5 | 724-729 | 1:18-4:25 | 434, 450 |
| 22:3 | 714, 716-717, 725 | 1:18 | 288, 479 |
| 22:15 | 234 | 1:23ff. | 257 |
| 22:18 | 130, 234 | 1:25 | 331 |
| 22:21 | 234 | 1:29-31 | 488 |
| 22:25ff. | 724 | 2:8 | 288 |
| 23:3 | 240 | 2:11 | 201, 480 |
| 23:6ff. | 787 | 2:12-16 | 466 |
| 23:6 | 716 | 2:12ff. | 467 |

| | | |
|---|---|---|
| 2:13 | 438 | 809, 1002 |
| 2:28f. | 754 | 5:12-19 | 932 |
| 2:28 | 472 | 5:12-14 | 493 |
| 2:29 | 438 | 5:13 | 466 |
| 3:1 | 434, 440 | 5:15 | 736 |
| 3:8 | 483 | 5:17 | 736 |
| 3:10-18 | 432-433, 444 | 5:20 | 457, 467 |
| 3:20 | 438, 457, 466, 472, 483 | 6 | 544 |
| | | 6:1-8:13 | 483-485, 487-494 |
| 3:21-4:25 | 433, 450 | 6:1-14 | 480 |
| 3:21-31 | 95, 106 | 6:1-13 | 938 |
| 3:21-24 | 431, 433, 435 | 6:1-11 | 499, 517 |
| 3:21-22 | 450 | 6:3-11 | 1002 |
| 3:21 | 479 | 6:3-5 | 446 |
| 3:25 | 932 | 6:4 | 939 |
| 3:27-28 | 472 | 6:5 | 792, 939 |
| 3:29f. | 201, 433, 440, 450 | 6:6 | 938, 939 |
| 3:31 | 754 | 6:7 | 939 |
| 4 | 203, 487 | 6:8 | 939 |
| 4:3-8 | 736 | 6:11 | 483, 939 |
| 4:5 | 450 | 6:12-13 | 480, 483 |
| 4:9-12 | 441-442 | 6:14-15 | 467 |
| 4:10-12 | 429-430 | 6:15-23 | 480 |
| 4:15 | 466 | 6:17 | 653 |
| 4:17 | 450-452 | 6:19 | 501 |
| 4:23-25 | 450-451 | 7-8 | 471 |
| 4:23-24 | 267, 452 | 7:1-25 | 1002 |
| 4:24 | 450-451 | 7:1-6 | 481, 483 |
| 4:25 | 451-452, 502, 628, 634 | 7:7-8:17 | 450 |
| | | 7:7-8:13 | 483 |
| 5-8 | 477-503 | 7:7-8:8 | 484 |
| 5:1-11 | 480, 483-484, 489-492, 498, 503 | 7:7-8:4 | 467-469 |
| | | 7:7-25 | 484, 487 |
| 5:3-5 | 495 | 7:7ff. | 488 |
| 5:5 | 490-491 | 7:7 | 481, 483-484 |
| 5:9f. | 736 | 7:13 | 466 |
| 5:10 | 567, 809 | 7:15-23 | 488 |
| 5:12-21 | 467-469, 472, 480, 487, 494, 497, 503, | 8:2 | 488 |
| | | 8:12-13 | 481, 488 |

| | | | |
|---|---|---|---|
| 8:14-39 | 483-485, 489-494, 496-498, 502-503 | 12:3-8 | 993 |
| | | 12:4-7 | 487 |
| 8:14-25 | 490 | 12:9-13 | 993 |
| 8:14-17 | 481, 491 | 12:14-21 | 993 |
| 8:15 | 419, 500-501, 503 | 12:17-21 | 418 |
| 8:16 | 503 | 12:19 | 394 |
| 8:18-27 | 495 | 13 | 979-995 |
| 8:19-23 | 473 | 13:1 | 979 |
| 8:23-25 | 299 | 13:1-7 | 981 |
| 8:23 | 293 | 13:8-10 | 440, 470 |
| 8:24-25 | 298 | 13:9 | 236 |
| 8:24 | 297 | 14:1-15:7 | 549 |
| 8:26-27 | 503 | 14:1-15:6 | 487 |
| 8:32 | 736 | 14:1-13 | 237 |
| 8:37 | 809 | 14:17 | 392 |
| 9-11 | 434, 743-761, 1010 | 15:2-3 | 933 |
| 9 | 750 | 15:7 | 933 |
| 9:3-5 | 716 | 15:9-12 | 432-433, 444 |
| 9:3 | 512 | 15:14-33 | 486 |
| 9:4f. | 744 | 15:19 | 728-729 |
| 9:5 | 331, 888 | 15:22-32 | 517 |
| 9:30-33 | 960 | 15:25-26 | 1003 |
| 9:31-32 | 470 | 15:25 | 702, 1002 |
| 9:32 | 472 | 15:27 | 1009 |
| 10 | 751 | 15:30-32 | 512, 1012 |
| 10:4 | 456, 472 | 15:31 | 1013 |
| 10:9 | 134, 419, 628 | 16:4 | 511 |
| 10:18 | 85 | 16:17 | 775 |
| 11 | 751-752 | 16:25-26 | 848 |
| 11:1 | 716, 719 | | |
| 11:12 | 736 | 1 Corinthians | |
| 11:20 | 260, 268-269 | 1:6 | 911 |
| 11:22 | 270 | 1:10 | 805 |
| 11:26f. | 752 | 1:11 | 783 |
| 11:28f. | 744 | 1:12 | 398 |
| 11:32 | 103 | 1:17-3:4 | 106 |
| 11:35 | 735 | 1:17ff. | 100 |
| 12-15 | 544 | 1:18-2:5 | 633 |
| 12:1-2 | 477, 993 | 1:18-25 | 803 |

| | | | |
|---|---|---|---|
| 1:18f. | 419 | 6 | 772 |
| 1:18 | 937 | 6:1-11 | 805 |
| 1:22 | 414, 419 | 6:2f. | 736 |
| 1:23-25 | 911 | 6:9-10 | 462, 807 |
| 1:23-24 | 267 | 6:12 | 258-259, 804 |
| 1:26-31 | 805 | 6:15 | 258 |
| 2:2 | 451, 911 | 6:18 | 263 |
| 2:6-3:4 | 293 | 7:1 | 22 |
| 2:6-16 | 908 | 7:2-6 | 1002 |
| 2:16 | 734 | 7:2 | 263 |
| 3 | 772 | 7:5 | 270 |
| 3:10-14 | 913 | 7:10 | 410 |
| 3:14 | 298 | 7:19 | 440, 446-447, 450 |
| 3:18 | 268, 735 | 7:25 | 22, 420 |
| 3:21-23 | 808 | 7:26 | 395 |
| 4 | 397 | 7:31 | 802 |
| 4:1-5 | 913 | 7:40 | 269, 420 |
| 4:5 | 290 | 8-10 | 803, 805 |
| 4:6 | 392, 803 | 8 | 268 |
| 4:8-13 | 802 | 8:1-13 | 259 |
| 4:8 | 391, 395, 791-792, 807 | 8:1-3 | 237 |
| | | 8:1 | 22, 258-259 |
| 4:9-13 | 803 | 8:3 | 294 |
| 4:10 | 258 | 8:4 | 258 |
| 4:12-13 | 935 | 8:5 | 777 |
| 4:12 | 393 | 8:6 | 639, 808 |
| 4:15 | 459 | 8:7ff. | 549 |
| 4:16 | 517 | 9:1 | 628 |
| 4:20 | 391-392, 807 | 9:6-15 | 1011 |
| 4:21 | 511 | 9:11 | 873 |
| 5 | 771-774 | 9:14 | 410 |
| 5:1 | 510 | 9:19-23 | 1010 |
| 5:2 | 768 | 9:20 | 1013 |
| 5:3 | 510 | 10:1-22 | 257 |
| 5:6-8 | 771 | 10:1-13 | 257-271 |
| 5:9-13 | 772 | 10:1-10 | 262-266 |
| 5:9 | 773, 775 | 10:1-4 | 262, 264 |
| 5:10 | 271 | 10:4 | 777, 938 |
| 5:11 | 767, 772-773, 775 | 10:6-10 | 264 |

| | | | |
|---|---|---|---|
| 10:7 | 257-271 | 13 | 275-300 |
| 10:8 | 258 | 13:1-3 | 284-287 |
| 10:11-13 | 266-271 | 13:4-7 | 287-289 |
| 10:11 | 292 | 13:8-13 | 289-292 |
| 10:14-22 | 258, 776-778 | 13:13 | 292 |
| 10:14 | 259 | 14:21 | 394 |
| 10:20-21 | 259 | 14:33 | 808 |
| 10:21 | 267 | 14:33a | 1002 |
| 10:23-31 | 258 | 14:33b-36 | 1002 |
| 10:23ff. | 549 | 14:37 | 1002 |
| 10:23 | 258 | 15 | 781-797, 901-809 |
| 10:24 | 935 | 15:1-11 | 781 |
| 10:27-29 | 259 | 15:1 | 413 |
| 10:27 | 774 | 15:3-23 | 915 |
| 10:28-31 | 237 | 15:3-8 | 912 |
| 10:32 | 753 | 15:3ff. | 628 |
| 10:33-11:1 | 933 | 15:3-4 | 634, 911, 915 |
| 11:1 | 517, 806, 937 | 15:3b-5 | 413 |
| 11:2-16 | 1002 | 15:3 | 653 |
| 11:3-16 | 436, 444 | 15:5-8 | 413 |
| 11:3-10 | 445 | 15:8 | 628 |
| 11:11 | 446 | 15:9 | 721 |
| 11:17-34 | 778, 805 | 15:12-17 | 451 |
| 11:17ff. | 705 | 15:12 | 781, 783-784, 791-792, 915 |
| 11:23-26 | 635 | | |
| 11:23ff. | 410 | 15:19 | 789 |
| 11:23 | 415 | 15:20ff. | 789 |
| 11:24-25 | 1007 | 15:21-22 | 809 |
| 11:25 | 656 | 15:22ff. | 792 |
| 11:26 | 1009 | 15:22 | 785 |
| 11:30 | 791 | 15:23-28 | 656, 801-809 |
| 12:1-14:40 | 276-280 | 15:23f. | 912 |
| 12:1 | 22 | 15:28 | 295, 567, 913 |
| 12:2 | 257, 422 | 15:29 | 785, 789, 793 |
| 12:3 | 134, 422 | 15:30-32 | 789 |
| 12:4 | 258 | 15:35 | 785, 788, 794 |
| 12:13 | 430, 445-446, 777, 938 | 15:36-41 | 794 |
| | | 15:36ff. | 795 |
| 12:31 | 275, 281 | 15:42-44 | 794 |

| | | | |
|---|---|---|---|
| 15:44-49 | 794, 809 | 5:14 | 446, 932 |
| 15:45-47 | 911 | 5:15 | 446, 634 |
| 15:50 | 392, 462, 794, 807 | 5:16 | 652 |
| 15:51ff. | 794 | 5:17 | 446, 939 |
| 15:51 | 793 | 5:18ff. | 960 |
| 15:54 | 735 | 5:21 | 632 |
| 16:1-4 | 1002, 1011 | 6:4 | 935 |
| 16:1 | 22 | 6:10 | 937 |
| 16:12 | 22 | 6:17 | 394 |
| 16:13 | 268-269 | 6:18 | 394 |
| | | 8-9 | 1012 |
| 2 Corinthians | | 8 | 705, 1002 |
| 1:3-7 | 331 | 8:1-4 | 1003 |
| 1:8-11 | 511 | 8:4 | 702, 1002 |
| 1:12 | 1010 | 8:5 | 1010 |
| 1:17 | 1010 | 8:7-9 | 933 |
| 1:22 | 293 | 8:8 | 937 |
| 1:24 | 268-269 | 8:9 | 912, 1003, 1010 |
| 2:1-11 | 511 | 8:13-15 | 706, 709 |
| 2:4 | 511 | 8:13-14 | 1010 |
| 2:6-7 | 776 | 8:21 | 1010 |
| 2:17 | 394 | 9 | 1002 |
| 3:6-11 | 656 | 9:1 | 1002 |
| 3:7-9 | 736 | 9:2 | 937 |
| 3:7 | 719 | 9:7 | 937 |
| 3:11 | 736 | 9:9 | 298 |
| 3:17 | 938 | 9:12 | 1005 |
| 4:1-15 | 633 | 9:13 | 702 |
| 4:3-4 | 753 | 9:14 | 937 |
| 4:3 | 394 | 10:1-13:10 | 511 |
| 4:7ff. | 935 | 10:1 | 510-511, 933 |
| 4:8 | 936 | 10:4 | 511 |
| 4:14 | 935 | 10:6 | 511 |
| 4:17 | 935 | 10:7 | 398 |
| 5:1-10 | 794 | 10:10 | 487, 511 |
| 5:1ff. | 786, 794-795 | 10:11 | 511 |
| 5:5 | 293 | 11:2 | 938 |
| 5:7 | 297-299 | 11:6 | 511 |
| 5:14-17 | 445, 939 | 11:21-22 | 716-717 |

| | | | |
|---|---|---|---|
| 11:22 | 434, 441, 720 | 3:6-7 | 432, 441 |
| 11:23 | 511 | 3:8-18 | 442 |
| 11:24 | 399 | 3:8 | 452, 457 |
| 11:25f. | 980 | 3:13 | 456, 632 |
| 11:31 | 331 | 3:15-4:7 | 493 |
| 11:32 | 460 | 3:16 | 457 |
| 13:2 | 511 | 3:18 | 457 |
| 13:9 | 937 | 3:19-4:11 | 457-465 |
| 13:10 | 511 | 3:19 | 460, 467 |
| | | 3:23-25 | 461 |
| Galatians | | 3:24 | 458 |
| 1:1 | 628 | 3:27-28 | 445-447 |
| 1:4 | 472 | 3:27 | 938 |
| 1:10 | 1010 | 3:28 | 545, 1002, 1017 |
| 1:11f. | 722 | 3:29 | 441 |
| 1:13ff. | 716-717 | 4:4 | 567 |
| 1:13f. | 722-724 | 4:6-7 | 491 |
| 1:13 | 721 | 4:6 | 419, 567 |
| 1:14 | 680 | 4:8-10 | 459 |
| 1:17 | 726, 730 | 4:8 | 257 |
| 1:18 | 728 | 4:12ff. | 633 |
| 1:22f. | 729-731 | 4:21-30 | 434 |
| 1:23 | 721 | 4:28-31 | 462 |
| 2:1-10 | 1003 | 5:1 | 269, 1002 |
| 2:1ff. | 728 | 5:2-6 | 489 |
| 2:6 | 612 | 5:4 | 523, 531 |
| 2:9 | 164, 612, 702 | 5:5 | 490-491 |
| 2:10 | 709, 1001-1917 | 5:6 | 432, 440, 446-447, 450 |
| 2:11-18 | 463 | | |
| 2:11-14 | 703, 778-779 | 5:7 | 432 |
| 2:11 | 510 | 5:13-6:10 | 490, 492 |
| 2:12 | 684, 767, 773 | 5:13-26 | 488, 489, 497 |
| 2:14-16 | 465 | 5:14 | 465 |
| 2:15-16 | 430 | 5:19-21 | 488 |
| 2:15ff. | 753 | 5:19 | 472 |
| 2:16 | 461, 472, 907 | 5:21 | 462 |
| 2:19-20 | 938 | 5:22 | 465 |
| 3 | 203 | 5:24 | 938 |
| 3:2-3 | 472 | 5:25 | 498 |

| | | | |
|---|---|---|---|
| 6:1-10 | 489, 497 | 2:6-11 | 628, 636, 639, 806, 915-916 |
| 6:1f. | 549 | | |
| 6:2 | 465 | 2:7 | 936 |
| 6:3 | 268 | 2:8 | 815, 935 |
| 6:11-18 | 490 | 2:12 | 512 |
| 6:12-13 | 472 | 2:13 | 512 |
| 6:13-15 | 939 | 2:25 | 511, 815 |
| 6:14ff. | 633 | 2:30 | 511, 815 |
| 6:14 | 938 | 3:2-14 | 433 |
| 6:15 | 440, 446-447, 450, 452, 472, 490, 753 | 3:3 | 434 |
| | | 3:4-6 | 716-722 |
| 6:16 | 719 | 3:5f. | 723 |
| | | 3:6 | 456, 723, 726 |
| **Ephesians** | | 3:7ff. | 633 |
| 1:3-14 | 320, 331 | 3:17 | 517, 937 |
| 1:4 | 856 | 3:18 | 512 |
| 1:9 | 142 | 3:20f. | 794 |
| 1:19 | 142 | 3:21 | 807 |
| 2:13-16 | 960 | 4 | 822-824 |
| 3:1-19 | 515 | 4:1 | 269, 815 |
| 4:4 | 661 | 4:2 | 815 |
| 4:13 | 567 | 4:7 | 460 |
| 4:20f. | 422 | 4:8 | 881 |
| 5:1-2 | 517 | 4:10-20 | 815 |
| 5:5 | 462 | 4:11-13 | 813 |
| | | 4:11 | 813-824 |
| **Philippians** | | 4:12f. | 814 |
| 1:4 | 815 | | |
| 1:5 | 815 | **Colossians** | |
| 1:7 | 815 | 1:1-2 | 514 |
| 1:18 | 815 | 1:4 | 513 |
| 1:20 | 511 | 1:5 | 514 |
| 1:21 | 511 | 1:7-8 | 513-514 |
| 1:27-30 | 512 | 1:8 | 514 |
| 1:27 | 511, 815 | 1:12 | 514 |
| 2:1 | 815 | 1:13-14 | 514 |
| 2:2 | 815 | 1:15-20 | 516, 639 |
| 2:3-12 | 933 | 1:16f. | 639 |
| 2:4 | 935 | 1:19f. | 960 |

| | | | |
|---|---|---|---|
| 1:21-23 | 516 | 2:9 | 1011 |
| 1:23 | 514-515 | 2:13-16 | 519-532 |
| 1:24-29 | 515 | 2:14-16 | 753 |
| 1:24 | 513 | 2:14 | 394, 517, 723 |
| 1:25 | 515 | 2:15-16 | 519-532 |
| 1:29 | 513 | 3:1 | 246 |
| 2:1-2 | 514 | 3:5 | 270 |
| 2:1 | 513 | 3:8 | 269 |
| 2:2-7 | 514 | 3:13 | 790 |
| 2:5 | 512-514 | 4 | 401, 544 |
| 2:11-15 | 516 | 4:9 | 775 |
| 2:12 | 792 | 4:10 | 393 |
| 2:18 | 639 | 4:11 | 393, 775 |
| 2:20 | 516 | 4:13-5:11 | 897 |
| 3 | 544 | 4:13-18 | 915 |
| 3:1-3 | 516 | 4:13-17 | 913 |
| 3:5-4:6 | 515 | 4:13ff. | 786, 790, 792 |
| 3:9-11 | 517 | 4:14 | 634 |
| 3:10 | 516 | 4:15ff. | 395 |
| 3:12-17 | 517 | 4:15 | 391, 393, 410 |
| 3:16 | 549 | 4:16 | 401, 410, 792 |
| 4:3-4 | 513 | 4:17 | 400 |
| 4:3 | 515 | 5:1-11 | 401 |
| 4:7-17 | 514 | 5:1 | 395 |
| 4:7-9 | 513 | 5:2-10 | 913 |
| 4:12 | 513-514 | 5:2 | 395, 521, 529 |
| 4:16 | 514-515, 668 | 5:9-12 | 824 |
| 4:18 | 513-516 | 5:10 | 634 |
| | | 5:14 | 549 |
| **1 Thessalonians** | | 5:23f. | 545 |
| 1:3ff. | 545 | 5:23 | 790 |
| 1:3 | 393 | 5:27 | 668 |
| 1:6 | 517, 935 | | |
| 1:7 | 449 | **2 Thessalonians** | |
| 1:9f. | 252 | 1 | 394 |
| 1:9 | 257 | 1:1-12 | 572 |
| 1:10 | 393, 567, 638, 642, 790, 913 | 1:7 | 401 |
| | | 1:10 | 523 |
| 2:1f. | 395 | 2 | 397-398, 400 |

| | | | |
|---|---|---|---|
| 2:1-12 | 394 | 2:5-9 | 401 |
| 2:1 | 401 | 3 | 308 |
| 2:3-4 | 88, 396 | 3:8-11 | 261, 266 |
| 2:3 | 83 | 4 | 308-309 |
| 2:5 | 395 | 4:14-7:19 | 894 |
| 2:7 | 395 | 4:1 | 549 |
| 2:8 | 396 | 5 | 309, 544 |
| 2:10 | 400 | 6 | 309-310 |
| 3:6-16 | 394 | 6:20-7:18 | 891 |
| 3:6-15 | 774-776 | 7 | 310 |
| 3:6 | 393 | 9 | 310-311 |
| 3:10 | 393 | 9:19 | 176 |
| 3:14 | 773 | 10 | 311-312 |
| | | 11 | 312, 894 |
| 1 Timothy | | 11:4-7 | 891 |
| 1:12-17 | 515 | 11:36-37 | 524 |
| 2:4 | 891 | 12 | 312-313 |
| | | 13 | 313-314 |
| 2 Timothy | | James | |
| | 545 | | 535-549 |
| 1:8-14 | 515 | 1:16 | 548 |
| 2:17f. | 786, 791 | 2:1-13 | 546 |
| 2:18 | 803 | 2:5 | 462 |
| 4:10 | 729 | 2:14-26 | 546 |
| | | 3:10 | 548 |
| Philemon | | 3:13-18 | 546 |
| 2 | 511 | 5:19f. | 549 |
| 16 | 1002 | | |
| Hebrews | | 1 Peter | |
| | 305-315 | | 544, 547-548, 827-845 |
| 1 | 307 | | |
| 1:1 | 887-898 | 1:1 | 830 |
| 1:1-4 | 887 | 1:3-2:10 | 833 |
| 1:1-2 | 887-898 | 1:3-7 | 331 |
| 1:3 | 628, 639 | 1:5-6 | 841 |
| 1:5 | 567 | 1:5 | 460, 837 |
| 2 | 307-308 | 1:14 | 830 |
| 2:2 | 460 | 1:17 | 833 |

| | |
|---|---|
| 1:22-24 | 837 |
| 2:4-10 | 827 |
| 2:5 | 829 |
| 2:8 | 960 |
| 2:11-3:12 | 833-834, 839 |
| 2:11-25 | 841 |
| 2:11-12 | 833 |
| 2:11 | 830 |
| 2:13-17 | 839, 981 |
| 2:13ff. | 986 |
| 2:17 | 839 |
| 2:25 | 837 |
| 3:1-12 | 841 |
| 3:7 | 834, 838 |
| 3:8-12 | 834 |
| 3:9-12 | 839 |
| 3:13-4:11 | 835 |
| 3:13-24 | 841 |
| 3:21 | 656 |
| 4:1-11 | 841 |
| 4:1-6 | 835 |
| 4:8 | 549 |
| 4:12-5:11 | 841 |
| 4:12-19 | 835 |
| 4:12 | 837 |
| 4:17 | 829 |
| 5:1-11 | 834, 839 |
| 5:2-4 | 837 |
| 5:3 | 837 |
| 5:8 | 837 |
| 5:9 | 839 |
| 5:12 | 842 |
| 5:14 | 838 |

**2 Peter**

| | |
|---|---|
| 1:5 | 881 |
| 1:17 | 567 |

**1 John**

| | |
|---|---|
| 1:1-4 | 154, 184 |
| 1:3 | 567 |
| 2:18 | 400 |
| 3:2 | 295 |
| 4:2f. | 422 |
| 5:16f. | 549 |

**2 John**

| | |
|---|---|
| 3 | 567 |
| 7 | 422 |

**Jude**

| | |
|---|---|
| 11 | 531 |
| 14-15 | 356 |

**Revelation**

| | |
|---|---|
| 1-3 | 403 |
| 1:1-3 | 21 |
| 1:3 | 668 |
| 1:19 | 41 |
| 2:5 | 1007 |
| 2:14 | 229, 235 |
| 2:18 | 567 |
| 2:20 | 229, 235 |
| 3:14 | 639-640 |
| 4:1 | 41 |
| 4:7 | 113 |
| 6:15-16 | 336 |
| 7:14 | 405 |
| 8-9 | 404 |
| 11 | 404 |
| 11:1-13 | 404-405 |
| 11:15 | 405 |
| 12:1-6 | 897 |
| 12:13-18 | 897 |
| 13:1-10 | 406 |
| 13:1-4 | 402 |
| 13:8 | 856 |
| 13:11-18 | 406 |

| 13:11 | 405 | 17:10 | 404 |
|-------|-----|-------|-----|
| 13:13 | 405 | 17:11 | 404 |
| 13:17f. | 406 | 20-21 | 656 |
| 14:4 | 405 | 22:17 | 403 |
| 17:3-13 | 402 | 22:18 | 668 |
| 17:8 | 856 | | |

## B. Apostolic Fathers and Other Early Christian Texts

Acts of Andrew

| | |
|-----|-----|
| | 876, 881 |
| 25 | 877 |
| 45 | 883 |
| 51-56 | 883-884 |

Acts of John

| | |
|-------|-----|
| 42 | 882 |
| 56-57 | 882 |

Acts of John in Rome

| | |
|-----|----------|
| 5-6 | 877, 882 |

Acts of Matthias

| | |
|---|-----|
| | 876 |

Acts of Paul and Thecla

| | |
|------|-----|
| 1-43 | 876 |

Acts of Paul, Martyrdom

| | |
|-----|-----|
| 1-5 | 878 |
| 3 | 878 |

Acts of Peter

| | |
|-------|-----|
| 7 | 877 |
| 23-29 | 881 |

Acts of Peter and Andrew

| | |
|-------|-----|
| 13-21 | 880 |

Acts of Philip

| | |
|------------|----------|
| V, 14-22 | 877 |
| VII, 7 | 877, 882 |
| VIII, 15-21 | 879 |
| XIII | 876 |

Acts of Philip, Martyrdom

| | |
|-------|-----|
| 23-48 | 879 |

Acts of Thomas

| | |
|------|-----|
| 1 | 875 |
| 5:45 | 971 |
| 6-8 | 881 |

Ambros of Milan
*Expositio in Lucam*

| | |
|-----------|-----|
| VII, 44-53 | 873 |
| VII, 54 | 874 |

Apostolic Constitutions

| | |
|--------|-----|
| 8:6.3-9 | 666 |

Ascension of Isaiah

| | |
|--------|-----|
| 4:2-16 | 572 |

Athenagoras
*Supplicatio*

| | |
|----|-----|
| 10 | 852 |

Barnabas

| | |
|---|---|
| 4:4-6 | 403 |
| 4:6 | 757 |
| 9:4 | 458 |
| 15:8 | 861 |
| 16:1-5 | 403 |
| 19:8 | 700 |

Bede the Venerable
*In Lucam*

| | |
|---|---|
| III, 1871-74 | 873 |
| III, 1921-6 | 882 |
| IV, 185-86 | 875 |

1 Clemens

| | |
|---|---|
| 5:5ff. | 399 |

Pseudo-Clementines
*Homiliae*

| | |
|---|---|
| 7. 3,2f. | 777 |
| 8. 6-7 | 757 |

*Recognitiones*

| | |
|---|---|
| 2. 71 | 777 |
| 4. 5 | 757 |

Cyrill of Alexandria
*Sermones in Lucam*

| | |
|---|---|
| 47 | 873, 881-882 |
| 60-64 | 873-874 |

Cyrill of Jerusalem
*Catecheses*

| | |
|---|---|
| 6:17 | 852 |

Didaché

| | |
|---|---|
| 1:2 | 21 |
| 1:3 | 21 |
| 4:8 | 700 |

| | |
|---|---|
| 4:14 | 21 |
| 5:1 | 21 |
| 7:1 | 21, 22 |
| 9:1 | 22, 59 |
| 11:1 | 21 |

Egeria
*Itinerarium*

| | |
|---|---|
| 24 | 666 |

Epiphanios
*Panarion*

| | |
|---|---|
| 30. 14,3 | 124 |
| 30. 14,4 | 124 |
| 31. 5,2 | 852 |

Epistle of the Presbyters and Deacons
of Achaea

| | |
|---|---|
| 12 | 883 |

Eusebios
*Historia ecclesiastica*

| | |
|---|---|
| 3. 5,3 | 84 |
| 3. 5,4 | 84 |
| 5. 8,4 | 157 |
| 5. 24,3 | 160 |

Gregor of Nyssa
*De hominis opificio*

| | |
|---|---|
| 2 | 378 |

Hermas

| | |
|---|---|
| 2:1 | 32 |
| 3:3 | 32 |
| 4:1 | 34 |
| 15:4 | 32, 38 |
| 16:1 | 32 |
| 18:1 | 34 |

Hippolytos
*Refutatio omnium haeresium*
7. 35.1-2            123

Ignatius
*Ephesians*
3:2                 859
6:1                 859
15:1-2              859-862
19:1                860

*Magnesians*
6:1                 858
7:2                 858
8-10                847-865
8:2                 847, 858, 860-862
9:2                 859

*Romans*
2:1                 860, 862

*Smyrnaeans*
6:2                 859

Irenaeus
*Adversus haereses*
1. 1,1              848, 852-853
1. 11,1             356
1. 13ff.            852
1. 13,6ff.          854
1. 14,1             851
1. 14,3             851
1. 23,5             791
1. 29               356
2. 12,5             853
3. 1,1              157
3. 10,5             114
3. 11,7             124
3. 11,8             113, 119

3. 16,3             114

Johannes Chrysostomos
*Homilia(e)*
in Matthaeum
33                  874, 884
in Johannem
15 on John 1:18     890
in 1 Cor 39:5-6     806

Justinus
*Apologiae*
1. 14.2             700
1. 26.4             791

*Dialogus cum Tryphone*
                    352
25:6-26:2           757
34:8                229, 235
45:2                757
90:1                580
134:3               757
138                 861

Origenes
*De oratione*
14:6                666

*De principiis*
4. 2,12             910
4. 2,13             910

Tertullianus
*Adversus Marcionem*
4. 21               872
4. 24               873

*Adversus Praxean*
5                   852-853

7 852

Theophilus Antiochenus
*Ad Autolycum*
2. 10,22 852

III. CLASSICAL TEXTS

A. Greek Texts

Ammonios
132 538

Apollonios Dyskolos
*De pronominibus*
77b 20

*De syntaxi*
98,26 20

Aristotle
*De interpretatione*
1. 16a 3-8 28
1. 16b 19 31

*Nicomachea ethica*
8. 3,1-9 821
8. 11 1539b
31-33 696
9. 8 1168b 6-8 696, 815

*De poetica*
11 136
14 144

*Protreptikos*
540

Corpus Hermeticum
I, 31 854

X, 5 854
XIII, 2 854

(Pseudo-)Demetrios
*De elocutione*
4:227 516

Dio Cassius
66. 19,3 402

Diodoros Siculus
2:55-60 698
5:45 698

Diogenes Laertios
5:20 815
8:10 697, 815
10:11 697
10:120 821

Dion Chrysostomos
*Orationes*
3:10 804
21:10 403
30:33 820
34:20 815
62:3 804

Dionysios of Halicarnassos                                    540
*Antiquitates Romanae*                      3-5               541
4. 20,4,2              815
7. 59,7,5              815                   *Epistolae*
                                            1. 1              510
Epiktetos                                   1. 2-3            510
*Dissertationes*
2:7,12                666                   Lukianos and Pseudo-Lukianos
1:1,27                820                   *Cyniscus*
1:16                  969                   15                819
22:15                 969
27:13                 969                   *Quomodo historia conscribenda sit*
                                            55                47

*Enchiridion*
19:16                 969                   *De morte peregrini*
                                            13                700

Galenos
*Protreptikos*                             *Toxaris*
2:4                   385                   7                 816

Hesiodos                                    Maximos Tyrios
*Theogonia*                                 *Dial.* ed. Hobein
671                   341                   6:1               385
713-726               341
                                            Plato and Pseudo-Plato
Homeros                                     *Apologia*
*Odysseia*                                  24b               249
11                    787                   29d               699
24:1-204              787
                                            *Criton*
Iamblichos                                  50e               724
*De mysteriis*                              51e               724
8:3                   854                   110cd             698

*De vita Pythagorae*                        *Definitiones*
167f.                 697                   413C              538

Isocrates and Pseudo-Isocrates              *Laches*
*Demonicea*                                  196E              376

*Lysis*
207C 815

*De re publica (Politeia)*
3. 416de 698
5. 457 698
5. 462 698
5. 464b-e 698

*Sophistes*
263E 376

*Theaitetos*
189E 376

Plutarchos
*De amicorum multitudine*
94E 822
95AB 815
96E 815

Porphyrios
*De exilio*
606D 820

*De abstinentia*
2:34 854

*Vita Pythagorae*
20 697

Prokopios of Caesarea
*Anecdota*
10. 1 724

Sextus Empiricus
*Pyrrhonei hypotyposeis*
1:62-77 376

*Sententiae*
427 854
578 854

Sophocles
*Oedipus tyrannus*
642 966

Stobaios
4. 7,66 820-821
4. 22,25 697

Strabo
*Geographica*
14. 5,13 716

Xenophon
*Memorabilia*
1. 1.1 249, 699

*Symposion*
4:42 820

## B. Latin Texts

Cicero and Pseudo-Cicero
*De Amicitia*
15-16 815
21 815, 822
22 816

23 822
26 816
27-28 821
30 822
31 818

| | |
|---|---|
| 33-34 | 815 |
| 51 | 822 |
| 58 | 816 |
| 64-65 | 815 |
| 69-73 | 815 |

*Pro Flacco*

| | |
|---|---|
| 68 | 694 |

*De inventione*

| | |
|---|---|
| 2. 39,116 | 215 |
| 2. 49,144-47 | 201 |

*De natura deorum*

| | |
|---|---|
| 2:133 | 379 |
| 154ff. | 379 |
| 154 | 385 |

*De officiis*

| | |
|---|---|
| 1:15.48 | 818 |
| 1:16.51 | 696 |
| 1:51 | 815 |

*De oratore*

| | |
|---|---|
| 3. 202-205 | 218 |

*Rhetorica ad Herennium*

| | |
|---|---|
| 1. 2,3 | 487 |
| 2. 10,15 | 201 |

Ovidius
*Tristia*

| | |
|---|---|
| 4. 10,3ff. | 724 |

Pliny the elder
*Naturalis historia*

| | |
|---|---|
| 2:25 | 403 |

Quintilian
*Institutionis oratoriae*

| | |
|---|---|
| 3. 6,60-62 | 200 |
| 9. 1,26ff. | 218 |

Seneca
*De beneficiis*

| | |
|---|---|
| 2. 1,2 | 816 |
| 4. 40,3 | 817 |
| 4. 40,5 | 816 |
| 7. 2,4-5 | 819 |

*Epistolae ad Lucilium*

| | |
|---|---|
| 9:3.5 | 822 |
| 9:17 | 821 |
| 55:9-11 | 515 |
| 89 | 540 |
| 89:13 | 539 |
| 90:38 | 698 |
| 95 | 540 |
| 95:1 | 539 |

Suetonius
*Nero*

| | |
|---|---|
| 57:2 | 403 |

Tacitus
*Historiae*

| | |
|---|---|
| 2. 8ff. | 403 |
| 2. 8,1f. | 400 |

Vergil
*Eclogae*

| | |
|---|---|
| 4:18-25 | 383 |

## IV. GNOSTIC TEXTS

### A. Nag Hammadi Texts

CODEX I
Apocryphon of James
*[I.2: 1,1-16,30]*
5,31ff.                    104

Gospel of Truth
*[I.3: 16,31-43,24]*
19,36-20,3          856
27,22-25            855
27,34-28,4          855
36,35-37,18         856
37,4-12             850
37,7-8              855

Tripartite Tractate
*[I.5: 51,1-138,25]*
55,37               853
57,3-8              852
60,1ff.             855
60,6-11             855
63,17-64,4          850
63,20-23            854
128,30-32           854

CODEX II
Apocryphon of John
*[II.1: 1,1-32,9]*
                    355-365, 410
2,25-4,6            364
11,15-22            361
13,20               361
22,22               361
23,3                361
24,15-31            362
25,2-7              362

29,6                361
27,21-30            364
27,31-28,32         359
28,32-29,15         359
29,16-30,11         360

*[BG 8502, 2]*
26,7-8              853

Gospel of Thomas
*[II.2: 32,10-51,58]*
14                  684
34                  677
40                  677
47:1-2              618
55                  104
55:1                618
76:3                618
78                  612, 615
78:1-3              614
89                  679
101                 104
101:1-3             618

CODEX III
Gospel of the Egyptians
*[III.2: 40,12-69,20]*
43,21-24            851

Eugnostos
*[III.3: 70,1-90,13]*
88,7ff.             852

CODEX IV
Gospel of the Egyptians
*[IV.2: 50,1-81,2]*
53,20-26              851

CODEX VI
The Thunder (Perfect Mind)
*[VI.2: 13,1-21,32]*
14,9-15              851

CODEX VII
Paraphrase of Shem
*[VII.1: 1,1-49,9]*
13,7                 853
17,6                 853

CODEX X
Marsanes
*[X.1: 1,1-68,18]*

4,21                 853
7,3-25               853
8,21-22              854
9,14-16              853
9,22-24              854
15,1                 853

CODEX XI
Allogenes
*[XI. 3: 45,1-69,20]*
61,20-22             853
63,35                853

CODEX XIII
Trimorphic Protennoia
*[XIII.1: 35,1-50,24]*
37,29-30             853
46,11-17             851

## B. Other Gnostic Texts

Excerpta ex Theodoto
29-30                852
41:2                 856

## V. VARIA

Asoka Inscription
                591-596

Papyrus Oxyrhynchus
1224 p. 176     418